"CLEAR, THOROUGH, AND METICULOUSLY RESEARCHED. AN INVALUABLE RESOURCE FOR OUR CHANGING WORLD."

—Elizabeth Kolbert, author of *Field Notes from a Catastrophe: Man, Nature, and Climate Change*

In May of 2008, polar bears were declared a threatened species under the Endangered Species Act. Scientists estimate that because of diminished Arctic sea ice, two-thirds of the world's polar bears will disappear by 2060. This eye-opening indication of change in our environment underlines the importance of understanding the forces driving that change. The *Companion* seeks that understanding and serves as an ideal reference for well-informed stewards of the planet, offering authoritative yet accessible scholarship that explains the natural phenomena and human activities transforming climates and landscapes around the globe.

Updating and adding to the research that went into an earlier multi-volume encyclopedia, *The Oxford Companion to Global Change* provides a concise guide to the realities of a planet in transition, covering such crucial topics as the threat of declining crude oil production, the status of coal-burning technology, and the future of nuclear power. Over 150 scientists and specialists, led by David J. Cuff and Andrew S. Goudie of Temple University and Oxford University respectively, contribute entries on key subjects, demonstrating the social, political, and technological interrelationships between them. We learn, for example, how the precautionary principle (in a nutshell, "Better safe than sorry") affects policymaking, and we see what developing nations are doing to respond to change. Articles on China and India, in particular, highlight threats to water supplies and clean air.

The topic that receives the most coverage in the *Companion*, global warming, is one of pressing urgency. In such entries as Arctic Warming, Regional Patterns of Climate Change, Greenland Ice Sheet, Sea-level Future and more, the authors investigate the reality and science of global warming from its origins to its impacts, adding a long-term perspective to the present debate. Human responses such as carbon taxes and the

USA $125.00

Continued on back flap

THE OXFORD COMPANION TO GLOBAL CHANGE

THE OXFORD COMPANION TO

GLOBAL CHANGE

DAVID J. CUFF AND ANDREW S. GOUDIE

OXFORD
UNIVERSITY PRESS
2009

OXFORD
UNIVERSITY PRESS

Oxford University Press, Inc., publishes works that further
Oxford University's objective of excellence
in research, scholarship, and education.

Oxford New York
Auckland   Cape Town   Dar es Salaam   Hong Kong   Karachi
Kuala Lumpur   Madrid   Melbourne   Mexico City   Nairobi
New Delhi   Shanghai   Taipei   Toronto
With offices in
Argentina   Austria   Brazil   Chile   Czech Republic   France   Greece
Guatemala   Hungary   Italy   Japan   Poland   Portugal   Singapore
South Korea   Switzerland   Thailand   Turkey   Ukraine   Vietnam

Published by Oxford University Press, Inc.
198 Madison Avenue, New York, NY 10016
www.oup.com

The Library of Congress Cataloging-in-Publication Data
Cuff, David J.
The Oxford companion to global change /
David J. Cuff and Andrew S. Goudie.
p. cm. Includes bibliographical references and index.
ISBN 978-0-19-532488-4
1. Global environmental change. 2. Environmental sciences. 3. Human ecology.
4. Nature--Effect of human beings on. I. Goudie, Andrew. II. Title.
GE149.C84 2008
363.7--dc22
2008013664

1 3 5 7 9 8 6 4 2

Printed in the United States of America
on acid-free paper

CONTENTS

Preface
vii

Introduction
ix

Abbreviations, Acronyms, and Symbols
xiii

Directory of Contributors
xix

Entries by Subject
xxvii

A-Z Entries
1

Resources for Citizens
651

Appendices
654

Index
661

PREFACE

Since publication of *The Oxford Encyclopedia of Global Change* in 2002, a number of events have pointed toward a new reference work.

There has been widespread recognition that global warming is no longer debatable. Al Gore's *Inconvenient Truth* and The Stern Report (see article, *Economics and Climate Change*) deserve much of the credit for raising awareness. The specifics of warming and the reality of the human acceleration of natural trends have been asserted by four reports during 2007 by the Intergovernmental Panel on Climate Change (IPCC). Although worded cautiously and toned down by some government representatives, the reports detail the science, the impacts of warming, and the need to reduce greenhouse gas emissions. New articles in this edition elaborate these three dimensions of global warming, with emphasis on impacts, especially in Arctic areas. One article defines the role of the IPCC, which has gained great prominence in recent years. Others explain the causes of warming, particularly the greenhouse effect.

Ironically, the recognition of global warming—caused largely by the burning of fossil fuels—coincides with reports of an impending shortage of crude oil, the source of gasoline, diesel fuel, and jet fuel that underpins our modern societies and contributes so heavily to global warming. Rising prices for crude oil in 2007 and 2008 seem to confirm that prediction, as demand soars because of rapid economic growth in developing nations. New articles examine that growth and its impact on the environment in India and China, while other articles clarify the assessment of mineral resources and the controversy surrounding the date of peak oil production.

In the last few years there has been a growing realization that transition to non-combustion energy sources, combined with new technologies and enlightened government policies during this transition, is essential. New articles explain carbon taxes versus emissions trading as competing policy measures, while other articles explore technologies for dealing with carbon dioxide emissions.

The impacts of global warming, combined with declining crude oil production and accelerating demand for resources by developing nations, can lead to alarming predictions about the state of the world. This subject is dealt with in an article on the Catastrophist-Cornucopian Debate, which lists many recent publications both gloomy and optimistic.

Altogether, there are over 250 entries, of which roughly one-third were written expressly for this edition, largely on topics of recent concern such as Greenland, Antarctica, sea level, biofuels, coal, nuclear power, and boreal and tropical forests. Although this edition highlights current concerns, it also preserves valuable principles in background articles from the original edition and deals with environmental change not dependent on global warming or energy choices. Land use, irrigation, population growth, and disease are enduring themes, as are mining and other human impacts on the landscape. And, for perspective on global warming, we examine natural climate change through articles on paleoclimate and the influence of solar variability. We also define the tools for investigating past climates and explain the climate models so vital for predicting climate change.

LINKS BETWEEN ARTICLES

Many broad subjects are explored through a skein or network of articles. A general article, such as *Energy Strategies*, will point to a number of more specific articles on the subject, and even when the structure is not so deliberate, most articles refer to related articles—either with an embedded reference (e.g., *See article: Climate Models*) or with a note at the end stating, for instance, *See Also: Dating Methods; and Proxy Data for Environmental Change*.

REFERENCES AND CURRENT INFORMATION

Few things change as rapidly as ideas and information on global change. Most articles here are enriched by references to books and professional journals. Many of those provide background to a subject, while some are sources of recent information. But none can provide current information; we thus urge the reader to use the listed government and private organizations whose websites explain research programs and offer latest data, revised annually in many cases. If a specific web address is for some reason not functional, the parent organization usually can be found by a web search.

In the Appendix we provide tabulations of data such as greenhouse gas emissions and rankings of nations on other key measures. Also in the final pages, for those who wish to improve the state of the world, is *Resources for Citizens*, a list of organizations (with websites) that undertake action in various ways.

UNCERTAINTY

Even the most current data on global change is not necessarily definitive, especially when the subject is man-induced change in climate and its projected impacts. Forecasts derived from climate models are tentative, particularly at regional and local levels; suggested ceilings on carbon dioxide concentrations, intended to avert dangerous climate change, necessarily are only informed estimates. Issues related to this theme are reviewed in the article *Uncertainty*.

OUTLINE OF CONTENTS

All entries in the *Companion* proper are arranged alphabetically. But in *Outline of Contents* the articles are grouped by category, so that the reader can browse categories and find relevant articles. Many articles appear in more than one group, indicating the nature of our subject. *Coal Gasification*, for instance, appears in *Energy and Mineral Resources* and also in *Industrial Activity*; and *Fisheries* appears in both *Oceans and Agriculture* and *Fishing*. This duplication lengthens the *Outline of Contents* but makes it, we hope, more useful.

ACKNOWLEDGMENTS

In the conception of the original *Encyclopedia of Global Change,* Sean Pidgeon played a vital role. For this edition Ben Keene, as project editor, provided remarkable knowledge, skill, and energy, as did Sara Lieber and Grace Labatt. Production was in the capable hands of Helen Mules. Alan Hartley improved the text immensely through his astute copyediting, sharp-eyed proofreaders headed off many errors, and Don Larson of Mapping Specialists, Ltd. executed a number of maps with great competence. As in the first edition, David Victor of Stanford University proved to be a valuable source of information and guidance. Finally, we salute all the authors who devoted their time and energy to this work.

—David J. Cuff

INTRODUCTION

Phrases like "global change" and "global environmental change" are much used but seldom rigorously defined. They are sometimes seen as synonymous, but the meanings of both have changed (and sometimes diverged) over time. Wide use of the term "global change" seems to have emerged in the 1970s, but in that period it was used principally, though by no means invariably, to refer to changes in international social, economic, and political systems (Price, 1989). The term included such issues as proliferation of nuclear weapons, population growth, inflation, and matters relating to international insecurity and decreases in the quality of life. As Pernetta (1995, p. 1) pointed out, the first use of the term was essentially anthropocentric.

Since the early 1980s, the concept of global change took on another meaning, which was much more geocentric in focus. As Price (1989, p. 20) remarked, "the concept has effectively been captured by the physical and biological sciences." He also indicated that such were the wide range of scales involved, whether spatial or temporal: "…it can be perceived to include almost any topic in the biological, Earth or atmospheric sciences." Price noted (p. 42) that the term has been used:

> "to describe changes in almost any variable that can be examined world-wide. These variables include the geological evolution of the Earth; human-induced changes in atmospheric composition and terrestrial ecosystems; urbanization, coastal erosion and volcanism; population growth and chemical pollution; as well as the resurgence of malaria and the rapid spread of AIDS. The periods encompassed by changes in these variables have varied from a single decade to billions of years."

The geocentric meaning of global change can be seen in the development of the International Geosphere–Biosphere Programme: a Study of Global Change. The IGBP was established in 1986 by the International Council of Scientific Unions "to describe and understand the interactive physical, chemical and biological processes that regulate the total Earth system, the unique environment that it provides for life, the changes that are occurring in this system, and the manner in which they are influenced by human actions."

The term "global environmental change" has in many senses come to be used synonymously with the more geocentric use of "global change." Its validity and wide currency were recognized when *Global Environmental Change* was established in 1990 as "an international journal that addresses the human ecological and public policy dimensions of the environmental processes that are threatening the sustainability of life of Earth. Topics include, but are not limited to, deforestation, desertification, soil degradation, species extinction, sea level rise, acid precipitation, destruction of the ozone layer, atmospheric warming/cooling, nuclear winter, the emergence of new technological hazards, and the worsening effects of natural disasters."

Likewise, the U.K. Research Councils established a U.K. Global Environmental Research Office, and recognized two scales of issues (*The Globe*, Issue 1, p. 1, March 1991): "(a) those that are truly global (e.g. ozone depletion, climate modification) and (b) local and regional problems which occur on a world-wide scale (e.g. acid rain)." The Research Councils recognized that global environmental change "has tended to become synonymous with understanding the complex interacting processes influencing the Earth's environment and the natural and man-induced factors, that affect them".

Beran (1995, p. 43), however, has suggested that there is a distinction between the two phrases:

> "Traditionally the term *Global Change* has referred to a branch of earth science which deals with the deep paleo. To most people *Global Environmental Change* comprises a set of issues such as climate change, ozone depletion, biodiversity reduction, desertification, eutrophication and so on. Scientists who study Global Change address major questions relating to how long the earth has had an atmosphere, or a magnetic field, or a salty ocean and why there are ice ages, soils and mountains."

The terminological confusion surrounding the two terms, as revealed by the statements outlined so far, is thus very profound. In this volume, we will use the term global change as being synonymous with global environmental change and take as our definition one that has been adopted in the United States (Munn, 1996):

> Global change is a term intended to encompass the full range of global issues and interactions concerning natural and human-induced changes in the Earth's environment. The [U.S.] Global Change Research Act of 1990 defines global change as 'changes in the global environment (including alterations in climate, land productivity, oceans or other water resources, atmospheric chemistry, and ecological systems) that may alter the capacity of the Earth to sustain life.'
>
> (*Our Changing Planet: The FY 1995 U.S. Global Change Research Program*, p. 2. A report of the U.S. National Science and Technology Council, Washington, D.C., 1994)

This definition is very similar to that used by the European Commission's European Network for Research in Global Change.

> "Global Change research seeks to understand the integrated Earth system in order to: (i) identify, explain and predict natural and anthropogenic changes in the global environment; (ii) assess the potential regional and local impacts of those changes on natural and human systems; and (iii) provide a scientific basis for the development of appropriate technical, economic and societal mitigation/adaptation strategies."

In this context, global change encompasses climate change; in atmospheric physics and chemistry (e.g., ozone depletion, tropospheric pollution); changes in land use and cover; variability in marine environments and ice cover; changes in biogeochemical cycles; impacts of these changes on natural balances (ecosystems), on natural resources (freshwater, forest products, crops, marine resources), and on socioeconomic balances (sustainable development, industrial development, human health, quality of life).

We therefore recognize the importance of both natural and anthropogenic factors in promoting environmental changes on a wide range of temporal scales. Anthropogenic changes can only be understood in the context of a whole range of past, present, and future natural changes.

However, it is also important to understand what we mean by "global." There are two components to this (Turner et al., 1990): systemic global change and cumulative global changes in climate caused by atmospheric pollution. In the systemic meaning, "global" refers to the spatial scale of operation and comprises such issues as global changes in climate brought about by atmospheric pollution. In the cumulative meaning, "global" refers to the areal or substantive accumulation of localized change. A change is seen to be "global" if it occurs on a worldwide scale or represents a significant fraction of the total environmental phenomenon or global resource. Both types of change are closely intertwined. For example, the burning of vegetation can lead to systemic change through such mechanisms as carbon dioxide release and albedo change, and to cumulative change through its impact on soil and biotic diversity (Table 1).

TABLE 1. Types of Global Environmental Change

Type	Characteristic	Examples
Systemic	Direct impact on globally functioning system	(a) Industrial and land use emissions of "greenhouse" gases. (b) Industrial and consumer emissions of ozone-depleting gases. (c) Land cover changes in albedo
Cumulative	Impact through world-wide distribution of change	(a) Groundwater pollution and depletion (b) Species depletion/genetic alteration (biodiversity)
	Impact through magnitude of change (share of global resource)	(a) Deforestation (b) Industrial toxic pollutants (c) Soil depletion on prime agricultural lands

SOURCE: from B. L. Turner et al., 1990, table 1.

This is an issue that has also been pursued by Talbot (1989, pp. 25–26) who indicates that environmental issues become global in a variety of ways:

"Some activities occur in a few places but may affect the biosphere as a whole. For example, large-scale combustion of fossil fuels may only occur in a few industrial areas but it may affect the climate as a whole. The same is true of the release of other greenhouse gasses.

Smaller-scale local activities, when repeated around the world, also may have global effects. Estuaries near coastal cities are heavily polluted, and, while each case is of local pollution, the wide repetition of the problem and its total impact make it global. The same is true, for example, of local changes in land use that cumulatively can affect the planet's albedo and the local clearance of forests, which can have major cumulative effects on species loss and CO_2 balance.

Species extinction is an important dimension of the problem. Although in former times the loss of species was considered to be a local problem, maintenance of biological diversity is now recognized to be of major global importance.

All environmental problems ultimately have social and economic impacts on people. Some global issues, like climate change, can have clear impacts on humans throughout the world. But with the increasing interdependence among nations and peoples, more apparently localized environmental problems have increasingly pervasive economic and social impacts in other parts of the world. The localized loss of a resource such as the Peruvian anchoveta can have an economic domino effect, causing economic dislocations in other nations across the world.

The socioeconomic impacts of environmental problems are particularly evident in the case of development assistance to Third World nations…. The size of the debt of many developing countries is staggering. Yet environmental degradation in many countries is reducing their capacity to support themselves much less to repay debts. This, in turn, affects other nations elsewhere in the world, developing as well as developed."

The present work aims to capture our current knowledge of natural and anthropogenic changes in the Earth's physical, chemical, and biological systems and resources and to examine the effects of those changes on human society. Anthropogenic and natural climate changes and their past and future impacts have become the focus of a great deal of recent comment (see, for example, Fagan, 2004; Diamond, 2005; Cox, 2005; Flannery, 2005; and Linden, 2006). The work focuses primarily on changes whose effects may be felt on human (rather than geological) timescales, although the Earth's natural rhythms and processes are discussed in sufficient detail that current or projected trends may be viewed against the appropriate background of natural change. Global warming, for instance, is placed in the context of longer-term climate change; predictions of sea-level rise are seen against coastlines that are rising and falling independent of global warming; and current glacier retreat is revealed as an acceleration of a trend begun roughly 15,000 years ago in the Northern Hemisphere at the end of the most recent ice age.

—Andrew S. Goudie

BIBLIOGRAPHY

Beran, M. "Education and Training of Global Environmental Change Scientists." In *Global Environmental Change in Science: Education and Training*, edited by D. Waddington, pp. 41–47. Berlin: Springer Verlag, 1995.

Cox, J. D. *Climate Crash*. Washington, D.C.: Joseph Henry Press, 2005.

Diamond, J. *Collapse*. London: Allen Lane, 2005.

Fagan, B. *The Long Summer. How Climate Changed Civilization*. London: Granta Books, 2004.

Flannery, T. *The Weather Makers*. London: Allen Lane, 2005.

IPCC. *Climate Change 2007: The Physical Science Basis. Contribution of Working Group I to the Fourth Assessment Report of the Intergovernmental Panel on Climate Change* (edited by S. Solomon et al.). Cambridge and New York: Cambridge University Press, 2007.

Linden E., *The Winds of Change*. New York: Simon and Schuster, 2006.

Munn, R. E. "Global Change: Both a Scientific and a Political Issue." In *Policy Making in an Era of Global Environmental Change*, edited by R. E. Munn, J. W. M. La Rivière, and N. van Lookeren Campagne, pp. 1–15. Dordrecht: Kluwer, 1996.

Pernetta, J. "What Is Global Change?" *Global Change Newsletter* 21 (1995), 1–3.

Price, M. F. "Global Change: Defining the Ill Defined." *Environment* 31(8) (1989), 18–20, 42–44.

Talbot, L. M. "Man's Role in Managing the Global Environment." In *Changing the Global Environment: Perspectives on Human Involvement*, edited by D. B. Botkin, M. F. Caswell, J. E. Estes, and A. Orio, pp. 17–33. Boston: Academic Press, 1989.

Turner, B. L., R. E. Kasperson, W. B. Meyer, K. M. Dow, D. Golding, J. X. Kasperson, R. C. Mitchell, and S. J. Patick. "Two Types of Global Environmental Change: Definitional and Spatial-Scale Issues in Their Human Dimensions." *Global Environmental Change* 1 (1990), 14–22. The most useful discussion of the definition of global environmental change.

ABBREVIATIONS, ACRONYMS, AND SYMBOLS

AABW	Antarctic Bottom Water
ABRACOS	Anglo-Brazilian Climate Observation Study
AC	alternating current
AGCM	atmospheric general circulation model
AIDS	acquired immune deficiency syndrome
AIJ	activities implemented jointly
AMIGO	America's Interhemisphere Geo-Biosphere Organization
AMIP	Atmospheric Model Intercomparison Project
AMS	accelerator mass spectrometry
ANC	acid-neutralizing capacity
AOU	American Ornithologists' Union
APEC	Asia-Pacific Economic Cooperation
AR	autoregressive
ASTER	Advanced Spaceborne Thermal Emission and Reflection Radiometer
ATP	adenosine triphosphate
ATSR	Along Track Scanning Radiometer
AU	astronomical unit (1 AU = 1.496×10^8 kilometers)
AVHRR	(NOAA) Advanced Very High Resolution Radiometer
BAP	Bureau of Animal Population
BASF	Badische Anilin- und Soda-Fabrik
BBSRC	(U.K.) Biotechnology and Biological Sciences Research Council
BCA	benefit–cost analysis
BCE	before the Common Era
BCG	bacille Calmette-Guerin
BLM	(U.S.) Bureau of Land Management
BNC	base-neutralizing capacity
BOREAS	Boreal Ecosystem-Atmosphere Study
BP	before the present
Btu	British thermal unit
CAD	computer-assisted design
CBD	Convention on Biological Diversity
CCAMLR	Convention on the Conservation of Antarctic Marine Living Resources
CCGT	combined-cycle gas turbine
CCN	cloud condensation nuclei
CDIAC	Carbon Dioxide Information Analysis Center
CDM	clean development mechanism
CE	Common Era
CEOS	Committee on Earth Observation Satellites
CEQ	(U.S.) Council on Environmental Quality
CERES	Clouds and the Earth's Radiant Energy System
CERLA	Comprehensive Environmental Response, Compensation, and Liability Act
CET	central England temperature
CFC	chlorofluorocarbon
CGIAR	Consultative Group on International Agricultural Research
CGIS	Canada Geographic Information System
CIA	cumulative impact assessment
CIESIN	Center for International Earth Science Information Network
CIM	computer integrated manufacturing
CIMMYT	Centro Internacional de Mejoramiento de Maiz y Trigo (International Maize and Wheat Improvement Center)
CIRAN	Centre for International Research and Advisory Networks
CITES	Convention on International Trade in Endangered Species of Wild Fauna and Flora
CLIVAR	Climate Variability and Prediction Program
CMS	Convention on the Conservation of Migratory Species of Wild Animals (or the Bonn Convention)
CN	condensation nuclei
CNRS	Centre National de la Recherche Scientific (France)
CoCP	Council of Contracting Parties
COM	cost of mitigation
COMECON	Communist Economic Community (or Council for Mutual Economic Assistance)
CoP	Conference of the Parties
CoP1	First Conference of the Parties, Berlin, Germany, March–April 1995
CoP3	Third Conference of the Parties, Kyoto, Japan, December 1997
CoP4	Fourth Conference of the Parties, Buenos Aires, Argentina, 2–13 November 1998
CPR	common-pool resource; contraceptive prevalence rate
CRED	Centre for Research on the Epidemiology of Disasters

CSD	(United Nations) Commission on Sustainable Development
CSERGE	Centre for Social and Economic Research on the Global Environment
DAAC	distributed active archive center
DARPA	(U.S.) Defense Advanced Research Projects Agency
DBMS	database management system
DDT	dichlorodiphenyltrichloroethane
DEM	digital elevation model
DGD	Decision Guidance Document
DHF	dengue hemorrhagic fever
DICE	dynamic integrated climate economy
DIF	Directory Interchange Format
DMS	dimethyl sulfide
DNA	deoxyribonucleic acid
DOC	dissolved organic carbon
DOD	(U.S.) Department of Defense
DSM	distributed shared memory
DSS	dengue shock syndrome
DU	Dobson unit
EA	environmental assessment
EBM	energy balance model
EC	European Community
ECC	electrochemical cell
ECE	(United Nations) Economic Commission for Europe
ECOSOC	(United Nations) Economic and Social Council
ED	electrodialysis
EDF	Environmental Defense Fund
EDR	electrodialysis reversal
EEA	environmental effects assessment
EEC	European Economic Community
EEZ	Exclusive Economic Zone
EIA	environmental impact assessment
EIS	environmental impact statement
EKC	environmental Kuznets curve
EM-DAT	Emergency Events Database: the OFDA/CRED International Disaster Database
ENMOD	Convention on the Prohibition of Military or Any Other Hostile Use of Environmental Modification Techniques
ENSO	El Niño–Southern Oscillation
EOS	(NASA) Earth Observing System
EOSDIS	EOS Data and Information System
EPA	(U.S.) Environmental Protection Agency
ERBE	(NASA) Earth Radiation Budget Experiment
ERS	(European) Earth Resources Satellite
ESA	Endangered Species Act
ESRC	(U.K.) Economic and Social Research Council

FAO	(United Nations) Food and Agriculture Organization
FCCC	(United Nations) Framework Convention on Climate Change
FFA	South Pacific Forum Fisheries Agency
FFT	fast Fourier transform
FGDC	U.S. Federal Geographic Data Committee
FIFE	First ISLSCP Field Experiment
FOE	Friends of the Earth
FoEI	Friends of the Earth International
FRG	Federal Republic of Germany
FRONTIERS	Forecasting Rain Optimised using New Techniques of Interactively Enhanced Radar and Satellite data
FS	(U.S.) Forest Service
FSU	former Soviet Union
FWS	(U.S.) Fish and Wildlife Service
G-7	Group of Seven (leading industrial nations)
GAC	Global Area Coverage
GARP	Global Atmospheric Research Program
GATS	General Agreement on Trade in Services
GATT	General Agreement on Tariffs and Trade
gC	grams of carbon
GCDIS	Global Change Data and Information System
GCM	general circulation model; global change model; global climate model
GCMD	Global Change Master Directory
GCOS	Global Climate Observing System
GDP	gross domestic product
GDR	German Democratic Republic (East Germany; now part of Germany)
GEC	global environmental change
GECHS	Global Environmental Change and Human Security
GEF	Global Environment Facility
GEWEX	Global Energy and Water Cycle Experiment
GFDL	Geophysical Fluid Dynamics Laboratory (NOAA)
GHG	greenhouse gas
GIS	Geographic Information Systems; Geographical Information Systems
GISS	Goddard Institute for Space Studies
GNP	gross national product
GONGO	governmental and nongovernmental organization
GPCP	Global Precipitation Climatology Project
GPS	Global Positioning System
GWP	global warming potential
HAP	hazardous air pollutants
HAPEX	Hydrological and Atmospheric Pilot Experiment

HCB	hexachlorobenzene
HCFC	hydrochlorofluorocarbon
HFC	hydrofluorocarbon
HIV	human immunodeficiency virus
HLW	high-level waste
HPLC	high-pressure liquid chromatography
IAA	International Association of Academies
IAEA	International Atomic Energy Agency
IAI	Inter-American Institute (for Global Change Research)
IARC	international agricultural research center
IARIW	International Association for Research in Income and Wealth
IAS	Institute for Advanced Study
IBAMA	Instituto Brasileiro do Meio Ambiente e dos Recursos Naturais Renováveis (Brazilian Institute of Environment and Renewable Natural Resources)
IBM	International Business Machines (Corporation)
ICAIR	International Centre for Antarctic Information and Research
ICAS	Interstate Council on the Aral Sea
ICBP	International Committee for Bird Protection (now BirdLife International)
ICCROM	International Centre for the Study of the Preservation and Restoration of Cultural Property
ICES	International Council for the Exploration of the Sea
ICESat	Ice, Cloud, and land Elevation Satellite
ICJ	International Court of Justice
ICOLD	International Commission on Large Dams
ICOMOS	International Council on Monuments and Sites
ICRW	International Convention for the Regulation of Whaling
ICSID	International Centre for Settlement of Investment Disputes
ICSU	International Council for Science (formerly the International Council of Scientific Unions)
ICZM	Integrated Coastal Zone Management
IDA	International Development Association
IDEAL	International Decade of the East African Lakes
IDGC	Institutional Dimensions of Global Change
IDN	(CEOS) International Directory Network
IDNDR	International Decade for Natural Disaster Reduction
IE	industrial ecology
IEA	International Energy Agency
IFAD	International Fund for Agricultural Development
IFAS	Interstate Fund for the Aral Sea
IFC	International Finance Corporation
IFOV	instantaneous field of view
IFPRI	International Food Policy Research Institute

IGBP	International Geosphere-Biosphere Programme
IGY	International Geophysical Year
IHDP	International Human Dimensions Programme on Global Environmental Change
IIASA	International Institute for Applied Systems Analysis
IISD	International Institute for Sustainable Development
ILW	intermediate-level waste
IM	industrial metabolism
IMF	International Monetary Fund
IMO	(United Nations) International Maritime Organization
IMS	Information Management System
INCD	Intergovernmental Negotiating Committee for the elaboration of an international convention to combat Desertification
INC5	Fifth Intergovernmental Negotiating Session for a Global POPs Treaty, Johannesburg, South Africa, 4–9 December 2000
INPA	Instituto Nacional de Pesquisas da Amazônia (National Institute for Research in the Amazon)
INPE	Instituto Nacional de Pesquisas Espaciais (Brazilian National Institute for Space Research)
INSEAD	European Institute of Business Administration
IPAT	I [environmental impact] = P [population] × A [affluence] × T [technology]; or FI = FP × FA × FT
IPCC	Intergovernmental Panel on Climate Change
IPF	Intergovernmental Panel on Forests
IPM	integrated pest management
IPP	independent power-producing
IPR	intellectual property rights
IR	infrared
IRC	International Research Council
ISCCP	International Satellite Cloud Climatology Project
ISLSCP	International Satellite Land Surface Climatology Project
ISO	International Organization for Standardization
ISSC	International Social Science Council
IT	Industrial Transformation (IHDP); information technology
ITCZ	intertropical convergence zone
ITO	International Trade Organisation
IUCN	International Union for the Conservation of Nature and Natural Resources (the World Conservation Union)
IWC	International Whaling Commission
IWRB	International Waterfowl Research Bureau
IWRM	integrated water resources management
JERS-1	Japanese Earth Resource Satellite-1
JI	joint implementation
K/T	Cretaceous-Tertiary

LAC	Local Area Coverage
LACIE	Large Area Crop Inventory Experiment
Landsat	system of U.S. land-surface observation satellites
LCA	life cycle analysis
LDC	less developed countries; London Dumping Convention
LEPA	low-energy precision application
LFG	landfill gas
LGM	last glacial maximum
LIS	Lightning Imaging Sensor
LLN	Louvain-la-Neuve
LRTAP	(Convention on) Long-Range Transboundary Air Pollution
LUCC	Land Use and Land Cover Change
LULC	Land Use and Land Cover
LWT	Lamb Weather Type
MAB	(United Nations) Man and the Biosphere Programme
MARC	Monitoring and Assessment Research Centre
MARPOL	negotiations of the International Convention for the Prevention of Pollution from Ships
MBIS	Mackenzie Basin Impact Study
MCA	multicriteria analysis
MDC	more developed countries
MDR	multidrug resistance
ME	multieffect evaporation
MIGA	Multilateral Investment Guarantee Agency
MIS	marine isotope stages
MM	Modified Mercalli intensity scale
MNC	multinational corporation
MOBILHY	(HAPEX) Mode'lisation du Bilan Hydrique (France)
MODIS	Moderate Resolution Imaging Spectrometer
MoP	Meeting of Montreal Protocol Parties
MOPITT	Measurement of Pollution in the Troposphere
MORECS	U.K. Meteorological Office Rainfall and Evaporation Calculation System
MPP	massively parallel processor
MSF	multistage flash
MSS	(Landsat) Multispectral Scanner
MSY	maximum sustainable yield
MTPE	Mission to Planet Earth (NASA)
NADW	North Atlantic Deep Water
NAFO	North Atlantic Fisheries Organization
NAFTA	North American Free Trade Agreement
NASA	(U.S.) National Aeronautics and Space Administration
NASA ER-2	NASA high-altitude research aircraft

NASDA	National Space Development Agency of Japan
NAT	nitric acid trihydrate
NATO	North Atlantic Treaty Organisation
NBII	(U.S.) National Biological Information Infrastructure
NCB	National Coal Board
NCDC	(U.S.) National Climate Data Center
NCP	(Montreal Protocol) Non-Compliance Procedure
NDVI	Normalized Difference Vegetation Index
NEP	net ecosystem production
NEPA	National Environment Policy Act
NERC	(U.K.) Natural Environment Research Council
NGO	nongovernmental organization
NHGRI	National Human Genomic Research Institute
NIEO	new international economic order
NMO	national member organization
NOAA	(U.S.) National Oceanic and Atmospheric Administration
NPP	net primary production; net primary productivity
NPS	(U.S.) National Park Service
NSF	(U.S.) National Science Foundation
NWT	North West Territories (Canada)
OCMIP	Ocean Carbon-Cycle Model Intercomparison Project
ODP	ozone depletion potential
OECD	Organisation for Economic Co-operation and Development
OEM	original equipment manufacturers
OFDA	Office of U.S. Foreign Disaster Assistance
OGCM	ocean general circulation model
OGI	old growth index
OH	free radical hydroxyl
OIES	(UCAR) Office for Interdisciplinary Earth Studies
OPEC	Organization of the Petroleum Exporting Countries
OSL	optically stimulated luminescence
OTA	Office of Technology Assessment
PAGES	(IGBP) Past Global Changes
PAH	polyaromatic hydrocarbon
PAM	plant available moisture
PAN	plant available nutrients
PAT	population, affluence, and technology
PC	personal computer
PCB	polychlorinated biphenyl
PCE	perchloroethylene
PCH	polychlorinated hydrocarbon
PDMS	postdepositional modification stratigraphy
PET	polyethylene terephthalate; potential evapotranspiration
pH	hydrogen ion concentration

PIC	prior informed consent
PNA	Pacific North American
POC	particulate organic carbon
POP	persistent organic pollutant
ppb	parts per billion
ppbv	parts per billion by volume
ppm	parts per million
ppmv	parts per million by volume
ppt	parts per trillion
pptv	parts per trillion by volume
PR	Precipitation Radar
PRA	probabilistic risk assessment
PSC	polar stratospheric cloud
PURPA	Public Utility Regulatory Policies Act of 1978
PVC	poly(vinyl chloride)
PVP	parallel vector processor
QA/QC	quality assurance and quality control
QRA	quantitative risk assessment
quad	a unit of energy; one quad equals one quadrillion Btu
RAID	redundant array of independent devices
RC	one-dimensional radiative-convective model
RD	relative dating
RECLAIM	Regional Emissions Clean Air Incentives Market (Southern California)
REE	rare-earth element
RIS	reservoir-induced seismicity
RMP	(IWC) Revised Management Procedure
RMS	(IWC) Revised Management Scheme
RNA	ribonucleic acid
RO	reverse osmosis
ROEC	Reed Odorless Earth Closet
R-strategists	Short-lived organisms characterized by short generation times and the ability to produce and disperse offspring efficiently and abundantly (e.g., dandelions, cockroaches)
SAGE	Semi-Automatic Ground Environment (U.S. Air Force)
SAR	Second Assessment Report; (JERS-1) Synthetic Aperture Radar
SBI	Subsidiary Body for Implementation
SBSTA	Subsidiary Body for Scientific and Technological Advice
SBUV	Solar Backscatter Ultraviolet Instrument
SCAQMD	South Coast Air Quality Management District (California)
SCICEX	Scientific Ice Expeditions
SCOPAC	Standing Conference on Problems Associated with the Coastline

SCOPE	Scientific Committee on Problems of the Environment
SD	statistical dynamical (model)
SEA	strategic environmental assessment
SEEA	system of integrated environmental and economic accounts
SFS	sea floor spreading
SIA	social impact assessment
SMART	Save Money and Reduce Toxics
SNA	system of national accounting
SOHO	solar and heliosphoric observatory
SPM	Summaries for Policymakers; suspended particulate matter
SPOT HRV-XS	Systeme Pour l'Observation de la Terre (SPOT) High-Resolution Visible (HRV) Multispectral (XS)
SQHW	small quantities of hazardous waste
SSP	Second Sulfur Protocol (to the Convention on Long-Range Transboundary Air Pollution)
SSS	sea surface salinity
SST	sea surface temperature
SSURGO	Soil Survey Geographic Database
STAP	Scientific and Technical Advisory Panel (of the Global Environment Facility)
START	The global change SysTem for Analysis, Research and Training
STATSGO	State Soil Geographic Database
STP	sewage treatment plant
SVD	singular-value decomposition
SWDA	Solid Waste Disposal Act
SWE	snow water equivalent
TAR	(IPCC) Third Assessment Report
TCE	trichloroethylene
TCP	Technical Cooperation Programme
TEK	traditional ecological knowledge
TEL	tetraethyl lead
TFR	total fertility rate
TL	thermoluminescence
TM	(Landsat) Thematic Mapper
TMI	TRMM Microwave Imager
TOA	top of the atmosphere
TOC	total organic carbon
TOGA	Tropical Ocean and Global Atmosphere program
TOMS	Total Ozone Mapping Spectrometer
TRMM	Tropical Rainfall Measuring Mission
TSCA	(EPA) Toxic Substances Control Act
TSS	total suspended solids
TVA	Tennessee Valley Authority

UARS	Upper Atmosphere Research Satellite
UCAR	University Corporation for Atmospheric Research
UKMO	U.K. Meteorological Office
UN	United Nations
UNCED	United Nations Conference on Environment and Development
UNCLOS	United Nations Convention on the Law of the Sea
UNCOD	United Nations Conference on Desertification
UNDP	United Nations Development Programme
UNEP	United Nations Environment Programme
UNESCO	United Nations Educational, Scientific, and Cultural Organization
UNFPA	United Nations Population Fund (formerly United Nations Fund for Population Activities)
UNICEF	United Nations Children's Fund
UNIDO	United Nations Industrial Development Organization
UPS	United Parcel Service
URL	Uniform Resource Locator
USAID	U.S. Agency for International Development
USGCRP	U.S. Global Change Research Program
USGS	U.S. Geological Survey
UTH	upper tropospheric humidity
UTM	Universal Transverse Mercator
UV	ultraviolet (radiation)
UV-B	ultraviolet-B (radiation)
VC	vapor compression; Vienna Convention for the Protection of the Ozone Layer of 1985
VIP	ventilated improved pit
VIRS	Visible and Infrared Scanner
VOC	volatile organic compounds
WCED	World Commission on Environment and Development
WCP	World Climate Programme
WCRP	World Climate Research Programme
WHO	World Health Organization
WIPO	World Intellectual Property Organization
WMO	World Meteorological Organization

WOCE	World Ocean Circulation Experiment
WRAP	Waste Reduction Always Pays
WTO	World Trade Organization
WWF	World Wide Fund for Nature (formerly World Wildlife Fund)
WWW	World Weather Watch; World Wide Web
YD	Younger Dryas

Measures and Conversions

centimeter	0.39 inches
foot	12 inches (0.3048 meters)
gram	0.0353 ounces
inch	2.54 centimeters
kilogram	1,000 grams (2.2046 pounds)
kilometer	1,000 meters (3,280.8 feet or 0.62 miles)

Prefixes for International System of Units

yotta (Y)	10^{24}
zetta (Z)	10^{21}
exa (E)	10^{18}
peta (P)	10^{15}
tera (T)	10^{12}
giga (G)	10^{9}
mega (M)	10^{6}
kilo (k)	10^{3}
hecto (h)	10^{2}
deca (da)	10^{1}
deci (d)	10^{-1}
centi (c)	10^{-2}
milli (m)	10^{-3}
micro (μ)	10^{-6}
nano (n)	10^{-9}
pico (p)	10^{-12}
femto (f)	10^{-15}
atto (a)	10^{-18}
zepto (z)	10^{-21}
yocto (y)	10^{-24}

DIRECTORY OF CONTRIBUTORS

Abdalati, Waleed
Research Scientist, Cryospheric Sciences Program, NASA Goddard Space Flight Center, Greenbelt, Maryland
Ice Sheets

Agnew, C. T.
Professor of Geography, Head of School of Environment and Development, University of Manchester, United Kingdom
Drought

Archibold, O. W.
Professor of Geography, University of Saskatchewan, Saskatoon, Canada
Biological Realms; *and* Wilderness and Biodiversity

Arnell, Nigel
Director of the Walker Institute for Climate System Research, Professor of Climate System Science, University of Reading
Impacts of Climate Change

Ayoub, Josef J.
Senior Planning Advisor in Energy Science and Technology, Natural Resources Canada, Varennes, Quebec
Desalination

Barendregt, Rene W.
Professor of Geography and Geology, University of Lethbridge; and Adjunct Professor of Geography, University of Calgary, Alberta, Canada
Dating Methods

Barker, Randolph
Senior Advisor to the Director General, International Irrigation Management Institute, Battaramulla, Sri Lanka
Irrigation; *and* Water

Barkin, J. Samuel
Associate Professor of Political Science, University of Florida, Gainesville
Globalization and the Environment

Barry, Roger G.
Director, World Data Center for Glaciology, Boulder; Former Director, National Snow and Ice Data Center; and Distinguished Professor of Geography, University of Colorado, Boulder
Snow Cover

Bird, Eric C. F.
Principal Fellow, Department of Geography, University of Melbourne, Parkville, Victoria, Australia
Emerging Coasts; Mangroves; *and* Sea Level Future

Bodansky, Daniel M.
Woodruff Professor of International Law, University of Georgia School of Law
Framework Convention on Climate Change; *and* Precautionary Principle

Boisson de Chazournes, Laurence
Professor and Director of the Department of Public International Law and International Organization, Faculty of Law, University of Geneva, Switzerland
Environmental Law

Botkin, Daniel B.
Professor Emeritus of Ecology, Evolution, and Marine Biology, University of California, Santa Barbara
Stability

Bowman, David
Professor of Forest Ecology, School of Plant Science, University of Tasmania, Hobart, Australia
Australia and Global Change

Boydak, Melih
Professor of Silviculture, Faculty of Forestry, Istanbul University, Turkey
Deforestation

Bradley, Robert
Director, International Climate Policy Initiative, World Resources Institute, Washington, D.C.
Sustainable Growth

Bridgman, Howard A.
Associate Professor of Environmental Science, University of Newcastle, Callagnan, New South Wales, Australia
Methane; *and* Pollution

Brimblecombe, Peter
Professor of Atmospheric Chemistry, University of East Anglia, Norwich, United Kingdom
Sulfur Cycle

Canney, Susan
Doctor of Zoology, University of Oxford, United Kingdom
Biological Feedback

Challinor, David
Senior Scientist Emeritus and Conservation and Science Directorate, Smithsonian Institution, National Zoo, Washington, D.C. (Deceased)
Hunting and Poaching

Chapman, Graham
Professor Emeritus of Human Geography, Lancaster University, United Kingdom
India and Environmental Change

Charnovitz, Steve
Associate Professor of Law, George Washington University Law School, Washington, D.C.
Trade and Environment

Coates, Peter
Professor of American and Environmental History, University of Bristol, United Kingdom
Parks and Preserves

Corell, Robert W.
Director, Global Change Program, H. John Heinz III Center for Science, Economics and the Environment, Washington, D.C.
Arctic Warming

Côté, Raymond P.
Professor, School for Resource and Environmental Studies, Dalhousie University, Halifax, Nova Scotia, Canada
Industrial Ecology

Cuff, David J.
Professor Emeritus of Geography, Temple University, Philadelphia, Pennsylvania
Carbon Footprint; Catastrophist-Cornucopian Debate; Chemical Wonders; Coal Gasification; Coal Liquefaction; Crude Oil Supply; Dendrochronology; Ecological Footprint; Economic Levels; Economics and Climate Change; Emissions Intensity; Energy and Environment; Energy Strategies; Environmental Performance Index; Externalities; Forests and Environmental Change; Fossil Fuels; Futurists; Globalization and the Environment; Greenhouse Gases; IPCC: Intergovernmental Panel on Climate Change; Kyoto Progress; Methane Hydrates; Oil Sands; Ozone Fluctuations in the Stratosphere; Renewable Sources of Energy; Resources; Stabilizing Carbon Emissions; Synfuels; Technology and Environment; Tragedy of the Commons; Urban Trends; Water; *and numerous vignettes*

Dando, William A.
Professor Emeritus of Geography, Geology, and Anthropology, Indiana State University, Terre Haute
Famine

DeSombre, Elizabeth R.
Frost Professor of Environmental Studies and Professor of Political Science, Wellesley College, Wellesley, Massachusetts
United Nations Environment Programme

Economy, Elizabeth
C.V. Starr Senior Fellow and Director of Asia Studies, Council on Foreign Relations
China and Its Environment

Ehrenfeld, John R.
Director of the Technology, Business and Environment Program and Senior Research Associate at the MIT Center for Technology, Policy, and Industrial Development, Massachusetts Institute of Technology, Cambridge
Chemical Industry

Emanuel, Kerry A.
Professor of Atmospheric Science, Massachusetts Institute of Technology, Cambridge
Extreme Events

Engelman, Robert
Vice President for Programs, Worldwatch Institute, Washington, D.C.
Population Policy

Fearnside, Philip M.
Research Professor, Department of Ecology, National Institute for Research in the Amazon (INPA), Manaus-Amazonas, Brazil
Amazonia and Deforestation

Fedorov, Alexey V.
Associate Professor, Department of Geology and Geophysics, Yale University, New Haven, Connecticut
Ocean-Atmosphere Coupling

Ferguson, Charles D.
Fellow for Science and Technology, Council on Foreign Relations, Washington, D.C.
Nuclear Power

Freestone, David
Deputy General Counsel, Advisory Services, Legal Vice Presidency, The World Bank, Washington, D.C.
Environmental Law

Friedland, Andrew J.
Professor and Chair of Environmental Studies, Dartmouth College, Hanover, New Hampshire
Acid Rain and Acid Deposition

Friedmann, S. Julio
Assistant Research Scientist, Department of Geology, University of Maryland, College Park
Carbon Capture and Storage

Geyer, L. Leon
Professor of Environmental and Agricultural Law and Economics, Virginia Polytechnic Institute and State University, Blacksburg
Ecotaxation

Gimingham, Charles H.
Professor Emeritus of Botany, University of Aberdeen, Scotland
Heathlands

Giorgi, Filippo
Head of the Physics of Weather and Climate Section, Coordinator of Scientific Programmes, The International Centre for Theoretical Physics, Trieste, Italy
Regional Patterns of Climate Change

Gleick, Peter H.
Co-Founder and President of the Pacific Institute for Studies in Development, Environment, and Security, Oakland, California
Dams; *and* Water

Golding, Dominic
Research Assistant Professor, George Perkins Marsh Institute, Clark University, Worcester, Massachusetts
Vulnerability

Goodchild, Michael F.
Professor of Geography, University of California, Santa Barbara
Geographic Information Systems

Goudie, Andrew S.
Professor of Geography, University of Oxford, United Kingdom
Anthropogeomorphology; Biomes; Causes of Climate Change; Climate Change and Societal Development; Dansgaard-Oeschger Cycles; Deltas and Global Warming; Desert Dunes in a Warmer World; Dust Storms; Earth System Science; El Niño-Southern Oscillation (ENSO); Extinction of Animals; Fire and Global Warming; Forests and Environmental Change; Glacier Retreat Since the Little Ice Age; Global Dimming; Ground Water; Heinrich Events; Holocene; Lakes; Land Surface Processes; Loess; Medieval Climate Optimum; North Atlantic Oscillation; Nuclear Waste; Ocean Acidification; Paleoclimate; Permafrost; Rivers: Impacts of Climate Change; Salinization; Thermohaline Circulation; Tipping Points; Transboundary Air Pollution; Tropical Climate Change; Tropical Cyclones in a Warming World; Twentieth Century Climate Change; Urban Climates; *and numerous vignettes*

Gould, W. T. S.
Professor Emeritus of Geography, University of Liverpool, United Kingdom
Human Populations

Grant, Lewis O.
Professor Emeritus of Atmospheric Science, Colorado State University, Fort Collins
Weather Modification

Griego, Fumie Yokota
Director of Domestic Policy Operations, Wittenberg Weiner Consulting, LLC, Former Health Economist and Decision Scientist, The Office of Information and Regulatory Affairs, Washington, D.C.
Regulation

Grieve, Richard A. F.
Chief Geoscientist, Earth Sciences Sector, Natural Resources Canada, Ottawa, Ontario
Extraterrestrial Impacts

Grove, Jean M.
Life Fellow, Girton College, Cambridge, United Kingdom (Deceased)
Little Ice Age in Europe

Hahn, Robert W.
Executive Director of the Reg-Markets Center, Senior Fellow at the American Enterprise Institute, Washington, D.C.
Regulation

Haigh, Joanna D.
Professor of Atmospheric Physics, Imperial College, London
Solar Variability and Climate

Hardy, Sheree
CarbonVentures, Environ, London
Emissions Trading

Harrison, Christopher G. A.
Professor of Marine Geology and Geophysics, University of Miami, Florida
Mobile Earth

Hassol, Susan Joy
Director, Climate Communication; Independent Climate Analyst, Basalt, Colorado
Arctic Warming

Hawkins, David G
Director, Climate Center at the Natural Resources Defense Council, New York, New York
Coal

Heerdegen, Richard G.
Honorary Research Associate in Geography, School of People, Environment and Planning, Massey University, Palmerston North, New Zealand
Value of Parks and Preserves

Hobbs, Richard J.
Professor of Environmental Science, Murdoch University, Western Australia
Heathlands

Huybrechts, Philippe
Professor of Climatology, Glaciology and Geodesy, Vrije Universiteit Brussel, Belgium
Greenland Ice Sheet

Jackson, Michael P.
Social Science Research Assistant, Program on Energy and Sustainable Development, Stanford University, California
Natural Gas

Jepma, Catrinus J.
Scientific Director, The Energy Delta Research Centre and Professor of Energy and Sustainability, University of Groningen, The Netherlands
Joint Implementation

Juday, Glenn Patrick
Professor of Forest Ecology, School of Natural Resources and Agricultural Sciences, University of Alaska, Fairbanks
Boreal Forests and Climate Change. *(This article represents University of Alaska SNRAS publication number 2008-001.)*

Kagbo, Robert B.
Senior Agricultural Advisor, USAID/WARP (West African Regional Program)
Pest Management

Kalm, Volli
Professor of Applied Geology, University of Tartu, Estonia
Dating Methods

Kammen, Daniel M.
Professor, Energy and Resources Group, Director, Renewable and Appropriate Energy Laboratory, University of California, Berkeley
National Energy Policy in the United States

Keith, David W.
Director, Energy and Environmental Systems Group, University of Calgary, Calgary, Alberta, Canada
Geoengineering

Kemp, David D.
Professor of Geography, Lakehead University, Thunder Bay, Ontario, Canada
Climate Models and Uncertainty; *and* Global Warming

Keys, Eric G.
Assistant Professor of Resource Conservation Geography, University of Florida, Gainesville
Agriculture and Agricultural Land; Carrying Capacity; *and* Land Use

Kimmins, J. P. (Hamish)
Professor of Forest Ecology, University of British Columbia, Vancouver, British Columbia, Canada
Forestation

Knight, C. Gregory
Professor of Geography, Pennsylvania State University, University Park
Regional Assessment

Leggett, Jeremy
Founder and Executive Chairman, Solarcentury, London, United Kingdom
Insurance

Lemons, John
Professor of Environmental Studies, University of New England, Biddeford, Maine
Ecological Integrity

Lenton, Tim
Professor of Earth System Science, University of East Anglia, Norwich, United Kingdom
Gaia Hypothesis

Loeb, Norman G.
Research Professor of Atmospheric Sciences, Hampton University/NASA Langley Research Center, Virginia
Albedo

Lonergan, Steve
Professor of Geography, University of Victoria, British Columbia, Canada
Security and Environment

Lu, Xianfu
Technical Advisor, The National Communications Support Programme, United Nations Development Programme-Global Environment Facility
IPCC: Intergovernmental Panel on Climate Change

Mahaney, William C.
Professor and Director of the Geomorphology and Pedology Laboratory, York University, Ontario, Canada
Dating Methods

Malone, Thomas F.
University Distinguished Scholar Emeritus, North Carolina State University, Raleigh
International Geosphere-Biosphere Programme

Marshall, Elizabeth
Senior Economist, World Resources Institute, Washington, D.C.
Biofuels; *and* Ethanol

Marty, Martin E.
Fairfax M. Cone Distinguished Service Professor Emeritus, University of Chicago Divinity School, Illinois
Religion

Mason, Robert J.
Associate Professor of Geography and Urban Studies, Temple University, Philadelphia, Pennsylvania
Land Preservation

Mastrandrea, Michael D.
Research Associate, The Center for Environmental Sciences and Policy, and Lecturer in the Interdisciplinary Graduate Program in Environment and Resources, Stanford University, California
Greenhouse Effect

Matthews, H. Damon
Assistant Professor, Department of Geography, Planning and Environment, Concordia University, Montreal, Quebec, Canada
Geoengineering

McIntyre, A. D.
Professor Emeritus of Fisheries and Oceanography, University of Aberdeen, Scotland
Marginal Seas

McManus, Phil
Senior Lecturer in Geoscience, University of Sydney, Australia
Environmental Impact Assessment

McNeely, Jeffery A.
Chief Scientist, The World Conservation Union, Gland, Switzerland
Agriculture and Biodiversity

Meadows, Michael E.
Professor of Biogeography and Head of the Department of Environmental and Geographical Science, University of Cape Town, Rondebosch, South Africa
Mediterranean Environments

Mégie, Gérard J.
Chairman of the Centre National de la Recherche Scientifique; Professor at the Université Pierre et Marie Curie; and Founder of the Pierre-Simon Laplace Institute for Environmental Sciences, Paris, France (Deceased)
Ozone

Meybeck, Michel H.
Senior Scientist, Centre National de la Recherche Scientifique, Laboratoire de Géologie Appliquée, Université de Paris VI, France
Water-Quality Trends

Meyer, William B.
Independent Scholar, Bradford, Massachusetts
Catastrophist–Cornucopian Debate; Global Change History; Human Ecology; Human Impacts on Earth; *and* Land Reclamation

Micklin, Philip
Professor Emeritus of Geography, Western Michigan University, Kalamazoo
Aral Sea

Mitchell, Peter B.
Senior Research Fellow of Environmental and Life Sciences, Department of Physical Geography, Macquarie University, New South Wales, Australia
Soils

Morgan, R. P. C.
Professor Emeritus of Soil Erosion Control, National Soil Resources Institute, Cranfield University, Bedford, United Kingdom
Erosion

Murphy, Peter E.
Associate Dean of Research, Department of Law and Management, La Trobe University, Victoria, Australia
Tourism

Nicholls, Roberta
Professor of Energy and Coasts, School of Civil Engineering and the Environment; and Leader of the Coastal Resesrach Programme at the Tyndall Centre for Climate Change Research, University of Southampton, United Kingdom
Impacts of Climate Change

Nordstrom, Karl F.
Professor of Marine and Coastal Sciences, Rutgers University, New Brunswick, New Jersey
Estuaries

Nunn, Patrick D.
Professor of Oceanic Geoscience, The University of the South Pacific, Suva, Fiji
Reefs

Oelschlaeger, Max
Professor, Department of Philosophy and Religion Studies, University of North Texas, Denton
Wilderness Debates

Oliver, Chadwick D.
Pinchot Professor of Forestry and Environmental Studies; Director, Yale Global Institute of Sustainable Forestry, Yale University, New Haven, Connecticut
Deforestation

O'Neill, John
Hallsworth Chair in Political Economy, University of Manchester, United Kingdom
Ethics

O'Riordan, Timothy
Professor of Environmental Sciences, University of East Anglia, Norwich, United Kingdom; and Fellow of the British Academy
Conservation

Ostrom, Elinor
Arthur F. Bentley Professor of Political Science; Co-Director of the Workshop in Political Theory and Policy Analysis, Indiana University, Bloomingtion; and Founding Director of the Center for the Study of Institutional Diversity, Arizona State University, Tempe
Commons

Pauly, Daniel
Professor and Director, Fisheries Centre, University of British Columbia, Vancouver, Canada
Fisheries

Penner, Joyce E.
Ralph J. Cicerone Distinguished University Professor of Atmospheric Science, University of Michigan, Ann Arbor
Aerosols

Peteet, Dorothy M.
Research Scientist, NASA Goddard Institute for Space Studies, New York; and Adjunct Senior Research Scientist, Lamont Doherty Earth Observatory, Palisades, New York
Younger Dryas

Peterson, Larry
Professor of Marine Geology and Geophysics, University of Miami, Florida
Climate Reconstruction

Pierrehumbert, Raymond
Louis Block Professor of Geophysical Sciences, University of Chicago, Illinois
Water Vapor

Plucknett, Donald L.
President and Principal Scientist, Agricultural Research and Development International, Annandale, Virginia (Deceased)
Pest Management

Posey, Darrell Addison
Director of the Working Group on Traditional Resource Rights, Mansfield College, Oxford, United Kingdom (Deceased)
Ethnobiology

Post, Wilfred M.
Senior Research Scientist, Oak Ridge National Laboratory, Tennessee
Carbon Cycle

Powell, Jane C.
Lecturer, School of Environmental Sciences, University of East Anglia, Norfolk, United Kingdom; and Director, Environmental Futures Ltd
Waste Management

Price, Martin F.
Director, Centre for Mountain Studies, Perth College, University of the Highlands and Islands, United Kingdom
Mountains

Pryde, Philip R.
Professor Emeritus of Geography, San Diego State University, California
Chernobyl

Ramani, Raja V.
Professor Emeritus of Mining and Geo Environmental Engineering, Pennsylvania State University, University Park
Mining

Ripley, Earle A.
Professor Emeritus of Plant Sciences, University of Saskatchewan, Saskatoon, Canada
Chlorofluorocarbons

Rolston, Holmes, III
University Distinguished Professor and Professor of Philosophy, Colorado State University, Fort Collins
Environmental Bioethics

Rosenblum, Daniel
Co-Founder, Carbon Tax Center; and Senior Attorney, Pace Law School Energy Project, New York, New York
Carbon Taxes

Rosier, Johanna
Senior Lecturer and Programme Coordinator, Resource and Environmental Planning Programme, Massey University, Palmerston North, New Zealand
Value of Parks and Preserves

Ruttenberg, Kathleen C.
Professor, Department of Oceanography, University of Hawai'i,
Phosphorus Cycle

Schlesinger, William H.
James B. Duke Professor Emeritus of Biogeochemistry, Duke University, Durham, North Carolina
Biogeochemical Cycles; Desertification; *and* Nitrogen Cycle

Schneider, Stephen H.
Professor of Biological Sciences, and Senior Fellow, Institute for International Studies; and Co-Director, Center for Environmental Science and Policy, Stanford University, California
Greenhouse Effect

Scott, Michael P.
Managing Director, Carbon Ventures, Environ, London
Emissions Trading

Seckler, David
Director, Winrock Water, Arlington, Virginia; and Former Director General of the International Water Management Institute, Battaramulla, Sri Lanka
Irrigation

Sedjo, Roger A.
Senior Fellow, Resources for the Future, Washington, D.C.
Deforestation

Self, Stephen
Professor of Volcanology, School of Ocean and Earth Science and Technology, University of Hawaii at Manoa, Honolulu
Volcanoes

Skeldon, Ronald
Professorial Fellow in Geography, University of Sussex, United Kingdom
Migrations

Smith, Keith
Professor Emeritus of Environmental Science, University of Stirling, Scotland
Natural Hazards

Soroos, Marvin S.
Professor of Political Science and Public Administration, North Carolina State University, Raleigh
Brundtland Commission

Sowers, Joseph K.
Market Analyst, U.S. Wheat Associates, Arlington, Virginia
Ecotaxation

Staley, Britt Childs
Research Analyst, International Climate Policy, World Resources Institute, Washington, D.C.
Transportation

Stephenson, Kurt
Professor of Resources and Environmental Economics, Department of Agricultural and Applied Economics, Virginia Polytechnic Institute and State University, Blacksburg
Ecotaxation

Stokes, Stephen
Vice President of Sustainability, AMR Research, Inc., Boston, Massachusetts
Proxy Data for Environmental Change

Stott, Philip
Professor Emeritus of Biogeography, School of Oriental and African Studies, University of London, United Kingdom
Savannas

Stroeve, Julienne
Research Scientist, National Snow and Ice Data Center, University of Colorado, Boulder
Arctic Sea-Ice

Swanson, Robert Lawrence
Director of the New York State Waste Reduction and Management Institute, State University of New York, Stony Brook
Ocean Disposal

Talbot, Lee M.
Professor of Environmental Science and Public Policy, George Mason University, Fairfax, Virginia
Exotic Species; *and* Wildlife Management

Thiele, Leslie Paul
Professor of Political Science, University of Florida, Gainesville
Environmental Accounting; *and* Environmental Movements

Thomas, David S. G.
Professor of Geography, University of Oxford, United Kingdom
Deserts

Thornbush, Mary J.
Senior Research Associate, School of Geography, University of Oxford, United Kingdom
Building Decay

Turco, Richard P.
Professor of Atmospheric Sciences and Founding Director, The UCLA Institute of the Environment, University of California, Los Angeles
Nuclear Winter

Turner, B. L., II
Director, Graduate School of Geography, and Milton P. and Alice C. Higgins Professor of Environment and Society, Clark University, Worcester, Massachusetts
Agriculture and Agricultural Land; Carrying Capacity; *and* Land Use

Turner, R. Kerry
Director, The Centre for Social and Economic Research on the Global Environment, and Professor of Environmental Science, University of East Anglia, Norfolk, United Kingdom
Intergenerational Equity

Vaughan, David G.
Principal Investigator, Glacial Retreat in Antarctica and Deglaciation of the Earth System, British Antarctic Survey
Antarctica and Climate Change

Victor, David G.
Director, Program on Energy and Sustainable Development, Professor of Law, and Freeman Spogli Institute for International Studies Senior Fellow, Stanford University, California
Kyoto Protocol; *and* Nongovernmental Organizations

Viles, Heather A.
Professor of Biogeomorphology and Heritage Conservation, University of Oxford, United Kingdom
Coastal Protection and Management; *and* Coastlines

Walbridge, Mark R.
Program Director, Ecosystem Science Cluster, Division of Environmental Biology, National Science Foundation, Arlington, Virginia; and Professor of Biology, West Virginia University, Morgantown
Ecosystems

Wallach, Bret
Professor of Geography, University of Oklahoma, Norman
Belief Systems

Warren, Rachel
Deputy Program Leader, Integrated Modelling, Tyndall Centre, School of Environmental Sciences, University of East Anglia, United Kingdom
Impacts of Climate Change

Weiss, Ray F.
Professor of Geochemistry, Scripps Institution of Oceanography, University of California, San Diego
Nitrous Oxide

Williams, Michael
Professor Emeritus of Geography, Distinguished Research Associate, University of Oxford, United Kingdom
Wetlands

Williamson, Douglas F.
Wildlife and Protected Area Management Officer, The United Nations Food and Agricultural Organization
International Human Dimensions Programme on Global Environmental Change (IHDP)

Wilson, Mary Elizabeth
Former Chief of Infectious Diseases, Mount Auburn Hospital; Associate Professor of Population and International Health, Harvard School of Public Health; and Associate Professor of Medicine, Harvard Medical School, Cambridge, Massachusetts
Disease

Zarin, Daniel J.
Professor of Tropical Forestry, University of Florida, Gainesville
Tropical Forests and Climate Change

Ziegler, Donald J.
Professor of Geography, Old Dominion University, Virginia Beach, Virginia
Urban Areas

Zelinsky, Wilbur
Professor Emeritus of Geography, Pennsylvania State University,
University Park
Global Change: Human Dimensions

Zwally, H. Jay
ICESat Project Scientist, Senior Research Scientist, Cryospheric Sciences
Branch, NASA Goddard Space Flight Center, Greenbelt, Maryland
Ice Sheets

ENTRIES BY SUBJECT

CATEGORIES

CONCEPTS OF GLOBAL CHANGE

EARTH AND ATMOSPHERIC SYSTEMS

Biosphere
Geologic Processes
Oceans
Atmosphere

CLIMATE CHANGE

RESOURCES

Water and Air
Land and Land Use
Energy and Minerals

HUMAN FACTORS

Human Populations
Agriculture and Fishing
Social, Cultural, and Ideological
  Factors
Industrial Activity
Hazards and Human Health

RESPONSES TO GLOBAL CHANGE

Scientific and Technological Tools
Economic and Social Policies

REGIONS AND CASE STUDIES

RESOURCES FOR CITIZENS

APPENDICES

ARTICLES

CONCEPTS OF GLOBAL CHANGE

Carbon Footprint
Carrying Capacity
Catastrophist-Cornucopian
  Debate
Commons
Conservation
Earth System Science
Ecological Footprint
Ecological Integrity
Economic Levels
Economics and Climate Change
Ecosytems
Ecotaxation
Energy and Environment
Energy Strategies
Environmental Accounting
Environmental Bioethics
Environmental Law
Environmental Performance
  Index
Ethics
Ethnobiology
Externalities
Extreme Events
Futurists
Global Change History
Human Dimensions of Global
  Change
Human Ecology
Human Impacts
Intergenerational Equity
Joint Implementation
Paleomagnetic Evidence of Crustal
  Movement
Pollution
Precautionary Principle
Resources
Stability
Technology and Environment
Tipping Points and Global
  Change
Tragedy of the Commons
Uncertainty
Vulnerability

EARTH AND ATMOSPHERIC SYSTEMS
Biosphere

Amazonia and Deforestation
Agriculture and Biodiversity
Biofuels
Biochemical Cycles
Biological Diversity
Biological Feedback
Biological Realms
Biomes
Boreal Forests and Climate Change
Carbon Cycle
Deforestation
Ethanol
Ethnobiology
Exotic Species
Extinctions of Animals
Fire and Global Warming
Forestation
Forests and Environmental
  Change
Heathlands
Hunting and Poaching
Mangroves
Nitrogen Cycle
Pest Management
Phosphorous Cycle
Reefs
Sulfur Cycle
Tropical Forests and Global
  Change
Wildlife Management

Geological Processes

Anthropogeomorphology
Building Decay
Deltas and Global Warming
Desert Dunes
Dust Storms
Emerging Coasts
Erosion

Extraterrestrial Impacts
Extreme Events
Glacier Retreat Since the Little Ice Age
Greenland Ice Sheet
Ice Sheets
Land Surface Processes
Loess
Mobile Earth
Permafrost
Rivers: Impacts of Climate Change
Sea Level Future
Volcanoes

Oceans

Arctic Sea Ice
Coastlines
Coastal Protection and Management
El Nino-Southern Oscillation
Emerging Coasts
Estuaries
Fisheries
Heinrich Events
Marginal Seas
North Atlantic Oscillation
Ocean Acidification
Ocean-Atmosphere Coupling
Ocean Disposal
Reefs
Sea Level Future
Thermohaline Circulation

Atmosphere

Acid Rain and Acid Deposition
Aerosols
Albedo
Carbon Cycle
Carbon Dioxide Emissions
Causes of Climate Change
Chlorofluorocarbons
El Nino-Southern Oscillation
Extreme Events
Global Dimming
Global Warming
Greenhouse Effect
Greenhouse Emissions
Greenhouse Gases
Nitrogen Cycle
Nitrous Oxide
North Atlantic Oscillation
Ocean-Atmosphere Coupling

Ozone
Ozone Fluctuations
Pollution
Snow Cover
Urban Climates
Weather Modification
Water Vapor

CLIMATE CHANGE

Aerosols
Antarctica and Climate Change
Arctic Sea Ice
Arctic Warming
Carbon Capture and Storage
Carbon Cycle
Carbon Dioxide Emissions
Carbon Emissions by Country
Carbon Footprint
Carbon Taxes
Causes of Climate Change
Climate Change and Societal
    Development
Climate Models and Uncertainty
Climate Reconstruction
Dansgaard-Oeschger Cycles
Dating Methods
Economics and Climate Change
Emissions Intensity
Emissions Trading
Extreme Events
Fire and Global Warming
Glacier Retreat Since the Little Ice Age
Global Dimming
Global Warming
Greenhouse Effect
Greenhouse Emissions
Greenhouse Gases
Greenland Ice Sheet
Heinrich Events
The Holocene
Impacts of Climate Change
IPCC: Intergovernmental Panel on
    Climate Change
Little Ice Age in Europe
Medieval Climatic Optimum
Nuclear Winter
Paleoclimate
Permafrost
Regional Patterns of Climate Change
Sea Level Future

Solar Variability and Climate Stability
Stabilizing Carbon Emissions
Thermohaline Circulation
Tipping Points and Global Change
Tropical Climate Change
Tropical Cyclones in a Warming
    World
Twentieth-Century Climate Change
Urban Climates
Water Vapor
Weather Modification
Younger Dryas

RESOURCES
Water and Air

Dams
Desalinization
Drought
Glacier Retreat Since the Little Ice Age
Ground Water
Ice Sheets
Irrigation
Lakes
Rivers: Impacts of Climate Change
Snow Cover
Watcr
Water Quality Trends

Land and Land Use

Agriculture and Agricultural Land
Amazonia and Deforestation
Desertification
Deserts
Deforestation
Dust Storms
Ethanol
Famine
Forestation
Forests and Environmental Change
Irrigation
Land Preservation
Land Reclamation
Land Use
Mediterranean Environments
Parks and Preserves
Salinization
Soils
Tropical Forests and Global Change
Wetlands
Wilderness and Biodiversity

Wilderness Debates
Wildlife Management

Energy and Mineral Resources

Biofuels
Coal
Coal Gasification
Coal Liquefaction
Chernobyl
Crude Oil Supply
Energy and Environment
Energy Strategies
Ethanol
Fossil Fuels
Methane
Methane Hydrates
Mining
National Energy Policy in the
    United States
Natural Gas
Nuclear Power
Nuclear Waste
Oil Sands
Renewable Sources of Energy
Resources
Synfuels

HUMAN FACTORS
Human Populations

Anthropogeomorphology
Human Impacts
Human Populations
Migration
Population Policy

Agriculture and Fishing

Agriculture and Agricultural Land
Agriculture and Biodiversity
Famine
Fisheries
Irrigation
Pest Management
Salinization
Soils
Water

Social, Cultural, and Ideological Factors

Belief Systems
Climate Change and Societal
    Development

Economic Levels
Economics and Environment
Environmental Accounting
Environmental Bioethics
Environmental Law
Environmental Movements
Environmental Performance Index
Ethics
Ethnobiology
Externalities
Globalization and Environment
Human Ecology
Insurance
Intergenerational Equity
Religion
Security and Environment
Sustainable Growth
Technology and Environment
Tourism
Trade and Environment
Transportation
United Nations Environment
    Programme
Urban Areas
Urban Climates
Urban Trends

Industrial Activity

Coal
Chemical Industry
Chemical Wonders
Chlorofluorocarbons
Externalities
Greenhouse Gases
Industrial Ecology
Mining
Nuclear Power

Hazards and Human Health

Building Decay
Chernobyl
Disease
Extraterrestrial Impacts
Fire and Global Warming
Natural Hazards
Nuclear Waste
Ocean Disposal
Pollution
Sea Level Future
Tropical Cyclones in a Warming World

Volcanoes
Waste Management

RESPONSES TO GLOBAL CHANGE
Scientific and Technical Tools

Carbon Capture and Storage
Climate Models and Uncertainty
Climate Reconstruction
Coal Gasification
Coal Liquefaction
Dating Methods
Dendrochronology
Desalination
Earth System Science
Environmental Impact
    Statements
Geographic Information Systems
Geoengineering
IPCC: Intergovernmental Panel on
    Climate Change
Pest Management
Proxy Data for Environmental
    Change
Regional Assessment
Stabilizing Carbon Emissions
Technology and Environment
Weather Modification

Economic and Social Policies

Bruntland Commision
Carbon Taxes
Economics and Climate Change
Ecotaxation
Emissions Trading
Environmental Impact Statements
Framework Convention on Climate
    Change
Industrial Ecology
International Geosphere-Biosphere
    Programme
International Human Dimensions
    Programme on Global
    Environmental Change
IPCC: Intergovernmental Panel on
    Climate Change
Kyoto Progress
Kyoto Protocol
Land Preservation
National Energy Policy in the United
    States

Nongovernmental Organizations
Regulation
Stabilizing Carbon Emissions
Sustainable Growth

REGIONS AND CASE STUDIES

Amazonia and Deforestation
Antarctica and Climate Change
Aral Sea
Arctic Sea Ice
Arctic Warming
Australia and Global Change
Chernobyl

Biomes
China and Environment
Coastlines
Coastal Protection and Management
Deserts
Estuaries
Greenland Ice Sheet
India and Environment Change
Little Ice Age in Europe
Mediterranean Environments
Mountains
Regional Patterns of Climate
  Change

Savanna
Tropical Forests and Climate Change

RESOURCES FOR CITIZENS

APPENDICES

Selected International Agreements
Nations Ranked by Environmental
  Performance Index, 2008
Nations Ranked According to Human
  Development Index, 2006
Total Greenhouse Gas Emissions and
  Emission Intensity, 2000

A

ACID RAIN AND ACID DEPOSITION

Acid rain is a colloquial term that refers to acids and associated compounds in rainfall, cloud water, snow, and airborne particles. Acid deposition is a more accurate and inclusive term. Acidity is the concentration of hydrogen ions in a substance; the negative logarithm of the hydrogen ion concentration (pH) is the common measure used for reporting the acidity of natural waters. Lower values correspond to greater acidity. Acid deposition has increased during this century as a result of human activity and has a variety of effects on natural and human systems, some of which have been well documented.

All rain is naturally somewhat acidic because the reaction between water and atmospheric carbon dioxide forms some carbonic acid:

$$H_2O + CO_2 \rightleftharpoons H_2CO_3 \tag{1}$$

The carbonic acid then partially dissociates, producing hydrogen ions and thus lowering the pH of precipitation to 5.65 (7.0 is neutral):

$$H_2CO_3 \rightleftharpoons H^+ + HCO_3^- \tag{2}$$

Acid rain refers to rainfall that has a pH lower than 5.65. Naturally generated acid compounds (from trees, fires and volcanoes, for example) can in some cases contribute to pH values as low as 5.0. Acid rain derived from human activity can result in rainfall with pH values as low as 2.6.

The precursors of acid deposition generated by human activity are the primary pollutants nitrogen oxide (NO) and sulfur dioxide (SO_2). Nitrogen oxides (NO_x) are released during combustion when atmospheric nitrogen (N_2) combines with atmospheric oxygen. The nitrogen contained in most fuels also combines with oxygen to form nitrogen oxide. When a compound containing sulfur is burned, the sulfur combines with atmospheric oxygen to form sulfur oxides. Mobile pollution sources such as automobiles generate one-third to one-half of nitrogen oxides. The combustion of coal, oil and other stationary sources (such as smelting) emits most of the sulfur oxides. Sulfur dioxide emissions vary according to the sulfur content of the fuel and the extent of pollution control at the source. Nitrogen oxide emissions vary according to the combustion temperature and the extent of pollution control.

Acid deposition is a more accurate term than acid rain because acids that are deposited from the atmosphere occur in a variety of forms: rain, snow, clouds, and as dry particles or vapors. In some cases, the amount of acidity contributed by dry deposition (fine particles, coarse particles, and vapors) can be greater than that contributed by precipitation. In a forest in Tennessee, dry deposition accounted for 55% of the hydrogen ions (acidity) and sulfate ions and 64% of the nitrate ions. There are two additional measures of the acid status of waters: acid-neutralizing capacity (ANC), which is roughly equivalent to alkalinity, and base-neutralizing capacity (BNC), which is roughly equivalent to acidity. Other substances contained in fuels are released during combustion and contribute to the overall or net acidity. For example, fly ash (noncombustible byproducts of combustion) usually has a high ANC and is released during combustion of oil and coal. In addition, coal and oil contain small quantities of lead, mercury, and other metals that are emitted during combustion. Although technically not part of acid deposition, fly ash and metals are often associated with the term acid rain.

In the presence of atmospheric oxygen and water, oxides of nitrogen and sulfur are transformed (primarily through oxidation) into nitric and sulfuric acid. Simplified equations for these reactions are:

$$2\,SO_2 + O_2 \rightarrow 2\,SO_3 \tag{3}$$

$$SO_3 + H_2O \rightarrow H_2SO_4 \rightarrow H^+ + HSO_4^- \rightleftharpoons 2\,H^+ + SO_4^{2-} \tag{4}$$

$$2\,NO + O_2 \rightarrow 2\,NO_2 \tag{5}$$

$$NO_2 + OH \rightarrow HNO_3 \rightarrow H^+ + NO_3^- \tag{6}$$

The conversion of the primary pollutants sulfur dioxide and nitrogen oxide into the secondary pollutants sulfuric acid and nitric acid occurs over a number of days. Once conversion occurs, the secondary pollutants are more readily washed out of the atmosphere and can contribute to acid deposition. If the reactions take place in a moving air mass, long-distance transport of the pollutants occurs. The reactions involving nitrogen occur more rapidly than those involving sulfur. Thus nitrogen compounds may be transported hundreds of kilometers while sulfur compounds may be transported more than a thousand kilometers before deposition occurs.

In the past four decades, many scientists have focused their research on the acid and sulfate compounds in acid deposition; more recently, nitrate has also been studied.

HISTORY

Acid deposition occurs whenever the precursors SO_2 and NO are present in the atmosphere. Thus acid rain has existed for as long as there have been lightning, forest fires, and volcanoes. But the term "acid rain" generally refers to excess acidity in wet and dry deposition caused by human activity. The earliest documented acid rain events occurred in London and Manchester, England, and Pittsburgh, Pennsylvania. Robert Angus Smith is usually credited with first describing acid rain near Manchester, in 1852. Similar events were probably occurring in many other cities around the world at this time. Referring to the contemporary scientific literature, Eriksson (1952) describes the sulfur concentration of rainfall for a variety of locations in Britain, France, Germany, Russia, Japan, and New Zealand during the late 1800s and early 1900s. Since all of these locations except some parts of Russia had sulfur levels above those of New Zealand, Eriksson described them as being impacted by "atmospheric pollution." Herman and Gorham (1957) first reported elevated sulfur and hydrogen ion concentrations in rainfall. Cogbill and Likens (1974) published the first thorough description of acid precipitation in the northeastern United States. They showed that prevailing winds carry acids from midwestern states toward the northeast. They also generated a series of pH isopleths (lines of equal pH) superimposed on a map, which has been widely used (Figure 1A).

Later studies showed that transboundary pollution has occurred from the United States to Canada. Similar transboundary transport has occurred in Europe, where the prevailing winds carry pollutants from England, Germany, and the Netherlands to Scandinavia (Figure 2).

During the 1970s and 1980s, acid deposition received a great deal of attention and was blamed for causing much environmental damage in many parts of the industrialized world. Persuasive evidence for acid rain damage has been found in many fewer systems than were originally thought, and today acid rain receives much less attention.

EXTENT

The pH isopleths (lines of equal pH) shown in Figure 1 document the extent of acid deposition in Europe and North America. There have been reports of regional acid deposition in West Africa, Japan, South America, and many areas in the former Soviet Union (Figure 2). It is reasonable to expect that there will be acid deposition downwind of any industrial activity or large concentration of motorized vehicles.

IMPACTS OF ACID DEPOSITION

There are many hypothetical or confirmed pathways and mechanisms by which acid deposition may affect aquatic and forest ecosystems, agricultural systems, human health, buildings and structures, and visibility. For some of these, it is important to distinguish between direct and indirect effects. In aquatic systems, for example, the lowering of the pH of lake water is a primary effect; the mobilization of toxic aluminum that results from the decrease in the pH is a secondary, or indirect, effect.

AQUATIC ECOSYSTEMS

Acid deposition has led to the documented acidification of lakes and streams in portions of northeastern North America,

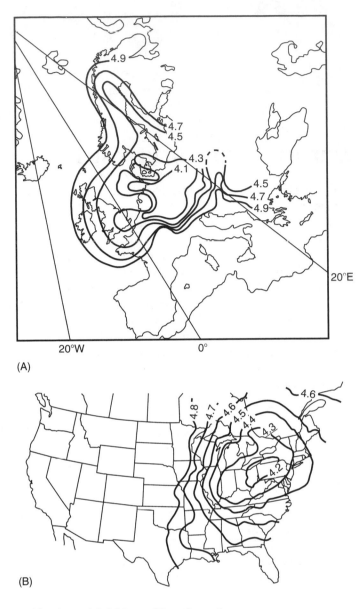

Acid Rain and Acid Deposition. FIGURE 1.

Long-term, volume-weighted averages of pH in precipitation in (A) Europe, 1978–1982, and (B) Eastern North America, 1980–1984

(After Spiro and Stigliani, 1996, p. 202.)

Scandinavia, and the United Kingdom. Decreases in the diversity of fish and crustacean species have been observed in acidified freshwater lakes and streams. Species diversity changes most between pH 3 and pH 6. Low pH interferes with the osmotic balance of certain aquatic organisms and can release metals into the water through a process called mobilization. These metals are normally bound in complex compounds in soils and sediments. Since the mobilization of many metals (such as aluminum and mercury) in water also affects the physiological function of aquatic organisms, it is not clear whether species changes are a direct or indirect effect of acid deposition.

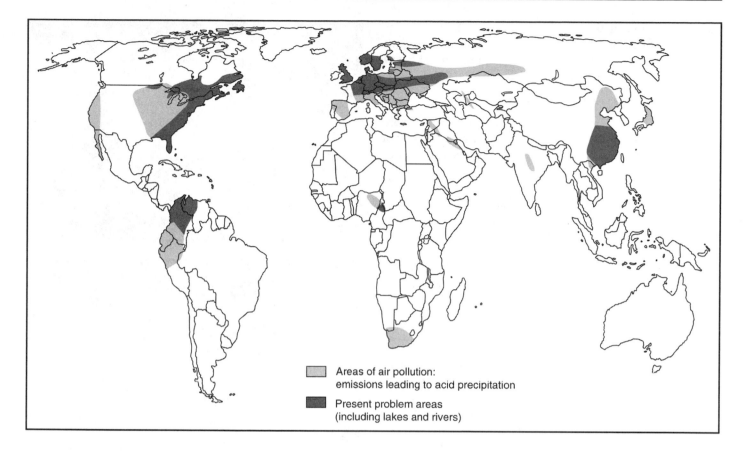

Acid Rain and Acid Deposition. Figure 2. Worldwide Extent of Acid Deposition and Acid Precursors.

(Adapted from Kaufman and Franz, 1993, p. 263.)

Differing responses in adults and juveniles have been observed in many species. Furthermore, a decrease in pH can affect the food sources of a fish before it affects the fish itself, further complicating the distinction between direct and indirect effects of acid deposition.

FOREST ECOSYSTEMS

Sulfur dioxide, a precursor to acid deposition, can affect plants directly by absorption through stomata. Sulfur dioxide is usually found close to a combustion source or smelter.

There are few observable effects of acid deposition on individual trees and seedlings at typical levels of acid deposition in North America. However, forest ecosystems are much more complex than individual trees, and we know little about the long-term effects of acid deposition on forests. In North America, there is only one widely accepted effect of acid rain on forests: a component of acid deposition—probably sulfate—has been shown to reduce the cold tolerance of red spruce at high elevations in the Northeast. This has led to a greater incidence of freezing injury to red spruce, seen especially from the 1960s to the 1980s. Acid deposition is believed

to have acidified some soils, indirectly affecting forests in central and eastern Europe. A lower pH in rainfall could lead to the mobilization of aluminum and accelerated chemical weathering of rock underlying soil. Excess sulfate deposition is believed to lead to excess leaching of sulfate (a mobile anion) and of cations such as calcium and magnesium. Some have considered this indirect effect—the mobilization of cation nutrients—to be more serious than any direct effect of acid deposition in forested ecosystems.

AGRICULTURAL SYSTEMS

Acid deposition is not one of the major pollutants affecting crop growth or yield. Most crop species are much more sensitive to ozone than acid deposition. Agricultural crops are highly managed and, in most cases, a farmer can compensate for any effects of acid deposition with additional fertilizer. Although there may be a financial cost, ambient levels of acidity are not known to have adverse effects on crop growth or yield, except for crops immediately adjacent to major emission sources. In some cases, nitrogen and sulfur components of acid deposition may even act as a fertilizer.

HUMAN HEALTH

Direct effects of acid deposition occur when asthma sufferers are exposed to sulfur dioxide or sulfuric acid vapor. Only areas in the immediate vicinity of large sources of sulfur pollution are of concern. In such areas, sulfuric acid and acid aerosol exposure can impair the respiratory function of children, the elderly, and those with preexisting health problems. Nitrogen oxide contributes to the formation of tropospheric ozone, which is also a respiratory irritant.

BUILDINGS AND OTHER STRUCTURES

Acid deposition has an adverse impact on metal-based and calcium carbonate (limestone and marble) building materials. The overall reaction between calcium-carbonate rock and acid precipitation is:

$$CaCO_3 + H_2O + CO_2 \rightarrow Ca^{2+} + 2HCO_3^- \qquad (7)$$

The water and carbon dioxide react as shown in equations (1) and (2) to create acidity (H^+). The calcium carbonate consumes H^+ and generates Ca^{2+}. Acids affect most exposed painted surfaces, possibly including automobile finishes. Some stone structures, such as the Acropolis in Athens, have deteriorated as a result of reactions with gaseous sulfur dioxide (SO_2).

VISIBILITY

Sulfuric acid and sulfate aerosols impair visibility significantly in many parts of the industrial world. This impaired visibility, sometimes called sulfate haze, occurs in dry climates and can be exacerbated by humidity. Annual haziness in the eastern United States increased by 25% between 1950 and 1985. Increasing haze in the eastern United States is strongly associated with increasing sulfur dioxide emission. Figure 3 illustrates the extent to which visibility has been reduced in the eastern United States. Ammonium nitrate, which can be formed from nitrogen oxide emissions, also contributes to impaired visibility.

ACID DEPOSITION IN A CHANGING GLOBAL ENVIRONMENT

Sulfate aerosol is the component of atmospheric acidity that most directly influences global climate. There is strong evidence that sulfate aerosols scatter solar radiation and change the reflective properties of clouds, both of which exert a cooling influence on global climate (Charlson et al., 1992). However, the continuing reduction in sulfate aerosols associated with the introduction of additional pollution control measures should cause a steady decrease in the influence of sulfate aerosol on global climate. [See Global Dimming.]

While acid deposition has been present in most industrialized areas for much of the twentieth century, there is good reason to believe that it has varied in its severity. During the early and middle years of the century, factories and power plants emitted more acid precursors, but they also emitted fly ash containing basic compounds that partially neutralized acidity. As factories increased their pollution-control measures, they emitted considerably less fly ash. The ANC of the emissions was therefore much less, and most acidity was neutralized by its reaction with soil minerals. In addition, as urban areas became more polluted, taller smokestacks were constructed. These taller stacks reduced urban air pollution, but increased the amount of nitrogen and sulfur oxides that was transported to distant areas.

A

B

Acid Rain and Acid Deposition. Figure 3. Clear visibility (A) and impaired visibility (B) over Grand Canyon National Park, Arizona.

(Photograph courtesy of Holle Photography.)

In the United States and many other industrialized countries, legislators have focused on sulfur rather than nitrogen emissions, in part because sulfuric acid, with its two hydrogen ions (compared to one in nitric acid) has been deemed to have greater potential for contributing to acidification. As a result, sulfur emissions in the United States (and other developed countries) have dropped since 1970, whereas nitrogen emissions have remained constant or increased during that time. The seriousness of acid rain caused by sulfur dioxide emissions in the western industrialized nations peaked in the mid-1970s or early 1980s. Changes in industrial technology, in the nature of economic activity, and in legislation caused the output of SO_2 in Britain to decrease by 35% between 1974 and 1990. However, there has been a shift in the geographical sources of sulfate emissions, so that whereas in 1980 60% of global emissions were from the U.S., Canada and Europe, by 1995 only 38% of world emissions originated from these regions (Smith et al., 2001). There are also increasing controls on the emission of nitrogen oxides in vehicle exhaust emissions, although emissions of NO$_x$ in Europe have not declined. A similar picture emerges from Japan (Seto et al., 2002) where sulfate emissions have fallen because of emission controls, whereas nitrate emissions have increased with an increase in vehicular traffic. This means that the geography of acid rain may change: it may become less serious in the developed world but increase in places like China, where economic development will continue to be powered by the burning of low-quality sulphur-rich coal in enormous quantities.

Since the 1980s, investigators in Europe and North America have begun to consider more closely the nitrogen component of acid deposition. The productivity of many terrestrial systems is limited by nitrogen, so it is often thought that the nitrogen added by air pollution may be beneficial. There is evidence from a number of ecosystems, however, that too much nitrogen has begun to impair ecosystem function. This nitrogen-saturation hypothesis has gained much attention in recent years.

As the global environment changes, acid deposition and its effects may change as well. For example, in a warmer climate, the conversion of sulfur oxides to sulfuric acid in the atmosphere might occur more rapidly, in which case acid rain may be offset and acid deposition distributed more widely. Greater rainfall volumes tend to dilute the acidity in rainwater, so regions subject to greater rainfall might receive less acidic rainfall. These projections are highly tentative and might be considered third-order effects of global change. To date, they have received little scientific attention.

BIBLIOGRAPHY

Barker, J.R., and D.T. Tingey, eds. *Air Pollution Effects on Biodiversity*. New York: Van Nostrand Reinhold, 1992.

Boyle, R.H., and R.A. Boyle. *Acid Rain*. New York: Schocken Books, 1983.

Charlson, R. J., et al. "Climate Forcing by Anthropogenic Aerosols." *Science* 255 (1992), 423–430.

Cogbill, C.V., and G.E. Likens. "Acid Precipitation in the Northeastern United States." *Water Resources Research* 10 (1974), 1133–1137.

Drabløs, D., and A. Tollan, eds. *Ecological Impact of Acid Precipitation*. Oslo: SNSF Project, 1980.

Eriksson, E. "Composition of Atmospheric Precipitation. II. Sulfur, Chloride, Iodine Compounds." *Tellus* 4 (1952), 280–303.

Godbold, D.L., and A. Hüttermann, eds. *Effects of Acid Rain on Forest Processes*. New York: Wiley-Liss, 1994.

Heij, G.J., and J.W. Erisman, eds. *Acid Rain Research: Do We Have Enough Answers?* Amsterdam and New York: Elsevier, 1995.

Herman, F.A., and E. Gorham. "Total Mineral Material, Acidity, Sulfur and Nitrogen in Rain and Snow at Kentville, Nova Scotia." *Tellus* 9 (1957), 180–183.

Irving, P. M., ed. *Acidic Deposition: State of Science and Technology*. Washington, D.C.: U.S. National Acid Precipitation Assessment Program, 1991.

Kaufman, D.G., and C.M. Franz. *Biosphere 2000: Protecting Our Global Environment*. Dubuque, Iowa: Kendall/Hunt, 2000.

Lindberg, S.E., et al. "Atmospheric Deposition and Canopy Interactions of Major Ions in a Forest." *Science* 231 (1986), 141–145. DOI: 10.1126/science.231.4734.141

Lucier, A.A., and S.G. Haines, eds. *Mechanisms of Forest Response to Acidic Deposition*. New York: Springer, 1990.

National Research Council. *Acid Deposition: Atmospheric Processes in Eastern North America*. Washington, D.C.: National Academy Press, 1983.

Rodhe, H., and R. Herrera, eds. *Acidification in Tropical Countries*. Chichester, U.K. and New York: Wiley, 1988.

Schindler, D. W. "Effects of Acid Rain on Freshwater Ecosystems." *Science* 239 (1988), 149–157.

Seto, S., et al. "Annual and Seasonal Trends in Chemical Composition of Precipitation in Japan during 1989–1998." *Atmospheric Environment*, 36 (2002) 3505–3517.

Smith, S. J., H. Pitcher, and T. M. L. Wigley. "Global and Regional Anthropogenic Sulfur Dioxide Emissions." *Global and Planetary Change* 29 (2001), 99–119.

Spiro, T. G., and W. M. Stigliani. *Chemistry of the Environment*. Upper Saddle River, N.J.: Prentice Hall, 1996.

U.S. Environmental Protection Agency. *National Air Pollutant Emission Trends, 1900–1995*. Research Triangle Park, N.C.: EPA, 1996.

—ANDREW J. FRIEDLAND

ACID RAIN IN ASIA

There has been progress in controlling sulfur dioxide emissions in many developed countries, but the problem is growing rapidly in Asia where energy use has surged, and sulfur-rich coal and oil are prevalent. Sulfur dioxide emissions in Asia could soar from 40 million metric tons per year in 1990 to 110 million metric tons per year by 2020 as Asian economic growth continues.

In Europe and North America, it is nitrogen oxides that are intractable: their levels, being closely linked to vehicles and electric power generation, have not fallen appreciably since 1980.

BIBLIOGRAPHY

Downing, R., R. Ramankutty, and J. Shah. *RAINS-ASIA: An Assessment Model for Acid Deposition in Asia*. Washington, D.C.: World Bank, p. 11, 1997.

Organisation for Economic Co-operation and Development. *Environmental Data Compendium*. Paris: OECD, 1997.

Swedish Secretariat. "The Swedish Secretariat on Acid Rain." *Acid News* 5 (1996), 14.

World Resources Institute. *World Resources 1998–99*. New York and Oxford: WRI, 1998, pp. 181–183.

— DAVID J. CUFF

AEROSOLS

An aerosol is a suspension of solid or liquid particles in a gas. By this standard, cloud droplets are technically aerosols, but it is common in the atmospheric sciences to use the term to refer to the fine particles in the atmosphere. These may be solid or liquid, and they are considered distinct from drops primarily because of their size. Drops grow to roughly 10–20 microns in radius and exist in regions of the atmosphere that have a relative humidity near or above 100%; aerosols are generally less than 10 microns in radius. Larger aerosols can be lifted into the air—soil grains lifted in dust storms, for example, or the bursting of whitecap bubbles or direct injection of drops creating particles of sea salt—but these larger particles are heavy enough to fall back to the surface within a few hours, so that they have no large-scale effects on the atmosphere.

ROLE OF AEROSOLS IN CLOUD FORMATION

Aerosols are intimately involved in the formation of clouds. It is generally difficult to form a cloud directly from water vapor—a process termed homogeneous nucleation—because water vapor molecules must first form clusters of sufficient size so that further growth is rapid. The formation of these clusters is generally very slow. In the atmosphere, water vapor condenses on aerosol particles. This process can occur under subsaturated conditions (relative humidity less than 100%) if the aerosol particle contains compounds that attract water and therefore decrease the equilibrium vapor pressure of water over the particle. However, as the relative humidity of an air parcel is raised above 100%, there comes a point at which the growth of the particle by condensation of vapor becomes unstable, allowing the particle to continue to take up water until the relative humidity is reduced again to near 100%. This is the mechanism by which warm cloud droplets form in the atmosphere. The particles that facilitate this process are called cloud condensation nuclei.

Ice clouds, on the other hand, may form by the deposition of vapor directly on particles (termed deposition ice nuclei), by the freezing of solution drops (termed homogeneous ice nuclei), or by the freezing induced by the presence of a solid particle (termed heterogeneous ice nuclei). The particles that are able to form ice nuclei are either very rare or require high supersaturations to reach the critical point at which ice nucleation occurs. Large regions of the atmosphere could therefore form ice clouds—that is, they have relative humidity above the saturated vapor pressure over ice—but do not do so because they lack sufficient nuclei of the appropriate type. Because the relative humidity of vapor over ice is less than the relative humidity of vapor over liquid water, once ice begins to form, ice clouds may grow rapidly from supercooled water clouds.

SOURCES AND SINKS OF AEROSOLS

Particles may be composed of sulfate, nitrate, organics, compounds associated with soil dust, compounds associated with the sea-salt aerosol, ammonia, soot or black carbon, and trace metals. The total trace metal mass is small and is therefore ignored in the following discussion. The sources of these components in the aerosol vary significantly with region. Thus, over the Amazon and in desert areas of the western United States, organic carbon is the most abundant fine-aerosol-particle component, whereas in rural continental areas of the eastern United States, sulfate accounts for more than 50% of the fine-particle mass.

Table 1 presents global average estimates for the sources of the atmospheric aerosol. The fine-particle fraction of the atmospheric aerosol (defined as that portion with a diameter of less than 2 microns) predominates and is, therefore, the most important to quantify in order to determine the effects of aerosol on the radiation balance and on clouds. Aerosol sources may be divided into gas-phase sources and primary particulate sources. Gas-phase sources are aerosol-precursor emissions that are converted through photochemical reactions to products that condense to the particulate phase. Primary particulate sources are emitted as particles at or near the source. The gas-phase sources include sulfate, nitrate, ammonia, and organic gases. Each of these has sources in both natural and anthropogenic gases. Estimates of the magnitude of the anthropogenic and natural sources, based on current estimates in the literature, are included in the table. Some of the aerosol components are volatile—that is, they exist in both the aerosol phase and the gas phase and adjust their concentrations in the aerosol phase, depending on the local aerosol concentrations of nonvolatile species as well as the local vapor pressure of the vapor compound. These components include nitrate, ammonium, the chloride in sea salt, and some organic compounds. As a result, the table assumes that approximately half of the airborne portion of nitric acid (HNO_3) is found as aerosol NO_3^-, and that half of the sources of ammonia (NH_3) become aerosol ammonium (NH_4^+). Volatile chloride and volatile organics were not considered in Table 1.

Primary particles are those that are associated with smoke from fires, wind-borne dust, sea salt from direct injection and bursting of bubbles, and biogenic particles (fungi, spores, plant waxes from leaf surfaces, etc.). Fires originate mainly from anthropogenic activity (burning for agriculture, to clear land, burning of fossil fuels). Dust outbreaks (Goudie and Middleton, 2006) have also been associated with anthropogenic activity (e.g., vegetation removal and desertification). Tegen and Fung (1995) estimated that about 50% of their total dust-source strength (emissions in teragrams per year) was associated with land-use changes. For

TABLE 1. Sources of Tropospheric Aerosols (radius less than 2 microns)

Type	Source Strength (teragrams per year)	
	Anthropogenic	Natural
Gas phase sources		
Sulfates	120	55
Ammonium	21	5
Nitrates	30	22
Organic aerosols	—	30
Primary particuate emissions		
Biomass burning for land clearing and agriculture	50	
Fossil fuel burning, industry	35	
Domestic fuels and bagasse burning	11	
Dust	160 (~750 for r < 10 microns)	160 (~750 for r < 10 microns)
Sea salt		140 (~12,000 for r < 10 microns)
Biogenic		50
Total (fine-particle fraction)	**430 (48 percent)**	**460 (52 percent)**

dust and sea salt, the table shows an estimate of the total source strength as well as that portion in the fine-particle fraction.

Nearly 50% of the total emissions of fine aerosol particles appear to derive from anthropogenic sources. This estimate is a factor of two to five times larger than previous estimates of the role of anthropogenic aerosols in the aerosol particle budget (see, for example, Prospero et al., 1983), in part because in the current analysis the fine-particle fraction of the aerosol mass has been emphasized. The estimates for all sources in Table 1 clearly demonstrate that atmospheric aerosol sources have a large anthropogenic component and may have changed over time.

When either liquid or ice clouds form precipitation, they also remove the aerosol from the atmosphere. This is the primary sink of atmospheric aerosols, although deposition, wherein aerosols are brought into contact with the surface and remain there, is also a (relatively minor) removal pathway.

ROLE OF AEROSOLS IN CLIMATE

Aerosols are important to climate because they scatter and absorb radiation in the atmosphere and because they change the microphysical structure and possibly the lifetime of clouds within the atmosphere. Radiation in the atmosphere is divided into solar and thermal radiation. The former has wavelengths up to about 4 microns, while the latter has wavelengths of 4–20 microns. Because most aerosols are smaller than 10 microns and because aerosol particles interact most strongly with wavelengths near their size, most of the scattering and absorption of radiation by aerosols takes place in the solar spectrum. An exception to this rule applies to the larger dust particles that interact strongly with both solar and infrared radiation. The scattering of solar radiation acts to cool the planet, while absorption of solar radiation by aerosols warms the air directly instead of allowing that sunlight to be absorbed by the surface. When sunlight is absorbed by the surface, the heat is transferred back to the atmosphere either by thermal (heat) radiation, by conduction of heat, or by evaporation of water which, when it condenses, releases the heat back to the atmosphere.

As a result of their abundance and the size of droplets, clouds both scatter solar radiation and absorb thermal radiation. Optical depth is a measure of the strength of interaction of clouds with radiation. Small changes in the size of cloud droplets, especially for clouds of intermediate optical depth, greatly increase their scattering of solar radiation while having little effect on their interaction with thermal radiation. The warm liquid clouds at low altitude mainly scatter solar radiation, while the ice clouds at high altitude mainly absorb thermal radiation. Thus, the former act mainly to cool the planet, while the latter act to warm it. Therefore, changes in aerosol concentrations over time have the potential to influence greatly the radiation balance, and therefore the climate (Ramanathan et al., 2007).

ICE-CORE RECORD OF AEROSOLS

Ice cores provide a proxy record of past climate changes, gas concentrations, and aerosol concentrations (Anderson et al., 2007, sections 2.4 and 9.3). Aerosol concentrations are recorded directly within the falling snow because these aerosols were either condensation nuclei or ice nuclei. The snow falls and is eventually transformed to ice under the pressure of overlying snow. As this compaction takes place, the porous snow and firn (partly consolidated snow) trap pockets of air which contain a record of past air composition. Oxygen-18 is the heavy isotope of oxygen, with a molecular weight of 18 instead of the normal 16. D is the heavy isotope of hydrogen, with a molecular weight of 2 instead of the normal 1. Because the heavy-isotope content of precipitation decreases as the condensation temperature decreases, the record of $HD^{16}O$ and $H_2^{18}O$ relative to $H_2^{16}O$ provides a proxy for the temperature at which the precipitation formed, which itself is a proxy for the atmospheric temperature, if the cycle of water evaporation, transport, and removal remained relatively constant over the period of interest.

Ice-core records going back some 800,000 years have been obtained from both Antarctica (EPICA Community Members, 2004; Jouzel et al., 2007) and Greenland. Each differs in the type of information it provides: Greenland is near two continents, and the proximity of human activity has allowed aerosols associated with the growth of industrial and anthropogenic activities to be recorded. Antarctica, on the other hand, is surrounded by ocean, and allows a study of cycles in natural aerosol concentrations. Unfortunately, it has been shown that at sites with low snow accumulation rates (such as Antarctica), the deposition of aerosols such as dust, sea salt, and sulfur is not closely tied to their concentration in falling snow because a variable amount of dry deposition leads to an impure signal in the snow. Thus a 10°C decrease in local temperature associated with the last ice age may have led to a drier atmosphere and to a reduction in the snow-accumulation rate. This would be recorded by roughly doubled concentrations of aerosols within the ice core without any associated increase in atmospheric concentrations. Nevertheless, concentrations of insoluble species such as dust were more than ten times higher during the last glacial maximum than they are now. In addition, sea salt concentrations were much higher during the last two glacial periods than they are now. These results have been interpreted as due either to higher wind speeds during glacial maxima or to a more efficient north-south transport in the Northern Hemisphere. In Antarctica, similar increases during the last glacial maximum have been interpreted as being associated with an expansion of arid areas and exposure of the continental shelves. Another aerosol species that was enhanced in Antarctica was sulfate. Because a similar enhancement of methane sulfonic acid (MSA)—which is associated with marine biological sources of sulfate—was also recorded, it is thought that the Antarctic increase was due to enhanced biological activity during the glacial maximum. No evidence of an increase in biological activity is evident in the ice cores from Greenland, however.

The increases in sea salt and sulfate aerosols would have led to additional cooling during ice ages (Overpeck et al., 1996). The increased dust, because of its ability to absorb solar and thermal radiation, could actually lead to regional warming events. This absorption might help to explain the abrupt warming events that took place as the glacial era was ending.

Changes in the concentrations of the various ions in ice cores have been used as indicators of sudden events of large magnitude. Thus volcanic events, which are a natural source of sulfate aerosol in the stratosphere and the troposphere, are recorded by large enhancements of sulfate, while forest fires are recorded by enhancements to ammonium, formate, and nitrate. If these events are screened out of the record for the last two hundred years, it can be seen that the Greenland ice core has substantially increased concentrations of sulfate (as well as nitrate), whereas the Antarctic ice core does not. The record for sulfate aerosol in Greenland is in broad agreement with the increasing emissions of anthropogenic sulfur dioxide. Decreased concentrations recorded since 1980 have been interpreted as being due to the reductions in emissions that have taken place in Europe and the United States. [*See* Acid Rain and Acid Deposition.]

ROLE OF AEROSOLS IN RECENT AND PROJECTED CLIMATE CHANGE

Because anthropogenic aerosols represent a relatively large fraction of the total source strength, it is important to try to understand the possible influence of these recently increasing aerosols on past and future climates. One method for estimating their possible climatic influence is to estimate the radiative forcing associated with the anthropogenic fraction of aerosol. Radiative forcing is the change in outgoing radiation at the top of the troposphere caused by a specific change in composition. It gives a first-order measure of the long-term steady-state response of the climate, because the global average change in surface temperature is related approximately linearly to the radiative forcing. Thus,

$$F \Delta T_s \approx \lambda \Delta F,$$

where λ is defined as the climate sensitivity and ΔF is the radiative forcing. The climate sensitivity depends on the change in water vapor (the most abundant greenhouse gas in the atmosphere), clouds, sea ice cover and snow, and may vary considerably between different climate models with different representations of physical processes.

Radiative forcing is only an approximate measure of climate effects. It relies on the assumption that the surface temperature change is effectively communicated throughout the troposphere by convective and radiative processes. However, because emissions into specific regions can alter the vertical profile of temperature and/or the response of clouds in different regions, the assumption is only approximately valid. Nevertheless, it provides a first-order estimate of the relative impacts of different emissions. Radiative forcing by aerosols may be compared to the forcing from greenhouse gases and from changes in solar radiation over the past one hundred years. These latter forcings were estimated as about 2.5 watts per square meter (W m^{-2}) in a recent scientific assessment.

Recent estimates for the direct forcing by anthropogenic sulfate aerosols and carbonaceous aerosols are between −0.3 and −0.9 W m^{-2} for sulfate, between −0.15 and −0.25 W m^{-2} for biomass aerosols (domestic fuels and land clearing), and between +0.15 and +0.2 W m^{-2} for fossil fuel and industrial sources of organic and soot aerosols. No specific estimates of climate forcing from anthropogenic nitrates or anthropogenic ammonia are yet available, but some authors consider that forcing by these aerosol compounds is small relative to the forcing aerosols. Anthropogenic sources of dust aerosols are estimated to have a global forcing of +0.09 W m^{-2} according to Tegen et al. (1996). The climate forcing associated with these estimates could offset a substantial fraction of the warming associated with greenhouse gases, and several climate models have simulated the effect of sulfate aerosols to show that the record and pattern of temperature change are consistent with the fact that the cooling caused by sulfate aerosols is mainly in the Northern Hemisphere. If the ratio of aerosol emissions to greenhouse-gas emissions remains constant, however, these impacts should decrease in the future, because the short lifetime of aerosols ensures that the future buildup of concentrations will not keep pace with the buildup of long-lived greenhouse gases.

While estimates of climate forcing by direct reflection and absorption of radiation are reasonably straightforward, estimating the indirect effects of aerosols has proven much more difficult. This is mainly because the indirect effects depend on natural as well as anthropogenic sources, the state of mixing of the aerosol components (i.e., whether the aerosol formed is a new cloud condensation nucleus or whether the aerosol adheres to a preexisting aerosol), and the capability of large-scale models to treat changes in cloudiness in response to increases in anthropogenic aerosols. The state of mixing has been shown to lead to uncertainties ranging from −0.4 to −1.5 W m^{-2} in forcing by sulfate aerosols associated with changes in drop size distributions (Chuang et al., 1997) and to uncertainties ranging from −1.1 to −4.8 W m^{-2} in forcing by sulfate aerosols associated with changes in cloudiness (Lohmann and Feichter, 1997). Changes in droplet concentrations due to carbonaceous aerosols from biomass burning, fossil fuels, and industry might also lead to large estimates of negative forcing (Penner et al., 1996). These estimates may be far too large, but if they are proven to be correct, then our explanations of recent climate changes and the match between the historical record of temperature change and the record of radiation forcing will need to be altered.

Finally, aerosols from aircraft have possibly been associated with increases in cirrus clouds (Jensen and Toon, 1997; Stordal et al., 2005). If cirrus cloudiness were to increase as a result of aircraft emissions, the likely impact would be a positive forcing leading to a warming, because the net influence of cirrus is to warm the planet. The radiative forcing of cirrus increase caused by aircraft emissions was estimated in the range of 0 to 0.02 W m^{-2}.

[*See also* Albedo; Dust Storms; Gaia Hypothesis; Global Dimming; Global Warming; Nuclear Winter; Pollution; Sulfur Cycle; *and* Volcanoes.]

BIBLIOGRAPHY

GENERAL REFERENCES

Chuang, C.C., et al. "An Assessment of the Radiative Effects of Anthropogenic Sulfate." *Journal of Geophysical Research* 102 (1997), 3761–3778.

Goudie, A.S., and N.J. Middleton. *Desert Dust in the Global System*. Berlin and New York: Springer, 2006. Includes a discussion of the role of dust in climate change and of the history of dust loadings in the atmosphere at different time scales.

Houghton, J.T., et al., eds. *Climate Change 1995: The Science of Climate Change: Contribution of Working Group I to the Second Assessment Report of the Intergovernmental Panel on Climate Change*. Cambridge: Cambridge University Press, 1996. A thorough summary.

Jensen, E., and O.B. Toon. "The Potential Impact of Soot Particles from Aircraft Exhaust on Cirrus Clouds." *Geophysical Research Letters* 24.3 (1997), 249–252.

Jouzel J., et al. "Orbital and Millennial Antarctic Climate Variability over the Past 800,000 Years." *Science* 317 (2007), 793–796. DOI: 10.1126/science.1141038.

Legrand, M., and P. Mayewski. "Glaciochemistry of Polar Ice Cores: A Review." *Reviews of Geophysics* 35 (1997), 219–243. A summary of what has been learned about aerosols and gases from ice cores.

Lohmann, U., and J. Feichter. "Impact of Sulfate Aerosols on Albedo and Lifetime of Clouds: A Sensitivity Study with the ECHAM-4 GCM." *Journal of Geophysical Research* 102 (1997), 13685–13700.

Penner, J.E. "Atmospheric Chemistry and Air Quality." In *Changes in Land Use and Land Cover: A Global Perspective*, edited by W.B. Meyer and B.L. Turner II, pp. 175–209. Cambridge and New York: Cambridge University Press, 1994. Sources and sinks of greenhouse gases and aerosols affecting atmospheric chemistry and climate.

Penner, J.E., C.C. Chuang, and C. Liousse. "The Contribution of Carbonaceous Aerosols to Climate Change." In *Nucleation and Atmospheric Aerosols 1996*, edited by M. Kulmala and P.E. Wagner, pp. 759–769. Oxford, U.K., and Tarrytown, N.Y.: Pergamon, 1996.

Prospero, J.M., et al. "The Atmospheric Aerosol System: An Overview." *Reviews of Geophysics and Space Physics* 21 (1983), 1607–1629.

Ramanathan, V., et al. "Warming Trends in Asia Amplified by Brown Cloud Solar Absorption." *Nature* 448 (2007), 575–578. DOI: 10.1038/nature06019.

Stordal F., et al. "Is There a Trend in Cirrus Cloud Cover Due to Aircraft Traffic?" *Atmospheric Chemistry and Physics* 5 (2005), 2155–2162.

Tegen, I., and I. Fung. "Contribution to the Atmospheric Mineral Aerosol Load from Land Surface Modification." *Journal of Geophysical Research* 100 (1995), 18707–18726.

Tegen, I., A. Lacis, and I. Fung. "The Influence on Climate Forcing of Mineral Aerosols from Disturbed Soils." *Nature* 380 (1996), 419–422. DOI: 10.1038/380419a0.

AEROSOLS AND CLIMATE CHANGE

Anderson D., A.S. Goudie, and A.G. Parker. *Global Environments through the Quaternary*. Oxford and New York: Oxford University Press, 2007.

EPICA Community Members. "Eight Glacial Cycles from an Antarctic Ice Core." *Nature* 429 (2004), 623–628.

Hegerl, G. C., et al. "Multi-Fingerprint Detection and Attribution Analysis of Greenhouse Gas, Greenhouse Gas-Plus-Aerosol and Solar Forced Climate Change." *Climate Dynamics* 13 (1997), 613–634.

Mitchell, J.F.B., and T.C. Johns. "On Modification of Global Warming by Sulfate Aerosols." *Journal of Climate* 10 (1997), 245–267.

Overpeck, J., et al. "Possible Role of Dust-Induced Regional Warming in Abrupt Climate Change during the Last Glacial Period." *Nature* 384 (1996), 447–449. DOI: 10.1038/384447a0.

Santer, B.D., et al. "Towards the Detection and Attribution of an Anthropogenic Effect on Climate." *Climate Dynamics* 12 (1995), 77–100. DOI: 10.1007/s003820050096.

Santer, B.D., et al. "A Search for Human Influences on the Thermal Structure of the Atmosphere." *Nature* 382 (1996), 39–46. DOI: 10.1038/382039a0.

Taylor, K.E., and J.E. Penner. "Response of the Climate System to Atmospheric Aerosols and Greenhouse Gases." *Nature* 369 (1994), 734–737. DOI: 10.1038/369734a0.

—JOYCE E. PENNER

AGRICULTURE AND AGRICULTURAL LAND

The use of land for the production of food, fiber, and fuel is the principal driver of land-use and land-cover change and, therefore, a key causal factor in global environmental change. Most agriculture involves the control and enhancement of nature to achieve production, leading to the modification and transformation of land covers (e.g., forests, grasslands, wetlands) and the manipulation of soil and water (e.g., fertilization, irrigation). As a result, changes in agricultural land and the strategies of production contribute significantly to so-called greenhouse gases and to impacts on the hydrologic cycle.

When the meaning of global change is expanded beyond climate warming, the reach of agriculture extends even further. Most of the humanly modified surface of the earth is connected in some way to agriculture. These changes alter the structure and function of ecosystems and reduce biotic diversity, while the production process pollutes the troposphere, primarily through the nitrogen cycle. These types of relationships make agricultural land and production susceptible not only to global climate change but also to geographically more restricted environmental feedbacks, and they heighten agriculture's role in a wide variety of environmental issues: to name a few, the migration of biota across disrupted and fragmented landscapes in the face of latitudinal and altitudinal climate shifts, the degradation of marine and lacustrine ecosystems from agricultural runoff, and soil and groundwater depletion.

Beyond these environmental impacts, agriculture is important for its role in a more crowded and consumption-driven world. A doubling of the world's population in the early part of the twenty-first century and the expectation of increasing "average" consumption, including increased emphasis on livestock, will significantly intensify the pressures on agricultural land and production. Adding to these pressures is the competition for urban, industrial, recreation, and preservation land uses, most of which outbid agriculture for land. It is expected, however, that technological and managerial improvements over the long run will increase production on land remaining in agriculture.

HISTORY OF AGRICULTURAL ATTRIBUTES

The role of agriculture and agricultural land in global environmental change is understood through the history of the key factors in land use and production: substitution and intensification, expansion, mechanization, crop diversity, and production-consumption linkages.

With few exceptions, agriculture manipulates and controls nature in order to achieve increased production and security from harvest losses. The technologies and strategies used to accomplish these goals vary considerably. They may be as simple as burning savanna grasses to enhance new shoots at the onset of the rainy season, thus providing a superior feed for livestock, or as complex as hydroponics, in which computer-controlled cultivation takes place in nutrient-loaded water, not soil. The former strategy relies almost entirely on nature to provide the inputs required for the output (feed), while the latter strategy substitutes fully for nature, even to the extent of controlling climate when undertaken in greenhouses.

Most systems of agriculture, of course, fit somewhere between these extremes, from slash-and-burn cultivation and pastoral nomadism to irrigated crops with satellite-informed fertilization and cattle feedlots. Systems that rotate cropping plots and grazing pastures (low-frequency use) generally rely on natural processes to replenish the critical elements lost in production (e.g., soil nutrients, pasture biomass). Increased frequency of use and increased yields require increased substitutes for nature—soil nutrient and moisture enhancement (fertilizers and irrigation), stabilization of soil on slopes (terraces), reduction of inundation (wetland fields and drainage)—and control of nature's vagaries—pests and weeds (pesticides and herbicides), frost and freezes (mounding and mulching), or drought (irrigation). Variants of these and other strategies abound throughout the world, giving rise to many agricultural ecosystems. Yet agriculture has always sought to increase yields and decrease labor inputs. The overall trend is toward increasing intensification through yields and frequency of cropping.

From the onset of domestication, agriculture expanded to include almost all types of arable land on Earth, and in some cases, such as the polders (tracts of land reclaimed from the sea) of the Netherlands, the creation of arable land where none existed. The global scale, therefore, reveals an ever-increasing portion of Earth placed under cropping and grazing production. This trend has not, however, been uniform from region to region. Before about 3,000 BP, agriculture was most widespread in tropical to midlatitude Eurasia and the Nile drainage. From 3,000 BP until 500 BP, significant areas of agriculture emerged everywhere, including the Western Hemisphere tropics. Subsequently, European colonialism profoundly altered agriculture globally through the huge scale of transcontinental species-exchanges, especially the movement of livestock to the Western Hemisphere. The twentieth century witnessed major expansion in the cultivation of grasslands in the Americas, Russia, and Australia, spurred by mechanization and irrigation, and of tropical forest biomes worldwide.

The global trend is full of counterexamples—regions that have witnessed major declines in cultivation. Salinization led to abandonment of ancient systems of desert irrigation, and population losses and relocation caused the large-scale abandonment of tropical forest and wetland agriculture in the Americas. More recently, much marginally arable land in Western Europe and North America has been taken out of cultivation, and urbanization has taken over prime agricultural lands.

Mechanization is the primary means of reducing labor and increasing production in agriculture. For example, the number of tractors in use worldwide per thousand hectares of arable land increased from 12 in the late 1960s to 19 by the beginning of the 1990s. Intensification does not, however, always require

mechanization. It is possible to achieve large yields and intensive production in labor-intensive systems. Mechanization dominates land-rich and labor-poor agricultural regions, such as the Great Plains of the United States. It also appears in land-poor and labor-rich conditions, such as South Asia, in concert with the use of high-yielding crop varieties. In either of these general cases, research and development aimed at improving mechanized tilling, crop-enhancing applications, and harvesting increases as well, even among relatively impoverished smallholders. For example, the powered "miniplow" has spread from China throughout Asia, diesel pumps lift irrigation water throughout the tropical world, and "backpack" sprayers are increasingly used to apply fertilizers, pesticides, and herbicides. Mechanization, coupled with high-yielding crops, increases the number of people fed per farmer. Agricultural productivity in the U.S. tripled between 1948 and 2004: a U.S. farmer now feeds or clothes roughly 120 persons at home and abroad.

The agricultural revolution some ten thousand years ago led to a proliferation of domesticates, many of them of very restricted geographic distribution. Subsequently, certain domesticates spread over large areas, becoming dominant staple crops for large regions: rice in lower-latitude Asia; wheat in Europe, North Africa, and Asia Minor; sorghum and millets in sub-Saharan Africa; maize in North and Central America; potatos in the Andes; and manioc in Amazonia. Individual localities bred numerous varieties of these and other major crops as well as retaining highly localized species.

The first global-level shock to this diversity coincided with the European colonization of much of the rest of the world from the sixteenth through the nineteenth centuries. The impacts of this colonization on population, settlements, land access, and political economies profoundly affected the global distribution of biota through intentional and unintentional exchange of plants, animals, and pathogens. Species favored by Europeans were privileged in these changes, leading to the spread of wheat, barley, and oats in suitable environments, and sheep, goats, and cattle to almost every agricultural region. And yet many other, non-European crops were also spread worldwide during this time: maize, manioc, potato, beans, tomato, and chile, to name a few. These exchanges began the process of lowering the diversity of domesticates everywhere, except in the most isolated locales. The second shock came in the middle of the twentieth century with the emergence of the "green revolution" and the high-yielding varieties emerging from it. The productivity of these crops, and the socioeconomic structures set in place to promote them, continues to reduce the varieties of staple crops everywhere and marginalizes knowledge about the many local species that were not favored for cropping. The intense focus on an increasingly small number of crops has raised concerns about the implications for genetic pools of domesticates.

Finally, the economic structure of agriculture continues to change. The long history of local production and consumption has given way to the spatial separation of the two. Few pure subsistence agriculturalists remain, including pastoralists.

Smallholders everywhere participate in the market, and the market increasingly is extralocal, serving national and international markets. These same markets, of course, serve the largeholder and corporate and state farms. Produce from anywhere is consumed everywhere, and the price received by the farmer is increasingly affected by international commodity exchanges. Hidden within this complex production-consumption network, however, is subsistence production, which persists in part because of the inability of many smallholders and pastoralists to gain sufficient and secure income from commodity production alone.

DISTRIBUTION OF MAJOR AGRICULTURAL TYPES

These broader trends in agriculture and their connections to global change and sustainability are best understood in terms of the types of systems in use. While no taxonomy of agriculture is accepted worldwide, typologies should be based on the plant or animal focus of production; the intensity of land use; the use of production for subsistence, market, or some combination of the two; and the technological/managerial strategies of production. These attributes blend into one another, making taxonomies difficult and often highly regional in applicability. In general, however, animal and crop production are typically separated, and their taxonomies are in turn subdivided.

LIVESTOCK PRODUCTION

Large stock (especially cattle, sheep, and goats) are overwhelmingly important in land use and global change because of the total amount of land devoted to their rearing and of the greenhouse gasses emitted by the increasing number of livestock globally. Three major types of large stock systems exist: pastoral nomadism, ranching/dairying, and feedlots. Pastoral nomadism is an ancient practice in which most or all of the human population moves seasonally with the livestock in search of natural feed. The importance of this practice should not be underestimated today, even if production increasingly is sold. Major areas throughout the arid and semiarid world—northern and eastern Africa, Asia Minor, and Central Asia—are dominated by pastoral nomadic activities, as are cold environments in the Hindu-Kush, the Himalayas, and northern Eurasia. Grasslands in the Americas, Australia, and southern Africa support ranching, characterized by commercial production of meat and stock by-products and, increasingly, improved pasture. Dairying uses cattle for commercial milk and cheese products and tends to be found near major urban markets. It is increasing worldwide. The most intensive stock-rearing activities are feedlots for cattle. While globally insignificant in area, feedlots are a major source of methane emissions.

CULTIVATION

Much of the Earth's surface has been or is being cultivated, mostly in rain-fed systems, which are overwhelmingly dominant both spatially and in total crops produced. These systems are coordinated with the seasonality of rainfall and focus on staple produce (cereals and root crops). Beyond these general shared qualities, rain-fed cultivation varies significantly. Subdivisions based on the frequency of cropping is significant for global change. Shifting cultivation refers to a variety of systems that rely primarily on the systematic movement of cropped plots. Minimal inputs are employed to enhance or maintain land productivity in the face of soil nutrient depletion and weed and pest invasion. Plots are abandoned, and nature regenerates the land. Shifting cultivation, therefore, requires access to much land, most of which is in some stage of regeneration at any given time. Associated overwhelmingly with subsistence production, shifting cultivation remains significant in the tropical world and is associated with burning forest lands and, in some cases, land degradation. Permanent rain-fed cultivation, by contrast, involves systems in which plots are cultivated annually or more often and are rested for only brief periods. The depletion of nature's resources are offset by human inputs. In the more intensive systems, land is tilled and weeded, and fertilizers, pesticides, and herbicides are applied to high-yielding varieties of crops. Many of the world's breadbaskets rely on mechanized, permanent cultivation, especially in the formerly glaciated soils of the middle latitudes, although irrigation may supplement precipitation.

Wetland cultivation, predicated on controlling water within otherwise naturally inundated lands, was practiced in large areas in the ancient Americas. Today, its significance is marked less by its total area (e.g., the Netherlands) than by its enormous costs, productivity, and impacts on local hydrologies and methane emissions. Investment in wetlands in the twentieth century focused on their drainage rather than on the use of wetland systems of production.

Irrigated cultivation, another ancient technology, continues to grow in spatial extent and environmental impacts. Based on the proper control and delivery of water, it is of several types. Wet rice irrigation requires infrastructures for field flooding and draining in addition to that for water delivery. Subsistence production once dominated wet rice production and remains important, especially in South and East Asia. Increasingly, however, wet rice cultivation has moved to commercial production throughout midlatitude and tropical Asia as well as California and Texas, where its cultivation is completely mechanized. The spread of wet rice agriculture contributes significantly to the emission of methane from its flooded fields.

Some irrigation is carried out without flooding. Often associated with semiarid and arid lands, it involves infrastructures of all sizes, from local streambed runoff to extensive canal systems and the pumping of deep groundwater. Irrigation enhances yields but, if improperly used, can lead to significant land degradation from salinization, as well as to the depletion of aquifers and destruction of downstream ecosystems, as is happening in the death of the Aral Sea. Areas of large-scale (non–wet-rice) irrigation include the Central Asian Republics and western China, the Nile and Tigris–Euphrates valleys, south-central

Australia, the southern High Plains and western United States, and northern Mexico.

Tree and shrub cultivation and horticulture range from house and orchard gardens to plantations and technologically advanced greenhouses. Production emphasizes high-value fruits, oils, condiments, ornamentals, and medicinal species. The house and orchard gardens tend to be used for subsistence or semisubsistence, focused on diverse species, and located adjacent to rural settlements and around urban areas. In contrast, the orchard, vineyard, and plantation (technically a specific labor arrangement) focus on the commercial monocropping of species requiring special conditions offered by the location. Market gardening, including the greenhouse, was once located adjacent to major markets (e.g., New Jersey and Long Island in the megalopolis of the Atlantic seaboard of the United States). Increasingly, however, the economics of modern transportation reduces the need for proximity and makes possible a long-distance trade in produce (e.g., the valleys of California, southern Mexico, and Morocco).

Finally, agroforestry is a historically important activity that has changed significantly. It once focused on the culling and manipulation of naturally occurring species to ensure a consistent production of food, resin, fiber, and wood, much like the present but waning subsistence sector of agroforestry. The timber plantation is focused on monocropping timber from naturally occurring or exogenous species. This form of agroforestry is growing significantly in the pinelands of the developed world and, increasingly, in parts of the developing world. Its impacts on biotic diversity are assumed to be large.

MAJOR AGRICULTURAL TRENDS

The significance of agriculture to humankind is attested by the antiquity of domestication and sophisticated means of production. The cultivation of virtually every environment, save those lacking a cropping season or access to water, has long been mastered, as have biotic means of enhancing production through the use of nitrogen-fixing species, night soil, crop rotations, and mounding and mulching, to name only a few ancient strategies. This knowledge diffused worldwide and was employed and expanded in step with population and settlement change. Prefossil-fuel agriculture, however, could not keep pace with the growing demands for produce triggered by the industrial revolution, especially with the exponential growth in global population from the middle of the twentieth century onward, accompanied in the latter portion of the century by major increases in global average consumption. These demands refocused the agriculture industry and agricultural science on the enhancement of production, giving rise to high-yielding hybrids (genetically manipulated crops) requiring increased applications of industrial-produced fertilizers, pesticides, and herbicides. Yields of major cultivars increased appreciably in the last half of the century, as hybrids of rice, maize, wheat, and potato poured from the Rockefeller-sponsored research-and-development centers created for this purpose. During this time, a staggering 170% increase in the production of staple foods

was achieved while adding only 1% to the area of land under cultivation (while population doubled). By the end of the century, however, the ability of this "green revolution" to push yields diminished, and attention is increasingly paid to the direct genetic manipulation of crops to enhance their resistance to diseases, pests, and droughts.

These advances in the science and technology of production take place within existing political economic structures. For example, sufficient food is produced to provide for all of humanity at relatively high rates of consumption, but world political and economic systems support highly skewed patterns of distribution and consumption. Not only is the distribution of global stocks of food skewed, but the success of the green revolution in achieving these stocks affects smallholders globally, creating winners and losers in terms of access to technological inputs for production and, ultimately, to land. Changes in agriculture and agricultural land use are thus intimately linked to much broader structural changes, especially in less wealthy economies where large rural labor pools must find new livelihoods, presumably in urban-industrial settings. The success of the green revolution followed, in part, from the realization that a technological solution that increased the total stock of produce globally was easier to achieve than a restructuring of the world political economy in order to alter patterns of distribution and consumption. This reality remains in force, despite international agendas calling it to question and asking for more "sustainable" or environmentally benign policies.

The first half of the twenty-first century is expected to include a staggering increase in the world's population as well as increases in per capita consumption, urban settlement, and the international exchange of people, services, and commodities. Under these conditions, more affluent locales with marginal agricultural lands will continue to follow the twentieth-century trend of deemphasizing agriculture, in many cases permitting forestation as in New England and Western Europe. Less affluent locales, in contrast, will increase agriculture for export, largely through the intensification process, as in the former Soviet Union. Urban-industrial centers will continue to consume the prime agricultural lands that gave rise to the centers in the first place, as in coastal Asia and exemplified by the changing periurban character of the delta of the Zhu (Pearl) River of China, once a breadbasket for rice. The environmental impacts of urban-industrial complexes on regional agriculture will increase, through land competition and tropospheric pollution. Moreover, boom-and-bust conditions will continue to dominate the remaining "open" agricultural lands of the world, such as Amazonia, leading to significant deforestation and land degradation. These trends, of course, are independent of any impacts that may follow from climate warming or environmental problems.

AGRICULTURAL IMPLICATIONS FOR GLOBAL ENVIRONMENTAL CHANGE

Agriculture and agricultural land use have played an important role in the modification and transformation of the biosphere and promise to do so well into the future. Deforestation for agriculture used to be the single largest contributor of human-induced carbon dioxide to the atmosphere, and the spread of wet rice cultivation was similarly important as a source of methane. Irrigation in general, especially the drawdown in aquifers and the drainage of wetlands, affected the hydrologic cycle. All these changes played significant roles in regional climates. The future will probably see continued agricultural expansion at the expense of tropical forests and woodlands, especially in Oceania, Southeast Asia, Africa, and Latin America, and increased irrigation globally. These changes will continue to fragment some of the most biotically diverse landscapes in the world, interfering with movements of fauna and decreasing biota in general.

Whatever the impacts from expansion, they will probably be exceeded by those of intensification. It is doubtful that major increases in production globally will be accomplished without sustained fossil fuel inputs and further genetic engineering of crops, which will be linked to increased applications of irrigation, fertilizer, herbicides, and pesticides. The use of nitrogenous fertilizers worldwide, for example, climbed to a staggering 57 kilograms per hectare of arable land by the 1990s. These inputs will affect trace gas emissions and the hydrologic cycle, just as the intensification of cattle production will increase methane emissions.

Intensification will also significantly affect biotic diversity and local environmental degradation. The enormous diversity in the varieties of domesticated plants continues to decrease in the face of the demand for production of a few major staples. We now speak of "lost" crops and preserving crop diversity in international seed banks. Poor agricultural practices are the primary cause of surface water pollution in many regions, and agriculture tends to violate one or more pollutant criteria, even where there is relatively strong enforcement of environmental policies. In the United States alone, it is estimated that farming and ranching are a source of water-quality impairment in 60, 50, and 34% of impaired river miles, lakes, and estuaries, respectively. Despite major improvements in soil tillage and grazing practices, agriculture remains a large cause of soil erosion and vegetation degradation and is the largest single consumer of fresh water.

GLOBAL CHANGE IMPLICATIONS FOR AGRICULTURE

Much uncertainty surrounds the impacts of potential climate change on agriculture and agricultural land use because of the uncertainty in global climate models, the role of enhanced atmospheric carbon dioxide—the fertilization effect—and adaptations that farmers might make. Various models suggest little impact through the end of the twenty-first century under the low-warming assumption (+1.5°C). Even the high-warming assumption (+4.5°C) may have only small impacts on global cereal production. Regional variations in the impacts, however, are significant, giving rise to clear winners and losers. The losers appear to be those parts of the tropical world where C4

crops (e.g., maize, sorghum, and millet) dominate. (C3 and C4 are classifications of crop plants based on the way they use carbon in photosynthesis.) C4 crops respond less well in experimental conditions to increased carbon dioxide concentrations. This effect, coupled with increased temperatures and hence increased evapotranspiration, bodes poorly for the non-wet rice regions of the tropics—much of Africa and the Americas. In contrast, these same models suggest that C3 crops (e.g., wheat, rice, soybean) will perform well with enhanced carbon dioxide levels, and warmer temperatures will allow the use of deeply glaciated soils to expand poleward, as on the Canadian plains and in parts of Russia. While the total area of cropped land is likely to increase for reasons that have little to do with climate change, significant changes will take place in lands put into and taken out of cultivation as the relative costs of production change.

Also important for agriculture are the feedbacks from production on tropospheric pollution. Prime crops lands are the source for more than half of the world's emissions of nitrogen oxide to the atmosphere. These lands are also near major urban-industrial complexes that generate ground-level ozone pollution, which reacts with nitrogen oxide to reduce crop yields. This pollution is becoming serious for major breadbasket zones around the world, such as the Ganges basin, and ozone pollution, if unabated, may have significant impacts on efforts to intensify production.

ADAPTATIONS TO GLOBAL CHANGE AND DEGRADATION

Perhaps the most important advance in understanding farming behavior and agricultural change in the past quarter century is the recognition that changes in cultivation practices, including the development and use of new technologies, maintain a strong endogenous character. Farmers, from impoverished smallholders to corporate largeholders, are not passive agents but are constantly innovating as conditions change. Agricultural research and development respond similarly. This recognition strongly suggests that, on average and globally, agriculture worldwide will adapt to climate change as well as to more localized environmental changes, such as land degradation. These adaptations could potentially lower agriculture's impacts on environmental change in general. For example, low- or no-tillage cultivation and organic farming have been shown to reduce air and water pollution, soil nutrient loss, and loss to pests. These practices currently involve increased costs to the farmer, however, and it is not clear how much of these costs can be passed on to the consumer or will be subsidized by society at large. Beyond these methods, conventional costs of inputs remain important to cultivation strategies. For example, the water-inefficient center-pivot irrigation used on the southern Great Plains of the United States has given way to more efficient irrigation methods as the depletion of the Ogalalla aquifer drives up the cost of pumping water. This raises an important environmental and economic issue: will the market mechanism take effect before agricultural land or critical production resources are irreparably damaged?

These kinds of adjustments are made by the agricultural sector on its own behalf. Climate change may, however, reduce or close down agriculture in certain regions or environments and expand it in others. In general, where water stress increases and cannot be efficiently alleviated, cultivation will be converted to other land uses, perhaps to livestock. Expansion is likely in higher latitudes where temperature currently limits the growing season. Regional economic impacts of less favorable agricultural conditions will vary by the political economy in question. In subsistence-oriented and economically poor regions, smallholders will be further marginalized, and movement to already crowded regions and urban areas will be exacerbated. In economically well-developed regions, however, the impacts will be masked by the much larger industrial and service sectors. In these cases, the burden of adjustment to other livelihoods will fall on the individual farmer.

This last scenario assumes, of course, that the agriculturalist confronts the changing physical and economic environment as an entrepreneur alone. There are many reasons to believe, however, that this confrontation will be fought politically, with the agrarian sector seeking support and subsidies to maintain agriculture. Confronted with inadequate water and international competition, agriculturalists in the western United States and Western Europe have leveraged their political clout for public financed and subsidized irrigation and guaranteed price support, respectively. These kinds of "adjustments" will surely become contested with climate change in the developed world.

[*See also* Biological Diversity; Deforestation; Desertification; Erosion; Fire and Global Warming; Forestation; Irrigation; Land Reclamation; Land Use; Nongovernmental Organizations; Pest Management; Salinization; Savannas; Soils; Sustainable Growth; Technology and Environment; *and* Water.]

BIBLIOGRAPHY

Chameides, W.L., et al. "Growth of Continental-Scale Metro-Agro-Plexes, Regional Ozone Pollution, and World Food Production." *Science* 264 (1994), 74–77.
Crosby, A.W. *Ecological Imperialism: The Biological Expansion of Europe, 900–1900.* Cambridge and New York: Cambridge University Press, 1986. Watershed but not first demonstration of the biological and ecological impacts of the era of European global dominace, focusing on the age of exploration and colonialism.
Darwin, R., et al. *World Agriculture and Climate Change: Economic Adaptations.* Agricultural Economic Report 703. Washington, D.C.: U.S. Department of Agriculture, 1995. Modeling the impact of climate change on world agriculture.
Ervin, D.E., et al. "Agriculture and the Environment: A New Strategic Vision." *Environment* 40.6 (1998), 8–15, 35–40. An assessment of the ability of the growth in global agriculture to keep up with expected increases in demand under conditions of environmental stress.
Frederick, K.D., and N.J. Rosenberg, eds. *Assessing the Impacts of Climate Change on Natural Resource Systems.* Special issue. *Climatic Change* 28.1–2 (1994). Reviews of major integrated modeling approaches for understanding climate change impacts on agriculture and other resource uses.
Galaty, J.G., and D.L. Johnson, eds. *The World of Pastoralism: Herding Systems in Comparative Perspective.* New York: Guilford Press, 1990. One of the few recent treatments of pastoralism and pastoralists in the contemporary world.
Grigg, D.B. *The Agricultural Systems of the World: An Evolutionary Approach.* Cambridge: Cambridge University Press, 1974. A geographical and historical review of agricultural production systems around the world.
Hayami, Y., and V.W. Ruttan. *Agricultural Development: An International Perspective.* Baltimore, Md.: Johns Hopkins University Press, 1985. An exemplary review of the neoclassical economics perspective on agricultural change and development embedded in an induced-innovation approach.
Henderson-Sellers, A., ed. *Future Climates of the World: A Modelling Perspective.* Amsterdam and New York: Elsevier, 1995. A state-of-the-art assessment of future-climate modeling illustrating links to such activites as land and agricultural change.
Lamb, H.H. *Climate, History, and the Modern World.* London and New York: Methuen, 1982. Classic assessment of the role of climate and climate change on human history.
Matson, P., et al. "Agricultural Intensification and Ecosystem Properties." *Science* 277 (1997), 504–509. DOI: 10.1126/science.277.5325.504. An example of the linkage between global change and socioeconomic conditions.
Meyer, W.B., and B.L. Turner II. "Human Population Growth and Global Land Use/Cover Change." *Annual Reviews in Ecology and Systematics* 23 (1992), 39–61. A review of human-induced changes in terrestrial land covers and uses.
Micklin, P. P. "Dessication of the Aral Sea: A Water Management Disaster in the Soviet Union." *Science* 241 (1988), 1170–1176. Documentation of the linkage between the demise of the Aral Sea and technologies of production and political economy.
National Research Council. *Lost Crops of Africa.* Washington, D.C.: National Academy Press, 1996. Crops and crop varieties that are decreasingly cultivated in Africa.
Parry, M.L. *Climate Change and World Agriculture.* London: Earthscan, 1990. Assesses various climate-change scenarios on global agriculture.
Pingali, P., Y. Bigot, and H.P. Binswanger. *Agricultural Mechanization and the Evolution of Farming Systems in Sub-Saharan Africa.* Baltimore, Md.: Johns Hopkins University Press, 1987. Induced innovation and intensification are found even in regions where agriculture seems to be on the decline.
Richards, J.F. "Land Transformation." In *The Earth as Transformed by Human Action: Global and Regional Changes in the Biosphere over the Past 300 Years*, edited by B.L. Turner II, et al, pp. 163–177. Cambridge and New York: Cambridge University Press, 1990. A historical reconstruction of global land use changes by regions of the world.
Rosenzweig, C., and M. Parry. "Potential Impact of Climate Change on World Food Supply." *Nature* 367 (1994), 133–138. DOI: 10.1038/367133a0. A synthesis of modeling outcomes of the impacts on global agriculture.
Sen, A. *Poverty and Famines: An Essay on Entitlement and Deprivation.* New York: Oxford University Press, 1981. A groundbreaking demonstration that malnutrition, hunger, and famine originate in the political economy.
Turner, B.L., II, and S.B. Brush, eds. *Comparative Farming Systems.* New York: Guilford Press, 1987. Reviews approaches to agricultural change and intensification largely outside neoclassical economics.
Turner, B.L., II, and K.W. Butzer. "The Columbian Encounter and Land-Use Change." *Environment* 43 (1992), 16–20, 37–44. Reviews misconceptions about ancient land and agriculture in the Americas and its meaning for global change.
Understanding Rural America. Agriculture Information Bulletin No. 710. Washington, D.C.: Economic Research Service, U.S. Department of Agriculture, 1995.
Waggoner, P.E., J.H. Ausubel, and I.K. Wenick. "Lightening the Tread of Population on Land: American Examples." *Population and Development Review* 22.3 (1996), 531–545. An examination of economic and population growth demands on agriculture with a positive spin.

—B. L. TURNER II AND ERIC KEYS

SAVING FARMLAND FROM URBAN SPRAWL

In the United States in an average year, over 400,000 hectares (1 million acres) of farmland is lost to urban sprawl. That is a significant portion of the nation's cropland, which totals 166 million hectares. Thus a farmland area roughly the size of the state of Delaware is being turned into housing developments, shopping centers, industrial parks, and roads every year. On an average day, the toll is about 1,100 hectares, or 4.2 square miles. Unhappily, much of the loss occurs on prime farmland: 19 million hectares of Class I soils and 89 million hectares of Class II soils, for a total of 108 million hectares, a large proportion of which is near urban areas because fertile soils and good water encouraged the original settlements that grew to become cities.

The loss of farmland to urban sprawl occurs across the nation because, as urban areas spread, the value of agricultural land soars. Farmers are faced with rising taxes, while working of the land is made more difficult by encroaching residences. When a developer offers an attractive price for his land, a farmer will often sell and retire. There are some devices, though, that can slow this process.

- Taxing the land at lower rates, as long as it is used for agriculture.
- Zoning laws, if enforced, can stipulate agricultural use of the land.
- Urban growth boundaries can limit the sprawl. The Green Belt around London, England, is a well-known application of the idea. In the United States, the state of Oregon leads in implementing growth boundaries.
- Land trusts or conservancies—private organizations that receive gifts of land, and also purchase land and development rights to preserve land that has scenic, recreational, or agricultural value.
- In the United States, state, county, or township governments may purchase development rights from the farmer. After appraisals are made, the farmer is paid a per acre easement value, which is the difference between the land's agricultural value and its value to a developer. The farmer remains owner of the property; but he and any subsequent owners must continue farming the land according to a deed of easement that specifies the land use. At county and local levels, funds may be raised by bond issues approved by taxpayers. Such programs have been popular mostly in northeastern states. (In England, private development rights were nationalized in 1947. For any development, other than farm buildings, a landowner must gain permission from the local government.)
[See also Land Preservation.]

BIBLIOGRAPHY

American Farmland Trust. *Farming on the Edge*. Northampton, Mass.: American Farmland Trust, 1997. Identifies the 20 most threatened agricultural regions in the United States, and areas in each state where strong development pressure coincides with high-quality farmland.
American Farmland Trust. *Saving American Farmland: What Works*. Northampton, Mass.: American Farmland Trust, 1997. A comprehensive guidebook for policy makers, planners, and concerned citizens working to save farmland at the local level.
Daniels, T., and D. Bowers. *Holding Our Ground: Protecting America's Farms and Farmlands*. Washington, D.C.: Island Press, 1997. A general review of the problem and its solutions. Includes extensive notes and bibliography.
Farmland Preservation Report. Street, Md.: Bowers, 1990–.

— DAVID J. CUFF

BIOREGIONALISM AND PERMACULTURE

Bioregionalism is a commitment to local places and local ecosystems, and to acting locally to improve the environment. Permaculture is a movement that aims to devise and recover cooperative and sustainable ways of living with the land: forms of agriculture that do not impoverish and destroy the soil; technologies that work with nature rather than against it; forms of social organization to accompany and support these agricultures and technologies.

BIBLIOGRAPHY

Jackson, W. *Rooted in the Land: Essays on Community and Place*. New Haven, Conn.: Yale University Press, 1996.
McGinnis, M. V. *Bioregionalism*. London and New York: Routledge, 1999.
Mollison, B. C. *Permaculture: A Practical Guide for a Sustainable Future*. Washington, D.C.: Island Press, 1990.
Sale, K. *Dwellers in the Land: The Bioregional Vision*. Athens, Ga.: University of Georgia Press, 2000.

— ANDREW S. GOUDIE

AGRICULTURE AND BIODIVERSITY

Agriculture, the art, science and business of raising livestock and cultivating soil to produce crops, is totally dependent on genes, species, and ecosystems and the variability inherent in them. This variability, known as biological diversity (or biodiversity for short) provides agriculture with the capacity to adapt to changing conditions. [*See* Biological Diversity.]

BIODIVERSITY AND THE GROWTH IN DEMAND FOR AGRICULTURAL PRODUCTS

Nearly a third of our planet's land is dominated by agricultural crops or planted pastures, thus having a profound ecological effect on the whole landscape. Another 10–20% of land is under extensive livestock grazing, and about 1 to 5% of food is produced in natural forests (Cassman and Wood, 2005). More than 1.1 billion people—most of them dependent on agriculture—now live within the world's 25 biodiversity "hotspots," areas described by ecologists as the most threatened species-rich regions on Earth (Cincotta and Engelman, 2000).

Human population is projected to grow from a little over 6 billion today to over 8 billion by 2030, an increase of about a third, with another two to four billion to come in the subsequent 50 years. But food demand may grow even faster, as a result of growing urbanization, rising incomes, and greater efforts to reduce hunger among the over 800 million people currently under-nourished (UN Millennium Project, 2005). Global consumption of livestock products is predicted to more than double from about 300 million metric tonnes in 1993 to over 650 million tonnes in 2020. More land will be required to grow crops and graze livestock, even more so as biofuels are expected to meet an increasing proportion of energy needs. In Africa alone, land in cereal production is expected to increase from over 100 million hectares in 1997 to about 135.3 million hectares in 2025, inevitably involving trade-offs among land devoted to crops, livestock, and other purposes.

Feeding a human population of 9 billion using current methods could require converting another one billion hectares of natural habitat to agricultural production, primarily in the developing world, together with a doubling or tripling of nitrogen and phosphorous inputs, a two-fold increase in water consumption and a three-fold increase in pesticide use. A serious limiting factor is expected to be water, as 70% of the freshwater used by people is already devoted to agriculture. Scenarios prepared by the Millennium Ecosystem Assessment thus suggest that agricultural production in the future will need to focus more explicitly on ecologically-sensitive management systems that give greater attention to biodiversity (Carpenter et al., 2005).

HOW BIODIVERSITY SUPPORTS THE GROWING DEMAND FOR AGRICULTURAL PRODUCTION

Virtually all domesticated species of plants and animals still have wild relatives whose genetic diversity can be valuable in enabling the domesticated species to adapt to changing conditions. While national and international seed banks contain much valuable genetic material, the wild relatives are especially valuable because they are living and adapting to changing climate conditions, competition with other species and predators, and new diseases. In many parts of Asia, farmers purposefully allow their domesticated chickens and pigs to cross-breed with wild relatives, adding new genes to the domesticated breeds. Efforts to conserve wild relatives of domesticated plants and animals have greatly increased over the past decades, international agreements now recognize their value, numerous projects have been launched in various countries, and institutional collaboration is expanding (Meilleur and Hodgkin, 2004).

Rural people everywhere rely on harvesting wild species. Wild greens, mushrooms, spices and flavorings enhance local diets, and in low-income regions many tree fruits and root crops serve to assuage "pre-harvest hunger" or provide "famine foods" when crops or the economy fails. Frogs, rodents, snails, edible insects and other small creatures have long been an important part of the rural diet in virtually all parts of the world. Bushmeat is the principal source of animal protein in humid West Africa,

Amazonia, and other forest regions, and efforts to replace this with domestic livestock have been disappointing. Fisheries are an important animal protein source, and the main supply of protein for the poor worldwide. But products from wild biodiversity provide far more than food. In Africa and many parts of Asia, more than 80% of medicines still come from wild sources, gathered wood remains the main fuel for hundreds of millions of people, and forests and savannas provide critical inputs for farming in the form of fodder, soil nutrients, fencing, and others (McNeely and Scherr, 2003). Achieving food security therefore requires the conservation of the ecosystems providing these foods and other products to agricultural production systems.

Conservation of wild biodiversity is considered by many to be an ethical imperative. At the same time, conservation also supports ecosystem services—ecological processes and functions that sustain and improve human well-being (Daily, 1997). Ecosystem services can be divided into four categories: provisioning services that provide food, timber, medicines and other useful products; regulating services such as flood control and climate stabilization; supporting services such as pollination, soil formation and water purification; and cultural services, which are aesthetic, spiritual, or recreational assets that provide both intangible benefits and tangible ones such as ecotourism attractions. Provisioning historically has been seen as the highest-priority service provided by agricultural landscapes, but even the main agricultural production areas of the world also deliver other important ecosystem services such as water supply and quality, pollination, and pest and disease control.

An especially important supporting service provided to agriculture by biodiversity is plant protection. Plants respond to insects feeding on their leaves by synthesizing and releasing complex blends of volatile compounds, which attract insects that are natural enemies of the insects who are feeding on the leaves, thereby helping defend the plant. If the biodiversity-based natural defenses of plants could be more effectively mobilized, safe and effective crop protection strategies could be designed that would significantly minimize the negative side effects of the current generation of chemical fertilizers.

Many of the world's most important watersheds are densely populated and under predominantly agricultural use, and most of the rest are in agricultural land use mosaics where crop, livestock and forest production influence hydrological systems. In such regions, agriculture can be managed to maintain critical watershed functions, such as maintaining water quality, regulating water flow, recharging underground aquifers, mitigating flood risks, moderating sediment flows, and sustaining freshwater species and ecosystems. Effective water management encompasses the choice of water-conserving crop mixtures, soil and water management (including irrigation), vegetation barriers to slow movement of water down slopes, year-around vegetative cover for soils, and maintenance of natural vegetation in riparian areas, wetlands, and other strategic areas of the watershed. Well-managed, biodiverse agricultural landscapes can also provide protection against extreme natural events. With water scarcity and extreme weather events predicted to increase in coming decades, the contribution of biodiversity to enhancing the capacity of agricultural systems to sustain watershed functions is likely to be one of the most important considerations in agricultural investment and management.

Agricultural landscapes can conserve a broad range of native terrestrial species, especially those that adapt well to habitat fragmentation and agricultural land use. The prospects for conserving biodiversity in agricultural landscapes depend on the degree of fragmentation and functional connectivity of natural areas, the habitat quality of those areas, the habitat quality of the productive matrix, and the extent to which farmers manage their land to conserve biodiversity. Forms of agriculture that successfully balance productivity, improved livelihoods, and biodiversity conservation at a landscape scale have been termed "ecoagriculture" (McNeely and Scherr, 2003).

Efforts to maintain natural habitats in farming areas are longstanding, principally through agricultural set-aside schemes, crop rotation, and leaving some land fallow. Land withdrawn from conventional production of crops has been shown unequivocally to enhance biodiversity in North America and Europe (van Buskirk and Willi, 2004). For many commercial crop monocultures, leaving field margins uncultivated for habitat protection does not reduce total yields, as inputs were applied more economically on the rest (Clay, 2004).

However, landscape-scale interventions specifically designed to protect habitats for biodiversity are much more effective than a farm-by-farm approach. A recent review of evidence from North America on how much wildlife habitat is "enough" in agricultural landscapes (Blann, 2006) concluded that habitat needs must be considered within the landscape history and context. Habitat patches must be large enough and connected to other patches, along rivers and streams or steep, hilly lands, for example. Smaller patches of natural habitat may be sufficient if adjacent agricultural patches are ecologically managed. A growing body of research shows that landscape connectivity between large patches of forest can be effectively maintained through retention of tree cover on the farm, such as live fences, windbreaks, and hedges in grazing lands and agricultural fields (Harvey et al., 2004). Biodiversity conservation efforts designed to adapt to changes in agricultural landscapes should therefore focus on protecting (or restoring) large areas of native habitat within agricultural areas, and retaining elements (such as hedgerows, isolated trees, riparian forests and other non-cropped areas) that enhance landscape connectivity, thereby ensuring heterogeneity at both field and landscape levels.

THE FUTURE OF BIODIVERSITY AND AGRICULTURE

From the perspective of wild-biodiversity conservation, ideal agricultural production systems mimic the structure and function of natural ecosystems (Blann, 2006; Jackson and Jackson, 2002). In humid and sub-humid forest ecosystems, farms would resemble forests, with productive tree crops, shade-loving understory crops, and agroforestry mixtures; in grassland ecosystems, production systems would rely more on perennial grains and grasses, and economically useful shrubs and dryland tree species. Annual crops could be cultivated in such systems, but as intercrops, or monoculture plots interspersed in mosaics of perennial production and natural habitat areas. Domesticated crop and livestock species diversity would be encouraged at a landscape scale, and genetic diversity within species would be conserved in situ at a large ecosystem scale, to ensure system resilience and the ecological diversity required to adapt to changing conditions.

Multistory agroforest systems, tree fallows and complex home gardens are especially rich in wild biodiversity. For example, canopy height, tree, epiphyte, liana, and bird species diversity, vegetation structural complexity, percent ground cover by leaf litter, and soil calcium, nitrate nitrogen, and organic matter levels in topsoils are all significantly greater in shade than in farms fully exposed to the sun, while air and soil temperatures, weed diversity, and percent of ground cover by weeds are significantly greater in farms without trees. In Central America, polyculture combinations and management systems significantly improve the productivity of coffee, cocoa, banana, timber, and other commercial tree products in these complex systems.

While coffee grown in monoculture plantations with full exposure to the sun has higher yields, coffee grown in the shade is far more beneficial for sustainable agriculture and conserving biodiversity. Shade coffee, especially in diverse systems, can support more than twice as many species of birds. Systems with multiple species of trees providing shade also help support beneficial insects, orchids, mammals, and other species, as well as protecting fragile tropical soils from erosion, providing nutrients, and suppressing weeds, thereby reducing or eliminating the need for chemical herbicides and fertilizers and thus reducing farming costs. Farmers also are able to harvest various species of fruits, firewood, lumber, and medicines from the shade trees.

In the Bahia State of Brazil, traditional shade plantations of cacao (known locally as *cabrucas*) also provide habitat for many forest-dwelling species, including a rich and abundant bat community that feeds on many species of insects and helps pollinate night-blooming species. But when the *cabrucas* are located more than one kilometer from native forests, the bat communities are less diverse than those found in forests. Therefore, the entire landscape should be considered for management, taking into account that maintenance of *cabrucas* together with the preservation and restoration of forest patches is essential to the conservation of bat diversity.

To replace crops that must be replanted each year (usually as monocultures, where a single species is planted over an extensive area), new and improved perennial crops, such as fruits, leafy vegetables, spices, and vegetable oils, are becoming more popular. Perennial crops can be more resilient and involve less soil and ecosystem disturbance than annual crops, and provide much greater habitat value, especially if grown in mixtures and mosaics (Jackson and Jackson, 2002). Breeding efforts are also underway to convert annual grains to perennial ones and to mimic ecosystem functions of natural grasslands, or to develop native perennial grains that can be grown more sustainably with much less environmental damage in dryland farming regions. The systems are not yet economically competitive, but yields are improving, while production costs are lower than current varieties; habitat value for wildlife is many times higher than in conventional wheat fields. Crops for biofuels are poised to become one of the fastest-growing segments of agricultural production, and although short-term investments have favored maize and canola in the developed world and sugarcane in the tropics, grasses, shrubs, and trees may be more economic and sustainable options once the technical challenges of processing cellulosic sources are overcome (Ragauskas et al., 2006).

Strategic planning for agricultural development has begun to focus on adaptation of systems to climate change, anticipating rising temperatures and more extreme weather events. With each one degree Centigrade increase in temperature during the growing season, the yields of rice, wheat and maize drop by about 10% (Brown, 2004). Cash crops such as coffee and tea, requiring cooler environments, will also be affected, forcing farmers of these crops to move higher up the hills, clearing new lands as they climb. Montane forests important for biodiversity are likely to come under increasing threat as a result. Effective responses to climate change will require changing varieties, modifying management of soils and water, and developing new strategies for pest management as species of wild pests, their natural predators, and their life-cycles change in response to climates. Increasing landscape and farm-scale diversity are likely to be an important response for reducing risks and adapting to change.

Since the 1960s both industrial agriculture in developed countries and the original green revolution in developing countries have depended on improved seeds, chemical fertilizers and pesticides, and irrigation. This production model involved a small number of crops, generally in monoculture stands (to increase efficiency in use of external inputs and mechanization). Wild flora and fauna were considered direct competitors for resources or harvested products, while water was diverted from wetlands and natural habitats for irrigation. But over the past two decades, research has demonstrated the value of agricultural biodiversity in all its forms, including crop and livestock genetic diversity, associated species important for production (for example, pollinators, soil microorganisms, beneficial insects, and predators of pests) and wild species that find their home in agricultural landscapes (Uphoff et al., 2006).

HOW DIFFERENT KINDS OF AGRICULTURAL SYSTEMS CONTRIBUTE TO BIODIVERSITY

Relatively benign approaches to production characterize many traditional systems that for ecological, cultural, or economic reasons have not been effectively incorporated into the industrial model. Such systems seek to build on, rather than replace, natural ecosystems. For example, shifting cultivation is a rotational system based on cutting living vegetation in early winter, letting the vegetation dry during the dry months, burning it late

in the dry season, and planting a crop of rice, corn, bananas, and a wide range of other plants in the fertile ash. After one or two crops, the field is left to fallow for at least 10 years, after which the cycle is repeated. An essential part of the system is the great diversity of crops which are grown, to some extent mimicking the diversity of natural forests. The Lawa (Lua) of northern Thailand, for example, grow about 120 crops, including 75 food crops, 21 medicinal crops, 20 plants for ceremonial or decorative purposes, and 7 for weaving or dyes; the fallow fields continue to be productive for grazing or collecting, with well over 300 species utilized. The most important crop is upland rice, and it is not unusual for a village to have 20 varieties of seed rice, each with different characteristics and planted according to soil type, fertility, and field moisture.

In South Africa, traditional agriculture in the form of contouring in a pesticide-free environment results in extensive edge habitat that provides food and cover for birds, leading to an increase in overall bird diversity. While not all species benefit from such edge habitats, the overall diversity of birds seems to increase with appropriate traditional agricultural practices.

Different modern approaches that encourage biodiversity have arisen from a variety of disciplines, philosophies, problem focus or geographic conditions. Biodiversity-friendly alternatives to industrial agriculture include agroecology (Altieri, 1995), conservation agriculture (FAO, 2001), organic agriculture (IFOAM, 2000), and sustainable agriculture (Pretty, 2005). They have tended to focus on maintaining the resource base for production through managing nutrient cycles, protecting pollinators and beneficial microorganisms, maintaining healthy soils and conserving water. They seek to reduce the ecological "footprint" of farmed areas and the damage to wild biodiversity from toxic chemicals, soil disturbance and water pollution.

Organic farming supports biodiversity by using fewer pesticides and inorganic fertilizers, and by adopting wildlife-friendly management of habitats where crops are not being grown. Strategies include not weeding close to hedges and mixing arable and livestock farming. Mixed farming particularly benefits some bird species, including those that nest in crops. Some argue that farms that adopt selected organic practices, such as replacing chemical weeding with mechanical methods, may encourage biodiversity as much as completely organic farms.

BIBLIOGRAPHY

Altieri, M.A. *Agroecology: The Science of Sustainable Agriculture.* Boulder, Colo.: Westview Press, 1995. A comprehensive coverage of the scientific basis of sustainable agriculture based on an understanding of the functioning of agroecosystems and the role biodiversity plays in them.

Blann, K. *Habitat in Agricultural Landscapes: How Much is Enough?* West Linn, Oreg.: Defenders of Wildlife, 2006.

Brown, L. *Outgrowing the Earth: The Food Security Challenge in an Age of Falling Water Tables and Rising Temperatures.* New York: W. W. Norton, 2004. A stimulating discussion of the relationship among water, food and climate, with global coverage and recommendations for addressing the challenges.

Carpenter, S.R., et al., eds. *Ecosystems and Human Well-Being: Scenarios.* Washington D.C.: Island Press, 2005. Another volume from the Millennium Ecosystem Assessment, this one looking at alternative futures and the role agriculture and biodiversity may play in them.

Cassman, K.G. and S. Wood. "Cultivated Systems." In *Ecosystems and Human Well-Being: Current State and Trends*, edited by R. Hassan, R. Scholes, and N. Ash, pp. 745–794. Washington D.C.: Island Press, 2005. Part of the report of the Millennium Ecosystem Assessment, the single most authoritative statement on the status of agroecosystems.

Cincotta, R.P., and R. Engelman. *Nature's Place: Human Population and the Future of Biological Diversity*. Washington, D.C.: Population Action International, 2000. The most useful reference linking biodiversity to the distribution of human population.

Clay, J. *World Agriculture and the Environment: A Commodity-By-Commodity Guide to Impacts and Practices*. Washington, D.C.: Island Press, 2004. A detailed overview of how each of the major agricultural commodities affects biodiversity.

Daily, G.C., ed. *Nature's Services: Societal Dependence on Natural Ecosystems*. Washington, D.C.: Island Press, 1997. The best available discussion of ecosystem services and the benefits these provide to humans.

Food and Agriculture Organization (FAO). *Conservation Agriculture: Case Studies in Latin America and Africa*. Rome: FAO, 2001.

Harvey, C.A., et al. *Assessing Linkages between Agriculture and Biodiversity in Central America: Historical Overview and Future Perspectives*. San José, Costa Rica: The Nature Conservancy, 2004.

IFOAM (International Federation of Organic Agriculture Movements). *Organic Agriculture and Biodiversity*. Bonn, Germany: IFOAM, 2000.

Jackson, D.L., and L.L. Jackson, eds. *The Farm as Natural Habitat: Reconnecting Food Systems with Ecosystems*. Washington, D.C.: Island Press, 2002. A comprehensive overview of the debate about agriculture and its impacts on the land, showing how farms can be managed as natural habitat.

McNeely, J.A., and S.J. Scherr. *Ecoagriculture: Strategies to Feed the World and Save Wild Biodiversity*. Washington D.C.: Island Press, 2003. Coined the term "ecoagriculture" to convey a vision of enhancing rural livelihoods, protecting or enhancing biodiversity and ecosystem services, and developing more sustainable and productive agricultural systems.

Meilleur, B., and T. Hodgkin. "In Situ Conservation of Crop Wild Relative: Status and Trends." *Biodiversity and Conservation* 13 (2004), 663–684. Provides a country-by-country summary on conservation of crop wild relatives and makes recommendations for future action.

Pretty, J.N., ed. *The Earthscan Reader in Sustainable Agriculture*. London: Earthscan, 2005. A comprehensive view of sustainable agriculture with chapters by many of the leading authorities in this field.

Ragauskas, A.J., et al. "The Path Forward for Biofuels and Biomaterials." *Science* 311 (2006), 484–489. DOI: 10.1126/science.1114736. A comprehensive and authoritative overview of biofuels and agriculture.

UN Millennium Project. *Investing in Development: A Practical Plan to Achieve the Millennium Development Goals*. New York: United Nations, 2005. The results of a three-year project carried out under the auspices of the Secretary-General of the United Nations to identify the key initiatives required to address major development issues in the new century.

Uphoff, N., et al., eds. *Biological Approaches to Sustainable Soil Systems*. Boca Raton, Fla.: CRC Press, 2006. Provides a comprehensive view of soil biodiversity and its contribution to agriculture.

Van Buskirk, J., and Y. Willi. "Enhancement of Farmland Biodiversity within Set-Aside Land." *Conservation Biology* 18 (2004), 987–994. Based on a meta-analysis of 127 published studies.

—Jeffrey A. McNeeley

ALBEDO

Albedo (derived from the Latin word albus, "white") is the fraction of incident solar radiation reflected by a surface. It can be defined over the entire spectrum of solar radiation (known as broadband albedo) or at a specific wavelength (known as spectral albedo). Averaged over the globe, the annual broadband planetary albedo at the top of the atmosphere (TOA) is approximately 0.3. Since clouds are highly reflective, with albedos ranging up to about 0.8, and cover approximately 60% of the

Earth, they have a dominant effect on planetary albedo. On average, clouds reflect approximately 20% of the solar radiation reaching the planet, compared with 6% reflected by gas molecules and aerosols and 4% by the Earth's surface.

THE GLOBAL PICTURE

Figure 1 illustrates TOA albedo over the globe for all sky conditions, as inferred from Earth Radiation Budget Experiment (ERBE) satellite measurements for September 1985 (Barkstrom and Smith, 1986).

Regions where clouds have a large influence on planetary albedo are areas of persistent low stratiform clouds over the eastern subtropical oceans (for example, off California, Angola, and Peru), in the tropics over regions of intense convective activity (central South America, the Congo Basin, India, and Indonesia), and in the midlatitudes over areas of cyclonic storm formation (eastern coasts of North America and Asia). Near the poles, the relative influence of clouds is not as pronounced because the clear-sky snow or ice background is already highly reflective.

In cloud-free regions, incoming solar radiation is reflected back to space by the atmosphere (gas molecules and aerosols) and the surface. The average planetary clear-sky TOA albedo is approximately 0.13. TOA albedos over ocean generally lie between 0.04 and 0.15. Subtropical desert regions (such as the Sahara and Arabian deserts) are much brighter, with TOA albedos between 0.25 and 0.35. As the amount of vegetation over land increases, the albedo decreases. Over forested regions, albedos are commonly between 0.05 and 0.20, while albedos over savannas and grasslands are typically between 0.15 and 0.25. In extreme conditions, such as dust outbreaks over ocean, forest fires, and volcanic eruptions, albedos over even dark surfaces can reach values comparable to those of clouds. By far the largest albedos observed on the planet occur over snow and ice. Just above the surface, albedos generally range between 0.65 and 0.75 for old snow, and can reach as high as 0.75–0.90 for fresh fallen snow. At the top of the atmosphere, albedos over snow are reduced slightly (by approximately 10–15%) because of absorption by the atmosphere (Warren, 1982).

THE IMPORTANCE OF SURFACE TYPE

The wavelength dependence of spectral albedo varies widely with surface type. Most surfaces (except snow) have very low albedos at ultraviolet wavelengths, and higher values in the visible and near-infrared. For vegetated surfaces it is especially maximized in wavelengths longer than 700 nanometers (Asrar, 1989). Albedos over soils have a more gradual increase with wavelength and are highly dependent upon the mineralogical composition of the soil and whether it is wet or dry. In contrast, albedos over snow are generally high at ultraviolet wavelengths, reach a maximum in the visible (400–500 nanometers), and decrease sharply at near-infrared wavelengths, where ice crystals strongly absorb solar radiation (Wiscombe and Warren, 1980).

Over most surfaces, albedo is also a function of the angle of solar incidence or, equivalently, the angle of the Sun above the horizon. The highest albedos tend to occur near sunrise and

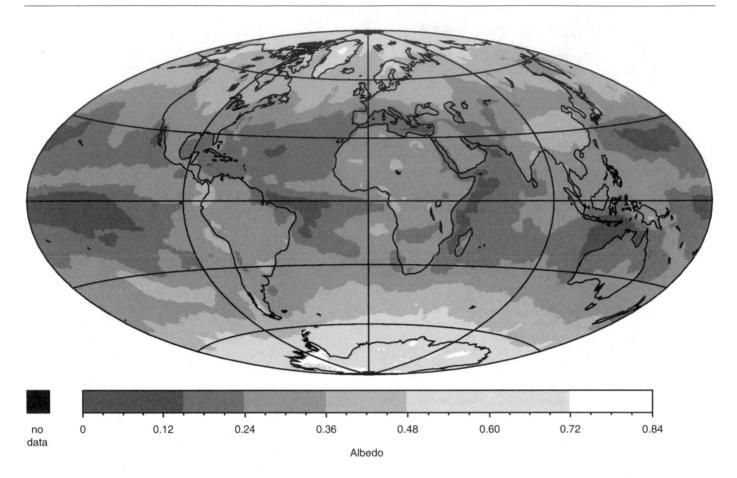

Albedo. Figure 1. Top-of-Atmosphere (TOA) Broadband Albedo Inferred from Earth Radiation Budget Experiment (ERBE) satellite measurements for September 1985 for all-sky conditions.

Scale shows the fraction of incident solar radiation.
(After Barkstrom and Smith, 1986.)

sunset, when the Sun is near the horizon. Because the angle of solar incidence decreases with latitude, albedos for a given surface type may also increase with latitude. How albedo varies with the angle of solar incidence depends on the physical properties and composition of the surface. Other factors, such as surface roughness, can also play an important role. For example, albedos over rough snow and wind-driven ocean surfaces are generally smaller than albedos over flat snow and ocean surfaces, and increase less rapidly when the Sun is near the horizon.

ASSESSMENT

The solar radiation absorbed by the Earth (which is the difference between the solar radiation intercepted by the planet and that reflected back to space) is the principal source of energy that drives the climate system. The Earth also emits radiation to space in the form of terrestrial infrared radiation. Over a year, a planetary radiation balance is approached, whereby the absorbed solar radiation is nearly balanced by outgoing terrestrial infrared radiation. A change in planetary albedo, brought about by such factors as a change in snow cover or by widespread deforestation could significantly modify this balance and alter climate. For example, an increase in albedo would mean less solar heating and a gradual cooling of the Earth. This cooling would continue until a new balance between emitted terrestrial infrared radiation and absorbed solar radiation was reached at some lower equilibrium temperature. Conversely, a decrease in

planetary albedo would result in a warmer climate. The prediction of global climate change due to natural or man-made perturbations requires an understanding of how the various components of the climate system influence the planetary radiation balance.

[*See also* Desertification; Global Warming; Greenhouse Effect; Pollution; *and* Snow Cover.]

BIBLIOGRAPHY

Asrar, G. *Theory and Applications of Optical Remote Sensing.* New York: Wiley, 1989.
Barkstrom, B. R., and G. L. Smith. "The Earth Radiation Budget Experiment: Science and Implementation." *Reviews of Geophysics* 24 (1986), 379–390.
Warren, S. G. "Optical Properties of Snow." *Reviews of Geophysical Space Physics* 20 (1982), 67–89.
Wiscombe, W. J., and S. G. Warren. "A Model for the Spectral Albedo of Snow. I. Pure Snow." *Journal of the Atmospheric Sciences* 37 (1980), 2712–2733.
—Norman G. Loeb

ALCOHOL

See Biofuels; *and* Ethanol.

AMAZONIA AND DEFORESTATION

The Amazon River watershed totals 7,350,621 km², of which 4,982,000 km² (67.8%) is in Brazil, 956,751 km² (13.0%) is in Peru, 824,000 km² (11.2%) is in Bolivia, 406,000 km² (5.5%) is in Colombia, 123,000 km² (1.7%) is in Ecuador, 53,000 km² (0.7%) is in Venezuela, and 5,870 km² (0.1%) is in Guyana. Depending on the definition used, Amazonia is 4–7 million km² in area, including in Brazil the Tocantins-Araguaia Basin (which drains into the Pará River, interconnected with the mouth of the Amazon) and the small river basins in Amapá that drain directly into the Atlantic. The forested area extends beyond the bounds of the river basin, especially on its northern and southern edges, but a number of enclaves of non-forest vegetation exist within the watershed. In addition, Greater Amazonia encompasses Suriname (142,800 km²), French Guiana (91,000 km²), and the

part of Guyana outside of the Amazon River watershed (205,369 km²), bringing the total area of "Greater Amazonia" to 7,789,790 km² (Figure 1).

In Brazil, the "Legal Amazon" (Portuguese, Amazônia Legal) is a 5 million km² administrative region comprising nine states. One million km² of the region was not originally forested, being covered by various kinds of savanna (especially the *cerrado,* or central Brazilian scrub savanna). The Legal Amazon was created in 1953 and slightly modified in extent in 1977. Because special subsidies and development programs apply within the region, its borders were drawn just far enough south to include the city of Cuiaba in Mato Grosso and just far enough east to include the city of São Luís in Maranhão, both outside of the Amazon River drainage basin.

Deforestation refers to the loss of primary (sometimes called "mature," "virgin," or "old-growth") forest. This is distinct from the cutting of secondary (successional) forests. In addition to clearing, as for agriculture or ranching, deforestation includes forest lost to flooding for hydroelectric dams. It does not include disturbance of forest by selective logging. In Amazonia, virtually

Amazonia and Deforestation. Figure 1. "Greater Amazon" and Brazil's Legal Amazon Regions.

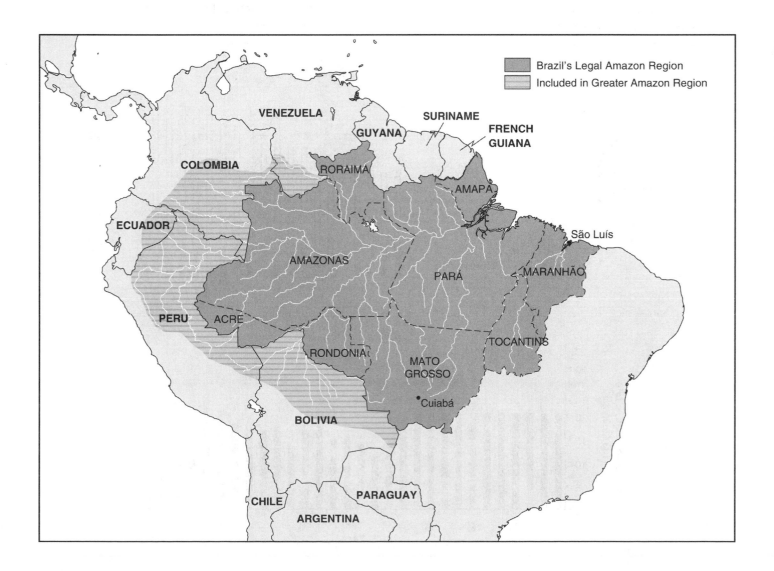

all logging is "selective" because only some of the many species of trees in the forest are accepted by today's timber markets.

Wide discrepancies in estimates for "deforestation" in Amazonia have often been the result of inconsistencies in definitions, including the delimitation of Amazonia, the inclusion or exclusion of the *cerrado* scrub savanna, classification of secondary forests as "forest" (versus already deforested), and the inclusion of flooding by hydroelectric dams. Differences among satellites and in interpretation of the data also contribute to discrepancies. Operationally, areas are classified as "deforested" if they are readily recognized as cleared on LANDSAT satellite imagery.

It is also important not to confuse deforestation with burning: not all land is burned when it is deforested, and many areas are burned that are either not originally forest (especially savanna) or have already been deforested (especially established cattle pastures). Amazonian forest can sometimes burn without being cleared first, as in the case of the Great Roraima Fire of 1998, but these events leave most trees standing and are not considered "deforestation."

EXTENT AND RATE OF DEFORESTATION

Much more complete information for the rate and extent of deforestation exists for Brazil than for the other Amazonian countries because of Brazil's monitoring capabilities at the National Institute of Space Research (INPE). The Food and Agriculture Organization of the United Nations (FAO) compiled estimates for the status of forests in 1990 and 2000 in all tropical countries. The FAO definitions of forest types are not entirely consistent with other classifications, particularly with regard to how much of the vast Brazilian *cerrado* should be considered a "forest." FAO (2001) estimated that for the 1991–2000 period 23.1×10^3 km² of forest were cleared annually in Brazil (including areas outside of Amazonia), 2.7×10^3 km²/year in Peru, 1.6×10^3 km²/year in Bolivia, 1.9×10^3 km²/year in Colombia, 1.4×10^3 km²/year in Ecuador, 2.2×10^3 km²/year in Venezuela, and 0.5×10^3 km²/year in Guyana. Deforestation rates in other parts of Greater Amazonia were minimal: deforestation in both Suriname and French Guiana was classified as "not significant" (FAO, 2001).

LANDSAT satellite data interpreted at INPE (Figure 2) indicate that by 2006 the area of forest cleared in Brazilian Amazonia had reached 712.6×10^3 km² (17.8% of the 4×10^6 km² originally forested portion of Brazil's 5×10^6 km² Legal Amazon Region),

Amazonia and Deforestation. Figure 2. Extent and Rate of Deforestation in the Brazilian Legal Amazon.

"Old" deforestation refers to pre-1970 clearing in Pará and Maranhão.

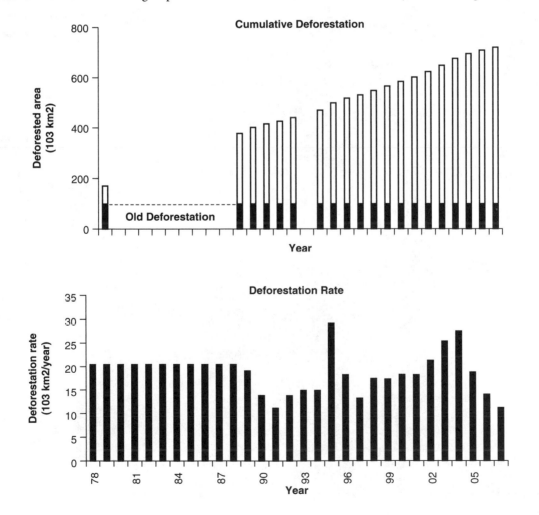

including approximately 100×10^3 km^2 of "old" (pre-1970) deforestation in Pará and Maranhão (Brazil, INPE, 2007). From 1978 to 1988, forest was lost at a rate of 20.4×10^3 km^2/yr (including hydroelectric flooding), the rate declined (beginning in 1987) to a low point of 11.1×10^3 km^2/yr in 1991, climbed gradually over the period 1992–1994 and then jumped to a peak of 29.1×10^3 km^2/yr in 1995. Following this the rate fell to 13.2×10^3 km^2/yr in 1997, after which it climbed again to a peak of 27.4×10^3 km^2/yr in 2004; the rate then fell to 14.0×10^3 km^2/yr in 2006 and preliminary results indicate a continued fall in 2007 (Brazil, INPE, 2007). Current values can be obtained from INPE's web site, http://www.inpe.br. Note, however, that the official explanations given by INPE as to *why* deforestation rates rise and fall (decrees affecting incentives and programs for inspection and levying fines) are unlikely to be correct (see below).

CAUSES OF DEFORESTATION

Amazonian countries differ greatly in the social factors driving deforestation. In Brazil, most clearing is done by large and middle-sized ranchers for cattle pasture, whereas the role of small farmers clearing for agriculture is relatively more important in the other countries. Brazil is by far the most important country in tropical forest matters in Amazonia and globally, both in terms of the extent of remaining forest and in terms of the area of forest being cleared each year.

The relative weight of small farmers versus large landholders in Brazilian Amazonia is continually changing as a result of changing economic and demographic pressures. The behavior of large landholders is most sensitive to economic changes such as the interest rates offered by money markets and other financial investments, government subsidies for agricultural credit, the rate of general inflation, and changes in the price of land. Tax incentives were a strong motive in the 1970s and 1980s. In June 1991 a decree suspended the granting of *new* incentives. However, the old (i.e., already approved) incentives continue to the present day, contrary to the popular impression that was fostered by numerous statements by government officials to the effect that incentives had been ended. Many of the other forms of incentives, such as large amounts of government-subsidized credit at rates far below those of Brazilian inflation, became much scarcer after 1984.

For decades preceding the initiation of Brazil's "Plano Real" economic reform program in July 1994, hyperinflation was the dominant feature of the Brazilian economy. Land played a role as store of value, and its value was bid up to levels much higher than what could be justified as an input to agricultural and ranching production. Deforestation played a critical role as a means of holding claim to land. Deforesting for cattle pasture was the cheapest and most effective means of maintaining possession of investments in land. The extent to which the motive for defending these claims (through expansion of cattle pasture) was speculative profits from increasing land value has been a matter of debate. Hecht et al. (1988) present calculations of the overall profitability of ranching in which the contribution from speculation is critical, while Mattos and Uhl (1994) show actual

production of beef has become increasingly more profitable, and that supplementary income from selling timber allows both deforestation and investment in recuperation of degraded pastures on the properties (Margulis, 2003). Progressive certification of Brazilian states as free of foot-and-mouth disease has opened Amazonia to the "hamburger connection" of international beef markets (Alencar et al., 2004; Arima et al., 2005; Kaimowitz et al., 2004). Selling off the timber can only be depended upon for a few years to subsidize the cattle-raising portion of the operations, since the timber harvest rates are virtually always above sustainable levels.

The decline in deforestation rates from 1987 through 1991 can best be explained by Brazil's deepening economic recession over this period. Ranchers simply did not have money to invest in expanding their clearings as quickly as they had in the past. In addition, the government lacked funds to continue building highways and establishing settlement projects. Probably very little of the decline can be attributed to Brazil's repression of deforestation through inspection from helicopters, confiscating chainsaws and fining landowners caught burning without the required permission from the Brazilian Institute of Environment and Renewable Natural Resources (IBAMA). Despite bitter complaints, most people continued to clear. Changes in policies on granting fiscal incentives also fail to explain the decline. The decree suspending the granting of incentives (Decree No. 153) was issued on June 25, 1991—after almost the entire observed decline in deforestation rate had already occurred (Figure 2). Even for the last year (1991), the effect would be minimal, as the average date for the LANDSAT images for the 1991 data set was August of that year.

The peak in 1995 was probably, in large part, a reflection of economic recovery under the Plano Real, which resulted in larger volumes of money suddenly becoming available for investment, including investment in cattle ranches. The fall in deforestation rates in the years after 1995 was a logical consequence of the Plano Real having sharply cut the rate of inflation. Land values reached a peak in 1995, and fell by about 50% by the end of 1997. Falling land values made land speculation unattractive to investors. Faminow (1998) analyzed state-level land price trends in Amazonia and concluded that speculative profits cannot explain the attraction of capital to investments in Amazonian ranches (see Fearnside, 2002).

Deforestation rates climbed steadily to another peak in 2004, after which they fell in the succeeding three years. While a repression campaign during this period undoubtedly had some effect, the decline in deforestation also coincides with falling international prices for soybeans and beef and a rise by about 50% in the value of the Brazilian real against the U.S. dollar, making Brazilian agricultural exports less profitable. The association of major swings in deforestation rate with macroeconomic factors such as money availability and inflation rate is one indication that much of the clearing is done by those who invest in medium and large cattle ranches, rather than by small farmers using family labor.

The distribution of clearing among the region's nine states indicates that most of the clearing is in states that are dominated by ranchers. For example, in 2006 the state of Mato Grosso alone accounted for 31% of the total, while the areas of large ranches in southern Pará accounted for most of the rest. Mato Grosso has the highest percentage of its privately held land in ranches of 1000 hectares or more: 84% at the time of the last (1985) agricultural census. The human significance of having 84% of the land in large ranches (and only 3% in small farms) should give anyone pause. By contrast, Rondônia—a state that has become famous for its deforestation by small farmers—had only 10% of the 1991 deforestation total, and Acre had 3%.

The number of properties censused in each size-class explains 74% of the variation in deforestation rate among the nine Amazonian states. Multiple regressions indicate that 30% of the clearing in both 1990 and 1991 can be attributed to small farmers (properties less than 100 hectares in area), and the remaining 70% to medium or large ranchers (Fearnside, 1993). This has been confirmed by interviews in the Arc of Deforestation where deforestation is concentrated along the eastern and southern edges of the region: only 25% of the clearing was in properties less than 100 hectares in area (Nepstad et al., 1999a). The social cost of substantially reducing deforestation rates would therefore be much less than is implied by frequent pronouncements that blame "poverty" for environmental problems in the region.

The question of who is to blame for tropical deforestation has profound implications for the priorities of programs intended to reduce forest loss. The prominence of cattle ranchers in Brazil (different from many other parts of the tropics) means that measures aimed at containing deforestation by, for example, promoting agroforestry among small farmers can never achieve this goal, although some of the same tools (such as agroforestry) have other important reasons for being supported.

IMPACTS OF DEFORESTATION

The deforestation of Amazonia affects biodiversity, greenhouse gases, and water resources.

Loss of biodiversity

Deforestation results in loss of biodiversity because most tropical forest species cannot survive the abrupt changes when forest is felled and burned and cannot adapt to the new conditions in the deforested landscape. The high degree of endemism (the presence of species that are only found within a small geographical range) can result in loss of species and loss of genetic variability within species even when the forest surrounding a cleared area appears to human observers to be identical to the forest that was lost.

The impact of deforestation extends beyond the area directly cleared because of edge effects and the impact of fragmentation of the formerly continuous forest into small islands that are unable to support viable populations of forest species, including their biological interactions (see Laurance and Bierregaard, 1997). In addition, fire and other disturbances (including

logging) are usually associated with the presence of nearby deforestation, thus further extending the impact beyond the edges of the clearings.

The impact of converting forest to a different land use depends not only on the patch of land for which conversion is being considered, but also on what has been done with the remainder of the region. As the cumulative area cleared increases, the danger increases that each additional hectare of clearing will lead to unacceptable impacts. For example, the risk of species extinctions increases greatly as the remaining areas of natural forest dwindle.

Biodiversity has many types of value, from financial value associated with selling a wide variety of products, to the use-value of the products, to existence-values unrelated to any direct "use" of a species and its products (Fearnside, 1999; Millennium Ecosystem Assessment, 2005). People disagree on what value should be attached to biodiversity, especially those forms of value not directly translatable into traditional financial terms by today's marketplace. While some may think that biodiversity is worthless except for sale, it is not necessary to convince such people that biodiversity is valuable; rather, it is sufficient for them to know that a constituency exists today and is growing, and that this represents a potential source of financial flows intended to maintain biodiversity. Political scientists estimate that such willingness to pay exceeds U.S.$20/hectare/year for tropical forest.

Greenhouse gas emissions

Carbon storage, in order to avoid global warming through the greenhouse effect, represents a major environmental service of Amazonian forests. The way that this benefit is calculated can have a tremendous effect on the value assigned to maintaining Amazonian forest. As currently understood in the United Nations Framework Convention on Climate Change (UNFCCC), maintaining carbon stocks is not considered a service—only deliberate incremental alterations in the flows of carbon (although this is excluded from credit under the Kyoto Protocol's Clean Development Mechanism for the period through 2012). Even considering only this more restrictive view of carbon benefits, the value of Amazonian forests is substantial. In 2006, Brazil's 14,039 km^2/year rate of deforestation was producing net committed emissions of 239 million metric tons of CO_2-equivalent carbon per year (updated from Fearnside, 1997a based on Nogueira et al., 2007). The benefit of slowing or stopping this emission is, therefore, substantial. All human activities in 2004 emitted approximately 14 billion tons of carbon, expressed as carbon equivalent from all greenhouse gases (IPCC, 2007). Of this, 8 billion tons was CO_2 from fossil-fuel combustion. Therefore, while slowing deforestation would be important in combating global warming, it cannot eliminate the need for major reductions in fossil fuel use throughout the world.

Although a wide variety of views exists on the value of carbon, already enacted carbon taxes of U.S.$45/ton in Sweden and the Netherlands and U.S.$6.1/ton in Finland indicate that the "willingness to pay" for this service is already substantial. This willingness to pay may increase significantly in the future when the magnitude of potential damage from global warming becomes more apparent to decision-makers and the general public. At the level indicated by current carbon taxes, the global-warming damage of Amazon deforestation at the 2006 rate already amounts to U.S.$1.4–10.8 billion/year. The amount of global-warming damage from clearing a hectare of forested land in Amazonia (U.S.$1,200–8,600) is much higher than the purchase price of land today. These calculations use U.S.$7.3/ton C as the value of permanently sequestered carbon.

Loss of water cycling

Water cycling is different from biodiversity and carbon in that impacts of deforestation in this area fall directly on Brazil rather than being spread over the world as a whole. About 20–30% of the rainfall in the Brazilian Amazon is water that is recycled through the forest, the rest originating from water vapor blown into the region directly from the Atlantic Ocean (Lean et al., 1996). Of the water entering the region, about 66% returns to the Atlantic via the Amazon River, the remainder being exported to other regions (Salati, 2001). Approximately half of the water vapor that remains airborne is transported southward (Correia, 2005), much of it to Brazil's Central-South Region, where most of the country's agriculture is located. Brazil's annual harvest has a gross value of about U.S.$65 billion, and dependence of even a small fraction of this on rainfall from Amazonian water vapor is a substantial value for Brazil. This water is also critical to hydroelectric power generated in south-central Brazil. Although movement of the water vapor is indicated by global circulation models, the amounts involved are still poorly quantified (Marengo et al., 2004).

The role of Amazonian forest in the region's water cycle also implies increasing risk with increasing deforestation: when rainfall reductions caused by losses of forest evapotranspiration are added to the natural variability that characterizes rainfall in the region, the resulting droughts would cross biological thresholds leading to major impacts (Foley et al., 2007). These thresholds include the drought tolerance of individual tree species and the increased probability of fire being able to propagate itself in standing forest. Fire entry into standing forest in Brazilian Amazonia already occurs in areas disturbed by logging (Cochrane et al., 1999). During the El Niño drought of 1997/1998, over 11,000 km² of undisturbed forest burned in Brazil's far northern state of Roraima (Barbosa and Fearnside, 1999). Large areas also burned in Pará (Alencar et al., 2006). In Amazonia, "mega-El Niño" events have caused widespread conflagrations in the forest four times over the past 2000 years (Meggers, 1994). The effect of large-scale deforestation is to make relatively rare events like these more frequent.

POTENTIAL COUNTERMEASURES

There are several strategies available to counteract the damaging effects of Amazonian deforestation.

Current efforts

Current efforts to contain deforestation include the Pilot Program to Conserve the Brazilian Rainforest, financed by the G-7 countries and administered by the World Bank and the Brazilian government. Components include the Demonstration Projects (PD/A, small projects carried out by NGOs), extractive reserves, indigenous lands, support for scientific research centers and directed research projects, natural resources policy (i.e., zoning), natural resources management (mainly forestry), várzea (floodplain) management, ecological corridors, fire and deforestation control (i.e., detection of deforestation and burning), and monitoring and analysis of Pilot Program activities in order to learn policy lessons.

In addition to the Pilot Program, the Brazilian government has a number of other programs aimed at controlling deforestation. These can be seen on the website of the Brazilian Institute for the Environment and Renewable Natural Resources (IBAMA, http:/www.ibama.gov.br). The ability of the Brazilian government to enforce environmental laws and restrain deforestation through command-and-control measures is essential, even though other more fundamental measures addressing the underlying causes of deforestation are also needed. Lack of confidence in the government's ability to control clearing has been at the root of the foreign ministry's longstanding reluctance to embrace avoided deforestation as a mitigation measure under the Kyoto Protocol. In this light, an experience with deforestation licensing and control by the state government of Mato Grosso over the 1999–2001 period has importance beyond the deforestation that was avoided in this period.

An important activity within the purview of the Ministry of the Environment is the creation of protected areas. The rapid expansion of the area in reserves of a variety of types has been, and continues to be, an important long-term restriction on deforestation (Ferreira et al., 2005). An important priority has been demarcation of indigenous lands, which comprise a much larger area of Amazonia than do protected areas. Indigenous areas are particularly effective because of the active defense by their indigenous inhabitants (Schwartzman et al., 2000). Nonetheless, progress on rewarding the environmental services of the reserves is needed if this protection is to be maintained over the long term.

Needed policy changes

The most basic problem in controlling deforestation is that much of what needs to be done falls outside of the purview of agencies such as IBAMA that are charged with mitigating environmental problems (Fearnside, 2005). Authority to change tax laws, resettlement policies, and road-building priorities, for example, rest with other parts of the government. The implications of infrastructure decisions are particularly important (Fearnside, 2007; Fearnside and Graça, 2006; Laurance et al., 2001; Soares-Filho et al., 2006).

The respite from deforestation pressure provided by economic factors such as unfavorable international commodity prices and exchange rates means that deforestation rates can be expected to increase again when these factors recover their strength, unless the government takes steps now to remove the underlying motives for deforestation. Steps needed include: assessing heavy taxes to take the profit out of land speculation, changing land-titling procedures to cease recognizing deforestation for cattle pasture as an "improvement" (*benfeitoria*), removing remaining subsidies, reinforcing procedures for Environmental Impact Reports (RIMAs), carrying out agrarian reform both in Amazonia and in the source areas of migrants, and offering alternative employment both in rural and in urban areas.

Although small farmers account for only about 30% of the deforestation, the intensity of deforestation within the area they occupy is greater than for the medium and large ranchers that hold 89% of the Legal Amazon's private land. Deforestation intensity, or the impact per unit area of private land, declines with increasing property size. This means that deforestation would increase if forest areas now held by large ranches were redistributed into small holdings. This indicates the importance of using already-cleared areas for agrarian reform, rather than following the politically easier path of distributing areas still in forest. Large as the area already cleared is, it falls far short of the potential demand for land to be settled. Indeed, even the Legal Amazon as a whole falls short of this demand. Recognizing the existence of carrying-capacity limits and then maintaining population levels within these is fundamental to any long-term plan for sustainable use of Amazonia.

Environmental services as development

At present, economic activities in Amazonia involve almost exclusively taking some material commodity and selling it. Typical commodities include timber, minerals, the products of agriculture and ranching, and non-timber forest products like natural rubber and Brazil nuts. The potential is much greater, both in terms of monetary value and in terms of sustainability, for pursuing a radically different strategy for long-term support: finding ways to tap the environmental services of the forest as a means of both sustaining the human population and maintaining the forest.

At least three classes of environmental services are provided by Amazonian forests: biodiversity maintenance, carbon storage, and water cycling. Various ways have been proposed to calculate the magnitude of the services and for the institutional arrangements that would reward them. The Kyoto Protocol, signed in December 1997, has been a substantial advance toward rewarding the forest's role in avoiding global warming, although political factors intervened to prevent granting carbon credit under the Protocol before 2013. Changes in the political context make some sort of credit for avoiding tropical deforestation much more likely from 2013 onwards. The Kyoto Protocol bases its carbon accounting on "additionality" (the incremental reduction in net emissions that results from a mitigation activity) as judged by comparison with a baseline scenario representing what would have been emitted without the project.

Additionality is not the only way to calculate the carbon benefits of avoided deforestation. A pre-Kyoto proposal for a system based on carbon stocks, rather than changes in flows, reappeared in 2007 as the basis of the "Amazonas Initiative"—a proposal by the government of Brazil's state of Amazonas for a system of payments based on stocks of environmental services. The original proposal for a stocks-based system included preliminary calculations of indicators of "willingness to pay" for the services lost from 1990 deforestation in the Brazilian Legal Amazon totaling U.S.$2.5 billion (assuming a 5% annual discount); maintenance of the stock of forest, if regarded as producing a 5%/year annuity, would be worth U.S.$37 billion annually (Fearnside, 1997b). The magnitude and value of these services are poorly quantified, and the diplomatic and other steps through which such services might be compensated are also in their infancy. These facts do not diminish the importance of the services nor of focusing effort on providing both the information and the political will needed to integrate these into the rest of the human economy in such a way that economic forces act to maintain rather than to destroy the forest.

On many fronts, one of the major challenges to finding rational uses for Amazonian forest lies in gathering and interpreting relevant information. Making environmental services of the forest into a basis for sustainable development is, perhaps, the area where information is most critical. Providing better understanding of the dynamics of deforestation, as well as understanding of deforestation's impacts on biodiversity, carbon storage and water cycling, is a necessary starting point on the long road to turning environmental services into a basis for sustainable development in Amazonia.

The term "development" implies a change, usually presumed to be an improvement. What is developed and whom the improvement should benefit are widely debated. This author holds that, in order to be considered "development," a change must provide a means to sustain the local population. Infrastructure that does not lead to production is not development, nor is a project that exports commodities from the region while generating minimal employment or other local returns. Aluminum processing and export provide the best example.

Production of traditional commodities often fails to benefit the local population. Conversion of forest to cattle pasture, the most widespread land-use change in Brazilian Amazonia, brings benefits that are extremely meager (although not quite zero). High priority must be given to redirection of development to activities with local-level returns that are greater and longer-lasting. Tapping the value of environmental services offers such an opportunity. Keeping benefits of these services for the inhabitants of the Amazonian interior is the most important challenge in turning these services into development.

BIBLIOGRAPHY

REFERENCES CITED

Alencar, A., et al. *Desmatamento na Amazônia: Indo além da emergência crônica.* Belém, Pará, Brazil: Instituto de Pesquisa Ambiental da Amazônia (IPAM), 2004.

Alencar, A., D.C. Nepstad, and M. del C. Vera Diaz. "Forest Understory Fire in the Brazilian Amazon in ENSO and Non-ENSO Years: Area Burned and Committed Carbon Emissions." *Earth Interactions* 10 (2006), 1–17.

Arima, E., P. Barreto, and M. Brito. *Pecuária na Amazônia: Tendências e implicações para a conservação ambiental*. Belém, Pará, Brazil: Instituto do Homem e Meio Ambiente da Amazônia (IMAZON), 2005.

Barbosa, R. I., and P. M. Fearnside. "Incêndios na Amazônia brasileira: Estimativa da emissão de gases do efeito estufa pela queima de diferentes ecossistemas de Roraima na passagem do evento 'El Niño' (1997/98)." *Acta Amazonica* 29.4 (1999), 513–534.

Cochrane, M.A., et al. "Positive Feedbacks in the Fire Dynamic of Closed Canopy Tropical Forests." *Science* 284 (1999), 1832–1835.

Correia, F.W.S. 2005. "Modelagem do impacto de modificaçoes da cobertura vegetal Amazonica no clima regional." PhD diss., Instituto Nacional de Pesquisas Espaciais (INPE), São José dos Campos, São Paulo, Brazil.

Faminow, M.D. *Cattle, Deforestation and Development in the Amazon: An Economic and Environmental Perspective*. New York: CAB International, 1998.

FAO (Food and Agriculture Organization of the United Nations). *Global Forest Resources Assessment 2000*. FAO Forestry Paper 140. Rome: FAO, 2001.

Fearnside, P.M. "Deforestation in Brazilian Amazonia: The Effect of Population and Land Tenure." *Ambio* 22.8 (1993), 537–545.

———. "Greenhouse Gases from Deforestation in Brazilian Amazonia: Net Committed Emissions." *Climatic Change* 35.3 (1997a), 321–360.

———. "Environmental Services as a Strategy for Sustainable Development in Rural Amazonia." *Ecological Economics* 20.1 (1997b), 53–70.

———. "Can Pasture Intensification Discourage Deforestation in the Amazon and Pantanal Regions of Brazil?" In *Deforestation and Land Use in the Amazon*, edited by C.H. Wood and R. Porro, pp. 283–364. Gainesville, Fla.: University Press of Florida, 2002.

———. "Deforestation in Brazilian Amazonia: History, Rates and Consequences." *Conservation Biology* 19.3 (2005), 680–688.

———. "Brazil's Cuiabá-Santarém (BR-163) Highway: The Environmental Cost of Paving a Soybean Corridor through the Amazon." *Environmental Management* 39.5 (2007), 601–614.

Fearnside, P.M. and P.M.L. de Alencastro Graça. "BR-319: Brazil's Manaus-Porto Velho Highway and the Potential Impact of Linking the Arc of Deforestation to Central Amazonia." *Environmental Management* 38.5 (2006), 705–716.

Ferreira, L.V., E.Venticinque and S.S. de Almeida. "O desmatamento na Amazônia e a importância das áreas protegidas." *Estudos Avançados* 19.53 (2005), 1–10.

Foley, J. A., et al. "Amazonia Revealed: Forest Degradation and Loss of Ecosystem Goods and Services in the Amazon Basin." *Frontiers in Ecology and the Environment* 5.1 (2007), 25–32.

Hecht, S.B., R.B. Norgaard, and C. Possio. "The Economics of Cattle Ranching in Eastern Amazonia." *Interciencia* 13.5 (1988), 233–240.

INPE (Instituto Nacional de Pesquisas Espaciais). *Projeto PRODES: Monitoramento da floresta Amazônica Brasileira por satélite*. São José dos Campos, São Paulo, Brazil: INPE, 2007.

IPCC (Intergovernmental Panel on Climate Change). *Contribution of Working Group III to the Fourth Assessment Report of the Intergovernmental Panel on Climate Change. Technical Summary*. Cambridge and New York: Cambridge University Press, 2007. http://arch.rivm.nl/env/int/ipcc/page_media/AR4-chapters.html (accessed May 24, 2008).

Kaimowitz, D., et al. *Hamburger Connection Fuels Amazon Destruction. Technical Report*. Bogor, Indonesia: Center for International Forest Research (CIFOR), 2004. http://www.cifor.cgiar.org/publications/pdf_files/media/Amazon.pdf (accessed May 24, 2008).

Laurance, W.F., and R.O. Bierregaard, Jr., eds. *Tropical Forest Remnants: Ecology, Management, and Conservation of Fragmented Communities*. Chicago: University of Chicago Press, 1997.

Laurance, W.F., et al. "The Future of the Brazilian Amazon." *Science* 291 (2001), 438–439. DOI: 10.1126/science.291.5503.438.

Lean, J., et al. "The Simulated Impact of Amazonian Deforestation on Climate Using Measured ABRACOS Vegetation Characteristics." In *Amazonian Deforestation and Climate*, edited by J.H.C. Gash, et al., pp. 549–576. Chichester, U.K., and New York: Wiley, 1996.

Marengo, J.A., et al. "Climatology of the Low-Level Jet East of the Andes as Derived from the NCEP-NCAR Reanalyses: Characteristics and Temporal Variability." *Journal of Climate* 17.12 (2004), 2261–2280.

Margulis, S. *Causas do desmatamento na Amazônia Brasileira*. Brasília, Brazil: The World Bank, 2003. http://www.ufra.edu.br/pet_florestal/downloads/desmatamento%20na%20amazonia.pdf (accessed May 24, 2008).

Mattos, M.M., and C. Uhl. "Economic and Ecological Perspectives on Ranching in the Eastern Amazon." *World Development* 22.2 (1994), 145–158.

Meggers, B.J. "Archeological Evidence for the Impact of Mega-Niño Events on Amazonia During the Past Two Millennia." *Climatic Change* 28.4 (1994), 321–338.

Millennium Ecosystem Assessment. *Ecosystems and Human Well-Being: Synthesis*. Washington, D.C.: Island Press, 2005.

Nepstad, D., et al. "Large-scale impoverishment of Amazonian forests by logging and fire." *Nature* 398 (1999), 505–508.

Nogueira, E.M., et al. "Wood Density in Forests of Brazil's 'Arc of Deforestation': Implications for Biomass and Flux of Carbon from Land-Use Change in Amazonia." *Forest Ecology and Management* 248.3 (2007), 119–135.

Salati, E. "Mudanças climáticas e o ciclo hidrológico na Amazônia." In *Causas e dinâmica do desmatamento na Amazônia*, edited by V. Fleischresser, pp. 153-172. Brasília, Brazil: Ministério do Meio Ambiente, 2001.

Schwartzman, S., A. Moreira, and D. Nepstad. "Rethinking Tropical Forest Conservation: Perils in Parks." *Conservation Biology* 14 (2000), 1351–1357.

Soares-Filho, B.S., et al. "Modelling Conservation in the Amazon Basin." *Nature* 440 (2006), 520–523.

SUGGESTED ADDITIONAL READINGS

Fearnside, P.M. "Human Carrying Capacity Estimation in Brazilian Amazonia as a Basis for Sustainable Development." *Environmental Conservation* 24.3 (1997), 271–282.

———. "Biodiversity as an Environmental Service in Brazil's Amazonian Forests: Risks, Value, and Conservation." *Environmental Conservation* 26.4 (1999), 305–321.

———. "Land-Tenure Issues as Factors in Environmental Destruction in Brazilian Amazonia: The Case of Southern Pará." *World Development* 29.8 (2001), 1361–1372.

———. "Saving Tropical Forests as a Global Warming Countermeasure: An Issue that Divides the Environmental Movement." *Ecological Economics* 39 (2001), 167–184.

———. "Deforestation Control in Mato Grosso: A New Model for Slowing the Loss of Brazil's Amazon Forest." *Ambio* 32.5 (2003), 343–345.

———. "Conservation Policy in Brazilian Amazonia: Understanding the Dilemmas." *World Development* 31.5 (2003), 757–779.

———. "A Água de São Paulo e a Floresta Amazônica." *Ciência Hoje* 34.203 (2004), 63–65.

———. "Indigenous Peoples as Providers of Environmental Services in Amazonia: Warning Signs from Mato Grosso." In *Global Impact, Local Action: New Environmental Policy in Latin America*, edited by A. Hall, pp. 187–198. London: University of London, School of Advanced Studies, Institute for the Study of the Americas, 2005.

———. "Mitigation of Climatic Change in the Amazon." In *Emerging Threats to Tropical Forests*, edited by W.F. Laurance and C.A. Peres, pp. 353–375. Chicago: University of Chicago Press, 2006.

———. "Dams in the Amazon: Belo Monte and Brazil's Hydroelectric Development of the Xingu River Basin." *Environmental Management* 38.1 (2006), 16–27.

Fearnside, P.M. and R.I. Barbosa. "Avoided Deforestation in Amazonia as a Global Warming Mitigation Measure: The Case of Mato Grosso." *World Resource Review* 15.3 (2003), 352–361.

—Philip M. Fearnside

ANTARCTICA AND CLIMATE CHANGE

Since the outset of scientific efforts to understand the natural climatic changes that the Earth has undergone in the past and the anthropogenic climate change we have now begun to recognize, Antarctica has been at the center of the debate. Today, Antarctica is at once a source of great insight into natural climate change in the Earth system over much of the last million years and a source of considerable confusion in the apparently counter-intuitive responses it is exhibiting today and may continue to display. Antarctic ice has yielded the best records of global climate during

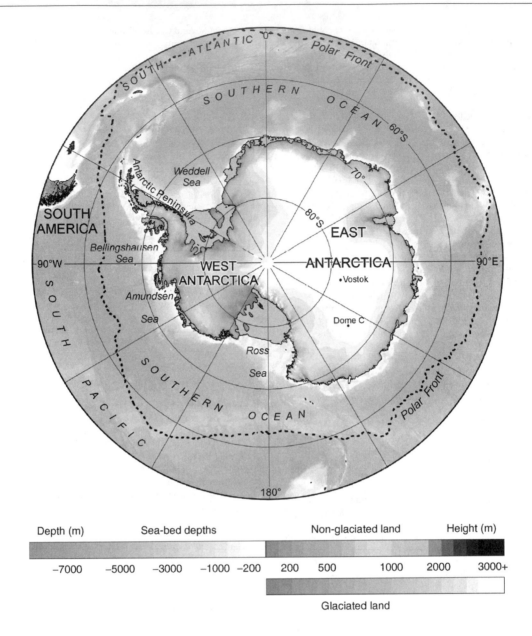

Depth (m)   Sea-bed depths   Non-glaciated land   Height (m)

-7000   -5000   -3000   -1000   -200   200   500   1000   2000   3000+

Glaciated land

the last half-million years and still contains a wealth of untapped climatic information which may go back more than one million years; the ice-sheet of Antarctica contains the greatest uncertainty in sea-level rise projections; and finally the Antarctic continent is a superb natural laboratory where the response of pristine natural systems to climate change can be studied in the absence of the confusion caused by direct human impacts.

THE "LAST CONTINENT"

Before the science-led exploration of the Antarctic continent that began during the International Geophysical Year of 1957–58, Antarctica was the sole domain of adventurers and explorers whose expeditions charted only a fraction of its surface. Even today, it would be untrue to say that every corner of Antarctica has been explored, but the entire continent has at least been mapped using satellites. Today Antarctica is governed by international treaty and is often described as a Continent for Science;

Antarctica and Climate Change. Figure 1. Map of Antarctica

it boasts many successes in cooperative international research. Tourists visit in ever increasing numbers; from several hundred visitors in 1967 to more than 30, 000 visitors a year today. And as images of the frozen south appear more frequently on our screens, far greater awareness, and concern, for the continent has developed in the general public. In science, attitudes are also changing. With a growing understanding of the global interdependence of physical processes, ecosystems, and human activities (collectively described as "earth system science"), the central role of Antarctica in maintaining Earth's environment is being established.

This article focuses on three particular areas of this science, and demonstrates this influence and the unique value of the last continent on our understanding of Earth and our influence upon it.

A WINDOW ON PAST CLIMATES

The dominant feature of the Antarctic continent is the ice. A continuous ice sheet covers 99.6% of the Antarctic continent. In places the ice sheet is over 4,500 m thick and the deepest layers perhaps millions of years old. It is the single largest solid object on the surface of the planet and contains around 90% of the Earth's fresh water. The ice sheet is nourished by snowfall and deposits of frost, which, because of the year-round cold environment, does not melt but accumulates year after year. As these surface snows are buried by new snowfall, they are compressed and eventually transformed into solid ice, ice that contains a chemical record of past climates and atmospheres. Eventually, glacial flow transports the ice back toward the sea, where it either calves in icebergs or melts directly into the coastal waters.

A vertical drill core into the ice sheet reveals that the snow near the surface is quite different from that near the bed. The near-surface snow has a low density and is highly porous, containing more air than ice. Close to the base of the ice is solid, clear-blue glacial ice. The transition from snow to ice, a process called firnification by glaciologists, results from the great pressure developed in the ice sheet by the mounting weight of new snowfall. Firnification includes many subtle changes, but the most important transition is one called pore close-off. This occurs at a depth of around 70 m, where the snow is already beginning to resemble ice but still contains a network of air bubbles. Above pore close-off, the air bubbles are still interconnected, and so essentially open to the atmosphere. Below pore close-off, the network shrinks and the air bubbles become isolated from one another and from the atmosphere above. At still greater depths, the air captured in bubbles at pore close-off remains captured and is eventually pushed by the weight of the ice above into the crystalline structure of the ice itself. If a sample of ice from below pore close-off is allowed to thaw, the air locked in the ice is released and can be captured for analysis. The archive of past climates that is available to scientists from ice cores is one of the most important sources of information about how Earth's climate has changed in the last million or so years. Not only does the air sample that can be obtained from an ice core tell us how the concentrations of greenhouse gases (carbon dioxide and methane) have changed through the glacial and interglacial cycles, but the relative concentrations of different isotopes, particularly oxygen and hydrogen, are a natural thermometer that records the changing temperature of the planet.

Ice cores from both Antarctica and Greenland reveal a broadly similar story. Carbon dioxide and methane concentrations have varied naturally from highs during warm interglacial periods to lows during the coldest glacial periods. These changes in greenhouse gases are closely matched by the isotope thermometers, indicating that on a naturally-regulated Earth, global changes in temperature and greenhouse gas concentrations have been inextricably linked. However, ice cores and direct measurements show that since the Industrial Revolution, when humans first began burning fossil fuels on an industrial scale, the concentration of carbon dioxide (and methane) has risen higher than it did during any of the natural fluctuations for many hundreds of millennia and is likely to rise faster in the coming century.

The most recent ice core extracted from Dome C in Antarctica shows that carbon dioxide is now 30% higher and methane 130% higher than at any time in the last 650,000 years. And the rates of rise in these concentrations are around 200 times the rate of natural changes over the same period. There is little doubt that such changes will cause rapid and irrevocable changes in the global climate and the natural and human systems it supports. There is a growing body of evidence that such changes are already underway.

Future work on ice cores will focus on several important areas of research: finding the best site to drill an ice core that will provide the longest record of climate change available, which is likely to be more than a million years; comparing northern hemisphere and southern hemisphere ice-core records, to understand whether there is any noticeable asymmetry in the response of north and south; and understanding the phasing between changes in greenhouse gases and global temperature, to understand the causal processes that link the two.

RECENT CLIMATE CHANGE IN ANTARCTICA

In most developed countries, including the United Kingdom, climate has been monitored at meteorological stations that have been in constant operation for many decades, and in a few cases for hundreds of years. In contrast, climate in Antarctica has been measured at manned scientific stations for only the 50 years since the IGY. The difficulties of interpreting these short records is compounded by the fact that the stations are very sparsely distributed. We have only around 20 long-term (existing for more than 30 years) climate-measuring stations across an entire continent whose greatest diameter is almost the same as the distance from London to New York (5,500 km), and these stations span several quite distinct climatic environments. In the cold, high continental climate of East Antarctica precipitation rates are so low that it can be classified as a desert. The more maritime West Antarctica sees more frequent storm activity, and the much warmer Antarctic Peninsula is unique in producing considerable rates of summer snow melt.

Given such a variety of climates and such a short-lived and sparse monitoring network, it is not surprising that our understanding of how recent global climate change has been represented in Antarctica is behind that which exists for the other continents. The most recent report from the Intergovernmental Panel on Climate Change (IPCC) noted that the "ability of coupled climate models to simulate the observed temperature evolution on each of six continents provides stronger evidence of human influence on climate" than was previously available, but they could not include Antarctica in this statement. This does not mean that evidence of climate change is not seen in Antarctica, but that perhaps as a result of a paucity of data due to real spatial and temporal complexity, we cannot see a clear representation of global climate change in Antarctica.

Outside the Antarctica Peninsula, there are 19 long-term Antarctic continental temperature records available, of which 12 show warming and 7 show cooling; but only two of these (one of each) are significant at the 10% level. The mean trend suggests that climate warming across Antarctica could be comparable to mean global warming, but while the Arctic shows clear evidence of "polar amplification" of climate change, there is no such evidence of a continent-wide amplification in Antarctica.

In contrast, there are on the Antarctic Peninsula several climate records spanning several decades. Each of these shows large and statistically significant warming trends. Indeed, over the past 50 years, the west coast of the Peninsula has been one of the most rapidly warming parts of the planet. Mean annual temperatures there have risen by nearly 3°C in the last 50 years; this is 5–10 times the mean rate of global warming. This regional warming has caused a host of changes in the area, from glacier and ice-shelf retreat, glacier acceleration, and increasing areas of exposed rock, to changes in flora and penguin distributions.

For some time the regional warming on the Antarctic Peninsula has appeared enigmatic, and considerable recent work has been done to determine if it is part of a natural cyclic change peculiar to this area, or whether the warming is a local magnification of human-induced global climate change; several lines of evidence now suggest it is the latter.

Ice shelves are floating extensions of the glaciers, and around the Antarctic Peninsula many ice shelves are retreating in response to atmospheric warming. Warmer summers create surface melt water that trickles down and warms the entire thickness of the ice shelf, making it more prone to fracture. The presence of ice shelves is recorded in the marine sediments that accumulate beneath them on the seabed. A record taken from beneath Larsen-B Ice Shelf shows that, before its final collapse in 2002, this ice shelf had existed continuously for at least 10,000 years. This showed that the climate has not been as warm as it is at present for a very long time, and present warming cannot be ascribed simply to natural oscillations. Similar retreat has been seen on around 10 other, similarly vulnerable, ice shelves along the Antarctic Peninsula. The likelihood of such events occurring over the same period by chance is very low and indicates that the present warming is not simply part of a natural cycle.

Recent climate models show that the Antarctic Peninsula is indeed part of the pattern of global climate change and that the changes in its climate can be attributed, at least in part, to anthropogenic causes. It has been shown that an increase in the strength of the dominant westerly atmospheric circulation over the Antarctic Peninsula is a predictable consequence of increased greenhouse-gas concentrations and ozone loss, and this provides a clear mechanism for bringing warmer air masses onto the Antarctic Peninsula. The question now is whether the elevated rates of climate warming we have seen on the Antarctic Peninsula will migrate further south in the coming decades. Such an occurrence over the rest of the Antarctic continent would have potentially dramatic consequences for the Antarctic ice sheet.

ANTARCTICA AND GLOBAL SEA LEVEL

Accumulation of new snow on the Antarctic ice sheet could not continue indefinitely without being balanced by loss of ice by glacial flow: eventually all the water from the oceans would be piled up in an impossibly thick ice sheet. Glacial flow exists essentially to regulate the amount of ice contained in the ice sheet. In simple terms, the Antarctic ice sheet can be thought of as an immense conveyor belt, transporting ice from the interior of the ice sheet to the sea. One must understand the balance between what is going into the conveyor and what is leaving it, because any imbalance implies a change in the volume of water in the world's oceans and thus a change in sea level. Since around 2 trillion metric tons of ice enters and leaves the Antarctic ice sheet each year, equivalent to 6 mm of global sea level, even small imbalances could have a significant impact on future sea-level rises.

Global sea-level rise has been measured with tide-gauges for more than 100 years, and with satellites for more than 20. It is clear from these records that global sea level is now rising at around 3 mm per year. This rise is the sum of many global processes, including thermal expansion of the oceans, melting of non-polar glaciers, and human changes in storage of water on and under the land. The 2007 report from the influential Intergovernmental Panel on Climate Change highlighted improved observation of sea-level rise and greater certainty in the projected impacts of global warming on non-polar glaciers and thermal expansion of the oceans. These advances heighten confidence in the most predictable components of sea-level rise, but the IPCC's projections specifically exclude the contribution that could arise from rapidly changing flow in ice sheets in the future, especially in Greenland and West Antarctica. The contribution to sea-level rise of ice sheets in Antarctica and Greenland is not well understood, but it could account for about one third of the present rate of sea-level rise and could grow substantially in the future.

Until a few years ago scientists had little idea whether or not the Antarctic ice sheet was contributing to global sea-level rise. The studies that addressed the question were generally simple efforts at accounting—summing algebraically the amount of snow falling on the continent and the amount leaving by iceberg production and melting. This may sound like a relatively straightforward task, but the uncertainties inherent in doing this over a continental area are inescapable. No such assessment of the continental contribution to sea-level rise has been precise enough to be useful, but in the last decade things have changed completely as new technology has provided glaciologists with satellite-borne altimeters that map the surface topography of ice sheets with great precision. These satellite altimeters are so precise that they can yield maps of the very small changes (around 1 cm per year) in the surface elevation of the Antarctic and Greenland ice sheets. The present generation of these maps shows thickening in some parts of the ice sheet and thinning in others. In less than a decade the emphasis of the science has changed radically, going beyond the conceptually simple question of whether any changes are occurring in the Antarctic ice sheet, to the much more difficult job of understanding what is causing the observed changes, and providing reliable predictions. Broadly, there are three parts of Antarctica where the evidence suggests that the ice sheet is changing, but each of these areas appears to be responding to different forces.

The northern Antarctic Peninsula

Over the last 50 years, the climate warming in this area (discussed earlier) has caused immediate changes in all of its glaciers. This warming reduces ice in coastal areas causing glaciers to both retreat and accelerate. Where ice shelves have retreated, the glaciers that once drained into them have accelerated dramatically. Finally, increased summer temperatures are producing more surface-melting and direct runoff of meltwater into the oceans. We expect these trends will continue.

East Antarctica

Despite very low rates of snowfall and low ice-flow rates, the huge area of the East Antarctic ice sheet means that even tiny changes in the thickness of ice in this region could have a substantial effect on sea-level rise. Recent evidence from satellite altimeters suggests that over the last decade there has been a thickening of a couple of centimeters per year and a little more in some limited areas. Debate concerning the exact distribution and magnitude of this change continues, but it is possible that this observation represents the emergence of a long-predicted consequence of anthropogenic climate change, that the rate of snowfall over East Antarctica will increase and act to slow the rate of sea-level rise. However, even if this is the case, and if climate change continues, current climate models predict that the increase in snowfall over East Antarctica could only marginally reduce the rate of global sea-level rise.

West Antarctica

The West Antarctic ice sheet is unique in that it rests on rock that is, in places, thousands of meters below sea level, and over large areas, the present ice sheet would not need to thin by much for the ice to begin to float. This means that the West Antarctic ice sheet may be uniquely capable of rapid deglaciation, and it is thus the focus of considerable concern. A decade of satellite measurements of the ice sheet surface in West Antarctica have shown that the portion of the ice sheet that drains into the Amundsen Sea is thinning at rates of several centimeters to several meters per year. Several neighboring glacier basins appear to be behaving similarly, and thinning is most concentrated on the fast-moving parts of those glaciers, suggesting that it is the result of a dynamic change in the ice sheet itself rather than a change in snowfall. All the glaciers affected drain into the same part of the Amundsen Sea, so it is likely that the cause of the change in the ice sheet across this region is to be found in those waters. At present, the timescales of the changes in the sea that might be driving the ice sheet are not clear, and there are too few measurements to establish whether change continues. Because ocean temperature and circulation are linked to climate, the oceans provide a plausible connection between anthropogenic greenhouse emissions and the changes occurring in this part of the Antarctic ice sheet. However, there are other, competing theories that attempt to explain this change; for example, it is possible that this is part of a millennia-long retreat of the ice sheet.

In recent years scientists have just begun to explore the key areas of the West Antarctic ice sheet, mapping its bed and monitoring imbalance in the ice flow. We may soon have a greatly improved understanding of the likelihood that West Antarctica could make an extra, as yet unpredicted, contribution to sea-level rise in the coming future.

In terms of exploration, Antarctica is the "last continent," but it is by no means the least important in the climate-change debate. There are lessons to be learnt by visiting Antarctica and by observing it from afar by satellites. Antarctica may be an icon of the unknowable, but in this changing world understanding Antarctic is essential and overdue.

BIBLIOGRAPHY

Solomon, S., et al., eds. "Summary for Policymakers." In *Climate Change 2007: The Physical Science Basis. Contribution of Working Group I to the Fourth Assessment Report of the Intergovernmental Panel on Climate Change.* Cambridge and New York: Cambridge University Press, 2007. http://www.ipcc.ch/pdf/assessment-report/ar4/wg1/ar4-wg1-spm.pdf (accessed May 24, 2008).

—DAVID G. VAUGHAN

ANTHROPOGEOMORPHOLOGY

Anthropogeomorphology is the study of the human role in creating landforms and modifying the geomorphological processes such as weathering, erosion, transport, and deposition (Goudie, 1993; Goudie, 2006a). Some features are produced by direct anthropogenic processes. These tend to be obvious in form and are frequently created intentionally. They include landforms produced by construction (e.g., mine dumps, embankments, sea walls), excavation (e.g., mines), hydrological interference (e.g., reservoirs, canals), and farming (e.g., terraces). Table 1 lists some of the major anthropogeomorphic processes.

By contrast, landforms produced by indirect anthropogenic processes are often more difficult to recognize because they involve the acceleration of natural processes rather than the creation of new ones. They result from environmental changes brought about inadvertently by human actions. Nonetheless, it is this indirect and inadvertent modification of processes and landforms that is the most crucial aspect of anthropogeomorphology. By modifying land cover, humans have accelerated erosion and sedimentation (James and Marcus, 2006; Wilkinson and McElroy, 2007). Sometimes the results will be spectacular and obvious, as when major gullies develop rapidly; other results may have less immediate effect on landforms (e.g., sheet erosion) but are nevertheless important. By other indirect means humans may create subsidence (Johnson, 1991), trigger

TABLE 1. Major Anthropogeomorphic Processes

Direct Anthropogenic Processes

Constructional

    tipping: molding, plowing, terracing, reclamation

Excavational

    digging, cutting, mining, blasting of cohesive or noncohesive materials

    craters

    tramping, churning

Hydrological interference

    flooding, damming, canal construction, dredging, channel modification, draining, coastal protection

Indirect Anthropogenic Processes

Acceleration of erosion and sedimentation

    agricultural activity and clearance of vegetation, engineering, especially road construction and urbanization

    incidental modifications of hydrological regime

Subsidence: collapse, settling

    mining (e.g., of coal and salt)

    hydraulic (e.g., groundwater and hydrocarbon pumping)

    thermokarst (melting of permafrost)

Slope failure: landslides, flows, accelerated creep

    loading

    undercutting

    shaking

    lubrication

Earthquake generation

    loading (reservoirs)

    lubrication (fault plane)

Weathering

    acidification of precipitation

    accelerated salinization

    lateritization

landslides, and even influence seismicity through the impoundment of reservoirs (Meade, 1991). Rates of weathering may be modified by the acidification of precipitation caused by accelerated nitrate and sulfate emissions or by accelerated salinization in areas of irrigation (Goudie and Viles, 1997). [*See* Building Decay.]

Finally, there are situations in which humans may, through a lack of understanding of the operation of processes and the links between different processes and phenomena, deliberately and directly alter landforms and processes and thereby set in train events that were not anticipated or desired. There have been many attempts to reduce coastal erosion which, in fact, only worsened it. Examples include dune-stabilization schemes in North Carolina (Dolan et al., 1973) and the role of sea walls in causing beach scour (Bird, 1979).

As so often with environmental change, it is difficult to disentangle anthropogenic changes from natural ones. There has, for example, been a long debate about the origin of incised valley-bottom gullies (arroyos) that developed in the southwestern United States between 1865 and 1915. Some workers have attributed them to human actions, citing such factors as timber felling, overgrazing, harvesting of grass, compaction along trails, channeling of runoff from trails and railroads, and disruption of valley-bottom sod by stock. Others have attributed them to natural environmental changes, noting that arroyo incision had occurred repeatedly before the arrival of Europeans. Among the natural changes that could promote the phenomenon are aridification (which depletes the cover of protective vegetation) and increased frequencies of intense storms (which generate erosive runoff) (Cooke and Reeves, 1976; Balling and Wells, 1990). Similar debates surround the incision of the Mediterranean valleys (Vitz-Finzi, 1969; Butzer, 1974) and the deposition of fills of freshwater carbonate (tufa) in European valleys (Goudie et al., 1993).

Anthropogeomorphology. Sand Quarry, United Arab Emirates.

Huge quantities of material are being excavated for the construction industry in this burgeoning, oil-rich country.

Another example of the complexity of causation in geomorphological change is that of the current loss of land to the sea in Louisiana (Walker et al., 1987). In addition to possible natural causes such as sea-level change, subsidence, progressive compaction of sediments, changes in the locations of deltaic deposition, hurricane attack, and degradation by marsh fauna, one must consider human actions, including the role that dams and levees have played in reducing the amount and altering the texture of sediment reaching the coast, the role of canal and highway construction, and subsidence caused by fluid withdrawals (especially by pumping hydrocarbons and fresh water).

The possibility of global warming has many implications for anthropogeomorphology. [*See* Rivers: Impacts of Climate Change.] While increased temperatures will have a direct impact on some landforms, they will also have an indirect effect through associated changes in precipitation regimes, rates of moisture loss by transpiration and evaporation, and the distribution and form of vegetation (Table 2).

Increased sea-surface temperatures may change the spread, frequency, and intensity of tropical cyclones, which are highly important geomorphological agents, particularly in terms of river channels and mass movements. Warmer temperatures will cause sea ice to melt and lead to the retreat of alpine glaciers and the melting of permafrost (permanently frozen subsoil). Vegetation types will change and show latitudinal and altitudinal migration that will also influence the operation of geomorphological processes. Changes in temperature, precipitation quantities, and the timing and form of precipitation (e.g., whether rain or snow) will have a range of important hydrological consequences (Goudie, 2006b). Some parts of the world may become moister (e.g., high latitudes and some parts of the tropics) while other parts (e.g., many drylands) may become drier. The latter would suffer from declines in river flow, lake desiccation, reactivation of dunes and increasing dust storms. [*See* Desert Dunes in a Warmer World *and* Dust Storms.] However, among the most important potential changes are those associated with rising

TABLE 2. Some Geomorphologic Consequences of Global Warming

Hydrologic

Increased evapotranspiration loss

Increased percentage of precipitation as rainfall at expense of winter snowfall

Increased precipitation as snowfall in very high latitudes

Possible increased risk of cyclones (greater spread, frequency, and intensity)

Changes in state of peatbogs and wetlands

Less vegetational use of water because of increased CO_2 effect on stomatal closure

Vegetational Controls

Major changes in latitudinal extent of biomes

Reduction in boreal forest, increase in grassland, etc.

Major changes in altitudinal distribution of vegetation types (ca. 500 m for 3°C)

Growth enhancement by CO_2 fertilization

Cryospheric

Permafrost, decay, thermokarst, increased thickness of active layer, instability of slopes, river banks, and shorelines

Changes in glacier and ice-sheet rates of ablation and accumulation

Sea ice melting

Coastal

Inundation of low-lying areas (including wetlands, deltas, reefs, lagoons, etc.)

Accelerated coast recession (particularly of sandy beaches)

Changes in rate of reef growth

Spread of mangrove swamp

Eolian

Increased dust storm activity and dune movement in areas of moisture deficit

Soil Erosion

Changes in response to changes in land use, fires, natural vegetation cover, rainfall erosivity, etc.

Changes resulting from soil erodibility modification (e.g., sodium and organic contents)

Subsidence

Desiccation of clays under conditions of summer drought

sea levels. [*See* Sea Level Future.] Low-lying areas (e.g., salt marshes, mangrove swamps, deltas, coral atolls) would be particularly susceptible, but rising sea levels could promote general beach erosion. [*See* Deltas and Global Warming.] Goudie (1996) introduced the term "geomorphological hotspots" for areas where the effects of global warming might be especially serious in highly sensitive landform environments.

Some landscapes will be especially sensitive because they are located where climate is expected to undergo greater than average change. This is the case in high latitudes where warming may be three to four times greater than the global average. It may also be the case in some critical areas where particularly large changes in precipitation may result from global warming. For example, various climatic-prediction models produce scenarios in which the interior of southern Africa will become markedly drier. Other landscapes will be especially sensitive because certain landscape-forming processes are closely controlled by climatic conditions. If such landscapes are close to particular climatic thresholds, modest climatic change may switch them from one state to another.

[*See also* Erosion *and* Land Surface Processes.]

BIBLIOGRAPHY

Balling, R.C., and S.G. Wells. "Historical Rainfall Patterns and Arroyo Activity within the Zuni River Drainage Basin, New Mexico." *Annals of the Association of American Geographers* 80 (1990), 603–617.

Bird, E.C.F. "Coastal Processes." In *Man and Environmental Processes*, edited by K. J. Gregory and D.G. Walling, pp. 82–101. Folkestone, U.K.: Dawson, 1979.

Butzer, K.W. "Accelerated Soil Erosion: A Problem of Man-Land Relationships." In *Perspectives on Environments*, edited by I.R. Manners and M.W. Mikesell. Washington, D.C.: Association of American Geographers, 1974.

Anthropogeomorphology. Man-made Structures.

The construction of engineering structures, such as this pier and marina at West Bay, Dorset, southern England, can have a whole series of impacts on sediment budgets, erosion and deposition.

Wilkinson, B. H., and B. J. McElroy, "The Impact of Humans on Continental Erosion and Sedimentation." *Bulletin of the Geological Society of America* 119 (2007), 140–156.

—ANDREW S. GOUDIE

Cooke, R.U., and R.W. Reeves. *Arroyos and Environmental Change in the American South-West.* Oxford: Clarendon, 1976.

Dolan, R., P.J. Godfrey, and W.E. Odum. "Man's Impact on the Barrier Island of North Carolina." *American Scientist* 61 (1973), 152–162.

Goudie, A.S. "Human Influence in Geomorphology." *Geomorphology* 7 (1993), 37–59.

———. "Geomorphological 'Hotspots' and Global Warming." *Interdisciplinary Science Reviews* 21 (1996), 253–259.

———. *The Human Impact on the Natural Environment.* 6th ed. Oxford: Blackwell, 2006a.

———. "Global Warming and Fluvial Geomorphology." *Geomorphology* 79 (2006b), 384–394.

Goudie, A.S., and H.A. Viles. *Salt Weathering Hazards.* Chichester, U.K.: Wiley, 1997.

Goudie, A.S., H.A. Viles, and A. Pentecost. "The Late-Holocene Tufa Decline in Europe." *The Holocene* 3 (1993), 181–186.

James L.A. and W.A. Marcus, eds. "The Human Role in Changing Fluvial Systems." *Geomorphology* 79 (2006), 143–506.

Johnson, A.I., ed. *Land Subsidence.* International Association of Hydrological Sciences Publication 200. Wallingford, U.K.: IAHS Press, 1991.

Meade, R.B. "Reservoirs and Earthquakes." *Engineering Geology* 30 (1991), 245–262.

Vita-Finzi, C. *The Mediterranean Valleys.* Cambridge: Cambridge University Press, 1969.

Walker, H.J., et al. "Wetland Loss in Louisiana." *Geografiska Annaler* 69A (1987), 189–200.

HUMANS VERSUS NATURE IN EARTHMOVING

Estimates of human earthmoving show that our efforts are comparable in scale to some natural geologic processes. Omitting the indirect effects of actions such as deforestation and cultivation, the following are the magnitudes of deliberate human earthmoving in the United States (Hooke, 1994).

	Billion metric tons per year
Excavation for housing and other construction	0.8
Mining	3.8
Road work	3.0
Total United States	7.6
World total (roughly four times the U.S. total)	30.0

HUMANS VERSUS NATURE IN EARTHMOVING

For comparison, the following figures represent estimated world totals due to natural earthmoving processes.

	Billion metric tons per year
River transport to oceans and lakes	14
Short-distance transport within river basins	40
Tectonic forces lifting continents	14
Volcanic activity elevating sea floor	30
Glacial transport	4.3
Wind transport	1.0

BIBLIOGRAPHY

Hooke, R.L. "On the Efficacy of Humans as Geomorphic Agents." *GSA Today* 9 (1994), 217–225.
Monastersky, R. "Earthmovers." *Science News* (December 24, 1994), 432–433.

— DAVID J. CUFF

ARAL SEA

The Aral Sea was, by area, the world's fourth largest lake in 1960. Though brackish, the lake was populated chiefly by fresh-water species. The sea supported a major fishery, directly and indirectly employing 60,000, and functioned as a key regional transportation route. The extensive deltas of the Syr Dar'ya and Amu Dar'ya, which flow into the Aral, sustained diverse flora and fauna and were very important economically.

The Aral has changed dramatically over the past 45 years. The sea has steadily shrunk and become more saline (Figure 2 and Table 1). The primary cause has been expanding irrigation that substantially diminished discharge from its two tributary rivers. The Aral separated into two water bodies in the late 1980s: the Small Aral in the north and the Large Aral in the south.

ENVIRONMENTAL, ECONOMIC, AND HUMAN CONSEQUENCES

Harm from the Aral's drying has been severe. Commercial fishing, which was a key regional industry, ended by the early 1980s as rising salinity drove native fish from the sea. The rich ecosystems of the Amu Dar'ya and Syr Dar'ya deltas also suffered from spreading desertification leading to ecological degradation and simplification. The area of lakes and wetlands, so important to permanent and migratory aquatic bird populations, shrank sharply. Irrigated agriculture, practiced in the deltas of the Amu Dar'ya and Syr Dar'ya for millennia, was severely harmed.

Salt and dust are blown as much as 500 km downwind from the increasingly large former sea bottom (over 53,000 km² by 2007). Natural vegetation and crops in the Amu Dar'ya delta have been most negatively impacted by this.

HOPE FOR THE ARAL SEA?

Returning the entire Aral to its pre-1960s state is not realistic for the foreseeable future, as it would require raising the average inflow to 55 km³/yr. But partial restoration/preservation of portions of the sea is feasible. A conservative estimate is that future average annual inflow would be at least 10 km³, 3.5 km³ going into the Small Aral from the Syr Dar'ya and 6.5 km³ into the Large Aral from the Amu Dar'ya. A U.S.$85 million project to raise and stabilize the Small Aral was completed in fall 2005. Funded by the World Bank and the Government of Kazakhstan, it created a 13-kilometer dike to block the flow from the Small to Large seas. By March 2007 the level of the Small Aral had risen to the design level of 42 meters, freshening the water body and improving its ecological condition as well as the fishery.

The Large Aral is a more difficult problem. It continues to shrink rapidly, with sea level falling below 30 meters by early 2007 and the sea separating into a western and eastern basin connected by only a narrow channel. Over several decades, the eastern basin will probably stabilize at about 28.3 meters, with an area of 4,300 km² and volume of 5 km³. The shallow residual lake would have a maximum depth of 2.5 meters. The western basin would probably stabilize at about 21 meters with an area near 2,100 km² and volume about 36 km³. It would be relatively deep (maximum 37 meters). Salinity in both basins would rise well above 100 g/1, far too high for fish, but optimal for brine shrimp (*Artemia*), which, if their eggs could be harvested, might provide some benefit.

There are, however, more optimistic scenarios for both the Small and Large Aral. If average annual inflow from the Syr Dar'ya could be maintained at 4.5 km³, which was slightly exceeded for the period 1990–2004 when discharge averaged 5 km³, the level of the Small Aral could be raised and stabilized at about 47 meters and the area expanded to about 4,300 km². This would not only improve ecological conditions and fishery prospects, but also allow reconnection of the sea via shipping channels to the former major port city of Aralsk.

Rehabilitation of the deep western basin of the Large Aral is also possible. Average annual flow to the Aral from the Amu Dar'ya would need to be raised to 8 km³. The flow of the Amu Dar'ya would be redirected from the eastern basin into the western via an existing diversion channel. The western basin could be maintained at a level of 33 meters and area of 6,200 km². A dike across the north end of the basin would control outflow to the eastern basin, averaging around 2.3 km³/yr. The western basin would gradually freshen as more salt is carried out of the lake than is brought in, allowing initial stocking with salt-tolerant fish and later with endemic Aral species. The eastern basin's level would stabilize at about 27.4 meters with an area around 2,600 km² and would become hypersaline (>200 g/1). This project would likely be more expensive and difficult than the recently completed project to rehabilitate the Small Aral Sea. Also, the range of potential negative environmental consequences is unknown.

BIBLIOGRAPHY

Aladin, N.V., I.S. Plotnikov, and R. Letolle. "Hydrobiology of the Aral Sea." In *Dying and Dead Seas: Climatic versus Anthropic Causes*, edited by C.J. Nihoul,

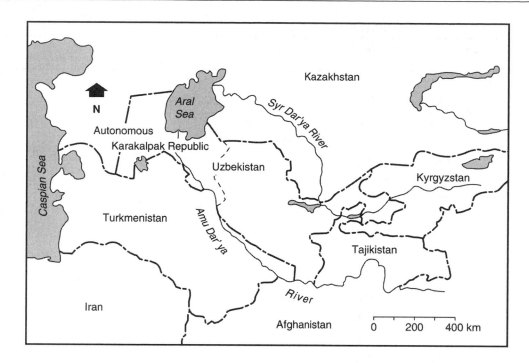

Aral Sea. FIGURE 1. Location of the Aral Sea.

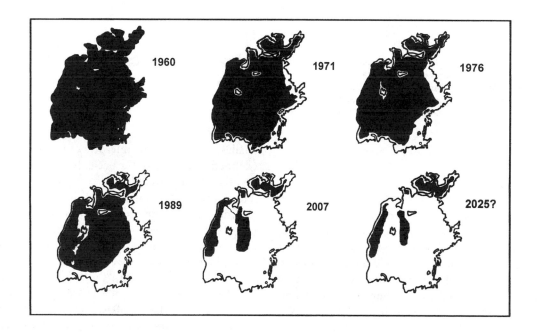

Aral Sea. FIGURE 2. The Shrinking Aral Sea, 1960–2025.

P. Zavialov and P. Micklin, pp. 135–259. Dordrecht, Netherlands, and Boston, Mass.: Kluwer, 2004.

CA Water Info (Information Portal for Water and Environmental Issues in Central Asia): http://www.cawater-info.net/index_e.htm (accessed May 24, 2008).

Cretaux, J.F., et al. "Evolution of Sea Level of the Big Aral Sea from Satellite Altimetry and Its Implications for Water Balance." *Journal of Great Lakes Research* 31.4 (2005), 520–534.

Micklin, P. *Managing Water in Central Asia*. London: The Royal Institute of International Affairs, Central Asian and Caucasian Prospects, 2000.

———. "The Aral Sea Crisis." In *Dying and Dead Seas: Climatic versus Anthropic Causes*, edited by C.J. Nihoul, P. Zavialov, and P. Micklin. Dordrecht, Netherlands, and Boston, Mass.: Kluwer, 2004, pp. 99–125.

———. "The Aral Sea Crises and Its Future: An Assessment in 2006." *Eurasian Geography and Economics* 47.5 (2006), 546–568.

TABLE 1. Hydrological and Salinity Characteristics of the Aral Sea, 1960–2025

Year (part of Aral Sea)	Level (m asl)	Area (km²)	% 1960 area	Volume (km³)	% 1960 Volume	Avg. Salinity (g/l)	% 1960 Salinity
1960 (Whole)[a]	53.4	67,499	100	1,089	100	10	100
Large	53.4	61,381	100	1,007	100	10	100
Small	53.4	6,118	100	82	100	10	100
1971 (Whole)	51.1	60,200	89	925	85	12	120
1976 (Whole)	48.3	55,700	83	763	70	14	140
1989 (Whole)		39,734	59	364	33		
Large	39.1	36,930	60	341	34	30	300
Small	40.2	2,804	46	23	28	30	300
2007 (Whole)[b]		13,958	21	102	9		
Large	29.4	10,700	17	75	8	East >100	>1000
						West 75–85	750–850
Small	42.0	3,258	53	27	33	12?	120
2025 (Whole)[b]		9,658	14	68	6		
Large[c]	21–28.3	6,400	10	41	4	>100 to >200	>1000 to >2000
Small	42.0	3,258	53	27	33	10?	100

[a]Annual average. [b]As of January 1. [c]The sea will consist of a western and eastern part with the west basin at 21 meters and the east at 28. Compiled from a variety of Russian and English sources as well as data and information gathered by the author.

———. "The Aral Sea Disaster." *Annual Review of Earth and Planetary Sciences* 35 (2007), 47–72. DOI: 10.1146/annurev.earth.35.031306.140120.

Sverskiy, I., et al. *Aral Sea: GIWA Regional Assessment 24.* Kalmar, Sweden: UNEP, 2005. www.giwa.net/publications/r24.phtml (accessed May 24, 2008).

Zavialov, P. *Physical Oceanography of the Dying Aral Sea.* Berlin: Springer, 2005.

—PHILIP MICKLIN

ARCTIC SEA-ICE

In the Northern Hemisphere, sea ice covers most of the Arctic Ocean and in winter can extend as far south as 40°N (e.g., Bo Hai Bay, China; Chesapeake Bay, United States). Figure 1 illustrates the strong seasonal cycle in Arctic sea-ice extent, ranging from an annual maximum of around 16×10^6 km² in March (solid black line) to a minimum of around 7×10^6 km² at the end of the summer melt season in September (solid dark gray line).

Remote sensing employing instruments in the microwave portion of the electromagnetic spectrum are well suited for studying changes in the Arctic sea-ice cover. These instruments are able to view the surface under cloud cover or at night, and because there is a large emissivity difference between ice and water, the presence of sea ice is easily distinguished from open water. Data from satellite-borne passive microwave instruments have been available since the late 1970s and provide the most accurate and consistent estimates of Arctic sea-ice cover.

CURRENT CHANGES IN ARCTIC ICE COVER

Both the extent and the age (and thickness) of the Arctic ice cover are affected by climate change.

Ice extent

Analysis of passive microwave-measured sea-ice extent (defined as the area of the ocean having at least 15% ice cover) reveals a rapid retreat in the extent of Arctic sea ice since the late 1970s. Based on data through 2006 the estimated rate of decline in annual ice extent is approximately 3.8% per decade (Figure 2). However, changes in the summer ice cover are much larger (e.g., Serreze et al., 2003; Stroeve et al., 2005). For example, Figure 4 shows the spatial extent of September sea ice in 2005, together with the median ice extent (dark gray line, based on data from 1979 to 2000). In 2005, the September ice cover was the smallest since 1979, with an average September ice extent of only 5.56×10^6 km², compared to the median ice extent of 7.04×10^6 km². Thus, in 2005 we saw a 21% reduction from normal in the area covered by sea ice. However, every year since 2002 has seen remarkable ice losses during the month of September, especially off the shores of Alaska and Siberia (e.g., Serreze et al., 2003; Stroeve et al., 2005). Before 2002, the decline in sea-ice extent at the end of the summer melt season was 6.5% per decade. In 2002 it jumped to 7.3% per decade and by 2006 it increased to 9.1% per decade (or at an ice loss rate of about 100,000 km² per year) (Stroeve et al., 2007).

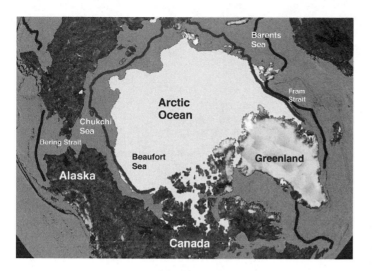

Arctic Sea-Ice. Figure 1. Sea-Ice Extent

Median ice extent based on the period 1979–2000 for September (dark gray line) and March (black line) illustrates the typical seasonal range of ice extent in the Arctic. The white area indicates sea-ice extent in September 2005. (National Snow and Ice Data Center, Boulder CO.)

Arctic sea-ice extent in September 2007 surpassed all previous September records for the lowest absolute minimum extent. Sea-ice extent retreated significantly in the East Siberian side of the Arctic (e.g., the Chukchi and East Siberian seas) and also in the Beaufort Sea north of Alaska. Ice conditions were also anomalously low in the Canadian Archipelago, resulting in an opening of the Northwest Passage (NWP) during the third week of August 2007. From Figures 2 and 3 it is clear that the 2007 summer ice cover shrank dramatically in relation to the previous record minimum year.

Although changes in winter have not been as dramatic as those in summer, the last three years have also witnessed large changes in the winter ice cover (e.g., Meier et al., 2005), with ice extents 6–8% below the long-term mean (1979–2000). These recent reductions have been observed in both the Pacific and Atlantic sectors, and winter 2006–2007 set record lows in ice extent over the satellite record. We are now in an era when statistically significant (at the 99% confidence level) downward trends in Arctic sea-ice extent occur in all calendar months.

Ice age and thickness

There is growing evidence for accompanying thinning of the ice pack. Rothrock et al. (1999) noted reductions of more than 1 m in late-summer ice-draft (the submerged depth of floating ice) over much of the Central Arctic Ocean from the period 1953–1976 to the period 1993–1997. The sparse sampling of the submarine sonar data used for making this assessment complicates interpretation, but there is other supporting evidence for a thinning Arctic ice pack. Thickness of the Arctic ice pack can be reduced through enhanced melt, reduced ice

growth, weaker ridging processes or export of sea ice from the Arctic Basin into the North Atlantic. Changes in the thickness distribution of the Arctic ice pack may also occur via transport of ice into other regions of the Arctic Basin, leaving some areas thinner and others thicker. Ice that has survived through at least one summer (multiyear ice) is typically thicker than first-year ice, and ice that has survived several summers is assumed to be thicker than second-year ice. Using satellite data and drifting buoys from 1979 on, Fowler et al. (2004) were able to assess the formation, movement, and melt of the ice, which in turn was used to estimate ice age. Results from this study show that the area of oldest ice (i.e., ice older than 4 years) is decreasing in the Arctic Basin, and being replaced by younger, and therefore thinner, ice. The oldest (and thus thickest) ice is now confined to a relatively small area north of the Canadian Archipelago.

FUTURE ARCTIC ICE CONDITIONS?

Zhang and Walsh (2006) note that all models used in the Intergovernmental Panel on Climate Change (IPCC) Fourth Assessment Report (AR4) show declining ice over the period of observations. These IPCC AR4 model simulations (under the A1B emissions scenario) suggest a seasonally ice-free Arctic may occur as early as 2050. The subsequent study of Stroeve et al. (2007), however, found that over the period 1953–2006 (using a sea-ice record extended back in time with earlier satellite data and other sources, such as aircraft and ship observations), none of 13 IPCC AR4 models examined shows a summer ice-loss trend as large as is observed (Figure 4). Considered as a group, the models simulate a loss of 2.5% per decade, whereas the observations indicate a loss of 7.8% per decade. This suggests that the transition to an ice-free summer Arctic Ocean may occur much earlier than many of these models predict, perhaps well within the twenty-first century.

Holland et al. (2006) suggest the transition to a seasonally ice-free Arctic might occur rather abruptly. Simulations based on one of the IPCC AR4 climate models (the Community Climate System Model, version 3 [CCSM3]) indicate that if the ice thins to a vulnerable state, natural climate variability may provide the extra push that would cause rapid summer ice loss through the ice-albedo feedback. [See Albedo.] In these simulations, abrupt transitions to a nearly ice-free summer Arctic were seen to occur in as little as 10 years.

EXPLANATIONS FOR THE OBSERVED ICE LOSSES

Almost all climate model simulations depict ice loss from the late twentieth through the twenty-first century as associated with rising greenhouse gas concentrations. However, the rates of decline vary widely between models. Rising surface air temperatures (SATs) help to explain the observed loss of ice. Comiso (2003) reports on an overall increase in SATs from satellite observations while Stroeve et al. (2006) note that the length of the melt season has increased by about two weeks per decade.

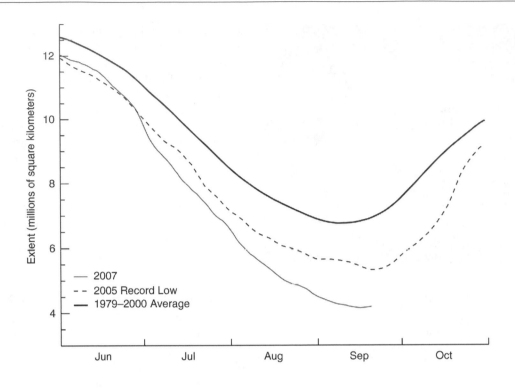

Arctic Sea-Ice. Figure 2. Arctic Sea-Ice Extent (Area of Ocean With at Least 15% Sea Ice).

(National Snow and Ice Data Center, Boulder CO.)

Variability in the atmospheric circulation has also played a strong role, especially through altering the circulation of the ice cover. Links with the North Atlantic Oscillation (NAO) and its hemispheric-scale counterpart, the Arctic Oscillation (AO), are especially prominent (e.g., Deser et al., 2000; Rigor et al., 2002; Zhang et al., 2003). [See North Atlantic Oscillation.] Rigor et al. (2002) showed that when the AO is positive in winter, altered wind patterns result in more offshore ice motion and ice divergence along the Siberian and Alaskan coastal areas, which leads to the production of thinner first-year ice in spring that requires less energy to melt in summer. Zhang et al. (2003) explained reduced summer ice cover during positive AO phases as a result of the spread of warmer air temperatures from Eurasia into the central Arctic. While this may have been the case in the 1990s, these hypotheses do not neatly explain the large ice losses that have occurred in the 2000s, which have seen the AO generally regress from its high positive phase to a more neutral phase.

There is evidence that the strongly positive phase of the winter AO in the early to mid 1990s led to the export of thick, multiyear ice out of the Arctic basin, leaving behind thinner ice that is more easily melted (Rigor and Wallace, 2004). Support for this view comes from tracking of ice age in the Arctic using satellite data that suggest the ice in the Arctic is younger now than it was in the 1980s (Fowler et al., 2004). However, Rigor and Wallace (2004) estimate that combined winter and summer AO-indices can explain less than 20% of the variance in summer sea-ice extent in the western Arctic, where most of the recent reduction in sea-ice cover has occurred. Maslanik et al. (2007) argue that atmospheric circulation patterns other than

the AO have contributed to this variance. A separate analysis of the combined effect of winds, radiative fluxes, and advected heat shows that atmospheric forcing can account for about half of the total variance in summer sea-ice extent in the western Arctic (Francis et al., 2005).

There are also potential impacts of changes in ocean heat transport. Maslowski et al. (2004) explored the role of oceanic forcing on sea-ice cover in the East Greenland Sea and found that oceanic heat fluxes associated with Atlantic water recirculating near Fram Strait can explain over 60% of the total variance in the summer ice cover over the Greenland shelf on an annual basis. There are recent observations showing warming of the Atlantic water flowing north into the Arctic through the eastern Fram Strait and the Barents Sea (Walczowski and Piechura, 2006), and showing changes in the transport of warm Pacific water that enters the Arctic Ocean through the Bering Strait (e.g., Shimada et al., 2006). The study by Holland et al., (2006) showed that a change in ocean heat transport could provide the trigger to initiate an abrupt loss of summer ice cover.

In the summer of 2007, a combination of high summer temperatures, clear skies, thinner ice and warming ocean temperatures contributed to the record ice losses. Air temperatures in June and July showed strong positive temperature anomalies over much of the Arctic Ocean, accelerating ice melt, with the largest temperature anomalies (3–5°C) occurring on the Siberian side

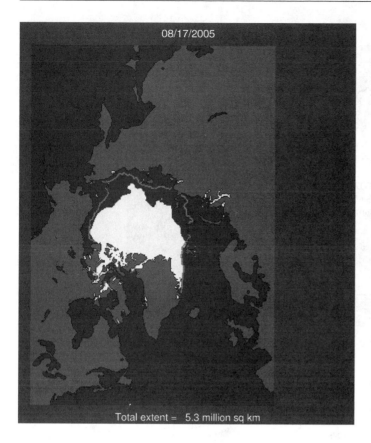

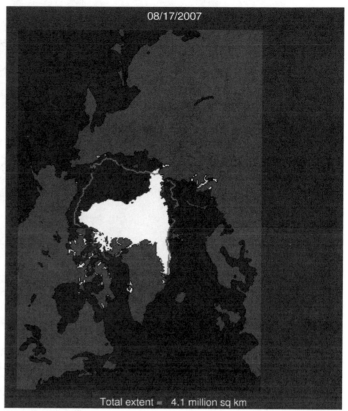

Arctic Sea-Ice. FIGURE 3. Sea-Ice Extent.

(National Snow and Ice Data Center, Boulder CO.)

where the largest ice losses were observed. However, at the same time, high pressure dominated the central Arctic Ocean, promoting very sunny conditions just at the time when the sun was highest in the sky over the far north. This led to unusually strong solar heating of the Arctic ice surface, further accelerating the melting process. Over Siberia, low pressure dominated during the same time period, which, when combined with the high pressure over the central Arctic Ocean, generated strong southerly winds over coastal Siberia that not only brought warm air into the region but also acted to push ice away from the coast and into the central Arctic Ocean, further reducing ice extent in the coastal areas. These atmospheric conditions, combined with an already thinner Arctic ice pack and increasingly warmer ocean temperatures were enough to result in record-breaking daily rates of sea-ice loss in June, July, and August 2007.

OUTLOOK

The Arctic is currently experiencing a dramatic reduction in its sea-ice cover, not only in its spatial extent, but also apparently in its volume. However, the causes of Arctic sea-ice decline are still not completely understood. Natural variability such as that associated with the AO and other circulation patterns will certainly continue to impact the Arctic sea-ice cover. However, results from the recent study by Stroeve et al. (2007) suggest the current summer ice losses are now too strong and persistent to be explained solely through natural processes and that the effects of greenhouse-gas loading are starting to emerge. It could also be that oceanic thermodynamic control of sea ice through under-ice ablation and lateral melt along marginal ice zones is playing a larger role than previously suspected and may be one of the reasons that current climate models underestimate how quickly the Arctic is currently losing its summer ice cover. Nevertheless, given the basic agreement between models and observations regarding the trajectory of ice loss, transition to a seasonally ice-free Arctic Ocean in summer seems increasingly certain.

BIBLIOGRAPHY

"Arctic Sea Ice News & Analysis." http://www.nsidc.org/arcticseaicenews/index.html (accessed May 25, 2008). Latest update of Arctic sea ice extent from the National Snow and Ice Data Center.

Comiso, J. "Arctic Warming Signals from Clear-Sky Surface Temperature Satellite Observations." *Journal of Climate* 16 (2003), 3498–3510.

Deser, C., J.E. Walsh, and M.S. Timlin. "Arctic Sea Ice Variability in the Context of Recent Atmospheric Circulation Trends." *Journal of Climate* 13 (2000), 617–633.

Fowler, C., W.J. Emery, and J.A. Maslanik. "Satellite-Derived Evolution of Arctic Sea Ice Age: October 1978 to March 2003." *IEEE Geoscience and Remote Sensing Letters* 1 (2004), 71.

Francis, J.A., et al. "Clues to Variability in Arctic Minimum Sea Ice Extent." *Geophysical Research Letters* 32 (2005), 21501. DOI:10.1029/2005GL024376.

Holland, M.M., C.M. Bitz, and B. Tremblay. "Future Abrupt Reductions in the Summer Arctic Sea Ice." *Geophysical Research Letters* 33, L23503 (2006). DOI: 10.1029/2006GL028024.

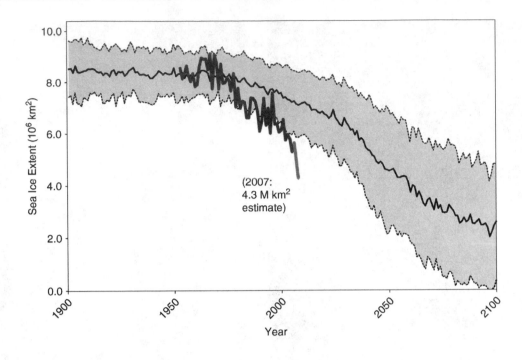

Arctic Sea-Ice. Figure 4. September Arctic Sea-Ice Extent.

September sea ice extent from observations (thick black line) and simulations from 13 IPCC AR4 climate models, with the multi-model ensemble mean indicated by the thin black line, and the one standard deviation by the dotted black line.

Maslanik, J., et al. "On the Arctic Climate Paradox and the Continuing Role of Atmospheric Circulation in Affecting Sea Ice Conditions." *Geophysical Research Letters* 34, L03711 (2007). DOI: 10.1029/2006GL028269.

Maslowski, W., et al. "On Climatological Mass, Heat, and Salt Transports through the Barents Sea and Fram Strait from a Pan-Arctic Coupled Ice-Ocean Model Simulation." *Journal of Geophysical Research* 109, C03032 (2004). DOI: 10.1029/2001JC001039.

Meier, W.N., et al. "Reductions in Arctic Sea Ice Cover No Longer Limited to Summer." *EOS* 86.36 (2005), 326.

Rigor, I.G., and J.M. Wallace. "Variations in the Age of Arctic Sea-Ice and Summer Sea-Ice Extent." *Geophysical Research Letters* 31, L09401 (2004). DOI: 10.1029/2004GL019492.

Rigor, I.G., J.M. Wallace, and R.L. Colony. "On the Response of Sea Ice to the Arctic Oscillation." *Journal of Climate* 15.18 (2002), 2648–2668 (http://iabp. apl.washington.edu/SesIceAO; accessed May 27, 2008).

Rothrock, D.A., Y. Yu, and G.A. Maykut. "Thinning of the Arctic Sea-Ice Cover." *Geophysical Research Letters* 26.23 (1999), 3469–3472.

Serreze, M.C., et al. "A Record Minimum Arctic Sea Ice Extent and Area in 2002." *Geophysical Research Letters* 30.3 (2003), 1110. DOI: 10.1029/2002GL016406.

Shimada, K., et al. "Pacific Ocean Inflow: Influence on Catastrophic Reduction of Sea Ice Cover in the Arctic Ocean." *Geophysical Research Letters* 33, L08605 (2006). DOI: 10.1029/2005GL025624.

Stroeve, J.C., et al. "Tracking the Arctic's Shrinking Ice Cover: Another Extreme September Minimum in 2004." *Geophysical Research Letters* 32, L04501 (2005). DOI: 10.1029/2004GL021810.

Stroeve, J., et al. "Recent Changes in the Arctic Melt Season." *Annals of Glaciology* 44 (2006), 367–374.

Stroeve, J., et al. "Arctic Sea Ice Decline: Faster than Forecast." *Geophysical Research Letters* 34 (2007). DOI: 10.1029/2007GL029703.

Walczowski, W., and J. Piechura. "New Evidence of Warming Propagating toward the Arctic Ocean." *Geophysical Research Letters* 33, L12601 (2006). DOI: 10.1029/2006GL025872.

Zhang, X., and J.E. Walsh. "Toward a Seasonally Ice-Covered Arctic Ocean: Scenarios from the IPCC AR4 Model Simulations." *Journal of Climate* 19 (2006), 1730–1747.

Zhang, J., et al. "Assimilation of Ice Motion Observations and Comparisons with Submarine Ice Thickness Data." *Journal of Geophysical Research* 108.C6 (2003), 3170. DOI: 10.1029/2001JC001041. (http://psc.apl.washington.edu/ zhang/Pubs/Zhang_assimilationIceMotion.pdf; accessed May 27, 2008).

—Julienne Stroeve

ARCTIC WARMING

Climate change is being experienced particularly intensely in the Arctic. The average temperature in the Arctic has, in the past few decades, risen at almost twice the rate as that of the rest of the world. Widespread melting of glaciers and sea ice and thawing of permafrost are additional evidence of strong arctic warming (ACIA, 2004, 2005). These changes in the Arctic provide an early indication of the environmental and societal significance of global warming.

An acceleration of these climatic trends is projected to occur during this century, caused by increases in the concentrations of greenhouse gases in the Earth's atmosphere. While greenhouse gas emissions do not originate primarily in the Arctic, they are projected to bring wide-ranging changes to the region. These Arctic changes will, in turn, impact the planet as a whole. For this reason, people outside the Arctic have a great stake in what is happening there. For example, climatic processes unique to the Arctic have significant effects on global and regional climate. The Arctic also provides important natural resources to the rest of the world (such as oil, gas, and fish) that will be affected by climate change. The melting of land-based ice in the Arctic is one of the factors contributing to global sea-level rise.

Climate change is also projected to have major effects inside the Arctic, some of which are already under way. Whether a particular impact is perceived as negative or positive often depends on one's interests. For example, the reduction in sea ice is very likely to have devastating consequences for polar bears, ice-dependent seals, and local people for whom these animals are a primary food source. On the other hand, reduced sea ice is likely to increase marine access to the region's resources, expanding opportunities for shipping and possibly for offshore oil extraction (although operations could be hampered initially by increasing movement of ice in some areas). Further complicating the issue, possible increases in environmental damage that often accompanies shipping and resource extraction could harm the marine habitat and negatively affect the health and traditional lifestyles of indigenous people.

Climate change is taking place concurrently with many other changes in the Arctic, including an increase in chemical contaminants entering the Arctic from other regions, overfishing, land-use changes that result in habitat destruction and fragmentation, an increase in ultraviolet radiation reaching the surface, rapid growth in the human population, and cultural, governance, and economic changes. Impacts on the environment and society result not from climate change alone, but from the interplay of all of these changes. The combination of climate change and other stresses presents a range of potential problems for human health and well-being as well as risks to other Arctic species and ecosystems.

Changes in Arctic climate including shorter warmer winters, increased precipitation, and substantial decreases in snow and ice cover, are projected to persist for centuries. Unexpected and even larger changes are also possible.

WHY THE ARCTIC WARMS FASTER THAN LOWER LATITUDES

First, as Arctic snow and ice melt, the darker land and ocean surfaces that are revealed absorb more of the Sun's energy, increasing warming. Second, in the Arctic, a greater fraction of the extra energy received at the surface due to increasing concentrations of greenhouse gases goes directly into warming the atmosphere, whereas in the tropics, a greater fraction goes into evaporation. Third, the depth of the atmospheric layer that has to warm in order to cause warming of near-surface air is much shallower in the Arctic than in the tropics, resulting in a larger Arctic temperature increase. Fourth, as warming reduces the extent of sea ice, solar heat absorbed by the oceans in the summer is more easily transferred to the atmosphere in the winter, making the air temperature warmer than it would be otherwise.

OBSERVED AND POSSIBLE FUTURE CHANGES IN ARCTIC CLIMATE

Increasing temperatures, melting glaciers, reductions in the extent and thickness of sea ice, thawing permafrost, and rising sea level all provide strong evidence of recent warming in the Arctic.

Increasing temperatures and precipitation

There are regional variations due to atmospheric winds and ocean currents, with some areas showing more warming than others and a few areas even showing a slight cooling; but for the Arctic as a whole, there is a clear warming trend. Annual average temperature changes range from a 2–3°C warming in Alaska and Siberia to a cooling of up to 1°C in southern Greenland. There are also patterns within this overall trend; for example, in most places, temperatures in winter are rising more rapidly than in summer. In Siberia, Alaska, and western Canada, winter temperatures have increased as much as 4°C in the past 50 years.

Precipitation has increased by roughly 8% across the Arctic over the past 100 years. In addition to the overall increase, there have been changes in the characteristics of precipitation. Much of the increase appears to be coming as rain, mostly in winter, and to a lesser extent in autumn and spring. The increasing winter rains, which fall on top of existing snow, cause faster snowmelt and, when the rainfall is intense, can result in flash flooding. Rain-on-snow events have increased significantly across much of the Arctic, for example, by 50% over the past 50 years in western Russia. Snow-cover extent over Arctic land areas has declined by about 10% over the past 30 years, with much of the decrease taking place in spring, resulting in a shorter snow-cover season.

Global climate model projections suggest that the Arctic will warm roughly twice as much as the globe over the course of the twenty-first century. Under one moderate emissions scenario run by five climate models, this would result in about 3 to 5°C of warming over land areas and up to 7°C over the oceans by 2100, averaged over the Arctic region (see Figure 1; the full set of emissions scenarios suggests a much wider range of possible outcomes). Winter temperature increases are projected to be substantially greater than the annual averages, with warming of 4 to 7°C over land areas and 7 to 10°C over the oceans for a moderate emissions scenario. Higher emissions scenarios yield larger increases.

Precipitation is also projected to increase significantly. Over the Arctic as a whole, annual total precipitation is projected to increase by about 20% by the end of the twenty-first century, with most of the increase coming as rain. The overall increase is projected to be most concentrated over coastal regions and in winter and autumn; increases in these seasons are projected to exceed 30%.

Snow-cover extent, which has already declined by 10% over the past 30 years, is projected to decline an additional 10–20% before the end of the twenty-first century. The decreases in snow-covered area are expected to be greatest in April and May, suggesting a further shortening of the snow season and an earlier pulse of river runoff to the Arctic Ocean and coastal seas. Important snow quality changes are also projected, such as an increase in thawing and freezing in winter that leads to ice formation which in turn restricts the access of some land animals to food and nesting sites.

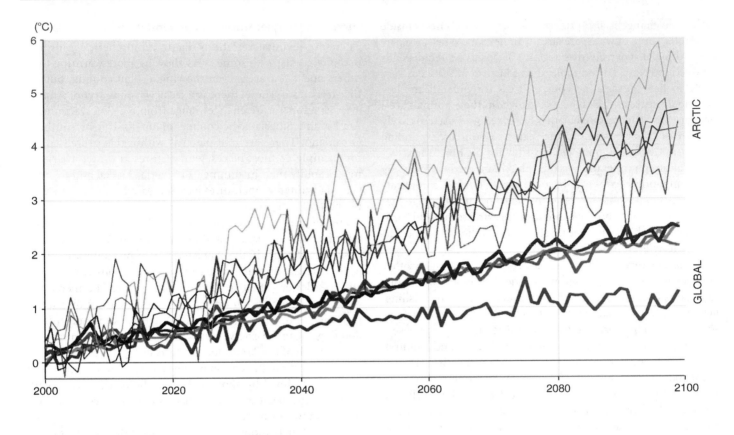

(°C)

Arctic Warming. FIGURE 1. Projected Average Surface Air Temperature Change (Change from 1981–2000 Average).

The graph shows annual average temperature projected by five climate models all using the same moderate emissions scenario (B2 from IPCC SRES). The heavy lines at the bottom are projected global average temperature increases and the thinner lines above are projected arctic temperature increases. As the results show, temperature increases are projected to be much greater in the Arctic than for the world as a whole. It is also apparent that the year-to-year variability is greater in the Arctic. Projected temperature increases for winter and over the oceans are much larger than these averages. ©ACIA, 2004.

Declining sea ice

Arctic sea ice is a key indicator and agent of climate change, affecting surface reflectivity, cloudiness, humidity, exchanges of heat and moisture at the ocean surface, and ocean currents. Changes in sea ice also have enormous environmental, economic, and societal implications. [See Arctic Sea Ice.]

Over the past 30 years, the annual average Arctic sea-ice extent has decreased by about 8%, or nearly one million square kilometers, an area larger than all of Norway, Sweden, and Denmark combined, and the melting trend is accelerating. Sea-ice extent in summer has declined far more dramatically than the annual average and is now declining at about 10% per decade or 72,000 square kilometers (28,000 square miles) per year. The rate of melting is accelerating. The 2007 record low sea-ice extent shattered the previous 2005 record low by 23%, and was 39% below the long-term average from 1970–2000. Scientists monitoring the sea ice now conclude the Arctic Ocean could be ice-free in summer by 2030 (NSIDC, 2007). Sea ice also has become thinner in recent decades, with Arctic-wide average thickness reductions estimated at 10–15%, and with particular areas showing reductions of up to 40% between the 1960s and the late 1990s.

Continuing declines in annual average sea-ice extent are projected, with the loss of sea ice in summer projected to be even greater (see projected shift in summer sea-ice boundary in Figure 2). Some recent analyses suggest a nearly complete disappearance of summer sea ice as early as the middle of this century.

IMPACTS OF ARCTIC CLIMATE CHANGE ON THE GLOBE

Because the Arctic plays a special role in global climate, Arctic changes have global implications. Here we focus on three of these: increased global warming due to a reduction in Arctic surface reflectivity, increases in global sea level due to melting of land-based ice in the Arctic, and possible releases of greenhouse gases from permafrost and ocean sediments. Arctic changes will also reverberate throughout the rest of

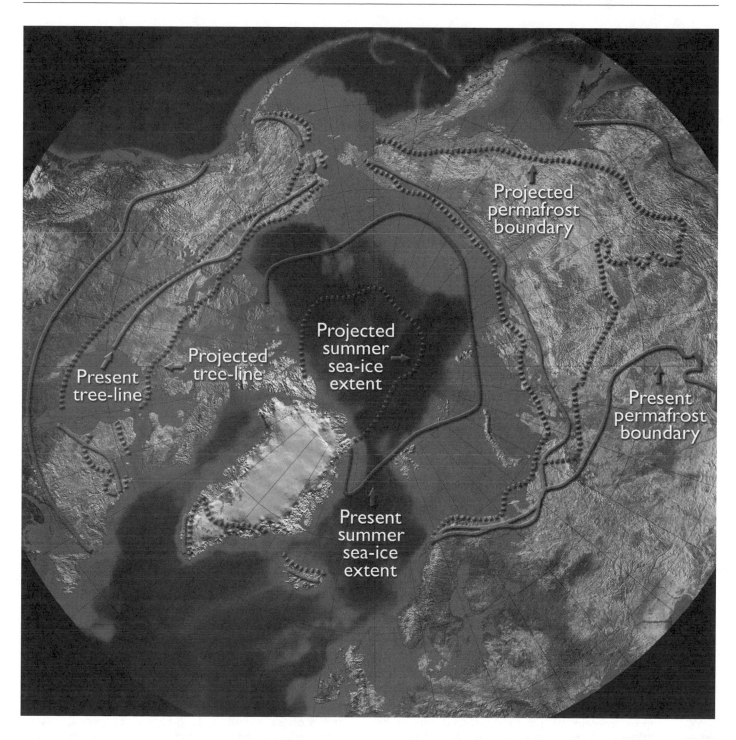

Arctic Warming. Figure 2. Projected Changes in the Arctic.

The indicated changes in summer sea-ice extent and tree-line are projected to occur during this century. The change in permafrost boundary assumes that present areas of discontinuous permafrost will be free of any permafrost in the future and this is likely to occur beyond the 21st century. ©ACIA, 2004.

the planet through potential alterations in ocean circulation patterns and changes in the availability of Arctic resources including oil, gas, fish, and migratory bird habitat.

Increased global warming due to reduced surface reflectivity

The bright white snow and ice that cover much of the Arctic reflect back to space most of the solar energy that reaches the surface. As greenhouse gas concentrations rise and warm the lower atmosphere and surface, snow and ice form later in the autumn and melt earlier in the spring. The melting of snow and ice reveals the land and water surfaces beneath, which are much darker and thus absorb more of the Sun's energy. This warms the surface further, causing faster melting, which in turn causes more warming, and so on, creating a self-reinforcing cycle that amplifies warming. This process is already underway in the Arctic, and accelerates global warming. [See Albedo.]

Sea-level rise

Climate change causes sea level to rise by affecting both the density and the amount of water in the oceans. First and most significantly, water expands as it warms, and less-dense water takes up more space. Second, warming increases melting of glaciers (land-based ice), adding to the amount of water flowing into the oceans.

The total volume of land-based ice in the Arctic corresponds to a global sea level equivalent of about eight meters. Most Arctic glaciers have been in decline since the early 1960s, with this trend accelerating in the 1990s. Projections from global climate models suggest that the contribution of arctic glaciers to global sea-level rise will accelerate over the next 100 years.

The Greenland ice sheet dominates land ice in the Arctic. [See Greenland Ice Sheet.] The area of surface melt on the ice sheet has been increasing rapidly in recent decades and studies suggest that Greenland is losing ice mass much more rapidly than anticipated.

Beyond this century, the Arctic contribution to global sea-level rise is projected to grow as ice sheets continue to respond to climate change and to contribute to sea-level rise for thousands of years. Climate models indicate that the local warming over Greenland is likely to be up to two to three times the global average. Ice sheet models project that sustained local warming of that magnitude would eventually lead to a virtually complete melting of the Greenland ice sheet, with a resulting sea-level rise of about seven meters.

Sea-level rise is projected to have serious implications for coastal communities and industries, islands, river deltas, harbors, and the large fraction of people living in coastal areas worldwide.

Release of greenhouse gases from permafrost and ocean sediments

Carbon is currently trapped as organic matter in the permafrost (frozen soil) that underlies much of the Arctic. Large amounts of carbon accumulate in the vast waterlogged peat bogs of Siberia and parts of North America. During the summer, when the surface layer of the permafrost thaws, organic matter in this layer decomposes, releasing methane and carbon dioxide to the atmosphere. Warming increases these releases, and can create an amplifying feedback loop whereby more warming causes additional releases, which causes more warming, and so on (see projected change in the permafrost boundary in Figure 2). The magnitude of these releases is affected by soil moisture and other factors.

Vast amounts of methane, in an icy form called methane hydrates or clathrates, are trapped at shallow depths in cold ocean sediments, and to a lesser extent in some permafrost areas on land. [See Methane Hydrates.] If the temperature of this permafrost or the water at the seabed rises beyond certain thresholds,

it could initiate the decomposition of these hydrates, releasing methane to the atmosphere and amplifying global warming.

IMPACTS OF CLIMATE CHANGE IN THE ARCTIC

Climate-induced changes in Arctic landscapes are important to local people and animals in terms of food, fuel, culture, and habitat. These changes may also have global impacts because many processes operating on Arctic landscapes affect global climate and resources. Some changes in Arctic landscapes are already occurring, and future changes are projected to be considerably greater.

Shifting vegetation zones

The major Arctic vegetation zones include the polar deserts, tundra, and the northern part of the boreal forest. [See Boreal Forests and Climate Change.] Climate change is projected to cause vegetation shifts because rising temperatures favor taller, denser vegetation and will thus promote the expansion of forests into the Arctic tundra (see the projected shift in treeline in Figure 2), and tundra into the polar deserts. The timeframe of these shifts will vary around the Arctic. Where suitable soils and other conditions exist, changes are likely to be apparent in this century. Where they do not, the changes can be expected to take longer. These vegetation changes, along with rising sea levels, are projected to shrink the area of tundra, greatly reducing the breeding area for many birds and the grazing areas for land animals that depend on the open landscape of tundra and polar desert habitats. Not only are some threatened species very likely to become extinct, some currently widespread species are projected to decline sharply.

Many animal species from around the world depend on summer breeding and feeding grounds in the Arctic, and climate change will alter some of these habitats significantly. For example, several hundred million birds migrate to the Arctic each summer, and their success in the Arctic determines their populations elsewhere. Important breeding and nesting areas are projected to decrease sharply as the treeline advances northward, encroaching on tundra, and because the timing of bird arrival in the Arctic might no longer coincide with the availability of their insect food sources. At the same time, sea-level rise will diminish the tundra extent from the north in many areas, further shrinking important habitat. A number of bird species, including several globally endangered seabird species, are projected to lose more than 50% of their breeding area during this century.

Forest disturbances: insects and fires

Increased insect outbreaks due to climate warming are already occurring and are almost certain to continue. Increasing climate-related outbreaks of spruce-bark beetles and spruce budworms in the North American Arctic provide two important examples. Over the past decade, areas of Alaska and Canada have experienced the largest and most intense outbreaks of spruce-bark beetles on record. There has also been an upsurge in spruce-budworm outbreaks, and the entire range of white-spruce forests in North America is considered vulnerable to such outbreaks under projected warming.

Fire will also have pervasive ecological effects. The area burned in boreal western North America has doubled over the past thirty years, and it is forecast to increase by as much as 80% over the next 100 years under projected warming. The area of boreal forest burned annually in Russia averaged four million hectares over the last three decades and more than doubled in the 1990s. As the climate continues to warm, the forest-fire season will begin earlier and last longer. Models of forest fire in parts of Siberia suggest that a summer temperature increase of 5.5°C would double the number of years in which there are severe fires, and increase the area of forest burned annually by nearly 150%.

Animal species

Many animal species will be affected by increasing arctic temperatures. In the marine environment, the sharp decline in sea ice is likely to be devastating to polar bears. Impacts have already been documented at James and Hudson Bays in Canada, the southern limits of the polar bear's distribution. The condition of adult polar bears has declined during the last two decades in the Hudson Bay area, as have the number of live births and the proportion of first-year cubs in the population. Polar bears in that region suffered 15% declines in both average weight and number of cubs born between 1981 and 1998. Other ice-dependent species at risk include ringed seals, walrus, and some species of marine birds.

Terrestrial animal species also face threats from warming. Caribou and reindeer herds depend on abundant tundra vegetation and good foraging conditions, especially during the calving season. Climate-induced changes are projected to reduce the area of tundra and the traditional forage (such as mosses and lichens) for these herds. Freeze-thaw cycles and freezing rain are also projected to increase, reducing the ability of caribou and reindeer populations to obtain food and raise calves. Future climate change could thus mean a decline in caribou and reindeer populations, threatening human nutrition and the whole way of life of some indigenous Arctic communities.

Warming also leads to other cascading impacts on Arctic land animals. For example, in winter, lemmings and voles live and forage in the space between the frozen ground of the tundra and the snow, almost never appearing on the surface. The snow provides critical insulation. Mild weather and wet snow lead to the collapse of the under-snow spaces, destroying the animals' burrows, while ice-crust formation reduces the insulating properties of the snow pack vital to their survival. Well-established population cycles are no longer seen in some areas. Declines in populations of lemmings, for example, would be very likely to result in even stronger declines in the populations of predators that specialize in preying on them, such as snowy owls, skuas, weasels, and ermine. More generalist predators, such as the Arctic fox, switch to other prey when lemming populations are low. Thus, a decline in lemmings can also indirectly result in a

decline in populations of other prey species such as waders and other birds.

Freshwater species face climate-related changes to their environments that include increasing water temperatures, thawing permafrost, and reduced ice cover on rivers and lakes. Southern species are projected to shift northward, competing with northern species for resources. The broad whitefish, Arctic char, and Arctic cisco are particularly vulnerable to displacement as they are fundamentally northern in their distribution. As water temperatures rise, spawning grounds for cold-water species will shift northward and probably diminish. As southern fish species move northward, they may introduce new parasites and diseases to which Arctic fish are not adapted. The implications of these changes for both commercial and subsistence fishing in far northern areas are potentially devastating, as the most vulnerable species are often the only fishable species present.

Coastal erosion

The effects of rising temperatures are already altering the Arctic coastline, and much larger changes are projected to occur during this century as a result of reduced sea ice, thawing permafrost, and sea-level rise. Thinner, less extensive sea ice creates more open water, allowing the wind to generate larger waves, thus increasing wave-induced erosion along Arctic shores. Sea-level rise, increasing storm surge heights, and thawing of coastal permafrost exacerbate this problem. Dozens of Arctic communities are threatened by these changes, and some are already planning to relocate. Hundreds more could be at risk in the future. The costs of protecting or relocating these communities will be enormous. Coastal erosion will also pose increasing problems for some ports, tanker terminals, and other industrial facilities around the Arctic.

Thawing permafrost

Transportation and industry on land, including oil and gas extraction and forestry, will be increasingly disrupted by the shortening of the periods during which ice roads and tundra are frozen sufficiently to permit travel. For example, warming has caused the number of days per year in which travel on the tundra is allowed under Alaska Department of Natural Resources rules to drop from over 200 to about 100 in the past 30 years, resulting in a 50% reduction in days that oil and gas exploration and extraction equipment can be used. In addition, as frozen ground thaws, many existing buildings, roads, and pipelines are likely to be destabilized, requiring costly repair and replacement (see the projected shift in permafrost boundary in Figure 2). Projected warming and its effects will need to be taken into account in the design of all new construction, thus increasing costs.

Marine access

Observed and projected reductions in sea ice suggest that the Arctic Ocean will have longer seasons of less sea-ice cover of reduced thickness, implying improved ship accessibility around the margins of the Arctic Basin. As summer sea ice retreats further from most Arctic landmasses, new shipping routes will open, and the period during which shipping is feasible via existing routes will expand (see the projected change in summer sea ice boundary in Figure 2).

The Northern Sea Route north of Eurasia could provide up to a 40% savings in distance for journeys from northern Europe to northeastern Asia and the northwest coast of North America compared to southern routes via the Suez or Panama canals. The navigation season for the Northern Sea Route is projected to increase from the current 20–30 days per year to 90–100 days by 2080; and for ships with ice-breaking capability the season could expand to 150 days. This could have major implications for transportation as well as for access to natural resources.

On the Canadian side of the Arctic, home to the fabled Northwest Passage, near-term benefits are less clear. Recent sea ice changes could, in fact, make the Northwest Passage less predictable for shipping. Studies indicate that sea ice conditions in the Canadian Arctic during the past three decades have had high year-to-year variability, making planning for transport very difficult. In addition, research suggests a warming climate could lead to more icebergs and greater ice movement in the Northwest Passage, presenting additional hazards to navigation. Thus, despite widespread retreat of sea ice around the Arctic Basin, the Canadian Arctic Archipelago is likely to have complex and challenging ice conditions for the decades ahead. [See Arctic Sea Ice.]

While increased marine access to Arctic resources will benefit some, it will also raise new issues relating to sovereignty, security, and safety. For example, the risk of oil spills and other industrial accidents in the challenging Arctic environment raises concerns.

Indigenous communities

Across the Arctic, indigenous people are already reporting the effects of climate change. Local landscapes, seascapes, and icescapes are becoming unfamiliar. Climate change is occurring faster than indigenous knowledge can adapt and is strongly affecting people in many communities. Unpredictable weather, snow, and ice conditions make travel hazardous, endangering lives. Impacts of climate change on wildlife, from caribou on land, to fish in the rivers, to seals and polar bears on the sea ice, are having enormous effects, not only on the diets of indigenous peoples, but also on their cultures and their very identities.

ASSESSMENT

Despite the fact that a relatively small percentage of the world's greenhouse gas emissions originate in the Arctic, changes in Arctic climate are among the largest on Earth. As a consequence, the changes already underway in Arctic landscapes, communities, and unique features provide an early indication for the rest of the world of the environmental and societal significance of global climate change. Changes in climate and their impacts in the Arctic are already being widely noticed and felt, and are projected to become much greater. These changes will also reach far beyond the Arctic, affecting global climate, sea level, biodiversity, and many aspects of human social and economic systems.

BIBLIOGRAPHY

ACIA. *Impacts of a Warming Arctic: Arctic Climate Impact Assessment.* Cambridge: Cambridge University Press, 2004. http://www.acia.uaf.edu (accessed May 25, 2008). Overview report.

ACIA. *Arctic Climate Impact Assessment.* Cambridge: Cambridge University Press, 2005. http://www.acia.uaf.edu (accessed May 25, 2008). Scientific report.

Nakicenovic, N., and R. Swart, eds. *IPCC Special Report on Emissions Scenarios.* Cambridge and New York: Cambridge University Press, 2000.

NSIDC. "Sea Ice Decline Intensifies." Boulder, Colo.: National Snow and Ice Data Center, 2005. http://nside.org/news/press/20050928_trendscontinue.html (accessed May 25, 2008).

NSIDC. "Arctic Sea Ice Shrinks as Temperatures Rise." Boulder, Colo.: National Snow and Ice Data Center, 2006. http://nside.org/news/press/2006_Seaiceminimum/20071003_pressrelease.html (accessed May 25, 2008).

NSIDC. "Arctic Sea Ice Shatters All Previous Record Lows." Boulder, Colo.: National Snow and Ice Data Center, 2007. http://nside.org/news/press/2007_Seaiceminimum/20071001_pressrelease.html (accessed May 25, 2008).

—SUSAN JOY HASSOL AND ROBERT W. CORELL

AUSTRALIA AND GLOBAL CHANGE

Australia serves as a model for understanding how human cultures cause environmental change and how environmental constraints drive cultural adaptation. Here most environments are biologically unproductive because of a constellation of geological, climatological, and biological factors. Landscapes are ancient, subdued, and based on sedimentary rocks rich in quartz. The few areas with fertile soils occur on floodplains or on an arc of highly localized, past volcanic activity on the east coast. During the ice ages, glaciers were limited to restricted mountainous areas in southeastern Australia and Tasmania. At this time most of the continent was affected by severe aridity, as evidenced by extensive networks of longitudinal dunes, deflated lake beds, and extensive sand-sheets. Presently, over two-thirds of the continental land mass (7.6×10^8 hectares) receives, on average, less than 500 mm of rainfall per year (Figure 1), a statistic that masks the enormous interannual rainfall variability that characterizes all Australian climates.

Aridity is a consequence of the absence of any great mountain ranges and the centering of the subtropical high-pressure belt over the continent. The highs also cause contrasting seasonal patterns in northern and southern Australia. In the austral summer months, southern Australian has a hot and dry climate that is conducive to episodic intense wildfires. Conversely, in northern Australia the climate is hot and wet due to the dominance of the summer monsoon, characterized by torrential rains and frequent intense tropical storms (called cyclones) that are occasionally very destructive. Some of these tropical low-pressure systems cross the continent, bringing to southern Australia summer rain or dry lightning storms that start bushfires. During the austral winter months, southern Australia receives westerly rain-bearing midlatitudinal fronts, while northern Australia has a rain-free hot "dry season" with steady southeasterly trade winds that spread extensive landscape fires set by humans or by lightning at the beginning of the wet season. El Niño–Southern Oscillation (ENSO) causes regular cycles of droughts and floods across southern and

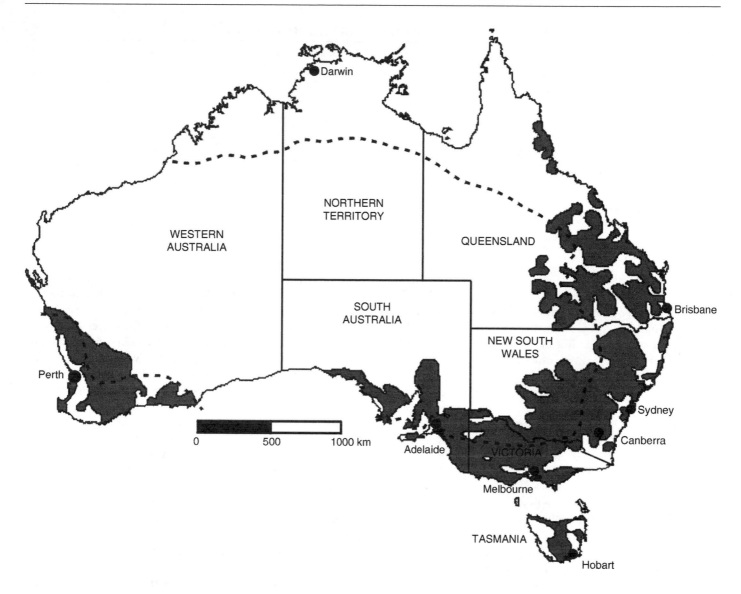

Australia and Global Change. FIGURE 1. Arid Zone and Land Clearance.

The dashed line bounds the area that normally receives less that 500 mm of rainfall per annum. Shading indicates areas of land clearance. (Derived from Australia: State of the Environment 1996, CSIRO, Melbourne, 1997.)

central Australia. The highly diverse Australian flora and fauna are superbly adapted to the largely infertile, climatically capricious, and fire-prone environment; the high level of endemism also reflects over 30 million years of geographic isolation (Table 1).

HISTORY

The ancestors of the Aborigines colonized Australia about 45,000 years ago. It is widely accepted that this first wave of human colonization was coincident with the extinction of large marsupials, birds, and reptiles, collectively known as megafauna.

The precise cause of these extinctions remains controversial, with hypotheses ranging from over-hunting to destruction of habitat due to sustained landscape burning, although there were probably multiple factors which varied in importance across different biomes. There is little doubt that when Aboriginal people entered the continent the vegetation had been adapted for millions of years to fires ignited by lightning storms associated with the summer monsoon. The first Australians would have used fire to hunt game and to increase the production of food, particularly of herbivores attracted to nutritious, resprouting grass. Such extensive use of fire would have changed the distribution and structure of vegetation, creating extensive savannas. However, during the extreme aridity at the height of the last ice age, 10,000–20,000 years BP, the skillful use of fire by Aboriginal people may have created firebreaks that conserved some fire-sensitive habitats such as rainforest, which would otherwise have been destroyed by a natural fire regime. Because of the long history of Aboriginal fire management, contemporary vegetation patterns can be considered as prehistoric legacies.

TABLE 1. Summary Statistics of the Flora and Fauna of the Australian Mainland and Offshore Islands

Group	No. of native species	% endemic species	No. native species extinct since 1788	No. native species in jeopardy	No. exotic species naturalised
Flowering plants	20 000	85	76	1009	1500–2000
Freshwater fish	195	90	0	17	21
Amphibians	203	93	3	29	1
Reptiles	770	89	0	51	2
Birds	777	45	20	50	32
Mammals	268	84	19	43	25

SOURCE: Derived from *Australia: State of the Environment* 1996, CSIRO, Melbourne, 1997.

At the time of the late-eighteenth-century European discovery and colonization of Australia there were 0.3 to 1.5 million indigenous hunter-gatherers on the whole continent. In 200 years the population has grown to over 21 million people. Most contemporary Australians live in urban areas comprising less than 1% of the land mass. Yet settlement has affected the whole of the continent with ecological impacts ranging from near complete destruction of ecosystems to support intensive agriculture on less than 10% of the continent, logging of nearly all commercially valuable forest, damming of rivers, establishment of plantations of eucalyptus species or exotic conifers, to subtler ecological changes such as altered wild-fire regimes and the introduction of exotic organisms in uncleared landscapes. The great rate of these ongoing changes and imperfect knowledge of the pre-colonization environment prevent precise conclusions, but negative trends are clearly apparent.

Habitat clearance has occurred in an arc from the humid tropics in northeast Queensland down the eastern seaboard and across to South Australia, with a disjunct area in southwestern Western Australia. This pattern corresponds to relatively moist climatic zones that form the hinterland of all major Australian cities (Figure 1). National parks, forestry areas, and water catchments provide the largest areas of uncleared vegetation within this agricultural zone. Since settlement, the proportion of the continent covered by forest and woodlands has shrunk from 30% to about 20%, with less than one quarter of the 1788 coverage (8×10^6 hectares) of rainforest remaining. Habitat clearance peaked after World War II, although clearing has only recently become controlled in Queensland, and there is mounting pressure to develop agriculture in the monsoon tropics where there are abundant unused water resources.

Land clearance has been highly focused, with habitats of little economic potential often being spared from destruction while more productive habitats have been systematically cleared. For instance, less than 0.5% of the original coverage (2×10^6 hectares) of native temperate grasslands remains in southeastern Australia, often in tiny fragments. Many fragments are too small to support viable populations of vertebrates, so even in regions where habitat destruction has abated there remains a significant "extinction debt." For example, there is a widespread and continuing population crash of scattered eucalyptus trees that escaped destruction during the initial phase of land clearance, with associated localized extinction of dependent fauna. These tree declines are in response to ecological changes associated with intensive agricultural land use, including increased soil nutrients, destruction of young trees by livestock, and population eruptions of leaf-eating insects. Fragmentation of habitats also affects highly mobile species, such as waterfowl, that require an archipelago of habitats. For example the drainage of over two-thirds of the wetlands in southern Australia so adversely affected the magpie goose (*Anseranas semipalmata*) that it is now restricted to northern Australia where wetlands are intact. Habitat destruction has also damaged catchments by the replacement of deeply rooted woody vegetation with shallow-rooted grasses which causes the watertable to rise by as much as 10 m, thereby mobilizing salt that has accumulated in the soil through geological time. About 9% of the cleared land in the wheat belt of southwestern Western Australian (14.6×10^6 hectares) is so affected.

Half of the continent supports native vegetation used for grazing of sheep and cattle, where it is standard practice to allow stock numbers to build up during moist periods to densities that are unsustainable when the inevitable drought arrives. Such boom-and-bust cycles cause severe overgrazing and trampling of soil with consequent degradation of habitats due to acceleration of water and wind erosion, fouling of springs and seeps, and destruction of riverine vegetation. Overgrazing is probably responsible for the contraction of the range of tropical seed-eating birds, such as the Gouldian finch (*Erythura gouldiae*). There appears to have been a marked increase in trees and shrubs on rangelands in response to severe overgrazing.

The cessation of Aboriginal landscape-burning has resulted in more intense and destructive forest fires, particularly where fire suppression has caused an increase in biomass of woody plants and associated build-up of fuels. The deliberate use of fire in Australian landscapes is controversial, signaling the incomplete adaptation of settlers to the highly fire-prone environment. Any return to Aboriginal landscape burning, however, is frustrated by habitat fragmentation, weeds, and the need to protect human life and property.

EXTINCTIONS AND HABITAT CHANGE

European colonists found the Australian continent alien and inhospitable; rather than adapting to the new environment, they sought to transform it into a facsimile of Europe, primarily by introducing plant and animal species and establishing European agricultural systems. This has resulted in the extinctions of native species and the naturalization of numerous exotic animal and plant species (Table 1). About 15% of the Australian flora comprises exotic species, and over 200 have become serious weeds in agricultural or natural landscapes. Although many weeds were accidentally introduced to Australia, some escaped from gardens and others were established in the hope of improving pasture production. Plant and animal pathogens have likewise escaped, causing significant ecological effects. For example, the root-rot fungus *Phytophthora cinnamomi* is likely to radically transform Australian mesic vegetation because most plants have no tolerance for this pathogen. Vermin, such as rats and mice, and domesticated animals (e.g., cats, pigs, buffalo, camels, horses, donkeys, and goats) have established wild populations throughout Australia, although some offshore islands remain relatively free of them. During the nineteenth century acclimatization societies actively promoted establishment of Northern Hemisphere animals to give a European character to Australia's environment and to provide game for recreational hunting; some have become serious pests, most notably fox and rabbit. The only naturalized amphibian, the cane toad (*Bufo marinus*), was introduced the middle of the twentieth century in the mistaken belief it would control an invertebrate pest of sugar cane. It is still aggressively expanding its range in the Australian tropics. There is some evidence that invertebrates that have been established intentionally (e.g., honeybees) or accidentally (e.g., ants, wasps, cockroaches, and fruit flies) have caused the decline of some native invertebrates, but the ecological consequences remain poorly understood.

Of all the native vertebrate groups, mammals have suffered the greatest species loss; this is particularly true for small marsupials and rodents adapted to the arid zone (Table 1). The extinction of these arid-zone mammals appears linked to their inability, unlike that of reptiles, to coexist with stock and other introduced herbivores and predators, especially during droughts. Cats and foxes have been devastatingly effective predators of native fauna as evidenced by the survival of otherwise extinct native animals on offshore islands which lack these carnivores. Exotic fish appear responsible for the decline and range contractions of over 20 native fish species. Only a few native species have been driven extinct by hunting, the most famous case being the Tasmanian marsupial wolf (*Thylacinus cynocephalus*). Nonetheless, unregulated hunting caused the near extinction of some vertebrate species such as crocodiles (e.g., saltwater crocodile, *Crocodylus porosus*) in northern Australia and seals (e.g., Australian sea lion, *Neophoca cinerea*) in southern Australia.

The complete destruction of habitats is now recognized as the most important threat to the survival of a number of plant and animal species; forestry operations in native forests are far less of a threat. For example, the survival of at least 35 reptile species, 32 bird species, 13 marsupial species and 3 rodent species is in jeopardy because of habitat destruction, yet logging is thought to threaten only three bird species and two marsupials. The negative effects of logging arise principally from the destruction of mature trees that serve as animal habitats and the establishment of pathways for the spread of exotic organisms. Some native species have benefited from agricultural activities: the galah (*Cacatua roseicapilla*), a native seed-eating bird, has been able to expand its range from the arid zone into agricultural landscapes. Installation of drilled wells and water troughs for cattle and sheep in rangelands has allowed increased abundances of some large native animals (e.g., kangaroos [*Macropus* spp.] and the emu [*Dromaius novaehollandiae*], a large flightless bird).

Most river systems in the agricultural zone have been modified to control floods and store water for irrigation and hydroelectric power. For example, over 80% of the water from the Murray-Darling system, Australia's largest catchment (14% of the continent), has been diverted for human use. The aquatic environment of the agricultural-zone rivers has been degraded by the combined effects of weed infestation, salinization, sedimentation, pollution with herbicides and fertilizers, modification of stream channels, regulation of flows by dams, and the dominance of introduced fish species such as European carp (*Cyprinus carpio*). In aggregate these changes have caused the contraction of the geographic ranges of native frog, fish, and invertebrate species and have caused recurrent blooms of blue-green algae (e.g., *Anabaena circinalis*) that cause fish-kills and make the water poisonous to livestock, wildlife, and humans. In contrast, catchments in the monsoon tropics that yield over 45% of the continent's mean annual runoff remain pristine, though there is increasing pressure to exploit the northern rivers because of the current sustained drying trend in southern Australia. Only a few river systems in Australia have been seriously polluted by mine tailings.

GLOBAL CLIMATE CHANGE IMPLICATIONS

The manifold environmental impacts of European colonization are being exacerbated by global climate change that is amplifying the inherently variable and extreme climate. There is serious concern for water security in southern Australia cities and the viability of agricultural enterprises in low-rainfall environments. The drying and warming trend also favors more frequent and extreme bushfire events. Australians are in the initial stages of adapting to climate change, with future responses likely to involve major changes in land use including the abandonment of some agricultural areas and the development of other areas (e.g., in northern Australia), and increased population densities in urban areas. Adaptation will also require new approaches to food production, improved water conservation, and a much sharper policy focus on ecosystem services (soil conservation, carbon storage, air quality, water security, and bushfire management), and less emphasis on the conservation of biodiversity as an end in itself.

BIBLIOGRAPHY

Alexander, N., ed. *Australia: State of the Environment 1996*. Melbourne: CSIRO Publishing, 1996. Compendium of information about critical Australian environmental issues.

Beeton, R.J.S., et al. *Australia State of the Environment 2006: Independent Report to the Australian Government Minister for the Environment and Heritage*. Canberra: Department of the Environment and Heritage, 2006. Up-to-date compendium of information about critical Australian environmental issues.

Flannery, T.F. *The Future Eaters: An Ecological History of the Australasian Lands and People*. Sydney: Read Books, 1994. A best-selling environmental history of Australia that serves as a useful introduction to debates surrounding human impacts and adaptation to Australia.

—DAVID BOWMAN

B

BELIEF SYSTEMS

The science of global change has become both so urgent and so technical in recent decades that a consideration of the development of the belief systems guiding social behavior may seem a frivolity, even a foolish distraction from the serious business of deciding how best to handle nuclear waste, protect biodiversity, or reduce global warming. The dominant culture on the planet—its mantra "progress," conceived in terms both of an ever more rapidly evolving technology and, presumably, of ever higher degrees of prosperity or social welfare—certainly does not need to study its own history in order to build new highways in China, shopping malls in India, or cell-phone systems in Africa. Nor is a study of that history necessary to find ways to reduce pollution, restore wildlife, or cope with increasingly frequent floods and droughts. The planet's dominant culture, in other words, is self-propelled: it does not require self-reflection either to continue on its course or to moderate its environmental footprint.

The depth of that footprint, however, depends on whether people in general believe that their happiness depends on maximizing their possession and use of things or upon living a less materialistic and consumptive life. This apparently quixotic alternative is, perhaps surprisingly, deeply incorporated in the planet's dominant culture—almost as deeply as its more familiar, more axiomatic cousin. This is why so many people shop for exotic products yet recycle, or agree to be taxed to recycle. This is why so many support the development of natural resources at the same time as they are eager to protect wilderness. How society strikes the balance between these historically twinned yet contradictory belief systems will either magnify or reduce the difficulty of maintaining global ecosystems. A consideration of belief systems, in short, reminds us of the practical importance of cultural values, which is to say, of the nonquantifiable, non-scientific factors in what otherwise may seem to be a purely technical domain best left to experts.

TWINNED HISTORIES

This, then, is the story of a tree with two trunks. It grows on a site—the planet Earth—already fully stocked, not only with tiny plants but other trees. The tiny plants are the world's tribal societies, much atrophied over the course of the last several centuries; the other trees are the civilizations that by the European Middle Ages had arisen on every continent and some of which have vanished, while others are gnarled survivors. This other vegetation still struggles to survive under the great shade cast by the tree that has become the world's dominant culture, and we shall return to it.

Now, however, consider the giant. Its roots reach deep into Periclean Athens, whose builders ventured, unlike their predecessors, to portray the gods as no more, or hardly more, than human. It was an act of shocking arrogance, but it anticipated by 2,000 years Hamlet's reflection on mankind: "How noble in reason! How infinite in faculties! . . . in apprehension how like a God!"

Whether it was hubris or common sense, Europeans began in the Renaissance to believe that people mattered as individuals and should be responsible for their own lives. Peasants would have rights, and serfs would be freed not only in a legal sense but in the existential sense that they, like everyone else, were no longer to be seen as the children—compliant or not—of mighty gods. The departure was huge and reverberates even today, when imams occasionally deplore democracy precisely because it allows society, not an almighty being, to set the limits within which people shall live.

An early sign of the new culture was the appearance in the 1400s of portraits painted by Jan van Eyck and Giovanni Bellini with almost photographic accuracy. This was a technical achievement to be sure, but it was also an expression of the subject's and perhaps the painter's belief in the importance of the sitter and, thus, of the importance of preserving a lifelike image of him or, at first only occasionally, her. The philosophy or mental outlook appropriate to that age became explicit in the early 1600s with the writings of Francis Bacon and René Descartes, radical skeptics who rejected traditional sources of authority, trusted empirical evidence, wanted to understand the physical world, and—particularly in Bacon's case—wanted to use that understanding to transform that world for the comfort of humankind. The works of Bacon and Descartes are not easily understood by most readers today, but the ideas of Bacon and Descartes permeate later works whose themes are not only easily understood today but accepted almost without question. In the 1760s, for example, Denis Diderot published a pictorial encyclopedia of the industries of his day, and its drawings are as fascinating now as then precisely because earlier writers like Bacon and Descartes had, directly or indirectly, inclined Europeans to appreciate clever solutions to technical problems.

Meanwhile, the other trunk was growing. Near the base is the work of Blaise Pascal, who was a contemporary of Descartes but who was deeply apprehensive about a world in which reason dominated the heart. The same uneasiness was expressed at about the same time in Rembrandt's *Anatomy Lesson of Dr. Tulp*, where the preening doctor and eager students group behind a cadaver and surround a central figure who stares at the viewer in shock at this objectification of the human body.

By the nineteenth century, the most popular European painters were those recalling a traditional, pre-industrial age. John Constable, the best known of these painters, remains a fount of popular imagery. The New World, meanwhile, had little bucolic countryside of the kind Constable painted, but it had sublime nature, whose portrayal was one of the chief themes of nineteenth-century American art, from Asher Durand through Thomas Cole, Frederick Church, Albert Bierstadt, and Thomas Moran. The reputation of these artists was in eclipse during the first half of the twentieth century, but now they are popular once more, probably because they express the love of nature that inspires the modern environmental movement and which, more broadly, grows from the second trunk of our cultural tree.

LIVING WITH CONTRADICTION

The classical world deplored barbarism but lamented the loss of a distant Golden Age inhabited, inevitably, by barbarians. Similarly, the early Christians tolerated the paradox that the inhabitants of Eden could live in paradise without the knowledge that alone could guarantee salvation. There were, in short, many precedents for Hamlet's vacillation between moments of inspiration—"how like a God!"—and moments of suicidal doubt—"to be or not to be." Similarly, Shakespeare's audience understood Macbeth's calling life "a tale told by an idiot, full of sound and fury, signifying nothing" precisely because that audience lived in a two-trunked culture, part confident in its godlike role but part afraid of living in a world without an external judge and, instead, one that people would have to shape for themselves, as best they could.

It comes as no surprise, then, that Charles Dickens and Victor Hugo, both hugely popular in their day, should have written books suffused with rage at the injustices of society yet read enthusiastically by—and indeed written by—members of the classes that prospered in that society. The same contradiction permeates the reform movements of the nineteenth century and Marxism itself, which began with humanist sympathy yet ended in a parody of European culture, where the pursuit of technological progress was almost deified but where, behind the mask of propaganda, politics were deeply corrupt, while industries were colossally inefficient.

By the late twentieth century, people in the dominant culture generally accepted, on one hand, the idea that human intelligence could be measured and reduced to a number while being prepared, on the other, to assume that the rich and powerful were guilty of almost any wrongdoing. The one cultural trunk was perhaps best symbolized by the fervent popular support for space exploration. The other was perhaps best symbolized by the popularity of Bambi (originally a German novel, by Felix Salten) or of science fiction, such as *The Terminator,* that postulated a future in which machines oppressed humanity.

PRIVATE AND PUBLIC INVOLVEMENT

The technological transformation of the world has been left largely to private enterprise. The textile mills of Ancoats, on the east side of Manchester, are quiet now, destroyed by the distant Asia that they once nearly obliterated. Henry Ford similarly devastated the wagon business, even as his company has now, though not yet silenced, been brought low by competitors, preeminently Toyota. The same drive for greater efficiency—and the same popular enthusiasm for the spectacle of this pursuit—can be seen today in the enthusiastic news coverage of the Airbus A380 as it slowly emerges, perhaps to devastate that giant of an earlier generation, the Boeing 747.

A steadfast support for technology runs as well, however, through the history of government policy in the nineteenth and twentieth centuries. The British in India rested their claim to rule on a utilitarian basis, with officials justifying themselves by developing railroads and irrigation systems. The countries that became predominantly European, such as the United States, Canada, and Australia, found themselves supporting the same things, beginning with the development of highly rational systems of land survey and proceeding to make the farmer a social icon, in whose name the government would support railroad construction, water-resource development, and educational systems from grade school to university, as well as government-funded agricultural research and extension programs. [*See* Technology and Environment.]

Yet this is only half the later story of this two-trunked culture, because at the same time as the private and public sectors were working to hasten material progress they were also doing the opposite. Perhaps the most dramatic example is the late nineteenth-century development of national parks, an American innovation that soon became almost universal, despite the implicit heresy that wild nature deserved protection. City parks, too, became commonplace. Significantly, their design tended away from the geometric gardens of Continental Europe and toward the English Garden, whose design was premised on the beauty of "unadorned nature," as Alexander Pope put it. Builders, meanwhile, did far more than construct proud skyscrapers: along with government built highways, they built the suburbs that promised a popular escape from domination by machines, not only by giving every house a garden but by making sure that the house, despite its modern materials and conveniences, was trimmed to evoke Tudor England or the French countryside or a Tuscan villa. The same builders have more recently turned away in their design of office and commercial buildings from the linear esthetic of modern architecture and toward allusions to traditional design, with purely ornamental columns and arches. Even so, the demand for escape remains unsatisfied, which explains the spectacular development of the world's tourism industry, which caters to the popular taste for traditional and natural landscapes, whether in Venice or the Lake District, Boston or Yellowstone, Quebec City or Banff.

THE CULTURAL ELEMENTS OF ENVIRONMENTAL POLICY

Environmental policy has itself grown around both cultural trunks. The early conservation movement, driven by a concern over deforestation in the United States, justified itself by appeals to efficiency, just as in a later day it aimed to develop water resources because they would otherwise be lost or wasted, as the dam builders argued, to the sea. Similarly, most of the entries in this volume could not have been written had it not been for the development of the sciences whose application society hopes will ameliorate the problems caused by development.

Yet the early soil conservationists, practical men, spoke of erosion as though it was not merely inefficient but unethical, and in doing so they echoed the views of eminent agriculturalists such as Liberty Hyde Bailey, author of the *The Holy Earth.* Rachel Carson's enormously influential *Silent Spring* was a cool analysis of the hazards of DDT but took wing with an emotive title and was dedicated to Albert Schweitzer because he had written of his fear of the consequences of losing what he called a "reverence for life."

A shelf of books—the best known probably being Carson's, Henry David Thoreau's *Walden,* and Aldo Leopold's *Sand County Almanac*—inspired in the 1960s the environmental movement and a wave of American legislation including the Wilderness Act, the Wild and Scenic Rivers Act, and the broad National Environmental Protection Act, which aimed to reduce the environmental impact of the federal government's own actions. Unlike earlier conservation legislation, these laws had no utilitarian justification: they rested instead on the ecocentric and still controversial idea that other species have rights to this planet. The same belief helped pass the Endangered Species Act of 1973, when, by no coincidence, the international Convention on the International Trade in Endangered Species was drafted. That convention now has 171 signatory nations. It has a utilitarian rationale—many species might be helpful in the development of new medicines—yet supporters have not been content with the preservation of species in zoos or gene banks, which suggests that their motivation is not purely utilitarian.

Many private organizations have taken up the challenge of protecting biodiversity. Among the oldest is the International Union for the Conservation of Nature (the World Conservation Union), a Swiss-based organization created in 1948. A few years later, the Nature Conservancy was established; in 1955 it made its first land purchase, and 50 years later it claims that, with more than a million members, it has protected more than 117 million acres worldwide. Deliberately and articulately bolstered by science, the Conservancy draws much of its funding—in fiscal year 2006 over $400 million, not counting land

donations—from people who are not scientists but believe they are doing the morally right thing in protecting nature. Even if those donors have not read Carson, Thoreau, or Leopold, their motivation is coming from the same cultural source, imbibed since childhood with Bambi and earlier works going back at least as far as *Black Beauty,* Anna Sewell's novel of 1877.

THE BROADER CONTEXT

Even in an age of globalization, the world's dominant culture does not stand alone on the planet, and though a powerful case may be made that this culture will grow stronger in the years to come, it is also true that the world's other cultures, particularly those grouped around or sustained by the world's major religions, are not fading nearly as quickly as was predicted even a few decades ago. The Catholic Church is in mortal danger in Western Europe, but Protestantism is flourishing in the Americas, as is Islam across North Africa and much of Asia, Hinduism in India, and Buddhism in East and Southeast Asia. Catholicism and Orthodox Christianity are growing forces in Eastern Europe, and even China appears to be making a place, once again, for traditional ideas—those of Confucius. There seems little doubt that this resurgence rests on the popular belief that reason alone, even with prosperity in its wake, cannot sustain a satisfying life.

Environmental policy makers have rarely sought common ground here: they have generally been secular and have wanted nothing to do with organized religion. Much religious teaching, moreover, has little or nothing to do with the environment, which would seem to reinforce the wisdom of keeping the two separate. The one exception has been tribal societies, whose animism has often inspired environmental writers.

Yet a fast-food company finds little operational difference between listening on the one hand to customers who object to animal cruelty and on the other, to those who have moral objections to eating particular foods. On the one hand the company pledges to buy its eggs and pork as far possible from producers whose animals can step outside cages and crates. On the other, the company makes sure that there is no beef or pork on the menu, or it goes out of its way to develop vegetarian dishes. These are small matters, though not so small from the perspective of a company facing outraged protesters. Much bigger ones are probably on the horizon, however, particularly as environmentalists realize that some of the biggest problems in the world today cannot be solved by Europeans and Americans alone—cannot be solved, to be blunt, without the participation of China and India. That buy-in requires plenty of technical innovation, but it is also true that solutions will come much more easily if society's material demands are moderated. The surest way for that to happen is for environmentalists—European, American, Asian, and others—to tap into the underlying, pre-European values of these societies. Western environmentalists, after all, were not the first to rail against materialism or to seek a materially simpler life, and they hold no copyright on discussions of the problems created by global change.

BIBLIOGRAPHY

Bailey, L. H. *The Holy Earth*. New York: Scribners, 1915.

Carson, R. *Silent Spring*. Boston: Houghton Mifflin, 1962.

Clark, K. *Civilization: A Personal View*. New York: Harper and Row, 1969.

Gillispie, C. C., ed. *A Diderot Pictorial Encyclopedia of Trades and Industry*. New York: Dover, 1959.

Hays, S. P. *Conservation and the Gospel of Efficiency: The Progressive Conservation Movement, 1890–1920*. Cambridge: Harvard University Press, 1959.

Hughes, R. *American Visions: The Epic History of Art in America*. New York: Knopf, 1997.

Leopold, A. *A Sand County Almanac*. New York: Oxford University Press, 1949.

Pascal, B. *Pensées*. Indianapolis: Hackett, 2005.

Rhodes, R. F. *Architecture and Meaning on the Athenian Acropolis*. Cambridge and New York: Cambridge University Press, 1995.

Salten, F. *Bambi: Lebensgeschichte aus dem Walde*. Berlin: Ullstein, 1923.

Sewell, A. *Black Beauty: His Grooms and Companions: The Autobiography of a Horse*. London: Jarrold and Sons, 1877.

Stokes, E. T. *The English Utilitarians and India*. Oxford: Clarendon, 1959.

Thoreau, H. D. *Walden*. Boston: Ticknor and Fields, 1854.

—Bret Wallach

BIOFUELS

The term "biofuels" covers a wide range of alternative transport fuels produced from organic materials, such as ethanol, methanol, and biodiesel. Prompted by high and volatile oil prices, concerns about energy independence, and a growing awareness of the irreversible impacts of climate change from fossil fuel combustion, both developed and developing countries are seeking alternatives to fossil fuels as liquid transportation fuels. Many are seeking to fill that niche with biofuels derived from traditional agricultural products. According to some projections, from traditional agricultural products is expected to nearly triple between 2006 and 2025 (Figure 1).

Biofuels, and potential feedstocks for them, vary around the globe, as do the environmental impacts of their production. The two major biofuels currently used are biodiesel and ethanol. Biodiesel is made from vegetable oil or animal fat and is suitable for use in diesel engines. Biodiesel is not the same thing as "waste vegetable oil" or pure vegetable oil, but it can be produced from those feedstocks through a relatively simple chemical process (transesterification). Unlike straight vegetable oil, transesterified oil has combustion properties very similar to those of petrodiesel and can therefore be used in most modern diesel engines with no modifications.

Ethanol is an alcohol that is blended into gasoline in volumetric proportions ranging from less than 10% to as high as 85% (E85). Low-level ethanol blends of up to 10% ethanol (E10) can be used in gasoline vehicles without modification to engine systems, and blends up to E85 can be used in specially configured cars called "flex-fuel" vehicles. Feedstocks for ethanol production tend to be starch- or sugar-rich crops such as sugar cane, sugar beets, corn, wheat, or cassava, while appropriate feedstocks for biodiesel production are oil-rich crops such as soybean, jatropha, palm seeds, rapeseed (canola), sunflower seeds, or cotton seeds. Biofuels made from these feedstocks are known

Biofuels. Figure 1. Projected Global Biofuel Production from Traditional Agricultural Products.
These projections exclude second-generation biofuels.
(FAO Projections (A. Prakash, Trade and Markets Division))

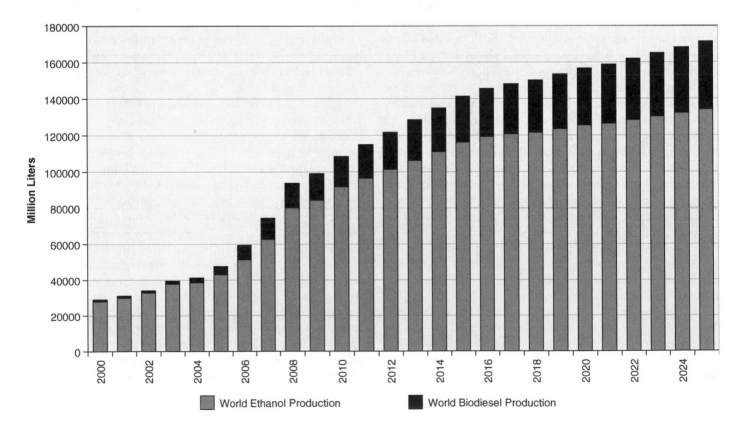

as first-generation biofuels, as they are produced using current, conventional technology. Figure 2 depicts the varying yields from several of these feedstocks. Second-generation biofuel technologies are in the research-and-development stages; those efforts seek to produce biofuels more efficiently using a wider range of technologies and feedstocks, including ethanol from cellulose, and biodiesel from alternative feedstocks such as algae or using alternative production pathways such as biohydrogen diesel or Fischer-Tropsch diesel. Other biofuels such as biobutanol and biomethanol are also being studied in an attempt to improve on fuel performance and reduce the infrastructure requirements for biofuel distribution.

BIOFUELS PRODUCTION

Although other bioenergy applications, particularly combustion of biomass to generate heat and power, have been commercially feasible in numerous markets, biofuel production in markets other than Brazil has rarely been cost-competitive with its intended substitute (Kojima et al., 2007). Development of biofuels markets has therefore relied heavily on government support. Such support generally either stimulates demand through fuel tax exemptions or blending mandates, such as the Renewable Fuels Standard in the United States, or supports biofuels production through producer subsidies, research and development support, and import tariffs.

The world's largest biofuels producers are the United States, Brazil, and the European Union (EU) (Figure 3), but several other countries such as Argentina, India, Malaysia, and the People's Republic of China are embarking on programs to rapidly expand their domestic biofuels sectors. The U.S. and Brazil are the world's major ethanol producers. Ethanol produced from sugar cane in Brazil accounts for about 30% of that country's gasoline demand (IEA, 2004), while the United States, which produces comparable volumes of ethanol from corn but has a much greater transport energy demand, satisfies less than 5% of its transport energy demand with ethanol.

Global production of biodiesel has been much smaller than that of ethanol, but is growing quickly due to national policies supporting development of the industry in several countries, including Indonesia, Malaysia, and Argentina. The EU has a non-binding biofuels directive calling for 5.75% of its transport energy demands to be met through biofuels by the year 2010; because the EU transport sector relies predominantly on diesel that region has quickly become the world's major producer and consumer of biodiesel, with 75% of its domestic biodiesel production using rapeseed as a feedstock. Most countries using biodiesel blend it into their diesel supply in proportions ranging from 2% to 20% (B2 to B20), though it is also used in its pure state (B100) in some truck fleets in Germany, where the majority of EU biodiesel is produced. Pending further research on performance and fuel quality for higher blends, most engine manufacturers support only the use of blends up to B5 in their engines.

Global trade in biofuels has been quite small and consists largely of ethanol exports from Brazil (Kojima et al., 2007). However, the EU's burgeoning demand for biodiesel is stimulating demand for imports of feedstocks as well, primarily for rapeseed oil from the U.S. and Canada, palm oil from southeast Asia, and soybean oil from South America. There is a global

Biofuels. FIGURE 2. Biofuel Yields of Selected Feedstocks.

(Data compiled from L.R. Brown and IEA, 2004.)

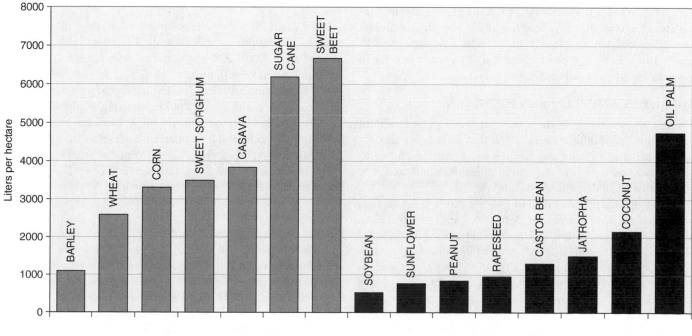

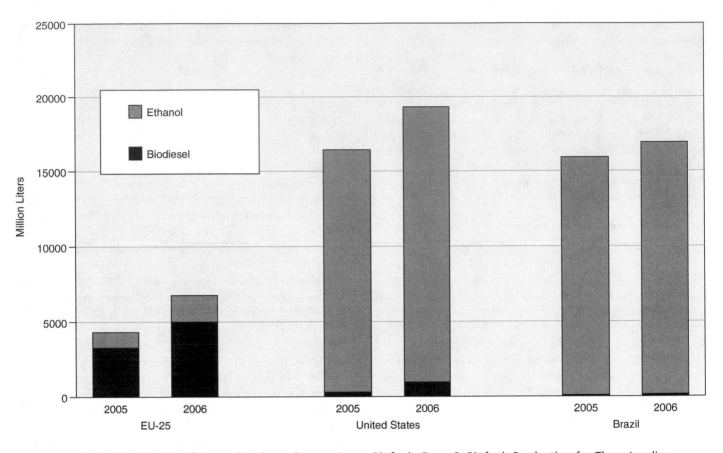

Biofuels. Figure 3. Biofuels Production for Three Leading Producers.

Note: Data for EU and US based on calendar years, Brazil based on marketing years 2005/2006 & 2006/2007 (May/April).

(Data compiled from USDA-FAS, Renewable Fuel Association, National Biodiesel Board, and Rainbow Energy Corp.)

asymmetry in the distribution of demand and supply capacity for biofuels; significant demand is likely to come from the heavily energy-dependent developed countries, while the less developed tropical and subtropical countries tend to have more land available, climates capable of supporting more productive feedstocks, and lower labor costs, and therefore a comparative advantage in supply. As international trade in biofuels and bio-feedstocks grows, so does concern about the environmental impacts associated with scaling up production of feedstocks and biofuels in both developed and developing countries to meet the transport needs of those markets.

BIOFUELS AND THE ENVIRONMENT

Biofuels are renewable in the sense that they can be produced from a number of different renewable sources, but they are only sustainable if feedstocks and biofuels are produced and combusted in a way that does not compromise the health and productivity of air, soil, and water resources.

One of the arguments made in favor of biofuels is that they burn cleaner than petroleum derivatives and will therefore improve air quality. Although it is generally agreed that ethanol blends do in fact result in a reduction of emissions of particulate matter, carbon monoxide (CO), and certain toxics such as benzene and toluene, emissions of other pollutants such as volatile organic compounds (VOC), nitrogen oxides (NO_x), and acetaldehyde actually increase relative to conventional gasoline (IEA, 2004). The net impact of low-level ethanol blends on smog, which is generated from VOC and CO in the presence

of NO_x, may therefore be positive under some atmospheric conditions, despite a reduction in direct emissions of CO (Yacobucci, 2006). Although earlier research on the smog-forming potential of high-level blends finds that E85 reduces smog production (Black et al., 1998), a recent report challenges that conclusion (Jacobson, 2007). Similarly, biodiesel exhaust contains fewer hydrocarbons, no sulfur oxides or sulfates, less carbon monoxide, and lower particulate matter than petrodiesel (Sheehan et al., 1998), but NO_x are generally found to slightly increase relative to petrodiesel (Figure 4). The potential impact of increased biofuels use on smog levels is therefore an open topic of debate, and is likely to vary regionally with climatic conditions.

The impact of biofuels production and use on greenhouse gas emissions has also generated a great deal of debate, but a consensus is emerging that most current, conventional methods of producing ethanol and biodiesel yield at least a moderate reduction in GHG emissions, with significantly larger reductions expected if cellulosic ethanol production technologies become commercially feasible (Farrell et al., 2006; Hill et al., 2006).

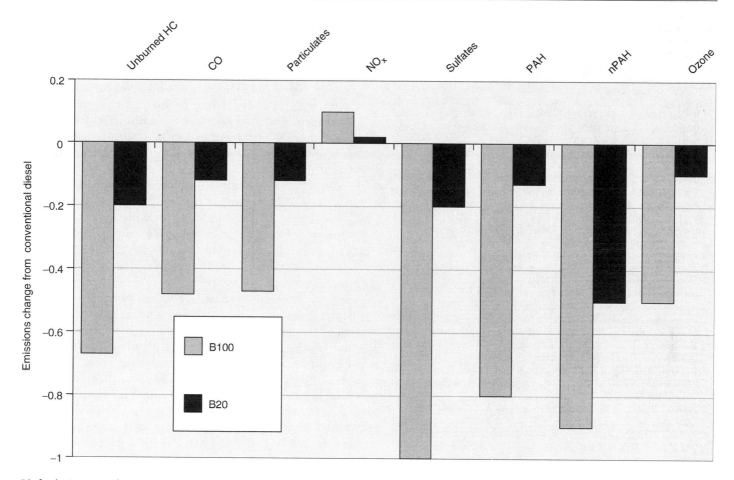

Biofuels. Figure 4. Change in Emissions Moving from Conventional Diesel to B100 and B20.

(U.S.D.O.E., Energy Efficiency and Renewable Energy.)

A comprehensive analysis of the benefits of displacing petroleum derivatives with biofuels would have to explore all of the environmental impacts of producing and processing the biofuels, not just the tail-pipe emissions. In the life cycle of a biofuel, a significant component of potential environmental impacts arises from production of the fuel's feedstock (Marshall and Greenhalgh, 2006; Farrell et al., 2006). Policies or technologies that stimulate demand for agricultural products can, in the absence of additional legislation, also intensify land-use change pressures and exacerbate existing problems associated with water demand, soil degradation, nutrient runoff, and erosion. Recent increases in the rate of biofuels production have raised the visibility of these issues and highlighted the need for greater understanding and quantification of the life-cycle impacts of biofuels production, and the trade-offs those impacts imply for national and global environment and development objectives. In Indonesia, for instance, native peat-soil forests are being replaced by palm-oil plantations to meet rising demand from the EU for palm oil despite the fact that burning the peat soils to prepare for the plantations releases significant amounts of carbon dioxide and degrades high-value habitat (Rosenthal, 2007). In the United States, increased production of nutrient-intensive corn to satisfy ethanol demand has exacerbated concerns about the impact of such production on the Gulf of Mexico's "dead zone"—a seasonally hypoxic area caused largely by nitrogen and phosphorus run-off from agricultural areas in the Midwest (Lambrecht, 2007; Turner and Rabalais, 2007).

To realize the potential environmental benefits associated with biofuels production, it will be critical to address the environmental concerns and trade-offs associated with their production as early as possible in the development of this burgeoning global industry. As a result, several international groups have convened to identify issues related to social and environmental sustainability in biofuels trade and production and to advance national and international policies that address those concerns (UN-Energy, 2007; GBEP, 2005; RSB, 2007).

BIBLIOGRAPHY

Black, F., S. Tejada, and M. Gurevich. "Alternative Fuel Motor Vehicle Tailpipe and Evaporative Emissions Composition and Ozone Potential." *Journal of the Air and Waste Management Association* 48 (1998), 578–591.

Farrell, A. E., et al. "Ethanol Can Contribute to Energy and Environmental Goals." *Science* 311 (2006), 506–508. DOI: 10.1126/science.1121416.

GBEP, 2005. "White Paper." Global Bioenergy Partnership (http://www.globalbioenergy.org/fileadmin/user_upload/docs/WhitePaper-GBEP_01.pdf).

Hill, J., et al. "Environmental, Economic, and Energetic Costs and Benefits of Biodiesel and Ethanol Biofuels." *Proceedings of the National Academy of Science* 103.30 (2006), 11206–11210. DOI: 10.1073/pnas.0604600103.

IEA, 2004. *Biofuels for Transport: An International Perspective.* Paris: International Energy Agency, 2004.

Jacobson, M. Z. "Effects of Ethanol (E85) versus Gasoline Vehicles on Cancer and Mortality in the United States." *Environmental Science and Technology* 41 (June 1, 2007), 4150–4157.

Juergens, I., and F. Nachtergaele. "Land Resources for Agriculture: Competing Demands and Major Trends." Presentation at Biofuel Assessment Conference, Copenhagen, June 4, 2007.

Kojima, M., D. Mitchell, and W. Ward. "Considering Trade Policies for Liquid Biofuels." Washington, D.C.: The World Bank, 2007 (http://siteresources. worldbank.org/INTOGMC/Resources/Considering_trade_policies_for_ liquid_biofuels.pdf; accessed May 27, 2008).

Lambrecht, B. "Fertilizer Runoff Creates 'Dead Zone' in Gulf." *St. Louis Post-Dispatch*, June 10, 2007.

Marshall, L., and S. Greenhalgh. *Beyond the RFS: The Environmental and Economic Impacts of Increased Grain Ethanol Production in the U.S.* World Resources Institute Policy Note, Energy: Biofuels no. 1. 2006 (http://www. wri.org/policynotes; accessed May 27, 2008).

Rosenthal, E. 2007. "Once a Dream Fuel, Palm Oil May Be an Eco-Nightmare." *New York Times*, January 31, 2007.

RSB, 2007. *Draft Global Principles for Sustainable Biofuels Production.* Roundtable on Sustainable Biofuels, Lausanne, Switzerland, 2007 (http://cgse.epfl. ch/webdav/site/cgse/shared/Biofuels/RSB%20Draft%20Principles%20-%20 June%205,%202007.pdf; accessed May 27, 2008).

Sheehan, J., et al. "An Overview of Biodiesel and Petroleum Diesel Life Cycles." U.S. Department of Energy, TP-580-24772. National Renewable Energy Lab, 1998.

Turner, R. Eugene, and N. Rabalais. "2007 Forecast of the Hypoxic Zone Size, Northern Gulf of Mexico." 2007 (http://www.epa.gov/gmpo/pdf/2007-hypoxia-pred-web-5.pdf; accessed May 27, 2008).

UN-Energy, 2007. "Sustainable Bioenergy: A Framework for Decision Makers." The United Nations, 2007 (http://esa.un.org/un-energy/pdf/susdev.Biofuels. FAO.pdf; accessed May 27, 2008).

Yacobucci, B. D. "Fuel Ethanol: Background and Public Policy Issues." Congressional Research Service, CRS Report for Congress. Order Code RL33290, 2006 (http://www.neseonline.org/NLE/CRSreports/06Nov/RL33290. pdf; accessed May 27, 2008).

—Elizabeth Marshall

BIOGEOCHEMICAL CYCLES

The chemical elements that compose the Earth are not held in static compartments. The components of the atmosphere and oceans are transported by the fluid movements of these bodies, which determine our daily weather patterns and the major ocean currents such as the Gulf Stream. Even the solid materials of the Earth—its crust and mantle—circulate by the processes that cause mountains to rise from the sea floor and rock materials to break down, delivering dissolved constituents to the sea. For every chemical element of the periodic table, we can outline a global cycle of its movement between the land, the atmosphere, and the oceans. We can compile measurements from studies around the world to estimate the annual transport of materials between these compartments, usually in units of millions of metric tons per year.

SEDIMENTARY CYCLES

There are two broad categories of global cycles, sedimentary and biological. Geologic processes determine the movement of elements in the sedimentary cycles. Elements circulating in sedimentary cycles typically have no gaseous forms; these are the common rock-forming elements, such as calcium, phosphorus, silicon, and most trace metals. Each year, these elements move from land to sea in the process of rock weathering, by which all crustal materials that are exposed above sea level are broken down mechanically and chemically. About 17,500 million metric tons of material are carried from land to sea each year. Some of the elemental constituents of this material, for example sodium, may spend a long time as a dissolved constituent of sea water, but eventually they are deposited on the sea floor. The deposition may be physical—for example, the deposition of river-borne sediments—or biological, as when a marine organism, with calcium carbonate ($CaCO_3$) in its skeleton, dies and falls to the sea floor.

If it were not for the internal movements of the Earth's crust and mantle, the movement of elements in sedimentary cycles would be unidirectional, not cyclic. However, tectonic movements of the Earth's crust carry marine sediments deep into the Earth, where they are transformed back into rock. The average age of the exposed sea floor is only about 150 million years—far less than the age of the Earth's oceans at 3.8 billion years. Older sediments have been recycled. Tectonic movements of the crust and mantle result in the uplift of marine sediments to form new mountainous areas on land, renewing rock weathering and rejuvenating the global sedimentary cycle of these elements. Elements moving in sedimentary cycles may spend only a fraction of their life near the Earth's surface, where they may be incorporated in organisms. The average lifetime of an atom of phosphorus in sea water is about twenty-five thousand years. When this atom of phosphorus is incorporated in a marine sediment, it is removed from the biosphere for about 400 million years.

BIOLOGICAL CYCLES

Elements moving in global biological cycles are typically found in one or more gaseous compounds that are produced by organisms. Carbon, oxygen, nitrogen, and sulfur are good examples. These elements are also found in rocks and also circulate in the sedimentary cycle. For example, a small amount of nitrogen is found in rocks (as ammonium ion, NH_4^+), and nitrogen derived from rock weathering is carried to the sea by rivers. But in contrast with the sedimentary cycles, biotic processes dominate the annual movement of elements with biological cycles. For example, relative to the total amount of nitrogen delivered to the oceans each year, very little is sequestered in marine sediments. The bulk of it, as much as 100 million metric tons per year, is released to the atmosphere as N_2 by the biological process of denitrification.

Biological processes dominate the global cycle of carbon. Each year the uptake of carbon by plant photosynthesis and the release of carbon dioxide by respiration result in a movement of carbon to and from the atmosphere that is more than 1,000 times greater than its movement in the underlying sedimentary cycle of carbon. The annual additions of oxygen to the Earth's atmosphere by photosynthesis and its removal by respiration also dwarf the movements of oxygen in the underlying sedimentary cycle, in which oxygen is consumed by rock weathering and carried to the sea, largely as sulfate (SO_4^{2-}). Thus, elements moving in global biological cycles have a relatively rapid circulation near the Earth's surface as a result of biotic activity.

Geochemists define the mean residence time of an element in any compartment of the Earth as the mass of the material in that compartment divided by the annual exchange between that compartment and other sectors of the Earth. For instance, the mean residence time of sodium in the world's oceans is about 75 million years—obtained by dividing the sodium content of all sea water by the annual delivery of sodium to the sea by rivers. In contrast, the mean residence time of bicarbonate (HCO_3^-), the major reservoir of carbon in sea water, is about 100,000 years. With its movements primarily determined by biological activity, carbon spends much less time in sea water. As a general rule, the mean residence time of elements moving in biological cycles is much shorter than those moving in sedimentary cycles at the Earth's surface.

HUMAN IMPACTS

One advantage to quantifying the global cycles of the elements, particularly the elements of life, is that we can evaluate the impact of humans on the cycles of individual elements (Steffen et al., 2004). In the mining of metals from the Earth's crust, humans expose buried rocks much more rapidly than would normally occur by erosion and rock weathering. Thus, humans accelerate the movement of the elements in the global sedimentary cycle. The annual transport of copper in the world's rivers is about three times greater than what one might estimate from the natural rate of rock weathering alone. The difference is largely attributed to the extraction and smelting of copper ores by humans. The mining of coal and the extraction of petroleum accelerate the natural rate at which these carbon-rich sediments would be exposed by rock weathering at the Earth's surface. The current rate of combustion of fossil fuel releases carbon dioxide to Earth's atmosphere about seventy times more rapidly than we would expect in nature. Humans have an enormous capacity to increase the rate of movement of materials in both the sedimentary and biological cycles.

[*See also* Acid Rain and Acid Deposition; Carbon Cycle; Nitrogen Cycle; Phosphorus Cycle; *and* Sulfur Cycle.]

BIBLIOGRAPHY

Bertine, K. K., and E. D. Goldberg. "Fossil Fuel Combustion and the Major Sedimentary Cycle." *Science* 173 (1971), 233 235. DOI: 10.1126/science. 173.3993.233.

Schlesinger, W. H. *Biogeochemistry: An Analysis of Global Change.* 2d ed. San Diego: Academic Press, 1997.

Steffen, W., et al. *Global Change and the Earth System.* New York and Berlin: Springer, 2004.

—WILLIAM H. SCHLESINGER

BIOLOGICAL DIVERSITY

Biological diversity is a huge topic and this article focuses on interactions of humans with biological diversity—how they perceive and measure biological diversity, why they value it, how they threaten and protect it. [*See* Agriculture and Biodiversity.]

WHAT IS BIOLOGICAL DIVERSITY?

Biological diversity, or biodiversity, refers to the myriad kinds of living things. Most obvious are the "charismatic megavertebrates" that have been the poster children for conservation campaigns—pandas, tigers, koalas, etc. But, biological diversity includes living things from all taxonomic groups and levels of biological organization. The vast majority are taken for granted—the bacteria, fungi, and invertebrates that decompose organic matter; the phytoplankton that fuel ocean productivity; the invertebrates and microorganisms that recycle nutrients from sediments. These inconspicuous taxa are rarely the focus of human concern. Even the larger vascular plants—grasses, herbs, trees—blend into a green backdrop, consuming carbon dioxide, and producing oxygen. Many organisms are overlooked, or even despised. These include agents of disease, pests and predators of domesticated plants and animals, and animals that are dangerous to humans. People find it difficult to embrace all living things under the umbrella of biodiversity.

Kinds of biological diversity

It is easiest to recognize biological diversity at the species level—the different kinds of organisms that are regarded as separate biological populations and separate units of evolution and given distinct scientific names. This focus belies the fact that biological diversity exists on a continuum ranging from genetic variation among individuals in the same population to the different biomes that cover the earth—tundra, freshwater lakes, polar oceans.

Genetic diversity usually refers to variation within species populations—among local populations of widely ranging species, and both among and within individuals in single populations. Genetic difference among populations of a single species can represent adaptation to local conditions. Genetic variation among individuals in a single population represents opportunities for adaptation to changing environmental conditions, especially important as the raw material for evolutionary response to global change. Genetic variation within individuals is thought to confer greater fitness in terms of enhanced reproduction and survival over individuals carrying two copies of the same genetic material. Above the species level, diversity among higher taxa (genera, orders, classes, phyla) represents further differentiation of genetic lineages and correspondingly different ways of making a living. All of these ways of classifying biological diversity rest on genetic connections—presumed evolutionary relationships ranging from close (individuals in the same local population) to distant (e.g., different animal phyla, as different as sponges and arthropods).

Another way of classifying biological diversity at different scales is to define an assemblage of organisms that occur in the same place at the same time, but have no particular genetic relationship. These are variously termed communities, ecosystems or biomes, defined geographically. They are usually named for their most conspicuous organisms, often vascular plants, and sometimes also for their biophysical locations—coral reefs, sea grass beds, dry tropical forest. Definitions of communities or ecosystems are more arbitrary than for taxonomic groupings, and the boundaries between neighboring communities or ecosystems are more difficult to delineate. The number and distribution of communities within a region contribute to its biological diversity. The fact that a freshwater lake has emergent aquatic vegetation and associated animals along the shoreline, plankton and fish in the open water, and invertebrates and microorganisms in the deepwater sediments makes it more diverse than it would be if the same populations of plants and animals were scattered evenly over the whole lake. The same is true on a global scale, where the major biomes (boreal forest, desert, grasslands) replace each other along altitudinal, latitudinal, precipitation, and soil gradients.

Measures of biological diversity

Measures of diversity incorporate both "richness," the number of species or communities in a given area, and "evenness," the relative abundance of those species or communities. Biodiversity may be expressed just in terms of richness or by using indices that combine richness and evenness. Areas with many species or communities, each about equally abundant, are considered more diverse than areas with fewer species or areas where a few species are very abundant and the rest much less abundant.

Patterns of biological diversity

Ecologists have detected patterns of biological diversity in space and in relation to biophysical features. One commonly observed pattern is a "species-area" relationship, where the number of species found in a given area increases as area increases, at first rapidly, then leveling off. Species-area relationships themselves show patterns in response to environmental gradients—more species in a given area in tropical regions than in higher latitudes; greater animal diversity in habitats with greater structural complexity (e.g., forests vs. grasslands); fewer species per area in "extreme" conditions, such as low precipitation. Some of these spatial patterns may reflect a correlation between higher productivity and higher diversity. These patterns can interact with human activities that threaten biodiversity—an area of tropical forest converted to pasture may affect far more species than an equal area of temperate forest.

Another aspect of spatial pattern in diversity concerns changes in species composition across the landscape. These patterns also interact with human activities. In the United States, national forest managers have sometimes argued that clear cutting enhances diversity at the level of a national forest by adding early successional species to those inhabiting mature forest stands. Opponents of clear cutting, looking at national forest land within a regional context where most surrounding land is already in early succession, have argued that regional diversity is enhanced by maintaining national forest land in mature stages to provide more habitat for late successional species. Ecotones, where two or more communities or ecosystems meet, are often highly diverse, combining species typical of the adjoining systems. Some wildlife managers have argued that creating more such edges, for example by cutting small patches in mature forest, will increase diversity. Again, taking a broader regional focus suggests that a mix of different types of habitats, some edge and some interior, supports the highest levels of diversity regionwide.

Ecologists have also noted patterns of biological diversity in relation to dynamic and functional features of ecosystems. More diverse systems are thought to exhibit greater stability and greater ability to recover from perturbations, including those caused by humans. Concern over oil spills in the high arctic is based partly on the expectation that systems with limited diversity in extreme environments will recover slowly, if ever. Biological diversity is thought to be higher in systems with intermediate frequencies of disturbance such as wildfire or hurricanes. Too frequent fires eliminate all but a few very fire-tolerant species; too few fires allow fire-intolerant species to dominate those adapted to survival or recovery after fires. Changing natural disturbance regimes is often a feature of human activities, with persistent consequences for biological diversity; widespread fire suppression in the United States has altered, and even eliminated, some fire-adapted communities such as that of longleaf pine. Some human activities mimic natural disturbance, but often with greater intensity and/ or greater frequency (e.g., clear cutting and blowdowns in forests), usually pushing ecosystems toward lower diversity. [See Fire and Global Warming.] The relationship between biodiversity and ecosystem stability continues to be a hot topic in ecology (Loreau et al., 2002; Kareiva and Levin, 2003). Some studies cast doubt on any simple relationship between biodiversity and stability (e.g. Pfisterer and Schmid, 2002), but there appears to be an emerging consensus that diversity is crucial to ecosystem operation (McCann, 2000). As Loreau et al. (2001, p. 807) write,

> There is consensus that at least some minimum number of species is essential for ecosystem functioning under constant conditions and that a larger number of species is probably essential for maintaining the stability of ecosystem processes in changing environments.

WHY IS BIOLOGICAL DIVERSITY IMPORTANT?

Because human activities often affect biodiversity, usually for the worse, questions about its value inevitably arise: What good is it? How much do we need? How should we trade off losses in biodiversity against gains in other areas, such as economic development? Are there ways of valuing biodiversity besides its importance to humans?

Use by humans

Utilitarian reasons for valuing biodiversity—focusing on what biodiversity provides to humans—have been the mainstay of arguments in favor of conserving biological diversity. These arguments view biological diversity as a source of goods, ecological services, aesthetic and spiritual benefits. An overused example of biological diversity as a good is biomedical prospecting for naturally derived compounds for new medicines. Other examples of raw materials include traditional products like timber or fish, but also chemical feedstocks for high-tech materials. In addition, genetic diversity in wild relatives of domesticated plants and animals is a potential source of improved protection against pests and diseases.

Less easily characterized are the ecological functions that biological diversity provides to humans. Biological organisms decompose waste products, remove impurities from water, generate oxygen, convert low-quality vegetable matter to high-quality protein, pollinate crops, and so on.

Still less tangible, but not necessarily less important, are the aesthetic, psychological, spiritual, and religious benefits of biological diversity. Humans derive satisfaction from experiencing beauty and order in natural systems. They may draw spiritual strength from wild places where nonhuman forces predominate. Religious and cultural practices in human societies incorporate landscapes, organisms and biologically derived products ranging from fungi to whales. [*See* Belief Systems.]

Monetary value

Questions about how much biodiversity we really need and how biodiversity should be weighed against human activities that threaten it have spurred attempts to express the utilitarian values of biodiversity in monetary terms. For biological products that are already traded in the marketplace, such as timber or ecotourism adventures, market value is a widely accepted way of monetizing worth, although many fear that market prices do not account fully for the side effects of exploiting biological resources. For biological products that might become market goods in the future, such as undiscovered medicines from tropical rainforests, economists have attempted to calculate an option value for preservation of this potential. For ecological services such as water purification, environmental economists have tried to assign monetary value by combining the estimated costs of replacing those natural services with engineered equivalents and the costs of environmental degradation (e.g., the manufacturing costs of using dirtier water for industrial processes). Even the less tangible ways of valuing biological diversity—the aesthetic and spiritual benefits—have been monetized using hypothetical questions where people are asked how much they would be willing to pay to preserve a particular biological feature. These monetary expressions of the value of biological diversity are apt to find their way into benefit-cost analyses, where proposals for human uses of biological systems are weighed against losses of biodiversity, or where opportunities to preserve biodiversity are weighed against expenditures for other social benefits. Many conservation-minded people wonder whether even the most comprehensive efforts to monetize the many uses of biodiversity by humans can capture its full value.

Intrinsic value

Even more skeptical are those who believe that biological diversity has intrinsic value, quite apart from its appreciation and use by humans. In this framework, biological diversity exists in its own right and should continue to do so unless there are compelling reasons for its destruction. This argument follows the same structure as the intrinsic value of human life, not to be traded off for economic gain or convenience, but to be safeguarded, except in very rare circumstances. The U.S. Endangered Species Act works this way on paper (although certainly not in practice), evaluating actions that jeopardize survival of endangered species without regard for socioeconomic consequences, unless there are extraordinary human needs that cannot be met without loss of endangered species. Some advocates for the intrinsic value of biodiversity attribute equal value to all biological organisms, regardless of aesthetic appeal or level of biological complexity. Under this framework, humans have the same moral obligations toward all living things, perhaps also including assemblages of organisms, such as ecosystems, or ecological phenomena, such as mass migrations of African wildlife. Other environmental ethicists attribute higher value to complex organisms that behave more like humans—exhibiting emotion, feeling pain. Advocates of this framework believe that humans have a greater obligation toward organisms that seem more like us, mainly birds and mammals.

Using any of these methods of valuing biological diversity in order to decide when to forgo other benefits to protect or restore biodiversity implies an answer to the question: how much diversity do we really need? The answer depends critically on which framework for valuation is used. Those who attribute the same intrinsic value to all living things would answer that we need all the diversity present at some previous time, usually assumed to be prior to the industrial revolution and perhaps prior to the agricultural revolution as well. Those who focus on the services that biological systems provide to humans would say that we need enough kinds and numbers of organisms to produce oxygen, purify water, or whatever the services of concern may be. Obviously, this latter view could be used to justify considerable losses of biodiversity, particularly over the short term. Think of the human-dominated landscapes of western Europe or Indonesia, which provide many ecological services and even aesthetic pleasures, but with a very depleted flora and fauna compared to prehistoric times.

THREATS TO BIOLOGICAL DIVERSITY

Loss of biological diversity has become a global concern. Although it is true that all species will become extinct (just as all individuals will die), there is little doubt that industrial humans have accelerated the rate of extinction 2 to 5 orders of magnitude above "background" levels. Even early hunter-gatherers extirpated many species of large mammals and birds, particularly on oceanic islands. Today the decline of one fishery after another to uneconomic levels continues this pattern of uncontrolled exploitation. But, as devastating as direct killing can be, destruction and fragmentation of habitats are undoubtedly the greater threats to biological diversity. Conversion of natural landscapes to agricultural and urban uses causes obvious loss of habitat. Less obvious loss results from human-induced changes in ecological processes, such as changes in productivity through addition of nutrients from fertilizers or wastewater. The spatial pattern of habitat loss can be as important as its extent—the same area of forest habitat broken into small patches sustains a different flora and fauna than larger patches; barriers to traditional migration routes created by road construction can degrade remaining habitat disproportionately to the area actually lost. [See Extinctions of Animals.]

The globalization of modern human society poses special threats to biological diversity. Humans have been transporting organisms beyond their natural ranges, wittingly and unwittingly, for millennia, causing extinctions of native species due to competition and predation by introduced species. With high-speed transport, pathogenic microorganisms can circle the globe in hours. Even slower-going ocean travel homogenizes nearshore ecosystems worldwide by transporting organisms on ship hulls and in bilge water. Once-local pollution has gone worldwide as well—acid emissions from power plants in Europe and the United States circulate in the upper atmosphere and rain down anywhere; heavy metals and pesticide residues appear in the tissues of animals from remote polar regions.

Some human actions have global repercussions, changing the chemical composition of the atmosphere and, probably, altering world climates. The interaction of global climate change with habitat destruction and fragmentation is particularly troubling—species that might adapt successfully to gradually changing climates by shifting their ranges will be unable to do so if contiguous habitat has been lost to development. Globalization has social implications that impinge on biodiversity as well. Uncontrolled borders facilitate smuggling of endangered species products, such as bear gallbladders for Oriental medicines. The homogenization of human cultures fostered by rapid transportation and electronic communication encourages people in all parts of the world to pursue the same patterns of development and material culture that have already devastated biological diversity in industrial societies. Rapid human population growth exacerbates these threats to biodiversity.

PROTECTION OF BIOLOGICAL DIVERSITY

Although the predominant impact of humans on biological diversity has been devastatingly negative, there are some encouraging efforts to slow the rate of loss and even to restore biodiversity. Although much could be said about how to conserve biodiversity, the discussion here will focus on methods of setting priorities and on examples of institutions and policies for biodiversity protection. [See Conservation.]

Species conservation

The job of conserving the world's biological diversity clearly exceeds the resources currently allocated to the task, requiring hard decisions about which species and ecosystems to protect first. For species, criteria for high priority include uniqueness (species with no close relatives), abundance (species with the lowest numbers and those that have suffered the greatest declines), distribution (species represented in only one or a few locations), threat (species facing the greatest immediate pressures), ecological function (species with functional importance disproportionate to their numbers, such as some key predators) and sometimes aesthetic or emotional appeal.

Habitat and ecosystem conservation

The futility of evaluating all threatened species in this manner and then implementing protection on a species-by-species basis, has led many conservationists to focus on habitat and ecosystem protection instead. A widely used tool for identifying areas with high priority for protection is "gap analysis." This analysis identifies "hot spots" of biological diversity—places where there are high levels of diversity (many species, habitats) and high levels of endemism (species not found elsewhere). Candidate areas for protection are then selected to form a complementary suite of areas that encompass the widest variety of resources. Sometimes gap analysis also includes areas where biodiversity is being lost especially rapidly (e.g., dry tropical forest) or where species and habitats are especially vulnerable to extinction (e.g., isolated areas such as oceanic islands). This kind of analysis has recently been extended to consider the cost of protecting candidate areas, in order to assemble a suite of areas that protect the most biological diversity for a given cost; this strategy may emphasize protection in developing countries, where land acquisition costs are lower.

Laws and institutions

Institutional and legal mechanisms for protecting biological diversity range from local to international and are too numerous to address here with more than a few examples. The Nature Conservancy (TNC) is a private nonprofit organization whose traditional focus has been species and habitat preservation through purchase of small areas. Recognizing that biodiversity protection on small parcels is affected by surrounding land uses and that successful protection must include multiple-use lands as well as those dedicated to conservation, TNC has begun working with both private landowners and public land managers toward conservation on regional scales. [See Environmental Law.]

The U.S. Endangered Species Act (ESA) is a federal law that constrains actions by public and, to a lesser extent, private entities that threaten the continued existence of species at risk of extinction. Implementation of the Act has been controversial, drawing criticism both from those who believe it does too little to list and then protect species in peril and from those who believe it interferes too often with legitimate activities of both public and private landowners. The ESA has been credited with some conservation successes, mainly for species facing single, fairly easily reversed threats, such as DDT contamination of bird eggs.

Internationally, the Convention on International Trade in Endangered Species (CITES) restricts trade in live organisms and products from species listed as endangered. In a recent CITES decision, continuing restrictions on the trade in elephant ivory have sparked criticism from a few countries where elephants have been protected successfully. As with most international agreements, compliance is voluntary, and some countries are notorious for their markets in banned products such as tiger parts and rhino horn.

Another international agreement, the Convention on Biodiversity, highlights the tension between industrialized and developing countries in balancing socioeconomic development and conservation of biological diversity. A major stumbling block to designing and ratifying the convention has been the allocation of financial benefits from commercial development of biologically derived products.

Development and biodiversity

The development/biodiversity struggle is particularly acute in developing countries, where much of the remaining biodiversity is found, but where means to conserve it are most limited and human needs most compelling. One organization concerned with this dilemma is the World Conservation Union (IUCN), a consortium of governmental and nongovernmental entities to protect and sustain the world's resources. Among its activities are publication of the "Red List" of threatened species and sponsorship of species survival plans for conservation of selected taxa. Institutional participants in these plans often include conservation organizations, such as WWF (formerly known as the World Wildlife Fund), and zoos from industrialized countries. The role of zoos in protecting biological diversity has been controversial, in part because zoos and countries with wild populations of endangered species may disagree about whether to emphasize captive breeding or protection in the wild, and in part because zoos historically have consumed biological diversity rather than protecting it.

Integrating human needs and biodiversity protection is a new challenge for international aid organizations such as the World Bank, after many years of coming down heavily on the side of economic development. Some innovative instruments have been developed for using the wealth of industrialized countries to support conservation in developing countries, including "debt for nature" swaps in which part of a country's foreign debt may be forgiven in return for dedication of land to protection of biodiversity.

Another approach to reconciling socioeconomic concerns with conservation is evident in the UNESCO Man and the Biosphere (MAB) reserves. These consist of a core area undisturbed by human activities, surrounded by a buffer of low-intensity, biodiversity-compatible human uses (e.g., extraction of nontimber forest products, such as thatch or nuts). Such systems view human societies, particularly traditional, resource-based economies, as part of nature, to be sustained along with the nonhuman components of the ecosystem. Globalization imperils these traditional societies, which are often linked with intimate knowledge of biological diversity as food, medicine, and religious artifacts. Losing their biodiversity base threatens these cultures, and loss of these cultures extinguishes their rich knowledge of biological diversity. Thus the preservation of human and nonhuman diversity is closely linked.

[*See also* Agriculture and Agricultural Land; Deforestation; Environmental Movements; Exotic Species; Global Change History; *and* International Geosphere-Biosphere Programme.]

BIBLIOGRAPHY

Daily, G. C., ed. *Ecosystem Services: Their Nature and Value*. Washington, D.C.: Island Press, 1997.

Kareiva, P. and S. A. Levin, eds. *The Importance of Species*. Princeton: Princeton University Press, 2003.

Leopold, A. *A Sand County Almanac, and Sketches Here and There*. New York: Oxford University Press, 1949. A classic source in environmental ethics, proposing a "land ethic" focused on ecosystem integrity rather than on human uses.

Loreau, M., et al. "Biodiversity and Ecosystem Functioning: Current Knowledge and Future Challenges." *Science* 294 (2001), 804–808. DOI: 10.1126/science.1064088.

Loreau, M., S. Naeem, and P. Inchausti, eds. *Biodiversity and Ecosystem Functioning: Synthesis and Perspectives*. Oxford: Oxford University Press, 2002.

Magurran, A. E. *Measuring Biological Diversity*. Oxford, U.K., and Malden, Mass.: Blackwell Publishing, 2004. A textbook.

McCann, K. S. "The Diversity-Stability Debate." *Nature* 405 (2000), 228–233. DOI:10.1038/35012234.

Meffe, G. K., and C. R. Carroll. *Principles of Conservation Biology*. 2d ed. Sunderland, Mass.: Sinauer Associates, 1997. A comprehensive textbook, with good attention to the human aspects of implementing conservation actions.

Myers, N. *The Sinking Ark*. Oxford: Pergamon Press, 1979. A forceful look at how humans are accelerating extinction.

Noss, R. F., and A. Y. Cooperrider. *Saving Nature's Legacy: Protecting and Restoring Biodiversity*. Washington, D.C.: Defenders of Wildlife and Island Press, 1992. Emphasis on U.S. examples of biodiversity loss and protection.

Pfisterer, A. B., and B. Schmid. "Diversity-Dependent Production Can Decrease the Stability of Ecosystem Functioning." *Nature* 416 (2002), 84–86. DOI:10.1038/416084a.

Stein, B. A., L. S. Kutner, and J. S. Adams, eds. *Precious Heritage: The Status of Biodiversity in the United States*. Oxford and New York: Oxford University Press, 2000. An edited survey.

Western, D., R. M. Wright, and S. C. Strum, eds. *Natural Connections: Perspectives in Community-Based Conservation*. Washington, D.C.: Island Press, 1994. Case studies on community involvement in sustainable development from around the world.

Wilson, E. O. *The Diversity of Life*. Cambridge, Mass.: Belknap Press of Harvard University Press, 1992. A beautifully written overview of biodiversity and its loss.

—LYNN A. MAGUIRE

BIOLOGICAL FEEDBACK

A feedback is the return of output to the input part of a system. The system may be the body of a living organism, a population, or the interacting biotic and abiotic components of an ecosystem. During negative feedback an output lessens the strength of a subsequent input thereby suppressing the original process. These help maintain stability provided time lags in response are short. Positive feedback occurs when the output adds effect to the input, amplifying a change and allowing the system to pass a "tipping point" and acquire a new state. As a result of such feedbacks, nature is frequently nonlinear, with responses to an environmental change being disproportionate to the change itself. The circularity, nonlinearity, and interconnectedness of feedbacks make their consequences difficult to analyze, quantify, and predict.

NEGATIVE FEEDBACKS

In an organism, negative feedbacks regulate such things as body temperature, and levels of glucose, water, and mineral salts.

Negative feedbacks in ecosystems are often due to density-dependent processes, whereby an increase in the abundance of the population generates pressures reducing further population growth. Such pressures include competition within and between species for food. One of the most common biological feedbacks may be increased disease transmission as host abundance increases.

Negative feedbacks may dampen a population at a stable level (regulation), or may lead to cycles within stable limits (as with hares and lynx in Canada). However, time lags before the feedback may lead to chaotic population changes.

During climate change, negative feedbacks include fertilization of plant and phytoplankton growth through increased carbon dioxide, and the spread of forests into high latitudes—both increasing uptake of carbon dioxide.

POSITIVE FEEDBACKS

Positive feedback in an organism is important for morphogenesis and growth, and allows for the fast mobilization particularly of elements of the endocrine and nervous systems where a rapid response is required. The fight-or-flight response to perceived danger is one example. The process of blood clotting involves several positive feedback loops that rapidly magnify the aggregation of blood platelets to form a clot. Once achieved, negative feedbacks regulate the process by the release of counter-signals to suppress or break the loop.

Positive feedback may occur in population growth or decline. The more adult organisms there are, the more there are to reproduce, as is the case in pest outbreaks and disease epidemics and when invasive species are introduced (e.g., rabbits and *Opuntia* [prickly pear] cactus in Australia). [*See* Exotic Species.] Introduced species may show "ecological release" from the negative feedbacks that naturally check the population. Some species, including our own, can grow at faster than exponential rates through adaptation. In humans, technological growth has increased the carrying capacity of the land for people. Increased populations have more potential inventors, which accelerate technological growth. Human activities require energy, much of which comes from the combustion of fossil fuels, making the increase in atmospheric CO_2 concentrations a measure with which to evaluate the rate and magnitude of human-driven change compared to natural variability. Similarly, feral pigs in the Galápagos are spreading their exotic food plants. Some social species (such as several seabirds and whales) breed less readily at lower densities (the Allee effect), so generating an "extinction vortex."

"Edge creep" is a feedback in landscape degradation. Before fragmentation, a habitat may have communities at its edge inimical to those at its core. As habitats are fragmented and penetrated by human agency, so the proportion of edge to core increases and a positive feedback may ensue, causing more fragmentation. Migrant birds in North America and forest-specialist birds of the tropics may be threatened by such changes.

Several positive feedbacks appear to be associated with climate change. Warming of soils induced by rising carbon dioxide increases decomposition in soils, releasing more carbon dioxide and is predicted to overtake the effect of CO_2 fertilization in the next few decades. The type of vegetation present influences the amount of water transpired back to the atmosphere and the absorption of reflection of the sun's radiation. Increase in boreal forest cover caused by warming at high latitudes decreases the effects of snow albedo and causes regional warming.

Evidence from studies of past glacial-interglacial cycles suggests that a cooler and drier climate leads to less vegetation cover on the land surface, which in turn leads to an increase in bare soil and thus dustiness. Iron-containing dust from the land is transported by wind over the oceans, where it acts as a fertilizer to phytoplankton, causing a bloom which removes CO_2 from the atmosphere, leading to a cooler and drier climate.

There is also evidence that the long-term cooling and drying over the past seven thousand years was triggered by subtle changes in the Earth's orbit but that abrupt desertification in the Sahara around 5,500 years ago was intensified by a series of positive feedbacks. Reduced vegetation and increased surface albedo resulted in decreased rainfall, which further reduced the vegetation cover.

IMPLICATIONS FOR THE SCIENCE OF GLOBAL CHANGE

Positive and negative feedbacks interact on a variety of spatial and temporal scales and can be thought of as linked in a complex interconnected web, because any organism or other entity in the Earth system is an integral part of many loops. Figure 1 shows a phytoplankton-climate link proposed by Charlson et al. (1987) that may exert a negative feedback on warming through the emission of dimethyl sulfide (DMS). Many of the features of this system have since been demonstrated, although the overall influence of cloud cover on algae (which could be either positive or negative) has been difficult to ascertain because of links to other complex biogeochemical cycles and climatic effects. Warmer surface waters, for example, increase the stratification of surface waters, thus reducing vertical mixing and the return to the surface of nutrients required for phytoplankton growth.

One of the greatest challenges of global change research is to establish the role played by the feedbacks within the Earth System. Feedbacks mean that climate change, for example, may not happen in the smooth manner envisaged by climate models. The balance between positive and negative feedbacks, and regional differences in their role, are major causes of uncertainty in climate predictions, as we do not have a strong basis for including their effects in climate models.

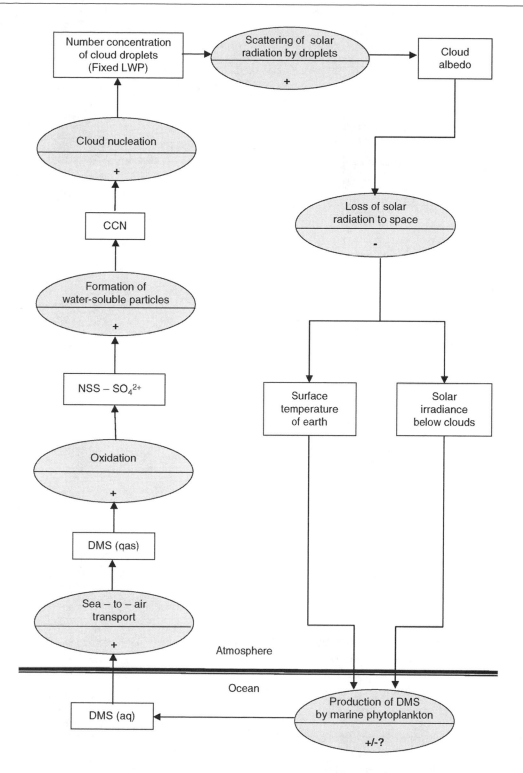

Biological Feedback. Figure 1. Diagram of the Proposed Phytoplankton-climate Feedback Loop.

The rectangles are measurable quantities, and the ovals are processes linking the quantities. The sign (+ or −) in the oval indicates the effect of a positive change of the quantity in the preceding rectangle. (Charlson et al., 1987.)

AN EMERGING GLOBAL PERSPECTIVE

Through the 1990s there was a shift in the understanding of the Earth System that owes much to the concept of Gaia, developed by James Lovelock. [*See* Gaia Hypothesis.] Several developments have led to this significant change in perception: the psychological impact of viewing the Earth from space; the development of global observation systems and

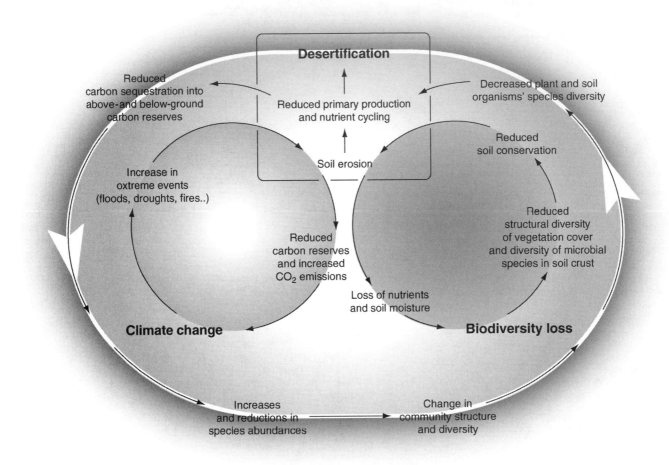

Biological Feedback. Figure 2. Interlinked Feedback Loops between Human-Induced Processes of Climate Change, Biodiversity Loss and Desertification.

(Millennium Ecosystem Assessment, 2005.)

databases; advances in the ability to understand Earth System processes in the past; and enhanced computing power that allows data assimilation and increasingly sophisticated modeling.

The emerging global perspective recognizes the Earth as a single system in which biological processes interact strongly with physical and chemical processes to create the planetary environment, through a combination of external forcing—primarily variations in solar radiation levels—and a complex array of feedbacks and forcings within the Earth's environment itself.

Evidence is mounting that human activities are changing the internal dynamics of the Earth System. Figure 2 shows some of the linkages and feedbacks between three such processes. Some fear that the Earth System's negative feedbacks may be overwhelmed by anthropogenically induced positive feedbacks, and that their multiple, interacting effects have the potential to switch the Earth System to alternative modes of operation that may prove to be less amenable to human life.

[*See also* Biological Diversity; Biogeochemical Cycles; Deforestation; Desertification; Earth System Science; Ecosystems; *and* Sustainable Growth.]

BIBLIOGRAPHY

Adeel, Z., et al. *Ecosystems and Human Well-Being: Desertification Synthesis: A Report of the Millennium Ecosystem Assessment.* Washington, D.C.: World Resources Institute, 2005.

Charlson, et al. "Oceanic Phytoplankton, Atmospheric Sulphur, Cloud Albedo, and Climate." *Nature* 326 (1987), 655–661. DOI: 10.1038/326655a0. A classic demonstration of the importance of life in climate change; hypothesizes that locally beneficial adaptations of algae might lead to global phenomena such as cooling and nutrient flow to the oceans.

Claussen, M., et al. "Simulation of an Abrupt Change in Saharan Vegetation at the End of the Mid-Holocene." *Geophysical Research Letters* 26 (1999), 2037–2040. DOI: 10.1023/A:1022115604225. An example of the importance of including biological feedbacks in models of climate change.

Cox, P. M., et al. "Acceleration of Global Warming Due to Carbon-Cycle Feedbacks in a Coupled Climate Model." *Nature* 408 (2000) 184–187. DOI: 10.1038/35041539.

Denman, K. L., et al. "Couplings Between Changes in the Climate System and Biogeochemistry." In *Climate Change 2007: The Physical Science Basis: Contribution of Working Group I to the Fourth Assessment Report of the Intergovernmental Panel on Climate Change*, edited by S. Solomon, et al. Cambridge and New York: Cambridge University Press, 2007. Summary of snow- and ice-cover data.

Kiene, R. P. "Ocean Biogeochemistry: Sulphur in the Mix." *Nature* 402 (1999), 363–365. DOI: 10.1038/46446. Summary of the state of knowledge regarding the DMS feedback.

Lovelock, J. E. *The Ages of Gaia.* 2d ed. Oxford: Oxford University Press, 1995.

Petit, J. R., et al. "Climate and Atmospheric History of the Past 420,000 Years from the Vostok Ice Core, Antarctica." *Nature* 399 (1999), 429–436. DOI: 10.1038/20859. Correlations between dust deposition, methane, and carbon dioxide concentrations through four glacial-interglacial cycles.

Ridgwell, A. J., and A. J. Watson. "Feedback between Aeolian Dust, Climate, and Atmospheric CO_2 in Glacial Time." *Paleoceanography* 17 (2002), 1059–2001. DOI: 10.1029/2001PA000729.

Soulé, M. E., ed. *Conservation Biology: The Science of Scarcity and Diversity.* Sunderland, Mass.: Sinauer Associates, 1986. See Section 3 for discussion of edge effects.

Steffen, W. A., et al. *Global Change and the Earth System: A Planet Under Pressure.* Berlin, and New York: Springer, 2004. A global perspective on change.

—SUSAN CANNEY

BIOLOGICAL REALMS

It has long been recognized that terrestrial biomes in different parts of the world support distinctive assemblages of plants and animals. These general patterns were originally attributed to differences in climate, but this explanation was increasingly questioned as more species were described by natural historians. Thus, in the mid-eighteenth century Buffon noted that environmentally similar regions in the Old and New World tropics supported very different fauna. In 1858 Sclater proposed six faunal regions based on the distribution of bird species; this arrangement is still widely used (Figure 1). The most extensive region is the Palearctic, which includes Europe, the Middle East and much of Asia. North America and the highlands of Mexico are represented by the Nearctic, which is linked to the Neotropical region of South America. Africa south of the Sahara Desert is included with Madagascar in the Ethiopian region. The Oriental region is bounded on the north and west by the Himalayan Mountains and the Tibetan Massif; it includes

---

Biological Realms. FIGURE 1. Zoological Regions of the World Based on the Distribution of Mammals.

(Modifed from Pielou, 1979.)

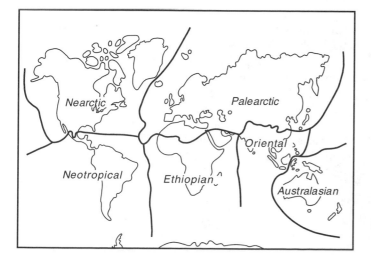

India, Ceylon and Malaysia. The Australasian region, which consists of Australia, New Zealand, New Guinea and several islands in the East Indies, is completely isolated and possesses many endemic species.

FLORISTIC REGIONS

Most families of flowering plants are restricted by general habitat conditions in much the same way as animals. Takhtajan (1986) described six floristic regions. In this scheme, the main divisions are based on the distributions of broadly endemic species that occur extensively, but exclusively, within a region. The temperate and arctic regions of the northern hemisphere are termed the Holarctic. Central America and much of South America are affiliated with the Neotropical region. The Paleotropics cover most of Africa south of the Sahara, Madagascar, India and S.E. Asia, with the distinctive flora of southern Africa incorporated into the Cape region. Australia is also recognized for its unusual flora. New Zealand, Patagonia and other land areas in the southern hemisphere are grouped together in the Antarctic region, although Antarctica itself is excluded. The recognition of an Antarctic temperate floristic region is an important difference between the distributions of plants and animals. The presence of podocarp gymnosperms and evergreen angiosperms (notably the genus *Nothofagus*, the southern beeches) provides the common link between these geographically isolated regions. Similarly, the Paleotropical floristic region extends to New Guinea, whereas zoogeographers include many of the islands of south-east Asia with Australia. The Cape flora of southern Africa is also treated as a distinct region by plant geographers.

FAUNA

The concept of biological realms is based on the distinctive biota found in each terrestrial region. Movement of organisms between realms is restricted by physiographic barriers. In many cases the realms are clearly isolated by the oceans, but mountain ranges and deserts also form insuperable barriers to dispersal. The change in biota can occur abruptly; the Palearctic fauna of northern Africa, for example, is very different from that found south of the Sahara. Elsewhere the boundaries are less distinct. This is the case in south-east Asia, where the separation of the Oriental and Australasian faunal regions has been the subject of much controversy (Figure 2).

In 1859 Wallace proposed a line of demarcation running through the Lombok Strait and coinciding with the deep-ocean region between Borneo and Sulawesi. Wallace's Line separates the placental mammals from the marsupials, although other faunal groups are more widely dispersed throughout the Malaysian archipelago. Physiographically significant are Huxley's Line proposed in 1868, which follows the Sunda Shelf, and Lydekker's Line (1896), which marks the limit of the Sahul Shelf. Lowering of sea level during the Pleistocene permitted land animals to move throughout these temporarily emerged marine platforms, although the two faunal realms remained separated by the deep water surrounding Sulawesi.

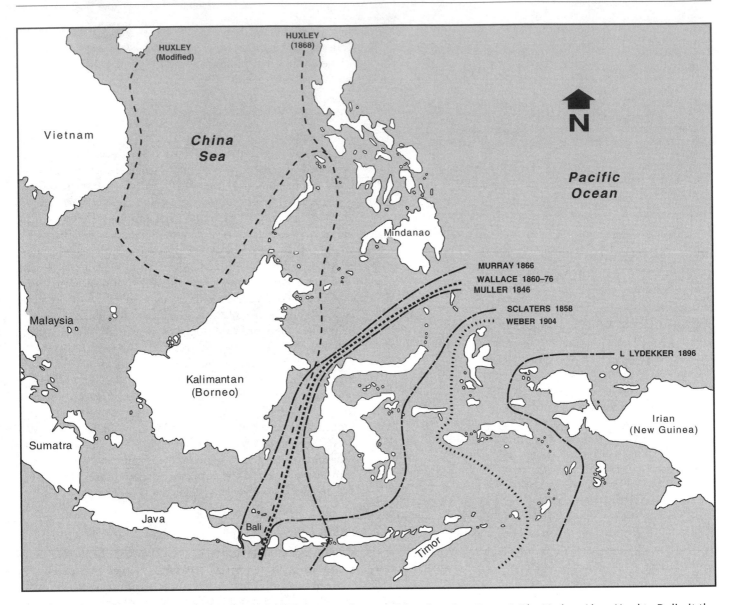

Biological Realms. FIGURE 2. The Various Lines Used to Delimit the Oriental and Australian Zoogeographic Regions.

(Adapted from Simpson, 1977.)

Zoologists recognize 89 families of terrestrial mammals (excluding bats). Three families are found worldwide because of human dispersal; these include rats and mice (family Muridae), rabbits and hares (Leporidae) and dogs and wolves (Canidae). The remainder varies in terms of their dispersal success. For example, ursids (bears), cervids (deer) and soricids (shrews) are found in all but the Australian region. Conversely, families including the kangaroos and wallabies (Macropodidae) and wombats (Phascolomidae) and platypus (Ornithorhynchidae) are restricted to the Australian region. About 58% of the families of terrestrial mammals are endemic to a single faunal region. The degree of endemism ranges from 91% in the Australian region to 3% in the Palearctic (Cox and Moore, 1993).

DISTRIBUTIONS

Although plants are motile during phases of dispersal, their geographic ranges are ultimately determined by adaptation to the environment. Consequently, many unrelated species exhibit similar patterns of distribution which typically reflect climate, topography, and soil conditions. Botanists recognize over 400 families of flowering plants ranging in size from the Asteraceae (composites), which contains more than 1,000 genera and 20,000 species to those which are represented by a single monotypic genus. Some families, for example the Asteraceae and Poaceae (grasses), are cosmopolitan in their distribution. Others, such as the Cruciferae (mustards) and Juncaceae (rushes), are predominantly found in temperate regions while the Rubiaceae (madders) and Euphorbiaceae (spurges) are mainly restricted to the tropics. Approximately 30% of plant families are endemic to specific areas. They include, for example, the Didiereaceae (spiny-stemmed succulents) of Madagascar, which is represented by 11 species, and the Xanthorrhoeaceae (grass trees) of Australia with 28 species.

In contrast, the Cactaceae (cacti), a much larger family represented by about 2,000 species, has a correspondingly greater geographic range and is endemic to the Americas. Some plant families are notable for their discontinuous distributions in that they are found in geographically separate parts of the world. For example, the Platanaceae (sycamores) are found in North America and western Eurasia, and the Strelitziaceae are native to Africa (five species, including the bird-of-paradise flower), Madagascar (one species, the traveler's palm, *Ravenala madagascariensis*) and South America (one species, *Phenakospermum guyanense*). The origin of such disjunct distributions has been a matter of much speculation.

FOSSIL EVIDENCE

Fossil evidence suggests that two distinct paleofloral regions had evolved by the early Mesozoic (230 million years BP). At this time ancestral conifers (Cordaitales) were widely distributed across the single northern landmass Pangea, with seed ferns, notably *Glossopteris*, occuring in Gondwanaland to the south. The subsequent breakup of Gondwanaland is inferred from present plant distributions; for example, the southern beeches (*Nothofagus*) are disjunct across the southern continents despite poor mechanisms for dispersal. The separation of South America and Africa probably began in the lower Cretaceous (127 million years BP); Madagascar and India broke away in the mid-Cretaceous (100 million years BP) with India becoming isolated in the late Cretaceous (80 million years BP). About this time New Zealand began to drift away from Antarctica, with the rift between Australia and Antarctica occurring in the Eocene (49 million years BP). The breakup of Pangea started with the opening of the North Atlantic in the late Triassic (180 million years BP), although links between Europe and North America probably persisted at high latitudes until the Eocene. A temporary connection between Africa and Europe is recognized in the early Paleocene (63 million years BP), with the present configuration of the Mediterranean Sea established in the Miocene (17 million years BP). Contact between India and Asia occurred in the Eocene. Finally, the connection of North and South America by a land bridge occurred in the Pliocene (6 million years BP).

Isolation and recombination of the continents over time have led to distinctive patterns of species distribution and areas of species richness. The most obvious pattern is that species richness decreases at higher latitudes so that tropical regions exhibit far greater diversity than temperate or polar regions. Superimposed on this general pattern are the effects of environmental factors such as elevation and precipitation, all of which augment habitat variability and increase the potential for species evolution and survival. Similarly, geographically isolated areas are important centres of species diversity because they invariably have large numbers of endemic species. Thus, in recent years more refined systems of classification have been devised. Ecozones, for example, are an extension of the concept of biological realms and have formed the basis of modern biogeographical and ecological classification since the 1970s (Udvardy, 1975). In this scheme the biogeographic realms were divided into 203 biogeographical provinces; it is now commonly used for intensive studies of regional biodiversity. Island ecosystems have been altered

dramatically since the mid-nineteenth century through the introduction of grazing animals and exotic plants. [*See* Exotic Species]. The problem of species loss is not confined to islands. Demands for food and natural resources have resulted in extensive loss of habitat. [*See* Human Impacts.] This is of paramount importance because extensive loss of habitat, together with accidental or deliberate introduction of exotic species, eradication of competitors, diseases and other pressures, is rapidly changing the faunal and floral distributions that are the natural legacy of ancient and complex evolutionary processes.

BIBLIOGRAPHY

Cox, C. B., and P. D. Moore. *Biogeography: An Ecological and Evolutionary Approach.* 5th ed. Oxford, U.K., and Cambridge, Mass.: Blackwell Science, 1993. The seventh edition was published in 2005.
Cracraft, J. "Continental Drift and Vertebrate Distribution." *Annual Review of Ecology and Systematics* 5 (1974), 215–261.
Fichman, M. *Alfred Russel Wallace.* Boston: Twayne, 1981.
George, W., and R. Lavocat, eds. 1992. *The Africa–South America Connection.* Oxford and New York: Oxford University Press, 1992.
Good, R. *The Geography of Flowering Plants.* 3d ed. London: Longman, 1964.
Groombridge, B., ed. *Global Biodiversity: Status of Earth's Living Resources.* London: Chapman and Hall, 1992.
Pielou, E. C. *Biogeography.* New York: Wiley, 1979.
Simpson, G. G. "Too Many Lines: The Limits of the Oriental and Australian Zoogeographic Regions." *Proceedings of the American Philosophical Society* 121.2 (1977), 107–120.
Takhtajan, A. *Floristic Regions of the World.* Translated by T. J. Crovello. Berkeley: University of California Press, 1986.
Udvardy, M. D. F. *A Classification of the Biogeographical Provinces of the World.* Morges, Switzerland: International Union for Conservation of Nature and Natural Resources, 1975.
Whitmore, T. C., ed. *Biogeographical Evolution of the Malay Archipelago.* New York: Oxford University Press, 1987.
Wolfe, J. A. 1975. "Some Aspects of Plant Geography of the Northern Hemisphere during the Late Cretaceous and Tertiary." *Annals of the Missouri Botanical Garden* 62.2 (1975), 264–279.

—O. W. ARCHIBALD

BIOMES

There is some variation in the use of the term "biome." Begon et al. (1986, p. 608) describe biomes as "communities characteristic of broad climatic regions." Cox et al. (1976, p. 36) recognize the existence of certain major climatic types, each of which "has a number of characteristic plant and animal communities that have evolved so that they are well-adapted to the range of environmental factors in them; such characteristic communities are called biomes." Walter (1985, p. 7), on the other hand, remarks that "the word biome on its own (without a prefix) is used for the fundamental unit of which larger ecological systems are made up," and (p. 2) that it is also a term for "a large and climatically uniform environment within the geo-biosphere." Clapham (1983, p. 244) suggests they are "generalised types of communities comprising several associations with similar community structure."

Some authors have divided biomes into different categories. Walter (1985) defines zonobiomes as major climatically defined zones, of which he identified nine:

ZBI   Equatorial with diurnal climate, humid.
ZBII Tropical with summer rains, humido-arid.

ZBIII	Subtropical-arid and summer drought, arido-humid.
ZBIV	Winter rain and summer drought, arido-humid.
ZBV	Warm temperate (maritime), humid.
ZBVI	Warm temperate with a short period of frost (nemoral).
ZBVII	Arid-temperate with a cold winter (continental).
ZBVIII	Cold-temperate (boreal).
ZBIX	Arctic (including Antarctic), polar.

Walter subdivided the large zonobiomes into subzonobiomes. Orobiomes are mountainous environments that can be subdivided into altitudinal belts. Pedobiomes are environments associated with a particular type of soil: stony, sandy, salty, swampy, nutrient-deficient, or waterlogged.

Figure 1 and Table 1 show the main terrestrial biomes that have been identified by a range of different biogeographers.

Biomes. FIGURE 1. The Pattern of World Biome Types in Relation to Mean Annual Temperature.

(Modified from Gates, 1993, Figure 1, p. 63. With permission of Sinauer Associates.)

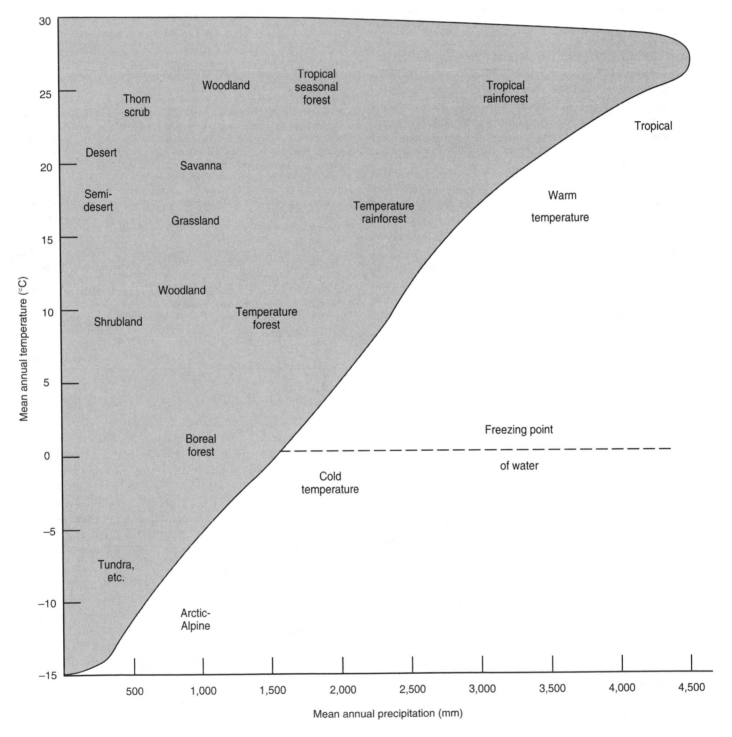

TABLE 1. Major Terrestrial Biomes as Identified by Different Biogeographers

Odum (1971)	Simmons (1979)	Cox et al. (1976)	Clapham (1983)
Tundra	Tundra	Tundra	Tundra
Northern conifer forest	Boreal forests	Northern coniferous forest (taiga)	Boreal conifer forests
Temperate deciduous and rainforest	Deciduous forests of temperate climate	Temperate forest	Temperate deciduous forests
Temperate grassland	Temperate grasslands	Temperate grassland	
Chaparral	Temperate sclerophyll woodland and scrub	Chaparral	Temperate evergreen woodland
Desert	Deserts	Deserts	Deserts
Tropical rainforest	Tropical rainforests	Tropical rainforests	Tropical rainforest
Tropical deciduous forest	Tropical seasonal forests		Tropical seasonal forests
Tropical scrub forest			Thorn woodland and scrubland
Tropical grassland and savanna	Tropical savannas	Tropical grassland or savanna	Tropical savanna Subtropical rainforests
Mountains	Mountains		

TABLE 2. Estimated Changes in the Areas of the Major Land Cover Types between Preagricultural Times and the Present*

Land Cover Type	Preagricultural Area	Present Area	Percent Change
Total forest	46.8	39.3	−16.0
Tropical forest	12.8	12.3	−3.9
Other forest	34.0	27.0	−20.6
Woodland	9.7	7.9	−18.6
Shrubland	16.2	14.8	−8.6
Grassland	34.0	27.4	−19.4
Tundra	7.4	7.4	0.0
Desert	15.9	15.6	−1.9
Cultivation	0.0	17.6	+1760.0

* Figures are given in millions of square kilometers.

SOURCE: From J. T. Matthews (personal communication), in Meyer and Turner (1994). With permission of Cambridge University Press.

[See Deserts; Forests and Environmental Change; Mediterranean Environments; and Savannas.]

Cox et al. (1976) identify three principal marine biomes:

1. The oceanic biome of open water, away from the immediate influence of the shore. This can be further subdivided into the planktonic sub-biome containing free-floating plankton, the nektonic sub-biome of active swimmers, and the benthic sub-biome whose fauna is especially adapted for life on the sea floor.
2. The rocky-shore biome.
3. The muddy- or sandy-shore biome.

Biomes have been transformed by human activities, particularly in the last few thousand years. As Simmons (1979, p. 92) says, maps of biomes are not maps "of contemporary reality." Most of the tundra, for example, is little altered; the deciduous forests of Eurasia have largely gone; the lowland tropical forests of the Congo and Amazon basins are shrinking fast. It is not simply

that biomes are being changed in extent by processes as deforestation; they are also continually being modified in character by such processes as fire. Table 2 shows changes in the area of the major land cover types between pre-agricultural times and the present. Such changes are reviewed in Meyer and Turner (1994).

There is increasing interest in the extent to which biomes will be transformed by warming and by changes in the concentrations of carbon dioxide in the atmosphere (see Gates, 1993, chap. 5; Joyce et al., 2001; Malhi and Phillips, 2005). Some models suggest that wholesale change will occur in the distribution of biomes. Theoretically, a rise of 1°C in mean temperature could cause a poleward shift of vegetation zones of about 200 km (Ozenda and Borel, 1990), but it is uncertain how fast plant species could move to and settle in new habitats suitable to the changed climatic conditions. Postglacial vegetation-migration rates appear to have been a few tens of kilometers per century. With a warming of 2–3°C, forest bioclimates could shift northward about 4–6° of latitude per century, which would require a migration rate of tens

Biomes. Tropical Rain Forest.
An aerial walkway spans the forest canopy in Kinabalu National Park, Sabah, Malaysia.

of kilometers per decade. Furthermore, migration could be hampered by natural barriers, zones of cultivation, etc.

Changes in forest composition or location could be slow, for mature trees are long-lived and resilient and so can survive long periods of marginal climate. However, it is during the stage of tree regeneration (seedling establishment) that they are most vulnerable to climate change. Seedlings are highly sensitive to temperature and may be unable to grow under altered climatic conditions. This means that if climate zones do shift more rapidly than trees migrate, established adults of appropriate species and genotypes will be separated from the place where seedling establishment will be required in the future. It is probable that future climate change will not cause catastrophic dieback of forests but that faster-growing tree species will enter existing forests over long periods.

Boreal forest will give way to other biomes (such as temperate forest) on its southern margins but will expand into tundra in the north (Chapin and Danell, 2001). Arctic and alpine tundra may suffer especially severe losses as a result of warming. As the tree line moves up mountains and migrates northward in the Northern Hemisphere, the extent of tundra will be greatly reduced, perhaps by as much as 55% (Walker et al., 2001). The alpine tundra zone may disappear completely from some mountain tops.

A precarious biome, located as it is at the southernmost tip of Africa with little room for displacement, is the very diverse and endemic-rich Fynbos Biome. It is a predominantly sclerophyll shrubland (consisting primarily of plants having leaves resistant to water loss). Modeling, using the Hadley Centre CM2 GCM model, indicates a likely contraction of the extent of Fynbos by about 2050 (Midgley et al., 2003).

In the U.K., the MONARCH program (U.K. Climate Impacts Programme, 2001) has investigated potential changes in the distribution of organisms caused by global warming. They identify as especially serious the loss of montane heaths in Scotland and the dieback of beech woodlands in southern Britain as summer droughts intensify.

Vegetation too will probably be changed by variations in the occurrence of extreme events that cause habitat disturbance, including fire, drought, wind storms, hurricanes (Lugo, 2000), and coastal flooding (Overpeck et al., 1990). Peterson (2000) has investigated the potential impact of climate change on the role of catastrophic winds from tornadoes and downbursts in causing disturbance in North American forests. It is possible that with warmer air masses over the middle latitudes, the temperature contrast with polar air masses will be greater, providing more energy and generating more violent storms, but more work needs to be undertaken before this can be said with any certainty. Other possible nonclimatic effects of elevated CO_2 levels on vegetation include changes in photosynthesis, stomatal closure, and carbon fertilization, though these are matters of controversy (Karnosky et al., 2001; Karnosky, 2003). It is possible that elevated CO_2 levels would have significant effects on tree growth, especially at high altitudes, by enhancing growth. Likewise, warm, drought-stressed ecosystems like chaparral scrub in the southwestern U.S. might be very responsive to elevated CO_2 levels. The frequency and intensity of fires are important factors in many biomes, and fires are strongly influenced by weather and climate. Fires, for example, are more likely to occur in drought years or when there are numerous lightning strikes or strong winds. An analysis by Flannigan et al. (2000) suggests that fire severity could increase over much of North America. They anticipate increases in the area burned in the U.S. of 25–50% by the middle of the twenty-first century, with most of the increases occurring in Alaska and the southeastern U.S.

Vegetation communities could be also be disturbed by changing patterns of insects and pathogens (Ayres and Lombardero, 2000). For example, in temperate and boreal forests, increases in summer temperatures could accelerate the development of insects and increase their reproductive potential, whereas warmer winter temperatures could increase overwinter survival. In addition, the ranges of introduced alien invasive species might change (Simberloff, 2000).

[*See also* Biological Realms; Ecosystems; Heathlands; Mangroves; Mountains; Reefs; Rivers: Impacts of Climate Change; *and* Wetlands.]

BIBLIOGRAPHY

Ayres, M. C., and M. J. Lombardero. "Assessing the Consequences of Global Change for Forest Disturbance from Herbivores and Pathogens." *The Science of the Total Environment* 262 (2000), 263–286.
Begon, M., J. L. Harper, and C. R. Townsend. *Ecology: Individuals, Populations and Communities.* Oxford: Blackwell Scientific, 1986. A particularly wide-ranging and conceptual treatment of all aspects of ecology.
Chapin, F. S., and K. Danell. "Boreal Forest." In *Global Biodiversity in a Changing Environment*, edited by F. S. Chapin III, O. E. Sala, and E. Huber-Sannwald, pp. 101–120. New York: Springer, 2001.
Clapham, W. B. *Natural Ecosystems.* 2d ed. New York: Macmillan, 1983.
Cox, C. B., I. N. Healey, and P. D. Moore. *Biogeography: An Ecological and Evolutionary Approach.* Oxford: Blackwell Scientific, 1976.
Flannigan, M. D., B. J. Stocks, and B. M. Wotton. "Climate Change and Forest Fires." *The Science of the Total Environment* 262 (2000), 221–229. DOI: 10.1016/S0048-9697(00)00524-6.

Gates, D. M. *Climate Change and Its Biological Consequences*. Sunderland, Mass.: Sinauer Associates, 1993.

Goudie, A. S. *Environmental Change*. 3d ed. New York: Oxford University Press, 1993.

Joyce, L., et al. "Potential Consequences of Climate Variability and Change for the Forests of the United States." In *Climate Change Impacts on the United States*, edited by National Assessment Synthesis Team, pp. 489–524. Cambridge, U.K., and New York: Cambridge University Press, 2001. The potential consequences of climate variability and change.

Karnosky, D. F. "Impacts of Elevated Atmospheric CO_2 on Forest Trees and Forest Ecosystems: Knowledge Gaps." *Environment International* 29 (2003), 161–169. DOI: 10.1016/S0160-4120(02)00159-9.

Karnosky, D. F., et al. *The Impact of Carbon Dioxide and Other Greenhouse Gases on Forest Ecosystems*. Wallingford, U.K., and New York: CABI Publishing, 2001.

Lugo, A. E. "Effects and Outcomes of Caribbean Hurricanes in a Climate Change Scenario." *The Science of the Total Environment* 262 (2000), 243–251. DOI: 10.1016/S0048-9697(00)00526-X.

Malhi, Y., and O. Phillips, eds. *Tropical Forests and Global Atmospheric Change*. Oxford and New York: Oxford University Press, 2005.

Meyer, W. B., and B. L. Turner, eds. *Changes in Land Use and Land Cover: A Global Perspective*. Cambridge: Cambridge University Press, 1994. A magisterial compendium on the human impact on the environment.

Midgley, G. F., et al. "Developing Regional and Species-Level Assessments of Climate Change Impacts on Biodiversity in the Cape Floristic Region." *Biological Conservation* 112 (2003), 87–97. DOI: 10.1016/S0006-3207(02)00414-7.

Odum, E. P. *Fundamentals of Ecology*. 3d ed. Philadelphia: Saunders, 1971. A classic consideration of key issues in ecology and biogeography.

Oechel, W. C., et al. "Direct Effects of Elevated CO_2 in Chaparral and Mediterranean-Type Ecosystems." In *Global Change and Mediterranean-Type Ecosystems*, edited by J. M. Moreno and W. C. Oechel, pp. 58–75. New York: Springer, 1995.

Overpeck, J. T., D. Rind, and R. Goldberg. "Climate-Induced Changes in Forest Disturbance and Vegetation." *Nature* 343 (1990), 51–53. DOI: 10.1038/343051a0.

Ozenda, P., and J. L. Borel. "Possible Responses of Mountain Vegetation to a Global Climatic Change: The Case of the Western Alps." In *Landscape-Ecological Impact of Climate Change*, edited by M. M. Boer and R. S. de Groot, pp. 221–249. Amsterdam: IOS Press, 1990.

Peterson, C. J. "Catastrophic Wind Damage to North American Forests and the Potential Impact of Climate Change." *The Science of the Total Environment* 262 (2000), 287–311. DOI: 10.1016/S0048-9697(00)00529-5.

Simberloff, D. "Global Climate Change and Introduced Species in United States Forests." *The Science of the Total Environment* 262 (2000), 253–261. DOI: 10.1016/S0048-9697(00)00527-1.

Simmons, I. G. *Biogeography: Natural and Cultural*. London: Edward Arnold, 1979. An early analysis of the main controls of biogeographical patterns and processes.

UK Climate Impacts Programme. *Climate Change and Nature Conservation in Britain and Ireland: MONARCH—Modelling Natural Resource Responses to Climate Change: Summary Report*. Oxford: UKCIP, 2001.

Walker, M. D., W. A. Gould, and F. S. Chapin III. "Scenarios of Biodiversity Changes in Arctic and Alpine Tundra." In *Global Biodiversity in a Changing Environment*, edited by F. S. Chapin III, O. E. Sala, and E. Huber-Sannwald, pp. 83–100. New York: Springer, 2001.

Walter, H. *Vegetation of the Earth*. 3d ed. Berlin: Springer, 1985.

—ANDREW S. GOUDIE

BOREAL FORESTS AND CLIMATE CHANGE

The boreal forest region is a circumpolar belt of the far northern hemisphere immediately south of the treeless tundra, occupying about 17% of the earth's land area. The region comprises a limited number of species of pine, spruce, larch, fir, birch, and poplar that are adapted to very cold temperatures, with conifers characteristically dominant. The boreal biome is striking for the abundance or even dominance of conifers and mosses.

The boreal forest is the least disturbed of the Earth's major forest regions. While the total area of all forest types remaining in the world today has been reduced to about half of that existing at the time of the emergence of human of civilization (UNEP-WCMC, 2007), the area of boreal forest has remained nearly stable (FAO, 2007). The boreal forest is the most ecologically entire and functional of the world's forest types, with many portions of the biome supporting substantial numbers of large area-demanding top predators generally not tolerated by humans.

The zone of latitude occupied by the boreal forest has experienced some of the greatest temperature increases on Earth during the past century, especially during the last quarter of the twentieth century. [*See* Arctic Warming.] While temperature regimes are highly variable over time in the boreal zone, the greatest climatic change in the last thousand years, at least, has already occurred there (Crowley and Lowery, 2000). Growing seasons have become longer, wildland fire and tree-killing insect outbreaks accelerated, permafrost temperatures warmed, tree growth rates altered, lake and pond surface area decreased in some regions, river ice-out dates moved earlier in the year, and river temperatures increased. Overall habitat suitability for migratory wildlife such as waterfowl, shorebirds, and songbirds has been reduced at least for a time of transition and, in many cases, perhaps permanently. Human cultures that had adapted to the predictable availability of subsistence resources have been disrupted, and human structures and developments face additional costs and risks as a result of climate change.

The boreal forest is not simply an object acted upon; it is a significant active component of the linked planetary climate and ecological systems. The surplus of plant growth over decomposition in the boreal zone has been a large terrestrial sink for carbon, which has so far mitigated the build-up of anthropogenically produced carbon dioxide in the atmosphere. Recent reduced tree growth rates and accelerated tree mortality suggest, however, that the annual level of carbon uptake from the atmosphere in large parts of the boreal zone may not be as great in the future as in the recent past. And now even carbon that has been in long-term storage in the far north may be beginning to return to the atmosphere.

Literate humans have not had the opportunity to record and document a climate change and its effects comparable to the scale and intensity of the one now underway. The early effects of climate warming are particularly visible in the boreal far north, and recent investigations provide a clearer picture of how the changes interact and reinforce one another. Climate-change effects in the boreal region may be instructive as an early warning and guide for other parts of the world.

CHANGES IN CLIMATE PARAMETERS AND SOME RESPONSES

Warming can occur in many different ways. Depending on the type of climate-forcing factor, it is possible for a given region to experience much of a temperature increase in one kind of warmth and not in another. For example, an increase in the concentration of greenhouse gases (with other factors constant), especially in early stages of warming, could cause a greater increase in nightly low temperatures than in daily high temperatures, because greenhouse gases act to decrease heat loss rather than augment high-temperature heat input. Such a pattern is detectable in much of the world but is especially significant in parts of the boreal world with a strongly continental climate (Figure 1). [See Global Warming.] Across most of the far north, winter warming is greater than summer warming, which likewise is consistent with greater reduction of heat loss in colder conditions rather than amplification of heat gain in warmer conditions.

Different aspects of increasing temperature in the boreal region elicit different biological responses. The number of days with extremely cold temperatures (e.g., −20 to −40°C) has decreased irregularly but systematically in nearly all the boreal region. Sustained periods of extreme low temperatures reduce the overwintering survival of many insect species, including wood-boring and tree-defoliating insects. When populations of these tree-damaging insects are reduced by extreme winter cold, the potential of population outbreaks the following warm season is limited. But with temperature increases above certain low-temperature thresholds or with the less frequent occurrence of severe winters, this low-temperature control of insect outbreaks is removed.

Some warming effects reinforce each other. Snow that crystallizes at warmer temperatures is denser than snow derived from crystals that form in the very cold temperatures (Libbrecht, 2005) typical of most boreal winters. (Boreal forests in maritime regions generally have denser snow.) Heavier snow places a greater load on the canopies of trees, especially evergreen conifers that retain snow-catching foliage throughout the winter. Heavy snow loads cause stem and tree breakage. Trees injured by snow breakage attract wood-boring beetles. Beetle populations start from a higher base after a warm winter and are more successful in reproduction during warm summers. Warm summers generate high moisture stress levels in trees and weaken their principal defense against wood-boring beetles, the resin manufactured out of surplus growth. The result of these compounding warming effects is elevated levels of insect-caused tree death, including unprecedented areas of tree death in Alaska (Werner et al., 2006) and northwestern Canada (Berg et al., 2006).

Other winter events can be important for forest health. Evergreen conifers are damaged when late winter warming produces air temperatures that induce the start of photosynthesis while the soil remains solidly frozen and unable to supply water. In the far north the onset of weather well below freezing is usually very rapid and decisive, especially because of rapidly decreasing daylength in the fall. But recent patterns of warming and delayed sea-ice formation now more frequently result in

Boreal Forests and Climate Change. Figure 1. Mean Daily Minimum Temperature, Fairbanks, Alaska.

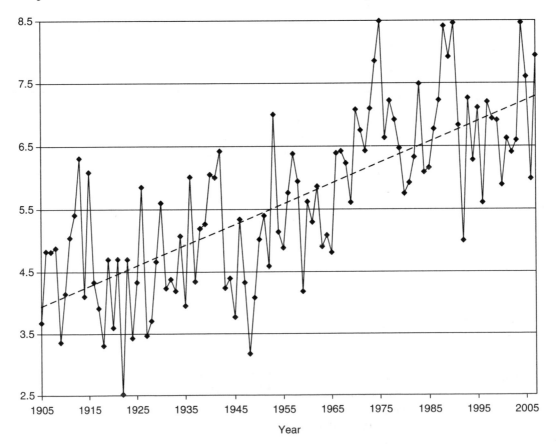

alternating peiods of above- and below-freezing temperatures at the usual time of dependable early-season snowfall. This can result in freezing rain at the start of winter that builds an ice crust over vegetation and ground surfaces. Instead of a fluffy, low-density snow cover that is easily pushed aside, animals seeking winter food, warmth, or concealment encounter thick, hard ice crusts for the remainder of the winter and may starve if they cannot relocate (Aanes et al., 2002).

Even though warm-season temperature increases are not as great as winter increases across most of the boreal region, they are large enough to have caused important biological effects. Spring arrives earlier across middle and high latitude regions, and the magnitude of the advance is particularly great at the latitude of the boreal forest. Occasionally, late winter or early spring warmth is enough to cause the loss of winter hardiness (resistance to freezing injury) well before the risk of occurrence of hard freezes has ended. Premature loss of winter hardiness followed by freezing can kill or injure expanding tender tissues such as buds, flowers, leaves, and shoots (Colombo, 1998). During the last century the date of ice breakup on rivers has moved earlier in the year (Figure 2), and initiation of snowpack begins later in the fall. Earlier springs and later fall freeze-ups extend the evaporation season.

In most of the boreal north, a plot of the coldest minimum temperature recorded during the warm season shows a steady and significant increase. Highly mobile species, such as flying insects or birds, that were previously excluded may now be able to survive and reproduce further north because their development will no longer be held back or eliminated by a few cold nights. The consecutive number of days with daily low temperatures warmer than 0°C (length of the frost-free season) has increased markedly in central Alaska from 60 to 90 days in the early twentieth century to about 120 days a century later (Figure 3). The longer and warmer evapotranspiration season that has occurred in recent decades in central and western Canada, Alaska, and central and eastern Siberia has reduced effective precipitation (available moisture surplus).

With a reduction of effective moisture and/or the thawing of permafrost, which forms an impermeable layer that maintains a high water table, the area of shallow, closed-circulation lakes and ponds has decreased in the parts of the boreal forest (Riordan et al., 2006). Decreases in water-surface area are particularly large in areas with marginal precipitation such as boreal western valleys and the lowlands east of the Rocky Mountains in North America and the southern boreal zone of central and mountainous Far East Russia. Wetlands of the boreal region are the breeding habitat of waterfowl and shorebirds, and this systematic reduction in surface water habitat directly reduces bird production.

Several of the great northward-flowing rivers of the far north, especially in central Eurasia, show clear and strong hydrologic effects from recent climate warming. In the Lena River, mid-winter stream flow has increased 25% to 90% and ice thickness decreased. Earlier (May) snowmelt has decreased June daily maximum discharge of the Lena River (Yang et al., 2002). Changes in permafrost are interacting with the changes in temperature and precipitation over the Lena River Basin to produce

Boreal Forests and Climate Change. FIGURE 2. Spring Ice Breakup Date, 1917–2007, Tanana River, Central Alaska.

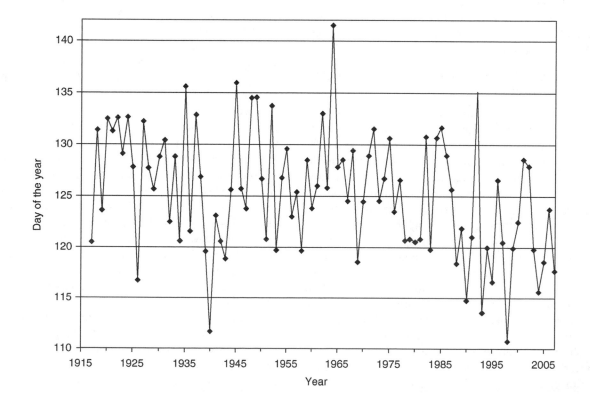

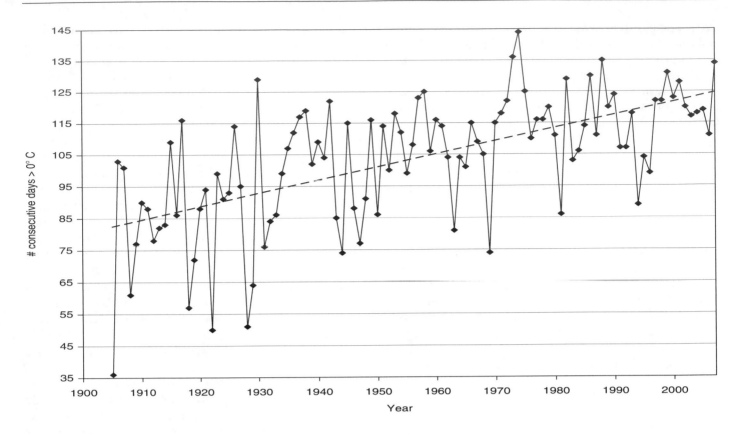

Boreal Forests and Climate Change. Figure 3. Frost-Free Season Length, Fairbanks, Alaska.

the hydrologic response. Increased water temperatures in the Yukon and Tanana rivers appear to be a factor in the increasing incidence of the wasting disease *Ichthyophonus* in Pacific salmon. Before 1985, *Ichthyophonus* was not reported in Yukon River salmon, but between 1999 and 2003 overall infection prevalence reached about 45% (Richard et al., 2004). These fish are a major source of food for rural people who live in a roadless region and must harvest natural products.

EFFECTS OF WARMING ON TREE GROWTH ON PRODUCTIVE SITES

Much of the boreal forest region is located far from potential moisture sources. The Arctic Ocean ice cap shuts off moisture from the north, although the ice cover has decreased markedly since 2003 (see National Snow and Ice Data Center, http://nsidc.org/). Cold marine surface waters of the North Pacific and North Atlantic also restrict moisture supply from those sources. Over long periods of time boreal conifer trees in particular adapted by adjusting the timing of their physiological activity to the most predictable supply of resources, especially water.

Most boreal trees achieve a disproportionate amount of their annual growth from the time of the introduction of snowmelt into the soil until that source of soil moisture is depleted and the trees first encounter moisture stress of sufficient severity to restrict physiological activity (Vaganov et al., 1999). When determinate-growth species, such as most evergreen conifers, first encounter their threshold level of moisture-stress they cease height-elongation, and in their lateral ring growth, switch from the production of large earlywood cells to the production of small latewood cells (Grossnickle, 2000). In many evergreen conifer species, that seasonal switch in growth appears to be one-way (Vaganov et al., 2006). If summer temperatures are consistently cool from the start of the season, then the initial moisture supply is depleted gradually and the active growth season is extended, allowing more annual growth. If the temperatures are high early in the growth season, the stress threshold is encountered quickly and less annual growth is accomplished (e.g., Bigras, 2000).

Growing-season length in much of central Alaska, western Canada, and portions of Far East Russia has increased 50–100%. Warm air triggers the beginning of tree growth in boreal evergreen conifers (Tanja et al., 2003). The associated earlier snowmelt then forces the annual water budget to be distributed over a longer warm evaporative season, in contrast to the cold season during which snow accumulates. This extension of the warm season leads to earlier and more acute shortages in soil-moisture supply, and lower early-season fuel moisture levels. These acutely dry conditions develop during the period of long days when solar-energy input is at its seasonal peak and is especially effective in warming ground-surface layers because it is no longer reflected by snow cover.

Following spring melt, summer rainfall in the boreal region is unreliable in timing and amount. White spruce trees in northern North America, at least, do not reactivate height growth or earlywood production no matter how abundant the mid- and late-season precipitation. By contrast, aspen and birch are capable of multiple flushes of height growth following repeated moist and dry episodes during the growth season. This warming-induced earlier seasonal induction of the one-way switch in growth is a significant limitation for determinate-growth species such as spruces and pines in their competition to emerge above broadleaf tree competitors.

Precipitation is relatively abundant in much of Scandinavia, northwest Russia, and eastern Canada. There and at many tree-line sites, boreal tree-growth is greater in warm summers and less in cool summers (D'Arrigo et al., 1996). In these tree populations, recent temperature increases have accelerated overall growth. But in the western North American boreal forest and the southern boreal forest of central and Far East Russia, many conifers and some broadleaf tree species are negatively sensitive to growing-season temperatures. In warmer years they achieve less tree-ring growth and in cooler years greater growth. This negative sensitivity of tree growth to temperature appears to be the result of moisture stress induced by temperatures elevated beyond the adaptive limits of the trees. On the most sensitive sites, index temperatures that best predict growth are nearing levels that empirical relations suggest would be associated with reduction of growth to zero—lethal temperatures in other words (Juday et al., 2005).

The cool, humid understory of conifer stands experiences needle-leaf litterfall rather than burial under a mat of fallen broad leaves. Needle-leaf litter is suitable for the development of a carpet of mosses. Broadleaf litterfall buries mosses and blocks light, restricting the microsites that can support moss growth.

Continued temperature increases are likely either to directly restrict or eliminate conifer growth (lethal high temperature limits), or to reduce conifer success in competition with broadleaf trees (one-way growth switch), which would in turn eliminate moss dominance of the forest understory. In these ways climate warming will undermine the definitional characteristic of the boreal forest—conifer and moss dominance—and these trends are already strongly established in large parts of the boreal zone.

FIRE AND INSECTS

Large-scale outbreaks of wood-boring and defoliating insects are long-term characteristics of the boreal forest (Kharuk et al., 2000; Bylund, 1999). The North American and parts of the Eurasian boreal forest are ecosystems driven by stand-replacement disturbance (Johnson, 1992). In such systems, trees originating from seed mostly sprout and grow up together and then mostly die together. Asexually reproducing plant species receive the stimulus to activate bud or other sprouting tissues from the death of the above-ground portion of the plant and the chemical and physical changes in soils from mass tree death.

These disturbances appear to be promoted by genetically fixed traits of the component forest species such as trees with flammable volatile oils and waxes in their foliage, or "ladder" structures of fuel arrangement that allow ground fire to quickly move into tree crowns (Hely et al., 2001). Such gene-based traits that facilitate disturbance can actually be regarded as an adaptive system. Disturbance reverses some of the cumulative effects of forest

development and maturation that inhibit tree growth and site productivity in cold regions, such as the accumulation of refractory (hard-to-decompose) organic matter and the cooling of soils (Van Cleve and Yarie, 1986). After disturbance, site productivity is renewed by soil warming and by leachates of forest-fire ash. The removal of the forest canopy also creates full sunlight at ground level, which is particularly suitable for tree regeneration.

The climatic regime of most of the boreal region during the past few millennia has been characterized by sustained periods of cool and moist growing seasons, punctuated by relatively infrequent periods (once to a few times per century) of extreme warm temperatures. Some of the same key features of warmth that facilitate the spread of wildfire also trigger periodic reproduction in some boreal trees (Juday et al., 2003). In that way the resulting insect outbreaks and extensive fires set the stage for forest renewal through disturbance.

Warm temperature anomalies in the far north are usually associated with solar-cycle maxima or with ocean-atmosphere coupling such as the Pacific ENSO system, and until recently tended to be spatially restricted. In the last several decades, however, warm summer-temperature anomalies have been more frequent or persistent—although not necessarily the most extreme in magnitude in the long-term record—and have become more widespread in the far north.

In the late twentieth and early twenty-first centuries, some especially large insect and fire disturbances in boreal North America and central and eastern Eurasia have altered the age structure of the forest over regions to such a degree that the overall age of the forest is now distinctly younger (Duffy et al., 2007; Balzter et al., 2007). The mountain pine beetle (MPB) outbreak in British Columbia in 2007–2008 is more extensive than

---

Boreal Forests and Climate Change. FIGURE 4. Spruce Budworm Larva. The budworm feeds on an expanding white spruce shoot early in the growing season.

Warm summers allow the budworm to complete a critical number of development stages before the foliage has hardened off and become unpalatable. Tree populations under stress favor population outbreaks of budworms.

Boreal Forests and Climate Change. FIGURE 5. **Drought Stress.**
Birch leaves from central Alaska show the characteristic 3-toned color of acute drought stress (leaf "scorch"). The margins of the leaves are necrotic (dead tissue), and bordered by a yellow band where the chlorophyll pigment has broken down prematurely. Green, normal leaf tissue is retained only along the principal veins which introduce water to the leaf. During extreme episodes of heat and drought these acute drought stress symptoms are the last stage before the death of branch axes or tree death. Such symptoms have been widespread in central Alaska in recent years.

any other beetle epidemic recorded in North America (Carrol, 2007; http://mpb.cfs.nrcan.gc.ca/index_e.html).

During the winter the MPB develops cold hardiness (in the form of antifreeze in its blood) as temperatures decline. The majority of larvae can withstand –40°C for short periods by mid-winter. But the sudden onset and persistence of early or late winter temperatures near –40° significantly reduces MPB population survival (http://cfs.nrcan.gc.ca/subsite/mpb/cold-froid). The occurrence of cold, and thus beetle-limiting, temperatures has decreased across large portions of southern, central, and even some areas of northern British Columbia in the last decade (Carroll et al., 2003). The preferred host of the beetle is lodgepole pine, the most abundant commercially-managed tree species in British Columbia. Projected rates of spread of the MPB outbreak indicate 50% of the mature trees of the species in the province will be dead in 2008. Recent temperature increases also raise the prospect of MPB spreading into vast new areas of Alberta's lodgepole pine forests and the jackpine stands of Canada's northern boreal forest.

In Siberia forest insect outbreaks are mainly caused by lepidopteran species, with areas damaged varying from 5,000 to more than 1 million hectares (Kharuk et al., 2000). Siberian silkmoth (*Dendrolimus superans sibiricus* Tschetw.) is the main agent of forest disturbance in southern boreal forest of central Eurasia, consuming the foliage of Siberian pine (the preferred food species), as well as fir, spruce, and larch (http://www.iki.rssi.ru/earth/pres2006/kharuk2.pdf). Major outbreaks have affected as much as 4.0 million hectares and are triggered by favorable weather, including warm temperatures and low levels of precipitation and humidity (Kharuk et al., 2003). Cold climate has, so far, limited outbreaks to areas generally south of 60°N latitude, but large areas of suitable host trees occur further north. The most recent outbreak was between 1994 and 1996 in the Priangar'e region between the Yenisey and Angara rivers; about 700,000 hectares of forest were affected (Kharuk et al., 2000). Completion of the full life cycle of the Siberian silkmoth usually takes two years, but in the southern parts of its natural range one generation can develop in a single year. Warmer temperatures in the northern portion of the silkmoth's distribution that allow a switch to this more rapid single-year life cycle development favor higher moth populations and greater forest damage (Vorontsov, 1995).

In some boreal regions the potential for further expansion of tree-killing insect outbreaks is limited now mainly by the supply of suitable (older) host trees rather than the temperature-induced outbreak potential of insect populations (annual reports of Alaska Forest Health Survey, http://www.dnr.state.ak.us/forestry/insects/survays.htm). It seems likely that such climate conditions will persist, meaning that the age structure and the species composition of the boreal forest itself essentially have been permanently altered. Large, older trees have systematically become rarer. In some cases, even the opportunity to establish and produce whole stands of now-vulnerable tree species has been eliminated.

Impressively large boreal fire disturbances have also occurred in connection with years of peak warmth during the overall period of increasing temperatures of recent decades. In 1987 several vast fires burned an estimated 14.4 million hectares in the Russian Far East and eastern Siberia (Cahoon et al., 1994). Following a very strong El Niño in 1997–1998, an estimated 9.4 million hectares burned in the Asian regions of Russia in 1998 (FAO, 2001).

Boreal wildland fires are a function of sustained periods with daily maximum temperatures above 25°C under high atmospheric pressure (the latter causing generally clear skies and low humidities), and sufficient ignitions by lightning strikes from dry thunderstorms. Exceptional fire years are characterized by a strong initial burning season near the summer solstice, and then the persistence of warmth and drought into a secondary and later (especially August) burning season. The typical season-ending precipitation event (rainfall sufficient to eliminate fire spread across the landscape) simply fails to occur.

In the spring and summer, the boreal forest hosts a huge influx of migratory forest-breeding birds, which then migrate south during the long boreal winter. Many of these species are cavity nesters dependent on older trees with disease and defects that make them suitable for excavation of cavities by primary excavators such as woodpeckers. Systematic decreases in the extent of older forests as the result of accelerated fire and insect disturbance triggered by warm temperature anomalies necessarily depress populations of wildlife species dependent on these older forest habitats and features (Usher et al., 2005).

CHANGES IN PERMAFROST

One of the unique features of the Arctic and boreal regions is the extensive growth of trees on permafrost. Permafrost is ground material that remains frozen for at least two years. Permafrost forms when mean annual temperatures are below freezing, generally in the range of 0 to −2°C. Differences in soil texture, water content, and site characteristics can allow permafrost to form at mean annual temperatures equal to freezing, or may require annual temperatures somewhat below freezing. The northern part of the boreal forest is within the discontinuous permafrost zone, where the presence or absence of the frozen state is influenced by local factors.

Surface-disturbing activities such as road and building construction and natural events such as wildfire can tip the thermal equilibrium toward thawing in warmer permafrost regions, and have for some time. But these surface disturbances are producing more widespread thawing effects in recent warmer conditions. Mean annual air temperatures above freezing now occur across large portions of the permafrost regions and are certain to thaw the permafrost if sustained. Permafrost temperatures in Alaska, Siberia, and northwestern boreal Canada have been trending upward (Osterkamp, 2005; Romanovsky et al., 2001) and are nearly all −0.5 to −2.0°C. Calculations indicate that a substantial fraction of existing permafrost in the boreal region has started or will start to thaw in the next several decades and that the process may take decades or centuries to complete to the full depths. [See Permafrost.]

Permafrost can be ice-rich, in which case thawing melts the frozen water content and causes ground subsidence, or it can be dry, leading to little surface change between the frozen and thawed conditions. Permafrost thawing at its southernmost limits in Canada (Camill, 2005) and central Asia (Cheng and Wu, 2007) is widespread. In warming ice-rich permafrost lowlands, forest land is filling with water and being converted to wetland. Decomposition often then proceeds in the absence of oxygen, putting stored carbon into the atmosphere as methane, a greenhouse gas that produces 21 times as much warming as a similar volume of carbon dioxide. Because water transfers heat to the soil much more effectively than does air, even subtle alterations of the movement or collection of water on landscapes well within the cold, continuous permafrost zone can initiate land subsidence from thawing. In a large landscape study-area of northern Siberia, rising temperatures have increased the area of permafrost-thaw lake-water surface by 14.7% from 1974 to 2000, with an associated increase in methane release of 58% (Walter et al., 2006).

In thawing soils that remain dry, the site itself usually becomes more fertile, as there is greater rooting volume and more rapid decomposition of organic matter leading to higher levels of available nutrient elements. Continued dominance of black spruce (North America) or small, slow-growing larches (Eurasia) on thawed former permafrost sites is not likely. Such a process, which is well underway, will most probably systematically change the future character of the boreal forest region as it has been known.

Permafrost and other cold soils hold an amount of carbon that, if it were entirely combusted, would nearly double atmospheric CO_2 content (McGuire et al., 1995). Further warming and/or thawing of cold northern and permafrost soils would move this carbon into the atmosphere in a variety of ways. Increased fire frequency and intensity will directly combust forest fuels that would otherwise likely have remained in storage. If soil moisture is not limiting, soils that are warmer after disturbance will allow faster rates of organic-matter decomposition by soil microbes. And if species that produce refractory litter (e.g., conifers) or high acidity (e.g., mosses) are replaced by broadleaf trees or shrubs and grasses characterized by rapidly decomposed litter, the net storage of carbon in the soils of the north will be diminished.

OUTLOOK FOR THE BOREAL FOREST

Among modeling scenarios of climate change driven by increases in atmospheric greenhouse gases, there is a strong consensus that temperature increases will accelerate over the next century. Most of the temperature increases exceed the temperature limits of many boreal species described by their current distribution or distribution during the past several thousand years.

As a result, and in addition to climate warming effects that have already occurred in today's boreal forest region, it is probable that there will be a complete shift of biome type near and within the boundaries of the boreal zone. Warmer portions of the boreal forest are susceptible to replacement by some form of grassland, parkland (Hogg and Hurdle, 1995; Tchebakova et al., 1995), or temperate forest in North America, north central Asia, and northeast Asia. Already, aspen stands along the southern margin of the central Canadian boreal forest have experienced large-scale dieback and tree growth-rate collapse (Hogg et al., 2002 and 2005), and these events are best correlated with drought severity (Hogg et al., 2007).

Temperatures suitable for tree growth now appear to be common in most years far north of today's northern treeline, although treeline movement has been extremely modest (tens to hundreds of meters) in the last few decades (Suarez et al., 1999; Shiyatov, 2003). Temperature increases of 1–2°C during the growing season at treeline increase the growth of white spruce on favorable sites (Danby and Hik, 2007a). If problems of long-distance transport of seed and the low receptivity of tundra as a tree seedbed are overcome, forest establishment and treeline movement occur suddenly where moisture is not limiting (Danby and Hik, 2007b). But even at some cold treeline sites, moisture is limiting, and the growth of many populations of trees is decreasing as the temperature increases (Wilmking and Juday, 2005). So, with accelerated warming, the treeline is likely to fragment rather than smoothly advance upward in elevation or northward. In many northern treeline landscapes, sites now able to support populations of trees appear to be mixed on a fine scale with sites that cannot. And human influences can become an important factor in treeline movement. In

---

Boreal Forests and Climate Change. Figure 6. Boreal Forest Wildland Fire.

Treeline white spruce in central Alaska shows the effects of the Boundary Fire 2004. Wildland fire in the boreal forest normally does not burn sites that are cooler and retain higher fuel moisture such as this alpine summit. Many parts of the boreal forest have recently experienced fires burning under extremely hot and dry conditions that have been non-selective and have burned vast areas from horizon to horizon (see background).

eastern Siberia, recent changes near the treeline include increased temperatures, steady or lower precipitation, and a reduced human capacity for fire suppression. The result is a considerable increase in human-caused fire, and a net conversion of 50 million hectares of forest to treeless vegetation, causing the treeline to actually move southward (Vlassova, 2002).

As climate-induced changes unfold, whatever remains of today's boreal forest could well assume characteristics, such as reduced conifer dominance, in the foreseeable future that would force a reappraisal of what constitutes boreal forest. The vast scale and comprehensive nature of the changes now underway or expected soon in the boreal forest under further warming present unprecedented challenges to natural resource management. The steady-state model of ecosystem development and sustainability in this region has been overtaken by events. Whole new management imperatives, such as relocation of human communities, timber salvage, assisted long-distance migration of unique plant genotypes, stabilization of stored carbon, and mitigation of effects produced by unstable thaw zones are just some of the challenges that are not just a near-term prospect, but issues of today.

BIBLIOGRAPHY

Aanes, R., et al. "The Arctic Oscillation Predicts Effects of Climate Change in Two Trophic Levels in a High-Arctic Ecosystem." *Ecology Letters* 5.3 (2002), 445–453. DOI: 10.1046/j.1461-0248.2002.00340.x.

Balzter, H., et al. "Coupling of Vegetation Growing Season Anomalies and Fire Activity with Hemispheric and Regional-Scale Climate Patterns in Central and East Siberia." *Journal of Climate* 20.15 (2007), 3713–3729. DOI: 10.1175/JCLI4226.

Berg, E. E., et al. "Spruce Beetle Outbreaks on the Kenai Peninsula, Alaska, and Kluane National Park and Reserve, Yukon Territory: Relationship to Summer Temperatures and Regional Differences in Disturbance Regimes." *Forest Ecology and Management* 227.3 (2006), 219–232. DOI: 10.1016/j.foreco.2006.02.038.

Bigras, F. J. "Selection of White Spruce Families in the Context of Climate Change: Heat Tolerance." *Tree Physiology* 20.18 (2000), 1227–1234.

Bylund, H. "Climate and the Population Dynamics of Two Insect Outbreak Species in the North." *Ecological Bulletins* 47 (1999), 54–62.

Cahoon, D. R. Jr., et al. "Satellite Analysis of the Severe 1987 Forest Fires in Northern China and Southeastern Siberia." *Journal of Geophysical Research* 99.D9 (1994), 18627–18638.

Camill, P. "Permafrost Thaw Accelerates in Boreal Peatlands during Late-20th Century Climate Warming." *Climatic Change* 68.1–2 (2005), 135–152. DOI: 10.1007/s10584-005-4785-y.

Carroll, A. L. "When Forest Management and Climate Change Collide: The Irruption and Spread of Mountain Pine Beetle Populations in Western North America." Abstract. In *Climate Change Impacts on Boreal Forest Disturbance Regimes*, VI International Conference on Disturbance Dynamics in Boreal Forests, p. 11. Fairbanks: University of Alaska-Fairbanks, School of Natural Resources and Agricultural Sciences, 2007.

Carroll, A. L., et al. "Effects of Climate Change on Range Expansion by the Mountain Pine Beetle in British Columbia." In *Mountain Pine Beetle Symposium: Challenges and Solutions*, edited by T. L. Shore, J. E. Brooks, and J. E. Stone, pp. 223–232. Canadian Forest Service, Pacific Forestry Centre, Information Report BC-X-399. Victoria, Brit. Col.: Natural Resources Canada, 2003.

Cheng, G., and T. Wu "Responses of Permafrost to Climate Change and Their Environmental Significance, Qinghai-Tibet Plateau." *Journal of Geophysical Research* 112, F02S03 (2007). DOI: 10.1029/2006JF000631.

Colombo, S. J. "Warming and Its Effect on Bud Burst and Risk of Frost Damage to White Spruce in Canada." *Forestry Chronicle* 74.4 (1998), 567–577.

Crowley, T. J., and T. S. Lowery. "How Warm Was the Medieval Warm Period?" *Ambio* 29.1 (2000), 51–54.

D'Arrigo, R. D., E. R. Cook, and G. C. Jacoby. "Annual to Decadal-Scale Variations in Northwest Atlantic Sector Temperatures Inferred from Labrador Tree Rings." *Canadian Journal of Forest Research* 26 (1996), 143–148. DOI: 10.1139/x26-015.

Danby, R. K., and D. S. Hik. "Responses of White Spruce (*Picea glauca*) to Experimental Warming at a Subarctic Alpine Treeline." *Global Change Biology* 13.2 (2007a), 437–451. DOI: 10.1111/j.1365-2486.2006.01302.x.

———. "Variability, Contingency, and Rapid Change in Recent Subarctic Alpine Treeline Dynamics." *Journal of Ecology* 95.2 (2007b), 352–363. DOI: 10.1111/j.1365-2745.2006.01200.x.

Duffy, P., D. Mann, and S. Rupp. "Aging Stands in the Alaska Boreal Forest Encounter Global Warming." Abstract. In *Climate Change Impacts on Boreal Forest Disturbance Regimes*, VI International Conference on Disturbance Dynamics in Boreal Forests, p. 11. Fairbanks: University of Alaska-Fairbanks, School of Natural Resources and Agricultural Sciences, 2007.

FAO, 2001. *Global Forest Resources Assessment 2000. Main Report.* Forestry Paper 140. Rome: UN Food and Agriculture Organization, 2001.

FAO, 2007. *Global Forest Resources Assessment 2005, Progress Towards Sustainable Forest Management.* Forestry Paper 147. Rome: UN Food and Agriculture Organization, 2007.

Grossnickle, S. C. *Ecophysiology of Northern Spruce Species: The Performance of Planted Seedlings.* Ottawa: NRC Reseach Press, 2000.

Hely C., et al. "Role of Vegetation and Weather on Fire Behavior in the Canadian Mixedwood Boreal Forest Using Two Fire Behavior Prediction Systems." *Canadian Journal of Forest Research* 31.3 (2001), 430–441. DOI: 10.1139/CJFR-31-3-430.

Hogg, E. H., and P. A. Hurdle. "The Aspen Parkland in Western Canada: A Dry-Climate Analogue for the Future Boreal Forest?" *Water, Air, and Soil Pollution* 82.1–2 (1995), 391–400. DOI: 10.1007/BF01182849.

Hogg, E. H., J. P. Brandt, and B. Kochtubajda. "Growth and Dieback of Aspen Forests in Northwestern Alberta, Canada in Relation to Climate and Insects." *Canadian Journal of Forest Research* 32.5 (2002), 823–832. DOI: 10.1139/x01-152.

———. "Factors Affecting Interannual Variation in Growth of Western Canadian Aspen Forests during 1951–2000." *Canadian Journal of Forest Research* 35.3 (2005), 610–622. DOI: 10.1139/x04-211.

Hogg, E. H., et al. "Impacts of Recent Drought on the Productivity, Health, and Dieback of Canadian Aspen Forests: Early Signs of Climate Change?" Abstract. In *Climate Change Impacts on Boreal Forest Disturbance Regimes*, VI International Conference on Disturbance Dynamics in Boreal Forests, p. 15. Fairbanks: University of Alaska-Fairbanks, School of Natural Resources and Agricultural Sciences, 2007.

Johnson, E. A. *Fire and Vegetation Dynamics: Studies from the North American Boreal Forest.* Cambridge and New York: Cambridge University Press, 1992.

Juday, G. P., et al. "A 200-Year Perspective of Climate Variability and the Response of White Spruce in Interior Alaska." In *Climate Variability and Ecosystem Response at Long-Term Ecological Research Sites*, edited by D. Greenland, D. G. Goodin, and R. C. Smith, pp. 226–250. Oxford: Oxford University Press, 2003.

Juday, G. P., et al. "Forests, Land Management, Agriculture." In *Arctic Climate Impact Assessment*, pp. 781–862. Cambridge and New York: Cambridge University Press, 2005.

Kharuk, V. I., et al. "NOAA/AVHRR Data in Detection of Insects Induced Catastrophic Changes in Siberian Taiga." In *Disturbance in Boreal Forest Ecosystems: Human Impacts and Natural Processes, Proceedings of the International Boreal Forest Research Association 1997 Annual Meeting*, edited by S. G. Connard. U.S. Forest Service General Technical Report NC-209, pp. 124–131. 2000.

Kharuk, V.I., et al. "Landsat-Based Analysis of Insect Outbreaks in Southern Siberia." *Canadian Journal of Remote Sensing* 29.2 (2003), 286–297.

Libbrecht, K. G. "The Physics of Snow Crystals." *Reports on Progress in Physics* 68 (2005), 855–895. DOI: 10.1088/0034-4885/68/4/R03.

McGuire, A. D., et al. "Equilibrium Responses of Soil Carbon to Climate Change: Empirical and Process-Based Estimates." *Journal of Biogeography* 22 (1995), 785–796.

Osterkamp, T. E. "The Recent Warming of Permafrost in Alaska." *Global and Planetary Change* 49.3–4 (2005), 187–202. DOI: 10.1016/j.gloplacha.2005.09.001.

Richard, K., P. Hershberger, and J. Winton. "Ichthyophoniasis: An Emerging Disease of Chinook Salmon in the Yukon River." *Journal of Aquatic Animal Health* 16 (2004), 58–72. DOI: 10.1577/H03-056.1.

Riordan, B., D. Verbyla, and A. D. McGuire. "Shrinking Ponds in Subarctic Alaska Based on 1950–2002 Remotely Sensed Images." *Journal of Geophysical Research* 111.G04002. 2006. DOI: 10.1029/2005JG000150.

Romanovsky, V. E., et al. "Permafrost Temperature Dynamics Along the East Siberian Transect and an Alaskan Transect." *Tohoku Geophysical Journal* 36.2 (2001), 224–229.

Shiyatov, S. G. "Rates of Change in the Upper Treeline Ecotone in the Polar Ural Mountains." PAGES News, 11.1 (2003), 8–10.

Suarez, F., et al. "Expansion of Forest Stands into Tundra in the Noatak National Preserve, Northwest Alaska." *Ecoscience* 6.3 (1999), 465–470.

Tanja, S., et al. "Air Temperature Triggers the Recovery of Evergreen Boreal Forest Photosynthesis in Spring." *Global Change Biology* 9.10 (2003), 1410–1426. DOI: 10.1046/j.1365-2486.2003.00597.x.

Tchebakova, N. M., et al. "Possible Vegetation Shifts in Siberia under Climate Change." In *The Impacts of Climatic Change on Ecosystems and Species: Terrestrial Ecosystems*, edited by J. Pernetta, et al., pp. 67–82. Gland, Switzerland: IUCN, 1995.

UNEP-WCMC, 2007. "Global Distribution of Original and Remaining Forests." United Nations Environmental Programme and World Conservation Monitoring Centre. http://www.unep-wcmc.org/forest/original.htm (accessed May 22, 2008).

Usher, M. B., et al. "Principles of Conserving the Arctic's Biodiversity." In *Arctic Climate Impact Assessment*, pp. 551–608. Cambridge and New York: Cambridge University Press, 2005.

Vaganov, E. A., et al. "Influence of Snowfall and Melt Timing on Tree Growth in Subarctic Eurasia." *Nature*, 400 (1999), 149–151. DOI: 10.1038/22087.

Vaganov, E. A., M. K. Hughes, and A. V. Shashkin. "Introduction and Factors Influencing the Seasonal Growth of Trees." In *Growth Dynamics of Conifer Tree Rings: Images of Past and Future Environments*. New York: Springer, 2006.

Van Cleve, K., and J. Yarie. 1986. "Interaction of Temperature, Moisture, and Soil Chemistry in Controlling Nutrient Cycling and Ecosystem Development in the Taiga of Alaska." In *Forest Ecosystems in the Alaskan Taiga: A Synthesis of Structure and Function*, edited by K. Van Cleve, et al., pp. 160–189. New York: Springer, 1986.

Vlassova, T. K. "Human Impacts on the Tundra-Taiga Zone Dynamics: The Case of the Russian Lesotundra." *Ambio Special Report* 12 (2002), 30–36.

Vorontsov, A. I. *Forest Entomology: Manual for Universities.* 5th ed. Moscow: Ecologia, 1995. In Russian.

Walter, K. M., et al. "Methane Bubbling from Siberian Thaw Lakes as a Positive Feedback To Climate Warming." *Nature* 443 (2006), 71–75. DOI: 10.1038/nature05040.

Werner, R. A., et al. "Spruce Beetles and Forest Ecosystems in South-Central Alaska: A Review of 30 Years of Research." *Forest Ecology and Management* 227.3 (2006), 195–206. DOI: 10.1016/j.foreco.2006.02.050.

Wilmking, M., and G. P. Juday. "Longitudinal Variation of Radial Growth at Alaska's Northern Treeline: Recent Changes and Possible Scenarios for the 21st Century." *Global and Planetary Change* 47.2–4 (2005), 282–300. DOI: 10.1016/j.gloplacha.2004.10.017.

Yang, D., et al. "Siberian Lena River Hydrologic Regime and Recent Change." *Journal of Geophysical Research* 107.D23, 4694 (2002). DOI: 10.1029/2002JD002542.

—GLENN PATRICK JUDAY

BRAZIL

See Amazonia and Deforestation.

BRUNDTLAND COMMISSION

The Brundtland Commission is the unofficial name of the World Commission on Environment and Development, which was chaired by Gro Harlem Brundtland, a former prime minister of Norway. Created as an independent commission in response to a United Nations General Assembly resolution of 1983, the body was given the general mandate of proposing ways in which the international community could achieve sustainable development that would both protect the environment and fulfill the aspirations of the poorer countries for economic development. Following in the tradition of the Brandt Commission on North-South issues and the Palme Commission on security and disarmament issues, the Brundtland Commission was convened at a time of growing concern over global environmental change and the mounting frustrations of the developing countries over their declining prospects for economic development and the failure of the West to enact key provisions of their proposals for a new international economic order.

The commission comprised twenty-three prominent individuals from around the world and was supported by an appointed group of expert advisors. The commission held public hearings at locations around the world to hear the views of governmental officials, scientists and experts, industrialists, representatives of nongovernmental organizations, and the general public. The commission's report, *Our Common Future* (1987), covered a wide range of topics, including the international economy, population and human resources, food security, species and ecosystems, energy, industry, the management of commons, and war and peace. The report emphasized that three global crises that arose during the preceding decade—a development crisis, an environmental crisis, and an economic crisis—were integrally related. The poverty and underdevelopment of much of the world's rapidly growing population were seen as factors contributing to a degradation of natural systems, which in turn deepened the economic crises faced by many societies. The report is also notable for promoting sustainable development, which it defined as meeting "the needs of the present without compromising the ability of future generations to meet their own needs." It contended that economic growth will be necessary for countries in which the majority are poor, and argues that such nations must also be ensured a fair share of the resources necessary to sustain such growth. The report offered numerous proposals to strengthen the national and international institutions that address economic and environmental problems, to engage the scientific community and nongovernmental organizations, and to foster cooperation with industry. To increase economic resources available to developing countries, the report proposed raising revenue from the use of international commons, such as the oceans and outer space, and taxing certain types of international trade.

Our Common Future was widely read and discussed in the years that followed its publication. It informed deliberations in the preparatory meetings for the United Nations Conference on Environment and Development that was held in 1992 in Rio de Janeiro and the drafting of Agenda 21, the elaborate plan of action that was adopted at the conference to be a blueprint for furthering sustainable development into the twenty-first century. In a broader sense it has provided the intellectual foundation for a sustained emphasis in the United Nations during the 1990s on reconciling environmental and developmental objectives.

BIBLIOGRAPHY

De la Court, T. *Beyond Brundtland: Green Development in the 1990s.* Translated by E. Bayens and N. Harle. New York: New Horizons Press, 1990. A critical analysis of the Brundtland report.
World Commission on Environment and Development. *Our Common Future.* New York: Oxford University Press, 1987. The full text of the Brundtland Commission Report.

—MARVIN S. SOROOS

Building Decay. Avenue of the Sphinxes.
Many of the monuments in Luxor, Egypt, show damage resulting from rising groundwater levels. Buildings and monuments in arid areas may, as a result of the spread of irrigation and leakage from urban sewers, suffer from accelerated weathering. Rising damp brings salts into their pores, effecting both chemical and physical changes such as damp patches and white areas of salt efflorescence.

BUILDING DECAY

Landscape change is driven by weathering, or the in-situ breakdown of material and its removal through erosion. Weathering affects the degradation and deterioration of stone, including building stone that is originally part of the landscape and covered with soil and sediments. Weathering causes changes in historical buildings and other structures, such as soiling and decay through color change and various associated features of decay (e.g., crusts, blisters, pitting). The main components of the weathering process are mechanical or physical, chemical, and biological.

Mechanical weathering occurs from physical stresses which induce strain in building materials, resulting in a weakening of the material and eventual breakdown. Heating and cooling, for instance, through insolation (solar radiation) may cause rock surfaces to expand with heating and contract with cooling, while the freezing of water or the crystallization of salts in rock pores may create stresses sufficiently large to cause fracturing. This can lead to the development of cracks at various scales, including

microcracks. Pressure and vibrations (from earthquakes or even from traffic) can affect the physical weathering of stone material and may trigger structural damage in buildings.

Chemical weathering is triggered by various agents in the biosphere, such as gases in the atmosphere and in solution in rainfall. Air pollution from combustion products emitted by industry and by vehicles contributes to surface changes that progress deeper into exposed rocks. Urban environments cycle pollutants deposited from the atmosphere in rainfall and dust. Surfaces react with these deposits to form acids (e.g., sulfuric acid) and salts (e.g., gypsum) that disintegrate building stone through various processes, including carbonation, hydration, hydrolysis, oxidation, and solution.

Biological weathering occurs on various scales, and microbiological impacts often operate on surfaces and within stone to disintegrate materials. Lichens, which consist of symbioses of algae and fungi, act upon rock surfaces by boring into the substrate—possibly even digesting the rock using excreted organic acids (e.g., oxalic acid, which forms deposits of calcium oxalate on surfaces).

The response of building material to the weathering process is affected by intrinsic properties of the substrate (e.g., chemical composition, pore size, and distribution). Human impacts can alter the process through contributions of air pollution from combustion, irrigation (including salinization and flooding), and mining. Irrigation and the rising of the water table may contain dissolved salts that can reach the Earth's surface and enhance chemical and biological weathering. [See Salinization.]

The building of dams (e.g., Aswan in Egypt, Three Gorges in China) is an example of how challenges of modern society, such as the production of and access to electricity, have the potential to impinge on geomorphology. Underground mining can destabilize the ground, causing localized subsidence and collapse of land surfaces. Shallow open-pit mining disturbs the surface layer of the Earth and releases dust into the atmosphere, which may soil buildings and other surfaces.

One of the greatest potential impacts of humanity is global warming. Pollutant gases (e.g., CO_2) produced by combustion and respiration are believed to create a "greenhouse effect" leading to global heating, melting of ice caps, sea-level rise, and associated global change. The production of carbonic acid by the carbonation of rain can accelerate the dissolution of stonework, especially that consisting of a carbonate-rich rock (limestone or marble). Pollution (e.g., CFCs) also thins the ozone layer, producing "holes" that allow unfiltered incoming solar radiation to enter into the troposphere thereby affecting insolation and possibly have some unforeseen synergisms. Not much is known about possible interactions in the context of global change in a polluted environment—for instance, whether there are any impacts of temperature on limestone dissolution from pollutant acidic gases (e.g., carbonic and nitric acids).

What will become of a significant part of humanity's cultural legacy on Earth—our historical artistic stoneworks? Some of these remain exposed outdoors (e.g., pyramids, remains of abbeys, standing stones) and are sensitive to external weather (temperature, rainfall and humidity), pollution, and impacts of climate change. In a developing world in which tourism is economically important, what will remain to market—except perhaps soiled and severely weathered slabs of stone, perhaps indistinguishable from natural stone lacking evidence of human culture? The alternatives are either to replace stone or to develop a cleaner environment with a stable climate in which stone weathering is controlled, though it cannot be eliminated.

BIBLIOGRAPHY

Brimblecombe, P. *The Effects of Air Pollution on the Built Environment.* London: Imperial College Press, 2003. Examines a range of materials in the built environment that are susceptible to damage from air pollution.
Fort, R., et al. *Heritage, Weathering, and Conservation.* London: Taylor & Francis, 2006. Proceedings, in two volumes, from an international conference in Madrid that focused on networks.
Gauri, K. L., and J. K. Bandyopadhyay. *Carbonate Stone: Chemical Behavior, Durability, and Conservation.* Chichester, U.K., and New York: Wiley, 1999. This is an essential text for anyone focusing on limestone.
Goudie, A. *The Human Impact on the Natural Environment: Past, Present, and Future.* 6th ed. Oxford, U.K., and Malden, Mass.: Blackwell Publishing, 2006. Provides a broad overview of human impacts and looks into their future ramifications.
Goudie, A., and H. Viles. *Salt Weathering Hazards.* Chichester, U.K., and New York: Wiley, 1997. This is an excellent source for specific case studies in a broader framework.
Siegesmund, S., T. Weiss, and A. Vollbrecht. *Natural Stone, Weathering Phenomena, Conservation Strategies, and Case Studies.* Geological Society Special Publication 205. London: Geological Society, 2002.
Viles, H. A. *Recent Advances in Field and Laboratory Studies of Rock Weathering.* Zeitschrift für Geomorphologie, Supplementband 120. Berlin and Stuttgart: Borntraeger, 2000. Contains many useful articles on experimentation in the field and laboratory.

—Mary J. Thornbush

C

CAP-AND-TRADE

See Emissions Trading.

CARBON CAPTURE AND STORAGE

Carbon capture and storage, or sequestration (CCS), is the long-term isolation of carbon dioxide from the atmosphere through physical, chemical, biological, or other engineered processes. This includes a range of approaches including soil-carbon sequestration (e.g., through no-till farming), terrestrial-biomass sequestration (e.g., through planting forests), direct injection of CO_2 onto the deep seafloor or into the intermediate depths of the ocean, injection into deep geological formations, and even direct conversion of CO_2 to carbonate minerals. [*See* Geoengineering]. All of these processes are considered in the 2005 special report by the Intergovernmental Panel on Climate Change (IPCC, 2005).

Geological carbon sequestration (GCS) appears to be the most feasible and economic option for major greenhouse-gas reduction in the next 10–30 years. Interest in GCS is based on several factors:

- The potential capacities are large. Formal estimates for global storage potential vary substantially, ranging between 800 and 3,300 billion metric tons (gigatons, Gt) of C (2,900–12,200 Gt of CO_2) with significant capacity located near large point-sources of the CO_2. The lower end of the range is roughly 100 times the 2005 annual global emission of CO_2 from the burning of fossil fuels.
- GCS can begin operations with demonstrated technology. Carbon dioxide has been separated from large point-sources for nearly 100 years and has been injected underground for over 30 years (below).
- Testing of GCS on an intermediate scale is feasible. In the U.S., Canada, and many other industrial countries, large CO_2 sources such as power plants and refineries lie near prospective storage sites. These plants could be retrofitted today and injection begun, while bearing in mind scientific uncertainties and unknowns. Three already functioning projects described here provide much information on the operational needs and field implementation of CCS.

When coupled with improvements in energy efficiency, renewable energy supplies, and nuclear power, CCS can help dramatically reduce emissions (US CCTP, 2005; MIT, 2007). If CCS is not available as a carbon-management option, it will be much more difficult and expensive to stabilize atmospheric CO_2 emissions. Recent estimates put the cost of carbon abatement without CCS at 30–80% higher than if CCS were to be available (Edmonds et al., 2004).

CARBON CAPTURE

CCS requires two separate but coupled steps. The first is the separation and concentration of CO_2 from industrial flue streams, chiefly in power plants. This first step, carbon capture, usually includes compression and transportation via pipeline. The second step, GCS, is the injection of CO_2 as a dense, supercritical (liquid-like) phase into deep geological formations. The cost of CCS lies mostly in the capture stage and the risk mostly in the sequestration stage.

The first step in CCS requires the separation of CO_2 and its concentration to purities of 95% or greater (Thambimuthu et al., 2005). This limits compression costs and makes efficient use of the available sequestration resource (the subsurface pore volume). Currently, three technologies exist for commercial CO_2 capture and separation:

- Post-combustion capture: the separation of CO_2 from nitrogen, commonly with chemical sorbents such as monoethanolamine (MEA).
- Pre-combustion capture: the conversion of fuel feedstocks (e.g., coal) into syngas via gasification, steam reformation, or partial oxidation, the conversion of the syngas chemically to hydrogen and CO_2, and then the separation of the hydrogen from CO_2. This last step is commonly done with physical sorbents (e.g., Selexol, Rectisol).
- Oxy-firing combustion: the combustion of fuels in a pure oxygen or O_2-CO_2-rich environment so that almost no nitrogen is present in the flue gas. Separation of O_2 from atmospheric nitrogen is required and creates the main cost.

Each of these approaches requires substantial power to run the adsorption and air-separation units, raising operating expenses and increasing the CO_2 emissions produced simply to drive the sequestration process. They also require more capital in plant construction and have differing operational costs and energy penalties. At present, the three processes appear equally viable economically and thermodynamically (Thambimuthu et al., 2005; Rao et al., 2006; MIT, 2007).

Industry has substantial experience with each of these processes, chiefly from the operation of hydrogen plants, fertilizer plants, refineries, and natural-gas processing facilities. CO_2 has been separated from industrial flue streams at scales much greater than 1 million tons CO_2 per year (270,000 tons of carbon). CO_2 has also been separated from small-scale power plants, and the technology to scale these operations up to plants of 200 megawatts or greater exists. Large pipelines transport millions of tons of CO_2 hundreds of kilometers; and millions of tons of CO_2 and other acid gases are compressed and injected into geological formations every year. Thus, a great deal is known about carbon capture, separation, and transportation, and many countries of the Organisation for Economic Co-operation and Development (OECD) have regulatory frameworks for the issuance of permits for separation facilities and pipelines.

Cost remains an important barrier to wider commercial deployment, but because the concepts for geological carbon sequestration are proven to be reliable for current power-plant technology, improved power-plant designs are expected to bring down sequestration costs dramatically. This year, several large pilot projects are testing pre-, post-, and oxy-fired combustion tests at the 4–5 megawatt scale, a necessary precursor to broad commercial deployment. A number of technologies claim to be able to capture and separate CO_2 at \$9–11/ton CO_2, less than half that for the best available technology. As the results from these and future tests are made public, decision-makers and investors will be able to plan better for plant economics and design.

GEOLOGICAL SEQUESTRATION

A number of geological reservoirs appear to have the potential to store many hundreds or thousands of Gt of CO_2 (Benson and Cook, 2005). The most promising reservoirs are porous and permeable rock bodies at depth:

- Saline formations contain brine in their pore volumes, commonly with salinities greater than 10,000 ppm.
- Depleted oil and gas fields have some combination of water and hydrocarbons in their pores. In some cases, economic gains can be achieved through enhanced oil or gas recovery (Stevens, 1999; Oldenburg et al., 2004; Jarrell et al., 2002). Substantial CO_2-enhanced oil recovery already occurs in the U.S. with both natural and anthropogenic CO_2. These fields provide much of our knowledge of issues related to CO_2 sequestration.
- Deep ("unmineable") coal seams are composed of organic minerals with brines and gases in their pores and fractures that can preferentially adsorb, bind, and store CO_2.

Because of their large storage potential and broad distribution, it is likely that most geological sequestration will occur in saline formations, though projects have been proposed to accompany enhanced oil recovery from depleted oil and gas fields because of the high density and quality of subsurface data and the potential for economic return. Although there remains some economic potential for enhanced coal-bed methane-recovery, much less is known about this type of sequestration (Benson et al., 2005; MIT, 2007; NPC, 2007; US DOE, 2007a). Even less is known about sequestration in basalts (a dense, fine-grained, often vesicular igneous rock). Many workers believe

sequestration projects in coal, basalts, or oil shales are not economically feasible given today's technology and understanding (US DOE, 2007b).

Storage of large CO_2 volumes in geological formations requires that the CO_2 be relatively dense in order that storage capacity be efficiently used. Given typical geothermal gradients and hydrostatic loads, CO_2 is likely to be in a supercritical state at most target sites at greater than 800 meters depth (e.g., Bachu, 2000). In the likely range of injection pressures and temperatures for most projects, CO_2 would be buoyant and would be pushed upward from the injection point. Trapping mechanisms are thus needed to store CO_2 effectively.

For depleted oil and gas fields or for saline formations, CO_2 storage mechanisms are reasonably well understood. CO_2 sequestration targets will require physical barriers to prevent CO_2 migration to the surface. These barriers will commonly take the form of impermeable layers (e.g., shales, evaporites) overlying the sequestration target. This storage mechanism is analogous to that of hydrocarbon trapping, natural gas storage, and natural CO_2 accumulations. The volume of CO_2 trapped as a residual phase is highly sensitive to pore geometry, and consequently is difficult to predict, but standard techniques can measure residual-phase trapping directly in the laboratory with rock samples.

Once in the pores, the CO_2 will dissolve into other pore fluids, including hydrocarbons (oil and gas) and brines. Depending on the fluid composition and reservoir condition, this may occur rapidly (seconds to minutes) or over a period of tens to hundreds of years. Once the CO_2 is dissolved in them, the CO_2-bearing brines are denser than the original brines, and the strong buoyant forces of free-phase gas are replaced by small downward forces. Over longer periods (hundreds to thousands of years) the dissolved CO_2 may react with minerals in the rock volume to dissolve or precipitate new carbonate minerals. For the majority of the rock volume and major minerals, this process is slow, and may take hundreds to thousands of years to achieve substantial storage volumes. Precipitation of carbonate minerals permanently binds CO_2 in the subsurface, and dissolution of minerals generally traps CO_2 as an ionic species (usually bicarbonate) in the pore fluid.

Although substantial work remains to be done to characterize and quantify these mechanisms, the current level of understanding can be used to estimate the percentage of CO_2 that can be stored over a given period of time. Confidence in these estimates is bolstered by studies of hydrocarbon systems, natural gas storage operations, hazardous waste injection, and enhanced recovery of crude oil. Evaluations based on our current understanding of trapping mechanisms estimate that more than 99.9% of injected CO_2 can be reliably stored over 100 years and that 99% of CO_2 can be reliably stored for 1,000 years (Benson et al., 2005). These estimates, predicated on the assumption of the careful choice of sites and due diligence before injection, reflect the view that the Earth's crust contains rocks that are generally appropriate for the effective storage of CO_2.

LARGE-SCALE COMMERCIAL DEPLOYMENT

In order to achieve substantial greenhouse-gas reductions, geological storage needs to be deployed at a large scale, there must be minimal leakage from the underground storage reservoirs back to the atmosphere, and there must be minimal impact on other uses of the subsurface environment and the resources it contains. The issue of scale dominates the deployment of GCS (Pacala and Socolow, 2004; Edmonds et al., 2004; McFarland et al., 2004; US CCTP, 2005). GCS would perhaps sequester 25–75 Gt C over 50 years, or 15–43% of the emissions reduction needed to stabilize atmospheric CO_2 levels at 550 ppm (Pacala and Socolow, 2004). [See Stabilizing Carbon Emissions.]

Today there are three well-established large-scale injection projects with ambitious scientific programs that include monitoring and verification (Table 1): Sleipner in Norway (Arts et al., 2004), Weyburn in Canada (Wilson and Monea, 2004), and In Salah in Algeria (Riddiford et al., 2004). Each project has injected CO_2 at the rate of about 1 million tons per year (270,000 t C). Each project has had a supporting science program or anticipates one. Summaries of the information available on these projects can be found in Benson et al. (2005).

These projects have sampled a wide array of geology with various trapping mechanisms, injection depths, reservoir types, and injectivity (capacity of the site to accommodate CO_2 injection). Each of these projects appears to have ample injectivity and capacity, and none has detected significant CO_2 leakage. In addition to the three sequestration projects, many industrial applications have injected large volumes of CO_2 underground. Enhanced oil-recovery operations in West Texas, New Mexico, Colorado, Wyoming, Oklahoma, Mississippi, Trinidad, Canada, and Turkey have individual injection programs as large as 3 million metric tons of CO_2 per year (810,000 t C) and cumulative injections of anthropogenic CO_2 of about 10 MM t CO_2/y (2.7 MM t C) (Kuuskraa et al., 2006). The monitoring and verification programs at these sites vary substantially (MIT, 2007). In many enhanced oil recovery projects, there is almost no monitoring beyond that required for CO_2-flood operations (Jarrell et al., 2002).

Several large-scale injection projects (Table 2) are expected to begin within the next five years: three in Australia, two in Norway, one in the U.K, and three in the U.S. [See Coal Gasification, section on FutureGen.] These will provide new

TABLE 1. Current Large CO_2 Injection Projects

Site	Location	Reservoir Class	Reservoir Type	Permeability	Seal Type	Start Date*
Sleipner	Norway	Offshore Saline Fm.	Deep-water sandstone	V. high	Thick shale	1996
Weyburn	Canada	Onshore EOR**	Ramp carbonate	Moderate	Evaporate	2000
In Salah	Algeria	Onshore Sandstone	Fluvial/tidal sandstone	Low	Thick shale	2004

* First injection or planned first injection of CO_2. ** EOR = Enhanced Oil Recovery

TABLE 2. Planned Large CO_2 Injection Projects

Site	Location	Reservoir Class	Reservoir Type	Permeability	Seal Type	Start Date*
FutureGen	U.S.	Onshore Saline Fm.	Fluvial sandstone or shelf carbonate	Moderate	Thick shales or evaporites	2012
ZeroGen	Australia	Onshore EOR*/Saline	Fluvial/deltaic sandstone	Low-moderate	Shale	2011
Snohvit	Norway	Offshore Saline Fm.	Fluvial sandstone	Moderate	Shale/evap.	2008
DF1/Miller	U.K.	Offshore EOR	Deep-water sandstone	Moderate–high	Thick shale	2011
DF2/Carson	U.S.	Onshore EOR	Deep-water sandstone	Moderate–high	Thick shale	2012
Latrobe Valley/ Monash	Australia	Offshore EOR/Saline	Fluvial/deltaic sandstone	High	Thin and thick shales	2011
Gorgon	Australia	Offshore Saline Fm.	Deep-water sandstone	Moderate	Thick shales	2009
Hauten/ Draugen	Norway	Onshore/Offshore Saline Fm.	Deep-water sandstone	High–v. high	Thick shales	2010
Phase III Regional Partnerships	U.S.	Varying, but mostly Saline Fm.	Varying	Varying	Varying	2010

* EOR = Enhanced Oil Recovery

opportunities to design, implement, and test new monitoring strategies in a wide range of geological environments.

SCIENCE AND TECHNOLOGY STATUS

Knowledge of trapping mechanisms and the successes of the three large current projects provide substantial information. These are augmented by studies of naturally occurring CO_2 systems, (IEA GHG, 2005), natural gas storage facilities, hazardous waste disposal, acid gas injection, and enhanced oil recovery (Benson et al., 2005). This knowledge provides a firm foundation for commercial action and a basis for the development of regulation, standards, and legal frameworks for sequestration (Wilson et al., 2003). GCS itself, however, drives the study of specific technical and scientific challenges associated with the central elements of site characterization, selection, operation, and monitoring (US DOE, 2007a; Wilson et al., 2007). Investigation of these topics will enhance the technical and operation understanding of commercial GCS.

KEY SCIENCE AND TECHNOLOGY GAPS

Despite the significant applied and basic knowledge already developed, there remain general and site-specific topics for investigation. From an applied perspective, the National Energy Technology Laboratory has written an annual plan to identify and address key technology gaps (US DOE, 2007a), while a recent report by the U.S. Department of Energy (DOE) Office of Science (US DOE, 2007b) is meant to focus on a set of basic science gaps and questions. While these documents are not meant to be comprehensive, they accurately reflect the current state of knowledge and potential to continue scientific investigations in GCS.

DEPLOYMENT CHALLENGES

Despite the current gaps in sequestration science and technology, commercial projects have begun. Today, we know enough to safely and effectively execute key tasks in single large-scale injection projects:

- Characterize a site.
- Design and operate the project.
- Monitor the CO_2 injection.
- Mitigate problems that might arise.
- Close down the project safely.

Although this knowledge is currently being brought to bear on specific injection projects around the world, greater scientific understanding is required to develop tools, regulations, and standards for the deployment of multiple million-ton injections in thousands of wells nationwide and worldwide in a range of geological settings (Friedmann, 2007; Wilson et al., 2003). Potential operators must execute a set of tasks to prepare for and execute injection permitting and operation. Potential regulators, investors, insurers, and public stakeholders likewise require information to make decisions. Part of the challenge is to provide a technical basis to enable all actors to make decisions concerning the minimal amount of information needed

to serve all stakeholders (Friedmann, 2007; Burton et al., 2007), but there are no broadly accepted standard measures of CCS site effectiveness. Characterizations must rely ultimately on conventional approaches in order to estimate injection rate and sustainability, total site capacity, geomechanical integrity, hydrodynamic stability, and seal continuity.

HAZARDS ASSESSMENT AND RISK MANAGEMENT

Supercritical CO_2 is buoyant and will seek the earth's surface; CO_2 injection therefore carries the possibility of leakage. Importantly, CO_2 leakage risk will not be uniform among sites, and CO_2 storage sites will have to demonstrate minimal risk in their site characterization plans (Bradshaw et al., 2004). Based on analogous experience in areas such as acid gas disposal and enhanced oil recovery, the risks of CO_2 injection appear to be less than those of current oil and gas operations (Benson et al., 2005).

The direct hazards associated with geologic sequestration fall into three categories:

- hazards associated with the release of CO_2 to the earth surface.
- hazards associated with release into groundwater and subsequent degradation.
- hazards associated with earth movement caused by the injection process itself.

The hazards are in turn associated with failure mechanisms and triggers (e.g., wellbore failure). Potential triggering of events associated with these hazards could lead to undesired consequences. While these hazards can be readily identified and managed, it is important to understand these hazards in order to avoid triggering such events in the first place. Protocols will be developed to inform operators and regulators on preparing and opening a site and will serve as the basis for operational standards. The development of these protocols based on studies at large-scale injection projects should be the highest priority of any decarbonization strategy for most OECD countries.

BIBLIOGRAPHY

Arts, R., et al. "Monitoring of CO_2 Injected at Sleipner Using Time-Lapse Seismic Data." *Energy* 29.9–10 (2004), 1383–1392. DOI: 10.1016/j.energy.2004.03.072.

Bachu, S. "Sequestration of CO_2 in Geological Media: Criteria and Approach for Site Selection in Response to Climate Change." *Energy Conversion and Management* 41.9 (2000), 953–970. DOI: 10.1016/S0196-8904(99)00149-1.

———. "Screening and Ranking of Sedimentary Basins for Sequestration of CO_2 in Geological Media in Response to Climate Change." *Environmental Geology*, 44.3 (2003), 277–289.

Benson, S.M., et al. "Underground Geological Storage." Chap. 5 of *Special Report on Carbon Dioxide Capture and Storage*, edited by B. Metz, et al. Prepared by Working Group III of the Intergovernmental Panel on Climate Change. New York: Cambridge University Press, 2005. www.ipcc.ch (accessed May 23, 2008).

Bradshaw, J., C. Boreham, and F. la Pedalina. "Storage Retention Time of CO_2 in Sedimentary Basins: Examples from Petroleum Systems." Proceedings of the 7th Conference on Greenhouse Gas Control Technologies (GHGT-7), Vancouver, British Columbia, 2004.

Burton, E.A., et al. 2007 "Geologic Carbon Sequestration Strategies for California: The Assembly Bill 1925 Report to the California Legislature." California Energy Commission, Systems Office. CEC-500-2007-100-SD (http://www.energy.ca.gor/2007_energypolicy/documents/index.html 100107; accessed May 27, 2008).

Edmonds J., et al. "Stabilization of CO_2 in a B2 World: Insights on the Roles of Carbon Capture and Disposal, Hydrogen, and Transportation Technologies." *Energy Economics* 26.4 (2004), 517–537.

Friedmann S. J. "Operational Protocols for Geologic Carbon Storage: Facility Life-Cycle and the New Hazard Characterization Approach." Abstract 034. 6th Annual National Energy Technology Laboratory (NETL) conference on Carbon Capture and Sequestration, 2007. Washington, D.C.: ExchangeMonitor, 2007.

FutureGen Alliance. *Final Request for Proposals for FutureGen Facility Host Site.* 2006. http://www.futuregenalliance.org/news/futuregan_siting-final_rfp_3-07-2006.pdf (accessed May 23, 2008).

Herzog, H., and J. Katzer. "The Future of Coal in a Greenhouse Gas Constrained World." Presented at the 8th International Conference on Greenhouse Gas Control Technologies, Trondheim, Norway, June, 2006. http://coal.mit.edu/pdf/GHGT8_Herzog_Katzer.pdf (accessed May 23, 2008).

Herzog, H., K. Caldeira, and J. Reilly. "An Issue of Permanence: Assessing the Effectiveness of Temporary Carbon Storage." *Climatic Change*, 59.3 (2003), 293–310. DOI: 10.1023/A:1024801618900.

Ide, S.T., S.J. Friedmann, and H.J. Herzog. "CO_2 Leakage Through Existing Wells: Current Technology and Regulatory Basis." Proceedings of the 8th International Greenhouse Gas Technology Conference, Trondheim, Norway, 2006.

IEA GHG, 2005. *A Review of Natural CO_2 Emissions and Releases and Their Relevance to CO_2 Storage.* International Energy Agency Greenhouse Gas R&D Programme, Report 2005/8, 2005. http://www.ieagreen.org.uk/ (accessed May 23, 2008).

IEA GHG, 2006. *2nd Well Bore Integrity Network Meeting.* International Energy Agency Greenhouse Gas R&D, Report 2006/12, 2006. http://www.co2captureandstorage.info/docs/WellBore2NP.pdf (accessed May 23, 2008).

IPCC, 2005. Intergovernmental Panel on Climate Change. IPCC Special Report on Carbon Dioxide Capture and Storage, Interlachen, Switzerland. http://www.ipcc.ch/ (accessed May 23, 2008).

Jarrell P.M., et al. *Practical Aspects of CO_2 Flooding.* Richardson, Texas: Society of Petroleum Engineers, 2002.

Keith D.W., H. Hassanzadeh, and M. Pooladi-Darvish. "Reservoir Engineering to Accelerate Dissolution of Stored CO_2 in Brines." Proceedings of the 7th International Greenhouse Gas Technology Conference (GHGT-7), Vancouver, Canada, 2004.

Kharaka, Y.K., et al. "Gas-Water-Rock Interactions in Frio Formation Following CO_2 Injection: Implications for the Storage of Greenhouse Gases in Sedimentary Basins." *Geology* 34.7 (2006), 577–580. DOI: 10.1130/G22357.1.

Knauss, K.G., J.W. Johnson, and C.I. Steefel. "Evaluation of the Impact of CO_2, Co-contaminant, Aqueous Fluid, and Reservoir Rock Interactions on the Geologic Sequestration of CO_2." *Chemical Geology* 217.3–4 (2005), 339–350. DOI: 10.1016/j.chemgeo.2004.12.017.

Kuuskraa V.A., P. DiPietro, and G.J. Koperna. "CO_2 Storage Capacity in Depleted and Near-Depleted U.S. Oil and Gas Reservoirs." 5th Annual National Energy Technology Laboratory (NETL) Conference on Carbon Sequestration, 2006. Washington, D.C.: ExchangeMonitor, 2006.

McFarland, J.R., J.M. Reilly, and H.J. Herzog. "Representing Energy Technologies in Top-Down Economic Models Using Bottom-Up Information." *Energy Economics* 26.4 (2004), 685–707. DOI: 10.1016/j.eneco.2004.04.026.

MIT, 2007. *Carbon Capture and Sequestration Technologies @ MIT.* Cambridge, Mass.: MIT Press, 2007. http://coal.mit.edu (accessed May 23, 2008).

NPC, 2007. "Facing Hard Truths about Energy: A Comprehensive View to 2030 of Global Oil and Natural Gas." Washington, D.C.: National Petroleum Council, 2007. www.npc.org (accessed May 23, 2008).

Oldenburg C.M., S.H. Stevens, and S.M. Benson. "Economic Feasibility of Carbon Sequestration with Enhanced Gas Recovery (CSEGR)." *Energy* 29 (2004), 1413–1422.

Pacala, S., and R. Socolow. "Stabilization Wedges: Solving the Climate Problem for the Next 50 Years Using Current Technologies." *Science* 305 (2004), 968–972. DOI: 10.1126/science.1100103.

Rao, A.B., et al. "Evaluation of Potential Cost Reductions from Improved Amine-Based CO_2 Capture Systems." *Energy Policy* 34.18 (2006), 3765–3772. DOI: 10.1016/j.enpol.2005.08.004.

Riddiford, F., et al. "Monitoring Geological Storage: In Salah Gas CO_2 Storage Project." Proceedings of the 7th Conference on Greenhouse Gas Control Technologies (GHGT-7), Vancouver, British Columbia, 2004.

Stevens, S. "Sequestration of CO_2 in Depleted Oil and Gas Fields: Barriers to Overcome in Implementation of CO_2 Capture and Storage (Disused Oil and Gas Fields)." IEA Greenhouse Gas R&D Programme, IEA/CON/98/31, 1999.

Thambimuthu, K., M. Soltanieh, and J.C. Abanades. "Capture of CO_2." Chap. 3 of *Special Report on Carbon Dioxide Capture and Storage*, edited by B. Metz, et al. Prepared by Working. Group III of the Intergovernmental Panel on Climate Change. New York: Cambridge University Press, 2005. www.ipcc.ch (accessed May 23, 2008).

US CCTP, 2005. *U.S. Climate Change Technology Program Strategic Plan.* Washington, D.C. 2005. http://www.dimatechnology.gov/stratplan/final/index.htm (accessed May 23, 2008).

US DOE, 2007a. *Carbon Sequestration Technology Roadmap and Program Plan 2006.* Morgantown, W.Va.: National Energy Technology Laboratory, 2007.

US DOE, 2007b. *Basic Research Needs for Geosciences: Facilitating 21st Century Energy Systems.* Washington, D.C.: Department of Energy Office of Basic Energy Sciences, 2007. http://www.sc.doe.gov/bes/report/list.html (accessed May 23, 2008).

Wilson, E., T. Johnson, and D. Keith. "Regulating the Ultimate Sink: Managing the Risks of Geologic CO_2 Storage." *Environmental Science and Technology* 37.16 (2003), 3476–3483. DOI: 10.1021/es021038+.

Wilson. M., and M. Monea, eds. *IEA GHG Weyburn CO_2 Monitoring & Storage Project Summary Report 2000–2004.* Regina: Saskatchewan Petroleum Technology Research Centre, 2004.

—S. Julio Friedmann

CARBON CYCLE

Carbon circulates among three distinct global reservoirs. These are the atmosphere, the oceans, and the terrestrial system. Of the three reservoirs, the oceans contain by far the greatest amount of carbon (40,000 petagrams; 1 petagram is 1 billion metric tons or 10^{15} grams). The terrestrial reservoir contains a much smaller amount of carbon (2,050 petagrams), mostly in the soil (1,500 petagrams). The atmospheric reservoir contains the smallest amount (currently 775 petagrams), and nearly all carbon in the atmosphere is in the form of the trace gas carbon dioxide. Nevertheless, the atmosphere plays an important role in the global carbon cycle as a conduit between the other two reservoirs. The concentration of carbon dioxide in the atmosphere is determined by dynamic exchanges between the oceans, the terrestrial system, and the atmosphere. Over geologic time, the concentration of carbon dioxide in the atmosphere has fluctuated as a result of shifts in the relative surface areas of ocean and land as well as changes in general climate regimes and the influences these have on marine and terrestrial ecosystems. The burning of fossil fuels is contributing carbon dioxide to the atmosphere at a rate that is increasing the atmospheric carbon dioxide concentration and altering the rates of carbon exchange between the three main reservoirs of the global carbon cycle. Figure 1 shows the major reservoirs in the global carbon cycle, their components, and the magnitudes of carbon exchange between them for preindustrial time (before 1860; Figure 1A) and conditions through 1997 (Figure 1B). There are other pools and fluxes that do not appear in these diagrams, including soil carbonates, the formation and dissolution of carbonates in the ocean, peat deposition, volcanic emissions, and groundwater and river transport of organic and inorganic carbon. While

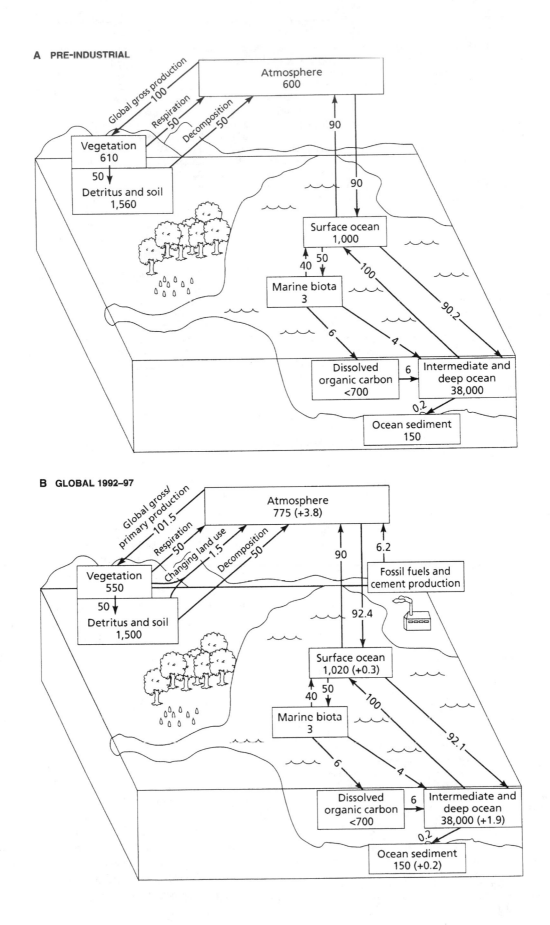

A PRE-INDUSTRIAL

Atmosphere
600

Global gross production
100

Respiration
50

Decomposition
50

Vegetation
610

50

Detritus and soil
1,560

90

90

Surface ocean
1,000

40 50

Marine biota
3

100

90.2

6

4

Dissolved
organic carbon
<700

6

Intermediate and
deep ocean
38,000

0.2

Ocean sediment
150

B GLOBAL 1992–97

Atmosphere
775 (+3.8)

Global gross/
primary production
101.5

Respiration
50

Changing land use
1.5

Decomposition
50

Vegetation
550

50

Detritus and soil
1,500

90

6.2

Fossil fuels and
cement production

92.4

Surface ocean
1,020 (+0.3)

40 50

Marine biota
3

100

92.1

6

4

Dissolved
organic carbon
<700

6

Intermediate and
deep ocean
38,000 (+1.9)

0.2

Ocean sediment
150 (+0.2)

important on geologic time scales, these pools and associated fluxes do not play a major role during the present, relatively short, fossil-fuel burning period.

The exchange of carbon between the atmosphere and the ocean is the result of diffusion of carbon dioxide across the ocean surface. The direction and rate of carbon dioxide diffusion vary from place to place and depend on the gas transfer coefficient for carbon dioxide and the difference in partial pressure of carbon dioxide between the atmosphere and the surface ocean waters. The gas transfer coefficient is a function of temperature and is very sensitive to wind speed over the ocean surface (greater wind speed enhances gas transfer by increasing mixed-layer thickness, wave action, and bubble formation). The difference in partial pressure of carbon dioxide between the atmosphere and the surface ocean water determines the magnitude and direction of the exchange. The partial pressure of carbon dioxide in sea water is a function of temperature, salinity, alkalinity, and, most importantly, total carbon dioxide concentration (dissolved bicarbonate and carbonate, as well as dissolved carbon dioxide). The effect of total dissolved carbon dioxide on the partial pressure of carbon dioxide in sea water is expressed as the Revelle factor. A global mean value is 10. This means that a 1% increase in total dissolved carbon dioxide causes a 10% increase in the partial pressure of carbon dioxide in sea water. The Revelle factor increases rapidly with increasing total dissolved carbon dioxide. A 10% increase in total dissolved carbon dioxide would increase the Revelle factor from 10 to 18. Thus, the more carbon dioxide surface ocean waters take up, the less effective they will become at taking up more carbon dioxide from the atmosphere.

The partial pressure of carbon dioxide in surface waters is affected by several ocean processes in addition to carbonate solution dynamics. The large-scale thermohaline circulation that results from the sinking of dense, cold, and salty water at high latitudes and the upwelling of nutrient- and carbon-rich deep waters along continental boundaries makes different ocean regions either sinks or sources of carbon dioxide to the atmosphere. Marine life also affects the uptake of carbon dioxide by the oceans. Photosynthesis carried out by phytoplankton in the well-lit surface layer (euphotic zone) of the ocean converts dissolved inorganic carbon dioxide into organic matter and calcium carbonate. A major portion of this primary production is consumed, decomposed, or remineralized in the surface waters, but a fraction escapes from the well-mixed surface ocean to the stratified deep ocean layers, where most is redissolved and only a minor fraction is deposited in the ocean sediments. This escaping fraction effectively lowers the concentration of dissolved carbon dioxide in the surface ocean, increasing its ability to take up atmospheric carbon dioxide and thereby reducing the atmospheric carbon dioxide concentration. Once carbon is transferred to the deep ocean it remains there, on average, for approximately 1,000 years until it is mixed into the surface layer or wells up in the global thermohaline circulation.

The terrestrial system, by virtue of the large amount of carbon in soil organic matter, is the second largest of the three global reservoirs. The flux between the atmosphere and the land surface results from the incorporation of atmospheric carbon dioxide into organic compounds during plant photosynthesis. Nearly all of this carbon is eventually returned to the atmosphere as carbon dioxide by the respiration of living organisms. Some is also returned by fires.

The rate at which carbon dioxide is taken up by plants, also called gross primary production (GPP), depends largely on the availability of light, water, and temperatures suitable for metabolic function. The availability of soil nutrients, particularly nitrogen, also influences the rate of photosynthesis and plant growth. Approximately half of the carbon fixed into organic compounds during photosynthesis is used directly by plants for growth and maintenance and is respired in a short time, returning carbon dioxide to the atmosphere. The remaining fraction, called net primary production (NPP), is the rate at which carbon is incorporated into plant tissues. Some of these tissues persist for only a short time before being shed and decomposed by soil organisms. For example, fine plant roots may last only a few weeks or months, and deciduous leaves less than a year. Other tissues, such as wood, can persist for several decades or even centuries, depending on the forest type and disturbance frequency. Soil organisms return most of the carbon in dead organic matter to the atmosphere as carbon dioxide. A smaller portion of this decomposing material is "humified" or converted by soil organisms into humic compounds that are more difficult to decompose because of chemical resistance or physical protection by soil minerals. Humic compounds can remain in soils for tens to thousands of years before being converted to carbon dioxide. As a result, most of the carbon in the terrestrial system is found in soils, rather than in living plant tissues. The rate of change in carbon storage in terrestrial ecosystems, or what is called net ecosystem production (NEP), is the difference between NPP and the rate of decomposition of shed and dead plant tissues. At equilibrium, NPP is balanced by the rate of decomposition, and NEP is zero. Of course, no single small plot of terrestrial vegetation is ever in equilibrium for long because of natural or human disturbances and subsequent plant regeneration. The notion that NEP

Carbon Cycle. Figure 1. Global Carbon Reservoirs (facing page).

(A) Preindustrial Global Carbon Cycle. The concentration of carbon dioxide in the atmosphere has been constant from the end of the last glacial period, approximately eleven thousand years ago, until the beginning of the Industrial Revolution in the mid-1800s, indicating that the carbon dioxide release from oceans and terrestrial systems was balanced by corresponding uptake. This is shown by the equal exchanges of carbon between the carbon pools in this diagram of the preindustrial global carbon cycle. All pools' units are petagrams of carbon (1 petagram = 1×10^{15} grams or 1 billion metric tons) and exchanges are in petagrams of carbon per year. (B) Global Carbon Cycle (1992–1997). The burning of fossil fuels and changing land use have resulted in human-induced alteration of the global carbon cycle. The magnitude of the perturbation in carbon fluxes can be determined by comparison with part (A). The rate of change in carbon pool sizes (in petagrams of carbon per year) is indicated by the numbers in parentheses. Land use change has resulted in a decrease of terrestrial vegetation and soil pool carbon content. Currently, losses due to land use change, largely in tropical regions, may be approximately balanced by increased rates of sequestration resulting from carbon dioxide fertilization in relatively undisturbed ecosystems.

TABLE 1. Carbon Dioxide Emissions From Fossil Fuel Consumption 2005

Country	Million Tons Carbon*	% of World	% Change in 2004	Per Capita Tons Carbon*
USA	1,697	22.38	unchanged	5.74
China	1,389	18.31	+ 9.10	1.06
EU (25)	1,130	14.91	unchanged	2.47
E. Europe	720	9.49	+ 1.74	2.15
Japan	368	4.85	+ 1.11	2.89
India	330	4.36	+ 2.34	0.31
Canada	164	2.16	+ 0.59	4.99
France	114	1.51	unchanged	1.89
Australia	99	1.31	+ 0.74	4.93
Brazil	94	1.24	+ 3.0	0.50
Rest of world	1,592	20.90	+ 3.2	0.61

* to convert tons of carbon to tons of carbon dioxide, multiply by 3.67.

Fossil fuel consumption: from *BP Statistical Review of World Energy*, 2005.

Populations mid-year 2005: from *CIA World Factbook*.

Calculations and analysis: John H. Walsh, Energy Advisor, Ottawa, Ontario.

See Carbon Dioxide Emissions 2005 online.

may be approximately zero requires an averaging over sufficiently large areas for long enough periods of time to include the effects of disturbances that result in losses of carbon to the atmosphere.

Over the last 150 years, as a result of the burning of fossil fuels, cement making, and the conversion of natural vegetation to agricultural use, there has been a large increase in the amount of carbon dioxide in the atmosphere. Since around 1850, the beginning of the Industrial Revolution, the amount of carbon dioxide added to the atmosphere has increased steadily. The preindustrial atmosphere held 600 petagrams of carbon in the form of carbon dioxide, equivalent to a concentration of 280 microliters per liter. The present atmosphere, with a concentration of 365 microliters per liter, contains 775 petagrams of carbon. The amount of carbon added from fossil fuel burning and cement production between 1992 and 1997 was 6.2 petagrams per year. Land-use conversion is estimated to contribute an additional 1.0 petagrams per year. (This estimate is a net flux that includes carbon from conversion of native vegetation to cultivation, at present mostly in tropical regions, and carbon uptake by the regrowth of forests on land no longer cultivated, largely in temperate regions.) Of this 7.2 petagrams of carbon per year emitted to the atmosphere, about 2.4 petagrams are taken up by the world's oceans and 3.8 petagrams remain in the atmosphere. Changes in atmospheric oxygen concentration, changes in carbon dioxide concentration in which the carbon is the stable isotope carbon-13, and the latitudinal distribution of atmospheric carbon dioxide suggest that terrestrial ecosystems take up the remaining one petagram per year and store it in plant tissues or soil.

Atmospheric carbon dioxide concentration is now 30% higher than in preindustrial times. This elevated carbon dioxide stimulates photosynthesis, and higher photosynthesis supports faster plant growth rates. In long-lived perennial species such as trees, increased growth implies an increase in carbon stored in wood, at least for several decades. In addition, increased plant production, when shed as dead litter, results in a larger amount of decaying organic matter. A portion of this decaying matter becomes humified and enters the soil carbon pool, where it may reside for several decades before undergoing further decomposition. This carbon dioxide fertilization effect may account for most of the current net storage of carbon annually in soil and plant tissues such as wood. For how long, and at what rates, terrestrial and ocean systems will take up carbon dioxide as the concentrations of atmospheric carbon dioxide continue to rise is the subject of considerable scientific investigation.

[*See also* Deforestation; Energy and Environment; Fossil Fuels; Global Warming; Greenhouse Effect; *and* Methane.]

BIBLIOGRAPHY

Barnola, J.-M., et al. "Vostok Ice Core Provides 160,000 Year Record of Atmospheric CO_2." *Nature* 329 (1987), 408–414. DOI: 10.1038/329408a0. This important paper contains a long history of atmospheric carbon dioxide concentration that provides a basis for current analyses and a glimpse into the dynamic nature of the carbon cycle.

Batjes, N.H. "Total Carbon and Nitrogen in the Soils of the World." *European Journal of Soil Science* 47.2 (1996), 151–163. An up-to-date analysis of the amount and location of soil carbon.

Broecker, W.S. "Paleocean Circulation During the Last Glaciation: A Bipolar Seesaw." *Paleoceanography* 13 (1998), 119–121. An explanation of the importance of the large-scale thermohaline circulation of the ocean and factors that determine its strength.

Ciais, P., et al. "A Three Dimensional Synthesis Study of $\delta^{18}O$ in Atmospheric CO_2. 1. Surface Fluxes." *Journal of Geophysical Research* 102.D5 (1997), 5857–5872.

TABLE 2. Carbon Dioxide Total Emissions by Country, 2003 Includes fossil-fuel burning, gas flaring, and cement production

Rank	Country	Total (thousand tons of carbon)	Rank	Country	Total (thousand tons of carbon)
1	UNITED STATES OF AMERICA	1580175	40	DEMOCRATIC PEOPLE'S REPUBLIC OF KOREA	21145
2	CHINA (MAINLAND)	1131175	41	PHILIPPINES	21007
3	RUSSIAN FEDERATION	407593	42	VIETNAM	20774
4	INDIA	347577	43	IRAQ	19893
5	JAPAN	336142	44	AUSTRIA	19192
6	GERMANY	219776	45	ISRAEL	18645
7	CANADA	154392	46	FINLAND	18519
8	UNITED KINGDOM	152460	47	BELARUS	17073
9	REPUBLIC OF KOREA	124455	48	CHILE	15965
10	ITALY (INCLUDING SAN MARINO)	121608	49	HUNGARY	15896
11	MEXICO	113542	50	PORTUGAL	15711
12	ISLAMIC REPUBLIC OF IRAN	104112	51	COLOMBIA	15158
13	FRANCE (INCLUDING MONACO)	102065	52	DENMARK	14873
14	SOUTH AFRICA	99415	53	SWEDEN	14378
15	AUSTRALIA	96657	54	NIGERIA	14244
16	UKRAINE	85836	55	LIBYAN ARAB JAMAHIRIYAH	13699
17	SPAIN	84401	56	FEDERAL REPUBLIC OF YUGOSLAVIA	13630
18	POLAND	83121	57	SYRIAN ARAB REPUBLIC	w13361
19	SAUDI ARABIA	82530	58	SINGAPORE	13048
20	BRAZIL	81445	59	QATAR	12605
21	INDONESIA	80544	60	NORWAY	12289
22	THAILAND	67131	61	BULGARIA	12001
23	TAIWAN	62720	62	TURKMENISTAN	11829
24	TURKEY	60057	63	IRELAND	11291
25	ALGERIA	44672	64	SWITZERLAND	11027
26	KAZAKHSTAN	43459	65	MOROCCO	10346
27	MALAYSIA	42692	66	HONG KONG	10317
28	VENEZUELA	39299	67	SLOVAKIA	10250
29	NETHERLANDS	38464	68	NEW ZEALAND	9487
30	EGYPT	38118	69	BANGLADESH	9452
31	UNITED ARAB EMIRATES	36862	70	OMAN	8804
32	ARGENTINA	34803	71	AZERBAIJAN	7963
33	UZBEKISTAN	33744	72	TRINIDAD AND TOBAGO	7820
34	CZECH REPUBLIC	31760	73	PERU	7138
35	PAKISTAN	31160	74	CUBA	6892
36	BELGIUM	28070	75	CROATIA	6496
37	GREECE	26268	76	ECUADOR	6334
38	ROMANIA	24875	77	BAHRAIN	5971
39	KUWAIT	21417	78	DOMINICAN REPUBLIC	5817

TABLE 2. (Continued)

Rank	Country	Total (thousand tons of carbon)	Rank	Country	Total (thousand tons of carbon)
79	TUNISIA	5697	119	NICARAGUA	1067
80	BOSNIA-HERZEGOVINIA	5221	120	UNITED REPUBLIC OF TANZANIA	1038
81	LEBANON	5177	121	GEORGIA	1017
82	ESTONIA	4976	122	REPUBLIC OF CAMEROON	965
83	JORDAN	4664	123	ARMENIA	935
84	YEMEN	4655	124	MAURITIUS	858
85	SLOVENIA	4205	125	ALBANIA	830
86	U.S. VIRGIN ISLANDS	3692	126	NEPAL	805
87	LITHUANIA	3459	127	PAPUA NEW GUINEA	685
88	ZIMBABWE	3130	128	MAURITANIA	682
89	JAMAICA	2926	129	REUNION	675
90	GUATEMALA	2918	130	MALTA	672
91	MACEDONIA	2873	131	MADAGASCAR	639
92	SRI LANKA	2812	132	NAMIBIA	635
93	LUXEMBOURG	2710	133	SURINAME	611
94	MYANMAR	2580	134	TOGO	599
95	SUDAN	2454	135	ZAMBIA	599
96	KENYA	2395	136	ICELAND	597
97	ANGOLA	2352	137	ARUBA	588
98	MONGOLIA	2176	138	PUERTO RICO	573
99	BOLIVIA	2155	139	BENIN	557
100	GHANA	2110	140	BAHAMAS	510
101	ETHIOPIA	2002	141	NEW CALEDONIA	510
102	CYPRUS	1987	142	MACAU	509
103	REPUBLIC OF MOLDOVA	1973	143	ZAIRE	488
104	LATVIA	1833	144	HAITI	474
105	EL SALVADOR	1785	145	GUADELOUPE	467
106	HONDURAS	1773	146	UGANDA	467
107	COSTA RICA	1728	147	GUYANA	445
108	PANAMA	1644	148	MOZAMBIQUE	428
109	CÔTE D'IVOIRE	1560	149	CONGO	376
110	KYRGYZSTAN	1452	150	MARTINIQUE	366
111	SENEGAL	1320	151	GUINEA	365
112	TAJIKISTAN	1270	152	LAO PEOPLE'S DEMOCRATIC REPUBLIC	342
113	BRUNEI (DARUSSALAM)	1242	153	GABON	334
114	URUGUAY	1193	154	NIGER	329
115	PARAGUAY	1129	155	BARBADOS	325
116	BOTSWANA	1123	156	FIJI	305
117	GUAM	1114	157	BURKINA FASO	284
118	NETHERLAND ANTILLES	1106			

TABLE 2. (Continued)

Rank	Country	Total (thousand tons of carbon)
158	FRENCH GUIANA	274
159	SWAZILAND	261
160	MALAWI	241
161	BELIZE	213
162	AFGHANISTAN	192
163	ERITREA	191
164	FRENCH POLYNESIA	189
165	FAEROE ISLANDS	180
166	SIERRA LEONE	178
167	RWANDA	164
168	GREENLAND	155
169	MALI	151
170	SEYCHELLES	149
171	CAMBODIA	146
172	BERMUDA	136
173	LIBERIA	126
174	MALDIVES	121
175	ANTIGUA & BARBUDA	109
176	BHUTAN	105
177	DJIBOUTI	100
178	GIBRALTAR	99
179	SAINT LUCIA	89
180	CAYMAN ISLANDS	83
181	AMERICAN SAMOA	80
182	GAMBIA	77
183	GUINEA BISSAU	74
184	CENTRAL AFRICAN REPUBLIC	69
185	PALAU	66
186	WESTERN SAHARA	65
187	BURUNDI	64
188	GRENADA	60
189	ST. VINCENT & THE GRENADINES	53
190	SOLOMON ISLANDS	49
191	EQUATORIAL GUINEA	45
192	EAST TIMOR	44
193	SAMOA	41
194	CAPE VERDE	39
195	NAURU	39
196	DOMINICA	38
197	ST. KITTS–NEVIS	34

Rank	Country	Total (thousand tons of carbon)
198	CHAD	32
199	TONGA	31
200	SAO TOME & PRINCIPE	25
201	COMOROS	24
202	VANUATU	24
203	BRITISH VIRGIN ISLANDS	21
204	ST. PIERRE & MIQUELON	18
205	MONTSERRAT	17
206	FALKLAND ISLANDS (MALVINAS)	12
207	COOK ISLANDS	8
208	KIRIBATI	8
209	WAKE ISLAND	5
210	SAINT HELENA	3

SOURCE: Gregg Marland, Tom Boden, and Bob Andres; Oak Ridge National Laboratory

A technically difficult but very clearly written paper demonstrating the significance of terrestrial systems in balancing the current global carbon cycle.

Falkowski, P.G. "The Role of Phytoplankton Photosynthesis in Global Biogeochemical Cycles." *Photosynthesis Research* 39.3 (1994), 235–258. DOI: 10.1007/BF00014586. A good general overview of the role of marine biology in the carbon cycle.

"Global Fossil Fuel CO_2 Emissions." Carbon Dioxide Information and Analysis Center, Oak Ridge National Laboratory, Oak Ridge, Tenn. http://cdiac.ornl.gov/trends/emis/meth_reg.html (accessed May 23, 2008). The standard source for annual data on release of carbon dioxide.

Houghton, R.A. "Land-Use Change and the Global Carbon Cycle." *Global Change Biology* 1.4 (1995), 275–287. DOI: 10.1111/j.1365-2486.1995.tb00026.x. A recent and authoritative summary of the impact of land use change on atmospheric carbon dioxide.

Keeling, R.F., and S.R. Shertz. "Seasonal and Interannual Variations in Atmospheric Oxygen and Implications for the Global Carbon Cycle." *Nature* 358 (1992), 723–727. DOI: 10.1038/358723a0. A key paper that demonstrates the usefulness of atmospheric oxygen measurements in separating ocean and terrestrial uptake of fossil-fuel carbon dioxide.

Keeling, C.D., et al. "Interannual Extremes in the Rate of Rise of Atmospheric Carbon Dioxide Since 1980." *Nature* 375 (1995), 666–670. DOI: 10.1038/375666a0. A detailed look at variations in atmospheric carbon dioxide concentrations with interesting suggestions on what this variation can reveal about carbon cycle processes.

Sarmiento, J.L., and M. Bender. "Carbon Biogeochemistry and Climate Change." *Photosynthesis Research* 39.3 (1994), 209–234. DOI: 10.1007/BF00014585. A good and up-to-date scientific summary of our knowledge of the global carbon cycle, with an emphasis on ocean processes.

Schimel, D.S., et al. "Climatic, Edaphic, and Biotic Controls over Storage and Turnover of Carbon in Soils." *Global Biogeochemical Cycles* 8.3 (1994), 279–293. An example of the use of a soil process model to obtain an understanding of soil carbon dynamics at a global scale.

Schimel, D.S., et al. "The Global Carbon Cycle." In *Climate Change 1994*, edited by J.T. Houghton et al., pp. 35–71. Cambridge: Cambridge University Press, 1996. A comprehensive explanation.

—WILFRED M. POST

CARBON FOOTPRINT

The carbon footprint represents the emissions of carbon dioxide that can be attributed to a person, company, or other organization. The emissions are calculated from knowledge of the energy used directly in the residence and in transportation (roughly 40% of a personal total) and indirectly in products and services used. The units are either tons of carbon per year or tons of carbon dioxide per year.

A number of organizations—among them An Inconvenient Truth Carbon Calculator, BP Global, Carbon Footprint Limited, The Carbon Trust, U.S. Environmental Protection Agency, and World Resources Institute—provide through their websites simple worksheets for calculations.

CARBON OFFSETS

Some companies that provide worksheets for calculating carbon footprint also arrange for the person or company to offset the emissions by participating in one or more activities intended to reduce the concentration of carbon dioxide in the atmosphere. These include:

- Paying, through a broker, for projects that plant trees. Growth of these new trees will consume and sequester carbon dioxide, though the decay of the trees will ultimately release the carbon dioxide.
- Buying carbon credits in the emissions trading market, in effect retiring carbon offsets that would otherwise be purchased by companies to help them meet their emissions targets. [See Emissions Trading.]
- Supporting renewable energy projects, such as wind-electric farms, by purchasing renewable energy certificates.

CARBON-NEUTRAL

The term is applied to an activity whose carbon footprint is completely offset by CO_2-reducing projects. A celebrity, for instance, may organize an extravagant birthday party, calculate its footprint, then support a project or activity at a scale that just offsets all CO_2-producing aspects of the event, including travel by guests and fuel used in cooking. A home owner may takes steps to make his home carbon-neutral by conserving energy, and then using the above strategies to offset the reduced footprint of the building. The concept has been adopted by some communities such as Newcastle, England, and the planned demonstration city, Dongtan, China.

SKEPTICS

Some critics attack the use of offsets because it delays the needed focus on actually reducing emissions by fundamental changes in fuel use and in transportation practice. Others point out that trees planted in mid-latitudes have little effect on global warming because the slow-growing forest will enhance the absorption of solar radiation and negate the benefit of capturing carbon dioxide.

BIBLIOGRAPHY

"The Carbon Neutral Myth: Offset Indulgences for Your Carbon Sins." Amsterdam: Transnational Institute, 2007. http://www.carbontradewatch.org/pubs/carbon_neutral_myth.pdf (accessed May 23, 2008).

"Another Inconvenient Truth." BusinessWeek, March 26, 2007. http://www.businessweek.com/magazine/content/07_13/b4027057.htm (accessed May 23, 2008).

—DAVID J. CUFF

CARBON TAXES

There is currently no cost charged to emit carbon into the atmosphere. The result is that the atmosphere is used as a free dumping ground for carbon dioxide (CO_2) emissions. A carbon tax puts a price on these emissions by taxing the carbon content of fuels. A carbon tax is a classic example of a pollution or Pigovian tax designed to internalize the negative externalities of a market activity. [See Ecotaxation and Externalities.] Internalizing those costs provides a market signal that reflects the true costs to society of the activity and, to the extent the demand for the product or service is responsive to price, will result in a reduction in that demand. To the extent the demand is not fully responsive to price, the revenues from such a tax can be used to counteract the impact on society of the externalities. The revenues from the tax can be used to reduce taxes on other, more productive activities; thus, revenue-neutral pollution taxes are designed to tax a "bad" such as pollution, while reducing taxes on a "good" such as employment. Carbon taxes, based as they are on sound economic theory, are supported across partisan and ideological lines (Carbon Tax Center A).

The rationale for a carbon tax is simple: the levels of CO_2 already in the Earth's atmosphere and being added daily are destabilizing established climate patterns and threatening the ecosystems on which we and other living beings depend. Carbon is present in every fossil fuel—coal, oil and gas. It is the primary source of the heat released in fuel combustion, and essentially all of it is converted to CO_2 when the fuel is burned. [See Global Warming; Greenhouse Effect; and Impacts of Climate Change.]

A carbon tax will not by itself stop global climate change—other, synergistic, actions to remove institutional barriers to low-carbon alternatives are required as well. But without a carbon tax, even the most aggressive regulatory mandates (e.g., high-mileage cars) and "enlightened" subsidies (e.g., tax credits for energy-efficiency investments and renewable solar and wind power) will fall woefully short of the necessary reductions in carbon burning and emissions. For every activity subjected to under efficiency mandates, dozens of others will elude regulatory control, either through industry "gaming" or due to the creative unruliness of consumer capitalism, forever finding new ways to burn fuels. Conversely, charging a price for carbon dumping will encourage individuals, firms, and institutions to adopt all cost-effective means of eliminating such dumping.

HOW A CARBON TAX WORKS

Currently, the prices of gasoline, electricity and fuels in general include none of the costs associated with climate change. This omission suppresses incentives to develop and deploy carbon-reducing measures such as energy efficiency (e.g., high-mileage cars and high-efficiency heaters and air conditioners), renewable energy (e.g., wind turbines, solar panels), low-carbon fuels (e.g., biofuels from high-cellulose plants), and conservation-based behavior such as bicycling, recycling, and overall mindfulness of energy consumption. Conversely, taxing fuels according to their carbon content will inject these incentives into every chain of decision and action—from individuals' choices and uses of vehicles, appliances, and housing, to businesses' choices of new-product design, capital investment, and facilities location, and governments' choices in regulatory policy, land use, and taxation.

The carbon content of every form of fossil fuel, from anthracite to lignite coal, from residual oil to natural gas, is precisely known. So is the amount of CO_2 released into the atmosphere when the fuel is burned. A carbon tax thus presents few problems of documentation or measurement. Administering a carbon tax should be simple; using existing tax collection mechanisms, the tax would be paid far "upstream" (e.g., at the point where fuels are extracted from the Earth and put into the stream of commerce, or imported into the U.S.). Fuel suppliers and processors would pass along the cost of the tax to the extent that market conditions allow.

Per unit of energy (calorie or BTU) produced, natural gas emits the least CO_2 of any fossil fuel when burned, and coal the most, with petroleum products in an intermediate position. Generally, one BTU from coal produces 30% more carbon dioxide than a BTU from oil, and 80% more than one from natural gas. A carbon tax would follow these proportions, taxing coal somewhat more heavily than petroleum products, and much more heavily than natural gas.

To the extent that carbon is included in a product like plastic, but is not burned, that carbon should not be taxed. Similarly, if carbon released in electrical generation is permanently sequestered rather than being released to the atmosphere, it should not be taxed—or a tax credit should be provided.

REVENUE-NEUTRALITY

Many carbon-tax proponents advocate a revenue-neutral carbon tax. Revenue-neutral means that little if any of the tax revenues raised by taxing carbon emissions would be retained by government. The vast majority of the revenues would instead be returned to the American people, with some small amount used to mitigate the otherwise deleterious impacts of carbon taxes on low-income energy users.

Two primary revenue-return approaches are being discussed. One would rebate the revenues directly through regular (e.g., monthly) equal dividends to all U.S. residents. Just such a program has operated in Alaska for three decades, providing residents with annual dividends from the state's North Slope oil revenues (Carbon Tax Center B).

In the other method, each dollar of carbon-tax revenue would trigger a dollar's worth of reduction in existing taxes such as the federal payroll tax or state sales taxes (Carbon Tax Center B). As carbon-tax revenues are phased in (with the tax rates rising gradually but steadily, to allow a smooth transition), existing taxes will be phased out and, in some cases, eliminated. This "tax-shift" approach, while less direct than the dividend method, would also ensure that the carbon tax is revenue-neutral.

Each individual's receipt of dividends or tax-shifts would be independent of the taxes he or she pays; no person's benefits would be tied to his or her energy consumption and carbon tax "bill." This separation of benefits from payments preserves the incentives created by a carbon tax to reduce use of fossil fuels and emit less CO_2 into the atmosphere. Of course, it would be extraordinarily cumbersome to calculate an individual's full carbon tax bill since to some extent the carbon tax would be passed through as part of the costs of various goods and services.

Other proponents of a carbon tax argue that some or all of the carbon-tax revenues should be used to fund some combination of energy efficiency, renewable energy, and research and development into the new technologies necessary to phase out carbon-based energy. Other potential uses of carbon tax revenues are limitless, and include expanding public transportation, stabilizing Social Security funding, financing universal health care and addressing high-profile political concerns such as the burgeoning alternative minimum tax.

EQUITY CONSIDERATIONS

A carbon tax by itself is, like any flat tax, regressive. Keeping the tax revenue-neutral in a way that protects the less affluent can minimize the regressivity (Carbon Tax Center B). To the extent necessary, a portion of the carbon tax revenues can be used to mitigate the impact of a carbon tax on those with low incomes.

The operative fact is that wealthier households use more energy. They generally drive and fly more, have bigger (and sometimes multiple) houses, and buy more things that require energy to manufacture and use (Carbon Tax Center B). As a result, most carbon tax revenues will come from families of above-average means, along with corporations and government.

Because income and energy consumption are strongly correlated, most poor households will get more back in carbon dividends than they will pay in the carbon tax. The overall effect of a carbon tax-shift could be equitable and perhaps even "progressive" (benefiting lower-earning households).

CARBON TAXES VS. CAP-AND-TRADE

A tax on carbon emissions is not the only way to "put a price on carbon" and thereby provide incentives to reduce use of high-carbon fuels. A carbon cap-and-trade system is an alternative approach supported by some prominent politicians, corporations, and mainstream environmental groups, many of whom have joined the United States Climate Action Partnership (USCAP).

A cap-and-trade system imposes a cap on emissions of a particular pollutant, makes emissions allowances available up to the cap and requires that each entity that emits the pollutant hold an allowance for each unit (generally tons) of the pollutant emitted. Companies that need additional allowances to cover their emissions can buy allowances from companies that have more than they need. If the market works properly, those companies that can reduce emissions at the lowest cost will do so and sell their allowances to the companies with higher costs. In theory, the costs to society of reducing pollution are minimized. [See Emissions Trading.]

The fact that electric utility companies in the United States have had positive experiences with cap-and-trade systems for other pollutants does not necessarily mean that cap-and-trade is a good approach for carbon dioxide. While the U.S. sulfur dioxide cap-and-trade system instituted in the early 1990s does deserve some of the credit for efficiently reducing acid-rain emissions from power plants, comparing sulfur dioxide trading to carbon dioxide trading is comparing apples to oranges. The most fundamental difference is that there are no readily available "technical fixes" for filtering or capturing CO_2, whereas a variety of technical fixes were available to reduce sulfur dioxide, most obviously switching to lower sulfur coal and using "scrubbers" to reduce sulfur dioxide emissions from the exhaust stream of electric generating plants.

Carbon taxes are superior to a carbon cap-and-trade program for six fundamental reasons:

- Carbon taxes will lend predictability to energy prices. With carbon taxes increasing over a number of years, energy and power prices can be predicted with reasonable confidence well ahead of time. This will make it possible for millions of decisions—from the design of new electricity generating plants to the purchase of the family car to the materials used in commercial airframes—to be made with full knowledge of carbon-appropriate price signals. In contrast, a cap-and-trade program will increase the volatility of energy prices because the price of carbon allowances will fluctuate as weather and economic factors affect the demand for energy (Shapiro, 2007). For example, the clearing prices of sulfur dioxide allowances moved up or down an average of more than 43% a year between 1997 and 2006 and an average of more than 80% a year during the last three years of that period (Shapiro, 2007). Price volatility in the first 22 months of the European Emissions Trading Scheme has been even greater, with monthly price shifts averaging 17% (Shapiro, 2007). Such volatility is anathema to the business community and precludes rational decisions by energy consumers to address future costs. The vaunted advantage of cap-and-trade—that future levels of carbon emissions can be known—is mostly notional, moreover, because most cap-and-trade systems under discussion include a "safety-valve" for auctioning off additional carbon allowances if the price of allowances exceeds a preset level. And even certainty in future emission levels is of questionable value, because there is no agreed-upon trajectory of emissions for achieving climate stability and preventing disaster. The real target for which the U.S. must aim is to reduce carbon emissions as much as possible, and then more. The value of "emissions certainty" under cap-and-trade was deflated by a recent newspaper article (Financial Times, 2007): "[Carbon cap-and-trade systems] fix the amount of carbon abated, not its price. Getting the amount of emissions a little bit wrong in any year would hardly upset the global climate. But excessive volatility or unduly high prices of quotas on carbon emissions might disrupt the economy severely. [Carbon] taxes create needed certainty about prices, while markets in emission quotas [i.e., cap-and-trade systems] create unnecessary certainty about the short-term quantity of emissions."

- Carbon taxes can be designed and adopted quickly. Cap-and-trade systems, by contrast, are highly complex and will take years to develop and implement. Thorny issues must be addressed intellectually and resolved politically: the proper level of the cap, timing, allowance allocations, certification procedures, standards for use of offsets, penalties, regional conflicts, inevitable requests for exceptions by affected parties and a myriad of other complex issues must all be resolved before cap-and-trade systems can be implemented. During this time, polluters will continue to emit carbon at no cost.

- Carbon taxes are transparent and are easier to understand than cap-and-trade. In a carbon tax, the government simply imposes a tax per ton of carbon emitted, which is easily translated into a tax per kilowatt-hour of electricity, gallon of gasoline, or therm of natural gas. By contrast, the prices for carbon set under a cap-and-trade system will vary with market fluctuations and be impossible even for big business (let alone small businesses or consumers) to predict. A cap-and-trade system will require a complex and difficult-to-understand market structure in order to balance the many competing interests and ensure that the trading system minimizes abuse and maximizes real carbon reductions.

- A carbon tax's simplicity inoculates it against the perverse incentives and potential for profiteering that will accompany cap-and-trade. In contrast to the simple and straightforward process of implementing a carbon tax, the protracted negotiations necessary to implement a cap-and-trade system will provide constant opportunities for the fossil-fuel industry and other invested parties to shape a system that maximizes their financial self-interests as opposed to an economically efficient system that maximizes societal well-being. If allowances are allocated based on some type of baseline reflecting past pollution (which has been the practice with NO_x and SO_2 trading programs), rather than being auctioned, polluters will have perverse incentives to maximize emissions before the cap-and-trade system goes into effect in order to "earn" those pollution rights. The voluntary carbon cap-and-trade system currently operating has already been criticized for questionable offsets that have produced huge profits but little environmental benefit, as described in a recent newpaper article (*New York Times*, 2006).

- Carbon taxes target carbon emissions in all sectors—energy, industry and transportation—whereas at least some cap-and-trade proposals are limited to the electric industry. It would be unwise to ignore the non-electricity sectors that account for 60% of U.S. CO_2 emissions.

- Carbon taxes can be used to fund progressive tax-shifting to reduce regressive payroll or sales taxes. The costs of cap-and-trade systems, both implementation and the costs incurred as more expensive technologies replace coal-fired combustion, are far more likely to be imposed upon consumers with less possibility of rebating or tax-shifting. Moreover, because cap-and-trade relies on market participants to determine a fair price for carbon allowances on an ongoing basis, it could easily devolve into a self-perpetuating province of lawyers, economists, lobbyists, and other market participants bent on maximizing their profits on each cap-and-trade transaction. The dollars that will be funneled into making the market work could be better spent reducing regressive taxes, protecting poorer households and/or helping consumers use less energy.

NATIONAL VERSUS INTERNATIONAL ACTION

Opponents of unilaterally reducing greenhouse gas emissions point to negative economic consequences from adverse terms of trade. However, any such consequences can be minimized by maintaining a "level playing field" via border-tax adjustments (Pauwelyn, 2007). This applies to any unilateral effort to address emissions, whether carbon taxes, cap-and-trade, or fuel efficiency standards.

Opponents of unilateral action also claim that such actions would be futile, given the huge emissions increase expected from industrializing nations such as China and India. This argument ignores several critical points:

First, the United States and the European Community will continue to be the world's biggest contributors to climate change long after China, or even India, surpasses us in annual emissions. That's because carbon dioxide molecules, once emitted, remain "resident" in the atmosphere for approximately a century. After the many decades in which carbon emissions from the United States dwarfed everyone else's, more than three times as much of the CO_2 now warming the Earth is the product of American emissions as Chinese emissions, but China has now surpassed the U.S. in annual CO_2 emissions.

Second, developed countries such as the United States will still be dumping the most CO_2 into the atmosphere on a per capita basis for years to come. The average American is responsible for emitting as much CO_2 in a day as do people in developing countries in an entire workweek.

Third, just as climate naysayers here use China's inaction on carbon to justify U.S. inaction, so too are industry and government in China using our temporizing on carbon to rationalize theirs. Breaking this cycle should be easier for the United States, insofar as our per capita use of energy (and emissions of carbon) is so much greater than China's, and given our well-developed political and administrative institutions.

Last, while it is true that only concerted action by all the world's nations and peoples can meet the climate crisis head-on, it is equally true that every action that reduces carbon emissions helps protect and stabilize climate. The injunction that the perfect must not become the enemy of the good has never been so apt as it is here and now, in Earth's climate emergency.

EXISTING CARBON TAXES

Carbon taxes are presently in place in parts of Europe and are being considered by various governments. For an up-to-date list of jurisdictions with carbon taxes, see the Carbon Tax Center Web site (Carbon Tax Center C).

[*See also* Energy Strategies *and* Stabilizing Carbon Emissions.]

BIBLIOGRAPHY

"Carbon Markets Create a Muddle." *Financial Times*, April 26, 2007.
Carbon Tax Center A. "Supporters." http://www.carbontax.org/who-supports (accessed May 24, 2008). A list of supporters of a carbon tax.
Carbon Tax Center B. "Managing Impacts." http://www.carbontax.org/issues/softening-the-impact-of-carbon-taxes (accessed May 24, 2008).
Carbon Tax Center C. "Where Carbon Is Taxed." http://www.carbontax.org/progress/where_carbon-is-taxed (accessed May 24, 2008).
Metcalf, G. "A Green Employment Tax Swap: Using a Carbon Tax to Finance Payroll Tax Relief." World Resources Institute. http://www.wri.org/publication/green-employment-tax-swap (accessed May 24, 2008).
"Outsize Profits, and Questions, in Effort to Cut Warming Gases." *New York Times*, December 21, 2006.
Pauwelyn, J. "U.S. Federal Climate Policy and Competitiveness Concerns: The Limits and Options of International Trade Law." Nicholos Institute for Environmental Policy Solutions, Duke University (April 2007). http://www.nicholas.duke.edu/institute (accessed May 24, 2008).
Shapiro, R. "Addressing the Risks of Climate Change: The Environmental Effectiveness and Economic Efficiency of Emissions Caps and Tradable Permits, Compared to Carbon Taxes." American Consumer Institute (February 2007). http://www.theamericanconsumer.org/shapiro.pdf (accessed May 24, 2008).

—DANIEL ROSENBLUM

CARRYING CAPACITY

That resource limits, including geographical space, set the maximum population size of a species was conventional wisdom at one time in ecology and maintains varying degrees of currency (for example, in conservation biology and ecological economics). Such relationships are referred to as "carrying capacity" and are measured by the number of an organism that can be supported by the requisite renewable resources of the environment. It would be a mistake, however, to assume that the application of the carrying-capacity concept to human-environment relationships was borrowed directly from the modern science of ecology. Phrased differently, the antecedents of its applications to human populations are old, traced back in western thought at least to the seminal population-resource theory of Thomas Robert Malthus's *An Essay on the Principle of Population* (1798)—that the technology of food production within a given environment, an assumed closed system—limits the numbers to which a human population can grow. Beyond these limits and without a change in technology, the resource base collapses, the environment degrades, and a Malthusian crisis ensues (Coleman and Schofield, 1986).

The application of the carrying-capacity concept to humans advanced to the forefront of research at least twice in the latter half of the twentieth century. The mid-1960s through the 1970s witnessed the first phase of interest, stimulated by two different research interests—cultural ecology and global population growth—that drew on ideas emanating from ecology, systems theory, and precursors to ecological economics. Cultural ecology emerged as a subfield of anthropology and geography and studied differences in the uses of land and other resources and the level of social and cultural development through the lens of the human-environment relationship. Global population concerns, in contrast, drew attention from diverse communities—not only the academic—which was focused on the then doubling of the world population to four billion and alarm about the ability of humankind to feed, clothe, and shelter its rapidly growing numbers.

Population-growth experts attempted to assess the carrying capacity of the earth at large (Meadows et al., 1972) and of regions and countries. These assessments projected that some areas would exceed their limits and experience Malthusian crises. Cultural ecologists, in contrast, used the concept less ambitiously, typically in terms of small areas and in reference to nonwestern peoples tied to subsistence livelihoods (Brush, 1975). In both cases, several concepts were common to various nomenclatures, definitions, and uses of carrying capacity: the native quality of a bounded unit of land (the environment); the resource response to a given set of technologies and use-strategies; and the maximum number of people sustainable in the environment. Conceptually, technology and use-strategies were thought to determine the quality and quantity of resources from a given environment; if they changed, so did the carrying capacity (Solow, 1970). This nod to human ingenuity was often lost in application, however, and some assessments of critical population densities were reduced to the basic environmental qualities of an area, raising the specter of environmental determinism.

Interest in carrying capacity waned during the late 1970s. Cultural ecology exhausted the reach of the concept's usefulness for understanding land-use change and cultural development; the fluidity of carrying capacity in regard to changing human-environment relationships was largely recognized; and attention turned to the issue of social structures that shaped the relationships. The global-population community's interest faded temporarily for several reasons. Famine (Malthusian crisis) was reinterpreted as having its origins in the political economy, not resource technology; the green revolution increased food production significantly through hybrid species; and, with the worldwide expansion of family planning, public attention moved toward economic development.

Finally, the concept implied an apparent internal contradiction: carrying capacity expanded or contracted as technology and resource use changed (Cohen, 1995). The principle of the substitutability of resources was difficult to refute, either historically or theoretically (Solow, 1970). If substitutions were exogenous or random in origin, then carrying capacity had a fallback position in terms of momentary capacities. Various works, however, demonstrated the role of endogenous technological change (Boserup, 1965; Turner and Ali, 1996) and the increasing diminution of geographical insularity because of the flows of energy, material, knowledge, and power across regions. Without this insularity and with endogenous technological change, what was the usefulness of carrying capacity?

The 1990s witnessed a second cycle of interest in carrying capacity, this time as embedded in the complementary concepts of sustainable development and global environmental change. These linkages purport to change the meaning of carrying capacity by shifting the processes and outcomes of concern and, as a result, the temporal and spatial scales of assessment (e.g., Brown and Kane, 1994; Daily and Ehrlich, 1992). Sustainable development and global environmental change increasingly refocus on the rights of future generations to experience existing nature—for example, biota, landscapes, and air quality—and to use the biosphere without endangering its structures and functions. In this view, worldwide access to high standards of consumption and quality of life must be met without endangering the ability of the biosphere to provide the life-support systems for humankind (Arrow et al., 1995) and, among deep ecologists, for nonhuman species.

In this iteration, carrying capacity focuses on critical flows of the biosphere, such as the carbon and nitrogen cycles, or on potential losses for humankind of biotic and habitat diversity (Vitousek et al., 1997). Changes in biogeochemical flows disrupt the state of the biosphere, with potential harmful consequences—for example, an atmosphere that permits ultraviolet radiation to penetrate to the Earth's surface unabated threatens biota with excessive levels of radiation and carries significant health implications for humans. Loss in biotic and ecosystem diversity, it is argued, constitutes losses of genetic stock and the resilience of nature to respond to perturbations.

The problems of substitution and geographical boundedness are challenged in this new version of carrying capacity (Daily and Ehrlich, 1992). Critical states and flows, at least by implication, are thought to be largely unsubstitutable and operate at global rather than local scales. Exogenous flows at the level of the biosphere are reduced by some to incoming solar radiation, funneled through human appropriation of net primary productivity, for example (Vitousek et al., 1997). Places and regions differ in their roles as sources and recipients of global change, and in their abilities to respond to change. They are, however, recognized as connected and their "carrying capacities" calculated through such measures as "ecological footprints" (Rees and Wackernagel, 1994). This change in usage may alleviate the problems inherent in the former meaning of carrying capacity, but it raises new criticisms, largely of a political nature. Reformulated in this way, it is suggested by some that the economically developed world seeks to assert a new kind of authority over the remainder of the world, potentially retarding development elsewhere.

The carrying-capacity principle remains in the cycle of interest that began in the 1990s. Other versions will no doubt emerge in future cycles. Its staying power rests in its centrality to the ultimate human-environment questions. Does the environment ultimately set limits on humankind? Or, can human ingenuity restructure nature as needed for human use? These questions and carrying capacity are central to the tensions surrounding the emergence of ecological economics and attempts to calculate the economic value of the biosphere (Costanza et al., 1997; Pearce, 1998).

[*See also* Agriculture and Agricultural Land; *and* Sustainable Growth.]

BIBLIOGRAPHY

Arrow, K., et al. "Economic Growth, Carrying Capacity, and the Environment." *Science* 268 (1995), 520–521. DOI: 10.1126/science.268.5210.520. An interdisciplinary view of carry-capacity applied to resource consumption in general.

Boserup, E. *The Conditions of Agricultural Growth*. Chicago: Aldine, 1965. The watershed argument that population determines the intensity of cultivation and behavior rationale for nonmarket farmers.

Brown, L.R., and H. Kane. *Full House: Reassessing the Earth's Population Carrying Capacity*. New York: Norton, 1994. A reassessment of global carrying capacity including damage to biosphere.

Brush, S.B. "The Concept of Carrying Capacity for Systems of Shifting Cultivation." *American Anthropologist*, n.s., 77.4 (1975), 799–811. A review of the meaning and use of carrying capacity in anthropology and the interdisciplinary field of cultural ecology.

Cohen, J.E. "Population Growth and Earth's Human Carrying Capacity." *Science* 269 (1995), 341–346. DOI: 10.1525/aa.1975.77.4.02a00040. A perspective questioning the presumed negative role of population growth on resources.

Coleman, D., and R. Schofield, eds. *The State of Population Theory: Forward From Malthus*. Oxford: Blackwell, 1986. A state-of-the-art review of population-resource relationships in demography and economics.

Costanza, R., et al. "The Value of the World's Ecosystem Services and Natural Capital." *Nature* 387 (1997), 253–260. An incipient attempt to place a monetary value on the biosphere. DOI: doi: 10.1038/387253a0.

Daily, G.C., and P.R. Ehrlich. "Population, Sustainability, and Earth's Carrying Capacity." *Bioscience* 42 (1992), 761–771. An update of the view that population and economic growth stress Earth resources.

Malthus, T.R. *An Essay on the Principle of Population*. London: J. Johnson, 1798.

Meadows, D.H., et al. *The Limits to Growth*. New York: Signet Books, 1972. A classic, controversial work attempting to model the global carrying capacity.

Pearce, D. "Auditing the Earth." *Environment* 40 (1998), 23–28. A neoclassical economist responds to attempts to place a value on the biosphere.

Rees, W.E., and M. Wackernagel. "Ecological Footprints and Appropriated Carrying Capacity: Measuring the Natural Capacity Requirements of the Human Economy." In *Investing in Natural Capital: The Ecological Economics Approach to Sustainability*, edited by A. Jansson, et al., pp. 362–390.

Washington, D.C.: Island Press, 1994. A methodology for assessing the environmental reach of consumption patterns in cities.

Solow, R.M. *Growth Theory: An Exposition*. New York: Oxford University Press, 1970. A neoclassical economic view of the economic implications of growth.

Turner, B.L., II, and A.M. Shajaat Ali. "Induced Intensification: Agricultural Change in Bangladesh with Implications for Malthus and Boserup." *Proceedings of the National Academy of Sciences* 93 (1996), 14,984–14,991. An elaboration of the applicability of a Boserupian model of agricultural change.

Vitousek, P.M., et al. "Human Domination of Earth's Ecosystems." *Science* 277 (1997), 494–499. DOI: 10.1126/science.277.5325.494. Ecologists' view of the human transformation of the Earth.

—B. L. TURNER II AND ERIC G. KEYS

CATASTROPHIST-CORNUCOPIAN DEBATE

"Catastrophist" and "cornucopian" are relatively neutral and descriptive names for two opposite points of view on the meaning and consequences of global environmental change and on relations between nature and society more generally. Synonyms for "catastrophist" are "ecocentric," "pessimist," "doomsday," "neo-Malthusian," and "Cassandra", and for "cornucopian," "technocentric," "optimist," "Polyanna," and "human exemptionalist."

The catastrophist maintains that there are natural limits to human exploitation and transformation of the Earth that cannot be transgressed without disaster and that the current scale and rate of human activity already exceed the globe's carrying capacity, defined as the maximum demand it can support without lessening the demand that it will be able to support in the future. The cornucopian dismisses human carrying capacity as a meaningless concept. It holds that human ingenuity and adaptation through technological and social responses, not natural limits, set the boundaries of human wealth and well-being. It envisions no resource shortage or pollution problem with which society cannot cope. In interpreting the history of human-environment relations, catastrophists emphasize the rise in human numbers, levels of consumption, and environmental transformation as evidence that pressures on the terrestrial environment are mounting to dangerous levels that threaten humankind's survival. Cornucopians point to rising human numbers, levels of consumption, and life expectancy as evidence of overall and steadily increasing success in the use and management of the Earth.

In academic debate, the catastrophist position is associated most strongly with the natural and especially the biological sciences, while cornucopianism usually finds its home in the social sciences, especially economics; there are many exceptions to both rules. Orthodox Western economics has long been called "the dismal science" for its insistence on the scarcity of everything and the costlessness of nothing. It is paradoxical that in the realm of environment and resources it is economists who have emerged as the voices of optimism and the questioners of limits to human expansion and well-being. Yet it also was an economic theorist, though a heterodox one in later terms, who offered the first compelling version of the pessimistic view.

THE IDEAS OF MALTHUS

Catastrophists and cornucopians, who agree on little else, generally concur that the work of the English clergyman and political economist Thomas Robert Malthus (1766–1834) was the starting point of the controversy. Malthus was not the first to question the adequacy of the Earth's resources to meet human demands, but his classic formulation of the problem had a profound influence on later debate.

When he first published *An Essay on the Principle of Population* (1798), Malthus was reacting to the confidence expressed by certain thinkers of his time who held the future of the human race to be one of unlimited progress in material well-being. Malthus responded with a model, famous in its own time and ever since, of the relation between population and food supply. It assumed an inherent human drive toward procreation, which ensured that numbers would always tend to increase more rapidly than the means of subsistence could be increased. Whereas population can grow geometrically by multiplication, food supply, Malthus assumed, could grow only arithmetically by the piecemeal cultivation of new lands; hence food supply will always limit the size and material welfare of the human population. This model formed the basis for a gloomy view of the human future which would consist not of a steady increase in the numbers of people enjoying ever higher levels of health, wealth, and happiness, but of population always approaching the limits of bare subsistence, its growth ever checked by one of the two means Malthus recognized, misery and vice.

The arguments of the *Essay* differ in several ways from those of modern environmental catastrophists. Malthus saw crises of subsistence not as a looming future consequence of excessive growth but as a factor constantly in operation, something that had always been a part of human life and always would be. He did not directly address environmental change as a constraint on growth in human population and wealth. He was not concerned with land degradation as it might affect food supply. In common with other political economists of his time, he treated the power of the soil to produce food as no more subject to degradation than to dramatic improvement. The ultimate problem for him was that the land and its productivity were finite. His importance for debates over environmental change stems from the broader message of his *Essay* and the compelling way in which he depicted the Earth's limited resources for its human inhabitants.

Malthusian reasoning was extended to the area of soil fertility and land exhaustion at the end of the nineteenth century by the British physicist Sir William Crookes (1832–1919). In a famous address to the British Association for the Advancement of Science in 1898 and in subsequent writings, he warned that the depletion of soil nutrients, especially nitrates, must eventually curb the world's food supply when the supply of mined nitrate fertilizers gave out. Crookes, however, is an ambiguous figure, as much hopeful cornucopian as worried catastrophist. He looked forward to a solution in the form of an efficient process for synthesizing fertilizers from atmospheric nitrogen, one that was indeed developed within a few years of his warning. By means of this and other advances, including agricultural mechanization and the breeding and dissemination of high-yield grain varieties, Malthus was, in a strict sense, proven wrong. Population expanded greatly during the twentieth century, but it was fed through dramatic increases in the output of land rather than through an equal expansion of the cultivated area.

New concerns, however, arose over soil erosion, the spread of deserts, and other forms of land degradation. A conservation movement that developed around the turn of the century in several countries blended concern over land degradation with the fear that a growing scarcity of natural resources such as energy and minerals would be a constraint on economic growth. It argued for regulation to ensure that such resources were not squandered but exploited for the maximum benefit of future generations. *The Coal Question* (1865) by the English economist William Stanley Jevons (1835–1882) was a classic early statement of this position. Variants of it appeared in the writings of a number of late-nineteenth- and early-twentieth-century theorists who proposed an economics based on energy rather than on monetary calculations. Conservationists' warnings about growing resource scarcity were countered by an influential set of studies published by the U.S. research institute Resources for the Future in the early 1960s. They showed that the real prices of key nonrenewable resources had not risen over time, as often predicted, but declined. To account for this result, the researchers proposed that early signs of scarcity stimulate a search for new sources, for substitutes, and for more efficient techniques of use, so that over the long run, abundance is likelier to increase than to diminish.

LIMITS TO GROWTH

The modern phase of the debate has seen both the catastrophist case and the cornucopian rebuttal extended to cover a wide range of human-induced environmental changes such as air, water, and soil pollution, species loss, and climate change. It has also seen a new emphasis on the possibility of comprehensive global-scale disaster brought on by the transgression of natural limits. *The Limits to Growth* (Meadows et al., 1972) brought the catastrophist perspective to wide public attention. It presented the results of a computer simulation of the world system that showed exponential growth in population and industrial output overwhelming within a century the earth's capacity to furnish food and nonrenewable resources and absorb pollutants. *Models of Doom* (Cole et al., 1973) promptly criticized *The Limits to Growth* for ignoring many processes—such as the adoption of substitutes and remedial and regulatory measures, the identification of new resources, and the more efficient use of resources as they become scarce—by which crises of supply and pollution are averted once they begin to develop.

Disagreements about how well these mechanisms work have been at the center of the debate ever since. The question of how far ingenuity can create substitutes for lost or degraded natural resources has been treated as a fundamental one in the new field of ecological economics. This field has many affinities with the catastrophist position in seeing many natural resources and services as unique and indispensable. Orthodox neoclassical economic analysis, on the other hand, echoes the cornucopian view of natural resources and services as themselves creations of human ingenuity and replaceable by further ingenuity should they grow scarce in their existing form. Cornucopians tend to regard natural inputs as merely one form of capital, for which nonnatural capital can be substituted. Ecological economists view many forms of natural capital as irreplaceable or at least very costly to replace and condemn as unsustainable growth that does not maintain natural capital undiminished. Differences in methodology reflect these conflicting assumptions. Catastrophists see measures of cost, scarcity, and efficiency as the best standards. Cornucopians prefer social measures, particularly market prices, as indicators of abundance or scarcity. Because of the tendency of markets to discount future values heavily in comparison to present consumption, catastrophists, far more than cornucopians, favor the use of lower-than-market discount rates when calculating the costs and benefits of conservation and preservation, particularly when the possibility exists of irreversible change or loss.

HUMAN POPULATIONS

The two sides take similarly opposed positions on many other questions of policy. Both profess concern for the well-being of future human generations while disagreeing as to what course of action in the present will bequeath a better world to them. Catastrophists see unrestrained growth in population, resource demand, and waste emissions as the chief problem. They therefore advocate limiting human numbers and resource use to levels that will be sustainable over the long term. A steady-state economy (a concept elaborated by the economist Herman Daly) holds out the hope that innovation will enable growth in affluence that depends not on greater resource consumption but on more efficient and economical use of a limited flow of material and energy. More rational planning guided by the "precautionary principle"—that society should proceed cautiously with a risky endeavor even when no cause-and-effect relationship has been positively established—is required in order to keep within environmental limits human activities that, unchecked, threaten to violate those boundaries with catastrophic consequences. Market mechanisms, even when operating perfectly, do not take account of such consequences and cannot alone be trusted to avert them. A key role is thus envisioned for state and society as custodians of the long-term interests of humankind. Uncontrolled technological development and affluence in the form of higher material consumption are viewed with suspicion.

Cornucopians see the problems, threats, and challenges of resource depletion and environmental degradation as largely self-correcting through the workings of markets and human creativity, if those operations are not unduly interfered with. If hubris and unregulated growth are, for catastrophists, the greatest dangers in human-environment relations, it is for cornucopians fear itself that is the greatest threat. What the catastrophist sees as necessary responses to impending crisis, the cornucopian believes that those responses hinder the very processes that can bring solutions while they raise the general quality of life. Where problems have not corrected themselves, it is because adaptation has been obstructed. The remedy is to remove the obstacles, such as excessive state regulation, that have prevented its smooth functioning. Planning for sustainability should be viewed with suspicion, excessive and stifling precaution avoided, individual decisions left as free as possible, and market transactions and private property rights expanded to ensure rational outcomes. Population, termed by the cornucopian economist Julian Simon "the ultimate resource," is part of the solution rather than the problem. Growth in human numbers increases the stock of knowledge and skills. Affluence likewise is viewed positively, as increasing demand for improved environmental quality and providing the means to achieve it.

CONCERNS OF THE TWENTY-FIRST CENTURY

Natural disasters such as earthquakes, tsunamis, volcanic eruptions, and asteroid impacts engage some thinkers, but the majority seem focused on human influence on the environment and on security.

The possible depletion of nonrenewable resources (i.e., minerals and fossil fuels) continues to be a matter of debate, although there is growing consensus that conventional crude-oil production will peak well before the middle of the twenty-first century. [See Crude Oil Supply and Resources.] The renewable resources—biodiversity, ecosystems, agricultural land, water supply, the oceans, human health and prosperity—are threatened, as before, by increasing population and growing affluence. Assessments such as the annual State of the World review published by Worldwatch Institute and United Nations Environment Programme (UNEP) provide a basis for agreement, but authors still differ on the severity of environmental problems and especially on the possibility of global warming which could so drastically constrain economic growth and damage the prospects for greater equality among nations.

Aside from resources, there are two twenty-first-century concerns that, while not engendering much debate, are at the fore in some pessimistic evaluations of the future—proliferation of nuclear and biological weapons and persistent spread of religious extremism and terrorist attacks around the globe.

BIBLIOGRAPHY

BASIC REFERENCES

Bailey, R., ed. The True State of the Planet. New York: Free Press, 1995. One of two collections (see Simon, below) of essays viewing a wide range of environmental issues from the cornucopian perspective.

Cole, H.S.D., et al. Models of Doom: A Critique of The Limits to Growth. New York: Universe Books, 1973.

Costanza, R., ed. Ecological Economics: The Science and Management of Sustainability. New York: Columbia University Press, 1991. A good collection of readings.

Ehrlich, P.R., and A.H. Ehrlich. The Betrayal of Science and Reason: How Anti-Environmental Rhetoric Threatens Our Future. Washington, D.C.: Island Press, 1996.

Hardin, G. *Living within Limits: Ecology; Economics, and Population Taboos.* New York: Oxford University Press, 1993. A forceful statement of many of the tenets of the catastrophist position.

Malthus, T.R. *An Essay on the Principle of Population.* New York: Oxford University Press, 1999. Available in many modern reprints.

Meadows, D.H., et al. *The Limits to Growth.* New York: Universe Books, 1972.

Simon, J.L, and H. Kahn. *The Resourceful Earth: A Response to Global 2000.* Oxford and New York: Blackwell, 1984.

Simon, J.L., ed. *The State of Humanity.* Oxford: Blackwell, 1996. One of two collections (see Bailey, above) of essays applying the cornucopian perspective to a wide range of environmental issues.

FURTHER READING

Begley, S. "The Truth About Denial." *Newsweek,* August 13, 2007. The author traces the history of statements denying the human role in global warming, and explores the roles of oil and coal industry organizations in promoting skepticism.

Deffeyes, K.S. *Hubbert's Peak: The Impending World Oil Shortage.* Princeton, N.J.: Princeton University Press, 2001.

Flannery, T.F. *The Weather Makers.* London: Allen Lane; New York: Atlantic Monthly Press, 2005.

Gore, A. *An Inconvenient Truth: The Planetary Emergency of Global Warming and What We Can Do About It.* Emmaus, Pa.: Rodale Books, 2006.

Grant, L. *The Collapsing Bubble: Growth and Fossil Energy.* Cabin John, Md.: Seven Locks Press, 2005. Asks how many people can be sustained at an acceptable standard by the energy sources available after the transition from fossil fuels.

Halpern, P. *Countdown to Apocalypse: A Scientific Exploration of the End of the World.* New York: Basic Books, 2000. Focuses on natural events.

Horner, C. *The Politically Incorrect Guide to Global Warming and Environmentalism.* Washington, D.C.: Regnery, 2007. Unabashed right-wing view, opposing government intervention.

Huber, P., and M. Mills. *The Bottomless Well: The Twilight of Fuel, the Virtue of Waste, and Why We Will Never Run Out of Energy.* New York: Basic Books, 2005. Expressing faith in technologies, especially nuclear.

Jaccard, M. *Sustainable Fossil Fuels: The Unusual Suspect in the Quest for Clean and Enduring Energy.* Cambridge and New York: Cambridge University Press, 2006.

Kolbert, E. *Field Notes from a Catastrophe: Man, Nature, and Climate Change.* London and New York: Bloomsbury, 2006.

Kunstler, J.H. *The Long Emergency: Surviving the End of Oil, Climate Change, and Other Converging Catastrophes of the Twenty-First Century.* New York: Grove Press, 2005.

Leeb, S. *The Coming Economic Collapse: How You Can Thrive When Oil Costs $200 a Barrel.* New York: Warner Business Books, 2006.

Linden, E. *The Winds of Change: Climate, Weather, and the Destruction of Civilizations.* New York: Simon and Schuster, 2006.

Lomborg, B. *Cool It: The Skeptical Environmentalist's Guide to Global Warming.* New York: Knopf, 2007.

Lovelock, J. *The Revenge of Gaia: Earth's Climate in Crisis and the Fate of Humanity.* New York: Basic Books, 2006. Lovelock, author of the Gaia Hypothesis, argues for nuclear fission as a bridge to sustainable energy sources and possibly to fusion power.

McBay, A. *Peak Oil Survival: Preparation for Life After Gridcrash.* Guilford, Conn.: The Lions Press, 2006.

McGuire, B. *A Guide to the End of the World: Everything You Never Wanted to Know.* Oxford and New York: Oxford University Press, 2004. Includes global warming.

Michaels, P.J. ed. *Shattered Consensus: The True State of Global Warming.* Lanham, Md.: Rowan and Littlefield, 2005. A collection of articles by Michaels and 9 others.

Pearce, F. *When the Rivers Run Dry: Water, the Defining Crisis of the Twenty-First Century,* Boston, Mass.: Beacon Press, 2006. Science journalist and editor, Pearce provides a remarkable tour of world areas where mismanagement of water is leading to crisis.

Pfeiffer, D.A. *Eating Fossil Fuels: Oil, Food, and the Coming Crisis in Agriculture.* Gabriola Island, B.C.: New Society Publishers, 2006.

Rees, M. *Our Final Hour: A Scientist's Warning: How Terror, Error, and Environmental Disaster Threaten Humankind's Future in This Century.* New York: Basic Books, 2004. Britain's Astronomer Royal gives civilization a 50% chance of surviving to 2100.

Roberts, Paul, *The End of Oil: On the Edge of a Perilous New World.* Boston, Mass.: Houghton Mifflin, 2005.

Simmons, M.R. *Twilight in the Desert: The Coming Saudi Oil Shock and the World Economy.* Hoboken, N.J.: Wiley, 2005.

Singer, S.F., and Avery, D.T. *Unstoppable Global Warming: Every 1,500 Years.* Lanham, Md: Rowman & Littlefield, 2007. Identifying natural cycles, benign and unstoppable.

Speth, J. G. *Red Sky at Morning: America and the Crisis of the Global Environment.* New Haven, Conn.: Yale University Press, 2004. See *Companion's* Appendix for Speth's "Resources for Citizens."

Tertzakian, P. *A Thousand Barrels a Second: The Coming Oil Break Point and the Challenges Facing an Energy-Dependent World.* New York: McGraw-Hill, 2006.

—WILLIAM B. MEYER AND DAVID J. CUFF

CAUSES OF CLIMATE CHANGE

Any explanation of the complex process of climate change must start with the ways in which the input of solar radiation into Earth's atmosphere can fluctuate (Anderson et al., 2007). The receipt of that radiation will be affected by the position of the Earth with respect to the Sun and by such factors as the amount of intervening interstellar dust. Once the radiation reaches the atmosphere its passage to the surface of Earth is controlled by the gases (including water vapor) and particulate matter (e.g., aerosols) in the air. These materials may be natural or man-made. The incoming radiation will be absorbed or reflected according to the reflectivity of the surface. [*See* Albedo.] The effect of the received radiation on climate also depends on the distribution and altitude of land masses and oceans. Continents may move to or from areas where ice-caps might accumulate, mountain belts may grow or subside and affect world wind-belts and local climates, and the arrangement of climatically important ocean currents may be controlled by changes in the depths of sills separating basins and by the width of the seas, oceans, and channels. The situation is complicated by feedback loops within and between the ocean, atmosphere, and land systems.

SOLAR RADIATION

Changes in the absorption of solar radiation at Earth's surface should cause changes in climate. [*See* Solar Variability and Climate Stability.] The Sun's radiation changes in quantity (associated with those intriguing blemishes on the face of the Sun, the sun-spots) and in quality (through changes in the ultraviolet portion of the solar spectrum). The problem is to establish causal connections between solar changes and changes in Earth's climate.

Short-term solar-activity cycles have been established, especially those with periods of 11 and 22 years. Cycles with periods of 80–90 years have also been postulated. One difficulty with solar-radiation hypotheses is the small range of solar-irradiance change associated with sunspot cycles. For instance, measurements of the solar constant (the rate at which solar energy impinges on a unit area at the top of the earth's atmosphere) over the most recent 22-year solar cycle indicate a variation of only 0.1% around the mean (Crowley and Kim, 1993) and through the Little Ice Age up to the present, variation has probably not exceeded 0.25%. Models suggest that even a 0.5% reduction in the solar constant would cause directly a cooling of only about 0.5°C (Rind and Overpeck, 1993). It is therefore necessary to invoke a variety of feedback mechanisms and nonlinear responses to explain the correlations between solar cycles and climate (see Stuiver and Brazinuas, 1993). For example, Svensmark and Friis-Christensen (1997) proposed that cooling associated with reduced solar radiation is amplified by the associated increase in the cosmic-ray flux which enhances cloud formation, thereby increasing planetary albedo.

Sunspot observations also give a measure of solar activity. A striking feature of the record is the near absence of sunspots between 1640 and 1710 CE (the Maunder Minimum). It is perhaps significant that this minimum occurred during some of the coldest years of the Little Ice Age (Shindell et al., 2001). Over a longer time-scale it is more difficult to show that the sun's output of radiation has changed sufficiently to affect the Earth's climate. However, some evidence comes from studies of the oscillation in the concentration of atmospheric carbon-14, which in turn depends partly upon variation in the emission of solar radiation (Magny, 1993; Karlén and Kuylenstierna, 1996).

ATMOSPHERIC TRANSPARENCY

The effects of incoming solar radiation may have been moderated by changes in the composition of Earth's atmosphere, especially of aerosols of various types, though there has been debate over whether they cause changes in temperature (Ramanathan et al., 2007). [See Aerosols.]

Volcanic dust may also play a role (see Chester, 1988). Greater amounts of dust in the atmosphere could increase the backscattering of incoming radiation, thus encouraging cooling. In addition, volcanic dust might further reduce solar gain by promoting cloudiness, because dust particles, by acting as nuclei, can promote the formation of ice crystals in subfreezing air saturated with water vapor. Emissions of sulfur dioxide gas from eruptions may also affect climate. This gas is converted into tiny sulfuric acid droplets which can block incoming radiation and so reduce atmospheric temperatures (Bluth et al., 1993).

The Toba super-eruption in Sumatra (ca. 73,500 BP) was so large that it created a dense stratospheric dust pall and aerosol clouds. A "volcanic winter" (Rampino and Self, 1992) may have accelerated the shift to the glacial conditions of the last ice age that was already under way, by inducing perennial snow cover and increased sea-ice extent in sensitive northern latitudes.

The ash emissions of Krakatoa in the 1880s and Katmai in 1912 produced a global decrease in solar radiation of 10 to 20% for one to two years, and many of the coldest and wettest summers recorded in Britain occurred at times of abundant volcanic dust in the stratosphere and upper atmosphere (Lamb, 1971). Moreover, the period of warming in the 1920s to 1960s coincides with a period when there were no major volcanic eruptions in the Northern Hemisphere, suggesting the possibility that the absence of a volcanic-dust pall in those decades was one factor in the warming process. [See Twentieth-Century Climatic Change.] More recent volcanic eruptions have also

caused short-term cooling (e.g., the eruption of Mount Pinatubo in the Philippines in 1991 [McCormick et al., 1995]).

A notable postglacial eruption was that of Thera (Santorini) in the Aegean shortly before 1600 BCE. (Friedrich et al., 2006). This devastated the Minoan civilization and caused significant cooling across the Northern Hemisphere. This cooling has been detected in the narrow growth rings of fossil Irish oak dating to the time of the eruption (Baillie and Munro, 1988). There were also two large postglacial eruptions of Hekla in Iceland (Hekla 3 between 1100 and 1200 BCE and Hekla 4 about 2300 BCE) which may have caused cooling across northwestern Europe.

Changes in atmospheric transparency might also be caused by desert dust or dust generated from glacial-outwash plains injected into the atmosphere by wind deflation of fine-grained surface materials. Such particles exert both direct and indirect influences on climate. One direct influence is the effect that dust has on radiation budgets. Indirect influences include those caused by the effects of dust on biogeochemical cycling (Moreno and Canals, 2004) and carbon dioxide levels in the atmosphere.

Radiative forcing by dust is complex (Tegen, 2003), because dust not only scatters but also absorbs incoming solar radiation, and also absorbs and emits outgoing long-wave radiation. Changes in the amount of dust in the atmosphere would cause changes in the radiation balance and thus also in surface temperatures, but the magnitude and even the sign of the resulting temperature change are uncertain (Arimoto, 2001). There is no clear consensus whether increased atmospheric dust during the Last Glacial Maximum might have caused either cooling or warming (e.g., Claquin et al., 2003). In addition, it is possible that dust additions to ice caps and glaciers could modify their albedo, leading to changes in their radiation budgets. Likewise, dust stimulation of phytoplankton production releases DMS (dimethyl sulfide) which may increase cloud albedo and so contribute to cooling. Dust loadings may be correlated with changes in atmospheric CO_2. Ridgwell (2002), for example, has argued that dust may affect climate by fertilizing ocean biota which remove CO_2 from the atmosphere, which in turn reduces the greenhouse effect.

Dust nuclei may modify clouds. Rosenfeld et al. (2001) argued that Saharan dust provides large concentrations of mostly small cloud condensation-nuclei, which give rise to clouds dominated by small droplets which have only a small tendency to coalesce. This results in suppressed precipitation, increased drought, and more dust emissions, thereby providing a possible feedback loop. Atmospheric dust and climate change have thus probably been connected in complex feedback loops (Harrison et al., 2001).

EARTH GEOMETRY: THE PACEMAKER

If the position of the Earth in relation to the Sun were to change, so might the receipt of solar radiation—the Croll–Milankovitch or orbital hypothesis. Such changes do take place, and there are three main astronomical factors that recur cyclically: changes in the eccentricity of the Earth's orbit (a 96,000-year cycle), the precession of the equinoxes (with a periodicity of 21,000 years), and changes in the obliquity of the ecliptic (the angle between the plane of the Earth's orbit and the plane of its rotational equator). This last has a periodicity of about 40,000 years.

There is substantial evidence to link this mechanism to the longer scales of climatic change (Goreau, 1980), and the influence of orbital fluctuations has been traced back in the geological record over millions of years (Kerr, 1987). While the amount of temperature change caused by these fluctuations may be small (about 1–2°C), the periodicity of these fluctuations seems to correlate with the periodicity of Quaternary ice advances and retreats.

Although there is good evidence for a close relationship between orbital forcing and major climatic changes during the Pleistocene (Kawamura et al., 2007), it is still necessary to inquire how the effects of the Milankovitch signal can be magnified to cause the observed magnitutdes and rates of climatic change. Carbon dioxide levels in the atmosphere are one possible intensifying mechanism. Another possibility is that the oceans respond in a nonlinear way to an initial climatic perturbation and switch from one circulation configuration to another (Broecker and Denton, 1989).

TERRESTRIAL GEOGRAPHY

Some longer-term climate changes, including the initiation of glaciation in parts of the world, may have resulted from changes in the positions of the continents and uplift of continents (Hay, 1996). The formation of the mountains and plateaus of High Asia and the southwestern U.S. has been accorded particular importance in this respect (Ruddiman et al. 1989). Tibet and the high Himalayas have undergone a net uplift of 2–3 km during the past 3 million years, so that, "As much as 75% of the net elevation of Tibet (an area approximately one third of the size of the contiguous United States) may have been attained during the time of Northern Hemisphere glacial inception and intensification" (Ruddiman and Raymo, 1988, p. 420). Significant uplift during the Pliocene and Pleistocene has also occurred in the southwestern U.S.

Such uplift has had two effects on Northern Hemisphere climate that could be relevant to glacial inception and intensification. One of these is to enhance albedo-temperature feedback on a globally significant scale (Ruddiman and Raymo 1988) by producing elevated regions that held large areas of highly reflective snow. The other is a change in the form of large waves (Rossby waves) in the upper atmosphere. The increased elevation of both the Tibetan-Himalayan area and the southwestern U.S. would have altered the planetary wave structure so as to cool North America and Europe and increase their susceptibility to orbitally driven insolation changes. Moreover, Raymo and Ruddiman (1992) argued that tectonically driven increases in chemical weathering may have resulted in a decrease of atmospheric CO_2 concentrations over the last 40 million years, contributing to the late Cenozoic climate decline and the development of glacial conditions.

Another tectonic event significant for the onset of Northern Hemisphere glaciation was the emergence of the Panama Isthmus and its closure of the connection between the Atlantic and Pacific. By ca. 4.6 million years ago the connection between the two oceans had become shallow enough to alter the circulation in the North Atlantic (Haug and Tiedemann, 1998). The effect of this was to intensify the north-south circulation of the Atlantic, and by 3.6 million years ago the thermohaline circulation had approached its Pleistocene state. The Gulf Stream and North Atlantic Drift had become established, and by transporting warmer waters towards the Arctic, the water vapor content of the atmosphere was increased, magnifying the potential for precipitation at high latitudes. This was an important precondition for the growth of Northern Hemisphere ice sheets about 2.7 million years ago when the ecliptic-obliquity cycle became stronger (Haug et al., 2005).

GREENHOUSE GASES

In recent years increasing attention has been paid to the role of carbon dioxide (CO_2) and various other trace gases (such as methane and nitrous oxide) in modifying the Earth's radiation budget (Weart, 2003) through the greenhouse effect. [*See* Global Warming; Greenhouse Effect; *and* Greenhouse Gases.]

The CO_2 levels in the atmosphere affect Earth's heat balance because CO_2 is virtually transparent to incoming solar radiation but absorbs outgoing terrestrial infrared radiation—radiation that would otherwise escape to space and result in heat loss from the lower atmosphere. In general, decreased levels of CO_2 in the atmosphere would be expected to lead to cooling.

Until recently there was no method for testing this hypothesis, but it has now become possible to retrieve carbon dioxide from bubbles in layers of ice of known age in ice cores. Analyses of changes in carbon dioxide concentrations in these cores have provided remarkable results. The pioneering work of Delmas et al. (1980) on the Dome C core in Antarctica showed that near the time of the last glacial maximum (ca. 20,000 BP) the level of atmospheric carbon dioxide was only about 50% that of the present. The Vostok core also shows that over the last four glacial cycles there was an apparent coincidence of cold temperatures and low CO_2 levels.

The explanation for this coincidence is still debated, and several models have been produced to explain the causes of the fluctuating atmospheric CO_2 levels. Because the oceans are such a large store of CO_2 in comparison with terrestrial sinks, the explanation probably lies in the oceans and changes in their circulation and turnover, or in changes in the productivity of the organisms inhabiting them. Broecker (1981) hypothesized that a possible cause of the high level of CO_2 during interglacials was a loss of phosphorus to continental shelf sediments during transgressions of the oceans. This would, he believes, reduce the amount of plant matter formed in the sea per unit area of upwelled water and would thereby increase the partial pressure of CO_2 in surface water and in the atmosphere. Regressions during glacials would tend to reverse this trend. Given that transgressions and regressions of the oceans are tied so closely to the decay and growth of ice caps, these CO_2 changes could amplify the effects of orbital variations.

Methane (CH_4) may have played a similar role in intensifying orbital effects, because molecule for molecule it is a highly effective greenhouse gas. As with CO_2, ice core studies show that CH_4 concentrations were higher during interglacials than during glacials (Raynaud et al., 1988). CH_4 concentrations have tended to be less than 400 parts per billion by volume during glacials, probably because of reduced biological activity on the colder, drier land surfaces, and over 600 ppbv in interglacials. Nisbet (1990) suggested that during glacials, many high-latitude bogs and wetlands (which are major sources of the gas) would have been covered by ice or rendered less productive by extensive permafrost. Moreover, many natural-gas fields which emit methane to the atmosphere would have been sealed off by ice sheets and permafrost. By contrast, in interglacials, wetlands would produce large amounts of methane, and at the transition between glacial and interglacial conditions the methane that had been trapped in and beneath ice would be released into the atmosphere as the ice cover decreased. The release of the gas would lead to warming which would in turn lead to more melting, and more gas release. Methane concentrations have also varied during the Holocene—by up to 15%—and this may reflect changes in the extent of tropical lakes and of northern wetlands (Blunier et al., 1995).

ABRUPT CLIMATE CHANGE

There has been a growing appreciation that climatic changes can occur rapidly. In other words, the world climate system may be less stable than was previously supposed (Cox, 2005). While the broad pattern of climatic changes through the Quaternary may be paced by Milankovitch orbital cycles, the actual climatic shifts between and during glacial cycles were far swifter than these cycles would predict, having occurred over sub-Milankovitch timescales.

The circulation of the North Atlantic Ocean probably plays a major role in triggering and/or amplifying rapid climate changes (Rahmstorf et al., 1996). Ocean-circulation models suggest that a relatively small increase in freshwater flowing into the Arctic Sea and the high-latitude North Atlantic could provide the trigger for a sudden switching off of deep-water formation in the usual circulation pattern in the North Atlantic. The drainage of fresh water from the melting of the Laurentide and Fennoscandian ice sheets, and in particular the drainage of massive ice-dammed lakes during the Late Glacial, are thought to have triggered the Younger Dryas. This event about 8,200 years ago is also thought to be related to an influx of fresh water into the North Atlantic from the catastrophic drainage of proglacial lakes with the waning of the Laurentide ice sheet. [See Holocene.]

ASSESSMENT

Our knowledge of the causes of climatic changes is still imperfect. It is clear that no process acting alone can explain all scales of climatic changes. The possible causes operate over a wide range of time-scales, and some factors will be more appropriate than others to account for a climatic change in a particular span of time.

Some combination of processes is probably required, and at different times in Earth's history there have been unique combinations of these factors. This makes it difficult to generalize about the causes of climate change. Moreover, numerous feedback loops may exist, and small triggers may set off a chain

of events that leads to substantial change. Some hypotheses appear to explain variations over a long period—for example, the Milankovitch hypothesis is applicable to the glacial-interglacial cycles of the Pleistocene—while others may appear more plausible for short-term fluctuations—changes in sunspots, for instance, may be a hypothesis relevant on the scale of a decade or more. We are dealing with an immensely complex series of interrelated systems: the solar system, the atmosphere, the oceans, biota, and the land. It is thus unlikely that any simple hypothesis or model of climatic change will be widely applicable in all locations and on all time-scales.

BIBLIOGRAPHY

Anderson, D.E., A.S. Goudie and A.G. Parker. *Global Environments through the Quaternary.* Oxford and New York: Oxford University Press, 2007.

Arimoto, R. "Eolian Dust and Climate: Relationships to Sources, Tropospheric Chemistry, Transport, and Deposition." *Earth-Science Reviews* 54.1 (2001), 29–42. DOI: 10.1016/S0012-8252(01)00040-X.

Baillie, M.G.L., and Munro, M.A.R. "Irish Tree Rings, Santorini, and Volcanic Dust Veils." *Nature,* 322 (1988), 344–346. DOI: 10.1038/332344a0.

Blunier, T., et al. "Variations in Atmospheric Methane Concentration during the Holocene Epoch." *Nature* 374 (1995), 46–49. DOI: 10.1038/374046a0.

Bluth, G.J.S., et al. "The Contribution of Explosive Volcanism to Global Atmospheric Sulphur Dioxide Concentrations." *Nature* 373 (1993), 399–404. DOI: 10.1038/366327a0.

Broecker, W.S. "Glacial to Interglacial Changes in Ocean and Atmosphere Chemistry." In *Climatic Variations and Variability: Facts and Theories,* edited by A. Berger, 111–121. Dordrecht, Netherlands, and Boston, Mass.: Reidel, 1981.

Broecker, W.S., and Denton, G.H. "The Role of Ocean-Atmosphere Reorganizations in Glacial Cycles." *Geochimica et Cosmochimica Acta* 53.10 (1989), 2465–2501. DOI: 10.1016/0016-7037(89)90123-3.

Chester, D.K. "Volcanoes and Climate: Recent Volcanological Perspectives." *Progress in Physical Geography* 12.1 (1988), 1–35. DOI:10.1177/030913338801200101.

Claquin, T., et al. "Radiative Forcing by Ice-Age Atmospheric Dust." *Climate Dynamics* 20 (2003), 183–202.

Cox, J.D. *Climate Crash: Abrupt Climate Change and What It Means for Our Future.* Washington, D.C.: Joseph Henry Press, 2005.

Crowley, T.J., and K.-Y. Kim. "Towards Development of a Strategy for Determining the Origin of Decadal-Centennial Scale Climate Variability." *Quaternary Science Reviews* 12.6 (1993), 375–385. DOI: 10.1016/S0277-3791(05)80003-4.

Delmas, R.J., J.-M. Ascencio, and M. Legrand. "Polar Ice Evidence That Atmospheric CO_2 20,000 yr BP Was 50% of Present." *Nature* 284 (1980), 155–157. DOI: 10.1038/284155a0.

Friedrich, W.L., et al. "Santorini Eruption Radiocarbon Dated to 1627–1600 B.C." *Science* 312 (2006), 548. DOI: 10.1126/science.1125087.

Goreau, T. "Frequency Sensitivity of the Deep-Sea Climatic Record." *Nature* 287 (1980), 620–622. DOI: 10.1038/287620a0.

Harrison, S.P., et al. "The Role of Dust in Climate Changes Today, at the Last Glacial Maximum, and in the Future." *Earth-Science Reviews* 54.1–3 (2001), 43–80. DOI" 10.1016/S0012-8252(01)00041-1.

Haug, G.H., and R. Tiedemann. "Effect of the Formation of the Isthmus of Panama on Atlantic Ocean Thermohaline Circulation." *Nature* 393 (1998), 673–676. DOI: 10.1038/31447.

Haug, G.H., et al. "North Pacific Seasonality and the Glaciation of North America 2.7 Million Years Ago." *Nature* 433 (2005), 821–825. DOI: 10.1038/nature03332.

Hay, W.W. "Tectonics and Climate." *Geologische Rundschau (International Journal of Earth Sciences)* 85.3 (1996), 409–437. DOI: 10.1007/BF02369000.

Karlén, W., and J. Kuylenstierna. "On Solar Forcing of Holocene Climate: Evidence from Scandinavia." *The Holocene* 6.3 (1996), 359–365. DOI: 10.1177/095968369600600311.

Kawamura, K., et al. "Northern Hemisphere Forcing of Climatic Cycles in Antarctica Over the Past 360,000 Years." *Nature* 448 (2007), 912–916. DOI: 10.1038/nature06015.

Kerr, R.A. "Milankovitch Climate Cycles through the Ages." *Science* 235 (1987), 973–974. DOI: 10.1126/science.235.4792.973.

Lamb, H.H. "Volcanic Activity and Climate." *Palaeogeography, Palaeoclimatology, Palaeoecology* 10 (1971), 203–230.

Magny, M. "Solar Influences on Holocene Climatic Cycles Illustrated by Correlations between Past Lake-Level Fluctuations and the Atmospheric ^{14}C Record." *Quaternary Research* 40.1 (1993), 1–9. DOI: 10.1006/qres.1993.1050.

McCormick, P.M., L.W. Thomason, and C.R. Trepte. "Atmospheric Effects of the Mt. Pinatubo Eruption." *Nature* 373 (1995), 399–404. DOI: 10.1038/373399a0.

Moreno, A., and M. Canals. "The Role of Dust in Abrupt Climate Change: Insights from Offshore Northwest Africa and Alboran Sea Sediment Records." *Contributions to Science* (Barcelona) 2.4 (2004), 485–498.

Nisbet, E.G. "The End of the Ice Age." *Canadian Journal of Earth Sciences* 27 (1990), 148–157.

Rahmstorf, S., J. Marotzke, and J. Willebrand. "Stability of the Thermohaline Circulation." In *The Warmwatersphere of the North Atlantic Ocean*, edited by W. Krauss, pp. 129–157. Berlin: Borntraeger, 1996.

Ramanathan et al., "Warming Trends in Asia Amplified by Brown Cloud Solar Absorbtion." *Nature* 448 (2007), 575–578.

Rampino, M.R., and S. Self. "Volcanic Winter and Accelerated Glaciation following the Toba Super-Eruption." *Nature* 359 (1992), 50–52. DOI: 10.1038/359050a0.

Raymo, M.E., and W.F. Ruddiman. "Tectonic Forcing of Late Cenozoic Climate." *Nature* 359 (1992), 117–122.

Raynaud, D., et al. "Climatic and CH_4 Cycle Implications of Glacial-Interglacial CH_4 Change in the Vostok Ice-Core." *Nature* 333 (1988), 655–657. DOI: 10.1038/333655a0.

Ridgwell, A.J. "Dust in the Earth System: The Biogeochemical Linking of Land, Air, and Sea." *Philosophical Transactions of the Royal Society* A 360 (2002), 2905–2924.

Rind, D., and J. Overpeck. "Hypothesized Causes of Decade-to-Century-Scale Climate Variability: Climate Model Results." *Quaternary Science Reviews* 12.6 (1993), 357–374. DOI: 10.1016/S0277-3791(05)80002-2.

Rosenfeld, D., Y. Rudich, and R. Lahav. "Desert Dust Suppressing Precipitation: A Possible Desertification Feedback Loop." *Proceedings of the National Academy of Sciences* 98.11 (2001), 5975–5980. DOI: 10.1073/pnas.101122798.

Ruddiman, W.F., and M.E. Raymo. "The Past Three Million Years: Evolution of Climatic Variability in the North Atlantic Region." *Philosophical Transactions of the Royal Society of London* B 318 (1988), 411–430.

Ruddiman, W.F., W.L. Prell, and M.E. Raymo. "Late Cenozoic Uplift in Southern Asia and the American West: Rationale for General Circulation Modeling Experiments." *Journal of Geophysical Research* 94.D15 (1989), 18379–18391.

Shindell, D.T., et al. "Solar Forcing of Regional Climate Change during the Maunder Minimum." *Science* 294 (2001), 2149–2152. DOI: 10.1126/science.1064363.

Stuiver, M., and T.F. Braziunas. "Sun, Ocean, Climate, and Atmospheric $^{14}CO_2$: An Evaluation of Causal and Spectral Relationships." *The Holocene* 3.4 (1993), 289–305. DOI: 10.1177/095968369300300401.

Svensmark, H., and E. Friis-Christensen. "Variation of Cosmic Ray Flux and Global Cloud Coverage: A Missing Link in Solar-Climate Relationships." *Journal of Atmospheric and Solar-Terrestrial Physics* 59.11 (1997), 1225–1232.

Tegen, I. "Modeling the Mineral Dust Aerosol in the Climate System." *Quaternary Science Reviews* 22.18–19 (2003), 1821–1834. DOI: 10.1016/S0277-3791%2803%2900163-X.

Weart, S.R. *The Discovery of Global Warming.* Cambridge, Mass.: Harvard University Press, 2003. A revised edition was published in 2008.

—ANDREW S. GOUDIE

CHEMICAL INDUSTRY

The chemical industry is the modern form of an ancient set of arts and sciences. Neolithic peoples produced copper by reducing minerals such as malachite with charcoal. Bronze, an alloy of copper and tin, perhaps the first synthetic substance invented by humans, appeared around 3,000 BCE, and iron emerged some 1,200 years later. The Egyptians had a rich chemical culture producing plaster, paper, glass, and potash, which they used to make a form of soap. Because they were local arts, based on tacit knowledge, none of these ancient chemical processes created an industry. The first signs of the emergence of what has become one of the world's largest industrial sectors came around the middle of the eighteenth century. As other industries such as textiles, metals, and glass-making outstripped their traditional sources of raw materials, a new market was created for firms supplying their basic building blocks. This pattern of providing the building blocks for other industries has persisted through much of the chemical industry's history.

The earliest examples of industrial chemical manufacture arose in Europe. Sulfuric acid plants were built in England and France to supply dye-making and metal-processing firms. Demand for alkali for glass and soap produced a thriving industry in France at the time of the Revolution. The French early dominance of this embryonic industry waned after the Revolution as the free-enterprise model that drove the Industrial Revolution in England spawned a growing basic chemicals industry. The mainstay was the manufacture of sodium carbonate (sal soda) via the heavily polluting Leblanc process, which produced copious emissions of hydrochloric acid. Regions around the plants were heavily damaged by an early form of acid rain. In perhaps the first instance of formal environmental legislation, the English Alkali Act of 1863 required firms to install absorbing towers to control the acid emissions and established a new bureaucracy to enforce the Act.

Very little of the European chemical technology and industry followed the American colonists to the New World. The free-trade policies of the new United States made it economical to import their basic chemical stocks from Europe. But for security reasons one important chemical substance, gunpowder, called for an industry independent of the potentially unfriendly European powers. In 1802, a French émigré, Éleuthère Irénée du Pont de Nemours, built a gunpowder plant near Wilmington, Delaware. DuPont remains today one the world's largest chemical firms and is considered a leader in environmental practices. The deeply acculturated safety consciousness of DuPont, an obvious outcome of their traditional product, is considered by many analysts to be the origin of their leadership in the industry. The chemical industry continued to develop during the first half of the eighteenth century as new technologies emerged. Electrochemical processes were discovered but waited in the wings for almost a century until cheap sources of electricity had been developed. Artificial fertilizers, fats, and rubber grew into important parts of the industry, and the earliest synthesis of organic chemicals was carried out by Wöhler in 1828 when he produced urea from ammonium cyanate and ammonium chloride.

The industry established itself as a major economic sector in the period from about 1850 to the beginning of World War I, following a spate of critically important scientific discoveries. Bringing back secrets of synthetic dye-making developed in England, German chemists established a powerful organic-chemicals industry around firms that remain dominant today—Hoechst, Badische Anilin- und Soda-Fabrik (BASF), and Bayer. New organic explosives brought both more power and more danger. Alfred Nobel learned the secret of stabilizing the powerful but ultrasensitive explosive nitroglycerin, thereby establishing his fortune. The photographic-arts industry arose in Europe and the United States, and the first synthetic fibers from petroleum were made in the United States.

The German industry continued to dominate the world up to the beginning of World War I but lost this position following Germany's defeat. The industry that grew rapidly after World War II is international in scope, well organized, and highly concentrated. Chemical manufacture continues to be capital intensive with large returns to scale. The industry has not only had to cope with costly and extensive regulations and a poor public image, but, since 1973, with more costly and less reliable feedstocks (such as petroleum). Much of the rapid growth of the global chemical industry following World War II was the direct consequence of abundant, cheap oil supplies that replaced coal. The 1970s saw a series of mergers and investments in new plants designed to gain market share and dominant positions, but oversupply and higher feedstock prices brought on a long period of poor economic performance. In the late 1980s and later, the global industry recovered and has continued to grow. Many of the giants like DuPont have, however, abandoned their basic commodity chemicals to independent producers and now focus on specialty chemicals and markets.

HAZARDS OF PRODUCTION

The industrial hazards of producing chemicals have always been of concern to laboratory chemists and plant operators. Nobel lost his younger brother in an explosion in 1864. An early BASF ammonia synthesis plant blew up in 1921 in Oppau, Germany, killing over 600 people. In 1946, a ship carrying ammonium nitrate exploded in Texas City, killing some 500 people. Dioxin, a new industrial hazard, gained notoriety from an explosion in Seveso, Italy, in 1978 which spread it through the surrounding community. And in 1984 an explosion and release of methyl isocyanate at an insecticide plant in Bhopal, India, killed over 2,000 people and injured hundreds of thousands more. Bhopal raised a global outcry that led to both government legislation and industry self-regulation. Various halogen-containing compounds have proved hazardous as well as very useful. [See Chemical Wonders.]

Other forms of hazard emerged as dangerous, unintended side effects were discovered in chemical products and in wastes from their production. Thalidomide, marketed by a German pharmaceutical firm, produced anomalies in newborns. It took three years to track down the cause of these birth defects to the drug that was being marketed as a palliative to the nausea that frequently accompanies pregnancy. An entire Japanese village was afflicted with similar teratogenesis (monstrous deformities in newborn children) that were eventually traced to organomercury compounds flowing from a company's outfall into Minamata Bay. The local diet depended heavily on fish from the bay, which had become contaminated by the polluted waters. Twenty-three years after fishing was declared off-limits in 1974, local fishermen are again allowed to fish Minamata Bay. Other chemical disposal practices led to widespread concerns over hazardous waste that had been placed in landfills. In New York, one community, Love Canal, was relocated following concerns that seepage from an abandoned and covered landfill had led to an unusually large number of childhood cancers and other diseases in the vicinity. Publicity of this event and similar problems at other chemical disposal sites eventually culminated in the passage of the Superfund Law in the United States in 1980.

LEGISLATION

The chemical industry has been the primary target of much environmental legislation in all of the developed industrial regions of the world. In the United States, the Toxic Substances Control Act (TSCA) was passed in 1976 to control the introduction of new chemicals into commerce. Some 70,000–80,000 chemicals are produced and sold in literally millions of products. TSCA requires chemical manufacturers to provide information on the safety of any new product prior to its market introduction. The original Act also banned polychlorinated biphenyls (PCBs). Pesticides are controlled by a related statute. European Community policy followed the U.S. pattern in its broad outlines. The first broad European policy came in 1967 with a Directive on dangerous substances, which set forth a set of requirements for labeling, classification, and handling of hazardous substances. The Directive's 6th Amendment set forth pre-market requirements very similar to those in TSCA.

Chlorine-based chemicals have been a particular target since the mid-1970s, when broad limits appeared in directives of the European Community designed to limit emissions into the aquatic environment. By 1990, groups such as Greenpeace, who had published a report entitled *The Product is the Poison: The Case for a Chlorine Phase-Out,* had called for a complete ban on chlorine-based chemicals and hoped to see this issue on the agenda at the 1992 United Nations Conference on Environment and Development in Rio de Janeiro. In North America, the International Joint Commission, an official U.S.–Canadian agency, called for the "virtual elimination of the input of persistent toxic substances into the Great Lakes."

The Superfund Law taxed the chemical and petroleum industries heavily and created a new and very expensive form of liability for actions—such as dumping of hazardous substances—that had been lawful in the past. The Law spurred companies to develop new strategies to prevent pollution. Companies such as 3M with its 3P program (Pollution Prevention Pays) had discovered that prevention could avoid investments in control equipment and other regulatory costs.

But even this theme could not insulate the industry from continuing regulatory pressures and public scrutiny. A series of newsworthy accidents such as Bhopal, coupled with concerns over the safety of many products, continued to expose chemical firms to legislative scrutiny and to pressures from advocacy groups to limit the marketing of broad classes of chemicals. In 1986, amendments to the Superfund Law required companies to disclose publicly the amounts of a long list of toxic substances being released. Realization of the magnitude of the releases created shock waves both in the public and in high executive levels of the industry.

INDUSTRY SELF-REGULATION

Faced with continuing regulatory and public pressure, the world chemical industry has created an elaborate self-regulatory system called Responsible Care. In 1988, the U.S. Chemical Manufacturers Association adopted a new self-governing system developed two years earlier by its neighbor to the north—the Canadian Chemical Producers Association. Responsible Care, now mandatory for member firms in the United States and adopted by sister associations around the world, sets forth a set of principles and codes of practice designed to improve environmental performance and to build public confidence in the industry. The codes include requirements for community preparedness, product stewardship, pollution prevention, process safety, distribution, and employee health and safety. Product stewardship sets forth new standards of care reaching forward through the life cycle of the chemicals beyond the traditional plant fence-line.

It is still too early to evaluate Responsible Care fully. Public opinion has changed only marginally. Investment in environmental management has increased. Public concerns still abound, having been kept alive by data showing anomalous development patterns in aquatic species (e.g., trout) that have been associated with chemicals that disrupt normal sexual traits. The industry's future looks rosy as the global economy continues its rapid growth, but the potential for future accidents and discoveries of harmful side effects will continue to focus public attention on the chemical industry and maintain the role of environment as an important strategic factor.

[See also Pest Management.]

BIBLIOGRAPHY

Aftalion, F. A History of the International Chemical Industry. Philadelphia: University of Pennsylvania Press, 1991.
Arora, A., R. Landau, and N. Rosenberg, eds. Chemicals and Long-Term Economic Growth: Insights from the Chemical Industry. New York: Wiley, 1998.
Fitzgerald, R. The Hundred-Year Lie: How to Protect Yourself from the Chemicals That Are Destroying Your Health. New York: Penguin, 2007.
Hester, R.E., and R.M. Harrison, eds. Chemicals in the Environment: Assessing and Managing Risk. Cambridge: Royal Society of Chemistry, 2006.
Nash, J., and J.R. Ehrenfeld. "Code Green: Business Adopts Voluntary Environmental Standards." Environment 38.1 (1996), 16–20, 36–45.
Russell, E. War and Nature: Fighting Humans and Insects with Chemicals from World War I to Silent Spring. Cambridge: Cambridge University Press, 2001.

—JOHN R. EHRENFELD

GREEN CHEMISTRY

As Anastas and Warner (1998, p. v) remark, chemists "possess the knowledge and skills to make decisions in the practice of their trade that can result in immense benefit to society or cause harm to life and living systems and they therefore have responsibility for the character of the decision made." The decision of chemists to minimize adverse impacts on the environment is summarized in the term "green chemistry," the twelve principles of which can be summarized thus (Anastas and Warner, 1998, p. 30, Figure 4.1):

1. It is better to prevent waste than to treat it or clean it up after it has been generated.
2. Synthetic methods should be designed to maximize the incorporation into the final product of all materials used in the process.
3. Wherever practicable, chemical systheses should be designed to use and generate substances that possess little or no toxicity to human health and the environment.
4. Chemical products should be designed to preserve efficacy of function while reducing toxicity.
5. The use of auxiliary substances (e.g., solvents, separation agents, etc.) should be made unnecessary wherever possible and innocuous when used.
6. Energy requirements should be recognized for their environmental and economic impacts and should be minimized. Synthesis should whenever feasible be conducted at ambient temperature and pressure.
7. Raw materials should be renewable rather than depleting wherever technically and economically practicable.
8. Unnecessary derivization (blocking group, protection/deprotection, temporary modification of physical/chemical processes) should be avoided whenever possible.
9. Catalytic reagents (as selective as possible), which can be reused, are superior to stoichiometric reagents, which are consumed in the reaction.
10. Chemical products should be designed so that at the end of their function they do not persist in the environment but break down into innocuous degradation products.
11. Analytical methodologies need to be further developed to allow for real-time, in-process monitoring and control prior to the formation of hazardous substances.
12. Substances and the form of a substance used in a chemical process should be chosen so as to minimize the potential for chemical accidents, including releases, explosions, and fires.

BIBLIOGRAPHY

Anastas, P. T., and J. C. Warner. Green Chemistry: Theory and Practice. Oxford and New York: Oxford University Press, 1998.

— ANDREW S. GOUDIE

CHEMICAL WONDERS

Many of the chemicals now banned or strictly controlled were at one time hailed as wonders that would benefit society. DDT has had two reversals. It had been viewed as the answer to one of humankind's greatest scourges, malaria, until Rachel Carson's Silent Spring made its harmful effects on fishing birds a cause célèbre in 1962. DDT was banned in all industrial countries; and in 2004 the global treaty on Persistent Organic pollutants (POP) banned the use of DDT worldwide. More recently, as malaria seems to be making a comeback, some public health officials are advocating the use of DDT again: in fact, the World Health Organization in 2006 endorsed the use of DDT for house spraying and for insecticide-impregnated bednets (WHO, 2006).

PCBs (polychlorinated biphenyls) offered a nonflammable alternative for use as a heat transfer agent and as a dielectric filler in electrical devices such as transformers. After decades of use, it was realized that PCBs in high doses caused tumors, birth defects, and other abnormalities in laboratory animals. Like DDT, the PCBs are persistent chemicals, remaining unaltered by reaction as they pass through a food chain, becoming more concentrated at each higher level. They were banned in 1976.

CFCs (chlorofluorocarbons) combine chlorine, fluorine, and carbon. Developed by DuPont in 1930, they have rare properties that make them uniquely suitable for certain applications: they are inert, stable, odorless, nonflammable, nontoxic, and noncorrosive; and they have physical characteristics appropriate for their use as working fluids in refrigerators, air conditioners, and heat pumps. In addition to their use as refrigerants, they were employed as cleaners for electronic components, fumigants for granaries and cargo holds, and propellants in aerosol cans. In addition, the closely related PFCs (perfluorocarbons) are the basis of special emulsions used to transport oxygen to the lungs of premature babies. When the scientific community recognized that CFCs were harmful to ozone in the stratosphere, a compelling irony became apparent. The same stability and inertness that make CFCs safe for use with foods, for instance, also allow their molecules to remain intact for years as they diffuse slowly through the atmosphere and eventually reach ozone-rich layers of the stratosphere, where ultraviolet radiation causes the molecules to dissociate, releasing chlorine atoms that begin the destruction of ozone. If the compounds were less stable, they would react with other chemicals in the lower atmosphere and never reach the stratosphere. The Montreal Protocol of 1987 initiated worldwide cooperation to reduce the use of CFCs and other chemicals harmful to the ozone layer.

Hydrofluorocarbons (HFCs) are widely used now instead of chlorofluorocarbons in refrigeration. They and perfluorocarbons, (PFCs), however, are potent greenhouse gases which occur in low concentrations in the atmosphere. [See Greenhouse Gases.]

BIBLIOGRAPHY

Carson, R. *Silent Spring*. Boston: Houghton Mifflin, 1962.
WHO. "WHO Gives Indoor Use of DDT a Clean Bill of Health for Controlling Malaria." World Health Organization Media Center, Sept. 15, 2006. http://www.who.int/mediacentre/news/releases/2006/pr50/en/indes.html (accessed May 25, 2008).

—David J. Cuff

CHERNOBYL

The most catastrophic accident ever to occur at a commercial nuclear power plant took place on April 26, 1986, in northern Ukraine at Chernobyl (Chornobyl' in Ukrainian). Intense radioactive fallout covered significant portions of several provinces in Ukraine, Belarus, and the Russian Federation, and lesser amounts fell out with precipitation in numerous other European countries. The resultant health and environmental consequences are ongoing, widespread, and serious.

The Chernobyl power station is one of several such complexes built in Ukraine. At the time, it was believed that nuclear energy would entail negligible damage to the environment. Four other large nuclear power complexes have been constructed and Ukraine has a major uranium-mining complex and numerous research facilities.

The Chernobyl reactors utilize a graphite-moderated type of nuclear reactor (Russian acronym, RBMK), with a normal output of 1,000 megawatts. These units are water-cooled and employ graphite rods to control core temperatures. Each reactor houses 1,661 fuel rods that contain mainly uranium-238 plus much smaller amounts of enriched uranium-235. There are several dangers inherent in the design of RBMK-1000 reactors, including the ability of the operators to disengage safety controls, the lack of a containment dome, and the possibility that, at very low power levels, a rapid and uncontrollable increase in heat can occur in the reactor's core and may result in a catastrophic explosion (Haynes and Bojcun, 1988, pp. 2–4).

This was what happened early in the morning of April 26, 1986. A series of violations of normal safety procedures, committed during a low-power experiment being run on reactor number 4, resulted in a thermal explosion and fire that destroyed the reactor building, exposed the core, and vented vast amounts of radioactive material into the atmosphere. Pieces of the power plant itself were found up to several kilometers from the site of the explosion.

This radiation continued to be released into the atmosphere over a period of nine days, with the prevailing winds carrying the radioactive material initially in a northwesterly direction over northern Europe. The winds later shifted to the northeast, carrying fallout southwestward into central Europe and the Balkan peninsula. The overall result was significant radioactive fallout (mainly associated with rainfall) in Austria, Czechoslovakia, Finland, Germany (mainly Bavaria), the United Kingdom, Hungary, Italy, Poland, Romania, Sweden, and Switzerland. Lower levels of radioactive deposition were reported in Denmark, France, the Benelux countries, Greece, Ireland, Norway, Yugoslavia, and several other European nations (Medvedev 1990, chap. 6). The republics of Estonia, Latvia, and Lithuania were also directly in the path of the initial plume.

In the Soviet Union, the regions that received the highest levels of radioactive contamination were in the northern Kiev and eastern Zhytomyr provinces in Ukraine, and in the Homyel' and Mahilyow provinces of Belarus (then Belorussia). In the Russian Federation, areas situated closest to the Belarus border, such as western Bryansk province, experienced the greatest radiation problems (NEA, 1995, p. 32). Lighter fallout, measured in terms of long-lived cesium-137, was recorded in parts of other Ukrainian provinces, as well as in the Baltic republics. Among the capital cities of these provinces, only Homyel' was in a region of high fallout, but other large cities, such as Orel, Mogilev, and Kiev, were right on the border of the danger zone (Bradley, 1997, p. 368; Marples, 2004, p. 598).

Large-scale evacuations were conducted in the most heavily affected sections of these provinces. The number of people who had to be resettled totaled around 107,000 in Belarus alone, plus approximately fifty thousand more in both Russia and Ukraine (International Atomic Energy Agency, 1996, p. 7). Another source cites a figure of over 84,000 people as having been relocated in the Russian Republic (Savchenko, 1995, p. 76), and other sources speak of over 100,000 evacuees in Ukraine. In many instances the displaced populations had to be moved quickly to places with inadequate housing, social services, and employment. For unknown reasons, thousands of people were not relocated from areas of high radiation until many years after the accident.

The effects on human health have been enormous. Around 600,000 people have been "significantly exposed" to radiation from the Chernobyl accident, and thousands of people have developed radiation sickness from exposure to contamination produced by the explosion and subsequent fire (Medvedev, 1990, pp. 129–130). Approximately 270,000 people still live in areas sufficiently contaminated to require ongoing protection measures (NEA, 1995, p. 12). Russia, like the former Soviet Union, still reports an official figure of around thirty-one deaths, but the actual number of Chernobyl-related fatalities is often suggested to be in the hundreds, if not the thousands (Marples, 1993, p. 282). In 1996, a senior Russian environmental official stated that "official [Chernobyl] statistics are incomplete and irreversibly falsified" (Yablokov, 1993).

Medical problems among the general population that are probably attributable to Chernobyl are a serious concern. The first wave of victims were workers at the plant, and the thousands of containment and cleanup personnel who needed treatment for radiation sickness. The workers' town of Pripyat' was not immediately evacuated nor the people even informed of the radiation danger, thereby placing many people, especially schoolchildren, at risk. The 30-kilometer-radius "exclusion zone" around the plant was not declared until May 3 and was inadequate in size. There is general agreement that there will be grave long-term cancer mortality from the accident but also vast disagreement over the magnitude of these carcinogenic consequences. The optimists suggest only a few hundred "excess deaths," all in the former Soviet republics, whereas the pessimists predict as many as 280,000 fatalities worldwide (Medvedev, 1990, p. 166).

The southeastern portion of Belarus received the plurality of fallout from Chernobyl; indeed, between half and two-thirds of all the radioactive fallout from Chernobyl fell on Belarusian territory. The environmental and human toll in this area has been at least as great as that experienced in Ukraine. The city of Homyel', with a population of around half a million, recorded the highest increase in background radiation of any major city in the Soviet Union. Many smaller towns in Belarus, especially those directly across the Pripyat' River from Chernobyl, received more. Approximately 20% of the country's agricultural land, possibly totaling in excess of a quarter million hectares, as well as 15% of the forests of Belarus, are no longer usable (Savchenko, 1995).

Perhaps the most tragic consequence of the accident has been the sharp increase in the incidence of thyroid cancer in children since 1989 in Ukraine, Belarus, and Russia. In Minsk (city and province) in 1986 there had been no such cancers, but by 1992 twenty-one cases had been recorded; in Homyel' province there had been one in 1986 but 97 more from 1987 to 1992. For all of Belarus, there had been two cases of thyroid cancer in children in 1986, but 172 cases were recorded in the period 1986–1992 (Marples, 1993, pp. 285–290; World Health Organization, 1995, pp. 20–24). By 1994, the total exceeded three hundred (NEA, 1995, p. 63). Since the breakup of the Soviet Union, little assistance in dealing with the consequences of Chernobyl has come from Moscow. Currently, a significant percentage of the national budget of Belarus must be devoted to dealing with the relocation, environmental, and public health costs of the accident.

The environmental consequences of the accident include large areas of contaminated soil, forests, and water. Soil and water pollution from the accident have been recorded in twenty-two provinces of the former Soviet Union, as well as in several foreign countries. In places, radionuclides have been measured in the soil at depths up to 25 centimeters, which is the vertical zone in which crop cultivation takes place. Because of radioactive contamination of soil, large areas of fertile farmland have had to be taken out of production. In northern Ukraine, over 100,000 hectares of agricultural land, which contain some of the world's richest soils, have had to be abandoned (Savchenko, 1995, p. 53). Meat and dairy products had to be destroyed, and deformed calves and pigs were born on nearby collective farms. The farmers have had to find work elsewhere, and lost agricultural output made up by increased production in other regions. The Nuclear Energy Agency (NEA, 1995, p. 81) has warned that forest products from the contaminated regions may present long-term radiation exposure problems.

Water supplies were not only contaminated by the immediate fallout, but also by the transport of radioactive sediments. Fishing was prohibited in the portions of the Pripyat' River and the Kiev Reservoir near the accident site, and outside sources of water for Kiev had to be developed quickly. The Pripyat' River flows through the power plant complex (and was the source of its cooling water), and thence flows into the Dnieper River, which runs through Kiev. Several million people living between Kiev and the Black Sea depend upon water from the Dnieper, and thus are potentially exposed to radiation moving through it. In the mid-1990s, though, contamination of drinking water was believed not to be a problem (NEA, 1995, p. 81). However, significant amounts of strontium-90 may be imbedded in the banks of the Pripyat' River. Bank collapse and shoreline erosion could eventually release this radiation.

A large concrete containment facility, termed a sarcophagus, was completed around the damaged Unit Number 4 in November 1986, finally halting the release of radiation. However, it was never viewed as a permanent containment structure, and because of the haste of its construction, serious doubts exist about its long-term viability. The sarcophagus covers hundreds of metric tons of nuclear fuel, which continue to produce high temperatures and radiation levels within the ruined reactor building. But the current structural stability of the sarcophagus is very questionable, and it will have to be replaced. The huge cost of this exceeds Ukraine's resources. As a result, at the 1997 economic summit meeting, the major world powers pledged U.S.$300 million to assist in the construction of a second concrete containment facility.

The health and environmental consequences of the accident have been sufficiently great that there was a widespread call to shut down the Chernobyl complex completely, and this was done in 2000. The Ukrainian government has linked the complete closure of the site to the receipt of foreign funding for cleanup assistance that was promised by multinational agreement in 1995.

The consequences of the Chernobyl disaster, including delayed health effects, will remain as significant problems for decades to come (Poyarkov, 2000). The huge costs of cleaning up the contaminated land and structures, caring for the displaced multitudes, and rebuilding the sarcophagus will have to be funded somehow, and may exceed the ability of Belarus and Ukraine to handle the costs (Pryde, 1995, chap. 10). In terms of future energy supplies, the accident has had a depressive effect on nuclear power in many parts of the world, most notably the United States, where no new development of nuclear power has taken place since 1986. Russia, on the other hand, plans to continue with its nuclear program and has announced plans to build a number of new units early in the twenty-first century. The ramifications of the Chernobyl accident are extensive and continuing, and it is likely that it will be remembered as one of the defining events of the twentieth century.

[See also Nuclear Power; and Nuclear Waste.]

BIBLIOGRAPHY

Bradley, D.J. Behind the Nuclear Curtain: Radioactive Waste Management in the Former Soviet Union. Columbus, Ohio: Battelle Press, 1997, pp. 345–370. The most comprehensive work to date on all aspects of commercial and military radioactive wastes in the former Soviet republics.
Haynes, V., and M. Bojcun. The Chernobyl Disaster. London: Hogarth Press, 1988. An early review of the disaster and its immediate effects.
International Atomic Energy Agency. One Decade after Chernobyl: Summing up the Consequences of the Accident. Vienna: IAEA, 1996. Summary report of the Joint EC/IAEA/WHO international conference, "One Decade After Chernobyl," held in Vienna, 8–12 April 1996.
Marples, D.R. "A Correlation between Radiation and Health Problems in Belarus?" Post-Soviet Geography 34 (1993), 281–292.
———. "Chernobyl: A Reassessment". Eurasian Geography and Economics 45 (2004), 588–607.
Medvedev, Z. The Legacy of Chernobyl. Oxford: Blackwell, 1990. A critical evaluation of Chernobyl and its aftermath by a Russian dissident.
NEA. Chernobyl: Ten Years on Radiological and Health Impact. Paris: Nuclear Energy Agency, 1995. A detailed study of the health and environmental consequences of Chernobyl.
Poyarkov, V., et al. The Chornobyl Accident: A Comprehensive Risk Assessment. Columbus, Ohio: Batelle Press, 2000.
Pryde, P.R., ed. Environmental Resources and Constraints in the Former Soviet Republics. Boulder, Colo.: Westview Press, 1995. Chapters 9, 10, and 11 are on environmental management problems in Ukraine and Belarus.
Savchenko, V.K. The Ecology of the Chernobyl Catastrophe. Paris, Casterton Hall, U.K., and New York: UNESCO and Parthenon Publishing, 1995.
World Health Organization. Health Consequences of the Chernobyl Accident. Geneva: WHO, 1995. This is the most recent United Nations report on this subject.
Yablokov, A.V., et al. "Facts and Problems Related to Radioactive Waste Disposal in Seas Adjacent to the Territory of the Russian Federation." Report to the President of the Russian Federation by the Government Commission on Matters Related to Radioactive Waste Disposal at Sea, 24 October 1992. Moscow, 1993. Yablokov was senior adviser on environmental matters to President Yeltsin.

—PHILIP R. PRYDE

CHINA AND ITS ENVIRONMENT

The rise of China as an economic power is one of the great stories of the latter half of the twentieth century and and the beginning of the twenty-first. Growing at 8–12% annually for more than two decades, China's economy is today the fourth largest in the world, and China exports more than any other country except the United States and Germany. This unfettered growth, building upon centuries of environmental degradation, has had devastating consequences for China's environment. Levels of air and water pollution have skyrocketed, and the process of desertification is advancing rapidly throughout China's north as deforestation and over-grazing take their toll.

These environmental problems are having a profound impact on the well-being of the Chinese people, limiting economic growth in some regions, harming people's health, and contributing to growing social unrest. Moreover, the implications of China's development and environmental practices for the rest of the world are increasingly worrying. China is either the first or second largest contributor to global environmental challenges, including climate change, the illegal timber trade, and marine pollution.

China's leaders recognize the damage that development has inflicted on the environment and have enacted many laws and regulations in an attempt to improve the situation, but real progress remains difficult. Investment in environmental protection remains low, demands on local authorities to expand their economies and maintain social stability keep environmental protection a distant priority for many officials, and economic incentives to protect the environment (e.g., accurate pricing of natural resources and heavy fines for failing to adhere to environmental regulations) remain elusive or are unenforced.

THE ENVIRONMENTAL LANDSCAPE

China today faces serious challenges to its air, land, and water resources. By several measures, it is the worst in the world in terms of these threats, and there is little indication of change in the near future.

The most visible of these challenges is China's heavily polluted air. According to Pan Yue, a senior Chinese environmental official, five of the world's ten most polluted cities are in China. Acid rain affects one-quarter of China's land and one-third of its agricultural land, diminishing agricultural output, eroding buildings, and contributing to respiratory problems. Regional haze results in 70% of crops yielding 5–30% less than their potential.

The preponderant source of this pollution is coal-fired power generation. China relies on coal for approximately 70% of its energy, consuming 2.1 billion tons in 2005. It is the largest consumer of coal in the world and consequently the largest emitter of sulfur dioxide. Coal consumption is expected to more than double from 2000 to 2020. Compounding the problem is that only 5% of China's power plants use desulfurization technologies to limit their pollution, believing them too expensive. Low utilization of energy-efficiency technologies in China's buildings and industries also means higher energy use: buildings in China consume 2–3 times the energy of those in developed countries in comparable climates, and industries are much less efficient than those in other countries.

China has plans to urbanize 300 million people by 2020. Because urban residents consume more than 250% more energy than their rural counterparts, overall energy consumption is likely to more than double, even if significant advances are made in energy conservation. Perhaps the greater challenge, however, rests in China's transportation sector. Chinese officials estimate that by 2050, China will have more vehicles on the road than the United States.

China also suffers from serious and increasing land degradation. Deforestation, along with the overgrazing of grasslands and over-cultivation of cropland, has dramatically altered the landscape of the country. Deforestation contributes to biodiversity loss, soil erosion, and local climatic change. Almost 40% of China's land is affected by soil erosion. The world's highest water-erosion rates occur in China in the Loess Plateau, where 1.6 billion tons of topsoil are washed into the Yellow River yearly.

In addition, China, which is roughly the same size as the United States, is now more than one-quarter desert, and desertification is advancing at a rate of roughly 1900 square miles annually. According to the country's State Forestry Administration, desertification affects 400 million people—tens of millions of whom become environmental refugees—and contributes to diminished agricultural and animal husbandry opportunities.

The most serious environmental challenge China confronts, however, is ensuring access to clean water. China has 7% of the world's water resources but 20% of the world's population. The country's annual per capita water supply is 25% of the global average, and by 2030, as demand increases, per capita water supply is expected to fall from 2,200 m³ to below 1,700 m³. According to one Chinese expert, cities in the Northeast could run out of water in 5–7 years.

Water pollution is also a significant problem. Of 44 Chinese cities surveyed, 42 had serious groundwater problems. More than three-quarters of the water flowing through China's urban areas is unsuitable for drinking or fishing, and 30% of the river water monitored by the Chinese government is worse than Grade 5 (not suitable for agriculture or industry). Agricultural runoff and untreated wastewater from rural industries have caused serious degradation of several of China's largest and most famous lakes, such as the Tai and Dianchi. In 2005, the State Environmental Protection Administration (SEPA) found that only 23% of 509 cities surveyed properly treated sewage before disposal.

IMPLICATIONS BEYOND THE ENVIRONMENT

These environmental challenges have also produced a range of economic, social, and political problems for China. The health of the Chinese people is endangered by the country's air and water quality. According to the Ministry of Water Resources, 190 million people drink water that is making them sick. In addition, an estimated 400,000 people die prematurely in China annually from respiratory diseases related to air pollution. There is growing evidence that environmental degradation and pollution are impinging on economic growth: polluted water ruins crops, acid rain harms fisheries, and water scarcity forces factories to close for extended periods. All told, SEPA estimates that environmental pollution and degradation cost the Chinese economy the equivalent of 10% of GDP annually. The environment has also become a source of China's growing social unrest. The Chinese media in 2006 reported that there were 50,000 environment-related disputes in China during 2005. Some of these engaged thousands of people and spiraled out of control, resulting in violence and even deaths.

A GROWING GLOBAL ENVIRONMENTAL FOOTPRINT

China's domestic economic and environmental practices also exert a profound impact on the global environment. China has become the first or second largest contributor to many of the world's most challenging environmental problems, among them global climate change, the illegal timber trade, and marine pollution.

Changing the world's climate

As a result of its reliance on coal to fuel its economy, China's emissions of CO_2, the greenhouse gas contributing most significantly to climate change, have tripled over the past 30 years and are now second only to those of the United States. China already uses more coal than the United States, the European Union, and Japan combined. Indeed, unless China takes dramatic action to decrease its reliance on coal and/or increases its use of advanced clean-coal technologies, the increase in global-warming gases from China's coal use will probably exceed that for all other industrialized countries combined over the next 25 years, surpassing by five times the reduction in such emissions that the Kyoto Protocol seeks.

For China itself, the impact of climate change is predicted to be significant. According to the World Bank, a one-meter rise in sea level will cost China's economy 2.4% of GDP. A 5-meter rise will cost 11%. Chinese scientists also predict that precipitation may decline by as much as 30% by 2040 in the Huai, Liao, and Hai river regions. In addition, the Tibetan glaciers are at risk of melting by 2100, which would be devastating not only for the 300 million farmers in China's western region but also for Beijing's plans to divert water to the Northeast.

China has taken several important steps to address the challenge of climate change. It has signed the Kyoto Protocol to the United Nations Framework Convention on Climate Change. (As an "Annex 2" country, it is not required to meet any targets or timetables for reducing its greenhouse gas emissions.) China joined the United States, Japan, and other Asian nations as a member of the Asia-Pacific Partnership on Clean Development and Climate; and it has introduced important domestic policy initiatives on energy efficiency and alternative-energy use.

Under the Kyoto Protocol, China has become active in Clean Development Mechanism (CDM) activities. In the CDM process, companies from around the world that face targets for emissions reductions from their home countries undertake activities in China (or other developing countries), to meet the companies' own emission-reduction targets. Doing so is often cheaper than changing the way these companies do business. Such activities might include investing in a wind-power firm, contributing to a reforestation effort, or paying for a Chinese company to install the most advanced technologies to capture a particular greenhouse gas so that it is not emitted into the atmosphere.

The Asia-Pacific Partnership on Clean Development and Climate includes six countries: Australia, China, India, Japan, the Republic of Korea, and the United States. The partnership is premised on the idea that a regulatory framework such as Kyoto is not the most effective way to meet the challenge of global climate change and stresses instead that developing and implementing "market-worthy technologies" will be more effective. To date, however, the partnership is primarily restricted to information-sharing, some capacity-building, and continued research into improving technologies. While these are all important in responding to climate change, they do not reduce emissions directly. It is also unclear what external incentives there will be for China to implement these new policy changes or technologies.

China's leaders have set out several goals to reduce the country's overall reliance on coal, even as it increases energy consumption. These measures include decreasing energy use per unit of GDP by 20% during 2005–2010, increasing the percentage of renewable energy in the overall energy mix to 10% by 2010, and implementing new energy-efficiency codes for construction throughout China. If achieved, these steps would represent an important demonstration of China's commitment to reducing its contribution to global climate change.

Felling the world's forests

China's role as a manufacturing center for the world, as well as its own rapidly growing need for construction materials, has made it a central player in the world's timber trade. China is the second largest importer of wood products in the world, and Chinese demand for timber and timber products is growing rapidly. From 1993 to 2005, imports more than tripled, and experts anticipate that China's demand for these products will increase by at least one-third during 2005–2010.

Unfortunately, much of China's timber demand, an estimated 50%, is met through illegal supplies. China is now the largest importer of illegally logged timber in the world. Chinese logging companies, active throughout Southeast Asia, Russia, Africa, and the Amazon basin, are a principal source of this illegal timber trade. In Africa, illegal timber exports to China have been soaring, with estimates as high as 70% of total timber exports from Gabon and as much as 90% from Equatorial Guinea. Even for African countries that have attempted to protect their forests, China poses a significant challenge. In the case of Mozambique, for example, Chinese middlemen contract with local license-holders to cut timber, then funnel it through informal ports and transfer it to Chinese ships offshore.

There are several reasons for the burgeoning illegal timber trade: there is typically poor government oversight in host countries, and there are few controls placed on loggers and virtually none at the point of cross-border trade—either by land or by sea into China's ports. Illegal practices such as logging without a license, logging in protected areas, taking protected tree species, and logging outside of concession boundaries are widespread practices wherever China does business.

Reining in the illegal timber trade and managing the world's forests sustainably are important because forests throughout the world are home to endangered species, guard against soil erosion and flooding, and play a critical role as a carbon sink, protecting against climate change.

China has in some instances pledged to improve its practices, signing a number of regional and global agreements to combat the illegal trade in timber, including the Santiago Declaration, the International Tropical Timber Agreement, an East Asian Forest Law Enforcement and Governance agreement, and a memorandum of understanding with Indonesia. However, China does not have any regulations in place to monitor effectively whether logs are imported legally or illegally. Without such enforcement mechanisms, there is little prospect for improvement.

Polluting the Pacific

The most prosperous and developed regions of China are the country's coastal provinces. Since the early 1980s, China's eastern seaboard has been the beneficiary of preferential treatment from a central government that has attracted significant domestic and foreign investment, raised the education level of the Chinese people, and lifted hundreds of millions of Chinese out of poverty to produce a vibrant middle class.

One of the downsides of this development has been that the Yangtze Delta—one of the wealthiest coastal regions—has become the biggest source of marine pollution in the Pacific Ocean. China has 18,000 km of coastline, and inspections by the SEPA and the State Oceanic Administration found that in nearly half of the 20 coastal cities inspected, more than 50% of the sewage is discharged into the sea untreated.

In some cases, the situation is dire. The State Oceanographic Administration has found that almost no river that flows into the Bo Hai Sea on the northeastern coast is clean, and predicts that the Bo Hai will become a dead sea in a dozen years if strong measures are not taken. Tests of the mud at the bottom of the Bo Hai indicate that the content of heavy metals is 2,000 times that of the national standard.

China is also polluting the waters of Cambodia, Malaysia, Thailand, and Vietnam. Over half of the nutrients that deoxygenate areas of sea shared by China and these countries originate in China.

China's own assessment of the roots of its large and growing contribution to marine pollution are not surprising: it pinpoints rapid growth of coastal areas and poor enforcement of marine protection and wastewater treatment laws. Despite understanding the nature of the challenge, China's leaders have been unable to address the problem effectively. The central government in Beijing has launched several large-scale but ineffective campaigns to improve waste treatment. Ambitious targets are undermined by lack of investment, water pricing that is too low to encourage conservation and treatment, local officials who ignore central directives, and the sheer scale and rapidity of economic development in these regions.

THE ENVIRONMENTAL FUTURE OF CHINA AND THE WORLD

China's rapid, unfettered development has produced vexing environmental challenges with significant social, economic, and political consequences for China and the rest of the world. There are great opportunities for China to transform its development practices—and in the process its contribution to global environmental degradation—as it continues to urbanize three to four hundred million people over the coming decades.

Taking advantage of new technologies and materials to enhance energy efficiency and energy conservation, providing greater levels of investment in environmental protection, and adopting policy approaches to limit the impact of China's development on global environmental problems such as deforestation are critical first steps.

Equally important, however, are measures to ensure that implementation of the country's environmental-protection laws and regulations is improved. This will mean strengthening the political power of local environmental protection officials, enacting political and economic incentives that make it easy for business and officials to do the right thing and obey environmental laws, and opening the door to greater transparency and rule of law. These are the underpinnings of an effective institutional infrastructure for environmental protection.

Certainly, the international community has both the opportunity and responsibility to assist China in transforming itself from one of the world's greatest environmental polluters to an environmental leader. Fundamentally, however, the choices and responsibility for meeting its own environmental needs and those of the rest of the world rest within China itself.

BIBLIOGRAPHY

Bradsher, K., and D. Barboza. "The Energy Challenge: The Cost of Coal: Pollution from Chinese Coal Casts a Global Shadow." *New York Times*, June 11, 2006, p. 1.
"China: A City Built on Mao's Order Fights an Encroaching Desert." *Inter Press Service*, November 8, 2006.
"China Admits to Marine Pollution Problem." *United Press International*, August 5, 2004.
Global Witness. "A Choice for China: Ending the Destruction of Burma's Northern Frontier Forests." October 2005, p. 24. http://www.globalwitness.org/media_library_get.php/323/a_choice_for_china_low_res.pdf (accessed May 26, 2008).
Griffiths, D. "Drought Worsens China Water Woes." *BBC News*, May 31, 2006. http://news.bbc.co.uk/2/hi/asia-pacific/474519.stm (accessed May 26, 2008).
Holland, T. "Pollution Woes Can Turn China into Green Industry Leader." *South China Morning Post*, April 3, 2006.
Pan Yue. "The Chinese Miracle Will End Soon." Interview by A. Lorenz. *Der Spiegel*, March 7, 2005. http://www.spiegel.de/international/spiegel/0,1518,345694,00.html (accessed May 26, 2008).
"Soil and Trouble." *Science* 304 (2004), 1614–1615. DOI: 10.1126/science.304.5677.1614.
Watts, J. "On the Water Front." *The Guardian*, November 11, 2004. http://www.guardian.co.uk/environment/2004/nov/11/water.china (accessed May 26, 2008).
Xinhua News Agency. "China Reports Cities Suffering from Severe Air Pollution." *People's Daily Online*, September 6, 2006. http://english.people.com.cn/200609/06/eng20060906_299854.html (accessed May 26, 2008).
———. "Less Greenhouse Gases to Help Balance Precipitation in China's Major Rivers." *People's Daily Online*, July 8, 2006. http://english.people.com.en.200607/08/eng20060708_171243.html (accessed May 26, 2008).
———. "One-Third of China's Land Areas Still Suffer from Soil Erosion." *People's Online Daily*, June 2, 2005. http://english.people.com.en.200506/02/eng20050602/_188151.html (accessed May 26, 2008).

—Elizabeth Economy

CHLOROFLUOROCARBONS

Chlorofluorocarbons (CFCs) are volatile compounds of chlorine, fluorine, and carbon that were first synthesized in the 1920s as a substitute for toxic refrigerants such as ammonia and methyl chloride, and patented under the trade name Freon. Because of their nontoxic, nonreactive, and nonflammable nature, they became widely used during the following decades, not only as refrigerants, but also as solvents, propellants, and foaming agents. Those very attributes also mean that they have very long residence times in the troposphere.

Molina and Rowland (1974) showed that these long-lived CFCs would eventually move up into the stratosphere where they would be broken down by ultraviolet radiation, releasing free chlorine and leading to the destruction of ozone in the stratosphere. Since stratospheric ozone absorbs most of the sun's ultraviolet wavelengths below 320 nanometers, the destruction of ozone would allow more medium-wavelength (UV-B) radiation to reach the earth's surface and cause damage to plants and animals. It has since been learned that several other substances are capable of destroying stratospheric ozone; these ozone-depleting substances (ODSs) are said to have ozone-depletion potential (ODP).

OZONE

Ozone (O_3) is a highly reactive form of oxygen having three atoms per molecule instead of the usual two. It occurs in both the troposphere and the stratosphere, but for different reasons. Over 90% of atmospheric ozone is produced in the stratosphere (20–30 km altitude) through the absorption of ultraviolet radiation which would otherwise reach the surface and affect plants and animals. The remainder is produced in the troposphere (0–10 km altitude) through the interaction of sunlight, volatile organic compounds (from natural as well as human sources), and nitrogen oxides (mostly human-made).

It is a key pollutant in the photochemical smog that plagues many urban areas and can cause severe injury to plants and animals. [See Ozone.]

The decrease in stratospheric ozone was first detected near the South Pole in the 1970s by the British Antarctic Survey, although its cause was not recognized until 1985. The phenomenon, called the "ozone hole," was found to be most pronounced during the polar spring. A decrease was later found also in the Northern Hemisphere, as much as 10% per decade in Europe and Canada since 1973. Ozone concentration at the South Pole, during October, dropped from about 325 Dobson units (DU) before 1970 to about 100 DU in the first decade of the twenty-first century.

HALOCARBONS AND THEIR GLOBAL-WARMING POTENTIAL

CFCs are one of a larger class of substances called halocarbons, which are compounds of carbon and one or more of the halogens (fluorine, chlorine, bromine, iodine, and astatine). Although not all halocarbons deplete stratospheric ozone, they are all greenhouse gases having global-warming potential (GWP). They include not only CFCs, but low-ODP substances that have been synthesized to replace CFCs and others that have a wide variety of industrial uses. The major halocarbons are listed in Table 1. Almost without exception these substances are man-made and were not present in the atmosphere prior to their synthesis a few decades ago. [See Greenhouse Gases.]

The most potent ODSs are the bromofluorocarbons or halons, compounds of bromine, chlorine, fluorine, and carbon used as fire-extinguishing agents. Although current concentrations of these substances in the atmosphere are about 0.6% those of CFCs, they are 50–100 times (per unit mass) more effective at destroying ozone. The CFCs, along with carbon tetrachloride, methyl chloroform, and methyl bromide, have intermediate ODPs (0.11–1.2). The hydrochlorofluorocarbons, which were synthesized as substitutes for the CFCs, have ODPs between 0.01 and 0.10, while the HFCs (hydrofluorocarbons) and PFCs (perfluorocarbons), which contain no chlorine or bromine, have zero ODP. Nearly all of the chlorine, and about half of the bromine, found in the stratosphere, comes from human sources. Virtually all of the substances in Table 1 have GWPs between several hundred and several thousand times that of carbon dioxide, and long atmospheric residence times, making them major threats as greenhouse gases.

STRATOSPHERIC OZONE DESTRUCTION

Ozone is produced in the stratosphere through the breakdown of oxygen molecules by solar UV radiation:

$$O_2 + UV \rightarrow 2O, \text{ and}$$
$$O_2 + O \rightarrow O_3.$$

At the same time, ozone molecules are destroyed naturally by radiation and by collisions with oxygen atoms:

$$O_3 + UV \rightarrow O_2 + O, \text{ and}$$
$$O_3 + O \rightarrow 2O_2.$$

A delicate balance between these production and destruction processes keeps the ozone concentration at a level appropriate for protecting the earth's surface from harmful UV radiation as well as raising the temperature of the upper stratosphere. It is believed that a number of man-made substances are capable of interfering with these processes and leading to ozone depletion, including nitrogen oxides from supersonic aircraft flying in the stratosphere, and some agricultural emissions. CFCs and their cousins appear to be even more dangerous than these, however, because of their large ODPs and very long residence times. While these substances are nonreactive in the troposphere, when they rise to the stratosphere and encounter intense ultraviolet radiation, they break down, releasing chlorine or bromine atoms which react with the ozone:

$$Cl + O_3 \rightarrow ClO + O_2, \text{ and}$$
$$ClO + O \rightarrow Cl + O_2.$$

Thus chlorine (or bromine) atoms are recycled through this process, and each one may remove as many as 100,000 ozone molecules before disappearing itself. The chlorine (or chlorine monoxide) ultimately reacts with nitrogen dioxide or methane to form chlorine nitrate ($ClONO_2$) or hydrochloric acid (HCl):

$$ClO + NO_2 \rightarrow ClONO_2, \text{ or}$$
$$CH_4 + Cl \rightarrow HCl + CH_3.$$

The chlorine nitrate and hydrochloric acid taking part in the above reactions act as long-lived carriers (or reservoirs) that release their chlorine efficiently on the surfaces of polar stratospheric cloud-particles. Nacreous (mother-of-pearl) clouds are distinctive by being visible after sunset or before sunrise, because of their high altitude (15–20 km). It was discovered in the 1980s that they are composed of a mixture of sulfuric and nitric acid particles, which form only at temperatures below -80°C, and are involved in ozone depletion in the polar regions. Volcanic emissions in the midlatitudes were found to play a similar role. Stratospheric ozone chemistry is much more complex than has been outlined here, and there are still some gaps in our understanding, particularly with regard to midlatitude ozone depletion.

HALOCARBON USE AND WORLD REACTION

World production of CFCs rose from 42,000 tons per year in 1950 to almost 1 million tons in 1974, when the first theory of ozone depletion was published. Production leveled off for a decade in response to this warning but then started to rise again. Increasing evidence of a cause-effect relationship between CFC production and ozone depletion, and the deepening ozone hole over Antarctica, finally led to the United Nations Environment Programme's Vienna Convention on the Protection of the Ozone Layer in 1985. This prompted 47 countries to sign the Montreal Protocol on Substances that Deplete the Ozone Layer in 1987, encouraging all countries to restrict and eventually eliminate the production of CFCs and halons and to replace them with less environmentally damaging chemicals. Its control provisions have

TABLE 1. Halogenated Alkanes and Similar Substances Released to the Atmosphere, with Their Ozone-Depletion Potentials (ODPs) and Global Warming Potentials (GWPs), Atmospheric Half-Lives, and Present Mass Concentrations and Trends

Name	Chemical Formula	Main Use or Source	Ozone-Depletion Potential	Global Warming Potential*	Half-Life (Years)	Present Level (per 10^{-12})	Trend
Chlorofluorocarbons (CFCs)		As solvents, refrigerants, propellants					
CFC-11	CCl_3F		1.0	4,000	60	270	Falling
CFC-12	CCl_2F_2		1.0	8,500	100	550	Level
CFC-13	$CClF_3$		1.0	11,700	640		
CFC-113	$C_2Cl_3F_3$		0.8	5,000	90	80	Level
CFC-114	$C_2Cl_2F_4$		1.0	9,300	200		
CFC-115	C_2ClF_5		0.6	9,300	400		
Hydrochlorofluorocarbons (HCFCs)		As substitutes for CFCs					
HCFC-22	$CHClF_2$		0.05	1,600	13		
HCFC-123	CF_3CHCl_2		0.02	90	2		
HCFC-124	CF_3CHClF		0.02	480	6		
HCFC-141b	CH_3CFCl_2		0.10	600	9		
HCFC-142b	CH_3CF_2Cl		0.06	2,000	19		
Hydrofluorocarbons (HFCs)		As substitutes for CFCs					
HFC-23	CHF_3		nil	11,700	250		
HFC-32	CH_2F_2		nil	650	6		
HFC-125	C_2HF_5		nil	2,800	30		
HFC-134a	CH_2FCF_3		nil	1,300	14	1.6	Rising
HFC-143a	CH_3CF_3		nil	3,800	40		
HFC-152a	CH_3CHF_2		nil	140	2		
Perfluorocarbons (PFCs)		From aluminum production and uranium enrichment					
Perfluoromethane	CF_4		nil	6,500	50,000	75	
Perfluoroethane	C_2F_6		nil	9,200	10,000	2.6	
Halons (Hs)		In fire extinguishers					
H-1211	$CBrClF_2$		4			3.5	Rising
H-1301	$CBrF_3$		12	5,600		2.3	Rising
H-2402	$C_2Br_2F_4$		6			0.5	Level
Carbon tetrachloride	CCl_4	As solvent	1.1	1,400	50	100	Level
Methyl chloroform	CH_3CCl_3	As adhesives and solvents	0.11	110	6	90	Falling
Methyl bromide	CH_3Br	Natural and as soil fumigant	0.6		1.3	10	Level
Sulfur hexafluoride	SF_6	For equipment insulation and cable cooling	nil	25,000	3,000	33	Rising

*GWPs are for a 100-year time horizon.

been amended and strengthened regularly since then in London (1990), Copenhagen (1992), Vienna (1995), and Montreal (1997). The Protocol set deadlines for the phase-out of CFCs, halons, methyl chloroform, carbon tetrachloride, and more recently, methyl bromide and the HCFCs (hydrochlorofluorocarbons).

The HCFCs and the HFCs (Table 1) were developed as substitutes for CFCs. The addition of hydrogen atoms to the molecules substantially reduced the ODP, GWP, and half-life of the HCFCs, while the subsequent removal of the chlorine atoms eliminated the ODP of the HFCs at the expense of increases in GWP.

Although production of the major ODSs has dropped dramatically since the Montreal Protocol was signed, their concentrations in the atmosphere, even 10 years later, had at best only leveled off. This is because of the long residence times of most of these substances, which indicate that it will be more than 100 years before there is a significant decline. However, concentrations of ODSs with shorter residence times, such as methyl chloroform, have already begun to decline.

The search for more environmentally friendly substitutes for these products continues. At present, the conservative use of zero-ODP substances such as the HFCs, together with effective recycling appears to offer the best alternative.

[*See also* Chemical Industry; Greenhouse Effect; Human Impacts; *and* Pollution.]

BIBLIOGRAPHY

Albritton, D.L., R.T. Watson, and R. J. Aucamp, eds. *Scientific Assessment of Ozone Depletion: 1994*. Geneva: World Meteorological Organization, 1995.
Bolin, B., et al., eds. *The Greenhouse Effect, Climatic Change, and Ecosystems.* SCOPE Report 29, Scientific Committee on Problems of the Environment. Chichester, U.K., and New York: Wiley, 1986.
Cunnold, D.M., et al. "Global Trends and Annual Releases of CCl_3F and CCl_2F_2 Estimated from ALE/GAGE and Other Measurements from July 1978 to June 1991." *Journal of Geophysical Research* 99.D1 (1994), 1107-1126.
Fraser, P., et al. "Lifetime and Emission Estimates of 1,1,2-trichlorotrifluoroethane (CFC-113) from Daily Global Background Observations June 1982–June 1994." *Journal of Geophysical Research* 101.D7 (1996), 12585-12599.
Houghton, J.T., B.A. Callander., and S.K. Varney, eds. *Climate Change 1992: The Supplementary Report to the IPCC Scientific Assessment*. Cambridge and New York: Cambridge University Press, 1992.
Houghton, J. T., G. J. Jenkins., and J. J. Ephraums, eds. *Climate Change: The IPCC Scientific Assessment*. Cambridge and New York: Cambridge University Press, 1990.
Houghton, J. T., et al., eds. *Climate Change 1995: The Science of Climate Change*. Cambridge and New York: Cambridge University Press, 1996.
Kaye, J. A., et al. *Report on Concentrations, Lifetimes and Trends of CFCs, Halons and Related Species*. NASA Reference Publication 1339. Greenbelt, Md.: NASA, 1994.
Molina M. J., and F. S. Rowland. "Stratospheric Sink for Chlorofluoromethanes: Chlorine Atomic-Catalysed Destruction of Ozone." *Nature* 249 (1974): 810–812.

—EARLE A. RIPLEY

CITIES

See Urban Areas; Urban Climates; *and* Urban Trends.

CLIMATE CHANGE AND SOCIETAL DEVELOPMENT

The many rapid and severe climate changes of the Quaternary have affected humans in many parts of the world (Table 1). Changes during the Upper Miocene (6–8 million years ago), such as the aridification in East Africa, set the scene for hominid evolution (Sepulchre et al., 2006), and it is evident that subsequent human evolution has been greatly affected by climate change (Vbra et al., 1995). Curiously, whereas hunter gatherers and foragers were able to move in response to changes in

TABLE 1. Examples of Recent Studies of Climatic Influences on Human History in the Holocene

Location	Approximate date	Source
Collapse of classic Mayan civilization	1000 AD	Hodell et al., 1995 & Neff et al., 2006
Expansion of cattle keepers into the Sahara	Early- to mid-Holocene	Petit-Maire et al., 1999
Abandonment of Greenland settlements	1300–1500 AD	Grove, 2004
Abandonment of highland settlement in SE Scotland	1300–1600 AD	Parry, 1978
Anasazi collapse, SW USA	End of 13th century AD	Grove, 2004
Economic decline in Gulf Region	4100 BP	Parker et al., 2004
Spread of cultivation into highland Britain	Medieval	Lamb, 1982
Decline of Middle Eastern empires (e.g., the Akkadian)	4200 BP	Weiss et al., 1993
End of Harappan (Indus) civilization	4200 BP	Staubwasser et al., 2003
Culture change in the Atacama Desert, Chile	Mid Holocene	Grosjean et al., 1997
Cultural change in coastal Peru	Mid Holocene	Wells and Noller, 1999
Domestication	Early Holocene/Late Pleistocene	Sherratt, 1997
Southwards expansion of Bantu in Africa	After c 4200 BP	Burroughs, 2005
Neolithic settlement in Harz Mountains	7600–4550 BP	Voigt, 2006
Mid-Neolithic decline in NE Morocco	6500–6000 BP	Zielhofer and Linstädter, 2006
Collapse of Tiwanaku State	c 1000 BP	Ortloff and Kolata, 1993
Emergence of Egyptian Dynastic state and of Pharaonic civilization	c 6000 BP	Brooks, 2006 & Kuper & Kröpelin, 2006.

climate, more advanced peoples have become increasingly anchored to particular locations and have been less able to adapt to changing conditions by means of migration (Linden, 2006).

There are many examples of the effects of climate change evident during the Holocene. [*See* Holocene.] The event about 8,200 years ago forced the abandonment of agricultural settlements in northern Mesopotamia and the Levant (Anderson et al., 2007). Conversely, the "greening of the Sahara" in the early to mid-Holocene led to an explosion of activity by Neolithic peoples in the Sahara (Petit-Maire et al., 1999). From about 6,000 years BP a reduction of rainfall and of monsoon strength in North Africa, the Near East, and Arabia forced people out of the deserts into other more favorable environments. Around 5,200 BP a rapid drying and cooling event in the Middle East may have led to the collapse of the Uruk culture in southern Mesopotamia. Around 4,200–4,100 BP another sharp climatic deterioration caused severe problems for many urban centers (Diamond, 2005; Fagan, 2004). In general, agricultural intensification and domestication may have been stimulated by episodes of increased aridity (Sherratt, 1997), and there was an association in the mid-Holocene between desiccation and increasing social complexity in the central Sahara and Egypt (Brooks, 2006). Enhanced aridity, Brooks argues, caused population agglomeration in environmental refuges located on bodies of fresh water (e.g., the Nile Valley).

Some of the cold phases of the Holocene (neoglaciations) had an enormous impact on peoples in high latitudes and at high altitudes (Grove, 2004), just as the Medieval Warm Epoch was seen as a time of economic progress in parts of Europe (Lamb, 1982). [*See* Little Ice Age in Europe; *and* Medieval Climate Optimum.]

BIBLIOGRAPHY

Anderson, D., A.S. Goudie, and A.G. Parker. *Global Environments through the Quaternary*. Oxford and New York: Oxford University Press, 2007.

Brooks, N. "Cultural Responses to Aridity in the Middle Holocene and Increased Social Complexity." *Quaternary International* 151 (2006), 29–49. DOI: 10.1016/j.quaint.2006.01.013.

Burroughs, W.J. *Climate Change in Prehistory*. Cambridge and New York: Cambridge University Press, 2005.

Diamond, J. *Collapse: How Societies Choose to Fail or Survive*. London: Allen Lane, 2005.

Fagan, B. *The Long Summer: How Climate Changed Civilization*. New York: Basic Books, 2004.

Grove, J.M. *Little Ice Ages: Ancient and Modern*. London: Routledge, 2004.

Kuper, R., and S. Kröpelin. "Climate-Controlled Holocene Occupation in the Sahara: Motor of Africa's Evolution." *Science* 313 (2006), 803–807.

Lamb, H.H. *Climate, History, and the Modern World*. London: Methuen, 1982.

Linden, E. *The Winds of Change*. New York: Simon and Schuster, 2006.

Neff, H., et al. "Climate Change and Population History in the Pacific Lowlands of Southern Mesoamerica." *Quaternary Research* 65 (2006), 390–400. DOI: 10.1016/j.yqres.2005.10.002.

Parker, A.G., et al. "Holocene Vegetation Dynamics in the Northeastern Rub' al-Khali Desert, Arabian Peninsula: A Pollen, Phytolith, and Carbon Isotope Study." *Journal of Quaternary Science* 19 (2004), 665–676.

Petit-Maire, N., et al. "Paléoclimats Holocènes du Sahara septentrionale, dépôts lacustres et terrasses alluviales en bordure du Grand Erg Oriental à l'extrême-Sud de la Tunisie." *Comptes Rendus Académie des Sciences*, Series 2, 312 (1999), 1661–1666.

Sepulchre, P., et al. "Tectonic Uplift and Eastern Africa Aridification." *Science* 313 (2006), 1419–1423. DOI: 10.1126/science.1129158.

Sherratt, A. "Climatic Cycles and Behavioural Revolutions: The Emergence of Modern Humans and the Beginning of Farming." *Antiquity* 71 (1997), 271–287.

Staubwasser, M., et al. "Climate Change at the 4.2 ka BP Termination of the Indus Valley Civilization and Holocene South Asian Monsoon Variability." *Geophysical Research Letters* 30 (2003). DOI:10.1029/2002GL016822.

Vbra, E.S., et al., eds. *Paleoclimate and Evolution, with Emphasis on Human Origins*. New Haven: Yale University Press, 1995.

Voigt, R. "Settlement History as Reflection of Climate Change: The Case Study of Lake Jues (Harz Mountains, Germany)." *Geografiska Annaler* 88.A (2006), 97–105.

Zielhofer, C., and J. Linstädter. "Short-Term Mid-Holocene Climatic Deterioration in the West Mediterranean Region: Climatic Impact on Neolithic Settlement Pattern?" *Zeitschrift für Geomorphologie* Supplement Band 142 (2006), 1–17.

—ANDREW S. GOUDIE

CLIMATE MODELS AND UNCERTAINTY

Climate models are designed to simulate the processes that produce climate. They take various forms and involve various levels of complexity depending upon the application for which they are designed. The earliest climate models were representative in nature, attempting to describe and explain the workings of the atmosphere rather than predict them. George Hadley's model of the circulation of the atmosphere developed in 1735 was a representative model, for example. Later refinements to this classic model, such as the introduction of seasonal variations plus an increased knowledge of the upper atmosphere, did add an element of prediction, but even into the middle of the twentieth century such representations of the earth's global winds and pressure belts remained essentially descriptive in nature.

The first effective predictive model was based on processes that were part of these systems but developed at a regional rather than a global scale: this was the mid-latitude frontal model of interactions among the various air masses involved in a low pressure system or cyclone. Developed between 1915 and 1920 by Norwegian weather forecasters, it remained an important forecasting tool in mid-latitudes for at least fifty years and the elements of the model—such as cold front, warm front, warm sector—continue to be part of the current weather forecasting vocabulary. The frontal model included elements of an analogue model in that future changes were predicted in part by comparing the existing situation with one that exhibited similar characteristics in the past; but it also introduced mathematical processes for predicting more accurately such elements as the speed and direction of the system as a whole, plus wind speeds and pressure changes within the system. With time and improved technology the numerical elements in the prediction became more and more effective. Modern weather forecasting techniques, as well as those used to predict climate, depend almost entirely on mathematical and computerized manipulation of data for their results.

Currently, the most common use of climate modeling is in the study of global warming. Since its inception, the Intergovernmental Panel on Climate Change (IPCC) has incorporated

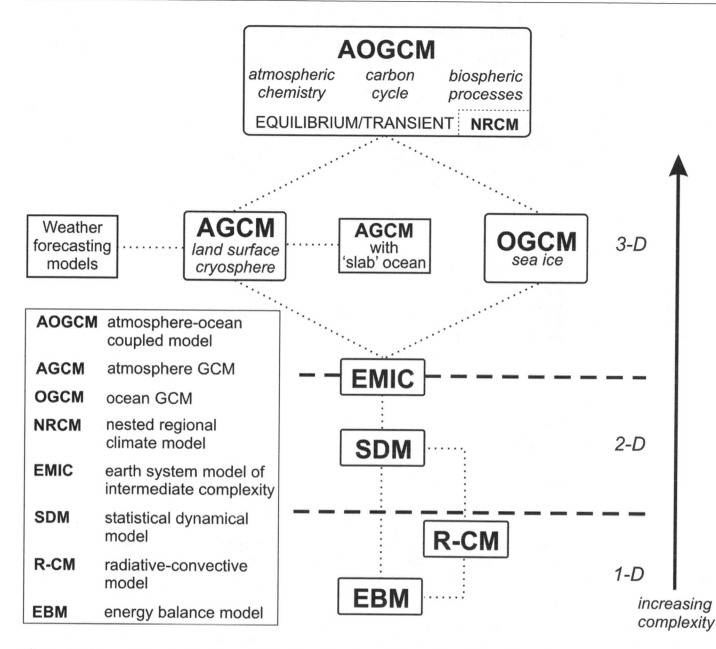

Climate Models and Uncertainty. FIGURE 1. The Hierarchy of Climate Models.

results from a variety of climate models in its predictions of future climate change, and in so doing has encouraged the evolution and development of modeling techniques. [*See* Global Warming.*]

MODEL TYPES

Climate models form a hierarchy that ranges from relatively simple one-dimensional models incorporating a single element such as radiation to highly sophisticated three-dimensional general circulation models that provide full spatial analysis of the earth-atmosphere system (see Figure 1). The simpler models include one-dimensional energy balance models (EBM), which predict variations in surface temperatures with latitude, and radiative-convective models (RC), which consider vertical radiative transfer through the atmosphere and the upward transfer of heat by convection, to provide a vertical temperature profile of the atmosphere. One-dimensional models have been used to investigate the effects of volcanic activity on radiative and convective processes at different levels in the atmosphere; in fact the concept of "nuclear winter" was based on results from an RC model (Turco et al., 1983). Slightly more complex are statistical dynamical (SD) models, which include zonally averaged horizontal energy transport as well as a vertically resolved atmosphere, creating a two-dimensional system (McGuffie and Henderson-Sellers, 1997). Although relatively fast and cheap to run, these models have serious limitations in the study and prediction of climate change. One-dimensional models treat the earth as a uniform surface with no geography and no seasons. As a result, they are unable to deal with uneven surface energy distributions such as those introduced by land and water. Two-dimensional models can include consideration of differences in heat capacity between land and ocean; but their ability to deal with the evolving dynamics of the atmosphere once change has been initiated remains limited. In part because of such inadequacies, and in part because of major advances in technology and analysis, these simple models have been superseded by a series of multidimensional, multifaceted models that attempt to provide full spatial analysis of the workings of the earth-atmosphere system.

GENERAL CIRCULATION MODELS

The most complex and sophisticated of current climate models are the general circulation models (GCMs). They represent the physics and dynamics of the earth-atmosphere system through a series of fundamental equations, such as those involving the conservation of energy, momentum, and mass, for example, or laws related to the pressure, density, and temperatures of gases. When these are solved repeatedly over short time steps, for a series of small incremental changes, they can forecast the state of the atmosphere over periods extending from decades to centuries.

The potential advantages of such techniques were recognized by weather forecasters in the early part of the twentieth century, but the complexity of the calculations and the existence of only rudimentary methods of mechanical computation meant that the predications could not keep ahead of changing weather conditions, and no real forecast could be made (Houghton, 2005). It was only in the 1950s and 1960s that advances in computer technology and improved methods of observation allowed the development of models capable of predicting changes in essential meteorological elements. Since then these methods have been universally adopted, and numerical modeling is the most common method of weather forecasting for periods of several hours to 5–6 days ahead.

Climate models incorporate similar methodologies when analyzing the atmosphere, but they differ in a number of important ways from weather-forecasting models. Over the short time periods—several days—covered by weather forecasting models, for example, environmental elements such as vegetation, oceans or ice sheets can be considered static or unchanging, therefore contributing nothing to atmospheric change. Over the longer time scales—decades to centuries—involved in climate models, however, these elements would be expected to change, and that change must be incorporated in the models (Figure 2). Complicating the situation is the fact that the changes are not always linear but incorporate feedback mechanisms that may enhance or diminish the original change. Climate models must also be capable of dealing with these feedbacks. Accommodating this increase in environmental variables and their changes, in addition to the longer timescales involved, increases the computer capacity and time required to run the model, which in turn increases costs. A reduction in the number of grid points at which calculations are made helps to keep time and cost requirements at a manageable level but produces a coarser resolution in the model. Typical climate models have a resolution that is three to six times coarser than that of weather forecasting models, for example: this provides adequate representation of large-scale climatic features but restricts the application to local climate change. To overcome this problem, regional climate models (RCMs) with higher resolution and shorter running times have been developed. They are imbedded within a global model and driven by that model. Since the extra information is required for only a restricted area, and running time is relatively short, demands on computer power and time are lessened and costs remain manageable.

State-of-the-art GCMs are capable of processing data at tens of thousands of points in a three-dimensional grid covering the earth's surface, and reaching through as many as 38 levels as high as 30 kilometers into the atmosphere. In the top 5 kilometers of the oceans they may sample at as many as 40 levels (Pope, 2007). Such detail and intensity provide a horizontal resolution of some 135 kilometers, which is sufficient to simulate major atmospheric processes but too coarse to allow the incorporation of processes that operate at a local or regional scale. These processes which operate at less than grid-scale—convective thundercloud formation, for example—are integrated into the models through parameterization, a technique that involves the establishment of a statistical relationship between grid-scale variables in the GCM and the smaller-scale processes. Calculations at the grid scale can then provide estimates of local or regional conditions. Cloudiness, net surface radiation, various elements of the hydrologic cycle, and land surface processes all require parameterization for inclusion in GCMs.

The earliest GCMs were component models that simulated conditions in one sector of the earth-atmosphere system. Atmospheric models (AGCM), for example, were designed to represent large-scale distributions of surface air temperature, precipitation, and mean sea level pressure, whereas oceanic models (OGCM) provided simulations of ocean temperatures, salinity, and sea-ice distributions. The constituents of the real environment, however, do not operate in isolation but as integrated elements of the earth-atmosphere system: in an attempt to emulate that, atmosphere and ocean models were combined or coupled to produce atmosphere-ocean general circulation models (AOGCM). These are the most complex GCMs in use, with some incorporating elements of biospheric processes, the carbon cycle, and atmospheric chemistry (Houghton, 2005). The IPCC used results from twenty-three AOGCMs in preparing its Fourth Assessment Report (FAR) and credits the large number of simulations available from these models for major advances in the assessment of climate-change projections available in the FAR (Randall et al., 2007). They show, for example, that following a doubling of CO_2, the global average surface-warming is likely to be in the range of 2°C to 4.5°C with a best estimate of 30°C. They are also able to project regional differences that show the greatest warming is to be expected at high latitudes over the continents.

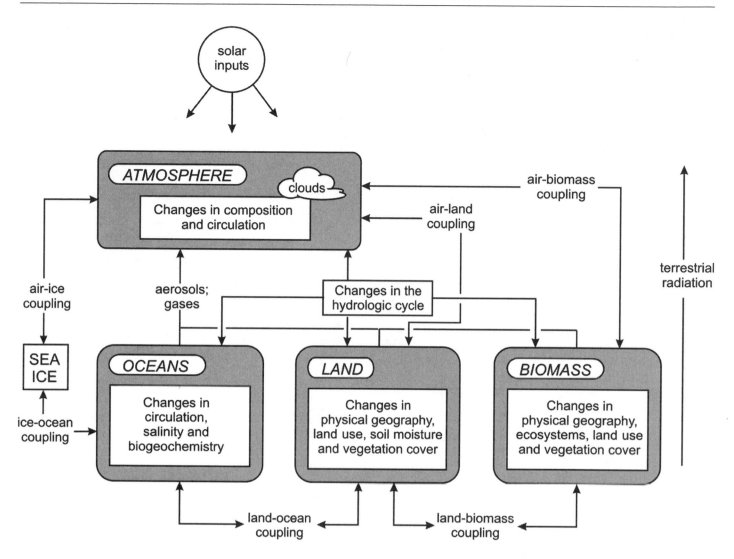

Climate Models and Uncertainty. Figure 2. The elements, processes and linkages that must be considered in developing models to emulate the integrated nature of the earth-atmosphere system.

In the development of GCMs, most of the initial effort was invested in producing equilibrium models. In these, instantaneous change is introduced into a model that represents existing climate conditions, and the model is then allowed to run until a new equilibrium is reached. The new model climate can then be compared with the original to establish the overall impact of the change. Many estimates of the global warming expected from a doubling of atmospheric carbon dioxide are of this type. They make no attempt to estimate changing climate conditions during the transient phase of the model run, although these changes may have important environmental impacts before equilibrium is reached. Transient or time-dependent models in which the change is apportioned over a specific time period were introduced to provide the intermediate information. Although requirements for increased computer power and additional informational data meant that their development initially lagged behind that of equilibrium models, they are now commonly employed in a range of climate change investigations, but particularly those involving global warming (e.g., Stier et al., 2006; Stott et al., 2006).

Models of intermediate complexity

Current AOGCMs are increasingly comprehensive in their consideration of components of the earth-atmosphere system and their dynamics. That comes with a high computational cost, however, and it has become apparent that the high level of complexity available in AOGCMs may in some cases exceed that required to investigate a specific issue. This has led to development of earth system models of intermediate complexity (EMIC) which incorporate most of the processes included in AOGCMs but at a reduced resolution and with some simplification of the atmospheric and oceanic components (Randall et al., 2007). The reduction in complexity reduces the computational costs of running EMICs, allowing them to provide results not normally available from AOGCMs. EMICs allow, for example, long-term climate simulation experiments—over several thousand years—which are not commonly run on AOGCMs because of prohibitive computational costs. Other EMICs attempt to simulate the natural integration of the components of the earth-atmosphere system by incorporating as many of these components as possible, while some include socioeconomic components (Claussen, 2002). EMICs differ in their levels of complexity, but the results they produce compare well with results from AOGCMs (Petoukhov et al., 2005) and they have been used to provide information on past and future climate change for the IPCC FAR (Randall et al., 2007).

EVALUATION AND RELIABILITY

Three to four decades of research and development have produced significant improvements in climate modeling, but deficiencies remain. Despite their overall sophistication and complexity, different models using the same data often produce different results. For example, they show a considerable range in their estimates of climate sensitivity—the equilibrium change in surface air temperature following a unit change in radiative forcing (as by an increase in carbon dioxide concentration). This is of some concern in the study of global warming, where despite ongoing improvements in the analytical abilities of the models the climate sensitivity range is not narrowing (Houghton, 2005). Inadequacies in the representation of complex climatic processes through parameterization or the incorporation of feedbacks involving clouds, oceans, sea-ice, and vegetation also limit the quality of simulations and require continued research. Since physical and statistical components differ from model to model, as do the quality of parameterization and the number and complexity of the feedbacks included, such variations are not unexpected.

Overall, there is growing confidence in the ability of models to provide credible predictions of climate change. When models are tested by comparing their results with observational data, such as twentieth-century global temperature records, for example, they perform increasingly well (Hengeveld, 2006). Comparisons with past climates provided by proxy data such as stable-isotope ratios show that models can reproduce the essential features of climate change back to the last glacial maximum with some reliability, while their ability to simulate short-term perturbations, such as major volcanic eruptions or the seasonal shifts of major monsoon systems, increases confidence in their accuracy (Randall et al., 2007). All climate models represent a compromise between the complexities of the earth-atmosphere system and the constraints imposed by such factors as data availability, computer power, and the cost of model development and operation—all of which limit the accuracy of the final product. The gap between climate simulation and climate reality will never be completely closed, but there is no doubt that climate models will continue to be important tools in improving our understanding of climate and the elements of the earth-atmosphere system with which it is involved.

BIBLIOGRAPHY

Claussen, M., et al. "Earth System Models of Intermediate Complexity: Closing the Gap in the Spectrum of Climate System Models." *Climate Dynamics* 18 (2002), 579–586.

Hengeveld, H. *CO2/Climate Report: 2003–2005 Science Review: A Synthesis of New Research Developments*. Toronto: Environment Canada, 2006.
Houghton, J. "Global Warming." *Reports on Progress in Physics* 68 (2005), 1343–1403. DOI: 10.1088/0034-4885/68/6/R02.
McGuffie, K., and A. Henderson-Sellers. *A Climate Modelling Primer*. 2d ed. Chichester, U.K., and New York: Wiley, 1997.
Petoukhov, V., et al. "EMIC Intercomparison Project (EMIP-CO$_2$): Comparative Analysis of EMIC Simulations of Climate, and of Equilibrium and Transient Responses to Atmospheric CO$_2$ Doubling." *Climate Dynamics* 25 (2005), 363–385.
Pope, V. (2007) "Models 'Key to Climate Forecasts.'" http://newsbbc.co.uk/2/hi/science/nature/6320515.stm (accessed May 29, 2008).
Randall, D.A., et al. "Climate Models and their Evaluation." In *Climate Change 2007: The Physical Science Basis. Contribution of Working Group I to the Fourth Assessment Report of the Intergovernmental Panel on Climate Change*, edited by S. Solomon, et al. Cambridge and New York: Cambridge University Press, 2007.
Stier, P., et al. "The Evolution of the Global Aerosol System in a Transient Climate Simulation from 1860 to 2100." *Atmospheric Chemistry and Physics* 6 (2006), 3059–3076.
Stott, P.A., et al. "Transient Climate Simulations with the HadGEM1 Climate Model: Causes of Past Warming and Future Climate Change." *Journal of Climate* 19.12 (2006), 2763–2782. DOI: 10.1175/JCLI3731.1.
Turco, R.P., et al. "Nuclear Winter: Global Consequences of Multiple Nuclear Explosions." *Science* 222 (1983), 1283–1292.

—David Kemp

CLIMATE RECONSTRUCTION

Our knowledge of climate history prior to the availability of instrumental records comes from two main sources: (1) historical observations, where information on past climatic conditions is contained either in direct accounts of the weather or in records that typically relate to agriculture and/or human health; and (2) the paleoclimatic record, where information is preserved by a wide array of physical, chemical, and biological proxies (Anderson et al., 2007).

HISTORICAL RECORDS

The barometer and thermometer were both invented somewhat before the middle of the seventeenth century. During the 1650s, distribution of the first standardized instruments in Europe made possible the collection of accurate instrumental data. The longest continuous time series of weather conditions for a single location is the Central England Temperature Record, which dates back to 1659. Early entries in this record of monthly temperatures for rural sites are based largely on weather diaries, but the record gradually integrated instrumental data as thermometers became more widely available. Several other long instrumental records exist, but the data are almost entirely restricted to Western Europe. Instrumental records with sufficient coverage to obtain a global-scale picture of climatic conditions only go back to about 1850. For information on climate before that time, one must turn to historical records and observations.

The earliest written records of climate come from Egypt, where stone inscriptions detailing Nile flood levels date back to about 5,000 BP. In China, the oldest preserved records date to the Shang Dynasty (3,700–3,100 BP) and appear to describe conditions warmer than those of the present. However, for the vast majority of areas on the continents and oceans, historical observations are only available for a few hundred years at most.

A great deal of the most useful historical information has come from written accounts of harvest yields and crop prices. An excellent example can be found in records of the harvest dates of grapes in the wine-making regions of northern and central France. A continuous series of wine-harvest dates from this region extends back to at least 1484. While longer-term variations in this record have to be viewed with caution—since tastes in wine have changed over the years and, with them, the date of harvesting—the year-to-year fluctuations in harvest dates have been shown to correlate closely with changes in summer growing temperature, and therefore provide an accurate measure of the weather.

Interpretations of the climatic significance of agricultural records must be made with caution and with an understanding of agricultural principles. Successful cereal culture in northwestern Europe, for example, requires a fine balance between adequate moisture and warmth. Wheat requires a higher summer temperature than barley or oats, and grows best when annual rainfall is less than about 900 millimeters. Thus, information on the type of grain as well as the yield is needed when trying to reconstruct summer growing conditions. In parts of the world where summers are typically hotter, such as in North America and India, drought plays a much more important role in the quality of harvests. Hot, dry summers in these regions are bad for most crops, while wetter, cooler summers produce the best harvests.

From feudal Europe there is plenty of evidence to suggest that the eleventh and twelfth centuries enjoyed a relatively benign climate, a period often termed the Medieval Climatic Optimum. By about 1300, however, it is clear from a variety of historical records that there was a marked deterioration in the weather. Two exceptionally severe winters gripped Europe in 1303 and 1306, followed in the years 1314–1317 by a string of very wet and cool summers. The devastating harvest failures of these years are probably the greatest weather-related disaster ever to hit Europe. In London, wheat prices in the early summer of 1316 were as much as eight times higher than in late 1313, while historical accounts indicate that starvation and pestilence were rampant. Cooler, wet conditions affected grain storage as well, and moldy grain resulted in widespread outbreaks of the dangerous skin condition known as erysipelas (Saint Anthony's fire). In the North Atlantic, the increased incidence of winter storms and the encroachment of sea ice prevented the resupply from Norway of the Viking colonies on Greenland and led to their abandonment by the mid-1300s.

As the discussion here illustrates, shifts in weather and climate have affected agriculture and human health throughout recorded history. Although one must not read too much into historical records because of the complex interactions between weather, economic activity, and social policies, historical data are a key source of meteorological information in the preinstrumental era.

PALEOCLIMATIC RECORDS

A wealth of information about past changes in the Earth's climate and environment is recorded in measures as diverse as tree rings, ice, and rocks and sediments that have formed in marine and terrestrial settings. To use these resources effectively, one must be able to extract information on past climatic conditions from the physical, chemical, and biological components preserved in the geologic record. Such information comes almost entirely from indirect measures, or what are known as *proxies*. Fortunately, there is a broad array of proxy types to choose from. [*See* Proxy Data for Environmental Change.]

Evidence of glaciation

In the mid-nineteenth century, observations of the wide distribution of physical deposits and features associated with modern alpine glaciers and ice sheets led to realization that the Earth had experienced a series of major ice ages in the recent geologic past. Some of the best evidence for past glacial activity comes from the debris deposited by moving glaciers. Drift comprises all types of glacial deposit, while till comprises deposits laid down directly by ice. The bulk of the material in tills is usually of clay, silt, or sand sizes, but pebbles and large boulders (known as erratics) may be present. A record of changes in the position of glacial fronts is generally derived from ridge-like features known as moraines (Figure 1) left at the leading edge of a glacier after its retreat. The problem with the record of moraines and with many other glacial deposits is that they are commonly incomplete, with more recent ice advances obliterating evidence of earlier, less extensive advances. Although careful stratigraphic studies will sometimes reveal evidence of weathering horizons and buried soils (paleosols) that effectively differentiate between successive ice episodes, the problems of accurately dating glacial deposits are acute. Radiocarbon dating of organic material in soils that have developed on or within glacial deposits is most frequently used, but this method can only be used for the last forty thousand years. Indeed, as recently as the early 1960s it was commonly believed that the most recent series of ice ages in the Pleistocene (the last 1.6 million years) totaled only four.

Deep-sea sediments and microfossils

The reconstruction of past climates took a major step forward with work on deep-sea sediments that began in earnest in the 1950s. Typical sediment accumulating on the ocean floor consists of a mixture of the fossil remains of marine microorganisms and terrigenous particles (mainly clays and silts) derived from the erosion and transport of materials from the continents. The biologically produced deposits can be divided into two major categories, depending on the mineralogy of the skeletal material: carbonate "oozes" are dominated by the fossil remains of foraminifera and calcareous nanoplankton, common plankton groups in the ocean that produce shells or skeletal elements made of calcite ($CaCO_3$), while siliceous oozes consist primarily of diatom and radiolarian remains composed of opal ($SiO_2 \cdot nH_2O$). Species of each of these major plankton

Climate Reconstruction. Figure 1. Glacial Moraine at Terminus of Modern Alpine Glacier Near Saas-Fee, Switzerland.

Moraines can be used to identify former positions of glacier fronts and usually mark the maximum extent of the ice.

groups live in the surface waters of the ocean and are distributed according to the physical and chemical characteristics of the upper water column. Many of the taxa show distinct biogeographies, with a distribution by latitude that is clearly related to sea surface temperature (SST) patterns (Figure 2).

Past expansions or contractions of the biogeographic ranges of temperature-sensitive species (Figure 3), which are traced and mapped through study of sediment cores, can be used to infer past changes in SST. More sophisticated approaches for estimating SST use equations that relate modern species abundances to historical SST data. Depending on the specific plankton group and ocean, most of the statistical techniques can estimate SST to within 1°–2°C. Problems with this approach can arise from imperfect preservation of the microfossil assemblage and from cases in which past assemblages cannot be matched with the modern calibration assemblages. The latter problem worsens as one moves back in time and faunal assemblages change naturally through evolution.

Oxygen and carbon isotopes

The measurement of stable oxygen and carbon isotope ratios (oxygen-18/oxygen-16, and carbon-13/carbon-12) in the $CaCO_3$ shells of foraminifera from marine sediments has proven to be one of the most powerful tools in the arsenal of the paleoclimatologist. Oxygen isotope records can be used to estimate past water temperatures, the size of ice sheets, and local salinity variations, while carbon isotope records can be used to reconstruct deep-ocean circulation patterns and provide estimates of past oceanic nutrient levels. Isotope ratios for each system are expressed in delta (δ) notation, which relates the isotopic composition of a sample to the known isotopic ratio of a standard. For oxygen isotopes,

$$\delta^{18}O = [(^{18}O/^{16}O_{sample} - {}^{18}O/^{16}O_{standard}) / (^{18}O/^{16}O_{standard})] \times 1,000,$$

with units of parts per thousand. Carbon isotope values, $\delta^{13}C$, are reported in the same form.

The use of stable oxygen isotope measurements as a proxy for paleotemperatures began in 1947 with Harold Urey's observation that the oxygen-18/oxygen-16 ratio in calcite should vary as a function of the temperature prevailing when the mineral precipitated. Experimental studies with mollusks confirmed this prediction and led to development of the first paleotemperature equation with the form:

$$T = 16.5 - (4.3 \times [\delta^{18}O_{calcite} - \delta^{18}O_{water}]) + (0.14 \times ([\delta^{18}O_{calcite} - \delta^{18}O_{water}])^2$$

where T and $\delta^{18}O_{water}$ are the temperature (°C) and oxygen isotope value of the water in which the organism lived, and $\delta^{18}O_{calcite}$ is the measured oxygen isotope value of the calcite.

Measurements of $\delta^{18}O$ in foraminifera, corals, and mollusks have been used routinely for forty years as a paleoclimatic tool and provide most of what is currently known about the evolution of Earth's climate over the past 100 million years. When inserted into the paleotemperature equation, measurements of $\delta^{18}O$ can give reliable paleotemperature estimates. Assuming no change in $\delta^{18}O_{water}$, a 0.23 parts per thousand increase in $\delta^{18}O_{calcite}$ corresponds to a 1°C decrease in temperature. However, $\delta^{18}O_{water}$ can vary substantially from place to place in the ocean and through time. Water molecules containing the heavier oxygen-18 isotope tend to evaporate less readily than those containing the lighter oxygen-16 isotope. Conversely, fractionation during condensation concentrates the heavier isotope in the precipitation (rain or snow), further enriching the clouds (water vapor) in the lighter $H_2^{16}O$ molecules. In the present hydrologic cycle, water evaporated from the ocean returns there relatively quickly through precipitation, summer melting, and continental runoff. During glacial periods, however, the oceans become enriched in the heavier $H_2^{18}O$ molecules at the expense of $H_2^{16}O$ molecules, which are preferentially stored in the ice sheets. During the recent Pleistocene ice ages, this effect has been shown to be the largest signal recorded at most locations in $\delta^{18}O_{calcite}$ records from deep-sea cores. The waxing and waning of ice sheets creates a whole-ocean $\delta^{18}O$ signal that provides a framework for making global correlations based on $\delta^{18}O$ variations

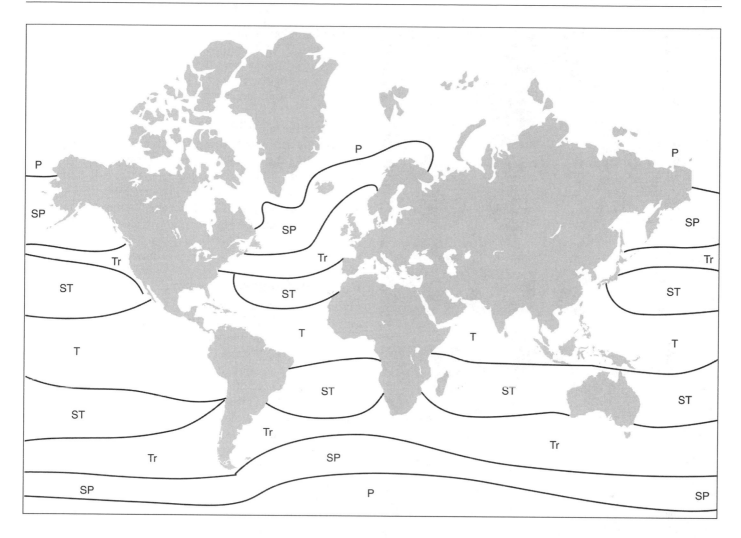

Climate Reconstruction. Figure 2. Modern Biogeographic Distributions of Planktic Foraminiferal Assemblages in the Ocean.

The latitudinal distribution pattern of this and other microplankton groups is largely controlled by sea surface temperature (SST). Those groups that leave a record of their distributions in the form of shells in the underlying sediment can be used to infer past changes in SST and other water properties through study of the expansions and contractions of their geographic ranges.
(T = Tropical assemblage; ST = Subtropical assemblage; Tr = Transitional Assemblage; SP = Subpolar assemblage; P = Polar assemblage.)
(Adapted from Bé and Tolderlund, 1971. With permission of Cambridge University Press.)

preserved in the sediment record. Pleistocene $\delta^{18}O$ stratigraphy is now well established, with chronological control coming from radiocarbon dating, the identification of key paleomagnetic reversals (for example, the Brunhes/Matuyama boundary at 0.78 million years BP), and the presence of marker horizons such as ash layers that can be traced to known volcanic eruptions. Unlike the incomplete continental record, the deep-sea $\delta^{18}O$ record indicates that there have been at least twenty major glaciations throughout the Pleistocene.

As with oxygen isotopes, variations in $\delta^{13}C$ result from fractionation of carbon-13 and carbon-12 during physical or chemical processes. In the ocean, the $\delta^{13}C$ of total carbon dioxide largely reflects the utilization and regeneration of organic matter. Phytoplankton in the surface ocean preferentially use isotopically light carbon to build soft tissues during photosynthesis. Remineralization of this soft tissue as the remains settle through the water column after death puts nutrients and light carbon back into the system at depth, a process often referred to as the biological pump. In the deep ocean, waters that have been longer removed from the surface typically exhibit higher concentrations of nutrients and lighter $\delta^{13}C$ because of their steady accumulation through time. The fractionation of $\delta^{13}C$ between the surface and deep ocean, and from place to place within the deep ocean, is reliably recorded in the shells of certain planktic and benthic (bottom-dwelling) foraminifera, as well as other calcareous organisms, and has proven to be a useful tool for reconstructing oceanic productivity and deep-water circulation patterns.

Trace elements

The oceanic distributions of certain trace elements reflect processes of climatic interest; many of these elements substitute readily for calcium in calcareous skeletal materials. Variations in

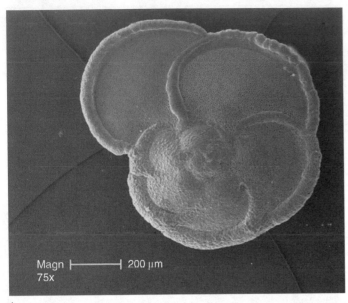

A

B

Climate Reconstruction. FIGURE 3. Electron Photomicrographs of Two Common Planktic Foraminifera that Inhabit the Modern Ocean.

(A) *Globorotalia menardii*, a common species found in tropical waters and sediments (magnification = 95×); and (B) *Neogloboquadrina pachyderma*, a dominant component of polar and subpolar foraminiferal assemblages (magnification = 110×).

cadmium/calcium (Cd/Ca) ratios in benthic foraminifera have provided important evidence for reorganization of deep-water circulation patterns during Pleistocene glacial-interglacial cycles. In the present ocean, cadmium concentrations are similar to those of the nutrient phosphorus, which increases with water-mass age because of the steady rain of organic matter to the deep sea and its subsequent remineralization. Changes in Cd/Ca concentration in foraminiferal shells therefore reflect

changes in the age of the water mass, in a manner generally consistent with $\delta^{13}C$. Foraminiferal Cd/Ca and $\delta^{13}C$ measured together in sediment cores from the Atlantic were among the first data to suggest that production rates of North Atlantic Deep Water were greatly reduced during the last glacial maximum.

In corals, the ratio of strontium to calcium (Sr/Ca) is strongly temperature dependent. Measurements of Sr/Ca in corals accurately capture the annual temperature cycle and allow for collection of high-resolution temperature time series in the tropical ocean. A relatively new paleothermometer is the ratio of magnesium to calcium (Mg/Ca). The value of this tool has been demonstrated with benthic marine ostracodes (small crustaceans that secrete a calcified bivalved carapace) and is currently being explored for corals and planktic foraminifera.

Depositional features

Marine sediments also preserve a wide variety of information on other climatic processes. Atmospheric circulation patterns can be assessed from study of the eolian, or wind-transported, material that reaches the deep sea floor. Wind direction and strength can be assessed through the character and pathways of particles transported offshore by the wind, the size and shape of the grains, and the occurrence of wind-derived higher plant materials and freshwater diatoms from dried lake deposits. In addition to eolian transport, mineral grains can reach the ocean floor by direct riverine input and by an assortment of gravity-driven processes that move materials downslope. The relative abundance of clay minerals and their degree of degradation and alteration provide information on the nature and amount of weathering on the adjacent land surface, while the presence of pollen and terrestrial organic matter can yield clues to continental climates recorded by vegetation types.

While the size of most terrigenous particles entering the ocean is limited by the carrying capacity of wind and water, larger and more poorly sorted mixtures of materials can be delivered to the deep sea by the melting of icebergs that have drifted away from land-based ice sheets. In the North Atlantic, sediments deposited during the last glacial are punctuated by distinct layers of ice-rafted materials that can be traced in a broad swath across the ocean. These layers, termed Heinrich layers after their discoverer, appear to reflect changes in the dynamics of the Laurentide Ice Sheet, the large ice mass centered over North America, during the last glacial. [*See* Heinrich Events.]

Ice cores

Just as the turn to deep-sea records in the 1950s led to major advances in understanding climate history, so did the systematic study of ice-core records that began in the 1970s. Ice sheets in Greenland and Antarctica have accumulated in place over the last several hundred thousand years and preserve a high-resolution record of climatic conditions; the age of the ice can be resolved in cores to within a few years by methods that include annual-layer counting in the uppermost section. The $\delta^{18}O$ record obtained from the ice is very similar to that obtained from deep-sea cores, although δ^{18}O variations in ice are interpreted in terms of air temperature at the site at which the ice accumulated. One of the most remarkable features of ice-core δ^{18}O records from Greenland is evidence for large and rapid fluctuations in temperature during the last glacial that are matched by variations in SST proxies in high-deposition-rate North Atlantic sediments. These changes appear to reflect massive reorganizations of the ocean-atmosphere system on time scales of a century or less, and were previously unknown. Another remarkable discovery has come from studies of gas inclusions in ice cores, which provide direct measurements of past atmospheric compositions (Figure 4). Measurements from both Greenland and Antarctic ice cores have shown that atmospheric carbon dioxide concentrations during the last glacial were some 75–80 parts per million less than preindustrial levels of about 280 parts per million, and that concentrations during the previous interglacial were as high or higher than preindustrial values. Concentrations of methane, another important greenhouse gas, were also reduced by half during the last glacial.

In addition to their unique record of atmospheric gas levels, the polar ice sheets contain a record of particle fallout from the atmosphere, mainly in the form of dust and ions such as chloride and calcium. Chloride is derived from sea

spray and provides an index of storminess and enhanced wind circulation, while calcium levels are dependent on the source of dust, especially that derived from glacial loess. High dust concentrations in glacial ice from both Greenland and Antarctica generally indicate more arid conditions during glacial maxima.

Pollen grains, spores, and tree rings

Although the record of glacial deposits on land is fragmentary, there are many other well-developed climate proxies for the continents. Pollen grains and spores that accumulate in lakes and bogs provide a record of an area's past vegetation (Figure 5). Abundance data need to be corrected for differences in pollen and spore production between plant taxa, as well as for differing rates of preservation and dispersal, but generally yield reliable estimates of the composition of the surrounding vegetation. Studies of modern pollen rain and modern vegetation patterns indicate that there is a good spatial correspondence between them. Such studies have led to synoptic mapping of inferred vegetation distributions at times in the past, as well as time series reconstructions from cores at single sites. While such vegetation reconstructions are relatively straightforward, the climatic inferences that can be drawn are often qualitative, with changes interpreted in terms of wetter/drier or warmer/colder conditions.

Variations in tree-ring width from year to year have long been recognized as a major source of chronological and climatic information. [See Dendrochronology.] The mean width of a ring in any one tree is a function of many variables, including the tree species, its age, the availability of stored nutrients in the tree and surrounding soil, and a host of climatic factors, including temperature, precipitation, and availability of sunlight. The extraction of useful climatic data usually follows calibration studies where local relationships are sought between tree-ring data and instrumental or historical data over the period in which they overlap. Tree ring methodologies have become very sophisticated and involve careful cross-dating, standardization, and analysis techniques. Although climatic information has most often been gleaned from tree ring width, variations in tree ring density and in the isotopic composition of the wood itself have proven useful as well.

Animal distributions, and continents in motion

Animal distributions on the continents, represented both by modern and fossil forms, also provide clues to past climatic states. Insects, for example, occupy virtually every type of terrestrial environment on Earth and produce chitinous exoskeletons that preserve well in sedimentary deposits. Most paleoclimatic work involving insects has focused on fossil beetles. Among larger animals, reptiles are useful because of their ectothermic (cold-blooded) nature. The presence of fossil alligators in sedimentary rocks of early Eocene age (55–50 million years old) on Ellesmere Island, west of Greenland, is a spectacular example of evidence for high-latitude warmth in this earlier geologic epoch.

Climate Reconstruction. Figure 4. Ice Core Data Spanning the Last Full Glacial–Interglacial Cycle (160,000 Years) from the Famous Vostok Site in Antarctica.

Atmospheric carbon dioxide content is determined from gas composition of air samples preserved in bubbles trapped in ice. Air temperature from the same site is derived from analysis of the deuterium isotope content of the ice itself.

(Data from Barnola et al., 1987; Jouzel et al., 1987.)

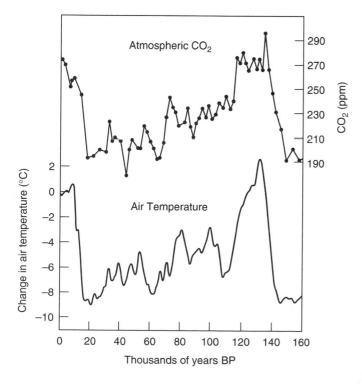

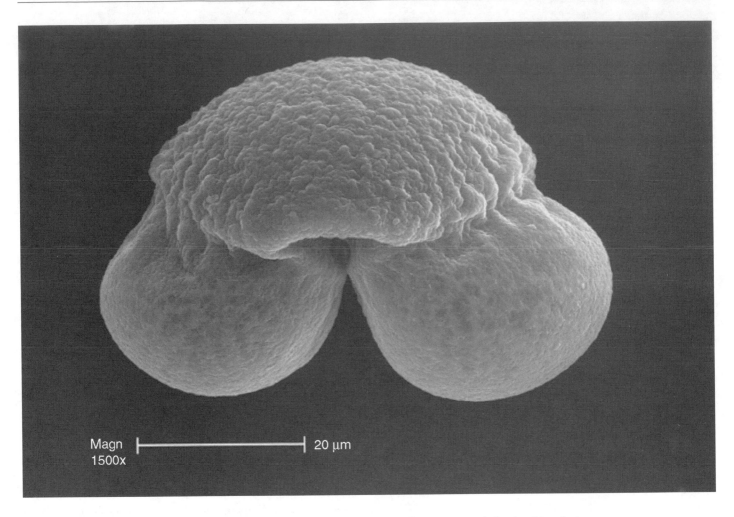

Climate Reconstruction. FIGURE 5. Photomicrograph of a Pine Pollen Grain Showing Its Distinctive Morphology.

Pollen, such as this specimen of *Pinus ponderosa*, preserved in sediments of lakes and bogs can be used to reconstruct vegetation patterns in the surrounding drainage basin (magnification = 1,500×).

As one moves back in time, the effects of plate tectonics and the physical rearrangement of the Earth's surface must be considered when one interprets paleoclimate data. The increased difficulty of establishing accurate time correlations inhibits the ability to develop global snapshots of climatic conditions, and biases introduced by physical and chemical postdepositional processes can obliterate or obscure original geochemical signals. Despite such problems, the geologic record contains a rich and diverse archive of information that offers our only means of deciphering the long history of climatic evolution on Earth.

[*See also* Dating Methods; Greenhouse Effect; Land Surface Processes; Loess; Paleoclimate; *and* Proxy Data for Environmental Change.]

BIBLIOGRAPHY

Anderson, D.E., A.S. Goudie, and A.G. Parker. *Global Environments through the Quaternary.* Oxford and New York: Oxford University Press, 2007. An introductory textbook on environmental change.

Barnola, J.M., et al. "Vostok Ice Core Provides 160,000-Year Record of Atmospheric CO_2." *Nature* 329 (1987), 408–414.

Bé, A.W.H., and D. S. Tolderlund. "Distribution and Ecology of Living Planktonic Foraminifera in the Surface Waters of the Atlantic and Indian Oceans." In *The Micropalaeontology of Oceans*, edited by B. M. Funnell and W. R. Riedel, pp. 105–149. Cambridge: Cambridge University Press, 1971.

Bradley, R.S. *Quaternary Paleoclimatology: Methods of Paleoclimatic Reconstruction.* Boston: Allen and Unwin, 1985. Contains a thorough and balanced summary of methods used in reconstructing past climates from proxy data series.

Burroughs, W.J. *Does the Weather Really Matter?: The Social Implications of Climate Change.* Cambridge and New York: Cambridge University Press, 1997. An up-to-date analysis of the debate on climate change, with abundant examples of historical climate data.

CLIMAP Project Members. "Seasonal Reconstructions of the Earth's Surface at the Last Glacial Maximum." *Geological Society of America, Map and Chart Series MC-36* (1981), 1–18. Presents detailed maps showing reconstructions of continental and sea surface conditions at the peak of the last ice age, 18,000 BP.

Crowley, T.J., and G.R. North. *Paleoclimatology.* New York: Oxford University Press, 1991. An excellent introduction to paleoclimatic data and observations, and the use of models in assessing our understanding of past climate change.

Flint, R.F. *Glacial and Quaternary Geology*. New York: Wiley, 1971. A bit dated, but still a classic introduction to the study of glacial deposits on the continents.

Grove, J.M. *The Little Ice Age*. London and New York: Methuen, 1988. A summary of historical and instrumental data that span the period of cooler climatic conditions between roughly 1450 and 1870 CE.

Imbrie, J., and K.P. Imbrie. *Ice Ages: Solving the Mystery*. Short Hills, N.J.: Enslow, 1979. An entertaining account of the history of ice-age theory with discussion of evidence that led to an understanding of the role of orbital variations in climate change.

Jouzel, J., et al. "Vostok Ice Core: A Continuous Isotope Temperature Record over the Last Climatic Cycle (160,000 Years)." *Nature* 329 (1987), 402–408.

Lamb, H.H. *Climate, History, and the Modern World*. London: Methuen, 1982. Presents an exhaustive compilation and discussion of historical climate records.

Le Roy Ladurie, E. *Times of Feast, Times of Famine: A History of Climate Since the Year 1000*. New York: Doubleday, 1971. Translated from the original French, this scholarly work by an economic historian contains detailed analyses of historical records.

Tuchman, B.W. *A Distant Mirror: The Calamitous 14th Century*. New York: Knopf, 1978. Contains an account of the effects of extreme weather events on European social structure in the fourteenth century.

—LARRY PETERSON

GRIP AND GISP2

Ice cores provide a wonderful storehouse of stratigraphical and paleoenvironmental information back to the last interglacial period. In the 1990s two deep cores were drilled into the Greenland Ice Sheet. The Greenland Ice Core Project (GRIP), a European enterprise, reached bedrock at 3,029 meters in 1992, while the Greenland Ice Sheet Project 2 (GISP2), a U.S. program located only 28 kilometers from the GRIP site, reached bedrock at a depth of 3,053 meters in 1993. The GRIP core is at the modern ice divide, whereas the GISP2 core is to its west. The GISP2 core is of large diameter—13.2 centimeters—and has been analyzed by 42 types of measurements. They include the gas content of air bubbles trapped in the ice, concentrations of major ions, cosmogenic isotopes, stable isotopes, dust content, electrical conductivity, and physical properties like crystal characteristics. Deep cores do, however, have problems, of which the disturbance of their lower portions by deformation is perhaps the most serious.

— ANDREW S. GOUDIE

COAL

Coal is the most abundant fossil fuel and is distributed broadly across the world. It has fueled the rise of industrial economies in Europe and the U.S. in the past two centuries and is fueling the rise of Asian economies today. Because of its abundance, coal is cheap and attractive to use in large quantities—if we ignore the harm it causes. However, per unit of energy delivered, coal today is a bigger global-warming polluter than any other fuel: double that of natural gas; 50% worse than oil; and, of course, enormously more polluting than renewable energy, energy efficiency, and, more controversially, nuclear power. To reduce the contribution to global warming from coal use, we can pursue efficiency and renewables to limit the total amount of coal we consume, but for the coal we use we must deploy and improve systems that will keep the carbon in coal out of the atmosphere, specifically systems that capture carbon dioxide (CO_2) from coal-fired power plants and other industrial sources for safe and effective disposal in geologic formations. [*See* Carbon Capture and Storage; Coal Gasification; *and* Coal Liquefaction.]

Today, the U.S. and other developed nations around the world run their economies largely with industrial sources powered by fossil fuel, and those sources release billions of tons of carbon dioxide (CO_2) into the atmosphere every year. There is national and global interest today in capturing that CO_2 for disposal or sequestration to prevent its release to the atmosphere. To distinguish this industrial capture system from removal of atmospheric CO_2 by soils and vegetation, the industrial system is referred to as carbon capture and disposal or CCD.

The interest in CCD stems from a few basic facts. We now recognize that CO_2 emissions from the use of fossil fuels result in increased atmospheric concentrations of CO_2, which along with other so-called greenhouse gases trap heat, leading to an increase in atmospheric temperatures. These increased temperatures alter the energy balance of the planet and thus our climate, which is nature's way of managing energy flows. Documented changes in climate today, along with those forecast for the next decades, are predicted to inflict large and growing damage on human health, economic well-being, and natural ecosystems.

GLOBAL COAL USE

Currently, the world consumes about 6 billion metric tons of coal per year (EIA, 2007b). The top five coal-consuming economies (China, U.S., European Union, India, and Russia) account for about 75% of global coal consumption (EIA, 2007b). Coal use is growing rapidly, with forecast global consumption in the year 2030 exceeding 9.5 billion metric tons per year (EIA, 2006b). Coal accounts for about 25% of total world energy use (EIA, 2006a) and is the dominant fuel in the electric-power sector, where it accounts for about 40% of total world electricity generation (EIA, 2007c).

THE TOLL FROM COAL

The use of coal is controversial because of the damages its production and use inflict today and skepticism that those damages can or will be reduced to a point where we can safely continue to rely on it as a mainstay of industrial economies. Coal is cheap and abundant compared to oil and natural gas, but the toll from coal as it is used today is enormous. From mining deaths and illness and devastated mountains and streams, to practices like mountaintop-removal mining, to accidents at coal-train crossings, to air emissions of acidic, toxic, and heat-trapping pollution from coal combustion, to water pollution from coal mining and combustion wastes, the conventional coal-fuel cycle is among the most environmentally destructive activities on earth. Certain coal production processes are inherently harmful, and while our societies have the capacity to reduce many of today's damages, to date, we have not done so adequately nor have we committed ourselves to doing so. These failures have created well justified opposition by many people to continued or increased dependence on coal to meet our energy needs.

Our progress in reducing harms from the mining, transport, and use of coal has been frustratingly slow, and an enormous amount remains to be done. Today mountain tops in the Appalachian region of the United States are destroyed to get at the coal beneath, and rocks, soil, debris, and waste products are dumped into valleys and streams, destroying them as well. Waste impoundments loom above communities—and in one particularly egregious case, above an elementary school—and thousands of miles of streams are polluted. In other areas surface-mine reclamation is incomplete, inadequately performed, and poorly supervised because of regulatory gaps and poorly funded regulatory agencies (Hawkins, 2006).

In the area of air pollution, although we have technologies to dramatically cut conventional pollutants from coal-fired power plants, in 2004 only one-third of U.S. coal capacity was equipped with scrubbers for sulfur dioxide control, and even less capacity applied selective catalytic reduction (SCR) for control of nitrogen oxides. In most other coal consuming countries the statistics are even worse (Hawkins, 2006).

THE NEED FOR CCD

Coal use and climate protection are on a collision course. Without rapid deployment of CCD systems, that collision will occur soon and with spectacularly bad results. The very attribute of coal that has made it so attractive—its abundance—magnifies the problem we face and requires us to act now, not a decade from now. Until now, coal's abundance has been an economic boon. But today, coal's abundance, absent corrective action, is more bane than boon.

Any significant additional use of coal that vents its CO_2 to the air is fundamentally in conflict with the need to prevent atmospheric concentrations of CO_2 from rising to levels that will produce dangerous disruption of the climate system. Given that an immediate world-wide halt to coal use is not feasible, analysts and advocates with a broad range of views on coal's role are increasingly coming to agree that, if it is safe and effective, CCD should be rapidly deployed to minimize CO_2 emissions from the coal that we do use.

Since the dawn of the industrial age, human use of coal has released about 150 billion metric tons of carbon into the atmosphere—about half the total carbon emissions due to fossil-fuel use in human history (Marland et al., 2006). But that contribution is the tip of the carbon iceberg. Another 4 trillion metric tons of carbon are contained in the remaining global coal resources (Metz et al., 2001). That is a carbon pool nearly seven times greater than the amount in our pre-industrial atmosphere. Using that coal without capturing and disposing of its carbon means a climate catastrophe.

And the die is being cast for that catastrophe today. Decisions being made today in corporate board rooms, government ministries, and legislative hearing rooms are determining how the next coal-fired power plants will be designed and operated. Power plant investments are enormous in scale, more than $1 billion per plant, and plants built today will operate for 60 years or more. The International Energy Agency (IEA) forecasts that more than $5 trillion will be spent globally on new power plants in the next 25 years (IEA, 2006). Under IEA's forecasts, over 1700 gigawatts (GW) of new coal plants will be built between 2005 and 2030—capacity equivalent to 3,000 large coal plants, or an average of ten new coal plants every month for the next quarter-century (IEA, 2006). This new capacity amounts to 1.5 times the total of all the coal plants operating in the world today (IEA, 2006).

The astounding fact is that under IEA's forecast, 7 out of every 10 coal plants that will be operating in 2030 don't exist today. That fact presents a huge opportunity: many of these coal plants will not need to be built if we invest more in efficiency; additional numbers of these coal plants can be replaced with clean, renewable alternative-power sources; and we can build the remainder to capture their CO_2, instead of building them the way our grandfathers built them.

If we decide to do it, the world could build and operate new coal plants so that their CO_2 is returned to the ground rather than polluting the atmosphere. But we are losing that opportunity with every month of delay—10 coal plants were built the old-fashioned way last month somewhere in the world and 10 more old-style plants will be built this month, and the next and the next. Worse still, with current policies in place, none of the 3,000 new plants projected by IEA is likely to capture their CO_2.

Each new coal plant that is built carries with it a huge stream of CO_2 emissions that will likely flow for the life of the plant—60 years or more. Suggestions that such plants might be equipped with CO_2-capture devices later in life might come true, but there is little reason to count on it. While commercial technologies exist for pre-combustion capture from coal-gasification plants, most new plants are not using gasification, and the few that are are not incorporating capture systems. Installing capture equipment at these new plants after the fact is impracticle for traditional coal plant designs and expensive for gasification processes.

If all 3,000 of the next wave of coal plants are built without CO_2 controls, their lifetime emissions will impose an enormous pollution lien on our children and grandchildren. Over a projected 60-year life these plants would probably emit 750 billion tons of CO_2, a total, from just 25 years of investment decisions, that is 30% greater than the total CO_2 emissions from all previous human use of coal (Hawkins, 2007). Once emitted, this CO_2 pollution remains in the atmosphere for centuries. Half of the CO_2 emitted during World War I remains in the atmosphere today.

In short, we face an onslaught of new coal plants with impacts that must be minimized without delay. The U.S. is forecast to build nearly 300 of these coal plants in the next two decades, according to reports and forecasts published by the U.S. Energy Information Administration (EIA, 2007a). China, the world's largest coal consumer, is adding new coal-generating plants at a rate of more than one per week. In 2006, China reportedly added over 90 GW of new coal capacity to its system (Pew, 2007). In the absence of policies to promote reduction of greenhouse-gas emissions, new coal plants will continue to be built using designs that are unsuitable for efficient and economical capture of CO_2. The result of this wave of construction of high-emitting plants will be to lock in very large streams of greenhouse-gas emissions for the operating lifetimes of these new plants—as long as 60–80 years—unless means are developed to capture emissions once these plants are built. To avoid this carbon lock-in, governments and industry are showing increased interest in accelerating the deployment of CCD systems.

To date most efforts have been limited to funding research, development, and limited demonstrations. Government subsidies are unlikely to be as effective as a real market for low-carbon goods and services. That market will be created only when requirements to limit CO_2 emissions are adopted.

POLICY ACTIONS TO SPEED CCD

Policies to deploy CCD are needed if new coal plants are to be designed to capture and dispose of their CO_2. While research and development funding is useful, it cannot substitute for the incentive that a genuine commercial market for CO_2 capture and disposal systems will provide to the private sector. That market will be created only when requirements to limit CO_2 emissions are adopted. The amounts of capital that the private sector can spend to optimize CCD methods will almost certainly always dwarf what legislatures will provide with taxpayer dollars. To mobilize those private-sector dollars, legislatures need a stimulus more compelling than the offer of modest handouts for research. Laws in the U.S. and elsewhere provide a model that works: intelligently designed policies to limit emissions cause firms to spend money finding better and less expensive ways to prevent or capture emissions.

Where a technology is already competitive with other emission control techniques, for example, sulfur dioxide scrubbers, a cap-and-trade program like that enacted by the U.S. Congress in 1990, can result in more rapid deployment, improvements in performance, and reductions in costs. Today's scrubbers are much more effective and much less costly than those built in the 1980s. However, a CO_2 cap-and-trade program by itself may not result in deployment of CCD systems as rapidly as we need. Many new coal-plant design decisions are being made today. Depending on the pace of required reductions under a global-warming bill, a firm may decide to build a conventional coal plant and purchase credits from the cap-and-trade market rather than applying CCD systems to the plant. While this may appear to be economically rational in the short term, it is likely to lead to higher costs of CO_2 control in the middle and longer term if substantial amounts of new conventional coal construction leads to a burgeoning demand for CO_2 credits.

Moreover, delaying the start of CCD until a cap-and-trade price is high enough to produce these investments delays the broad demonstration of the technology that the U.S. and other countries will need if we continue substantial use of coal, as seems likely. The more affordable CCD becomes, the more widespread its use will be throughout the world, including in rapidly growing economies like those of China and India. But the learning and cost reductions for CCD that are desirable will come only from the experience gained by building and operating the initial commercial plants. The longer we wait to ramp up this experience, the longer we will wait to see CCD deployed in mature industrial economies and in countries like China.

In the U.S., interest is developing in a hybrid program that combines the breadth and flexibility of a cap-and-trade program with well-designed performance measures focused on key technologies like CCD. Such performance measures can serve two purposes. First, they insure that no new coal plants are built without operating CCD systems. New coal plants with uncontrolled CO_2 emissions will increase costs for others now and/or in the future. Second, they provide a stimulus for early and significant deployment of CCD systems. These two purposes may appear to be the same, but they are not. Prohibiting construction of new coal plants without CCD will not assure early deployment of CCD if no new coal plants are built for some time. And policies that do not require each new coal project to meet a performance standard will not necessarily prevent the construction of new coal plants that lack CO_2 controls. But a combination of performance measures can achieve both of these objectives.

One such policy is a CO_2 emissions standard that applies to new power-generation investments. In the U.S., California has enacted such a measure. It requires new investments for sale of power in California to meet a performance standard that is achievable by coal with a moderate amount of CO_2 capture. Similar standards are proposed in legislation pending in the U.S. Congress (S 309, 2007).

A second measure is a low-carbon generation obligation for coal-based power (S 309, 2007). Similar in concept to a renewable performance standard, the low-carbon-generation obligation requires an initially small fraction of sales from coal-based power to meet a CO_2 performance standard that is achievable with CCD. The required fraction of sales would increase gradually over time and the obligation would be tradable. Thus, a coal-based generating firm could meet the requirement by building a plant with CCD, by purchasing power generated by another source that meets the standard, or by purchasing credits from those who build such plants. This approach has the advantage of speeding the deployment of CCD while avoiding the "first-mover penalty." Instead of causing the first builder of a commercial coal plant with CCD to bear all of the incremental costs, the tradable low-carbon-generation obligation would spread those costs over the entire coal-based generation system. The builder of the first unit would achieve far more hours of low-carbon generation than required and would sell the credits to other firms that needed credits to comply. These credit sales would finance the incremental costs of these early units. This approach provides the coal-based power industry with the experience with a technology that it knows is needed to reconcile coal use and climate protection and does it without large consumer rate increases.

These two measures can work together to achieve a result that neither could accomplish alone. The new source-performance standard prevents the construction of new coal plants without CCD, something that could happen with a low-carbon-generation obligation by itself. The low-carbon-generation obligation, because it can be met through trading with other coal-based generators, avoids placing the entire incremental cost of the first CCD units on the customers of the companies that build the plants. This cost spreading avoids significant rate impacts from implementation of the new source-performance standard. The low-carbon-generation obligation also assures that CO_2 pollution from America's coal-power plants, whatever their number, is reduced at a predictable minimum rate—something that would not be assured with a new source-performance standard by itself if the industry delayed construction of new coal plants.

BIBLIOGRAPHY

"CO_2 Capture and Storage." IEA Greenhouse Gas R&D Programme. http://www.co2capture and storage.info/ (accessed May 26, 2008).

Deutch, J., et al. *The Future of Coal*. Cambridge, Mass.: MIT Press, 2007. http://web.mit.edu/coal/ (accessed May 29, 2008).

EIA. *International Energy Annual 2004*. Washington, D.C.: U.S. Energy Information Administration, 2006a.

EIA. *International Energy Outlook 2006*. Washington, D.C.: U.S. Energy Information Administration, 2006b.

EIA. *Annual Energy Outlook 2007*. Washington, D.C.: U.S. Energy Information Administration, 2007a.

EIA. *International Energy Annual 2005*. Washington, D.C.: U.S. Energy Information Administration, 2007b.

EIA. *International Energy Outlook 2007*. Washington, D.C.: U.S. Energy Information Administration, 2007c. See fig. 6.

Goodell, J. *Big Coal*. Boston: Houghton Mifflin, 2006.

Hawkins, D. G. Testimony to U.S. Senate Committee on Energy and Natural Resources, Washington, D.C., April 24, 2006.

———. Testimony to U.S. Senate Committee on Environment and Public Works, Washington, D.C., June 28, 2007.

Hawkins, D. G., D. A. Lashof, and R. H. Williams. "What to Do about Coal." *Scientific American* (September, 2006).

IEA. *World Energy Outlook 2006*. Paris: International Energy Agency, 2006.

Marland, G., T. A. Boden, and R. J. Andres. *Global, Regional, and National Fossil Fuel CO_2 Emissions*. CDIAC, 2006. http://cdiac.ornl.gov/trends/emis/em_cont.htm (accessed May 29, 2008).

Metz, B., et al, eds. 2001. *Climate Change 2001: Mitigation*. Cambridge and New York: Cambridge University Press. p. 6. DOI: 10.2277/0521015022.

Metz, B., et al., eds. *Carbon Dioxide Capture and Storage*. Prepared by Working Group III of the Intergovernmental Panel on Climate Change. Cambridge and New York: Cambridge University Press, 2005.

Natural Resources Defense Council. "Coal in a Changing Climate." http://www.nrdc.org/globalWarming/coal/contents.asp (accessed May 29, 2008).

Pew. *Coal and Climate Change Facts*. Pew Center on Global Climate Change, 2007. http://www.pewclimate.org/global-warming-basics/coalfacts.cfm (accessed May 29, 2008).

S.309. "Global Warming Pollution Reduction Act." Washington, D.C.: U.S. Senate, introduced January 16, 2007.

U.S. Department of Energy, National Energy Technology Laboratory. "Coal and Power Systems." http://www.netl.deo.gov/technologies/coalpower/index.html (accessed May 29, 2008).

U.S. EPA. "Inventory of U.S. Greenhouse Gas Emissions and Sinks: 1990–2005." http://epa.gov/climatechange/emissions/usinventoryreport07.html (accessed May 29, 2008).

—D. HAWKINS

COAL GASIFICATION

Production of gas from coal was revived in the 1970s when U.S. supplies of natural gas seemed to be waning. Now, the Great Plains Coal Gasification Plant in Beulah, North Dakota, built with federal government support, uses local lignite coal to produce methane which is fed by pipeline to natural gas markets. Carbon dioxide from the process is piped across the border to southern Saskatchewan where it is injected into oil reservoirs in the Weyburn field to enhance production—demonstrating, incidentally, the feasibility of storing (sequestering) carbon dioxide in porous and permeable reservoir rock. When government price controls on natural gas were lifted, more natural gas became available and no more coal-gasification plants for this purpose have been built in the United States.

More recently, concern about air pollution from coal-fired power plants engendered interest in using coal-gas in electrical generation by using a gas-fired turbine. Gas turbines are very efficient in converting fuel-energy into electricity, especially when they use the "combined cycle" in which natural gas is burned at high temperature in a turbine that drives a generator and yields exhaust gases near the boiling point of water. That exhaust is used to raise steam for a second turbine that generates electricity. Ideally, waste heat from that second turbine is used to heat buildings or for process-heat in a factory; but even without that final application the efficiency can exceed 50% compared to 35–40% in a single-stage fuel-burning power plant. Most new gas-fired power plants are built this way.

A technology now being demonstrated joins coal gasification to the front end of a combined-cycle plant and is called, therefore, Integrated Gasification and Combined Cycle (IGCC). In the gasification process, powdered coal is combined with steam and air or oxygen to yield a synthetic gas containing hydrogen, carbon monoxide, and other gases. Virtually all sulfur dioxide and mercury can be removed from the synthetic gas stream, and with the right technology carbon dioxide can be captured.

In Europe there are five such power plants operating, and in the United States the Department of Energy has built four demonstration plants in Kentucky, Florida, Nevada, and Indiana. One completed in 1995 is the Wabash River Coal Gasification Repowering Project near Terre Haute, Indiana. It is the first full-sized commercial IGCC plant built in the United States: rated at 292 megawatts, it has roughly one-third the generating capacity of a typical coal-burning or nuclear power plant.

The U.S. Department of Energy's 10-year FutureGen program aims for a zero-emissions power plant by means of sequestering the carbon dioxide removed from the synthetic gas stream of an IGCC plant. The program comprises a government-industry consortium of 12 industry partners, some of which are foreign-based (FutureGen Alliance, 2006). As of July, 2007, the program had selected four candidate sites, two in Illinois and two in Texas, that are underlain by rock that can accommodate injected carbon dioxide.

[*See also* Coal Liquefaction; Fossil Fuels; Natural Gas; *and* Synfuels.]

—David J. Cuff

COAL LIQUEFACTION

Converting coal to liquid fuel may be unwise because the conversion process emits carbon dioxide and the synthetic fuel emits more when it is burned. The abundance of coal and the need for transportation fuels have nevertheless revived interest in technologies that have existed for many years. Today the U.S. Department of Energy refers to these as coal-to-liquid (CTL) processes.

The original process is considered indirect coal liquefaction because it first converts coal to synthetic gas which then is fed to the Fischer-Tropsch process that yields a synthetic crude oil which then can be refined for diesel fuel and other liquids. This process has been used for decades in South Africa, where production in 2006 was roughly 150,000 barrels per day (compared with daily Alberta oil-sands production of 1.2 million barrels). In the U.S., no commercial-scale plants exist, but the U.S. Department of Energy projects that by the year 2030 there may be 0.8 million barrels of daily domestic production (reference scenario), and 1.7 million (high-price scenario), mostly in coal-producing areas of the U.S. Midwest (EIA, 2006).

Direct coal liquefaction reacts coal with hydrogen at high temperature to produce a synthetic crude. This process is used only in pilot plants now, but China plans to have two commercial-scale plants operational sometime after 2008 (*Business China*, 2005).

BIBLIOGRAPHY

EIA. *Annual Energy Outlook 2006*. Washington, D.C.: U.S. Energy Information Administration, 2006, p. 55. http://www.eia.doe.gov/ioaf/archive/ae006/index.html (accessed May 29, 2008).
"Shenhua Coal Liquefaction Project Planned for Execution in Inner Mongolia." *Business China*, Jan. 24, 2005.

—David J. Cuff

COASTAL PROTECTION AND MANAGEMENT

It has been claimed that half the population of the industrialized world lives within one kilometer of the coast and that roughly 75% of the world's population lives within 60 km of the coastline. Coasts are by their nature dynamic areas, with hot spots prone to particularly rapid changes due to interrelated natural and physical causes. Such hot spots include sandy coasts (beaches and dunes), coastal wetlands, coastal cliffs composed of weak, easily eroded sediments, and coral reefs. Coastal change costs money. A recent estimate suggests that one-quarter of the coastline of the United States is significantly affected by coastal erosion, costing around $300 million per year in the loss of property and the construction of protective structures. Coastal change also constitutes a direct hazard to human populations. In Bangladesh, for example, erosion and flooding caused by cyclones are major causes of loss of life and disruption to agricultural production. As sea-level rise induced by global warming increases the threat to the environment, it is likely that coastal protection and management will become an increasingly important challenge for many societies.

Coastal change is caused by natural and/or human factors. The types of change most threatening to human use and enjoyment of the coastal zone are erosion and deposition of sediment, deterioration in coastal ecosystems (e.g., loss of species), and pollution of coastal land and waters. It is becoming increasingly apparent that successful management of these coastal problems must be integrated—that is, all aspects of often multiple problems must be addressed, and the problems themselves must be seen in a wider context of other linked environments.

In the past, coastal protection and management schemes have often been piecemeal, localized attempts to deal with coastal change, often based on a limited scientific understanding of the rates and processes of change. In Britain, for example, coastal protection schemes historically were planned and implemented at the local government level, with adjacent parishes sometimes enacting conflicting solutions to the same problem. Over the past few decades, local, national, and international coastal management plans have been proposed, and there has been a growth in integrated coastal-zone-management (ICZM) ideas; the UNCED meeting in Rio de Janeiro in 1992 laid out an important role for ICZM in aiding national sustainable development plans. ICZM, as generally practiced, involves three major components: environmental conservation, sea defense, and development planning. Thus coastal protection should be seen as part of coastal management. The first attempt at comprehensive coastal zone management was probably the U.S. Coastal Zone

Coastal Protection and Management. Major concrete coastal protection structures at Arica, northern Chile.

Management Act of 1972, which provided for the development of coastal planning and management schemes by state authorities. More recently, in 1995, Australia enacted its Commonwealth coastal policy, designed to facilitate ICZM across the whole country.

Coastal-zone management needs to reconcile different uses of the coastal zone through legislation and zoning, while also ensuring that coastal geomorphologic and ecological changes are minimized. A prerequisite of any successful management scheme is thus good scientific understanding of the coastal system involved, how and why it has changed in the past, and how it will react in the future. This is in itself a difficult task, but once the system is broadly understood, the human ownership and use of the coastal zone also need to be determined, before management strategies can be proposed and debated.

A good example is the management of the Dorset, Hampshire, and Sussex coast in southern Britain. Here scientists have been involved for many years in studying the dynamics of the coast, while engineers and managers have been trying to design better coastal protection in an area of great natural beauty. Responsibility for coastal protection and sea defense in England and Wales is shared by district councils and the Environment Agency, which, together with other interested bodies, formed

SCOPAC (Standing Conference on Problems Associated with the Coastline) to coordinate expert advice on coastal management. Scientists provided evidence used to produce scenarios involving options of retreat, accommodation, and protection against future sea-level rise. Such scenarios have been proposed for many other coastal areas facing the prospect of rising sea levels and thus increased coastal erosion and flooding. The retreat option involves developing legislation to prevent further development along vulnerable coasts within a certain distance (bounded by the set-back line) of the coast and encourage relocation of currently occupied property. This option can be costly and difficult to implement in highly built-up areas. The accommodation option involves adapting to the changes by changing agricultural practices, modifying building construction, and taking out better insurance to live with the coastal changes. Finally, the protection option involves increasing both hard

Coastal Protection and Management. Sea Wall.

This stretch of coastline at Weymouth in southern England has in theory been protected by the construction of a whole series of engineering structures, including a large sea wall. However, sea walls, in addition to being expensive, can also accelerate beach scour and impede drainage of water from the cliffs behind, thereby causing cliff instability.

methods (as in structural methods of coastal protection such as sea walls, groins, dikes, and tidal barriers) and soft methods (such as beach nourishment and wetland creation) of protecting the coast from higher sea levels.

All three of these strategies have advantages and disadvantages in any particular situation, and all should be seen as ongoing rather than one-off solutions. Ownership of coastal land can be very fragmented, making coherent planning difficult. The location of key, highly valuable industrial plants (such as power stations or oil terminals) can bias decisions in favor of protection. Hard engineering schemes are costly and can often fail, or produce secondary effects down the coast. Soft engineering schemes also often fail, and require costly long-term management. In most coastal areas, sea-level rise is not the only problem that needs to be dealt with, so such management plans also need to include consideration of issues such as pollution, species loss, and human-induced subsidence (through removal of ground water and other fluids).

[See also Coastlines; Global Warming; Land Reclamation; and Sea Level Future.]

BIBLIOGRAPHY

Beatley, T., D.J. Brower., and A.K. Schwab. *An Introduction to Coastal Zone Management.* 2d ed. Washington, D.C.: Island Press, 2002. A simple and clear introduction to the U.S. coastal management situation.

Bray, M., J. Hooke, and D. Carter. "Planning for Sea-Level Rise on the South Coast of England: Advising the Decision-Makers." *Transactions of the Institute of British Geographers* 22 (1997), 13–30. Review of issues and possible solutions along one area of coast.

French, P.W. *Coastal and Estuarine Management.* London and New York: Routledge, 1997. A readable and wide-ranging introduction to coastal management issues and strategies, with many case studies.

———. *Coastal Defences: Processes, Problems and Solutions.* London and New York: Routledge, 2001. A presentation of the methods used to protect coastlines and a consideration of the issues these methods raise.

—HEATHER A. VILES

COASTLINES

Coastlines are a dynamic interface where waves, currents, and tides influence landforms, which in turn affect the movement of water. It is difficult to measure the length of coastline on the Earth today; it is in any case perhaps better to talk about the coastal zone as an area rather than as a mere line running around the edge of continents and islands. The influence of marine or lacustrine waters often extends several kilometers inland, especially where rivers produce estuaries or deltas.

TYPES OF COASTLINE

The world's coastline can be divided into several types. The fundamental factor influencing the large-scale location and shape of coasts is plate tectonics. Collision or active-margin coasts, such as those of western North America, are typified by a mountainous hinterland, producing coarse debris in streams, with a narrow continental shelf. In contrast, trailing-edge, or passive-margin, coasts like those along eastern South

America are fed by extensive river systems that contribute huge volumes of fine-grained sediment to wide, gently sloping continental shelves. The major deltas of the world have developed on such passive-margin coasts, where barrier island development is also common. In marginal-sea coasts, such as in the Gulf of Mexico and the South China Sea, the coast, although near a collision plate-boundary, is protected from its effects by a marginal sea, allowing it to behave like a trailing-edge coast. [See Mobile Earth.]

On a smaller scale, coasts vary according to the oceanographic setting, sediment size and availability, climate, and sea-level history. The latter is a particularly important control on the nature of today's coasts, especially in areas where the vast changes wrought by the last ice age on both land and sea continue to exert an influence. For example, where an ice sheet once depressed a land mass, the land has gradually rebounded (in a process called isostasy) as the ice has melted and may still be rising, producing an emerging coast characterized by falling sea level. In many areas, the major sources of coastal sediment were glacial debris that was swept up from the sea floor as sea levels rose at the end of the last glaciation. Now this source of sediment has been largely used up, leading to sediment-limited coastlines.

The present-day setting also affects the characteristics of today's coasts. Wave environments, tidal range, sediments, and climate are all important in determining whether coasts are characterized by extensive beaches backed by dunes, rocky coasts with pocket beaches, muddy coasts such as salt marshes and mangrove swamps, or biogenic features such as coral reefs. In many situations, these different coastal types are found close together. Barrier islands, for example, which front much of the coastline of the eastern United States and parts of the Nigerian coast, consist of beach, dune, marsh, and back-barrier lagoon (a lagoon behind a barrier island) environments. Similarly, along many tropical coasts, coral reefs are found close to beaches and mangrove swamps. The coastal zone is characterized by dynamism over a range of temporal scales, producing nearly continuous changes in topography, vegetation, and water flow.

COASTAL CHANGE

Coastlines act as systems in which sediments, water, and organisms are linked by flows and cycles. This means that change in one factor (e.g., the removal of vegetation) can influence other parts of the system. One approach used by coastal scientists to define coastal systems has been to identify coastal sediment cells. Such cells are a convenient way of delimiting areas of coast that function together, linked by flows of sediment along the shore as well as between onshore and offshore zones.

Dynamism in coastlines is produced by various factors, including, on a large scale, tectonic activity and sea level change (on a scale of decades or centuries, or longer), with El Niño–Southern Oscillation (ENSO) events, storms, and other climatic perturbations producing change on a medium time scale (annual to decadal), and variations in wave energy, tidal height, and currents causing changes on a subannual time scale. The dynamic nature of coastlines is determined primarily by sea level, as it is at the intersection of the sea surface with land that wave, tidal, and current energy is concentrated and that most morphological change occurs. Any change in sea level, or in the energy conditions at that level, will produce some change in coastal morphology. Plate tectonics sets the coastal scene, but it can also produce vertical and horizontal movements along coastlines, influencing the level of the sea relative to the land. Such changes operate over a range of time scales, from millions of years down to seconds (as in uplift associated with earthquakes). Sea level also depends on the volume of water held in the ocean basins, which itself is controlled by tectonic and climatic factors. Over the past thousand years, sea level has been rising globally at 0.1–0.2 millimeters per year because of continuing (if diminishing) isostatic crustal adjustments following deglaciation. Most studies estimate global sea level to have risen by about 1.0–2.0 millimeters per year over the last 100 years or so, probably as a result of the warming of ocean water (producing expansion and thus a volume increase) and the melting of ice stored on land. Recent predictions by the Intergovernmental Panel on Climatic Change (IPCC) suggest that, over the next century or so, sea level will rise at an accelerated rate of 4–5 millimeters per year, in response to increased global air temperatures. Much uncertainty surrounds such predictions, and local sea-level changes may differ greatly from the global average, depending upon natural coastal processes and on human activities (e.g., the pumping of ground water, which causes subsidence).

On the annual to decadal time scale, coasts respond dynamically to changes in oceanographic and climatic regimes. Thus, for example, extreme storms (such as Hurricane Andrew, which affected the Caribbean in 1992) produce catastrophic changes in coastal sediment regimes. The intensely studied ENSO events have also produced extensive coastal change, especially on Pacific-island coral-reef coasts where elevated sea-water temperatures, coupled with lower sea levels, have wrought considerable damage to the coral ecosystem. Such extreme events may have a range of impacts on the coastline, and in several cases it is the intensity of local human impacts that determines whether change will be acute or not. On a daily to seasonal scale, coastlines are prone to change as wave energy, climate, vegetation, and sediment volume vary. Many British beaches, for example, have distinct summer and winter states. The summer beach is characterized by increased sediment supply, often in association with vigorous growth of backshore and dune vegetation. In winter, frequent storms produce a reduction in sediment volume. The causes of coastal change at different scales can be difficult to disentangle—even in circumstances in which there is no human impact—and assessment of the rates of change is also a complex task, the rates themselves being scale-dependent.

RATES OF COASTAL CHANGE

How can we assess natural rates of coastal change? Several techniques are available, from stratigraphic methods, which provide information about long-term (millennial) variations in the positions of land and sea, through a range of historical sources of information (such as old maps, photographs, and documents of known dates, which can be compared to construct a picture of coastal change over the centuries), to short-term monitoring (over months or years) of the volume of sediment on, for example, beach and dune coasts. All such methods have their limitations, but they can provide some indication of the rate and nature of coastal change in a particular area. For example, much work has been done by Robert Morton and his coworkers (e.g., Morton 1979; Morton et al. 1993) on the dynamism of sandy coastlines of the Texas gulf using comparisons of maps and air photographs from 1850 onwards coupled with increasingly precise measurements of month-by-month changes. For many areas of the world, however, our knowledge of rates of coastal change is patchy at best.

Rates of coastal change vary greatly depending on environmental conditions and on rock, sediment, and vegetation characteristics. On exposed coasts constructed of weakly cohesive glacial sediments, where wave energies are high and materials are prone to erosion, rates of erosion (i.e., horizontal retreat of the coastline) of up to 10 meters per year can be found. Conversely, on plunging clifflines composed of hard rock in low-energy coastal environments, no discernible erosion at all may be produced for a century. Spectacular long- and short-term changes can occur along delta coasts. The Yellow River delta in China, covering a total area of 15,000 square kilometers, illustrates this well. Between 1128 and 1855 CE it formed a large delta, but after that the mouth of the river migrated north, and erosion has begun to dominate the delta because no new sediment is being delivered. Shoreline retreat has reached 110 meters per year in places and around 44 billion cubic meters of sediment has been eroded into the ocean since the mid-nineteenth century.

Coastal change can also be positive, with the building out of coastlines. In tropical mangrove swamp environments, for example, increased supply of muddy sediment coupled with colonization of suitable plant species can produce spectacular accretion. In peninsular Malaysia a study of maps, aerial photographs, and soil-augering surveys showed that the area of mangroves increased by 26.7 square kilometers between 1914 and 1969, with accretion rates of 18–54 meters per year in places. The cause of this accretion seems to have been onshore mining and agricultural activities that resulted in increased river sediment loads. In global terms, however, erosion seems to dominate. Bird (1985) has coordinated a worldwide survey of coastal change and concludes that of the roughly 20% of global coastline that is sandy, more than 70% has shown net erosion over the past few decades.

Coastal changes can thus be measured or estimated in terms of the relative position of land and sea in both vertical and horizontal dimensions, changes in the volume of sediment within the coastal zone, and/or changes in ecosystem characteristics. Many such investigations, especially of short-term coastal change, are carried out within the framework of coastal sediment cells. It is possible to identify coastal hot spots or areas prone to high rates of coastal change, including deltas and other areas prone to subsidence.

HUMAN INFLUENCES ON COASTAL CHANGE

Human activities have become an increasingly important component of coastline change within the last hundred or so years, often working with natural processes to produce spectacular change (Nordstrom, 2000). Human activities can influence physical, chemical, and/or biological characteristics of coastal systems in a variety of direct and indirect, deliberate, and accidental ways. Table 1 gives some examples.

The table shows that important deliberate and direct changes can be made through land reclamation, an ancient process whereby new land is won from the sea. In the Netherlands dikes have been constructed from 10 CE onward, and in China coastal modifications may date back to earlier than 4,000 BCE. In Singapore, reclamation has occurred since 1820 CE, with the land area of the island increasing from 582 square kilometers in 1962 to 641 square kilometers in 1992. More widely, coastal engineering schemes also have direct impacts on the coastline, as they attempt to reduce coastal changes through "hard" and "soft" alterations to coastal sediment movements. In many areas, however, activities within the coastal zone itself can have unintended impacts on coastal change. The quarrying of rock and sediment can upset sediment budgets in the local area, a famous example being the erosion of the coast near the village of Hallsands in Devon, England, as a result of the dredging of offshore sediment for use in protecting other areas of the coast.

Removal or introduction of vegetation in the coastal zone can also produce coastal change. In many parts of the tropics, mangrove trees are an important component of the local economy and thus are often felled. Furthermore, the mangrove swamps are increasingly being converted to other uses (e.g., agriculture and aquaculture), as in Indonesia where brackish-water fishponds dug into coastal wetland soils now cover approximately 269,000 hectares, or 6.5% of the former mangrove area. Such conversion can have geomorphologic and ecological consequences, as fishpond areas are prone to erosion and pollution.

Conversely, the introduction of species can also have important effects on coastal change. Along much of the British coast, for example, salt marshes have been affected by the spread of the marsh grass *Spartina anglica,* which now covers 10,000 hectares. This species encourages the accretion of mud, thus increasing the area of coastal wetland, but it reduces biological diversity and is prone to die-back. Along many coastlines, pollution within the coastal zone can contribute to coastal change through its effects on vegetation and animal life. On fringing coral reefs, for example, sewage is often discharged directly onto the reef, where it may kill reef-building coral species and encourage the growth of less desirable species, thereby threatening the fabric of the entire reef.

Indirect human activities are probably responsible for a vast amount of coastal change, whereby activities upstream, offshore, and alongshore have secondary effects on coastal systems. Human impacts on river systems, whereby sediment and pollutants are introduced into rivers and dumped in the coastal zone, are particularly important. The reduction of sediment load associated with the damming of major rivers has had a huge impact on many coasts. In the Ebro delta in northeastern Spain, for example, dams have reduced sediment-discharge from roughly 4 million metric tons per year before 1965 to less than 400,000 metric tons per year, producing changes in the depositional environments of the delta with secondary effects on wetland ecology. Finally, the withdrawal of ground water and oil from coastal aquifers, potentially leading to subsidence, is also a potent agent of coastal change. Venice was particularly prone to such subsidence from the 1950s until groundwater pumping was banned, and it has been estimated that the withdrawal of groundwater caused 12–14 centimeters of subsidence, which combines with the rising level of the Adriatic to endanger the city and the ecology of the entire lagoon.

[*See also* Coastal Protection and Management; Estuaries; Global Warming; Ocean-Atmosphere Coupling; *and* Sea Level Future.]

BIBLIOGRAPHY

Bird, E.C.F. *Coastline Changes: A Global Review.* Chichester, U.K., and New York: Wiley, 1985.
Carter, R.W.G. *Coastal Environments: An Introduction to the Physical, Ecological and Cultural Systems of Coastlines.* London and New York: Academic Press,

TABLE 1. Human Impacts on Coastline Change

	Physical Change	*Biological Change*	*Chemical Change*
Direct and deliberate action	Land claim; coastal engineering		
Direct/largely unplanned action	Quarrying of material from within the coastal zone	Accidental introduction of species (e.g., *Spartina* grass); vegetation clearance; Aquaculture	Introduction of pollutants onto beaches, or nearshore coastal waters
Indirect but deliberate action	Coastal protection and modification schemes influencing nearby coastline		
Indirect/largely unplanned action	Sediment delivery changes consequent on damming rivers; subsidence of coast following removal of ground water or oil	Sediment influx from eroding agricultural land damaging coral reef ecosystems	Pollution from offshore, upstream, and other sources entering a coastal system and producing knock-on biological effects

1988. An extensive and informative survey of coastal processes and management.

Davis, R.A. *The Evolving Coast.* New York: Scientific American Library, 1994. A readable briefing on coastlines and coastal change.

Morton, R.A. "Temporal and Spatial Variations in Shoreline Changes and Their Implications, Examples from the Texas Gulf Coast." *Journal of Sedimentary Research* 49 (1979), 1101–1111.

Morton, R.A., et al. "Monitoring Beach Changes Using GPS Surveying Techniques." *Journal of Coastal Research* 9 (1993), 702–720.

Nordstrom, K.F. *Beaches and Dunes of Developed Coasts.* Cambridge and New York: Cambridge University Press, 2000. Discusses the role of humans in transforming coastal landscapes.

Trenhaile, A.S. *Coastal Dynamics and Landforms.* Oxford: Clarendon Press, 1997. An advanced, comprehensive account of coastal geomorphology.

Viles, H.A., and T. Spencer. *Coastal Problems: Geomorphology, Ecology and Society at the Coast.* London: Edward Arnold, 1995. A wide-ranging introduction to coastal environments and human impacts upon them.

—HEATHER A. VILES

COMMONS

The "tragedy of the commons" has been a famous metaphor for problems related to common-pool resources ever since Garrett Hardin (1968) wrote his evocative article in *Science*, referring to a "common" or "commons," which is a hypothetical grazing land shared by a number of herders. Common-pool resources (CPRs) are natural or human-made resources that share two attributes, substantial difficulty (but not impossibility) of devising ways to exclude individuals from benefiting from these resources, and the subtractability of benefits consumed by one individual from those available to others (Ostrom et al., 1994, p. 6). CPRs share the first attribute with public goods and the second attribute with private goods. [*See* Externalities; *and* Tragedy of the Commons.]

COMMON-POOL RESOURCES

Natural CPRs can range in size from global phenomena, such as the ocean's fisheries and migratory wildlife, to very small-scale local commons such as irrigation systems, small lakes, grazing lands, or inshore fisheries. Human-made CPRs may also range in size from the global (e.g., the Internet) to the local (a mainframe computer used by multiple researchers). One must distinguish between the resource system itself and the resource units generated by such a system. The resource units of a CPR are finite and can be overused, leading to externalities including congestion and higher costs of production. For a groundwater basin, the resource system is the physical aquifer that has the potential of storing up to a certain maximum amount of water. The resource units from a groundwater basin are the quantities of water that are withdrawn for household, agricultural, or industrial uses.

Because CPRs face problems related to exclusion, those who may benefit from their improvement will be strongly tempted to free-ride on the efforts of others if they can. When a group of fishers agree to abide by a plan to share a conservatively estimated safe yield from a fishery, all benefit. They benefit from the preservation of their fishery over time, from the lowered cost of fishing, and from the increased quality of their catch. They all pay a short-term cost amounting to the immediate income forgone by following the agreed-upon conservative strategy in their fishing efforts. Unless the fishers find a way to exclude those who did not agree to the plan (as well as monitoring those who agreed), those who pay a short-term cost in order to receive long-term benefits may be "suckered" into paying short-term costs and not receiving the long-term benefits. Solving the problems of exclusion is difficult; they are essential if any highly valued commons is to be governed and managed effectively over the long term.

Because CPRs face problems related to subtractability, users always face potential problems of congestion and higher production costs. It is a much discussed problem for contemporary users of the Internet. Users at key times of the day find that they cannot get information rapidly because so many other users are also accessing the Internet and it has become very congested. Various plans to increase the capacity of the Internet, as well as regulating the amount of use through pricing or rationing, are under discussion.

PROPERTY-RIGHTS SYSTEMS

In order to effectively govern and manage a CPR, some form of property-rights system must be developed. Property-rights systems can be thought of as a bundle of rights related to who can access the CPR, whether they can withdraw resource units and how much, who can invest in and manage the CPR, who has the right to exclude users, and what type of rights can be transferred to others under what circumstances (Schlager and Ostrom, 1992). When these rights are given to a private individual or corporation, one has a private-property system. When these rights are held by a local, regional, or national government, one has a public property-rights system. A common-property or communal-property system is involved when an association of individuals or firms holds at least access, management, and exclusion rights even though they may not be able to alienate these rights to others. Many CPRs exist without well-defined property-rights systems having been designed. The most severe problems of the commons exist for open-access regimes as a result of free-riding and overuse.

Much contemporary policy analysis has presumed that state ownership or private ownership are the only modes of effectively managing CPRs. Since a major study by a National Academy of Sciences panel was conducted in the mid-1980s, however, common-property regimes of diverse kinds have been found to be as effective as, or more effective than, some state or private-property systems (NRC, 1986, 2002; Feeny et al., 1990). For global commons that cross national boundaries, state ownership is not even an option. Thus, various kinds of international regimes are essential ingredients of any effort to govern and manage a global commons (Keohane and Ostrom, 1995).

There are no easy solutions to the problems of the commons. Given the complexity of ecological systems, it is always a struggle to find effective means of governing them (Dietz et al., 2003). It is dangerous for the resource and for the people using it to adopt a uniform blueprint that is recommended in the literature as a panacea. Unfortunately, there are no panaceas for this complex set of problems.

BIBLIOGRAPHY

Bromley, D.W., et al., eds. *Making the Commons Work: Theory, Practice, and Policy.* San Francisco: ICS Press, 1992.

Dietz, T., E. Ostrom, and P. Stern. "The Struggle to Govern the Commons." *Science* 302 (2003), 1907–1912. DOI: 10.1126/science.1091015.

Feeny, D., et al. "The Tragedy of the Commons: Twenty-Two Years Later." *Human Ecology* 18 (1990), 1–19. DOI: 10.1007/BF00889070.

Hardin, G. "The Tragedy of the Commons." *Science* 162 (1968), 1243–1248. DOI: 10.1126/science.162.3859.1243.

Keohane, R.O., and E. Ostrom, eds. *Local Commons and Global Interdependence: Heterogeneity and Cooperation in Two Domains.* London: Sage, 1995.

NRC (National Research Council). *Proceedings of the Conference on Common Property Resource Management.* Washington, D.C.: National Academy Press, 1986.

NRC (National Research Council). *The Drama of the Commons.* Committee on the Human Dimensions of Global Change. E. Ostrom, et al., eds. Washington, D.C.: National Academy Press, 2002.

Ostrom, E. *Governing the Commons: The Evolution of Institutions for Collective Action.* Cambridge and New York: Cambridge University Press, 1990.

Ostrom, E., R. Gardner, and J. Walker. *Rules, Games, and Common-Pool Resources.* Ann Arbor: University of Michigan Press, 1994.

Schlager, E., and E. Ostrom. "Property-Rights Regimes and Natural Resources: A Conceptual Analysis." *Land Economics* 68 (1992), 249–262.

—ELINOR OSTROM

CONSERVATION

Conservation is a social movement that aims to alter the attitudes and practices of the human race toward its use of the life-supporting materials and processes of the planet. Conservation is the antidote to the universal tendency of humans to alter their surroundings in order to compete and survive. The term "conservation" is used here generically for any act of environmental protection or other behavior that promotes the sustained well-being of ecosystems and social cohesiveness. This interpretation is close to that of Aldo Leopold, the famous U.S. environmentalist, that conservation is an act and a way of thinking that leads to the continued integrity of ecological functions. Ecosystem integrity also requires a democratically functioning society that links social care to ecological care. If Leopold had not been writing as a naturalist, he too would surely have linked the two.

Without conservation, the tendency to self-destruction would go unchecked. All societies, to a greater or lesser extent, have had philosophies and practices of conservation. These philosophies change with the nature of the economy, the character of communication, and the state of science and of education in ethical awareness.

Whether the institutionalization of conservation changes anything depends on the extent to which the conservation ideal is accepted. If conservation is seen as altruistic or self-sacrificial, then regulation will always have to act against the social current, and penalty rather than reward will drive regulation. But if conservation comes to be accepted as a private and a social good combined, then conservation becomes ecologically constructive and socially bonding. We are not there yet, but we could still move in that direction.

Historians and anthropologists have long held that no society is immune from a drive to act in a manner that overuses resources and otherwise exploits nature. Despite a widespread belief that the life-ways of indigenous people are sustainable, even those societies have to rely on sophisticated cultural taboos to maintain sustainability. Taboos, societal regulations, and moral codes are all part of conservation. Some societies appear to have succumbed to the ravages of resource scarcity or disease because they never accomplished the conservation readjustment, but such conclusions may be too simplistic. Cultural collapse often arises as much from the social order in effect as from the mismanagement of the planet. [*See* Belief Systems.]

Conservation has four main manifestations:

- The preservation movement wants to protect particular ecosystems, cultural heritages, or life-ways. Some of the justification for preservation is self-serving: the desire to protect amenities in one's neighborhood, to maintain property values, or to exclude undesirable intruders. This is rightly the most criticized effect of preservation, because it relies on prejudice and political muscle for its operation. Another motive is to protect habitats, ecosystems, or natural processes that are critical for the health of a life-supporting planet. In this case, the advocates are acting more from a global interest than for personal gain, as in biodiversity-protection strategies aimed at safeguarding species and their habitats that are regarded as essential for life-support processes.

- The ecomanagement movement seeks to intervene in "unruly" ecosystems to harness their functions for the good of humanity. This is largely a utilitarian approach seeking to maximize the value of natural resources while leaving them sustainable for future use. The techniques used include those of maximum sustained yield in forestry and maximum allowable catch in fisheries. These approaches are largely failing because scientific knowledge is not sufficiently developed to recognize the limits. More to the point, the managers rarely have the power to control property rights, price signals, and political interference by vested interests. Fisheries, for example, are being overwhelmed world-wide because governments have neither the authority nor the will to control the fishing industry so that it takes only the allowable catch. [*See* Fisheries.]

- The precautionary approach in conservation applies different rules. First, it seeks to create a society that is more ecocentric than technocentric, in that its adherents respect nature and find pleasure in giving the natural world room to breathe. Second, it recognizes that science is fallible, that outcomes cannot be predicted—in part because the processes being interfered with are nonlinear—and that the interests of future generations are served better if they are given a say in today's management decisions. The criticism implicit in the precautionary principle is based partly on ethics but more importantly

TABLE 1. The Spectrum of Environmentally Related Political Activity

Passive					Active
Ordinary Political Participation	Passive Lobbying	Active Support	Activism	Direct Action	Revolutionary Action
Following events in the media	• Letter writing	• Attending meetings and demonstrations	• Organizing events, boycotts, and lobbying efforts	• Picketing and committing acts of obstruction	• Engaging in complete civil disobedience, sabotage, and terrorism
	• Signing petitions	• Leafleting and collecting money	• Doing research and writing	• Engaging in ethical shoplifting	
• Voting in local and national elections	• Joining groups	• Boycotting goods, companies, or institutions	• Organizing campaigns and fund-raising	• Lecturing and public speaking	
• Responding to surveys and questionnaires	• Making donations				

These categories are intended to reflect the different degrees of commitment to environmental change. The particular category in which an activity is placed is necessarily somewhat arbitrary. For example, although boycotting could be considered a form of direct action, it is placed under "Active Support" because it is essentially nonconfrontational. Also, although some individuals and groups may fall within a single category, many will not.

SOURCE: O'Riordan (1995, p. 28)

on a concern for a different approach to justice and the intrinsic rights of natural things. [*See* Precautionary Principle.]

• Modern societies are characterized by violence, fragmentation, disobedience to laws, distrust of authorities, especially governments, and a slim sense of do-it-yourself civic activism. Some direct action is illegal, dangerous, and violent and is pursued by a minority comprising zealots, high-minded and sincere protesters, and criminal troublemakers. It is dangerous to pigeonhole direct action: it comes in many forms for many reasons (Table 1). Peaceful direct action is of growing importance in the modern conservation movement because society is increasingly active civically and because protest is often led by articulate and well-connected nongovernmental organizations. The rise of the World Wide Web has considerably increased the cohesion and effectiveness of these organizations. [*See* Environmental Movements.]

Conservation is a profound movement, rooted in human nature and triggered by economic change, technological transformation, political fragmentation, and ethical concern. It is its adaptability that is its enduring strength.

[*See also* Agriculture and Biodiversity; Biological Diversity; Deforestation; Erosion; Industrial Ecology; Land Reclamation; Land Use; Parks and Preserves; Resources; Salinization; Tourism; Water; *and* Wilderness and Biodiversity.]

BIBLIOGRAPHY

Easterbrook, G. *A Moment on the Earth: The Coming of Age of Environmental Optimism.* London: Penguin Books, 1996.

O'Neill, J. *Ecology, Policy, and Politics.* London and New York: Routledge, 1993.

O'Riordan, T. "Frameworks for Choice: Core Beliefs and the Environment." *Environment* 37.8 (1995), 4–9, 24–29.

Pepper, D. *Modern Environmentalism: An Introduction.* London and New York: Routledge, 1995.

—TIMOTHY O'RIORDAN

CRUDE OIL SUPPLY

A future without cheap oil has been portrayed in a number of recent books and news stories, some of which estimate the year in which world oil production will peak and begin to decline. The reality of expensive oil was demonstrated in May 2008 when the price of crude on world markets exceeded $125 per barrel.

This impending shortage of oil commands our attention just as we grasp the reality of global warming—which is caused in large part by the burning of petroleum products, natural gas, and coal. A further coincidence is the rapid economic growth in nations such as China and India, which until recently were not making great demands on crude oil supplies: their ascendance now accompanies the projected decline in petroleum and forces large consuming nations to compete for the remaining crude.

The decline of a nonrenewable resource like crude oil is inevitable, but its urgency is debated in two respects. First is the fundamental difference between earth scientists and economists: geologists study the resource, while many economists believe that shortages will raise prices, spur more intense exploration, and allow exploitation of oil accumulations not considered economical at the former price. The principle is valid, but the current supply picture does seem drastically different from that of the past. The second debate is among various geologists who agree on the decline coming in the twenty-first century but disagree on its imminence because of different estimates of remaining resources. [*See* Resources.]

Especially compelling is the history of discoveries versus production rates for the world (Figure 1). Since the 1970s the rate of discovery has fallen steadily, while production (use) has continued to climb at nearly 2% per year. The gap between the two, when projected beyond 2005 with the assumption of no major discoveries, leads to a peak in production in the year 2010.

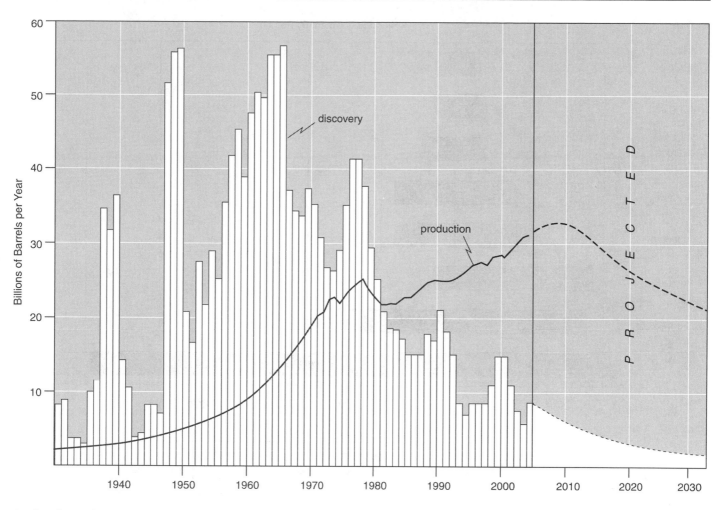

Crude Oil Supply. Figure 1. Conventional Crude Oil Discovery and Production Rates to 2005, with Projections to 2030.

Production peaks in 2010. (Data from Colin J. Campbell in a graph in *The Oil Age: World Oil Production 1859–1950*.)

The date of peak production is not determined simply by applying an annual production rate to proven reserves. Instead, following the example of a Shell oilman (Hubbert, 1956) geologists estimate the year in which half the world's total recoverable endowment of oil will have been produced. This ultimate recovery is defined as the sum of oil produced to date, proven reserves, and expected recovery from oil fields as yet undiscovered. There is no doubt about oil produced to date, there are small differences in interpreting reserve data, and there are large differences in estimates of what may be recovered from fields still hidden in sedimentary rock in less-explored regions. If the concept is applied region by region, it reveals some useful contrasts (Figure 2). If the left side of a bar (past production) is longer than the right, as in North America, that region is already past its peak. Latin America and Europe appear to be at the halfway mark at the time of the estimate. The Gulf region of the Middle East, on the other hand, has remaining resources that are much greater than amounts produced.

In such a summary, for regions or for the world as a whole, the undiscovered recoverable component is debatable, as is seen in Table 1 in which the estimates are for conventional oil and therefore exclude oil from oil sands, heavy oil deposits, and oil shales.

Campbell's low estimate of undiscovered recoverable may be due to his excluding polar oil and deepwater oil from his definition of conventional oil. That leads to a reduced ultimate recovery number and a peak production date of 2005 (which differs by five years from the date inferred from Figure 1).

The analysis by Wood et al. (2004) states some assumptions and statistical probabilities that further illuminate their estimates. The authors identify three values for ultimate recovery: Low (95% probability), Mean (their expected value), and High (5% probability). They assume annual demand growth of 2%, and a reserve/production ratio of 10 in the post-peak years; and they note the peak production rate for each scenario. Their key tabulation, which is the basis for their entry in Table 1, is simplified here as Table 2.

In Table 2, production rates in the years of peak production range from 117 to 178 billion barrels of oil per day. That is remarkable because in 2006 world daily production averaged around 84 billion barrels. Their numbers are derived from the 2% annual growth in demand and the assumption that demand

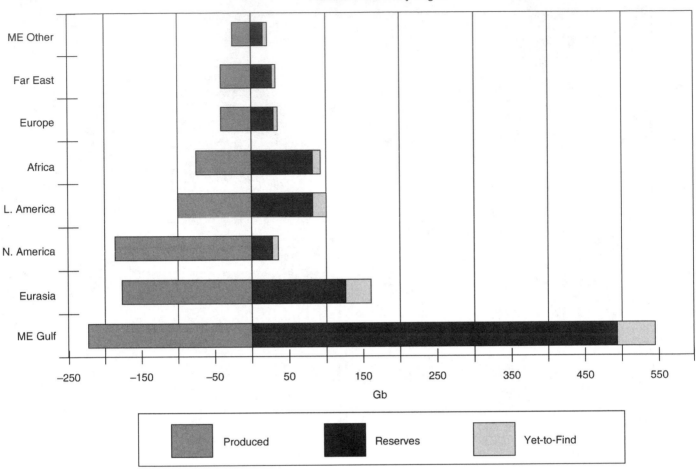

Crude Oil Supply. Figure 2. Ultimate Recovery of Conventional Crude Oil by Region.

(From Colin J. Campbell, Feb, 2002.)

Table 1. Recent Estimates of Ultimate Recovery and Year of Peak Production for Conventional Crude Oil (billions of barrels)

	Cumulative Production	Proven Reserves	Undiscovered Recoverable	Ultimate Recovery	Peak Production Year
Masters et al., 1994	800	1,103	471	2,272	2005–2020
Edwards, 1997	800	1,111	1,005	2,836	2020
Campbell, 2002	873	928	149	1,950	2005**
Wood et al., 2004	—	900*	700*	low 2,248	2026
				mean 3,003	2037
				high 3,896	2047

* estimated from authors' diagram ** from Campbell and Laherrere (1998)

will somehow be met. To balance the gloomier picture in Figure 1, the projection by Wood et al. is shown in Figure 3, using only the Low and Mean scenarios, and showing production peaks in 2026 and 2037 respectively.

In the spring of 2007 some announcements from industry leaders and geologists reinforced the prediction of decline. Geoscientists reporting on a November 2006 conference suggest conventional crude production will peak in 2020–2030 at a rate

TABLE 2. USGS/DOE/EIA World Oil Production Forecast 2004 (billion barrels)

	Ultimate Recovery	Annual Growth in Demand	Peak Year	Peak Production Rate (million bopd)
Low	2,248	2%	2026	117
Medium	3,003	2%	2037	146
High	3,896	2%	2047	178

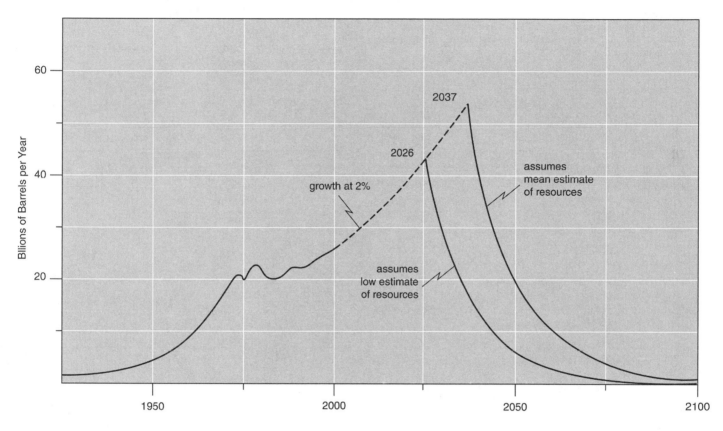

Crude Oil Supply. FIGURE 3. US Geological Survey/DOE Production Scenarios for Low and Mean Estimates of Ultimate Recovery.

(From Wood, Long, and Morehouse, 2004.)

of 90–100 million barrels per day, a number much less optimistic than the 117–178 million proposed by Wood et al. (*Oil and Gas Journal*, April 4, 2007). Following this, the CEO of Shell Oil wrote that "supplies of conventional oil and natural gas . . . will struggle to keep up with accelerating demand. Just when energy demand is surging, many of the world's conventional oilfields are going into decline" (van der Veer, 2007). He suggests that depending on renewables to fill the gap is unrealistic: instead, we must focus on more efficient use of energy and reduce the demand for crude oil. Fatih Birol, Chief Economist of the International Energy Agency, voiced the same opinion and noted the explosive growth in China together with the fall in non-OPEC oil production. He, too, called for tough policies to curb the growth in oil demand (*Le Monde*, June 27, 2007).

It seems unlikely that we will run completely out of oil in the twenty-first century, because before that happens it will become so expensive that other sources of primary energy will be more attractive. Also, the mitigation of greenhouse gas emissions will reduce the use of petroleum products and possibly slow the demand growth assumed in Table 2 and Figure 3 (if population growth and economic growth do not reverse that slowdown). In any case, the world will face more expensive crude oil and alternative liquid fuels that are costly and less convenient than gasoline and diesel fuel. The impacts on wealthy and developing societies are developed in a number of publications, some of which are listed in the bibliography.

[*See also* Fossil Fuels; *and* Oil Sands.]

BIBLIOGRAPHY

REFERENCES CITED

Campbell, C. J. "Peak Oil: An Outlook on Crude Oil Depletion." Feb. 2002. http://www.greatchange.org/ov-combell,outlook.html (accessed May 29, 2008).

Campbell, C.J., and J.H. Laherrere. "The End of Cheap Oil." *Scientific American* (March, 1998), 78–83.

Edwards, J.D. "Crude Oil and Alternate Energy Production Forecasts for the Twenty-First Century; The End of the Hydrocarbon Era." *American Association of Petroleum Geologists Bulletin* 81.8 (August 1997), 1292–1305.

Hubbert, M.K. *Nuclear Energy and the Fossil Fuels.* Publication 95. Houston: Shell Development Company, June 1956.

Masters, C.D., E.D. Attanasi, and D.H. Root. "World Petroleum Assessment and Analysis." *Proceedings of the 14th World Petroleum Congress.* Stavanger, Norway: Wiley, 1994.

The Oil Age: World Production 1859–2050. Poster showing past and projected oil production by region. http://www.oilpaster.org/posterlarge.html (accessed May 29, 2008).

Van der Veer, J. "High Hopes and Hard Truths Dictate Future." *Times* (London), June 25, 2007.

Wood, J.H., G.R. Long, and D.F. Morehouse. "Long-Term World Oil Supply Scenarios: The Future Is Neither as Bleak or Rosy as Some Assert." U.S. Energy Information Adminstration (EIA), 2004.

FURTHER READING

Campbell, C.J. *The Coming Oil Crisis.* Brentwood, U.K.:Multi-Science Publishing, 1997.

Deffeyes, K.S. *Beyond Oil: The View from Hubbert's Peak.* New York: Hill and Wang, 2005.

Jaccard, M. *Sustainable Fossil Fuels: The Unusual Suspect in the Quest for Clean and Enduring Energy.* Cambridge and New York: Cambridge University Press, 2005.

Kunstler, J.H. *The Long Emergency: Surviving the End of Oil, Climate Change. and Other Converging Catastrophes of the Twenty-First Century.* New York: Atlantic Monthly Press, 2005.

Leeb, S. *The Coming Economic Collapse: How You Can Thrive When Oil Costs $200 a Barrel.* New York: Warner Business Books, 2006.

Roberts, P. *The End of Oil: On the Edge of a Perilous New World.* Boston: Houghton Mifflin, 2005.

Simmons, M.R. *Twilight in the Desert: The Coming Saudi Oil Shock and the World Economy.* Hoboken, N.J.: Wiley, 2005.

—DAVID J. CUFF

D

DAMS

Dams and reservoirs have long been an integral part of water management. They store water in wet periods for use in dry periods for agriculture and cities; they produce electricity by tapping the energy of falling water; they reduce the risks of disastrous flooding; they create reservoirs used for recreation; and they assist navigation by leveling during high-flow and low-flow periods. Recently, however, dams have become the focus of intense international debate because of their negative, and often ignored, impacts on both people and natural ecosystems.

Humans have been building dams since the earliest days of human civilization. There are examples over five thousand years old from Mesopotamia and Egypt. Examples of ancient dams can also be found in China, South Asia, Medieval Europe, and North America before the arrival of Europeans.

Despite this long history, the widespread construction of large dams did not begin until the middle of the twentieth century, when improvements in engineering and construction skills, hydrologic analysis, and technology made it possible to build them safely. Much of the initial large-dam construction occurred in the United States (Graf, 1999). The government built about 50 large dams between 1900 and 1930. Between 1930 and 1980 it built a thousand more, together with tens of thousands of smaller ones. The first of the massive dams was the Hoover Dam, built by the U.S. Bureau of Reclamation on the Colorado River in the 1930s. By 1945, the five largest dams on Earth had been completed, all in the western United States. Today, dammed reservoirs store 60% of the entire average annual river flow of the United States (Hirsch et al., 1990).

Other countries also saw large dams as vital for national security, economic prosperity, and agricultural survival. In the Soviet Union, Stalin dreamed of transforming that country's massive rivers into controlled projects to provide electricity for Soviet industries and "transform nature" into a machine for the communist state. By the 1970s, the total area flooded by dams in the former U.S.S.R. greatly exceeded that of the United States, and the world's tallest dam—the 300-meter-tall Nurek—was completed in 1980 in Tajikistan. In India, the program of dam construction initiated by the British colonial government was quickly adopted after independence in 1947 by the independent government, which built thousands of dams and associated facilities. Following the Chinese revolution in 1949, more than 600 dams were built every year for three decades, with both wondrous and disastrous results.

Today nearly 500,000 square kilometers of land worldwide are inundated by reservoirs capable of storing 6,000 cubic kilometers of water (Shiklomanov, 1993, 1996; Collier et al., 1996). This redistribution of fresh water is so large that scientists reported that it is responsible for a small but measurable change in the orbital characteristics of the Earth (Chao, 1995). Today's dams produce roughly 20% of the world's total supply of electricity. Table 1 shows the breakdown of hydroelectric production by region for 2005. Much of the hydropower generation is concentrated in a few countries, including Canada, the United States, Brazil, and China.

The construction of large dams continues today. In Asia, China is pursuing an ambitious hydropower development program, including the massive and controversial Three Gorges project. India has 10,000 megawatts approved or under construction and another 28,000 megawatts planned. Laos, Nepal, Malaysia, Russia, and the Philippines all have major construction projects under way. In Latin America, Brazil has the most ambitious plans, with more than 10,000 megawatts under construction and plans for another 20,000 megawatts. Honduras, Mexico, and Ecuador all have major projects under consideration. In Europe, projects for new or rehabilitated hydroplants are being pursued in Albania, Bosnia, Croatia, Greece, Iceland, Macedonia, Portugal, Slovenia, and Spain.

IMPACTS

Many of these dams may never be built. Serious opposition to large dams is growing throughout the world because of their environmental, social, and cultural consequences. Among the many impacts are land inundation, loss of riparian (river-related) habitat, adverse effects on aquatic species, and reservoir-induced

TABLE 1. Hydroelectric Generation by Region, 2005

	Billion Kilowatt hours
North America	657.66 (Canada 359.88)
Central and South America	613.16 (Brazil 334.88)
Europe	539.57 (Norway 134.44)
Eurasia	244.73 (Russia 172.86)
Middle East	20.98 (Iran 15.94)
Africa	88.66 (Mozambique 13.13)
Asia and Oceania	735.27 (China 396.99)
World	2,900.03

seismicity, as well as social impacts on local populations and people who must be uprooted and resettled from reservoir areas (Goldsmith and Hildyard, 1986; White, 1988; Covich, 1993; McCully, 1996).

Only a small fraction of land-area worldwide has been lost to reservoirs, but this land is often of special value as fertile farmland, riparian woodland, or wildlife habitat. River floodplains are among the world's most diverse ecological systems, balancing aquatic and terrestrial habitat, species, and dynamics. In addition to the area lost to the reservoir behind a dam, there are often secondary impacts on surrounding lands, as humans are required to move to build new homes and farms. Wildlife populations displaced by the dam must seek new habitat. Access roads built in remote areas where many dams are built also bring in loggers and others searching for quick economic gains.

Dams can also destroy dramatic scenery when they are located in mountainous terrain. The Itaipú Reservoir inundated the spectacular waterfall of Sete Quedas on the Paraná River. The dam that provides water for the city of San Francisco flooded the Hetch Hetchy Valley in California, which was considered comparable in beauty to the famous Yosemite Valley. In an ironic twist, the dam that created Lake Powell along the Colorado River was named for a magnificent remote desert canyon that the rising waters destroyed—Glen Canyon. Indeed, massive public opposition to additional dams along the Colorado

resulted in large part from the desire to prevent the destruction of the Grand Canyon, one of the most important symbols of natural beauty in the United States.

Dams radically alter natural river systems and put pressure on aquatic ecosystems and species. There is often an immediate decline in the diversity of native fishes after dam construction because the new environment is so different from the original river ecosystem or because nonnative species outcompete native species. Dams interrupt the seasonal upstream migration of many species and alter the flow, sediment regime, dissolved oxygen content, and temperature of the habitat, all of which affect reproduction and survival. They alter the hydrology of a basin and the dynamics of riverine ecosystems through changes in nutrient retention, water levels, and water chemistry. Large fluctuations in reservoir levels during droughts or seasonal drawdowns alter the habitat along the margins where fish feed and spawn. Temperature differences in reservoirs often result in completely different aquatic flora and fauna.

The ecological impacts of dams on rivers extend all the way to the sea. Many of the world's major fisheries depend on the

---

Dams. Hydroelectric Generation.

The Kariba Dam, on the Zambezi River in central Africa, is a major source of hydro-electric power. However, large dams such as this have a whole series of ecological consequences, as well as causing displacement of people.

volume and timing of fresh water and nutrient flows from large rivers into estuaries or the ocean. Almost all of the fish caught in the Gulf of Mexico, the Grand Banks of Newfoundland, the Caspian Sea, the eastern Mediterranean, and off the western coast of Africa depend on river discharges. The vast salmon fisheries of the eastern Pacific along the coasts of Canada and the United States rely on the ability of the fish to spawn in freshwater streams. Dams in all of these areas, combined with overfishing and fisheries mismanagement, have led to great declines in many anadromous (freshwater-spawning) fish populations.

Partly as a consequence of large dams, more than 20% of all freshwater fish species are now considered threatened or endangered, and many of the most severe impacts have been felt by amphibians, insects, waterfowl, and plants. The western coast of the U.S. once boasted 400 separate salmon and steelhead stocks, but a century of habitat loss, dam construction, changes in flow regimes, and overfishing have eliminated nearly 50% of them, and many of the remainder are at high risk of extinction. Other examples of aquatic species threatened by dams include several species of river dolphins in Latin America and Asia, sturgeon in North America, China, and Russia, and commercial and noncommercial fisheries at the mouth of almost every major river, including the Nile, Colorado, Volga, and Indus, and in the Black, Azov, and Caspian seas.

Another consequence of some dam construction is earthquakes caused by the filling of a large reservoir. For most cases the intensity of seismic activity increases with the size of a reservoir and the speed the reservoir is filled. The strongest shocks normally occur as the reservoir approaches maximum volume, and earthquakes may continue for a few years after initial filling. The effect has occurred near at least 200 reservoirs around the world, but the mechanism is not well understood. Of the 11 reported cases of earthquakes greater than 5.0 on the Richter scale associated with filling of reservoirs, 10 of them occurred in dams higher than 100 meters.

One of the most serious concerns about large dams has been the involuntary displacement and resettlement of people living in areas to be flooded by reservoirs. Often entire villages are destroyed, with generations of history and culture lost, churches and burial grounds flooded, and homes and farmlands inundated. Limited and often contradictory data are available on populations displaced by dam construction and the creation of reservoirs. According to a World Bank study (1994), approximately 40 million people were displaced by dams between 1986 and 1993, an average of about five million people a year. Others estimate that this many people have been displaced by dams during the twentieth century (McCully, 1996). The vast majority of people displaced by dam construction are in India and China, two countries with extremely high population densities and aggressive dam-development programs. In China, over 10 million people were officially displaced by water projects between 1960 and 1990, and the Three Gorges Dam project

DAMS AND EARTHQUAKES

Perhaps the most important human-induced seismicity results from the creation of large reservoirs. Reservoirs impose stresses of significant magnitude on crustal rocks at depths rarely equaled by any other human construction. With the increasing number and size of reservoirs the threat rises. There are at least six cases—Konya (India), Kremasta and Marathon (Greece), Hsinfengkiang (China), Kariba (Zambia and Zimbabwe), Hoover (Arizona and Nevada)—where earthquakes of a magnitude greater than 5 on the Richter scale, accompanied by a long series of foreshocks and aftershocks, have been related to reservoir impounding. There are many more locations where the filling of reservoirs behind dams has led to appreciable, though less dramatic, levels of seismic activity. Detailed monitoring has shown that earthquake clusters occur in the vicinity of some dams after their reservoirs have been filled, whereas before construction activity was less clustered and less frequent. Similarly, there is evidence that there is a correlation between the storage level in the reservoir and the frequency of shocks. Dams induce earthquakes partly because of the pressure exerted by the mass of the water impounded in the reservoir and the changing water pressures across the contact surfaces of faults in the underlying rock. Because the deepest reservoirs provide surface loads of only 20 bars or so, direct activation by the mass of the impounded water seems an unlikely cause, and the role of changing pore pressure assumes greater importance.

Our ability to prove a cause-and-effect relationship between reservoirs and earthquakes is limited by our ability to measure stress below depths of several kilometers, and some examples of induced seismicity may have been built on the false assumption that because an earthquake occurs in proximity to a reservoir it has to be induced by that reservoir (Meade, 1991).

BIBLIOGRAPHY

Meade, R.B. "Reservoirs and Earthquakes." *Engineering Geology* 30 (1991), 245–262.

—ANDREW S. GOUDIE

now under construction will displace between one and two million more. The resettlement issue is complicated to address; it involves restoring and improving living standards as well as trying to resolve a host of problems usually ignored by traditional economic solutions.

NEW DEVELOPMENTS

The negative environmental and social impacts resulting from past dam projects have given rise to opposition to new ones. Few major dams are now moving forward without public scrutiny and analysis, and several major projects have been canceled or postponed. Many more have been redesigned to address public concerns and interests.

While many new construction plans are well along and may fill a vital need, serious obstacles will limit the actual level of development and lead to the cancellation of some projects. Growing public opposition on environmental and social grounds, more comprehensive regulatory procedures, and new complexities in the financing of major dam projects are all working to slow development. The World Bank, long a major international funder in this area, is rethinking guidelines and environmental requirements for major dam projects.

Public debate and opposition to major dam projects have appeared in Nepal, India, South Africa, Latin America, and even China, where active dissent from government policies is a dangerous and courageous act. Laws in the United States, Norway, and Sweden limit development on pristine rivers. Opposition comes from local grassroots efforts and, internationally, from nongovernmental organizations. Local communities are no longer willing to accept immediate social and environmental disruption for a promise of hypothetical future benefits. Moreover, the frequent disregard for the civil rights of people living in rural areas affected by some dam projects has led to a widespread distrust of all dam projects.

Major projects are likely to be successful only if local populations are fully consulted, involved, and represented in decisions about a project and its alternatives. Yet planning for almost all major dam projects is still usually conducted behind closed doors by a small number of engineers and water experts. In most countries, dam developers solicit little or no public feedback, and decisions are made by a small group of water managers or governmental organizations, together with international funding agencies (Oud and Muir,

WHAT IS A LARGE DAM?

There is no single definition of a large dam. According to criteria set by the *International Journal on Hydropower and Dams*, there are more than 300 major dam projects that meet at least one of the following criteria:

- dam height exceeding 150 meters
- dam volume exceeding 15 million cubic meters
- reservoir volume exceeding 25 billion cubic meters, or
- installed electrical capacity exceeding 1,000 megawatts.

The International Commission on Large Dams (ICOLD) defines large dams less restrictively. According to ICOLD criteria, there are roughly 40,000 large dams and over 800,000 small ones (McCully, 1996). A large dam is one whose height is 15 meters or greater; or whose height is between 10 and 15 meters if it meets at least one of the following conditions:

- A crest length of not less than 500 meters
- A spillway discharge potential of at least 2,000 cubic meters per second
- A reservoir volume of not less than one million cubic meters.

—PETER H. GLEICK

ENVIRONMENTAL IMPACTS OF LARGE VERSUS SMALL DAMS

While much has been written about the environmental impacts of large dams, there is still uncertainty about the impacts of single small dams and the cumulative impacts of many small dams. Moreover, there are many different types of dam, built and operated for many different purposes in a variety of environments, making generalizations unreliable and misleading.

Single large dams have attracted the most attention from the environmental science and environmental advocacy communities because they often create enormous reservoirs, flood large land areas, displace large populations, and form significant barriers to aquatic species and navigation. Smaller dams may be built on smaller river systems, be designed to either create a reservoir or operate in "run-of-river" mode without storing water, generate small amounts of electricity, or divert small amounts of irrigation water. They thus tend to avoid the more obvious environmental and social disruption of large projects, but they produce fewer benefits as well. Proper comparison of impacts is therefore extremely difficult.

Appropriate measures of the environmental consequences of dams must include not only their size, but how they are designed and operated. In a comparison of large and small dam systems in the western United States, multiple small dams were shown to have some impacts that exceeded those of a single large dam (Gleick, 1992). In particular, while many large hydroelectric dams with large reservoirs flood a substantial amount of land and lose water to evaporation, certain kinds of small dam may actually flood more land or lose more water to evaporation per unit of energy produced. Another factor relevant to determining net impacts is how dams are operated. Dams operated in "run-of-river" mode—independent of size—have less impact on natural riverine ecosystems than dams that store water in large reservoirs and alter the timing, quality, and character of streamflow.

This area requires further analysis. No comprehensive study has been done, for example, on the numbers of people displaced by dams as a function of energy produced, land flooded, or water supplied. Few analyses of the net impact to natural ecosystems have been done as a function of either the size of a dam, or the number of dams built on a single river. And information is especially limited on impacts in developing countries, where baseline environmental data, reliable social indicators, and environmental assessments are less commonly available.

—PETER H. GLEICK

1997). Such lack of consideration for the public has also contributed to growing opposition to dams around the world.

While new dams that will improve the quality of life for many people will be built in the future, there are signs that the philosophy of dam construction is changing.

More attention is finally being paid to understanding and mitigating the environmental and social impacts of dams and to soliciting the participation of local people in making decisions about new facilities. And in some places, some bad decisions made over the past century may finally be reconsidered. In late 1997 the U.S. government for the first time refused to relicense a hydroelectric dam and ordered the structure—the 16-meter-high Edwards Dam on the Kennebec River in Maine—destroyed on the grounds that its costs as a barrier to migratory fish significantly exceed its hydroelectric benefits. Other dams that have environmental or social costs exceeding their benefits also face removal. While they are not large, they symbolize many of the problems facing all dam projects. The precedent set by their destruction may herald a new generation of hydrologic engineers and ecological scientists whose field of expertise is the removal of large dams (Graf, 2001).

[See also Ecosystems; Irrigation; and Water.]

BIBLIOGRAPHY

Chao, B.F. "Anthropogenic Impact on Global Geodynamics Due to Reservoir Water Impoundment." *Geophysical Research Letters* 22 (1995), 3529–3532.

Collier, M., R.H. Webb, and J.C. Schmidt. *Dams and Rivers: A Primer on the Downstream Effects of Dams.* Tucson, Ariz. and Denver, Colo.: United States Geological Survey, 1996.

Covich, A.P. "Water and Ecosystems." In *Water in Crisis: A Guide to the World's Fresh Water Resources*, edited by P.H. Gleick, pp. 40–55. Oxford and New York: Oxford University Press, 1993.

Gleick, P.H. "Environmental Consequences of Hydroelectric Development: The Role of Facility Size and Type." *Energy* 17.8 (1992), 735–747.

———. *The World's Water: 1998–1999.* Washington, D.C.: Island Press, 1998.

Gleick, P.H., et al. *California Water 2020: A Sustainable Vision.* Oakland, Calif.: Pacific Institute For Studies in Development, Environment, and Security, 1995.

Goldberg, C. "Fish Are Victorious over Dam as U.S. Agency Orders Shutdown." *The New York Times*, November 26, 1997, A12.

Goldsmith, E., and N. Hildyard, eds. *The Social and Environmental Impacts of Large Dams.* Worthyvale Manor Camelford, Cornwall, U.K.: Wadebridge Ecological Centre, 1984.

Goodland, R. *Ethical Priorities in Environmentally Sustainable Energy Systems: The Case of Tropical Hydropower.* World Bank Environment Working Paper 67, 1994.

Goodland, R. "Environmental Sustainability in the Hydro Industry: Disaggregating the Debates." In *Large Dams: Learning from the Past, Looking at the Future*, edited by T. Dorcey, et al., pp. 69–102. Washington, D.C.: World Bank, 1997. Proceedings of IUCN and World Bank Group Workshop, Gland, Switzerland, April 11–12, 1997.

Graf, W. "Dam Nation: A Geographic Census of American Dams and Their Large-Scale Hydrologic Impacts." *Water Resources Research* 35 (1999), 1305–1311.

———. "Damage Control: Restoring the Physical Integrity of America's Rivers." *Annals of the Association of American Geographers* 91 (2001), 1–27. DOI: 10.1111/0004-5608.00231.

Hirsch, R.M., et al. "The Influence of Man on Hydrologic Systems." In *The Geology of North America*, v. O-1, *Surface Water Hydrology*, edited by M.G. Wolman and H.C. Riggs, pp. 329–359. Boulder, Colo.: Geological Society of America, 1990.

McCully, P. *Silenced Rivers: The Ecology and Politics of Large Dams.* London: Zed Books, 1996.

McPhee, J. *Encounters with the Archdruid.* New York: Farrar, Straus, and Giroux, 1971.

Murty, K.S. *Soil Erosion in India*, vol. 1, *River Sedimentation.* Beijing: International Research and Training Center on Erosion, 1989.

Ortiz, A., ed. *Handbook of North American Indians.* Vol. 9. *Southwest.* Washington, D.C.: Smithsonian Institution, 1979.

Oud, E., and T.C. Muir. "Engineering and Economic Aspects of Planning, Design, Construction, and Operation of Large Dam Projects." In *Large Dams: Learning from the Past, Looking at the Future*, edited by T. Dorcey, et al., pp. 17–39. Washington, D.C.: World Bank, 1997. Proceedings of IUCN and World Bank Group Workshop, Gland, Switzerland, April 11–12, 1997.

Reisner, M. *Cadillac Desert: The American West and its Disappearing Water.* New York: Penguin, 1993.

Rouse, H., and S. Ince. *History of Hydraulics.* Ames: Iowa Institute of Hydraulic Research, State University of Iowa, 1957.

Scudder, T. "Recent Experiences with River Basin Development in the Tropics and Subtropics." *Natural Resources Forum* 18.2 (1994), 101–113.

Scudder, T. "Social Impacts of Large Dam Projects." In *Large Dams: Learning from the Past, Looking at the Future*, edited by T. Dorcey, et al., pp. 41–68. Washington, D.C.: World Bank, 1997. Proceedings of IUCN and World Bank Group Workshop, Gland, Switzerland, April 11–12, 1997.

Sewell, W.R.D. "Inter-Basin Water Diversions: Canadian Experiences and Perspectives." In *Large Scale Water Transfers: Emerging Environmental and Social Experiences*, edited by G.N. Golubev and A.K. Biswas, pp. 7–35. Oxford: Tycooly, 1985.

Shiklomanov, I.A. "World Fresh Water Resources." In *Water in Crisis: A Guide to the World's Fresh Water Resources*, edited by P. H. Gleick, pp. 13–24. Oxford and New York: Oxford University Press, 1993.

Shiklomanov, I.A. "Assessment of the Water Resources and Water Availability in the World." Draft Report to the Comprehensive Assessment of the Freshwater Resources of the World. St. Petersburg, Russia: State Hydrological Institute, 1996.

Stanford, J.A., and J.V. Ward, eds. "Stream Regulation in North America." In *The Ecology of Regulated Streams*, pp. 215–236. New York: Plenum, 1979.

White, G. "The Environmental Effects of the High Dam at Aswan." *Environment* 30.7 (1988), 4.

World Bank. "Resettlement and Development: The Bankwide Review of Projects Involving Involuntary Resettlement 1986–1993." Washington, D.C.: World Bank, 1994.

World Bank. *Resettlement Remedial Action Plan For Africa.* Washington, D.C.: World Bank, 1995.

—Peter H. Gleick

DANSGAARD-OESCHGER CYCLES

The fine-resolution climate record provided by the deep ice-core record from the poles has indicated the rapid and frequent "flickering" of climate during a glacial–interglacial cycle. The oxygen isotopic study of the cores for the last glacial period shows 24 intervals of relatively high and low $\delta^{18}O$ (oxygen-isotope values). Variations are of the order of 4–6 per thousand, which implies a temperature change of 7–8°C. The intervals of less-negative $\delta^{18}O$ values, representing warmer interglacials, lasted between five hundred and two thousand years. An important element of this pattern of change is the abruptness of the shift (within a few decades) from cold to warm temperatures at the onset of these interstadials (warmer intervals). In contrast, the initial part of the return of colder stadial conditions is more gradual. There is thus a characteristic sawtooth form of very rapid warming to interstadials followed by slower cooling to the next stadial. This is termed a Dansgaard-Oeschger cycle, after the pioneers of ice-core drilling.

BIBLIOGRAPHY

Anderson, D., A.S. Goudie, and A.G. Parker. *Global Environments through the Quaternary*. Oxford and New York: Oxford University Press, 2007.

Bond, G., et al. "Correlations between Climate Records from North Atlantic Sediments and Greenland Ice." *Nature* 365 (1993), 143–147. DOI: 10.1038/365143a0.

—Andrew S. Goudie

DATING METHODS

The reconstruction of past climates (paleoclimatology) depends on highly refined stratigraphy and dating methods. [*See* Paleoclimate.] Stratigraphy includes the composition, sequence, age, and correlation of rock strata or deposits; as a field of study it also includes fossil content, geochemical, chemical, mineralogical, and magnetic properties, mode of origin, and all physical properties and attributes that mark rock or other deposits as strata. Strata are organized or distributed according to superposition: younger strata overlie older strata (Steno's law), or are sequentially distributed across the land surface in accordance with episodic geologic activity (e.g., moraines deposited by various glacial episodes, or dunes deposited by eolian activity occurring at various times). All geologic history and paleoclimatic and paleoenvironmental reconstruction is based on the physical, mineralogical, chemical, and biological variations that occur within and between strata in a sequence. Lateral changes within strata may be as important as vertical changes in a stratigraphic column in terms of assessing regional variations in paleoclimate.

The geologic time scale (Figure 1) is a chronological sequence of geologic events that serves as a measure of the relative or absolute age of a part of geologic time. Geologic time units are subdivided into eons, eras, periods, and epochs; in recent time (less than sixty-five million years ago), where erosion has not removed much chronological evidence, epochs are used to subdivide periods of time (for example, the Pleistocene Epoch or Holocene Epoch during the Quaternary Period). Older units in pre-Cenozoic time are subdivided into periods, and occupy much wider time slots based on relative or absolute dating methods.

STRATIGRAPHY

Stratigraphic or chronological indicators include any material that provides relative or absolute age control. Tills (glacial sediment), for example, provide evidence for drastic changes in climate, but are considered time transgressive—the process, in this case glaciation, does not begin and end at the same time in every place. Tephra (volcanic ash or dust), on the other hand, can be dated by potassium/argon (K/Ar) or fission-track methods and is time-parallel—the process begins and ends at the almost the same time everywhere and thus may be globally nearly synchronous.

Lithostratigraphy is based on particular homogeneous lithologic characteristics that are used to recognize rocks or depositional units in unconsolidated, unweathered, and undifferentiated material and consolidated, cemented, and indurated material (rock). Both unlithified deposits and solid rock are recognized by physical characteristics and/or the presence of certain lithic materials that dominate a unit. A lithostratigraphic unit (also called rock stratigraphic unit) is named from a type area, should be described from a type stratigraphic section representative of the unit, and should be labeled with a descriptive lithologic name (e.g., Trenton limestone). The formation is the fundamental lithostratigraphic unit; other units include group, member, lentil, tongue, and bed. In many glaciated areas, lithostratigraphic units all have the same lithology, so weathering characteristics and differences in soil expression are used to help differentiate the units (Birkeland et al., 1979; Birkeland, 1984; Mahaney, 1990). Because the beginning and end of deposition may have occurred earlier or later in different areas, the morphological character of the unit may be used for recognition (morphostratigraphy) but should be secondary to its lithic character.

It is common in Quaternary stratigraphy to use the morphology of the deposit as a major criterion in placing it within a sequence. Frye and Willman (1962) defined morphostratigraphic units in the U.S. Midwest as a body of rock (especially unconsolidated surficial deposits) identified by its surface form. Over thirty morainic units have been named in the Midwest, and they are identified solely on surface form. These moraines may also be grouped together as geologic-climatic units, but in that case each individual moraine is undifferentiated.

Geologic-climatic units are defined from the rock or soil record, and boundaries within a local area are isochronous (simultaneous), though over a wide region they may not be isochronous. The major unit is a glaciation (a climatic episode in which glaciers expanded, developed their maximum volume, and ultimately receded); interglaciations are episodes during which the climate favored glacial stagnation or retreat. Subdivisions include stades, which are climatic episodes within a glaciation in which secondary advances occurred; interstades are climatic episodes within a glaciation in which secondary recessions occurred. A geologic-climatic unit may be named after a rock-stratigraphic and/or a soil-stratigraphic unit. In the type locality of a geologic-climatic unit, the record of its major climatic characteristics should be manifest, for instance, glacial till or a record of climatic deterioration in paleosols below and above the lower and upper limits of the unit (e.g., Pinedale Glaciation with overlying interglacial [Holocene] or interstadial [later Pleistocene] paleosol). Fossil life forms found in some of the rocks may provide a means of differentiation on a biostratigraphic basis. While generally not important for Quaternary rocks or deposits, discrimination of sedimentary rock is often achieved on the basis of fundamental units called biozones. If fossil content is high and is lithologically important, biostratigraphic units become, in essence, lithostratigraphic units.

A chemostratigraphic unit is recognized on the basis of its chemical homogeneity; physical and lithic properties often dominate in the field, and chemical properties are determined

RELATIVE GEOLOGIC TIME				ABSOLUTE TIME (million years)	LIFE FORMS
EON	ERA	PERIOD	EPOCH		
Phanerozoic (evident life)	Cenozoic (recent life)	Quaternary	Holocene		Rise of mammals and appearance of modern marine animals
			Pleistocene		
		Tertiary	Pliocene	2	
			Miocene	5	
			Oligocene	24	
			Eocene	37	
			Paleocene	58	
				66	
	Mesozoic (middle life)	Cretaceous	Late		Abundant reptiles (including dinosaurs); more advanced marine invertebrates
			Early	144	
		Jurassic	Late		
			Middle		
			Early	208	
		Triassic	Late		
			Middle		
			Early	245	
	Paleozoic (ancient life)	Permian	Late		
			Early	286	
		Carboniferous – Pennsylvanian	Late		First reptiles
			Middle		
			Early		
		Carboniferous – Mississippian	Late		
			Early	360	
		Devonian	Late		First terrestrial vertebrates - amphibia
			Middle		
			Early	408	
		Silurian	Late		
			Middle		
			Early	438	
		Ordovician	Late		First vertebrates - fish
			Middle		
			Early	505	
		Cambrian	Late		Primitive invertebrate fossils
			Middle		
			Early	570	
	Precambrian			3800+	Meager evidence of life

Dating Methods. FIGURE 1. Geologic Time Scale.

(After Birkeland and Larson, 1989. With permission of Oxford University Press.)

after laboratory analysis. Chemostratigraphy often provides information on the source of sediment in lithostratigraphic units, on the chemical and mineral homogeneity of sediments, and on the changes that have occurred in the sediments since their deposition (e.g., chemical alteration, cementation, and induration). Perhaps most importantly, chemostratigraphy provides geochemical profiles of the rare-earth elements (REEs) that are important in the differentiation of strata (Hancock et al., 1988).

Soil stratigraphic units are formed by the weathering of lithostratigraphic, biostratigraphic, and/or chemostratigraphic units during a hiatus in deposition. A soil stratigraphic unit has physical features and stratigraphic relationships that allow consistent recognition of mappable units. A soil stratigraphic unit differs from a lithostratigraphic unit in that it forms in the latter as a result of pedologic (soil-related) processes acting from the surface downward. The soil may change laterally in the landscape, for example, from a well-leached one to a carbonate-rich one. A soil stratigraphic unit should be named after a lithostratigraphic unit using the prefix "post-" to avoid terminological proliferation (Mahaney, 1990).

Postdepositional modification stratigraphy (PDMS) as advocated by Birkeland et al. (1979) is a "hybrid of time stratigraphic and rock stratigraphic units and contains elements of both age and physical properties." Subdivision and correlation of deposits in a geologic sequence is achieved by using multiple relative-dating (RD) methods, including rock-weathering parameters, soils, landform morphometry, and lichens wherever and whenever possible. Despite the number of RD studies in different areas, we still do not know the minimum number of parameters that should be used in age determination (Mahaney, 1990; Birkeland et al., 1979).

Time stratigraphy (chronostratigraphy) describes material units that comprise all rock formed in a particular interval of time. Time-stratigraphic boundaries are based on geologic time; that is, they are isochronous surfaces based on objective criteria that are nearly time-parallel. Such criteria for Quaternary successions include some, but not all, faunal and floral zone boundaries, shorelines controlled by worldwide sea-level changes, and tephra; evidence for climatic change is excluded because it is time-transgressive. Time stratigraphic units for the midwestern U.S. are based on paleosols representing interglacial stages separating glacial stages, as in the case of the Lake Michigan glacial lobe (Morrison and Frye, 1965).

RADIOMETRIC DATING

Many dating tools are available to provide absolute or relative-age controls. Radiometric methods include radiocarbon, potassium-argon (K/Ar), U-series (using uranium isotopes), and rubidium-strontium (Rb/Sr); each method is best suited to specific materials. The radiocarbon method, developed by W. F. Libby of the University of Chicago (Libby et al., 1949), is based on the rate of decay of carbon-14. There are three isotopes of carbon, carbon-12 and carbon-13, which are stable, and carbon-14, which is unstable (radioactive). The latter is formed in the upper atmosphere by the effect of cosmic-ray neutrons on nitrogen-14:

$^{14}N + n \rightarrow {}^{14}C + p$, where n is a neutron and p is a proton (Figure 2). Radiocarbon is oxidized to carbon dioxide (CO_2) and enters through photosynthesis and the food chain into plant and animal tissues, ocean waters, and biogenic carbonate minerals (Nydal, 1995; Figure 2). An equilibrium is established between the carbon-14 concentration in the atmosphere and that in organic tissues.

When plants or animals die, carbon-14 uptake ends and decay proceeds. The radioactive carbon-14 decays at a constant rate, which is expressed in terms of its half-life value, 5,730 ± 40 years. After every 5,730 years, half of the remaining carbon-14 will have decayed. During the decay, carbon-14 emits a beta particle (β^-, an electron) and the decay can be written as follows:

$^{14}C \rightarrow {}^{14}N + \beta^-$.

The number of β^- emissions per unit time allows the determination of the amount of carbon-14 remaining in the carbon-containing material. Assuming that the carbon-14 concentration of the atmosphere (and in the food chain) has been constant through the history of the sample, the elapsed time since the start of decay can be established by measuring the amount of carbon-14 left in the sample. All the carbon-14 dates are are expressed with reference to 1950 CE. Materials commonly dated by carbon-14 are charcoal, wood, seeds, bone, peat, lake mud, humus-rich soil, and mollusk shells.

Because the carbon-14 concentration fluctuates with time, the calibration of radiocarbon dates against historically dated materials becomes important (Stuiver and Pearson, 1986). Radiocarbon dates of sequential dendrochronologically dated wood or annual increments of marine and lacustrine sediments and corals produce a calendar-year–radiocarbon-year calibration-curve that extends back over 12,000 years, enabling radiocarbon dates to be calibrated to calendar dates over that period. [*See* Dendrochronology.] The way radiocarbon dates and absolute dates relate to each other differs in three periods: back to 12,400 calendar-years BP, radiocarbon dates can be calibrated with tree rings, and the calibration curve in this form should soon extend back to 18,000 cal BP. Between 12,400 and 26,000 cal BP, the calibration curves are based on marine records, and are thus only an estimate of atmospheric concentrations (Bronk Ramsey et al., 2006).

Potassium-argon (K/Ar) can be used to date tephra, many igneous rocks, and some metamorphic rocks. U-series is used to date peat, tufas (spring deposits), and coral. Rubidium-strontium (Rb/Sr) is used to date volcanic rock. Both U-series and K/Ar dates span the entire age of the solid Earth, while the radiocarbon method is limited to 40,000 BP, although the accelerator–mass-spectroscopy (AMS) radiocarbon method has the potential to reach to about 90,000 BP.

PALEOMAGNETIC DATING

Paleomagnetism is used in Quaternary stratigraphic studies as a tool for correlation and relative dating of strata and in some cases can be used for the absolute dating of deposits. Magnetic stratigraphy organizes rock strata into identifiable units based on stratigraphic intervals with similar magnetic characteristics. The method is based on the detection of changes in the Earth's magnetic field—especially changes of polarity—that are recorded by ferromagnetic minerals at the time of their formation. The polarity is referred to as normal where the north-seeking magnetization gives a Northern Hemisphere pole, as it does today, or reversed where the north-seeking magnetization gives a Southern Hemisphere pole.

The dating of Quaternary sediments and rocks by geomagnetic-polarity history and by paleomagnetic parameters such as field declination and inclination, secular variation, and susceptibility is now commonplace (Evans and Heller, 2003; Opdyke and Channel, 1996; Barendregt, 1995). The large-scale features of the Earth's magnetic field have been well worked out for the past five million years or so, using lava flows and deep-sea sediments. These have been used to construct the geomagnetic-polarity time scale (Figure 3). The detailed (albeit short-lived) features

Dating Methods. FIGURE 2. Production and Decay of Carbon-14 in Nature.

(Adapted from Nydal, 1995. With permission of PACT, Belgium.)

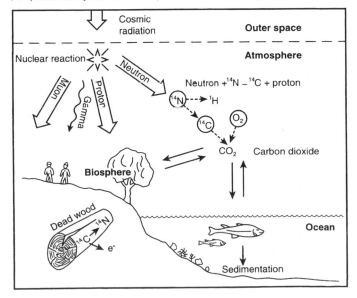

for this period are still being discovered and defined through analysis of marine and terrestrial sediments where high sedimentation rates have continued for long periods of time. It is likely that more of these short-lived events, which provide a record of the excursions and perturbations of the Earth's magnetic field, will ultimately become useful correlative tools (Lund et al., 2001).

Fine-grained (clay- and silt-sized) sediments, lava flows, and baked pottery are the media most frequently used for magnetic dating. Because reversals have occurred repeatedly in the past, their identification within incomplete sedimentary records is possible only through comparison with other stratigraphic or radiometric data collected for similar or related sedimentary sequences. Continuously-deposited marine or terrestrial sediments that show a high sedimentation rate provide records of polarity that can be used for worldwide correlation.

The only practical way of demonstrating the validity of magnetostratigraphy is to show that results are reproducible in widely separated sections with different lithologies and sedimentation rates. A long-standing problem of magnetostratigraphy has been the correlation of the terrestrial and marine records (Cooke, 1983). Since geomagnetic polarity reversals are recorded globally, magnetic stratigraphy provides ample opportunity to correlate between the two contrasted sedimentary environments. Recent work (e.g., Parfitt, et al., 2005; Barendregt and Duk-Rodkin, 2004) has shown the usefulness of magnetostratigraphy in establishing the chronology of glacial sequences where few absolute dates are available. Other studies (e.g., Heller and Liu, 1982) have established magneto-biostratigraphies for lake-sediment and loess sequences, motivated largely by a desire to understand continental responses to climatic change, and to late Cenozoic glaciations in particular.

Marine isotope stages shown in Figure 3 are correlated with the geomagnetic polarity timescale for the last 3.3 million years. The oscillation of cold and warm events is indicated, and at several points in the time scale, isotope stages coincide with warming and cooling events. For example, isotope stage 5 coincides with the last interglaciation when the climate was even warmer than present; the last glaciation coincides with isotope stages 4 and 2; isotope stage 3 coincides with a time of ice recession and relative warmth but not total loss of ice cover; and isotope stage 1 coincides with the Holocene.

Oxygen-16 (^{16}O) and oxygen-18 (^{18}O) are stable isotopes found in earth's atmosphere, waters, and ice masses. Evaporation from the oceans and subsequent storage of this water on land (in ice masses) increases the relative amount of the heavy isotope (^{18}O) in ocean water. The $^{18}O/^{16}O$ ratio is therefore an indicator of global temperature. This ratio is generally expressed as delta (δ) ^{18}O given in units per mil (‰), where the $^{18}O/^{16}O$ ratio of the sample is measured relative to that of mean standard ocean water (MSOW). In the oceans, during warm periods, lower concentrations of ^{18}O (negative ^{18}O) are incorporated into the tests (shells) of invertebrates (mainly foraminifera); higher concentrations

(positive ^{18}O) are incorporated during cold periods when more ^{16}O is locked up in land ice, thus enriching ocean water in ^{18}O. This global temperature signal is also reflected in an opposite sense in glacial ice where the $^{18}O/^{16}O$ ratio decreases in cold climates (^{18}O becomes more negative) and increases in warm climates (^{18}O becomes less negative).

The ocean cores used to construct the marine isotope record are also suitable in most cases for paleomagnetic study, so the isotopic and polarity data can be reported in tandem, reliably dating the cold and warm peaks of the paleotemperature curve.

VARVE CHRONOLOGY

The clay varve chronology, the first absolute dating method to be developed, was introduced in Sweden by Gerard De Geer in 1884, and was used to estimate the timing of the disappearance of the Scandinavian Ice Sheet. Laminations in lake sediments are usually referred to as rhythmites or—where the lamination develops because of annual variations in sedimentation—as varves. Annual laminations (O'Sullivan, 1983) in lacustrine sediments are formed as a consequence of seasonal, rhythmic changes in biogenic production, water chemistry, and the inflow of mineral matter (Saarnisto, 1986). Glaciolacustrine varves—alternating layers of coarse and fine sediment—develop in proglacial lakes (just beyond glacial margins) as a result of summer and winter contrasts in sediment input. Counting of varves allows a precise dating of the start of, changes in, and end of deposition in lakes. By using distinctive annual layers or groups of layers (marker layers characterized by their thickness, texture, and composition), it is possible to correlate sediment sections from different lakes and to establish long varve chronologies. For example, the Swedish Time Scale covers more than 13,300 varve years (Wohlfarth et al., 1995) and is correlated with dendrochronological and ice-core records and high-resolution AMS-dated lacustrine deposits (Björck et al., 1996).

[*See also* Climate Reconstruction; *and* Proxy Data for Environmental Change.]

BIBLIOGRAPHY

Barendregt, R.W. "Paleomagnetic Dating Methods." In *Dating Methods for Quaternary Deposits*, edited by N.W. Rutter and N. Catto, pp. 24–49. St. John's, Nfld: Geological Association of Canada, 1995.

Barendregt, R.W. and A. Duk-Rodkin. "Chronology and Extent of Late Cenozoic Ice Sheets in North America: A Magnetostratigraphic Assessment." In *Quaternary Glaciations-Extent and Chronology, Part II*, edited by J. Ehlers and P.L. Gibbard, pp. 1–7. Amsterdam and San Diego: Elsevier, 2004.

Berger, G.W., B.J. Pillans, and A.S. Palmer. "Dating Loess up to 800 ka by Thermoluminescence." *Geology* 20 (1992), 403–406.

Birkeland, P.W. *Soils and Geomorphology*. New York: Oxford University Press, 1984.

Birkeland, P.W., and E. Larson. *Putnam's Geology*. 5th ed. New York and Oxford: Oxford University Press, 1989.

Birkeland, P.W., et al. "Nomenclature of Alpine Glacial Deposits, Or, What's in a Name?" *Geology* 7 (1979), 532–536.

Björck, S., et al. "Synchronized Terrestrial-Atmospheric Deglacial Record around the North Atlantic." *Science* 274 (1996), 1155–1160. DOI: 10.1126/science.274.5290.1155.

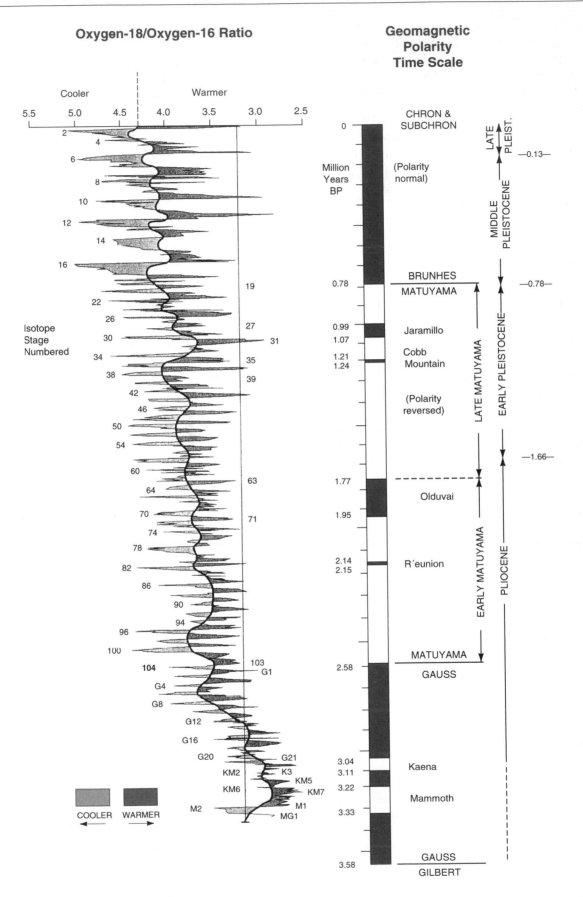

Oxygen-18/Oxygen-16 Ratio

Cooler   Warmer

5.5   5.0   4.5   4.0   3.5   3.0   2.5

Isotope
Stage
Numbered

COOLER   WARMER

Geomagnetic Polarity Time Scale

CHRON &
SUBCHRON

0

Million
Years
BP

(Polarity
normal)

0.78   BRUNHES
        MATUYAMA

0.99   Jaramillo
1.07
1.21   Cobb
1.24   Mountain

        (Polarity
        reversed)

1.77   Olduvai
1.95

2.14   R'eunion
2.15

        MATUYAMA
2.58   GAUSS

3.04   Kaena
3.11
3.22   Mammoth
3.33

3.58   GAUSS
        GILBERT

LATE
PLEIST.   —0.13—

MIDDLE
PLEISTOCENE

        —0.78—
EARLY PLEISTOCENE

LATE MATUYAMA

        —1.66—

EARLY MATUYAMA

PLIOCENE

Bronk, R.C., et al. "Developments in Radiocarbon Calibration for Archaeology." *Antiquity* 80 (2006), 783–798.

Cande, S.C., and D.V. Kent. "Revised Calibration of the Geomagnetic Polarity Timescale for the Late Cretaceous and Cenozoic." *Journal of Geophysical Research* 100.B4 (1995), 6093–6095.

Cooke, H.B.S. "Recognizing Different Quaternary Chronologies: A Multidisciplinary Problem." In *Correlation of Quaternary Chronologies*, edited by W.C. Mahaney, pp. 1–14. Norwich, U.K.: Geobooks, 1983.

Evans, M.E., and F. Heller. *Environmental Magnetism: Principles and Applications of Enviromagnetics.* Amsterdam and Boston: Academic Press, 2003.

Frye, J.C., and H.B. Willman. "Morphostratigraphic Units in Pleistocene Stratigraphy." *American Association of Petroleum Geologists Bulletin* 46 (1962), 112–113.

Hancock, R.G.V., W.C. Mahaney, and A.M. Stalker. "Neutron Activation Analysis of Tills in the North Cliff Section, Wellsch Valley, Saskatchewan." *Sedimentary Geology* 55 (1988), 185–196.

Hang, T. "Clay Varve Chronology in the Eastern Baltic Area." *Geologiska Föreningens I Stockholm Forhandlingar* 119 (1997), 295–300.

Heller, F., and T.S. Liu. "Magnetostratigraphical Dating of Loess Deposits in China." *Nature* 300 (1982), 431–433. DOI: 10.1038/300431a0.

Hillhouse, J.W., T.E. Cerling, and F.H. Brown. "Magnetostratigraphy of the Koobi Fora Formation, Lake Turkana, Kenya." *Journal of Geophysical Research* 91 (1986), 11581–11595.

Libby, W.F., E.C. Anderson, and J.R. Arnold. "Age Determination by Radiocarbon Content: World-Wide Assay of Natural Radiocarbon." *Science* 109 (1949), 227–228. DOI: 10.1126/science.109.2827.227.

Lund, S. P., et al. "Brunhes Chron Magnetic Field Excursions Recovered from Leg 172 Sediments." In *Proceedings of the Ocean Drilling Program, Scientific Results*, vol. 172, edited by L.D. Keigwin, et al. http://www.odp.tamu.edu/publications/172_SR/chap_10/c10_.htm (accessed May 29, 2008).

Mahaney, W.C. *Ice on the Equator.* Sister Bay, Wisc.: William Caxton, 1990.

Morrison, R.B., and H.E. Wright, Jr., eds. *Means of Correlation of Quaternary Successions.* Salt Lake City: University of Utah Press, 1968.

Nydal, R. "The Early Days of ¹⁴C in Scandinavia, and Later Development." *PACT* 49 (1995), 9–27.

Opdyke, N.D., and J. Channell. *Magnetic Stratigraphy.* San Diego: Academic Press, 1996.

O'Sullivan, P.E. "Annually-Laminated Lake Sediments and the Study of Quaternary Environmental Changes: A Review." *Quaternary Science Reviews* 1 (1983), 245–313.

Parfitt, S.A., et al. "The Earliest Record of Human Activity in Northern Europe." *Nature* 438 2005, 1008–1012. DOI: 10.1038/nature04227.

Raymo, M.E. "Global Climate Change: A Three Million Year Perspective." In *Start of a Glacial*, edited by G.J. Kukla and E. Went. Berlin and New York: Springer, 1992.

Ruddiman, W.F., M.E. Raymo, and A. McIntyre. "Matuyama 41,000-Year Cycles: North Atlantic Ocean and Northern Hemisphere Ice Sheets." *Earth and Planetary Science Letters* 80 (1986), 117–129.

Saarnisto, M. "Annually Laminated Lake Sediments." In *Handbook of Holocene Palaeoecology and Palaeohydrology*, edited by B.E. Berglund, pp. 343–370. Chichester, U.K., and New York: Wiley, 1986.

Shackleton, N.J., M.A. Hall, and D. Pate. "Pliocene Stable Isotope Stratigraphy of Site 846." In *Proceedings of the Ocean Drilling Program, Scientific Results*, vol. 138, edited by N.G. Pisias, et al., pp. 337–353. College Station, Tex.: Ocean Drilling Program, 1995.

Stuiver, M., and G.W. Pearson. "High Precision Calibration of the Radiocarbon Time Scale, AD 1950–500 BC." *Radiocarbon* 28.2B (1986), 839–862.

Wohlfarth, B., S. Björk, and G. Possnert. "The Swedish Time Scale: A Potential Calibration Tool for the Radiocarbon Time Scale During the Late Weichselian." *Radiocarbon* 37.2 (1995), 347–359.

—WILLIAM C. MAHANEY, RENÉ W. BARENDREGT, AND VOLLI KALM

Dating Methods. FIGURE 3. Geomagnetic Polarity Time Scale and Oxygen-18/Oxygen-16 Paleotemperature Record (Facing Page).

Isotope stages: even numbers are cold, odd numbers are given where they coincide with Chron and Subchron boundaries. Letters and numbers used before isotope stage 104 (Matuyama/Gauss boundary) follow Shackleton et al., 1995. (Paleotemperature record from Ruddiman et al., 1986; Raymo, 1992. Geomagnetic polarity time scale after Cande and Kent, 1995.)

DEFORESTATION

Deforestation is the removal (or killing) of all trees and conversion of the land to desert, agricultural or grazing land, buildings, eroded barrens, or other nontreed conditions. Removing, or killing, all trees by natural or human disturbances, is not considered deforestation if the area grows back to trees. This temporary removal of trees simply places the forest in a different structural stage—the "open" (stand initiation) structure. For the purposes of this article, the practice of harvesting the trees, cultivating the area for agriculture for several years, and then allowing regrowth to forests in "shifting agriculture" will not be considered deforestation, because the net effect is a return of the land to a forested condition. Similarly, harvesting native forests and regrowing the area with plantations of exotic tree species will not be considered deforestation, although there may be environmental consequences of this change. Rates of deforestation are difficult to determine because of variations in the way data are collected and monitored in different countries; information in this article is based on United Nations Food and Agriculture Organization data, which have possible shortcomings, as described later.

Deforestation can occur naturally when the climate changes at the forested extremes of cold, dry, or water-saturated conditions so that forests can no longer survive or regenerate. Continental and mountain-glacier advances during the Pleistocene (1.5 million to 10,000 years BP) removed forests from vast areas of Europe, North America, and Asia, and as these glaciers melted, rising sea levels removed forests from the inundated areas. More recent cooling trends, the past few thousands and hundreds of years, have caused forests to disappear in high altitudes and polar latitudes. At other times, warming trends have reduced the area of forests as deserts expanded Gates, 1993). Likewise, sinking land surfaces have caused forests to disappear, as in southern Louisiana, where forests are being inundated with salt water (DeLaune et al., 1983).

Timber harvesting, land clearing, and/or grazing as well as natural disturbances such as fires, windstorms, or flooding can increase the rate of deforestation that is associated with these geologic changes. In some cold areas, natural or human disturbances can prevent or reverse the change of forests to peat bogs by draining the bogs and/or mixing the mineral and organic soils.

RATES AND LOCATIONS OF DEFORESTATION

Recent, rapid deforestation seems to be caused directly by people and is a major concern of the international forestry community. The world's forests are estimated to have covered 8 billion hectares in 2,000 BCE (Food and Agriculture Organization, 1993) and to have been reduced to 3.45 billion hectares by 1995. Deforestation began in parts of the Mediterranean and Chile about 10,000 years ago (Aschmann, 1973). Humans have accelerated deforestation in the past few centuries in parts of Europe, temperate and tropical Asia, North America, and tropical Central and South America. Following changes in cultures in tropical Asia (as at the abandoned temple sites of Angkor Wat and Borobodor) and tropical Central and South America (e.g., Mayan, Inca; Turner and Butzer, 1992; von Kooten et al., 1999), forests regrew. Recently, forests have been regrowing in more developed regions such as North America and Europe (Allan and Lanly, 1991; Food and Agriculture Organization, 1997).

Deforestation is now occurring at a net rate globally of 10.8 million hectares per year (0.3% per year, 1990–1995 average). The loss of forests is currently higher than this in less-economically-developed-regions of the world but is offset by net increases in forest area in more-developed regions. The increase in some forest areas compensates statistically for the decrease in others, but this does not necessarily mean that the species diversity, habitats, and socioeconomic benefits are similarly offset.

The highest rates of deforestation appear to be in tropical forests of Asia, Africa, and Central and South America. [See Amazonia and Deforestation.] It is argued that net deforestation is actually lower in these areas because abandoned agricultural land, which regrows to forests, may not be adequately incorporated into the data. It is estimated that 90% of the recent tropical deforestation has occurred since 1970 (Skole et al., 1994). In 1990, the tropical forests of the world were estimated to cover about 1.7 billion hectares, compared with 1.9 billion hectares in 1981—an annual tropical deforestation rate of about 0.8% (Food and Agriculture Organization, 1993). [See Tropical Forests and Global Change.]

Land deforested by poorly managed agriculture or grazing activities in arid, erosive, or otherwise disruptive conditions can result in damage to the soil structure, depletion of the nutrient pool, erosion, and/or desertification, so that forests will not grow again. As trees become scarcer for firewood, animal dung is often used instead. This dung and its nutrients are not allowed to replenish soil nutrients, and the soil productivity for agriculture is further depleted. Consequently, other areas are cleared for agriculture or grazing and the deforestation is continued.

In arid areas, some previously forested regions have been changed to "anthropogenic steppes" through deforestation (Boydak and Dogru, 1997). Further degradation can lead to desertification (Aubreville, 1949)—a relatively nonreversible process by which the area loses its ability to sustain forest growth, biological diversity, and most human values. It is uncertain how much of the presently degraded arid land was once forested; Africa and Asia have the most degraded land,

while much of the drylands of Africa, Europe, and Asia has been degraded.

During desertification, the topsoil and associated soil nutrients, structure, organic matter, and water-holding capacity are lost when the forest is harvested and it and other vegetation are prevented from growing, through a combination of inappropriate cultivation, grazing, and burning. With the loss of topsoil, wind and water erosion often remove the lower soil layers and deposit them in streams, residential areas, and other unwanted locations. The inability of the area to support forests (or other vegetation) means that the area's capacity to provide forest biodiversity and forest products is gone, as is its ability to sequester carbon through forest growth and forest-product use. If large areas are converted to deserts, the result may be local climate changes and movement of people to other areas where, if not managed appropriately, they can cause further desertification. In areas of sufficient rainfall, vegetation and ultimately forests usually will regrow after the grazing, burning, cultivation, and/or other pressures are removed, but in arid areas the land may remain as a relatively permanent desert once the vegetation has been removed. [See Desertification.]

Most developed regions have a net increase in forests, although within a region there may be deforestation in some places compensated for by reforestation in others. Historically, the rise of civilization has been associated with expanding deforestation, as growing populations and industrialization consumed more fuelwood and cleared more land for agriculture and grazing (Perlin, 1989). The lack of forests has been suggested as a cause of the decline of some civilizations. Events of the past two centuries, however, suggest that a new relationship between economic development and deforestation is emerging. Technological advances in transportation and farming mean that more food can be produced on the very productive areas, fewer people are employed to do the farming, and the products are shipped longer distances than before. As these events occur, the less productive farming and grazing lands are being abandoned and allowed to regrow to trees, and the unneeded farm labor moves to cities. Also, as societies develop, they are now typically substituting fossil fuel for fuelwood and thus decreasing pressure on the forest. The result is a reversal of the deforestation trend, although forests will probably never cover as much area as they could.

As regions develop, deforestation is caused by building construction in expanding urban areas; by clearing of forests on the most productive soils for agricultural use; by construction of roads, reservoirs, and similar structures; and sometimes by pollution of the air and soil. The area deforested is generally less than the reforested area—but local deforestation can threaten or cause extinction of species that occupy the specific areas and ecosystems being deforested. Deforestation can sometimes have the beneficial effect of providing productive farm and residential areas, thus providing food and shelter and allowing more forests to grow on less productive lands. However, even these cases create negative trade-offs such as loss of species habitats in the productive, deforested areas.

CAUSES OF DEFORESTATION

The causes of deforestation are complex and often misunderstood (Williams, 2003). Commercial timber-harvesting in the tropics is rarely a significant cause of deforestation, although it can change the forest to the "open" structure until it regrows. Commercial logging, however, can increase road access and remove large trees and so can make forest areas more accessible for conversion to agricultural cultivation and grazing—and hence deforestation.

Shipment of wood (in the form of timber and timber products), from less developed to more developed regions of the world, does not appear to be occurring in such vast quantities that it is a significant cause of deforestation. It may, however, affect the forest composition, the wood quality, and the socio-economic conditions of the exporting country, and thereby indirectly affect deforestation. Overseas shipment causes forests and wood products to become valued by the exporting country as a promising economic sector, and the emphasis on protection, reforestation, and management of forests increases, although this reforestation may consist of plantations of exotic tree species.

Deforestation is also commonly attributed to population growth. As populations rise, the pressures on the forests might be expected to increase, but it has been difficult to link population and economic growth directly to all deforestation (Skole et al., 1994, Table 4). A population increase accompanying certain lifestyles (e.g., subsistence agriculture and grazing), may account for deforestation in some regions.

Government policies that encourage people to move to rural lands to avoid urban congestion, to strengthen territorial security or claims, or to provide other benefits often promote deforestation. Much tropical deforestation is driven by the replacement of forests through agricultural activities similar to the deforestation that occurred in temperate North America between 1700 and about 1930 CE. In addition, substantial native tropical forests have been replaced by the introduction of tree crops such as rubber, palm oil, and coconut. Fertile bottomland forests have gradually been converted to agriculture, and recent water-development projects remove forests where water is impounded and allow agriculture to replace forests in areas previously too arid for effective cultivation.

Industrial chemical pollutants released into the air and water can kill trees and soil organisms, thus causing deforestation (Gordon and Gorham, 1963; Rykowski, 1995). In most developed countries, pollution-control measures and laws now minimize or prevent this chemical pollution, but these pollutants can still cause deforestation where these laws are not strict or are ignored, or when accidents happen.

Much of the present deforestation is closely related to subsistence agriculture and pastoral systems and associated large uses of trees for fuelwood. Subsistence agriculture and grazing limit areas in which new trees can grow. The net effect is to provide little wood, so wood is cut over larger areas, which are then cultivated and grazed—and deforestation spreads. Forty-eight percent of the world's harvested wood is used for fuel, and 72% of the wood harvested in regions with net deforestation is used for fuel. Forest growth for fuelwood does not necessarily promote deforestation. For example, a well managed coppice forest can be harvested for firewood, and new sprouts will grow to a new forest. If, however, the harvesting is followed by grazing and/or fires that prevent new sprouts, local people often dig out the tree roots and cut new forests for fuelwood—and the newly cut areas are then burned and/or grazed. In addition, when trees are cut for fuelwood before their rapid growth stage, large areas are needed to provide a modest wood volume and the trees are kept so small that they cannot be used for other products such as building materials.

EFFECTS OF DEFORESTATION

Often, especially in less developed regions of the world, deforestation results in a loss of soil productivity and thus a reduced ability to grow any useful products. This deforestation can eliminate species directly through harvest and indirectly through destruction of habitats. It can eliminate the forested habitat or part of the habitat of species that use both forest and nonforest areas, and it can interrupt the migration routes of other species that travel through forests.

Elimination of old-growth forests—forests containing very old or large trees (also known as late successional forests, ancient forests, ancient woodlands, precolonial forests, and climax forests)—was a particular concern when it was assumed that old growth was the condition in which all forests existed and that all species survived before the forest was altered by humans. Deforestation does eliminate such forests, but the old-growth condition was only one of many natural conditions of the forests as they changed through disturbances and regrowth. And there are species that depend on open forests, savannas, and dense forests, as well as those that depend on old growth (Oliver and Larson, 1996). Deforestation eliminates all of these conditions and threatens the species that depend on them. Elimination of the old forests through deforestation or other harvest is also of concern, because these forests sequester large amounts of carbon. By not harvesting these forests, the carbon stored is much less than the carbon that is added to the atmosphere by using substitute products such as steel, aluminum, brick, and concrete if wood is not available (Kershaw et al., 1993). Although these old-growth forests have many values, these values must be balanced against the increased carbon dioxide added to the atmosphere if substitute products are used because these forests are not harvested. It must also be remembered that harvesting of old-growth forests is not synonymous with "deforestation" if forests regrow after the harvest. However, certain habitats and other values are lost for a long time in both cases.

Deforestation alters the water-flow over and within the soil as well. Elimination of the trees reduces the evapotranspiration, and so allows more water to flow into groundwater reservoirs and aquifers as long as the soil structure is maintained. Because there are no trees to regenerate, the soil organic matter and structure degenerate shortly after deforestation. In fine-textured soils such as clays, the soils become compact and easily eroded. Rainfall flows over the land-surface rather than through the soil, causing severe erosion and stream deposition, as well as flash floods. In coarse-textured soils such as sands, rainfall can penetrate the soil rather than flow overland, even when the soil profile has been disrupted, but the soils often eroded by wind, and the nutrients are leached into the groundwater reservoir.

The increase in atmospheric carbon dioxide during the early Industrial Revolution is attributed to the burning of wood for energy and the associated deforestation. Since about 1930, the increase is largely attributable to fossil-fuel use. [See Global Warming.] Deforestation affects carbon dioxide in the atmosphere both during the process and afterward. During deforestation, the carbon in the trees is released to the atmosphere as carbon dioxide through burning or rotting. After deforestation, there is no forest to regrow and to absorb carbon dioxide from the atmosphere through photosynthesis (Sampson and Hair, 1992, 1996). In addition, deforestation prevents forest products from being put to use; and so steel, concrete, brick, and other substitute products are used; these consume far more fossil fuel in their manufacture and so add much more carbon dioxide to the atmosphere than if wood were used. Energy produced from wood also emits less carbon dioxide than energy produced from fossil fuels; however, burning of wood for energy does not save as much fossil fuel (and store as much carbon dioxide) as does using wood for substitute products (Kershaw et al., 1993; Koch, 1991). For most efficient carbon dioxide sequestration, wood energy should be generated from the residuals of other wood products of higher carbon-substitute value.

Deforestation can also have more direct effects on climate patterns at local levels. Locally, trees reduce wind speeds and direct sunlight to the ground surface and so reduce the surface dryness, extreme heat, and wind chill near the ground. Tree shade also reduces extreme daytime heat and nighttime cold, which can occur at the ground surface in deforested places.

Large-scale deforestation may also change global climate patterns, although our ability to discern these effects is confounded by other strong influences on global climate patterns (Gash et al., 1996). Large-scale deforestation can change global-climate patterns by reducing the humidity and causing hotter days and colder nights, thus changing rainfall, precipitation, and wind patterns. The lack of trees means less evapotranspiration and less humid air blowing from a deforested area. The hotter surfaces can also be focal points for convection and resulting thunderstorms.

Deforestation may cause drier climates and more extreme temperature fluctuations downwind. There may be less humidity for rainfall, and temperatures may be colder at high altitudes and hotter in low areas in mountainous terrain without moisture to modify the extremes. Forests also release terpenes and

other particulate-forming substances into the atmosphere that form "seeds" for water condensation for clouds and precipitation. These terpenes are less common in deforested areas.

[See also Agriculture and Agricultural Land; Amazonia and Deforestation; Biological Diversity; Biomes; Erosion; Extinctions of Animals; Forestation; Global Warming; Greenhouse Effect; International Geosphere-Biosphere Programme; Human Impacts; Migrations; and Urban Areas.]

BIBLIOGRAPHY

Allan, T., and J.P. Lanly. "Overview of Status and Trends of World's Forests." In *Technical Workshop to Explore Options for Global Forestry Management*, edited by D. Howlett and C. Sargent, pp. 17–39. London: International Institute for Environment and Development, 1991.

Aschmann, H. "Man's Impact on the Several Regions with Mediterranean Climates." In *Mediterranean Type Ecosystems, Origin and Structures*, edited by F. di Castri and H.A. Mooney, pp. 363–371. Berlin and New York: Springer, 1973.

Aubréville, A. *Climats, Forêts, et Désertification de l'Afrique Tropicale*. Paris: Société des Éditions Géographiques, Maritimes, et Coloniales, 1949.

Boydak, M., and M. Dogru. "The Exchange of Experience and State of the Art in Sustainable Forest Management (SFM) by Ecoregion: Mediterranean Forests." In *Proceedings of the Eleventh World Forestry Congress*, vol. 6, pp. 179–204. Ankara: Ministry of Forestry of Turkey, 1997.

DeLaune, R.D., et al. "Relationships among Vertical Accretion, Coastal Submergence, and Erosion in a Louisiana Gulf Coast Marsh." *Journal of Sedimentary Research* 53 (1983), 147–157.

Eleventh World Forestry Congress. "Antalya Declaration of the XI World Forestry Congress: Forestry for Sustainable Development: Towards the XXI Century." Antalya, Turkey, 1997. Resolution published, approved, and distributed at the Congress; available from the Ministry of Forestry of Turkey, Ankara, Turkey.

Food and Agriculture Organization. *Role of Forestry in Combating Desertification*. Proceedings of the FAO Expert Consultation held in Saltillo, Mexico, June 24–28, 1985. Rome: FAO, 1985.

———. "Forest Resources Assessment 1990: Tropical Countries." FAO Forestry Paper 112. Rome: FAO; 1993.

———. *State of the World's Forests*. Rome: FAO, 1997. http://www.fao.org/docrep/w4345E/W4345E/W4345E00.htm (accessed May 29, 2008).

Gash, J.H.C., et al., ed. *Amazonian Deforestation and Climate*. Chichester, U.K., and New York: Wiley, 1996.

Gates, D.M. *Climate Change and its Biological Consequences*. Sunderland, Mass.: Sinauer, 1993.

Kershaw, J.A., Jr., et al. "Effect of Harvest of Old Growth Douglas-Fir Stands and Subsequent Management on Carbon Dioxide Levels in the Atmosphere." *Journal of Sustainable Forestry* 1 (1993), 61–77.

Koch, P. "Wood vs. Nonwood Materials in U.S. Residential Construction: Some Energy-Related International Implications." CINTRAFOR Working Paper 36. Seattle: College of Forest Resources, University of Washington, 1991.

Odera, J., ed. "The Present State of Degradation of Fragile Ecosystems in Dry Lands and the Role of Forestry in Their Restoration." International Expert Meeting on Rehabilitation of Degraded Forest Ecosystems Secretariat Note No. 1, Lisbon, Portugal, 1996.

Perlin, J. *A Forest Journey: The Role of Wood in the Development of Civilization*. New York: Norton, 1989.

Sampson, R.N., and D. Hair. *Forests and Global Change*. Vol. 1. *Opportunities for Increasing Forest Cover*. Washington, D.C.: American Forests, 1992.

———. *Forests and Global Change*. Vol. 2. *Forest Management Opportunities for Mitigating Carbon Emissions*. Washington, D.C.: American Forests, 1996.

Skole, D.L., et al. "Physical and Human Dimensions of Deforestation Amazonia." *BioScience* 44.5 (1994), 314–322.

Thomas, D.S.G., and N. Middleton. *World Atlas of Desertification*. London and Baltimore, Md.: Edward Arnold, 1992.

Turner B.L., II, and K.W. Butzer. "The Columbian Encounter and Land-Use Change." Environment 34.8 (1992), 16–20, 37–44.

Von Kooten, G.C., R. Sedjo, and E. Bulte. "Tropical Deforestation: Issues and Policies." In *International Yearbook of Environmental and Resource Economies:*

1999–2000: A Survey of Current Issues, edited by P. Teitenburg and H. Folmer, vol. 3, pp. 198–249. Cheltenham, U.K.: Elgar, 1999.

Williams, M. *Deforesting the Earth: From Prehistory to Global Crisis*. Chicago: University of Chicago Press, 2003. An overview by a distinguished historical geographer.

Williams, M. *Deforesting the Earth: From Prehistory to Global Crisis: An Abridgement*. Chicago: Chicago University Press, 2006. An abridged and accessible edition.

World Resource Institute. *World Resources 1996–1997*, p. 204.

—CHADWICK D. OLIVER, MELIH BOYDAK, AND ROGER SEDJO

DELTAS AND GLOBAL WARMING

Deltaic coasts and their environs are home to large numbers of people and also have great ecological value. They are likely to be threatened by submergence as sea levels rise, especially where there is no compensating sediment accretion. Many deltas are subsiding at 1–10 mm per year because of the weight of the sediments from which they are formed. This will compound the effects of eustatic sea-level rise (Milliman and Haq, 1996), which is estimated to be 4–6 mm per year.

Deltas will not be affected only by sea-level changes. The delta lands of Bangladesh (Warrick and Ahmad, 1996) for example, receive very heavy sediment loads from the Himalayan rivers that feed them, so it is the relative rates of accretion and inundation that will be crucial (Milliman et al, 1989). Land-use changes upstream, such as deforestation, could increase rates of sediment accumulation, while groundwater and gas extraction could accelerate subsidence. Deltas could also be affected by changing tropical-cyclone activity. [*See* Tropical Cyclones in a Warming World.]

Broadus et al. (1986), for example, calculated that if sea level were to rise by just one meter in 100 years, 12–15% of Egypt's arable land would be lost, and 16% of its population would have to be relocated. With a 3-meter rise the figures would be 20% and 21% respectively. The cities of Alexandria, Rosetta, and Port Said are at particular risk, and a sea-level rise of even 50 centimeters could mean that 2 million people would have to abandon their homes (El-Raey, 1997). In Bangladesh, a 1-meter rise would inundate 11.5% of the total land area of the country and affect 9% of the population directly, while a 3-meter rise would inundate 29% of the land area and affect 21% of the population. Approximately half of Bangladesh's rice production is in the area that is less than 1 meter above sea level. Many of the world's major conurbations might be flooded in whole or in part, sewers and drains rendered inoperative (Kuo, 1986), and peri-urban agricultural productivity reduced by saltwater incursion (Chen and Yong, 1999).

Even without an accelerating sea-level rise, the Nile Delta has been suffering accelerated retreat because of sediment retention by dams. The Nile's sediment, on reaching the sea, used to move eastward with the general counterclockwise current in that part of the eastern Mediterranean, generating sandbars and dunes that contributed to delta accretion. About a century ago the delta began to recede. The Rosetta mouth of the Nile lost about 1.6 kilometers of its length between 1898 and 1954.

The imbalance between sedimentation and erosion appears to have started with the delta barrages (1861) and been continued by later works including the Aswan High Dam. In addition, large amounts of sediment are retained in an extremely dense network of irrigation and drainage channels that has been developed in the Nile Delta itself (Stanley, 1996). Much of the Egyptian coast is now "undernourished" with sediment, and as a result of this overall erosion of the shoreline, the sandbars bordering Lake Manzala and Lake Burullus on the seaward side are eroded and likely to collapse. If this were to happen, the lakes would be converted into marine bays, allowing saline water to come into direct contact with low-lying cultivated land and freshwater aquifers. The future of our large deltas looks grim (Ericcson et al., 2006).

BIBLIOGRAPHY

Broadus, J., et al. "Rising Sea Level and Damming of Rivers: Possible Effects in Egypt and Bangladesh." In *Effects of Changes in Stratospheric Ozone and Global Climate*, edited by J.G. Titus, pp.165–89. Washington, D.C.: UNEP/USEPA, 1986.

Chen, X., and Y. Zong. "Major Impacts of Sea-Level Rise on Agriculture in the Yangtze Delta Area around Shanghai." *Applied Geography* 19 (1999), 69–84.

El-Raey, M. "Vulnerability Assessment of the Coastal Zone of the Nile Delta of Egypt to the Impact of Sea Level Rise." *Ocean and Coastal Management* 37 (1997), 29–40.

Ericcson, J.P., et al. "Effective Sea-Level Rise and Deltas: Causes of Change and Human Dimension Implications." *Global and Planetary Change* 50 (2006), 63–82. DOI: 10.1016/j.gloplacha.2005.07.004.

Kuo, C. "Flooding in Taipeh, Taiwan and Coastal Drainage." In *Effects of Changes in Stratospheric Ozone and Global Climate*, edited by J.G. Titus, pp. 37–46. Washington, D.C.: UNEP/USEPA, 1986.

Milliman, J.D., and B.U. Haq, eds. *Sea Level Rise and Coastal Subsidence*. Dordrecht, The Netherlands, and Boston, Mass.: Kluwer, 1996.

Milliman, J.D., J.M. Broadus, and F. Gable. "Environmental and Economic Impacts of Rising Sea Level and Subsiding Deltas: the Nile and Bengal Examples." *Ambio* 18 (1989), 340–345.

Stanley, D.J. "Nile Delta: Extreme Case of Sediment Entrapment on a Delta Plain and Consequent Coastal Land Loss." *Marine Geology* 129 (1996), 189–195.

Warrick, R.A. and Q.K. Ahmad, eds. *The Implications of Climate and Sea-Level Change for Bangladesh*. Dordrecht, The Netherlands, and Boston, Mass.: Kluwer, 1996.

—ANDREW S. GOUDIE

DEMOGRAPHY

See Human Populations.

DENDROCHRONOLOGY

Because the widths of annual tree rings reveal changes in temperature or moisture in the region where the tree grows, tree rings are important in the study of recent climate change in one region versus another. An essential part of such work is assigning absolute calendar dates to specific tree rings that then serve as historical markers. Dendrochronology makes use of periods of distinctive oscillations or patterns in the record of rings. When these appear in records from both a younger and an older tree (or from a living tree and dead wood) the two records can be overlapped to make a composite history. Using a series of

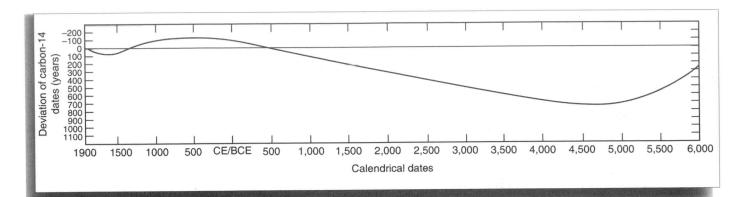

Dendrochronology. Figure 1. Deviation of Carbon-14 Dates from Absolute Calendrical Dates Established by Tree Ring Study.

(From Ralph, E.K. and Henry N. Michael.)

Dendrochronology. Figure 2. Bristlecone Pines in the White Mountains of Southern California.

(Photo by Henry N. Michael, University of Pennsylvania Museum.)

such overlaps, a sequence of dates can be extended backward for thousands of years on the basis of a few trees whose dates of cutting or coring provide the calendar dates. The result is a clear record of changes in climate.

Dendrochronology has another vital function—correcting the dates obtained from radiocarbon (carbon-14) dating. While that method can provide a date for charcoal, bone, or other organic materials (or scraps of wood without suitable tree rings) the result is uncertain because the concentration of carbon-14 isotope in the Earth's atmosphere has not been constant through time. (It varies with the strength of the Earth's magnetic field, which affects cosmic radiation.) [See Mobile Earth.] This discrepancy was revealed by carbon-14 dates that failed to coincide with known calendar dates at Egyptian sites. Because archaeologists must know how to correct (calibrate) their carbon-14 dates for samples of various ages, the solution has been to obtain a large number of wood samples ranging in age from present to thousands of years BCE, to date each one by radiocarbon and by dendrochronology, and then to assemble the resulting dates in a plot that reveals any discrepancy (Figure 1). Researchers from the University of Arizona and the University of Pennsylvania have constructed the sequence of dual-dated samples, collecting wood from sequoia trees in California, and, more recently, from bristlecone pine in the White Mountains of California (Figure 2). These bristlecones are the world's oldest trees: one living tree is 4,700 years old, and pieces of dead wood from the forest floor have extended the record back beyond 6,000 BCE. The plot shows that for the period from 6,000 BCE to 500 BCE, carbon-14 dates are too old by as much as 700 years; for 500 BCE to 1300 CE they are too young by as much as 100 years; and for 1300 CE to 1900 CE they are too old by as much as 75 years.

BIBLIOGRAPHY

Cohen, M.P. A Garden of Bristlecones: Tales of Change in the Great Basin. Reno: University of Nevada Press, 1998.
Fritts, H.C. Tree Rings and Climate. London and New York: Academic Press, 1976. Reprinted 2001 by Blackburn Press.
McGraw, D.J. Andrew Ellicott Douglass and the Role of the Giant Sequoia in the Development of Dendrochronology. Lewiston, N.Y.: Mellen Press, 2001.
Ralph, E.K., and H.N. Michael. "Twenty-Five Years of Radiocarbon Dating." American Scientist 62.5 (1974), 553–560.
Stokes, M. A., and T.L. Smiley. An Introduction to Tree-Ring Dating. Tucson: University of Arizona Press, 1996.
Vaganov, E. A., M.K. Hughes, and A.V. Shaskin. Growth Dynamics of Conifer Tree Rings: Images of Past and Future Environments. New York: Springer, 2006.

—DAVID J. CUFF

DESALINATION

Humans have practiced the desalting of seawater to obtain potable water for centuries. Greek sailors on board ships used to boil seawater and condense its vapor—a process known as distillation—in the fourth century BCE. Romans, in the first century CE, were reported to have filtered seawater through a clay soil to obtain drinking water. By the fourth century distillation had become the preferred method of desalination (Popkin, 1968). Today, a wide variety of desalination technologies is available on the commercial market (Lauer, 2006).

The first known patent for a desalination process through steam distillation was granted in England in 1869. In the same year, British colonists in Aden built a distillation plant to supply fresh water to merchant and naval vessels stopping at the port. The first large desalting plant may have been the one installed in Aruba, Netherlands Antilles, in 1930, producing 1,000 cubic meters of fresh water per day (Hornburg, 1987). It was not until the mid-1950s, however, that the use of large land-based desalination plants, particularly those using multistage flash distillation, became economically feasible for nonindustrial purposes. This spurred intensive research and development into a variety of desalination processes. By the mid-1960s much of the work in desalination remained experimental, improving on earlier designs of plants that failed to meet expectations.

The arid oil-producing countries of the Middle East stimulated the development of desalination technology and encouraged the growth of the desalination industry. Oil revenues enabled these countries to use desalination as their most reliable and secure solution to the problem of providing fresh water to their populations (WRI, 1993; Ayoub and Alward, 1996).

WORLDWIDE DESALINATION CAPACITY

Countries such as Saudi Arabia, Kuwait, and the United Arab Emirates are the major users of desalination technology, along with the middle- and high-income regions in the United States, such as the states of Florida and California, whose residents are able to pay the high costs of desalted water.

The slow adoption of desalination technology in the early 1960s was reflected in the gradual increase in desalination capacity. A sharp rise began toward the end of the 1960s, however, with an average annual increase in cumulative capacity in the order of 125,000 cubic meters per day. This rate jumped threefold in the early to mid-1970s and sixfold by 1990 (Wangnick, 1992). Since 1960 the worldwide capacity of installed desalination plants has likewise increased enormously. The number of desalination units producing fresh water in excess of 100 m^3/day increased from 3,527 units in early 1987 to 8,886 in early 1992, to operating in some 120 countries with a total or contracted capacity of about 21 million m^3/day in 1997 (Wangnick, 1992; Wangnick, 1998). The total installed capacity by 2004 was over 35 million m^3/day (Wangnick, 2005).

A large plant using wind-electric power opened early in 2007 near Perth, Australia. At the time it was the largest plant in the world to rely on renewable electricity, and is expected to supply 17% of Perth's electrical needs (www.water-technology.net/projects/perth/).

DESALTING PROCESSES

There are two main desalination processes currently in use, characterized by the quality of input-energy required: thermal (in which a phase-change occurs in the feedwater, e.g., distillation), and membrane (in which no phase-change occurs). In some thermal processes, such as multistage flash (MSF), multieffect evaporation (ME), and vapor compression (VC) distillation, a relatively high thermal energy input is required to bring about a phase change in the seawater. These processes are generally cost effective and commercially viable in large-scale plants supplying municipal drinking water because the unit cost of product water is lower (Ayoub and Alward, 1996). Other thermal processes such as freezing, membrane and solar distillations usually have a lower-quality energy requirement (e.g., thermal energy from such sources as industrial waste heat and solar collectors) and are cost effective in small- to medium-scale systems used to supply community or family drinking water needs.

In membrane processes such as reverse osmosis (RO), electrodialysis (ED), and electrodialysis reversal (EDR), high-grade electrical or mechanical energy is required to produce potable water without a phase change in the sea water or brackish water (Nilsson, 1995). These processes can be scaled to meet various applications, including supplying industrial process water, treating municipal waste water, and supplying potable water for communities (Table 1).

Very large plants, such as the 1 million m³/day plant in Saudi Arabia, typically use the distillation process of seawater desalination. While the major distillation process, multistage flash distillation, has declined in market share from 79% in total capacity in 1969 to slightly above 30% in 1991, it still is used in a significant share of the very large plants and dual-purpose plants coupled with power generation. Smaller plants typically use the membrane-separation process of reverse osmosis. RO plants accounted for about 45% of global capacity by 1991, compared with 10% in 1969. Approximately two-thirds of all plants worldwide are converting sea water, and the remaining one-third is treating brackish water. Desalination plants are being used increasingly for applications other than the production of potable water, such as for the treatment of effluent water and polluted groundwater sources, and in the production of ultrapure water for the electronics industry (WRI, 1992).

COST OF DESALINATED WATER

The costs of desalinated water vary depending on the specific desalination processes chosen, the scale of the operation, and site conditions. In large-scale systems, optimization of energy costs and plant performance are major determinants in the choice of desalination technology, whereas technical, physical, social, and economic factors determine the design of small-scale systems. Although the MSF process has been operating commercially for much longer than RO, significant improvements in membrane technology over the last two decades have made the latter process much more economically attractive for large-scale seawater desalination (Malek et al., 1992).

ASSESSMENT

There is a growing need to find solutions to the problems of freshwater supply. The technology of seawater and brackish-water desalination for the production of potable water is well established. In terms of large-scale desalination systems, multistage flash distillation and reverse osmosis are presently the dominant processes technically and economically. Newer and more efficient membranes provide real possibilities of reducing the cost of water obtained from large-scale seawater desalination in the future.

[See also Deserts; Irrigation; and Water.]

TABLE 1. Commercially Available Desalination Processes

Process	Feedwater	Capacity (M³/DAY)	Power Source	Market Share (%)*	Total Installed or Contracted Desalting Capacity (%)*
Major Processes					
Thermal					
MSF					
ME	Sea	4,000	Natural gas	32	52
VC	Sea	30,000		†	†
Membrane	Sea	2,000–10,000	Natural gas	†	†
RO					
ED	Sea/brackish	20–2,000	Electric	50	33
EDR	Sea/brackish	Various	Electric		†
Minor Processes	Sea/brackish	Various	Electric		†
Vacuum freezing	Sea	38–750	Electric	Negligible	
Solar humidification	Sea/brackish	1 m² of collector area produces 41/day of potable water	Solar	Negligible	

* 1991 figures.
† ME, VC, ED, and EDR share the remaining 18% of market share and 15% of total installed or contracted desalting capacity. RO, ED, and EDR are amenable to a wide variety of desalting capacities from 0.10 m³/day to virtually any capacity. However, large-size membrane plants do not have the economies of scale that are achieved by distillation plants.
SOURCE: Ayoub and Alward (1996).

BIBLIOGRAPHY

Ayoub, J., and R. Alward "Water Requirements and Remote Arid Areas: The Need for Small-Scale Desalination." *Desalination* 107.2 (1996), 131–147. DOI: 10.1016/S0011-9164(96)00158-0.

Hornburg, C.D. "Desalination for Remote Areas." In *Developing World Water*, pp. 230–232. London and Hong Kong: Grosvenor Press International, 1987.

Lauer, W.C., ed. *Desalination of Seawater and Brackish Water.* Denver, Colorado: American Water Works Association, 2006.

Malek, A., M.N.A. Hawlader, and I.C. Ho. "Large-Scale Seawater Desalination: A Technical and Economic Review." *ASEAN Journal of Science and Technology Development* 9.2 (1992), 41–61.

Narayanan, P.K., et al. "Performance of the First Seawater Electrodialysis Plant in India." In *Desalination and Water Re-Use: Proceedings of the Twelfth International Symposium*, edited by M. Balaban, vol. 4, pp. 210–211. Rugby: Institution of Chemical Engineers, 1991.

Natarjan, R., W.V.B. Ramalingam, and W.P. Harkare. "Experience in Installation and Operation of Brackish Water Desalination Plants in Rural Areas of India." *IDA Conference on Desalination and Water Reuse: "Water: The Challenge of the 90s," Washington, D.C., August 25–29, 1991*, vol. 2, p. 13.

Nilsson, S. *A Review of Desalination Processes and Future Water Needs.* New York: Energy and Atmosphere Programme, BPPS/SEED, United Nations Development Programme, 1995.

Pappas, C.A. "Why Desalination is Not in Common Use Worldwide." *Desalination and Water Reuse* 3.4 (1993), 34–39.

Popkin, R. *Desalination: Water for the World's Future.* New York: Praeger, 1968.

Wangnick, K. *1992 International Worldwide Desalting Plants Inventory.* Report No. 12. Gnarrenburg, Germany: Wangnick Consulting, 1992.

———. *1998 IDA Worldwide Desalting Plants Inventory.* Report No. 15. Gnarrenburg, Germany: Wangnick Consulting, 1998.

———. *2004 Worldwide Desalting Plants Inventory.* Oxford: Global Water Intelligence, 2005.

World Resources Institute (WRI). *World Resources 1992–93: Towards Sustainable Development.* New York: Oxford University Press, 1993.

Woto, T. *The Experience with Small-Scale Desalinators for Remote Areas Dwellers of the Kalahari, Botswana.* Kanye, Botawana: Rural Industries Promotion/Rural Industries Innovation Centre, 1987.

—JOSEF AYOUB

DESERTIFICATION

Desertification is land degradation in arid, semiarid, and dry subhumid areas resulting from various factors, including climatic variations and human activities. The term, first introduced by A. Aubréville in his 1949 book, *Climats, Forêts et Désertification de l'Afrique Tropicale,* has been used to refer to a wide variety of ecological problems in dryland habitats throughout the world. Although desertification is usually associated with drought, it is quite common for land degradation to occur without changes in rainfall, as when humans remove vegetation, and bare soil is eroded by wind and water. Desertification is often associated with the loss of desirable plant species and their replacement by species of lesser economic importance, and with a permanent loss in the productive capacity of the land.

The term "desertification" should not be used to describe cyclic phenomena, as when decadal variations in precipitation lead to periods of drought and to losses of vegetation that are fully restored when the rains return. For example, desertification has been used to describe land degradation along the southern border of the Sahara, where a 1975 survey by the

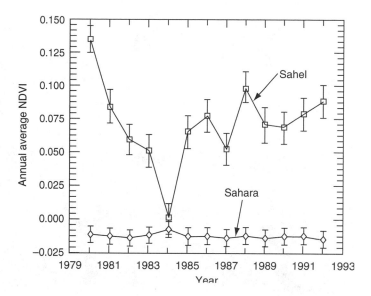

Desertification. FIGURE 1. Normalized Difference Vegetation Index (NDVI) for Lands Bordering the Sahel Zone and for the Sahara Itself, during a 10-Year Period.

(From Tucker et al., 1994, with permission from Taylor and Francis Ltd.)

United Nations found the desert to be expanding southward at 5.5 kilometers per year in the Sudan. In fact, the southward expansion of the Sahara, having reached its peak in 1984, was effectively reversed with a return to a period of greater rainfall in more recent years (Figure 1), and in most areas there was no long-term loss in the productive capacity of the land. [*See* Drought.]

About 30% of the world's land surface, 6,150 million hectares (15,200 million acres), is classified as arid or semiarid. About 16% of that area (mostly in the Sahara, but including also the Atacama and the Namib) is considered hyperarid and not subject to further desertification. The remaining 5,200 million hectares, mostly classified as semiarid, is vulnerable to degradation. These areas are mostly grasslands and savannas at the boundaries of arid regions. [*See* Biomes.] The 1991 United Nations assessment of desertification estimated that 3,600 million hectares, or nearly 70% of the vulnerable land, was already in some stage of degradation. This was an increase of 117 million hectares over an earlier (1984) UN assessment, or 3.4% in seven years. The largest changes were seen in Africa and Asia. Geist (2005) reviews current trends.

Overgrazing is perhaps the leading cause of desertification worldwide. Overgrazing occurs when improper timing, intensity, or frequency of herbivory (grazing and browsing) causes damage to plants. Historically, the intensity of herbivory by livestock has been too high for many arid lands. A survey of grazed lands in South America showed that they often contained about ten times more herbivore biomass than found in adjacent ungrazed lands. The consequences of improperly managed grazing can be devastating to soil resources. In southern New Mexico, overgrazing of semiarid grasslands dominated by black

Desertification. Figure 2. Crescent Dunes Developing toward the Front of the Shelter Belt in Gonghe County, Quinghai, China.

(From Ministry of Geology & Mineral Resources, P.R.C., State Science & Technology Commission, P.R.C, and State Planning Commission, P.R.C., 1991.)

grama (*Bouteloua eriopoda*) has led to the invasion of mesquite (*Prosopis glandulosa*) and creosote bush (*Larrea tridentata*) in less than 100 years. When shrubs replace semiarid grasses, most of the fertility of the remaining soils is isolated in patches that persist under the shrubs, while the barren soils between shrubs may be nearly devoid of biotic activity. It is often impossible to remediate degradation of these lands by replanting the native vegetation.

Other human activities also cause desertification. In many areas, desertification is linked to excessive harvesting of fuel wood from semiarid habitats. Dryland soils that are used for irrigated agriculture are subject to degradation as a result of a buildup of salinity in the soil profile. Lands in both irrigated and rain-fed agriculture are subject to wind erosion during seasons when the soils are left bare. Desertification in the many areas of China stems from the encroachment of sand dunes into agricultural areas (Figure 2).

Areas of desertification are vulnerable to wind erosion. As the cover of vegetation is reduced by cattle grazing or agriculture, barren soils are subjected to wind erosion, because the threshold velocity to initiate the movement of fine soil materials is lower on a barren, unprotected surface. Wind erosion also increases when human activities and cattle disrupt the crust of algae and lichens that often forms on the surface of desert soils.

The infiltration of soil moisture is lower on barren soils, so desertified landscapes are subject to high rates of runoff and soil erosion during infrequent heavy rains. In many construction projects, humans channelize and reroute the natural drainageways of arid landscapes, also lowering the effective infiltration of moisture into the soil and leading to a reduction in the cover of vegetation. Rain-use efficiency—the proportion of incident rain that is used by plants for growth—is often lower in areas of desertification, and changes in rain-use efficiency are indicative of land degradation.

Areas of reduced vegetation cover often reflect a greater portion of solar radiation. [*See* Albedo.] Despite absorbing less incident radiation, barren landscapes have higher soil and air temperatures. The conversion of water from liquid to vapor consumes 540 calories per gram (the latent heat of vaporization), which can result in significant evaporative cooling of the landscape from the uptake and evapotranspiration of soil moisture by plants. In areas of reduced vegetation, there is less evaporative cooling. In northern Mexico, soil and air temperatures average about 3°C higher than those in southern Arizona, where grazing has been less severe. Thus, an increase in the Bowen ratio—the ratio of the amount of incoming radiation dissipated by sensible heat to that dissipated by latent heat—is a good index of desertification. A small proportion, perhaps 1%, of the Earth's recent increase in temperature is thought to derive from increasing desertification.

Changes in the area and borders of arid lands are easy to monitor by remote sensing. Since 1980, NASA scientists have used a high-resolution radiometer to examine changes in the greenness of the Sahel zone in Africa. Vegetation greenness is quantified by the normalized difference vegetation index (NDVI), which is based on the differential absorption of red and infrared radiation by plants. Plants absorb red radiation, but they reflect infrared radiation, whereas bare soils reflect both forms equally. Thus, an index of greenness is calculated as:

$$NDVI = \frac{(Infrared\ Reflectance)-(Red\ Reflectance)}{(Infrared\ Reflectance)+(Red\ Reflectance)}$$

The index is most useful when the cover of vegetation is greater than 50%. On areas with lesser amounts of plant cover, the reflectance of bare soils dominates the radiation received by the satellite, and it is more difficult to see changes in vegetation. The record of vegetation greenness in the Sahel shows a cyclic pattern that is associated with recent changes in regional rainfall, whereas NDVI for the Sahara over the same period shows consistent low values that are unrelated to annual rainfall (Figure 1).

Land degradation often does not follow a smooth progression during desertification. An existing cover of semiarid grassland may persist for many years despite high levels of livestock grazing. Then, within just a few years, perhaps coincident with reduced rainfall, the grasses may disappear entirely from the landscape. In such rapid transitions, ecologists suggest that the landscape has passed a threshold—a level of stress that pushes the ecosystem to a new stable state. Desertification is analogous to a teeter-totter, in which human impact tips the balance of the landscape to a new, degraded state.

The frequency of drought is expected to increase during the next century as global climate change warms the Earth's land surface more rapidly than the ocean surface, where most precipitation is generated. Thus an increasing proportion of the world's land surface is likely to experience greater potential evapotranspiration, with little or no increase in precipitation. Soil dusts generated from desertified areas reflect incoming solar radiation, so a greater area of desertified land may influence global climate. Dust from barren desertified soils in Africa is transported across the Atlantic Ocean and deposited in the southeastern United States (Figure 3). Airborne dusts tend to cool the atmosphere over ocean waters, which otherwise absorb

Desertification. FIGURE 3. Transport of Desert Dust from the Sahara across the Atlantic Ocean.

(From Perry et al., 1997. Copyright by the American Geophysical Union.)

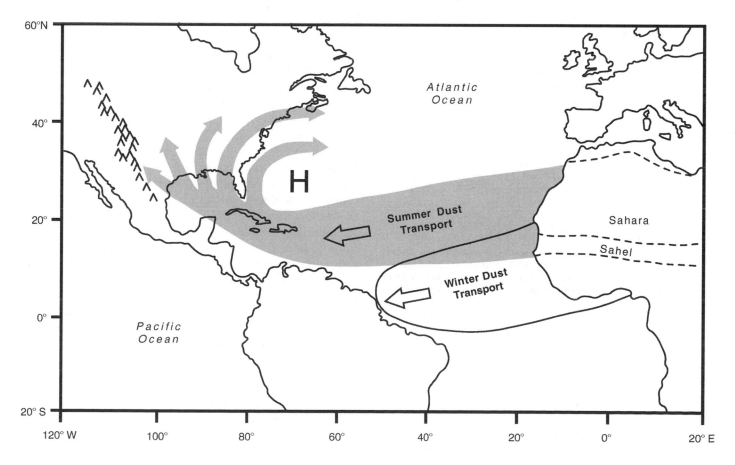

a large proportion of incoming solar radiation. Ironically, an increasing amount of soil dust over the oceans, a likely consequence of an increasing global area of desertified lands, may reduce the rate of greenhouse warming of Earth. Ice core records show that desert dust was more widespread during the last glacial epoch, when the Earth's temperature was 6°C lower than at present. [*See* Dust Storms.]

Drought is linked to the downfall of great historic civilizations, including that of early Mesopotamia in 2200 BCE and that of the Maya in Mexico around 900 CE. Today about 20% of the world's people live in environments at or near the border of desert regions. Concern about the increasing degradation of semiarid lands and an expansion of deserts has led the United Nations to host a number of meetings to assess and combat desertification. The first, the UN Conference on Desertification (UNCOD), was held in Nairobi, Kenya, in 1977, when the world's attention was focused on drought and famine in central Africa. More recently, a convention that followed the Earth Summit in Rio de Janeiro in June 1992 produced an international agreement of cooperation that was signed in Paris in 1994. Parties to this convention pledge to combat desertification and reclaim desertified land, with a special focus on Africa, of which 66% is dryland.

[*See also* Aerosols; Deforestation; Deserts; *and* Salinization.]

BIBLIOGRAPHY

Dregne, H.E. "A New Assessment of the World Status of Desertification." *Desertification Control Bulletin* 20 (1991), 6–18.

Geist, H. *The Causes and Progression of Desertification.* London: Ashgate, 2005.

Guo, X. *Geological Hazards of China and Their Prevention and Control.* Beijing: Geological Publishing House, 1991.

Laycock, W.A. "Stable States and Thresholds of Range Condition in North American Rangelands: A Viewpoint." *Journal of Range Management* 44 (1991), 427–433.

Le Houérou, H.N. "Rain Use Efficiency: A Unifying Concept in Arid-Land Ecology." *Journal of Arid Environments* 7 (1984), 213–247.

Perry, K.D., et al. "Long-Range Transport of North African Dust to the Eastern United States." *Journal of Geophysical Research* 102, D10 (1997), 11225–11238.

Rind, D., et al. "Potential Evapotranspiration and the Likelihood of Future Drought." *Journal of Geophysical Research* 95 (1990), 9983–10004.

Schlesinger, W.H., et al. "Biological Feedbacks in Global Desertification." *Science* 247 (1990), 1043–1048. DOI: 10.1126/science.247.4946.1043.

Tegen, I., and I. Fung. "Contribution to the Atmospheric Mineral Aerosol Load from Land Surface Modification." *Journal of Geophysical Research* 100 (1995), 18707–18726. DOI: 10.1029/95JD02051.

Tucker, C.J., W.W. Newcomb, and H.E. Dregne. "AVHRR Data Sets for Determination of Desert Spatial Extent." *International Journal of Remote Sensing* 15 (1994), 3547–3565.

Verstraete, M.M., and S.A. Schwartz. "Desertification and Global Change." *Vegetatio (Plant Ecology)* 91.1–2 (1991), 3–13. DOI: 10.1007/BF00036043.

West, N.E. "Structure and Function of Microphytic Soil Crusts in Wildland Ecosystems of Arid to Semi-Arid Regions." *Advances in Ecological Research* 20 (1990), 179–223.

—WILLIAM H. SCHLESINGER

DESERTS

Deserts, or drylands, are known to experience significant environmental changes at time scales ranging from the geologic (millions of years) to decadal and annual. Short-term changes (ten years or less) are part of the natural changes associated with climatic variability or, increasingly, with human activities. Information on significant environmental changes that have occurred in deserts and drylands during the Quaternary geologic period (the last two million years) is important not only to identify the response of these areas to past global climate changes, but to use in predicting changes that might be expected to occur as a result of anthropogenic global warming. To understand the nature, timing, and magnitude of changes in deserts, it is necessary to define what these areas are, assess their current extent, examine proxy data that allow past changes to be assessed, and then evaluate the likely status of deserts and drylands in the future.

DEFINING DESERTS AND DRYLANDS

Most definitions of desert relate directly or indirectly to moisture deficiency. Deserts do, however, experience significant intense rainfall events, albeit on an irregular, unreliable basis, and some deserts are crossed by perennial rivers with sources in wetter regions—for example the Nile, which waters areas of Egypt and Sudan with extremely low rainfall. Deserts are not totally devoid of plant and animal life; most species have adaptive strategies that permit the accumulation and retention of available moisture, and/or physiologies that allow biological functions to be slowed or shut down at times of acute moisture stress.

Deserts are characterized primarily by aridity, which has four main causes: tropical and subtropical atmospheric stability; continentality (distance from oceans); topographically induced rain shadows; and, in some coastal situations such as Chile and Namibia, cold ocean currents which limit evaporation from the sea surface. Scientific definitions of desert have been based on criteria that include the nature and development of drainage systems, the prevailing types of rock weathering, ecological communities, and the potential for crop growth (see Thomas, 1997, chap. 1). Attempts to quantify aridity have focused on the balance between atmospheric moisture inputs (through precipitation) and losses (through evapotranspiration, determined in part by temperature). Two further factors have been included in definitions of aridity. First, attempts to define deserts and aridity since 1950 have tended to be concerned with human use of the environment. Most definitions since that of Meigs (1953) for UNESCO have excluded areas that are too cold for the production of crops, so polar deserts and extreme high-altitude deserts are excluded. Second, different degrees of moisture deficit have been identified. Hyperarid, arid, semiarid, and now even dry-subhumid areas are all regarded as drylands, with hyperarid areas being viewed as true deserts. However, the term "desert" is sometimes also applied to regions that do not experience such extreme aridity; for example, the Kalahari Desert in southern Africa comprises areas that range from arid to dry-subhumid. Deserts must therefore be considered in the context of the full range of dryland environments.

THE EXTENT OF DESERTS AND DRYLANDS

The most recent attempts to determine the extent of deserts and drylands on the basis of moisture availability have used an aridity or moisture index in the form P/PET, where P is the annual precipitation and PET is the potential evapotranspiration. Meigs's moisture index used annually-aggregated monthly moisture-surplus and deficit data instead of P, with PET calculated by the Thornthwaite method, which requires only inputs of mean monthly temperature and daylight hours and is therefore suitable for use in drylands where climate data may be sparse. The most recent widely available assessment (by Hulme for UNEP; in Middleton and Thomas, 1997) has used the same method of calculating PET. To further rationalize values, Hulme used meteorological data for a defined time period (1951–1980) to calculate P/PET, rather than simply taking mean values from each station supplying data. This overcomes the problem that, in some developing parts of the world, mean values calculated from data runs of a few decades would be treated as equal to those derived from several centuries of data from parts of the developed world. It also recognizes an important climatological characteristic of drylands, namely, high interannual and interdecadal climatic variability. This also makes it possible to construct dryland climate-surfaces for different decades, and to identify spatial changes in their extent (Hulme, 1992). Table 1 shows the global extent of drylands by different aridity zones, as represented in different sources.

IDENTIFYING DESERTS AND DRYLANDS

Figure 1 shows the global distribution of desert biomes. The identification of deserts and dryland types on the ground cannot always be done easily or precisely. While plant-cover densities in true desert areas may be extremely low and, in extreme cases, limited to microorganisms, the mesophytes (which can tolerate moderate moisture deficiencies) and xerophytes (which can cope with extreme moisture deficiencies) that do occur in different dryland areas have distributions influenced by a range of environmental factors in addition to gross climate. Semiarid and dry-subhumid areas include the savanna regions of the Americas, Africa, and Australia, but in all drylands, high interannual and decadal variability in moisture has significant effects on the plant communities present at any particular time. On an intradecadal scale, El Niño–Southern Oscillation (ENSO) events in the Pacific are now known to be linked through teleconnections (distant but simultaneous changes in the atmosphere) to significant droughts and to intensified aridity in dryland areas as far afield as northeastern Brazil, southeastern Africa, and Australia. Gross seasonal and annual changes in biomass can be estimated using satellite-derived normalized difference vegetation index (NDVI) data, and although there are doubts about the biological interpretation of NDVI, these data have been used to chart fluctuations in the desert front in response to moisture-regime variability (see Tucker et al., 1991), demonstrating effectively the short-term dynamism of desert biomes. [See El Niño–Southern Oscillation.]

Deserts and drylands also include a wide range of landscape systems, demonstrating that such areas are far more complex than the popular images of seas of sand dunes. Even in the Sahara, which includes many other named desert areas, over 40% of the terrain is mountainous and under 30% comprises sand seas (Clements et al., 1957).

It is clear that deserts and drylands are complex biomes that are only now receiving the depth of scientific investigation that more temperate and polar regions have received in the past. Three factors complicate the interpretation and prediction of global changes affecting deserts and drylands: our limited understanding of environmental processes that affect them; the short-term natural variability inherent in key climate-forcing factors; and the growing role of humans, with drylands today supporting 17% of the global—and nearly 50% of the African—population.

PAST CHANGES IN DESERTS AND DRYLANDS

The major climatic changes that have affected the Earth in the Quaternary period are known on theoretical and empirical grounds to have affected the distribution and extent of drylands. The rock record has also been used to identify the existence of desert sand-seas and dune deposits as far back as the Proterozoic (up to 2,500 million years ago; Glennie, 1987). The distribution and occurrence of such deposits reflects not only climatic changes that affected the Earth in earlier geologic times, but the changing location of land masses relative to aridity-inducing climate systems, caused by plate tectonic movements.

TABLE 1. The Extent of Global Drylands, Expressed as a Percentage of the Global Land Area, According to Different Classification Schemes

Classification	Dry-subhumid	Semiarid	Arid	Hyperarid	Total
Köppen (1931)	—	14.3	12.0	—	26.3
Thornthwaite (1948)	—	15.3	15.3	—	30.6
Meigs (1953)	—	15.8	16.2	4.3	36.3
Shantz (1956)	—	5.2	24.8	4.7	34.7
UN (1977)	—	13.3	13.7	5.8	32.8
Middleton and Thomas (1997)	9.9	17.7	12.1	7.5	47.2

SOURCE: From Thomas, 1997, chap. 1. With permission of John Wiley and Sons.

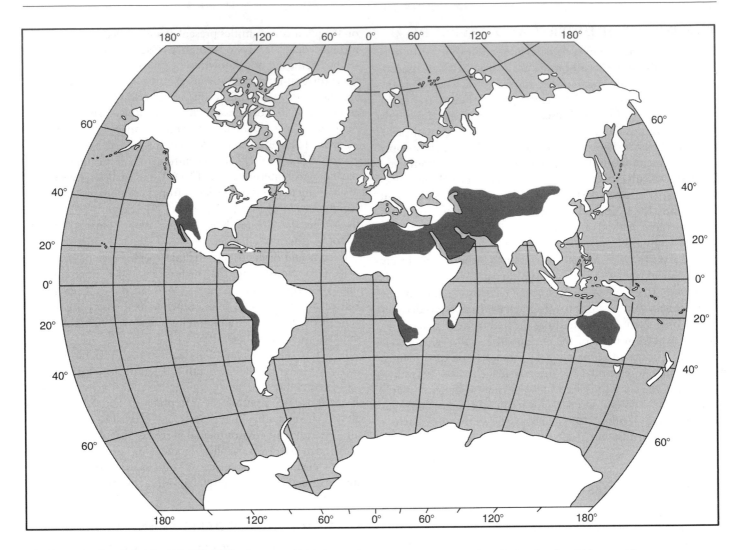

Deserts. Figure 1. Global Distribution of Desert Biomes.

At the scale of Quaternary glacial-interglacial cycles, changes in the extent of deserts and drylands can be expected to have occurred as a result of changes in the partitioning of moisture in the global hydrologic cycle and changes in the positions of major climatic systems. Evidence for dryland changes comes from deep-sea core sediments, which may contain dust and sand eroded and transported by wind during conditions of expanded aridity, or may reflect changes in fluvially derived sediments indicative of changed catchment weathering environments and landforms, and in terrestrial sediments. Terrestrial evidence points not only toward larger deserts at times during the Quaternary but also—in the form of palaeolake shorelines, significant fluvial deposits, and cave speleothems in present-day deserts—to times of reduced desert extent.

RECONSTRUCTING QUATERNARY DESERTS

Major advances have recently been made in understanding past dryland and desert changes (Goudie, 2002), particularly using terrestrial proxy data, but Stokes (see Thomas, 1997, chap. 27) notes that reconstruction of Quaternary desert and dryland conditions is hindered by a number of factors:

- The episodic rather than continuous sediment accumulation characteristic of drylands.
- The low biomass productivity of the driest areas, limiting the accumulation of pollen and the application of radiocarbon dating.
- Groundwater movements contaminating weathering products that might otherwise yield datable materials.
- The slow accumulation and poor development of soils.
- The long exposure of some arid-landscape features at the ground surface, making the determination of the time of development/accumulation difficult.

In addition, some drylands are deficient in closed sites that preserve longer sediment accumulations that might record fluctuating desert conditions; Thomas and Shaw (1991) note that this is a particular problem in central southern Africa. Together, these limitations make it difficult in many parts of the world to identify both subtle changes that have occurred in the distribution of different dryland zones, and the climatic parameters that contribute to the formation of desert conditions. Notable exceptions do exist, and in North America, South Africa, and Australia the pollen preserved in urine-cemented rat middens provides valuable data on biological changes in the arid realm.

One of the most widely used lines of evidence for more extensive Quaternary deserts is fossil, relict, or degraded sand-dune systems located in areas that today are not conducive to the operation of eolian processes. Anderson et al. (2007) has identified such features in many parts of Africa, and in India, Australia, and North and South America. One study by Sarnthein (1978) suggested that 50% of the land area between 30° north and 30° south latitude was covered by active dune fields at the last glacial maximum, compared with only 10% today. The resolution and paleoenvironmental utility of Quaternary dune systems is now being enhanced by the application of luminescence techniques to date phases of sand accumulation directly, and by studies of the interaction of environmental parameters that control eolian processes and the accumulation of various dune types in dryland environments (see Thomas, 1997, chap. 26). As a result, the apparent coincidence of the great desert expansions worldwide at the last glacial maximum is being questioned, and more complex models of climatic changes affecting drylands are being proposed. New studies show that the sediments of dune systems that are inactive today may possess evidence of multiple phases of accumulation in the late Quaternary, and that the focus of enhanced desert conditions was not necessarily at the last glacial maximum. Stronger, more consistent winds, rather than simply drier climatic conditions, may have been important for late-Quaternary dunefield development.

THE IMPACT OF HUMANS

The ability of humans to alter desert and dryland environments is not new. Human actions in deserts and drylands are often viewed as detrimental; salinization in Mesopotania around 2500 BCE, for instance, was attributed by Jacobson and Adams (1958) to agriculture, and O'Hara et al. (1993) have recently shown that significant soil erosion in dryland areas of central Mexico was caused by pre-Colombian societies. These and other studies show that even early civilizations degraded dry environments. During the last century or so, the growth and changing distributions of dryland populations, and developments in technologies and land uses, have increased this ability; while desertification is by no means a new phenomenon, it has today attained a new significance (Thomas and Middleton, 1994). Many concerns about human-induced changes in drylands relate to enhanced rates of soil degradation and total vegetation loss, but studies are now beginning to elucidate their impact on desert and dryland biodiversity on a global scale and the potential use to humankind of various plant species.

Deserts. A Rocky, Hyper-Arid Desert.

Located near Iquique in Chile. The annual rainfall is less than 1 mm.

Deserts. Sossus Vlei, Namib Desert, Namibia.
These are among the world's largest dunes.

Several environmental factors contribute to the susceptibility of deserts and drylands to degradation by humans. These do not necessarily relate to the sometimes supposed fragility of their ecosystems—which, as Behnke et al. (1993) show, is disputable for many dryland areas—but to the nature of environmental dynamics and human activities. First, the inherent natural variability of dryland climates and ecosystems tends to be overridden today when human activities employ technologies and methods imported from temperate environments that enjoy more consistent conditions. Second, many geomorphologic processes in deserts and drylands are characterized by significant periods of quiescence, punctuated by abrupt episodes of activity. Areas cleared of natural vegetation by grazing, or bare in the period immediately following harvesting, are thus particularly susceptible to rapid erosion by high-intensity rainstorms or strong winds. Third, the rapid growth of urban areas in deserts and drylands since World War II has placed significant pressures on limited water resources and options for waste disposal. In dryland areas of the developing world, rural depopulation resulting from migration to urban centers can lead to the failure of traditional soil- and vegetation-conservation techniques. Tiffen et al. (1994) have shown that more people on the land can in certain circumstances halt and reverse environmental degradation.

FUTURE CHANGES

Deserts and drylands will inevitably continue to evolve in response to the twin pressures of natural climatic change and direct human impacts. [*See* Desert Dunes in a Warmer World.] Anthropogenic global warming is also likely to have marked impacts. While drylands are themselves net contributors of an estimated 5–10% of enhanced greenhouse gases (Williams and Balling, 1995), Ojima et al. (1993) estimate that this proportion will grow dramatically if human activities in drylands are not managed better.

According to OIES (1991), deserts and drylands are expected to be among the biomes that respond most rapidly to global warming. Williams and Balling (1995) assess current modeled predictions of climate changes affecting deserts and drylands under a doubled level of atmospheric carbon dioxide, which are summarized in Table 2. The sequestration of atmospheric carbon will be increasingly important in mitigating the impacts of global warming, and deserts and drylands can, according to Squires and Glenn (see Middleton and Thomas, 1997, pp. 140–143), play a vital role. Opportunities exist for both enhanced dryland soil and biomass carbon storage, in large part because drylands contain about 75% of global-soil carbonate carbon, which participates less in the global carbon flux than does organic carbon. Squires and Glenn note that if the antidesertification land-restoration measures proposed by the United Nations were to be implemented, the sequestered carbon would be equivalent to 15% of current annual carbon dioxide emissions. This clearly demonstrates the significant linkages between different aspects of dryland environmental changes and their global significance.

[*See also* Desertification; Drought; Dust Storms; *and* Salinization.]

BIBLIOGRAPHY

Anderson, D.E., A.S. Goudie, and A.G. Parker. *Global Environments through the Quaternary.* New York and Oxford: Oxford University Press, 2007. Chapter 4 contains a general study of Quaternary changes in lower latitudes.

Behnke, R.H., et al., eds. *Range Ecology at Disequilibrium: New Models of Natural Variability and Pastoral Adaptation in African Savannas.* London: Overseas Development Institute, 1993. A collection of papers that show developments in understanding the ecological dynamics of drylands.

Clements, T., et al. *A Study of Desert Surface Conditions.* Natick, Mass.: United States Army Environmental Protection Research Division, 1957.

Glennie, K.W. "Desert Sedimentary Environments, Present and Past: A Summary." *Sedimentary Geology* 50 (1987), 135–165. Includes evidence of desert environments during different geologic periods.

Goudie, A.S. *Great Warm Deserts of the World.* Oxford and New York: Oxford University Press, 2002. A review of the environmental history of the world's arid lands.

Hulme, M. "Recent Climatic Change in the World's Drylands." *Geophysical Research Letters* 23.1 (1996), 61–64. An analysis of climate surface data, exploring decadal-scale variations in the extent of drylands.

Jacobson, T., and R.M. Adams. "Salt and Silt in Ancient Mesopotamian Agriculture." *Science* 128 (1958), 1251–1258. DOI: 10.1126/science.128.3334.1251.

Meigs, P. "World Distribution of Arid and Semiarid Homoclimates." In *Arid Zone Hydrology*, pp. 203–209. Paris: UNESCO, 1953.

Middleton, N.J., and D.S.G. Thomas, eds. *World Atlas of Desertification.* 2d ed. London: Arnold, 1997. An analysis of UNEP's most recent survey of desertification, supplemented by valuable articles on key social and environmental aspects of change in drylands.

O'Hara, S., F.A. Street-Perrott, and T.P. Burt. "Accelerated Soil Erosion around a Mexican Highland Lake Caused by Prehispanic Agriculture." *Nature* 362 (1993), 48–51. DOI: 10.1038/362048a0.

Office of Interdisciplinary Environmental Science. *Arid and Semi-Arid Regions: Response to Climate Change.* Boulder, Colo.: OIES, 1991.

Ojima, D.S., et al. "Assessment of Carbon Budget for Grasslands and Drylands of the World." *Water, Air, and Soil Pollution* 70 (1993), 95–109.

Sarnthein, M. "Sand Deserts during Glacial Maximum and Climatic Optimum." *Nature* 272 (1978), 43–46. DOI: 10.1038/272043a0.

Stokes, S., D.S.G. Thomas, and R. Washington. "Multiple Episodes of Aridity in Southern Africa since the Last Interglacial Period." *Nature* 388 (1997), 154–158. Uses luminescence dating to show how multiple phases of aridity can be detected in the Quaternary record, and climate modeling to assess the causal factors.

TABLE 2. Predicted Changes in the Climate of Selected Dryland and Desert Areas, Based on Three Different Climate Models, Assuming a Doubling of the Atmospheric Carbon Dioxide Content

	Europe	North Africa	Southern Africa	Asia	Middle East and Arabia	North America	South America	Australia
Areas included	Drylands bordering the Mediterranean	Sahara and surrounding areas	Kalahari, Karoo, and Namib	From Iran to China, including Thar	Arabia, and eastern Mediterranean	North Mexico, western United States, and Great Plains	Atacama, Peru, Chaco, Patagonia	
Summer temperature change (°C)	+4–6	+4–6	+2–4	+6	+4–6	+4–6 in United States; +2–4 in Mexico	+2–4, +2–6 in Atacama, Patagonia	+2–4
Winter temperature change (°C)	+2–6	+4–6	+4–6	+4–8 in east; +4–6 in west	+2–4	+4–6 in United States; +2–4 in Mexico	+2–4	+2–4
Summer precipitation change	Decrease	Decrease	Decrease	Highly varied, increase in Thar	Decrease	Highly varied	Slight decrease; possible increase in Peru	Variable, mainly increased
Winter precipitation change	Varied decrease	Decrease	Slight decrease	Slight decrease	Decrease	Highly varied	Slight decrease	Increase in east; decrease in west
Soil moisture change	Significant decrease	Decrease	Significant decrease	Slight increase (winter); general decrease (summer); increase in Thar	Decrease	Highly varied	General decrease	General increase in east; decrease in west

SOURCE: From Thomas, 1997, chap. 30, using information from Williams and Balling, 1995, and other sources. With permission of John Wiley and Sons.

175

Thomas, D.S.G., ed. *Arid Zone Geomorphology: Process, Form, and Change in Drylands.* 2d ed. Chichester, U.K.: Wiley, 1997. A textbook containing 30 chapters by international authorities on the characteristics and environmental processes operating in deserts and drylands, including reconstruction of past environmental changes, and accounts of deserts and drylands in each continent.

Thomas, D.S.G., and N.J. Middleton. *Desertification: Exploding the Myth.* Chichester, U.K.: Wiley, 1994. A critical assessment of desertification that includes coverage of the natural variability of deserts and drylands.

Thomas, D.S.G., and P. Shaw. *The Kalahari Environment.* Cambridge and New York: Cambridge University Press, 1991.

Tiffen, M., et al. *More People, Less Erosion: Environmental Recovery in Kenya.* Chichester, U.K., and New York: Wiley, 1994. Challenges the conventional wisdom that more people on the land inevitably leads to degradation in drylands.

Tucker, C. J., et al. "Expansion and Contraction of the Sahara Desert from 1980 to 1990." *Science* 253 (1991), 299–300. Uses satellite-derived data to show how the desert area varies naturally in response to seasonal and annual rainfall variability. DOI: 10.1126/science.253.5017.299.

Williams, M.A.J., and R.C. Balling, Jr. *Interactions of Desertification and Climate.* London: Edward Arnold, 1995. Includes coverage of the linkages between climate change and desertification, including assessment of predictions of future climate changes due to global warming.

Williams, M.A.J., et al. *Quaternary Environments.* London: Arnold, 1993. One of several good texts covering Quaternary environmental reconstruction; this one has a chapter specifically devoted to deserts.

—David S. G. Thomas

DESERT DUNES IN A WARMER WORLD

Desert sand dunes, because of the crucial relationships between vegetation cover and sand movement, are highly susceptible to the effects of changes of climate. Some areas, such as the southwestern Kalahari or portions of the High Plains of the United States may have been especially prone to the effects of changes in precipitation, evapotranspiration, and/or wind velocity because of their location in climatic zones that are close to a climatic threshold between dune stability and activity.

A remarkable recent discovery, arising from the explosive development in the use of thermoluminescence and optical stimulated luminescence of sand grains, and studies of explorers' accounts (Muhs and Holliday, 1995), is the realization that such marginal dune fields have undergone repeated changes at decadal and century time scales in response to extended drought events through the Holocene. [*See* Dating Methods.]

The mobility of desert dunes (M) is directly proportional to the sand-moving power of the wind but indirectly proportional to their vegetation cover (Lancaster, 1995, p. 238). An index of the wind's sand-moving power is given by the percentage of the time (W) the wind blows above the threshold velocity (4.5 meters per second) for sand transport. Vegetation cover is a function of the ratio between annual rainfall (P) and potential evapotranspiration (PE). Thus, $M = W/(P/PE)$. Empirical observations in the United States and southern Africa indicate that dunes are completely stabilized by vegetation when M is less than 50, and are fully active when M is greater than 200.

Muhs and Maat (1993) used the output from general circulation models (GCMs) combined with this dune mobility index to show that sand dunes and sand sheets on the Great Plains are likely to become reactivated over a significant part of the region as a result of global warming, particularly if the frequencies of wind speeds above the threshold velocity were to increase even moderately. The methods used to estimate future dune field mobility are, however, still full of problems, and much more research is needed before we can have confidence in them (Knight et al. 2004). Stetler and Gaylord (1996) have suggested that with a 4°C warming, vegetation in Washington State would be greatly reduced and that sand-dune mobility would consequently increase by over 400%. For the Canadian prairies, Wolfe (1997) found that while most dunes were currently inactive or only had active crests, most dunes would become more active under conditions of increased drought, as occurred in 1988 and are likely to occur in the future.

Perhaps the most detailed scenarios for dune remobilization by global warming have been developed for the Kalahari in southern Africa (Thomas et al., 2005). Much of the Mega Kalahari, a desert that was much larger during past dry phases than it is today, is currently vegetated and stable, but GCMs suggest that by 2099 all dunefields, from South Africa in the south to Zambia and Angola in the north will be reactivated. This could disrupt pastoral and agricultural systems.

BIBLIOGRAPHY

Knight, M., Thomas, D.S.G., and Wiggs, G.F.S. "Challenges of Calculating Dunefield Mobility over the 21st Century." *Geomorphology* 59.1–2 (2004), 197–213. DOI: 10.1016/j.geomorph.2003.07.017.

Lancaster, N. *Geomorphology of Desert Dunes.* London and New York: Routledge, 1995.

Muhs, D.R., and P.B. Maat. "The Potential Response of Eolian Sands to Greenhouse Warming and Precipitation Reduction on the Great Plains of the United States." *Journal of Arid Environments* 25 (1993), 351–361.

Muhs, D.R., and V.T. Holliday. "Evidence of Active Dune Sand on the Great Plains in the 19th Century from Accounts of Early Explorers." *Quaternary Research* 43 (1995), 198–208.

Stetler, L.L., and D.R. Gaylord. "Evaluating Eolian-Climatic Interactions Using a Regional Climate Model from Hanford, Washington (USA)." *Geomorphology* 17.1–3 (1996), 99–113.

Thomas, D.S.G., M. Knight, and G.F.S. Wiggs. "Remobilization of Southern African Desert Dune Systems by Twenty-First Century Global Warming." *Nature* 435 (2005), 1218–1221. DOI: 10.1038/nature03717.

Wolfe, S.A. "Impact of Increased Aridity on Sand Dune Activity in the Canadian Prairies." *Journal of Arid Environments* 36.3 (1997), 412–432. DOI: 10.1006/jare.1996.0236.

—Andrew S. Goudie

DISEASE

Infectious diseases have shaped human history. They are dynamic, and will continue to influence where and how humans live—and human activities will alter the paths and expressions of infectious diseases. A broad range of societal, biological, and physicochemical factors influence the distribution, incidence, and burden of infectious diseases. In recent years, patterns of infectious disease have changed. These changes are reflected in the description of diseases caused by pathogens (disease-causing agents) long present but not previously identified, recognition of seemingly new microbes, changes in old pathogens (e.g., changes in distribution, incidence, virulence, resistance to drugs), new interactions among diseases, and the spread to humans of organisms never previously known to be human pathogens.

Infectious diseases remain the single most common cause of death in low-income countries, where nearly a third of all deaths are among children under 14 years of age. The burden is spread unevenly by population and geographic region. Infectious diseases have a disproportionate impact on the poor and undereducated, and in developing regions of the world. In 2001, of the approximately 56 million deaths globally, 10.6 million were children, 99% of them in low and middle income countries. In 2001 more than half of deaths in children aged 0–4 years were from infections: acute respiratory infections, measles, diarrhea, malaria, and HIV/AIDS (Lopez, 2006). Undernutrition is a leading risk factor in health loss (Ezzati et al., 2002). The probability of death between birth and age 15 is 22% in sub-Saharan Africa versus 1.1% in established market economies.

Although much media attention has focused on remote tropical locations and on exotic viral infections such as Ebola, the changing pattern of infections involves all geographic regions and all classes of pathogen (such as viruses, bacteria, fungi, helminths [parasitic worms], and protozoa). Most of the major global causes of death from infectious disease are common, widely distributed infections, such as tuberculosis, measles, HIV, influenza, pneumococcus, and rotavirus.

Infections kill and disable in many ways. Many pathogens cause acute disease, but infectious diseases also impose a burden through chronic diseases, including cancer. Chronic diseases may be a consequence of persistent infection (for example, hepatitis B virus) or may result from tissue damage caused by past infection. Many cancers have been linked to infections. The World Health Organization (WHO) estimates that more than 1.5 million cancers each year, or about 15% of the total, are related to microbes. The three that lead the list (and their pathogens) are gastric (*Helicobacter pylori*), cervical (papillomaviruses), and liver (hepatitis B and C viruses) cancers.

Many factors are contributing to the changing patterns of infectious disease. Those commonly identified are microbial adaptation and change, human demographics and behavior, international travel and commerce, climate and weather, ecosystem changes, technology and industry, economic development and land use, breakdown of public-health measures, poverty and social inequality, war and famine, and lack of political will. (Smolinski et al., 2003). How these influence the appearance, reappearance, and spread of infections will become apparent in the discussion of specific disease examples. Typically, multiple factors interact, leading to changes in a disease. The emergence of a disease may be an unintended consequence of what is otherwise viewed as progress: the building of a dam, clearing of lands, mass processing and wide distribution of foods and water, medical interventions (transfusions of blood and blood products, tissue and organ transplantation, cancer chemotherapy), and use of antimicrobial agents.

The burden of disease in humans can increase through increased contact between pathogen and host, increase in virulence or resistance of the pathogen, increase in the vulnerability of the host, or limited access to effective prevention or therapy. A human or a population can be completely or relatively invulnerable to some infections because of immunity (past infection or immunization), genetic factors, or a whole range of barriers (such as shoes, screens, good housing) or interventions (provision of clean water and adequate waste disposal, control of organisms responsible for transferring pathogens between hosts) that prevent contact between human and pathogen. Good nutrition, including adequate intake of micronutrients, can lead to an improved outcome in at least some infections.

MICROBES

It is useful to take a broad view of microbial life before focusing on microbes that harm humans. Only a tiny fraction of microbes that exist on Earth have been identified and characterized. Of those identified, most do not infect humans, and some are essential for shaping and sustaining life as we know it. Microbes are old, diverse, abundant, and resilient. They live in communities, send signals to communicate with each other, and change in response to changes in the environment. Microbial communities living deep in the Earth metabolize organic materials bound to rocks and sediments and shape the physical environment. Some microbes have short generation times (for example, twenty to thirty minutes for an organism like staphylococcus, compared with twenty to thirty years for a human), and hence can undergo rapid change. Such organisms change via mutation but also by a variety of molecular maneuvers that involve the acquisition and exchange of genetic information (e.g., transfer, reassortment, recombination, conjugation). These can alter microbial traits relevant to human health—virulence, resistance to drugs, and even transmissibility.

The source of microbes causing infections in humans is typically another human, an arthropod or other animal, or soil or water. Globally, about 65% of infections that lead to death are spread from person to person (such as respiratory tract infections, tuberculosis, HIV, and measles); almost a quarter are carried in food, water, or soil (e.g., infections such as cholera and hookworm); and about 13% are vector-borne (malaria and leishmaniasis) (World Health Organization, 1997). Increasingly, animals are being recognized as a source of human infections. Prominent contemporary examples include SARS, Nipah virus, and avian influenza (bird flu).

To cause disease, a microbe must find a way to enter the human host and reach appropriate cells or tissues where it can replicate. Microbes typically enter the body via ingestion, inhalation, or through the skin or mucous membranes. Many important pathogens, including the malaria parasite, are carried to the human host by a mosquito and inoculated through the skin. Some pathogens have complicated cycles that involve one or more intermediate hosts, typically animals that support one stage of development of the pathogen. Other microbes, such as hantaviruses, reside in an animal, known as a reservoir host. Humans can become infected if they enter the habitat of the animal or if they come into contact with them or their secretions/excretions through other activities. The human may be irrelevant to the maintenance of the microbe in nature, although the human, if infected, may die as a result of the infection.

VECTORS OF INFECTION

Many viruses, protozoa (e.g., malaria, trypanosomes, leishmania), and a few bacteria (especially rickettsia) and helminths (many filarial [thread-like] parasites) require the assistance of an arthropod to deliver the pathogen to the human host. These arthropods and other organisms that shuttle pathogens from one host to another are called "vectors." Vectors are important in carrying pathogens to animals and plants, as well as to humans. Many animal pathogens can also infect humans—as an essential part of the cycle or as an occasional unhappy event if the human happens to be the source of the arthropod's blood meal. Sometimes an insect will simply serve as a mechanical carrier of microbes that stick to its feet, hairs, or body, transporting microbes to food, for example. Organisms can also be carried passively on biting mouthparts or in the gut of the insect, but these means of transmission are probably infrequent and do not work for many infections.

In most instances, the arthropod (such as mosquito, tick, sandfly, reduviid bug, louse), in the process of taking a blood meal needed for its own reproduction, will ingest a pathogen along with the blood. The pathogen replicates (sometimes to high levels) or undergoes development to a more mature stage inside the arthropod during a period called extrinsic incubation. When the arthropod feeds again, the pathogen can be inoculated into the new host. In a few instances (as with Chagas' disease or American trypanosomiasis) the pathogen is found in the feces of the insect (e.g., a reduviid bug), which defecates after feeding, allowing the pathogens to enter through the bite site or via other surfaces (e.g., conjunctivas).

Pathogen-vector interactions may be very specific. Only certain types of mosquito are biologically competent to support the development of a given pathogen. Vectors vary greatly in their capacity to carry pathogens to humans, by virtue not only of their abundance, but also of their biting preferences, with some mosquitoes, for example, preferring nonhuman hosts and biting humans only if no animals are available. The likelihood of being bitten is also strongly influenced by human activities, clothing, habits, recreation, and housing.

ENVIRONMENT AND CLIMATE

Environmental and climatic factors strongly influence the distribution and incidence of many infectious diseases directly and indirectly. In general, infections that are carried by the human host and can be transmitted from one person to another (such as influenza, HIV, measles, chicken pox, and tuberculosis) can and do appear anywhere in the world, unless a population is geographically isolated or immune (because of past infection or immunization). Other infections require certain environmental or climatic conditions or the presence of a specific arthropod vector, animal, or other intermediate host in order to persist in an area. These are the infections that are geographically focal, although the area of distribution can expand or contract in response to a variety of factors, including the weather and environmental changes.

Many infections that are widespread still have striking fluctuations that correspond to the seasons. These may reflect seasonal human activities and also the ambient temperature and humidity as they affect the viability, duration of survival, replication, and transmissibility of the microbe. Influenza, for example, is seen primarily in the winter months in temperate regions, although it occurs throughout the year in tropical environments. Rapid and wide transmission has occurred in special habitats (for example, airplanes, cruise ships, air-conditioned barges, air-conditioned nursing homes) outside of the usual transmission season. In many temperate areas, salmonella, campylobacter, and some other food-borne infections tend to increase in summer months, perhaps reflecting food handling (grilled foods, picnics, higher ambient temperatures, and inadequate refrigeration) and other human activities during those months.

Environmental change, considered broadly for the microbe, includes the application of chemicals and other agents such as antimicrobials. Microbes that have or can acquire resistance mechanisms are more likely to survive. Today a variety of antiseptic, antibacterial, antiviral, antifungal, and other kinds of antimicrobial agents made by humans permeate the environment—in soaps, hand creams, cutting boards, toys, animals feeds, aquafarming, and antibiotics given to humans to treat and prevent infections. Of the 23 million kilograms of antibiotics used annually in the United States, more than 40% is used in animals (Levy, 1998). Increasingly, microbes, including many important human pathogens, are becoming resistant to antimicrobials in common use. Insect vectors also adapt to changes in the chemical environment and can become resistant to insecticides.

The physicochemical environment influences the pathogen, the vector, intermediate and reservoir hosts, vegetation, and human behavior and activities. For each biological species, the physicochemical environment influences the distribution, abundance, and duration of survival. Temperature (not just mean, but also minimum, maximum, and amplitude), humidity, rainfall (pattern as well as amount), types of vegetation, animal life, and distribution of water (such as ponds, rapidly flowing streams) may determine whether a region can support a vector. For an insect vector, the environment also determines its capacity to support the maturation of a pathogen, its biting activity, flight patterns, and shedding or transmission pattern. Hence the epidemiology of many vector-borne infections is characterized by seasonality through influences of weather patterns on host, vector, and microbe.

Seasonal events, such as human and animal migration, vacation, social, and school activities, and occupational work (e.g., harvesting of crops), can all influence patterns of infectious disease. The epidemiology of infections may also show periodicity or cyclical patterns extending over many years. This may be related cyclical weather patterns (for example, periodic climate perturbations such as El Niño–Southern Oscillation, which causes fluctuations in temperature and rainfall) or the number of susceptible people through birth or migration into an area (as with measles in the prevaccination era).

MALARIA

An ancient disease, malaria remains a major killer in many tropical regions. A protozoan infection, it is transmitted by mosquitoes, which require moisture for breeding. Malaria, along with other vector-borne infections, is strongly affected by rainfall and temperature, although the relationship is not a simple one. Increased rainfall can be associated with expansion of malaria

GLOBAL WARMING AND MALARIA

Vector-borne diseases and climatic factors are often closely linked. For example, the *Anopheles* mosquito, which transmits malaria, does not survive easily when the mean winter temperature drops below approximately 15°C. It survives best where the mean temperature is 20°–30°C and humidity exceeds 60%. Higher temperatures speed up the malaria parasite's developmental cycle; the parasite cannot survive below a temperature of around 14°–16°C for *Plasmodium vivax* and 18°–20°C for *Plasmodium falciparum*. By improving the conditions for both the vector and the parasite, unusually hot and humid weather in endemic areas could cause a marked rise in malaria incidence.

Models that relate annual average temperatures and rainfall to malaria incidence worldwide found that for five different climatic-change scenarios, the land area affected by malaria would increase by 7–28%. Cities at a sufficiently high altitude to be above the "mosquito line" (e.g., Nairobi and Harare) might be especially susceptible, and the vulnerability of newly affected populations could initially lead to high case-fatality rates because of their lack of natural immunity. Some models predict a potential climate-induced increase of around 25% in malaria cases worldwide.

Climatic change is not the only factor in the changing incidence of malaria. In sub-Saharan Africa (where 90% of all malaria deaths in the world occur), its incidence has worsened over the past three decades. This can be attributed to a number of factors, including drug and insecticide resistance, declining health service and control infrastructure, increased population movements (migrants and refugees), and land-use changes.

BIBLIOGRAPHY

Martens, W.J.M., et al. "Potential Impact of Global Climate Change on Malaria Risk." *Environmental Health Perspectives* 103.5 (1995), 458–464.
Martin, P.H., and M.G. Lefebvre. "Malaria and Climate: Sensitivity of Malaria Potential Transmission to Climate." *Ambio* 24.4 (1995), 200–207.
McMichael, A.J., et al., eds. *Climatic Change and Human Health.* Geneva: World Health Organization, 1996.

ANDREW GOUDIE

breeding sites and an increase in malaria in arid areas. In humid areas, drought can improve breeding conditions for mosquitoes, leading to outbreaks.

Natural predators of vectors influence their abundance. If the reproductive cycle of a predator is longer than that of the mosquito, a mosquito population could surge before the predator population could expand to control it. Temperature, rainfall, and vegetation also affect the abundance of food and the behavior of predators.

Increased rainfall can provide more breeding sites, but excess rain can also destroy breeding sites. Increased temperature, to a point, can speed the maturation of the mosquito through its various stages and may decrease the extrinsic incubation period (the time inside the vector required for the pathogen to develop to an infective stage) for the parasite in the arthropod. Yet excessive temperature may kill or inhibit growth. Very warm temperatures may shorten the survival of adult mosquitoes and immature forms.

Changes in weather patterns or in land use may have varying effects on different vectors. In an area of northern Sarawak (Malaysia) undergoing oil-palm development, mosquitoes were surveyed during major changes in the habitat. In association with forest clearing, *Anopheles* mosquitoes decreased and the risk of malaria transmission dropped by 90% over a four-year period. During the same period, however, vectors of dengue virus increased (Chang et al., 1997).

Interventions can have unexpected consequences. The use of bed nets has been advocated in highly malarial regions as a way to reduce the number of bites by infective mosquitoes and hence the morbidity and mortality from malaria. In Gambia, West Africa, a national program of impregnated bed nets was introduced in 1992. A follow-up study to assess the impact on malaria found that malaria prevalence was inversely related to vector density. Bed-net usage was strongly influenced by the density of biting mosquitoes. Prevalence rates of malaria were reduced in areas where nuisance biting of mosquitoes was sufficient to lead people to use bed nets. The highest rates of malaria were found in villages with low bed-net usage.

CHOLERA

A bacterial infection acquired by ingesting food or water contaminated with *Vibrio cholerae*, cholera has long caused dramatic epidemics and invokes fear because of its capacity to kill quickly through massive diarrhea. It has a striking seasonal pattern in Bangladesh and in some endemic areas where outbreaks tend to recur.

Vibrio cholerae lives in close association with marine life—algae, phytoplankton, copepods, and aquatic plants. It can bind to chitin in crustacean shells. A single copepod can contain up to ten thousand cells of the bacterium. Special techniques can document its continued presence in marine life even when the organism cannot be grown with ordinary culture techniques in the laboratory.

Under unfavorable conditions the organism can enter a dormant state, in which it requires decreased oxygen and nutrients.

In response to changing environmental factors, such as warming of water temperature, increase in pH and nutrients, and decrease in salinity, its population may expand (and become culturable), increasing the risk of human infection, especially in areas where sanitation is poor and drinking water is untreated. Environmental factors such as increase in sea water temperature and influx of organic nutrients can also trigger plankton blooms that provide a favorable milieu for the proliferation of *V. cholerae*.

History is full of examples of introductions of cholera via ships carrying people infected with *V. cholerae* and excreting it with their feces. Carried in the ballast and bilgewater of ships, it can also contaminate waters in new ports. Infected people can be a source of infection in a community, but an aquatic reservoir of the bacterium can be a long-term source for periodic introductions into human populations. Shellfish become colonized with *V. cholerae* in their water habitats and can infect humans if inadequately cooked before being eaten.

The bacterium can survive for up to fourteen days in food and for weeks in shellfish, and can persist indefinitely in an aquatic environment. Although environmental factors can trigger an expansion of bacterial populations, human living conditions and activities determine whether and how often human disease occurs. The discharge of untreated human waste into surface water used by humans for preparation of food, bathing, etc., allows continuing contact between *V. cholerae* and humans. Chlorination of water can kill the bacterium, and filtering of untreated water, which removes copepods, can reduce the number of viable bacteria.

War and other conflict leading to population displacement and disruption of basic sanitation systems can lead to cholera epidemics. For example, in 1994 when refugees fleeing genocide in Rwanda settled in camps with poor sanitation, a massive outbreak of El Tor cholera in Goma, Zaire, caused 70,000 cases and 12,000 deaths. Extreme weather events, such as flooding, can also precipitate cholera epidemics by making land uninhabitable and displacing populations. Flooding can also disperse microbes and allow sewage contamination of water sources used by humans.

A new strain of cholera, *V. cholerae* 0139 Bengal, appeared in Asia in 1992 and caused explosive epidemics in Bangladesh, India, and other nearby countries, temporarily displacing the resident *V. cholerae* strains. Its virulence was similar to that of typical cholera strains, but it could infect people who were relatively immune to *V. cholerae* 01. This meant that the organism had the capacity to cause high rates of infection and illustrates how a change in the pathogen can abruptly alter the epidemiology of an old, familiar infection. Such shifts have important implications for vaccine development. Existing cholera vaccines did not protect against this new strain.

HIV/AIDS

Perhaps more than any infection in recent history, AIDS shows the vulnerability of humans to new infection. The appearance of an infection that would claim 2.6 million lives in 1998 was unimaginable a few decades ago. Human behaviors and technology have fueled the spread of HIV throughout the world. Rapid, widespread travel; injections and intravenous drug use; multiple sexual partners (heterosexual and homosexual); other sexually transmitted diseases; blood transfusions and use of factor-concentrates to treat hemophilia; and, to a much lesser extent, artificial insemination and tissue and organ transplantation have aided the spread of the virus.

The consequences of HIV infection include progressive, profound depletion of the immune system. Death is often a result of opportunistic infection or malignancy. The appearance of HIV and its subsequent study have led to major advances in immunology and also the recognition of new clinical syndromes caused by well-known pathogens. In addition, the presence of HIV has contributed to the characterization of organisms not previously well defined (e.g., cryptosporidium, *Bartonella* species, and microsporidia). HIV has also been an important factor in the resurgence of tuberculosis in many regions of the world.

As HIV has moved into rural and tropical regions, its overlap with the distribution of geographically focal infections, such as Chagas' disease, *Penicillium marneffei*, and leishmaniasis, has made diagnosis and treatment of these infections even more difficult. HIV has altered every aspect of medicine—clinical expression of disease, pathologic findings, interpretation of diagnostic tests, and treatment approaches.

TUBERCULOSIS

Mycobacterium tuberculosis, the bacterium that causes tuberculosis, infects one-third of the human population. As a single agent it kills about 1.5 million people each year. As with so many infections, tuberculosis is unevenly distributed by geographic region and population. More than 95% of the cases and 99% of the deaths from tuberculosis are in developing countries.

Tuberculosis spreads from person to person via droplet nuclei, tiny particles less than 10 microns in diameter that are expelled by people with active infection. These droplet nuclei are dispersed widely in the air after coughing, singing, or talking, and remain airborne for hours. Their small size allows them to pass easily into the bronchioles of the lung.

Most people who are infected with *M. tuberculosis* have "silent" infection that may remain unrecognized for a lifetime. In most populations, only 5–15% of people infected with *M. tuberculosis* develop active disease. In contrast, HIV-infected people are more likely to become infected and to progress to active disease. Their annual risk of progressing to active tuberculosis is 7–10%. The interaction between HIV and tuberculosis is bidirectional. Tuberculosis in HIV-infected people increases viral replication and leads to more rapid progression of HIV disease. There is extensive overlap of the populations infected with HIV and *M. tuberculosis*. HIV is spreading rapidly in many areas of the world where latent infection with tuberculosis is common.

Although drugs that are effective for treating tuberculosis have been available since the middle of the twentieth century, prospects for control of global tuberculosis in the near term are poor. About 50% of people with untreated active tuberculosis will die from the infection. The death rate is higher in people with AIDS and other conditions associated with poor immune response. Infection with multidrug-resistant (MDR) strains of tuberculosis becomes untreatable if effective drugs are unavailable or inaccessible because of cost.

MDR strains, and more recently extensively drug-resistant strains (XDR), emerge as a consequence of inappropriate treatment of tuberculosis. All bacterial populations of *M. tuberculosis* contain rare bacilli that are resistant to drugs commonly used for treatment. Therapy with too few drugs or for too short a period of time can allow drug-resistant bacilli to emerge and become the predominant infecting strain. Not only can infection persist and progress in the individual, but drug-resistant strains can spread to others who live and work nearby. People with untreated active tuberculosis (whether sensitive or resistant strains) transmit infection, on average, to 10–15 people per year.

Many habitats in today's world facilitate the transmission of tuberculosis. These include prisons, homeless shelters, hospitals, refugee camps, and nursing homes. Vulnerable people are brought together and often share the same air-circulation system. One habitat that is especially worrisome is the hospital in regions where tuberculosis is common and facilities for respiratory isolation are limited or nonexistent. Hospitals have been the site of many outbreaks of MDR tuberculosis. Hospital workers as well as patients and visitors become infected— although HIV-infected people are especially vulnerable. In Argentina, more than one hundred HIV-infected people acquired MDR tuberculosis in a hospital. The attack rate of MDR tuberculosis among hospitalized HIV-infected people was an extraordinary 37%.

A survey published by the World Health Organization in 1997 found that drug resistance to one or more drugs was present in all countries surveyed and exceeded 40% in some areas. As of early 2007, XDR tuberculosis had been documented in 17 countries on six continents. In an outbreak of XDR tuberculosis in South Africa, 52 of 53 patients with the infection died from tuberculosis. Drugs that are active against many MDR strains do exist, but treatment is difficult (requiring multiple drugs, many with unpleasant and toxic side effects that require careful monitoring) and extremely expensive. Fewer agents are available to treat XDR tuberculosis.

Crowded living conditions enhance the spread of tuberculosis. Increasing urbanization and poverty, along with the other potent forces of HIV infection and expansion of MDR strains, make for a gloomy forecast. Many researchers are working to develop safe and highly effective vaccines. The currently available vaccine, bacille Calmette Guérin (BCG), continues to be widely used. Most newborns in the world receive the vaccine. For example, 85% of children born worldwide in 1990 received BCG as infants, according to WHO statistics. WHO continues to recommend BCG, preferably at birth, for all infants born in high-risk countries, including those at high risk for HIV infection. A meta-analysis of major studies found an overall protective effect against tuberculosis of about 50% and protection against death and disseminated disease in the range of 60–75%. While BCG may have reduced deaths from tuberculosis, it is not the answer to global control.

Because of its ease of transmission, tuberculosis anywhere in the world is a concern for everyone. Molecular fingerprinting has allowed the tracing of particular strains of tuberculosis that have been carried across continents and oceans. In western Europe, Canada, and the United States, a significant and rising proportion of the tuberculosis cases are in immigrant populations. In the United States in 2005, 54% of the tuberculosis cases were in the foreign-born. Tuberculosis-control efforts must be global. Many populations still lack access to reliable diagnostic testing and effective drugs. Changes in the microbe can also alter the epidemiology and expression of infection. In 1995, a strain of tuberculosis with high transmissibility was identified in an outbreak in the southern United States. Extensive transmission followed contact, often brief, with people infected with this strain. In two instances, active disease developed after very limited exposure. This strain, when studied in the laboratory, grew much faster than other clinical isolates of *M. tuberculosis*. It is postulated that the more rapid growth could allow this strain to establish infection before an effective immune response could develop (Valway et al., 1998).

Disease. Vector Control.

Workers in the southern United States practice "vector control," a procedure that aims to decrease contacts between humans and vectors of human disease. The workers dig a drainage ditch in order to disperse standing water, a frequent breeding ground for the *Anopheles* mosquito. Malaria is one of several diseases that may be prevented through mosquito control; others include the West Nile virus and dengue. (From Centers for Disease Control and Prevention. www.cdc.gov.)

DENGUE

Dengue fever, also known as breakbone fever, is a viral infection transmitted to humans by the bite of an infective mosquito, usually *Aedes aegypti*. In recent years the mosquito vector and the virus have spread into new geographic regions. Dengue virus has caused major outbreaks in the Americas, and it continues to be a major pathogen in Asia. An estimated two billion people live in tropical and subtropical regions at risk for dengue fever, and about 150 million cases occur each year. Although some primates can be infected with the virus, humans are the primary host and the usual source for human infections. An initial infection with the dengue virus typically causes fever, chills, headache, and muscle aches, and is followed by complete recovery. There is no vaccine yet available and no specific therapy, although supportive care in the severe forms of infection can be lifesaving.

Dengue fever is caused by four antigenically distinct RNA viruses, designated dengue types 1, 2, 3, and 4. Infection with one dengue virus is followed by immunity to that serotype but not to others. Infection with a second dengue serotype can lead to severe disease—dengue shock syndrome (DSS) or dengue hemorrhagic fever (DHF). Mortality in untreated DSS/DHF can reach 20%, but falls to less than 1% with aggressive supportive treatment. Although an initial infection with dengue can be severe, the relative risk of severe disease is 100 times higher after a second infection than after primary dengue infection.

In contrast to many vector-borne infections, dengue fever is an urban disease. The primary vector, *Aedes aegypti,* is an urban mosquito, well adapted to human habitats. It rests indoors, sleeps in bedrooms, and prefers human blood. Humans have provided it with many suitable breeding sites—water storage containers, flowerpots, discarded plastic containers, used tires, and tin cans, among others. *Aedes aegypti* is also the principal urban vector for yellow-fever virus.

Many factors have contributed to the striking increase in dengue. Rapid and frequent travel means that humans who are viremic (have the virus in their bloodstream) regularly carry the virus from one geographic region to another. Expansion of the mosquito populations because of inadequate vector control programs and increasing resistance of the mosquito to insecticides means that many areas will be receptive to the introduction of the virus by a traveling human. Infection can spread rapidly when vectors are abundant and have frequent contact with humans. Poor housing, lack of screens or air conditioning, and dense human populations also favor spread of infection. Epidemics can be huge, sometimes involving a million or more people.

More people live in urban areas today than ever before in history. Seventy-five percent of the world population is in developing countries, and more than 90% of the population growth is occurring in these regions. Increasingly, growth of large urbanized centers is taking place in tropical regions. Of the 25 megacities (urban areas with more than 8 million people) in the year 2000, 19 were in developing regions. Huge peri-urban slums surround many of these cities in tropical and subtropical areas and provide the ideal environment for the appearance and rapid spread of a number of infectious diseases, including dengue fever. It has been estimated that a population of somewhere between 150,000 and one million is needed to sustain the cocirculation of more than one dengue serotype, thus setting the stage for severe and complicated dengue infections. More urban centers in tropical regions are reaching this size and are increasingly linked to the world via international air travel. With expansion of the populations in which multiple dengue serotypes circulate simultaneously or sequentially, the risk for DSS/DHF increases greatly. Larger human populations can also potentially influence viral evolution. Over the last two centuries, the number of viral lineages has been increasing roughly in parallel with the growing human population. Will an expanding human population lead to increasing rates of viral evolution? Increases in viral diversity could lead to more transmissible or pathogenic lineages (Zanotto et al., 1996).

Mosquitoes typically take some meals from plants (whose sugars provide energy) but require blood meals for the nutrients necessary for reproduction. *Aedes aegypti* mosquitoes that feed only on human blood have a reproductive advantage and hence can spread viruses more effectively. Dense human populations provide more blood meals for mosquitoes.

Weather patterns also affect the distribution and incidence of dengue through their impact on the mosquito vector. Studies in Thailand in the 1980s showed the strong influence of temperature on vector efficiency for dengue virus. When mosquitoes were incubated at 30°C, the extrinsic incubation period for dengue-2 virus was 12 days, but dropped to 7 days at 32° and 35°C (Watts et al., 1989).

Interventions must be carried out with clear understanding of the potential consequences. In general, larger mosquitoes are more easily infected with the dengue virus and hence more likely to transmit it. Reducing larval density in breeding sites leads to larger mosquitoes. A control measure that reduced but did not eliminate larvae in breeding sites could have the perverse outcome of increasing dengue transmission to humans.

COCCIDIOIDOMYCOSIS

The soil-associated fungus *Coccidioides immitis* is found in arid and semiarid areas with alkaline soils, hot summers, and short moist winters. Humans become infected when they inhale airborne arthroconidia (spores) of the fungus. Activities and events that disturb the soil (for example, excavation, construction, earthquakes) can lift arthroconidia into the air. Infections are typically acquired only in areas where the appropriate environmental conditions support the growth of the fungus in the soil. Weather patterns can influence risk and can partially explain periodic increases. Heavy rains followed by drought can allow the fungus to thrive—and then to be dispersed during dry, dusty days. In 1977, a major windstorm in the southern extreme of the San Joaquin

Valley in California carried aloft soil from this coccidioidomycosis-endemic region and dispersed it over an area encompassing approximately 87,000 square kilometers, an area larger than Austria. This resulted in an epidemic outside the usual endemic area.

HANTAVIRUSES

In 1993, in the southwestern part of the United States, a cluster of deaths in previously healthy young adults led to the identification of a hantavirus as the cause of the disease—later named hantavirus pulmonary syndrome. Hantaviruses, a large group of rodent-associated viruses, had long been known to be important pathogens in other parts of the world but had not been known to cause pulmonary disease in the United States. Rodents infected with hantaviruses shed the virus in urine, feces, and saliva but do not become ill.

Subsequent studies yielded important insights. The virus was not new to the area; infections in humans that had occurred decades earlier could be confirmed retrospectively by studying saved serum and tissues from people who had died of undiagnosed illnesses. Infections were not localized to the area in which the first cases were identified. Once physicians became aware of the infection and had techniques to diagnose it, they identified infections from the same or related hantaviruses from many other parts of the Americas, from Canada to southern South America. As of early 1998, infections had been documented in at least twenty-nine states in the U.S. This poses the question, why an infection that kills about half of the humans who become infected had gone unrecognized for so long—and why was it finally recognized and characterized in 1993.

Because of favorable weather conditions that supported abundant food for rodents, the rodent population increased more than tenfold between 1992 and 1993 in the area where the outbreak occurred. An expanded rodent population allowed increased contact between rodents and humans. A cluster of deaths in highly visible, young, healthy adults attracted the attention of astute clinicians. The rapid identification of the hantavirus drew on past research and new molecular techniques. Although the hantavirus pulmonary syndrome has characteristic findings, it shares many features (fever, aches, shortness of breath, pulmonary infiltrates [the infilling of air spaces in the lungs with fluids, inflammatory exudates, or cells]) with many other more common diseases. Hence, occasional, sporadic cases in the past did not raise alarms.

Hantavirus researchers expect that these viruses will be found to cause at least occasional human cases in areas where human disease has not yet been reported. Many cases have now been identified in South America. As humans clear lands and change habitats in ways that increase human–rodent contact, the number of human cases will probably increase. A survey of rodents in national parks in the United States in 1994 and 1995 found that antibodies to Sin Nombre (Spanish, "unnamed") virus (the hantavirus found in the southwestern United States) were also widespread in eastern and central regions of the country (Mills et al., 1998). Many factors influence rodent-human contact, including agricultural activities, season of the year, housing, abundance of rodents, and changes in land use, which can change rodent habitats.

[*See also* Global Warming; Impacts of Climate Change; *and* Migrations.]

BIBLIOGRAPHY

Centers for Disease Control and Prevention. *CDC Health Information for International Travel 2008*. Atlanta: CDC, 2007.
Chang, M.S., et al. "Changes in Abundance and Behaviour of Vector Mosquitoes Induced by Land Use During the Development of an Oil Palm Plantation in Sarawak." *Transactions of the Royal Society of Tropical Medicine and Hygiene* 91.4 (1997), 382–386.
Colditz, G.A., et al. "Efficacy of BCG Vaccine in the Prevention of Tuberculosis: Meta-Analysis of the Published Literature." *Journal of the American Medical Association* 271.9 (1994), 698–702.
Colwell, R.R. "Global Climate and Infectious Disease: The Cholera Paradigm." *Science* 274 (1996), 2025–2031. DOI: 10.1126/science.274.5295.2025.
Ezzati, M., et al. "Selected Major Risk Factors and Global and Regional Burden of Disease." *Lancet* 360 (2002), 1347–1360.
Levy, S.B. "Multidrug Resistance: A Sign of the Times." *New England Journal of Medicine* 338.19 (1998), 1376–1378.
Lopez, A.D., et al. "Global and Regional Burden of Disease and Risk Factors, 2001: Systematic Analysis of Population Health Data." *Lancet* 367 (2006), 1747–1757.
McNeill, W.H. *Plagues and Peoples*. Garden City, N.Y.: Anchor Press, 1976.
Mills, J.N., et al. "A Survey of Hantavirus Antibody in Small-Mammal Populations in Selected United States National Parks." *Amerian Journal of Tropical Medicine and Hygiene* 58.4 (1998), 525–532.
Morell, V. "How the Malaria Parasite Manipulates its Hosts." *Science* 278 (1997), 223. DOI: 10.1126/science.278.5336.223.
Raviglione, M.C., et al. "XDR Tuberculosis: Implications for Global Public Health." *New England Journal of Medicine* 356.7 (2007), 656–659.
Reeves, W.C., et al. "Potential Effect of Global Warming on Mosquito-Borne Arboviruses." *Journal of Medical Entomology* 31.3 (1994), 323–332.
Scott, T.W., et al. "A Fitness Advantage for *Aedes Aegypti* and the Viruses it Transmits when Females Feed Only on Human Blood." *American Journal of Tropical Medicine and Hygiene* 57.2 (1997), 235–239.
Smolinski, M.S., et al., eds. *Microbial Threats to Health: Emergence, Detection, and Response*. Washington D.C.: National Academies Press, 2003.
Travis, J. "Africa's Latest Scourge." *Science News* (July 17, 1999), 40–42.
Valway, S.E., et al. "An Outbreak Involving Extensive Transmission of a Virulent Strain of Mycobacterium Tuberculosis." *New England Journal of Medicine* 338 (1998), 633–639.
Watts, D.M., et al. "Effect of Temperature on the Vector Efficiency of *Aedes Aegypti* for Dengue 2 Virus." *American Journal of Tropical Medicine and Hygiene* 36.1 (1987), 143–152.
Whalen, C., et al. "Accelerated Course of Human Immunodeficiency Virus Infection after Tuberculosis." *American Journal of Respiratory and Critical Care Medicine* 151.1 (1995), 129–135.
Wilson, M.E. *A World Guide to Infections: Diseases, Distribution, Diagnosis*. New York: Oxford University Press, 1991.
———. "Travel and the Emergence of Infectious Diseases." *Emerging Infectious Diseases* 1.2 (1995a), 39–46.
———. "Infectious Diseases: An Ecological Perspective." *British Medical Journal* 311 (1995b), 1681–1684.
Wilson, M.E., R. Levins, and A. Spielman, eds. *Disease in Evolution: Global Changes and Emergence of Infectious Diseases*. New York: New York Academy of Sciences, 1994.
Wolfe, N.D., C.P. Dunavan, and J. Diamond. "Origin of Major Human Infectious Diseases." *Nature* 447 (2007), 279–283. DOI: 10.1038/nature05775.
World Health Organization. *Anti-Tuberculosis Drug Resistance in the World: Third Global Report: The WHO/IUATLD Global Project on Anti-Tuberculosis*

Drug Resistance Surveillance, 1999–2002. Geneva: World Health Organization, 1997.

Zanotto, P.M. de A., et al. "Population Dynamics of Flaviviruses Revealed by Molecular Phylogenies." *Proceedings of the National Academy of Sciences* 93.2 (1996), 548–553.

—MARY ELIZABETH WILSON

DROUGHT

Drought is a shortage of water, but there is no universal definition of drought. A shortage of water can be brought about by a reduction in supply (e.g., a decline in rainfall), or by an increase in demand (caused by a change in land use, for example), or by a combination of the two. Drought can be defined as a period of below-average precipitation (meteorological drought), as a shortage of soil moisture in the root zone of crops that affects their productivity (agricultural drought), or as a low river discharge that impacts the ecosystem adversely (hydrological drought). There are also climatological definitions of drought and those dealing with its ecological and economic aspects.

Drought is a creeping phenomenon, with an uncertain start, characterized by its intensity, location, impact, and duration. Drought should not be confused with aridity, which is a measure of the lack of water in a region based on observations averaging data over 30 years or more. Warren and Khogali (1992), in their assessment of desertification and drought in the Sudano–Sahelian region, distinguish drought, in which moisture is supplied in below-average amounts for short periods (one to two years); desiccation, aridization lasting decades; and land degradation, a persistent decrease in the productivity of vegetation and soils.

Each of these environmental problems prompts different environmental strategies. Drought requires food storage and short-term relief; desiccation demands more radical measures such as resettlement and changing land use patterns; land degradation is more amenable to corrective and preventive measures. It is essential to distinguish between a short-term reduction in rainfall (i.e., drought), and the process of longer-term climate change. [*See* Climate Change and Societal Development.]

DROUGHT IMPACTS AND FREQUENCY

Drought is a worldwide phenomenon. Drylands in India experience drought once every four years, and a similar frequency is observed in Israel, southern Africa, and parts of China, although in the North China Plain there have been thirty-five reported droughts in the last forty years. Australia and the United States have both experienced major droughts this century: California suffered consecutive years of low rainfall between 1987 and 1992, and Australia was completely free of drought for only one year in the same five-year period. In northeastern Brazil, droughts occur eight out of every ten years, often accompanied by floods. Drought has been blamed for death and economic disruption on all inhabited

---

INFECTIOUS DISEASES

A broad range of societal, biological, and physicochemical factors influence the distribution, incidence, and burden from infectious diseases.

- Infectious diseases are dynamic; they will continue to change.
- Many diseases that appear to be new are not truly new but are only newly recognized and characterized.
- Changes in infections are global in distribution and involve all classes of organisms.
- Infection is a universal phenomenon, affecting plants and animals as well as humans.
- Human activities are a potent force in changing patterns in infectious diseases.
- Infections can cause chronic diseases and are involved as one of the causes in at least 15% of human cancers.
- The physicochemical environment affects the distribution, abundance, and dispersal of many human pathogens. Its role is especially prominent in vector-borne and animal-associated infections.
- Animals are the source of many new microbial threats to humans.

—MARY ELIZABETH WILSON

THE WORLD'S TOP FIVE INFECTIOUS KILLERS IN 2002

1. Pneumonia and other lung infections: 3.9 million deaths. Major killer of children in developing countries. Undernutrition and micronutrient deficiencies and indoor air pollution, and poor access to care contribute to burden. Many are treatable with antibiotics; some are preventable with vaccines.

2. AIDS: about 3 million deaths. Sub-Saharan Africa thought to have two-thirds of world's cases. Transmissible through body fluids such as blood and semen. No cure or vaccine, but a combination of drugs can prolong life.

3. Diarrheal diseases, including cholera: more than 1.5 million deaths. Contaminated water and foods are primary causes. Most victims are under five years of age and live in developing countries. Deaths can be reduced with oral rehydration, proper nutrition, and antibiotics. Wide use of rotavirus vaccine in low-income countries could reduce deaths.

4. Malaria: 1.5 million deaths. Endemic in 100 countries; highest incidence in sub-Saharan Africa. Transmitted by infected female *Anopheles* mosquitoes. Curable with early diagnosis and prompt treatment, but protozoa are developing increasing resistance to drugs.

5. Tuberculosis: more than 1 million deaths. Airborne transmission. Ninety-five percent of cases are in developing countries. Treatable with antimicrobials, but multidrug-resistant and extensively drug-resistant strains have emerged. Overlap with HIV infection in many areas. Current vaccine widely used but not very effective.

Source: World Health Organization, 2007, www.who.int/mediacentre/factsheets/en.

—MARY ELIZABETH WILSON

continents; in 1985–1988, for example, 28 million people are believed to have been affected by drought in India in the period, although Africa appears to have been the worst affected. The droughts of the mid-1980s created millions of environmental refugees in Africa and enormous suffering for those left behind. Three major droughts occurred in the Sahel region in the twenty-first century—during the 1910s, 1940s, and 1970s. The last is of most concern because it appears to have heralded the onset of generally drier conditions that have affected 80% of the population of the Sahel.

CAUSES OF DROUGHT

Drought is often considered to be strictly a climatological phenomenon, but to ascribe the problem solely to a lack of rainfall ignores the impacts of human activity—if not in causing drought, then at least in exacerbating its impacts. Publications with titles such as "Nature Pleads Not Guilty" and "Drought the Scapegoat" illustrate the importance attached to nonclimatological causes, a perspective taken by many writing on drought in Africa. It is therefore necessary when discussing the causes of drought to discuss the role of the impacts of human activities as well as that of climate.

DROUGHT AS A CLIMATOLOGICAL PHENOMENON

The primary characteristic of meteorological drought is a reduction in precipitation. There are many definitions of the phenomenon, including threshold values (in the United Kingdom, drought is fifteen consecutive days without rain) and statistical values (in South Africa, 70% of normal rainfall; in India, twice the standard deviation below the average rainfall). These approaches have the advantage of precision but they often lack an assessment of impact.

Detailed analyses of the Sahel region with respect to meteorological drought have provided evidence of a persistent decline in annual rainfall since the 1970s. This has been linked to local land-use changes, but regional and global phenomena such as El Niño–Southern Oscillation (ENSO) and global warming may offer an alternative mechanism. [See El Niño–Southern Oscillation (ENSO); and Global Warming.]

It has been suggested that local causes of rainfall reduction are related to the impacts of land degradation on the energy balance of the atmosphere. This idea has been prevalent since the 1970s, when it was proposed as a biogeophysical feedback initiated by overgrazing leading to increased surface albedo, reduced heating of the atmosphere, and hence a reduction in rainfall. [See Albedo.] This model has been criticized for ignoring the lack of evidence of extensive overgrazing, the observed increases in surface temperatures in drylands, and changes in latent heat flux. More recently, the importance of surface moisture content (and hence vegetation cover) has been demonstrated for areas such as the Sahel, where rainfall is produced by convection, but the latest climate models suggest that there is no clear link between land degradation and rainfall.

On a worldwide scale, the interlinking (teleconnection) of climate and oceanic circulations has been examined as a possible explanation of drought. [See Ocean-Atmosphere Coupling.] Changes in rainfall in Africa have been coupled to sea surface temperature anomalies in the Atlantic, while sea-surface temperature changes in the southern Atlantic and southwestern Indian oceans appear to be significant for rainfall in southern Africa. The most widely discussed coupling is that of ENSO with monsoonal rainfalls. During the 1983 El Niño, Australia experienced one of the worst droughts this century, followed by unusually heavy rainfall in 1988 when the normal (Walker) circulation was reestablished. [See El Niño–Southern Oscillation.] Drought in India and northeastern Africa has similarly been related to El Niño. The association with Sahelian rainfall is less clear, however, and for northeastern Brazil there is only a weak correlation between rainfall and El Niño. Caution must therefore be exercised before accepting the assumption that an El Niño heralds the worldwide onset of drought conditions, a point made by Wuethrich (1995), who reported that the El Niño phenomenon was becoming increasingly unpredictable and appeared to follow a more complex pattern than previously believed.

There are also concerns that drought, especially agricultural drought, will become more frequent as a result of global warming. Higher temperatures may cause an intensification of the hydrological system, but more detailed analyses of seasonal changes suggest an increase in drier periods; England, for example, is expected to experience milder winters and drier summers. General circulation models have indicated that drought will become more frequent in the United States and much of Europe. In the tropics, agriculture is particularly vulnerable in situations where crops are grown near their tolerances of heat and water supply; hence yields may decline under global warming unless water is used more efficiently. Even where an increase in rainfall is predicted, it may not result in higher production. Monsoonal precipitation is expected to increase in northern Australia, for example, encouraging better rangeland production and improvements in cattle ranching. But since plant growth is limited also by low levels of soil phosphorus, a reduction in drought will not necessarily lead to greater productivity unless fertilizers are applied.

DROUGHT AND ENVIRONMENTAL MISMANAGEMENT

The changes that took place in rural communities during the twentieth century and assumed links between agricultural production, rainfall, and famine have generated much debate over the relationship between environmental mismanagement and drought. Vulnerability is the key issue with respect to mismanagement. Rainfall is highly variable in space and time, and it is inevitable that any region will have periods during which rainfall is significantly below average. Whether this has an impact on human activities or the ecosystem and is regarded as drought will depend upon the resilience or vulnerability of that system. Rural communities in developing countries have become less resilient with the opening up of their economies to world market forces during the latter half of the twentieth century. The intensification of agriculture and greater water demands for irrigation and urban expansion creates an environment that is more sensitive to rainfall variations (Glantz, 1994). A reduction in rainfall is seen as a trigger mechanism for drought, but the broad phenomenon is explained in terms of social and economic change. Such explanations are not merely the province of the developing countries. The United Kingdom has recently experienced a number of droughts, and blame has been apportioned variously to rainfall, consumer demand, and even the recent privatization of the water supply companies.

IMPORTANT FEATURES OF DROUGHT

* The appropriate definition for drought in any particular instance must be stated at the outset.
* Meteorological drought is a normal feature of any climate and should be expected from time to time.
* Economic or agricultural drought arises through an imbalance between supply and demand, and can be the result of a reduction in supply, an increase in demand, or a combination of the two.
* Because drought may be caused by a reduction in rainfall or an increase in demand for water, solutions to drought may include supply enhancement (desalination, interbasin transfers, cloud seeding) or demand management (short-term water restrictions or longer-term economic measures and education).
* We must move from responding to drought (with tactical measures) to a more proactive approach (using strategic measures) for drought management and mitigation.

[*See also* Deserts; Desert Dunes in a Warmer World; Desertification; *and* Famine.]

BIBLIOGRAPHY

DROUGHT DEFINITIONS

Agnew, C.T. "Sahel Drought, Meteorological or Agricultural?" *International Journal of Climatology* 9.4 (1989), 371–382. DOI: 10.1002/joc.3370090404.
Agnew, C.T., and E. Anderson. *Water Resources in the Arid Realm*. London and New York: Routledge, 1992.
Le Houérou, H.N. "Climate Change, Drought and Desertification." *Journal of Arid Environments* 34.2 (1996), 133–185. DOI: 10.1006/jare.1996.0099.
Wilhite, D.A., ed. *Drought Assessment, Management, and Planning*. Boston: Kluwer, 1993.

CLIMATE AND DROUGHT

Glantz, M.H. *Currents of Change: El Niño's Impact on Climate and Society*. Cambridge and New York: Cambridge University Press, 1996.
Glantz, M.H., R.W. Katz, and N.Nicholls, eds. *Teleconnections: Linking Worldwide Climate Anomalies*. Cambridge and New York: Cambridge University Press, 1991.
Gordon, A.H. "The Random Nature of Drought: Mathematical and Physical Causes." *International Journal of Climatology* 13.5 (1993), 497–507. DOI: 10.1002/joc.3370130503.
Marsh, T.J., et al. *The 1988–92 Drought*. Wallingford, U.K.: Institute of Hydrology, 1994.
Nicholson, S.E., and I.M. Palao. "A Re-evaluation of Rainfall Variability in the Sahel." *International Journal of Climatology* 13.4 (1993), 371–389. DOI: 10.1002/joc.3370130403.
Wuethrich, B. "El Niño Goes Critical." *New Scientist* 145.1963 (February 4, 1995), 32–35.

DROUGHT IMPACTS

Binns, T., ed. *People and Environment in Africa*. Chichester, U.K., and New York: Wiley, 1995.
Cannel, M.G.R., and C.E.R. Pitairn. *Impacts of the Mild Winters and Hot Summers in the UK in 1988–1990*. London: Department of the Environment, HMSO, 1993.
Downing, T.E. *Climate Change and Vulnerable Places: Global Food Security and Country Studies in Zimbabwe, Kenya, Senegal, and Chile*. Environmental Change Unit Report 1. Oxford: University of Oxford, 1992.
Glantz, M.H., ed. *Drought and Hunger in Africa*. Cambridge: Cambridge University Press, 1987.
Glantz, M.H. *Drought Follows the Plow*. Cambridge: Cambridge University Press, 1994.
Mortimore, M. *Adapting To Drought: Farmers, Famines, and Desertification in West Africa*. Cambridge: Cambridge University Press, 1989.
Rozenzweig, C., and M.C. Parry. "Potential Impact of Climate Change on World Food Supply." *Nature* 367 (1994), 133–138. DOI: doi:10.1038/367133a0.
Thomas, D.S.G. "Sandstorm in a Teacup? Understanding Desertification." *Geographical Journal* 159.3 (1993), 318–331.
Wilhite, D.A., ed. *Drought*. 2 vols. London: Routledge, 2000.

—C. T. AGNEW

DUST STORMS

Dust storms, events in which visibility is reduced to less than 1 kilometer by wind-blown particles, are important environmental phenomena and have shown great variability in their incidence through time in response to environmental changes (Goudie, 1983). The consequences of dust-storm activity are legion, but particular interest has arisen recently in the possible role of atmospheric dust in modifying Pleistocene climates (Overpeck et al., 1996) and in contributing to future climatic changes (Andreae, 1996). Atmospheric dust affects air temperatures through absorption and scattering of solar radiation. [*See* Aerosols.] In addition, they may influence marine primary productivity and the drawdown of carbon dioxide from the atmosphere. Changes in atmospheric temperatures and in concentrations of potential condensation nuclei may affect convection and cloud formation, thereby modifying rainfall and possibly intensifying drought.

Dust deposition provides considerable quantities of nutrients to ocean surface waters and the seabed. Eolian (wind-blown) dust contains iron, the addition of which to the oceans may increase plankton productivity. Dust aerosols originating in the Sahara influence the nutrient dynamics and biogeochemical cycling of terrestrial and oceanic ecosystems. Moreover, the influence of dust extends as far as northern Europe, Amazonia, and the coral reefs of the Caribbean. African dust may be an efficient medium for transporting spores that can cause epidemics that diminish coral reef vitality, a good match having been found between times of coral-reef die-off and peak dust deposition. Dust storms also have many direct effects on humans. They can, for example, transport allergens and pathogens, create respiratory problems, and disrupt communications. They may also be a manifestation of desertification and of accelerated soil erosion.

DUST MOVEMENTS IN THE QUATERNARY

At certain times during the Pleistocene, the world was very dusty, as indicated by extensive deposits of loess, and the presence of large amounts of eolian dust in ocean cores and in ice cores from the poles and elsewhere. This dustiness, especially during cold glacial periods, may relate to a larger sediment source (e.g., areas of glacial outwash), changes in wind characteristics both in proximity to icecaps and in the trade-wind zone (Ruddiman, 1997), and the expansion of low-latitude deserts.

It is possible to obtain a long-term measure of dust additions to the oceans by studying the sedimentology of deep-sea cores (Rea, 1994). On the basis of cores from the Arabian Sea, Sirocko et al. (1991) suggested that dust additions were around 60% higher during glacials than in postglacial times. Likewise, also working in the Arabian Sea, Clemens and Prell (1990) found a positive correlation between global ice-volume and the accumulation rate and sediment size of dust material. Venkatarathnam and Biscaye (1977) confirmed this picture for a larger area of the Indian Ocean, and indicated that large dust inputs came from Arabia and Australia during the last glacial. In the Atlantic west of the Sahara at around 18,000 BP the amount of dust transported into the ocean was augmented by a factor of 2.5 (Tetzlaff et al., 1989, p. 198).

On a longer time scale there is some evidence that dust activity has increased as climate has deteriorated during the last few million years. In the Atlantic off West Africa, Pokras (1989) found clear evidence for increased dust input at 2.3–2.5 million years ago, while Schramm (1989) found that the largest increases in mass accumulation rates in the North Pacific occurred 2–3 million years ago. This coincides broadly with the initiation of Northern Hemisphere glaciation. However, no such link has been identified in the southern Pacific Ocean (Rea, 1989). The most comprehensive analysis of dust deposition in the oceans has been undertaken by Leinen and Heath (1981) using the sediments of the central part of the North Pacific. They have demonstrated that there were low rates of dust deposition from 50 to 25 million years ago. This, they believe, reflects the temperate, humid environment that appears to have been characteristic of the early Tertiary, and the lack of vigorous atmospheric circulation at that time. From 25 million to 7 million years ago, the rate of eolian accumulation on the ocean floor increased, but it accelerated greatly from 7 to 3 million years ago. However, it was around 2.5 million years ago that the most dramatic increase in eolian sedimentation occurred. This accompanied the onset of Northern Hemisphere glaciation.

DUST DEPOSITION AS RECORDED IN ICE CORES

Another major source of long-term information on rates of dust accretion is the record preserved in long ice cores retrieved from the polar icecaps (Fischer et al., 2007) or from high-altitude ice domes at lower altitudes.

Because they are generally far removed from source areas, the rates of accumulation are generally low, but studies of variations in microparticle concentrations with depth do provide insights into the relative dust loadings of the atmosphere in the last glacial and during the course of the Holocene. Thompson and Mosley-Thompson (1981) collected much of the published material available at the time they wrote and pointed out the great differences in microparticle concentrations between the late glacial and the postglacial. The ratio at Dome C ice core (East Antarctica) was 6:1, for the Byrd Station (West Antarctica) it was 3:1, and for Camp Century (Greenland) it was 12:1. Briat et al. (1982) maintained that at Dome C there was an increase in microparticle concentrations by a factor of 10–20 during the last glacial stage, and they attribute this to a large input of continental dust. The Dunde ice core from High Asia (Thompson et al., 1990) also shows very high dust loadings in the Late Glacial and a sudden falloff at the transition to the Holocene.

LOESS ACCUMULATION RATES

By measuring and dating sections in a silty, wind-blown material called loess it has been possible to estimate the rate at which dust accumulated on land during the Quaternary (see Table 1). [See Loess.] The data may somewhat underestimate total dust fluxes into an area because even at times of rapid loess accumulation there would have been concurrent losses of material as a result of fluvial and mass movement processes. Solution and compaction may also have occurred. The data show a range of values between 22 and 4,000 millimeters per thousand years, but Pye (1987, p. 265) believes that, at the maximum of the last glaciation (at about 18,000 BP), loess was probably accumulating at a rate of between 500 and 3,000 mm per thousand years, a rate he suggests was possibly unparalleled in previous Earth history. By contrast, he suggests that during the Holocene, dust deposition have been too low for significant thicknesses of loess to accumulate even though eolian additions to soils and ocean sediments have been appreciable. Pye also hypothesizes that rates of loess accumulation showed a tendency to increase during the course of the Quaternary. Average loess accumulation rates in China, Central Asia, and Europe were of the order of 20–60 mm per thousand years during the Matuyama epoch (2.60–0.78 million years ago), and of the order of 90–260 mm per thousand years during the Brunhes epoch (since 0.78 million years ago). He also points out that these long-term average rates disguise the fact that rates of loess deposition were one to two orders of magnitude higher during Pleistocene cold phases, and one or two orders of magnitude lower during the warmer interglacial phases when soil formation predominated.

DUST STORMS IN THE TWENTIETH CENTURY

The changes in temperature and precipitation conditions in the twentieth century influenced the development of dust storms. Probably the greatest incidence of dust storms occurs when climatic conditions and human pressures combine to make surfaces susceptible to wind attack.

Possibly the most famous case of soil erosion by deflation (wind removal) was the Dust Bowl of the 1930s in the United States (see Figures 1 and 2). This was caused in part by a series

TABLE 1. Loess Accumulation Rates for the Late Pleistocene

Location	Rate (millimeters per thousand years)
Negev (Israel)	70–150
Mississippi Valley (United States)	100–4,000
Uzbekistan	50–450
Tajikistan	60–290
Lanzhou (China)	250–260
Luochaun (China)	50 70
Czech Republic	90
Austria	22
Poland	750
New Zealand	2,000

From various sources in Pye, 1987, and Gerson and Amit, 1987.

of hot, dry years that depleted the vegetation cover and made the soils dry enough to be susceptible to wind erosion. The effects of this drought were gravely exacerbated by years of over-grazing and poor farming techniques, but perhaps the primary cause of the event was the rapid expansion of cereal cultivation in the Great Plains.

Dust storms remain a serious problem in various parts of the United States. In the San Joaquin Valley of California in 1977, for example, a dust storm caused extensive damage and erosion over an area of about 2,000 square kilometers. More than 25 million metric tons of soil was stripped from grazing land in 24 hours. While the combination of drought and a very high wind (as strong as 300 kilometers per hour) provided the predispos-ing natural conditions for the stripping to occur, overgrazing and the general lack of windbreaks in the agricultural land played a more significant role. In addition, broad areas of land had recently been stripped of vegetation, leveled, or plowed up prior to planting. Elsewhere in California, dust yield has been increased considerably by mining operations in dry lake beds (Wilshire, 1980).

A comparable acceleration of dust storm activity occurred in the former Soviet Union. After the Virgin Lands program of agricultural expansion in the 1950s, dust storm frequencies in the southern Omsk region increased on average by a factor of 2.5 and locally by factors of 5 to 6.

The increasing frequencies of Saharan and Sahelian dust events since the mid-1960s is revealed by data on dust storms observed at meteorological stations, satellite observations, and data on atmospheric dust concentrations and dust-deposition rates monitored at a distance from source areas (Goudie and Middleton, 1992; Goudie and Middleton, 2001). As rainfall has diminished, the frequency of dust haze has increased (Figure 3a). The frequency of dust events also depends on the deflational power of the wind. In the Sahel there is some evidence that this increased between 1970 and 1984. Another climatic forcing-factor that has attracted recent attention is the

North Atlantic Oscillation (NAO) (Figure 3b). Between 1982 and 1996 there was a similarity in trends between atmospheric optical depth, dust concentrations, and the NAO index (Chiapello et al., 2005).

Australia experiences considerable variation in dust-storm activity from year to year, and agricultural degradation of land surfaces in areas like the Mallee may have had an impact on dust storm frequencies. The variability of storm frequency over the last four decades of the twentieth century was high (Figure 4). There is a close relationship between years of high dust-storm frequency and the occurrence of drought (McTainsh et al., 2005). The decline in dust storm activity over central eastern Australia, which commenced in the mid-1970s, was due to a decrease in postfrontal south to southeast winds, and such cir-culation changes are themselves related to changes in the Pacific Decadal Oscillation (PDO).

Various anthropogenic reasons have also been forwarded to explain the low frequencies of the 1970s and early 1980s, includ-ing a reduction in rabbit numbers, the adoption of minimum-tillage techniques, and an increase in land cover as a result of the invasion of woody weeds. Nevertheless, the occurrence of drought seems likely to be a stronger determinant of dustiness, the 1970s and 80s having been decades with relatively few drought periods. The droughts of 1994–95 and 2002 were clearly reflected in increased dust storm activity.

The changing frequency of dust storms during the period of meteorological observations has been discussed by a number of authors in the context of East Asia (Figure 5). In Mongolia, an increasing trend from the 1960s to the 1980s has been identified (Natsagdorj et al., 2003), with an approximately threefold increase over that period, followed by a downward trend in the 1990s. Human activities accounted for the first of these two phases, but an increase of precipitation may have caused the reversal in trend during the latter phase. For the period since 1954, the highest frequency of severe dust storms in China occurred in the 1950s, and the lowest in the 1990s. From the 1950s to the 1970s dust storms were twice as prevalent as they were after the mid-1980s (Zhou and Zhang, 2003). This can be attributed to a reduced meridional temperature gradient, result-ing in a lower cyclone frequency in Northern China. On the other hand, some workers have attributed the negative trend in dust storm frequency to the planting of a vast belt of forests— "The Great Green Wall"—across the northern arid lands of China. In the early twenty-first century reduced precipitation and concomitant decrease in vegetation cover caused a resur-gence of dust events. There also appears to have been greater atmospheric instability, leading to stronger winds and thus more dust storms.

THE EOLIAN ENVIRONMENT IN A WARMER WORLD

Given the impact that past climatic variability has had on soil erosion by wind, it is likely that global warming will have a major impact as well. Changes in precipitation and

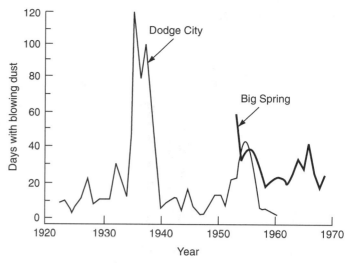

Dust Storms. FIGURE 2. Frequency of Dust-Storm Days at Dodge City, Kansas (1922–1961) and Big Spring, Texas (1953–1970).

(After Gillette and Hanson, 1989.)

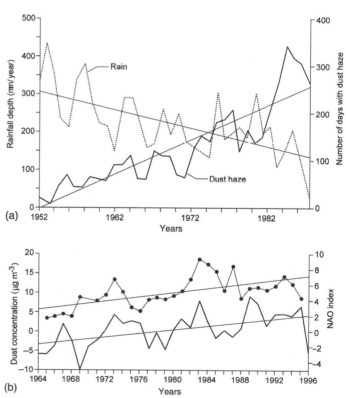

Dust Storms. FIGURE 3. Changes in dust conditions in the Sahara and Sahel.

(a) The increase in dust haze conditions as rainfall has decreased, at Gao.
(b) The relationship between atmospheric dust concentrations at Barbados and the strength of the North Atlantic Oscillation. (From Goudie and Middleton, 2006, fig. 7.7.)

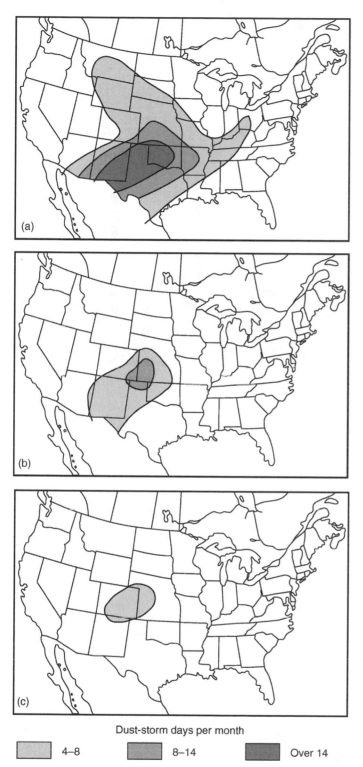

Dust-storm days per month

4–8 8–14 Over 14

Dust Storms. FIGURE 1. The concentration of dust storms (number of days per month) in the United States in 1936, illustrating the extreme localization over the high plains of Texas, Colorado, Oklahoma, and Kansas: (a) March, (b) April, and (c) May.

(After Goudie, 1983.)

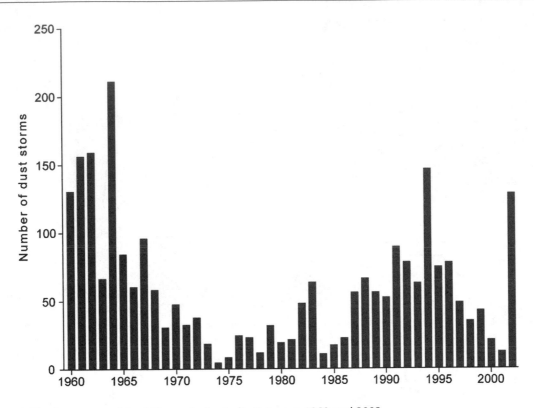

DUST STORMS. FIGURE 4. The Frequency of Dust Storms in Australia Between 1960 and 2002.
(Modified after McTainsh et al. 2005, fig. 5.)

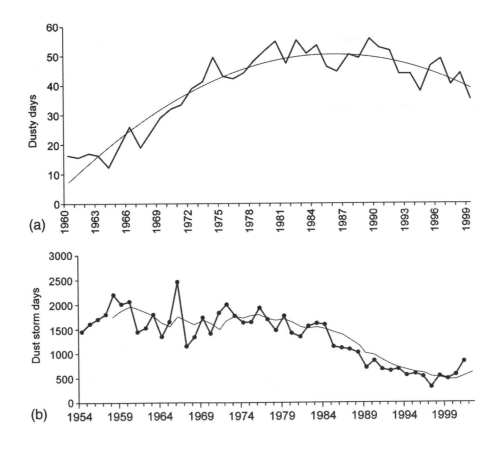

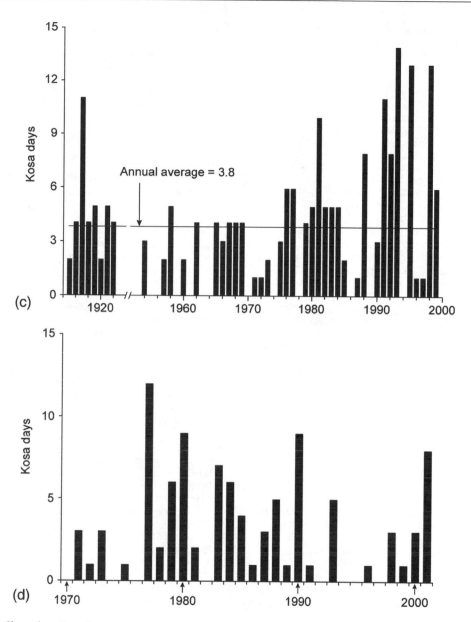

Dust Storms. FIGURE 5. Changing Dust Storm Frequencies in East Asia.

(a) Number of dusty days in Mongolia, (b) number of dusty days in China, (c) Asian dust observed in Seoul, Korea, (d) Asian dust observed in Yamanashi, Japan. (From various sources in Goudie and Middleton, 2006, fig. 7.15.)

evapotranspiration rates will probably have a marked impact on the eolian environment. Rates of deflation, and sand and dust entrainment are closely related to soil moisture conditions and the extent of vegetation cover. Areas that are marginal in terms of their stability with respect to eolian processes will be particularly susceptible; this is evident, for example, in recent studies of the semiarid portions of the United States (e.g., the High Plains). Repeatedly through the Holocene these areas have switched from states of vegetated stability to states of drought-induced surface instability.

It is apparent from the general circulation models that, with global climate change, there are likely to be substantial changes in eolian activity (Muhs and Matt, 1993; Stetler and Gaylord, 1996), with dust-storm incidence in the High Plains and the Canadian Prairies (Wheaton, 1990) being comparable to that of the devastating Dust Bowl years of the 1930s.

[*See also* Aerosols; Climate Models; Desertification; Global Warming; *and* Soils.]

BIBLIOGRAPHY

Andreae, M.O. "Raising Dust in the Greenhouse." *Nature* 380 (1996), 389–390. DOI: 10.1038/380389a0.

Briat, M., et al. "Late Glacial Input of Eolian Continental Dust in the Dome C Ice Core: Additional Evidence from Individual Microparticle Analysis." *Annals of Glaciology* 3 (1982), 27–31.

Chiapello, I., C. Moulin, and J.M. Prospero. "Understanding the Long-Term Variability of African Dust Transport across the Atlantic as Recorded in Both Barbados Surface Concentrations and Large-Scale Total Ozone Mapping

Spectrometer (Toms) Optical Thickness". *Journal of Geophysical Research* 110, D18S10 (2005). DOI: 10.1029/2004JD005132.

Clemens, S.C., and W.L. Prell. "Late Pleistocene Variability of Arabian Sea Summer Monsoon Winds and Continental Aridity: Eolian Records from the Lithogenic Component of Deep Sea Sediments." *Palaeoceanography* 5.2 (1990), 109–145.

Fischer H., et al. "Glacial/Interglacial Changes in Mineral Dust and Sea-Salt Records in Polar Ice Cores: Sources, Transport, and Deposition. *Reviews of Geophysics* 45, RG1002 (2007). DOI: 10.1029/2005RG000192.

Gerson, R., and R. Amit. "Rates and Modes of Dust Accretion and Deposition in an Arid Region—The Negev, Israel." In *Desert Sediments Ancient and Modern*, edited by L.E. Frostick and I. Reid, pp. 157–169. Oxford: Blackwell Scientific, 1987. DOI: 10.1144/GSL.SP.1987.035.01.11.

Gillette, D.A., and K.J. Hanson. "Spatial and Temporal Variability of Dust Production Caused by Wind Erosion in the United States." *Journal of Geophysical Research* 94.D2 (1989), 2197–2206.

Goudie, A.S. "Dust Storms in Space and Time." *Progress in Physical Geography* 7.4 (1983), 502 530. DOI: 10.1177/030913338300700402.

Goudie, A.S., and N.J. Middleton. "The Changing Frequency of Dust Storms through Time." *Climatic Change* 20.3 (1992), 197–225. DOI: 10.1007/BF00139839. A study of meteorological records of dust in the past few decades.

———. "Saharan Dust Storms: Nature and Consequences." *Earth-Science Reviews* 56.1–4 (2001), 179–204. DOI: 10.1016/S0012-8252(01)00067-8.

———. *Desert Dust in the Global System*. Berlin and New York: Springer, 2006. A comprehensive, modern review.

Leinen, M., and G.R. Heath. "Sedimentary Indicators of Atmospheric Activity in the Northern Hemisphere during the Cenozoic." *Palaeogeography, Palaeoclimatology, Palaeoecology* 36.1–2 (1981), 1–21. DOI: 10.1016/0031-0182(81)90046-8.

McTainsh, G.H., et al. "The 23rd October 2002 Dust Storm in Eastern Australia: Characteristics and Meteorological Conditions." *Atmospheric Environment* 39.7 (2005), 1227–1236.

Muhs, D.R., and P.B. Maat. "The Potential Response of Eolian Sands to Greenhouse Warming and Precipitation Reduction on the Great Plains of the U.S.A." *Journal of Arid Environments* 25.4 (1993), 351–361.

Natsagdorj, L., D. Jugder, and Y.S. Chung. "Analysis of Dusts Storms Observed in Mongolia during 1937–1999." *Atmospheric Environment* 37.9–10 (2003), 1401–1411. DOI: 10.1016/S1352-2310(02)01023-3.

Overpeck, J., et al. "Possible Role of Dust-Induced Regional Warming in Abrupt Climate Change during the Last Glacial Period." *Nature* 384 (1996), 447–449. DOI: 10.1038/384447a0.

Pokras, E.M. "Pliocene History of South Saharan/Sahelian Aridity: Record of Freshwater Diatoms (Genus *Melosira*) and Opal Phytoliths, ODP Sites 662 and 664." In *Paleoclimatology and Paleometeorology: Modern and Past Patterns of Global Atmospheric Transport*, edited by M. Leinen and M. Sarnthein, pp. 795–804. Dordrecht, Netherlands, and Boston, Mass.: Kluwer, 1989.

Pye, K. *Aeolian Dust and Dust Deposits*. London: Academic Press, 1987. A comprehensive general review.

Rea, D.K. "Geologic Record of Atmospheric Circulation on Tectonic Time Scales." In *Paleoclimatology and Paleometeorology: Modern and Past Patterns of Global Atmospheric Transport*, edited by M. Leinen and M. Sarnthein, pp. 841–857. Dordrecht, Netherlands, and Boston, Mass.: Kluwer, 1989.

Rea, D.K. "The Paleoclimatic Record Provided by Eolian Deposition in the Deep Sea: The Geologic History of Wind." *Reviews of Geophysics* 32.2 (1994), 159–195.

Ruddiman, W.F. "Tropical Atlantic Terrigenous Fluxes Since 25,000 Yrs BP." *Marine Geology* 136 (1997), 189–207.

Schramm, C.T. "Cenozoic Climatic Variation Recorded by Quartz and Clay Minerals in North Pacific Sediments." In *Paleoclimatology and Paleometeorology: Modern and Past Patterns of Global Atmospheric Transport*, edited by M. Leinen and M. Sarnthein, pp. 805–839. Dordrecht, Netherlands, and Boston, Mass.: Kluwer, 1989.

Sirocko, F., et al. "Atmospheric Summer Circulation and Coastal Upwelling in the Arabian Sea during the Holocene and the Last Glaciation." *Quaternary Research* 36.1 (1991), 72–93. DOI: 10.1016/0033-5894(91)90018-Z.

Stetler, L.L., and D.R. Gaylord. "Evaluating Eolian-Climatic Interactions Using a Regional Climate Model from Hanford, Washington (USA)." *Geomorphology* 17.1–3 (1996), 99–113.

Tetzlaff, G., W. Janssen, and L.J. Adams. "Aeolian Dust Transport in West Africa." In *Paleoclimatology and Paleometeorology: Modern and Past Patterns of Global Atmospheric Transport*, edited by M. Leinen and M. Sarnthein, pp. 1985–2203. Dordrecht, Netherlands, and Boston, Mass.: Kluwer, 1989.

Thompson, L.G., and E. Mosley-Thompson. "Microparticle Concentration Variations Linked with Climatic Change: Evidence from Polar Ice Cores." *Science* 212 (1981), 812–815. DOI: 10.1126/science.212.4496.812.

Thompson, L.G., et al. "Glacial Stage Ice-Core Records from the Subtropical Dunde Ice Cap, China." *Annals of Glaciology* 14 (1990), 288–297.

Venkatarathnam, K., and P.E. Biscaye. "Distribution and Origin of Quartz in the Sediments of the Indian Ocean." *Journal of Sedimentary Petrology* 47.2 (1977), 642–649.

Wheaton, E.E. "Frequency and Severity of Drought and Dust Storms." *Canadian Journal of Agricultural Economics* 38 (1990), 695–700.

Wilshire, H.G. "Human Causes of Accelerated Wind Erosion in California's Deserts." In *Thresholds in Geomorphology*, edited by D. R. Coates and J. D. Vitek, pp. 415–433. London, U.K., and Boston, Mass.: Allen and Unwin; Stroudsburg, Pa.: Dowden, Hutchinson, and Ross, 1980.

Wilshire, H.G., et al. "Field Observations of the December 1977 Wind Storm, San Joaquin Valley, California." In *Desert Dust: Origin, Characteristics, and Effect on Man*, edited by T.L. Péwé, pp. 233–251. Boulder, Colo.: Geological Society of America, 1981.

Zhou, Z., and G. Zhang. "Typical Severe Dust Storms in Northern China during 1954–2002." *Chinese Science Bulletin* 48.21 (2003), 2366–2370. DOI: 10.1360/03WD0029.

—Andrew S. Goudie

E

EARTH SYSTEM SCIENCE

Earth System Science (ESS) seeks to understand major patterns, processes, and interactions of the main components of planet Earth—the atmosphere, oceans, fresh water, rocks, soils, and biosphere (Lawton, 2001). It also assesses the involvement and importance of human activities (Steffen et al., 2004).

ANTECEDENTS

Geography has long been a holistic discipline concerned with the interactions with the natural environment and their relationship to human (Pitman, 2005). However, certain developments have recently occurred in science as a whole that have contributed to the development of ESS. These include:

- An increasing appreciation of the pervasiveness of human activities in modifying the natural environment, especially over the last 300 years (Turner et al., 1990; Goudie, 2006).
- A global view of the planet provided since the 1960s by the development of remote sensing from space. This provides not only a global perspective on climate patterns, land cover, etc., but also enables monitoring of global change.
- The development of systems thinking (e.g. Chorley, 1964) and our ability, following the development of information technology, to analyze huge quantities of data and to develop models (e.g., general circulation models) at the global scale. [See Climate Models and Uncertainty.]
- The adoption since the 1960s of plate tectonics as a major global model.
- The recognition of the importance of the Gaia hypothesis based on the work of Lovelock and collaborators (Lovelock, 1979).
- A growing appreciation of global connections in the ocean-atmosphere system, through a study of such phenomena as teleconnections and the thermohaline circulation.
- The development of high-resolution, securely dated, long-term records of environmental change derived from the analysis of ocean and ice cores (Anderson et al., 2007).
- Social, economic, and political globalization.
- A series of global programs such as the International Geosphere Biosphere Programme and the Intergovernmental Panel on Climate Change.

AN EXAMPLE

An example of one component of ESS is dust derived from desert surfaces. It is blown off old lake beds and alluvial spreads depending on the availability of susceptible materials, moisture conditions of the surface, wind strength, land cover and the degree of human disturbance. It rises into the atmosphere and is transported as far as several thousand kilometers to locations as distant from source as the poles, rainforests, and ocean islands. It settles out as a result of dry and wet depositional processes, creating loess sheets, modifying soil characteristics, and fertilizing vegetation and ocean waters. It may transport various pathogens and allergens that can affect the health of coral reefs and of human populations. It modifies the radiative budget of the atmosphere, provides cloud condensation nuclei, and delivers nutrients (such as iron) to plankton, which in turn draws down carbon dioxide from the atmosphere and affects dimethyl sulfide (DMS) levels, thereby affecting the climate. Such climate change may itself change dust emissions at their source. This illustrates the interactions and feedbacks that have global implications (Goudie and Middleton, 2006).

THE AMSTERDAM DECLARATION

A conference in July 2001 produced the Amsterdam Declaration on Global Change (Steffen et al., 2004, p. 298). It stresses that the Earth System operates as a single, self-regulating system, that human impacts may be equal to the great forces of nature in their extent and impact, that global change cannot be understood in terms of a simple cause-effect paradigm, that Earth System dynamics are characterized by critical thresholds and abrupt changes, and that changes currently taking place are unprecedented.

BIBLIOGRAPHY

Anderson, D.E., A.S. Goudie and A.G. Parker. *Global Environments through the Quaternary*. Oxford: Oxford University Press, 2007.
Chorley, R.J. "Geomorphology and General Systems Theory." U.S. Geological Survey Professional Paper 500B, 1964.
Goudie, A.S. *The Human Impact on the Natural Environment*. 6th ed. Oxford, U.K., and Malden, Mass.: Blackwell, 2005.
Goudie, A.S., and N.J. Middleton. *Desert Dust in the Global System*. Berlin and New York: Springer, 2006.
Lawton, J. "Earth System Science." *Science* 292 (2001), 1965. DOI: 10.1126/science.292.5524.1965.
Lovelock, J. *Gaia, a New Look at Life on Earth*. Oxford and New York: Oxford University Press, 1979.
Pitman, A.J. "On the Role of Geography in Earth System Science." *Geoforum* 36.2 (2005), 137–148. DOI: 10.1016/j.geoforum.2004.11.008.
Steffen, W., et al., eds. *Global Change and the Earth System*. Berlin and New York: Springer, 2004.
Turner, B.L., et al., eds. *The Earth as Transformed by Human Action: Global and Regional Changes in the Biosphere over the Past 300 Years*. Cambridge and New York: Cambridge University Press, 1990.

—ANDREW S. GOUDIE

TABLE 1. Ecological Footprint and Biocapacity

	Total Ecological Footprint	*Biological Capacity*	*Ecological Deficit (−) or Reserve (+)*
World	2.2 ha/person	1.8 ha/person	−0.5
High Income	6.4	3.3	−3.1
Mid Income	1.9	2.1	+0.2
Low Income	0.8	0.7	−0.1

SOURCE: Global Footprint Network (http://www.footprintnetwork.org) [*See also*: Carbon Footprint; Ecosystems; Environmental Performance Index; Fisheries; *and* Sustainable Growth]

ECOLOGICAL FOOTPRINT

The ecological footprint is a measure of how much biologically productive land and water an individual, population, or activity requires in order to produce all the resources it consumes and all the wastes it generates (using prevailing technology and resource management practices). The measure, indirectly, reveals the magnitude of consumption of food and manufactured products. The units used are global hectares and hectares per person.

According to the organization Global Footprint Network, most countries—and especially the more industrialized countries—show ecological deficits, as does the world as a whole: that means their footprints exceed their biological capacity, which is defined as the capacity of ecosystems to produce useful biological materials and to absorb waste materials generated by humans.

If a country shows an ecological deficit, that country is either importing biocapacity (e.g., grain) through trade or is liquidating biological assets.

For the world as a whole there is, of course, no possibility of trading. In 1961 the world used only 49% of its biological capacity, and therefore showed ecological reserves, but in 2001 it used 121% of capacity, an ecological deficit of 21%. In 2003 the deficit was over 22%.

For more on the Global Footprint Network and its methodology, see the website below. It includes a comprehensive table, "Ecological Footprint and Biocapacity, 2006," that lists regions and countries, their footprints deduced from a number of agricultural and other activities, their biological capacities, and the net result for each, expressed as ecological deficits or reserves. Highlights from that compilation (Table 1) show the heavy impact of countries in the high-income group.

—DAVID J. CUFF

ECOLOGICAL INTEGRITY

Recent recommendations have been that environmental public policies should be based on concepts of ecological integrity. The recommendations come from scientists and others concerned about the threats of human activities to ecosystems and species, and from philosophers attempting to derive a more suitable ethic for the relationships between humans and the nonhuman environment. Proponents of "ecological integrity" believe that it offers a better prospect for the management of human and environmental systems than do the concepts of "environmental health" or "sustainable development," which they view as too strongly oriented toward human-dominated systems.

Although ecological integrity has been proposed as a norm for public policies and decision-making, the concept is relatively new, and therefore the scientific and philosophical rationales undergirding it have not been fully developed. Hence, proponents of ecological integrity are attempting to relate ecosystem-management approaches and the goal to restore integrity to moral principles, that they might serve as a basis for public policy.

Despite recent interest in ecological integrity, the concept is not defined succinctly or precisely. Kay (1991) has proposed that ecological integrity encompasses three facets of ecosystems: the ability to maintain optimum operations under normal conditions, the ability to cope with changes in environmental conditions (i.e., stress), and the ability to continue the process of self-organization, that is, the ability to continue to evolve, develop, and proceed with the cycle of birth, death, and renewal.

By "optimum operations," Kay means the situation in which a balance is maintained between the external environmental fluctuations that tend to disorganize ecosystems and the organizing thermodynamic forces that make ecosystems more effective. It is not clear what Kay means by "normal conditions" and hence to what extent ecological integrity can or should refer to human interventions in ecosystems. He does, however, believe that integrity includes nonlinear ecosystems whose properties or behavior cannot be explained or predicted by knowledge of lower levels of hierarchical organization within them. These ecosystems have multiple organizational states and processes based on nonequilibrium paradigms that include the following notions: ecosystems are open, processes rather than end points are emphasized, various temporal and spatial scales are emphasized, and episodic disturbances are recognized.

Westra (1994) proposes a definition wherein ecosystems are said to have ecological integrity when they can maintain operations under conditions as free as possible from human intervention, the ability to withstand anthropocentric changes in environmental conditions (i.e., stress), and the ability to continue the process of self-organization on an ongoing basis.

She argues that concepts inherent in ecological integrity emerge from continuing scientific, legal, and ethical analysis and that while they correspond in her mind to more or less "pristine nature," they cannot be described or predicted precisely because ecosystems are constantly evolving. Westra's definition includes the following: ecosystem health, which may apply to some nonpristine or degraded ecosystems provided they function successfully; ecosystems' abilities to regenerate themselves and withstand stress, especially nonanthropogenic stress; ecosystems' optimum capacity for undiminished developmental options; and ecosystems' abilities to continue their ongoing change and development unconstrained by human interruptions past or present. One of the problems with Westra's definition is that it is impossible to determine either theoretically or practically what constitutes a "natural" ecosystem (Callicott, 1991). Cairns (1977) defines ecological integrity as "the maintenance of the community structure and function characteristic of a particular locale or deemed satisfactory to society." Karr (1992) defines ecological integrity as "the capability of supporting and maintaining a balanced, integrated, adaptive community of organisms having a species composition, diversity, and functional organization comparable to that of natural habitats of the region."

While recognizing that the characterization of ecological integrity in more precise terms is difficult, Noss (1995) nevertheless proposes that the concept can be made operational by selecting measurable and quantifiable indicators that correspond to the ecological qualities we associate with integrity.

According to Kay and Schneider (1995), ecosystems can respond to environmental changes in five qualitatively different ways: after undergoing some initial structural and functional changes, they can operate in the same manner as before the changes; they can operate with an increase or decrease in the same structures they had before the changes; they can operate with the emergence of new structures that replace or augment existing structures; different ecosystems with significantly different structures can emerge; and ecosystems can collapse with little or no regeneration. Although ecosystems can respond to environmental changes in one of these ways, there is no inherent or predetermined state to which they will return. Further, none of the above ways indicates a priori whether a loss of integrity has occurred. One problem with this view is that it would not be helpful to decision makers because it accepts all ecosystem responses to change as constituting integrity, with the exception of total collapse, which occurs rarely and is clearly undesirable. Consequently, while in theory science can inform decision makers about the responses of ecosystems to environmental change, it cannot provide a scientific or so-called objective basis for deciding whether one change is more desirable than another. In other words, the selection of criteria to use in such a decision must be based on human judgment regarding the acceptability of a particular change.

Regier (1993) provides an abstract definition stating that ecological integrity exists when an ecosystem is perceived to be in a state of well-being. In part, Regier stresses that a more precise definition of ecological integrity is dependent on people's perspectives of what constitutes complete ecosystems, as many of the aforementioned definitions demonstrate. In addition to reflecting the concerns and values of scientists, definitions of ecological integrity also must reflect various social and ethical values relevant for public-policy decisions regarding the protection of ecosystems. One reason for the inclusion of these various values is that there is no a priori scientific definition of ecological integrity, and therefore the concept encompasses perspectives or ways of viewing the world that inevitably reflect value judgments. The ambiguity of ecological integrity is a recognition that its definition, like that of many other ecological concepts, is determined in part on the basis of value judgments and not solely on so-called value-free or precisely defined scientific criteria.

While apparently sympathetic to the attempt to use concepts of ecological integrity as a basis for public policy and decision-making, several commentators have questioned the extent to which this can be done at present. Shrader-Frechette and McCoy (1993), Shrader-Frechette (1995), and Lemons (1996) maintain that the methods and tools of ecology are too general and limited in their precision and predictive capabilities. They argue that the value of ecology is primarily heuristic and capable of providing useful information for decision-making if studies are based on practical case studies and not on generalizable theories. Unless the problem of scientific uncertainty is overcome, concepts of ecological integrity probably will remain largely philosophical. In any case, before using ecological integrity as a basis for public policies, further work is required to clarify the concept's scientific, philosophical, and practical dimensions.

BIBLIOGRAPHY

Cairns, J. "Quantification of Biological Integrity." In *The Integrity of Water*, edited by R. K. Ballentine and L. J. Guarraia, pp. 171–187. Washington, D.C.: U.S. Environmental Protection Agency, Office of Water and Hazardous Materials, 1977.

Callicott, J.B. "The Wilderness Idea Revisited: The Sustainable Development Alternative." *The Environmental Professional* 13 (1991), 235–247.

Karr, J.R. "Ecological Integrity: Protecting Earth's Life Support Systems." In *Ecosystem Health*, edited by R. Costanza, B. G. Norton, and B. D. Haskell, pp. 223–238. Washington, D.C.: Island Press, 1992.

Kay, J. "A Nonequilibrium Thermodynamics Framework for Discussing Ecosystem Integrity." *Environmental Management* 15.4 (1991), 483–495. DOI: 10.1007/BF02394739.

Kay, J.J., and E. Schneider. "Embracing Complexity: The Challenge of the Ecosystem Approach." In *Perspectives on Ecological Integrity*, edited by L. Westra and J. Lemons, pp. 49–59. Dordrecht, The Netherlands, and Boston, Mass.: Kluwer, 1995.

Lemons, J., ed. *Scientific Uncertainty and Environmental Problem-Solving*. Cambridge, Mass.: Blackwell, 1996.

Lemons, J., L. Westra, and R. Goodland, eds. *Ecological Sustainability and Integrity: Concepts and Approaches*. Dordrecht, The Netherlands, and Boston, Mass.: Kluwer, 1998.

Noss, R.F. "Ecological Integrity and Sustainability: Buzzwords in Conflict?" In *Perspectives on Ecological Integrity*, edited by L. Westra and J. Lemons, pp. 60–76. Dordrecht, The Netherlands, and Boston, Mass.: Kluwer, 1995.

Regier, H.A. "The Notion of Natural and Cultural Integrity." In *Ecological Integrity and the Management of Ecosystems*, edited by S. Woodley, J. Francis, and J. Kay, pp. 3–18. Delray Beach, Fla.: St. Lucie Press, 1993.

Shrader-Frechette, K. S., and E. D. McCoy. *Method in Ecology*. Cambridge and New York: Cambridge University Press, 1993.

Shrader-Frechette, K. S. "Hard Ecology, Soft Ecology, and Ecosystem Integrity." In *Perspectives on Ecological Integrity*, edited by L. Westra and J. Lemons, pp. 125–145. Dordrecht, The Netherlands, and Boston, Mass.: Kluwer, 1995.

Westra, L. *An Environmental Proposal for Ethics: The Principle of Integrity.* Lanham, Md.: Rowman and Littlefield, 1994.

—John Lemons

ECOLOGICAL VALUE OF PARKS AND PRESERVES

Today in parks and preserves we expect to continue our traditional uses of: harvesting timber and using nature's products (for example, bark and seeds); hunting game animals and grazing domesticated animals, which may be indigenous or introduced species; researching, studying, and photographing plants and animals in a "living museum"; hiking as individuals or conducting group tours led by amateur or professional guides; and continuing our lives without visiting an area, but content in the knowledge that it is there for others to enjoy and for the benefit of future generations. However, all of these uses are dependent on maintaining viable ecological functions of parks and preserves and ensuring that biological diversity is protected. We also need to understand the dynamics of natural systems and the influence of human-induced environmental change.

THE ECOLOGICAL FUNCTION OF PARKS AND PRESERVES

Parks and preserves provide important ecological functions that make them an indispensable element in the conservation of global biodiversity. First, parks and preserves play significant roles in maintaining those ecological processes that depend on natural ecosystems, such as purifying water and air by natural ecological processes. In addition, the natural functioning of nutrient cycles and energy flows is facilitated by parks and preserves. Some of these products may also move outside the protected area and benefit the surrounding landscape, for example the movement of a wildlife population or the flow of rivers through catchments. The role of protected areas in maintaining ecological processes is crucial since it is almost impossible to study ecological relationships within ecosystems that are under constant stress from human activities in areas beyond the boundaries of parks and preserves.

Second, parks and preserves help to preserve species diversity and genetic variations within species. Protected areas therefore play an important part in preserving representative samples of plant and animal populations. This role is especially important when considering global change, since genetically poor species are highly vulnerable to environmental changes. Hence parks and preserves help prevent irreversible damage to natural ecosystems.

Third, parks and preserves provide benchmarks by which the impact of humans on the environment can be better understood and compared. Natural or near-natural parks and preserves provide ecological baselines for measuring change within parks and in nearby areas.

Finally, protected areas maintain the productive processes of ecosystems and safeguard habitats critical for the sustainable use of species. Thus the natural productive processes in parks and preserves can be used as models for developing sustainable utilization strategies outside park boundaries.

Our expectations of activities and opportunities in parks, however, are changing as technology changes. For example, the use of four-wheel-drive vehicles has increased the ability to intrude into previously inaccessible landscapes, with resultant effects such as weed and pest introduction, erosion of tracks, and petrochemical pollution of waterways. Now we have the capacity to "tread more lightly" by using helicopters to reach remote places, even though there are new adverse effects (such as noise). The development of new technology often means that traditional approaches to calculating carrying capacity of areas need to be rethought.

Other changes are occurring because indigenous people want recognition of the need to link their identity to place and history. They also want to be partners in managing parks and preserves or species of importance to their traditional ways of life.

Business is becoming increasingly involved in management of protected areas—concessions to provide transport, food, and accommodation; revenue-generating activities along with operational services such as management of water supply, sewerage, and road/path systems. Sponsorship of places and species for protection or research is also important to cash-strapped government management systems.

EFFECTS OF HUMAN ACTIVITIES

Some activities have local or regional effects on the environment: for example, lakes polluted by boating activity, poor management of facilities, and overharvesting of local species. However, environmental effects on national parks and preserves are becoming increasingly global in nature as the Earth's landscapes are extensively transformed, including systemic changes in water, vegetation, soil, atmosphere, and energy- and material-flows. Collectively, these changes are referred to as global change. Global change should not be equated with climate change because the former encompasses both changes in climate and large-scale changes in land use associated with industrialization, urbanization, ozone depletion, deforestation, and large-scale agriculture.

Global change presents enormous challenges to the conservation of parks and preserves and to the protection of biodiversity generally. While we are already observing the effects of landscape change on parks and preserves, the impacts of climatic change on these protected areas are generally only predictions (for example, the estimate that a 1°C change in temperature is equivalent to a 2° change in latitude in the mid-latitudes). As more land is exploited and suffers land-use change from population pressure, parks and preserves are becoming increasingly insular "habitat islands" in a sea of human-dominated or human-altered landscapes. This trend is expected to intensify as global population increases. Possible impacts on parks and preserves from the insularization process include elimination of potential sources of immigrant species; a reduction in immigrant species by conversion of natural landscapes between habitat patches and preserves; and the removal of vital resources outside reserve boundaries upon which species depend for survival. The insularization process may also create a situation in which much of the world's terrestrial biota is confined to national parks and preserves.

Scientists investigating the implications of climate change for species survival predict that the resulting changes in habitats would cause the ranges of many species to shift outside the boundaries of parks and refuges now established to protect them. For instance, climatic changes in the drier critical Mediterranean regions in southern Europe, the Levant, and North Africa could accelerate the desertification process, causing a rapid shift of the subdeserts and desert biomes far into the Mediterranean region of Israel and elsewhere. A. P. Dobson (1996) points out that climatic changes may already be apparent in the Everglades National Park in Florida, where the area of the park decreases by 25 square kilometers for every 30 centimeters of mean sea level rise. As a result, endangered marshland species of the park are being trapped between the rising sea and the large human settlements inland.

It is certain that species and ecosystems contained within protected areas will be affected by climate change (for example, since many protected areas are now "islands" of habitat to which species are closely adapted, climate change could cause extinctions among reserve species without being compensated by the immigration of "new" species). It is also unrealistic to expect boundaries of existing protected areas to change very much because they are usually surrounded by more intensive human land uses that limit changes.

CONSERVING BIODIVERSITY IN PARKS AND PRESERVES

The protection of habitats is considered the best approach to protecting species and thus conserving global biodiversity. Most nations have established legal means for protecting habitats that are important for conserving biodiversity, and these protected areas include national parks and preserves. The growth in the number and area of formally protected areas during the past thirty years has been considerable, although the rate of growth has slowed significantly since 1980. J. A. McNeely and J. Harrison (1994) have compiled a detailed inventory of formally protected areas for the International Union for Conservation of Nature (IUCN) and classified them in terms of international criteria.

The extent of protection varies greatly from one region to another: from 2.8% of land area in North Africa and the Middle East to 12.6% in North America. Although these percentages are regional generalizations and therefore conceal variations within a region, there are significant gaps in the extent of protected areas and in the protection of global biodiversity. For instance, in *Global Biodiversity Assessment* (Heywood and Watson, 1996), several authors estimate that the total worldwide extent of protected areas needs to be increased by at least three times if global biodiversity is to be managed over the long term in an environmentally sound way.

Furthermore, efforts by the IUCN to establish a global protected-area system that would ensure adequate representation of the full range of biome types have shown that particular attention should be paid to further development of protected areas in temperate grassland regions and in the major lake systems. Studies of the extent of parks and preserves in South America and East Africa have shown that the area of land set aside to protect biodiversity is only a small fraction of the total area of natural habitat (including tropical forests, savannas, and wetlands) that is being converted to agriculture or harvested for timber. Furthermore, most of the parks and preserves in these continents are only around 10–30 square kilometers in size, and some of the largest parks and preserves in those areas are located in desert or mountain areas that contain unique collections of species but at very low densities. Dobson believes that only 3.5% of those parks and preserves and only 5–10% of national parks in tropical areas may be large enough to maintain their present level of biodiversity. Such statistics highlight the need for more national parks and preserves of sufficient size throughout the world for the protection of global biodiversity.

Much of the current research has concentrated on terrestrial biodiversity, despite the fact that 71% of the Earth's surface and much of its biodiversity is found in oceans, coastal waters, and estuaries. About 60% of the human population lives within 60 kilometers of the coast, and much of the oceans' productive coastal margin has been strongly affected by human exploitation (for example, many marine fisheries are unsustainable because of overexploitation). The critical need to conserve and sustainably use marine and coastal biological resources was recognized by IUCN, the United Nations Environment Programme, and the World Wildlife Fund (World Conservation Union, 1991). All of the marine regions have inadequate representation of biogeographic variation and detailed levels of biodiversity. For instance, in the Mediterranean region, where only 6% of the coastline is protected, some of the most crucial ecosystems—the seagrass meadows and the wetlands—urgently require protection (McNeely and Harrison, 1994).

However, the setting aside of parks and preserves, both terrestrial and marine, does not necessarily protect biodiversity. Many parks and wilderness areas are bordered by other public lands, which are open to consumptive development, or by unregulated private lands. Since this trend is expected to intensify, parks and preserves will succeed only to the extent that the areas themselves are managed effectively, and to the extent that the management of the surrounding landscape is compatible with the objectives of the protected areas. This will require an integrated approach to the management of parks and preserves in which protected areas become part of larger regional schemes to ensure biological and social sustainability.

Integrated management would provide for the successful protection of marine biodiversity. Often, coastal environmental and resource policies and management approaches have concentrated on specific activities and resources or the environment generally, and they have therefore failed to reflect the linkages between all issues. Integrated management aims to address the conflicting uses and interrelationships between physical processes and human activities, and to promote linkages and cooperation between coastal activities among different domains. This approach will therefore facilitate the sustainable use of coastal and marine resources while providing for the protection of marine biodiversity.

In recognition of the issues associated with global change, other approaches for the integrated management of biodiversity have been offered that require protected areas to be managed not as isolated systems, but as part of the whole landscape. The ecosystem management approach, for example, requires park and preserve managers to shift away from setting aside special sites toward the creation of interconnected systems linking various types of conservation areas along protected corridors. The integrated management of protected areas and their surrounding landscapes is crucial because the ecological health of a park depends on the natural processes in its surroundings near and far.

INTEGRATED APPROACHES TO LANDSCAPE MANAGEMENT

Examples of integrated systems include the "multiple use modules" suggested by R. F. Noss and A. Y. Cooperrider (1994), in which a graduation of buffer zones around reserves can insulate natural areas from external influences, and "greenways" consisting of landscape linkages designed to connect open spaces form protected corridors that may follow natural or man-made terrain features and embrace ecological, cultural, and recreational amenities where possible. The application of the greenway concept is shown in the European Ecological Network, in which national networks of ecologically important areas are being built throughout Europe so that the individual protected areas are strengthened and connected.

In Australia, subnational governments are adopting the bioregion as the unit of management in planning. The basis of the bioregion is one whole or several nested ecosystems that are identified by the community and government and managed via a collaborative planning process. The key criteria of success are the extent to which the planning and management process increases the capacity of people living in the bioregion to identify ecological priorities, the effects of people's activities, and the technical, financial, and management ability to deal with the issues. Essential components of Australia's *National Strategy for the Conservation of Australia's Biological Diversity* (Commonwealth of Australia, 1996) are to increase the representativeness of terrestrial and marine protected areas and to integrate, within the next ten years, management plans for protected areas with plans for resource management in surrounding landscapes.

[*See also* Biological Diversity; Biomes; Carrying Capacity; Land Preservation; *and* Wilderness and Biodiversity.]

BIBLIOGRAPHY

Commonwealth of Australia. *National Strategy for the Conservation of Australia's Biological Diversity*. Canberra: Department of the Environment, Sport, and Territories, 1996.
Dearden, P., and R. Rollins, eds. *Parks and Protected Areas in Canada: Planning and Management*. Toronto and Oxford: Oxford University Press, 1993. A collection of articles concerned with protected-area management.
Dobson, A. P. *Conservation and Biodiversity*. New York: Scientific American Library, 1996. The second edition was published in 2002.
Heywood, V. H., and R. T. Watson, eds. *Global Biodiversity Assessment*. Cambridge and New York: Cambridge University Press, 1996.
Lewis, C. *Managing Conflicts in Protected Areas*. Gland, Switzerland: IUCN, 1996. A useful resource for people who play a role in resolving conflicts in protected-area management, including examples of comanagement with indigenous peoples and nongovernmental organizations.
Local Greening Plans: A Guide for Vegetation and Biodiversity Management. Canberra: Greening Australia, 1995. Demonstrates how practical local outcomes can be achieved in biodiversity management using cooperative methods, existing data, and available resources.
Long, F. J., and M. B. Arnold. *The Power of Environmental Partnerships*. Fort Worth, Tex.: Dryden Press, 1994. An essential guide to establishing and maintaining successful partnerships between government, business, and nongovernmental organizations to achieve positive ecological outcomes in national parks and surrounding lands.
McNeely, J. A., J. Harrison, and P. Dingwall, eds. *Protecting Nature: Regional Reviews of Protected Areas*. Gland, Switzerland: IUCN, 1994.
Meyer, W. B., and B. L. Turner II, eds. *Changes in Land Use and Land Cover: A Global Perspective*. Cambridge and New York: Cambridge University Press, 1994. A collection of essays examining land transformation over the long term and presenting information about data modeling and analysis of global change and its consequences.
Noss, R. F. "Landscape Connectivity: Different Functions at Different Scales." In *Landscape Linkages and Biodiversity: Defenders of Wildlife*, edited by W. E. Hudson, pp. 27–39. Washington, D.C.: Island Press, 1991. An analysis of the spatiotemporal scales of conservation problems and issues related to the establishment of regional corridors.
Noss, R. F., and A. Y. Cooperrider. *Saving Nature's Legacy: Protecting and Restoring Biodiversity*. Washington, D.C.: Island Press, 1994.
Noss, R. F., and J. M. Scott. "Ecosystem Protection and Restoration: The Core of Ecosystem Management." In *Ecosystem Management*, edited by M. S. Boyce and A. Haney, pp. 239–264. New Haven: Yale University Press, 1997. A critique of piecemeal environmental management and a guide to using ecosystem management to conserve ecosystems and ecological integrity.
Organization for Economic Co-operation and Development. *Investing in Biological Diversity*. Proceedings of the OECD International Conference on Incentive Measures for the Conservation and Sustainable Use of Biological Diversity, Cairns, Australia, March 25–28, 1996. Paris: OECD, 1997. Papers outlining methodologies for setting conservation priorities, estimating biodiversity costs and benefits, and providing information about experiences and concerns regarding the appropriate combination of incentives and strategies for supporting biodiversity incentives in non-OECD nations.
Solbrig, O. T., H. M. van Emdem, and P. G. W. J. van Oordt, eds. *Biodiversity and Global Change*. Wallingford, U.K.: CAB International, 1994. Essays on types of biodiversity and issues of identifying and protecting terrestrial and marine biodiversity, with emphasis on the transformation of natural landscapes, subsequent losses of habitats and fauna, and analysis of the long-term implications of global change.
World Conservation Union. *Caring for the Earth: A Strategy for Sustainable Living*. Gland, Switzerland: IUCN/UNEP/WWF, 1991.

—JOHANNA ROSIER AND RICHARD G. HEERDEGEN

ECONOMIC LEVELS

For millennia, there have been contrasts between the advanced and the less advanced, the developed and the less developed. Around 3,000 BCE, before agriculture was widely spread, the advanced nations included China and those areas on the eastern fringe of the Mediterranean Sea, while western and northern Europe were relatively backward. Much later, the Industrial Revolution triggered the rapid spread of another advance that has affected the world unevenly, bringing wealth to the more industrialized nations rather than to those that remained primarily agricultural. At the beginning of the twenty-first century, the dichotomy between more- and less-developed nations is a crucial factor in dealing with global changes in the environment and bringing about a transition toward lower and more stable rates of population growth.

DEFINING AND TRACKING ECONOMIC LEVELS

To highlight differences between developed and less-developed nations, gross domestic product (GDP) is often used as a surrogate for more specific indicators of quality of life. Energy use per capita correlates strongly with GDP, confirming the industrial character of the wealthier nations. The United Nations Development Programme (UNDP) has devised the Human Poverty Index, an aggregate measure that recognizes low life expectancy, illiteracy, and reduced access to health services, safe water, and adequate nutrition.

The Human Development Index (HDI) is a composite measure used by the UN Development Programme (UNDP) since 1993 in its annual Human Development Report. It is an alternative to simply reporting measures of income, such as the GDP or the gross national product (GNP). It uses three dimensions, and applies them to 177 member states: to represent health, life expectancy at birth; to represesent education, the adult literacy rate and gross school enrollments; and to represent the standard of living, gross domestic product per capita. For the 2006 Human Development Report, data from 2004 was used (UNDP, 2006). The Appendix to the *Companion* contains a complete list of the states and their rankings.

The high-index states (0.80 to 1.0) include developed countries in North America, western Europe, temperate South America, and Oceania. The top ten countries are, in descending order, Norway, Iceland, Australia, Ireland, Sweden, Canada, Japan, United States, Switzerland, and the Netherlands. In the medium category (0.50 to 0.79) are countries in tropical South America, northern and southern Africa, and most of Eurasia. In the lowest category (0.30 to 0.49) are mostly African nations straddling the equator: 29 of the 31 countries in this category are in Africa.

This three-part division justifies the use of the term "third world" for the least advanced nations. Describing the wealth contrast as a North-South divide, however, is not justified: it perhaps arises from a comparison of North America and Europe on the one hand and sub-Saharan Africa on the other, but it fails to recognize that the most prosperous countries of South America and Africa are at their southern tips, and that Australia and New Zealand are well south of the less prosperous nations of south and southeast Asia. If a generalization is needed, higher-versus lower-latitude would fit the global pattern better.

Since the mid-1970s almost all regions have progressively increased their HDI scores. East Asia and South Asia have accelerated their progress since 1990. Central and Eastern Europe, including the Commonwealth of Independent States, recovered after an abrupt decline in the first half of the 1990s. The major exception to the trend is sub-Saharan Africa: since 1990 it has stagnated, partly because of economic reversal, but principally because of the catastrophic effect of HIV/AIDS on life expectancy. Eighteen countries have lower HDI scores than in 1990, and most of them are in sub-Saharan Africa.

Progress in human development is sometimes taken as evidence of convergence between the developed and developing worlds, but that is not always the case. Child mortality, for instance, is rising in developing nations at a greater rate than in high-income countries. Child-mortality rates demonstrate that increases in income do not always correspond to progress in human development. Measured by wealth generation, India is one of the successes of globalization, having increased its per capita GDP by 4% a year since 1990, but reduction of child mortality has slowed from 2.9% per year in the 1980s to 2.2% since 1990. Bangladesh does not match India in average income, but has maintained a 3.4% decline in child-death rates since 1990 (UN Human Development Report 2006, pp. 265–267).

The United Nations Millennium Development Goals, adopted in September, 2000 by the UN Department of Economic and Social Affairs, identifies targets to be achieved by the year 2015 with regard to eight aspects of welfare: poverty and hunger, education, gender equality, child mortality, maternal health, HIV/AIDS and malaria, environmental sustainability, and a global partnership for development (aid from wealthy nations). The agency publishes annual reports with statistics showing progress and estimating the odds of reaching the stated goals by 2015. The report for 2007 includes a progress chart, with comments on the eight goals and the prospects in ten world regions (Millennium Development Goals Report, 2007).

POVERTY AND THE ENVIRONMENT

Regarding environment quality, there still is a contrast between the more and the less developed nations, the latter being distinguished typically by problems of water supply and sanitation, and by erosion, desertification, and other threats to agricultural landarising partly from overuse and population pressure. The more industrial nations typically must deal with chemical and other industrial wastes, and with regional and urban air pollution due largely to vehicle emissions. The distinction between the more and less developed nations is blurring, however, as many cities in poor nations now growing economically have industrial pollution and large fleets of vehicles, whose emissions pollute the urban air to levels beyond those in many developed nations. [*See* China and Its Environment.] More importantly, the fates of rich and poor nations are linked, now that combustion emissions affect the global atmosphere.

GLOBAL WARMING

The matter of carbon-based fuels now divides the less and the more developed nations as they try to establish timetables to deal with emissions of greenhouse gases. [*See* Global Warming; Kyoto Progress; Greenhouse Effect; *and* Kyoto Protocol.] Developing nations such as India and China understandably wish to power their growth with fossil fuels, as did the now-industrial nations, but the economic development of their large populations will require huge quantities of energy, much of which will probably be supplied by coal. [*See* Coal; Energy and Environment; *and* Fossil Fuels.] As that occurs, developing nations begin to rival the industrial nations in their emissions of greenhouse gases. The developed nations should perfect and promote technologies that will allow less-developed nations to use fossil fuels efficiently and to move gradually to more benign energy sources.

Recent reports and projections point to serious impacts of global warming and highlight the conflicting positions of industrial versus less-developed nations. The United States and western European nations have contributed roughly two-thirds of the greenhouse gases responsible for global warming, and continue to emit at the highest rates, though China is second in the world and closing fast on the U.S. [*See* Greenhouse Gases and Carbon Dioxide Emissions, Appendix.] At the same time, wealthy nations are making plans to adapt to predicted warming by building desalinization plants in Australia and the U.S. to deal with drought, strengthening the Thames flood barrier, and testing floating residences in The Netherlands.

Poor nations, like many in the continent of Africa, account for a miniscule portion of past and current greenhouse gas emissions yet face some of the most serious risks—drought in East Africa, floods from rising sea levels in Bangladesh and Vietnam—and do not have the resources to adapt to these changes. Ironically, the wealthy nations gained their wealth largely through industry fueled by coal and petroleum.

In addition to the threat of drought and floods in certain regions, there are health threats that accompany changes in climate. There will likely be an increase in intensity, duration and frequency of heat waves. Warming may expand the range of mosquito-borne diseases such as malaria, dengue fever, and encephalitis: in fact, there is evidence now that malaria is moving into higher altitudes in Africa, Asia, and Latin America (U.S. Department of Health and Human Services, Feb., 2007). [*See* Disease.] The areas most affected are in poorer nations whose health-care systems are not equipped to deal with the changes.

POPULATION GROWTH

The history of world population growth and the evolving pattern of vital rates (births, deaths, natural increase) testify to the principle that as a population attains higher economic levels, death rates fall and, sooner or later, birth rates follow. Now, all nations in the wealthiest category have slow-growing populations typical of nations that have undergone the European-style transition from high birth and high death rates to low birth and low death rates (with small natural increase) that accompanied the shift to more industrial and more urban societies. When modern medicines were introduced to some less-developed regions after World War II, the result was an immediate drop in death rates, birth rates that resisted lowering, and a demographic transition that was incomplete. The resulting growth in less wealthy areas has been a major feature of world population

patterns in the past 50 years and is responsible for a progressive imbalance in numbers, roughly 80% of the population now being in the lower two HDI categories. Today, not all poor nations have rapid population growth: some are beset by high death rates, especially those African nations afflicted by AIDS. Remarkable declines in fertility have taken place recently in rapidly-developing countries such as Thailand, the Republic of Korea, and Singapore, confirming the association between fertility decline and economic growth. However, it is not higher income itself that lowers fertility, but social change. Lowered fertility is the result of improved health care, access to family planning, and better education, especially for women.

[*See also* Climate Change and Societal Development; Economics and Climate Change; Environmental Accounting; Global Warming; Greenhouse Effect; Human Populations; Impacts of Climate Change; Sustainable Growth; *and* Technology and Environment.]

—David J. Cuff

ECONOMICS AND CLIMATE CHANGE

Recent ideas on economic aspects of climate change center on a few themes:

- The effects of global warming—rising sea levels, severe droughts, loss of agricultural land, spread of tropical diseases, invasion of forest pests—all threaten dislocations and significant cost.
- Much of the economic impact will be in less-developed nations that are not able to guard against the effects or adapt to them readily. Their economic growth and their attainment of U.N. Millennium Development Goals will be compromised.
  [*See* Economic Levels.]
- Developing and implementing technologies such as renewable sources of electricity could be an opportunity for economic growth in the nations that engage in their research, development, and manufacture.
- Reducing carbon dioxide emissions will save enough fuel and electrical energy to lower costs and confer economic benefits, though fuel and electricity prices per unit will be higher.
- Proponents of intervention see very large economic benefits to the world in return for relatively modest investments in methods and technologies that reduce greenhouse gas emissions. Skeptics suggest the funds would be better spent in direct aid to poor nations, providing agricultural aid, education, and improved health.

THE STERN REPORT

Although much has been written on the subject (for instance, Cline [1992] and Nordhaus [2001]), attention has been intensified by a large and influential study commissioned by Britain's chancellor, and written by Nicholas Stern, head of the Government Economic Service. Known as *The Stern Review on* the Economics of Climate Change, it is available online and in paperback as *The Economics of Climate Change: The Stern Review* (Cambridge University Press, 2007).

The report has six parts dealing with these topics: the science of climate change and global warming; impacts of climate change on world regions and the prospects for economic development; the challenge and the costs of stabilizing greenhouse gas emissions; policies and strategies needed to reduce emissions; the costs and relevant policies for adapting to climate change effects; and the need for international collective action. The review makes the important observation that "the impacts of unabated climate change could be equivalent to 20% of world gross domestic product, while the costs of actions to avoid the worst impacts can be limited to around 1% of global GDP per year" (HM Treasury Press Release, 2006).

Stern identifies three elements of policy for an effective response: carbon pricing, to include taxation, emissions trading, or regulation; technology policy to drive development and deployment of a range of low-carbon and high-efficiency products; and removing barriers to energy efficiency, and educating individuals about how they can respond to climate change. His second point, regarding new technologies, is underlined by the possibility of significant profits and large numbers of productive jobs that will be enjoyed by nations that seize the opportunities. Stern sees very large markets for low-carbon technologies—a view reinforced by a more recent study focusing on that aspect (Dumas, 2006).

APOLLO ALLIANCE

The economic motivation for moving toward energy independence and noncarbon energy sources is stressed also by the Apollo Alliance, which is organized by the Institute for America's Future and the Center on Wisconsin Strategy. It brings together environmentalists—Carl Pope of the Sierra Club is one of the founders—businesses, and labor unions in an effort to improve the nation's infrastructure, to develop renewable energy technologies, and to manufacture the associated equipment. The Alliance hopes to create over 3 million high-wage jobs in the process and to add $95 billion in new income (http://www.apolloalliance.org/).

[*See also* Carbon Capture and Storage; Carbon Taxes; Emissions Trading; *and* Stabilizing Carbon Emissions.]

BIBLIOGRAPHY

Cline, W. R. *The Economics of Global Warming*. Washington, D.C.: Institute for International Economics, 1992.
Dumas, L. J. *Seeds of Opportunity: Climate Change: Between Complacency and Panic*. Newton Center, Mass.: Civil Society Institute, 2006.
Lomborg, B. "Stern Review: The Dodgy Numbers behind the Latest Warming Scare." *Wall Street Journal*, Online Edition, November 2, 2006.
Nordhaus, W. D. "Global Warming Economics." *Science* 294 (2001), 1283–1284. DOI: 10.1126/science.1065007.
Pew Center on Climate Change. http://www.pewclimate.org/global-warming-basics (accessed May 29, 2008).
Samuelson, R. J. "The Worst of Both Worlds?" *Newsweek*, November 13, 2006.
Simms, A., J. McGrath, and H. Reid. *Up In Smoke? Threats from, and Responses to, the Impact of Global Warming on Human Development*. London: New Economics Foundation, 2004.
U.S. Congressional Budget Office. *The Economics of Climate Change: A Primer*. Washington, D.C.: Congressional Budget Office, 2003. http://www.cbo.gov/doc.cfm?index=4171&type=0 (accessed May 29, 2008).
U.S. Congressional Budget Office. *Evaluating the Role of Prices and R and D in Reducing Carbon Dioxide Emissions*. http://www.cbo.gov/doc.cfm?index=7567 (accessed May 29, 2008).

—David J. Cuff

ECOSYSTEMS

An ecosystem is an ecological community—the living organisms inhabiting an area—and its associated physical (nonliving) environment. The term was introduced in 1935 by A. G. Tansley (1935). Before that, scientists had begun to approach the idea through such concepts as the "biocoenose" (Möbius, 1887); limnologists S. A. Forbes (1887); and A. Thienemann (1931) had discussed food chains, trophic structure, and organic nutrient cycling in lakes; A. J. Lotka (1925) had applied thermodynamic principles to food webs and chemical cycles; and E. Transeau (1926) had studied primary production and energy budgets in land plants. Since 1935, ecosystem ecology has developed into an important subdiscipline of ecology, with direct links to the fields of biogeochemistry and global change biology (Golley, 1993).

Ecosystems perform two basic functions, capturing and processing energy, and cycling and regenerating nutrients. Each function involves interactions between the ecological community (biotic component) and the physical environment (abiotic component). Performing these functions requires an interacting group of organisms including producers (autotrophs), who capture energy, and consumers/decomposers (heterotrophs), who degrade wastes and regenerate nutrients. Because no single species does both, ecosystems are the smallest ecological units capable of sustaining life (Morowitz, 1979). Recognition of the importance of ecosystems to the sustainability of life on Earth is the basis of ecosystem management, a management approach in which the conservation of biodiversity is achieved by conserving ecosystems. Relationships among producer, consumer, and decomposer organisms constitute an ecosystem's trophic structure (Figure 1).

The ecosystem concept is independent of scale. At one extreme, model ecosystems (called Folsom bottles) can be created by sealing algae, bacteria, water, and sediments inside small flasks. Exposed only to sunlight as an energy source, these bottles have been known to sustain life for twenty years (Biosphere 2 is an application of this approach on a larger, more complex scale). At the other extreme, the planet Earth can be viewed as one large ecosystem (Lovelock, 1979). Despite the disparity in size, Folsom bottles and planet Earth have a number of common features as ecosystems. In particular, both are sustained by the same energy source—the sun. Because all ecosystems require an external energy source, no ecosystem is totally self-sustaining. Similarly, interconnections between ecosystems are the rule rather than the exception, and for that reason, defining ecosystem boundaries can be problematic (Reiners, 1986).

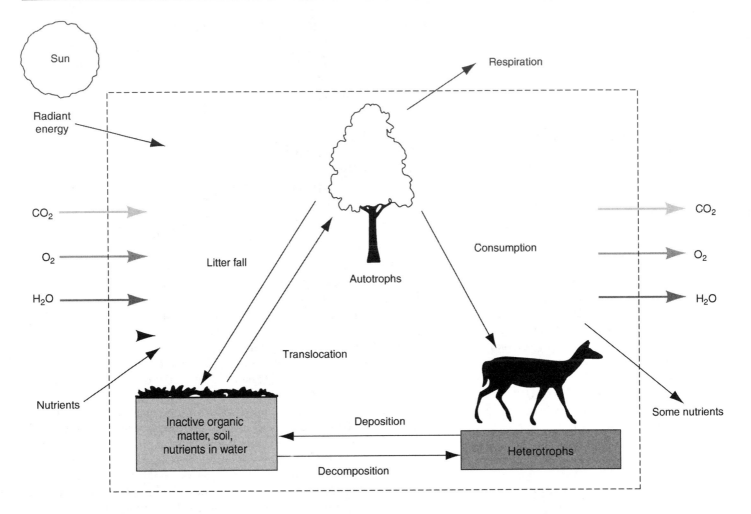

Ecosystems. Figure 1. A Simple Ecosystem and Its Food Web.

Primary producers (plants) use radiant energy from the sun to drive photosynthesis, fixing inorganic carbon (CO_2) in organic (reduced) form. Both producers and consumers use organic carbon to drive biologic processes through metabolism, resulting in the respiration (oxidation) of organic carbon back to the atmosphere as carbon dioxide. As carbon cycles from producer to consumer organisms, energy is dissipated as heat. Thus an external energy source is required for the continued operation of ecosystem processes. Nutrients, in contrast, cycle continually among ecosystem compartments. Additionally, nutrients may be imported or exported from the ecosystem via atmospheric and hydrologic pathways.
(Adapted from O'Neill, 1976, as modified in Smith, 1996. With permission of Harper Collins.)

Most ecosystems use solar energy to power their processes. Through photosynthesis, primary producers (most plants and algae and some bacteria) capture light energy (by means of photosynthetic pigments), using it to split water molecules and generate chemical energy in the form of free electrons, and releasing molecular oxygen as a byproduct. The free electrons are attached to carbon dioxide, thereby converting inorganic carbon to an organic (reduced, electron-rich) form. Organisms access the energy in organic carbon by metabolizing it through respiration (in gross terms the reverse of photosynthesis), using this energy to drive biological processes and regenerating inorganic carbon dioxide and water as byproducts. At the ecosystem level, the total amount of inorganic carbon converted to organic form per year is called annual gross primary production (GPP).

Primary producers use a portion of this fixed carbon to support their own biological processes. The remainder accumulates as biomass or net primary production (NPP, equal to GPP minus primary-producer respiration). At the ecosystem level, NPP represents energy available to support consumer populations. Energy transfer is accomplished by the consumption and respiration of organic carbon by consumer/decomposer populations. Organisms are functionally classified by the trophic level on which they feed. Herbivores feed on primary-producer (plant) biomass, carnivores feed on animal biomass, omnivores feed on both, and detritivores feed on dead organic matter. Diagrams of the feeding relationships within ecosystems, called food chains or webs, identify links between producer and consumer organisms and can be used to track the flow of matter and energy through the ecosystem. Ultimately, fixed carbon either accumulates within the ecosystem as net ecosystem production (NEP; equal to GPP minus community respiration) or is recycled back to the atmosphere through respiration. [*See* Carbon Cycle.]

As carbon cycles through ecosystems, energy flows from one trophic level to the next. The transfer of energy across trophic levels has been estimated to be 5–20% efficient at best. Thus productivity and trophic complexity (i.e., the number of links in the food chain) are intimately associated ecosystem properties. Keeping ecosystems operating requires a constant input of energy from an external source (usually the sun). In contrast, carbon and other chemical elements cycle constantly within the ecosystem. Both inorganic and organic forms can be assimilated by living organisms; metabolism of organic matter by consumer/decomposer organisms releases chemical elements back to the environment in inorganic form. This second function of ecosystems (nutrient regeneration) is closely linked to NEP, because rates of energy capture and carbon assimilation can be limited by the availability of other chemical elements, particularly nitrogen and phosphorus. Nitrogen is a key component of the photosynthetic enzymes that control carbon fixation, and in the form of adenosine triphosphate (ATP), phosphorus serves as the energy currency of the cell. Both nitrogen and phosphorus are also important components of nucleic acids (e.g., DNA). [See Phosphorus Cycle.]

There is some controversy over the use of the term "ecosystem." Some ecologists prefer to think of the community as the highest level of ecological organization (e.g., Begon et al., 2005). Ecosystem processes are viewed simply as interactions between the community and the physical environment. In the reductionist view, the whole is explained simply as the sum of its parts. In the alternative holistic view, ecosystem properties and processes transcend those of ecosystem components. An intermediate view defines ecosystems in a simple, operational manner, as the list of species in an area and their nonbiological environment. Regardless of which view one holds, the utility of the systems approach to ecological analysis lies in the fact that organisms are grouped according to function rather than taxonomy. Functional analysis can provide insights into competitive relationships among organisms with similar functional roles. Quantifying rates of energy flow and nutrient cycling can identify factors that control energy assimilation by ecological communities. The ecosystem concept may be most appropriate to understanding the dynamics of Earth's environment, where numerous and varied component ecosystems interact with a constantly changing physical environment over long time scales to produce the phenomenon known as global change.

[See also Biogeochemical Cycles; Biological Diversity; Biological Realms; and Biomes.]

BIBLIOGRAPHY

Begon, M. J., J. L. Harper, and C. R. Townsend. *Ecology: Individuals, Populations, and Communities*. 4th ed. Oxford, U.K., and Cambridge, Mass.: Blackwell, 2005.

Botkin, D. B., and E. A. Keller. *Environmental Science: Earth As a Living Planet*. New York: Wiley, 1995. The sixth edition was published in 2007.

Forbes, S. A. "The Lake as a Microcosm." *Bulletin of the Peoria [Illinois] Scientific Association* 52 (1887), 77–87. A seminal work reprinted in 1925 in Bulletin 15 of the Illinois Natural History Survey, pp. 537–550.

Golley, F. B. *A History of the Ecosystem Concept in Ecology*. New Haven, Conn.: Yale University Press, 1993.

Likens, G. E. *The Ecosystem Approach: Its Use and Abuse*. Oldendorf/Luhe, Germany: Ecology Institute, 1992.

Lotka, A. J. *Elements of Physical Biology*. Baltimore: Williams and Wilkens, 1925.

Lovelock, J. E. *Gaia: A New Look at Life on Earth*. Oxford and New York: Oxford University Press, 1979.

Möbius, K. A. *Die Auster und die Austernwirtschaft*. Berlin: Wiegandt, Hempel, und Parey, 1887.

Morowitz, H. J. *Energy Flow in Biology*. Woolbridge, Conn.: Oxbow Press, 1979.

O'Neill, R. V. "Ecosystem Persistence and Heterotrophic Regulation." *Ecology* 57.6 (1976), 1244–1253.

Reiners, W. A. "Complementary Models for Ecosystems." *American Naturalist* 127 (1986), 59–73.

Ricklefs, R. E. *Ecology*. 3d ed. New York: Freeman, 1990. The fourth edition, coauthored by G. L. Miller, was published in 2000.

Smith, R. L. *Ecology and Field Biology*. 5th ed. New York: HarperCollins, 1996.

Stiling, P. D. *Ecology: Theories and Applications*. 3d ed. Upper Saddle River, N.J.: Prentice Hall, 1999. The fourth edition was published in 2002.

Tansley, A. G. "The Use and Abuse of Vegetational Concepts and Terms." *Ecology* 16.3 (1935), 284–307.

Thienemann, A. "Der Produktionsbegriff in der Biologie." *Archiv für Hydrobiologie* 22 (1931), 616–622.

Transeau, E. N. "The Accumulation of Energy by Plants." *Ohio Journal of Science* 26.1 (1926), 1–10.

—MARK R. WALBRIDGE

ECOTAXATION

Ecotaxation, also known as pollution, Pigovian (or Pigouvian), or green taxation, is an economic instrument using taxes to encourage behavior that reduces pollution or otherwise directs private activities toward actions that are deemed environmentally and ecologically favorable.

Taxation of polluting activities is designed to give firms and individuals an economic disincentive to create externalities. An externality exists when an activity of a firm or individual imposes a cost on another party for which the firm or individual is not charged by the price system of a market economy. The sufferer of the externalized cost can be a private citizen, firm, or society at large. A common example of an externality is pollution experienced by residents on a river downstream from a industrial-production facility. The residents downstream of the industry might suffer from diminished water quality for drinking, swimming, or fishing as a result of the pollution emitted from the factory. The industry is externalizing the cost of pollution to another party.

The taxation of polluting activities is based on the "polluter pays" principle, or the belief that the polluter does not have rights to discharge pollutants into the environment. The "polluter pays" principle is generally accepted internationally as a verifiable rule. The OECD (Organisation for Economic Co-operation and Development) adopted the principle in 1972 as the foundation of its pollution policy, calling it a "fundamental principle of allocating costs of pollution prevention and control measures." A subsidy, on the other hand, is a payment to a polluter to reduce polluting activites. Subsidies are usually paid on the assumption that the discharger has authority or privilege to discharge pollutants and the society must provide incentives for prevent or reduce these activities.

Ecotaxation entails setting a price per unit of pollution emitted. This "marginal price" is either charged for each unit of pollution emitted or rewarded as a subsidy for reducing pollution by one unit. The marginal unit tax can be applied directly to pollution emissions or indirectly by taxing the use of products whose production causes pollution.

Pollution taxes can be in the form of direct or indirect taxes. A direct tax places a per-unit charge or tax on the amount (pound, kilogram, ton, etc.) of the damaging pollutant being discharged. An indirect tax is a charge on either an input or output of the production process that gives rise the the pollution. Carbon dioxide, a cause of the greenhouse effect and global warming, could be taxed both directly and indirectly. Governments could tax firms according to the number of units of carbon dioxide pollution they emit. The direct tax is levied on the amount of the pollutant that is emitted from the production facility. A direct tax on pollution emissions increases the discharger's cost of production. The producer reacts to increased production costs by reducing production or installing a pollution abatement technology to avoid the tax. The discharger will find it in their financial interest to avoid the tax as long as the per-unit pollution-abatement costs associated with the next pollution-prevention investment (marginal abatement cost) is less than the tax rate. The tax also creates a constant long term financial incentive to research, develop, and implement pollution prevention strategies.

Carbon-dioxide pollution can be indirectly taxed by taxing the fuel or the carbon content of fuel used during production. For the electric-power industry, an tax is sometimes proposed on the carbon content of fossil fuels used to generate power. Such a tax would provide an incentive for power generators to switch to lower carbon sources of power. Similarly a tax could be levied on the end product. A tax levied per kilowatt-hour of energy used, for instance, increases the price of energy to the consumer, thus lowering overall power consumption and thus emissions.

Indirect taxes, however, can eliminate some pollution-prevention options and contribute to unintended outcomes. For instance, a carbon-fuel tax provides no financial incentives for a coal-burning power plant to invest in carbon-capture technologies. A tax on synthetic fertilizer to reduce nutrient runoff into a body of water is another example of an indirect tax. Since the tax does not place a charge on the total quantity of nitrogen being discharged to the stream, economic forces might cause farmers to substitute the use of manure for the synthetic fertilizers. If the manure is not applied correctly, it may exhibit higher leaching and runoff characteristics than fertilizers, thus compounding the nutrient pollution. Another example is the European refuse-bag tax, in which garbage bags carry a tax. Instead of increasing investment in recycling and reduction of consumption, the tax induces many citizens to dump their refuse illegally, causing much worse pollution.

Specific examples of ecotaxation are product charges, pollution taxation, and energy taxation. Many countries tax products such as soft drinks and other beverages in order to internalize the cost of disposal of the used containers in which they are sold. Other examples of product charges are taxes on water consumption, automobile tires, and batteries. Product charges generally exemplify indirect taxation. Governments place direct taxes on the generation of hazardous wastes, household wastewater, chlorofluorocarbons, halons, carbon dioxide, and sulfur.

Examples of ecotaxation subsidies are recycling tax credits, direct payments for pollution abatement, and reduction in real-estate taxes to encourage environmentally friendly land use, such as preserving stream banks with vegetative cover, or wetlands protection. Subsidies are often used in the agricultural sector. Governments reward farmers for reducing pesticide and fertilizer runoff, fencing cattle out of streams, and reducing soil erosion. Agricultural subsidies are more common in more developed countries and are generally indirect subsidies encouraging the adoption of specific conservation practices or technologies (as opposed to direct payment for environmental outcomes such as a per-pound reduction of pollutants). Less developed countries often do not have sufficient funds in their treasuries to subsidize environmentally sound agricultural practices and are reluctant to raise food prices to do so. These countries are hesitant to levy taxes on farmers because large percentages of the population work in agriculture, often earning low incomes.

Critical to the the environmental effectiveness of ecotaxation is setting the level of the tax. Ecotaxation is often linked to the famous British economist Arthur C. Pigou and his 1920 book *The Economics of Welfare*. Pigou observed that polluting enterprises create external costs to third parties and proposed that an externality tax be imposed on the polluter in order to internalize the costs. The magnitude of a Pigovian tax is is based on the damages imposed on others by the polluting activities. Such an approach is computationally challenging and rare in practice. More generally, tax levels are set to modify behavior or to achieve some socially determined environmental objective. For example, a carbon-dioxide tax could be set so as to achieve target aggregate emission levels for a particular industry. Setting the tax so as to achieve a specific environmental outcome is difficult in practice because the government officials setting the tax have incomplete information about costs and pollution-control options and behavior.

The effects of pollution often cross political boundaries, one region suffering from pollution produced in another. The environmental policy of one country therefore has a large impact on the environmental quality of another. There are economic implications for inconsistent ecotax policies as well. One country, for example, may levy a large tax on its industries in order to diminish the production of greenhouse gases. The environmental quality the country's industries are paying for is shared by the entire planet. Another country may not tax greenhouse gases at all, counteracting the benefits of the efforts of other countries' environmentally friendly policies. Furthermore, if industries in both countries produce the same commodity, the industry that is not taxed will probably be more competitive on a global market. However, the relatively modest levels of ecotaxation and the relatively small share of product costs associated with environment protection means that this may not be a significant contemporary issue.

Governmental intervention in externalities has historically consisted of command-and-control regulation. This form of pollution control entails a pollution standard mandated by the government, either by specifying the exact pollution-control technology required to comply with the policy using the best available technology, or by allowing individual firms to find technologies that meet the pollution standard at the lowest cost possible. While least-cost compliance provides incentives for technological innovation of pollution reduction, governmental enforcement costs tend to be higher.

A major criticism of standard-setting policies is the disincentive for polluters to reduce emissions as low as possible, but instead to emit exactly the mandated minimum amount of pollution. Furthermore, command-and-control regulation has been ineffective in addressing nonpoint-source pollution (pollution that cannot be attributed to a single source because many sources are responsible for emissions, such as pesticide runoff from farmland).

Many economists believe that a centralized regulatory policy structure will neither provide desired environmental outcomes at least cost nor create incentives for pollution prevention. Current economic theory suggests that a marketlike alternatives may lower pollution-control costs and induce technological change. Ecotaxation is one such market mechanism. Ecotaxation is an economic instrument that has emerged from natural resource and environmental economics policy. [See Economics and Climate Change.] The market mechanisms differ from command-and-control regulation. The decentralized dischargers or individuals, rather than a central authority, determine how and to what extent individual behavior will change. Cap-and-trade market mechanisms place a mass-load cap on a group of dischargers. The cap is then divided into authorized permissions to discharge (called allowances) which are distributed to dischargers. Individual dischargers are allowed to increase their emissions by buying allowances from dischargers whose emissions are lower than permitted levels and who thus have surplus allowances. The price of an allowance (i.e., the cost to discharge) is determined by market forces. Because the total allowable amount of pollution is fixed, such programs are called quantity-based market mechanisms. Ecotaxation on the other hand is a price-based market mechanism because the price of a undesirable activity is fixed, and actual physical outcomes (total discharge for example) may vary.

Ecotaxation also has the potential of producing a "double dividend." In addition to reducing pollution (the first dividend), ecotaxes also generate tax revenue. Such taxes can then be used to offset taxes levied on capital and labor. Increasing taxes on "social bads" can reduce the distorting and welfare-reducing effects associated with taxes on social goods (the second dividend). Recently, economists have pointed out that this double-dividend may not be as large as many would suspect, because ecotaxes have their own distorting effects on the polluting industries. For example, ecotaxes can drive up production costs and product prices in the polluting industries. Higher prices in turn can reduce household income and thus reduce welfare

As concern over environmental degradation has grown in the last twenty years, countries are trying to mitigate the damage caused by pollution. Countries are generally moving away from centralized regulatory systems and toward market mechanisms. Ecotaxation is proving to be a viable means of pollution reduction and externality compensation. Empirical evidence suggests that ecotaxation could be economically viable in less developed countries as well. However, many of these countries currently lack regulatory institutions that allow for the effective implementation of market mechanisms in pollution control.

[See also Carbon Taxes.]

BIBLIOGRAPHY

Andersen, M. S. The Use of Economic Instruments for Environmental Policy. Available at http://www.iisd.ca/linkages/consume/stou.html (accessed May 29, 2008). Although advocatory, an insightful essay detailing the international linkages of economic instruments.

Cornwell, A., and J. Creedy. Environmental Taxes and Economic Welfare: Reducing Carbon Dioxide Emissions. Cheltenham, U.K., and Lyme, N.H.: Elgar, 1997. Mathematical models illustrating sector responses to public policy implementation of pollution taxes.

Goodstein, E. "The Death of the Pigovian Tax? Policy Implications from the Double-Dividend Debate." Land Economics 79.3 (2003), 402–414.

Hanson, C., and D. Sandalow. Greening the Tax Code. Washington, D.C.: World Resources Institute and Brookings Institution, 2006.

Organization for Economic Co-operation and Development (OECD). Climate Change: Designing a Practical Tax System. Paris: OECD, 1992. International collection of OECD representatives' papers on tax-policy design.

Organization for Economic Co-operation and Development (OECD). Taxation and the Environment: Complementary Policies. Paris: OECD, 1993. Concise text on international implications of ecotaxation.

Organization for Economic Co-operation and Development (OECD). Environmental Taxes in OECD Countries. Paris: OECD, 1995. Tables listing specific taxes and their annual revenue.

Organization for Economic Co-operation and Development (OECD). Agriculture and the Environment: Issues and Policies. Paris: OECD, 1998.

Parry, I., R. Williams, and L. Goulder. "When Can Carbon Abatement Policies Increase Welfare? The Fundamental Role of Distorted Factor Markets." Journal of Environmental Economics and Management. 37.1 (1999), 52–84.

Pearce, D. W., and R. K. Turner. Economics of Natural Resources and the Environment. Baltimore: Johns Hopkins University Press, 1990. Comprehensive text on the subject.

Pigou, A. C. The Economics of Welfare. London: Macmillan, 1920. Pioneering work on the subject of pollution taxes, yet of predominantly historic significance.

Sullivan, T.F.P. Environmental Law Handbook. 14th ed. Rockville, Md.: Government Institutes, 1997. General environmental law text.

—L. Leon Geyer, Joseph K. Sowers, and Kurt Stephenson

EL NIÑO–SOUTHERN OSCILLATION (ENSO)

ENSO is the primary global mode of climatic variability on a 2–7 year time-scale and is an example of a coupled ocean-atmosphere phenomenon. El Niño is an extensive warming of the upper ocean in the equatorial eastern Pacific lasting as long as a year or longer. The cooling phase is called La Niña. El Niño events are linked with a change in atmospheric pressure known as the Southern Oscillation (SO). Because the SO and El Niño are so closely linked, they are known collectively as the El Niño–Southern Oscillation (ENSO). The system oscillates between warm and neutral (or cold) conditions approximately every three to four years.

Precipitation and temperature anomalies characterize El Niño warm episodes and can be summarized thus:

- The eastward shift of thunderstorm activity from Indonesia to the central Pacific results in abnormally dry conditions over northern Australia, Indonesia, and the Philippines.
- Drier-than-normal conditions are also observed over southeastern Africa and northern Brazil.
- The Indian summer-monsoon rainfall tends to be lower than normal, especially in the northwest.
- Wetter than normal conditions are usual along the west coast of tropical South America, and in the subtropical latitudes of North America (the Gulf Coast) and South America (southern Brazil to central Argentina).
- El Niño conditions are thought to suppress tropical-storm and hurricane development in the Atlantic but to increase it over the eastern and central Pacific Ocean.
- In all, there were around 25 warm events of differing strengths in the twentieth century, with that of 1997–1998 being especially strong (Changnon, 2000). ENSO was, however, relatively quiescent from the 1920s to 1940s (Kleeman and Power, 2000). The frequency and intensity of ENSO was unusual between the mid 1970s until 1998, in comparison with earlier in the century, with more frequent, persistent, and intense warm phases and less frequent La Niña conditions (Houghton et al., 2001).

HISTORY

ENSO has a history back into the Holocene and earlier. The Holocene history of El Niño has been a matter of some controversy (Wells and Noller, 1999), but Grosjean et al. (1997) have discovered more than 30 debris-flow events caused by heavy rainfall between 6,200 and 3,100 years BP in the northern Atacama Desert of Chile. The stratigraphy of debris flows has also been examined by Rodbell et al. (1999), who have been able to reconstruct their activity over the last 15,000 years. Between 15,000 and 7,000 years BP, the length of time between deposition events was at least 15 years and then progressively increased to 2–8.5 years. The modern periodicity of El Niño may have been established about 5,000 years ago, possibly in response to orbitally-driven changes in solar radiation (Liu et al., 2000). Archival materials give a picture of the El Niño history back to the sixteenth century (Ortlieb, 2000).

Going back still further, studies of the geochemistry of dated *Porites* corals from the last interglacial in Indonesia have shown that at that time there was an ENSO signal with frequencies nearly identical to the instrumental record from 1856 to 1976 (Hughen et al., 1999).

RAINFALL AND TROPICAL CYCLONES

Severe El Niños, like that of 1997–1998, have a remarkable effect on rainfall. This was shown in Peru where normally dry locations

suffered huge storms. At Paita (mean annual rainfall 15 mm) there was 1,845 mm of rainfall, while at Chulucanas (mean annual rainfall 310 mm) there was 3,803 mm. Major floods resulted (Magilligan and Goldstein, 2001). ENSO also affects tropical cyclone activity. In some regions an El Niño phase brings increases in tropical cyclone formation (as in the South Pacific and the North Pacific between 140°W and 160°E), while others tend to see decreases (as in the North Atlantic, the Northwest Pacific and the Australian region). La Niña phases typically bring opposite conditions. Landsea (2000) sees several reasons that ENSO should relate to cyclone activity: modulation of the intensity of the local monsoon trough, repositioning of the location of the monsoon trough, and alteration of the tropospheric vertical shear.

The differences in cyclone frequency between El Niños and La Niñas are considerable (Bove et al., 1998). For example, the probability of at least two hurricanes striking the U.S. is 28% during El Niño years, 48% during neutral years, and 66% during La Niña years. There can be very large differences in hurricane landfalls from decade to decade. In Florida, between 1851 and 1996, the number of hurricane landfalls ranged from 3 per decade (1860s and 1980s) to 17 per decade (1940s) (Elsner and Kara, 1999).

RELATED OSCILLATIONS IN CLIMATE: PACIFIC DECADAL OSCILLATION (PDO) AND INTERDECADAL PACIFIC OSCILLATION (IPO)

In addition to ENSO, other modes of climatic variability operating at decadal to multidecadal time scales occur in the Pacific Ocean. The Pacific decadal oscillation (PDO) is a long-lived El Niño–like pattern. According to Houghton et al. (2001, p.151) "the Interdecadal Pacific Oscillation is likely to be a Pacific-wide" manifestation of the PDO and shows three major phases in the twentieth century. From 1922 to 1946, and again from 1978 to 1998, it was positive, while between 1947 and 1976 it was in a negative phase. During positive phases, sea surface temperatures (SSTs) over much of the southwestern Pacific and the extratropical northwestern Pacific are cold, while SSTs in the central tropical Pacific are warm (but not as warm over the equatorial far-eastern Pacific as in ENSO). The IPO and PDO modulate ENSO variability over vast areas (e.g., the South Pacific and teleconnections across North America) (Salinger et al., 2001) and are part of a continuous spectrum of ENSO variability. Since 1900, El Niño (and La Niña) events have been more prevalent during positive (negative) phases of the IPO. Dendrochronological studies have indicated decadal-scale reversals of Pacific climate throughout the last four centuries (Biondi et al., 2001). Such variability in the PDO is important for understanding precipitation changes in the western U.S. (McCabe and Dettinger, 1999).

THE FUTURE

There has been much recent debate over whether ENSO is influenced by global warming, the severe El Niño of 1997–1998 perhaps having been enhanced by global warming. The latest report of the Integovernmental Panel on Climate Change (IPCC, 2007,

p. 780) is cautious on this matter, remarking that after examining the results from a whole series of models "there is no consistent indication at this time of discernible future changes in ENSO amplitude or frequency."

BIBLIOGRAPHY

Biondi, F., A. Gershunov, and D. R. Cayan. "North Pacific Decadal Climate Variability since 1661." *Journal of Climate* 14.1 (2001), 5–10. DOI: 10.1175/1520-0442(2001)014<0005:NPDCVS>2.0.CO;2.

Bove, M. C., et al. "Effect of El Niño on U.S. Landfalling Hurricanes, Revisited." *Bulletin of the American Meteorological Society* 79.11 (1998), 2477–2482.

Changnon, S. A., ed. *El Niño 1997–1998.* Oxford and New York: Oxford University Press, 2000.

Elsner, J. B., and A. B. Kara. *Hurricanes of the North Atlantic: Climate and Society.* New York: Oxford University Press, 1999.

Grosjean, M., et al. "Mid-Holocene Climate and Culture Change in the Atacama Desert, Northern Chile." *Quaternary Research* 48.2 (1997), 239–246. DOI: 10.1006/qres.1997.1917.

Houghton, J. T., et al., eds. *Climate Change 2001: The Scientific Basis: Contribution of Working Group I to the Third Assessment Report of the Intergovernmental Panel on Climate Change.* Cambridge: Cambridge University Press, 2001.

Hughen, K. A., et al. "El Niño during the Last Interglacial Period Recorded by a Fossil Coral from Indonesia." *Geophysical Research Letters* 26.20 (1999), 3129–3132.

Kleeman, R., and S. B. Power. "Modulation of ENSO Variability on Decadal and Longer Timescales." In *El Niño and the Southern Oscillation*, edited by H. F. Diaz and V. Markgraf, pp. 413–441. Cambridge and New York: Cambridge University Press, 2000.

Landsea, C. W. "El Niño–Southern Oscillation and the Seasonal Predictability of Tropical Cyclones." In *El Niño and the Southern Oscillation*, edited by H. F. Diaz and V. Markgraf, pp. 149–181. Cambridge and New York: Cambridge University Press, 2000.

Liu, Z., J. Kutzbach, and L. Wu. "Modeling Climate Shift of El Niño Variability in the Holocene." *Geophysical Research Letters* 27.15 (2000), 2265–2268.

Magilligan, F. J., and P. S. Goldstein. "El Nino Floods and Culture Change." *Geology* 29.5 (2001), 431–434.

McCabe, G. J., and M. D. Dettinger. "Decadal Variations in the Strength of Enso Teleconnections with Precipitation in the Western United States." *International Journal of Climatology* 19.13 (1999), 1399–1410.

Ortlieb, L., and J. Machare. "Former El Niño Events: Records from Western South America." *Global and Planetary Change* 7 (1993), 181–202.

Rodbell, D. T, et al. "An ~15,000-Year Record of El Niño-Driven Alluviation in Southwestern Ecuador." *Science* 283 (1999), 518–520. DOI: 10.1126/science.283.5401.516.

Salinger, M. J., J. A. Renwick, and A. B. Mullan. "Interdecadal Pacific Oscillation and South Pacific Climate." *International Journal of Climatology* 21.14 (2001), 1705–1721.

Solomon, S., et al., eds. *Climate Change 2007: The Physical Science Basis: Contribution of Working Group I to the Fourth Assessment Report of the Intergovernmental Panel on Climate Change.* Cambridge and New York: Cambridge University Press, 2007.

Wells, L. E., and J. S. Noller. "Holocene Coevolution of the Physical Landscape and Human Settlement in Northern Coastal Peru." *Geoarchaeology* 14.8 (1999), 755–789. DOI: 10.1002/(SICI)1520-6548(199912)14:8<755::AID-GEA5>3.0.CO;2-7.

—ANDREW S. GOUDIE

EMERGING COASTS

Emerging coasts are found where sea level is falling relative to the land. This can be the result of coastal land uplift (isostatic or seismic), an actual (global, eustatic) lowering of sea level, or some combination of land and sea movement. A rising sea level can be demonstrated when changes in mean sea level are calculated from tide-gauge records over a period of at least two decades. This duration is necessary to exclude variations related to waves, weather, and long-term tidal cycles such as the oscillation related to the 18.6-year Saros eclipse cycle, which peaked in 1987 and 2006.

Analyses by Pirazzoli (1986) of long-term tide-gauge records from 229 stations showed that while over 70% registered a mean sea-level rise, 28% showed a mean sea-level fall, indicating coastal emergence. However, the geographical distribution of the 229 stations was uneven, with strong northern hemisphere midlatitude clustering, and only six in the southern Hemisphere. There is also the problem that most tide gauges are located at ports and may not be reliable indicators of mean sea-level changes along the coastline. Emery and Aubrey (1991) reviewed records from 664 tide-gauge stations and obtained similar results.

The Intergovernmental Panel on Climate Change used evidence from satellite altimetry to measure global average sea-level changes between 1993 and 2003 (IPCC, 2007), but this is too brief a period to determine mean sea-level trends. In addition to evidence from tide-gauge records, the following are indications of an emerging coast:

- Abandonment of cliffs as they are cut off from marine erosion and become subaerially degraded to bluffs.
- Formation of river-mouth rapids.
- Incision of streams in deltas and coastal plains.
- Widening of beaches (if this is not due simply to increased accretion of beach sediment where sea level has remained stable, or even risen).
- Widening of coastal salt marshes or mangrove swamps (if this is not due simply to an increased sediment supply).
- Dissection of salt marshes and mangrove swamps by incised tidal creeks.
- Shallowing and shrinking of estuaries and coastal lagoons.
- Revival and upward growth of corals and other marine organisms on reefs or shore platforms.

The global distribution of emerging coasts is shown in Figure 1. Emerging coasts are found in two situations. The first, in polar and subpolar regions, is where land that was depressed by the weight of Pleistocene ice sheets is now rising after the removal of the glacial load (Figure 1A). This postglacial isostatic rebound is seen on the coasts of Canada and northern Britain, and in Scandinavia, where the coasts of Sweden and Finland, bordering the Gulf of Bothnia, are rising by up to a centimeter annually. There is little information on vertical movements on the coasts of arctic and eastern Russia, but it is likely (as in northern Alaska) that these include sectors where isostatic rebound has been offset by subsidence beneath the load of sediment on accreting deltas and coastal plains.

Coastlines emerging because of isostatic uplift of the land are usually backed by sequences of uplifted terraces, as on the southern shores of Hudson Bay in Canada, where Holocene beaches have been raised by up to 315 m. On Skuleberget, a mountain in northeastern Sweden, a hilltop beach marks a

Emerging Coasts. Figure 1. World Map of Emerging Coasts.

(A) Postglacial isostatic rebound. (B) Neotectonic zones with emerging coasts locally. (C) Combination of A and B with emerging coasts locally.

coastline 8,600 years old that has been raised 286 m above the present level of the Gulf of Bothnia by Holocene isostatic rebound. Much of Scotland is still rising isostatically, but the Outer Hebrides are undergoing submergence. Northern Ireland has a low postglacial (Holocene) terrace that diminishes in altitude and disappears southward, indicating tilting related to isostatic recovery. Similar features occur around Puget Sound in the northwestern United States.

Emerging coasts are also found in regions of tectonic activity, marked by recurrent earthquakes and volcanic eruptions (Figure 1B), notably around the Pacific basin, in the Mediterranean and in Iran, Pakistan, Bangladesh, and Burma. In contrast with the gradual emergence produced by postglacial isostatic rebound, most emerging coasts result from sudden uplift during earthquakes, particularly in zones where tectonic plates are converging and mountain-building is occurring.

Emerging coasts occur locally (on sectors too small to be shown on a world map), interspersed with coasts that have remained stable or subsided. Thus the Alaskan earthquake in 1964 raised a shore platform on Montague Island by up to 11 m while subsidence of up to 2 m occurred in Turnagain Inlet and Kachemak Bay. Similar examples of emergence and subsidence during earthquakes have been reported from the Pacific coast of the United States and South America. In the Mediterranean region neotectonic movements have raised parts of the coasts of Algeria, Crete, and southern Turkey, while several ancient ports, notably Carthage (in present-day Tunisia), have subsided. Emerging and submerging coasts are also found in earthquake-prone areas of the North Island of

New Zealand, in New Guinea and Indonesia, the Philippines, Taiwan, and Japan.

Examples of recently emerged coasts are seen around Tokyo Bay, where raised beaches were elevated during earthquakes in 1703 and 1923. In the vicinity of Wellington, New Zealand, parts of the coastline were uplifted by as much as a meter during the 1855 earthquake, forming emerged shore platforms. An earthquake at Hawke Bay, New Zealand, in 1931 raised the coastal plain near Napier by up to 2 m and drained a lagoon. Similar neotectonic features have been reported from sectors of the Antarctic coastline.

There is overlap between isostatic rebound and tectonic movements on the coasts of southern Alaska, British Columbia, and Washington State in North America (Figure 1C). Here some emerging coasts are the outcome of a gradual isostatic rise complicated by intermittent earthquakes resulting from movements along the offshore subduction zone. In southern Alaska, Holocene uplift has proceeded at an average rate of at least 3.5 cm per year, as indicated by glaciomarine sediments now 230 m above sea level near Juneau.

The coast bordering the Caspian Sea were emerging between 1930 and 1977, a period when sea level fell about 3 meters, but then the sea began to rise and emergence has given place to submergence. [*See* Sea Level Future, Fig. 1.]

According to the Intergovernmental Panel on Climate Change (2007) average global sea level is expected to rise during the twenty-first century. This will reduce the extent of emerging coasts and the rate of emergence of those that survive. [*See* Sea Level Future.*]

BIBLIOGRAPHY

Emery, K. O., and D. G. Aubrey. *Sea Levels, Land Levels, and Tide Gauges.* New York: Springer, 1991.
Pirazzoli, P. A. "Secular Trends of Relative Sea-Level (RSL) Changes Indicated by Tide-Gauge Records." *Journal of Coastal Research,* Special Issue 1 (1986), 1–26.
Solomon, S., et al., eds. *Climate Change 2007: The Physical Science Basis: Contribution of Working Group I to the Fourth Assessment Report of the Intergovernmental Panel on Climate Change.* Cambridge and New York: Cambridge University Press, 2007.

—Eric C. F. Bird

EMISSIONS INTENSITY

Carbon dioxide emissions per unit of economic output, such as gross domestic product (GDP).

As a country develops, intensity tends to decline because GDP increases more rapidly than emissions. Relatively low numbers in an advanced country sometimes are used to justify that country's large total emissions. Often those low numbers are due to the value of services and other activities that swell the GDP but contribute low emissions. For a list of nations by CO_2 emissions and emission intensity, see Appendix.

—David J. Cuff

EMISSIONS TRADING

Market mechanisms such as emissions trading are increasingly being used to achieve cost-effective reductions in greenhouse gas (GHG) emissions and are being introduced by a number of developed countries to help them meet their emission-reduction commitments under the Kyoto Protocol. A good example of this is the introduction of the Emissions Trading Scheme by the European Union (EU) as a key measure to assist the governments of EU Member States to meet their emission-reduction commitments under the Kyoto Protocol. This article provides an overview of emissions trading and explains how the two types of trading schemes, cap-and-trade and project-based baseline-and-credit, function. The key design elements of emissions trading are outlined, including the scope of emissions trading schemes in terms of sectors and emission sources covered; distributing allowances and setting baselines; banking and borrowing; methodologies, monitoring, and verification; and enforcement and penalties. The article also briefly reviews some of the emissions-trading schemes currently in use and emerging worldwide.

Emissions trading can be described simply as a market whereby parties buy or sell allowances to permit greenhouse gas emissions or carbon credits for making reductions in greenhouse gas emissions. Emissions trading can occur within a country or on a regional or international basis and involve all types of participants, including individuals, companies, and governments. Regulators play a key role in the emissions-trading market in determining the overall emission limits, the allocation of permits and eligibility of carbon offset projects, and penalties for noncompliance.

THE PURPOSE OF EMISSIONS TRADING

The overall purpose of emissions trading is to reduce greenhouse gas emissions. Emissions trading provides a cost-effective means of doing this by allowing participants with low-cost GHG emission-reduction opportunities to exceed their targets and sell their additional allowances (carbon credits) to participants whose reductions are more burdensome and costly. Overall, this leads to the lowest overall cost.

Consider for example Company A and Company B who each emit a significant quantity of GHGs. In a circumstance where the regulators require a certain reduction of GHGs by each company, Company A may find it cost-prohibitive to implement abatement measures to reduce its GHG emissions, whereas Company B may be able to make cost-effective reductions easily. If Company B agrees to make the additional GHG reductions instead of Company A, and provided Company A can pay for such additional reductions (rights to emit) above the cost to Company B but below what it would cost Company A, reductions in GHG emissions can be made in a cost-effective way.

The same considerations apply to industrial sectors and countries as well as to individual companies. This point is well illustrated in an analysis by McKinsey & Co. of the relative costs of abating GHGs in various industrial sectors (power, manufacturing, transportation, residential and commercial buildings, forestry, agriculture, and waste disposal) on a regional basis including developing countries. The resulting "cost curves" show marked differences in the relative costs of abatement in different industrial sectors and regions. For example, improvements in new building insulation and lighting systems or planting, protecting, or replanting tropical forests were viewed as relatively low-cost options compared with other abatement options, for example, switching from coal to gas as a fuel. These differences in abatement costs underline the need for policy change to promote lowcost emission reductions and also identify opportunities for emissions trading.

Unlike a traditional command-and-control approach to environmental regulation, the nature of emissions trading means that regulators defer most decisions about compliance to participants in the system and focus on the "back end" of the system design, the details of which are explained in more detail below.

SO_2 TRADING IN THE U.S.

One of the first broad scale applications of emissions trading was the trading of SO_2 allowances under the U.S. Acid Rain Program. The Acid Rain Program, regulated under the Clean Air Act 1990, aimed to reduce annual SO_2 emissions by 10 million tons below 1980 levels. The program has been implemented in two phases (1995–1999, and 2000 and beyond) and targets the emissions of SO_2 from fossil-fuel power-generators.

Reductions of SO_2 emissions are facilitated through a cap-and-trade emissions trading system. Power generators that reduce their emissions below the number of allowances they hold may trade allowances with other participants in the system or bank them to cover emissions in future years. In this way, power generators regulated under the Acid Rain Program can decide the most cost-effective way to use available resources to comply with the requirements of the Clean Air Act. (See the U.S. Environmental Protection Agency's "SO_2 Reductions and Allowance Trading Under the Acid Rain Program," http://www.epa.gov/airmarkets/progsregs/arp/s02.html.)

HOW DOES EMISSIONS TRADING WORK?

There are two main types of emission trading systems, cap-and-trade systems and project-based systems, commonly referred to as baseline-and-credit.

Cap-and-trade

Under a cap-and-trade system, the regulator prescribes a limit on the level of GHG emissions that can be emitted (the emissions cap) and then distributes emissions allowances equal to the emissions cap to the participants in the system.

During the compliance period, the participants in the system are required to surrender allowances for the GHG emissions emitted—participants whose emissions exceed their allowance quota must buy additional allowances (or incur a penalty) and participants whose emissions are less than their allowance quota can sell surplus allowances. The relative supply and demand for emission allowances determines their market value.

Prominent examples of cap-and-trade emissions-trading systems include the European Union Emissions Trading Scheme (EU ETS) for GHGs and the U.S. Acid Rain Program for SO_2.

Baseline-and-credit

Under a project-based baseline-and-credit system, the regulator approves a GHG emissions baseline for the project in question; such projects are sometimes referred to as offset projects. The baseline is the amount of GHG emissions that would have been emitted in the absence of any future GHG reductions made by the project. Carbon credits are earned by participants for the reductions of GHG emissions made below the baseline. Importantly, emission reductions must be additional to what is considered business as usual and not simply the result of what would have happened as a matter of course. This can be a controversial issue in establishing project eligibility.

The Clean Development Mechanism (CDM) and Joint Implementation (JI) under the Kyoto Protocol are examples of baseline-and-credit systems and are based on individual GHG abatement projects where a baseline is established and the carbon credits are a result of the emission reductions achieved by the project.

CDM and JI

The Clean Development Mechanism is a mechanism under Article 12 of the Kyoto Protocol by which Annex I Parties (i.e., developed countries and economies in transition listed in Annex I of the United Nations Framework Convention on Climate Change [UNFCCC]) may finance GHG reduction or removal projects that contribute to sustainable development in developing countries, and receive credits (certified emission reductions) for doing so. These credits may be applied towards meeting mandatory limits on their own emissions.

Joint Implementation is a mechanism under Article 6 of the Kyoto Protocol through which an Annex I Party that satisfies certain eligibility requirements can receive credits (emissions reduction units) when it helps to finance projects that reduce net GHG emissions in another Annex I Party (in practice, the recipient state is likely to be a country with an "economy in transition"). Like CDM, the investing developed country may use the credits towards meeting mandatory limits on their own emissions.

Design elements

The design of any emissions-trading system is fundamental to its successful operation. Some of the key design considerations are set out below.

Scope. An emissions trading system must specify the types of GHG emissions to be included, the sources and industry sectors that are covered, and whether the system applies to both direct and indirect emission sources.

First, there are several GHG gases besides carbon dioxide and numerous sources of GHG emissions. The Kyoto Protocol applies to the following six GHGs: carbon dioxide (CO_2); methane (CH_4); nitrous oxide (N_2O); hydrofluorocarbons (HFCs); perfluorocarbons (PFCs); and sulfur hexafluoride (SF_6). These gases vary substantially in their relative global warming potential (GWP), which is a measure of how much a given mass of greenhouse gas is estimated to contribute to global warming and is reported in terms of carbon dioxide equivalent (CO_2e). Typically, emissions-trading systems include emissions of CO_2 and exclude emissions that are small or difficult to monitor. For example, the first phase of the EU ETS cap-and-trade system (2005–2007) includes CO_2 only, whereas project-based systems such as JI and CDM include the six GHGs regulated by the Kyoto Protocol.

Second, emissions trading systems are particularly suited to sectors where emissions can be estimated and reported accurately at low cost, which have a relatively large number of emitters, and where the transaction costs of covering those emitters are not unreasonably high. For example, the nonmobile energy and industrial manufacturing sectors generally fulfill these requirements and are the main candidates for emissions trading systems worldwide. Conversely, more diffuse sources associated with transportation and energy efficiency have tended not to be covered.

Third, direct emissions are those that occur from a source owned or controlled by the participant or are located at the site in question. Indirect emissions, on the other hand, are emissions due to the participant's activity but which do not arise from sources owned or controlled by the participant or are not located at the participant's site. For example, indirect emissions arise from the production of purchased electricity or from the use of products manufactured by the participant.

Distributing allowances and setting baselines. The allocation of allowances in a cap-and-trade system and the setting of baselines in a project-based baseline-and-credit system are fundamental distinctions between the two systems. While the baseline is determined in advance for project-based schemes, participants do not know the extent of their emissions-capture opportunities until the end of the compliance period, when emission reductions are verified and carbon credits are assigned. In cap-and-trade schemes, the amount of the cap is known in advance, so allowances can be allocated with certainty at the start of the compliance period.

In a cap-and-trade system, allowances can be allocated to participants by auction or may be issued free of charge. The latter approach is embedded in the Kyoto Protocol in the allocation of assigned amount units to Annex I Parties (assigned amount units or AAUs are emission "allowances" under the Kyoto Protocol); these AAUs can be exchanged with other Annex I countries through emissions trading and also in the EU ETS. As a general matter, allowances can also be distributed using a hybrid approach. For example, in the EU ETS, allowances are distributed without charge based on National Allocation Plans developed by each member state and can also be auctioned by each member state up to a set cap—in Phase 1 of the scheme (2005–2007) the cap is 5% and in Phase 2 of the scheme (2008–2012) the cap is 10%.

The quantity of allowances distributed can be made with reference to several factors including current or historical direct emissions; indirect emissions such as electricity or fuel consumption; consideration of those participants that are most disadvantaged by the introduction of GHG abatement policy; or allocated on the basis of industry-wide emissions.

Banking and borrowing. Some emissions trading systems allow participants to bank and borrow allowances between different compliance periods.

In banking, participants are able to save any surplus allowances or credits for use during a future compliance period. While there is a possibility of short term increases in GHG emissions beyond the overall GHG reduction target as the banked allowances or credits are redeemed, from an economic point of view banking creates flexibility for participants in achieving compliance and accordingly more price flexibility for participants to sell surplus allowances or credits.

In borrowing, participants are able to use allowances or credits from a future compliance period during the current compliance period. Again, while borrowing creates flexibility for participants in achieving compliance it may lead to an overall increase in GHG emissions if for example a participant ceases operation before the borrowed allowances or credits are paid back.

Methodologies, monitoring, and verification. For the project-based baseline-and-credit schemes, there is typically a requirement that the emission reductions be achieved by use of a standardized methodology. For example, as part of the CDM process, methodologies have been developed for projects in a broad range of sectors including the manufacturing, chemical, and energy industries, as well as in waste handling and agriculture.

In addition, to promote the correct reporting of GHG emissions and emission reductions, a comprehensive monitoring and verification system is an essential part of the design of an emissions trading system. Typically, emissions trading systems prescribe the use of the most accurate monitoring available and require GHG emissions (and emissions reductions) to be verified by an independent third party. The general principles that form the basis for the accounting of emission reductions under most emissions-trading schemes are set forth in the GHG Protocol published by the World Resources Institute and World Business Council for Sustainable Development. The California Climate Action Registry and the European Pollutant Emission Register are two examples of registries that have used the GHG Protocol in establishing their own accounting and reporting standards.

In the voluntary markets, where no formalized regulatory framework applies, the absence of standardized methodologies has led to criticism about the quality of project-based emission reductions. In response to this criticism a number of standards are emerging to provide a basis for improved quality and accountability. Examples include the Voluntary Carbon Standard developed by the International Emissions Trading Association (IETA), The Climate Group, and the World Economic Forum (WEF); and the Gold Standard developed by the WWF (formerly the World Wildlife Fund) and other nongovernment organizations.

Enforcement and penalties. Enforcement of compliance with the specific rules of an emission trading system and penalties to deter noncompliance are both critical to the successful operation of emissions trading. For example, under the EU ETS cap-and-trade system, the penalties for noncompliance are substantial; in addition to paying a fine (40 per metric ton CO_2e from 2005–2007 and 100 per ton CO_2e from 2008 onward), participants need to make up the shortfall in the next year. These penalties are considerably higher than the level most commentators predict the price of allowances will reach, thereby encouraging "over-emitters" to participate.

Under a project-based baseline-and-credit approach such as the CDM and JI, penalties may be incorporated into the contracting mechanisms for the delivery of carbon credits by the project developer to the buyer and tend to be project-specific. For example, some buyers of credits from CDM or JI projects impose stringent nondelivery penalties on sellers if a project fails to achieve the emissions reductions projected.

Infrastructure to support the marketplace. The development of emissions-trading markets is moving rapidly thanks to the support of governments and participation by the private sector. In addition to underlying regulations dictating the design elements of trading schemes, the carbon markets have created opportunities for specialist organizations, including project developers and technology providers, validators and verifiers, carbon funds that invest in emission reduction projects, and brokers and exchanges that support trading activities.

EMISSIONS TRADING EXPERIENCE

In 2006 a reported 1.6 billion tons of CO_2e was traded under cap-and-trade schemes, worth an estimated 22.5 billion. The key mandatory and voluntary schemes are highlighted below.

Mandatory emissions trading schemes

- The European Union Emissions Trading Scheme (EU ETS) began on January 1, 2005, and is the world's first large-scale GHG trading system, covering approximately 12,000 installations in 25 countries across 6 industrial sectors.
- The NSW [New South Wales, Australia] Greenhouse Gas Abatement Scheme (GGAS)—GGAS began on January 1, 2003, and imposes mandatory greenhouse gas benchmarks on all NSW electricity retailers and certain other "benchmark participants."
- The Norwegian Emissions Trading Scheme, a domestic cap-and-trade emissions trading system was instituted in 2005, coinciding with the implementation of the EU ETS and adopting a similar coverage of industries and emitted gases.

Voluntary emissions trading schemes

- The Chicago Climate Exchange (CCX) is a voluntary exchange in North America with global membership. Emitting members are required to make a but legally binding commitment to meet annual GHG emission-reduction targets. Those who reduce below the targets have surplus allowances to sell or bank; those who emit above the targets comply by purchasing carbon credits.
- The voluntary United Kingdom Emissions Trading Scheme (UKETS) commenced in April 2002. The scheme ran until December 2006, when it was superseded by the EU ETS. Under the scheme, participants could choose to enter through either Climate Change Levy Agreements (baseline-and-credit approach) or as Direct Participants with absolute targets (cap-and trade-approach).
- In 2005, the Japanese Ministry of the Environment selected 34 companies and corporate groups as participants in Japan's Emissions Trading Scheme. Under the scheme, the ministry subsidizes the installation cost of CO_2 emissions-reduction equipment to help businesses that are actively attempting to reduce greenhouse gas (GHG) emissions. In exchange for the subsidy, the participants are required to commit to a specified reduction in their CO_2 emissions.

Trading of emissions has not been restricted to cap-and-trade schemes. The Kyoto Protocol anticipates a global emissions trading market for "assigned amount units" (AAUs) to start in 2008 (for the first commitment under the Kyoto Protocol, i.e., 2008–2012). In addition, the CDM and JI has resulted in several hundred projects registered with the CDM Executive Board and JI Supervisory Committee (the respective regulating bodies) leading to hundreds of millions of CO_2e emissions reductions. Also, increasing activity is occurring through bilateral trades in the voluntary emission reduction markets by companies willing to take the risk that such verified emission reductions (VERs) can be used in future compliance schemes, or to offset their own GHG emissions in pursuit of carbon neutrality and/or as part of their corporate social responsibility commitments.

In addition, voluntary emissions trading has been conducted internally within some large corporations. For example, both Shell and BP, two of the world's largest energy corporations, have developed internal emissions-trading schemes to help meet their own emission reduction targets and to better understand the mechanics of trading.

CRITICS OF EMISSIONS TRADING

Some commentators, in particular environmental NGOs, see emissions trading as eco-capitalism—a move of the private sector and free market into environmental policy-making where the right to pollute is sold to the highest bidder, and they have suggested that a carbon tax may be less subject to manipulation. Others have argued that the opportunity costs of projects may outweigh the environmental benefits, or point to the failure of "carbon accounting." For example, the National Allocation Plans by member governments of the EU ETS were criticized when some member states issued more carbon allowances than the actual quantity of emissions during Phase I of the scheme. This was a result of the allocation process being based on forecast CO_2 emissions (which are inherently inaccurate) rather than historic CO_2 emissions. There have also been concerns expressed regarding the quality of the carbon credits traded in the voluntary unregulated markets where there is as yet no single universally recognized standard for establishing the validity of the emission reductions, and there is often confusion amongst consumers about the quality of offset projects.

On the other hand, emissions trading can give emitters maximum flexibility and control over the way they reduce their GHG emissions and achieve emission reductions in a cost-effective way. Most importantly, the overall cap on emissions ensures that the environmental objective of reducing GHG emissions is met. Also, for those developing countries whose environmental policies and regulations are not advanced enough to support a trading system, project-based mechanisms such as the CDM provide an opportunity for emission reductions to be generated in a sustainable way and incorporate third-party verification of emission reductions.

EMERGING EMISSIONS TRADING SCHEMES

Several emissions-trading schemes are currently under development at a federal and state level worldwide by countries to help achieve their emission reduction commitments under the Kyoto Protocol or for other reasons (for example the schemes developing in Australia and the United States, who have not ratified the Kyoto Protocol). Emerging schemes include:

- The Regional Greenhouse Gas Initiative (RGGI) in the northeastern United States will establish a cap-and-trade program for power plants with provision for offset projects.
- The California Global Warming Solutions Act (AB32) will include a cap-and-trade scheme and provision for offset projects.
- Several bills before the 110th U.S. Congress, both in the House and Senate, containing proposed cap-and-trade schemes and provision for offset projects.
- A National Emissions Trading System (NETS) in Australia.
- The Carbon Reduction Commitment in the U.K. for large commercial and public sector organizations.

ASSESSMENT

Emissions trading is an important and powerful tool to help large emitters reduce GHG emissions in a cost-effective way and encourage investments in innovative clean technologies. Cap-and-trade schemes are currently being advocated by many developed countries as part of a broader policy to reduce GHG emissions. For developing countries and countries in transition where institutional capacity and environmental regulation may not be as advanced or rigorous, baseline-and-credit schemes such as JI and CDM projects are being developed and in general appear to be operating successfully.

While the successes and failings of GHG emissions trading schemes have received widespread attention in recent times, actual experience in trading carbon credits is relatively recent. Emerging schemes will probably incorporate architecture similar to that of existing schemes but will address "lessons learned" to overcome perceived failings and improve operational issues. In the future, it will be interesting to observe how emissions trading schemes operate together on a global, regional, and national basis and what rules regarding the linking of schemes worldwide will develop.

[*See also*: Carbon Taxes.]

BIBLIOGRAPHY

Capoor, K., and P. Ambrosi. *State and Trends of the Carbon Market 2006*. Geneva: IETA; Washington, D.C.: World Bank, 2006.

Enkvist, P. A., T. Nauclér, and J. Rosander. (2007) "A Cost Curve for Greenhouse Gas Reduction." *McKinsey Quarterly*, No.1 (2007).

Haefeli-Hestvik, S., et al. *Programmatic CDM: What is New?* IETA Greenhouse Gas Market Report 2006, p.106. Geneva: IETA, 2006.

Pew Centre on Global Climate Change. (2006) *The European Union Emissions Trading Scheme (EU-ETS) Insights and Opportunities*. Arlington, Va.: Pew Centre on Global Climate Change, 2006. http://www.//Pewclimate.org/docUploads/EV%2DETS%20White%20Paper%2Epdf (accessed May 29, 2008).

Philibert, C., and J. Reinaud. *Emissions Trading: Taking Stock and Looking Forward*. Paris: Organization for Economic Co-operation and Development, 2004.

Roine, K., and H. Hasselknippe, eds. *Carbon 2007: A New Climate for Carbon Trading*. Oslo: Point Carbon, 2007. htttp://www.pointcarlom.com (accessed May 29, 2008).

—MICHAEL P. SCOTT AND SHEREE HARDY

ENERGY AND ENVIRONMENT

Humans with modern technology engage in massive reordering of the landscape through mining and construction projects, and emit pollutants into waterways and the atmosphere in quantities that grow rapidly every year as less advanced nations modernize and adopt the industrial way—employing vast amounts of coal and petroleum to power machinery, factories, and vehicles. This is the fundamental connection between energy and environment in the modern world: cheap and readily available fossil fuels have made our industrial societies possible and have empowered humankind for the first time to change the physical environment on a worldwide scale with effects that will persist for centuries. In poor economies the impacts are very different: burning of wood and manure for cooking and light cause unhealthful air and deforestation—effects that are mostly local but significant to those populations.

Concern with environmental impacts of production and use of fuels has been with us ever since coal burning fouled the air in thirteenth-century England. Now, many universities boast institutes, departments, or programs that concentrate on the energy-environment connection: in the United States these include MIT, Stanford University, the University of California at Berkeley, Johns Hopkins University, and Princeton University; in the U.K. they include Bristol University, the University of East Anglia, Imperial College (London), University of Leeds, and the University of Oxford. Much research at such institutions focuses necessarily on specifics such as new technologies and energy policies. This broad overview will provide background for narrower concerns and for a number of articles in this volume.

ENERGY CONCEPTS AND TERMS

A useful distinction is that between primary and end-use energy, primary being in many cases the raw material, or fuel, which serves various needs. Using the United States as an example, about 90% of coal goes into electrical generation, after which the electricity goes to myriad end-use applications in lighting, electric motors, industrial processes, and electronics. Crude oil is converted into many products, but the transportation sector accounts for 68% of all petroleum products used in the United States, while electrical generation uses only 3%. Only 3% of all electrical generation in the United States relies upon oil.

Recent concern about crude-oil supply has encouraged a loose and general use of the term "energy" and a reluctance to say "electricity." In the face of uncertain oil supplies, it is not helpful to observe that vast resources of coal can be used to "produce energy." Since coal energy is almost entirely converted to electricity, it is no substitute for gasoline or diesel fuel—unless a fleet of vehicles is designed around electric motors (ignoring the remote possibility that coal can be converted on a large scale to liquid fuels).

Nuclear power, hydropower, and alternative sources such as solar-electric and wind-electric occupy a special place in a nation's energy supply as they yield electricity directly without burning fuel. But stimulating the growth of nonfuel electricity generation will not lead to energy independence for a nation if transportation depends upon liquid fuels; furthermore, nuclear electricity will not save petroleum immediately because only small quantities of oil are now used to generate electricity in the United States and most other industrial nations.

ENVIRONMENTAL IMPACTS OF PRIMARY SOURCES

All the primary energy sources affect the environment in specific ways.

Combustion

Certain fuels yield air pollutants that depend on the fuel's composition: coal that is rich in sulfur, for instance, yields sulfur oxides. But, regardless of the fuel—be it pure ethanol or sulfur-rich coal—combustion with air yields nitrogen oxides because abundant nitrogen (78% of air by volume) is swept into the process and combines with oxygen. Ironically, when combustion temperatures are raised to improve efficiency and reduce carbon monoxide in the exhaust, the production of nitrogen oxides is increased. As nitrogen dioxide is a greenhouse gas and other nitrogen oxides contribute to acid deposition and smog, it would be ideal if combustion in vehicles were eventually phased out in favor of electric motors whose batteries are charged by clean sources of electricity. [See Greenhouse Gases; and Pollution.]

Coal. Mining of coal is famously destructive to the earth's surface, though mined areas can be reclaimed and planted with grass or trees. Runoff from mining waste pollutes local streams. Sulfur oxides, nitrogen oxides, and particulate matter can be controlled at the smokestack—and have been dealt with effectively in more advanced countries—but mercury in stack emissions still is prevalent.

Carbon dioxide is the big problem because coal is used in vast quantities for electrical generation in advanced and in developing nations, and because burning coal releases more CO_2 per unit of heat energy produced than does fuel oil or natural gas. CO_2 contributes heavily to ocean acidification and, as the most important greenhouse gas, it enhances the greenhouse effect and causes global warming. There is thus great interest in technologies that can capture CO_2 when burning or otherwise processing coal, then store (sequester) the gas securely to prevent it from entering the atmosphere. [See Carbon Capture and Storage; China and Its Environment; Coal; Global Warming; and Greenhouse Effect.]

The burning of coal for electrical generation will continue for decades, despite efforts to develop clean sources of electricity. This makes new coal-burning technologies and conservation of electricity imperative. The fact that 65% of primary fuel energy is wasted in power plants (whose efficiency is roughly 35%) is a compelling argument for optimizing the efficiency of motors and appliances, and for conservation programs in lighting and air conditioning.

Petroleum and natural gas. These, the other two fossil fuels, contribute CO_2 when burned as gasoline, diesel fuel, fuel oil, and gas in electrical generation and heating of buildings. Exploration and production of petroleum and natural gas have impacts on ecosystems; and, of course, the transportation of crude oil and petroleum products entails spills from tankers and pipelines. Natural gas (dominantly methane, CH_4) is relatively rich in hydrogen and lean in carbon, so its contribution of CO_2 per energy unit is lower than that of coal or petroleum products. On that basis alone (ignoring supply issues) substituting gas for the other fuels is desirable. Some leakage and venting of natural gas occurs in production of oil and gas and in coal mining: this is significant because methane is a greenhouse gas.

Reducing the use of petroleum products depends heavily on transportation technologies and policies. In advanced nations, the burning of gasoline and diesel fuel now makes a massive contribution to world greenhouse gases. As vehicle fleets in China, India, and other developing nations grow rapidly, the local and regional air quality decline, and carbon dioxide and nitrogen oxides from combustion accelerate global warming. The need for alternative automotive fuels or drastically different technologies is obvious. [See Greenhouse Gases; and Transportation.]

Alternative liquid fuels. Although liquid fuels can be manufactured from coal, it is biofuels—and ethanol in particular—that receive the most attention today. One environmental concern is the land area required in competition with food crops. In the United States, production of ethanol from corn is being promoted by the federal government and is expanding rapidly. In Brazil, ethanol from sugarcane has proven much more efficient. Expansion of that production and export of ethanol may ultimately displace large quantities of gasoline and diesel fuel, reducing CO_2 emissions greatly. A negative impact would be further cutting of tropical rainforest if sugarcane acreage is obtained that way. [See Biofuels; and Ethanol.]

Nuclear power

Concerns about global warming and the undeniable role of coal-fired electric plants have led to the reevaluation of nuclear power. The attraction of nuclear-electric generation is that it releases no greenhouse gases, though it leaves the society with growing stockpiles of hazardous wastes and raw materials that can be used for nuclear weapons. Ideally, these plants would not be needed if drastic conservation of electricity were achieved. It can be argued that such conservation is unlikely, that the waste problem is manageable, and that weapons-grade fuel can be controlled by an international system that manages the nuclear fuel cycle. [See Nuclear Power.]

Renewable energy sources

Renewable sources of heat and electricity are easy on the environment because they involve no combustion and add little waste to the atmosphere. They do entail some construction and manufacturing, however—using fossil fuels, metals, other materials, and electrical energy—all of which should be included in a thorough analysis of life-cycle impacts on the environment.

Some applications of solar energy, namely photovoltaic electric, solar water heating, and passive-solar building design do not require significant land areas: typically, solar collectors are mounted on the buildings they serve. Others, like wind-electric and high-temperature solar electric, do occupy large areas and have some impact on the Earth's surface and on wildlife. [See Renewable Energy Sources.]

Hydropower is a special and controversial case. Construction of a dam requires great amounts of material and energy; and its reservoir floods areas that may be important historically and as habitat. Furthermore, dams often interfere with fish migration and thus indirectly affect wildlife such as grizzly bears. These impacts must be balanced against decades of electrical generation free of greenhouse gases. Significant hydroelectric capacity can be installed with less environmental impact if small dams are employed, or if generators are driven by river currents without dams.

APPRAISAL

Every effort to gather and use nonanimate energy has some effect on the environment, but renewable sources, especially those that do not entail combustion, are the most sustainable. Mineral fuels impact land and water when they are produced and when they are burned pollute the air locally and regionally, cause acid deposition on land, acidify the oceans, and enhance the greenhouse effect.

Global warming with its wide-ranging impacts on ecosystems, agriculture, water supply, human health, and coastlines will drive us to reduce emissions from fossil-fuel burning, and to adopt electrical generation and transportation technologies that are free of emissions.

[See also Crude Oil Supply; Energy Strategies; Fossil Fuels; Impacts of Climate Change; and Sustainable Growth.]

BIBLIOGRAPHY

Cleveland, C. J., ed. Encyclopedia of Energy. Amsterdam: Elsevier, 2004.
Hentzman, A., and E. Solomon. Fueling the Future: How the Battle over Energy Is Changing Everything. Toronto: House of Anansi Press, 2003.
Mallon, K. Renewable Energy Policy and Politics: A Handbook for Decision-Making. London: Earthscan Publications, 2006.
Smil, V. Energy at the Crossroads: Global Perspectives and Uncertainties. Cambridge, Mass.: MIT Press, 2003.
United Nations Development Program (UNDP). The Sustainable Difference: Energy and Environment to Achieve the MDGs [Millennium Development Goals]. New York: UNDP, 2005. http://www.undp.org/energy and environment/Sustainable difference; accessed May 29, 2008.

—DAVID J. CUFF

ENERGY STRATEGIES

Two motives now drive the quest for effective energy strategies in the United States and other countries. First is the need for more secure supplies of primary energy, especially crude oil. Second is the threat of global warming, which dictates the reduction of carbon dioxide emissions. [See Global Warming and Greenhouse Effect.] The strategies mentioned briefly here are, with the exception of "Conservation, or Energy Efficiency," developed in related articles in this volume.

CONSERVATION, OR ENERGY EFFICIENCY

Both of the above goals will be served by reducing demand for electricity and for transportation fuels. The reduction will be accomplished by a combination of individual actions, new technologies, and government policies that mandate more efficient power plants, vehicles, appliances, and electric motors, and also establish energy-saving building standards.

STABILIZING CARBON DIOXIDE EMISSIONS

One article is often cited because it illuminates the daunting scale of the problem of achieving substantial reductions in carbon-dioxide emissions, while at the same time laying out solutions attainable using today's technologies (Pacala and Socolow, 2004). [See Stabilizing Carbon Emissions.]

EMISSIONS TRADING

One way to encourage modernization of power plants and other industries—and thereby reduce their carbon-dioxide emissions—is to institute a system of emission trading driven by caps placed on emissions (cap-and-trade system).

An industrial plant that can modernize readily and keep its emissions below the limit will earn credits which can be sold to the owners of a plant that cannot meet its emission standard. The result is to provoke the use of new technologies or other upgrades and to realize emission reductions that would not otherwise have occurred. [See Emissions Trading.]

CARBON TAXES

In this system the relevant government imposes taxes directly on carbon-dioxide emissions from a power plant or a cement manufacturing facility, for instance. This approach may be less complex than emissions trading and may yield more predictable reductions in carbon-dioxide emissions. [See Carbon Taxes.]

DEVELOPING ALTERNATIVE ENERGY SOURCES

These include biofuels for vehicles, and electricity from constant-flow sources such as solar radiation, the wind, river flow (hydro) and tidal-hydro. Clean generation of electricity will make it possible to reduce fuel combustion significantly. [See Biofuels; Energy and Environment; Ethanol; and Renewable Sources of Energy.]

NEW TECHNOLOGIES

Because coal-fired and gas-fired power plants are being planned and built around the world, their potential for carbondioxide emissions must be dealt with, using technologies that convert coal to gas and methods that capture and store (sequester) the carbon dioxide. [See Carbon Capture and Storage; and Coal Gasification.]

Assuming greenhouse-gas concentrations will continue to rise in the immediate future, some suggest technologies that will either draw carbon dioxide from the atmosphere into natural sinks in earth or ocean, or offset the greenhouse effect by intercepting solar radiation in the atmosphere and reflecting it to space. [See Geoengineering.]

ROLE OF GOVERNMENTS

Impatient with the federal government, a confederation of eight states (Connecticut, Delaware, Maine, Massachussetts, New Hampshire, New Jersey, New York, Vermont) in 2003 created the Regional Greenhouse Gas Initiative with its own cap-and-trade system. In 2007, Maryland joined that group, and five western states (Arizona, California, New Mexico, Oregon, and Washington) announced a similar program; by that year 431 mayors had signed on to a program to reduce emissions in their cities across the United States. [*See* Emissions Trading.]

In addition to levying taxes and approving cap-and-trade systems, governments can initiate conservation measures, collaborate with utility companies to build demonstration plants, and grant funds for research and development of alternative energy technologies. Some see great potential in an enlightened U.S. federal energy program. [*See* Coal Gasification; *and* National Energy Policy in the United States.]

BIBLIOGRAPHY AND OTHER RESOURCES

CONSERVATION

Alliance to Save Energy. www.ase.org/consumers

American Council for an Energy-efficient Economy. www.aceee.org

Willam J. Clinton Foundation. www.clintonfoundation. *Program to reduce energy use in buildings worldwide*

Energy Efficient Building Association. www.eeba.org

MacKinsey Global Institute Books. www.mickinsey.com/mgi. *Curbing Global Energy Demand Growth: The Energy Productivity Oppourtunity.* May 2007. *Wasted Energy: How the U.S. Can Reach Its Energy Productivity Potential.* July 2007

U.S. Department of Energy. www.energy.gov/energyefficiency. Energy Efficiency and Renewable Energy

U.S. Green Building Council. www.usgbc.org. Leadership in Energy and Environmental Design (LEED) rating system

ROLE OF GOVERNMENT

Regional Greenhouse Gas Initiative. www.rggi.org/about

STABILIZING CARBON DIOXIDE EMISSIONS

Pacala, S., and R. Socolow. "Stabilization Wedges: Solving the Climate Problem for the Next 50 Years with Current Technologies." *Science* 305 (2004), 968–972. DOI: 10.1126/science.1100103.

CARBON TAXES

Nordhaus, W.D. "To Tax or Not to Tax: Alternative Approaches to Slowing Global Warming." *Review of Environmental Economics and Policy* 1 (2007), 26–44. DOI: 10.1093/reep/rem008.

Parry, I.W.H. "Should We Abandon Cap and Trade in Favor of a CO_2 Tax?" *Resources*, Resources for the Future, No. 166 (Summer 2007), 7–10.

ALTERNATIVE ENERGY SOURCES

Sedjo, R. A. "From Oilfields to Energy Farms: A Brief Look at the Environmental Consequences of Biofuels." *Resources*, Resources for the Future, No. 166 (Summer 2007), 16–19.

—DAVID J. CUFF

ENVIRONMENTAL ACCOUNTING

Environmental accounting (EA) is the systematic effort to assess the ecological significance of economic activity and the economic worth of natural resources. It is employed by businesses, nonprofit organizations, and governments. Businesses may employ EA to control and reduce the costs of managing waste, remediating contaminated sites, paying environmental fines,

penalties and taxes, or purchasing pollution prevention technologies. Various national and international organizations employ EA to facilitate ecolabeling. Germany's "Blue Angel" and the U.S. "Green Seal" programs, for example, identify for consumers those goods whose production, use, and disposal are less environmentally harmful than those of noncertified products. When employed by governments, EA is grounded on the premise that measures of (national) welfare should include assessments of: available natural capital (stocks of natural resources); the depletion or degradation of natural capital and the collateral costs associated with such depletion or degradation; and expenditures for environmental protection and restoration. Here EA may expose the subsidization of environmentally harmful corporate practices and the environmentally destructive tax loopholes given to industries. Standard measures of economic welfare such as gross domestic product (GDP), which simply calculate the monetary value of all market transactions, disregard environmental impacts.

The most ambitious goal of EA is full-cost pricing. Full-cost pricing is based on the premise that the price consumers pay for goods and services should factor in long-term environmental (and social) costs. Businesses often "externalize" these costs. They may not clean up the waste streams produced by their operations, for example, effectively passing along the risks of pollution and expenditures for its mitigation to residents living "downstream." Alternately, a natural resource may be depleted without recompense to future generations that would otherwise benefit from its availability. Were full-cost pricing implemented, goods and services would be priced to include the environmental costs associated with their production, distribution, use, and disposal.

The use of "green taxes" approaches this goal. Many environmental groups endorse a tax on gasoline that would pay for the costs of building and maintaining highways and abating the pollution caused by vehicle exhausts. Pollution taxes for industrial facilities are also widely endorsed, as are taxes on resource and energy use and waste production. [*See* Ecotaxation.] In each case, EA is the first step of the process. Certain components of national EA—the valuation of natural resource stocks and use, for instance—are becoming mainstream. Incorporating other features that cannot easily be measured in economic transactions, such as the depletion of nonmarket goods (e.g., scenic views, wildlife), remains controversial.

THE HISTORY OF ENVIRONMENTAL ACCOUNTING

In the early 1970s, E. F. Schumacher observed that the modern industrial system was treating its irreplaceable natural capital as if it were income. Viewing the capacity of the biosphere to absorb pollution as a type of natural capital itself, Schumacher maintained that the saturation of the biosphere with pollution constituted an unsustainable depletion of resources. Schumacher's concerns were shared by many environmental scholars of the time, including economist Herman Daly. Only in the late 1980s, however, did EA gain widespread attention and undergo extensive conceptual clarification, empirical measurement, and practical implementation. Today many scholars, nongovernmental organizations, national and regional governments, and international agencies engage in and promote EA.

In 1991, a Special Conference on Environmental Accounting organized by the International Association for Research in Income and Wealth (IARIW) was held for scientists and practitioners in Baden, Austria. The conference produced a draft manual, later issued by the United Nations Statistics Division (UNSD) as a handbook entitled *Integrated Environmental and Economic Accounting*. That same year, a colloquium held by the U.S. National Academy of Sciences investigated the relation of EA to the emerging field of "industrial ecology," which employs lifecycle analysis of products and "design for environment" strategies. The 1992 United Nations Conference on Environment and Development held in Rio de Janeiro, also known as the "Earth Summit," produced a consensus view on the merit of public policies oriented toward sustainable development. The conference action plan, Agenda 21, endorsed environmental accounting as a component of sustainable development strategies.

In 1993, the findings of the Baden conference were partially incorporated into the revised edition of the globally-adopted system of national accounting (SNA). A system of integrated environmental and economic accounts (SEEA) was produced to accompany the SNA. In 2001 (revised 2003), UNSD and the United Nations Environment Program published this as the *Handbook of National Accounting*. A gathering of experts from national statistical agencies and international organizations, known as the London Group on Environmental Accounting, meets annually to develop and refine various protocols for EA. In 2007, the London Group focused on revisions to the SEEA handbook.

GREENING BUSINESS

Support within the business community for EA has been reserved. In part, this is because EA can be a complex and potentially costly enterprise; the internalization of externalities threatens profit margins. Were the full-cost pricing implemented, for example, the cost of monocropped fruits and vegetables produced by agribusiness and sold on distant supermarket shelves, despite industrial efficiency and economies of scale, might rise well above the cost of local organic produce purchased at farmers' markets. Full-cost pricing is also a time-consuming exercise that entails the discovery and disclosure of the complete life cycles of products. Determining the full-cost price of commercially produced fruits or vegetables would entail assessing: the environmental costs of their agricultural production, including soil erosion, the eutrophication of water sources caused by the use of synthetic fertilizer, and the bioaccumulation of contaminants caused by pesticide applications; the environmental costs of their delivery to consumers, including the pollution caused by trucking to market and the energy depletion caused by refrigerated transport and storage; and the environmental costs of their waste streams, including spoilage, discarded packaging, and noncomposted remains. The present total unpriced environmental costs of the U.S. food system are estimated at $150 billion to $200 billion per year. Whereas traditional accounting methods of agricultural production estimate an average profit of $80 per acre, full-cost pricing studies have estimated a loss of $26 per acre (Faeth et al., 1991). Full-cost pricing of imported foodstuffs may yield an even greater deficit.

The full-cost pricing of automobile use would also increase its costs significantly, making public transportation much more economical. Current gasoline taxes, vehicle taxes, and road tolls in the United States cover less than two-thirds of the total capital and operating costs of highways. Operating costs not covered each year by these user fees generally come out of state and local (income, property, or sales) taxes. In turn, the indirect costs associated with automobile travel, such as highway law enforcement, tending to accident victims, and smog abatement, amount to billions of dollars each year. Were these expenditures figured in to the price of motor-vehicle fuel, the cost of gasoline per gallon would double. If other collateral effects were assessed, the price would rise even higher. The destructive effects of car emissions on the nation's roadside crops are extensive. Motor vehicle pollution also adds billions of dollars to annual healthcare expenditures, and causes thousands of premature deaths. In turn, the cost of outfitting a large military force to secure foreign oil is substantial. With these expenditures included, the full-cost price of gasoline could mount to as much as $15 per gallon (International Center for Technology Assessment, 2005). Environmental accounting, advocates conclude, would have the effect of "taking cars off welfare."

Along with public transport, alternate forms of energy production would become more economically feasible were EA applied to fossil-fuel consumption. Greenhouse gases produced by the burning of fossil fuels are now understood to be responsible for significant global warming. Mitigating the effects and paying for the repercussions of climate change will be exorbitantly expensive. In addition, thousands of deaths from heart and lung disease are caused each year in the United States by particulate air pollution. If the cost of mitigating and paying for the repercussions of global warming, the cost of caring for particulate-pollution patients, and the cost of lost productivity and premature deaths were added to the price of burning coal or oil, these fossil fuels might become significantly more expensive than many forms of renewable energy.

GREENING THE GDP

Environmental organizations were quick to publicize the fact that the 1989 Exxon Valdez disaster, which dumped 11 million gallons of oil into Alaska's coastal waters, actually raised the GDP. That is because the cleanup efforts were formally recorded as contributions to the nation's economic productivity. Less controversial but no less significant examples abound: walking, biking, or taking mass transit to work contributes less to the GDP than the private use of an automobile. Wearing a sweater on winter nights contributes less than raising the thermostat. In short, the environmental imperative to "reduce, reuse, and recycle" is undermined by standard measures of economic productivity. Greening the GDP would necessitate counting the depletion and degradation of natural resources as a debit, not a credit to national accounts. A more comprehensive measure of quality of life would include various indicators of environmental welfare, such as human morbidity and mortality rates; ecological health indicators for forests, rivers, lakes, coastal regions, and agricultural land; levels of air and water purity; presence of wildlands; and biological diversity. Environmental accounting is a component of and prerequisite for all indices of national welfare.

BIBLIOGRAPHY

Ahmad, Y., S. El Serafy, and E. Lutz. *Environmental Accounting for Sustainable Development*. Washington, D.C.: World Bank, 1989. A brief account with an international focus.

Chertow, M.R., and D.C. Esty, eds. *Thinking Ecologically: The Next Generation of Environmental Policy*. New Haven, Conn.: Yale University Press, 1997. A very informative collection of essays.

Daly, H.E., and J.B. Cobb Jr. *For the Common Good: Redirecting the Economy toward Community, the Environment, and a Sustainable Future*. 2d ed. Boston: Beacon Press, 1994. A readable yet comprehensive introduction.

Dryzek, J.S. *Rational Ecology: Environment and Political Economy*. Oxford and New York: Blackwell, 1987. A critical look at standard economic practices and an endorsement of sustainable economics.

Faeth, P., et al. *Paying the Farm Bill*. Washington, D.C.: World Resources Institute, 1991.

Friends of the Earth and the National Taxpayers Union Foundation. *The Green Scissors Report: Cutting Wasteful and Environmentally Harmful Spending and Subsidies*. Washington, D.C., 1997. An example of environmental accounting in practice.

Hardin, G. *Living within Limits: Ecology, Economics, and Population Taboos*. New York: Oxford University Press, 1993. A hard-nosed assessment of ecological constraints to economic and population growth.

Hawken, P. *The Ecology of Commerce: A Declaration of Sustainability*. New York: HarperBusiness, 1993. An overview of environmental business practices and possibilities.

Hecht, J.E. "Environmental Accounting: Where We Are Now, Where We Are Heading." *Resources*, Resources for the Future, No. 135 (1999), 14–17.

International Center for Technology Assessment. *Real Price of Gasoline*. http://www.icta.org/pubs/ (accessed May 27, 2008).

MacKenzie, J.J., R.C. Dower, and D. Chen. *The Going Rate: What It Really Costs to Drive*. Washington, D.C.: World Resources Institute, 1992. An informative, empirical assessment.

Roodman, D.M. *Paying the Piper: Subsidies, Politics, and the Environment*. Worldwatch Paper 133. Washington, D.C.: Worldwatch Institute, 1995. An informative, empirical assessment.

Schmidheiny, S. *Changing Course: A Global Business Perspective on Development and the Environment*. Cambridge, Mass.: MIT Press, 1992. A useful overview of corporate environmentalism.

Schumacher, E.F. *Small Is Beautiful: Economics as If People Mattered*. New York: Harper and Row, 1973. A classic introduction to environmentally grounded economic thought.

United Nations. *Handbook of National Accounting: Integrated Environmental and Economic Accounting*. New York: United Nations, 2003. A useful summary account.

Uno, K., and P. Bartelmus, eds. *Environmental Accounting in Theory and Practice*. Dordrecht, The Netherlands, and Boston: Kluwer Academic, 1998. A well-organized anthology.

Welford, R., and R. Starkey, eds. *Business and the Environment*. Washington, D.C.: Taylor and Francis, 1996. A helpful introduction.

—LESLIE PAUL THIELE

ENVIRONMENTAL BIOETHICS

Environmental bioethics, or environmental ethics, is the theory and practice of values and duties concerning the natural world. A recurrent issue is whether ethics should be applied to the environment in the same anthropocentric way it is applied to business, medicine, engineering, law, and technology—the concern being that humans are helped or hurt by the condition of their environment. A naturalistic ethics is more radical, holding that animals, plants, endangered species, ecosystems, and even Earth as a whole ought to be the direct objects of moral concern. If so, environmental bioethics is unique in moving beyond human interests.

Perhaps the most urgent issue arises from global warming, because it threatens all life on Earth. Climate change affects human welfare, through melting ice caps, shifting rainfall, agricultural crises, flooded shorelines, and altered ocean currents. Biodiversity is equally threatened. Furthermore, the burning of fossil fuels confers benefits on some groups of people while harming others. The magnitude of the problem and the need to deal with with lag times require long-term self-discipline and revised political and economic institutional structures on a scale unprecedented in human history. This threat is so comprehensive that it renders the anthropogenic/naturalistic issue to some extent moot.

Environmental ethics and philosophy arose in the second half of the twentieth century under the impetus of the dramatically escalating power of humans to affect nature. Industrialization, advanced technologies, global capitalism, consumerism, ecological and evolutionary sciences, and exploding populations have all contributed to a concern that humans are not now in a sustainable relationship with their natural environment and that they have not been sensitive enough to the welfare of the myriads of other species.

A concern also arose for animal welfare. Sometimes ethicists advocated animal rights, typically for domestic animals (e.g., food animals, pets), but they also considered wild animals. These ethicists found common interests with environmentalists but also many differences. An animal-welfare ethics seeks to be "humane," and its adherents may be vegetarian. An ecocentric ethics has more concern for ecosystems, soil and water conservation, or wilderness preservation, and some of its advocates are hunters. Aldo Leopold termed this a land ethic, where "land" means the regional biotic community of life.

Biocentrism is sometimes used as a generic term for any naturalistic or nonanthropocentric ethics: more specifically, it refers to an ethics of respect for life and is focused on individuals. Going beyond animal welfare, biocentrism holds that any living thing can count morally, though plants, insects, animals, and humans need not count equally. Animals and plants must use each other as resources, which justifies some human uses of the environment. But human uses can be unjustified if they fail to consider the worth, or intrinsic value, of living things—cutting old-growth forests and threatening spotted owls, for example, instead of recycling or using tree plantations to meet our needs for paper and wood.

An axiological environmental ethics identifies various values carried by nature. Humans value nature as their life-support system, economically, recreationally, scientifically, aesthetically, and religiously, and for genetic diversity and as cultural symbols. Such values may be assigned to natural things by humans, or they may come into existence in human interactions with nature. Further, many values in nature are independent of human valuations: these are autonomously intrinsic values. Plants and animals alike defend their own lives; they belong to millennia-old lineages. Ecosystems are the sources and systems of life. An adequate ethics should optimize all relevant values, humanistic and naturalistic. Moral concern needs to focus on the relevant survival unit, not always the individual—often the species, the ecosystem, or, ultimately, the planet Earth.

Some values carried by nature are said to be "subjective," found only in the experiences of psychological subjects interacting with the world, as contrasted with "objective" values that are independent of such experiences, particularly those of humans. The issue is whether, apart from humans, animals and plants embody any values on their own, and whether these, too, ought to figure in environmental ethics (animal pain, the flourishing of a sequoia tree, or an endangered insect species). Some, adopting sentient environmental ethics, think that higher animals (vertebrates, mammals) with developed central nervous systems, are capable of such valuing experiences, but lower animals and plants are not; mere objects, such as mountains or rivers, have no values of their own.

"Deep ecology" emphasizes the ways in which humans, although individual selves, ought to extend those selves through a web of connections, taking a model from ecology. In this view, humans have destinies so entwined with the natural world that their richest quality of life involves a larger identification with these communities, human and natural, by which they are surrounded.

Human or social ecology focuses on the institutions of society, its politics, business, development plans, population policies, legal systems, and patterns of resource distribution. What is needed is not some revised metaphysics of nature sbut a criticism and reformation of human patterns of social behavior regarding nature. Though these follow from the worldviews of individuals, an environmental ethics must be corporate, because action must be taken collectively. Thus, an environmental policy, or a political ecology, sometimes called green politics, is needed. Bioregionalism argues that such human–nature relationships can best be worked out at regional levels, as in the U.S. Southwest or the Scandinavian Arctic.

Since the United Nations Conference on Environment and Development (UNCED) at Rio de Janeiro in 1992, there has been growing interest in sustainable development ethics. Third World nations argued that environmental conservation should not be separated from development, which involves environmental justice as well as environmental preservation. About four-fifths of the world's population, including most nations, produce and consume only about one-fifth of the world's goods. About one-fifth of the world's population produce and consume four-fifths of the goods. That is, according to many, neither fair nor sustainable. They observe that consumption by the rich is a greater problem than increasing populations in the developing nations, while global warming is produced by industrial nations, not developing ones. They call for an ethics of ecojustice.

Sustainable development, however, has proved an elastic concept, which may aim to sustain growth, profit, resource-base, opportunity, or communities. Those inclined to a more ecological ethics argue that ultimately humans ought to strive for a sustainable biosphere (which is seriously threatened by global climate change).

An ecofeminist ethics finds an alliance between the forces that exploit nature and those that exploit women, and may observe that women tend to care for nature, while men tend to dominate it, expressing a patriarchal bias present in many societies but especially in the modern West.

Many argue that a religious environmental ethics is essential, because religion is globally more influential than philosophy, and religion, misunderstood, has contributed to environmental problems. Monotheistic religions, such as Christianity, Judaism, and Islam, urge stewardship of creation, and they may speak of reverence for life. A creation spirituality has a strong sense of the divine presence in nature. Others argue that Eastern religions have something to offer, such as the harmoniously balanced *yang* and *yin* of Taoism, or the *ahimsa* (noninjury and respect for life) traditions in Hinduism and Buddhism. Native Americans and indigenous peoples in Africa, Australia, and South America have claimed that their traditions respect the natural world better than the modern West.

A postmodern environmental ethics doubts whether human knowledge of nature can be independent of the various cultural schemes used to interpret it: our worldview is more a social construction than an objective account of nature. These views can be better or worse—judged by their sustainability, or equitable distribution of resources, or quality of life—and that is all that is needed for an environmental ethics. Pluralist environmental ethics recognizes these cultural differences, while communitarian ethics emphasizes both human and biotic communities and how values differ at different ecological levels and different scales. These various ethics are unified when humans see themselves as Earthlings, with their home planet as their responsibility.

[*See also* Ethics; *and* Intergenerational Equity.]

BIBLIOGRAPHY

Armstrong, S., and F. Botzler, eds. *Environmental Ethics: Divergence and Convergence.* 3d ed. New York: McGraw-Hill, 2003.
Attfield, R. *The Ethics of the Global Environment.* Edinburgh: Edinburgh University Press, 1999.
Callicott, J. B. *Earth's Insights: A Survey of Ecological Ethics from the Mediterranean Basin to the Australian Outback.* Berkeley: University of California Press, 1997.
Dallmeyer, D., and A. Ike, eds. *Environmental Ethics and the Global Marketplace.* Athens, Ga: University of Georgia Press, 1998.
Devall, B., and G. Sessions. *Deep Ecology.* Salt Lake City: Smith, 1985.
Gardner, S. M. "A Perfect Moral Storm: Climate Change, Intergenerational Ethics and the Problem of Moral Corruption." *Environmental Values* 15 (2006), 397–413.
Gottlieb, R. S., ed. *The Oxford Handbook of Religion and Ecology.* Oxford and New York: Oxford University Press, 2006.
Light, A., and H. Rolston III, eds. *Environmental Ethics: An Anthology.* Malden, Mass., and Oxford: Blackwell, 2003.
Pojman, L. P. *Global Environmental Ethics.* Mountain View, Calif.: Mayfield, 2000.
Rolston, H., III. *Environmental Ethics: Values in and Duties to the Natural World.* Philadelphia: Temple University Press, 1988.

————. *Conserving Natural Value.* New York: Columbia University Press, 1994.

Schmidtz, D., and E. Willott, eds. *Environmental Ethics: What Really Matters, What Really Works.* New York: Oxford University Press, 2002.

Zimmerman, M. J., et al, eds. *Environmental Philosophy: From Animal Rights to Radical Ecology.* 4th ed. Upper Saddle River, NJ: Prentice-Hall, 2005.

—HOLMES ROLSTON III

ENVIRONMENTAL IMPACT ASSESSMENT

Environmental impact assessment (EIA) was introduced in the United States through the 1969 National Environmental Policy Act (NEPA), which came into effect on January 1, 1970. A previous attempt to introduce EIA failed after President Eisenhower opposed the Resources and Conservation Bill of 1959. Since its introduction NEPA has given rise to over 25,000 environmental impact statements that are used to influence decision-making and to provide a base of environmental information in the U.S. (Glasson, Therivel, and Chadwick, 2005).

EIA is a process of systematically identifying and assessing expected environmental impacts before the implementation of a proposed project, policy, program, or plan. The identification of significant negative impacts may prevent the proposal—which, until recently, has often been a project—from going ahead. However, the original proposal is generally modified, or measures are introduced to mitigate the anticipated negative environmental impacts. The EIA process should also consider the possibility that a proposal may generate positive environmental impacts, particularly on sites that are currently degraded.

EIA is now a legal requirement in the European Union, in many countries and provinces/states, and sometimes in individual cities. International institutions such as the United Nations Environment Programme (UNEP), the Asian Development Bank, the World Bank, and international aid agencies also require EIA for particular development proposals. The focus of these institutions is usually on capacity-building in individual countries so that they can develop the structures, skills, and motivation necessary to undertake EIA themselves (Lee and George, 2000).

Thomas and Elliot (2005) defined EIA as an environmental impact statement (EIS) plus an assessment report. Increasingly, environmental concerns are addressed as much as possible before the formal assessment. This may be achieved by the use of strategic environmental assessment (SEA) at the policy, program, or plan stage before a project is proposed. EIA requirements vary between jurisdictions, and different countries also use different terminology, which often causes confusion. For example, in some places an EIA is simply known as "impact assessment" because it covers more than the physical environment. In other locations it is known as an environmental assessment (EA) or, in the Australian state of Victoria, as environmental effects assessment (EEA). The word "impact" is sometimes perceived to have negative connotations. In the United States, an environmental assessment is a preliminary study undertaken as part of the EIA process to identify the likelihood of significant impacts, which then require the preparation of a full EIS.

EIA has expanded beyond NEPA's initial coverage of U.S. government projects. Wood's (2002) comparison of EIA systems in six countries and the states of California and Western Australia shows that EIA may include provincial and/or state development proposals and private development proposals, depending on the local legislation. The introduction of EIA in many countries has been based on the NEPA model, although attempts have been made in Canada and in the European Union to move away from the legal focus in the NEPA approach.

EUROPE

The European Economic Community (EEC) adopted EIA for all member countries in 1985 through Directive 85/337/EEC, which covered the types of project that required assessment, the scope of the assessment, and the public consultation requirements for all EEC member countries. Before the issuance of this directive, some European countries were advanced in EIA while other countries lagged in the introduction of EIA. The 1985 Directive left member states to implement the requirements of the Directive in legislation that they considered appropriate. This resulted in significant variations in the number of EIA reports prepared annually. Changes made to the 1985 Directive in 1997 included extending the assessment requirements to cover more projects and expanding the notion of public consultation to include consultation in a neighboring member-country, if people there are likely to be impacted by a proposed project, policy, plan, or program. This resulted in some countries continuing their high rate of EIAs per annum (notably France), some countries undertaking more EIA activity per annum between 1999, when the changes came into effect, and 2003—notably Denmark, Spain, and the U.K.—and some countries making few changes, notably Finland, The Netherlands, Portugal, and Sweden (Glasson, Therivel, and Chadwick, 2005). The 2003 review recommended further changes to EIA legislation and practice, especially by linking it to the Aarhus Convention on public participation. In countries such as Canada, the participation of indigenous people (First Nations) is being recognized in EIA, and particularly in the "upstreaming" of EIA into strategic environmental assessment (SEA), which was done because EIA has often come too late in the planning process (Lajoie and Bouchard, 2007).

CHANGES

EIA has also evolved from its initial focus on environmental protection to include the idea of sustainable development, which was introduced in the World Conservation Strategy in 1980 and popularized by the World Commission on Environment and Development (the WCED or Brundtland Commission) in 1987. The WCED's expert group on environmental law reported that states should undertake, or require, EIA (referred to as "prior environmental assessments") on proposed activities that may have significant effects on the environment, including the use of natural resources.

In addition to the above changes, forms of impact assessment have developed as extensions or critiques of EIA. Social impact assessment (SIA) considers the likely social and cultural impacts of a proposed project, plan, policy, or program. Strategic environmental assessment (SEA) recognizes the importance of decisions taken at the level above individual projects: that is, at policy, plan, and program levels. A European Union Directive on SEA came into effect in July 2004. The World Bank in 1989 required SEA of regional and sectoral activities (Therivel and Partidario, 1996). SEA, like other forms of impact assessment, needs to be understood in the context of environmental policy, planning, and management (Marsden and Dovers, 2002). Cumulative impact assessment (CIA) recognizes the existence of a range of cumulative impacts, such as time-crowding, space-crowding, time lags in the onset of impacts, compounding effects on a single site, which result in the whole being far greater than the sum of the individual parts. While SIA and CIA are now frequently incorporated into an expanded form of EIA, the treatment of social and cumulative impacts is often unsatisfactory.

EFFECTIVENESS

There is a range of opinion about the effectiveness of EIA. Supporters see EIA as an important process that discourages the environmentally worst projects from being undertaken and prevents the most undesirable aspects of some submitted proposals from being implemented. Most supporters recognize, however, that EIA by itself does not necessarily guarantee high-quality development, environmental protection, or sustainable development.

Some opponents perceive the EIA process as a way of legitimizing controversial development proposals while doing little to maintain environmental quality. They argue that few projects are refused because of the findings of the EIA process. However, this is not a good measure of effectiveness because projects may be substantially revised during the EIA process, and the mere existence of a process may prevent some environmentally damaging projects from being advocated. Opponents of EIA also argue that many key decisions have previously been taken at the policy level, and that individual project-based EIA also fails to consider the cumulative impacts of each development. These concerns are being addressed in part by strategic environmental assessment (SEA) at the policy and program level, and by cumulative impact assessment (CIA).

Between these extremes, there are those who believe that EIA has both strengths and weaknesses, and that the weaknesses could be addressed given political will. Current work includes a focus on EIA follow-up, because it is recognized that EIA predictions need to be monitored, and the effectiveness of mitigation and whether additional action was required to deal with unanticipated impacts need to be known (Morrison-Saunders and Arts, 2004).

EIA has changed significantly since its introduction in NEPA. Such evolution is evidence that this traditional project-based form of impact assessment is capable of being extended to newer forms of assessment (e.g., SEA, CIA, SIA) and of embracing ideas such as sustainable development. However, the effectiveness of the EIA process in practice, as opposed to an EIA legislative framework, is dependent upon the values, motivation, and skills of people involved at all stages in this process.

[See also Environmental Law; and Human Impacts.]

BIBLIOGRAPHY

Glasson, J., R. Therivel, and A. Chadwick. *Introduction to Environmental Impact Assessment.* 3d ed. London and New York: Routledge, 2005. Comprehensive coverage of the history, methods, and issues of EIA. It emphasizes the U.K., but has a chapter on comparative practice from various countries and looks at future prospects.

Lajoie, G., and M. A. Bouchard. "Native Involvement in Strategic Assessment of Natural Resource Development: The Example of the Crees Living in the Canadian Taiga." *Impact Assessment and Project Appraisal* 24.3 (2006) 211–220. DOI: 10.3152/147154606781765174.

Lee, N. and C. George, eds. *Environmental Assessment in Developing and Transitional Countries.* Chichester, U.K., and New York: Wiley, 2000. Includes coverage of the principles, processes, and practices of EIA followed by case studies of EIA undertaken by and for countries and institutions.

Marsden, S., and S. Dovers, eds. *Strategic Environmental Assessment in Australasia.* Annandale, New South Wales: Federation Press, 2002. Coverage of SEA in Australia with reference to the New Zealand experience.

Morrison-Saunders, A., and J. Arts, eds. *Assessing Impact: Handbook of EIA and SEA Follow-Up.* London: Earthscan, 2004. Covers process, countries (The Netherlands, Canada, Hong Kong), and issues such as dams, fisheries, and energy.

Thérivel, R., and M. R. Partidário, eds. *The Practice of Strategic Environmental Assessment.* London: Earthscan, 1996. A good overview of SEA, with five sectoral case study chapters and three regional case studies drawn from Europe, the United States, and Nepal.

Thomas, I., and M. Elliot. *Environmental Impact Assessment in Australia: Theory and Practice.* 4th ed. Annandale, New South Wales: Federation Press, 2005. A useful, if somewhat dated, guide to EIA in Australia. It is suitable for an international audience because it includes chapters on the history of EIA, forms of impact assessment, public participation, and it compares EIA systems in a range of countries.

Wood, C. *Environmental Impact Assessment: A Comparative Review.* 2d ed. Upper Saddle River, N.J.: Prentice Hall, 2002. Comprehensive coverage and comparison of many facets of EIA in the U.K., U.S., the Netherlands, Canada, Australia, New Zealand, and South Africa.

—PHIL MCMANUS

ENVIRONMENTAL LAW

Sophisticated legal systems have existed since early times, including the code of Hammurabi in Babylonia in the eighteenth century BCE and the laws of Manu in India (200 BCE). In modern societies, law is the primary instrument through which policies are implemented, and it can express minimum standards of morality or reflect the aspirations of a society. Law is a manifestation of society's values and adapts as those values change while helping to assure that change occurs in an orderly fashion.

Diverse legal traditions coexist in the world today. The common-law tradition evolved from judge-made law in medieval England and is now used by most former British possessions including the United States. The civil-law tradition is characterized by the enactment of law codes that integrate and organize all legal rules pertaining to a particular subject. This tradition has its roots in Roman law, was revitalized by the enactment in France of the Napoleonic Code in 1804, and is now used in most countries in Western Europe and Latin America, as well as in some Asian countries like Japan.

Other legal traditions are based on religious beliefs and include Jewish, Hindu, Muslim, and (Christian) canon law.

Sources of law vary among the legal traditions, but they usually include judicial decisions rendered by courts and tribunals. Another important source is the body of statutes or acts that are adopted by the state—in democracies, by an elected legislature. These statutes and acts are in turn implemented by detailed regulations promulgated by the national administration. Additional sources of law include custom, general principles of law, and legal writing by scholars. The science of law is divided into contract, tort, property, criminal, administrative, and constitutional law, as well as admiralty, corporate, intellectual property, and environmental law.

DOMESTIC ENVIRONMENTAL LAW

Domestic, or national, law is the legal system applicable to a defined territory over which a sovereign power has jurisdiction. International law, on the other hand, regulates the conduct of states and other international actors. Over the years, domestic and international law systems have evolved in parallel. In certain subject areas and regions of the world, international law has shaped and significantly contributed to the development of domestic environmental law, but international environmental law also reflects domestic experiences considered successful by the community of nations. The result is a complex relationship in which the two spheres of environmental law reinforce each other.

Early developments

Environmental law is a relatively new field, and other branches of law have historically been used to remedy environmental problems. In the common-law system, tort law—which provides remedies for harm caused by one individual to another—provided the necessary legal foundation in early cases. Nuisance actions were the most popular because they allow a successful claimant to receive not only compensation but also a court order to abate the nuisance, such as a smell or smoke. In the civil-law system, claimants invoked tort and property law generally in the same way. Historically, however, tort law, based as it is on the protection of individual's rights and the need to prove specific injury, has not been an effective means of preventing environmental degradation.

This inadequacy of tort and property law convinced governments, including local authorities, to adopt measures to tackle the most pressing environmental problems. There is some debate regarding the true nature of the first local ordinances regulating odors, smoke, and wastewater. Some scholars argue that they are early environmental statutes, while others consider that they are simply health-based policies having the effect of regulating environmental problems. Most of these early measures were in fact enacted following sporadic crises that endangered public health.

Modern environmental law

Division of powers and institutional arrangements. Since the 1970s, environmental law has experienced unprecedented growth in many countries. This was made possible through the enactment of new statutes and regulations that provide for higher standards of environmental protection. The level of government that has enacted these instruments varies from one country to another. In federal states like Canada, jurisdiction over the environment is shared between the provincial and federal governments. In the United States, the federal government has adopted most of the important environmental statutes, but their implementation is delegated to the states through a complex system of incentives and responsibilities. The European Union has a developed system of environmental law, the legal basis for which is to be found in the 1992 Maastricht Treaty on European Union. Although implementation is the responsibility of the individual EU Member States, European law permits individuals as well as other Member States and the European Commission, to pursue actions for breach of these rules before the European Court of Justice in Luxembourg.

Most countries have created institutions that handle environmental matters and enjoy varying degrees of independence, power, and jurisdiction. The primary function of these institutions is to coordinate domestic efforts aimed at the protection of the environment. This normally involves statute and regulation development, environmental-law enforcement, integration of environmental concerns in governmental decision-making and general environmental education. The nature of the institutions also differs greatly from one country to another; there is no ideal arrangement. Many countries have created an independent environment ministry, or have established a specialized agency, such as the U.S. Environmental Protection Agency, which was created by executive order and reports directly to the president. Some countries, such as the U.K., have both. Another approach, adopted widely in Latin America is the creation of an environmental commission that comprises representatives of many other ministries and departments.

Organization of environmental statutes. Environmental statutes have traditionally been drafted and organized around important themes like nature conservation and protection of the principal natural substances, air, water, and soil. This allows the elaboration of rules of limited application that are easier to manage and enforce but may not acknowledge the importance of a holistic approach or deal with important natural relationships such as the effects of air pollution on water quality. Other countries have adopted different approaches. New Zealand has a seminal 1991 Resource Management Act that integrates all sectors and relevant activities, while Canada has consolidated five of its main environmental statutes into a single act of general application. A similar technique is also used in countries like Chile that have adopted environmental framework laws, under which sectoral laws can be promulgated in an integrated way.

Legislative techniques. Despite the particular organization of a country's environmental laws, a law-making body will resort to a number of legislative techniques to attain its policy objectives.

A general *prior-authorization* requirement prohibits any person from engaging without prior permission in any activity that could harm to the environment. This essentially establishes a permit or license system whereby any activity that constitutes a potential source of pollution requires the permission of a central authority. This technique can be adapted to serve different policy goals. The scope of the permitting-system can be made broad to cover almost any component of the biosphere or narrow to regulate only certain types of activities.

Environmental standards are mostly command-and-control measures whereby a central authority mandates specific requirements to be followed by the regulated community. As such, authors distinguish them from "economic instruments" which rely on market-based approaches and which will be analyzed below.

The objective of standards is to prescribe specific quantitative and qualitative limits to be followed by the regulated community. They may take at least five different forms. First, health standards are normally based on risk-assessment analysis that identifies safe tolerance levels. These are used to control pesticides and similar substances and may be enacted without taking into account the compliance costs for the regulated community. Second, ambient environmental standards are used widely in the control of water- and air-pollution. These standards prescribe specific limits on the concentration of certain designated pollutants that will be tolerated, for example, in the ambient air or water. They may be used for the control of non-point (diffuse) pollution sources like the nitrate carried by runoff from agricultural land. Compliance with such standards may require major changes in agricultural or commercial practice. Third, emission and discharge standards are also used to combat air and water pollution. Instead of specifying limits applicable to the ecosystem, the standards place limits regarding the composition of the actual emissions or discharge by a specific source.

Two further forms of standards relate to technology. The most commonly used standard is technology-based. A statute may prescribe the use of the "best available technology." Through a cost/benefit analysis, the environmental agency will then specify for each class of industry the specific technology that it considers the "best available" and which is therefore mandated. Such standards may be relatively easily upgraded. More progressive are "technology-forcing" standards that cannot be met by the regulated community under the current state of technology. The intention, however, is that the obligation to meet this type of standard will stimulate and "force" technological innovation. This technique has been used in the United States to regulate motor-vehicle emissions.

Liability is the condition of being actually or potentially subject to a legal obligation. Under civil liability, a person will be liable if he or she was negligent, that is, if his or her conduct fell below the objective standard of a reasonable person. Criminal liability is more serious and requires proof beyond reasonable doubt of an unlawful act as well as of the defendant's specific intent. Strict liability is an intermediary concept that is commonly used in environmental laws. It relieves the state of the obligation to prove that the unlawful act resulted from negligence (civil liability) or that the defendant's conduct was intentional (criminal liability). In other words, the state need only prove that the particular defendant committed an unlawful act (e.g., the illegal discharge of wastewater). Another important liability concept is that of joint and several liability, under which violators will be held liable together and individually. In this case, the government can sue all violators or any one of them separately to recover, for example, cleanup costs. This technique is very useful when it can be proved that each defendant contributed to an unlawful activity, but the exact contribution of each is difficult to demonstrate, or when the injury is simply indivisible.

Retroactive liability is the hallmark of modern soil statutes and constitutes an exception to general principles of law. Under these principles, one should not be held liable for the acts of another or for actions that were lawful when they were taken. Many governments have invoked this exception as a solution to the contamination of land by hazardous wastes. In urban areas the contamination of land often results from decades of intensive industrialization that has occurred without any meaningful preexisting environmental standards. Under some soil statutes, current and past owners of contaminated land may be held liable for cleanup costs, even if they have not personally contributed to the contamination. Under certain circumstances, operators, transporters and, to a limited extent, lenders can also be held liable. Retroactive liability is still controversial and has raised some problems. It has important economic consequences as the value of such land may drop so far as to become negative in cases where cleanup costs exceed the property's value. In the long term, retroactive liability can also result in new investments going only to pristine "greenfield" sites to avoid contaminated areas that are often situated in disadvantaged communities. Despite these difficulties, the harshness of the liability provision has in some countries coerced industries into better environmental behavior and has substantially minimized major health risks.

Among modern environmental statutes, *environmental impact assessment* (EIA) laws represent a preventive approach to environmental protection because they integrate environmental considerations in decision-making processes. Generally, EIA laws require the preparation of an environmental impact assessment for any proposed development to review and assess its environmental impacts. The requirement can be applicable to a broad range of actions and include issuance of a permit or prior authorization, the funding of a project, and the adoption of a new statute or policy. The first step under EIA laws (known as screening) is the determination of whether or not the proposed activity is likely to cause environmental impacts beyond a certain threshold. If such a determination is positive, the proposer must proceed with the preparation of a formal assessment. Depending on the apprehended impacts, the general public will be notified and public consultations will be held. The environmental assessment may be required to identify appropriate mitigation measures or alternatives to the proposed action which minimize environmental impacts. The key issue is whether EIA statutes oblige the proposer to implement the mitigation measures and alternatives previously identified. Without such a mitigation requirement, EIA laws may render decision-making more transparent, but they do not provide effective safeguards to protect the environment.

[*See* Environmental Impact Assessment.]

Enforcement of environmental law. Enforcing environmental law is critical to ensure that the regulated community complies with the policies embodied in a statute. The goals of a good enforcement program are to achieve general environmental compliance through deterrence and to identify environmental violators efficiently and prosecute them diligently. Compliance can be achieved through general education and outreach to the regulated community, backed by effective prosecution procedures. In addition, government bodies may conduct inspection activities periodically or on the basis of probable cause. In some countries, the regulated industry is obliged to make their monitoring data publicly available. This information may also allow nongovernmental organizations to play an important role in identifying violators.

The government, through its administrative agency, is normally the entity responsible for prosecuting violations of environmental law. In some countries, individuals or nongovernmental organizations can also sue violators and recover a share of the awarded penalty as a reward for their initiative, through procedures known as citizen suits or public interest actions. In addition, national constitutions or environmental statutes may protect the right of an individual to a clean environment. In India, for example, such provisions have allowed the courts to take a highly proactive role in the protection of the environment.

New trends in environmental law

Two new trends are currently shaping environmental lawmaking. The first is integrated pollution control (IPC) that allows for the regulation of an ecosystem as a whole, instead of approaching it on a sector-by-sector basis. This specifically avoids the transfer of pollution from one medium (such as water) to another (such as air) and helps in controlling pollution from non-point sources. This approach has been pioneered in the U.K. and now in the EU.

The second trend is the use of economic instruments that complement command-and-control measures. Under this approach, the government sets targets and allows members of the regulated community to allocate among themselves the burden of compliance. Theoretically, if the price of noncompliance is set at an appropriate level, the desired abatement of pollution will be achieved. The advantage is that sources with lower compliance costs will overcomply and receive economic benefits from those with higher compliance costs. The result is the attainment of pollution abatement at a lower net cost to society than would be the case under strict command-and-control measures. Other economic instruments include the use of taxes, environmental auditing, ecolabeling (to assure consumers that a product meets certain environmental standards), and the reduction of subsidies that allow the regulated community to play a role in shaping new practices.

INTERNATIONAL LAW

Modern international law has its roots in the sixteenth- and seventeenth-century public law of Europe that was created to govern the diplomatic, commercial, military, and other relations of the society of Christian states. With the growing penetration of Europe into Asia in the late eighteenth and early nineteenth centuries, other subjects were included in the community of states, but it was only with the formation of the League of Nations in 1920, of which any state could be a member, that the international system began to aspire to be truly global.

Doctrinal foundations of international law

International law rests on the doctrine of sovereignty and equality of states. This doctrine enshrines the principle that national states are sovereign and have equal rights and duties as members of the international community, notwithstanding economic, social, political, or other differences. This fundamental feature of international law has created systemic limitations: the absence of an established central legislative authority comparable to a nation system; the absence of a compulsory, or even widely used, judicial system coupled often with the absence of effective enforcement machinery for breaches of international law. It is no surprise, then, that after several centuries of international law, many still ask what has been described as the standard cocktail-party question, "Is international law really law?" Despite its systemic limitations international law does exist. States make it and follow it—and occasionally break it. Certain breaches are spectacular but overshadow the general everyday pattern of compliance.

Sources of international law

The international community, in the face of the rudimentary character of international law-making institutions, has developed its own system for creating norms and making international law. These are basically twofold, treaties and customary international law. Treaties can only be binding on those who consent to them; they are solemn binding agreements between subjects of the international legal order, principally states. They originate in a framework of international negotiation over matters of common interest and result in an agreement, in the form of a text, that usually reflects mutual advantage. Once the text is agreed upon (and at that stage often signed), the process of ratification commences. This is the process by which the parties ensure, by their various constitutional means, that when the treaty comes into force, the legal, financial, and administrative mechanisms by which the parties will be able to honor their new obligations will be in place. Only after these national measures have been enacted will the state be in a position to notify the depository (the state or institution formally holding the list of parties) that it wishes to be bound by the treaty; this is the act of ratification. Once the treaty has received the agreed number of ratifications it will come into force. This is not an easy process. Pressures of government time, changing priorities, or simple second thoughts, can cause dramatic delays. The larger the enterprise, the more intransigent the problems often are.

For example, it was not until November 16, 1994, that the Law of the Sea Convention signed in Jamaica in December 1982 finally came into force. It had taken twelve years and considerable legal ingenuity in the negotiation of an amending agreement for this major international legislative act to receive the 60 ratifications it required to enter into force.

International customary law is defined by the founding Statute of the International Court of Justice as general practice accepted by states as law. In simple terms it is something that states do because they regard themselves as legally obliged to do it.

Treaties and custom constitute "hard law," law that nation states are obliged to follow under pain of sanction from the international legal system and community. "Soft law," in contrast, comprises nonbinding instruments which lay down guidelines or desiderata for future action, or through which states commit themselves politically to meeting certain objectives. Soft law is largely based on international diplomacy and customs, and dependent on moral suasion or fear of diplomatic retribution. The 1972 Stockholm Declaration and the 1992 Rio Declaration, which embody a series of widely revered environmental principles, constitute good examples of soft law, although a number of those principles may be said to have crystallized into "harder" obligations representing customary law. There are also subsidiary sources of international law such as doctrine, judicial decisions, resolutions of the UN General Assembly, and opinions of international jurists.

Development of international environmental law

While the status of international environmental law is disputed by a few international scholars who believe that no autonomous "international law" exists apart from the general international law, it appears well established that environmental perspectives and concerns have stimulated international legal development. The growth of international environmental law is premised on the globalization of environmental problems and concerns, attributable to two crucially interlinked factors, ecological and economic interdependence.

Huge conceptual leaps were made in international environmental law in the last quarter of the twentieth century. Environmental problems have progressed from being tackled in a bilateral, coexistence framework to being dealt with in a multilateral, cooperative framework. Further, international environmental law has gone from being merely reactive, as in the negotiation of treaties to address the threats of marine oil pollution, to being proactive, as in the case of the UN Framework Convention on Climate Change (UNFCCC) which is an anticipatory response to the possibility of anthropogenic global climate change.

The development of international environmental law can be traced through two main phases: 1972–1992, which was the period of burgeoning international environmental consciousness during and after the UN Conference on the Human Environment in Stockholm in 1972; and from 1992 onward. The latter period, initiated by the negotiations leading up to the 1992 UN Conference on Environment and Development in Rio de Janeiro, is distinguished by concerns for sustainable development and includes the current phase of experimentation with market-based instruments to achieve environmental compliance.

From Stockholm to Rio (1972–1992). The Stockholm Conference, held in 1972, catalyzed several environmental initiatives. It resulted in a declaration containing a series of normative environmental principles, a 109-point Environmental Action Plan, and a resolution recommending institutional and financial implementation by the UN. The result of these recommendations was the creation of the United Nations Environment Programme (UNEP), established by a resolution of the UN General Assembly and based in Nairobi. UNEP plays an active role in convening meetings to negotiate global environmental treaties. The Convention on the Control of Transboundary Movements of Hazardous Wastes and their disposal, signed in Basel, Switzerland, March 22, 1989, is a case in point. The Basel Convention is built around two basic principles—that of proper waste management and that of prior informed consent. UNEP was also directly responsible for the development of the important Regional Seas Program which has resulted in a network of regional framework conventions protecting the marine environment, each with protocols developed to meet the special requirements of the region.

This era also witnessed the birth of several other international environmental treaties. Of particular significance is the 1985 Vienna Convention for the Protection of the Ozone Layer. The real and apparently imminent threat of depletion of the ozone layer by commercially produced chemicals, principally chlorofluorocarbons (CFCs), prompted the convening of the 1985 conference. The format chosen was a framework convention: general obligations and institutional framework were laid down by the treaty, to be made more specific in the future by the negotiation of detailed protocols (or subtreaties open to the parties to the main convention). The discovery of the ozone hole over Antarctica led to intense intergovernmental negotiations resulting in the Montreal Protocol on Substances that Deplete the Ozone Layer in 1987. The protocol called for a freeze on the production and consumption of CFCs and halons at 1986 levels, followed by a 50% reduction in CFC use by industrialized countries over a ten-year period. Developing countries were allowed to increase their CFC consumption for ten years. The protocol was deliberately designed as a flexible and dynamic instrument; countries were allowed to select the most economical combination of reductions and incentives to reduce the most harmful chemicals.

A follow-up to the Stockholm Conference held in 1982 in Nairobi spurred the UN to set up the World Commission on Environment and Development, chaired by Gro Harlem Brundtland, then prime minister of Norway. Its 1987 report "Our Common Future" placed the concept of sustainable development in the realm of international environmental law. At the suggestion of the Commission, preparations began for the Rio Summit, officially the Conference on Environment and Development, thus marking the end of the era of emphasis on the human environment and the beginning of the era of emphasis on environment and development.

Rio and beyond. The United Nations Conference on Environment and Development held in Rio de Janeiro twenty years after the Stockholm Conference was popularly perceived as an attempt at environmental planning on a grand scale. In addition to a tremendous surge in environmental consciousness, the Rio Summit resulted in:

* Agenda 21, a plan for action into the twenty-first century.
* The Rio Declaration on the Environment and Development.
* The 1992 United Nations Framework Convention on Climate Change, which was to provide a framework for the negotiation of detailed protocols on further issues such as controls on the emissions of greenhouse gases—particularly carbon dioxide—and deforestation.
* The 1992 Convention on Biological Diversity, which was aimed at arresting the alarming rate at which species were disappearing through pollution and habitat destruction.
* A legally nonbinding Declaration on Forests.

Despite the obvious significance of these environmental initiatives, perhaps the most enduring legacy of the Rio Summit lies in its contribution to the development of a framework of international environmental law principles. If the maturity of international environmental law is to be assessed by the development of discrete discipline-specific principles, then the Rio Declaration heralded its coming of age. [*See* Biological Diversity; *and* Framework Convention on Climate Change.]

Principles of international environmental law

Several principles of international environmental policy, some first enunciated in the Stockholm Declaration, were crystallized through the Rio process. Among them, were the principles of precaution, polluter-pays, sustainable development, common but differentiated responsibility, and environment impact assessment (EIA). Some of these concepts such as polluter-pays and environment impact assessment have their roots in domestic environmental law. EIA, for instance, was first established in the domestic law of the United States under the 1972 National Environment Protection Act. Other principles, such as that of common but differentiated responsibility are products of international thought and action. International lawyers still dispute whether any or all of these concepts remain policy principles or have hardened into binding principles of customary international law.

Precautionary. Enshrined in Principle 15 of the Rio Declaration, the precautionary principle asserts that where serious harm is threatened, positive action to protect the environment should not be delayed until irrefutable scientific proof of harm is available. It represents an important tool for decision-making in uncertainty, which a significant body of opinion argues is now a legal principle. In its strongest formulations this principle requires a reversal of the normal burden of proof so that a potential actor would need to prove that a proposed activity will not cause harm before it can be sanctioned. It has been endorsed by virtually all recent environmental treaties, including regional treaties such as the 1992 Maastricht Treaty on European Union, the 1992 Paris Convention for the Protection of the Marine Environment of the North-East Atlantic, the Helsinki Convention on the Baltic Sea Environment and global environmental treaties such as the UNFCCC, the Convention on Biological Diversity, and the 1995 United Nations Agreement on Straddling Fish Stocks and Highly Migratory Fish Stocks. [*See* Precautionary Principle.]

Environment impact assessment, public participation, and access to information. Related to the precautionary principle is the concept of environment impact assessment. It is based on the premise that rational planning constitutes an essential tool for reconciling development and environment. EIA provides an important means of implementation of the precautionary principle. Though first debated at Stockholm, the concept of environment impact assessment was not formally expressed until the Rio Declaration. Agenda 21 calls on countries to assess the suitability of infrastructure in human settlements, ensure that relevant decisions are preceded by environment impact assessments, take into account the costs of any ecological consequences, and integrate environmental considerations in decision-making at all levels and all ministries. The Environment Impact Assessment requirement is embodied in several international instruments, notably the 1991 UN Economic Commission for Europe (ECE) Convention on Environmental Impact Assessment in a Transboundary Context, the 1992 Biodiversity Convention, and the 1991 World Bank Operational Directive 4.01. The value and legitimacy of environment impact assessment has in recent times been strengthened by the evolution of the right of access to information on the environment and the right of public participation. The Rio Declaration recognizes in Principle 10 that environmental issues are best handled with the participation of all concerned citizens. It has recently been validated in the UN ECE Convention on Access to Information, Public Participation in Decision-Making, and Access to Justice in Environmental Matters, signed on June 25, 1998, by 37 countries. The Convention recognizes that "every person has the right to live in an environment adequate to his or her health and well-being, and the duty … to protect and improve the environment" and that "citizens must have access to information, be entitled to participate in decision-making, and have access to justice in environmental matters." In order for people to enjoy these rights and fulfill these responsibilities, the Convention obligates signatory states to, among other provisions: make environmental information available "as soon as possible," and "without an interest having to be stated" by the solicitor; take specific measures to ensure complete public participation in decisions of specific activities, plans, programs, policies, and other regulations related to the environment; and ensure that any person who feels the state has not met specific environmental commitments has access to review before a court. The value of such participation is enhanced by the right of access to information, a right which has found its way into various international instruments. The ECE Directive 90/313 on Access to

Environmental Information assures the public free access to and dissemination of all environmental information held by public authorities throughout the ECE.

Common but differentiated responsibility. Articulated as Principle 7 in the Rio Declaration, this principle requires states to cooperate in a spirit of global partnership to protect the environment. Yet, because states have contributed differently to global environmental problems, the principle recognizes that though they should have common responsibilities, those responsibilities should be apportioned rationally among the states. Article 4 of the 1992 UNFCCC, for instance, places an obligation on developed countries to take the lead in meeting the required reductions in greenhouse-gas emissions and on developing-country parties only to implement those commitments to the extent that developed countries have met their commitments to provide financial resources and to transfer technology. The principle of common but differentiated responsibility is sure to govern further negotiations on the UNFCCC. The structure of the 1997 UNFCCC Kyoto Protocol mirrors the philosophy of common but differentiated responsibility. The developed countries are committed to reducing their overall emissions of greenhouse gases to at least 5% below 1990 levels between 2008 and 2012. The developing nations have no such commitments. Although every nation state has the responsibility of reducing global greenhouse-gas emissions, only the OECD and economies-in-transition countries are required to meet specific quantified emission limitations. The limitations, even among these countries, vary in order to account for differing domestic circumstances. Developing countries are provided with an opportunity to participate through the Clean Development Mechanism that allows countries to cooperate on specific projects to reduce greenhouse gas emissions. [See Kyoto Protocol.]

Polluter-pays. This requires that the costs of pollution be borne by the party responsible. The practical implications of this principle lie in its allocation of economic obligations in environmentally damaging activities. This seemingly intuitive principle has not received the broad support that the precautionary principle has. Principle 16 of the Rio Declaration, for instance, supports the "internalization of environmental costs" taking into account the polluter-pays principle but only "with due regard to the public interest and without distorting international trade and investment." An example of an international instrument that refers expressly to the polluter-pays principle is the 1972 OECD Council recommendation on Guiding Principles Concerning the International Economic Aspects of Environmental Policies, which endorses the polluter-pays principle to allocate costs of pollution-prevention and control measures so as to encourage rational use of environmental resources.

Sustainable development. Defined by the 1987 Brundtland Committee Report as "development that meets the needs of the present without comprising the ability of future generations to meet their own needs," this principle is at the heart of many environmental initiatives. It recognizes the need for intergenerational equity, sustainable and equitable use of resources held in common by the current generation, and the integration of environmental considerations into economic and other development initiatives. This principle is also reflected inter alia in the Framework Convention on Climate Change in Article 3(4). Although specifically recognized as a legal principle in the separate opinion of International Court of Justice (ICJ) Judge Weeramantry in the *Gabcikovo-Nagymaros* case (1997), the very breadth of the concept means that considerable controversy still surrounds this argument. [See Brundtland Commission; and Sustainable Growth.]

Compliance and enforcement of international environmental law

The term "enforcement" in the context of international environmental law refers to the measures to ensure the fulfillment of international legal obligations or to obtain a ruling by an appropriate international body that obligations are not being fulfilled.

Initially, only the general principles of state responsibility and dispute settlement guided efforts at enforcement of international environmental law. As the principal subjects of international law, states assume the obligation to enforce international environmental law. Enforcement by states arises primarily in situations of transboundary environmental harm and involves a determination by an international body such as the ICJ in The Hague. The ICJ, the principal judicial organ of the UN, rules on questions of international law, including, potentially, issues of international environmental law. In fact, however, its contribution to the development of international environmental law principles has been slight.

A range of techniques and a wide array of international actors are today involved in the enforcement of international law. Enforcement includes a panoply of tools including diffusion of information, monitoring, verification, and inspection. For example, it is increasingly common for international-law agreements to mandate their Conferences of Parties, the permanent plenary body of environmental agreements, to conduct implementation reviews. This review mechanism monitors national compliance with the obligations undertaken under the environmental agreement. Such a review is based primarily on national self-reporting, though some conventions do provide for independent means of gathering information.

Other conventions may use incentives or disincentives, the carrot-and-stick approach, to obtain participation and ensure compliance. For example under the Montreal Protocol, trade restrictions can be imposed on imports to and exports from states not party to the protocol, and a fund has been created to assist countries in complying with their obligations under the protocol, thereby encouraging participation. Recently negotiated conventions use creative, dynamic, and flexible means to obtain environmental compliance. The UNFCCC Kyoto Protocol provides a number of "flexibility mechanisms" (including cooperative implementation, emissions trading, and technology transfer) to assist parties in meeting their commitments.

Among the concerned actors are also international organizations and nongovernmental organizations. International organizations have a small but useful role to play in the enforcement of international environmental obligations. States have traditionally been reluctant to endow international organizations with enforcement powers, but some recent instruments do provide certain bodies with limited enforcement authorities. For instance the 1982 UNCLOS (United Nations Convention on the Law of the Sea) provides the International Seabed Authority with the power to supervise implementation of parts of the Convention, invite attention of the Assembly to cases of noncompliance, and institute proceedings for noncompliance. Nongovernmental actors often play the role of self-appointed watchdogs against the national governments and can thus help in the enforcement of international law through political means or public interest litigation to ensure that governments keep to their international environmental commitments. The individual as an actor in the international arena also deserves mention. With the increasing emphasis on public participation and provision of access to environmental information, in international discourse, the individual's role in ensuring international environmental compliance is becoming increasingly relevant.

BIBLIOGRAPHY

Ball, S., and S. Bell. *Environmental Law: The Law and Policy Relating to the Protection of the Environment.* 2d ed. London: Blackstone, 1994. First book to provide a systematic exposition of English environmental law, also incorporating European Union policies and requirements.

Birnie, P. W., and A. E. Boyle. *International Law and the Environment.* Oxford: Clarendon, 1992. An outstanding work of scholarship and reference, providing an invaluable map of the emerging field of international environmental law.

Boisson de Chazournes, L., R. Desgagné, and C. Romano. *Protection internationale de l'environnement: Recueil d'instruments juridiques.* Paris: Pedone, 1998. The first comprehensive French language collection of international legal materials on the protection of the environment. Contains useful thematic summaries and analytical bibliographies.

Boisson de Chazournes, L. "La mise en oeuvre du droit international dans le domaine de la protection de l'environnement: Enjeux et defies." *Revue Générale de Droit International Publique* 99 (1995), 37. Analysis of the role played by traditional means and new procedures for ensuring compliance and enforcement of international environmental law.

Boyle, A.E., and M. Anderson, eds. *Human Rights Approaches to Environmental Protection.* Oxford: Clarendon Press, 1996.

Chertow, M.R., and D.C. Esty, eds. *Thinking Ecologically: The Next Generation of Environmental Policy.* New Haven, Yale University Press, 1997.

Churchill, R., and D. Freestone, eds. *International Law and Climate Change.* London: Graham and Trotman/Martinus Nijhoff, 1991.

David, R., and J.E.C. Brierley. *Major Legal Systems in the World Today.* 3d ed. London: Stevens, 1985.

Freestone, D. "The Road from Rio: International Environmental Law after the Earth Summit." *Journal of Environmental Law* 6 (1994), 193–218. DOI: 10.1093/jel/6.2.193. An assessment of the impact of the UN Conference on Environment and Development on the development of international environmental law.

Freestone, D., and E. Hey, eds. *International Law and the Precautionary Principle: The Challenge of Implementation.* The Hague and London: Kluwer Law International, 1996.

Harris, D.J. *Cases and Materials on International Law.* 4th ed. London: Sweet and Maxwell, 1991.

Huglo, C. and de Malafosse, J., eds. *Juris-classeur environnement.* Paris: Éditions du Juris-Classeur, 1998. 3 vols. The most comprehensive source on French domestic environmental law.

Kamto, M. *Droit de l'environnement en Afrique.* Vanves, France: EDICEF/AUPELF, 1996. Very good analysis of domestic and regional environmental law in Africa.

Kiss, A., and Shelton, D. *International Environmental Law.* New York: Transnational Publishers, 1991. The first and still classic exposition of the new subject area of international environmental law.

Krämer, L. *Focus on European Environmental Law.* London: Sweet and Maxwell, 1992.

———. *European Environmental Law: Casebook.* London: Sweet and Maxwell, 1993.

Kummer, K. *International Management of Hazardous Wastes: The Basel Convention and Related Legal Rules.* Oxford: Clarendon Press, 1995.

Lyster, S. *International Wildlife Law.* Cambridge: Grotius, 1985. Although dated, this is an excellent and highly readable account of the various international treaty regimes which aim to protect wildlife.

Reitze, A. W. Jr. *Air Pollution Law.* Charlottesville, Va.: Michie Butterworth, 1995.

Rodgers, W. H. Jr. *Environmental Law.* 2d ed. St. Paul, Minn: West, 1994. Provides a comprehensive overview of domestic environmental law in the United States.

Sand, P. H., ed. *The Effectiveness of International Environmental Treaties.* Cambridge: Grotius, 1992. This volume brings together expert reports prepared for UNCED assessing the success of international environmental treaty law in meeting its declared objectives.

Sands, P. *Principles of International Environmental Law.* Manchester, U.K.: Manchester University Press, 1995. First of three volume collection provides a stimulating scholarly and highly readable exposition of international environmental law. The remaining two volumes, edited jointly with Richard Tarasofsky and Mary Weiss, provide an invaluable collection of primary materials on international and European Environmental law.

UNEP. *Handbook of Environmental Law.* Nairobi: UNEP, 1992.

—DAVID FREESTONE AND LAURENCE BOISSON DE CHAZOURNES

ENVIRONMENTAL MOVEMENTS

Environmental movements are networks of groups and individuals that hold common ecological values. Movement members seek to shape sensibilities, commitments, and practices within the general public as well as to influence business practices and government policy. To achieve these ends, members of environmental movements may organize themselves into political parties or form nonprofit organizations.

There are currently about 75 national green political parties worldwide. The earliest were organized in the early 1970s in New Zealand and the United Kingdom. The United States Green Party formed in the mid-1980s, by which time West German Greens had already gained significant representation in government. Most environmental groups are not political parties but nongovernmental organizations (NGOs). Environmental NGOs engage in scientific research, public education, political advocacy, and hands-on environmental protection, preservation, and restoration. They strategically exploit the resources of the media, government, the legal system, and public opinion to further their goals. While most environmental groups are organized locally, regionally, or nationally, many have global orientations and international memberships. There are tens of thousands of these groups worldwide. This article focuses primarily on the North American environmental movement and its most popular organizations. [*See* Nongovernmental Organizations.]

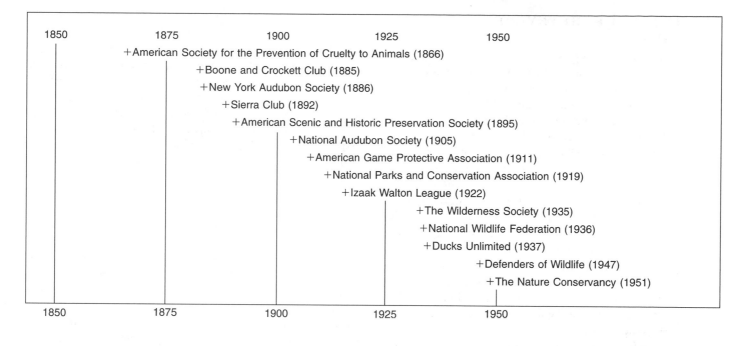

| 1850 | 1875 | 1900 | 1925 | 1950 |

+American Society for the Prevention of Cruelty to Animals (1866)
+Boone and Crockett Club (1885)
+New York Audubon Society (1886)
+Sierra Club (1892)
+American Scenic and Historic Preservation Society (1895)
+National Audubon Society (1905)
+American Game Protective Association (1911)
+National Parks and Conservation Association (1919)
+Izaak Walton League (1922)
+The Wilderness Society (1935)
+National Wildlife Federation (1936)
+Ducks Unlimited (1937)
+Defenders of Wildlife (1947)
+The Nature Conservancy (1951)

| 1850 | 1875 | 1900 | 1925 | 1950 |

| 1950 | 1975 | 2000 |

+World Wildlife Fund (1961)
+Environment Defense Fund (1967)
+Zero Population Growth (1968)
+Friends of the Earth (1969)
+National Resources Defense Council (1970)
+Environmental Action (1970)
+League of Conservation Voters (1970)
+Sierra Club Legal Defense Fund (1971)
+Clean Water Action (1971)
+Greenpeace (1971)
+Cultural Survival (1972)
+Negative Population Growth (1972)
+Cousteau Society (1973)
+Environmental Policy Institute (1974)
+Worldwatch Institute (1975)
+Sea Shepherd Conservation Society (1977)
+People for the Ethical Treatment of Animals (1980)
+Earth First! (1980)
+Citizens Clearinghouse for Hazardous Waste (1981)
+Co-op America (1982)
+Earth Island Institute (1982)
+National Toxics Campaign (1984)
+Rainforest Action Network (1985)
+The Conservation Fund (1985)
+Rainforest Alliance (1986)
+Conservation International (1987)

| 1950 | 1975 | 2000 |

Environmental Movements. Figure 1. Founding Dates of Selected Environmental Organizations.

THE HISTORY OF THE ENVIRONMENTAL MOVEMENT

As the environmental dangers of industrialization became evident in the nineteenth century, the popularity of nature writing and natural history grew in America and Europe. In the late 1820s, John James Audubon began publishing his *Birds of America*. Ralph Waldo Emerson wrote his famous essay "Nature" in 1836. In 1854, Henry David Thoreau published *Walden*, America's most famous tribute to the harmony of humanity and nature. In the early 1870s, the first popular magazines advocating nature conservation were published. By the late 1800s, the goal of protecting nature and conserving natural resources was gaining public and governmental support. A conservation movement formed. Early conservationists are often divided into two categories: resource conservationists and nature preservationists. Resource conservationists promoted the efficient management of natural resources for human benefit, with an eye to the welfare of future generations. Preservationists focused on the intrinsic value of nature, arguing for the preservation of wilderness for its own sake.

The first citizen conservationists were members of regional mountaineering or birdwatching clubs. These citizen groups had both resource conservationist and preservationist tendencies. They concerned themselves not only with the efficient management of natural resources for human use and recreation, but with the preservation of wildlife for its aesthetic and spiritual benefits. George Bird Grinnell, editor and publisher of *Forest and Stream*, was the founder in 1886 of America's first popular conservation organization, the Audubon Society. Its primary mission was the protection of plumage birds from the millinery industry and the protection of certain game birds from unregulated sport hunting. Many women, including former suffragette Rosalie Edge, played an important role in maintaining the organization's preservationist orientation. In Europe, similar efforts to protect wildlife, forests, and wilderness were well under way, particularly in Britain.

The most famous preservationist of the time was John Muir (1838–1914), a Scottish-born immigrant who spent much of his life hiking and climbing in America's wilds. Muir founded the Sierra Club in 1892 and remained its president until his death. Muir and his fellow Sierrans promoted recreational enjoyment of the forests, canyons, and mountains of California's Sierra Nevada and opposed extensive logging and livestock grazing.

Resource conservationists, maintaining anthropocentric (human-centered) values, had the upper hand in the first wave of environmentalism. They formed the backbone of the early conservation movement and were most persuasive in government circles. Yet preservationists, with biocentric (nature-centered) perspectives, were not without influence. Moreover, because the natural resources that early conservationists aimed to husband often included wildlands and wildlife, their policies, if not their principles, frequently dovetailed with those of preservationists.

Aldo Leopold (1887–1948), a U.S. Forest Service employee, exemplified the tension between anthropocentric and biocentric perspectives within the early conservation movement. After observing the pitfalls of shortsighted forestry practices and predator-extirpation programs, Leopold came to understand the human economy as part of an overarching ecological balance. He cofounded the Wilderness Society with Bob Marshall in 1936. In *A Sand County Almanac*, published posthumously in 1949, Leopold developed the first formalized environmental ethic. Leopold's "land ethic" extended moral concern to the biotic community as a whole.

In the 1960s, and more markedly by the early 1970s, a second wave of environmentalism arose. Previously, both resource conservationists and nature preservationists had placed their activities under the rubric of nature conservation. The words "environment" and "environmentalism" were not yet in general circulation. By the mid-1970s, talk of environmental protection was widespread in the media, in schools, and in the halls of government.

Not unlike their predecessors, second-wave environmentalists were concerned with managing natural resources efficiently to satisfy human needs, but they were also troubled by the growth of these needs and the ecological costs of satisfying them on a global scale. With mounting unease, the general public learned that humankind was becoming the victim of its own environmental abuses. Consumerism and the mass-production of goods had yielded a tremendous increase in litter. Waste-disposal and energy-resource problems were mounting. Rapid suburban development led to the paving over of green spaces. Urban air quality was deteriorating noticeably; many cities suffered from deadly inversions that trapped heavily polluted smog. Oceans were often used as dumping grounds, and many streams and rivers were clogged with effluent that made their waters undrinkable and frequently unfit for swimming or fishing. The public began to worry about the planetary effects of accelerating human production and reproduction.

The rapid growth of second-wave environmentalism was sparked by the publication of Rachel Carson's *Silent Spring* (1962). In scrupulous detail, Carson documented the widespread use of pesticides and their devastating effects on bird populations. America, Carson predicted, would soon face a spring wholly deprived of its beloved avian singers. *Silent Spring* also foretold a time when chemicals recklessly introduced into nature in the pursuit of profit would take a significant human toll. After reading *Silent Spring*, President Kennedy appointed a special panel of the Science Advisory Committee to study pesticide use. The panel largely corroborated Carson's findings. A group of private citizens inspired by Carson's work demonstrated that the use of the pesticide DDT to control mosquitoes was the cause of a sharp decline in the osprey populations on Long Island. They founded the Environmental Defense Fund (EDF). By 1972, the EDF had succeeded in having the use of DDT banned nationwide.

In 1968, Paul R. Ehrlich published *The Population Bomb*. It quickly became a best seller. Ehrlich argued that overpopulation was the chief obstacle to resolving many of the world's most pressing economic and ecological problems. He prophesied that humankind would breed itself into oblivion. After publishing his book, Ehrlich founded Zero Population Growth, an organization with a mandate to stem the tide of human numbers.

Widespread concern about environmental degradation in the United States and the growth in the world's population burst into a true mass movement in 1970. On April 22 of that year, the first Earth Day was celebrated. An estimated twenty million Americans participated. In the following year, biologist Barry Commoner accomplished for the issue of technology what Ehrlich had achieved for population. In *The Closing Circle* (1971), Commoner raised concerns about the social and ecological effects of a centralized, technological way of life. Commoner argued that ecological devastation was directly tied to the way society was organized and the manner in which its productive capacities were designed.

Employing complex computer-aided analyses, the authors of *The Limits to Growth* (1972) brought overconsumption, the third agent of environmental degradation, to the public eye. This detailed study described the accelerating rate of natural resource depletion that modern technology, increasing human numbers, and rapid resource consumption had produced. If growth trends in world population, industrialization, food production, pollution, and resource depletion continued unabated, its authors predicted, the planetary limits to growth would be reached within the next one hundred years, with catastrophic results. While some predictions proved exaggerated, public concern for the environment grew steadily in light of such forecasts and in the wake of the widely observed degradation of the air, water, and land.

Between 1901 and 1960, an average of three conservation groups formed each year in the United States. Between 1961 and 1980, an average of 18 new groups were founded each year. These organizations expanded the environmental agenda and radicalized its operations. In 1971, Greenpeace was formed. Originally organized in Canada to oppose nuclear testing carried out by the United States off the coast of Alaska, Greenpeace quickly became involved in a wide array of environmental issues, including well-known campaigns to end seal hunting and whaling. Greenpeace inaugurated an era of environmental "direct action." Although eschewing violence and the destruction of property, Greenpeace members frequently engaged in civil disobedience to publicize or prevent environmental misdeeds. Activists climbed smokestacks to release banners decrying pollution, positioned their rubber dinghies between whales and harpoon-armed whaling ships, and sailed into nuclear testing zones. More radical groups such as the Sea Shepherd Conservation Society and Earth First! engaged in ecological sabotage—sinking whaling ships or destroying tree-harvesting machinery—to protect wildlife and wilderness.

The vast majority of environmental groups adopted legal means to protect the environment and gained widespread public support for their efforts. Indeed, by the early 1980s certain segments of the environmental movement were actively courted by business interests and the political establishment. Environmentalism was no longer a "fringe" movement; it had become mainstream. Many of the larger environmental groups, with memberships in the millions and annual budgets over U.S.$100 million, were now run by professional administrators who controlled entire departments of scientists, lobbyists, lawyers, public relations personnel, fundraisers, and membership recruiters. Many grassroots environmentalists objected to the national organizations' professionalism, commercialism, and reliance on corporate donations. Beginning in the late 1980s, the mainstream groups were also criticized for catering exclusively to the needs and concerns of the middle and upper classes. In the United States and many other countries, an "environmental justice" movement formed to challenge the disproportionate suffering of minorities and the poor from the effects of environmental degradation. In the 1990s and 2000s, many environmental groups adopted the broad goal of sustainability as their mandate. Sustainability links the pursuit of social justice with ecological preservation and environmental health, while paying heed to the requirements of a human economy.

PUBLIC SUPPORT AND PROSPECTS FOR THE FUTURE

Support for environmentalism rises and falls periodically as the public's economic and security concerns wax and wane. Support for movement organizations typically swells in the wake of large-scale environmental catastrophes. The disaster of leaching toxic wastes at Love Canal (1978), the evacuation of Times Beach, Missouri, as a result of dioxin contamination (1982), and the pesticide leak at the Union Carbide plant in Bhopal, India (1984), vastly heightened environmental concerns and stimulated the development of a "toxics" movement. Massive environmental degradation caused by oil and fuel spills have had similar effects. In March of 1989, for example, the *Exxon Valdez* oil tanker ran aground on Bligh Reef in Alaska's Prince William Sound, spilling eleven million gallons of oil and creating an 80-kilometer-wide slick that contaminated over a thousand miles of formerly pristine coastline. Movement membership rose dramatically following the spill.

Growing environmental values and increased membership in movement organizations do not result directly in widespread changes to the lifestyles of supporters. As many as four out of five Americans claim to be environmentalists and endorse increased environmental protection. The movement's success in gaining such widespread support is significantly offset, however, by the general public's reluctance to translate its proclaimed values into environmentally responsible behavior.

For the foreseeable future, environmental movements will be defined by many different voices. The movement remains divided, for example, on the benefits and dangers of free trade; animal rights activists continue at odds with environmentally oriented hunters and fishermen; biocentric preservationists have sharp differences with mainstream resource conservationists. Such diversity could fragment the environmental movement. At the same time, environmentalists are learning to value diversity in their movement for the same reason that they value diversity in nature: it fosters the resilience needed to adapt and succeed in a quickly changing world.

[See also Conservation.]

BIBLIOGRAPHY

Brown, M., and J. May. *The Greenpeace Story*. New York: Dorling Kindersley, 1991. A readable, illustrated account.

Bryant, B., ed. *Environmental Justice: Issues, Policies, and Solutions*. Washington, D.C.: Island Press, 1995. A concise summary.

Dalton, R. *The Green Rainbow: Environmental Groups in Western Europe*. New Haven, Conn.: Yale University Press, 1994. A detailed, social scientific examination.

Dowie, M. *Losing Ground: American Environmentalism at the Close of the Twentieth Century*. Cambridge, Mass.: MIT Press, 1995. A critical challenge to mainstream environmentalism.

Dunlap, R., and A. Mertig, eds. *American Environmentalism: The U.S. Environmental Movement 1970–1990*. New York: Taylor and Francis, 1992. A comprehensive empirical assessment.

Fox, S. *John Muir and His Legacy: The American Conservation Movement*. Boston: Little, Brown, 1981. A classic history.

Hays, S. P. *Conservation and the Gospel of Efficiency: The Progressive Conservation Movement*. Cambridge, Mass.: Harvard University Press, 1958. A detailed assessment of the early resource conservationists.

Kamieniecki, S., ed. *Environmental Politics in the International Arena: Movements, Parties, Organizations, and Policy*. Albany: State University of New York Press, 1993. A useful summary of global environmental groups.

Kempton, W., et al. *Environmental Values in American Culture*. Cambridge, Mass.: MIT Press, 1995. A useful analysis of environmental opinions and commitments.

Leopold, A. *A Sand County Almanac, with Essays on Conservation from Round River*. New York: Ballantine Books, 1966. A classic of ecological thinking and environmental ethics.

Manes, C. *Green Rage: Radical Environmentalism and the Unmaking of Civilization*. Boston: Little, Brown, 1990. An insider's view of Earth First!

Sale, K. *The Green Revolution: The American Environmental Movement 1962–1992*. New York: Hill and Wang, 1993. A brief, readable account.

Thiele, L. P. *Environmentalism for a New Millenium: The Challenge of Coevolution*. Oxford and New York: Oxford University Press, 1999. A detailed history and analysis of environmentalism.

Wapner, P. *Environmental Activism and World Civic Politics*. Albany: State University of New York Press, 1996. An informative exploration of transnational environmental groups.

—Leslie Paul Thiele

ENVIRONMENTAL PERFORMANCE INDEX

At the World Economic Forum in Davos, Switzerland, in early 2006 a new global survey was unveiled. The Environmental Performance Index (EPI) was developed by the Center for Environmental Law and Policy at Yale University and the Center for International Earth Science Information Network (CIESIN) at Columbia University.

Like the Human Development Index (HDI) it is intended to supplement the popular gross domestic product (GDP) as a measure of the quality of life of the world's nations. The HDI assigns a numerical ranking to 133 countries on the basis of their environmental practices and outcomes. Switzerland heads the list in 2008, followed by Sweden, Norway, Finland, Costa Rica, and Austria. Japan is ranked number 21, the Netherlands 55, and the United States 39 (its low ranking due largely to greenhouse-gas policy and emissions). The Dominican Republic is ranked 33, while Haiti, its neighbor on the island of Hispaniola, is ranked 119.

For the entire list, see the Appendix. For a full report on the index and the methodology employed, see http://www.epi.yale.edu/Home.

—David J. Cuff

EROSION

Erosion is a natural process by which flowing water, wind, and ice remove soil and weathered material from land surfaces. By acting on rocks of different resistance, erosion shapes the hills and valleys that make up our landscape. The study of the nature and evolution of landforms is known as geomorphology, and erosion is a geomorphologic process.

Erosion comprises the detachment of individual soil particles from the soil mass, the pick-up or entrainment of those particles by the flow, and the transport of the particles over the land. When the energy of the eroding agent is no longer sufficient to move the particles, they are deposited. Erosion thus connects the source areas of sediment, where the weathering takes place, to sediment sinks where the deposition occurs. Studies of sediments in partially enclosed environments such as lakes can often be used to interpret erosion rates on the surrounding land. Erosion rates are normally expressed as a weight of soil removed from a unit area of land over a given period of time, typically in units of metric tons per hectare per year.

The main impact of erosion is on the surface material or soil. Under well vegetated conditions such as forests and grasslands, a balance exists between the rate of soil erosion and the rate of soil formation. The vegetation cover protects the soil from erosion. It intercepts rainfall, reducing the amount that reaches the ground surface by some 20–30% annually. It increases the amount of water that infiltrates the soil because the plant roots open up passages in the soil through which water can move. Overall, the amount of water flowing as runoff over the land surface is reduced. The percentage of the annual rainfall contributing to runoff varies from less than 1% in densely vegetated areas to nearly 60% in urban areas and on bare soil. By determining the fate of the rainfall, the vegetation cover directly influences the erosion by raindrop impact and surface runoff.

RAINDROP IMPACT

Raindrop impact on bare soil is a powerful agent of particle detachment. Norman Hudson (1934–1996) carried out a simple but classic experiment in the 1950s in Zimbabwe to show the importance of covering the soil against falling raindrops. Soil loss was measured from two experimental plots over a ten-year period. Both were kept free of vegetation by hand-weeding. One plot was open to the rainfall, while the other was covered by a double layer of fine-mesh wire gauze. The gauze allowed rain to pass through but broke up the falling raindrops so that they reached the soil surface in small droplets. Over a ten-year period, an average annual soil loss of 127 tons per hectare was recorded on the bare plot but only 0.9 tons per hectare on the plot covered with the gauze. The experiment thus demonstrated the importance of cover in controlling the rate of erosion by reducing the rate of soil-particle detachment.

The maximum effect of a vegetation cover in controlling raindrop impact occurs when the cover is at the ground surface. When rainfall is intercepted by a plant canopy, its properties are altered. First, the rainfall at the ground becomes concentrated beneath individual drip points. Second, the raindrops coalesce on the leaves to form larger drops. Typically, natural rainfall has a median drop size of about 2.0 millimeters; in contrast, the median drop size of leaf drips is about 4.8–5.0 mm. Although the energy of the rainfall is absorbed by the plant canopy, the drips gain energy again as they fall from the leaves. With vegetation canopies on or close to the ground surface, this gain is very small, but once the canopy rises to 0.5 meters or more above the ground, the drip energy is sufficient to detach soil particles. Detachment rates on bare soil under forest canopies can be 2–4 times higher than those on open ground. Fortunately, in most forested areas the soil is protected by a litter layer of decaying plant matter. On agricultural land, however, no such protection exists, and detachment rates under crops such as maize and cassava can be two or more times that of uncropped bare land. Since detachment is the first phase of the water erosion process, its control is important. If few or no soil particles were detached, there would be no material for eroding agents to transport and erosion rates would therefore be low.

RUNOFF

Ground-level vegetation imparts roughness to the surface, reducing the velocity of the flowing water and therefore its capacity to erode the soil. Runoff will detach soil particles from the soil mass and entrain them in the flow when its velocity exceeds a critical value that depends upon the resistance of the soil material. The critical velocity is higher for coarse materials (sands, gravels), which weigh more, and for fine particles (clay), which are held together by cohesion. It is lowest for silts and fine sands, which explains why silty and loamy soils are more prone to erosion than other soil types. Once a soil particle has been picked up by the flow it can be carried at much lower velocities than those required for detaching it. This is particularly true for clay particles which, once detached, can be transported considerable distances (tens of meters to kilometers) before coming to rest at a point in the landscape where velocity is reduced and deposition occurs.

Surface runoff initially takes the form of a shallow (1–2 millimeter) sheet-like flow spreading out over the slope surface. Its velocity is low because of the roughness of the ground surface and any vegetation present, and it is not able to detach soil

particles. It can, however, transport material splashed into it by raindrop impacts. As the water flows down the slope it becomes concentrated into flow paths, its velocity increases, and it is able to cut small channels or rills into the land surface. Dense rill networks can be formed on bare farmland during intense rainstorms; they are also a feature of road cuttings, embankments, industrial sites, and residential areas left bare of vegetation while construction work is in progress.

In many situations, rills do not cut very deeply because the underlying material is less weathered, more compact, and therefore more resistant to erosion. Sometimes, however, the reverse is the case, and once the rill has cut through the surface soil it can continue to develop, forming gullies 20–30 meters deep and 20–40 meters wide. Such features are common in many tropical and subtropical areas where the bedrock is chemically weathered to form a layer of saprolite (a soft, earthy decomposed rock which is much weaker than the overlying soil) 5–20 meters or more thick. The spectacular gullies or *lavakas* of Madagascar originate in this way, and similar features are found in the southeastern United States, southern Brazil, West Africa, Zimbabwe, Swaziland, and South Africa. Gullies can also develop in soils that are prone to subsurface water flow in natural pipes or tunnels. As erosion proceeds, the pipes enlarge until their roofs collapse, uncovering a network of deep channels or gullies.

WIND

Some of the most catastrophic examples of soil erosion are associated with wind acting on bare soil, following clearance of the vegetation cover. Wind is able to detach and transport large quantities of material, carrying the finer particles in suspension high into the atmosphere. Clouds of dust can affect people hundreds or even thousands of kilometers away, blotting out the sun, creating respiratory problems, and polluting the air. The best known example is the Dust Bowl that occurred in the Great Plains of the United States in the 1930s. During the 1920s, rainfall was above average and the prairie grasslands were plowed up for wheat cultivation, but cereal production was not sustainable when drought conditions returned. The first great "blow" occurred on May 11, 1934, and within a few hours the sun was obscured over a large area including Chicago, New York, and Washington, D.C. Over the next five years some 350 million tons of soil were eroded, and in some areas over 1 meter of soil was removed.

A similar episode occurred in Kazakhstan in the 1950s, following the extension of agriculture on to marginal lands under the U.S.S.R.'s Virgin Lands program. Wind erosion is also a major problem in the drier parts of Argentina, the Middle East, the Sahel, India, Pakistan, China, and Australia. Its association with semiarid areas means it is often associated with desertification. In reality, however, it is the lack of vegetation cover rather than climatic conditions that control its distribution. For example, in Iceland the rainfall is more than sufficient to support vegetation, yet wind erosion is a major environmental issue. Largely as a result of overgrazing, vegetation occupies only some 25% of the country today, compared with 65% when the first settlers arrived in the eighth century CE.

HISTORICAL PERSPECTIVES

Given the protective effect of vegetation, it is not surprising that erosion rates are sensitive to the ways in which the type and amount of plant cover have changed over time. Sedimentation studies in lakes show that mean annual erosion rates were relatively high (greater than 1.3 tons per hectare) in the immediate postglacial period (up to 10,000 BP). As the climate warmed and forest cover grew more extensive between 10,000 and 2,500 BP, mean annual erosion rates fell to less than 0.5 tons per hectare. Since then, erosion rates have been locally highly variable, depending on the level of human impact. Where deforestation took place and the land was plowed, rates increased by about 500 CE to around one ton per hectare, but elsewhere they remained low. The Middle Ages saw a further extension of the land under farming as a result of demographic pressure as well as an increase in the use of spring-sown crops, so that land was bare for the autumn and winter seasons. This, coupled with clearing of the forests for fuelwood, charcoal production, and shipbuilding, led to an increase in erosion which, locally, reached 10 tons per hectare. Fluctuations in erosion over time and space were common, however, with rates decreasing wherever war, famine, and disease reduced population numbers. In the late Middle Ages (1350–1400), very high rates were recorded in parts of central Europe as a result of catastrophic rainfall events; for example, deep gullies developed in parts of Lower Saxony in Germany, where rates locally exceeded 2,000 tons per hectare. In contrast, the period 1400–1750 was less extreme and the gullying ceased.

The late eighteenth and early nineteenth centuries saw the introduction of new crops on fallow land, improved manuring, and overall improved agricultural practices. As a result, erosion declined further until the late nineteenth century, when a second phase of gullying took place, also related to a greater frequency of intense rain events. Erosion rates increased locally to 100–200 tons per hectare before falling again in the early part of the twentieth century. Between the 1950s and the 1980s the intensification of agriculture, the concentration on cereals, oil seeds, and root crops with consequent decline in rotational grass, and the removal of hedgerows and field banks to enlarge fields all contributed to higher erosion rates. More recently, erosion rates have started to decrease again with the promotion of soil protection and agri-environment programs.

CONSEQUENCES

Since soil, along with water and air, is one of the resources needed to support human life, the rate at which it is removed is important. Soil is required for growing crops for food and industrial use and fodder for livestock. The loss of soil by erosion has effects both on site, where the erosion occurs, and off site, at the places downstream or downwind where sedimentation takes place. The main effects on site are loss of soil and, more importantly, decline in soil fertility. The two effects are separated because the first relates to the mass of soil material, the second to its composition. When erosion occurs, it is a selective process in which the finer particles are removed preferentially and the coarser material left behind. The fine particles (clays) contain in readily available form the nutrients, particularly nitrogen and phosphorus, required for plant growth. The material that remains is not only less fertile but retains less water. Erosion caused a decline in wheat yields in Australia of 6–52% in the decade 1973–1983, equivalent to A$13–155 per hectare. In the 1980s, the annual cost to Zimbabwe of nitrogen and phosphorus loss due to erosion was estimated at U.S.$1.5 billion.

Off-site effects relate to silting of rivers, canals, and reservoirs, damage to roads and property from burial by sediments during muddy floods, and pollution of water bodies through increased concentrations of sediment particles and transfer of chemicals, particularly phosphorus, adsorbed on the clay particles. The overall costs of erosion, both on- and off-site, are considerable, amounting to U.S.$30–44 billion annually in the U.S. and £90 million annually in the U.K.

Over time, if no remedial measures are taken, accelerated soil erosion can lead to a self-perpetuating system in which the loss of soil fertility results in poorer vegetation cover, hence reduced soil protection, more erosion, and, in turn, less vegetation. Under these extreme conditions, land can become desert-like. In areas of low but intense rainfalls, erosion can be a major contributing factor leading to desertification.

SOIL CONSERVATION

Soil erosion has long been recognized as one of the leading environmental issues threatening our ability to meet world needs for food. W. C. Lowdermilk, an American archaeologist of the 1930s, documented evidence that erosion was a major factor contributing to the decline of the ancient civilizations in Mesopotamia and the Middle East. The remains of terracing from these times illustrate a very early understanding of erosion control. The foundation of soil conservation as a worldwide movement dates from the establishment in 1935 of the United States Soil Conservation Service (now the Natural Resources Conservation Service), with H. H. Bennett as its first director. The basis of soil conservation is wise land use and good land management. The Soil Conservation Service pioneered a system of land evaluation to determine the suitability of the land for agriculture. All land was assigned to one of seven classes, depending on the type and severity of limitations for arable farming. With increasing severity of limitation, a greater level of soil conservation is required.

Soil conservation measures can be divided into three broad groups, defined as agronomic, soil management, and engineering. Agronomic measures relate to the way the land cover is managed and include the growing of grasses and legumes in rotation with other crops, the use of cover crops, and agroforestry. Soil management relates to the way the land is tilled. Soil conservation tillage retains the residue from previous crops to help provide a surface mulch to protect the soil. Engineering measures include various forms of terracing and bunding (embankments), contour grass barriers, shelterbelts, and purpose-built waterways to convey excess runoff to safe outlets. In many cases, these measures are integrated into a coherent system of soil and water management.

Erosion. Erosion Effects.

Badlands, locally called dongas, produced by erosion of colluvial deposits in the Middleveld of Swaziland, southern Africa.

Throughout the 1950s and 1960s, soil conservation was promoted in many countries through local equivalents of the United States Soil Conservation Service. This resulted in a top-down approach in which conservation staff proposed and designed erosion-control measures and the farmers were expected to implement them. Although there were examples of successful conservation projects, they often had to be supported by financial incentives to farmers from national and local governments. Implementation of the measures usually increased a farmer's costs without any appreciable short-term gain in income, and it was the community rather than the individual farmer who benefited. The need to subsidize conservation in this way is unsustainable, and over the last decade a new "bottom-up" approach has been adopted. Farmers are encouraged to be involved in decisions on how their land is managed. The emphasis is on improving all aspects of land husbandry, including erosion control, rather than dedicating resources specifically to soil conservation, and on recognizing the role played by indigenous conservation methods. The Land Care Program in Australia is a successful pioneer of this approach.

[*See also* Agriculture and Agricultural Land; Anthropogeomorphology; Deforestation; Desertification; Land Surface Processes; *and* Soils.]

BIBLIOGRAPHY

Boardman, J., and J. Poesen. *Soil Erosion in Europe.* Chichester, U.K., and New York: Wiley, 2006. Papers on the status of soil erosion in several European countries followed by papers on erosion and its control at a pan-European scale.
Bork, H. R. "The History of Soil Erosion in Southern Lower Saxony." *Landschaftgenese und Landschaftsökologie* 16 (1989), 135–163.
Hudson, N. W. *Land Husbandry.* London: Batsford, 1992. Modern approaches to land use and land degradation issues in developing countries.
Hudson, N. W. *Soil Conservation.* 3d. ed. London: Batsford, 1995. A practical guide to modern soil conservation.
Johnson, D. L., and L. A. Lewis. *Land Degradation: Creation and Destruction.* Oxford: Blackwell, 1995. Case studies from the developing and developed world emphasizing interactions between physical and human environments.
Morgan, R. P. C. *Soil Erosion and Conservation.* 3rd ed. Oxford: Blackwell, 2005. A general introduction to the subject.
Pimental, D., ed. *World Soil Erosion and Conservation.* Cambridge: Cambridge University Press, 1993. Papers on soil erosion in different countries and regions of the world.
Stocking, M. "How Eroding Soils Lose Money." *International Agricultural Development* 8.1 (1988), 11–12.
van Vliet-Lanoë, B., et al. "Soil Erosion in Western Europe: From the Last Interglacial to the Present." In *Past and Present Soil Erosion: Archaeological and Geographical Perspectives,* edited by M. Bell and J. Boardman, pp. 101–114. Oxford: Oxbow Books, 1992.

—R. P. C. MORGAN

ESTUARIES

An estuary is the lower portion of the river or an arm of the sea, where saline sea water is diluted with fresh water. Estuaries are inherently dynamic as a result of short-term fluctuations in water level and water masses due to tides, storm surges, and runoff from tributary streams as well as long-term changes in water level and sediment inputs that change the size of the basins and the rate of migration of the shorelines. The characteristics of many present-day estuaries result from a slowing of the rate of sealevel rise several thousand years ago that allowed sediment to accumulate and create beaches, shallow-water subtidal flats, and intertidal land that developed into salt marshes. These diverse environments and the tidal creeks that traverse them provide valuable habitat and feeding areas for fauna. Estuaries also provide fish and shellfish for human consumption and sheltered harbors and navigation corridors for boating and shipping. The favorable location of estuaries for human activity causes them to be foci of human settlement. Many of the world's largest cities are located on estuaries, and many are subject to the most intensive levels of use applied to any marine water area.

RECENT CHANGES

The expansion of industrial and commercial activity in the nineteenth century and recreational activity in the twentieth greatly modified the character of natural estuaries, and human development is still increasing in intensity and spatial coverage. Human modifications affect biological processes by altering photosynthetic production, nutrient cycling, food supply, activity patterns, and mortality rates. The introduction of exotic or cultured species has changed biota. The construction of dams and levees and the alteration of tributaries for flood control or use of water for human consumption or agricultural production alter the migratory patterns of fish, change the distribution of salinity and nutrients, change the range of predators, and change the amount of sediment delivered to the estuaries, which, in turn, alters siltation rates and shoreline locations.

The size and shape of estuaries is altered by land reclamation for agricultural and residential use and for the building of causeways and bridges, leading to loss or fragmentation of habitat. The dredging of channels for navigation and disposal of the dredge spoil changes turbidity levels, circulation patterns, and zones of sediment erosion and accretion. The construction of generating plants for electricity has caused thermal pollution of the waters. The use of fertilizers and inputs of human waste from ever-increasing populations contributes to organic enrichment in estuaries (eutrophication), which leads, in turn, to excessive growth of algae, increasing metabolism, which causes changes in the structure of biological communities. Toxic substances such as heavy metals, petroleum products, and pesticides cause direct chronic or lethal effects to primary ingestors, and are passed through the food chain to predators. There are also positive impacts, including the restoration of natural habitat and the creation of recreational beaches using artificial fill.

SENSITIVITY AND RESILIENCE OF ESTUARIES

Estuaries are resilient natural features because their physical environments and biota are adapted to continuous inputs from rivers and from the sea that renew the supply of water, food, larvae, and other essential elements to small damaged areas, aiding recovery and protecting long-term net stability. The organisms that are adapted to estuaries have great tolerance to the rapid changes in temperature and salinity that are helpful in resisting external forces, although some adverse human inputs are exceeding the capacity of some estuaries to absorb them.

One of the greatest threats to the viability of estuaries is the effect of accelerated sea level rise, coupled with human attempts to reduce the threat of flooding or to retain a stable shoreline position by using protective structures. A rise in sea level will tend to cause the land/water boundary of an estuary to shift inland, bringing about more frequent inundation of land that was less affected previously. [See Sea Level Future.] The extent to which estuaries can adapt by creating new natural shoreline environments will depend on the rate of sea level rise, the amount of sediment available, and the actions of humans to protect developed land. Coastal marsh systems are one of the landscape types most threatened by sea level rise. Valuable salt marshes will be lost in places because sediment inputs will be insufficient to allow marshes to build up as fast as they are inundated. Estuaries may become deeper and more marine as well.

ESTUARINE MANAGEMENT

Programs have been implemented in many countries at national, state and provincial, and local levels of government to improve water quality and enhance resources that have been threatened by pollution, development, and overuse. Regulations include waterfront development laws, wetland and tideland management acts, water quality planning and maintenance programs, health regulations, dredge-and-fill permit programs, critical area laws requiring site plan reviews, erosion-control setback lines, shore-protection programs, and parks and recreation programs. Environmentally oriented restrictions on development have prevented the filling of marshes in many countries, but other habitats that are not protected by legislation, including beaches and naturally functioning upland margins, are still being eliminated through human development. Much of this development has occurred at locations where new marsh would otherwise be created as a result of sea level rise. The amount of salt marsh will be reduced where losses due to wave erosion and inundation cannot be replaced by the creation of new marsh on the landward side because the land is developed for human use. This loss of estuarine habitat has been called the "coastal squeeze." Management plans for overcoming the coastal squeeze include adding sediment to existing marsh surfaces to allow them to keep pace with inundation, or introducing managed retreat, whereby low-lying upland that is not intensively developed will be allowed to revert to marsh. Creation of marsh by reshaping the land, reintroducing tidal flow, and planting marsh vegetation is also possible, and a number of projects have been attempted with varying success.

[See also Coastlines and Ecosystems.]

BIBLIOGRAPHY

Cronin, L. E. "The Role of Man in Estuarine Processes." In *Man's Impact on the Environment*, edited by T. R. Detwyler, pp. 266–294. New York: McGraw-Hill, 1971. A landmark article in a landmark volume.

Cronin, L. E., ed. *Estuarine Research*. 2 vols. New York and London: Academic Press, 1975.

Day, J. W., Jr., et al. *Estuarine Ecology*. New York: Wiley, 1989. A comprehensive synthesis that serves as a text and standard reference.

Kennedy, V. S., ed. *Estuarine Perspectives*. New York and London: Academic Press, 1980.

Kennish, M. J. *Practical Handbook of Estuarine and Marine Pollution*. Boca Raton, Fla.: CRC Press, 1997. A recent, comprehensive review of problems of pollution and programs for monitoring and controlling them.

Lauff, G. H., ed. *Estuaries*. Washington, D.C.: American Association for the Advancement of Science, 1967. The first of a series of edited volumes representing the state of the art in estuarine research. Selected representative volumes in this series, resulting from research results presented at meetings of the Estuarine Research Federation, include Cronin (1975), Kennedy (1980), Wiley (1976), and Wolfe (1986).

Nordstrom, K. F., and C. T. Roman, eds. *Estuarine Shores: Evolution, Environments, and Human Alterations*. Chichester, U.K., and New York: Wiley, 1996. Contributions in this book focus on horizontal changes to estuarine shores, in contrast to the many existing evaluations of vertical changes or processes and biota in deeper waters.

Reed, D. J. "The Response of Coastal Marshes to Sea-Level Rise: Survival or Submergence." *Earth Surface Processes and Landforms* 20 (1995), 39–48. A good review of the literature. Companion articles in the same issue assess effects of sea level rise on other coastal environments.

Wiley, M., ed. *Estuarine Processes*. 2 vols. New York: Academic Press, 1976.

Wolfe, D. A., ed. *Estuarine Variability*. Orlando, Fla.: Academic Press, 1986.

—Karl F. Nordstrom

ETHANOL

Ethyl alcohol, or ethanol, is a colorless liquid with the chemical formula CH_3CH_2OH. Ethanol is one of the best-known of the alcohols because it has a wide variety of uses—as a solvent, an antifreeze, an ingredient in alcoholic beverages, an octane booster in gasoline, and, most recently, as a transport fuel. As shown in Figure 1, global production of ethanol climbed slowly until the year 2000, when an expanding market for ethanol as a transport fuel sparked the beginning of an exponential increase in global production. Ethanol production more than doubled between 2000 and 2005 and is likely to continue to climb as more countries, faced with the twin problems of improving domestic energy security and combating global climate change, turn to ethanol to meet rising transportation fuel demands.

ETHANOL AS A MOTOR FUEL

In the last thirty years, interest in ethanol as a motor fuel has been reinvigorated in the United States and abroad by concerns about the volatility of oil markets, the realization that greenhouse-gas emissions from fossil-fuel combustion are a key causal factor for climate change, and an interest in supporting farmers and agricultural communities through stronger agricultural markets. All vehicles can accommodate low-level blends, up to 10% ethanol (E10), without modification to engine systems. "Flex-fuel" vehicles, however, are designed to accommodate up to 85% ethanol (E85). Ethanol has a higher octane rating than gasoline but a lower heat content, and its use may therefore result in a drop in fuel efficiency. In low blends the effect is quite small (1.5–2%), but the use of E85 blends can result in a 10–25% drop in mileage. Although flex-fuel vehicles can accommodate E85, they are not optimized to burn E85 blends; should dedicated ethanol vehicles emerge that are optimized specifically to ethanol's high octane levels, those differences in fuel efficiency may decline or even reverse.

In the United States, ethanol has been used extensively since 1980 as a gasoline additive to boost gasoline's octane level and improve engine performance. Brazil has aggressively promoted ethanol to replace gasoline since 1975, and by 2005 ethanol held a greater than 40% share of the fuel market for spark-ignition vehicles (ESMAP, 2005). More recently, several other countries have established national policies to promote ethanol production and use, including Australia, Canada, China, and Japan. Although trade in biofuels has historically been small, significant demand for imports is likely to emerge from the heavily energy-dependent developed countries. This demand will likely be met by exports from the less developed tropical and subtropical countries, which tend to have more land available, climates capable of supporting more productive feedstocks, and lower labor costs, and therefore a comparative advantage in supply. Despite a $0.54/gallon import tariff, ethanol imports into the United States have increased dramatically since 2002 (Table 1), with more than 50% of supply coming from Brazil.

CURRENT AND FUTURE ETHANOL PRODUCTION TECHNOLOGIES

Ethanol can be produced from a variety of feedstocks; regionally appropriate feedstocks depend on the climate and local conditions for crop production. Feedstocks for ethanol production tend to be starch- or sugar-rich crops such as sugar cane, sugar beets, corn, wheat, or cassava. Because available sugar content varies by crop, ethanol yield per acre varies widely between feedstocks (Figure 2). The two largest ethanol producers in the world—the United States and Brazil—rely on very different feedstocks with different conversion effiencies. Brazil uses primarily sugar cane for its ethanol production, while the U.S. relies on corn. Sugar cane is a very efficient feedstock because it has a high simple, or monomeric, sugar content, yielding an estimated 650–700 gallons of ethanol per acre. Additional energy-use efficiencies arise because the fibrous bagasse that remains once the sugar has been extracted from the cane can be burned to provide the process energy used to drive the conversion process, thereby obviating the need for additional sources of energy. In contrast, using corn as a feedstock provides an average ethanol yield of 400 to 450 gallons per acre and generally requires the use of coal or natural gas for process energy.

The majority of ethanol investment in the U.S. and abroad continues to be for conventional technologies that convert simple sugars (or easily broken-down sugar polymers such as starch) to

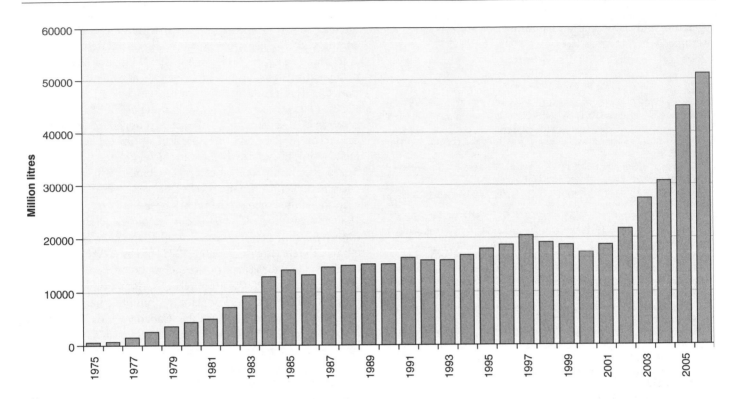

Ethanol. Figure 1. Historic World Fuel Ethanol Production.

(Data compiled from Earth Policy Institute and Renewable Fuels Association)

alcohol through fermentation. However, conventional technologies are inherently inefficient because much of the sugar in biomass is stored in more tightly bonded complex sugars known as cellulose (a glucose polymer) and hemicellulose (a mixed polymer of 6-carbon sugars such as glucose and 5-carbon sugars such as xylose), which together with lignin (a complex organic polymer in plant cell-walls) make up the majority of biomass. The sugars bound in cellulose and hemicellulose are not available for fermentation to ethanol using conventional technologies.

The "state of the art" in ethanol production, therefore, refers to cellulosic ethanol, which is produced using technologies that allow the conversion of cellulose to alcohol (Figure 3). Fermentation of cellulosic feedstocks involves an additional first step that uses enzymes called cellulases to break cellulose down into glucose, which conventional methods can then ferment to ethanol. Because cellulose comprises 40–60% of a plant's dry weight, such technology would allow a much greater portion of biomass to be converted to ethanol, resulting in higher land-use efficiency in ethanol production. It would also greatly broaden the variety of feedstocks that could be used for ethanol production, as conversion would no longer be limited to those crops that are rich in starches and simple sugars; cellulosic ethanol technology would allow the conversion of biomass feedstocks such as stalks, leaves, perennial grasses, trees, and even wood waste into ethanol.

Hemicellulose also comprises a significant portion of a plant's dry weight, with estimates ranging by crop from 20 to 40%. Research is also being conducted on the most efficient way of breaking down and converting hemicellulose; this task is slightly more difficult even than conversion of cellulose, because breaking down hemicellulose yields several different types of sugars, including 5-carbon sugars, which have not traditionally been fermentable to alcohol.

The residue remaining once all the sugars have been extracted from the cellulose and hemicellulose in biomass is called lignin; it is the biomass component that provides plants' structural support. Although lignin does not contain sugars that can be made available for fermentation, it plays an important role in cellulosic ethanol production because it can be burned to generate process energy. Most ethanol processing plants today combust coal or natural gas to generate the energy needed to power the conversion process. Cellulosic biorefineries generate their own power by burning nonfermentable lignin byproducts from their biomass feedstock, thereby considerably reducing their dependence on fossil fuels in ethanol production.

Cellulosic technology therefore promises to deliver greater environmental and economic returns than grain-based ethanol technology, but obstacles to commercialization of cellulosic conversion technology remain. These include technical barriers such as the design of efficient and low-cost enzymes for the breakdown of complex sugars, as well as nontechnical barriers such as the high cost of financing plants constructed using untested technology. To expedite commercialization, the U.S. Department of Energy in 2007 awarded 6 grants to companies interested in constructing medium-scale biorefineries (10–40 million gallons per year) using a number of different cellulosic feedstocks including wheat straw, wood chips, and orange peels.

TABLE 1. U.S. Fuel Ethanol Demand (millions of gallons)

	2002	2003	2004	2005	2006
U.S. Production	2,130	2,800	3,400	3,904	4,855
Imports	46	61	161	135.0	653.3

SOURCE: Renewable Fuels Association

The sugar fermentation, or biochemical, platform described above is currently the most widely used for the production of ethanol, but several other technology platforms exist or are under development for the production of ethanol from biomass. Thermochemical conversion technologies, including fast pyrolysis and gasification, involve heating biomass, either with or without oxygen, to produce oils or synthetic gases that can then be combusted directly or chemically converted into a variety of chemicals or liquid fuels, including ethanol. In addition to the wider variety of outputs, thermochemical technologies have the advantage of being able to process a more diverse array of feedstocks and feedstock mixes than do biochemical, enzyme-based technologies, which must be more closely customized to feedstocks. Technical barriers remain to commercialization of thermochemical conversion, however, including issues related to feedstock handling, waste-stream management, and system integration.

As described above, the raw material for ethanol is generally a renewable plant material, but thermochemical conversion technologies also allow the production of "synthetic ethanol" from petroleum precursors. Synthetic ethanol is chemically identical to bio-ethanol, but because its feedstock is a fossil fuel, it is less desirable as a gasoline substitute from a greenhouse gas perspective.

ETHANOL AND GLOBAL WARMING

Ethanol supporters argue that displacing gasoline use with ethanol use may help balance atmospheric carbon dioxide and reduce the magnitude of global warming from transport energy use. Although the tailpipe carbon dioxide emissions are similar for ethanol and gasoline (301.1 grams per vehicle mile traveled and 272.4 gms/VMT, respectively [EIA, 1996]), the carbon that is released when ethanol is combusted is carbon that was captured in the growing system when the biomass was produced. The carbon that is released when gasoline is combusted, on the other hand, is fossil carbon that was captured through photosynthesis eons ago, prior to the establishment of current climate patterns, and is in a sense "new" to the climate system. Whereas it is theoretically possible to balance extraction and reintroduction of carbon into the climate in a closed loop through ethanol combustion, such balance is not possible with fossil fuel combustion unless the fossil carbon is captured and neutralized through technologies such as carbon capture and storage, which is in its infancy.

Ethanol. FIGURE 2. Ethanol Yields from Selected Feedstocks.
(Data compiled from L.R. Brown and IEA, 2004)

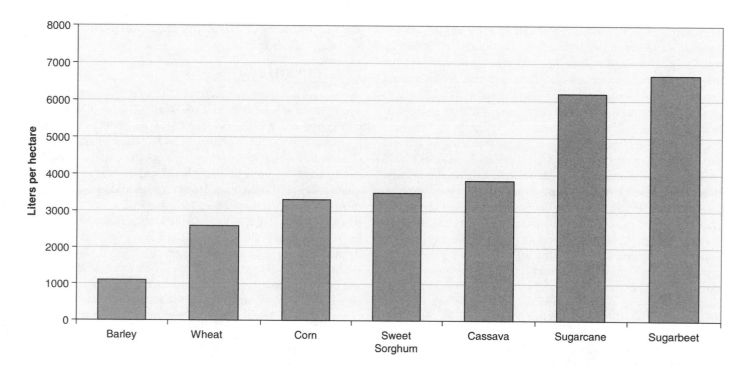

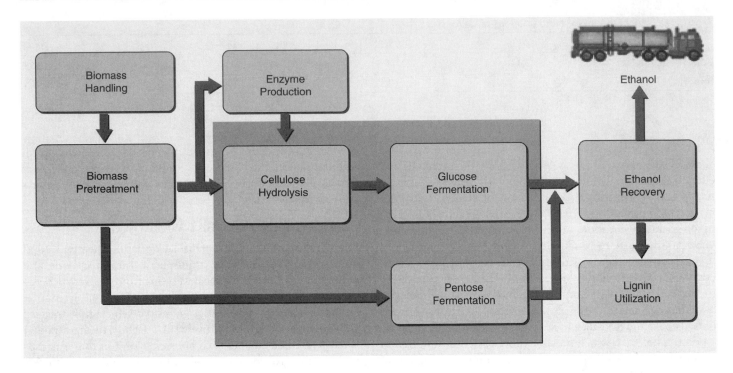

Ethanol. Figure 3. The Production of Ethanol from Cellulosic Biomass.

(Source: National Renewable Energy Laboratory.)

Although it is theoretically possible, ethanol use is in practice not carbon-neutral, or closed-loop, because fossil fuels are used throughout the production process. Ethanol's contribution to global warming therefore comes through the fossil carbon that is released over the production life-cycle of the fuel rather than through combustion of the fuel. This life-cycle carbon includes the carbon released when natural gas is converted to fertilizer for feedstock production, when diesel fuel is combusted to power the harvest and cultivation machinery and transporting the feedstock to the refinery, and when coal or natural gas is burned to produce process energy for ethanol conversion. Therefore, ethanol's fossil carbon content, or the amount of fossil carbon released in the production of a gallon of ethanol, varies widely depending on how the feedstock is produced (i.e., the intensity of fertilization and tillage), how far the feedstock and the ethanol are transported before conversion and delivery to the consumer, and what type of energy input is used for generation of the process energy.

Life-cycle calculations based on current scenarios for ethanol production suggest that most current ethanol use does have a moderate greenhouse-gas benefit relative to gasoline because most conventional ethanol production technologies result in less carbon released per unit of energy than does the production, transport, and combustion of gasoline (Farrell, 2006). This greenhouse gas benefit is expected to be significantly larger when production scenarios include cellulosic production, because lignin combustion would replace fossil-fuel combustion in the generation of process energy, which is the largest single source of fossil carbon emissions in ethanol's production life-cycle. Other greenhouse-gas benefits may also emerge if cellulosic technologies become more widely available. Due to the variety of potential feedstocks, it might be possible to locate cellulosic ethanol processing plants closer to the point of actual use, thereby reducing the fossil carbon released in transporting the product to the consumer. In the United States, for example, greater dispersal of cellulosic refineries could eliminate the need to transport ethanol from the corn-growing regions of the Midwest to the more populated coasts where larger ethanol markets are likely to exist.

THE FLIP SIDE

Not everyone agrees that ethanol is "the fuel of the future." Many question the feasibility and advisability of large-scale ethanol production, citing issues ranging from energy efficiency to environmental impact. One argument widely cited by critics is that ethanol has a negative energy balance—that more fossil fuel energy is used to create ethanol (both corn-based and cellulosic) than is displaced by its use. However, the studies that reached these conclusions have been widely criticized as relying on flawed and out-of-date data, and the argument has lost traction in most scientific circles. Recent studies and reviews by the Argonne National Laboratory, the University of California at Berkeley, and the U.S. Department of Agriculture all find a positive net energy balance per gallon of ethanol using current corn-based technology and predict significantly more favorable energy returns from cellulosic technology (Shapouri, 2002; Wang, 1999; Farrell et al., 2006). Farrell et al. (2006) review a number of published studies and normalize the assumptions made about energy inputs and outputs to calculate adjusted energy inputs and outputs with a consistent methodology. Although they derive estimates ranging from 0.88 to 1.38, their "best estimate" of a net energy ratio using today's technology is 1.22. That is to say, ethanol contains 22% more available energy than is contained in the fossil fuel inputs used directly and indirectly to produce it. Their analysis also predicts a much-improved net energy ratio of 8.2 from cellulosic technology.

The prospect of diverting large amounts of corn into the ethanol market has also generated a debate about "food versus fuel" in the use of agricultural resources. The United States currently provides about 60% of the world's corn exports, which is largely imported by countries in Southeast Asia, Mexico, and Egypt. These imports help keep corn prices low in those countries. Diverting U.S. corn from export to ethanol might cause food prices to increase in those importing countries. Although cellulosic technology would allow ethanol production from parts of the plant, such as corn stalks or wheat straw, not generally used for food, production of dedicated energy crops such as switchgrass or hybrid poplar may simply shift the "food vs. fuel" tension upstream to a competition for production resources such as land and labor rather than competition for the agricultural product itself.

There are also significant environmental concerns related to the production of ethanol, especially when potential impacts are considered at an international scale. Although ethanol's rapid degradation in the environment makes the fuel itself relatively environmentally benign, there are environmental impacts associated with the production of its feedstock that must be considered in a full, life-cycle accounting of the fuel's impact (Farrell, 2006). Of particular concern is the quantity of land required for feedstock production and the associated impacts on habitat, biodiversity, and water, air, and soil quality (Marshall, 2007; UN-Energy, 2007). In the United States, for instance, increased production of nutrient-intensive corn to satisfy ethanol demand has exacerbated concerns about the impact of such production on the Gulf of Mexico's "dead zone"—a seasonal hypoxic area caused largely by nitrogen and phosphorus run-off from agricultural areas in the Midwest (Lambrecht, 2007; Turner and Rabalais, 2007). In Brazil, the areas in which sugar cane is grown do not overlap with the Amazon, and deforestation is therefore not directly attributable to sugar cane production. A 2006 report on the sustainability of Brazilian ethanol production, however, emphasizes the importance of greater understanding of the impacts of indirect or induced land-use change, as other land uses are diverted from cane-growing areas into forest areas, and how such impacts can be addressed in sustainability criteria (Smeets et al., 2006).

Ethanol skeptics argue that the environmental costs associated with ethanol production may be prohibitive and that we are simply trading off the health of our planet's soil and water for a modest displacement of greenhouse-gas emissions. Conversion technologies under development, however, promise substantial gains in ethanol production efficiency and associated reductions in emissions and land-use impacts. To advance development of the ethanol industry in a sustainable direction, several groups have convened to identify and establish sustainability criteria for ethanol production and to advocate for their application in national and international policy (UN-Energy, 2007; GBEP, 2005; RSB, 2007).

BIBLIOGRAPHY

Berg, C. "World Fuel Ethanol Analysis and Outlook." April, 2004. http://www.distill.com/world-Fuel-Ethanol-A&O-2004.html (accessed on May 28, 2008).

Brown, L. R. *Plan B 2.0: Rescuing a Planet Under Stress and a Civilization in Trouble.* New York: Norton, 2006. http://www.earth-policy.org/Books/PB2/Contents.html (accessed on May 28, 2008).

EIA. "Alternatives to Traditional Transportation Fuels 1994: Vol. 2, Greenhouse Gas Emissions." Washington, D.C.: Energy Information Administration, 1996. http://tonto.eia.doe.gov/FTPROOT/alternativefuels/0585942.pdf (accessed May 28, 2008).

ESMAP. "Potential for Biofuels for Transport in Developing Countries." Report 312/05. Washington, D.C.: Energy Sector Management Assistance Program, The World Bank, 2005. http://www.esmap.org/filez/pubs/31205BiofuelsforWeb.pdf (accessed May 28, 2008).

Farrell, A. E., et al. "Ethanol Can Contribute to Energy and Environmental Goals." *Science* 311 (2006), 506–508. DOI: 10.1126/science.1121416.

Fulton, L. "Biodiesel: Technology Perspectives." Geneva UNCTAD Conference. November 30, 2006. http://r0.unctad.org/ghg/events/EnergySector2006/Lew%20Fulton.pdf (accessed May 28, 2008).

GBEP. "Global Bioenergy Partnership: White Paper." Global Bioenergy Partnership, October, 2005. http://www.globalbioenergy.org/fileadmin/use_upload/docs/WhitePaper-GBEP_01.pdf (accessed May 28, 2008).

IEA. "Biofuels for Transport: An International Perspective." Paris: International Energy Agency, 2004. http://www.iea.org/textbase/nppdf/free/2004/biofuels2004.pdf (accessed May 28, 2008).

Lambrecht, B. 2007. "Fertilizer Runoff Creates 'Dead Zone' in Gulf." *St. Louis Post Dispatch*, June 16, 2007.

Marshall, L. "Thirst for Corn: What 2007 Plantings Could Mean for the Environment." WRI Policy Note. 2007. http://www.wri.org/publication/thirst-for-corn (accessed May 28, 2008).

RSB. "Draft Global Principles for Sustainable Biofuels Production: Discussion Document for Global Stakeholder Feedback." Roundtable on Sustainable Biofuels, 2007. http://cgse.epfl.ch/page65660-en.html (accessed May 28, 2008).

Shapouri, H., J. A. Duffield, and M. Wang. *The Energy Balance of Corn Ethanol: An Update.* USDA-814. Washington, D.C.: U.S. Department of Agriculture, 2002.

Smeets, E., et al. "Sustainability of Brazilian Bio-ethanol." Utrecht, The Netherlands: Copernicus Institute, 2006. http://www.bioenergytrade.org/downloads/sustainabilityofbrazilianbioethanol.pdf (accessed May 28, 2008).

Turner, R. E., and N. Rabalais. "2007 Forecast of the Hypoxic Zone Size, Northern Gulf of Mexico." NOAA Center for Sponsored Coastal Ocean Research, Coastal Oceans Program, 2007. http://www.epa.gov/gmpo/pdf/2007-hypoxia-pred-web-5.pdf (accessed May 28, 2008).

UN-Energy. "Sustainable Bioenergy: A Framework for Decision Makers." United Nations, 2007. http://www.esa.un.org/un-energy/pdf/susdev.Biofuels.FAO.pdf (accessed May 28, 2008).

Wang, M., C. Saricks, and D. Santini. "Effects of Fuel Ethanol Use on Fuel-Cycle Energy and Greenhouse Gas Emissions." Argonne National Lab ANL/ESD-38, 1999.

—Elizabeth Marshall

ETHICS

Environmental decisions are ethical choices. Different ethical theories offer conflicting views of the values to which decisions should appeal, of equity in the distribution of benefits and burdens, and of the extent of the ethical reference class—who should count.

The utilitarian holds that we should aim at the decision that maximizes the welfare of affected parties. Hedonist utilitarianism takes welfare to consist in pleasure and the absence of pain, preference utilitarianism in the satisfaction of preferences. The utilitarian approach can allow direct preferences for environmental goods to be a component of welfare. It need not involve a narrow definition of welfare such that nature is just a resource for the production of consumer goods.

Objections to utilitarianism include the following: distributions of benefits and burdens matter as such, not just as a means of increasing total welfare—a decision that placed all burdens, for example health hazards, on a particular minority might be inequitable even if it maximized the total welfare; the rightness of an action is not determined solely by its consequences—some acts, for example torture, are wrong no matter what the consequences.

Rights-based theories assert that beings have certain claims and rights that are not open to being traded against increases in the total welfare. There are two distinct justifications for this position. The first appeals to respect for the intrinsic value of individuals: individuals possess a special value that is not reducible to their value to others. The second appeals to contract: ethical rules are those that would be agreed between rational persons about the conditions under which they will cooperate, rather than compete in pursuing their interests; rational contractors would agree to their essential interests being guaranteed from interference through the institution of rights.

These different approaches have implications for the constituency of ethics—who is to count. For the utilitarian, if a being has welfare interests then it counts—as such it classically involves an extension to incorporate all sentient beings, human and nonhuman, present and future. Intrinsic-value rights theorists allow any being that is an end in itself to be included. They differ on whom that incorporates: Kantians extend rights to persons, animal-rights theorists to sentient beings, biocentric rights theory to all living things. Contract theory has more difficulty in extending the ethical constituency beyond those capable of entering into contracts: future generations and nonhumans can be included if rational contractors have an interest in their well being.

For utilitarian and rights theorists only individuals count. Ecocentric holist positions include collective entities such as biological communities as direct objects of ethical concern. Typical is Aldo Leopold's land ethic, according to which actions are right if they tend "to preserve the integrity, stability, and beauty of the biotic community."

Different approaches have implications for the size of human populations. If each new individual has a positive welfare, for the utilitarian, paradoxically, population increase may be one way of augmenting total welfare. In contrast, some ecocentric positions entail a radical reduction in human population.

[*See also* Belief Systems; Conservation; Environmental Bioethics; Environmental Law; Gaia Hypothesis; Human Impacts; *and* Intergenerational Equity.]

BIBLIOGRAPHY

Attfield, R. *The Ethics of Environmental Concern.* New York: Columbia University Press, 1983. A clear overview of basic positions in environmental ethics.
Leopold, A. *A Sand County Almanac.* New York: Oxford University Press, 1949. The most influential source for many recent ecocentric perspectives.

ECOTHEOLOGY

Ecotheology explores the links between religious thought and ecological concerns. It has sometimes been argued that Judeo-Christian thought is at the base of the environmental crisis, though others argue that Christian thought requires stewardship rather than domination. Other religions have different attitudes to the environment and may, for example, promote a respect for animal life or for the conservation of trees.
[*See also* Religion.]

BIBLIOGRAPHY

Gottlieb, R. *This Sacred Earth: Religion, Nature, Environment.* New York: Routledge, 1996.
Kinsley, D. *Ecology and Religion: Ecological Spirituality in Cross-Cultural Perspective.* Englewood Cliffs, N.J.: Prentice Hall, 1995.

— ANDREW S. GOUDIE

O Neill, J. *Ecology, Policy, and Politics: Human Well-Being and the Natural World.* London and New York: Routledge, 1993. A defense of a virtues-based approach that is critical of utilitarian, rights-based, and ecocentric positions.
Singer, P. *Practical Ethics.* Cambridge and New York: Cambridge University Press, 1979. An overview of ethical positions and defense of a utilitarian perspective.
Taylor, P. W. *Respect for Nature: A Theory of Environmental Ethics.* Princeton, N.J.: Princeton University Press, 1986. A biocentric rights-based approach to environmental ethics.

—JOHN O'NEILL

ETHNOBIOLOGY

Ethnobiology (Ellen, 2006) is the comparative study of human beliefs about, and perceptions, categorizations, uses, conservation, and management of, the visible and invisible worlds (bios) that provide a context for "life." The term is roughly synonymous with "ethnoecology," although some practitioners use ethnobiology as the more general term referring to all living things, leaving ethnoecology as the study of how humans understand interactions between elements of ecosystems and landscapes (Toledo, 1992). Hardesty (1977, p. 291) defined ethnoecology as "the study of systems of knowledge developed by a given culture to classify the objects, activities, and events of its universe." These differences are semantic and reflect variations in the different use of "ecology" and "biology" in different languages. Generally, the terms are used interchangeably and in the broadest sense (namely, the human perception of all living things). Subcategories of ethnoecology/ethnobiology are common and mirror the fragmented subdisciplines of Western science (for example, ethnobotany, ethnozoology, ethnopedology, ethnoastronomy, ethnomedicine, and so forth) more than they do the holistic cosmic visions of other traditions (Ellen, 1993).

The continuum of research and methodologies that comprises ethnoecology extends from the perception of phenomena (cognition), to the ordering of cognitive categories (ethnotaxonomy), the social expression of the system (culture), the impact of cultural systems on physical surroundings (anthropogenic and cultural landscapes), the management of those landscapes (conservation and resource management), the exploitation of knowledge and resources for wider use and application (applied research), and the moral concerns of how to apply such research equitably while protecting the rights of knowledge holders (ethics and intellectual property rights). Thus, ethnobiology and ethnoecology inevitably draw from disciplines such as cognitive psychology, linguistics, anthropology (including ethnology and biological and social anthropology), geography, ecology, biology, history of science, philosophy, ethics, and additional areas of study such as forestry and plant sciences, zoology, agriculture, and medicine.

Each phase of the continuum evokes problems of epistemology, terminology, and methodology, because there is no general agreement between disciplines on how to view this spectrum of concerns (Atran, 1990). In practical terms, ethnobiology requires crossdisciplinary and interdisciplinary methodologies that are sensitive to profound differences between cultures, especially in relation to sacred categories, places, or domains that may restrict or prohibit access to researchers. Thus, ethnobiologists are constantly torn between maintenance of the rigors of their Western scientific discipline and respect for and understanding of the metaphysical, aesthetic, and spiritual dimensions that define and encompass the societies of the peoples they study.

Conklin (1957) became a pioneer in ethnobiological research when he described the extensive knowledge of natural history of the Hanuno'o people of the Philippines, as did Bateson (1979) in his thesis on the "unity of mind and nature." Levi-Strauss (1962) provided the modern framework for understanding the links between the "savage mind" and the environment, and drew inspiration from the early (1900) work of Barrows on the Coahuila Indians' knowledge and use of the edible and medicinal plants of the Southern California desert. Berlin et al. (1966) set the current standard for comparative studies of ethnobiological classification systems based on their studies of the Tzeltal Maya of Mexico (also see Berlin, 1992). Majnep and Bulmer provided another classic standard on the Kalam of New Guinea in *Birds of My Kalam Country* (1977). Debates still rage over whether cognitive, or utilitarian, factors underlie folk classification systems (Hunn, 1993). More recently, ethnobiological studies have tended to focus on more practical aspects of ethnobiological knowledge, especially its application to conservation, natural resource management, and environmental change and management (Berkes, 1989; Martin, 1995; Warren et al., 1989).

One goal of ethnobiology is to stimulate dialogue between scientists and local-knowledge specialists so that a common scientific language can eventually emerge for the discussion and study of what is generally known as traditional ecological knowledge, or TEK (Slikkerveer, 1998). Historically, ethnobiology has concentrated on, but not been limited to, studies of indigenous and traditional peoples (such as peasants, hunters, gatherers, fisherfolk, and small farmers). Today, however, there is increasing interest in knowledge systems of urban dwellers, suburban and periurban communities, and peoples in industrial societies.

Since the 1992 Convention on Biological Diversity (CBD), global interest in the "wider use and application" of traditional peoples' "knowledge, innovation and practices" has accelerated. The search for new products and genes for biotechnology (bioprospecting) has highlighted ways in which the knowledge and genetic resources of indigenous and local peoples have been exploited without compensation (biopiracy), despite requirements of the CBD for equitable benefit-sharing with and protection of the "holders" of TEK. Thus, a debate on the ethics of science and industry in their study and exploitation of "traditional resources" has ensued (Posey, 1996). It is no longer possible to undertake ethnoecological research without dealing with full disclosure of research intentions and outcomes, prior informed consent from affected communities, equitable benefit-sharing from any products or derivatives of research, and other ethical issues in research and dissemination (such as publication, films, and photos). The application of intellectual property rights (IPRs) has become a particularly contentious ethical issue, since industrial "discoveries" can be protected by law, but collective knowledge of indigenous, traditional, and local communities cannot. The CBD has initiated a process, in conjunction with the Food and Agriculture Organization (FAO) and the World Intellectual Property Organization (WIPO), to investigate sui generis (unique or specially developed) options for the protection of traditional genetic resources and the TEK associated with them. This process builds upon a long-standing attempt within FAO to develop farmers' rights to guarantee just compensation for traditional farmers who have developed and conserved for millennia the folk varieties and landraces from which high-yielding domesticated crop plants were developed— and upon whose future improvement and adaptation these crops still depend (Posey and Dutfield, 1996).

Ethnobiologists and ethnoecologists have become leaders in the struggle to prevent extinction of plant and animal species and the loss of languages and cultures that encode knowledge about biodiversity and management strategies that conserve it. The International Society for Ethnobiology meets biennially and has developed, together with indigenous and traditional peoples, a model code of conduct to guide "equitable partnerships" between experts in TEK and Western scientists. Many countries (such as the United States, India, Mexico, Brazil, Thailand, and China) have their own societies or associations of ethnobiologists. There are several journals that deal specifically with ethnobiology and ethnoecology, including the *Journal of Economic Botany* and *Journal of Ethnobiology* (both published in the United States), and *Etnoecológica* (Mexico).

[*See also* Biological Diversity; Ethics; *and* Extinctions of Animals.]

BIBLIOGRAPHY

Atran, S. *Cognitive Foundations of Natural History*. Cambridge and New York: Cambridge University Press, 1990. A fundamental study of the underlying perceptual elements of ethnobiology.

Bateson, G. *Mind and Nature: A Necessary Unity*. New York: Dutton, 1979. Sequel to the author's *Steps to an Ecology of the Mind* (1972), which established the link between cognition, society, and nature.

Berkes, F., ed. *Common Property Resources: Ecology and Community-Based Sustainable Development*. London and New York: Belhaven Press, 1989. A broad collection of studies on the relationship between property systems and environmental management by communities.

Berlin, B. *Ethnobiological Classification: Principles of Categorization of Plants and Animals in Traditional Societies*. Princeton, N.J.: Princeton University Press, 1992. Provides an outline of the general principles of ethnobiological classification, followed by an exemplary case study of indigenous Mayans of Chiapas, Mexico.

Berlin, B., D. E. Breedlove, and P. H. Raven. "Folk Taxonomies and Biological Classification." *Science* 154 (1966), 273–275. DOI: 10.1126/science.154.3746.273. One of the foundation works on the universal principles of folk classification.

Conklin, H. "Hanunoo Agriculture: Report of an Integral System of Shifting Cultivation in the Philippines." Forestry Development Paper No. 5. Rome: FAO, 1957. The historic study of traditional agriculture that helped fuel the early interest in traditional knowledge and ethnobiology.

Ellen, R. *The Cultural Relations of Classification*. Cambridge and New York: Cambridge University Press, 1993. One of the primary theoretical studies on ethnobiology and classification, building upon extensive field data and case studies.

Ellen, R., ed. *Ethnobiology and the Science of Humankind*. Oxford: Blackwell, 2006.

Ford, R. I., ed. *Ethnobiology at the Millennium: Past Promise and Future Prospects*. Ann Arbor: University of Michigan Museum, 2001. An edited survey of a maturing field.

Hardesty, D. *Ecological Anthropology*. New York: Wiley, 1977. A foundation study on the role of culture and environment in molding human societies.

Hunn, E. "The Ethnobiological Foundation for TEK." In *Traditional Ecological Knowledge: Wisdom for Sustainable Development*, edited by N. Williams and G. Baines. Canberra: Centre for Resource and Environmental Studies, 1993.

Levi-Strauss, C. *La Pensée Sauvage*. Paris, 1962. (English translation: *The Savage Mind*, Chicago: University of Chicago Press, 1996.) A classic work that lays out the importance of biology and nature in shaping human society and the universal perceptions of nature that are influenced by biological function.

Majnep, I., and R. Bulmer. *Birds of My Kalam Country*. Auckland: Auckland University Press, 1977. One of the most influential studies in ethnoornithology and ethnobiology.

Martin, G. J. *Ethnobotany*. London: Chapman and Hall, 1995.

Posey, D. A. *Traditional Resource Rights*. Gland, Switzerland: IUCN, 1996.

Posey, D. A., and G. Dutfield. *Beyond Intellectual Property Rights*. Ottawa: IDRC Books, 1996.

Slikkerveer, J. "Traditional Ecological Knowledge: An Introduction." In *Cultural and Spiritual Values of Biodiversity*, edited by D. Posey. London: UNEP and IT Press, 1999.

Toledo, V. "What is Ethnobiology? Origins, Scope, and Implications of a Rising Discipline." *Etnoecológica* 1.1 (1992), 5–21.

Warren, D. M., et al, eds. *The Cultural Dimension of Development*. London: Intermediate Technology Publications, 1995.

—DARRELL ADDISON POSEY

EXOTIC SPECIES

An exotic species is one that is found in a habitat in which it did not evolve. Also called alien or nonnative species, or invaders, exotic species comprise all forms of life, including plants, higher animals, invertebrates, and lower forms such as parasites and pathogens. Throughout the history of life on Earth, the movement of species into new niches or habitats has been intimately connected with the spread of life forms and the creation of new species and new assemblages of species and ecosystems. Exotics may colonize empty habitats or niches (for example, following major disturbances such as storms, volcanic activity, and ice ages), or may move into already occupied areas and create new conditions through such processes as predation, competition, and coevolution. Historically, most exotics, along with associated life forms, have become extinct, but often only after they have contributed genetically and ecologically to the biota and ecosystems that followed. In a sense, the Earth's present biodiversity is at least partly the result of over three billion years of exotic species.

One of the best known examples of this process is provided by the finches of the Galápagos Islands, made famous by Charles Darwin's study that gave him insights into evolution that later appeared in his *On the Origin of Species by Natural Selection* (1859). Following the arrival of one species of finch on an island, the birds spread to other islands. On each island the finches changed dramatically in form and habit to enable them to survive under the different islands' varying supplies of food and other environmental conditions. In the process, they created new finch species and modified species associations and ecosystems.

While the invasions of exotic species have been an integral part of the development of life on Earth, the process has been altered significantly and the rate of invasions greatly accelerated by human activities. As a result, exotic species in large part have ceased to be a "natural" part of the development of biological diversity and instead represent a growing ecological disaster and a major threat to that biological diversity. Exotic species now cost the U.S. economy $100 billion a year. [*See* Biological Diversity.]

Today there are still some invasions of exotic species that may not be caused by human intervention. In the United Kingdom, for example, around 80% of the invading species of birds during the past century apparently arrived without help from humans. In North America, again apparently without help from humans, the nine-banded armadillo is rapidly extending its range northward. In both of these cases, human alteration of the environment may be playing some role by creating suitable habitats, but the invasions are basically a natural process. In the case of the armadillo, at least, it appears that the species is in the process of following a warming that has been proceeding since the last ice age but which has been accelerated by the recent global warming. Other species of animals and plants are also gradually extending their range northward for the same reason.

INTRODUCTION OF EXOTIC SPECIES

Most exotic invasions are now due to human activities. There are many examples of intentional introductions. Crop plants and commercial timber trees have been introduced intentionally on a global scale. Some of these have proven beneficial, while others have had dramatically negative impacts. Throughout the world, especially in developing nations, indigenous forests have been cleared to plant fast-growing eucalyptus or pine trees. This process is still actively promoted by international development agencies. These plantations have often proven uneconomic or, at best, short lived, and usually fare worse than indigenous species in terms of erosion control, wildlife habitat, and maintenance of biodiversity and ecological services.

To provide sport fishing, trout have been introduced into mountain streams, rivers, and lakes worldwide. These introductions have often provided the desired fishing. In the rare cases where no native fishes were present, these exotic trout represented a net benefit. In most cases, however, the trout preyed on or outcompeted indigenous fishes, depleting the biodiversity and changing the aquatic ecosystem.

Fish hatcheries are a major source of exotic species. In North America, hatcheries have been developed for decades as a way to restock streams that had been overfished and to augment the fish catch for both commercial and sport fisheries. The hatchery programs have been politically popular and many millions of dollars have been spent on them. In recent years, however, research has increasingly shown that exotic hatchery fish have a host of negative effects and often no demonstrable benefits. Among other problems, they dilute the genetic makeup of the native fish, in many cases leading to depletion or loss; they introduce diseases; and, when subjected to careful scientific analysis, most have not proven to increase the fishery yields.

Deer have been introduced in many areas for sport hunting and have often become a major threat to indigenous plants and the habitats of some forms of native wildlife. Efforts to protect indigenous biodiversity have often pitted conservation authorities against the hunters. The impacts of the exotic deer and the resultant controversies are most acute in island situations such as Hawaii and Mauritius.

Exotic game birds have also been widely introduced for sport hunting, but in general their impact has been more benign than that of introduced mammals. Some have been introduced to fill a habitat niche that was not being used by native game birds. The ring-neck pheasant (*Phasianus colchicus*), introduced in 1881 from Asia, has become successful as a game bird in much of the United States. Since it usually occupies agricultural lands, it appears generally to coexist rather than compete with native wildlife.

Kudzu (*Pueraria thunbergiana*), a very fast-growing vine, was introduced from China into the United States as an ornamental plant in the 1870s, and it was reintroduced widely in the 1930s for soil erosion control. It can grow a foot a day and it covers anything in its path with a green blanket, blocking out the Sun and killing trees and other vegetation in its way. It is now regarded as a major menace to most forms of land use and to biological diversity conservation. The U.S. Forest Service estimates the area of kudzu infestation in the United States at about 2.8 million hectares (7 million acres), from southern Florida to Massachusetts, and expanding rapidly. In a similar manner, rhododendrons introduced as ornamental plants into Ireland from the Himalayas now rate as a major threat to many native plants, especially in southwestern Ireland where they are taking over forest areas and shading out smaller plants and tree reproduction.

Goats and mongooses are intentional exotic introductions that disrupt island environments worldwide. In a process that started centuries ago, fishermen and other sailors have put goats on islands to provide a source of meat. This is still being done, for example, in the Galápagos Islands. The voracious goats eat virtually anything, removing native vegetation and preventing its regeneration, causing erosion, and damaging the habitat for indigenous plants and animals. Goats are also regarded as one of the major agents by which humans denuded the vegetation of much of the Middle East. Mongooses were introduced onto islands in the Pacific and the Caribbean to control the rats and, in some cases, snakes. However, they found the indigenous birds, mammals, and reptiles easier prey, and they have depleted the native biota on many islands, without much affecting the rats.

Many exotics have been imported for specific uses, such as pets, but have escaped and become established. The state of Florida has been particularly afflicted by tropical birds, fishes, and plants that have escaped from intended captivity. The Asian walking catfish was recently introduced as a pet but has escaped, evading control efforts, and threatening native Floridian freshwater fishes. The African "killer bee" was introduced into Brazil by a beekeeper for breeding experiments with domestic bees, but it escaped. This particularly aggressive bee has killed or interbred with more placid native or domesticated bees, spreading north through South and Central America, and is now entering the southern United States (see Figure 2). The gypsy moth was introduced onto Cape Cod a century ago as the basis of a planned American silk industry, but it escaped and has become a major pest, threatening forests throughout the eastern U.S.

UNINTENTIONAL INTRODUCTIONS

Most problems with exotics probably stem from unintentional introductions. Many ships carry water as ballast, which is discharged in or near port, introducing whatever organisms are carried in it from the place the ballast water was taken on board. In this manner, for example, the zebra mussel (*Dreissena polymorpha*) was introduced to the Great Lakes in about 1988. It has spread throughout most of the Great Lakes and many rivers, including most of the Hudson River basin, and in the first decade after its introduction it is estimated to have cost industry over U.S.$15 billion.

Wherever they have gone, people have carried pests, parasites, and diseases. Europeans coming to the Americas brought smallpox, chicken pox, and other European diseases that caused fatal epidemics among the indigenous inhabitants. Rats (*Rattus* species) and the house mouse (*Mus musculus*), carried as stowaways on boats, have been introduced throughout the world.

Very serious damage has been caused by parasites and diseases carried by exotic species that were intentionally introduced. Rinderpest, a viral disease, was introduced to Africa in the late 1800s in cattle brought from Asia, where the disease was endemic. In less than four years, it swept through the continent, devastating the herds of domestic cattle and many wild ungulates. A few years later, some nursery stock brought from Asia to the United States carried a parasitic fungus that attacked the American chestnut trees. Although the chestnut had been a dominant tree in eastern U.S. forests, it had virtually disappeared by the 1930s.

IMPACTS OF EXOTICS

Predatory exotics can wreak particular havoc on native prey species, particularly when no such predator existed prior to the exotic's introduction, so that the native species have not developed defenses against the predation. Cats, dogs, rats, and mongooses,

Exotic Species. Australian Acacias in South Africa.

This species was introduced into the Fynbos Heathlands of the Cape Region of South Africa. It has spread explosively and has overwhelmed the native flora over wide areas. (Modified after Texas Agricultural Station, in *Christian Science Monitor*, September 1991.)

particularly when introduced into island habitats, have decimated native prey species, especially small mammals and ground-nesting birds. In Mauritius, for example, dogs were a major factor in the extinction of the dodo, whose eggs were laid on the ground. The brown tree snake (*Boiga irregularis*) was accidentally introduced onto the island of Guam after World War II, presumably in shipments of derelict vehicles and equipment salvaged from the Pacific war zone. This snake is a formidable predator, and by 1985 most of Guam's bird species were either isolated in small pockets or were exterminated, the native lizards and mammals were decimated, poultry and other small livestock had been reduced, and over 160 cases of serious snake bites had been reported, most of them babies bitten while they slept. [*See* Extinctions of Animals.]

COMPETITION

The principle of competitive exclusion states that complete competitors (that is, species that compete directly for the same resource or niche) cannot coexist: one will always exclude the other. Where the introduced species is a superior competitor, this principle operates to the detriment of the native species, with the exotic expanding its numbers and range rapidly and, in the process, threatening the native competitors with extinction. The zebra mussel, noted above, is one such example. Another is the sea lamprey (*Petromyzon marinus*), which was in Lake Ontario as

early as the 1820s and had invaded all the Great Lakes by the 1930s after the opening of the modern Welland Canal. The Mediterranean annual grasses that were introduced into California in packing materials at the time of the gold rush so completely replaced the native perennials that they created a whole new ecosystem. The exotic kudzu, also noted above, is rapidly outcompeting native vegetation in much of the eastern and southeastern United States, as are the rhododendrons introduced to Ireland.

NEW HERBIVORE NICHES

Another form of competition is that of herbivorous species filling a new niche, as when deer and goats have been introduced into islands where no such hoofed herbivore previously existed. The native plants have no defenses against such an animal, and these animals' feeding has decimated native species. The same thing occurred when, in 1839, the Asian water buffalo was introduced into northern Australia as a beast of burden. There were no native grazers of this magnitude nor any predators of

THE AFRICANIZED HONEYBEE

Exotic Species. The spread of the Africanized honeybee in the Americas between 1957, when it was introduced in Brazil, and 1990.

The growth of world trade and communications has caused a great increase in the number of accidental introductions and subsequent explosions of fauna and flora. Indeed, as C. S. Elton (1958, p. 31) put it, "We are seeing one of the great historical convulsions in the world's fauna and flora."

A recent example of the spread of an introduced insect in the Americas is provided by the Africanized honeybee (*Apis mellifera scutellata*). Some of these bees were brought to Brazil from South Africa in 1957 as an experiment, and some escaped. Since then, they have moved north to Central America and the United States, spreading at a rate of 300–500 kilometers per year and competing with established populations of European honeybees. They reached Texas in 1990, Arizona and New Mexico in 1993, California in 1994, and Nevada in 1998.

The Africanized honeybee, popularly known as the "killer bee," defends its nest (by stinging) far more than does the European honeybee, swarms more frequently, and is far less selective about where it will nest.

— Andrew S. Goudie

eruption followed by a crash is characteristic of introductions of exotic ungulates. [*See* Australia and Global Change.]

DISEASES AND PARASITES

In the case of diseases such as smallpox, the population in which the exotic disease was endemic, in this case the Europeans, had developed significant resistance to it, but when it was introduced to human populations that had no such resistance, the results were catastrophic. The same thing happened with rinderpest. The Asian cattle had developed resistance or even immunity to the disease, but, when it was introduced to African livestock and wildlife that had no such resistance, the results were devastating.

In the same way, parasites such as the chestnut fungus, gypsy moth, and hemlock adelgid (an insect that feeds on the sap of North American hemlock trees) were of little concern in their native lands. The chestnut fungus, for example, had little impact on its native European chestnut trees because they had developed resistance to it. But when it was introduced to the United States, where the American chestnut had no such resistance, it virtually exterminated that species.

WHAT DETERMINES THE IMPACT OF EXOTICS?

Some exotics are successful invaders, usually causing serious impacts, while others apparently never get a foothold or appear to be benign. Several factors combine to create conditions in which an exotic is a successful invader. The species must have characteristics that fit the conditions into which it is introduced, and the recipient ecosystem must be in some way vulnerable to such introductions. The vulnerability of ecosystems varies over time, and stress of some sort can predispose an ecosystem to invasion. A closed forest may be resistant to exotics that require sunlight until the necessary open light conditions are created by a forest fire, a storm blowdown, or even a falling tree. Apparently the factors that determine the success or failure of invaders include the interrelations between the biology of species, the properties of the ecosystems at the time, and perhaps pure chance.

Most species have existed for a long period in their native habitats and have evolved together so that the predators, parasites, prey, competitors, and symbionts (species that provide each other mutual advantages) have adjusted to one another. There are limiting factors in such an ecosystem that assure that relations among the species involved seldom gets far out of balance. The prey species develop defensive strategies and adaptations to protect themselves from the predators, so that there is a dynamic balance between them. Similar mechanisms are developed between plants, animals, diseases, and parasites. However, when exotic species are introduced into a new habitat where such limiting factors are not present, they have the opportunity to increase without their previous limitations, usually with devastating results for the native biota.

In general, the exotics that have been benign or beneficial have been domestic species of plant or animal that required human care to survive, such as most field crops, or that fitted into an

such a large animal, and the buffalo population increased very rapidly. It soon exhausted the native vegetation and there were periodic die-offs from starvation. This process of population unoccupied niche. But, even in these cases, domestic exotics have escaped and become pests, or their diseases or parasites have done so. People still believe that introductions can bring substantial benefits, and intentional and unintentional introductions continue to expand. With the exception of certain domestic species, however, exotic introductions continue to cause far more problems than they solve and, on a global basis, exotic species represent one of the greatest threats to biodiversity and to related human welfare. Global warming promises to increase this threat manifold. A warming climate will destabilize ecosystems, creating fertile habitats across the globe for exotic species.

[*See also* Biological Diversity; Biological Realms; *and* Biomes.]

BIBLIOGRAPHY

Elton, C. S. *The Ecology of Invasions by Animals and Plants.* London: Chapman and Hall, 1958.
Mooney, H. A., and J. A. Drake, eds. *The Ecology of Biological Invasions of North America and Hawaii.* New York: Springer, 1986.
Office of Technology Assessment. *Harmful Non-Indigenous Species in the United States.* Publication No. OTA-F-565. Washington, D.C.: U.S. Government Printing Office, 1993.
Simberloff, D. "Why Do Introduced Species Appear to Devastate Islands More than Mainland Areas?" *Pacific Science* 49 (1995), 87–97.
U.S. Geological Survey. *Status and Trends of the Nation's Biological Resources.* Reston, Va.: U.S. Department of the Interior, 1999.
Wilcove, D. S., et al. "Quantifying Threats to Imperiled Species in the United States." *Bioscience* 48.8 (1998), 607–615.

—LEE M. TALBOT

EXTERNALITIES

Generally, the term refers to unintended effects of an activity or a process. Persons or communities affected are unwilling participants who may be affected positively or negatively.

Positive externalities include a property owner who landscapes his acreage, and raises the value of neighboring properties; car owners who maintain their vehicles and contribute to cleaner air for all drivers; and civic-minded individuals who argue for reforms in government policy and improve the lot of other citizens.

Negative externalities, in an environmental context, include logging, which can inadvertently cause soil erosion and affect water quality and wildlife; mining and smelting, which can degrade both air and water and be detrimental to health; and coal-fired generating plants, which can affect the atmosphere on local, regional, and world scales.

In such activities the product's price typically does not reflect the external costs. In effect, the product is too cheap: the industry may prosper while society suffers the air pollution or other wastes; these are the social costs of the production.

When many individuals pump groundwater without controls and reduce the supply for other users, the water is recognized as a common-pool resource. The atmosphere, the oceans, and a given stretch of river may also be considered common-pool resources. [*See* Commons; *and* Tragedy of the Commons.]

The internalization of externalities is the imposition of fines or taxes on the polluting activity to discourage pollution and raise the product's price so it reflects external costs—a strategy sometimes called full-cost pricing. [*See* Environmental Accounting.] If gasoline or coal-fired electricity were subject to full-cost pricing, the higher prices would make renewable technologies more competitive.

—DAVID J. CUFF

EXTINCTIONS OF ANIMALS

Spectacular examples of extinction are known from the geological record, but extinction continues today, accelerated by the expansion of human influence over the nonhuman natural world.

PREHISTORIC TIMES

Some workers believe that the human role in animal extinctions goes back to the Paleolithic (Stone Age) in the Late Pleistocene. They believe that the chronology of extinction closely follows that of the spread of humans and the development of hunting. They also maintain that there are no known continents or islands in which accelerated extinction definitely pre-dates the arrival of humans. Martin (1982) argued that the global pattern of extinctions of large land mammals follows the spread of Palaeolithic humans. He suggested that Africa and parts of Southern Asia were affected first, with substantial losses at the end of the Acheulean, around 200,000 years ago. Europe and northern Asia were affected between 20,000 and 10,000 years ago, while North and South America lost their large herbivores between 12,000 and 10,000 years ago. Megafaunal extinctions in Australia may have occurred around 41,000 years ago, shortly after humans arrived (Roberts et al., 2001). Extinctions continued into the Holocene on oceanic islands. In the Galápagos Islands, for example, virtually all extinctions took place after the first human contact in 1535 CE (Steadman et al., 1991). Likewise, the complete deforestation of Easter Island between 1200 and 800 years BP led to the eradication of much of the native flora and fauna and precipitated the decline of the megalithic culture that had erected the famous statues (Flenley et al., 1991).

The nature of the human impact on animal extinctions can conveniently be classified into three types (Marshall, 1984): the "blitzkrieg effect," which involves rapid spread of humans with hunting technology resulting in the very rapid demise of animal populations; the "innovation effect," whereby long-established human population groups adopt new hunting technologies and erase fauna that have already been stressed by climatic changes; and the "attrition effect," whereby extinction takes place relatively slowly after a long history of human activity because of loss of habitat and competition for resources. Haynes (1991) has suggested that about 11,000 years ago conditions were dry in the interior of the U.S. and that Clovis hunters may as a result have found large game animals easier prey when they were concentrated around waterholes and under stress.

Extinctions of Animals. African Elephants.

Animals with long gestation times that produce limited numbers of offspring are highly prone to extinction if hunting reaches high levels. Elephants have disappeared from large tracts of Africa, but in locations like the Etosha National Park in Namibia, they are protected and their numbers have grown.

There are several arguments for an anthropogenic interpretation. In North America massive extinction appears to have coincided in time with the arrival of humans in sufficient numbers and with sufficient technological skill in making suitable artefacts (Clovis blades) to be able to kill many animals (Krantz, 1970). Also, animals unfamiliar with people are often tame in their presence, and it would have taken them time to learn to flee or hide. Moreover, humans, in addition to hunting animals, may have competed with them for food or water or may have introduced predators (especially dogs) which then competed with native fauna (Johnson and Wroe, 2003). In addition, Coe (1982) suggested that the supposed preferential extinction of larger mammals could also support the role of human actions. He argued that while large body size has its advantages, especially in terms of avoiding predation and being able to cover vast areas of savanna in search of food, it also means that these herbivores are required to feed almost continuously to sustain their large body mass. Furthermore, as the size and generation time of a mammal increases, the rate at which it turns over its biomass decreases. This means that, because large mammals can only turn over a small percentage of their population biomass each year, the rate of slaughter that such a population can sustain in the face of even a primitive hunter is very low.

An alternative interpretation is that the Late Pleistocene extinctions were caused by the rapid and large changes of climate at the end of the last glacial (Martin and Klein, 1984). Certain objections have been leveled against the climatic-change model which therefore tend to support the anthropogenic model. Changes in climatic zones are generally gradual enough for animals to be able to follow the shifting biomes of their choice. It can also be argued that earlier climatic changes do not seem to have caused the same striking degree of extinction as those in the Late Pleistocene. A further difficulty with the climatic theory is that animals like the mammoth occupied a broad range of habitats from arctic to tropical latitudes, so it is unlikely all would have perished as a result of a climatic change (Martin, 1982).

This is not to say, however, that the climatic hypothesis lacks foundation. Animal migration in response to rapid climatic change could be halted by barriers such as high mountain ranges or seas. Climatic change might also have caused extinction through its influence on disease transmission. It has been suggested that during glacial periods animals were split into discrete groups cut off by ice sheets but that, as the ice melted, contacts between groups would be reestablished, enabling diseases to which immunity might have been lost during isolation to spread rapidly.

The detailed dating of the European megafauna's demise lends some support to the climate model (Reed, 1970). The Eurasian boreal mammals, such as mammoth and woolly rhinoceros, were adapted to the cold steppe that was the dominant environment in northern Europe during the glacial phases of the last glaciation. Each of these animals, especially the mammoth and the steppe bison, had been hunted by humans for tens of thousands of years yet managed to survive the last glacial. They appear to have disappeared, according to Reed, within the space of a few hundred years when warm conditions associated with the Allerød interstadial led to the restriction and near disappearance of their habitat.

Grayson (1977) expressed further doubts about the anthropogenic hypothesis. He suggested that the overkill theory required terminal-Pleistocene generic extinctions of large mammals to have been relatively greater than those within other classes of vertebrates at that time. However, when he examined bird extinctions he found that a proportion comparable to that of the megafauna became extinct at the end of the Pleistocene. Moreover, as the dates for early societies in countries like Australia are pushed back, it becomes increasingly clear that humans and several species of megafauna lived together for long periods, thereby undermining the notion of rapid overkill (Gillespie et al., 1978).

Actual extinction may have occurred during or after a substantial decrease in mammalian body size, though this is a subject of controversy (Guthrie, 2003). On the one hand, the dwarfing might have resulted from a reduction in food availability brought about by climatic deterioration. On the other, it can be argued that small animals, being more adept at hiding and a less attractive target for a hunter, are more likely to survive human predation, so that reduced body size is favored genetically.

MODERN-DAY EXTINCTIONS

As their populations have grown and their technology has developed, humans have been responsible for the extinction of many species of animals and a reduction in biodiversity, "the only truly irreversible global environmental change the Earth faces today" (Dirzo and Raven, 2003). Indeed, there is an apparent close correlation between population growth since the mid-seventeenth century and the number of species that have become extinct. Although it is likely that European expansion overseas during that time has indeed led to many extinctions, the apparent dramatic increase in the rate of extinctions over the last few centuries may partly be a result of the increasingly thorough documentation of natural phenomena.

Some modern extinctions are natural. Extinction is a biological reality, a part of the process of evolution. In any period, including the present, there are species that are doomed to disappear, either because of overspecialization or an inability to adapt themselves to climatic change and the competition of others, or because of natural cataclysms such as earthquakes, eruptions, and floods.

One of the fundamental ways in which humans are causing extinction is by the reduction of the area of available natural habitat and its fragmentation (Fahrig, 2003). Habitat fragmentation divides once large, continuous populations into many smaller ones, which are more or less isolated. The small size and isolation of populations is associated with various negative consequences, including susceptibility to natural disasters, to genetic drift (random fluctuations in gene frequencies), and to inbreeding (Lienert, 2004). Even wildlife reserves tend to be small islands in an inhospitable sea of anthropogenically modified vegetation or urban sprawl. We know from classic studies in island biogeography that the number of species living in a place is related to area; islands support fewer species than do similar areas of mainland, and small islands have fewer species than do large ones. Space is therefore an important consideration, especially for those animals that require territories. For example, the population density of the wolf is about one adult per 20 square kilometers, and it has been calculated that to maintain a viable population to exist, there should be 600 individuals ranging over an area of 12,000 square kilometers. This is significant because most nature reserves are small: 93% of the world's national parks and reserves have an area less than 5,000 square kilometers, and 78% less than 1,000 square kilometers.

Reduction in area leads to a reduction in numbers, which leads in turn to genetic impoverishment through inbreeding (Frankel, 1984). The effect on reproductive performance appears to be particularly marked. Inbreeding degeneration is not the only effect of small population size because, in the longer term, the depletion of genetic variance is more serious since it reduces the capacity for adaptive change. Range loss, the shrinking of the geographical area in which a given species is found, likewise often marks the start of a downward spiral towards extinction.

Another important cause of extinction is the introduction of competitive species. When they are deliberately or accidentally introduced to an area, they can cause the extermination of local fauna by preying on them or by outcompeting them for food and space. The World Conservation Monitoring Centre, in its analysis of the known causes of animal extinctions since 1600 CE, found that 39% were caused by species introductions, 36% by habitat destruction, 23% by hunting, and 2% by other factors (*World Resources*, 1994–1995, p. 149).

Some environments particularly important in terms of their species diversity—biodiversity hot-spots—need to be made priorities for conservation. They include coral reefs, tropical forests (which support well over half the planet's species on only about 6% of its land area), and some of the Mediterranean types of biomes (such as the extraordinarily diverse Fynbos heathlands of the Cape region of South Africa). Myers (2000) has argued that as many as 44% of all species of vascular plants and 35% of all species in four groups of vertebrate animals are confined to just 25 hotspots that comprise a mere 1.4% of Earth's land surface.

Finally, it is possible that climate change will be a major cause of extinctions in coming decades, and a major threat to biodiversity (Thomas et al., 2004). Many habitats will change markedly, leaving many nature reserves in the wrong place for the species they are meant to protect. For instance, mountaintop habitats that harbor biological communities we now consider typical of high altitudes may simply disappear.

BIBLIOGRAPHY

Coe, M. "The Bigger They Are..." *Oryx* 16 (1982), 225–228.
Dirzo, R., and P. H. Raven. "Global State of Biodiversity and Loss." *Annual Review of Environment and Resources* 28 (2003), 137–167.
Fahrig, L. "Effects of Habitat Fragmentation on Biodiversity." *Annual Review of Ecology, Evolution, and Systematics* 34 (2003), 487–515. DOI: 10.1146/annurev.ecolsys.34.011802.132419.
Flenley, J. R., et al. "The Late Quaternary Vegetational and Climatic History of Easter Island." *Journal of Quaternary Science* 6 (1991), 85–115.
Frankel, O. H. "Genetic Diversity, Ecosystem Conservation, and Evolutionary Responsibility." In *Ecology in Practice*, vol. 1, edited by F. D. Castri, F. W. G. Baker, and M. Hadley, pp. 4315–4327. Dublin: Tycooly, 1984.
Gillespie, R., et al. "Lancefield Swamp and the Extinction of the Australian Megafauna." *Science* 200 (1978), 1044–1048. DOI: 10.1126/science.200.4345.1044-a.
Grayson, D. K. "Pleistocene Avifaunas and the Overkill Hypothesis." *Science* 195 (1977), 691–693. DOI: 10.1126/science.195.4279.691.
Guthrie, R. D. "Rapid Body Size Decline in Alaskan Pleistocene Horses before Extinction." *Nature* 426 (2003), 169–171. DOI: 10.1038/nature02098.
Haynes, C. V. "Geoarchaeological and Paleohydrological Evidence for a Clovis-Age Drought in North America and Its Bearing on Extinction." *Quaternary Research* 35 (1991), 438–450.
Johnson, C., and S. Wroe. "Causes of Extinction of Vertebrates during the Holocene of Mainland Australia: Arrival of the Dingo, or Human Impact?" *The Holocene* 13 (2003), 941–948. DOI: 10.1191/0959683603hl682fa.
Krantz, G. S. "Human Activities and Megafaunal Extinctions." *American Scientist* 58 (1970), 164–170.
Lienert, J. "Habitat Fragmentation Effects on Fitness of Plant Populations: A Review." *Journal for Nature Conservation* 12 (2004), 53–72. DOI: 10.1016/j.nc.2003.07.002.
Marshall, L. G. "Who Killed Cock Robin? An Investigation of the Extinction Controversy." In *Quaternary Extinctions*, edited by P. S. Martin and R. G. Klein. Tucson: University of Arizona Press, 1984.
Martin, P. S. "The Pattern and Meaning of Holarctic Mammoth Extinction." In *Paleoecology of Beringia*, edited by D. M. Hopkins, et al., pp. 399–408. New York: Academic Press, 1982.
Martin, P. S., and R. G. Klein, eds. *Quaternary Extinctions*. Tucson: University of Arizona Press, 1984.
Myers, N., et al. "Biodiversity Hotspots for Conservation Priorities." *Nature* 403 (2000), 853–858.
Reed, C. A. "Extinction of Mammalian Megafauna in the Old World Late Quaternary." *BioScience* 20 (1970), 284–288.
Roberts, R. G., et al. "New Ages for the Last Australian Megafauna: Continent-Wide Extinction about 46,000 Years Ago." *Science* 292 (2001), 1888–1892. DOI: 10.1126/science.1060264.

Steadman, D. W., et al. "Chronology of Holocene Vertebrate Extinction in the Galápagos Islands." *Quaternary Research* 36 (1991), 126–133.

Thomas, C. D., et al. "Extinction Risk from Climate Change." *Nature* 427 (2004), 145–148. DOI: 10.1038/nature02121.

—ANDREW S. GOUDIE

EXTRATERRESTRIAL IMPACTS

Throughout the history of the solar system, planets have been impacted by asteroids and comets. Approximately 170 impact craters have been identified on earth. They range in diameter to more than 250 km and in age from thousands to approximately 2 billion years. On impact, vast amounts of energy are transferred to the target rocks by an ultra-high-pressure shock wave, which blasts out a crater and creates shock-metamorphic effects in rocks. In some cases, a small chemical anomaly, representing material from the impactor, can be detected in rocks melted by the impact.

EARLY EARTH EVOLUTION

Planetary formation involved up to one trillion asteroid-sized bodies growing rapidly by collisions to form about 20–30 embryonic planets, each about 10% of the mass of the Earth. This was followed by giant collisions between these embryos, until a few planet-sized bodies were formed. On the early Earth, the last major collision may have been the impact of a Mars-sized body that produced an orbiting disk of impactor and terrestrial material from which our Moon formed. This giant impact would also have caused massive remelting of the Earth and the loss of its original atmosphere.

The subsequent bombardment by the remaining tail of debris following planetary formation is best recorded on the Moon, where at least 6,000 craters with diameters greater than 20 kilometers formed during the following 700 million years. They include about 45 collisions that produced impact basins ranging in diameter from 300 km, to 2,500 kilometers (the South Pole Aitken basin), to 3,500 kilometers (the possible Procellarum basin). It is estimated that several hundred such impact basins may have been formed on the Earth from 4.5 to about 3.8 billion years ago. The effect of such a bombardment on the surface of the Earth is unknown. Few terrestrial surface rocks are likely to have survived intact through this period of heavy bombardment.

These impacts would have affected the Earth in other ways as well. For example, the impact of a body about 500 km in diameter would release sufficient energy to vaporize the present world's oceans. It would envelope the Earth in a rock-vapor atmosphere that would radiate heat downward, raising the surface temperature to over 2,000°C. Impacts by bodies of around 200 km in diameter would be sufficient to evaporate the entire upper zone of the oceans in which photosynthesis occurs. Life could have survived in a deep marine setting as early as 4.2–4.0 billion years ago, but smaller impacts would continue to make the surface inhospitable until 4.0–3.8 billion years ago.

As the impact rate stabilized, major basin-forming impacts no longer occurred, but there were still occasional impacts resulting in craters hundreds of kilometers in diameter. For example, the terrestrial record contains remnants of the Sudbury (Ontario) and Vredefort (South Africa) structures, with estimated original diameters of 200–300 kilometers and ages of about two billion years.

MORE RECENT IMPACTS

A number of large craters have been preserved on Earth from Phanerozoic time (the most recent 550 million years), among them Manicouagan (Quebec), diameter 100 kilometers, age 212±2 million years (Figure 1), and Popigai (Siberia), 100 kilometers, 35±5 million years. Impact events resulting in craters in the 100 kilometer size-range release, in seconds, energies equivalent to the explosion of tens to a hundred million megatons of TNT and create destructive surface blast-waves over a million square kilometers.

There is evidence for a major impact 65 million years ago, at the so-called Cretaceous-Tertiary (K/T) boundary, which is associated with a mass extinction in the terrestrial biosphere. The evidence consists of shocked and melted materials and a chemical anomaly indicative of meteoritic material at the stratigraphic boundary between the Cretaceous and the Tertiary. The buried 180-kilometer Chicxulub crater, on the Yucatán peninsula of Mexico, was formed by the K/T event.

Early models for the global devastation of life focused on the effects of the vast amounts of ejected dust in the atmosphere, resulting in the cessation of photosynthesis and below-freezing temperatures on land. More recent models suggest that the

Extraterrestrial Impacts. FIGURE 1. Extent of Airblast Produced by the Manicouagan Impact.

Near the impact site wind speeds would have exceeded 1000 kilometers per hour. The white circle (radius 560 kilometers) represents the limit of overpressures that have the capacity to severely damage and kill plants and animals.

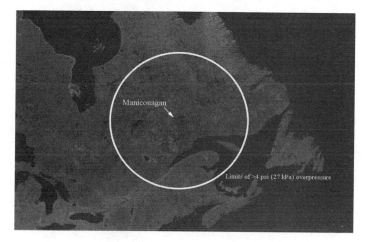

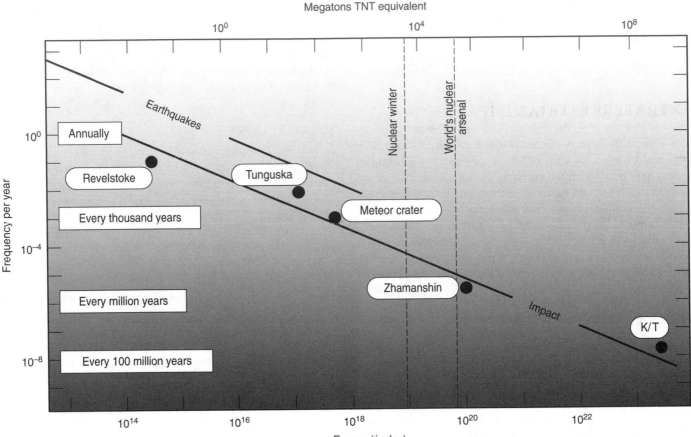

Extraterrestrial Impacts. Figure 2. Frequency of Impact Plotted against Energy Released, in Joules and Megatons of TNT Equivalent.

A number of specific impact and atmospheric explosion events are indicated. For comparison, the frequency and energy of earthquakes are shown. Earthquakes are more common than impacts but are limited in the amount of energy they release. Also shown (dotted vertical lines) are the energies required to produce a global "nuclear winter" and the world's nuclear arsenal.

oceans might have offset land surface cooling and that subfreezing temperatures occured only in some areas.

Soot too is found in K/T deposits. Models of the thermal radiation produced by the atmospheric reentry of K/T ejecta indicate a strong thermal pulse, up to 50–150 times the present solar input, which radiated down onto the Earth's surface for several hours. Calculations indicate that this thermal radiation is at the lower end of that required to ignite living plant materials. If massive wildfires, in addition to the effect of atmospheric dust, are required to produce mass extinction, that may explain why impacts that result in 100-kilometer craters do not result in mass extinctions. The accompanying thermal radiation is insufficient to result in the ignition of plant materials.

A considerable thickness of rock containing the mineral anhydrite ($CaSO_4$) occurs in the target rocks at Chicxulub. The impact would have driven off sulfur dioxide from the anhydrite, producing about one trillion metric tons of sulfur aerosols in the atmosphere. From the study of volcanic eruptions, the effects of sulfur aerosols on atmospheric cooling are known to be greater than those of dust particles. Ultimately, the aerosols will rain out as sulfuric acid, which would further severely damage the biosphere. It may be that the devastating effects of the K/T impact are due, in part, to the unusual composition of the target rocks at Chicxulub. This temporal association of a large impact crater with a worldwide ejecta layer and a global mass extinction is well established. The cause-and-effect relationships are less well established. Modeling of the atmospheric and biospheric effects of large impacts is in its infancy.

FUTURE IMPACTS

K/T-sized impact events occur every 100±50 million years. Smaller impact events occur more frequently. They will not produce mass extinctions but will affect the global climate and biosphere to varying degrees. Potentially climate-changing impacts occur every 2 or 3 million years (e.g., the 15 kilometer diameter Zhamanshin crater in Kazakhstan at about 700,000 BP). Such impacts will not have a serious effect on the overall biosphere, because climatic disruptions are of limited severity and duration. The most fragile component of the environment, however, is our civilization, which is highly dependent on an organized and technologically complex infrastructure. While we seldom think of civilization in terms of millions of years, there is little doubt that there is potential for it to suffer severely or even be destroyed by an impact event.

Impact risk involves rare events with extreme consequences. When will the next large impact take place? NASA began the Spaceguard Survey in 1998 to find 90% of the so-called near-Earth asteroids larger than 1 kilometer, which would result in 15–20 kilometer craters if they impacted the Earth. It is estimated that 60% of these bodies have so far been found, and none is known to be on a collision-course with Earth. Beyond this telescopic search, little serious effort has been devoted to the mitigation of an impact. Most approaches so far discussed center on nudging an incoming body into a less threatening orbit, but this requires warning times of years or even decades.

If some comfort can be taken from the fact that civilization-threatening impact events occur only every half million years or so, it must be remembered that impact is a random process in time. "Impact" events have occured on human time scales. The Tunguska event in 1908 was caused by the atmospheric explosion of a body several hundred meters in diameter at an altitude of 10 kilometers or less. The energy released is estimated to have been the equivalent of 10–100 megatons of TNT, and the blast resulted in the devastation of about 2,000 square kilometers of Siberian forest (Figure 2). There was no recorded loss of human life because of the very sparse population. Events such as Tunguska occur at intervals of hundreds of years, and the next Tunguska-sized event could occur over an urban center.

The lunar and planetary exploration programs provided the impetus and rationale for the study of terrestrial impacts. Impacts, however, can no longer be considered of interest only to the planetary community. Impacts have changed the course of terrestrial evolution in fundamental ways. Without the K/T impact and the extinction of the dominant dinosaurs, the present-day biosphere might not have included mammals—and, in particular, humans—as an important component. Similarly, without a Mars-sized impact forming the Moon, with its accompanying tidal forces, one can only speculate as to how the intertidal zone, one of the most important parts of the terrestrial ecosystem, would have evolved and been populated. Impacts have happened throughout geologic time and will happen again. Although the occurrence of a large impact has a low probability on the scale of human history, its consequences would be globally disastrous.

[See also Extinctions of Animals; and Volcanoes.]

BIBLIOGRAPHY

Alvarez, W. *T. Rex and the Crater of Doom*. Princeton, N.J.: Princeton University Press, 1997. An account of the development of the impact hypothesis for the K/T boundary and mass extinctions and the discovery of the Chicxulub crater. Written by the son of Nobel laureate L. Alvarez, the primary author of the initial scientific article presenting chemical evidence for the involvement of impact at the K/T boundary.

Bobrowsky, P. T. and Rickman, H., eds. *Comet/Asteroid Impacts and Human Society*. Berlin and New York: Springer, 2007. A compendium of papers dealing with impacts, their physical effects, and communication and mitigation strategies for dealing with the risk associated with impact events.

Gehrels, T., ed. *Hazards Due to Comets and Asteroids*. Tucson: University of Arizona Press, 1994. A compendium of scientific papers by 120 authors dealing with a range of subjects related to impact hazards.

Remo, J. L., ed. *Near-Earth Objects: The United Nations International Conference*. New York: New York Academy of Sciences, 1997. A compendium of scientific papers dealing with near-Earth objects. A follow-up and update to some of the topics covered in Gehrels (1994).

—RICHARD A. F. GRIEVE

EXTREME EVENTS

Among the possible consequences of global climate change are changes in the severity and frequency of extreme events such as floods, droughts, tropical cyclones, and severe thunderstorms. [See Drought *and* Tropical Cyclones in a Warming World.] These events entail large societal costs, including injury, loss of life, property loss, and impairment of business; changes in their intensity and frequency are therefore of special concern. In developing nations, loss of life from such events can be extreme. For example, a tropical cyclone in Bangladesh in 1970 killed nearly half a million people, while more than three million have perished in single flooding events in China (Southern, 1979). In developed nations, sophisticated warning technology has greatly reduced loss of life from extreme weather, but the rapidly expanding technological infrastructure has at the same time vastly increased economic vulnerability to extreme events (Landsea and Pielke, 1998). For example, Hurricane Andrew (1992) was one of the costliest national disasters in United States history, with insured losses in excess of U.S.$15 billion (in constant 1990 dollars), while the cost of the Florida hurricane of 1926, normalized to 1990 dollars, exceeded U.S.$70 billion (Landsea and Pielke, 1998). Hurricane Katrina (2005) cost at least U.S.$81.2 billion. This article reviews our present understanding of the response of the frequency and intensity of extreme events to global climate change.

FLOODS

There are two broad categories of flood, river floods that result from weeks or months of unusually heavy rainfall over large portions of drainage basins, and flash floods that typically result from a single convective storm of a few hours' duration. Such events are related to climate in many ways.

Global precipitation patterns are intimately related to the atmospheric greenhouse effect. When water condenses and falls out of the atmosphere, latent heat of vaporization is released to the air. Over long periods of time worldwide, this heat release must be compensated by radiative cooling of the atmosphere. If we ignore absorption of sunlight by atmospheric constituents and dry turbulent heat fluxes, the cooling of the atmosphere is the difference between the net outgoing longwave radiative flux at the Earth's surface and that at the top of the atmosphere. This is a gross measure of the greenhouse effect. Thus an increasing greenhouse effect implies increasing precipitation and a more active hydrologic cycle. The effect is quantitatively small, however: doubling carbon dioxide, for example, is predicted to cause about a 7% increase in global precipitation.

In addition to changes in global precipitation, changes in the distribution of precipitation in space and time are of concern.

Such changes may be brought about by changing atmospheric circulation patterns and changing atmospheric stability with respect to convection. There are several reasons that global warming might lead to the concentration of precipitation into more localized and intense events. [See Global Warming.] First, it has been shown by Emanuel and Bister (1996) that the average convective instability in the atmosphere depends on the thermodynamic efficiency of the atmospheric heat engine, that is, the rate of conversion of thermal energy into the energy of convection depends on the difference between the surface temperature and the average temperature at which the atmosphere loses heat to space. Greenhouse warming increases this temperature difference and so increases the kinetic-energy density of convective clouds. Precipitation from such clouds should therefore be more intense even though precipitation episodes would be less frequent on average. Quantitatively, however, the effect is slight. For example, a radiative-convective equilibrium-model based on a 2°C rise in surface temperature caused by greenhouse warming shows an increase in the average vertical velocity in clouds of about 5%.

There is some indication that global precipitation is becoming increasingly concentrated in more episodic, high-intensity events (Tsonis, 1996). It has not been established, however, that this results from anthropogenic global warming.

Theory and several numerical modeling studies suggest that major atmospheric circulation systems in the tropics would increase in intensity in response to global warming. These circulations greatly affect the distribution of precipitation in the tropics and subtropics, enhancing precipitation in equatorial regions and decreasing it in subtropical regions such as the Sahara Desert. Increases in the intensity of such circulations would have the effect of increasing rainfall in regions where it is already plentiful and decreasing it elsewhere. Taken together, these results point to an increase in the occurrence of flash floods, river floods, and drought in association with global warming, but the magnitude of such an increase is difficult to estimate at present, as is the magnitude of global warming itself.

TROPICAL CYCLONES

Changes in the frequency, intensity, or geographic distribution of tropical cyclones would have major consequences for society.

Because we do not understand what controls the intensity of individual tropical cyclones, we have almost no ability to forecast storm intensities even over periods as short as 24 hours (DeMaria and Kaplan, 1997). On the other hand, we can calculate the definite upper limit of tropical-cyclone intensity from our knowledge of the temperatures of the ocean surface and of the overlying atmosphere.

Studies of the variations of tropical cyclone frequency and potential intensity have been summarized recently by Henderson-Sellers et al. (1998). There is a general consensus that potential maximum wind speed (V_m) increases with global warming. Estimates of the magnitude of possible increases of V_m vary widely, however. A doubling of atmospheric carbon dioxide is estimated to increase V_m by 5–20%. This could have serious consequences. For example, an increase in the upper bound on intensity from 60 to 70 meters per second would increase the frequency of storms with winds greater than 50 meters per second by almost 70%, keeping the total frequency of all storms constant.

Estimates of the change in frequency of occurrence of all tropical cyclones have been made principally by integrating global climate models with increased greenhouse gases. They range from modest decreases to modest increases, depending on the model and on how the model's climate is altered. It is thus impossible at present to make useful estimates of how total storm frequency might change. This also reflects our substantial ignorance of the factors determining global tropical cyclone frequency in the present climate.

Theoretical calculations and modeling show decisively that the total geographic area affected by tropical cyclones will neither expand nor contract appreciably as a result of climate change. This is because tropical cyclones occur almost exclusively in parts of the tropical atmosphere undergoing very slow, large-scale ascent, and are largely absent in regions of large-scale sinking. The dynamics of the tropical atmosphere dictate that roughly half of the tropical atmosphere is ascending and half descending, and this will not change appreciably with modest climate change. This result counters the naive view that the area affected by tropical cyclones expand simply because tropical cyclones occur where sea-surface temperatures exceed 26°C and global warming would expand the area of water with temperatures above this value. (In essence, the 26°C threshold value also increases with global warming; it is not a constant threshold.)

Notwithstanding the constant total surface area affected by tropical cyclones, one might expect some change in the distribution of tropical cyclones within those regions currently affected by them. Unfortunately, global climate models reveal no consistent picture of such changes, because they may depend on comparatively subtle changes in the general circulation of the atmosphere.

Finally, individual ocean basins, especially the Atlantic, experience large decadal fluctuations in tropical cyclone activity, independent of global climate change (Landsea and Gray, 1992). The magnitude of such decadal changes is so large as to mask any changes that might be attributable to global warming, so policies and procedures related to tropical cyclone preparedness must naturally be more concerned with such decadal fluctuations. [See Tropical Cyclones in a Warming World.]

SEVERE WINTER STORMS

We are interested in possible changes in the frequency, intensity, and distribution of winter storms, which provide much of the precipitation that falls outside the tropics and which are associated with rainstorms, blizzards, ice storms, and severe coastal and marine windstorms. Winter cyclones are powered by the energy that resides in the general pole-to-equator temperature gradient in the lowest 10 kilometers or so of the atmosphere, although they are also influenced by atmospheric stability, condensation of water vapor, and surface exchanges of heat, momentum, and moisture. Cyclonic storms are concentrated in a few relatively narrow belts, or storm tracks.

One universal feature of global warming simulations in climate models is the relatively large warming that takes place at the poles compared with the tropics. Thus the average pole-to-equator temperature gradient is reduced. While this is true at the Earth's surface, the opposite is the case high in the atmosphere, where equatorial warming exceeds polar warming in most simulations. Because the growth rate of winter storms depends on temperature gradients at the surface and in the upper troposphere, it is not obvious whether storms will increase or decrease with greenhouse warming.

That the intensity of winter storms might increase as a result of greenhouse warming is borne out by the few studies that have been performed using general circulation models of the atmosphere. Lambert (1995) found that the frequency of intense winter storms increased in a global-climate model based on a doubling of carbon dioxide, even though the frequency of all cyclones diminished. Similarly, Lunkeit et al. (1996) found an increase in extreme wind events in a coupled ocean-atmosphere climate model subjected to rising greenhouse-gas concentrations. Neither study found appreciable shifts in storm tracks.

SEVERE THUNDERSTORMS, HAIL, AND TORNADOES

Hail, tornadoes, and local damaging winds are associated with atmospheric convective systems whose horizontal dimensions are far too small to be simulated by global climate models. Such models thus cannot make direct predictions of the frequency, intensity, or geographical distribution of such events. We must at present rely on indirect inferences about changes in such phenomena, based on explicit simulation of the large-scale conditions known to be conducive to them.

We know from direct observation and from numerical simulation (with specialized, cloud-resolving numerical models) that the severity of convective storms depends on certain combinations of atmospheric stability and the vertical shear of the horizontal wind. Large amounts of convective instability coupled with strong vertical shear, particularly in the lowest 2–3 kilometers of the atmosphere, are conducive to severe thunderstorms. These conditions arise from regional circulations, so it is unlikely that their global averages will prove useful in assessing changes in severe convective storm activity. More important are changes in regional circulations and thermodynamic conditions in certain regions such as central North America which are unusually prone to severe thunderstorms.

Unfortunately, global models are mutually inconsistent in their predictions of regional responses to anthropogenic climate change. Thus, models cannot yet be regarded as credible in their predictions of regional change, even if they are reliable in their forecasts of global changes. It is also difficult to detect changes in the frequency of small-scale events from past observations. Thunderstorms are too small to be detected systematically with the standard observational network, and one must rely on meteorological radar for such systematic detection. In the United States, a comprehensive network of radars has been in place since the 1950s, but little attempt has been made to detect trends in convective radar echoes. Over the past decade, these radars have been replaced by modern Doppler radars, which are more accurate and can detect air motion within thunderstorms.

Severe thunderstorms, hail, and tornadoes in the United States are heavily concentrated in the Midwest and Plains states. Changing demography and levels of education have had such strong effects on reporting of tornadoes and hail that reliable inferences about any long-term trends in such phenomena are impossible. The advent of satellites, Doppler radar, and trained storm spotters over the past three decades, however, now assures that almost every significant tornado or hail event in the United States will be detected, which will allow the tracking of long-term trends in such activity.

[*See also* Climate Models; Natural Hazards; Rivers: Impacts of Climate Change; *and* Sea Level Future.]

BIBLIOGRAPHY

DeMaria, M., and J. Kaplan. "An Operational Evaluation of a Statistical Hurricane Intensity Prediction Scheme (SHIPS)." Preprint, 22d American Meteorological Society Conference on Hurricanes and Tropical Meteorology, pp. 280–281. Fort Collins, Colo.: AMS, 1997.

Emanuel, K. A. *Influence of Climate Processes on Tropical Cyclone Potential Intensity.* Preprint, 23d American Meteorological Society Conference on Hurricanes and Tropical Meteorology, pp. 1073–1076. Boston: AMS, 1999.

Emanuel, K. A., and M. Bister. "Moist Convective Velocity and Buoyancy Scales." *Journal of the Atmospheric Sciences* 53 (1996), 3276–3285.

Henderson-Sellers, A., et al. "Tropical Cyclones and Global Climate Change: A Post-IPCC Assessment." *Bulletin of the American Meteorological Society* 79 (1998), 19–38.

Lambert, S. J. "The Effect of Enhanced Greenhouse Warming on Winter Cyclone Frequencies and Strengths." *Journal of Climate* 8 (1995), 1447–1452.

Landsea, C. W., and W. M. Gray. "The Strong Association Between Western Sahelian Monsoon Rainfall and Intense Atlantic Hurricanes." *Journal of Climate* 5 (1992), 435–453.

Landsea, C. W., and R. A. Pielke, Jr. "Trends in U.S. Hurricane Losses, 1925–1995." Preprints of the American Meteorological Society Symposium on Global Change Studies, pp. 210–212. Boston: AMS, 1998.

Lunkeit, F., et al. "Cyclonic Activity in a Warmer Climate." *Contributions to Atmospheric Physics* 69 (1996), 393–407.

Southern, R. L. "The Global Socio-Economic Impact of Tropical Cyclones." *Australian Meteorological Magazine* 27 (1979), 175–195.

Tsonis, A. A. "Widespread Increases in Low-Frequency Variability of Precipitation over the Past Century." *Nature* 382 (1996), 700–702. DOI: 10.1038/382700a0.

—KERRY A. EMANUEL

F

FAMINE

Famine is a protracted total shortage of food in a restricted geographical area, political unit, or cultural group, causing widespread disease and mass deaths from starvation. In most instances, a famine sequence—crop failure, lack of food, social disruption, moral degeneracy, migration, epidemics, and death from starvation—is triggered by restriction of food imports to food-deficit areas or crop failures in traditional food-surplus areas (Figure 1). The primary human factors have been war, political decisions, poverty, and inadequate transportation infrastructure. The primary natural factors have been crop failures resulting from frost, floods, drought, violent natural events, insects, and plant diseases. Throughout history, famine has rivaled pestilence and war as a scourge of humankind.

The locations of high-frequency famine regions have shifted globally as civilizations or nations emerged, flourished, and declined and as food demands in certain places exceeded food production or the ability to import food. Case studies on critical regions (Figure 2) have proven that acute food crises, starvation, and famine are not short-term critical events but the results of longer-term processes. The seeds of famine require time to mature. The threat to certain groups of humans increases slowly, and the possibility for successful food-crisis management becomes more and more limited. The famine process goes through site-specific stages of development that are characterized by the growing vulnerability of social groups to food shortages, up to the point at which mass starvation becomes famine.

Famine affects people of all ages, sexes, and nationalities. The first to die are those who live in poverty, in inequitable societies, in cultures that do not encourage education, and in placeswith unsustainable populations. Famines have appeared in the world's best agricultural regions and in all natural zones and climatic regions, and have not been restricted to one cultural area, nation, or racial group. The map of world famine regions in Figure 2 shows the areas affected by more than 800 famines spanning four millennia. Although famines occurred throughout the famine zones in all time periods, the highest percentage of total famines in each time period occurred in very specific regions. The map identifies the location of six major famine regions and the "Future Famine Zone."

MODERN "FOUR HORSEMEN"

Concerns over world food production, problems of chronic hunger, undernutrition, and malnutrition problems, and unstable world food reserves are compounded by fear of the "Four Horsemen" of famine in the twenty-first century: abrupt climatic perturbations and climatic change; uncontrolled population growth in food-deficit regions; changing dietary expectations and increased food needs for an enlarging world population; and misguided political decisions by self-centered and culturally biased religious leaders and national heads of state. Famines have claimed the lives of more people between 1981 and 2007 than in any other period since World War II. Famines have taken place in the Sahel and Ethiopia, Mozambique, Bangladesh and northeastern India, Cambodia, Vietnam, North Korea, Central America, and the highlands of eastern Africa. With high population growth in areas of political and economic instability, illiteracy, disease, pollution, massive rural-to-urban migration, and gross inequalities in food production and food-purchasing capability, humankind faces an unending struggle against famine.

SEEDS OF FAMINE

It is conservatively estimated that at least 800 million people in developing countries are chronically undernourished, and possibly 200 million people in developed countries suffer from mild undernourishment and aspects of malnutrition. Per capita daily caloric intake in developing countries averages about 2,200, compared with 3,400 calories in developed nations. (The average minimum daily requirements vary according to physical size, climate, type of work performed, and sex of the individual.) The International Food Policy Research Institute (IFPRI) estimates that 90% of those who suffer from chronic undernutrition live in sub-Saharan Africa, South Asia, East Asia, Latin America, the Caribbean, the Near East, and North Africa.

WORLD FOOD PRODUCTION

Improved agricultural technology, practices, and policies, have enabled the world's agriculturalists to produce more than twice as much food per year in 2000 as they did in the 1950s. World grain production increased 60% between 1969 and 1990, and grain supplies could provide every person on Earth with at least 2,800 calories per day. World food production per capita also increased but not equally in all countries of the world; production per capita was lower in underdeveloped countries than in developed countries. The amount of arable land that is under cultivation varies markedly from one continent or one country to another, and there are opportunities for increased productivity. World food trade and food imports have mitigated food problems in many underdeveloped countries and are not necessarily evidence of internal national agricultural failures. For

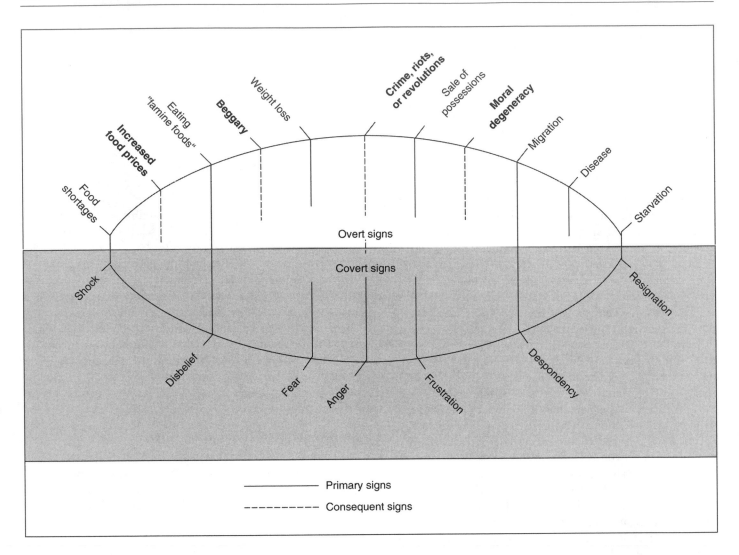

Famine. Figure 1. The Modern Starvation Sequence.

(Modified after Dando, 1980. With permission of Edward Arnold.)

many developing countries, it is economically efficient to allocate portions of total agricultural investment for the enhanced production of high-value indigenous export commodities that command hard currency, while importing low-value, high-bulk supplemental food commodities. Moreover, both developed and underdeveloped countries that import and export food commodities are capable of substantial increases in food production and reductions in food losses. What has caused (and will cause) famine crises in many countries of the world is not a global shortfall in food. Famine in the future will be related to political decisions; poverty; an unprecedented and accelerating worldwide demand for food; civil strife; religious prejudice; ethnic antagonisms; and a pervasive urban bias in national food policies.

A MODERN POLITICAL FAMINE: CHINA 1959–1961

Agriculture in China was socialized in the 1950s. The Stalinist model of agricultural development was put into effect in three phases: (1) land, animal, and tool redistribution, 1949–1952; (2) cooperative-socialist stage, 1953–1957; and (3) commune stage, 1958–1961. Social disruption associated with the collectivization of agriculture, the commune system, and abuses associated with the zeal generated by the "Great Leap Forward" campaign of 1958 upset China's intricate traditional farming system. Peasant apathy and indifference, diversion of nearly 40% of the agricultural workforce to nonagricultural activities, removal of one-third of the agricultural land from food production, and a severe drought created a catastrophic agricultural crisis.

Grain production dropped from more than 200 to 150 million metric tons, and the vast country experienced the horrors of its first socialist, nearly nationwide famine. Food shortages in urban areas, serious in late 1959, reached a critical point during April and May 1961. Twenty million urban residents were ordered into the countryside to ease food shortages in urban areas; food rationing (below human dietary requirements) was ordered for urban dwellers in noncritical occupations. Threatened with the first nationwide famine in Chinese history, the Chinese Communist Party (not Mao Zedong) acted to

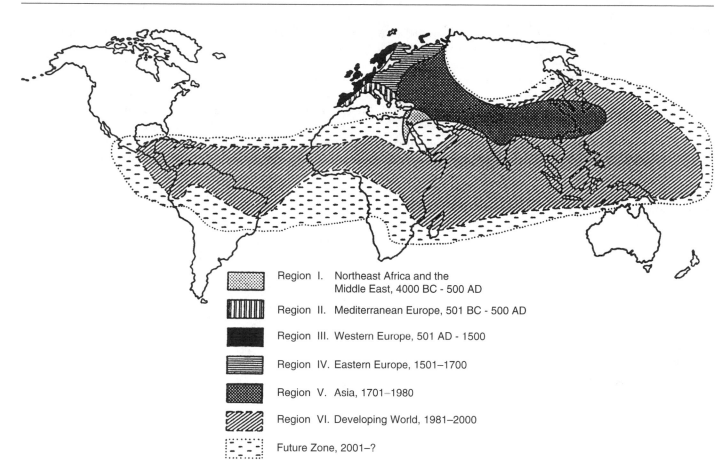

Region I. Northeast Africa and the Middle East, 4000 BC - 500 AD

Region II. Mediterranean Europe, 501 BC - 500 AD

Region III. Western Europe, 501 AD - 1500

Region IV. Eastern Europe, 1501–1700

Region V. Asia, 1701–1980

Region VI. Developing World, 1981–2000

Future Zone, 2001–?

Famine. FIGURE 2. World Famine Regions, 4000 BC–2000 AD.
(Modified after Dando, 1980. With permission of Edward Arnold.)

rectify the errors in national agricultural decision-making, to conserve food, and to save as many lives as possible.

Domestic food supplies provided less than 1,800 calories per day to each working citizen. Grain imports were increased from 2.6 million metric tons in 1960–1961 to 5.8 million in 1961–1962. Stringent food rationing was enforced, military food rations cut, and food quality reduced. Malnutrition and undernutrition caused widespread night blindness, famine edema, famine diarrhea, liver disorders, tuberculosis, amenorrhea, beriberi, and a general rise in mortality. The natural population increase (births minus deaths) in China in 1960 dropped to zero, famine-related deaths exceeded 6.8 million, and the calculated total loss of population as a result of the 1959–1961 famine was 32.1 million.

In the millennia of Chinese history, famines have always been regional or local, never nationwide. Of the three major causes of massive loss of life in China (famine, pestilence, and war), famine remains the most amenable to social control and elimination. Mao stressed that the state could organize the nation's resources for the common good. It was only when the agricultural disaster of 1959 was followed by a second monumental setback in 1960 and millions of people had died, that the Communist Party leadership modified Mao's plan, implemented drastic measures to feed those in need, and restored agricultural productivity. The Chinese famine of 1959–1961 was an unintentional, state-created, social catastrophe. This famine was the precursor of future "political" famines in developing nations led by a dictator or driven by an ideology.

A MODERN MEDIA FAMINE: ETHIOPIA 1984–1985

In the mid-1980s millions of Africans living in the Sahel—a narrow semiarid zone stretching 3,000 miles from Senegal to Sudan—were confronted with death, as were hundreds of thousands of inhabitants of countries outside this zone. What began as a series of local food shortages became a multinational human catastrophe. The Great African Famine of 1984–1985 claimed the lives of at least 300,000 people in Ethiopia, and probably millions there have not been accounted for. At the same time, at least 200,000 people died in Mozambique, 50,000 in Senegal, and thousands in Chad. An estimated 2.5 million suffered from malnutrition and related diseases in Mali, and one million Sudanese suffered acute food deprivation. The precise dimensions of this human tragedy are unknown because governments have been unwilling or unable to provide accurate statistics. The triggering physical factor that led to this international famine was two vast belts of drought that spread across the continent;

the basic cultural factors were overpopulation in marginal agricultural areas, pervasive poverty, abuse of a delicate physical environment, government mismanagement, and civil strife. Warnings of impending disaster were issued by many scholars, international development agencies, and national planners but were ignored by government leaders in most countries.

[*See* Drought.]

Thousands of emaciated refugees from famine-stricken Ethiopia streamed across the border into neighboring Sudan each day, placing an intolerable strain on the Sudanese government and people. More than one million Ethiopian refugees sought food, fuel, and medicines in Sudan. Sudan soon faced a threat of famine among its own people—a horrendous price to pay for its open-door policy and concern for those in need. The threat of a continent-wide famine was averted by the actions of national and international relief agencies stimulated by television reports. Yet insensitive national leaders, inexperienced government administrators, political expediency, cultural pride, and religious intolerance have created the setting for further famines in Africa.

A MODERN SILENT FAMINE: NORTH KOREA 1995–1999

A xenophobic political system, a faltering state-controlled food-production system, a crippled industrial economy, and a series of devastating natural disasters have produced a modern "silent" famine in the Democratic People's Republic of Korea. It is estimated that 16 million out of a population of 23 million suffered from malnutrition and undernutrition, 2–5 million were considered to be at high risk of death, and at least 800,000 were killed by famine. Many of those who died were elderly, children, individuals or groups considered nonessential to the communist government, and urban inhabitants who had no access to foraging off the bleak land. The famine reached its most devastating stage in late 1996 and early 1997. It led to acute malnutrition and stunted the growth of two out of every three children under the age of five. North Korean authorities were successful in maintaining order and preventing large refugee movements, yet at least 400,000 fled the famine-torn nation for China. A precursor of the North Korean famine was the great Ukrainian famine of 1946–1947 (under Stalin's rule) and the Chinese famine of 1959–1961 (Mao's famine) during the "Great Leap Forward," when political control prevented movement of refugees, external fact-finders were denied entry to the country, and the state assumed control of famine mitigation activities. Because the world knew little of these two famines, they too are called "silent." The silent North Korean famine can also be termed a national "carpet" famine, because 90% of North Koreans survived on a state-determined food ration insufficient to maintain human health. Ubiquitous suffering and chronic malnourishment still threaten millions.

The Democratic People's Republic of Korea retains a Stalinist type of communist system under the leadership of Kim Jong II. Since the Korean War in the 1950s and the collapse of communism in the former Soviet Union and Eastern Europe, North Korean leaders have chosen a path of national isolation and self-reliance, or *chuch e*. It maintains an armed force of 1.04 million, and the military accounts for 25% of the nation's annual budget. Causes of the famine were multifaceted and resulted from human-made and natural disasters. Food shortfalls arose from years of economic mismanagement, failed collective-farming practices, political posturing, and redirection of resources toward the military. Coupled with antiquated political decision-making, one natural disaster after another has plagued the country. Hail destroyed much of the food crop in 1994, floods reduced yields in 1995 and 1996, and a severe drought and typhoon destroyed most of the corn crop and much of the rice crop in 1997. After four consecutive years of reduced food production, loss of life, and human suffering, the leaders of North Korea realized the gravity and far-reaching repercussions of the food-supply situation. The government increased efforts to import food from Thailand, Vietnam, and China, and from relief agencies in the developed world; 3.5 million metric tons of donated food raised national diets to subsistence nutritional levels. The survivors, weakened and malnourished, will have difficulty resisting disease and infections. The extent of death and suffering in North Korea may never be known; the famine's victims have died in silence, out of view of the world's media.

HOW MANY PEOPLE CAN THE EARTH FEED?

Thomas Robert Malthus wrote in *An Essay on the Principle of Population* (1798), "the power of population is indefinitely greater than the power in the earth to produce subsistence for man." Malthus concluded that unless family size was regulated, famines would eventually become a global epidemic and over time result in the destruction of civilization. He could not foresee the agrotechnical revolution, transportation innovations, global migrations, and a global food economy. Nevertheless, world population estimates and projections to the year 2100 raise deep concern. Population in the developed countries of the world is increasing slowly and in some cases actually declining. Unfortunately, in most developing countries of the world, population growth continues at a rate that threatens the quality of life; in these countries hunger is a way of life for millions, poverty harms family life, women's rights are minimal, and many people are migrating internally and internationally. The world's population is increasing by over 90 million people annually. Demographers believe that the world's population in the year 2050 will be about 9–10 billion, approximately 40% more than the estimated 6.2 billion people on Earth in 2000. In 2100, the world's population is projected to reach 12–15 billion, a 100% increase over the population of the Earth in 2000. To the dismay of all who are concerned with human physical, mental, and economic development, most of the population growth in the future will occur in developing countries.

Demographers disagree about the maximum number of people the Earth can support. Food consumption is expected to double by the year 2050 and then double again by 2100. Predictions of the world's carrying capacity depends on assumptions of future food production. The world's carrying capacity is subject to uncertain aspects of climatic change which alter physical and biological conditions, technical and logistical deficiencies, ecological constraints and feedbacks, economic problems and limitations, and political and cultural restrictions. The United Nations Food and Agriculture Organization estimated in the 1980s that under optimal conditions the world could support 33 billion people. A more recent estimate, considered more reasonable, is that sufficient food could be produced to support 10 to 15 billion people, under favorable political and socioeconomic conditions.

FAMINE MITIGATION

To eliminate famine, the world's leaders must accept that an adequate diet is a basic human right, strive to implement means to continually increase food supplies, insure that all households have adequate incomes to purchase necessary foods, develop regional and international systems to provide early famine-warning and emergency amelioration activities, and maintain resilience and flexibility in famine-relief programs. No social or economic problem facing the world today is more urgent than famine. While these distressing events are not new, their persistence despite the remarkable technical and productive advances of the twentieth century is difficult to understand.

A successful program to reduce famine includes an international early-warning system. Four key components of a successful system are: (1) detecting and predicting widespread food shortages; (2) forecasting or informing decision-makers in regions, nations, or subnational areas of the impending threat; (3) communicating to the world a warning of an impending famine and needed relief; and (4) creating global food reserves and a means to deliver food quickly to needy famine victims. Unfortunately, any early-warning system is a response to symptoms rather than to causes. Effective famine mitigation is always problematic in societies that lack resources and those in which politics or religion dictate who will live and who will die.

URBAN FAMINES OF THE TWENTY-FIRST CENTURY

Millions of new urbanites exist on the edge of survival in large cities in the developing world—a phenomenon that can be termed "subsistence urbanization." Even a small reduction in food consumption means, for many, a decline from acute malnutrition to death by starvation or disease. Traditional local foodstuffs are becoming scarce and expensive. The rural elite generally have moved to cities, and the agricultural sector has lost a critical portion of its ability to feed those who live in cities. Urbanization without rural development eventually forces urban leaders to rely on imported food to maintain the urban population. Any disruption in food deliveries from developed countries could result in food shortages, food riots, revolution, mass starvation, or urban famine.

PROSPECTS OF FUTURE FAMINES

The twenty-first century will be the climate century. Despite the technological advances in agriculture that have dramatically increased crop yields, food production is highly dependent upon weather and climate. Since the industrial revolution, humans have been changing the weather and climate of places, then regions, and now the world. Removal of natural vegetation for agricultural purposes, paving over vast areas for urban and transportation use, and changing the composition of gases in the atmosphere have resulted in changes in the way short-wave solar radiation behaves at the surface of the Earth and long-wave terrestrial radiation behaves as it is passes from the surface of the Earth to the atmosphere. The world is experiencing higher global temperatures, changing hydrologic regimes, and increasing climatic variability and violent weather. The enhanced greenhouse effect over the next century will have a significant effect on world food production. How great an impact, where the greatest reduction will take place, and whose food security will be affected most by climatic change are questions that scientists and policy-makers must address.

[See also Agriculture and Agricultural Land; Carrying Capacity; Catastrophist-Cornucopian Debate; Climate Change and Societal Development; Desertification; Global Warming; Human Populations; and Migrations.]

BIBLIOGRAPHY

Avery, D. T. Global Food Progress 1991. Indianapolis, Ind.: Hudson Institute, 1991.
Bhatia, B. M. Famines in India: A Case Study of Some Aspects of the Economic History of India, 1860–1965. Bombay and New York: Asia Publishing House, 1967.
Brown, L. R., and H. Kane. Full House. New York: Norton, 1994.
Cartledge, B., ed. Population and the Environment. Oxford and New York: Oxford University Press, 1995.
Dando, W. A. "Man-Made Famines: Some Geographical Insights from an Exploratory Study of a Millenium of Russian Famines." Ecology of Food and Nutrition 4 (1976a), 219–234.
———. "The Soviet Famines of 1946–47." The Great Plains-Rocky Mountain Journal 5.3 (1976b), 15–21.
———. The Geography of Famine. London: Edward Arnold, 1980.
———. "Famine in China, 1959–1961: Some Geographical Insights." In China in Readjustment, edited by C.K. Leung and S.S.K. Chin, pp. 231–249. Hong Kong: Centre of Asian Studies, University of Hong Kong, 1983a.
———. "Biblical Famines, 1850 B.C.–A.D. 46: Insights for Modern Mankind." Ecology of Food and Nutrition 13 (1983b), 231–249.
———. World Hunger and Famine. Indiana State University, Department of Geography, Geology, and Anthropology, Professional Paper 20. Terre Haute: Indiana State University Press, 1995.
Dando, W. A., and C. Z. Dando. A Reference Guide to World Hunger. Hillside, N.J.: Enslow, 1991.
Dando, W. A., and V. Lulla. "Agriculture and Food Provisioning, A.D. 2100." In Climatic Change and Variation: A Primer for Teachers, edited by W.A. Dando, pp. 29–43. Manhattan: National Council for Geographic Education and The Kansas State University Press, 2007.
Food and Agricultural Organization. Urbanization and Hunger in the Cities. Madrid, Spain: FAO, 1986.
Gaffin, S. et al. Mapping the Future of World Population. Washington, D.C.: Population Action International, 2006.
Greenough, P. R. Prosperity and Misery in Modern Bengal: The Famine of 1943–44. Oxford and New York: Oxford University Press, 1982.
Lanagan, K. "Hungry Nations in a World of Plenty." Farmline 4.8 (1983), 16.

Maass, W.B. *The Netherlands at War: 1940–1945.* London and New York: Abelard-Schuman, 1970.

Malthus, T.R. *First Essay on Population, 1798.* London: Macmillan, 1926.

Ruowang, W. *Hunger Trilogy.* Armonk, N.Y.: M. E. Sharp, 1991.

World Bank. *Population and Development.* Washington, D.C.: World Bank, 1994.

World Resources Institute. *World Resources: A Guide to the Global Environment.* Oxford and New York: Oxford University Press, 1996.

—WILLIAM A. DANDO

FEEDBACK

See Biological Feedback *and* Tipping Points and Global Change.

FIRE AND GLOBAL WARMING

The frequency and intensity of fires may change with future warming and associated environmental changes. For example, an analysis by Flannigan et al. (2000) suggests that future fire severity could increase over much of North America. They anticipate a 25–50% increase in the area burned in the U.S. by the middle of the present century, with most of the increase occurring in Alaska and the southeastern U.S. In Canada, the area burned is expected to increase by 74–118% by the end of this century with a tripling of atmospheric CO_2 (Flannigan et al., 2005). In addition there is some evidence that warmer temperatures in recent decades have contributed to an increase in the duration and intensity of the wildfire season in the western U.S. Since 1986 there has been a fourfold increase in major wildfires and a sixfold increase in the area of forest burned, compared to 1970–1986 (Westerling et al., 2006). One of the reasons for this is that mountain snowpacks, which help depress fire danger, have been melting earlier in the year.

BIBLIOGRAPHY

Flannigan, M.D., B.J. Stocks, and B.M. Wotton. "Climate Change and Forest Fires." *The Science of the Total Environment* 262.3 (2000), 221–229. DOI: 10.1016/S0048-9697(00)00524-6.

Flannigan, M.D., et al. "Future Area Burned in Canada." *Climatic Change* 72.1–2 (2005), 1–16. DOI: 10.1007/s10584-005-5935-y.

Westerling, A.L., et al. "Warming and Earlier Spring Increase Western U.S. Forest Wildfire Activity." *Science* 313 (2006) 940–943. DOI: 10.1126/science.1128834.

—ANDREW S. GOUDIE

Fire and Global Warming. Healthland.

Fire was one of the earliest, and is still one of the most powerful means of environmental change available to humans. Many ecosystems, such as this heathland at Studland in southern England, owe much of their character to fire. It is likely that fire characteristics will change in the face of climate change.

FISHERIES

Fishing, in the inclusive sense of the catching of fish, other aquatic vertebrates, and aquatic invertebrates—all referred to here as "fish" unless otherwise noted—is conducted in both fresh and marine waters, and there is evidence for a considerable antiquity of both. Here, we shall deal only with marine fisheries, because of their size and because inland fisheries are strongly affected by habitat modifications. In the marine realm, on the other hand, it is mainly fisheries which affect the ecosystems, and hence the habitat of resource species.

Marine fisheries, in virtually all of the world's maritime countries, consist of large-scale, or industrial fisheries, and small-scale, or artisanal fisheries. Industrial fisheries tend to use fuel-intensive, active gear, deployed from large vessels (e.g., trawlers), and/or to fish far offshore (e.g., tuna longliners), often as parts of distant-water fleets. Artisanal fisheries tend to use passive gear (set nets, traps) set from small vessels within tens of kilometers of their landing place.

Industrial and artisanal marine fisheries generate combined catches (including discards) in excess of 100 million metric tons (Figure 1), with a value (as unloaded from the vessel) of about U.S.$80 billion. Industrial and artisanal fisheries land similar quantities for human consumption (25–30 million tons). Industrial fishing lands, additionally, about 35–40 million tons of small pelagic fish (e.g., anchovies, sardines, mackerels, capelins) destined to be ground up for fishmeal and fish oil, used in equal proportions in animal husbandry (e.g., chicken feed) and aquaculture (e.g., salmon farming).

Industrial and artisanal fisheries contribute very unequally to the discard (and by-catch) problem of fisheries, which is caused by the nonselective operation of trawls, longlines, and now-banned driftnets, which annually catch and kill millions of tons of nontargeted bony fish, plus large numbers of turtles, seabirds, and marine mammals, which are then discarded, along with the carcasses of about 50 millions of sharks whose dried fins are exported to East Asian markets.

Industrial and artisanal fisheries, finally, probably contribute equally to the IUU (illegal, unregulated, and unreported) catch of the world (Figure 1), with industrial fisheries probably responsible for the bulk of the illegal and undocumented catch and small-scale fisheries for most of the unreported catch.

The combined capacity of the world's fleet is estimated to be 2–3 times what is needed to generate the catches mentioned above (Pauly et al., 2002), the result of the U.S.$30–34 billion of subsidies they are given annually. These are given by governments ignoring the fact that when fisheries resources are as overfished as they are now, subsidies reduce catch because they enable fishing to continue on collapsed stocks, and create uncompetitive, fragile fisheries, likely to become even more dependent on subsidies in the future.

Subsidies and the resulting overcapacity have led to targeted and by-catch species undergoing precipitous declines throughout the world (Myers and Worm, 2003), and since the late 1980s global fish landings have been declining as well (Watson and Pauly, 2001). In addition to reducing food security, this has begun to endanger marine biodiversity, especially the survival of the large, long-lived species that have sustained fisheries for centuries.

FISHERIES EXPANDING

The depletion of easily accessible coastal stocks (Jackson et al., 2001) caused the fisheries to expand simultaneously in three ways: toward deeper water (farther offshore); toward new fishing grounds; and toward smaller fish at the base of marine food webs.

Fishing deeper, farther offshore

This was enabled by development of larger, more capable craft, and of gear capable of exploiting deeper waters. Foremost among those is the bottom trawl. This gear was inverted in the Middle Ages, but its ruthless effectiveness became manifest only with the invention of the steam trawler in the late nineteenth century, later to be replaced by more efficient diesel-powered trawlers. Indeed, factory trawlers now exist capable of fishing at depths below 1,000 meters and of catching and processing hundreds of tons per day.

The ecosystem impact of these, and even of smaller trawlers, is tremendous because they destroy all biogenic structure and sessile (bottom-attached) animals in the path of their gear (Watling and Norse, 1998). Also, the sediment resuspended in the "mudtrails" they generate has an impact on both the surviving benthic (bottom-dwelling) animals and the water column. The demersal (near-bottom-dwelling) fish that trawlers exploit are thus, increasingly, deep sea fish, that is, fish that because of their extremely long life and delayed maturity, are very vulnerable to fishing.

The geographic expansion of fisheries

Large-scale expansion began in the 1960s, when most traditional fishing grounds in the North Atlantic and other areas adjacent to the industrialized maritime countries became seriously depleted by new, post–World War II fishing fleets. These countries, located mostly in north temperate latitudes, thus shifted an increasing fraction of their fishing capacity to lower latitudes and began to operate along the coast of developing countries. This trend has not been slowed by the creation, in the early 1980s, of 200-mile-wide exclusive economic zones (EEZ). Countries instead used their economic power to negotiate unequal fishing-access agreements (see, e.g., Kaczynski and Fluharty, 2002).

Catches from new, southern fishing grounds had earlier masked the collapse of catches from traditional, northern fishing grounds. This southward expansion of fisheries has now

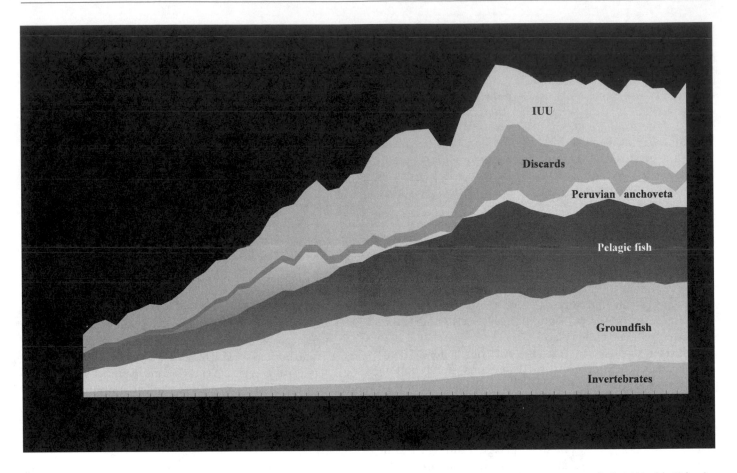

Fisheries. FIGURE 1. Key Components of the World Fisheries Catches, 1950–2004.

The landings of named groups (mainly from FAO; see www.fao.org) is adjusted for overreporting by China (Watson and Pauly, 2001). The discarded bycatch is from Zeller and Pauly (2005), while the rough estimate of IUU (illegal, unregulated and unreported) catch is from Pauly et al. (2002). (Courtesy Sea Around Us Project, www.seaaroundus.org.)

reached its natural limits in Antarctic waters, and global catches are declining (Watson and Pauly, 2001).

Fishing down marine food webs

Generally, fisheries are described in terms of their target species (e.g., the North Sea cod fishery, or the Greenland shrimp fishery), but these labels are as misleading as identifying our ancestors as giant-elk hunters. Rather, as is now evident from all over the world, ancient hunters killed all large herbivores they encountered when they arrived in a new area. Indeed, given these hunting patterns, Alroy (2001) found that in his simulations of North American extinctions that "the only way to prevent a size-selective mass extinction is to assume that humans strongly prefer to hunt small game."

Similarly, when fishing starts in a new area, it is the large fish that go first because they are easier to catch than small fish (e.g., with harpoons), and they give a better return on energy expended, be it in form of muscle power or fuel. Large fish, such as tuna or grouper, usually fetch higher prices than an equivalent weight of small fish.

Large fish, with their low natural mortalities and relatively high age at sexual maturity cannot sustain much fishing pressure, and their numbers decline, forcing the fishers to move on to smaller fishes and/or to other, previously unexploited areas. Because larger fish tend to occupy higher trophic levels than smaller fish—indeed, the latter are usually the prey of the former—this process, now called "fishing down marine food webs," invariably leads to declining trends in the mean trophic level of of the fish landed (Pauly et al., 1998). This suggestion was initially challenged, but subsequent work, reviewed in Pauly and Watson (2005), shows the "fishing-down" phenomenon to be ubiquitous.

Essentially, fishing down is an ecological succession, consisting of a gradual loss of large organisms and species diversity and a gradual replacement of recently evolved groups (marine mammals, bony fishes) by more primitive groups, that is, invertebrates (notably jellyfishes), and bacteria. This is best seen when distinguishing three phases of the fishing-down sequence, and by characterizing, for each phase, the main features of the fish and other nektonic (free-swimming) organisms and their effect on processes in the water column.

The first phase, which may be called "pristine," is that which prevailed before humans strongly impacted ocean ecosystems. A few parts of the oceans, notably outlying areas of the South Pacific, may be still pristine, But for most of the world, pristine abundances must be reconstructed from historical accounts and anecdotal evidence or inferred from archaeological data (Jackson et al., 2001).

Such a pristine state is invariably characterized by numerous marine mammals and large fish as top predators, the latter with biomasses often exceeding their present abundance ten- to hundredfold (Jackson et al., 2001). Elevated biomass of top predators implies moderate to large biomass of small productive prey fish and invertebrates, though not necessarily of those opportunistic groups (shrimp, squid) which now support increasingly valuable fisheries.

In the pristine environment, benthic life is dominated by an abundant, structure-forming, and sessile fauna, composed of filter- and deposit-feeders, which keep down the biomass of phytoplankton (planktonic plants), and prevent resuspension of sediments. As a result, the water column, even in shallow areas, tends to free of suspended particles and of nutrients leaching from them.

The second phase, here called "exploited," is the one we are presently in. It is best characterized by declining biomasses of large fish, declining sizes and diversity of fish in fisheries catches, and declining trophic levels of the same (the fishing-down phenomenon). Initially, these declines are compensated for by cascade effects, manifest in the emergence of new fisheries for squid and other invertebrates, but these eventually decline as well.

Life on the sea floor is also modified: oyster and other reefs built over centuries by filter-feeders and detritus-feeders are increasingly destroyed by bottom trawling. This leads to an increased turbidity of the overlying water column because of the absence of the organisms that were filtering the water, and by bottom mud stirred up by storms and by trawling itself.

The third phase, here called "fully degraded," is that which will follow from the continuation of present trends—though in some places, as in estuaries such as Chesapeake Bay, many of these features associated with that stage have already developed. There, fishing has eliminated not only virtually all animals above the size of striped bass, the current top predator, but also the benthic filter-feeders. Indeed, the oysters, which until 150 years ago formed giant reefs, were capable of filtering the water of Chesapeake Bay in a few days (Jackson et al., 2001). Their absence, a result of fishing, is the ultimate reason that pollution from effluents can now have such strong effects, including harmful algal blooms.

The end result of ecosystem degradation is a "dead zone," that is, an area that is seasonally or nearly continuously free of oxygen and of multicellular life, because of excess nutrients in the water column, and bacteria, rather than benthic animals that process the resulting abundance of marine snow and other detritus. There is a growing number of seasonal dead zones throughout the world, from the northern Gulf of Mexico to the Benguela Current, off Namibia.

THE OUTLOOK

Increasing fishing effort in the absence of an effective global network of large marine reserves—similar in scope to the national parks that now protect the large mammals of Africa—will mean that large marine fishes, both pelagic (open-sea-dwelling, including some tuna, many sharks, and billfish), and demersal (groupers, large croakers, etc.) will be fished to extinction in the next decades. The fisheries impacting these species would go bankrupt in the process, though they would last for a while if propped up by sufficient subsidies. The good news is that we know in principle how to avoid overcapitalization of fisheries and the collapse of their underlying stocks.

Most fisheries research, however, still follows traditional lines, performing assessments for single-species fisheries to reestimate their annual total allowable catch (TAC). At the same time both managers and scientists are coming under increasing pressure from conservationists who assert that industrial-scale fisheries are destroying ecosystems. While the claims of the conservationists are sometimes exaggerated, there is strong scientific evidence, as documented above, for large-scale ecosystem impacts of fishing in general and bottom trawling in particular.

The measures taken to mitigate climate change may help reduce global fleet capacity through the reduction of their greenhouse-gas emissions. This may sharpen the focus on small-scale fisheries, which have so far been neglected but whose adjacency to the resources they exploit and frequent use of fuel-efficient, passive gear offer a real prospect of sustainability.

Ecosystem-based considerations will also play a part. Here, "no-take" marine reserves will have to be perceived not as scattered small concessions to conservationist pressure, but as a legitimate management tool to prevent entire areas of exploited species being made inaccessible to fishing. Indeed, avoiding the extinction of species previously protected because they were out of reach of fishing gear should become a major goal of management. This would link fisheries scientists with the vibrant community of researchers now working on marine biodiversity issues.

The formal adoption of the FAO Code of Responsible Fishing by virtually all fishing nations has created favorable conditions for the changes suggested here, by shifting the burden of proof onto those who claim that fishing does not harm stocks and ecosystems. Time will tell if "responsible fishing" is sufficient to halt the decline of marine fisheries resources.

WEB RESOURCES FOR FISHERIES

FishBase (http://www.fishbase.org) and SeaLifeBase (http://www.sealifebase.org) provide the scientific and common names, as well as key biological information on all species of marine fishes, and on other marine organisms, respectively, whether exploited or not.

The website of the Sea Around Us project (http://www.seaaroundus.org) provides time series (1950–present) of the marine catch in the exclusive economic zones of all maritime countries of the worlds, and on the high seas, by fleets and gear types, and in terms of tonnage or value. It also provides key biological data and distribution ranges of all species reported in the fisheries statistics of the world's maritime countries (see Pauly, 2007). These Web resources rely mainly on fisheries statistics from the Food and Agriculture Organization of the UN (http://www.fao.org).

BIBLIOGRAPHY

Alroy, J. "A Multispecies Overkill Simulation of the End-Pleistocene Megafaunal Mass Extinction." *Science* 292 (2001), 1893–1896. DOI: 10.1126/science.1059342.

Jackson, J.B.C., et al. "Historical Overfishing and the Recent Collapse of Coastal Ecosystems." *Science* 293 (2001), 629–637. DOI: 10.1126/science.1059199.

Kaczynski, V.M., and D.L. Fluharty. "European Policies in West Africa: Who Benefits from Fisheries Agreements?" *Marine Policy* 26.2 (2002), 75–93. DOI: 10.1016/S0308-597X(01)00039-2.

Myers, R.A., and B. Worm. "Rapid Worldwide Depletion of Predatory Fish Communities." *Nature* 423 (2003), 280–283. DOI: 10.1038/nature 01610.

Pauly, D., et al. "Fishing Down Marine Food Webs." *Science* 279 (1998), 860–863. DOI: 10.1126/science.279.5352.860.

Pauly, D., et al. "Towards Sustainability in World Fisheries." *Nature* 418 (2002), 689–695. DOI: 10.1038/nature 01017.

Pauly, D., and R. Watson. "Background and Interpretation of the 'Marine Trophic Index' as a Measure of Biodiversity." *Philosophical Transactions of the Royal Society B* 360 (2005), 415–423.

Watling, L., and E.A. Norse. "Disturbance of the Seabed by Mobile Fishing Gear: A Comparison to Forest Clearcutting." *Conservation Biology* 12.6 (1998), 1180–1197. DOI: 10.1046/j.1523-1739.1998.0120061180.x.

Watson, R., and D. Pauly. "Systematic Distortions in World Fisheries Catch Trends." *Nature* 414 (2001), 534–536. DOI: 10.1038/35107050.

Zeller, D., and D. Pauly. "Good News, Bad News: Global Fisheries Discards Are Declining, but So Are Total Catches." *Fish and Fisheries* 6 (2005), 156–159. DOI: 10.1111/j.1467-2979.2005.00177.x.

—Daniel Pauly

FORESTATION

Forestation (or reforestation) is the renewal of the trees on a forest area from which the trees have recently been harvested or removed by natural disturbance (e.g., fire, insects, wind, disease, or landslide). The term implies forest replacement by some means other than natural regeneration (natural seed-fall, germination, and seedling establishment). Afforestation is forestation on lands that have not previously supported forest plant communities, or not for a long time.

Forestation is undertaken when the natural processes of forest renewal are not working, are expected to work unacceptably slowly, or will result in a new forest that does not have the desired species mixture or genetic constitution. These processes may fail for a variety of reasons. It may be because there is no source of seed close enough for natural seed-dispersal processes to deliver seed of desired species to the site in sufficient density and at an acceptable speed. This may be the result of large wildfires, extensive clear-cut logging that left no seed trees, or the absence of seed trees of the desired tree species in the surrounding forest. The natural processes of reforestation may not work because the surface of the soil (the seedbed) is not in a suitable condition for seed germination and seedling establishment. Consumption of seed by insects, rodents, or other seed-eating animals, or the killing of seed by fungal pathogens in the soil may prevent natural generation or make it unreliable. Unfavorable microclimatic conditions (temperature, moisture, and exposure to frost) that kill newly germinated seedlings will also influence natural processes of forest renewal. Finally, competition from grass, other herbs, and shrubs may prevent new seedlings from becoming established. The purpose of forestation, then, is to assist or replace natural processes that are not achieving forestation objectives.

Forestation is associated mainly with even-age forestry (in which the trees are all of the same age) that uses clear-cutting, but it may also be used in uneven-age forestry and with other silvicultural (forest-culture) systems. Forestation may be used in partially harvested forests to change the tree-species composition or to sustain species that have been removed by harvesting or that do not have reliable natural regeneration.

STAGES IN THE DEVELOPMENT OF FORESTRY

Forestry generally develops over time through a series of predictable stages. Very different forestation strategies have been associated with these different stages.

Unregulated exploitation before the development of forestry

The earliest relationship between humans and forests is simply the use of the values of the forest without any explicit activity to ensure their renewal (i.e., without any management of those values). When people are few and lack powerful technology, humans are generally unable to take more from the forest than natural processes can replace. This level of exploitation has little effect on the forest and the future availability of values. But as the numbers of humans and the power of their technology increase, the demands on the forest exceed nature's regenerative capacity, the forest begins to change, and the resource values begin to be depleted. If this continues unchecked, it may lead to deforestation. [*See* Deforestation.]

Administrative forestry

In an effort to ensure continued supplies of wood for fuel, commerce, war, and other uses, societies that have experienced forest depletion generally institute taboos, religious edicts, laws, policies, or regulations concerning forest use and renewal. Similar mechanisms have been used to protect and conserve the many other values and services forests provide. These early attempts to ensure forest sustainability, or the sustainability of specific values, were not generally based on knowledge of the ecological character of the forest and thus frequently failed. Rigid administrative approaches to the conservation and management of dynamic and spatially variable forests almost never succeeds in sustaining the functions and structures of local forest ecosystems or of forested landscapes. Forest alteration and sometimes degradation continue.

Ecologically-based forestry

In contrast to "eco-forestry," which frequently involves a more spiritual than scientific approach, ecologically based forestry takes into account both the ecological diversity of the forest landscape (climates, soils, geology, topography) and the associated biological diversity (the interaction between the physical environments and the region's animals, plants, and microbes, as well as the processes of ecosystem disturbance and recovery). Once this overall ecosystem diversity has been recognized, policies and regulations are developed that respect the ecology of the forest values and services that are to be sustained. [*See* Biological Diversity.]

Social forestry

Where ecologically based forestry is designed to sustain a wide range of values, it may provide the foundation for the sustainable forest management that today's society wants. In many situations, this has not been the case. Aesthetic, spiritual, recreational, and various nonwood products and nonconsumptive values have often received less attention and may have been impaired, even when overall ecosystem function and integrity have been conserved and sustained. Consequently, ecosystem-based forestry may evolve into "social forestry," which is based on a strong ecological foundation but recognizes and sustains a much wider range of forest values.

In the exploitative, preforestry stage, nature is eventually unable to renew forests and their values as fast as they are exploited. In the administrative stage, an initial reliance on natural regeneration is often unsuccessful because the bureaucratic approach to management and harvest does not respect the ecology of the natural regeneration process. The predictable result is an increasing dependence on planting, seeding, or other methods of assisted forestation. This in turn encourages the use of harvesting methods, such as clear-cutting, that are easier and generally more economical. Such methods may be biologically superior for the planting and establishment of a new forest of light-demanding species that are adapted to ecosystem disturbance and are often the desired timber species.

As forestry becomes ecologically based, clear-cutting and planting may continue to dominate forestation strategies in ecosystems where they are ecologically appropriate, but there is a closer matching of the tree species planted to the ecological conditions of the site, and greater care is taken that the planted seedlings are in appropriate physiological condition. There is also increasing use of modified clear-cutting and of other silvicultural systems that make natural regeneration more successful as well as more feasible. In the social forestry stage, there is often strong public pressure to move away from clear-cutting and planting. The public generally favors the visually more acceptable minimal disturbance, partial harvesting. Where forestry is economically marginal, there may also be economic pressure to accept "free" natural regeneration, and to use more economic partial harvesting systems. Unfortunately, this often regresses into exploitive selective harvesting (high-grading). Thus unless forestation remains based on the ecology of forest renewal, social forestry can return to the earlier, unsustainable stages of forestry.

PLANTED FORESTS AND NATURALLY REGENERATED FORESTS

Most people think of plantation forests (i.e., forests that have been planted) as straight rows of a single species of tree, all of similar height and diameter, in dense dark stands with little or no understory vegetation. Forests established primarily for short-rotation timber production on previously agricultural land, or on land deforested long ago, often look like this. The public tends to compare this almost agricultural tree-production system with "natural," unmanaged forests, which they think of as consisting of many species of different sizes and ages, arranged in more or less random patterns of dense patches interspersed with gaps, and with a well-developed understory of herbs, shrubs, possibly mosses, and tree seedlings. [*See* Agriculture and Agricultural Land.]

In reality, where forestation occurs by planting in sustainable, managed, naturally mixed-species forests, the planting is often done merely to ensure that the planted species will be present in the developing "seminatural" forest, which is created as much by natural regeneration of the other species in the surrounding forest as it is by planting. "Plantations" in this type of forest are quite different from the agriculture-like stands normally associated with the term.

There is thus a continuum in the ecological character of the forest: from plantation afforestation, to planted seminatural forest, to natural, unmanaged forests. The last will differ ecologically from either of the former in a number of ways, but this generally has little to do with whether or not the forest was renewed by planting or natural processes.

CAN PLANTED FORESTS SUBSTITUTE FOR "OLD GROWTH"?

There is understandable confusion about plantation forests and "old growth" forests which results from a lack of understanding of the two forest types.

With growing public interest in clear-cutting and old growth, an evaluation was made of the differences between recently harvested areas, young forests established by planting, mature forests established by natural regeneration, and old-growth coastal forests in Vancouver Island, western Canada. The comparison included several measures of biological diversity, species composition, and forest structure. The result revealed far fewer statistically significant differences than had been expected. This is not because there are no ecological differences between these different forest ages and conditions, but because any one of these stages in forest development can exhibit such a wide range of ecological conditions. There is no simple, easy-to-recognize division of forests into "old growth" and not "old growth," and no single forest-ecosystem condition described by the term "planted forest."

"Old growth" has been defined by tree age, tree size, variability in age and size, the presence of large dead trees (snags) and logs on the ground in various stages of decay, patchiness (gaps in the canopy), many different canopy layers, and a variety of other characteristics. Because so many characteristics are attributed to the old-growth condition, few forests conform perfectly to the definition. Instead, we should think of forests as having an index of "old-growthness," or simply an old growth index (OGI); the degree to which they resemble the ideal "old growth" condition. A particular forest can be evaluated for each of the many characteristics that define this condition for that kind of forest ecosystem. By summing the individual evaluations, one can assess the degree to which that forest exhibits the "ideal" condition.

Forests vary greatly in their OGI. Agricultural-type tree plantations have a very low OGI. Ancient forests that have not been affected by natural disturbance or human impacts for many centuries often have a very high OGI. Many forests planted following the harvest of a forest with a high OGI have quite high OGI values themselves, due to a biological legacy carried over from the preharvest forest to the managed forest. The extent of this legacy depends on the OGI of the original forest, how it was harvested, the type of ecosystem, and how the new forest has been managed. The legacy declines over successive rotations of managed forest, unless they are managed to maintain the stand structures that are associated with high-OGI forest. Intensively managed, short-rotation, single-species plantation forests grown to maximize timber values generally have few "old growth" characteristics and so do not provide habitat for those plants, animals, and microbes that depend on these characteristics. In contrast, a planted forest that is managed to have a medium to high OGI may provide habitat for, and support healthy populations of, many species that people normally associate with unmanaged old-growth forest.

NATURAL PROCESSES OF SUCCESSION

The ecological process of succession is the successive occupancy of a particular area by different plant communities and their associated animal and microbial communities following the removal or modification of the previous communities by natural disturbance or forest harvesting. Herbaceous plants may invade open areas created by disturbance and may in the course of time be replaced by shrubs. These may then give way to invading light-demanding tree species, which may in turn eventually be replaced by shade-tolerant tree species. The different living communities in this sequence are called "seral stages."

Several different mechanisms are involved in this process of replacement of one living community by another. One of the key processes is the arrival and establishment of the seeds or spores of the plants of the next seral stage. Forestation affects succession by establishing seedlings or providing seeds. Where these are of species that are characteristic of the next seral stage, forestation will result in natural patterns of succession. Where they are of a much later seral stage, it accelerates succession. Where they are of the same or an earlier seral stage, forestation may cause a particular seral stage to be repeated or create an earlier seral plant community.

In some environments, the sequence of seral stages is predictable, and succession may require a particular sequence of stages if it is to proceed. This is especially true of succession in harsh environments. In most forests the sequence of stages is naturally more variable and less predictable. One or more stages may be missing. There is thus no single "natural" successional pattern to follow. This natural variation has its limits, however, and the long-term health and productivity of the forest may depend on there being a sequence of seral stages. Forestation policies should respect this requirement in those forests where it exists. The biological diversity of a forested region will also depend on the existence of a range of seral stages and forest ages across the landscape.

Where forest managers wish not only to sustain a particular forest condition over several tree-crop rotations but also to sustain the biodiversity and other benefits provided by a series of seral stages, they may be able to do so by managing mixed-species forests. By using forestation practices that sustain mixtures of species from different seral stages, some of the ecological attributes of several stages may be combined in a single seral stage, but this may also require intensive stand management that may not be economically feasible. It will also generally require the retention at time of harvest of permanent or semipermanent patches of old trees and standing dead trees (snags) to provide in the developing new forests some of the structural elements and associated habitat values of older seral stages.

FORESTATION, SUSTAINABLE FOREST MANAGEMENT, AND ECOLOGICAL ROTATIONS

One of the most fundamental characteristics of forests is that they change over time by the processes of disturbance and succession. Sustainability in most forests is therefore related not to unchanging conditions but to a nondeclining pattern of change. The sustainability of this pattern is defined by the degree of ecosystem change caused by disturbance, the frequency of this disturbance, and the rate of ecosystem recovery from the disturbance.

A high degree of disturbance may be sustainable because the ecosystem recovers rapidly (is resilient), or because the disturbance is infrequent, or both. Frequent harvests may be sustainable if the harvest does not change ecosystem conditions greatly, or the ecosystem is resilient, or both. Frequent, severe ecosystem disturbance will make it difficult to maintain ecological conditions that develop under lower-intensity or less-frequent disturbances. The combination of intensity and frequency of disturbance and rate of ecosystem recovery that will sustain a nondeclining pattern of change in some ecosystem condition is called the "ecological rotation" for that condition.

Forestation can promote the sustainability of tree growth and timber production by speeding succession and thereby increasing the resilience of the forest ecosystem. By ensuring prompt establishment of a new forest, it may render combinations of rotation lengths and silvicultural systems sustainable that are unsustainable when based on unreliable natural regeneration. Prompt forestation, however, may shorten or eliminate seral stages that are needed for long-term site productivity and for nontimber values. The shortened rotations that may be possible with forestation may result in the loss of certain ecosystem structures and conditions. Ecological rotations should be evaluated for all the different values that are to be sustained.

Forestation is a key component of sustainable forest management, but it should complement rather than replace natural regeneration. It should be used to help achieve management objectives, rather than as a means to shorten rotations, especially where this results in the loss of desired ecosystem values.

[*See also* Ecosystems; *and* Forests and Environmental Change.]

BIBLIOGRAPHY

Nyland, N.D. *Silviculture: Concepts and Applications.* New York: McGraw-Hill, 1996. The second edition was published in 2001.
Smith, D.M., et al. *The Practice of Silviculture.* 9th ed. New York: Wiley, 1997.

—J. P. (Hamish) Kimmins

FORESTS AND ENVIRONMENTAL CHANGE

The importance of forests in environmental change was appreciated by George Perkins Marsh (*Man and Nature,* 1864), who argued that some of the most important differences between landscapes in the Old World and the New were caused by the long history of forest clearing in the former. He believed that forest removal could trigger a cascade of changes that include the denudation of slopes, flooding, alluviation of bottomlands, and silting of estuaries.

SOILS, HYDROLOGY, AND HABITAT

Forest removal can lead to loss of nutrients from soils, especially in tropical forests where much of the nutrient is cycled through trees and the upper (humus) layer of the soil. [*See* Deforestation.] Removal also can cause a rise in groundwater levels that leads to salinization of low-lying areas. In addition, there is some evidence that tree removal can hasten the process of the formation of lateritic hardpans (hard soil layers formed from a weathered rocky residuum rich in iron and aluminum oxides) in some tropical soils. Likewise, in cool, temperate areas forest removal can contribute to soil acidification, the formation of podzols (soils typical of moist regions under a coniferous or mixed forest or heath land), and peat development.

With regard to soils, the most important role of forests is in controlling rates of erosion and mass movement (the movement of a body of earth, usually in response to gravity). A tree canopy protects the soil from direct rainfall, shortening the fall of raindrops, decreasing their velocity, and thus reducing their kinetic energy. The humus in forest soils helps to absorb the impact of raindrops and confers on the soil an improved structure that facilitates infiltration and reduces runoff. Furthermore, roots stabilize slopes and reduce mass movement. [*See* Anthropogeomorphology; *and* Land Surface Processes.]

From a hydrological standpoint, forests are important because they transpire large amounts of moisture, intercept rainfall, promote infiltration rather than runoff, enhance the recharge of groundwater reservoirs, and lower the peak flows of streams and generally make their hydrologic behavior less variable. The most important hydrologic effect of forests (or deforestation) is on flooding: where highlands have been stripped of forest, heavy rains will be followed by extreme flow volumes causing gullying, increased sediment load, erosion of stream banks, and loss of farmland. The resulting pools of stagnant water can promote diseases such as malaria. Even stream chemistry is influenced by forests, because removal of trees releases nutrients that increase the concentration of dissolved ions such as nitrates in river water (Anderson and Spencer, 1991).

Forests, especially tropical forests, are the habitat of countless species, and the removal or fragmentation of forests is a crucial threat to biodiversity.

CLIMATE CHANGE

Forests and climate change are closely linked: forests play an important role in moderating global warming, and changes in climate have significant impacts on forests.

As they grow, trees remove carbon dioxide from the atmosphere, converting it through photosynthesis to carbon which they store as wood and vegetation. Trees are about 20% carbon by weight, and together with dead wood and organic matter in forest soils, store very large amounts of carbon. By one estimate, forests and forest soils currently store twice the amount of carbon that is contained in atmospheric carbon dioxide (FAO, 2006). Destruction of forests ends the sequestration of carbon dioxide and releases more when the debris is burned: in fact, tropical deforestation may be responsible for 20% of total human-caused carbon-dioxide emissions each year, the balance being generated by the combustion of coal, natural gas, and petroleum products (UCS).

The effects of climate change can be mitigated by reducing the cutting of forests and by new plantings, particularly in tropical forests where growth is rapid. Such plantings are being encouraged now by arrangements that allow carbon-dioxide emissions to be offset by the funding of forestation projects. [*See* Carbon Footprint.] The benefit of new forest growth is less clear in the middle latitudes where (relatively slow) growth is offset by the tendency of dark forest to absorb sunlight more effectively than light-colored grasslands. [*See* Albedo.]

Forests can be affected by the higher temperatures and reduced moisture that accompany climate change in some areas. Warming, especially in high-latitude areas, will shift forest boundaries poleward and upslope and will encourage new pests: higher temperatures have already allowed the spruce budworm to invade latitudes and altitudes where it has never previously been recorded. [*See* Arctic Warming *and* Boreal Forests and Climate Change.] In low latitudes, tropical forests might expand at the expense of neighboring savanna lands (Archibold, 1995), though there are also fears that tropical forests could suffer from increasing droughts. [*See* Tropical Forests and Global Change.]

[*See also* Carbon Cycle; Forestation; Global Warming; *and* Greenhouse Gases.]

BIBLIOGRAPHY

REFERENCES CITED

Anderson, J.M., and T. Spencer. *Carbon, Nutrient, and Water Balances of Tropical Rain Forest Ecosystems Subject to Disturbance. Man and Biosphere Digest 7.* Paris: UNESCO, 1991.

Archibold, O.W. *Ecology of World Vegetation.* New York: Chapman and Hall, 1995. See pp. 425–428.

FAO. UN Food and Agricultural Organization. FAO Newsroom: *Forests and Climate Change.* www.fao.org/newsroom/en/focus/2006 (accessed May 29, 2008).

UCS. Union of Concerned Scientists. *Recognizing Forests' Role in Climate Change.* www.ucrusa.org/global_warming/solutions (accessed May 29, 2008).

ADDITIONAL READING

Noss, R.F. "Beyond Kyoto: Forest Management in a Time of Rapid Climate Change." *Conservation Biology* 15.3 (2001), 578–590.

Schimel, D.S., et al. "Recent Patterns and Mechanisms of Carbon Exchange by Terrestrial Ecosystems." *Nature* 414 (2001), 169–172. DOI: 10.1038/35102500.

—ANDREW S. GOUDIE AND DAVID J. CUFF

FOSSIL FUELS

Fossil fuels remain the energy foundation for most of the world—still inexpensive, compact, convenient, transportable—and irresistible, were it not for their serious effects on the environment. Because the most significant greenhouse gases are produced by burning fossil fuels, these fuels must be phased out at soon as possible, or must at least (in the case of coal) be burned in a way that prevents the release of carbon dioxide. That realization and the public awareness of impending crude oil shortage have focused attention on the fossil-fuel era as a period enjoyed by industrial societies but not by our descendants. [*See* Crude Oil Supply.]

How quickly combustion will give way to to more sustainable primary energy is difficult to say. Our dependence upon fossil fuels is so ingrained institutionally and commercially that it is difficult to see an early end to their dominance, especially if new technologies prove able to mitigate the impact of coal on the environment. Alternative sources of primary energy will make significant inroads only if the fuels become much more expensive, either through deliberate energy policies or through the decline of fossil fuel resources. That decline is inevitable, but even crude oil, the least plentiful of the fossil fuels, will not near exhaustion until late in the twenty-first century. Enlightened energy policy is essential. [*See* Energy and Environment *and* Energy Strategies.] While most analysts urge a rapid transformation from fossil fuels to alternative forms of primary energy, a minority believes that fuel resources are still abundant and that technological advances make it possible to exploit them in good conscience (Jaccard, 2005).

FOSSIL FUELS DEFINED

Coal, crude oil, and natural gas are called fossil fuels because they originated in plant or animal life that grew millions of years ago. Unlike firewood, which can be replaced by tree growth in a few decades, these fuels accumulated and formed in sedimentary rock over millions of years, storing vast quantities of solar energy. Humankind promises to spend that inheritance in a few hundred years.

The fossil-fuel era began with large-scale use of coal in the late eighteenth century. Coal and petroleum fueled the process of industrialization and now fuel virtually all space-heating, industrial processes, private transportation, and over 60% of electrical generation, world-wide.

In 1850 the major fuel in the United States was wood, although coal had made an impact with the advent of steam power. By 1900, coal had displaced wood from most applications and accounted for three-quarters of the nation's raw energy, only 9% of which came from the young oil industry. By 1950, oil and gas supplied 55% of all raw energy needs, while coal's share had shrunk to about 35%. At the beginning of the twenty-first century, over 85% of raw energy for the United States comes from coal, oil, and natural gas. A similar dependence is seen in most regions of the world and is greater in developing nations where nuclear power does not contribute a large proportion of the total energy consumed.

FOSSIL FUELS AND THE ENVIRONMENT

In addition to the impact of coal mining on the surface of the land and on nearby streams, the combustion of coal, petroleum products, and natural gas produces emissions that directly affect the atmosphere and indirectly affect water bodies and forests.

Because these fuels contain carbon, their combustion produces carbon dioxide—the greenhouse gas most strongly implicated in global warming. While there is a slight uncertainty about the link between temperature trends and anthropogenic emissions, there is no doubt about the rise in carbon dioxide concentrations in the atmosphere. Nor is there any doubt that the increase is due to the burning of fossil fuels. A second greenhouse gas, methane, is added to the atmosphere in small amounts by coal-mining operations and by oil refineries and natural gas production. A third, nitrous oxide, is added in small amounts by the combustion of all fuels. [*See* Greenhouse Effect; *and* Greenhouse Gases.]

The various fossil fuels are not equivalent in their contribution of carbon dioxide. Coal, because it is so rich in carbon, contributes the most carbon dioxide per unit of energy delivered. Petroleum products such as gasoline and fuel oil (which have about twice as many hydrogen atoms as carbon) are intermediate. Natural gas, predominantly methane (CH_4), is much richer in hydrogen and contributes the least carbon dioxide per unit of energy delivered. The emissions can be expressed as kilograms of carbon added to the atmosphere: for example, a coal-fired generating plant will add roughly 0.3 kilograms of carbon for every kilowatt-hour of electrical energy generated, while a gas-fired two-stage turbine and boiler combination will—because of the efficiency of the design as well as the different fuel—contribute only 0.1 kilograms of carbon for the same electrical output. [*See* Natural Gas.]

The prevalence of carbon in the world's fuel (amount of carbon per unit of energy) has actually diminished through the industrial period, as wood has been displaced by coal, and coal by oil, gas, and alternatives such as nuclear fuels and hydropower. While total carbon emissions have increased along with increases in global energy use, the average carbon emission per unit of primary (raw) energy has declined (decarbonization). Future increases in renewable energy will displace fossil fuels still further, but rapid growth in the use of coal in developing nations will probably offset any gains due to decarbonization. [See Carbon Cycle.]

Global warming aside, air and water pollution generated by the combustion of fossil fuels is a significant problem. The combustion of the sulfur in coals produces sulfur oxides, which ultimately form sulfuric acid, which is harmful to the lungs and a key constituent of acid rain and acid deposition. Lead in gasoline, which is widely banned in the developed world but still used in developing regions, finds its way into the air and water. Nitrogen oxides add significantly to acid rain and acid deposition and contribute to urban smog. If our response to the threat of global warming is to slow the burning of fossil fuels, reduced pollution will be a significant dividend. [See Energy and Environment.]

COAL

The nature and depth of a coal deposit dictate whether it can be mined by surface or underground methods, and the coals themselves differ in purity and energy content, both of which can be explained the evolution of a coal bed. Certain ancient bogs where plant materials collected and became peat were, by virtue of their location and surrounding bedrock, apt to be enriched in sulfur or other impurities such as arsenic and selenium. Coals derived from these peat accumulations are correspondingly rich in those impurities and therefore of lower *grade.*

Distinct from grade is *rank,* which depends on how drastically the original peat has been transformed (metamorphosed) into coal. Through millions of years of heat and the pressure of overlying younger sediments (and ultimately sedimentary rock), peat gradually loses moisture and gains energy content in a maturing process (coalification) that, incidentally, releases methane. Coal that is immature and low in energy content is lignite. More mature are subbituminous coals. Next in rank are bituminous. The most completely altered and generally highest in energy content by weight are anthracite coals. The lower two ranks are called *soft coals* and the higher two *hard coals.* Worldwide, the most extensive coal-forming materials were deposited during the Carboniferous period, 250–300 million years ago, when Northern Hemisphere continents were located in warmer climates that favored prolific plant growth and widespread swamps where peat accumulated. Continents now in the Southern Hemisphere did not accumulate as much coal-forming material during this period but did accumulate coal materials during the Cretaceous period, roughly 100 million years ago. Because the large Carboniferous deposits are so old, their coals are mature and of higher rank; hence over 60% of the world's coal is bituminous or anthracite, while less than 40% is subbituminous or lignite.

Because grade and rank are independent, the all-important trait of low sulfur-content does not always occur in a particular rank of coal, but an anthracite that happens to have a low sulfur-content is extremely desirable. For the production of coke, bituminous coals are ideal. Soft coals are less valuable from the standpoint of energy content, but that characteristic is offset in some deposits by low sulfur-content. Coals of lower rank usually occur in thick near-horizontal beds that are easily mined—often by surface-mining methods—whereas anthracites are in beds contorted and tightly folded by the same compressive forces that pushed coalification beyond the bituminous stage.

The uses of coal are changing. Bituminous coal continues to be used for coke, but new methods of steel production require less coke. Coal as a boiler fuel for heating buildings has largely been displaced by oil and natural gas: its major use now is in electrical generation. In 2004 coal accounted for 26% of total world energy consumption, 65% in electrical generation and 31% in industry, and coal consumption is projected to rise by 74% from 2004 to 2030, largely because of increases in China and India (DOE/EIA, 2007). India's use will probably mirror that in most world regions, the growth being for electrical generation. But in China, where alternative energy sources are scarce, much of the growth may be in nonelectrical uses, such as steam and heat for industrial processes and coke for steel plants.

Over half the world's coal reserves are in three regions—the United States, the former Soviet Union, and China. Four other countries, Australia, India, Germany, and South Africa, account for an additional 27% (Table 1). The leading exporters of coal in 2005 were Australia, Indonesia, China, Canada (coking coal) and the United States (coking coal). Projections to 2030 suggest Australia will be the dominant coal exporter (DOE/EIA, 2007).

These reserves, defined as economically feasible to recover at today's prices, total 997 billion tons according to the Energy Information Agency. At the 2006 production rate of roughly 6 billion tons per year, the reserves may be expected to last over 165 years, but both reserve amounts and production rates are uncertain. Ideally, as shortages develop, prices rise and currently-unmineable coal becomes classified as reserves but this has not been reflected in national estimates of coal reserves. [See Resources.] At the same time, production rates are beginning to soar with the rapid growth of industry and electrical generation in China and India: between 2000 and 2006 global coal production rose 35%. A further complication is that world demand is largely for for bituminous coal, while much of the reserve total is in lower ranks. While coal is widely regarded as a stopgap fossil fuel in the face of declining crude oil supplies, its future contributions will not be clear without knowing the prospects for growth in reserves of desirable ranks and projected rates of production from those deposits. If the relevant resource is bituminous and anthracite coals, and the annual production rate rises to 10 billion tons per year, the life of current reserves will be only 50 years. (For an alarming analysis, see Strahan, 2008).

TABLE 1. Coal Reserves (Billion Short Tons)

	Bituminous & Anthracite	Subbituminous	Lignite	Total
World	528.8	298.1	170.9	997.7
U.S.A.	123.7	110.3	33.5	267.8
Former Soviet Union	54.1	107.4	11.5	173.1
China	68.6	37.1	20.6	126.2
India	99.3	0.0	2.6	101.9
Non-OECD in Europe and Eurasia	50.1	18.7	31.3	100.1
Australia and New Zealand	42.6	2.7	41.9	87.2
African Continent	55.3	0.2	0.0	55.5
OECD Europe	19.5	5.0	18.8	43.3
Non-OECD Asia	1.4	2.0	8.1	11.5
Brazil	0.0	11.1	0.0	11.1
Other Central & South America	8.5	2.2	0.1	10.8
Canada	3.8	1.0	2.5	7.3
Other	1.8	0.4	0.1	2.3

SOURCE: DOE/EIA International Energy Outlook, 2007

CRUDE OIL AND NATURAL GAS

Like coal, crude oil and natural gas originated in ancient plant and animal life that accumulated along with sediments and was eventually transformed into oil or gas, which in turn became trapped and preserved in sedimentary rock such as sandstone or limestone. Unlike coal, most petroleum originated in marine rather than continental sediments, and the plants and animal remains were of microscopic size, while the materials in coal show obvious leaves and stems. The chronology too is different: coal deposits were not formed until land plants had colonized the continents; the first economic coal beds are in rock of late Devonian age (370 million years old). Though petroleum has been found in rock of Cambrian age (500 million years old) at the beginning of the Paleozoic era, roughly 70% of the world's crude oil occurs in rock of Cenozoic age, that is, less than 100 million years old. With regard to exploration for and definition of resources, the major difference between petroleum and coal is that coal beds are more continuous and more predictable than are accumulations of crude oil or natural gas.

Crude oil and natural gas occur as fluids in the pore spaces and fractures of rock, where the accumulation depends upon some form of trap that has interrupted the upward migration of oil or gas from a source rock. The source is usually a shale, rich in organic matter, thick beds of which are usually found in the column of sedimentary rock that includes oil and gas accumulations.

For a sizable accumulation to form, there must be a source rock buried deeply enough to provide the temperature and pressure needed to convert organic material to petroleum, porous and permeable rock to allow migration and accumulation of oil or gas, and a suitable trap with overlying impermeable rock to block the upward migration and cause the fluids to accumulate. Finally, the trap must form before the migration occurs: oil or gas may escape if the trap is disturbed by subsequent folding, faulting, or tilting. This is one reason that most of the world's oil and gas resources are in relatively young rock. Some traps (and hence some fields) hold just crude oil, some just natural gas, and others a combination of the two. Natural gas alone usually forms at greater depths and higher temperatures than does crude oil, although the separation into oil accumulations in one area and gas in another can occur during migration of the fluids.

Exploration for oil and gas begins by identifying regions with thick layers of marine sedimentary rock, preferably with evidence of rocks such as sandstone or ancient coral reefs that are porous and permeable to fluids. Then, drilling sites are selected on the basis of geologic and geophysical evidence that suggests structures that will serve as traps. Whether the structure is there, and whether the potential trap holds petroleum or just ancient salt water, can be determined with certainty only by drilling.

When a field is discovered and then delineated by development wells, the thickness and areal extent of rock saturated by petroleum can be estimated from drilling records. Core samples from the reservoir rock reveal how much pore space exists to hold oil or gas. These measures allow an estimate of the volumes of oil-in-place or gas-in-place. The reservoir rock's permeability indicates the proportion that will be recovered: for natural gas that may be as high as 85%; for crude oil, the proportion is much lower, 35 or 40% on a historical average. New technologies can greatly enhance the recovery and inrease the estimates of how much oil a given field may produce, using assumptions about prices. These recoverable amounts, calculated for each field and summed for a state or a region, constitute reserves. As with any mineral resource, reserves are in the rock awaiting production; they are not a stockpile at the surface. [*See* Resources.] One exception is the U.S. Strategic Petroleum Reserve, which is oil already produced, then purchased by the U.S. government and stored in underground caverns.

CONVENTIONAL AND UNCONVENTIONAL OIL AND GAS

Conventional crude oil is that which is sufficiently thin (of low viscosity) that it will flow from its reservoir rock into a drillhole and can be pumped to the surface. Unconventional crude oil sources include the Alberta oil sands of Canada, the Orinoco heavy oil of Venezuela, and smaller or poorly defined deposits of oil sands in Colombia, Jordan, and the United States. Whereas oil sands are beds of bituminous sand, much of which can be mined and processed at the surface, the Orinoco deposit is thick tarry oil that must be dissolved in solvent underground in order to be pumped out. [*See* Oil Sands.]

Oil shales are rich in kerogen, a substance that can be converted to a crude oil by heating the crushed rock. These organic shales appear to be potential source rock that was never subjected to extreme depth and heat, and therefore still contains the original raw material. The world's largest deposits are in the United States and Brazil, and in the former Soviet Union where

some oil has been produced from the shales. Oil shales are generally very expensive to process and are excluded from most summaries of crude oil sources.

Conventional natural gas is in permeable rock that allows gas (or oil containing the gas) to flow readily into a drillhole in response to pressure within the rock. Some unconventional gas accumulations in the United States are in tight sands or organic shales that must be fractured artificially before they yield gas. The amounts are relatively small compared with resources of conventional gas and are roughly comparable to the amounts of methane that could be recovered by drilling into coal beds before mining. Larger amounts of unconventional gas reside in deeply buried sandstones in the Gulf Coast region of the United States: these geopressured zones will be tapped only if a safe use can be found for the hot brines that would flow to the surface along with the gas. Very unconventional is the gas in methane hydrates that occur in deep-water ocean sediments and in Arctic permafrost. [*See* Methane Hydrates.]

DISTRIBUTION OF RESOURCES

Oil and gas fields occur only in areas with thick sedimentary rock, but some sedimentary basins (areas where sediment accumulated and rock was formed) are richer in petroleum than others. Oil and gas fields of the Middle East, the U.S. Gulf Coast, Mexico, Venezuela, and North Africa are in regions that are now subtropical in climate. According to one interpretation, these favored areas were, at a critical period during the migration of continental plates, in equatorial or near-equatorial latitudes, a setting that favored the accumulation of organic material in source rock, as well as the deposition of carbonate rock and reefs, which would serve eventually as reservoir rock (Klemme and Ulmishek, 1991). Furthermore, these conditions led to deposition of evaporite rocks, such as salt and gypsum, which serve as cap rocks for reservoirs and also deform under pressure to cause structural traps such as those in the U.S. Gulf Coast.

TABLE 2. Proved Reserves of Conventional Crude Oil As of End of 2006

	Billion Barrels
Asia–Pacific	40.5
North America	59.9
South and Central America	103.5
Africa	117.2
Europe and Eurasia	144.4
Middle East	742.7
Total	1,208.2

SOURCE: BP Statistical Review of World Energy, 2007

TABLE 3. World Coal Energy Versus That in Conventional Crude Oil and Natural Gas

Coal	Estimated reserves (1)	998 billion short tons
	Average energy value per ton	22 million BTU
	Energy content	25,146 Quads
Crude Oil	Estimated Reserves (2)	1,000 billion barrels
	Average energy per barrel	5.56 million BT
	Energy content	5,560 Quad
Natural Gas	Estimated Reserves (3)	6,410 cu.ft.
	Average energy per cu. ft.	1,035 BTU
	Energy content	6,635 Quads

(1) DOE/EIA *International Energy Outlook 2007* (2) DOE/EIA *Long-term World Oil Supply Scenarios*, Aug. 2004 (3) BP *Statistical Review of World Energy* 2007

Whatever the mechanisms, the world's remaining conventional crude oil is now concentrated in the Middle East, which holds roughly half the identified reserves (Table 2).

ENERGY CONTENT OF COAL, OIL, AND NATURAL GAS RESOURCES

When the three fossil fuels are tabulated separately in their own peculiar units—imperial tons for coal, barrels for oil, and cubic feet for natural gas—their relative importance as energy sources is obscured, but they can be compared directly by translating resource amounts into British Thermal Units (BTU) or Quads (one quadrillion BTU). For simplicity, undiscovered amounts of oil and gas are ignored here, as are hypothetical resources of coal: only recoverable reserves of coal are compared with reserves of conventional crude oil and natural gas (Table 3). World crude-oil and natural-gas reserves appear to be roughly equivalent in energy content, but coal reserves contain five times the energy in crude oil, and more than twice the energy in oil and gas combined.

[*See also* Crude Oil Supply; Greenhouse Effect; Greenhouse Gases; Global Warming; Natural Gas; Stabilizing Carbon Emissions; *and* Sustainable Growth.]

BIBLIOGRAPHY

Jaccard, M.K. *Sustainable Fossil Fuels: The Unusual Suspect in the Quest for Clean and Enduring Energy*. Cambridge and New York: Cambridge University Press, 2005.
Kavalov, B., and S.D. Peteves. "The Future of Coal." Petten, The Netherlands: European Commission DG JRC [Directorate-General, Joint Research Centre] Institute for Energy, 2007. http://www.jrc.nl/downloads/file.php?id=75 (accessed May 29, 2008).
Klemme, H.D., and G.F. Ulmishek. "Effective Petroleum Source Rocks of the World: Stratigraphic Distribution and Controlling Depositional Factors." *American Association of Petroleum Geologists Bulletin* 75.12 (1991), 1809–1851.
Strahan, D. "The Great Coal Hole." *New Scientist* (Jan. 19, 2008), 38–41.
"Coal: Resources and Future Production." Berlin: Energy Watch Group, 2007. http://www.energywatchgroup.org/fileadmin/global/pdf/EWG_Report_Coal_10-07-2007ms.pdf (accessed May 29, 2008).

—DAVID J. CUFF

FRAMEWORK CONVENTION ON CLIMATE CHANGE

Adopted in 1992 under the auspices of the United Nations, the Framework Convention on Climate Change (FCCC) establishes the basic system of governance for the emerging global climate change regime (Table 1). Given the substantial uncertainties and complicated politics of the greenhouse-warming issue, the FCCC requires very little by way of actual mitigation or adaptation measures. Instead, it creates a long-term evolutionary process to encourage further research, promote national planning, increase public awareness, and help create a community of states. As of May 11, 2000, the FCCC had 182 parties, making it one of the most widely accepted international environmental agreements. Pursuant to the FCCC, on December 11, 1997, the Third Conference of the Parties adopted the Kyoto Protocol, which establishes more stringent emission limitation commitments for developed countries. [*See* Kyoto Protocol.]

HISTORY

In 1985, an expert meeting held in Villach, Austria, sponsored by World Meteorological Organization (WMO) and United Nations Environment Programme (UNEP), concluded that significant anthropogenic climate change is highly probable and first suggested the development of a global convention to address the problem. In 1990, following the First Assessment Report of the Intergovernmental Panel on Climate Change (IPCC) and the Second World Climate Conference, the UN General Assembly established the Intergovernmental Negotiating Committee for a Framework Convention on Climate Change (INC/FCCC) with the mandate of negotiating a convention containing "appropriate commitments" in time for signature at the June 1992 Earth Summit in Rio de Janeiro.

The INC/FCCC held five negotiating sessions between February 1991 and May 1992, when it finalized the text of the Framework Convention on Climate Change. The two principal issues were quantified targets and timetables to limit greenhouse gas emissions (advocated by, among others, the European Union and the Alliance of Small Island States (AOSIS), but opposed by the United States), and financial assistance. On the latter issue, developing countries sought new and additional funds for their incremental costs of implementation, as well as the creation of a new financial mechanism, while developed countries wished to give more limited assistance, administered by the recently established Global Environment Facility (GEF). The final text of the FCCC reflects compromise on both issues.

The Convention was opened for signature at the 1992 Earth Summit, where it was signed by 154 nations. It entered into force on March 21, 1994, following its ratification by 50 nations. One year later, the first Conference of the Parties (COP-1) concluded that the commitments contained in the FCCC were inadequate and adopted the Berlin Mandate, which called for the negotiation of additional commitments by industrialized countries. The Berlin Mandate negotiations concluded in December 1997 at COP-3, with the adoption of the Kyoto Protocol, which establishes emissions limitation commitments for each industrialized country, as well as market mechanisms that parties can use to meet these commitments, including emissions trading and the Clean Development Mechanism. Detailed rules elaborating the provisions of the Protocol are being negotiated pursuant to the 1998 Buenos Aires Plan of Action, which was scheduled for completion at COP-6 in November 2000. The Kyoto Protocol entered into force on February 16, 2005.

FRAMEWORK VS REGULATORY CONVENTION

As its name suggests, the FCCC establishes a general framework of governance rather than a detailed regulatory regime. Because of the difficulty of gaining agreement on substantive commitments, framework conventions have been widely used in international environmental law. Agreement proved particularly difficult in the climate-change context given the uncertainties about the science of climate change, the potentially high economic stakes, and divergent national

TABLE 1. Landmarks of the Emerging Climate Change Regime

Event	Date	Organizer	Outcomes, Conclusions, Recommendations
Villach Conference	1985	WMO and UNEP	Significant climate change highly probable
			States should initiate consideration of a global climate convention
Toronto Conference	1988	Canada	States should cut global CO_2 emissions by 20 percent by 2005
			States should develop a comprehensive framework convention on the law of the atmosphere
UN General Assembly	1988	UN	Climate change a "common concern of mankind"
Hague Summit	1989	Netherlands, France, Norway	New institutional authority should be developed within the UN involving nonunanimous decision-making
Noordwijk Conference	1989	Netherlands	Industrialized countries should stabilize greenhouse gas emissions as soon as possible
			"Many" countries support stabilization of emissions by 2000
IPCC First Assessment Report	1990	WMO and UNEP	Global mean temperature likely to increase by 0.3°C per decade under business-as-usual scenario
Second World Climate Conference	1990	WMO and UNEP	Countries need to stabilize greenhouse gas emissions
			Developed states should establish targets and/or national programs or strategies to limit emissions
UN General Assembly	1990	UN	Establishment of INC/FCCC
INC 5	1992	UN	Adoption of FCCC
UNCED	1992	UN	FCCC opened for signature; 154 signatories
FCCC's entry into force	1994		Entry into force on 21 March, 1994, ninety days after the fiftieth ratification
Berlin Conference (COP-1)	1995	FCCC	Berlin Mandate for negotiations to strengthen FCCC commitments
Kyoto Conference (COP-3)	1997	FCCC	Kyoto Protocol adopted
COP-4	1998	FCCC	Buenos Aires Plan of Action adopted

SOURCE: From Bodansky (1995).

interests—for example, between big emitters of greenhouse gases such as the United States, rapidly developing countries such as China, oil-producing states, and small-island developing states. Other examples of framework conventions include the 1979 Long-Range Transboundary Air Pollution Convention (LRTAP), which addresses the problem of acid rain in Europe, and the 1985 Vienna Convention on the Protection of the Ozone Layer. The rationale of the framework convention approach is to proceed in steps, beginning with the creation of a framework of institutions and mechanisms, which draws nations in without requiring them to make detailed commitments, and only later elaborating more substantive regulations, generally in separate protocols such as the Montreal Protocol on Substances that Deplete the Ozone Layer (1987) or, in the case of the climate change regime, the Kyoto Protocol.

KEY PROVISIONS OF THE FCCC

The framework of governance set forth in the FCCC and the Kyoto Protocol include the provisions set out in Tables 2 and 3, respectively.

Objective and principles

To guide the evolution of the climate-change regime, the FCCC defines its ultimate objective as the stabilization of atmospheric concentrations of greenhouse gases at safe levels (that is, levels that would "prevent dangerous anthropogenic interference with the climate system"). The elaboration of the regime will require the determination of what concentrations levels are safe and what emission reductions are necessary to achieve these concentrations. The FCCC also sets forth several general principles, including the principles of "common but differentiated responsibilities" (e.g., different countries may have different obligations to regulate their emissions that cause global warming), inter- and intragenerational equity, precaution, cost-effectiveness, and sustainable development.

Commitments

As a framework convention, the FCCC imposes limited obligations, although industrialized (and in particular Western) countries have somewhat more stringent obligations than do developing countries. All parties to the FCCC have general obligations aimed at promoting long-term planning through the

TABLE 2. Key Provisions of the FCCC

Objective	Stabilize atmospheric greenhouse gas concentrations at a level that would prevent dangerous anthropogenic interference with the climate system, within a time-frame sufficient to (i) allow ecosystems to adapt naturally, (ii) protect food production, and (iii) allow sustainable economic development (art. 2)
Principles	Intra- and intergenerational equity; differentiated responsibilities and respective capabilities; right to promote sustainable development; precaution; cost-effectiveness; comprehensiveness; and free trade (art. 3)
Commitments	All countries—general commitments to: develop national greenhouse gas inventories; formulate national mitigation and adaptation programs; promote and cooperate in scientific research, education, training, and public awareness (arts. 4(1), 5, 6)
	Developed countries (listed in Annex 1)—recognize that a return to earlier emission levels of CO_2 and other greenhouse gases by the end of decade would contribute to modifying long-term emission trends, and will report with aim to return to 1990 emission levels (art. 4(2))
	OECD countries (listed in Annex 2)—commitments to: fully fund developing country inventories and reports; fund the incremental costs of agreed mitigation measures; provide assistance for adaptation; and facilitate, promote, and finance technology transfer (art. 4(3)–(5))
Institutions	Conference of the Parties (art. 7), Secretariat (art. 8), Subsidiary Body for Scientific and Technological Advice (SBSTA) (art. 9), Subsidiary Body for Implementation (SBI) (art. 10), financial mechanism (art. 11)
Reporting ("communication of information")	All countries—communication of information on national greenhouse gas inventories and on steps taken to implement the Convention (art. 12(1))
	Developed countries (listed in Annex 1)—detailed description of policies and measures to limit greenhouse gas emissions and enhance sinks, and a specific estimate of their effects on emissions
Adjustment mechanism	Reviews of the adequacy of commitments every three years, based on the best available scientific information (art 4(2)(d))

SOURCE: From Bodansky (1995).

TABLE 3. Key Provisions of the Kyoto Protocol

Emission reduction commitments	Specific emission limitation commitments for each industrialized country set forth in Annex B. Commitments apply to basket of six greenhouse gases (carbon dioxide, methane, nitrous oxide, and three trace synthetic gases.
	First five-year commitment period runs from 2008–2012. Negotiations on second commitment period to begin no later than 2005.
Sinks	Emissions and removals due to afforestation, reforestation, and deforestation since 1990 count toward emission targets. Other sink activities can be added by decision of the Parties.
Emissions trading	Industrialized countries may trade their emission allowances.
Joint implementation	Industrialized countries may receive credit toward their emission reductions, resulting from projects undertaken in another industrialized country.
Clean Development Mechanism	Industrialized countries may receive credits toward their targets for emission reductions resulting from projects undertaken in developing countries. CDM governed by an executive board, with specific projects overseen by "operating entities" (for example, multinational accounting firms).
Institutions	Generally the same as FCCC institutions. Conference of the Parties serves as meeting of the Protocol Parties (COP/MOP).
Reporting and reviewing	Industrialized parties must have "national systems" to monitor and report on their greenhouse gas emissions. Emission inventories must follow IPCC inventory guidance. National inventories reviewed by expert review teams, which can recommend adjustments to inventory numbers that fail to follow IPCC guidelines.
Compliance	As of June 2000, compliance institutions and rules under negotiation pursuant to Buenos Aires Plan of Action.

development of national programs to mitigate and adapt to climate change, and international review of national actions. In addition, industrialized country parties (identified in Annex I of the Convention) agreed to a nonbinding working target and timetable to return greenhouse gas emissions to 1990 levels by the year 2000, and western industrialized countries (identified in Annex II) agreed to provide financial assistance to developing countries, primarily to fund the preparation of national inventories and reports. The 1997 Kyoto Protocol sets forth legally binding emission-limitation commitments for each industrialized country, ranging from a reduction of 8% to an increase of 10% compared to 1990 emission levels. These commitments apply to a group of six greenhouse gases, for a five-year commitment period from 2008 to 2012.

Joint implementation

A controversial issue has been whether states must implement their commitments to limit greenhouse gas emissions at home, or whether they can do so through actions in other countries. The Kyoto Protocol includes mechanisms that allow industrialized countries to meet their commitments through emission reductions in other countries, including trading of emission allowances; undertaking emission reduction projects in another industrialized country (joint implementation); and undertaking emission reduction projects in developing countries through the Clean Development Mechanism. The Kyoto Protocol states that reductions through these mechanisms must supplement domestic action but does not specify quantitative limits on their use.

Institutions

The Conference of the Parties (COP) meets yearly and is the principal decision-making body of the FCCC. It is assisted by the Subsidiary Body on Scientific and Technological Advice (SBSTA) and the Subsidiary Body on Implementation (SBI). The convention also establishes a secretariat and a financial mechanism, currently operated by the Global Environment Facility (GEF). The IPCC has no formal role under the FCCC, but has continued to serve as the main source of scientific information relating to climate change.

Reporting and review

To promote transparency, provide information needed for the elaboration of the regime, and build trust among the parties, nation parties must submit periodic reports on their greenhouse-gas inventories and national policies and measures. The reporting requirements are differentiated: developed countries have more stringent requirements than developing countries with respect to the content and timing of reports. The national reports are reviewed by experts, who provide in-depth analyses of individual reports as well as synthesis reports. The Kyoto Protocol sets forth more stringent requirements to monitor and report on emissions, as well as an expert review process and the development of a procedure to determine compliance with its binding emissions limitation commitments.

[See also Global Warming; IPCC: Intergovernmental Panel on Climate Change; and Joint Implementation.]

BIBLIOGRAPHY

Bodansky, D. "The Emerging Climate Change Regime." *Annual Review of Energy and Environment* 20 (1995), 425–461. DOI: 10.1146/annurev. eg.20.110195.002233. General overview.
Bodansky, D. "The United Nations Framework Convention on Climate Change: A Commentary." *Yale Journal of International Law* 18.2 (1993), 451–558. A detailed history and legal analysis of the FCCC.
Churchill, R., and D. Freestone, eds. *International Law and Global Climate Change.* London and Boston, Mass.: Graham and Trotman, 1991. An older but useful collection of essays on legal issues relating to climate change.
Grubb, M. *The Kyoto Protocol: A Guide and Assessment.* London: Royal Institute of International Affairs, 1999.
Mintzer, I.M., and J.A. Leonard, eds. *Negotiating Climate Change: The Inside Story of the Rio Convention.* Cambridge and New York: Cambridge University Press, 1994. Interesting accounts of the FCCC negotiations by key participants.
Oberthür, S., and H.E. Ott. *The Kyoto Protocol: International Climate Policy for the 21st Century.* New York: Springer, 1999.
Paterson, M. *Global Warming and Global Politics.* London and New York: Routledge, 1996. An excellent survey of political-science analyses of the FCCC negotiations.
Susskind, L.E. *Environmental Diplomacy: Negotiating More Effective Global Agreements.* New York: Oxford University Press, 1994. Criticisms of the framework convention/protocol approach.
Victor, D.G., and J.E. Salt. "From Rio to Berlin: Managing Climate Change." *Environment* 36.10 (1994), 6–15, 25–32. A perceptive analysis of post-Rio developments.

—DANIEL M. BODANSKY

FUTURISTS

Prominent among organizations concerned about the future is the World Future Society, founded in 1966. The organization is concerned with how social and technological developments are shaping the future and has approximately 25,000 members world wide.

The organization issues three major publications in addition to electronic newsletters and reports to members: *The Futurist,* a bimonthly popular magazine; *Future Survey,* a monthly that alerts members to recent books, articles, and reports; and *Futures Research Quarterly,* a scholarly journal.

The society sponsors an annual meeting, usually covering a number of themes. At the July, 2007 meeting, themes included Resources and the Environment (specifically the Green Revolution), and Technology and Science (specifically Nanotechnology).

[See also Catastrophist-Cornucopian Debate.]

BIBLIOGRAPHY

Cornish, E. *Futuring: The Exploration of the Future.* Bethesda, Md.: World Future Society, 2004.
Didsbury, H.F., ed. *21st Century Opportunities and Challenges: An Age of Destruction or an Age of Transformation?* Bethesda, Md.: World Future Society, 2003.
———. *Thinking Creatively in Turbulent Times.* Bethesda, Md.: World Future Society, 2004.
Mack, T., ed. *Creating Global Strategies for Humanity's Future.* Bethesda, Md.: World Future Society, 2006.
———. *Hopes and Visions for the 21st Century.* Bethesda, Md.: World Future Society, 2007.
Wagner, C.G., ed. *Foresight, Innovation, and Strategy: Toward a Wiser Future.* Bethesda, Md.: World Future Society, 2005.

—DAVID J. CUFF

G

GAIA HYPOTHESIS

The Gaia hypothesis postulates that the Earth's surface environment is maintained in a habitable state by self-regulating feedback mechanisms involving organisms tightly coupled to their environment. The Earth's atmospheric composition, climate, much of the chemical composition of the ocean, and the cycling of many elements essential to life are hypothesized to be regulated. The idea arose from the involvement of the British independent scientist and inventor James Lovelock in the 1960s space program and was developed during the early 1970s in collaboration with the American microbiologist Lynn Margulis.

Lovelock was employed by NASA as part of the team that aimed to detect whether there was life on Mars. Lovelock's interest in atmospheric chemistry led him to seek a general, physical basis for detecting the presence of life on a planet. He recognized that most organisms shift their physical environment away from equilibrium. In particular, organisms use the atmosphere to supply resources and as a repository for waste products. In contrast, the atmosphere of a planet without life should be closer to thermodynamic equilibrium, in a state attributable to photochemistry (chemical reactions triggered by solar ultraviolet radiation). Thus, the presence of abundant life on a planet might be detectable by atmospheric analysis.

Such analysis can be conducted from Earth using an infrared spectrometer (which detects the characteristic absorption of infrared radiation by specific gases) linked to a telescope. Using this technique, it was discovered that the atmospheres of Mars and Venus are dominated by carbon dioxide and are relatively close to chemical equilibrium, suggesting that they are lifeless. In contrast, the atmosphere of the Earth is in an extreme state of disequilibrium because of the activities of life, in which highly reactive gases such as methane and oxygen coexist many orders of magnitude from the photochemical steady state. Remarkably, despite this disequilibrium, the composition of the Earth's atmosphere was known to be fairly stable over geologic periods of time. Lovelock concluded that life must regulate the composition of the Earth's atmosphere.

Interestingly, the composition of the Earth's atmosphere is particularly suited to the dominant organisms. For example, nitrogen maintains much of the atmospheric pressure and serves to dilute oxygen, which at 21% of the atmosphere is just below the level at which fires would disrupt land life. Yet oxygen is sufficiently abundant to support the metabolism of large respiring organisms such as humans. Both oxygen and nitrogen are biological products—oxygen is the product of past photosynthesis, while the gaseous nitrogen reservoir is largely maintained by the actions of denitrifying organisms (which use nitrate as a source of oxygen and release nitrogen gas). Furthermore, the oxygen content of the atmosphere has remained within a narrow range for over 350 million years.

It is also remarkable that life on Earth has persisted despite major changes in the input of matter and energy to the Earth's surface. Most notably, the Sun is thought to have warmed by about 25% since the origin of life on Earth over 3.8 billion years ago. This increase in solar output alone should raise the Earth's surface temperature by about 20°C. Yet the current average temperature is only 15°C. The continuous habitability of the Earth in the face of a warming Sun suggested to Lovelock that life may have been regulating the Earth's climate in concert with its atmospheric composition.

The idea was named "Gaia" after the Greek goddess of the Earth and was first published in 1972. Lovelock then sought an understanding of the organisms that might be involved. Lynn Margulis was already developing the theory of symbiogenesis—that eukaryotic cells (those with genetic material contained within a distinct nucleus) evolved from the symbiotic merger of previously free-living prokaryotes (organisms, including bacteria, whose genetic material is not enclosed within a cell nucleus). Margulis contributed her intimate knowledge of microorganisms and the diversity of chemical transformations that they mediate to the development of what became the Gaia hypothesis of "atmospheric homeostasis by and for the biosphere."

The Gaia hypothesis was used to make predictions (for example, that marine organisms would make volatile compounds that can transfer essential elements from the ocean back to the land). Lovelock and colleagues tested this ancillary hypothesis on a scientific cruise between England and Antarctica in 1972. They discovered that the biogenic gases dimethyl sulfide and methyl iodide are the major atmospheric carriers of the sulfur and iodine cycles. Later, the Gaia hypothesis was extended to include regulation of much of the chemical composition of the ocean.

DAISYWORLD

The Gaia hypothesis was greeted with hostility from many scientists and leading scientific journals, partly because of its mythological name. The first scientific criticism of the hypothesis was that it implies teleology, some conscious foresight or planning by the biota. Most subsequent criticisms have focused on the need for evolutionary mechanisms by which regulatory feedback loops could have arisen or been maintained. As Richard Dawkins pointed out (Dawkins, 1983) the Earth is not a unit of

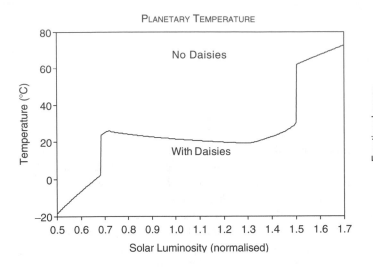

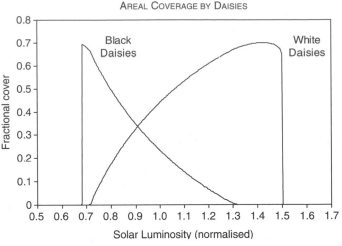

selection, so Gaian properties cannot be adaptations in a strict neo-Darwinian sense since they cannot be refined by natural selection. This poses the challenge of explaining how such properties could arise.

The Daisyworld model (Figure 1) was formulated to demonstrate that planetary self-regulation does not necessarily imply teleology. It provides a hypothetical example of climate regulation emerging from competition and natural selection at the individual level. Daisyworld is an imaginary gray world orbiting, at a similar distance to the Earth, a star like our Sun, which gets warmer with time. The world is seeded with two types of life, black and white daisies. These share the same optimum temperature for growth, 22.5°C, and limits to growth of 5°C and 40°C. When the temperature reaches 5°C, the first seeds germinate. The paleness of the white daisies makes them cooler than their surroundings, hindering their growth. The black daisies, in contrast, warm their surroundings, enhancing their growth and reproduction. As they spread, the black daisies warm the planet. This further amplifies their growth and they soon fill the world. At this point, the average temperature has risen close to the optimum for daisy growth. As the sun warms, the temperature rises to the point where white daisies begin to appear in the daisy community. As it warms further, the white daisies gain a selective advantage over the black daisies and gradually take over. Eventually, only white daisies are left. When the solar forcing gets too high, regulation collapses.

Daisyworld illustrates that both positive and negative feedback are important for self-regulation. While the solar input changes over a range equivalent to 45°C, the surface of the planet is maintained within a few degrees of the optimum temperature for daisy growth. The initial spread of life is characterized by positive feedback—the more life there is, the more life it can beget. This is coupled to an environmental positive feedback—the warming due to the spread of black daisies enhances their growth and reproduction rates. The long period of stable, regulated temperature on Daisyworld represents a predominance of negative feedback. If the temperature of the planet is greatly perturbed by the removal of a large fraction of the daisy

Gaia Hypothesis. FIGURE 1. The Daisyworld Model.

A thought experiment to demonstrate that planetary self-regulation can emerge from natural selection at the individual level between types of life with different environment-altering traits. In this case the traits are "darkness" (albedo = 0.15) and "paleness" (albedo = 0.65) of black and white daisies on a gray planet (albedo = 0.4). Left panel: Planetary temperature as solar luminosity increases. The bold line is within daisies and the faint line without daisies. Right panel: Areal cover of black and white daisies.

population, then positive feedback acts rapidly to restore comfortable conditions and widespread life. The end of regulation on Daisyworld is characterized by a positive feedback decline in white daisies—solar warming triggers a reduction in their population that amplifies the rise in temperature.

The modeling approach pioneered in Daisyworld provided the beginnings of a mathematical basis for understanding self-regulation. It was soon adapted to study the regulation of atmospheric composition and climate on the early Earth. With this work, Lovelock began to refer to Gaia as a theory, in which self-regulation is understood as a property of the whole system of life tightly coupled to its environment. This replaced the original suggestion that regulation is "by and for the biota" (which is often interpreted as teleological, although never intended as such). The term "homeostasis," which refers to regulation around a fixed set point, has also been revised: more appropriate is Margulis's suggestion of "homeorrhesis," which describes regulation around an evolving set point.

The Gaian view of Earth history is one of periods of stability of the environment and life, coupled together—with intervening periods of rapid change. Such a pattern of punctuated equilibria appears consistent with the geologic record of both environmental proxies (accessible data used to represent less readily measurable characteristics of a system) and species. Furthermore, evidence that the Earth has remained habitable despite major, periodic disruptions, including the impact of planetesimals and massive volcanic outbursts, supports the notion that the Earth is self-regulating. These events appear to have caused mass extinctions and climate change and yet, in all cases, diverse, widespread life and a tolerable climate soon returned.

CLIMATE REGULATION

Climate feedbacks somewhat analogous to those in Daisyworld can be found in the real world. For example, the trees of the boreal forests can be likened to the dark daisies. They possess the traits of shedding snow and dark foliage that give them a low albedo (reflectivity) and make them warmer than their surroundings. The presence of forest warms the high northern latitudes by approximately 4°C in winter. Over much of the surface of the Earth and over longer time scales, the Gaia theory predicts, given the relatively high solar input at present, that the predominant effect of organisms should be to cool the planet. [See Albedo.]

A Gaian mechanism for long-term climate regulation, involving the biological amplification of rock weathering, was proposed in the early 1980s. Over million-year time scales, the carbon dioxide content of the Earth's atmosphere and the resulting greenhouse effect on the Earth's temperature is determined by the balance of carbon dioxide input and removal fluxes. Removal occurs in the process of weathering of silicate rocks on land and the subsequent formation of carbonate rocks in the ocean. A chemical negative-feedback mechanism exists whereby, for example, increases in planetary temperature are counteracted by increases in the rate of rock weathering and the uptake of carbon dioxide. However, the rate of rock weathering is greatly enhanced by the activities of soil microbes, plants, and lichens. This offers the potential for more responsive stabilization of the Earth's temperature. For example, rising temperature may trigger increased plant growth and microbial respiration, which reduces the carbon dioxide content of the atmosphere. The evolution of biological amplification of rock weathering is estimated to have progressively reduced the level of carbon dioxide in the Earth's atmosphere and counteracted the warming Sun, so that this process now cools the Earth by roughly 20°C. [See Carbon Cycle.]

In the mid-1980s, Gaian thinking led to the hypothesis that production of dimethyl sulfide (DMS) by marine phytoplankton also cools the climate. DMS is oxidized in the atmosphere to form sulfate aerosol particles that can grow, often in combination with ammonium (NH_4^+, another biological product), to become cloud condensation nuclei (CCNs). Increases in the number density of CCNs make clouds more reflective, increasing the scattering of solar radiation back to space and thus causing cooling. Temperature affects phytoplankton growth directly and also determines the degree of stratification in the ocean water-column and hence the supply of nutrients to the surface layers. Hence there is potential for climate feedback involving the growth of DMS-emitting phytoplankton. The nature of this feedback is the subject of intensive ongoing research.

A regional example of self-regulation is the Amazon rainforest, where the trees, by generating a high level of water cycling, maintain the moist environmental conditions in which they can persist. Nutrients are also effectively retained and recycled, in contrast to the nutrient-poor soil. If too much forest is removed, the water-regulation system can collapse, the topsoil is washed away, and the region reverts to arid semidesert. Such change may be irreversible.

CURRENT WORK

In recent years, the implications of Gaian feedback for ecology and evolution have been explored. The Daisyworld model has been extended to include different types of "daisy" as well as herbivores and carnivores. Studies of biodiversity within this context (of plant life tightly coupled to climate) suggest that the potential for biodiversity is an essential part of an ecosystem's capacity to respond to perturbation. Different herbivore-feeding strategies have been found to have different effects on the self-regulating capacity of the system. Increases in the number of connections in a Daisyworld food web have been found to increase the stability of both population dynamics and climate, as has the introduction of carnivores to a model with only herbivores and plants. Simulations of habitat fragmentation in Daisyworld have revealed that a critical threshold exists at which the plants become geographically isolated and regulation breaks down. This emphasizes the importance of spatial interaction for self-regulation.

The challenge of reconciling the theories of Gaia and natural selection is now being addressed again, and evolutionary biologists are showing renewed interest in Gaia. When random mutation of the albedo of the daisies is incorporated in Daisyworld, the range of temperature regulation is extended. However, Daisyworld represents only one special case of a direct connection between the effect of a trait on its bearer and on the global environment. To test further the effect of natural selection on environmental regulation, new models are being developed that incorporate the random generation of environment-altering traits.

Fresh emphasis is also being placed on the importance of life in increasing the cycling of nutrient elements, both on land and in the ocean. For example, it has long been recognized that phosphate and nitrate are available in ocean waters in just the ratio required by phytoplankton. The effects of nitrogen fixation, denitrification, preferential recycling of phosphorus from ocean sediments, and the resultant feedbacks are being modeled to test whether they can account for such regulation. This is generating a new focus on the molecular biology of Gaia—the enzymes responsible for the regulation and the trace elements crucial to their functioning.

Gaian hypotheses concerning the mechanisms responsible for gradual onset and rapid termination of ice ages have been put forward and modeled. These may help us to understand and predict the biosphere's response to global change. Contemporary observations indicate that members of both the marine and terrestrial biota are involved in removing a significant fraction of the excess carbon dioxide released to the atmosphere by human activities. However, this negative feedback is not sufficient to prevent the carbon dioxide content of the atmosphere from rising. Furthermore, Lovelock has predicted that increasing temperature and resultant stratification of the ocean will trigger a decline in phytoplankton and their cooling effect via DMS emissions, providing a positive feedback on global warming. [*See* Global Warming.]

The Gaia hypothesis has contributed greatly to our understanding of the Earth as a unitary system. The previous view that life is merely a passenger on a dead planet has largely been replaced with recognition of the coevolution of organisms and their environment. The degree to which organisms are involved in regulating conditions at the surface of the Earth remains a subject of controversy, but the concept has proved its worth in stimulating valuable research. It may thus offer a new paradigm for environmental science.

BIBLIOGRAPHY

GENERAL REFERENCES

Bunyard, P., ed. *Gaia in Action: Science of the Living Earth*. Edinburgh: Floris Books, 1996. Collected papers from three meetings on the scientific and philosophical implications of the Gaia hypothesis.

Lovelock, J. E. *Gaia: A New Look at Life on Earth*. New York and Oxford: Oxford University Press, 1979. The classic exposition of the hypothesis, born out of the frustration of censorship from scientific journals. A rare and inspiring blend of science and poetry.

———. *The Ages of Gaia: A Biography of our Living Earth*. New York and Oxford: Oxford University Press, 1988. The definitive scientific exposition of what the author now describes as the Gaia theory. A thorough response to the criticisms triggered by the original hypothesis, seeking consistency with natural selection, and replete with suggested and, to a lesser degree, tested regulatory mechanisms.

———. *Gaia: The Practical Science of Planetary Medicine*. London: Gaia, 1991. An accessible and well-illustrated introduction to the subject for the general reader.

———. *The Revenge of Gaia: Earth's Climate in Crisis and the Fate of Humanity*. New York: Basic Books, 2006.

Margulis, L., and D. Sagan. *Microcosmos: Four Billion Years of Evolution from Our Microbial Ancestors*. London: Allen and Unwin, 1987. The history of microbial life and evolution. Stresses the importance of microbes in regulating the Earth's surface environment.

———. *Slanted Truths: Essays on Gaia, Symbiosis, and Evolution*. New York: Copernicus/Springer, 1998. Provides a varied introduction to the work and thought of Lynn Margulis and colleagues.

Schneider, S. H., and P. J. Boston, eds. *Scientists on Gaia*. Cambridge, Mass.: MIT Press, 1991. Scientific and philosophical papers from the 1988 Chapman Conference on the Gaia hypothesis, sponsored by the American Geophysical Union. Covers a broad spectrum of views on the subject.

Volk, T. *Gaia's Body: Toward a Physiology of the Earth*. New York: Copernicus/Springer, 1998. Emphasizes the greatly amplified cycling of essential elements resulting from the existence of life.

Williams, G. R. *The Molecular Biology of Gaia*. New York: Columbia University Press, 1996. Focuses on the biochemistry of the enzymes that catalyze matter transfers between organisms and their environment as a route to understanding the regulation of global biogeochemical cycles.

SCIENTIFIC PAPERS

Charlson, R. J., et al. "Oceanic Phytoplankton, Atmospheric Sulphur, Cloud Albedo and Climate." *Nature* 326 (1987), 655–661. A much cited paper, proposing both a mechanism of climatic cooling due to phytoplankton and (more speculatively) a resulting regulatory feedback. DOI: 10.1038/326655a0.

Kump, L. R., and J. E. Lovelock. "The Geophysiology of Climate." In *Future Climates of the World: A Modelling Perspective*, edited by A. Henderson-Sellers, pp. 537–553. Amsterdam, Oxford, and New York: Elsevier, 1995. An accessible review of postulated climate feedback mechanisms involving life.

Lovelock, J. E. "Gaia as Seen through the Atmosphere." *Atmospheric Environment* 6.8 (1972), 579–580. The first "Gaia" paper. DOI: 10.1016/0004-6981(72)90076-5.

Margulis, L., and J. E. Lovelock. "Biological Modulation of the Earth's Atmosphere." *Icarus* 21 (1974), 471–489. One of a collection of jointly authored papers that clarified the Gaia hypothesis and proposed regulatory mechanisms.

Watson, A. J., and J. E. Lovelock. "Biological Homeostasis of the Global Environment: The Parable of Daisyworld." *Tellus* 35B (1983), 284–289. Gives the equations, mathematical analysis, and an interesting variant of the Daisyworld model.

Whitfield, M. "The World Ocean: Mechanism or Machination?" *Interdisciplinary Science Reviews* 6 (1981), 12–35. A comprehensive review that extends the Gaia hypothesis to include biological control of aspects of the chemical composition of the ocean.

CONTRASTING VIEWS

Dawkins, R. *The Extended Phenotype*. Oxford and New York: Oxford University Press, 1983.

Doolittle, W. F. "Is Nature Really Motherly?" *CoEvolution Quarterly* 29 (1981), 58–63. A thoughtful critique of Lovelock's first book (Lovelock, 1979). The author argues that the Gaia hypothesis is inconsistent with natural selection. For a response, see Watson and Lovelock, 1983, and Lovelock, 1988.

Holland, H. D. *The Chemical Evolution of the Atmosphere and Oceans*. Princeton: Princeton University Press, 1984. A thorough textbook on the Earth's geochemical history. The author also argues that the Gaia hypothesis is not necessary to explain the continuity of life on Earth for 3.8 billion years.

RECENT WORK

Lenton, T. M. "Gaia and Natural Selection." *Nature* 394 (1998), 439–447. DOI: 10.1038/28792. A review and synthesis; clarifies the types of environmental feedback and explores their implications at levels from the individual to the global.

—TIM LENTON

GEOENGINEERING

Geoengineering is the intentional large-scale manipulation of the global environment. The term has usually been applied to proposals to manipulate the climate with the primary intention of reducing undesired climatic change caused by human influences. These geoengineering proposals seek to offset the effect of fossil-fuel combustion on the climate without reducing fossil-fuel use—for example, by placing shields in space or reflective particles in the atmosphere to reduce the sunlight incident on the Earth.

Possible responses to the problem of anthropogenic climate change fall into three broad categories, abatement of human impacts on the climate system by reducing the climate forcings, adaptation to reduce the impact of altered climate on human systems, and deliberate intervention in the climate system to counter the human impact on climate—geoengineering. The first of these is generally defined as "mitigation"—alleviating the effects of climate change by, for example, decreasing human emissions of greenhouse gases. In contrast to mitigation, the goal of geoengineering is to offset the effects of greenhouse gases by additional climate interventions rather than by reduced emissions.

It is central to the common meaning of geoengineering that the environmental manipulation be deliberate and be a primary goal rather than a side effect. This distinction is at the heart of the substantial moral and legal concerns about geoengineering. The current climate modifications which are occurring as a result of greenhouse-gas emissions from fossil-fuel combustion are inadvertent; the use of fossil fuels for energy production

TABLE 1. Summary Comparison of Geoengineering Options

Geoengineering Scheme	Technical Uncertainties	Risk of Side Effects	Nontechnical Issues
Solar shields to generate an increase in the Earth's albedo.	Costs are large and highly uncertain.	Does not exactly counteract the effect of increased carbon dioxide. Possible indirect carbon cycle effects.	Security, equity, and liability if system used for weather control.
Stratospheric SO_2 to increase albedo by direct optical scattering.	Uncertain lifetime of stratospheric aerosols.	Effect on ozone depletion and lifetime of other greenhouse gases uncertain. Also, as above.	Liability if ozone destruction occurs.
Tropospheric aerosols to enhance cloud formation.	Scale and technology required to achieve a measurable effect is uncertain.	Regional effects would not counteract global effect of greenhouse gases. Possible effects on atmospheric circulation and ocean biology.	Unlike other albedo modification schemes, this scheme is local and could be applied regionally.
Injection of carbon dioxide into the ocean or in underground geologic reservoirs.	Costs are much better known than for other geoengineering schemes. Uncertainty about fate of carbon dioxide in ocean.	Possibility of damage to local benthic community. Small risk of leakage from poorly chosen geologic sites.	Like abatement, this scheme is local with costs associated with each source. Potential legal and political concerns over oceanic disposal.
Ocean fertilization to stimulate carbon uptake.	Field tests have not demonstrated additional carbon sequestration to the deep ocean.	Possible oxygen depletion may cause methane release. Impacts on ocean biota and adjacent land areas.	Legal concerns: Law of the Sea, Antarctic Treaty. Liability concerns arising from effect on fisheries.
Intensive forestry to capture carbon in harvested trees.	Uncertainty about rate of carbon accumulation. Potential loss of soil carbon.	Serious consequences for soils and ecological communities. Use of genetically modified crops could affect natural vegetation.	Political questions: How to divide costs? Whose land is used? Likely unacceptable environmental impacts.

does not constitute geoengineering, as there is no intent to modify climate. Continued reliance on fossil-fuel energy despite an increasing awareness of the climatic consequences may well be unwise and short-sighted, but is nevertheless not geoengineering.

There is a substantial body of literature that considers the possibility of human modification of the global climate. One of the earliest such discussions came from the Swedish scientist Svante Arrhenius, who suggested that the CO_2 and resultant warming from fossil-fuel combustion might benefit plant growth and allow agriculture to extend northward (Arrhenius, 1908). Sporadic analysis of the potential for global climate modification continued through the first half of the twentieth century. The 1950s and 1960s saw increasing interest in controlling weather and climate for human benefit. Discussion of climate engineering as a means of counteracting destructive human influences began in the 1970s at a time of growing awareness of the negative effects of global climate change. Geoengineering has recently become more prominent in climate policy discussions as concerns about the possibility of dangerous climate change have increased among scientists and the general public alike.

EXAMPLES OF GEOENGINEERING PROPOSALS

Proposals to engineer the climate may be classified by their mode of action. Some aim to offset climate warming by managing solar radiation in such a way that less solar radiation is absorbed by the climate system, while others aim to manage the carbon cycle to decrease atmospheric concentrations of carbon dioxide and consequently increase the amount of outgoing terrestrial radiation. The few proposals that do not directly address the global radiation budget typically involve modification of ocean currents (e.g., Johnson, 1997). Geoengineering has also occasionally been proposed to deal with nonclimatic problems such as ozone depletion. Table 1 summarizes various geoengineering ideas.

Solar radiation management

Schemes to manage solar radiation aim to increase the planetary albedo (the Earth's reflectivity) so as to offset the effect of increasing carbon dioxide on the global radiative balance, and thus on average surface temperatures. An albedo increase of roughly 1.5% is needed to offset the effect of doubled carbon dioxide. [See Albedo.] However, even if perfect compensation of the radiative balance could be achieved, the resulting climate might still be significantly altered by differences in the vertical and latitudinal distributions of atmospheric heating; it is likely that regional climate changes would persist in a globally geoengineered climate.

Increases in carbon dioxide would continue in these scenarios, with additional nonradiative effects on the climate system. For example, increasing carbon dioxide could have substantial effects on terrestrial vegetation, affecting both growth rates and the use of soil water. Precipitation patterns might be altered by changes in vegetation transpiration under elevated carbon dioxide, with the result that changes in the hydrological cycle would remain in a geoengineered climate. The oceans would continue to take up atmospheric carbon, with the potential for negative consequences on marine ecosystems from ocean acidification (Royal Society, 2005). Albedo modification schemes might also increase ocean uptake of carbon dioxide by decreasing surface ocean temperatures, which would in turn increase the solubility of carbon dioxide in the ocean. Geoengineered global cooling with continued rises in atmospheric carbon dioxide might thus increase the rate of ocean acidification

Stratospheric aerosols. Aerosols in the stratosphere influence radiation fluxes by direct optical scattering and by re-radiation of incoming sunlight. It appears that anthropogenic sulfate aerosols in the lower atmosphere may currently decrease absorbed solar radiation by about 1 watt per square meter—enough to counter about one-third of the effect of increased greenhouse gases. Budyko (1977) was the first to suggest increasing the albedo of the planet by injecting sulfur dioxide into the stratosphere, mimicking the action of large volcanoes on the climate. Crutzen (2006) recently proposed that stratospheric aerosols could be used to replace the current cooling effect of anthropogenic aerosols, allowing a reduction of lower-atmosphere pollution without a corresponding cost in terms of unmasked climate warming. Several technologically straightforward options exist for injecting the required sulfate into the stratosphere at a trivial cost compared with other methods of climate modification (National Academy of Sciences, 1992).

The most serious problem with this scheme may be the effect of the aerosols on atmospheric chemistry. The Antarctic ozone hole has clearly demonstrated the complexity of chemical dynamics in the stratosphere and the resulting susceptibility of ozone concentrations to aerosols. Changes in atmospheric chemistry caused by stratospheric aerosols might increase the lifetime of other greenhouse gases, thus partly offsetting the intended cooling effect. Recent elaborations of this scheme have focused on tailoring the optical scattering properties of the particles, and on choosing particles that would be chemically inert. Depending on the size of particles used, an aerosol layer might also cause significant whitening of the daytime sky, with additional potential impacts on plants caused by an increase in diffuse, as opposed to direct, sunlight.

Space-based shields. The possibility of shielding the Earth with orbiting mirrors is the most technologically extravagant geoengineering scheme. While expensive, it has clear advantages over other geoengineering options. Because solar shields affect a clean alteration of the solar constant, their side effects would be both less significant and more predictable than those of other albedo modification schemes. Assuming that the shields were steerable, their effect could be eliminated at will. Additionally, steerable shields might be used to direct radiation at specific areas; this could offer the possibility of weather control, but also the potential of aggressive military application.

Most discussion of solar shields has assumed that they would be placed in low Earth orbit; however, such shields would act as solar sails and would be rapidly pushed out of orbit by the sunlight they were designed to block. This problem was recognized by Seifritz (1989), who proposed using a single shield of 2,000-kilometer radius near the Lagrange point between the Earth and the Sun. (Objects at that Lagrange point can have quasi-stable orbits that remain on a line between the Earth and the Sun.) Such a shield could be kept stable with weak active control. A recent elaboration on this idea was proposed by Angel (2006), who envisioned a solar shield comprised of many small spacecraft in the form of meter-sized reflective disks. Such schemes are constrained by the cost of lifting the required mass into orbit. Angel (2006) proposed using electromagnetic acceleration as a way of reducing transportation cost to as little as $50/kg (compared to current costs of about $20/gram). Nevertheless, his proposal carries a total cost of a few trillion dollars.

Enhanced marine cloud formation using tropospheric aerosols. Marine stratocumulus clouds are among the Earth's most reflective cloud types, and they act to cool the ocean surface. There is evidence that aerosols from human activities sometimes influence cloud properties in such a way that the lifetime and brightness of clouds increase; for example, ship tracks can be seen in satellite images as long streaks of bright clouds generated by the interaction between aerosols from ship exhaust and the formation of cloud droplets. This has led some scientists to speculate that the intentional introduction of aerosols into the lower atmosphere might increase the number of droplets in—and hence the reflectivity of—marine stratocumulus clouds.

Proposals for how to achieve this have focused on the development of wind-powered seagoing vessels which would generate a fine spray of seawater and sea-salt aerosols. Such ideas are at present untested, however, and there are questions about the effectiveness of the transfer of aerosols to the height needed for cloud formation. There have also been suggestions that iron fertilization of ocean phytoplankton could increase the production of dimethyl sulfide (DMS), which might also increase regional cloud cover. If it were possible to achieve a significant increase in cloud reflectivity by such methods, the cooling generated would be regional; it might thus be possible to use this method to restrict warming over sensitive marine locations such as coral reefs. Further research would, however, be required to assess the effects on atmospheric circulation, as well as the implications of increased cloud cover and consequent decreased light availability for marine ecosystems.

Carbon management

Proposals to manage the global carbon cycle for the purpose of reducing atmospheric carbon dioxide concentrations occupy an intermediate area between the solar radiation management proposals outlined above and more conventional forms of climate mitigation by promoting natural carbon sinks. For example, avoided deforestation, or reforestation for the purposes of promoting biodiversity (with the added potential of increased carbon storage) is not geoengineering, but large-scale afforestation with intensive harvesting or the use of genetically engineered crops to capture the stored carbon would be considered geoengineering. In general, carbon management schemes can be labelled geoengineering if they are proposed at a planetary scale and use technological intervention for the explicit purpose of removing carbon dioxide from the atmosphere.

Carbon capture and storage. The climatic impact of fossil energy use may be reduced by capturing the resulting carbon and sequestering it away from the atmosphere. Carbon can be captured from fossil fuels by separating carbon dioxide from the products of combustion or by reforming the fuel (using catalytic cracking and dehydrogenation) to yield a hydrogen-enriched fuel stream for combustion and a carbon-enriched stream for sequestration.

As carbon capture and storage emerges as a plausible near-term option for reducing carbon dioxide emissions, the degree to which it constitutes geoengineering has become controversial. Like other forms of carbon management, carbon capture and storage occupies an uncertain place in the conventional abate/adapt/geoengineer taxonomy outlined above. The term "geoengineering" was coined in the early 1970s by Marchetti (1977), who proposed that carbon dioxide from combustion could be disposed of in the ocean. Oceanic sequestration would constitute a deliberate intervention in the carbon cycle, thus is seems reasonable to label it geoengineering. However, proposed "zero emission" power plants, which would emit nothing to the atmosphere and would sequester their carbon dioxide emissions in stable geologic formations, may be seen as a novel form of mitigation rather than as geoengineering. [*See* Carbon Capture and Storage.]

Ocean surface fertilization. Carbon could be removed from the atmosphere by fertilizing the biological pump that transports carbon from the surface to the deep ocean by the sinking of organic carbon-containing detritus. Proponents of ocean fertilization have suggested that the addition of limiting nutrients such as iron to the surface ocean could increase biological production and stimulate the biological pump, resulting in a net uptake of CO_2 from the atmosphere. However, small-scale experimental tests have not been able to demonstrate the practical effectiveness of this approach, and the effect of large-scale ocean fertilization on both marine and adjacent terrestrial ecosystems is unknown. There is also the possibility of decreased oxygen concentrations in the surface ocean, leading to the production of methane, itself a greenhouse gas.

Afforestation. Large-scale forest management for the purpose of removing atmospheric carbon dioxide is a form of geoengineering. It appears that terrestrial forests are currently sequestering a significant fraction of anthropogenic carbon emissions, but there is uncertainty about the long-term effectiveness of this carbon sink under continued changes in atmospheric CO_2, climate, and land use. Capturing a substantial fraction of fossil-fuel carbon in forests over an extended period of time would require intensive management of forests on a very large scale; it would be necessary to harvest the trees continually and sequester their carbon so that it could not return to the atmosphere. Fertilization would be also required to replace the nutrients removed with the trees, and there would probably be substantial ecosystem-carbon loss over time through erosion and the degradation of soil-carbon pools. Intensive forest management on this scale would have a substantial impact on forest ecosystems. Furthermore, changes in surface albedo that result from forest-cover changes would have to be considered so as not to offset any carbon gains by increased surface radiation absorption.

EVALUATING GEOENGINEERING

Most discussions of geoengineering have focused on assessments of technical feasibility and cost. However, it is likely that issues of risk, politics, and ethics will prove more decisive in implementation. Many geoengineering proposals elicit strong negative reactions from climate scientists and the public, and we will probably continue to see strong sentiments expressed about the morality of deliberate control of the climate system. There is real concern that geoengineering treats the "symptoms" of climate change rather than the cause, and that focusing on geoengineering in research and policy discussions might detract from mitigation efforts.

Proponents of geoengineering themselves have widely divergent perspectives on when and how geoengineering should be considered and ultimately implemented. Some have argued that current and anticipated climate changes are more dangerous than the likely side effects of geoengineering and that the costs of reducing fossil-fuel emissions are higher than the costs of geoengineering. Geoengineering should thus be actively researched, and implemented as soon as it is technically feasible to do so. This is the "have-our-cake-and-eat-it-too" perspective, in which geoengineering is seen as an alternative to emissions reductions. This approach leads to a dangerous scenario in which a geoengineered climate would become increasingly divergent from the climate consistent with the level of greenhouse gases in the atmosphere. Any failure of geoengineering technology, or forced cessation on account of unacceptable side-effects, could lead to very rapid warming as the climate rebounds to its non-geoengineered state. We could become completely reliant on geoengineering without the capacity to adapt to potentially rapid climate changes, or to implement the necessary emissions reductions quickly enough to replace the effect of geoengineering.

Others have suggested that geoengineering be used as a near-term intermediate measure that could slow the rate of climate change and allow more time to reduce greenhouse gas emissions: a "buy-us-time" perspective. Such an approach might facilitate a more cost-effective and smooth transition to a carbon-free economy, while restricting near-term dangerous climate change. It is also possible that concentration on geoengineering might itself delay research and development of clean-energy technology, and that "buying time" might turn into the "have-our-cake" scenario. This is again a dangerous scenario in which we could become increasingly reliant on geoengineering technologies without the incentive to focus on the more important and possibly more difficult task of reducing emissions.

Still other experts believe that geoengineering is worthy of cautious evaluation and research, given current uncertainty about the extent of future climate changes. This is a "fallback strategy" in which geoengineering could be held in reserve should climate change prove to be more extensive and more severe than expected. In such a case it would be important to understand the full costs and risks of geoengineering so they could be weighed against the risks of climate warming at a time when such risks are unavoidable by other means. There is still the concern in this scenario that mitigation efforts might be weakened by the existence of a possible technological "silver bullet." However, it is unlikely that consideration of geoengineering schemes will abate, and it is clear that the discussion of the merits and risks of such schemes would benefit from increased scientific understanding. The notion of geoengineering as a fallback option provides a central—and perhaps the only—justification for taking large-scale geoengineering seriously.

Political considerations

The cardinal political reality of geoengineering is that, unlike other responses to climate change (e.g., abatement and adaptation), geoengineering could be implemented by one or a few countries acting alone. Moreover, geoengineering could be implemented by large corporate entities, or attempted by for-profit companies in the business of providing carbon offsets to consumers. There is also the potential for covert geoengineering, which at present would be very difficult to either detect or monitor. Various political concerns arise from this with respect to security, sovereignty, and liability.

Some geoengineering schemes raise direct security concerns; solar shields, for example, might be used as offensive weapons. A subtler but perhaps more important security concern arises from the growing links between environmental change and security. Whether or not they were actually responsible, the operators of a geoengineering project might be blamed for harmful climatic events that could plausibly be attributed—by an aggrieved party—to the geoengineering scheme. Given the current political disputes arising from issues such as the depletion of fisheries and aquifers, a unilateral geoengineering project might well lead to significant political tension.

As in the current negotiations under the Framework Convention on Climate Change, geoengineering would raise questions of equity. In this case, geoengineering might simplify the politics. As Tom Schelling (1996) pointed out, geoengineering "totally transforms the greenhouse issue from an exceedingly complicated regulatory regime to a simple—not necessarily easy but simple—problem in international cost sharing." It is also possible that geoengineering itself might come into conflict with the stated goal of the Framework Convention on Climate Change to "prevent dangerous anthropogenic interference with the climate system" (United Nations, 1992), as some geoengineering schemes may themselves be considered "dangerous anthropogenic interference."

But should we do it?

Questions about the advisability of geoengineering revolve around risk: risk of failure and risk of side effects. Recent studies have illustrated the possibility of rapid climate changes in the case of geoengineering failure, as well as the potential for alterations to the global hydrological cycle, and there is ongoing research on the potential for other side effects, such as the effect of stratospheric aerosols on ozone chemistry. Further research is clearly needed to understand more fully the potential risks involved in any deliberate human intervention in the climate system. However, risk assessment does not formally address questions of whether geoengineering is the "right thing to do."

Discussion of geoengineering commonly elicits strong negative reactions, often for emotional or moral reasons. Within the policy-analysis community, for example, there has been vigorous debate about whether discussion of geoengineering should be included in public reports that outline possible responses to climate change. Preceding Paul Crutzen's (2006) publication, a number of scientists were opposed to publishing this paper, even after peer review and revisions. Fears have been voiced that active scientific investigation of geoengineering could influence policy makers to take it too seriously and perhaps to defer action on abatement and mitigation given the possibility of geoengineering as an alternative. (See Schneider [1996] for discussion of the debate over geoengineering in the 1992 National Academy of Sciences panel, and Cicerone [2006] for a description of the opposition to Crutzen's 2006 editorial.)

These debates raise the questions of whether geoengineering is an appropriate course of action and whether geoengineering is even an appropriate focus of scientific research and attention. On the one hand, it can be argued that carrying out scientific research is an implicit endorsement of the concept of geoengineering, regardless of the research findings. On the other hand, some opponents of geoengineering have acknowledged a need for careful research on geoengineering proposals, either to prevent the proliferation of scientifically flawed or even dangerous ideas, or simply to demonstrate the risks of geoengineering.

Society will inevitably have to grapple with the fundamental question of whether it is morally right to attempt to control the climate system. Many objections to geoengineering have been and will continue to be raised: from pragmatic concerns that it will open the door to future systematic efforts to alter the global environment to suit human needs—or that it is inappropriate to impose an "end-of-the-pipe" technical fix rather than to seek a solution to the root cause of the problem—to more ethical concerns about the appropriateness of intentional interference with a complex, poorly understood system, the results of which we cannot reliably predict. Ultimately, the debate may come down to the question of whether the problem of climate change should be solved by minimizing human influence on the environment or by treating the global environment as a system to be managed by humans. It is difficult to predict how such a debate would be resolved.

BIBLIOGRAPHY

HISTORICAL WORKS ON DELIBERATE CLIMATE MODIFICATION

Arrhenius, S. *Worlds in the Making*. New York and London: Harper, 1908. Published 12 years after Arrhenius first calculated the effect of carbon dioxide on climate, this extraordinary general exposition of planetary science includes discussion of deliberate climate modification.

Budyko, M. I. *Climatic Changes*. Washington, D.C.: American Geophysical Union, 1977. This wide-ranging treatment of the interrelationship of humans and climate discusses geoengineering using sulfates in the stratosphere (originally published in Russian in 1974; based on work from the mid-1960s).

Kellogg, W. W., and S. H. Schneider. "Climate Stabilization: For Better Or for Worse?" *Science* 186 (1974), 1163–1172. An early summary of various geoengineering schemes that discusses their uncertainty and their political ramifications. DOI: 10.1126/science.186.4170.1163.

Marchetti, C. "On Geoengineering and the CO_2 Problem." *Climate Change* 1.1 (1977), 59–68. DOI: 10.1007/BF00162777. The term "geoengineering" was coined in this paper.

GENERAL WORKS ON GEOENGINEERING

Bengtsson, L. "Geo-Engineering to Confine Climate Change: Is It at All Feasible?" *Climatic Change* 77.3–4 (2006), 229–234. DOI: 10.1007/s10584-006-9133-3.

Bodansky, D. "May We Engineer the Climate?" *Climatic Change* 33.3 (1996), 309–321. DOI: 10.1007/BF00142579. A review of the legal implications of geoengineering.

Cicerone, R. J. "Geoengineering: Encouraging Research and Overseeing Implementation." *Climatic Change* 77.3–4 (2006), 221–226. DOI: 10.1007/s10584-006-9102-x.

Jamieson, D. "Ethics and Intentional Climate Change." *Climatic Change* 33.3 (1996), 323–336. DOI: 10.1007/BF00142580. The only paper on the ethics of geoengineering.

Kiehl, J. T. "Geoengineering Climate Change: Treating the Symptom over the Cause?" *Climatic Change*, 77.3–4 (2006), 227–228. DOI: 10.1007/s10584-006-9132-4.

Keith, D. W, and H. Dowlatabadi. "A Serious Look at Geoengineering." *EOS* 73.27 (1992), 289–293. DOI: 10.1029/91EO00231. A general review of geoengineering.

Keith, D. W. "Geoengineering the Climate: History and Prospect." *Annual Reviews of Energy and Environment* 25 (2000), 245–284.

———. "Engineering the Planet." In *Climate Change Science and Policy*, edited by S. H. Schneider and M. Mastrandrea. Washington, D.C.: Island Press, forthcoming.

Lane, L., et al., eds. *Workshop Report on Managing Solar Radiation*. NASA/CP–2007-214558. Moffett Field, Calif.: NASA Ames Research Center, 2007.

Lawrence, M. G. "The Geoengineering Dilemma: To Speak or Not to Speak." *Climatic Change* 77.3–4 (2006), 245–248. DOI: 10.1007/s10584-006-9131-5.

MacCracken, M. C. "Geoengineering: Worthy of Cautious Evaluation?" *Climatic Change* 77 (2006), 235–243. DOI: 10.1007/s10584-006-9130-6.

National Academy of Sciences. *Policy Implications of Greenhouse Warming*. Washington, D.C.: National Academy Press, 1992. The chapter on geoengineering contains many detailed cost estimates.

Office of Technology Assessment. *Changing by Degrees: Steps to Reduce Greenhouse Gases*. Report OTA-O-482. Washington, D.C.: Congress of the U.S., Office of Technology Assessment, 1991. This report contains substantial treatment of geoengineering, particularly afforestation.

Schelling, T. C. "The Economic Diplomacy of Geoengineering." *Climatic Change* 33.3 (1996), 303–307. DOI: 10.1007/BF00142578.

Schneider, S. H. "Geoengineering: Could—or Should—We Do It?" *Climatic Change* 33.3 (1996), 291–302. DOI: 10.1007/BF00142577. Contains a summary of the intellectual history of geoengineering.

Watts, R. G., ed. *Engineering Response to Global Climate Change*. Boca Raton, Fla.: CRC Lewis, 1997. This book includes an up-to-date chapter on geoengineering.

WORKS ON SPECIFIC GEOENGINEERING METHODS

Angel, R. "Feasibility of Cooling the Earth with a Cloud of Small Spacecraft near the Inner Lagrange Point (L1)." *Proceedings of the National Academy of Science* 103.46 (2006), 17184–17189. DOI: 10.1073/pnas.0608163103.

Bower, K., et al. "Computational Assessment of a Proposed Technique for Global Warming Mitigation via Albedo-Enhancement of Marine Stratocumulus Clouds." *Atmospheric Research*, 82.1–2 (2006), 328–336.

Brewer, P. G. "Evaluating a Technological Fix for Climate." *Proceedings of the National Academy of Sciences* 104.24 (2007), 9915–9916.

Crutzen, P. J. "Albedo Enhancement by Stratospheric Sulfur Injections: A Contribution to Resolve a Policy Dilemma?" *Climatic Change* 77.3–4 (2006), 211–220. DOI: 10.1007/s10584-006-9101-y.

Dickinson, R. "Climate Engineering: A Review of Aerosol Approaches to Changing the Global Energy Balance." *Climatic Change* 33.3 (1996), 279–290. DOI: 10.1007/BF00142576.

Herzog, H., B. Eliasson, and O. Kaarstad. "Capturing Greenhouse Gases." *Scientific American* 282.2 (February 2000), 72–79.

Johnson, R. G. "Climate Control Requires a Dam at the Strait of Gibraltar." *EOS* 78.27 (1997), 277, 280–281. DOI: 10.1029/97EO00180.

Latham, J. "Amelioration of Global Warming by Controlled Enhancement of the Albedo and Longevity of Low-Level Maritime Clouds." *Atmospheric Science Letters* 3.2–4 (2002), 52–58. DOI: 10.1006/asle.2002.0099.

Lawrence, M. G. "Side Effects of Oceanic Iron Fertilization." *Science* 297 (2002), 1993. DOI: 10.1126/science.297.5589.1993b.

Monastersky, R. "Iron Versus the Greenhouse." *Science News* 148 (1995), 220–222. A good review of iron fertilization for the nonspecialist.

Parson, E. A., and D. W. Keith. "Fossil Fuels without CO_2 Emissions." *Science* 282 (1998), 1053–1054. DOI: 10.1126/science.282.5391.1053. A summary of recent developments in carbon sequestration.

Schneider, S. H. "Earth Systems Engineering and Management." *Nature* 409 (2001), 417–421. DOI: 10.1038/35053203.

Seifritz, W. "Mirrors to Halt Global Warming?" *Nature* 340 (1989), 603. DOI: 10.1038/340603a0. Describes a stable solar-shield scheme that involves a large shield at the Lagrange point.

Turner, S. M., et al. "Iron-Induced Changes in Oceanic Sulfur Biogeochemistry." *Geophysical Research Letters* 31, L14307 (2004). DOI: 10.1029/2004GL020296.

WORKS ON THE CLIMATE RESPONSE TO GEOENGINEERING

Govindasamy, B., and K. Caldeira. "Geoengineering Earth's Radiation Balance to Mitigate CO_2-Induced Climate Change." *Geophysical Research Letters* 27.14 (2000), 2141–2144.

Govindasamy, B., et al. "Impact of Geoengineering Schemes on the Terrestrial Biosphere." *Geophysical Research Letters* 29.22 (2002), 2061. DOI: 10.1029/2002GL015911.

Matthews, H. D., and K. Caldeira. "Transient Climate-Carbon Simulations of Planetary Geoengineering." *Proceedings of the National Academy of Sciences* 104.24 (2007), 9949–9954. DOI: 10.1073/pnas.0700419104.

Trenberth, K. E., and A. Dai. "Effects of Mount Pinatubo Volcanic Eruption on the Hydrological Cycle as an Analog of Geoengineering." *Geophysical Research Letters*, 34, L15702 (2007). DOI: 10.1029/2007GL030524.

Wigley, T. M. L. "A Combined Mitigation/Geoengineering Approach to Climate Stabilization." *Science* 314 (2006), 452–454. DOI: 10.1126/science.1131728.

OTHER CITED WORKS

Royal Society. *Ocean Acidification Due to Increasing Atmospheric Carbon Dioxide*. London: Royal Society, 2005.

United Nations. *Earth Summit Convention on Climate Change*. New York: UN Department of Public Information, 1994.

—H. Damon Matthews and David W. Keith

GEOGRAPHIC INFORMATION SYSTEMS

Geographic information systems (GIS) apply computer technology to the capture, storage, manipulation, analysis, modeling, and display of information about the surface of the Earth and its phenomena. They have emerged over the past four decades as a distinct form of computer use, with its own software industry and products, directed at applications ranging from management of the resources of utility companies, to support global-change science. Worldwide sales of GIS software in the early twenty-first century were about U.S.$1 billion annually, with much larger investments in associated digital geographic data.

GIS deal with information that is geographically or spatially explicit, representing the spatial variation of phenomena over the Earth. Although many forms of software can handle such information in limited ways, GIS is the only form designed expressly for this purpose, with a full range of necessary data structures and functions. Global-change science is also inherently geographically explicit, concerned as it is with spatial dynamics and differentiation over the surface of the planet. GIS is thus uniquely suitable as a tool for the computing functions needed to support global-change science.

It is helpful to think of a GIS as a computer containing maps. One of the simplest reasons for manipulating maps with computers is to make them easier to construct and draw, and GIS are often used for this purpose. By computerizing the map-making process it is possible to edit easily, manipulate the map's contents without the labor-intensive task of redrafting, transmit maps electronically, and create output in any convenient form. GIS makes it possible for anyone to be a cartographer who has the necessary software, a computer to run it on, and a suitable printer.

This view of a GIS as an automated mapping system is, however, much too limited. The first GIS is generally agreed to have been the Canada Geographic Information System (CGIS), a project developed in the Canadian government in the 1960s, under the direction of Roger Tomlinson. At the time there were no printers capable of making acceptable maps, even in black and white, and the design of CGIS did not include map output. Instead, the project was justified entirely on the basis of the need to analyze geographic information obtained from maps. Its original design included a thorough cost-benefit analysis that is still a model for the industry; it found substantial net benefits to computerization despite the high costs and crude technology of the time.

The case for computerizing the analysis of geographic information rests on two propositions: first, that the few traditional tools that exist are very labor intensive and crude; and second, that once geographic information is in digital form there are massive economies of scale because of the many forms of analysis that are possible. For example, there are two traditional ways of measuring area from a map, with a mechanical planimeter, and by counting dots on a transparent overlay; both are tedious and inaccurate. But the measurement of area from a digital representation of a map is trivial, and virtually as accurate as the representation. Once a representation has been created, it is easy to add functions to the software to perform almost any analysis imaginable.

Today's GIS software includes functions that support the analysis of digital data by manual or automated digitizing of paper maps; functions to convert between map projections; functions to integrate data from different sources by converting formats or removing spurious differences; functions to make mapped output more publishable and pleasing to the eye; and links to specialized software for modeling physical processes or conducting statistical analyses. All of these are relevant to global-change science, and GIS has become one of that science's most valuable analytical tools.

PRINCIPLES

There are two main competing forms of digital representation in GIS. The *vector* approach builds a database from digital representations of points, lines, and areas. The location of each primitive object is recorded using an appropriate combination of coordinates referenced to the Earth's surface, often in latitude and longitude but also in standard coordinate systems such as UTM (Universal Transverse Mercator, a world standard initially developed for military applications). The characteristics of each object are termed its attributes, and a vector GIS will accommodate large numbers of these, in the form of names and measurements of various kinds. Objects are grouped into classes, each member of a class having the same dimensionality (e.g., all points) and the same group of characteristics. It is convenient to think of the attributes of a class of objects as forming a table, and many vector GIS incorporate relational-database management-systems to handle the tables.

The *raster* approach, on the other hand, covers the relevant part of the Earth's surface with an array of rectangular cells and describes variation by allocating a value to each cell. Almost all designs allow only one value per cell, so representations of multidimensional variation are built by constructing several layers of cells, each describing the variation of one variable. A cell can contain a digital representation of a number, as in digital images of Earth from space (remote sensing) or representations of the variation of elevation (digital elevation models or DEMs); or a digital representation of a class, as in layers of land cover, vegetation classification, or land use. The fixed cell-size gives the raster representation the appearance of constant spatial resolution, whereas vector representations have resolutions that are unlimited in principle but limited in practice by the nature of the data.

Vector GIS originated in applications where this representation is most appropriate. For example, it is clearly more reasonable to represent the links in a connected river or water-supply network as lines than as collections of cells. This is particularly apparent in the management of telephone networks, where the connectivity in the system is apparent only at the most detailed spatial resolution. Vector data is also dominant in social, economic, and demographic data, and thus in the human aspects of global-change science, because of the practice of collecting such data for irregularly shaped regions. On the other hand it is more reasonable to process information gathered by remote sensing in a raster GIS, because the data are collected in that form. Raster GIS are similar in many ways to the image-processing systems developed for handling remotely sensed data, but they add functions that allow these data to be integrated with other, possibly vector data. Vector GIS are similar in many ways to computer-assisted design (CAD) systems, but add functions and capabilities that reflect the special needs of users of Earth-referenced data. Modern GIS attempt to integrate raster and vector approaches, though with only partial success, and many systems still reflect their earlier roots in one approach or the other.

RECENT TRENDS

GIS is a new and rapidly developing technology, positioned to take advantage of broader trends in computing. At the same time, its origins in the paper map have established a legacy that is on the one hand an advantage, because it allows the user of a GIS to understand its potential in terms of a familiar metaphor, but on the other hand limiting, because it fails to acknowledge the true potential of GIS. In recent years much work has gone into developing GIS in directions that go beyond the metaphor of a map inside a computer. Today, GIS users can expect functions that process data that have significant temporal elements (maps are inherently static); that deal effectively with complexity and uncertainty (maps present the world as simpler than it really is); and that handle the third spatial dimension (paper maps are inherently two-dimensional). A development of particular significance to global-change science is the ability to analyze data distributed on the curved surface of the Earth; early GIS took for granted the distortions introduced by map projections and processed information as if it were planar. Such distinctions are unimportant over small areas but become very important if GIS is used on a larger scale, as in estimating the mean of the global temperature field.

Of particular significance for global-change science is the role of GIS in facilitating the integration of data. Integrated assessments require access to both physical and human geographic data, ranging from demographic and economic statistics to climate, soil class, and land cover. Often the only way to integrate such data is within a common geographic framework implemented in a GIS. The data of a particular discipline inevitably adopt that discipline's conventions, which may be very different from those of another discipline. Point records of climate, for instance, must be merged with raster databases from remote sensing and statistics for the irregularly shaped reporting zones commonly used by statistical agencies. Scales vary widely, as do map projections. The impact of GIS on global-change science has been greatest in two areas, where data must be integrated across such displinary differences, and where the results and predictions of global-change science must be integrated with other concerns in support of policy decisions. GIS is thus as likely to be used in a policy agency as in a global-change science laboratory.

BIBLIOGRAPHY

Bugayevskiy, L. M., and J. P. Snyder. *Map Projections: A Reference Manual.* London, U.K., and Bristol, Pa.: Taylor and Francis, 1995. An excellent compendium on the geometric basis of mapping.

Burrough, P. A., and R. A. McDonnell. *Principles of Geographical Information Systems.* 2d ed. Oxford and New York: Oxford University Press, 1998. An early and influential text, with particular focus on applications to environmental science.

Clarke, K. C. *Getting Started with Geographic Information Systems.* 4th ed. Upper Saddle River, N.J.: Pearson Education, 2003. An excellent introduction.

DeMers, M. N. *Fundamentals of Geographic Information Systems.* 3d ed. New York: Wiley, 2005. Another introduction; a fourth edition is in preparation.

Ehleringer, J. R., and C. B. Field, eds. *Scaling Physiological Processes: Leaf to Globe.* San Diego: Academic Press, 1993. An ecological perspective on the issue of scale in global change science.

Goodchild, M. F., B. O. Parks, and L. T. Steyaert, eds. *Environmental Modeling with GIS.* New York: Oxford University Press, 1993. A compendium of applications of GIS to the modeling of various elements of environmental systems at local to global scales.

Longley, P. A., et al. *Geographic Information Systems and Science.* 2d ed. Chichester, U.K., and Hoboken, N.J.: Wiley, 2005. The most popular GIS text.

Longley, P. A., et al., eds. *Geographical Information Systems: Principles, Techniques, Management, and Applications.* 2d ed., abridged. Hoboken, N.J.: Wiley, 2005. A comprehensive, commissioned state-of-the-art review of GIS.

Quattrochi, D. A., and M. F. Goodchild, eds. *Scale in Remote Sensing and GIS.* Boca Raton: Lewis, 1997.

Rhind, D. W., ed. *Framework for the World.* Cambridge: GeoInformation International; New York: Wiley, 1997. A recent collection on the issues impeding comprehensive global mapping.

Star, J. L., J. E. Estes, and K. C. McGwire, eds. *Integration of Geographic Information Systems and Remote Sensing.* Cambridge and New York: Cambridge University Press, 1997. A review of the issues at the interface of these two geographic information technologies, of particular interest to global-change scientists.

Worboys, M. F., and M. Duckham. *GIS: A Computing Perspective.* 2d ed. Boca Raton, Fla.: CRC; New York and London: Taylor and Francis, 2004. An excellent introduction to GIS from two computer scientists.

Zhang, J., and M. F. Goodchild. *Uncertainty in Geographical Information.* London and New York: Taylor and Francis, 2002.

ADDITIONAL SOURCES: JOURNALS

International Journal of Geographical Information Science
Computers, Environment, and Urban Systems
Transactions in Geographic Information Science
Journal of Geographical Systems
Environment and Planning B
GeoInformatica
Geographical Analysis
Annals of the Association of American Geographers

ADDITIONAL SOURCES: GIS SOFTWARE

Environmental Systems Research Institute, www.esri.com
Intergraph Corporation, www.intergraph.com
MapInfo Corporation, www.mapinfo.com
Manifold GIS, www.manifold.net
Idrisi GIS, www.clarklabs.org

—MICHAEL F. GOODCHILD

GLACIER RETREAT SINCE THE LITTLE ICE AGE

Many of the world's alpine glaciers have retreated as a consequence of the climatic changes, especially warming, that have occurred in the last hundred or so years since the end of the Little Ice Age (Oerlemans, 1994). [*See* Twentieth-Century Climate Change] Changes in the positions of the snouts of glaciers permit estimates to be made of the rate at which

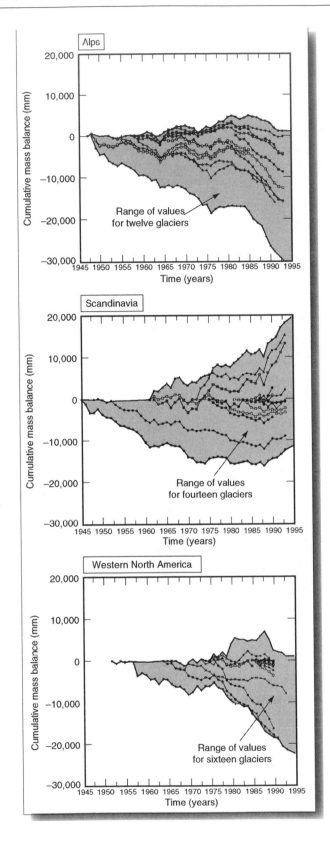

retreat can occur (Slaymaker and Kelly, 2007). The rate has not been constant nor the process uninterrupted. Indeed, some glaciers have advanced during part of the recent warm period. Among those glaciers that have shown a tendency for a general retreat there is, as with most geomorphologic phenomena, a wide range of values, the variability of which is probably related to such factors as topography (especially slope), size, altitude, accumulation rate, and ablation rate. The rates of retreat can be very high, on the order of 20–70 meters per year over extended periods of some decades in the case of the more active examples, and alpine glaciers in many areas have retreated by several kilometers in the last 100 years or so.

Current glacier tendencies for selected regions are shown at left (from Hoelzle and Trindler, 1998) using mass balance, which is defined as the difference between gains and losses (expressed in terms of water equivalent). In the European Alps there has

Glacier Retreat Since the Little Ice Age. Pedersen Glacier, Alaska, 1920.

(National Snow and Ice Data Center. Photographer unknown.)

Pedersen Glacier, Alaska, 2005.

(National Snow and Ice Data Center, B. F. Molnia.)

Glacier Retreat. Figure 1. Current Glacier Tendencies.

been trend toward mass loss, with some interruptions in the mid-1960s, late 1970s, and early 1980s. Scandinavian glaciers close to the sea have seen a strong mass gain since the 1970s, but the more continental glaciers have undergone mass losses. The mass gain in western Scandinavia might be due to an increase in precipitation, which more than compensates for an increase in ablation caused by rising temperatures. Western North America shows a general mass loss near the coast and in the Cascade Mountains (Hoelzle and Trindler, 1998).

The positive mass balance (and advance) of some Scandinavian glaciers in recent decades, notwithstanding rising temperatures, has been attributed to increased storm activity and precipitation coincident with a high index of the North Atlantic Oscillation in winter months since 1980 (Zeeberg and Forman, 2001; Nesje et al., 2000). In the case of Nigardsbreen (Norway) there is a strong correlation between mass balance and the NAO index (Reichert et al. 2001). A positive mass balance phase in the Austrian Alps between 1965 and 1981 has been correlated with a negative NAO index (Schoner et al., 2000). Indeed, the mass balances of glaciers in the north and south of Europe are inversely correlated (Six et al., 2001). [*See* North Atlantic Oscillation.]

Glaciers on tropical mountains (Kaser and Osmaston, 2002) and those that calve into the sea appear to be undergoing particularly rapid thinning and retreat, as in the Andes and the Antarctic respectively (Pritchard and Vaughan, 2007).

BIBLIOGRAPHY

Goudie, A. S. *The Changing Earth: Rates of Geomorphological Processes*. Oxford, U.K., and Cambridge, Mass.: Blackwell, 1995.

Hoelzle, M., and M. Trindler. "Data Management and Application." In *Into the Second Century of Worldwide Glacier Monitoring: Prospects and Strategies*, edited by W. Haeberli, M. Hoelzle, and S. Suter, pp. 53–72. Paris: UNESCO, 1998.

Kaser, G., and H. Osmaston. *Tropical Glaciers*. Cambridge and New York: Cambridge University Press, 2002.

Nesje, A., Lie, Ø., and Dahl, S. O. "Is the North Atlantic Oscillation Reflected in Scandinavian Glacier Mass Balance Records?" *Journal of Quaternary Science* 15 (2000), 587–601.

Oerlemans, J. "Quantifying Global Warming From the Retreat of Glaciers." *Science* 264 (1994), 243–245. DOI: 10.1126/science.264.5156.243.

Pritchard, H. D., and D. G. Vaughan. "Widespread Acceleration of Tidewater Glaciers on the Antarctic Peninsula." *Journal of Geophysical Research* 112, F03S29 (2007). DOI: 1029/2006JF000597.

Reichert, B. K., L. Bengston, and J. Oerlemans. "Midlatitude Forcing Mechanisms for Glacier Mass Balance Investigated Using General Circulation Models." *Journal of Climate* 14 (2001), 3767–3784. DOI: 10.1175/1520-0442(2001)014<3767:MFMFGM>2.0.CO;2.

Schöner, W., I. Auer, and R. Böhm. "Climate Variability and Glacier Reaction in the Austrian Eastern Alps." *Annals of Glaciology* 31.1 (2000), 31–38. DOI: 10.3189/172756400781819806.

Six, D., L. Reynaud, and A. Letreguilly. "Bilans de masse des glaciers alpins et scandinaves, leurs relations avec l oscillation du climat de l' Atlantique nord." *Comptes Rendus Academie des Sciences, Science de la Terre et des planètes*, 333 (2001), 693–698.

Slaymaker, O., and R. E. J. Kelly. *The Cryosphere and Global Environmental Change*. Oxford, U.K., and Malden, Mass.: Blackwell, 2007.

Zeeberg, J., and Forman, S. L. "Changes in Glacier Extent on North Novaya Zemlya in the Twentieth Century." *The Holocene* 11.2 (2001), 161–175. DOI: 10.1191/095968301676173261.

—ANDREW S. GOUDIE

GLOBAL CHANGE HISTORY

The phrase "global environmental change" has come into wide use only within the past few decades. Attention to such change has never been stronger or more widespread than it is today, yet it existed in more scattered and fragmentary form before talk about global change as such became common. To what extent it existed and how it differed from current awareness are important questions that await satisfactory answers, and an adequate history of thought regarding global environmental change has still to be written.

Such thought takes two forms, beliefs about what changes have taken place or might take place and how, and evaluations of the changes (e.g., whether they are for the better or for the worse). A full intellectual history of global change would include many ideas of the first sort that would now be judged untenable, in cases incorrectly attributed to human-induced. It would also include many past evaluations of most real or imagined human-induced changes as improvements upon nature—part of the remodeling of the Earth from its bleak, hostile, and forbidding primeval state into one better suited to its human occupants. This point of view, though not typical of contemporary discourse, is part of the wider history of global change. A history shaped too restrictively by present-day concerns is apt to overlook earlier viewpoints.

Such a history is also apt to distort the significance of much of what it does include. Many possibilities of misinterpretation arise when earlier ideas are examined only in the framework of contemporary ones. One of the most common is that of paying undue attention to ideas similar to today's just because of that similarity and ascribing them more importance in earlier thought than they actually had. In the field of global change, it is dangerously easy to declare past thinkers who expressed concern over any perceived human-induced environmental change ahead of their time and necessarily more insightful than contemporaries who did not share their concerns. At an extreme, it can mean lauding marginal figures whose views were absurd by the standards of the best science of their time but whose errors led them to express worries in some way similar to those of the present.

Documenting what has been thought about global change is made difficult by the uneven and unrepresentative nature of the primary source material. Though much of past and present awareness consists of popular as well as scientific beliefs, the character, extent, and distribution of those beliefs—even as they exist today—are little known. Scientific and explicit understandings of global change are far more thoroughly recorded than are nonprofessional and tacit ones. As a result, little can be said with confidence about what views of global change prevailed in the past and among what groups. Because they may have differed greatly with respect to such factors as location, ethnicity, age, class, race, and gender, one must be wary of generalizing about the beliefs of a population or a period without recognizing how narrowly a generalization may apply even within the domain for which it is advanced.

As the geographer Clarence Glacken has shown (1967), observations and discussions of human influence on the environment stretch back to classical antiquity and beyond. It is difficult and arbitrary to establish when awareness of environmental change became awareness of global change. Much was said in classical texts about the decay or the improvement of the Earth that could be considered global environmental theorizing, yet it was based on scant empirical knowledge of the Earth's surface. It reached global conclusions mainly by abstract reasoning rather than by thorough analysis and synthesis of observed phenomena. So too, many premodern Christian theologians viewed the Fall of Man and the Deluge as cases in which human misdeeds led to the physical degradation of the entire Earth, shaping its current forms and functions, from its geomorphology to its climate. These conclusions about global change likewise derived more from reasoning or revelation than from detailed knowledge established by observation or report. To be sure, many such thinkers did appeal to the evidence provided by the Earth's surface—which they read to support their case—and they linked, as many environmentalists do today, human misdeeds with environmental degradation in a call for reform. Inasmuch as the link they invoked between misdeeds and degradation was a supernatural one and the reforms for which they called were not in behavior toward the environment as such, it would be wrong to overemphasize their kinship with the mainstream of present environmental thought. It would also be an error to ignore the extent to which similar views persist and even thrive today, albeit in areas such as fundamentalist religion which are little known to intellectual historians or environmental activists.

Through the end of the nineteenth century, most discussions of human impact through means other than supernatural emphasized land-cover changes that were usually viewed as improvements: the clearing of forests, the draining of wetlands, and the cultivation of the soil. But the work of authors collating and comparing observations of these processes and their effects in different regions represents another point where concern over environmental change could be said to have become global. It is also an awareness that merits the term "environmental" in the modern sense, for it drew attention not only to the direct and deliberate effects of human action but to their possible secondary, inadvertent, and harmful consequences. The eighteenth century, as the historian Richard Grove has demonstrated (1995), saw the emergence of a school of thought comprising scientists, travelers, and government officials who linked deforestation in Europe's far-flung tropical colonies to disastrous climatic change in the form of lessened rainfall. The thesis gained further adherents and credibility during the first half of the nineteenth century and helped to shape the forestry policies of many colonial governments. It marks an important point at which emerged a coordinated and politically influential concern for the widespread and evidently harmful effects of human alteration of the land cover. Many of the connections that the desiccation theorists invoked, though, would be judged scientifically dubious by modern standards, and many of their claims

about human impact were overblown. They somewhat resemble current thought but were by no means its lineal ancestors.

Such theorizing about deforestation and desiccation developed alongside the growth of Western knowledge about other parts of the world, a growth hastened by the formal and informal efforts of governments and learned societies to promote the systematic exploration of the Earth and its human occupants, including observations on human alteration of the environment. In the latter part of the eighteenth century, the French savant Count Buffon (1707–1788) produced the period's most ambitious synthesis of global geography and natural history. His *Histoire Naturelle* (44 vols. 1749–1804) devoted much attention to humankind as a powerful force altering the Earth. Buffon judged most of these changes—from forest clearance to species transplantation to soil drainage—to have been for the better. He expressed an Enlightenment confidence in the steady improvement of the environment as part of the progressive perfection of the human race.

For Buffon and even for later compilers and interpreters of global geographic knowledge, human impact had been only one theme among many. The first full-length work devoted entirely to a survey of the impacts of human activity on the Earth came in 1864. *Man and Nature, or Physical Geography as Modified by Human Action* was the work of the American diplomat, legislator, linguist, and historian George Perkins Marsh (1801–1882). Marsh more aptly titled later editions (published in 1874, in 1882, and posthumously in 1885) *The Earth as Modified by Human Action*, for he did not consider all types of relations between man and nature or between society and the environment. Marsh declared himself not concerned with deliberate and successful changes. Hence he offered only a partial assessment of human-induced change, and one limited still further by his scant knowledge of many regions of the world. He dealt chiefly with land-cover change, especially deforestation, but also wetland drainage, changes in surface and underground water, the creation and spread of deserts, and the transfer of plant and animal species.

Its limitations notwithstanding, the book is a landmark in the history of global change. It was based factually on the best evidence yet collected, drawn from his wide reading in many languages and enriched by personal observations in North America and the Mediterranean lands. Throughout, Marsh emphasized what he called the "secondary and collateral" effects of human actions, their unforeseen and often distant, surprising, and dismaying consequences. In places, he overemphasized these effects, ascribing too large a role to land-cover modification in climate change, the spread of deserts, and the flooding of rivers.

Marsh, while challenging some of the assumptions current in his time, accepted others. He tended to view nature in the absence of humans as harmonious and unchanging (or changing only gradually). He thus tended to attribute any sudden or profound change occurring during the human period to human action. Like many of his contemporaries, he took an anthropocentric view that placed humankind outside of and above nature and focused on the significance of the environment for human life and livelihood. He questioned, however, the widespread optimism—the equation of environmental alteration with progress that prevailed in his time—by documenting the damage that had been done and the mass of unintended environmental consequences that could flow from human actions. He emphasized the immense power of human agency in the environment and the havoc that it could produce if it were not restrained and informed by a better understanding of its possible effects on the complex web of natural processes.

Marsh's influence on later thought is difficult to define. He stated clearly and forcefully many of the themes that have become central to concern about human impact on the environment in the early twenty-first century. How far did he help to shape that concern, and how far has he simply been rediscovered because of his congeniality to later opinion? Certainly he was widely read in his day. Among the most important of several writers who closely followed Marsh was the Russian meteorologist and geographer Aleksandr Ivanovich Voeikov (1842–1916). In 1901 he published an extensive evaluation of human alteration of land and land cover and its repercussions for such realms as climate, water balance, and sediment flows. Voeikov was one of a number of European scholars around the turn of the century who echoed Marsh in their concern with what the German geographer Ernst Friedrich termed *Raubwirtschaft* (plunder economy), the destructive exploitation of the land. Similar concerns took shape in many countries in a forest- and soil-conservation movement that was advanced by the catastrophe of the American Dust Bowl and similar disasters elsewhere in the 1930s. A 1955 conference held at Princeton University on the theme of "Man's Role in Changing the Face of the Earth" was defined by its organizers—the geographer Carl Sauer, the social theorist Lewis Mumford, and the biologist Marston Bates—as a "Marsh Festival" dedicated to the memory of the author of *Man and Nature*. Published in 1956, the papers and proceedings of the conference updated Marsh's analysis in light of nearly a century of further scholarship and of further human-induced environmental change.

They also dealt with some newer themes, one of which had developed separately from the Marsh tradition that concerned the adequacy of vital natural resources (e.g., coal, timber, minerals) and the possibility that waste and overuse would exhaust them. The late nineteenth century had also seen the earliest serious attention to the ways in which coal consumption might affect human life on a global scale, not only by depleting the supply but by releasing waste products into the environment. Work published in 1896 by the Swedish chemist Svante Arrhenius (1859–1927) suggested that the temperature of the Earth might be increased by several degrees if releases from coal combustion doubled the atmospheric concentration of carbon dioxide. Arrhenius's work is another landmark in the understanding of global change, making as it did the first credible forecast of substantial human impact on a system that might affect the entire planet.

It is, however, a work susceptible of misinterpretation when viewed too much in relation to present-day concerns. As his biographer Elisabeth Crawford points out (1997), Arrhenius was not the first to suggest that human activities might raise the atmospheric level of carbon dioxide and thereby affect the global climate, and he was concerned primarily with explaining the mechanism by which continental glaciation had occurred in the geological past. He was no more than incidentally concerned with human impacts in the future. Finally, Arrhenius, in common with contemporaries who took up his suggestion, looked on a warming induced by carbon dioxide as an unqualified good that would make agriculture more productive, life more comfortable, and another ice age less likely. Throughout the first half of the twentieth century, Arrhenius's suggestions failed to win general acceptance. Many meteorologists believed that the oceans would absorb any additional carbon dioxide released by fuel combustion and that any added to the atmosphere would cause only a small increase in the amount of heat trapped. What would come to be known as the greenhouse effect was not seriously discussed at Princeton in 1955.

More general than Arrhenius's speculations but almost as optimistic in tenor, were those of the Russian chemist Vladimir Ivanovich Vernadsky (1863–1945), the most significant early theorist of biogeochemistry as a major factor in global environmental change. Vernadsky believed the central fact of modern Earth history to be the emergence of humankind as an almost geological force shaping the transformation of the planet's material and energy flows. He described its central process as the reshaping of the biosphere—the envelope of soil, air, and water at the Earth's surface capable of supporting life—into a noosphere dominated by the power of human consciousness. Language and cultural barriers meant that Vernadsky's ideas were slow to diffuse into other countries save in the somewhat altered form in which they were adapted by the French philosopher Teilhard de Chardin. There was little of admonition or pessimism in Vernadsky's work, which nonetheless was of fundamental importance in assessing the human impact on the Earth's biogeochemical fluxes as comparable in importance to the land-cover transformations treated by Marsh and his successors.

Attention to the human impact on the biogeochemical cycles flowered in the decades following World War II under the stimulus of a much-improved capacity to monitor and detect change in the environment. Technological advances in the gathering and analysis of data made it possible to record trends in a far wider range of environments than before, and with increasing precision. Year-by-year monitoring of the carbon dioxide content of the troposphere begun at the Mauna Loa observatory in Hawaii in the 1950s clearly demonstrated a steady increase as fossil-fuel combustion and land-cover change released carbon, at the same time that scientists began to consider anew the idea that it and other trace gases could significantly warm the global climate.

The data thus accumulated testified less to the increasing rational human control over the biosphere that Vernadsky had foreseen than to a growing variety of impacts arising by chance and inadvertence from novel human activities. The discovery of radioactive fallout from the atmospheric testing of nuclear weapons brought the dark side of the picture to popular and scientific attention in the 1950s. It was further dramatized by Rachel Carson's (1907–1964) *Silent Spring*, published in 1962. By linking declines in bird populations to the widespread use of the pesticide DDT, Carson vividly illustrated how human interventions in the biosphere could produce consequences vastly more varied, wide-reaching, and undesirable than those originally conceived. Her polemic gave urgent expression and wide currency to a sense of the environment as Marsh had portrayed it—a complex, interconnected system in which surprises and unforeseen effects were always possible and even likely—but one now threatened by a far wider array of stresses and impacts than existed in Marsh's time. It marks the emergence of full-blown concern for the global environment. The fears that it helped to arouse were kept alive by many further well-publicized examples of increases in concentrations of metals and chemical compounds in air, water, soil, and biota often quite distant from their points of release. The most dramatic and far-reaching was the conclusion by scientists that the release of chlorofluorocarbons, synthetic organic chemicals used in refrigeration and other processes, was significantly depleting the ozone of the upper atmosphere that reduces the incidence of high-energy (UV) solar radiation on the Earth's surface. [*See* Chlorofluorocarbons.]

One other undeniably global human impact attracted even more scientific and public attention. Climatic warming through greenhouse-gas accumulation was increasingly seen as a potential catastrophe rather than as a net benefit to the world, as it had been in the early twentieth century. The new and more pessimistic assessment arose from a greater awareness of the manifold probable second- and third-order consequences of climate change, such as possible sea-level rise from melting of the Antarctic and Greenland ice sheets, biodiversity loss through ecosystem disruption, and impacts on human health through rising heat stress and changes in the distribution of infectious diseases.

Modern thought about global change is thus characterized by a much wider range of concerns than in the past. Another inventory of human impact, *The Earth as Transformed by Human Action* (1990), was a catalog as much larger than that of the 1955 Princeton conference as the latter's was than Marsh's *Man and Nature*. Its core consisted of chapters on eighteen major realms and fluxes of the global environment, documenting the often multiple changes that had taken place in each, many of them unrecognized in 1956. Another dozen chapters explored the further combinations and interactions of changes occurring in particular regions and producing diverse impacts.

Discussion and debate have proliferated in public forums of all sorts. Public opinion has always been an element of global-change thought, but with the rapid popularization of the topic it has become more important than in the past. Scientific beliefs about global change often differ profoundly from nonprofessional beliefs. The contemporary public understanding of almost every aspect of global climate change, from its physical mechanisms to its likely impacts, differs widely from the models generally accepted by climate scientists and those who study the impacts of global change. These differences are sometimes described as being between scientific understanding on the one side and lay misunderstanding on the other, and sometimes as the expression of different but equally legitimate concerns. The question arises why public concern over global change is so substantial if the public has not assimilated the scientific reasons for thinking it a matter for concern.

Concern is not universal, as witnessed by the rancorous debates that surround almost every important environmental issue. There is a striking lack of consensus, both globally and within any country, on almost all issues. This absence of consensus is most apparent in differing evaluations of human impact and disagreements over the need to regulate it. Influential perspectives in today's environmental debate span the range from radical Green and doomsday perspectives to a radical questioning of the reality of almost any environmental threat, with many variations between those extremes.

[*See also* Environmental Movements; Global Warming; *and* Greenhouse Effect.]

BIBLIOGRAPHY

Asimov, I. *Asimov's Chronology of the World.* New York: HarperCollins, 1991.
Chandler, T. *Four Thousand Years of Urban Growth: An Historical Census.* Lewiston, N.Y.: St. David's University Press, 1987.
Thomas, W. L., Jr., ed. *Man's Role in Changing the Face of the Earth.* Chicago: University of Chicago Press, 1956.

—WILLIAM B. MEYER

GLOBAL DIMMING

Variations in global radiation, which is the total short-wave irradiation from sun and sky, can affect climate, the hydrological cycle, and plant photosynthesis. There is some evidence that the amount of solar radiation that reached the Earth's surface declined by about 0.2–0.3% per year between between about 1960 and 1990—a phenomenon called "global dimming" (Stanhill and Cohen, 2001). Possible causes include changes in clouds, increasing amounts of anthropogenic aerosols, and reduced atmospheric transparency after explosive volcanic eruptions (Pinker et al., 2006). Air pollution may have worked in two ways—by reflecting sunlight back into space, and by making clouds more reflective. Global dimming may to a certain degree have masked the greenhouse effect. Since about 1990, the trend has been reversed and is referred to as "global brightening" (Wild et al., 2005). This may have made the effects of rising greenhouse-gas loadings more evident during the 1990s (Wild et al., 2007). The reason for this change may be that some atmospheric pollutants, particularly sulfur dioxide and black carbon, have declined in many regions (e.g., over eastern Europe) (Streets et al., 2006).

BIBLIOGRAPHY

Pinker, R. T., B. Zhang, and E. G. Dutton. "Do Satellites Detect Trends in Surface Solar Radiation?" *Science* 308 (2005), 850–854. DOI: 10.1126/science.1103159.

Stanhill, G., and S. Cohen. "Global Dimming: A Review of the Evidence for a Widespread and Significant Reduction in Global Radiation with Discussion of Its Probable Causes and Possible Agricultural Consequences." *Agricultural and Forest Meteorology* 107.4 (2001), 255–278. DOI: 10.1016/S0168-1923(00)00241-0.

Streets, D. G., Y. Wu and M. Chin. "Two-Decadal Aerosol Trends as a Likely Explanation of the Global Dimming/Brightening Transition." *Geophysical Research Letters* 33, L15806 (2006). DOI: 10.1029/2006GL026471.

Wild, M., et al. "From Dimming to Brightening: Decadal Changes in Solar Radiation at Earth's Surface." *Science* 308 (2005), 847–850. DOI: DOI: 10.1126/science.1103215.

Wild, M., A. Ohmura, and K. Makowski. "Impact of Global Dimming and Brightening on Global Warming." *Geophysical Research Letters* 34, L04702 (2007). DOI: 10.1029/2006GL028031.

—Andrew S. Goudie

GLOBAL WARMING

Global warming has become the dominant environmental issue of modern times, receiving an unprecedented level of attention from scientists, politicians, business organizations, the media and the general public. Anecdotal, documentary, and instrumental evidence supports the widely held perception that the twentieth century was a period in which global temperatures rose to unprecedented levels.

Periods of warming earlier in the century had been recognized by climatologists, but the current major warming only became evident to a wider audience in the 1980s, the warmest decade on record up to that time. [*See* Twentieth-Century Climate Change Uncertainty.] Temperature records were broken into the 1990s, and 1998 gained the distinction of being the warmest year since instrumental records began. The warming trend has continued into the twenty-first century. In 2005, the global average surface temperature surpassed that for 1998 (Henson, 2005), and eleven of the twelve years between 1995 and 2006 ranked among the twelve warmest years in the instrumental record (Solomon et al., 2007). Analysis of the instrumental climate record over the past century indicates that global

mean temperatures increased by 0.74°C between 1901 and 2005 (Solomon et al., 2007). That trend has not been even, however. Warming occurred mainly in two periods, 1920–1945 and after 1975, separated by three decades of cooling (see Figure 1).

Other elements such as real or perceived changes in unusual weather patterns (Shabbar and Bonsal, 2003), a potential increase in more severe weather conditions such as hurricanes and tornadoes (Emanuel, 2005) or the melting of ice in the Arctic (ACIA, 2004) have been explained by or blamed on global warming. Studies prepared by the Intergovernmental Panel on Climate Change (IPCC) and reports from government environmental agencies and a host of non-governmental environmental organizations have helped to keep global warming in the public eye.

PAST TRENDS

Exceptional as the current warming seems to be, the Earth has experienced similar periods of rising temperatures in the past. Since the retreat of the ice from the maximum of the most recent ice age some 20,000 years ago, the earth has experienced several periods of rising temperatures. Major global warming began in the Holocene about 10,000 yr BP during the immediate postglacial period and is commonly thought to have peaked between 7,000 and 5,000, with some regional variations in timing, during the so-called Climatic Optimum. Temperatures at that time were estimated to be between 1–3°C above early-twentieth-century normals (Folland et al., 1990). [*See* Holocene *and* Paleoclimate.]

Much later, between about 750 and 1300 CE, rising temperatures in Europe, North America, and elsewhere, produced the Medieval Warm Period (MWP, also known as the Medieval Climatic Optimum) characterized by fewer storms, a reduction in sea ice in the North Atlantic, glacier retreat in the Alps, rising treelines, better harvests, and improved living conditions for the human population. The warming originally was thought to be global, but the emerging consensus is that in the period between about 750 and 1300 CE warming was restricted to several periods of higher temperatures lasting no more than 20–30 years each, moderately warmer than the centuries preceding or following them, and local or regional in their extent. Modern interpretations of the data also indicate that at no time were medieval temperatures greater than those during the current warming (Crowley and Lowery, 2000; Osborn and Briffa, 2006). [*See* Medieval Climatic Optimum.]

Global Warming. Figure 1. Changes in Global Average Surface Temperatures.

(Based on data in IPCC 2007a.)

In addition to periods of climatic amelioration such as the Climatic Optimum and the MWP, the earth's climatic history also includes periods of cooling. Each of these warm spells was followed by a cooling episode, raising concerns that the current warming will also be followed by cooling. In the case of the Climatic Optimum, the early Holocene temperature rise following the end of the last ice age was disrupted by cooling some 8,000 years ago. The cooling that followed the MWP has been named the Little Ice Age (LIA), and as with the MWP, most of the initial evidence for the change was obtained from Europe and North America. It was originally identified as a period of cooling that lasted for about 300 years from the mid-sixteenth to the mid-nineteenth century, but modern interpretations view it as a combination of local or regional, relatively short cooling episodes, rather than a major cold spell (Ogilvie and Jonsson, 2001; Matthews and Briffa, 2005). [See Little Ice Age in Europe.]

Will there be a repetition of the cooling that followed these earlier warm spells? For some time it has been recognized that such cooling was associated with the disruption of the thermohaline circulation of the oceans, particularly in the North Atlantic (Broecker, 1997), with a consequent reduction in heat transport into higher latitudes via the Gulf Stream (Lund et al., 2006). There is evidence that an increase in the amount of cold, fresh water released into the northern parts of the ocean, as might be produced by the increased melting of snow and ice in northern latitudes, for example, could be sufficient to initiate such a disruption (Teller et al., 2002; Jennings et al., 2006). The mechanisms involved remain imperfectly understood, but some researchers see the potential for such a situation to develop as a result of global warming in the coming decades. Freshening of the waters in the North Atlantic is already evident, and modern measurements indicate that the thermohaline circulation is again weakening (Hansen et al., 2004). As yet the changes appear to be within the range of natural variability in the system (Kerr, 2005), and some scientists think it highly unlikely that northern latitudes will face a period of cooling initiated by a decline in the North Atlantic thermohaline circulation (Merali, 2006).

One of the problems of dealing with climate change in the pre-instrumental era is the availability and quality of data. Identifying the timing, extent, and magnitude of earlier episodes depends on a wide variety of proxy data. They include, for example, stratigraphical records (including varves), tree rings, pollen sequences, ice cores, archaeological records, and historical documents, which reflect, to a greater or lesser degree, the climatic conditions that prevailed at the time they were developing or being recorded. Applying that indirect evidence and using multiple, cross-referenced sources, scientists have reconstructed the climatic history of the last 10,000 years with considerable reliability. [See Proxy Data for Environmental Change.]

Multi-proxy reconstructions have been criticized, especially when they are used as evidence that late-twentieth-century warming is unprecedented in the last several thousand years of the earth's climatic history (Mann et al., 1998). Questions involving the quality of the original data, calibration methods and the techniques used in statistical analysis have cast some doubt on that conclusion (McIntyre and McKitrick, 2005) and have been used to suggest that temperatures in the past were higher than, or at least as high as, those in the current warming. This implies that natural processes are capable of producing the level of warming currently being experienced and that the role of human activities may be less than widely assumed. Ongoing development of analytical techniques for the treatment of proxy data, however, as well as the construction of more sensitive climate models support the anomalous nature of the twentieth century warming (Andronova et al., 2004). Given the contribution of natural processes to past climate change, it is unlikely that they will remain quiescent while only anthropogenic inputs contribute to change (Moberg et al., 2005). Although any modern change is likely to include both natural and anthropogenic elements, the consensus is that the latter makes the greater contribution to current warming: the IPCC has calculated there is a 90% probability that the current warming is the result of human activity (Solomon et al., 2007).

CURRENT WARMING

It is the human impact that makes the current warming different from past episodes, and to understand the nature of that impact, it is necessary to consider the way in which the earth warms naturally. The energy that heats the earth/atmosphere system comes from the sun, but the processes involved are quite complex. The ability of the atmosphere to be selective in its response to radiation is critical: it is transparent to the incoming high-energy, short-wave solar radiation—with the exception of the ultraviolet absorbed by the ozone layer—but partially opaque to the outgoing lower-energy long-wave terrestrial radiation. The latter is trapped in the atmosphere, thus raising its temperature. The capture of the outgoing terrestrial radiation is accomplished largely by water vapor and carbon dioxide, along with methane and traces of about twenty other gases. These are called greenhouse gases, and the whole process is named the greenhouse effect because the gases, by trapping the heat, have much the same effect as the glass in a greenhouse. Without the greenhouse effect global mean temperature would be much lower than it is, $-17°C$, compared to the current $+15°C$. [See Greenhouse Effect.]

Given their ability to warm the atmosphere, any increase in greenhouse gases should lead to additional warming. There is strong evidence for that during the twentieth century, when the earth's surface temperature increased at a rate broadly consistent with that expected from the measured rise in atmospheric greenhouse-gas levels (Houghton, Jenkins, and Ephraums, 1990). The process involved is an example of radiative forcing in which an agent is capable of changing the average net radiation—incoming solar radiation compared to outgoing terrestrial radiation, usually expressed in watts per square meter—at the tropopause. Forcing can be negative or positive. Aerosols, which reduce the flow of incoming radiation, for example, generally have a negative impact whereas greenhouse gases are positive radiative forcing agents. According to the Fourth Assessment Report (FAR) of the IPCC, the combined radiative forcing of three greenhouse gases—carbon dioxide, methane, and nitrous oxide—and their rates of increase since about 1750 is very likely (i.e., at least a 90% probability) to have been greater than at any other time in the last 10,000 years. Carbon dioxide forcing alone increased by 20% between 1995 and 2005 (Solomon et al., 2007), indicating the importance of that gas to global warming.

There are some twenty greenhouse gases capable of contributing to increased radiative forcing. Water vapor is the most common, but it normally receives less attention than the other gases in the study of global warming, because its life span in the atmosphere is relatively short and its distribution in time and place varies considerably, more often as a result of natural processes than human activities. Carbon dioxide, methane, and nitrous oxide are recognized as the most important greenhouse gases making an increasing contribution to global warming as their atmospheric concentrations continue to rise. Chlorofluorocarbons (CFCs) and halons are also very effective greenhouse gases, but as a result of the restrictions placed on their production and use by the Montreal Protocol, their concentrations in the atmosphere have stabilized or declined. Because all these gases differ in their ability to promote global warming, the concept of global-warming potential (GWP) was incorporated in the first IPCC Scientific Assessment as a means of indicating or comparing these differences (Houghton, Jenkins, and Ephraums, 1990). The values represent a comparison with carbon dioxide: if the GWP for carbon dioxide over a given period is 1, for example, the GWP for methane over the same period would be 21. Comparable values for nitrous oxide and CFC-11 are 290 and 3,500 respectively (Shine et al., 1990). [See Greenhouse Effect.]

Greenhouse-gas levels in the past rose and fell as a result of natural processes, but current values are considered to reflect the results of human activities over the past 250 years or so. During that time the world has felt the ongoing effects of industrialization with its growing reliance on fossil fuels and the release of higher volumes of carbon dioxide, methane, nitrous oxide, and other gases into the atmosphere. As a result, present concentrations are well above the pre-industrial values of the mid-eighteenth century. Carbon dioxide concentrations, for example, grew increasingly rapidly from about 280 parts per million in 1750 to reach 379 ppm by 2005, a level that far exceeds its maximum over the past 650,000 years (300 ppm). The bulk of the increase is the result of fossil-fuel use, with land-use change—deforestation, for example—also contributing (Solomon et al., 2007).

Over the past 250 years, atmospheric concentrations of methane and nitrous oxide have also increased. Pre-industrial levels of methane were about 715 parts per billion in 1750 and had risen to 1774 ppb in 2005. As with carbon dioxide, that latter level is far beyond the natural range for the past 650,000 years (320–790 ppb), although growth rates have declined since the 1990s. The IPCC considers it very likely (i.e., at least a 90% probability) that the increase in methane concentrations is the result of anthropogenic activities, including agriculture and fossil fuel use. Agricultural activities also make a significant contribution to the increase in nitrous oxide concentration, which has risen from 270 ppb in 1750 to 319 ppb in 2005, with a growth rate that has been almost constant since 1980 (Solomon et al., 2007). [See Nitrous Oxide.] For some purposes the concentrations of individual gases are combined and expressed as carbon dioxide equivalents, the current value being 425 ppm compared to carbon dioxide alone at 375 ppm.

DETECTION AND MEASUREMENT

Given the elevated levels of greenhouse gases and their ability to cause positive radiative forcing, it is not surprising that global temperatures have risen since the beginning of the twentieth century. The observational record indicates that mean global temperatures rose 0.3–0.6°C between 1900 and the 1990s, but the change was not even, and the values were considered to be well within the range of normal natural variation in global temperatures. The main increase took place between 1910 and 1940 and again after 1975. Between 1940 and 1975, despite rising greenhouse levels, mean global temperatures declined, particularly in the northern hemisphere (Jones and Moberg, 2003). From the mid-1970s, however, the rate of warming increased, particularly in the 1980s, and near the end of that decade Hansen and Lebedeff (1988) were already suggesting that the so-called global greenhouse signal might be emerging from the background noise. In its first Scientific Assessment in 1990, the IPCC did not endorse an enhanced greenhouse effect in the observations; but sufficient progress was made in techniques of observation and analysis in the five years between the first and second Assessments to allow the IPCC to conclude that "the balance of the evidence suggests a discernible human influence on global climate" (Houghton et al., 1996). That position was reinforced in the Third Assessment Report (TAR) with new evidence indicating that most of the observed warming in the second half of the twentieth century was attributable to human activities (Houghton et al., 2001). By the fourth report in 2007, the scientists of the IPCC claimed that "warming of the climate system is unequivocal" and that recent improvements in the understanding of anthropogenic warming and cooling influences on climate leads to "very high confidence" (i.e., at least a 90% probability) that the globally averaged net effect of human activities since 1750 has been one of warming. The FAR also concluded that it is extremely unlikely (less than 5% probability) that the warming over the last half century can be explained by natural forcing and identified the observed increase in anthropogenic greenhouse gases as the agent responsible (Solomon et al., 2007).

Analysis of the instrumental record provides evidence not only that temperatures are rising but that they are rising at an increasingly rapid rate. In the TAR, the 100-year linear warming trend (1901–2000) for global surface temperatures was 0.6°C. Only five years later the equivalent trend (1906–2005) had increased to 0.74°C, while the decadal increase over the past 50 years was nearly twice that for the last 100 years. Temperatures in the Arctic have increased at about twice the global average over the past century (Solomon et al., 2007). Because they are

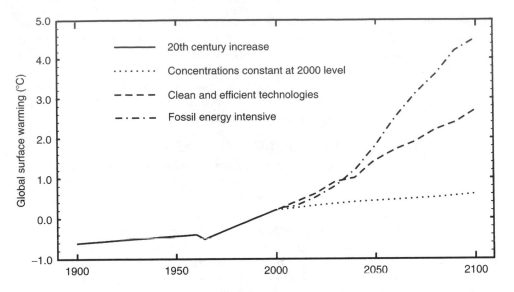

Global Warming. FIGURE 2. Potential Global Surface Warming (relative to 1980–1999) for Different Energy-Use Scenarios. (Based on data in IPCC 2007a.)

global mean values, these numbers may not seem impressive, and significant trends may be obscured by seasonal and annual variability of the climate system. In most cases it is the maximum, minimum, and extreme temperatures that receive most attention, and they too reflect the overall warming. At the low end of the scale, for example, cold days and nights and sub-zero temperatures below freezing have become less common over the past 50 years, whereas, over the same time period, hot days and nights and heat waves have become more frequent. Improved measurement and analysis shows that temperatures in the mid-troposphere are rising at rates similar to those at the surface, thus reconciling apparent discrepancies that existed between the two levels at the end of the twentieth century (Solomon et al., 2007). In addition, although "global warming" is obviously associated with temperature change, other climatic elements were also affected. Warmer air can hold more water vapor, for example, and the average water content of the atmosphere has increased since the 1980s at a rate broadly consistent with the rate of warming. More intense and longer droughts have been observed over some areas, although the frequency of heavy precipitation events has also increased. Over the oceans, changes in evaporation and precipitation patterns have brought about changes in salinity, and there is some evidence that increased sea-surface temperatures in the tropics have led to an increase in intense tropical-cyclone activity in the North Atlantic (Solomon et al., 2007). [See Tropical Cyclones in a Warming World.]

Sea-level change involves both temperature and moisture. This has been the source of mixed and often unreliable information in the past with estimates of sea level rise ranging from a few centimeters to several meters over a period of 50–100 years. Measurements using tide gauges and satellite altimetry indicate that sea level is currently rising, but at only a few millimeters per year. Contributions to the rise come from the expansion of the oceans as they warm, the melting of glaciers and icecaps, and losses from the Greenland and Antarctic ice sheets. The Greenland ice sheet appears to be particularly vulnerable and is melting at an increasingly rapid rate (Chen et al., 2006). Sea level rose 1.8 mm per year between 1961 and 2003 but 3.1 mm per year from 1993 to 2003. The overall rise in the twentieth century is estimated at 0.17 meters and may reach 1.4 meters by 2100 (Rahmstorf, 2007), but there are uncertainties in estimating the contributions from sources other than climate change (Solomon et al., 2007). [See Sea Level Future.]

PREDICTION

In addition to study of past and current climate change, considerable effort has gone into forecasting the magnitude and rate of global warming (see Figure 2). Estimates are commonly obtained from computer models—general circulation models (GCMs). These represent physical processes in the earth-atmosphere system through a series of fundamental equations which are solved repeatedly for small but incremental changes during the run of the model to produce a forecast of the future state of the system. [See Climate Models.] The early GCMs were developed to provide information about change in the atmosphere, but the essential interaction between the atmosphere and surface conditions led to the incorporation of ocean circulation processes to create atmosphere-ocean general circulation models (AOGCMs). Later, ice and land-surface changes were added to create a full climate model (Houghton, 2005). Current climate models are remarkably sophisticated, although such issues as the incorporation of feedback mechanisms require further refinement, and most are considered to be less than adequate at a regional scale. Models tested by comparing their results with observational data—global temperature records for the twentieth century, for example—perform increasingly well (Hengeveld, 2006). All models represent a compromise between the complexities of the earth-atmosphere system and the constraints imposed by such factors as data availability, computer size and speed, and the cost of computer development and operation, which limit the accuracy of the simulations. The inadequacies inherent in modeling something as complex as the earth-atmosphere system continue to be addressed by a large body of scientists, and in its FAR the IPCC noted that improvements in understanding physical processes and their simulation in models had contributed to progress in the understanding of global warning since the TAR in 2001 (Solomon et al., 2007).

IMPACTS: CURRENT AND FUTURE

The environmental impact of climate change was apparent in some areas before the nature, magnitude, or causes of the warming were identified. Retreating glaciers, melting permafrost, less extensive sea ice, increased drought frequency, shifts in plant and animal ranges, and earlier spring migrations of birds and fish have been observed in some areas since at least the 1980s. In the TAR the IPCC concluded that there was a high confidence (an 80% probability) that these physical and biological impacts were brought about by rising temperatures (Houghton et al., 2001). Subsequent ecological studies showed a correlation between range shifts for plants and animals and climate change (Parmesan and Yohe, 2003). The Arctic Climate Impact Assessment recognized the role of global warming in existing and potential physical and ecological changes in the Arctic (ACIA, 2004). [See Arctic Warming.] The high confidence in such relationships expressed in the IPCC TAR has been reaffirmed in the FAR, with the confidence level increasing to very high (at least a 90% probability) for impacts such as earlier bird migrations or poleward and upward shifts in plant and animal ranges. Plants and animals unable to respond quickly enough to the warming will be at increased risk of extinction, which in turn will diminish biodiversity (Parry et al., 2007).

Hydrology

Some of the physical and ecological impacts of global warming can be observed in the disruption of the hydrologic cycle by melting of snow and ice and by rising sea levels. These disruptions involve complex patterns, and it is often difficult to identify the contribution of global warming. The apparent increase in drought episodes in Africa, Australia, and parts of central North America, for example, may well be part of normal regional fluctuations associated with variations in atmospheric or oceanic circulation patterns—within which any global warming signal remains hidden. Studies have linked changes in current precipitation, runoff, and soil moisture patterns to warming, however, (Solomon et al., 2007) and model projections indicate that these changes are likely to continue into the future, with considerable regional variation. [See Regional Patterns of Climate Change.] It is projected, for example, that runoff over the next 50 years will show an increase of 10–40% in eastern equatorial Africa, high latitude North America, and Eurasia, with decreases of 10–30% in southern Africa, southern Europe, the Middle East, and mid-latitude western North America (Milly et al., 2005). On a global scale the impact of global warming

will be to increase water supply in those areas that already have sufficient and reduce it in those areas currently suffering deficits (Hengeveld, 2006).

Natural vegetation

Because the most obvious element in many landscapes is the vegetation cover, global plant communities or biomes are likely to provide a strong indication of the impacts of warming through their changing structure and distribution. Global ecosystems are complex, so it is difficult to isolate the impacts of individual climate elements, but changes will be driven in large part by a combination of increased carbon dioxide levels, temperature increases, and changes in water availability. The stimulation of photosynthesis by higher carbon dioxide concentrations raises productivity in some plants (carbon dioxide fertilization) although the magnitude of the increase will in many cases be constrained by water and nutrient availability. Some forest ecosystems have already responded to change: In Amazonia, tropical forest growth has been accelerating in recent years probably due to a combination of carbon dioxide fertilization, solar radiation increases, and temperature increases, but such trends may be transitory (Malhi and Phillips, 2004). Globally, changing climatic conditions are expected to bring about wholesale changes in the distribution of forests. The expansion of the boreal forest in North America and Eurasia into the tundra biome has long been expected (Bruce and Hengeveld, 1985). Plant communities migrate only slowly, however, and if the climate changes take place more rapidly than forests can respond, as seems likely, the rapid die-off of trees is a distinct possibility before some degree of equilibrium is again attained.

Agriculture

Conditions that alter the distribution and productivity of natural vegetation are likely to change the nature and extent of cultivated vegetation. For agriculture, warming will have both positive and negative impacts. Longer, warmer growing seasons will lead to increased crop yields in some areas and allow cultivation to expand into higher latitudes and to greater altitudes in others. All crops have temperature limits beyond which growth is curtailed by heat stress, moisture stress, or both: warming of only 1–3°C may be sufficient to bring about a decline in productivity in cereal crops, for example. Insect pests and plant disease may increase in some areas (Parry et al., 2007). Agricultural productivity also depends on a number of nonclimatic variables such as suitable soil conditions and a variety of economic inputs. The IPCC has projected that, on balance, crop production in mid to high latitudes will increase slightly, at least where local mean temperature increases do not exceed 1–3°C. Crop productivity in the tropics and subtropics is expected to decline for even relatively small temperature increases. This, together with a projected increase in drought and flood frequency, would increase the risk of hunger in many low latitude subsistence economies (Parry et al., 2007). The full effects of the projected impacts may be ameliorated by adaptation to changing conditions, through the introduction of new cultivars or alterations to cropping patterns, for example.

Industry

Industries such as forestry, fishing, shipping, and tourism which depend on natural resources, will experience considerable disruption over the next 50 to 100 years. Changes in the northern boreal forest economy, for example, will have significant effects on the national and regional economies of Canada, Sweden, Finland, and Russia, which depend on the harvesting of softwood from the boreal forest. Further disruption will be caused by the increase in forest fires (Westerling et al., 2006).

The fishing industry, already under major threat from overfishing, is expected to suffer further damage as a result of warming. Rising water temperatures will alter the distribution of preferred habitats for different species, as will changes in water circulation and salinity patterns. The flooding of coastal areas by rising sea level will change the distribution of existing spawning and feeding grounds with resulting ecological and economic impacts. Given the likelihood that sea level will continue to rise at least for the next century, the IPCC projects an increase in adverse effects for the fishing industry as a result of global warming (Parry et al., 2007).

Any change in the physical nature of the oceans will also impact the shipping industry and may bring both benefits and costs. Warmer winters will be beneficial for shipping in northern waters, for example, allowing longer ice free travel in the Arctic and on inland waterways such as the Great Lakes, but flooding at port terminals as a result of sea-level rise, will be highly disruptive. In those sea areas affected by more severe weather, ocean travel will become more hazardous, increasing potential losses and insurance rates.

Tourism involves a wide variety of activities, many of which are susceptible in whole or in part to global warming, because of their dependence on natural climatic resources. From mountains to beaches, from season to season, the impacts are likely to be significant. Winter snow-based activities such as skiing in the Alps have felt the effects of reduced snow fall and a rising snow line (Elsasser and Messerli, 2001), while the use of beaches for recreation is already suffering from increased coastal erosion in some areas. That will only continue as sea level rises and stormy conditions become more common, with beaches in the Caribbean and the Indian and Pacific oceans particularly vulnerable (Solomon et al., 2007).

Settlement and Human Health

As the warming continues many communities will no longer be sustainable. Survival will require some form of adjustment. In some cases that may be relatively easily done through settlement relocation, for example, or changes in agricultural activities, but in others more radical change may be required. The most vulnerable communities are likely to be in coastal areas in tropical and subtropical latitudes where the combination of rising sea level and more frequent severe weather will place the lives and livelihood of millions of people in jeopardy. In Bangladesh, for example,

more than 6 million people will be at risk if the sea level rises by 0.5 meters (Houghton, 2005). Similar effects, compounded by increasing storminess, would be felt in all low-lying coastal plains and deltas around the world: some of the small island states in the Pacific and Indian oceans would disappear completely. Although in direct human terms these changes will be greatest in the developing world, where millions of people are already living on the margin, no part of the world is immune. Coastal cities everywhere will experience the physical and socioeconomic impacts of rising sea level through the disruption of sewage and industrial waste disposal facilities, road and rail networks, and harbor activities. Although the cities of the developed world are in a better position to adapt or take preventive measures, they are no less vulnerable, as the impact of the severe hurricane season of 2005 on New Orleans and the U.S. Gulf Coast have shown.

Migration

One response to environmental change has always been migration. Already, as many as 25 million people in the world have been forced to leave their homelands because of drought, desertification, flooding, soil erosion, and other environmental problems. The number of environmental refugees will increase by perhaps as many as 200 million as a result of coastal flooding, drought, and other environmental disruption brought by global warming (Myers, 2002). Many will be accommodated locally, as in Asia (Hugo 2006), but there is likely to be an increase in global international migration in the twenty-first century.

Health

In addition to the trauma of flooding or extreme weather events, some individuals will be exposed to increasing health risks, from malnutrition to a variety of infectious diseases. Rising temperatures and changing weather patterns will alter the distribution of infectious disease vectors. The ranges of West Nile virus and Lyme disease have already expanded in North America, and the spread of other insect-borne diseases, such as malaria are also projected (Watson et al., 2005; Parry et al., 2007). Deaths from heat stress caused by extreme high temperatures will increase, particularly in large cities where higher concentrations of ground-level ozone will also cause health problems. In higher latitudes, there will be a decline in the number of deaths from hypothermia (cold exposure).

RESPONSES AND SOLUTIONS

Although there are some parts of the world and some activities that will benefit from global warming, the consensus is that detrimental effects will far outweigh the benefits. As a result, the search for solutions has intensified, particularly in recent years as enough evidence has accumulated to show that the health and welfare of the world's population is at risk. Most of the options being considered involve either adaptation or mitigation, and sometimes a combination of the two. Adaptation is designed to reduce a specific impact caused by global warming by adjusting to changes it has caused, whereas mitigation involves responses that will prevent the impact from occurring in the first place or at least reduce its severity. Adaptation might involve changing agricultural activities in response to rising temperatures, for example. Reducing greenhouse gas emissions to reduce temperature rise is the major example of mitigation.

Adaptation is an integral part of the earth-atmosphere system, in which natural adjustments maintain some degree of dynamic equilibrium among its components. Throughout history, humans have also displayed an ability to adapt to changing conditions: current warming is already producing examples of that same adaptability. Farmers have begun to plant or consider planting different crops, or to develop new cultivation techniques. Other industries are likely to adapt also. With time and continued warming, however, the costs of adaptation may eventually become prohibitive, or the cumulative effects of changes may surpass the capacity of society to adjust. Preventive measures will be required.

The Kyoto Protocol

The first global attempt to reduce greenhouse gas emissions through cooperative mitigation came in the 1990s with a series of agreements that produced the Kyoto Protocol. Seen by many as a major step forward, it has had some success in Europe, but many of the nations that signed it are unlikely to meet their targets. Developing nations, some of which—China and India, for example—are major greenhouse gas emitters, were not required to reduce emissions, and the United States, at that time the world's leading producer of greenhouse gases, refused to ratify the accord. The Protocol was signed in 1997 and came into effect in 2005. It established greenhouse-gas emission reductions based on levels that existed in 1990, with signatories agreeing to specific reduction goals, with no constraints on the methods they use to reach them. The targets agreed on by the signatories of the protocol are legally binding, but sanctions for failing to meet the targets are weak, with little incentive for the offending nations to comply. Some flexibility has been introduced into the system through the creation of emissions-trading permits. In their simplest form these allow countries that cannot reduce their emissions to their targeted level to purchase the emissions credits of countries that have surpassed their targets. [*See* Emissions Trading; Kyoto Progress; *and* Kyoto Protocol.]

The debate continues on the necessity for the Kyoto Protocol. Some do not accept the existence of human-induced global warming. They question the science on which it is based and see no need for the protocol (*see, e.g.,* Essex and McKitrick, 2002). Many of the scientific uncertainties upon which these climate skeptics based their arguments have, however, been addressed in the latest IPCC FAR (Hopkin, 2007). Even some who accept global warming question the benefits that Kyoto might bring. They see the costs of implementing the protocol as likely to be greater than the costs of adjusting and adapting to the changes that would accompany warming. The most comprehensive consideration of the economics of climate change—the Stern Report—disputes such thinking, employing economic models to show that the benefits of strong and early action easily exceed the costs of taking little or no action (Stern, 2006). The IPCC has also indicated that mitigation through the stabilization of greenhouse-gas levels can be done at a reasonable cost, with variations according to the level and timing of the targets (IPCC, 2007c).

Mitigation in the energy sector

Since the primary source of increased atmospheric concentrations of carbon dioxide is the burning of carbon-based fuels, the energy sector has received considerable attention in the search for mitigation options. Much energy is used inefficiently, with some studies indicating that, in developed nations, improvements in energy efficiency of at least 30% could be achieved at little or no overall cost to the consumer (Houghton, 2005). Proposals to encourage greater efficiency have included fiscal measures such as taxation. A carbon tax, based on fuel consumption, has been promoted as a means of reducing fossil-fuel use, for example. The resulting higher fuel prices would in theory encourage increased efficiency and the revenue generated could be used for technological development of alternative energy resources or to deal with some of the existing negative impacts of warming. The adoption of renewable-energy technology is still limited on a global scale but gaining momentum, with wind and solar power now widely available, and biomass, tidal, and geothermal energy important regionally.

Carbon sequestration

The atmosphere's natural ability to recycle carbon dioxide during photosynthesis maintained a near equilibrium in the environment's greenhouse gas levels for thousands of years. Photosynthesis absorbs carbon dioxide, retains (sequesters) the carbon, and releases oxygen into the atmosphere. In that way, plant communities became carbon sinks, keeping carbon out of circulation until they died, were harvested, or burned. Emission levels are now so high that photosynthesis cannot keep up. Some of the problems arise from deforestation, which reduces the volume of carbon dioxide that can be recycled. It has therefore been suggested that widespread reforestation and the planting of trees on previously nonforested land would provide a natural method of increasing the rate of recycling and therefore sequestration. The capture of carbon dioxide from fossil-fuel power plants and its subsequent sequestration by injection into geological formations is a new technology that has considerable potential to contribute to future mitigation (IPCC, 2007c). [*See* Carbon Capture and Storage.]

Geoengineering

Among suggestions for dealing with global warming are some that fall into the realm of global environmental engineering, which combines natural environmental processes with the application of technology on a global scale. One such approach is based on the well established observation that increased atmospheric turbidity following major volcanic eruptions reduces the amount of solar radiation reaching the earth's surface and causes lower temperatures. It has been suggested that deliberate injection of particulate matter into the atmosphere would have the same effect (Crutzen, 2006). Simple as it appears on paper—apart from the ethical question of trying to mitigate one atmospheric effect induced by human activities by introducing another—there are serious doubts about the feasibility of the approach (Bengtsson, 2006). While the impact of sulfate injections on global warming should be positive, the impacts in other areas would be negative: potential damage to the ozone layer, for example (Deshler et al., 1992), and an increase in acid rain falling on oceans already experiencing increase acidification from higher carbon dioxide and nitrous oxide concentrations (Solomon et al., 2007). [*See* Geoengineering.]

Manipulation of the oceans to increase their ability to absorb carbon dioxide has also been considered as a means of combating warming. Experiments have shown that fertilizing the oceans with iron would encourage phytoplankton growth and increase the rate of photosynthesis. Additional carbon would be sequestered, but the amounts involved, the scale of the operation required for any real impact, and the high costs mean that it is not a feasible option for reducing or slowing global warming (Buesseler and Boyd, 2003).

STABILIZATION, TARGETS, AND THRESHOLDS

The aim of mitigation is to stabilize greenhouse gas concentrations in the atmosphere and thus control the rise in global temperatures. Specific target concentrations required to control the rising temperature are not well established, but there is increasing recognition that stabilization must take place at carbon dioxide equivalent levels below 550 ppm (Houghton, 2005), while a temperature rise of 2°C above pre-industrial levels is regarded by many as a threshold beyond which major impacts could not be avoided (Hengeveld, 2006). To manintain the increase at less than 2°C, greenhouse-gas concentrations will have to be stabilized at a carbon dioxide equivalent of 450 ppm (IPCC, 2007c). Given the current level of 425 ppm carbon dioxide equivalent, some response is obviously required in the very near future. Financial, behavioral, and institutional barriers to mitigation still exist in some countries, but according to the IPCC, society has a portfolio of technologies, available now or in the near future, with which it can begin the process of stabilization (IPCC, 2007c). A claim that appropriate technology already exists to begin the process of stabilization has also been made by Pacala and Socolow (2004). They envision "stabilization wedges," activities that reduce greenhouse emissions by zero at the outset to one gigaton of carbon per year after 50 years. It is the graphical representation of that increased reduction that provides the concept of the wedge. A combination of wedges using different technologies—some promoting energy efficiency while others reduce deforestation—would be sufficient to stabilize carbon dioxide levels at 500 ppm in 50 years. [*See* Energy Strategies *and* Stabilizing Carbon Emissions.]

Many predictions of future temperatures and their impacts assume a gradual change which can be slowed and eventually reversed by stabilizing and then reducing greenhouse-gas emissions over the next 50 or 100 years. The reality may be much more complex. The IPCC (2007a) has projected, for example, that even if emissions could be stabilized at 2000 levels, warming would continue because of thermal inertia in the system. Some researchers also point to the possibility of rapid, nonlinear responses when certain environmental equilibria (tipping points) are exceeded (Schneider and Lane, 2005). [*See* Tipping Points and Global Change.] Such changes have produced abrupt cooling in Greenland in the past (Hengeveld, 2006). Their causes are not well understood, and the specific temperatures or gas concentrations with which they are associated are as yet unknown. Until research clarifies some of these issues, the possibility exists that the environment might be approaching a threshold beyond which continuing temperature increases will cause dramatic and perhaps irreversible change.

BIBLIOGRAPHY

ACIA. *Impacts of a Warming Arctic: Arctic Climate Impact Assessment.* Cambridge and New York: Cambridge University Press, 2004.

Andronova, N. G., M. E. Schlesinger, and M. E. Mann. "Are Reconstructed Pre-Instrumental Hemispheric Temperatures Consistent with Instrumental Hemispheric Temperatures?" *Geophysical Research Letters* 31, L12202 (2004). DOI: 10.1029/2004GLO19658.

Bengtsson, L. "Geo-Engineering to Confine Climate Change: Is It at All Feasible?" *Climatic Change* 77.3–4 (2006), 229–234. DOI: 10.1007/s10584-006-9133-3.

Berkelmans, R., et al. "A Comparison of the 1998 and 2002 Coral Bleaching Events on the Great Barrier Reef: Spatial Correlation, Patterns, and Predictions." *Coral Reefs* 23.1 (2004), 74–83. DOI: 10.1007/s00338-003-0353-y.

Broecker, W. S. "Thermohaline Circulation, the Achilles Heel of Our Climate System: Will Man-Made CO$_2$ Upset the Current Balance?" *Science* 278 (1997), 1582–1588. DOI: 10.1126/science.278.5343.1582.

Bruce, J., and H. G. Hengeveld. "Our Changing Northern Climate." *Geography* 14.1 (1985), 1–6.

Buesseler, K. O., and P. W. Boyd. "Will Ocean Fertilization Work?" *Science* 300 (2003), 67–68. DOI: 10.1126/science.1082959.

Chen, Z., et al. "Holocene Climate Fluctuations in the Yangtze Delta of Eastern China and the Neolithic Response." *The Holocene* 15.6 (2005), 915–924.

Clausen, M., et al. "Climate Change in Northern Africa: The Past is Not the Future." *Climatic Change* 57.1–2 (2003), 99–118. DOI: 10.1023/A:1022115604225.

Crowley, T. J., and T. S. Lowery. "How Warm Was the Medieval Warm Period?" *Ambio* 29.1 (2000), 51–54.

Crutzen, P. "Albedo Enhancement by Stratospheric Sulfur Injections: A Contribution to Resolve a Policy Dilemma?" *Climatic Change* 77.3–4 (2006), 211–220.

Deshler, T., et al. "Volcanic Aerosol and Ozone Depletion within the Antarctic Polar Vortex during the Austral Spring of 1991." *Geophysical Research Letters* 19 (1992), 1819–1822.

Donner, S. D., T. R. Knutsen, and M. Oppenheimer. "Model-Based Assessment of the Role of Human-Induced Climate Change in the 2005 Caribbean Coral Bleaching Event." *Proceedings of the National Academy of Sciences* 104.13 (2007), 5483–5488. DOI: 10.1073/pnas.0610122104.

Elsasser, H., and Messerli, P. "The Vulnerability of the Snow Industry in the Swiss Alps." *Mountain Research and Development* 21.4 (2001), 335–339.

Emanuel, K. "Increasing Destructiveness of Tropical Cyclones over the Past 30 Years." *Nature* 436 (2005), 686–688. DOI: 10.1038/nature03906.

Essex, C., and R. McKitrick. *Taken by Storm: The Troubled Science, Policy, and Politics of Global Warming.* Toronto: Key Porter Books, 2002. A revised edition was published in 2007.

Folland, C. K., T. R. Karl, and K. Y. Vinnikov. "Observed Climate Variations and Change." In *Climate Change: The IPCC Scientific Assessment*, edited by J. T. Houghton, G. J. Jenkins and J. J. Ephraums, pp. 195–238. Cambridge and New York: Cambridge University Press, 1990.

Gadd, A. J. "Scientific Statements and the Rio Earth Summit." *Weather* 47 (1992), 294–315.

Hansen, B., et al. "Already the Day after Tomorrow?" *Science* 305 (2004), 953–954. DOI: 10.1126/science.1100085.

Hansen, J., and S. Lebedeff. "Global Surface Air Temperatures Update through 1987." *Geophysical Research Letters* 15.4 (1988), 323–326.

Haug, G. H., et al. "Southward Migration of the Intertropical Convergence Zone through the Holocene." *Science* 293 (2001), 1304–1308. DOI: DOI: 10.1126/science.1059725.

Hengeveld, H. *CO₂/Climate Report: 2003–2005 Science Review: A Synthesis of New Research Developments.* Toronto: Environment Canada, 2006.

Henson, R. "The Heat Was on in 2005." *Nature* 438 (2005), 1062. DOI: 10.1038/4381062a.

Hopkin, M. "Climate Skeptics Switch Focus to Economics." *Nature* 445 (2007), 582–583. DOI: 10.1038/445582a.

Houghton, J. "Global Warming." *Reports on Progress in Physics* 68.6 (2005), 1343–1403. DOI: 10.1088/0034-4885/68/6/R02.

Houghton, J. T., G. J. Jenkins, and J. J. Ephraums, eds. *Climate Change: The IPCC Scientific Assessment.* Cambridge and New York: Cambridge University Press, 1990.

Houghton, J. T., et al., eds. *Climate Change 1995: The Science of Climate Change.* United Nations Intergovernmental Panel on Climate Change. Cambridge and New York: Cambridge University Press, 1996.

Houghton, J. T., et al., eds. *Climate Change 2001: The Scientific Basis.* Cambridge and New York: Cambridge University Press, 2001.

Hughes, M. K., and H. F. Diaz. (1994) "Was There a 'Medieval Warm Period,' and If So, Where and When?" *Climatic Change* 26.2–3 (1994), 109–142. DOI: 10.1007/BF01092410.

Hugo, G. J. "Immigration Responses to Global Change in Asia: A Review." *Geographical Research* 44.2 (2006), 155–172. DOI: 10.1111/j.1745-5871.2006.00382.x.

Jennings, A. E., et al. (2006) "Freshwater Forcing from the Greenland Ice Sheet during the Younger Dryas: Evidence from Southeastern Greenland Shelf Cores." *Quaternary Science Reviews* 25. 3–4 (2006), 282–298. DOI: 10.1016/j.quascirev.2005.04.006.

Joerin, U. E., T. F. Stocker, and C. Schlüchter. "Multicentury Glacier Fluctuations in the Swiss Alps during the Holocene." *The Holocene* 16.5 (2006), 697–704. DOI: DOI: 10.1191/0959683606hl964rp.

Jones, P. D., and A. Moberg. "Hemispheric and Large-Scale Surface Air Temperature Variations: An Extensive Revision and Update to 2001." *Journal of Climate* 16.2 (2003), 206–223.

Lamb, H. H. *Climate, History, and the Modern World.* 2d ed. London and New York: Routledge, 1995.

Lund, D. C., J. Lynch-Stieglitz, and W. B. Curry. "Gulf Stream density structure and transport during the past millennium." *Nature* 444 (2006), 601–604. DOI: 10.1038/nature05277.

Mackay, A. W., D. B. Ryves, and P. Rioual. "1000 Years of Climate Variability in Central Asia: Assessing the Evidence for the Medieval Warm Period and Little Ice Age Signals using Diatom-Inferred Snow Depth Model from Lake Baikal (Russia)." *Geophysical Research Abstracts* 7 (2005), 4429.

Malhi, Y., and O. Phillips. "Tropical Forests and Global Atmospheric Change: A Synthesis." *Philosophical Transactions of the Royal Society B* 359.1443 (2004) 549–555.

Mann, M. E., R. S. Bradley, and M. K. Hughes. "Global-Scale Temperature Patterns and Climate Forcing over the Past Six Centuries." *Nature* 392 (1998) 779–787. DOI: 10.1038/33859.

Matthews, J. A., and K. R. Briffa. (2005) "The 'Little Ice Age': Re-evaluation of an Evolving Concept." *Geografiska Annaler, Series A: Physical Geography* 87.1 (2005), 17–36. DOI: 10.1111/j.0435-3676.2005.00242.x.

McIntyre, S., and R. McKitrick. "Hockey Sticks, Principal Components, and Spurious Significance." *Geophysical Research Letters* 32, L03710 (2005). DOI: 10.1029/2004GL021750.

Milly, P. C. D., K. A. Dunne, and A. V. Vecchia. "Global Pattern of Trends in Streamflow and Water Availability in a Changing Climate." *Nature* 438 (2005), 347–350. DOI: 10.1038/nature04312.

Moberg, A., et al. (2005) "Highly Variable Northern Hemisphere Temperatures Reconstructed from Low- and High-Resolution Proxy Data." *Nature* 433 (2005), 613–617. DOI: 10.1038/nature03265.

Myers, N. "Environmental Refugees: A Growing Phenomenon of the 21st Century." *Philosophical Transactions of the Royal Society B* 357.1420 (2002), 609–613.

Ogilvie, A. E. J., and T. Jónsson. "Little Ice Age Research: A Perspective from Iceland." *Climatic Change* 48.1 (2001), 9–51.

Osborne, T. J., and K. R. Briffa. "The Spatial Extent of 20th-Century Warmth in the Context of the Past 1200 Years." *Science* 311 (2006), 841–844. DOI: 10.1126/science.1120514.

Pacala, S., and R. Socolow, "Stability Wedges: Solving the Climate Problem for the Next Fifty Years with Current Technologies." *Science* 305 (2004), 968–972.

Parmesan, C., and G. Yohe. "A Globally Coherent Fingerprint of Climate Change Impacts across Natural Systems." *Nature* 421 (2003), 37–42. DOI: 10.1038/nature01286.

Parry, M., et al., eds. *Climate Change 2007: Climate Change Impacts: Impacts, Adaptation, and Vulnerability: Contribution of Working Group II to the Fourth Assessment Report of the Intergovernmental Panel on Climate Change.* Cambridge and New York: Cambridge University Press, 2007.

Rahmstorf, S. "A Semi-Empirical Approach to Projecting Future Sea-Level Rise." *Science* 315 (2007), 368–370. DOI: 10.1126/science.1135456.

Sarnthein, M., et al. "Centennial-to-Millennial-Scale Periodicities of Holocene Climate and Sediment Injections of the Western Barents Shelf, 75°N." *Boreas* 32.3 (2003), 447–461. DOI: 10.1080/03009480310003351.

Schneider, S. H., and J. Lane. "An Overview of 'Dangerous' Climate Change." In *Avoiding Dangerous Climate Change,* edited by H.J. Schellnbhuber, et al., pp. 7–23. Cambridge and New York: Cambridge University Press, 2005.

Shabbar, A., and B. Bonsal. "An Assessment of Changes in Winter Cold and Warm Spells over Canada." *Natural Hazards* 29.2 (2003), 173–188. DOI: 10.1023/A:1023639209987.

Shine, K., et al. "Radiative Forcing of Climate." In *Climate Change: The IPCC Scientific Assessment,* edited by J. T. Houghton, G. J. Jenkins, and J. J. Ephraums, pp. 41–68. Cambridge: Cambridge University Press, 1990.

Solomon, S., et al., eds. *Climate Change 2007: The Physical Science Basis: The Physical Science Basis: Contribution of Working Group I to the Fourth Assessment Report of the Intergovernmental Panel on Climate Change.* Cambridge and New York: Cambridge University Press, 2007.

Stern, N. *The Economics of Climate Change: The Stern Review.* Cambridge and New York: Cambridge University Press, 2007.

Teller, J. T., D. W. Leverington, and J. D. Mann. "Freshwater Outbursts to the Oceans from Glacial Lake Agassiz and Their Role in Climate Change during the Last Deglaciation." *Quarternary Science Reviews* 21.8–9 (2002), 879–887. DOI: 10.1016/S0277-3791(01)00145-7.

Van Kooten, G. C., L. M. Arthur, and W. R. Wilson. "Potential to Sequester Carbon in Canadian Forests: Some Economic Considerations." *Canadian Public Policy* 18.2 (1992), 127–138.

Watson, R. T., et al. "Environmental Health Implications of Global Climate Change." *Journal of Environmental Monitoring* 7 (2005), 834–843. DOI: 10.1039/b504683a.

Westerling, A. L., et al. "Warming and Earlier Spring Increase Western U.S. Forest Wildfire Activity." *Science* 313 (2006), 940–943. DOI: 10.1126/science.1128834.

Yang, B., et al. "General Characteristics of Temperature Variation in China during the Last Two Millennia." *Geophysical Research Letters* 29.9 (2002), 1324. DOI: 10.1029/2001GL014485.

—David D. Kemp

GLOBALIZATION AND THE ENVIRONMENT

Global commerce has been an important feature of the growth of the capitalist system for half a millennium. Trade three or four centuries ago involved the shipment of luxury goods and bulk commodities, such as basic foodstuffs, thousands of miles. The last century saw a rapid increase in international efforts to encourage and manage the global economy, and in the number of transnational and international organizations that participate in it. The last few decades have seen a rapid growth in globalization, with international trade, finance, investment, and production consistently growing much faster than total economic output.

International commerce has always had an impact on the environment. Long-distance trade and investment allowed resources to be extracted at far greater rates than local populations could have done, and agricultural production for international markets displaced native ecosystems. The impact of contemporary globalization, however, is different in both scale and kind. The scale of the contemporary global economy magnifies the traditional environmental effects of economic production, while technologies create global environmental hazards, such as global warming and widespread extinctions, that were unknown to previous generations. Yet globalization also helps create the surplus wealth that is necessary for environmental protection and makes countries more willing to participate in international efforts to protect the environment.

CONTEMPORARY GLOBALIZATION

Globalization means an unprecedented increase in economic integration. Globalization is often taken at its most basic to refer to increases in trade and capital flows across borders. Both of these are measures of scale, and while they suggest a level of integration higher than it was half a century ago but perhaps not qualitatively different from that of a century ago. Yet there are a number of aspects of contemporary globalization that suggest basic structural changes in the international political economy.

One of the most notable aspects of the global economy since World War II has been its continual expansion. Even through the crises of the 1970s and 1980s, average income per capita has continued to increase, and international trade has increased even faster. Parts of the world have seen their growth slow for significant periods, but overall global economic activity and output have increased steadily and will continue to do so. The rise in average per capita income has been so great that, by the middle of the 1990s, average global per capita GNP (i.e., the average for all countries) was roughly the same as the per capita GNP of the richest country in the world a century earlier.

The contemporary global economy is becoming increasingly postindustrial. It is conventional wisdom that, as countries develop economically, agriculture as a proportion of the total economy decreases while industry's share increases. This is still the case in many lower- and middle-income economies; between 1980 and 1995, agriculture's share of low-income economies decreased from 34 to 25%, while industry's share increased from 32 to 38%. In wealthier countries, however, there is a different trend. In these countries, the importance of industry is declining, and many of the wealthiest economies are becoming dominated by services. In the United States, for example, roughly three-quarters of the economy is generated by services.

The distinction between low- and high-income countries highlights a disturbing feature of the contemporary global economy that is not apparent from figures on aggregate international economic growth, namely, the increasing disparity between the richest countries and the poorest. The per capita income of the richest countries in the world is 400–500 times greater than the per capita income of the poorest. Most of the world's industrialized countries show slow but consistent economic growth. Elsewhere, growth rates across and within regions vary dramatically. Some countries in sub-Saharan Africa are poorer, on a per capita basis, than they were two or three decades ago. At the same time, other countries, primarily in the Asia-Pacific region but also in South America, have transformed themselves from primarily agrarian to primarily industrial countries over the same period. This has had the effect of making generalizations like "third world countries" and "developing countries" less meaningful; an industrializing country such as South Korea has far more in common economically with the United States than it does with countries that remain agrarian and poor.

GLOBALIZATION AND ECONOMIC INTEGRATION

Several other factors contribute to contemporary globalization. Some of these, notably the globalization of production, are purely economic. Whereas until recently goods were usually made in one country and then traded internationally as finished goods, it is increasingly the case that the various parts of a product are made and assembled wherever it is most cost-efficient, blurring the concept of a product's country of origin. An automobile may be designed in the U.S., for example, and assembled in Japan from parts manufactured in Southeast Asia. A related phenomenon is the increasing degree to which international commerce happens within companies rather than between them. Trade between two countries now often consists of one part of a multinational corporation (MNC) transferring goods or services to another part of the same corporation rather than one national firm selling a finished good or service to another.

This globalization of production allows MNCs to perform each specific economic function wherever it can be done most cost-effectively, but it also makes it difficult for governments to regulate production processes. At the same time, private international capital flows can now swamp the efforts of governments and central banks to manage their currency exchange rates. This means that government policy that is not interpreted as market-friendly by the international capital markets can result in rapid and sharp depreciations of national currencies, which is a major added cost of adopting such policies. The globalization of both production and capital thus has the effect of limiting the ability of states to manage their own economies and to adopt policies that are not seen as market-friendly. Global economic forces such as MNCs and capital markets are increasingly important relative to states as sources of economic governance.

Along with this globalization of production and decision-making comes a globalization of consumption. With increased flows of trade and capital come increasing flows of technology, innovation, and culture. On the one hand this kind of globalization makes new technologies available worldwide, improving living standards and increasing the pace of innovation as new ideas spread at the unprecedented speed of modern communication. On the other hand, it homogenizes cultures, as the cultural identity of individual places is replaced by companies, goods, and services that are the same worldwide, creating a homogenized world culture based on the lowest common denominator of Western multinational exports. This latter phenomenon is often referred to as cultural colonialism or cultural imperialism, because most of the culture being internationalized comes from a few developed countries, particularly the United States.

PROBLEMS OF GLOBALIZATION

Other criticisms relate to the effects of globalization on local governance. As suggested above, increased globalization of finance and production diminish the decision-making autonomy of states. The broader phenomenon of the geographical separation of the production of goods and services from their consumption diminishes local empowerment and governance to the extent that local economic production is held captive by the effects of markets abroad. This phenomenon is exacerbated by advances in telecommunications and transportation. Day-to-day decisions on local production can now for the first time be made abroad, further reducing the need for local input in decision-making. Decreases in the costs of transportation increasingly tie local production to conditions elsewhere. At the same time, much of the local decision-making power that is lost is gained by MNCs, whose priorities are often very different from those of local communities. Because these communities often have far fewer resources than MNCs with which to lobby (or bribe) governments, they find it difficult to compete with MNCs for governmental attention.

Another adverse effect of the globalization-driven separation of production from consumption is the protection of consumers from the effects of production. The most straightforward example of this phenomenon is the demand from the industrialized world for resources from the developing world. The depletion of local resources has often provided a check to economic excesses, but overconsumption can now deplete resources on a global rather than just a local scale. If a resource is depleted locally, it is lost only to that local community; if it is depleted globally, it is lost to humankind forever. A second example is the international trade in pollution. If richer countries can export pollution to poorer countries, then a natural check on local pollution levels is lost, and problems of pollution threaten to become global.

Proponents of globalization argue that it allows more and faster economic growth than would otherwise be the case. Some opponents agree but suggest that such untrammeled growth is a serious problem. These critics believe that globalization promotes a culture of consumption, at the expense of other potential social and cultural values, that unlimited consumption must necessarily eventually deplete available natural resources and diminish the ability of the environment to absorb pollution,

and that globalization thus accelerates the rate at which we approach natural limits to economic growth.

THE GLOBAL ECONOMY AND THE GLOBAL ENVIRONMENT

All countries impose some regulation on commerce and industry for environmental reasons, but the extent of that regulation varies widely and in some developing countries is clearly inadequate. Some experts argue that globalization forces better-regulated countries to deregulate to the international lowest common denominator of environmental management. To the extent that environmental regulations impose costs on businesses, increased regulation makes production more expensive and thus less competitive internationally, while decreasing regulation makes production cheaper and thus more competitive. In a global economy in which MNCs can easily move production facilities wherever costs are lowest, there is an incentive for governments to weaken environmental regulation, either to attract foreign businesses into the country, or to discourage domestic businesses from moving to less-regulated countries. Globalization can thus discourage environmental regulation in favor of maintaining a country's international competitiveness.

Others argue, however, that while it makes sense for companies to worry about competitiveness, it does not make sense for countries. By this logic, environmental regulations do create costs, as they would in a nonglobalized economy, but they do not result in a loss of national competitiveness. They suggest that there is little evidence that MNCs are being drawn to countries with laxer environmental regulation and that increased environmental regulation can create new environmental management industries in a country that would not otherwise have developed them. Globalization can also give environmentally conscious governments the tools to encourage increased environmental regulation abroad, tools they might otherwise not have.

Many governments, particularly of developing countries, are limited in their freedom to protect their environments by their foreign debt. High debt requires that countries ensure strong growth in exports in order to service that debt. This can force governments to promote higher, less sustainable rates of resource extraction and to focus on environmentally damaging cash crops in order to generate the needed exports. Such export industries (e.g., unsustainable logging) are often damaging to the environment.

GLOBAL COMMONS

The global commons includes those areas of the planet that are not within national jurisdictions, those environmental goods and bads that cross national boundaries as a matter of course, and elements of the ecosystem that are part of the common heritage of humanity. Examples include the high seas and the upper atmosphere, migrating species, and biodiversity. The economic expansion associated with globalization has given the human economy a far greater ability than it has ever had to exploit the global commons. It is in the nature of commons resources that they are difficult to manage, because even though the community of users has an incentive to manage the commons in a sustainable way, individual users have an incentive to overuse it. This was not a problem on a planetary scale until well into this century, when new technologies made possible the depletion of fisheries on an oceanic scale, the injection of sufficient chemicals into the air to deplete the ozone layer on a global scale, and the extinction of species at an unprecedented rate.

Commons problems are difficult to deal with, but not impossible. Successful international action has been taken on ozone-depleting substances, on a number of fisheries issues, and on the trade in endangered species, all of which are discussed elsewhere in this encyclopedia. The climate-change issue shows signs of meaningful international action; whether this will lead to successful abatement of the problem remains to be seen. Yet global economic expansion will inevitably increase pressures on the global commons, and multilateral efforts may be insufficient to cope with these mounting pressures.

The international community has come increasingly to recognize that issues of economy and environment are intimately and necessarily related; that recognition has arisen from and in turn reinforced the movement for sustainable development. Most countries have signed the Rio Declaration, formally committing themselves to that principle, and many of the international organizations, such as the World Trade Organization, that regulate the global economy officially recognize its centrality to the global economy. Skeptics suggest that this recognition is meaningless in the absence of specific limitations on behavior and that it is in any case unclear exactly what sustainable development means and how it might be put into operation. Optimists believe that the adoption of the term indicates a broader trend toward the incorporation of environmental sensibilities into the management of global economic affairs. The truth probably lies somewhere in between.

[*See also* Economic Levels; Industrial Ecology; *and* Trade and Environment.]

BIBLIOGRAPHY

Brecher, J., and T. Costello. *Global Village or Global Pillage.* Boston: South End Press, 1995. A radical contemporary critique of globalization, whose second edition was published in 1998.

Caves, R., J. Frankel, and R. Jones. *World Trade and Payments: An Introduction.* 7th ed. New York: Harper Collins, 1996. A classic introductory international economic text, whose tenth edition was published in 2007.

Fuller, K. "Globalization and the Environment." Speech, April 2, 2003. http://www.worldwildlife.org. (accessed May 30, 2008).

Helleiner, E. *States and the Reemergence of Global Finance: From Bretton Woods to the 1990s.* Ithaca, N.Y.: Cornell University Press, 1994. A discussion of the globalization of finance.

Keohane, R. O., and J. S. Nye. *Power and Interdependence: World Politics in Transition.* Boston: Litttle, Brown, 1977. One of the earliest statements of the globalization hypothesis.

Krasner, S., ed. *International Regimes.* Ithaca, N.Y.: Cornell University Press, 1983. A collection of approaches to the study of international economic institutions and governance.

Krugman, P. *The Age of Diminished Expectations: U.S. Economic Policy in the 1990s.* 3d ed. Cambridge, Mass.: MIT Press, 1997. Collection of essays for nonspecialists.

Najam, A., D. Runnalls, and M. Halle. "Environment and Globalization: Five Propositions." Winnipeg: Manitoba: International Institute for Sustainable Development, 2007. http://www.iisd.org (accessed May 30, 2008).

Spero, J. E., and J. A. Hart. *The Politics of International Economic Relations.* 5th ed. New York: St. Martin's Press, 1997. A good undergraduate survey.

Speth, J. G., ed. *Worlds Apart: Globalization and the Environment.* Washington, D.C.: Island Press, 2003.

World Bank. *The World Development Report.* New York and Oxford: Oxford University Press, various years. A source for various analyses of contemporary global economic issues and for comparative statistics.

OTHER RESOURCES

Economic Globalization and the Environment Program at the Pacific Institute (http://www.pacinst.org; accessed May 30, 2008).

Globalization and the Environment, Department of Economics, University of Birmingham (http://www.economics.bham.ac.uk; accessed May 30, 2008).

"Understanding the Face of Globalization." University of Wisconsin, Milwaukee, Center for International Education (http://www.uwm.edu/Dept/CIE/Resources/globalization/index.html; accessed May 30, 2008).

—J. SAMUEL BARKIN, REVISED BY DAVID J. CUFF

GREENHOUSE EFFECT

The potential of the atmosphere to trap solar radiation was proposed as early as 1827 by the mathematician and physicist Joseph Fourier. This mechanism is called the greenhouse effect, a term coined by Svante Arrhenius in 1896, who was the first to argue that changes in the level of carbon dioxide in the atmosphere could have a significant effect on surface temperature. The greenhouse effect is now scientifically well established and is rooted in basic thermodynamics. The natural greenhouse effect makes our planet much more habitable, 33°C warmer than it would otherwise be. Also scientifically well-established is the intensification of the greenhouse effect by human-induced emissions of greenhouse gases.

Since the second half of the nineteenth century, the global average surface temperature has risen approximately 0.75°C. Through 2006, eleven of the last twelve years rank among the twelve warmest years on record. Many of the findings referred to in this article are taken from the peer-reviewed, government-approved Intergovernmental Panel on Climate Change (IPCC; Solomon et al., 2007, and Parry et al., 2007) Assessment Reports, which present the best approximation of a worldwide consensus on climate-change science every five to six years. There is now overwhelming scientific evidence that the primary driver of this observed warming, particularly the rapid warming of the last 40 years, is emissions of greenhouse gases from human activities. Warming has been linked to other changes that can already be seen around the world, including melting mountain glaciers and polar ice, rising and increasingly acidic seas, increasing severity of droughts, heat waves, fires, hurricanes, and changes in the life cycles and ranges of plants and animals.

ENERGY BALANCE

What keeps a house warm in the winter? Heat is continually flowing out through the walls and roof, through the windows and doors, so what stops the house from getting colder and colder? Some source—a gas furnace, a woodstove, electric heaters—must supply heat to replace what is being lost. If energy enters the house at the same rate at which it is being lost, the house is said to be in energy balance, creating an equilibrium in temperature inside the house.

The same holds for the Earth and other planets. Energy, virtually all of it in the form of sunlight, arrives at the Earth. In turn, Earth loses energy to the cold vacuum of space. The rate at which Earth loses energy is given by a law of physics stating that all objects lose energy to their surroundings in the form of radiation. The higher the temperature, the greater the loss rate. Suppose Earth were so hot that it was losing energy at a greater rate than incoming sunlight could replace it. Then there would be a net loss of energy and the planet would cool. As it cooled, the energy loss rate would drop. Eventually the loss would become equal to the energy supplied in the incoming sunlight, and Earth would be in energy balance at a new, lower equilibrium temperature. If the planet became too cool, it would lose energy at a lower rate than the incoming solar energy replaced it, and Earth would experience a net energy gain and heat up. As it heated, the loss rate would increase until it just balanced the incoming sunlight. Again, Earth would achieve energy balance at a new, higher temperature. When there is a balance between the incoming sunlight and the energy lost to space, Earth's temperature remains constant.

Not only is the energy-loss rate dependent on temperature, but so is the form of the energy being lost. Any object surrounded by a vacuum loses energy by electromagnetic radiation. The hotter an object, the higher the frequency and shorter the wavelength of the dominant radiation it emits. Radio waves have the lowest frequency and longest wavelength, followed by microwaves, infrared, visible light, ultraviolet, X-rays, and gamma rays. The Sun, at 6,000°C surface temperature, emits primarily visible light. A hot stove burner glows a dull red and emits a mix of infrared and visible light. And Earth itself, a cooler object, emits primarily infrared radiation.

Knowing the rate at which solar energy reaches Earth and the mathematical relationship between temperature and infrared radiant energy loss, it is a simple matter to calculate this equilibrium temperature and obtain a reasonable estimate of the global average temperature measured from space. The result, for Earth, is about −18°C. Our simple energy balance model predicts a temperature that seems cold, since most of Earth's surface is well above freezing. In fact, Earth's average surface temperature is about 15°C, some 33°C higher than the predicted equilibrium from energy balance alone. The discrepancy arises from the natural greenhouse effect.

THE GREENHOUSE EFFECT

On average, the rate at which solar energy arrives at the top of Earth's atmosphere is approximately 1,368 watts on every square meter oriented at right angles to the incoming sunlight. Accounting for Earth's spherical shape and the fact that only the daytime half of the planet faces the Sun, this is an average of 342 watts per square meter of solar energy for Earth's entire surface averaged over a full day. For energy balance, Earth must return energy to space at the same rate. Around 31% of incoming sunlight is reflected back into space,

most of it by clouds but some by ice, snow, deserts, and other light-colored surfaces. Another 20% or so of the incident solar energy is absorbed in the atmosphere, directly heating it. The remainder—nearly 50% of the total—penetrates the atmosphere and is absorbed directly by Earth's surface. The surface warms, and re-emits energy, primarily as infrared radiation. (The evaporation of water is an additional source of energy that leaves the surface and is absorbed in the atmosphere when water vapor condenses into clouds.) The atmosphere is much less transparent to infrared radiation. Certain naturally occurring gases and particles—most notably greenhouse gases and clouds—absorb 80–90% of the infrared radiation emitted at the surface and re-emit it in all directions, both up to space and back down toward the surface, hindering its ability to escape from the atmosphere. This trapping of infrared energy heats the lower layers of the atmosphere, warming the surface further, which emits infrared radiation at a still greater rate, and so on, until the infrared radiation emitted to space is in balance with the absorbed energy from sunlight and the other forms of energy coming and going from the surface (e.g., rising plumes of convective energy or of water vapor which carry a great deal of energy from the surface to the clouds where it is released by condensation). The result is an Earth in energy balance but with a surface temperature significantly higher than it would be in the absence of greenhouse gases.

Comparing Earth to Mars and Venus demonstrates the importance of greenhouse gases in creating a climate conducive to life. A simple energy-balance calculation neglecting Mars' atmosphere suggests a surface temperature around −60°C. In fact, Mars' surface temperature is only a little warmer, about −50°C, because its atmosphere is so thin that it provides little greenhouse warming. Venus, on the other hand, is closer to the Sun, and the simple calculation suggests a surface temperature around 50°C, but Venus's surface temperature is much hotter, about 500°C. Venus' atmosphere is composed primarily of the greenhouse gas carbon dioxide (CO_2). Consequently, Venus has a "runaway" greenhouse effect that greatly increases its temperature.

HUMANS ACTIVITIES AND THE INTENSIFYING GREENHOUSE EFFECT

Human activities, predominantly the burning of fossil fuels, are increasing the concentrations of greenhouse gases in the atmosphere and intensifying the greenhouse effect. Climatologists characterize the effect of a given atmospheric constituent by its radiative forcing, the rate at which it alters absorbed solar or outgoing infrared energy. Emissions of greenhouse gases add to the "blanket" of heat-trapping gases, increasing the Earth's temperature, a positive radiative forcing. Water vapor is the most important greenhouse gas, though it is not changed very much directly by human activities—only indirectly by global warming that changes rates of evaporation and evapotranspiration, and thus the amount of water vapor in the atmosphere. This indirect effect on water-vapor concentrations can have a large feedback effect on heat trapping.

CO_2 is the most important of the greenhouse gases emitted by human activities in terms of its direct effect on climate, but other gases play a significant role too. Human-induced, or anthropogenic, emissions of greenhouse gases also include methane, nitrous oxide, a host of industrial gases that do not appear naturally in the atmosphere, and, indirectly, ozone in the lower atmosphere, formed as a component of smog. On a molecule-for-molecule basis, most other greenhouse gases are far more potent absorbers of infrared radiation than CO_2, but they are released in much smaller quantities, so their overall effect on climate is also smaller.

The second most prevalent anthropogenic greenhouse gas is methane. One methane molecule is roughly 30 times more effective at heat-trapping than one CO_2 molecule, although this comparison varies with the timescale involved and the presence of other pollutants. Whereas CO_2 increases tend to persist in the atmosphere for centuries or longer, methane typically disappears in decades, making its warming potential relative to that of CO_2 lower on longer time scales. Currently, the radiative forcing from anthropogenic methane is slightly less than one-third that of CO_2.

Together, nitrous oxide and halocarbons account for approximately the same level of radiative forcing as methane. Halocarbons include chlorofluorocarbons (CFCs), which are also the leading cause of stratospheric ozone depletion. Newer halocarbons do not cause severe ozone depletion but are still powerful greenhouse gases. They are hundreds to thousands of times more potent than carbon dioxide, molecule for molecule, and remain in the atmosphere for centuries to millennia but appear in much lower concentrations than carbon dioxide and methane. A number of other trace gases contribute a small amount of additional forcing. All the gases mentioned so far are well mixed, meaning that they persist long enough to be distributed in roughly even concentrations throughout the troposphere, the lowest 10 km of the atmosphere.

Finally, ozone itself is also a greenhouse gas. Ozone occurs naturally in the stratosphere and absorbs incoming UV radiation. Ozone in the troposphere, however, is a potent component of smog, resulting largely from motor vehicle emissions. Tropospheric ozone contributes about one-fourth of the radiative forcing of CO_2, although unlike the well-mixed gases, tropospheric ozone tends to be limited to industrialized regions, and is of great concern for is negative health impacts as well as its climatic influences. Often, ozone depletion and climate change are conflated, but the two are distinct problems. Ozone depletion in the upper atmosphere eventually will come under control because of the 1987 Montreal Protocol, an international agreement that bans the production of the CFCs, while large-scale changes to our energy and transportation systems will be needed to mitigate climate change.

Fossil-fuel combustion, and to a lesser extent agricultural and other industrial processes, also produce emissions that create particulate matter. Coal-fired power plants burning high-sulfur coal, in particular, emit gases that become sulfate aerosols that reflect incoming solar energy and produce a cooling effect (negative radiative forcing). Natural aerosols that produce a cooling effect are also produced during volcanic eruptions and the evaporation of sea water producing salt crystals, as well as from emissions of hydrocarbons in forested areas. Conversely, diesel engines and some biomass burning produce black aerosols such as soot, which absorb the Sun's energy and, depending on circumstances, can warm the climate. Aerosol particles also affect radiative forcing indirectly. For example, they act as "seeds" for the condensation of water droplets to form clouds, affecting the color, size and number of cloud droplets and thus, in aggregate, probably temporarily offsetting some greenhouse warming. Finally, land-use activities such as deforestation contribute to greenhouse gas emissions, a positive forcing, and can change the Earth's albedo, or reflectivity, by, for example, replacing "dark" forest by "light" agricultural land, a negative forcing. [See Albedo.] The aggregate effects of land use changes on temperature trends is not yet well established because of the complexity of the system in which different processes have opposite effects.

Current estimates make the overall influence of human activities roughly equivalent to the positive radiative forcing of increased carbon dioxide concentrations alone, with the positive forcing of other gases and dark aerosols roughly offset by the negative forcing of direct and indirect aerosol effects and land-use changes. While scientists are very confident that the net forcing is positive, they are still uncertain of its magnitude and the magnitude of various components, particularly the net negative forcing from aerosols.

Another important influence on the climate system, one which is not affected by human activities, is the variation in the Sun's energy output. Long-term variations in solar output, from variability in the Sun itself or from changes in the Earth's orbit and tilt (known as Milankovitch cycles), have substantially affected Earth's climate over periods of tens of thousands of years. The sunspot cycle also has a small effect on solar output (about 0.1%). There are many hypotheses for Sun-driven climate change, but none is a plausible explanation of the recent climate warming. [See Solar Variability and Climate].

HUMAN AND NATURAL RESPONSES TO CLIMATE CHANGE

The greenhouse effect and its intensification by human-induced emissions of greenhouse gases are well-understood and solidly grounded in basic science. Likewise, observed warming is now unequivocal, and many impacts of that warming can already be observed around the world. Nevertheless, the future effects of climate change are highly uncertain, compounded by the global scale of the problem and by the fact that climate change is not just a scientific topic but also a matter of public and political debate. There are two general sources of uncertainty in projecting future climate change: what we do, and how the natural climate system responds. Uncertainty over what we do incorporates a broad range of social factors: the world population, the standards of living they will demand, and the extent to which development goals will be achieved through greenhouse gas-emitting energy systems and land-clearing activities. The second component of uncertainty is the response of the climate system to increasing greenhouse gas concentrations—the extent of warming, the effect of warming on cloudiness and the natural uptake of carbon by the ocean and growing vegetation, and so on.

Policy decisions can strongly influence the first source of uncertainty (future emissions) but will have little influence on the second source (climate response to emissions). We cannot know precisely how severe the impacts will be for a specific trajectory of future emissions, but we can confidently say that the severity will be reduced if emissions are reduced. In general terms, climate policy manages risk: assessing the potential impacts of climate change, judging how likely it is that various impacts will occur, and ultimately making judgments about which risks to avoid—by adaptation for those climate changes that cannot be prevented, and by mitigation of emissions to reduce the likelihood of more dangerous impacts.

[*See also* Climate Models and Uncertainty; Greenhouse Gas Emissions; Greenhouse Gases; Global Dimming; *and* Global Warming.]

BIBLIOGRAPHY

Bard, E., and M. Frank. "Climate Change and Solar Variability: What's New under the Sun?" *Earth and Planetary Science Letters* 248.1–2 (2006), 1–14. DOI: 10.1016/j.epsl.2006.06.016.
Lockwood, M., and C. Fröhlich. "Recent Oppositely Directed Trends in Solar Climate Forcings and the Global Mean Surface Air Temperature." *Proceedings of the Royal Society A* 463 (2007), 2447–2460. DOI: 10.1098/rspa.2007.1880.
Parry, M., et al., eds. *Climate Change 2007: Climate Change Impacts: Impacts, Adaptation, and Vulnerability: Contribution of Working Group II to the Fourth Assessment Report of the Intergovernmental Panel on Climate Change.* Cambridge and New York: Cambridge University Press, 2007.
Solomon, S., et al., eds. *Climate Change 2007: The Physical Science Basis: The Physical Science Basis: Contribution of Working Group I to the Fourth Assessment Report of the Intergovernmental Panel on Climate Change.* Cambridge and New York: Cambridge University Press, 2007.

—MICHAEL D. MASTRANDREA AND STEPHEN H. SCHNEIDER

GREENHOUSE GAS EMISSIONS

See Appendix.

GREENHOUSE GASES

These are the gases that absorb infrared radiation thereby reducing the loss of heat from Earth to space. A full accounting would include water vapor, but it is usual to discuss only those gases, natural and unnatural, that are influenced by human activity.

Warming of the lower atmosphere is caused by what in climate-change models is called radiative forcing, the change in net radiation at the top of the troposphere because of a change in either incoming solar short wave radiation or outgoing infrared radiation. [*See* Greenhouse Effect.] Radiative forcing is caused

naturally by changes in such factors as solar radiation, planetary albedo, and atmospheric aerosol concentration, and while these factors still exist, they have been surpassed by anthropogenic forcing agents such as greenhouse gases emitted by human activities. Since increasing greenhouse gas concentrations contribute to the retention of energy in the troposphere, they are considered positive forcing agents. The potency or effectiveness of a greenhouse gas in this regard is expressed by global warming potential (GWP) which compares the rate of radiative forcing that would result from emission of one kilogram of the greenhouse gas to that from emission of one kilogram of carbon dioxide over a given period of time. The GWP of a greenhouse gas over 100 years, for instance, will be called its 100-year GWP. On this scale, carbon dioxide is assigned a value of one.

For comparative purposes it is sometimes appropriate to express the contribution of all greenhouse gases as CO_2 equivalent, that is, the CO_2 concentration alone that would have the same effect as all greenhouse gases combined.

THE GASES

Under the Kyoto Protocol, there are six gases or groups of chemicals whose concentrations are monitored. [*See* IPCC: Intergovernmental Panel on Climate Change *and* Kyoto Protocol.] They are listed below roughly in order of their contributions to the greenhouse effect: that contribution depends upon the abundance (concentration) of the gas as well as its GWP.

Carbon dioxide (CO_2), GWP 1

This comes mainly from combustion of fossil fuels, trees, and other biomass, but it released also from limestone ($CaCO_3$) in the manufacture of cement. Land-use change and forestry practice can affect concentrations of CO_2 in the atmosphere—directly, by the burning of trees, and indirectly by the removal of forest that would otherwise serve as a carbon sink by absorbing CO_2 as trees grow.

Methane (CH_4), GWP 21

This is the main constituent of natural gas and occurs naturally in coal beds, so some is released during the production of coal, crude oil, and natural gas. (Gas wasted in crude-oil production usually is burned off in flares, releasing CO_2 as a combustion product which has a lower GWP than methane.) The gas is also produced by decomposition of organic materials in landfills and in swamps and is emitted by belching livestock.

Nitrous oxide (N_2O), GWP 310

Much is produced by high-temperature combustion in motor vehicles and power plants where the nitrogen in air combines with oxygen. Another major source is chemical fertilizers rich in nitrates. [*See* Nitrogen Cycle.]

Hydrofluorocarbons (HFCs), GWP up to 11,700

This is a family of chemicals produced artificially as replacements for chlorofluorocarbons (CFCs) which have been found

TABLE 1. Various Greenhouse Gases as Proportion of Total Emissions

	Developed	Developing	Least Developed
CO_2	81%	41%	5%
N_2O	6	10	12
CH_4	11	16	21
Fluor gases	2	0	0
LUCF	0	33	62

SOURCE: World Resources Institute, 2005 (data for year 2000)

to damage the ozone layer in the stratosphere and are banned in developed countries. They are used as refrigerants, propellants, and foaming agents for plastics.

Perfluorocarbons (PFCs), GWP 7,000–9,000

These chemicals are largely byproducts of aluminum production and semiconductor manufacturing.

Sulfur hexafluoride (SF_6), GWP: 23,900

This is produced for use as an insulator in various kinds of electrical equipment. This, together with the previous two man-made chemical categories, despite their very high GWP values, contribute roughly 2% of the world's greenhouse gas impact.

EMISSIONS AND ECONOMIC LEVEL

In agrarian economies with little heavy industry or electrical generation, methane is often the predominant greenhouse gas. In such countries, land-use change and forestry practice (LUCF) such as tropical deforestation account for a large share of emissions. In more industrial countries, electrical generation, transportation, industry, and heating of buildings contribute carbon dioxide, methane, and nitrous oxide, while CO_2 from land-use change is not significant (see Table 1).

Concentrations and GWPs for the six gases can be combined to yield one value expressed as million metric tons of CO_2 equivalent to make comparisons possible. On this basis—using data for the year 2000 (the most recent available in 2007)—the U.S. accounts for roughly 21% of world total, China 15%, and the European Union roughly 14%. The top ten countries account for 75% of emissions, while the top 25 account for 83%. [See Total Emissions and Emission Intensity, Year 2000, in Appendix.]

BIBLIOGRAPHY

Navigating the Numbers: Greenhouse Gas Data and International Climate Policy. Washington, D.C: World Resources Institute, 2005. http://www.wri.org/publication/navigating-the-numbers (accessed May 31, 2008).

—DAVID J. CUFF

GREENLAND ICE SHEET

The Greenland ice sheet is the second largest ice mass on Earth and is about one-tenth the volume of the Antarctic ice sheet. It is the only significant ice mass in the Arctic today. [See Antarctica and Climate Change; and Ice Sheets.] It is an ice-age relict that overlies a bowl-shaped continent almost completely fringed by coastal mountains.

PHYSICAL-GEOGRAPHIC SETTING

The ice sheet extends from about 60° to 83°N over a distance of 2,400 km in the North Atlantic Ocean. The ice sheet covers 1.71 million km^2, or roughly 80% of the surface of Greenland. It consists of a northern dome and a southern dome, with maximum elevations of 3,230 m and 2,850 m, respectively, linked by a long saddle with elevations around 2,500 m. Its total volume is about 2.85 million km^3, which, if it were to melt entirely, would raise global sea level by about 7.2 m. The ice sheet has an average thickness of 1,670 m and reaches a maximum of 3,300 m in the center. The bedrock surface below the ice sheet is an extensive flat area near sea level, which would rebound by as much as 1,000 m if the ice sheet were removed (Figure 1).

Precipitation over Greenland generally decreases from south to north, ranging from about 2,500 mm per year in the southeast to less than 150 mm per year in interior northeastern Greenland. The southern high precipitation zone is largely determined by the Icelandic low and the resulting onshore flow which is forced to ascend the surface of the ice sheet. In contrast to Antarctica, summer temperatures on Greenland are high enough to cause widespread summer melting. This results in an ablation zone with negative mass balance all around its perimeter. Ablation rates are highest over the southwestern part of the ice sheet where they typically reach values on the order of 5 m per year. Most of the meltwater flows into the sea, either by surface runoff or by draining to the glacial bed via crevasses. The equilibrium line, which separates the ablation zone from the accumulation zone, ranges in elevation from 1,600–1,800 m in the southwest to less than 1,000 m along the northern coast. This setting makes the ice sheet sensitive to a warming climate. Surface melting is already an important component of its mass budget, and higher temperatures will raise both the amount of melting and the area over which the melting takes place.

Because of its comparatively high coastal temperatures, Greenland has no major ice shelves, only a few small ones along the northern and northeastern coasts. Ice not lost by ablation is discharged into the ocean by the calving of icebergs from outlet glaciers, in roughly the same amount as runoff. Iceberg calving takes place where the ice flow channelled into fast moving outlet glaciers reaches the oceans. Some glaciers flow at speeds of up to several km per year. Jakobshavn Isbræ on the western side of the ice sheet is the fastest glacier on Earth, with velocities of up to 12 km per year or 32 m per day. Changes in oceanic temperature are suspected to control the calving dynamics and flow speeds at the margin.

The Greenland ice sheet affects the global environment through its high albedo and its elevated topography. These act as cooling surfaces for the atmospheric heat balance and are an effective barrier to atmospheric circulation patterns. The loss of meltwater and icebergs to the ocean plays an important role in the freshwater balance of the North Atlantic Ocean and potentially in

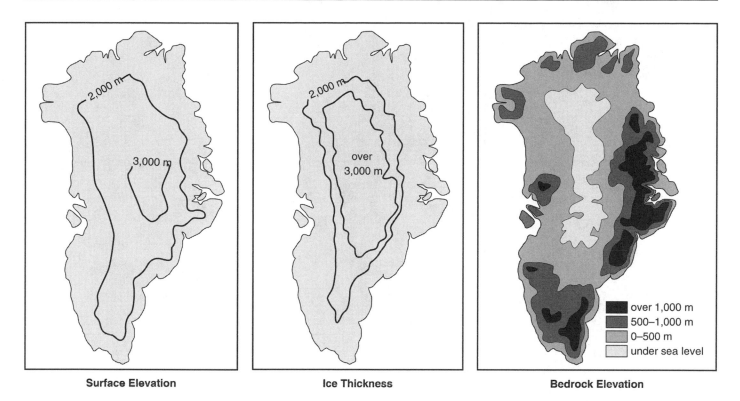

Surface Elevation   **Ice Thickness**   **Bedrock Elevation**

over 1,000 m
500–1,000 m
0–500 m
under sea level

variations in the meridional (north-south) overturning circulation, and hence, in the strength and position of the Gulf Stream.

RECENT GLACIAL HISTORY

Glacier ice probably appeared first on Greenland in the late Miocene some 7 million years ago, but a continent-wide ice sheet did not form until the late Pliocene or early Pleistocene after about 3 million years ago. Greenland's glacial history is known best for the period since the ice sheet retreated from its Last Glacial Maximum position between 22,000 and 14,000 years ago. At that time, the ice sheet extended to the margin of the continental shelf over a distance of up to 200 km offshore. It joined the Laurentide ice sheet flowing out of Canada in the northwest over the Nares Strait and into the Kane Basin. The Greenland ice sheet was in full retreat between 13,000 and 8,000 years ago in response to rising sea levels, causing retreat of ice grounded on the sea floor, and to a warming climate, causing more surface melting. The ice sheet retreated to approximately the present coastline by 10,000 years ago and melted back further inland to near its present position by about 6,000 years before present. In central western Greenland, the ice sheet eventually retreated to a position at least 15 km behind its present position between 6,000 and 3,000 years ago following the mid-Holocene Climatic Optimum. The Neoglacial advance culminated with the Little Ice Age between 100 and 300 years ago.

CURRENT EVOLUTION

The current evolution of the Greenland ice sheet is dominated by continuing retreat from its Little Ice Age maximum

Greenland Ice Sheet. Figure 1. Configuration of the Present-day Greenland Ice Sheet.

Determined from a combination of satellite and airborne laser altimetry, barometric altimetry, and airborne radar (radio-echo) sounding.
Pictures reproduced from: Huybrechts P, and H. Miller (2005).

combined with a slower trend resulting from older climate changes and from continuing changes in basal-ice properties. On these are superimposed the direct effects of recent changes in surface mass-balance and ice dynamics. Until recently, it was not possible to determine with any confidence whether the Greenland ice sheet was growing or shrinking. Over the last decade, however, improved remote sensing techniques combined with accurate GPS positioning have made it possible to estimate more precisely the mass balance of the ice sheet for the period since the early 1990s. These data show a consistent picture of a small thickening of the accumulation zone offset by larger thinning rates at lower altitudes, with a total mass balance that became increasingly negative up to 2005 (Figure 2).

The slow thickening at high elevations since the early 1990s at rates that increased to about 4 cm per year after 2000 is consistent with expectations of increasing snowfall in a warming climate. Total loss from the ice sheet, however, exceeded mass gains, and the total volume deficit more than doubled between the early 1990s and 2005 from a few tens of billions of tons per year to more than 200 billion tons per year, equivalent to a global sea-level rise of 0.5 mm per year or 5 cm per century. These increasing losses are associated partly with recent warm

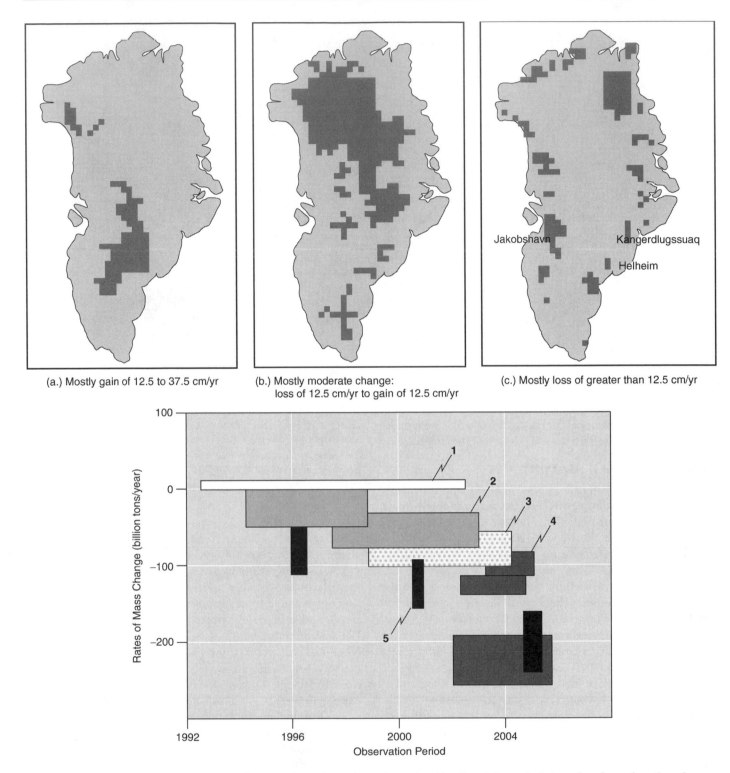

(a.) Mostly gain of 12.5 to 37.5 cm/yr

(b.) Mostly moderate change: loss of 12.5 cm/yr to gain of 12.5 cm/yr

(c.) Mostly loss of greater than 12.5 cm/yr

summer temperatures causing more melting, and partly with increased discharge of ice from outlet glaciers into the ocean. The summers of 1998, 2003, and 2006 were record runoff years at levels not seen since an earlier warm period in the 1930s and 1940s. In addition, the speeds of three of Greenland's fastest glaciers have approximately doubled since 2000, although the two glaciers in the east (Helheim and Kangerdlugssuaq) again slowed to near their previous rates in 2006. The third glacier, Jakobshavn Isbræ, increased its speed to about 14 km per year after the rapid thinning and breakup of its floating ice tongue, and has shown no signs of slowing.

Greenland Ice Sheet. FIGURE 2. Rates of surface-elevation change, late 1990s to 2003, derived by comparing satellite and aircraft laser-altimeter surveys.

Maps are generalized: in areas of +12.5 cm/yr loss, large parts exceed 37.5 cm/yr loss. The graph shows rates of change according to five kinds of evidence through time: (1) satellite radar-altimeter, (2) airborne laser-altimeter, (3) airborne/satellite laser-altimeter, (4) temporal changes in gravity, (5) mass-budget calculations. Jakobshavn, Helheim, and Kangerdlugssuaq are fast glaciers that doubled in speed recently, though the latter two returned to near their previous flow speeds in 2006. (Picture reproduced from: *Global Outlook for Ice & Snow*, United Nations Environment Programme, 2007.)

The mechanisms for these observed speed-ups are not well understood. The glaciers mentioned above have in common that their calving fronts are in deep bedrock troughs, indicating a strong linkage between bed topography and glacier vulnerability to change, possibly by oceanic erosion from higher water temperatures. In addition, marked increases in ice velocity occurring soon after periods of high surface melting suggest that meltwater making its way to the base of the ice lubricates glacier sliding. Such a mechanism provides near-instantaneous communication between surface forcing and basal-ice dynamics and may make the Greenland ice sheet more sensitive to a warmer climate with more surface melting.

The short records for which elevation changes and flow speeds are available are of concern. The recent slowdown of the Helheim and Kangerdlugssuaq glaciers suggests that there is a significant short-term variability in glacier flow-rates. Whereas the recent mass loss from Greenland parallels global-warming trends seen elsewhere, the interpretation of mass-balance estimates is complicated by high natural variability on a range of time scales. The separation of long-term trends in ice mass from the effects of short-term variability requires observations over longer time periods than are currently available.

OUTLOOK

Compared to its volume and potential to raise sea-level, the average contribution of the Greenland ice sheet to global sea-level rise has so far been very small. According to the Fourth Assessment Report of the Intergovernmental Panel on Climate Change (IPCC AR4), Greenland ice contributed no more than 0.05 mm per year to the observed 1.8 mm per year for the period between 1961 and 2003, and 0.21 mm per year to the higher rate of 3.1 mm per year of total sea-level rise observed between 1993 and 2003.

Because of the poor understanding of the ice-dynamic changes currently taking place and the known variability of surface mass balance, the short-term evolution of the Greenland ice sheet is hard to predict. Observations over the last 5 years reveal that the current generation of ice-sheet models cannot simulate the rapid changes taking place at the margin today. These flow changes may simply represent natural variability hitherto undetected, in which case they would not matter much. On the other hand, they may also be a function of the climate warming itself, in which case the future mass loss from the ice sheet might be significantly larger than most predictions suggest. Climate and surface mass balance models generally predict that in a warmer climate the increase in runoff will generally outweigh the concomitant increases in snowfall, so that the ice sheet will shrink in a warmer climate. But such a relation is less evident on time scales shorter than 10 years.

For the next few decades, the evolution of the Greenland ice sheet will be largely locked in by past climatic changes and therefore will not be strongly dependent on twenty-first-century greenhouse-gas emissions. For the full range of emission scenarios, the IPCC AR4 predicts that the Greenland contribution to global sea-level rise will be between 1 and 13 cm by 2090–2099. This range takes into account changes in surface mass balance and assumes that the ice-dynamic imbalance from accelerating glaciers observed between 1993 and 2003 holds constant. If these accelerations were to scale with the warming, the Greenland ice sheet might contribute an additional 5 cm or more, but our understanding of these effects is too limited to assess their likelihood or provide a good estimate or an upper bound for sea-level rise. If the current accelerations are transient, the sea-level contribution from Greenland will be 1–2 cm less.

The evolution of the Greenland ice sheet over centuries and longer is, however, critically dependent on future greenhouse-gas emissions. If global average temperatures increase more than 1.9–4.6°C above pre-industrial values, loss by surface melting will exceed precipitation. Under these circumstances, the ice sheet must contract, even when iceberg production falls to zero as the ice sheet retreats from the coast. This threshold at which melting exceeds accumulation will already be crossed, according to most global-warming scenarios, in the second half of the twenty-first century. Depending on the strength and duration of the warming, the ice sheet may nearly disappear over a period of a few millennia, except for residual glaciers in the mountains (Figure 3). Without the ice sheet, the climate of Greenland would be much warmer because the land surface would be at lower altitude and, with less snow cover, would reflect less sunlight. Several model studies suggest that even if global climate were to return to pre-industrial conditions, the ice sheet might not regrow, in which case the demise of the Greenland ice sheet and the associated sea-level rise might be irreversible. For this reason, the Greenland ice sheet is often described as a relict ice mass. It survived the current Holocene interglacial solely because it creates its own cold surface-climate because of its elevation.

The last time Greenland temperatures were several degrees higher than today was the last interglacial 125,000 years ago. Ice-core evidence for a smaller ice sheet is consistent with the observation that sea level then was several meters higher than today. At that time, the ice sheet did not disappear completely, probably because the warming was not strong enough and did not last long enough. The ice sheet was probably saved from extinction by the onset of the last glacial period several thousand years later.

BIBLIOGRAPHY

Alley, R. B., et al. "Ice-Sheet and Sea-Level Changes." *Science* 310 (2005), 456–460. DOI: 10.1126/science.1114613.

Gregory, J. M., P. Huybrechts, and S. C. B. Raper. "Threatened Loss of the Greenland Ice Sheet." *Nature* 428 (2004), 616. DOI: 10.1038/428616a.

Gregory, J. M., and P. Huybrechts. "Ice-Sheet Contributions to Future Sea-Level Change." *Philosophical Transactions of the Royal Society of London A* 364 (2006), 1709–1731.

Howat, I. M., I. Joughin, and T. A. Scambos. "Rapid Changes in Ice Discharge from Greenland Outlet Glaciers." *Science* 315 (2007), 1559–1561. DOI: 10.1126/science.1138478.

Huybrechts, P., and H. Miller. "Flow and Balance of the Polar Ice Sheets." In *Observed Global Climate*, edited by M. Hantel, pp. 13.1–13.13. Landolt-Börnstein/ New Series (Numerical Data and Functional Relationships in Science and Technology), vol. 6. Berlin, Heidelberg, and New York: Springer, 2005.

Meehl, G. A., T. F. Stocker, et al. "Global Climate Projections." In *Climate Change 2007, The Physical Science Basis, Contribution of Working Group I to the Fourth Assessment Report of the Intergovernmental Panel on Climate Change*, edited by S. Solomon et al., pp. 747–846. Cambridge and New York: Cambridge University Press, 2007.

Otto-Bliesner, B. L., et al. "Simulating Arctic Climate Warmth and Icefield Retreat in the Last Interglaciation." *Science* 311 (2006), 1751–1753. DOI: 10.1126/science.1120808.

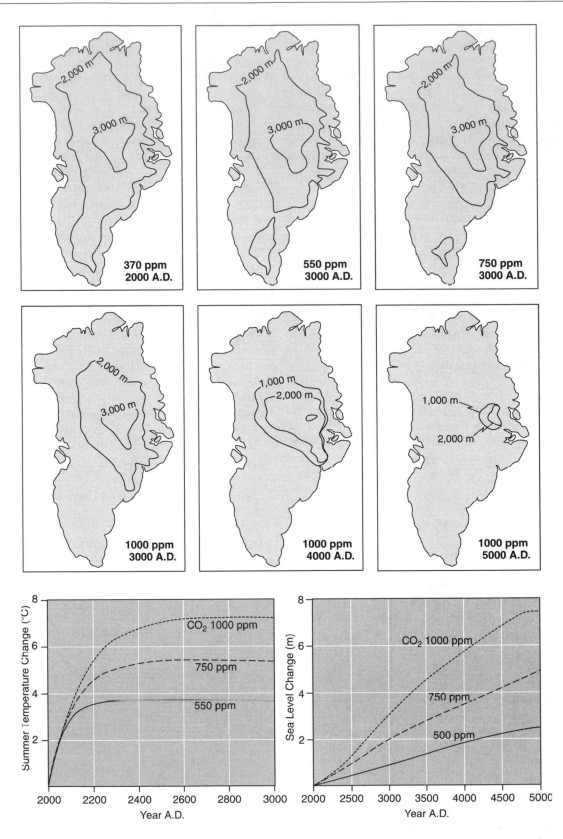

Greenland Ice Sheet. Figure 3. Future of the Greenland Ice Sheet

Calculated from a 3D ice-sheet model forced by three greenhouse gas stabilization scenarios. The warming scenarios correspond to the average of seven IPCC models in which the atmospheric carbon dioxide concentration stabilizes at levels between 550 and 1000 ppm after a few centuries. For a sustained average summer warming of 7.3°C (1000 ppm), the Greenland ice sheet is shown to disappear within 3000 years, raising sea level by about 7.5 m. (Picture reproduced from: Alley, R.B., et al., 2005.)

Shepherd, A., and D. Wingham. "Recent Sea-Level Contributions of the Antarctic and Greenland Ice Sheets." *Science* 315 (2007), 1529–1532. DOI: 10.1126/science.1136776.

Thomas, R., et al. "Progressive Increase in Ice Loss from Greenland." *Geophysical Research Letters* 33, L10503 (2006). DOI: 10.1029/2006GL026075.

Toniazzo, T., J. M. Gregory, and P. Huybrechts. "Climatic Impact of a Greenland Deglaciation and Its Possible Irreversibility." *Journal of Climate* 17.1 (2004), 21–33.

—Philippe Huybrechts

GROUND WATER

In some parts of the world, ground water is the main source of water for industrial, municipal, and agricultural use. Some rocks, including sandstones and limestones, have characteristics that enable them to hold and transmit large quantities of water, which can be reached by installing pumps and boreholes.

Considerable reductions in ground-water levels have been caused by abstraction. The rapid increase in the number of wells tapping ground water in the London area from 1850 until after World War II caused substantial changes in groundwater conditions. The water level in the confined chalk aquifer (water-bearing stratum) fell by more than 60 meters over hundreds of square kilometers.

In some industrial areas, recent reductions in industrial activity have led to less ground water being withdrawn and groundwater levels have begun to rise, a trend worsened by considerable leakage from ancient, deteriorating pipe and sewer systems. This is happening in British cities such as London, Liverpool, and Birmingham. In London, a 46% reduction in ground-water withdrawal has caused the water table in the Cretaceous chalk and younger Tertiary beds to rise by as much as 20 meters. Such a rise has numerous effects:

- increased spring and river flows
- reemergence of flow from dry springs
- surface flooding
- pollution of surface and underground waters
- flooding of basements
- increased leakage into tunnels
- reduction in stability of slopes and retaining walls
- reduction in the weight-bearing capacity of foundations and pilings
- increased hydrostatic uplift and swelling pressures on foundations and other underground structures
- swelling of clays as they absorb water
- chemical attack on building foundations.

—Andrew S. Goudie

GROUNDWATER DEPLETION IN SAUDI ARABIA

Most of Saudi Arabia is desert, so climatic conditions are unfavorable for the rapid large-scale recharge of aquifers, and much of the groundwater that lies beneath the desert is a fossil resource, created during more humid conditions—pluvials—that existed in the Late Pleistocene, between 15,000 and 30,000 BP. In spite of these unfavorable circumstances, Saudi Arabia's demand for water is growing inexorably as its economy develops. In 1980, the annual demand was 2.4 billion cubic meters. By 1990 it had reached 12 billion cubic meters (a fivefold increase in just a decade), and it is expected to reach 20 billion cubic meters by 2010. Only a very small part of the demand can be met from desalinization plants or surface runoff; over three-quarters of the supply is obtained from predominantly non-renewable groundwater resources. The drawdown on aquifers is thus enormous. It has been calculated that, by 2010, the deep aquifers will contain 42% less water than in 1985. Much of the water is used ineffectively and inefficiently in the agricultural sector (Al-Ibrahim, 1991) to irrigate crops that could easily be grown in more humid regions and imported.

BIBLIOGRAPHY

Al-Ibrahim, A.A. "Excessive Use of Ground-Water Resources in Saudi Arabia: Impacts and Policy Options." *Ambio* 20 (1991), 34–37.

—Andrew S. Goudie

GULF STREAM

See Thermohaline Circulation.

H

HEATHLANDS

In everyday language the word "heathland" signifies a variety of open, largely treeless, uncultivated landscapes, usually on acidic soils of low fertility. Defined more technically, it is a type of vegetation or biome in which the prominent plants are sclerophylls, mostly evergreen subshrubs with small tough leaves. Trees and tall shrubs, if present, are sparse, and grasses are either absent or are subordinate to the subshrubs. The dominant species belong to a small number of botanical families—e.g., Ericaceae (heath), Epacridaceae (Australian heath), Myrtaceae (myrtle), Proteaceae, and Vacciniaceae—not necessarily closely related but sharing certain structural features described as "ericoid" (heathlike). They are usually much-branched, woody subshrubs, seldom more than about 1–1.5 meters tall and sometimes less than 10 centimeters, often forming a rather dense low canopy composed of the numerous small or very small, often narrow leaves.

Heathland soils are almost universally low in plant nutrients (notably phosphorus and calcium) and usually acidic. They include freely drained sands, gravels and podzols, on which dry heaths develop, and moist or seasonally saturated such as peats and gleys, which support humid or wet heaths. Where such soils occur under oceanic or seasonally moist climatic conditions, rang-ing from subarctic through cool temperate to Mediterranean-type climates, heathlands may develop. Hence they occur chiefly on the margins of continents (for example, western and eastern North America, the Cape Province of South Africa, southwest and southern Australia, and in much of the subarctic tundra). They are absent where continental climates prevail, but are found on mountains in many parts of the world (including tropical regions) under suitable combinations of soil and climatic conditions. However, arid lands, wet tropical and warm temperate lowlands, permanently waterlogged habitats, and very fertile soils are all unsuitable for heathlands.

Heathland vegetation is made up of a number of characteristic plant communities that include, in addition to the subshrubs, a variety of (mostly perennial) herbaceous species, bryophytes (mosses, liverworts, hornworts), and lichens. In each of the regions in which they are present, the floristic composition of these communities is distinctive and often of great ecological interest and visual attractiveness, especially when the heath plants are in bloom. Furthermore, some heathland areas, notably the *fynbos* of South Africa and the kwongan of southwestern Australia, have become centers of spectacular evolutionary radiation, producing flora of amazing diversity

and beauty. Heathlands also support important invertebrate and vertebrate fauna.

NATURAL AND SEMINATURAL HEATHLANDS

The absence of a dominant tree or tall shrub stratum may be a result of purely natural (i.e., nonhuman) causes, as in the case of tundra heaths, heaths above the treeline on mountains, and heaths on exposed clifftops or on certain dry and extremely nutrient-deficient soils. Here tree growth may be inhibited by climatic factors, including very strong winds and low temperatures, or by soil conditions. Naturally occurring fire, when frequent, may also prevent forest growth and permit the development of heath.

Heathland also develops naturally as a stage in a plant succession prior to the entry of tree species, for example, on some acid sand dunes and some peat bogs subject to surface drying. Such heathland plant communities usually give place in time to scrub or woodland.

In addition to these types of heathland, however, there are also (or have been in the past) very extensive lowland or middle-altitude heathlands in locations entirely suitable for forest or woodland vegetation. Such heathlands may make a major contribution to the landscape, as in the heath region of west Europe (from western Norway, through southwestern Sweden, Denmark, the North German Plain, the Low Countries, and northern and western France, to northern Spain, and including the British Isles). These heathlands have replaced former forest and owe their origin and maintenance largely to human activities, including clearance of trees and subsequent management by cutting or burning the vegetation, turf stripping, or the use of grazing animals. However, the plant communities consist of naturally occurring, not cultivated, species, so the vegetation may be described as "seminatural."

FIRE

A factor generally associated with heathland is periodic fire, which may be caused naturally, as by lightning or sparks from falling rocks, or through human agency. Some heathland areas have long been subject to natural fires, but many have in addition a history of occasional or frequent burning related to human use. In the South African *fynbos,* the pine plains of New Jersey and Long Island (North America), and the Australian heaths, although fire has always been an integral component of the ecosystem, its frequency has been much increased by mankind from early times. Fire has also contributed in some regions to forest clearance, creating areas open to colonization by heathland vegetation.

Where frequent, fire has led to selection of a flora composed of species that regenerate vigorously after burning, either vegetatively from protected buds or subsurface perennating structures, or by seed from a soil seed-bank or contained in woody fruits which disperse their contents only when heated by a fire. [*See* Fire and Global Warming.]

ORIGINS OF HEATHLANDS

Purely natural heathlands may have a long history, dating sometimes from the Pleistocene period or earlier. Few of them, however, have escaped modification by human influence from early times: the South African *fynbos*, for example, was subject to "firestick farming" at least 10,000 years ago and in places has been used for grazing by domestic stock for some 2,000 years.

At many different times in the past, heathlands have evidently replaced former forest. In such instances, studies of Quaternary forest history almost invariably demonstrate direct links between human activity and reductions in forest cover, with its replacement by grassland in the more fertile areas and heathland on poorer soils. This is especially true of the western European heathlands, and because they were formerly extensive and their origins have been intensively researched, the following summary concentrates on this area.

WESTERN EUROPE

At first, inroads into the forest, which date from late Neolithic times (more than 4,000 years ago), were small and temporary, representing a form of shifting cultivation. After cropping for a few seasons, the cleared patches were abandoned, allowing the heath plants especially heather (*Calluna vulgaris*), already present as part of the forest flora on poor, acidic soils, to colonize from a buried seed-bank or dispersal from nearby. If no further use was made of these patches, however, trees quickly reinvaded, and the area reverted to woodland.

Later, especially during the Bronze Age (about 3,500 years ago) and Iron Age (about 2,500 years ago), heathland came to be valued as grazing for the increasing numbers of domestic herbivores (sheep, cattle, goats, horses), and return to forest was delayed or prevented. Heather proved to be a useful grazing plant where the more palatable and nutritious grasses were scarce, particularly in winter when other forage was unavailable. The herbivores themselves tended to stimulate the production of edible green shoots by the heather plants and to prevent the establishment of tree seedlings. Where grazing intensity was insufficient for these purposes, fire was sometimes used.

Hence most heathlands in western Europe were anthropogenic. Although only a few have an unbroken history extending over 3,000 years or more, the process of forest clearance continued at intervals because of the demand for timber for buildings, ships, and fuel (including charcoal for iron smelting), and because of increasing needs for arable and grazing lands. Heather proved to have other uses, including thatch, animal bedding, resilient foundations for tracks and roads, and as a source of dyes and honey. The areas of open heathland grew, and they were maintained and managed until their extent reached a peak in most countries of the heathland region in the late nineteenth century. In Britain, extensive midaltitude and upland heathlands became important for hill-sheep farming, particularly in the late eighteenth and early nineteenth centuries, and later for sporting purposes because they provided a habitat for large populations of the red grouse (*Lagopus lagopus scoticus*, a game bird) and the red deer (*Cervus elaphus*). Hill-sheep and grouse rely on the young green shoots of heather for a large proportion of their diet, and they are also grazed by deer.

Rotational burning was adopted as the regular method of heathland management. This was carried out in small strips and patches, such that each patch was burned at intervals of, usually, between ten and fifteen years. The branching pattern of the heather bush is such that, as long as it is not allowed to get too old, it responds well to burning or cutting and will resprout from buds at the stem base, which are protected from damage by surface litter or vegetation.

THE DECLINE OF HEATHLANDS

In many regions the area of heathland declined over the past 100 to 300 years because of the transformation for agriculture and other land uses. In places its disappearance has been rapid, so that there is now little left outside nature reserves or other protected areas. For example, it has been estimated that the extent of *fynbos* in South Africa has declined by some 60% and that of heath and scrub heath in the southwest botanical province of Australia by between 40 and 60%. Even greater losses have occurred in the lowland heathland regions of western Europe: losses as high as 95% of the area covered by heath around 1850 have been quoted for Denmark and the Netherlands, and 90% in the province of Halland in southern Sweden. Similar trends are reported in Belgium and parts of northern Germany and France. In southern England, six of the main heathland areas have decreased in extent in the same period by 72% overall, the figures ranging from 50 to 90% in different localities. In the uplands and North of Britain the decline has been rather less, but in Scotland between the 1940s and 1980s there has been a contraction in the area of "heather moorland" of at least 23%. In a few localities there has been limited gain, however, caused by the change toward heathland on bog surfaces that have been drained, or where former forest has been cleared.

THE CAUSE OF LOSS OF HEATHLAND VEGETATION

In northern Europe many factors are contributing to this decline in the extent of heathland, most of them associated with the disappearance of traditional forms of management and the demands on land for alternative uses. Increased production on better land has made the use of heathland for grazing domestic herbivores relatively unprofitable, and there is now little interest in harvesting cut vegetation or peat for fuel or other purposes.

Where management has ceased, heathland may quickly be invaded by shrubs and trees, or by other aggressive competitors such as bracken fern (*Pteridium aquilinum*). In Europe and elsewhere, however, most of the losses of heathland have been due to conversion to arable land, grassland, or plantation forestry, accompanied by soil improvement, including the use of fertilizers. For example, nearly 50% of the area of fynbos in South Africa has been transformed by afforestation or agriculture, mainly in the period following colonial settlement from the late seventeenth century onward, while much of the loss and fragmentation of southwestern Australian heaths has also been a consequence of land use change, mainly during the past one hundred years. In Europe, conversion of heath to plantation forest has been the major change in countries such as Sweden and Scotland, while "reclamation" for agriculture was predominant in Denmark, the Netherlands, Germany, and southern England.

In Australia, heathlands have suffered in many places from the effects of the introduced root-rot fungus *Phytophthora cinnamomi*, while in northwestern Europe damage to heather has been caused by plant-eating insects such as the heather beetle (*Lochmaea suturalis*) and (very recently in northern Scotland) the winter moth (*Operophtera brumata*). Heathlands have also disappeared under urban expansion, industrial development, roads, airports, and other artifacts. Some have given place to invasive plants, especially trees, as in the fynbos, where some 36% of the total area of this vegetation type has changed in this way.

In many places, heathlands have survived only where protected or where they retain some economic or social value, for example, as open countryside for hunting (e.g., in Britain, red grouse or red deer), as grazing land for ponies (northern France, southern England), or as a source of cut flowers for export (South Africa). Pastoral use of heathlands continues in some areas, including to some extent the fynbos and, more especially, Scotland, where sheep and red deer are the chief grazers. In parts of these regions, grazing pressure has increased and become excessive in recent years, in contrast to its cessation elsewhere, and this too has damaged the vegetation, usually causing change to rough, relatively unproductive grassland.

In many heathlands there is a delicate balance between heath and grassland species. The heath vegetation belongs to infertile soils, and any significant increase in nutrient status leads to change toward grassland or other vegetation types. Traditional forms of management in Europe, such as grazing, burning, and peat harvesting have always had the effect of periodically depleting the ecosystem of a proportion of the nutrient fund, thus maintaining conditions suitable for the heath. Abandonment of this management may allow some accumulation of nutrients in soil and vegetation, improving conditions for competitor species. Change of this kind has been greatly accelerated in recent times in areas such as the Netherlands, northern Germany, and southeastern England by the input of nutrients, especially nitrogen and phosphorus, from atmospheric pollution. In the Netherlands, for example, since the 1980s inputs of

nitrogen have exceeded 40 kilograms per hectare per year, and in places more than 60 kilograms. This development has been clearly linked to the decline of heath species such as heather (sometimes associated with increased attacks of heather beetle) and their replacement by dominant grasses such as wavy hair grass (*Deschampsia flexuosa*) or purple moor grass (*Molinia caerulea*). Throughout much of the heathland region of western Europe inputs of nitrogen now exceed 15 kilograms per hectare per year, which is said to be beyond the ecological tolerance of most heath species. These heathland ecosystems must therefore be regarded as endangered.

Climatic warming and increased carbon dioxide concentrations in the atmosphere are also possible causes of change. A somewhat precarious biome, located as it is at the southernmost tip of Africa and so with little scope for displacement, is the very diverse Fynbos Biome. Modeling, using the Hadley Centre CM2 GCM (general circulation model), indicates a likely contraction of the extent of Fynbos by about 2050 (Midgley et al., 2003). In Europe, heather occurs over a wide temperature range and might therefore be affected by climatic warming only at the margins of its geographical area, though changes in precipitation and atmospheric humidity regimes might prove more important. Other species of heathland communities have narrower temperature ranges and in some cases might be significantly affected by global warming. There is experimental evidence of a positive growth response in heather to increased carbon dioxide levels, but such an increase is quickly limited by the nutrient supply in typical nutrient-poor habitats. Flowering, however, is strongly enhanced and advanced in season under increased carbon dioxide concentrations. The ecological significance of these responses, however, is unknown. In Australia, as elsewhere, it is a general view that land use changes are, at least now and in the foreseeable future, of greater significance in regard to loss of heathland than is climate change.

IS THERE A FUTURE FOR HEATHLANDS?

The global extent of heathlands has never been large compared other biomes, and its rate of decline in the past 200 years makes it an endangered type, except in a very few areas. The scientific and aesthetic value of heathlands, however, is great, especially where they are seminatural, managed ecosystems and where they have high biodiversity. Conservation of heathlands must therefore have high priority. The disappearance of traditional uses of heathlands in Europe poses problems because conservation there depends on continued management, which must perpetuate their ecological effects (such as preventing nutrient accumulation), although not necessarily by the use of traditional methods. In view of the drastic reductions of area and fragmentation of heathland in many countries, attention is also turning now to the restoration of heath vegetation in places from which it has disappeared and to the creation of corridors to link surviving fragments. Continuing and increasing interest in the conservation and restoration of heathland suggests that there is indeed a future for heathlands.

BIBLIOGRAPHY

Cowling, R. M., ed. *The Ecology of Fynbos: Nutrients, Fire, and Diversity.* Cape Town: Oxford University Press, 1992. An authoritative, multiauthor account of the Fynbos Biome Project.

Forman, R. T. T., ed. *Pine Barrens: Ecosystem and Landscape.* New York: Academic Press, 1979. A thorough coverage of all aspects of the ecology of these areas, including the heaths of the "pine plains."

Gimingham, C. H. *Ecology of Heathlands.* London: Chapman and Hall, 1972. Covers the origins, history, structure, ecology, and uses of heathlands, with emphasis on the western European heathland region.

Gimingham, C. H., and J. T. de Smidt. "Heaths as Natural and Seminatural Vegetation." In *Man's Impact on Vegetation,* edited by W. Holzner, M. J. A. Werger, and I. Ikusima, pp. 185–199. The Hague and London: Junk, 1983. Reviews the origins, uses, and management of European heaths, with special reference to grazing, burning, and *plaggen* (turf stripping).

Hobbs, R. J., ed. *Biodiversity of Mediterranean Ecosystems in Australia.* Chipping Norton, New South Wales: Surrey Beatty, 1992. Includes much material on Australian heathlands.

Hobbs, R. J., and C. H. Gimingham. "Vegetation, Fire, and Herbivore Interactions in Heathland." In *Advances in Ecological Research,* vol. 16, edited by A. Macfadyen and E. D. Ford, pp. 87–173. London: Academic Press, 1987. A review of research and its bearing on management and conservation in northwestern Europe, especially Scotland and northern England.

Midgley, G. F., et al. "Developing Regional and Species-Level Assessments of Climate Change Impacts on Biodiversity in the Cape Floristic Region." *Biological Conservation* 112 (2003), 87–97. DOI: 10.1016/S0006-3207(02)00414-7.

Pate, J. S., and J. S. Beard. *Kwongan: Plant Life of the Sand Plain.* Nedlands, Western Australia: University of Western Australia Press, 1984. A comprehensive review of southwestern Australian heathlands.

Smidt, J. T. de. "Phytosociological Relations in the North West European Heath." *Acta Botanica Neerlandica* 15 (1967), 630–647. Analyzes the variation in floristic composition of European heathland vegetation.

Specht, R. L., ed. *Heathlands and Related Shrublands.* 2 vols. *Ecosystems of the World.* Amsterdam: Elsevier, 1979. Indispensable source books of information on the world's heathlands, divided into descriptive studies (Vol. A), and analytical studies (biological, physiological, and ecological, including conservation; Vol. B).

Thompson, D. B. A., A. J. Hester, and M. B. Usher, eds. *Heaths and Moorland: Cultural Landscapes.* Edinburgh: Her Majesty's Stationery Office and Scottish National Heritage, 1995. Twenty-four contributions to a conference, providing an up-to-date source of information on dynamic processes and changes in heathlands in the U.K.

Webb, N. R. *Heathlands.* The New Naturalist Series. London: Collins, 1986. An excellent, readable account of the history, natural history, and ecology of heathlands, especially the lowland heaths of England.

Woodin, S. J., et al. "Nutrient Limitation of the Long Term Response of Heather [*Calluna vulgaris* (L.) Hull] to CO_2 Enrichment." *New Phytologist* 122.4 (1992), 635–642. An experimental study relevant to the possible effects of CO_2 enrichment and global warming on *Calluna* heathland.

—CHARLES H. GIMINGHAM AND RICHARD J. HOBBS

HEINRICH EVENTS

In the 1980s, the German paleoceanographer Hartmut Heinrich (Heinrich, 1988) extracted samples at regular increments from northeastern Atlantic sediment cores that had been retrieved by drilling into the ocean floor. He analyzed his samples and determined their lithic content and their content of planktonic foraminifera fragments. He found that the relative numbers of lithics (sand, stones, etc.) and foraminifera fluctuated in a surprising manner and that the transitions between lithic-dominated (light-colored) and foraminifera-dominated (dark-colored) sediments were unexpectedly abrupt. These phases with sudden increases in the amount of lithics have subsequently been termed "Heinrich events" (Broecker et al., 1992). The key features of sediment delivery during Heinrich events are the presence of icebergs, meltwater plumes, and massive gravity flows (turbidites). The iceberg-rafted debris accumulated on the ocean floor every 5–10 thousand years during the last glacial period. These processes, which are associated with cold events (stadials), produce sediments with a high lithic content, whereas the foraminifera-rich non-Heinrich sediments were deposited during warmer (interstadial) periods.

The lithic sediments of Heinrich events, which contain iceberg-rafted detritus, have a high carbonate content that is probably derived from the source region of Paleozoic limestones and dolomites in eastern Canada and possibly northwestern Greenland (Bond et al., 1992). This suggests that the lithic sediments of the Heinrich events were excavated by the Hudson Strait ice stream, which drained a large part of the former Laurentide ice sheet. Rapid fluctuation in this ice stream not only produced the sudden Heinrich events (of which there have been 6 over 60 thousand years) but also led to the creation of plumes of extremely fresh glacial meltwater. These flowed into the normally salty North Atlantic and so would have affected the thermohaline circulation in the North Atlantic, which could in turn cause abrupt climatic changes far afield. Abrupt dusty events at low latitudes appear to have been broadly synchronous with high-latitude Heinrich events (Jullien et al., 2007).

BIBLIOGRAPHY

Anderson, D., A. S. Goudie, and A. G. Parker. Global *Environments through the Quaternary.* Oxford and New York: Oxford University Press, 2007.

Bond, G., et al. "Evidence for Massive Discharges of Icebergs into the North Atlantic during the Last Glacial Period." *Nature* 360 (1992), 245–249.

Broecker, W. S., et al. "Origin of the Northern Atlantic's Heinrich Events." *Climate Dynamics* 6.3–4 (1992), 265–273. DOI: 10.1007/BF00193540.

Bryant, E. *Climate Process and Change.* Cambridge and New York: Cambridge University Press, 1997.

Heinrich, H. "Origin and Consequences of Cyclic Ice Rafting in the Northeast Atlantic Ocean during the Past 130,000 Years." *Quaternary Research* 29.2 (1988), 143–152. DOI: 10.1016/0033-5894(88)90057-9.

Jullien, E., et al. "Low-Latitude 'Dusty Events' vs. High-Latitude 'Icy Heinrich Events.'" *Quaternary Research* 68.3 (2007), 379–386. DOI: 10.1016/j.yqres.2007.07.007.

—ANDREW S. GOUDIE

THE HOLOCENE

The period after the Late Glacial Oscillation has traditionally been divided into the Late Glacial (Pleistocene) and the postglacial (Holocene, Recent, or Flandrian). [*See* Younger Dryas.] The classic terminology was established by two Scandinavians, Blytt and Sernander, who, in the late nineteenth and early twentieth centuries, introduced the terms Preboreal, Boreal, Atlantic, Subboreal, and Subatlantic for the various environmental fluctuations that took place. This is essentially a scheme of vegetation change, not a scheme of climate change, for the bulk of the evidence used by Blytt and Sernander was provided by plant remains. Inaccuracies may thus creep into climatic reconstructions because of nonclimatic factors affecting vegetation associations. Such factors include the intervention of humans (Ruddiman, 2005), the evolution of soils, and the passage from pioneer to climax species during vegetation succession.

Though the terminology may still be used, there have been substantial changes in interpretation of the classic Blytt-Sernander model in recent decades. Mangerud et al. (1974) suggested using the traditional terms (correlated with paleoclimatic divisions based on pollen stratigraphy) with the following radiocarbon dates (in carbon-14 years BP):

- Preboreal (pollen zones IV and V) 10,000–9,000
- Boreal (pollen zones VIa and VIb) 9,000–8,000
- Atlantic (pollen zones VIc and VIIa) 8,000–5,000
- Subboreal (pollen zone VIIb) 5,000–2,500
- Subatlantic (pollen zone VIII) 2,500 to the present.

EARLY HOLOCENE CLIMATE

From radiocarbon dating of early Holocene deposits, the start of the Holocene (the Preboreal) has long been placed at approximately 10,000 carbon-14 yr BP, but the radiocarbon-based estimates are younger than the calendar-year estimates spanning the early Holocene. Counting of annual ice layers in the GRIP and GISP2 ice cores yielded ages of 11,550–11,640 and 11,640–11,890 cal yr BP respectively for the transition from the Younger Dryas

---

The Holocene. Dakhla, Egypt.

In the early to mid Holocene, some lower latitude areas were more humid than today. At Dakhla, currently hyper-arid, a freshwater lake accumulated, as represented by dark, flat lying lake sediments, which are now being excavated by wind attack.

(Late Pleistocene) to the Holocene (Johnsen et al., 1992; Alley et al., 1993). Similar estimates between 11,500 and 11,600 cal yr BP have also been made by dendrochronology and the study of annually laminated lake sediments (varves) in northern Europe (Gulliksen et al., 1998).

A rapid increase in temperature occurred at the beginning of the Holocene during the Preboreal. From the Greenland Dye 3 ice core Dansgaard et al. (1989) suggested that the mean annual temperature increased by 7°C in 50 years or less, and from the GISP2 record Alley et al. (1993) found that ice accumulation doubled in just three years. A large shift in the deuterium (hydrogen isotope) ratio, indicating a major change in the source region of water vapor reaching Greenland, occurred in just one year. This points to an abrupt reorganization of atmospheric circulation in the North Atlantic region which was linked to the reestablishment of a vigorous density-driven thermohaline circulation and the delivery of warm waters to high northern latitudes. A similar abrupt shift is also seen in temperature-dependent oxygen-isotope data from a varve sequence in Poland (Goslar et al., 1995) and from beetle-based reconstructions for Britain in which mean annual temperature increased rapidly by over 10°C (Atkinson et al., 1987).

Following the abrupt temperature increase at the start of the Holocene, the Greenland ice-core records show that temperatures continued to increase (but at a slower rate) until reaching a maximum between 9,000 and 8,000 years ago. Indeed,

Holocene temperatures probably reached their maximum in the early Holocene over most parts of the globe, with the exception of those regions that were close to the decaying residual ice sheets (COHMAP, 1988).

Superimposed on the early Holocene warming trend were some short, minor oscillations. The Greenland ice cores show minor temperature declines at 11,300 and at 9,300 years ago (Johnsen et al., 2001), and a more marked decline at about 10,300 years ago. A core from the North Atlantic suggests a contemporaneous decline in the average sea-surface temperature (SST) around the Faeroe Islands of over 2°C within a 200-year period (Koç Karpuz and Jansen, 1992), This correlates with a brief decline of similar magnitude recorded in a core from the Atlantic off West Africa (deMenocal et al., 2000).

THE 8,200 CAL YR BP EVENT

Temperature records derived from Greenland ice cores display a significant temperature anomaly centered on 8,200 cal yr BP that lasted for about 400 years (Alley et al., 1997; Clark et al., 2001). The data suggest a cooling of as much as 6°C. The generally accepted explanation for this is that there was a catastrophic meltwater release into the North Atlantic which disrupted the thermohaline circulation and its associated northward heat transport. [See Thermohaline Circulation.] This proposal has been supported by dating of the final outburst drainage of proglacial Lake Agassiz-Ojibway in Canada during the final melting of the Laurentide ice sheet (von Grafenstein et al., 1998; Teller et al., 2002).

The 8,200 cal yr BP event has been detected across the world, for example in pollen data from eastern North America (Shuman et al., 2005). Dating of a pronounced glacier advance in the Silvretta Mountains (Austria) yielded ages ranging from 8,010 ± 360 to 8,690 ± 410 years, with a mean age for moraine construction of 8,410 ± 690 years. The 8,200 cal yr BP event has also been identified in proxy records from monsoonal regions (Hughen et al., 1996). A broad Holocene minimum is found, for instance, in the lake-sediment record at Awafi, in the United Arab Emirates, which shows an abrupt lowering in water level and an influx of aeolian sand (Parker et al., 2006).

POSTGLACIAL SPREAD OF VEGETATION IN EUROPE

The warming of climate in the postglacial set off successive returns of trees with different tolerances of cold and different powers of colonization. At first there were a few Arctic tree species in Britain, then larger numbers of more tolerant species arrived, and the composition of the woodlands became more complex (Rackham, 1980). The trees did not, in general, stream in from the south in successive waves. Rather, each crept up in small numbers and became widespread (though rare) long before reaching its full abundance.

Birks (1990) has synthesized the changes that occurred across Europe in response to Holocene warming. At 12,000 carbon-14 yr BP Pinus (pine) was mainly in southern and eastern Europe but by 6,000 carbon-14 yr BP was abundant in northern,

central, and Mediterranean Europe though absent from much of the western European lowlands. Quercus (oak) spread progressively northward from southern Europe and reached its maximum range limits by 6,000 carbon-14 yr BP. Ulmus (elm), Corylus (hazel), and Tilia (linden) had also reached their present-day range limits by that time. However, not all forest trees had reached these limits by 6,000 carbon-14 yr BP. Picea (spruce) has spread westward through Finland, across Sweden, and into central and eastern Norway in the last 6,000 years. Fagus had a small range in southern and central Europe by 6,000 carbon-14 yr BP, which is in contrast to its extensive range in western Europe today. Similarly, Carpinus, which is today widespread in lowland Europe was, at 6,000 carbon-14 yr BP, largely confined to Bulgaria, Italy, Yugoslavia, Romania, and Poland.

By about 6,000 years ago, most tree species had reached their maximum Holocene range limits in Europe. From then on the vegetation changes became more complex because of increasing human influence. Instead of the broad regional trends seen in tree-spread during the early to mid-Holocene, the later Holocene saw increased fragmentation of woodland and a great diversity of local changes superimposed on a general trend of deciduous-forest retreat from the earlier established range maxima. From the Neolithic onwards it becomes increasingly difficult to distinguish in pollen diagrams between climate-related and human-caused vegetation changes. However, by about 5,000 years ago agriculture exerted significant effects on the landscape in most of Europe.

By 3,000 years ago mixed forest had expanded in the north, and boreal (coniferous) forests in the mountains, at the expense of deciduous forest. Compared with 3,000 years ago, the present range limit of deciduous forest is farther south in Scandinavia and northeastern Europe. However, mixed forest has expanded at the expense of boreal forest in the Alps since 3,000 years ago, and over the same time period Mediterranean vegetation has expanded in southern Europe.

Another important vegetation trend through the late Holocene was the expansion of peatlands and heaths, particularly in the more maritime parts of Europe. It has been argued by some that peat deposition in many areas of Britain was begun by human actions that changed catchment hydrology and surface wetness, as by the reduction of evapotranspiration by deforestation. However, there is also evidence from parts of Europe for peatland expansion caused by shifts to wetter and/or cooler climatic conditions, predominantly after 5,000 years ago (Barber and Charman, 2005).

THE NORTH AMERICAN HOLOCENE

Bernabo and Webb (1977) showed the nature of vegetation changes in northeastern North America by summing the observed changes in the pollen record from multiple sites. One of the most important events was the decline of spruce from 11,000 to 8,000 carbon-14 yr BP as it gradually moved northwards. Another important feature of the Holocene vegetation history of North America has been the fluctuating position of the boundary between prairie and forest. Signs of prairie development in the western Midwest are visible in the pollen record over 11,000 years ago as the vast region formerly occupied by the Late Glacial boreal forest began to shrink. The largest eastward shift of the prairie took place between 10,000 and 9,000 carbon-14 yr BP. It reached its maximum eastward extent in about 8,000 carbon-14 yr BP, then receded somewhat from 7,000 to 2,000 carbon-14 yr BP (Webb et al., 1983).

Other evidence of Holocene vegetation and climatic fluctuations comes from a study of eolian stratigraphy in the drier areas of the U.S. In the central Great Plains, periods of rapid loess (windblown silt) accumulation indicate episodes of extensive wind activity. [See Loess.] Optical dating methods such as optically stimulated luminescence indicate that loess deposition in this region was occurring in the early Holocene and ended shortly after 6,500 years ago. This corresponds with other proxy data from the Great Plains indicating an early- to mid-Holocene dry period (Miao et al., 2005). In Wyoming, for example, Gaylord (1990) identified pronounced aridity and dune activity from 7,545 to 7,035 years ago and from 5,940 to 4,540 years ago. Indeed, one of the most interesting recent developments in the study of dune fields in the western U.S. is the recognition that dry phases or very extended droughts have caused repeated dune reactivation during the Holocene (see, for example, Arbogast, 1986, and Madole, 1995).

HUMANS AND THE HOLOCENE

In the Holocene, and particularly from the mid-Holocene onward, humans were increasingly potent agents of change. A striking example is the extinction of many species of large mammals (and the associated ecological changes) that occurred as humans spread through the Americas during the Late Glacial and early postglacial. Likewise, Li et al. (2006) describe how agricultural and pastoral activities affected the Holocene landscape of China and can be identified by paleoecological techniques.

Of particular interest in Britain is the decline of the linden (*Tilia*), the pollen of which disappears in many sites at the same time as charcoal and other evidence of human activity appears, c. 3,700 BP (Hone et al., 2001). The elm decline in many parts of Europe at about 5,000 carbon-14 yr BP has been attributed by some workers to the use of elm leaves for livestock feed. This phase was followed by more intensive clearances for shifting agriculture. Certainly, this was the most marked and rapid vegetation change in the European Holocene record, with elm pollen falling drastically in just a few hundred years. There has been much debate about its causes, with disease (carried by the elm bark beetle) currently thought by many to be the primary cause. In a recent review Parker et al. (2002) scrutinized the elm decline as represented in pollen diagrams from sites across Britain and Ireland and found that the event occurred from about 6,300 to 5,300 calendar years ago. They also proposed that reductions in elm pollen during this time were the result of a unique combination of interrelated factors, including climate change, disease, and human activity.

A dramatic event in the British pollen record was the decline of Scots pine (*Pinus sylvestris*) pollen, which occurred throughout the northwest Highlands of Scotland at about 4,000 carbon-14 yr BP (Gear and Huntley, 1991). Studies of buried pine stumps in peatlands suggest that this decline in *Pinus* pollen was associated with a large-scale reduction in the northerly range of Scots pine forests. It has been postulated that this indicates a shift towards cooler and wetter conditions, possibly associated with a shift in the jet stream which brought a greater frequency of Atlantic storms into Scotland (Anderson, 1998). On the other hand, human activities including the use of fire, soil deterioration, the role of unknown pathogens, and climatic consequences of a massive eruption of the Iceland volcano Hekla c. 4,000 carbon-14 yr BP, have also been discussed as possible triggers (e.g., Blackford et al., 1992).

POSTGLACIAL CLIMATIC OPTIMA AND NEOGLACIATIONS

That climatic conditions were appreciably warmer earlier in the Holocene than in recent times was discovered by Praeger (1892) in connection with his investigation of the fauna of the estuarine clays of Ireland. Scandinavian workers subsequently showed that the pine forest had at some stage in the postglacial moved into zones which are now dominated by birch or alpine associations. This period of extended forest distribution has been called the postglacial climatic optimum. In a classic study of ivy, holly, and mistletoe pollen in Denmark, Iversen (1944) suggested that summers there were 2–3°C warmer in the mid-Holocene than in recent times. The pollen-based vegetational reconstructions of Huntley and Prentice (1988, 1993) yield similar estimates: mean July temperatures over most of continental Europe were probably around 2°C warmer than today at 6,000 carbon-14 yr BP.

The record from the NorthGRIP ice core shows that air temperatures over Greenland peaked about 8,600 years ago and remained relatively high, though with some variation, until about 4,300 years ago. Since then, temperatures have declined (Johnsen et al., 2001). The coolest conditions over Greenland since the 8,200 cal yr BP event occurred between 2,500 and 2,100 calendar years ago. Much recent paleoclimatic research has supported the interpretation of widespread climate change around this time (e.g., the evidence for cooling in northwestern Europe and elsewhere at about 2,700 cal yr BP presented by van Geel et al. [1996]).

In medieval times there may have been a return to more favorable conditions, particularly in North America and Europe—the so-called Little Optimum or Medieval Warm Period. [See Medieval Climatic Optimum.]

In 1973, Denton and Karlén postulated that the Holocene had been punctuated by at least three phases of Alpine glacial expansion: the Little Ice Age of the last few centuries, the period 3,300–2,400 carbon-14 yr BP, and the period 4,900–5,800 carbon-14 yr BP. They believed that in general the periods of glacier expansion lasted 600 to 900 years and that they were separated by periods of contraction lasting up to 1,750 years. More recently, taking the last 11,000 years as a whole, Koch and Clague (2006) suggested that broadly synchronous periods of glacier advance around the world took place at 8,600–8,100, 7,300–5,900, 5,140–4,200, 4,200–1,900, 1,900–900 cal yr BP and also during the past millennium (the Little Ice Age). The Little Ice Age—a term first introduced by Matthes (1939) to describe an "epoch of renewed but moderate glaciation which followed the warmest part of the Holocene" (the Medieval Climatic Optimum)—is now more widely used "to describe the period of a few centuries between the Middle Ages and the warm period of the first half of the twentieth century, during which glaciers in many parts of the world expanded and fluctuated about more advanced positions than those they occupied in the centuries before or after this generally cooler interval" (Grove, 1988, p. 3). More recently, the validity and value of the Little Ice Age concept has been questioned (see Matthews and Briffa, 2005, for a review). Nonetheless, Grove (1996) stoutly defended the concept and suggested that its effects can be seen world-wide. [*See* Little Ice Age In Europe.] Climate changes have also taken place in the twentieth century. [*See* Twentieth-Century Climate Change.]

The Holocene experienced abrupt and relatively brief climatic changes. In addition to the changes in high and mid-latitudes outlined above, there were alternations of pluvials and intense arid phases in the tropics and subtropics. The Holocene in lower latitudes was unstable, and it is possible that a climatic deterioration around 4,000 years ago was a cause of the nearly simultaneous collapse or eclipse of civilizations in Egypt, Mesopotamia, and northwestern India (Dalfes et al., 1997).

BIBLIOGRAPHY

Alley, R. B., et al. "Abrupt Increase in Greenland Snow Accumulation at the End of the Younger Dryas Event." *Nature* 362 (1993), 527–529. DOI: 10.1038/362527a0.

Alley, R. B., et al. "Holocene Climatic Instability: A Prominent, Widespread Event 8200 Yr Ago." *Geology* 25.6 (1997), 483–486.

Anderson, D. E. "A Reconstruction of Holocene Climatic Changes from Peat Bogs in North-West Scotland." *Boreas* 27 (1998), 208–224.

Arbogast, A. F. "Stratigraphic Evidence for Late-Holocene Aeolian Sand Mobilization and Soil Formation in South-Central Kansas, U.S.A." *Journal of Arid Environments* 34 (1996), 403–414. DOI: 10.1006/jare.1996.0120.

Atkinson, T. C., K. R. Briffa, and G. R. Coope. "Seasonal Temperatures in Britain during the Past 22,000 Years, Reconstructed Using Beetle Remains." *Nature* 325 (1987), 587–592. DOI: 10.1038/325587a0.

Barber, K., and D. Charman. "Holocene Palaeoclimate Records from Peatlands." In *Global Change in the Holocene*, edited by A. Mackay, et al., pp. 210–226. London: Arnold, 2005.

Bernabo, J. C., and T. Webb III. "Changing Patterns in the Holocene Pollen Record of North-Eastern North America: A Mapped Summary." *Quaternary Research* 8.1 (1977), 64–96. DOI: 10.1016/0033-5894(77)90057-6.

Birks, H. J. B. "Changes in Vegetation and Climate during the Holocene of Europe." In *Landscape-Ecological Impact of Climatic Change*, edited by M. M. Boer and R. S. de Groot, pp. 133–158. Amsterdam: IOS Press, 1990.

Blackford, J. J., et al. "Icelandic Volcanic Ash and the Mid-Holocene Scots Pine (*Pinus sylvestris*) Pollen Decline in Northern Scotland." *The Holocene* 2.3 (1992), 260–265. DOI: 10.1177/095968369200200308.

Clark, P. U., et al. "Freshwater Forcing of Abrupt Climate Change during the Last Glaciation." *Science* 293 (2001), 283–287. DOI: 10.1126/science.1062517.

COHMAP members. "Climatic Changes of the Last 18,000 Years: Observations and Model Simulations." *Science* 241 (1988), 1043–1052. DOI: 10.1126/science.241.4869.1043.

Dalfes, H. N., G. Kukla, and H. Weiss, eds. *Third Millennium BC Climate Change and Old World Collapse*. Berlin and London: Springer, 1997.

Dansgaard, W., J. W. C. White, and S. J. Johnsen. "The Abrupt Termination of the Younger Dryas Climate Event." *Nature* 339 (1989), 532–534. DOI: 10.1038/339532a0.

DeMenocal, P. B., et al. "Abrupt Onset and Termination of the African Humid Period: Rapid Climate Response to Gradual Insolation Forcing." *Quaternary Science Review* 19 (2000), 347–361.

Denton, G. H., and W. Karlén. "Holocene Climatic Variations: Their Pattern and Possible Cause." *Quaternary Research* 3.2 (1973), 155–205.

Gaylord, D. R. "Holocene Palaeoclimatic Fluctuations Revealed from Dune and Interdune Strata in Wyoming." *Journal of Arid Environments* 18 (1990), 123–138.

Gear, A. J., and B. Huntley. "Rapid Changes in the Range Limits of Scots Pine 4000 Years Ago." *Science* 251 (1991), 544–547. DOI: 10.1126/science.251.4993.544.

Goslar, T., et al. "High-Resolution Lacustrine Record of the Late Glacial/Holocene Transition in Central Europe." *Quaternary Science Reviews* 12 (1993), 287–294.

Goslar, T., M. Arnold, and M. F. Pazdur. "The Younger Dryas Cold Event: Was It Synchronous over the North Atlantic Region?" *Radiocarbon* 37.1 (1995), 63–70.

Grove, J. M. "The Century Time-Scale." In *Time-Scales and Environmental Change*, edited by T. S. Driver and G. P. Chapman, pp. 39–87. London and New York: Routledge, 1996.

———. *The Little Ice Age*. London: Methuen, 1988.

Gulliksen, S., et al. "A Calendar Age Estimate of the Younger Dryas-Holocene Boundary at Kråkenes, Western Norway." *The Holocene* 8.3 (1998), 249–259. DOI: 10.1191/095968398672301347.

Hone, R., et al. "Holocene Vegetation Change at Wytham Woods, Oxfordshire." *Quaternary Newsletter* 94 (2001), 1–15.

Hughen, K. A., et al. "Rapid Climate Changes in the Tropical Atlantic Region during the Last Deglaciation." *Nature* 380 (1996), 51–54. DOI: 10.1038/380051a0.

Huntley, B., and I. C. Prentice. "July Temperatures in Europe from Pollen Data, 6000 Years Before Present." *Science* 241 (1988), 687–690. DOI: 10.1126/science.241.4866.687.

———. "Holocene Vegetation and Climates of Europe." In *Global Climates since the Last Glacial Maximum*, edited by H. E. Wright Jr., et al., 136–168. Minneapolis: University of Minnesota Press, 1993.

Iversen, J. "*Viscum, Hedera*, and *Ilex* as Climate Indicators: A Contribution to the Study of the Post-Glacial Temperature Climate." *Geologiska Föreningens i Stockholm Förhandlingar* 66 (1944), 463–483.

Johnsen, S. J., et al. "Oxygen Isotope and Palaeotemperature Records from Six Greenland Ice-Core Stations: Camp Century, Dye-3, GRIP, GISP2, Renland, and NorthGRIP." *Journal of Quaternary Science* 16 (2001), 299–307.

Johnsen, S. J., et al. "Irregular Glacial Interstadials Recorded in a New Greenland Ice Core." *Nature* 359 (1992), 311–313. DOI: 10.1038/359311a0.

Koç Karpuz, N., and E. Jansen. "A High-Resolution Diatom Record of the Last Deglaciation from the SE Norwegian Sea: Documentation of Rapid Climatic Changes." *Paleoceanography* 7 (1992), 499–520.

Koch, J., and J. J. Clague. "Are Insolation and Sunspot Activity the Primary Drivers of Holocene Glacier Fluctuation?" *PAGES News* 14.3 (2006), 20–21.

Li, Y. Y., et al. "The Impact of Ancient Civilization on the Northeastern Chinese Landscape: Palaeoecological Evidence from the Western Liaohe River Basin, Inner Mongolia." *The Holocene* 16.8 (2006), 1109–1121. DOI: 10.1177/0959683606069403.

Madole, R. F. "Spatial and Temporal Patterns of Late Quaternary Eolian Deposition, Eastern Colorado, U.S.A." *Quaternary Science Reviews* 14.2 (1995), 155–177. DOI: 10.1016/0277-3791(95)00005-A.

Mangerud, J. "The Chronostratigraphic Subdivision of the Holocene in Norden: A Review." *Striae* 16 (1982), 65–70.

Matthes, F. E. "Report of Committee on Glaciers." *American Geophysical Union Transactions* 20 (1939), 518–523.

Matthews, J. A., and K. R. Briffa. "The 'Little Ice Age': Re-Evaluation of an Evolving Concept." *Geografiska Annaler* 87.1 (2005), 17–36. DOI: 10.1111/j.0435-3676.2005.00242.x.

Miao, X., et al. "Loess Record of Dry Climate and Aeolian Activity in the Early- to Mid-Holocene, Central Great Plains, North America." *The Holocene* 15.3 (2005), 339–346. DOI: 10.1191/0959683605hl805rp.

Parker, A. G., et al. "A Review of the Mid-Holocene Elm Decline in the British Isles." *Progress in Physical Geography* 26.1 (2002), 1–45. DOI: 10.1191/0309133302pp323ra.

Parker, A. G., T. J. Wilkinson, and C. Davies. "The Early-Mid Holocene Period in Arabia: Some Recent Evidence from Lacustrine Sequences in Eastern and Southwestern Arabia." *Proceedings of the Seminar for Arabian Studies* 36 (2006), 243–255.

Praeger, R. Ll. "Report on the Estuarine Clays of the North-East of Ireland." *Proceedings of the Royal Irish Academy* 2 (1892), 212–289.

Rackham, O. *Ancient Woodland.* London: Arnold, 1980.

Ruddiman, W. F. *Plows, Plagues, and Petroleum: How Humans Took Control of Climate.* Princeton, N.J., and Oxford, U.K.: Princeton University Press, 2005.

Shuman, B., P. J. Bartlein, and T. Webb III. "The Magnitudes of Millennial- and Orbital-Scale Climatic Change in Eastern North America during the Late Quaternary." *Quaternary Science Reviews* 24.20–21 (2005), 2194–2206. DOI: 10.1016/j.quascirev.2005.03.018.

Van Geel, B., J. Buurman, and H. T. Waterbolk. "Archaeological and Palaeoecological Indications of an Abrupt Climate Change in The Netherlands, and Evidence for Climatological Teleconnections around 2650 BP." *Journal of Quaternary Science* 11.6 (1996), 451–460.

Webb, R. S., et al. "Influence of Ocean Heat Transport on the Climate of the Last Glacial Maximum." *Nature* 385 (1997), 695–699. DOI: 10.1038/385695a0.

—ANDREW S. GOUDIE

HUMAN DIMENSIONS OF GLOBAL CHANGE

Human beings have played a crucial role in recent global change, either by modifying or by redirecting natural terrestrial processes—while also carrying out certain economic, social, and cultural activities on a global scale—or as subjects of the good or ill effects of such changes.

THE HISTORICAL PERSPECTIVE

Complex interactions among people and places have been going on for many millennia, sometimes resulting in important local or regional transformations, but it is only with the dawn of the modern age that we begin to discern some truly global aspects to the behavior of our species. This article is therefore limited to developments taking place since the late fifteenth century.

The Columbian Encounter

The pivotal event was the abrupt Columbian Encounter: the mutual discovery by the inhabitants of the two hemispheres of the existence of the transoceanic other, resulting in the immediate establishment of close connections between the peoples and biotic and other resources of the Americas on the one hand, and Europe, Africa, and Asia on the other. Australia, New Zealand, and the Pacific Islands were to enter this extended community two to three hundred years later.

There is botanical, linguistic, and archaeological evidence of sporadic human contacts across the Atlantic and Pacific long before 1492, but the impacts of such interchanges were minor or local. The only actual colonizations we can be sure of, those of the Norse in Greenland, Newfoundland, and perhaps other places in northeastern North America, were tiny and short-lived. But it was in that same homeland of wanderers—northwestern and western Europe, a region that had long lagged behind the civilizations of Asia and the Mediterranean—that our great enterprise in globalization was to be launched. It was also there, as documented by Fernand Braudel (1981–1984), that we find the earliest decisive stirrings of the capitalist system, arguably the most essential component of modernization.

As the first chapter in the chronicle of human-induced global change, the Columbian Exchange had many immediate and long-term effects, but perhaps none more sudden or dramatic than those in the biotic realm. On balance, the interhemispheric exchange of domesticated plants and animals was beneficial to the affected parties. The introduction of maize, the white potato, manioc (cassava), peanuts, tomato, cacao, sunflowers, pineapple, and various New World squashes and beans into Eastern Hemisphere farms generated major demographic and economic change and had a mostly positive impact on the diet and welfare of their Old World cultivators and their communities. But perhaps the ideal exemplar of biological globalization—albeit of dubious benefit to human well-being—is tobacco, which spread rapidly from its American homeland to the most remote inhabited tracts of Eurasia and Africa during the sixteenth and seventeenth centuries.

Perhaps equally impressive is the westward flow of domesticated plants and animals into the Americas. The arrival—then veritable population explosion—of horses, cattle, sheep, goats, swine, and poultry brought not only the creation of wholly new rural economies but also drastic impacts on indigenous biota, forests, grasslands, and hydrology, even though the changes occurred at different times and rates in various regions. These effects were compounded by the importation of virtually the entire repertory of cultivated Eurasian and African plants. The major grains—wheat, barley, oats, rye, rice, and sorghum—may have been the most consequential, but there were also many vegetables, fruits, nuts, and such plantation crops as sugarcane, coffee, bananas, and various spices. There were less welcome transatlantic passengers in the form of weeds and insects that proved to be successful in their aggression against native competition. For reasons that are unclear, American species were unable to retaliate in the Eastern Hemisphere.

The transfer of Old World technologies also had major consequences for American ecosystems. Metallurgical knowledge was introduced into societies in which metal objects had previously been rare. That introduction was to have vast repercussions for the habitat through the universal availability of guns and iron-shod plows.

The early intercontinental sharing of artificially bred and managed species inaugurated an era of genuine globalization of economic activity that has yet to run its course. An ideal example of the process is the massive cultivation and refining of sugarcane in nearly every place in the world where climate, terrain, soil, labor supply, and other economic considerations render the practice profitable. There has likewise been a worldwide dispersal of wine grapes. Both cultures were being pursued vigorously in the Americas by the early 1500s, although the sugar plantation was to have much the greater economic, social, and geopolitical impact. In subsequent periods, these two agricultural items, along with other globalized plantation crops, were to be established in many parts of Africa, Asia, Australia, and the Pacific Islands as well as the Americas.

On balance, the Columbian Exchange of domesticated life forms and various technologies seems to have benefited the affected populations. The opposite is true of the exchange of disease organisms between two worlds previously isolated from one another. Indeed, for too many indigenous American peoples the consequences were sudden and catastrophic. For reasons related to prehistoric patterns of migration of small bands of human beings along high-latitude routes from Eurasia into the Americas, the millions of pre-Columbian Americans lacked immunity to the various infectious and parasitic ailments that had been acquired over many generations by Eurasians and Africans. [See Migrations.] The outcome was a series of devastating epidemics among susceptible populations, whose numbers were reduced by 50–90% in just a few years, a holocaust chronicled by William Denevan (1992). Indeed, exotic pathologies seem to have been the principal factor in the total extinction of many communities. The phenomenon was to be repeated later among isolated groups in the Pacific and Siberia and is still being played out today in the remote reaches of Amazonia.

Syphilis is the only likely candidate for retribution, a lethal disease apparently originating in the Americas and subsequently diffusing throughout the world, but that hypothesis is still subject to scholarly dispute. Horrific as the intercontinental exchange of certain microorganisms may have been, the resulting losses were continental or regional in scope; these were not global pandemics. However, with the gradual universalization of immunities and low-level infections, the stage was set for the genuine worldwide pandemics that were to become an inescapable feature of modernization.

One of the more unfortunate results of universal intensification of contact among peoples and places is the occurrence of global pandemics. The greatest of these so far has been the influenza pandemic of 1918–1919 that caused more than 20 million deaths worldwide, far exceeding the toll of later outbreaks of flu viruses or the earlier cholera episodes. The ongoing AIDS pandemic will almost certainly not be the last such event.

The most crucial development in modernization was the appearance of a new mind-set among a critical, interactive mass of human beings. It involved the notions of rapid, perpetual change and material progress, individualism, scientific rationality, a devout belief in technology, and a mechanistic vision of the world; a loosening of the claims of traditional religion, new ways of regarding space and time, and the ascendance of impersonal relationships. These new sensibilities are compatible with the rise of capitalism and, later, state socialism. Such symptoms of the new regime as industrialization, urbanization, and advanced communication systems should be regarded not as causes of modernization but rather as concomitants or consequences of an unprecedented mode of dealing with the challenges of a globalizing, humanized planet. Also vital to the modern age are

that extraordinarily important fifteenth century invention, the printing press, and the massive, widespread exploitation, beginning some generations later, of fossil fuels. The emergent new order would have been unthinkable without an abundance of cheap printed matter—supplemented eventually by universal literacy and (often compulsory) mass education—and, in the material realm, cheap and abundant energy.

Europeanization of the world

From its opening episodes until recently, the modern age was characterized by the "Europeanization" of the world. From the mid-1400s onward, western European mariners and explorers availed themselves of steadily improving vessels, charts, and other navigational aids to penetrate all the seas of the world and to scout their shores. They were followed soon by explorers of continental interiors, soldiers, merchants, administrators, clerks, missionaries, teachers, curious scientists, and, where conditions looked inviting, European settlers. Eventually, by the early twentieth century, the entire inhabited world, with only a few exceptions such as China and Japan, was occupied or governed directly or indirectly by Europeans. A series of imperial regimes of global reach came into being—the Spanish, Portuguese, Dutch, French, and, most far-flung of all, the British. All were managed with a degree of sophistication, systematic exploitation, and racism unknown in the premodern era.

The globalization of the spiritual realm was especially noteworthy. Proselytizing activity kept pace with advancing flag and weaponry, sometimes even preceding it. The claims of a universal (Western) Christian church were being realized, even though dominion was divided between Roman Catholics and their Protestant competitors. Although success in conversion varied greatly from place to place, only a few localities were spared the attentions of European and North American missionaries. These evangelists often introduced Western languages, schooling, medicine, and much other cultural baggage, as well as the gospel. The worldwide program of Christianity would later be emulated by Buddhists and Muslims, whose previous range had been regional.

From its outset, European hegemony brought about redistributions of population on a scale and over distances previously unknown. Initially, the transfers overseas of Europeans in their various imperial capacities were much smaller than the forced movements of slaves and indentured laborers. The largest such stream of migrants was that of enslaved Africans shipped to the plantations and mines of the West Indies and parts of South and North America. This process began in the early 1500s and lasted well into the nineteenth century, involving an estimated 15 million captives. On a much smaller scale, but also producing major alterations in the human geography of the receiving areas, was the recruitment, often under false pretenses, of laborers from India, Malaya, China, the Philippines, the Pacific Islands, and elsewhere for farm labor in various European colonies lacking adequate local labor forces.

European emigration began in the 1600s and peaked in the early twentieth century. Reaching a total of perhaps 60 million, this was the largest migration in human history. The United States absorbed most of these migrants, but Canada, Argentina, Uruguay, Brazil, South Africa, Australia, New Zealand, Siberia, and Central Asia also received substantial immigration. The extermination or displacement of indigenous peoples commonly accompanied these migrations. Many of the pioneers settled in areas that had been thinly occupied by the indigenous peoples, and too frequently the ecological well-being of the colonized territories was imperiled by new modes of land use.

The initial wave of European settlement was generally followed by substantial natural population growth, bringing about a radical transformation of the world's population. There were also diasporas of certain ethnic groups who served the economy as middlemen in commerce or various crafts or services in places where neither Europeans nor the subordinated population could fill vital niches. Thanks to modern modes of transportation and communication, these scattered communities of Chinese, East Indians, Jews, Lebanese, Armenians, and Gypsies, for example, were able to maintain their cultural integrity and global connections.

Among the unintended consequences of these great population movements was an increase in miscegenation, that is, mating between members of different "races" and the resulting hybrid offspring. This had gone on for millennia at a low level, for even in premodern times human populations were rarely completely isolated. Within the past few centuries, however, some new mixed-blood populations have been formed, for example, Mexican mestizos and South Africa's *Cape Coloured*. Perhaps even more important ultimately is the recent, steady increase in the frequency of interracial marriages world-wide. If this trend continues, the Earth may come to be populated by a human species with few group differences in visible physical ("racial") attributes—a consummation of the globalization process.

DEMOGRAPHIC AND SETTLEMENT TRANSFORMATION

More immediately consequential for the welfare of humans and the ecological health of the planet has been the enormous growth in population during the modern period. After a major spurt following the adoption of agriculture and animal husbandry in the Neolithic, there was probably a gradual buildup of total global population through the Middle Ages, despite occasional setbacks. [See Agriculture and Agricultural Land.] The modern era has brought at least a twelve-fold increase in the world's population, from an estimated half-billion in the late 1600s to more than six billion at the close of the twentieth century. This population explosion began with death-control—the first phase of the Demographic Transition—initially among European populations, then spreading to other communities, with improvements in food supply, hygiene, housing, and, later, prevention and effective medical treatment of disease and injuries. The globalization of death-control was responsible for the 2% annual rate of growth in world population in the climactic decade of the 1960s. A universal fall in death rates was followed

eventually by a parallel decline in birth rates, beginning once again in developed countries, then spreading to developing countries. Several developed nations are now reporting an excess of deaths over births, while others are approaching zero natural population growth. The global human population may stabilize by the end of the twenty-first century, but certainly at a level above ten billion.

Urbanization has been a significant result of modernization. In premodern times, cities were to be found only in where complex civilizations existed, but the modern era has witnessed the creation of cities large and small over vast areas where they were previously unknown, notably North America, the West Indies, most of Central and South America, Africa south of the Sahara, Siberia, and Australia. Moreover, many new cities sprouted in such historically advanced areas as China, India, Russia, and Europe, and many older towns and cities experienced substantial growth. Almost everywhere, internal and international migrants flocked to the bright lights and economic opportunities of these centers. Although there is no uniformly accepted definition of "urban," it seems probable that more than half of the world's people in the early twenty-first century are city dwellers. This widespread urbanization brings a wide variety of commercial and manufacturing enterprises, as well as service industries and complex social and cultural activities.

The modernization of the world also entailed a novel reordering of its political-geographic arrangements. Following the process begun in western Europe, all of the Earth's land surface (except Antarctica) was divided up into nominally sovereign states, now numbering more than 150. The most avidly sought-after political situation, albeit one seldom fully achieved, is that of the perfected nation-state, an entity within which a political apparatus coexists with a single national or ethnic group, to the exclusion of other groups or loyalties. After the decolonization of the European empires, which began haltingly after World War I and accelerated rapidly after World War II, the former colonies have tried, with only limited success, to emulate the European model.

GLOBALIZED SOCIETY TODAY

The existence of a globalized world is the paramount social fact of the early twenty-first century. The concept of globalization combines two related phenomena: a worldwide sharing of various political, economic, social, and cultural patterns and modes of behavior as suggested above; and a close-knit interdependency among all the geographic and other components of humankind, a set of indispensable working interrelationships. Contrary to the general misconception, globalization cannot be equated with homogenization. Although there are many obvious examples of standardized items replicated worldwide, we are not undergoing simple convergence toward a universal cultural sameness, however inexorable may be the progress toward biological homogeneity. In fact, the forces of globalization, while obliterating some differences among places, are also breeding wholly new varieties of places and people. Furthermore, the operation of the current world-system has yielded highly uneven levels of development, and the gaps between centers of power and dominance in the developed world and a huge less-developed periphery show no signs of narrowing. Similarly, the developmental disparities within a number of countries—for example, Italy, Argentina, Brazil, and China—refuse to disappear under the present advanced form of capitalism.

Advanced modes of transportation and communication—railroads, automobiles, trucks, and aircraft—have vastly reduced the burden of distance and costs for passengers and commodities, while the instantaneous transmission of information and money—by telegraph, telephone, recordings, radio, television, video cassettes, and rapidly evolving electronic and computer networks—has transformed work and leisure. These innovations have enabled the creation and growth of immensely powerful, geographically fluid multinational firms. This revolution in information, travel, and business has been greatly facilitated by the adoption of English as the world language. Routing such early competitors as Latin, French, and German, English in its various dialects has become the first or second language of a majority of countries and the unrivaled medium for commerce, finance, diplomacy, science, and scholarship.

A uniquely modern development has been the emergence of popular culture, something that was manifested by the late nineteenth century as spectator sports and mass-circulation periodicals gained popularity. Since then, with the compression of space and time, there has been a worldwide sharing of movies, comics, television programs, gadgets, popular music and dance, dress, cuisines, other forms of entertainment, and much else.

The recent boom in human numbers has been accompanied by a marked rise in territorial mobility. International migrations of the conventional type persist, but the outward streaming of Europeans has dropped precipitously and has been largely replaced by flows of Asians, Latin Americans, West Indians, Middle Easterners, and Africans gravitating toward prosperous destinations. In addition, there is now a brisk circulation of temporary labor migrants among countries, and new transnational communities are taking shape. The latter phenomenon, with its interesting political, economic, and social implications, involves both the working class and the elite of society, people moving facilely among countries without a definitive attachment to any of them. The expansion of tourism, both domestic and international, into a leading industry has been tremendous and shows no signs of abating. Few places fall outside the realm of tourism, and the social and environmental impacts, while undoubtedly substantial, are still poorly understood. A related recent development has been the growth of vacation trips and retirement migration. Less welcome is the proliferation of refugees, a chronic crisis of the modern world. At a conservative estimate, at least 15 million refugees and asylum-seekers have been displaced from their homes by warfare, civil and ethnic strife, and natural and industrial disasters.

The massive growth of population and its complex redistribution have implications for environmental change at the global scale, but they are difficult to enumerate. The impact of humans on all aspects of the habitat is obvious, especially in those burgeoning cities and conurbations with 10 million inhabitants or more, but it would be too simplistic to equate environmental change on a global scale with population densities measured in regional or national terms. Patterns of activity, consumption, and organization are more relevant. Thus, through its purchases and trips of all sorts, a single affluent household in Frankfurt or Los Angeles may inflict more ecological harm throughout the world than a score of families in rural Bangladesh or the Philippines.

The most successful of nation-states lack the means to cope with economic, environmental, and other problems that transcend its borders. Whatever the strengths or weaknesses of individual states, the globalization of human affairs has necessitated intergovernmental treaties and other arrangements for postal, navigational, aeronautical, meteorological, medical, criminal, intellectual property, humanitarian, and other functions. Along with the creation of a growing number of official international organizations since the late nineteenth century, a vast array of nongovernmental organizations (NGOs) and special-interest associations have come into being. The range of their interests is endless, including sports, technology, science, hobbies, philanthropy, social issues, and much else.

As the ultimate evidence of the impotence of the sovereign state, the world has witnessed the founding of the League of Nations in the aftermath of World War I and its successor, the United Nations, a quarter-century later. Although neither institution has lived up to the hopes of its creators, their very existence testifies to the stubborn reality of an interactive, globalized human community.

At the beginning of the twenty-first century the human species inhabits a planet radically transformed. It is truly a global community, however troubled by internal tensions and conflicts. Our contemporary world is one in which there is universal sharing of modes of production and consumption, of values, amusements, anxieties, and ways of behaving—even though the flow of influences may be much stronger from developed to less-developed lands than the reverse. It is a place in which distant events can cause instantaneous perturbations throughout the system. It is, finally, also a world increasingly unified in its worries over the viability of an ecosystem so strongly modified by human activities that have both local and planetary consequences.

[See also Economic Levels; Environmental Movements; Globalization and the Environment; Human Populations; International Environmental Agreements; International Human Dimensions Programme on Global Environmental Change (IHDP); and Urban Areas.]

BIBLIOGRAPHY

Appadurai, A. *Modernity at Large: Cultural Dimensions of Globalization.* Minneapolis: University of Minnesota Press, 1996. The nine chapters in this volume are varied in focus and uneven in value, but *in toto* this is a most significant exploration of transnationalism, diasporas, and the postnational idea.

Barber, B. R. *Jihad vs. McWorld*. New York: *Times Books*, 1995. A highly readable, popular survey of the apparent contradiction between global cultural convergence and localized, militant new social identities in the contemporary world.

Barnet, R. J., and J. Cavanagh. *Global Dreams: Imperial Corporations and the New World Order*. New York: Simon and Schuster, 1994. An excellent account of the rising power of multinational firms and their impact upon culture and demography as well as the economy.

Blaut, J. M. *The Colonizer's Model of the World: Geographical Diffusionism and Eurocentric History*. New York: Guilford Press, 1993. A persuasive polemic that not only attacks the conventional Eurocentric view of history and geography but also presents a plausible, if iconoclastic, hypothesis for the rise of Europe and the origin of the modern world-system.

Braudel, F. *Civilization and Capitalism, 15th–18th Century*. 3 vols. London: Collins; New York: Harper and Row, 1981–1984. A rich, magisterial treatment of the many dimensions of the European genesis of capitalism.

Butzer, K. W., ed. "The Americas before and after 1492: Current Geographical Research." *Annals of the Association of American Geographers* 82.3 (1992), 343–568. A dozen articles that provide an excellent conspectus of what is known and what remains to be discovered about this enormous hemispheric transformation.

Crosby, A. W. *The Columbian Exchange: Biological and Cultural Consequences of 1492*. Westport, Conn.: Greenwood, 1972. A pioneering study, one with special emphasis on the effects of the Columbian Encounter on the peoples and ecologies of the New World.

——. *Ecological Imperialism: The Biological Expansion of Europe, 900–1900*. Cambridge and New York: Cambridge University Press, 1986. A superb treatment of the changes wrought in the non-European world by the introduction of European organisms, with special attention to disease.

Denevan, W. M. *The Native Population of the Americas in 1492*. 2d ed. Madison: University of Wisconsin Press, 1992. A study of precontact human numbers and subsequent depopulation that is as nearly definitive as is feasible given difficult data problems.

Fishman, J. A., R. L. Cooper, and A. W. Conrad. *The Spread of English: The Sociology of English as an Additional Language*. Rowley, Mass.: Newbury House, 1977. The most extensive coverage of the topic to date.

Goudie, A. *The Human Impact on the Natural Environment*. 4th ed. Cambridge, Mass.: MIT Press, 1994. Details the kinds of biophysical impacts that humankind has made on Earth. The fifth edition was published in 2000.

Grübler, A. *Technology and Global Change*. Cambridge and New York: Cambridge University Press, 1998. Assesses the role of technological change in global environmental change, focusing on the history of that change in the twentieth century.

Hopkins, T. K., and I. Wallerstein, eds. *The Age of Transition: Trajectory of the World-System, 1945–2025*. London ,U.K., and Atlantic Highlands, N.J.: Zed Books, 1997. Nine essays, looking before and after, that examine issues of politics, production, labor, and welfare at the world scale.

Kotkin, J. *Tribes: How Race, Religion, and Identity Determine Success in the New Global Economy*. New York: Random House, 1993. A breezy, semipopular account of how traditional "tribes" (Jewish, Chinese, Japanese, English, Armenian) and nascent ones (East Indian, Mormon, Palestinian) operate effectively at a global or quasi-global level. The author claims that tribalism will be a major ingredient in the new global order.

McCrum, R., et al. *The Story of English*. Rev. ed. New York: Penguin, 1993. The final chapters of this excellent volume deal with the worldwide diffusion of the language. The third revised edition was published in 2003.

McEvedy, C., and R. Jones. *Atlas of World Population History*. Harmondsworth, U.K., and New York: Penguin, 1978. Although far from definitive, this atlas—the only one of its kind—remains useful.

Meinig, D. W. *The Shaping of America: A Geographical Perspective on 500 Years of History*. Vol. 1. *Atlantic America, 1492–1800*. New Haven: Yale University Press, 1986. This volume, the first of four, deals masterfully with the genesis and development of the Atlantic World, the core of the emergent modern world-system.

Meyer, W. B. *Human Impact on the Earth*. Cambridge and New York: Cambridge University Press, 1996. Traces the human impact on the biosphere, including causes and regional variations, all placed in historical context.

Meyer, W. B., and B. L. Turner II, eds. *Changes in Land Use and Land Cover*. Cambridge and New York: Cambridge University Press, 1994. A set of essays documenting the role of human-induced land changes in global environmental change.

Schiller, H. I. *Mass Communications and American Empire*. 2d ed. Boulder, Colo.: Westview, 1992. An acerbic but well-informed overview of the ways in which modern media have saturated the world and the effects and implications thereof, with special attention to the role of the United States.

Socolow, R., et al., eds. *Industrial Ecology and Global Change*. Cambridge and New York: Cambridge University Press, 1994. A set of 36 essays offering a variety of useful perspectives on the ecological implications of worldwide industrialization.

Thomas, W. L., ed. *Man's Role in Changing the Face of the Earth*. Chicago: University of Chicago Press, 1956. A monumental, highly influential work consisting of 52 essays and complementary discussion. Still indispensable for people seeking understanding of the effect of human activities on major categories of the natural environment.

Turner, B. L., II, and K. W. Butzer. "The Columbian Encounter and Land-Use Change." *Environment* 43.8 (1992), 16–20. Connects the European conquest of the Western Hemisphere with current global environmental change.

Turner, B. L., II, et al. *The Earth as Transformed by Human Action: Global and Regional Changes in the Biosphere over the Past 300 Years*. Cambridge and New York: Cambridge University Press, 1990. A sequel to the preceding item, this massive, richly informative volume devotes pp. 19–141 to "Changes in Population and Society."

Wallerstein, I. *The Modern World-System: Capitalist Agriculture and the Origins of the European World-Economy in the Sixteenth Century*. New York: Academic Press, 1976. A brief summary of research by an influential author concerning a crucial period in the development of the modern world-system.

Wills, C. *Children of Prometheus: The Accelerating Pace of Human Evolution*. Reading, Mass.: Perseus Books, 1998.

—WILBUR ZELINSKY

HUMAN ECOLOGY

Human ecology is the study of the relations between human beings and their biophysical environment, or between nature and society, though the term is also used in many narrower senses.

The word "ecology" is derived from *Oekologie,* introduced in 1866 by the German biologist Ernst Haeckel. He coined the term to denote the relations of the organism with its environment, a topic he held no less deserving of scientific study than the organism's internal anatomy and physiology. In the late nineteenth and early twentieth centuries, "ecology" became the accepted English-language name for a subfield of biology examining the ways in which climate, soil, other environmental conditions, and interactions among organisms influence the distribution of plant and animal species and species assemblages. Biological ecology developed a number of highly influential terms and concepts: among them, those of community and ecosystem emphasizing the close relations and interdependencies of different components of the landscape. Those of succession and climax described an orderly evolution of species assemblages toward an end state determined largely by local conditions of climate and soil. [*See* Ecosystems.]

The approach and the concepts developed by ecologists proved attractive to some social scientists as well. A subfield of sociology that developed in the 1920s under the name of "human ecology" transferred them into the social realm to address the relations between human individuals and their social—economic, institutional, and technological—surroundings. Its name notwithstanding, sociological human ecology paid and has continued to pay little attention to human relations with the biophysical environment. But it is not the only school of thought to take that name or a similar one, and the term "human ecology" and similar coinages have also been attached to the study of particular aspects of human interaction with the biophysical world. A subfield of medicine addressing the environmental relations of disease was dubbed human ecology; so was the study of the physiological and psychological influence of weather on human beings. Anthropologists and geographers interested in "cultural ecology"—a term that dates back to the 1940s—have focused on human use of resources in rural and especially premodern settings. More recently, the term "political ecology" has been used to describe similar work with a stronger emphasis on the role of class and power in shaping and constraining resource use. Still more recent coinages include those of "feminist cultural ecology" and "feminist political ecology," denoting a particular interest in gender relations. Concern among economists for such matters as the material and energy dimensions of transactions has given rise to the field of ecological economics. "Industrial ecology" has recently been proposed as a name for the study of the entire set of relations between industry and the environment, from the consumption of resources to the emission of byproducts and wastes. A radical school of environmental ethics associated with the Norwegian philosopher Arne Naess has taken the name of "deep ecology." [See Industrial Ecology.]

As used here, "human ecology" takes in many of these partial senses. It was defined in its full breadth as early as 1922 by the American geographer Harlan H. Barrows as denoting "the mutual relations between man and his natural environment." It is used in this wider meaning by, among others, the U.S.-based journal Human Ecology, the international Society for Human Ecology, and a Library of Congress cataloging-class for books dealing with human-environment relations.

Taken in this sense, "human ecology" is one of several possible umbrella terms comprising the study of relations between humankind and the biophysical world. Other terms in the same sense are "human-environment relations," "nature-society relations," "environmentalism," "environmental studies," and "environmental science." "Human ecology" is the crispest and least clumsy of the available terms, and it carries few of the political connotations of "environmentalism." Not only is the literal meaning of the term apt, but because the concepts of integration, complexity, systems, and feedback central to biological ecology are basic to the contemporary understanding of the nature of human-environment relations and especially of global environmental change, its connotations are equally appropriate.

The name also has liabilities. It is sometimes argued that a human ecology, so-called, must tend to emphasize the elements that human beings share with plants and animals, thus reducing social science to a form of biological determinism; that it must focus on such variables as population numbers and means of subsistence while neglecting what is distinctively human, including relations with the environment: reflexivity, values and ethics, institutions, and culture. It has also often been suggested that classical plant and animal ecology places such emphasis on the notions of equilibrium and climax states that any social science drawing upon it must have conservative or reactionary political implications. It has been suggested too that any importation of natural science into social analyses must have the effect of justifying all social relations as "natural" and therefore beyond criticism. But many counterexamples suggest that this need not be the case, nor is there the full range of distinctively human characteristics cannot be brought into a field called human ecology. The danger of reductionism indeed exists and must be guarded against, though a social science that ignores the biophysical dimension of human life offers no less distorted a picture of reality than one that overemphasizes it. The objection that drawing upon ecology implies a bias toward stability carries less weight now than it once might have, for biological ecology has undergone such change in this regard that many now speak of a "new ecology" that has abandoned the steady-state and climax dogmas of its past.

If "human ecology" is defined as encompassing human relations with the biophysical environment, it covers a much wider field than "global environmental change" or its human dimensions. Global changes are one possible consequence of human use of the environment, and they are one possible source of change in human-environment relations. They are far from the only factor in those relations, nor are they necessarily the most important one at any particular time and place. Human ecology is the whole of which the human dimensions of global change form a part. Under any logical organization of inquiry, therefore, an encyclopedia of human ecology would incorporate an entry or entries on "global environmental change," not the other way around. Yet human ecology does not exist, under that or any other name, as an organized, comprehensive academic field. The study of global change and its human dimensions, on the other hand, is increasingly approaching that status, with its own journals, academic organizations, professional meetings, and budget lines with funding agencies. How this state of affairs arose, and how the narrower focus has flourished at the expense of the broader—how the study of global environmental change has taken precedence over the wider study of environment—has much to do with the history of attitudes in twentieth-century social thought toward the biophysical dimensions of human existence.

The first important grand theory of human ecology in modern social science was that of "environmental determinism," in which the biophysical "environment also played a partial role, in this case chiefly as something affecting rather than affected by humankind. In the early twentieth century, determinism dominated the academic field of geography in many countries and influenced work in every other discipline as well. Its best-known proponents included the American geographers Ellen Churchill Semple and Ellsworth Huntington. Both emphasized the role of the biophysical environment in shaping individual behavior and collective social attributes alike. Semple, for instance, proposed that the inhabitants of mountains, mountain passes, islands, seacoasts, wetlands, and other physiographic zones had certain fixed psychological and social characteristics impressed upon them by their surroundings. Huntington sought the sources of such characteristics mainly in climate. He tried to identify the ideal and the substandard climates and seasons for civilization, mental and manual labor, and social progress, and he attempted to explain the rise and decline of ancient civilizations as the consequence of shifts in storm tracks that had stimulated or sapped human energies. Not even Semple and Huntington were environmental determinists in the strictest sense. Both paid frequent lip service (and sometimes more) to ways in which social and cultural differences affected the significance of environmental features. Huntington in some of his writings emphasized race and diet as factors ranking with climate as forces in human life. But both did regard environment as a powerful and sometimes the dominant external and independent influence, and to call their work deterministic is not misleading.

By the 1920s, criticisms of environmental determinism in the social sciences were already widespread and effective. Within a few decades, it had almost entirely ceased to be a significant presence even within those disciplines, such as geography and anthropology, most closely concerned with human relations to the environment. The most constructive reaction against determinism came to be known as "possibilism." Expounded most influentially by the French historian Lucien Febvre, it held that environments never impose any characteristics or any particular way of life on those who dwell in them. Instead, they offer a broad range of possibilities. Any particular society, depending on its own characteristics and activities, will recognize and exploit only some of those possibilities as resources and encounter and suffer from only some of them as hazards or obstacles. Thus the environment is never an entirely independent variable in possibilist human ecology; its significance can never be defined except with relation to the goals, technological capacity, internal organization, and external relations typical of the society that occupies it. Over time, the possibilities offered by the environment can be altered by changes in the environment itself, whether natural or human-induced (and, if the latter, whether deliberate or inadvertent). They are likewise altered, even if the environment remains stable, by any changes occurring in human society, from technological innovation to cultural and political change to shifts in settlement patterns to the expansion of trade to the development or decay of property rights, exchange institutions, or social safety nets, that affect the range of possibilities and problems that the environment offers.

The possibilist approach to human ecology emphasized detailed attention to the full array of characteristics of both peoples and environments as necessary for understanding their interactions. It drew empirical support from research in anthropology, geography, and history contradicting the claims of environmental determinists and showing that similar environments had been and continued to be inhabited by very different societies and cultures and used by them in quite varied ways. A French-based approach to history associated with Febvre and his colleague Marc Bloch came to be known, after the name of the journal on which it centered, as the Annales school. It devoted much attention to climate, terrain, soils, biota, and other aspects of the human environment and to the changing conditions under which societies exploited them as resources or experienced them as hazards. Possibly the most influential single work it produced was Fernand Braudel's *La Méditerranée et le monde méditerranéen à l'époque de Philippe II* (1949). Braudel dealt at the outset with the human ecology of the Mediterranean region—the biophysical environment and the technology and institutions that governed its use—as intimately intertwined with its economic and political history.

Equally within the possibilist tradition, the German-trained, American-based economist Erich Zimmermann laid out what he called "the functional theory of natural resources." He defined resources not through their inherent physical qualities alone but through the roles that those qualities can play in particular human activities. The usefulness of a resource, Zimmermann argued, is therefore dependent on the social conditions, including technology and institutions and culture, that allow the activity in which it is useful to be profitably carried on. A natural substance can thus cease to be a resource, though itself remaining physically unchanged, when changes in activities put an end to its usefulness, or it may become a resource in a new way, as, for instance, the chief use of petroleum shifted from lighting in the nineteenth century to transportation in the twentieth. Environmental change in the form of physical depletion or exhaustion through overuse is only one possible end to a resource. Mines are not abandoned only when the ore runs out or becomes too difficult to extract. Product substitution may render the ore valueless. Ruinous competition may arise from other and richer mines opened elsewhere. Declines in ore prices or in protective tariffs may make extraction uneconomical. Changes in labor relations may raise wages, or changes in markets raise energy prices beyond what extraction can profitably cover, and so on.

The American geographer Gilbert F. White pioneered an analogous social-science approach to environmental hazards. Rather than seeing certain natural events or phenomena as inherently hazardous to human activity, White described losses from hazards as the result of the interaction between natural events and human activities that effectively invite or avoid loss from them. The former approach implied that only altering or controlling a feature of the environment could make it less hazardous. What White called the "range of choice" perspective, on the other hand, called attention to the many ways in which changes in human use and occupation of the environment could make natural agents more or less threatening and harmful without those agents themselves undergoing any change. Subsequent hazards research has defined the vulnerability of different groups, individuals, and activities exposed to the same natural agents as the differences in ability to cope with its effects that make losses greater for some than for others. [See Natural Hazards.]

Mid-twentieth-century research into the role of culture and technology in the adaptation of peoples to their habitats came to be known through the writings of the American anthropologist Julian Steward as "cultural ecology." One of its key concerns has been the role of indigenous environmental knowledge in resource management and its relation to the pressures of the economic and political context. Similar interests, including a local scale of study and an emphasis on field research in rural settings, characterized the Berkeley school of Carl O. Sauer. Apart from natural hazards research, it represented the chief nature-society subfield in the discipline of geography. All of these approaches were broadly representative of a possibilist human ecology.

It was not possibilism, however, but rather a nearly total disregard for the biophysical environment that became the rule in the Western social sciences by midcentury. Questions of human ecology in any form disappeared from teaching and research save in a few subfields and the work of scattered individuals. This state of affairs came about for several reasons. A strong contributing factor was a reaction against the excesses and the distasteful political affiliations of much of environmental determinism that sometimes went to the extreme of disregarding the biophysical world altogether. Many social scientists may also have supposed, consciously or not, that technology had become so powerful and culture and society so intricate as to deprive the environment of most of its significance for modern human life, however much it might have mattered in the past. The American sociologists William Catton, Jr., and Riley Dunlap have described this belief as the "human exemptionalist paradigm" and found it reflected in most mainstream social science of the latter half of the twentieth century. But it was the organization of academic research and instruction into separate realms devoted to natural and social phenomena respectively that perhaps did the most to discourage work on topics necessarily involving both. That separation allowed social scientists to establish their independence from the natural science disciplines and allowed and encouraged them to insist that social phenomena in their causes and consequences be discussed only in terms of other social phenomena. Equally, it diverted Earth and biological scientists from any close or sophisticated consideration of the possible human role in the patterns and processes they studied.

When human ecological concerns began to reappear widely in academic research and teaching on both sides of the divide, it was largely because of events occurring outside of academia. The rise of popular environmental consciousness and concern affected social and natural scientists no less than it did the lay public. What has resulted from their reawakened interest is a body of research displaying several characteristics shaped by the circumstances under which it developed. Its origin in a sense of crisis and a wish to contribute to the solution has colored it in such a way as to leave it open to the suspicion of being less than dispassionate and even-handed. It is often accused of a predisposition to judge human impact to be harmful and its regulation to be necessary, allowing those who do not agree to dismiss it out of hand. Also, as the product not of a discipline of its own but of researchers trained in the established natural and social

science disciplines, it lacks a unifying body of theory and methods. Most of the concepts it uses are simply those central to various other, nonenvironmental fields transplanted and applied to environmental issues as if fully adequate to deal with them. As a result, environmental research is kept intellectually fragmented into subschools of thought originating in the various social and natural science disciplines. There exist few concepts and theories truly indigenous to human ecology. Last and most strikingly, arising as it did out of concern over human impact, it has tended to deal with the effects of environmental changes, and particularly global ones, to the exclusion of other aspects of human-environment relations. Yet because of the previous neglect of human ecology, it has been in the position of doing applied science before the basic science has been done; of asking, that is, what role environmental change might play in human life before knowing what role environment plays in human life. [See Human Impacts.]

The fields of global change and the human dimensions of global change do not constitute a full-fledged human ecology because of their partial focus. Environmental change, global or otherwise, can make any feature of the environment more or less valuable as a resource and more or less threatening as a hazard, but so too can social change that leaves that feature physically unaffected. The increasingly large-scale and rapid social changes that contribute to an unprecedented rate of alteration in the global environment also make for an unprecedented rate of change in human relations with aspects of the environment in which the role of environmental change is modest. The most worrisome of the projected consequences of human-induced stratospheric ozone depletion is an increase in the incidence of skin cancer in the human population. But incidence has already increased dramatically during the twentieth century for other reasons: chiefly migration, especially of fair-skinned peoples of northern European descent, to lower latitudes and changes in dress and behavior increasing exposure to sunshine. Dry and sunny climates during the late twentieth century have become much more valuable a resource than ever before, not because of any changes in climate but thanks to factors increasing the potential for their exploitation by tourism and "sunbelt" migration, and as a result they have become a more deadly hazard. The role of stratospheric ozone depletion in the increase in skin cancer is a matter of the human dimensions of global change. The role of all factors together, including but not limited to ozone depletion, that contribute to the increase is a question of human ecology. It is the human dimensions of global change that have been the most closely studied, despite their small relative importance to date, because anything having to do with environmental change is guaranteed attention that other processes of human ecology are not. Likewise, agricultural land abandonment can sometimes be traced to environmental change, such as climatic change or soil degradation or pest infestation. But it often occurs for other reasons entirely: changing tastes, increases in labor and energy costs, and the abandonment of tariffs, import quotas, and other restrictions on trade that lessened competition from elsewhere, for instance. A complete understanding of the process will not be obtained from analyzing the role of stress from environmental change alone.

But as its relevance to the human dimensions of global change becomes clearer, such a wider perspective may well be developed. The urgency associated with many global change issues may finally overcome the barriers to environmental research more generally and make possible the emergence of a human ecology equally attentive to natural and social processes. Much of the research and many of the ideas developed in the global change field may form some of its building blocks. Studies prompted by concern about the effects of global climatic change have greatly, if incidentally, enlarged our understanding of society-climate relations more generally. The recently popularized concept of "natural services" has been elaborated by ecological economists to capture the point that ecosystems, climate, and other biophysical realms provide services that are vital or valuable to human society but are often taken for granted rather than being ascribed their real value and protected accordingly. The concept expands the notion of "direct environmental value" beyond the classical notion of "natural resources" to include many services that are useful without being consciously exploited and whose importance may be neglected until they disappear or decay through mismanagement. The parallel concept of natural disservices, broadening the classical one of natural hazards, could be developed to catalog and value the sources of human loss in nature-society relations. In either case, a key insight of earlier resource and hazards work must not be lost: that the services and disservices rendered by any aspect of the environment are not inherent in its physical qualities. Rather, they emerge from the interaction of those qualities with human arrangements and can be altered by a change on either side, or both.

[*See also* Environmental Movements.]

BIBLIOGRAPHY

Barrows, H. H. "Geography as Human Ecology." *Annals of the Association of American Geographers* 13.1 (1923), 1–14.
Burton, I., R. W. Kates, and G. F. White. *The Environment as Hazard.* 2d ed. New York: Guilford Press, 1993. A standard work on the nature of natural hazards.
Daily, G., ed. *Nature's Services.* New York: Island Press, 1997.
Ellen, R. *Environment, Subsistence, and System: The Ecology of Small-Scale Social Formations.* Cambridge and New York: Cambridge University Press, 1982. A solid assessment of anthropological human ecology.
Febvre, L. *La Terre et l'évolution humaine.* Paris: La Renaissance du Livre, 1922. (Translated by E. G. Mountford and J. H. Paxton as *A Geographical Introduction to History.* Boston, 1925.) The classic statement of possibilism.
Human Ecology. Journal, 1966–. Features as wide a range as any journal of scholarly research on environment and society.
Huntington, E. *Mainsprings of Civilization.* New York: Wiley, 1945. A classic treatise of environmental determinism.
Worster, D. *Nature's Economy: A History of Ecological Ideas.* Cambridge and New York: Cambridge University Press, 1985. An outstanding if controversial analysis of the emergence and evolution of ecological thought. The second edition was published in 1994.
Zimmermann, E. W. *World Resources and Industries.* 2d ed. New York: Harper, 1951.

—WILLIAM B. MEYER

HUMAN IMPACTS

This article deals with all anthropogenic changes in the terrestrial environment, whether their effects be harmful or beneficial.

HUMAN IMPACTS ON EARTH

Few of the major systems of the biosphere have escaped the impacts of human activity. A 1990 inventory and assessment of impacts concluded that we live already on an Earth fundamentally transformed by human action (Turner et al., 1990), and it is likely that the scale and variety of human impacts will continue to grow.

Some human impacts are the intended results of human actions, while some are the incidental and inadvertent results of actions taken for altogether different purposes. Some losses in biodiversity, for example, are the result of deliberate efforts to exterminate unwanted species, but most are the unforeseen consequences of other practices. Some forms of weather modification have had modest success locally, but most human impacts on weather and climate are inadvertent. Unintended impacts are numerous and frequent in human-environment relations. The biosphere and its overlapping ecosystems are such complexly woven systems of interacting and interdependent elements—of climate, soil, and biota and of flows of water, material, and energy—that it is nearly impossible for one part to be altered without affecting many others. The ways in which they are affected are often—at least at first—unexpected and even counterintuitive. These secondary impacts are less likely than the deliberate and intentional changes to be beneficial. Human-induced environmental change tends to be viewed as harmful today more often than it was previously—as "impact" rather than as improvement—because much more is now known about the wider results of human actions, the repercussions that may spread far from their point of origin.

A second difference between the present and the past offers reason for greater concern. As human activities grow in scale and variety, so do the environmental impacts that they may produce on a planet that has not itself grown larger. As a result, it more likely that the integrity of the biosphere and the necessary conditions for human existence on Earth may be disrupted by the totality of human impacts. Throughout most of human history, excessive demands on resources might place local and regional environments under stress, but the Earth is so vast in comparison as never to seem fundamentally threatened. It was, on the contrary, Earth's impacts on humans that were, justifiably, of more concern.

The change in the scale and type of human actions has caused impacts amounting to global environmental change. "Global change" and "human impact" are overlapping but not synonymous terms. There are many significant human impacts on the environment, past and present, that do not constitute global change. Those that do are of two different sorts. Some changes achieve global magnitude by affecting a realm of the environment that operates as a fluid global system. Examples are the release of carbon dioxide and other stable trace gases into the atmosphere and the possible change in sea level resulting from climatic change produced by increased concentrations of such gases. These are globally systemic changes. Globally cumulative changes, on the other hand, are those that reach a global magnitude either by occurring widely across the Earth's surface or by significantly affecting the total stock of some resource, however geographically restricted its distribution may be.

Some human impacts can also be described as cumulative in a temporal rather than spatial sense. They are impacts that are essentially irreversible and therefore steadily cumulative, as opposed to those that can be reversed by natural or human-aided processes. Species extinction and nonrenewable resource extraction are cumulative in this sense. Other changes, such as the pollution or depletion of ground water, may be reversible, but over so long a time that for most human purposes they are irreversible. Cumulative impacts of this sort are a particular cause for concern because they represent a permanent alteration and/or impoverishment of the terrestrial environment.

Human impacts on individual aspects of the environment are dealt with in detail in other articles in this encyclopedia, as are questions about their causes and their significance for society. The present article focuses on themes common to many of them and on their overall character and briefly discusses some of the chief difficulties and sources of uncertainty in documenting human impacts, reviews the chief realms of the environment affected by human impact, and describes the overall character, magnitude, spatial pattern, and chronology of human impact.

DOCUMENTING HUMAN IMPACT

It is often difficult to assess the degree of human impact in the environment. Doing so requires a knowledge of both the previous and the current state of affairs and of any contribution that natural processes may have made to a particular change. These requirements are more easily satisfied in some forms of change and some aspects of the environment than in others.

The original, preimpact state of the environment can be reconstructed from documentary sources, on the indirect evidence of what are called "proxy" indicators, or on the even more indirect basis of theories and assumptions. Documentary sources range from government tax and land survey records to maps and detailed scientific observations. But such sources do not exist for most of the human past. Even where they do, they are often not accurate, reliable, or comprehensive. Much of the information they offer must be treated with caution, and much interpolation may be needed to fill the gaps left by available written sources.

To supplement them, scientists have employed proxy indicators as varied as oxygen isotopes present in the sediments of the deep sea floor and pollen in terrestrial sediments; these have been used with much success in reconstructing climates of the geological and recent past, and their use has been steadily refined. It has proven possible to reconstruct long-term changes in many marine fish populations by measuring the abundance of fish scales in ocean sediments and changes in land use from the patterns of soil erosion and deposition in streambeds.

Human activities also may offer proxies for environmental change. Harvest times and traces of the abandonment of human settlements have been used to document climatic conditions during the past millennium. Such data must be used with caution, for such changes may have occurred for social reasons having nothing to do with environmental changes. [See Climate Reconstruction; and Erosion.]

Uncertainty about the past remains a great obstacle to impact-assessment. In some areas, human-induced environmental changes have turned out to have a much longer history than was once assumed. As a result, a pristine, preimpact state has proven difficult to define. In other realms, the knowledge of the preimpact baseline is seriously incomplete because the necessary knowledge is particularly costly. The extent of known deposits of many mineral and fossil fuel resources in the Earth's crust depends on the economic incentives to search for the deposits: shortages that arise from the depletion of known sources encourage the discovery of more. Over the course of human history, known stocks of nonrenewable resources have steadily grown as a result of exploration at the same time that they have been reduced by extraction and use. The proportion of the total resource judged usable for human wants also depends on evolving technology and economics. In such cases, it is difficult to define precisely the initial size of a resource that has subsequently been depleted and how much of it remains, even though it may be a reasonably simple task to calculate roughly what amount has been extracted to date. It cannot be assumed that discovery has come to an end and that what is currently known is the total of what exists. The gaps can be filled by estimates made using theoretical assumptions, but the results tend to be controversial.

Theoretical models of species size and distribution are often used in assessing human impact on plants and animals. Our knowledge of many species and populations is far sketchier than that of ore and energy resources because little or no direct use is made of them and little effort has been made to determine their numbers. It is generally agreed that more species exist that have not been identified and named than that have been, but how many is very uncertain. Biogeographical theory has been invoked to provide estimates, but its results are inevitably less compelling and more controversial than those based on observation. The resulting uncertainty affects both the baseline number of species and the number that have been extinguished by human action.

For current land-use and land-cover changes, documentary sources, especially statistics, are much more abundant than for the past, but many are of questionable accuracy, and standard definitions and measures that would permit the comparison of figures from different times and places are rare. Nonetheless, much progress has been made. Remote sensing technologies have greatly expanded data archives and the possibilities for reliable assessments of land cover. There are now many observing stations for the regular collection of data on atmospheric composition, climate, streamflow, and other variables of interest, and sophisticated techniques of chemical analysis permit the detection of trace substances in tiny quantities in the environment.

Natural change must be distinguished from contemporaneous anthropogenic change. The last ice age, ending about 10,000 years ago, was one of natural upheavals in climate, biotic patterns, hydrology, and landforms across the globe at a time when *Homo sapiens* was already a significant presence in many regions. Natural changes, though less dramatic and profound than continental glaciation, have have continued in the subsequent (postglacial) period of accelerated human impact.

The problems of separating anthropogenic from natural change are nowhere greater than in the area of climate and related realms. The reconstructed record of global climate through geological time shows many fluctuations caused by forces that continue to operate even as human activities such as the release of greenhouse gases have reached a point at which they are capable of affecting the global climate. Natural climatic variations may explain, in whole or in part, a number of environmental changes that have been attributed to human impact. Vegetation decline in arid and semiarid zones, part of the process of desertification, can be the work of human actions or of climatic changes. [*See* Desertification.] Abrupt declines in marine fish populations may be caused by overharvesting, but there is evidence that such declines, probably triggered by climate, also occurred long before any significant human impacts. The task of determining causes and separating human and natural processes is complicated especially by important synergies between them. The two forces, moreover, may work at cross purposes, as with some types of climatic change, thereby masking each other's effects.

The question of natural change is not always a major one. Human impacts may be far more rapid or powerful than similar natural processes, or the possibility of nonanthropogenic variations can be dismissed because the changes are novel ones that do not occur in environments not affected by humans. Changes that fall into the first category include certain kinds of land-cover alteration, such as forest clearance and wetland drainage (which do occur naturally but where human impact is generally not difficult to identify), and such modern processes as the large-scale mining and release of heavy metals, such as lead, mercury, and cadmium, which are mobilized by human action in quantities far exceeding their flows in nature. The second category includes the presence in the environment of nonnatural substances such as synthetic organic chemicals, plastics in the oceans, and artificial radionuclides.

HUMAN IMPACTS

The Earth's land cover—the soil, vegetation, and structures on the land surface—displays the most obvious marks of human impact—and many that are not so obvious. Cultivated land now covers about 15 million square kilometers of the Earth's surface. It has expanded at the expense of other land-cover types. The global area of forest has diminished by 15–20% since preagricultural times. Grassland has undergone a smaller net decline. It has grown through the conversion of forest to pasture and

shrunk through conversion to cultivation and other uses. The global area of coastal and freshwater wetlands has declined, mostly as a result of drainage for cultivation and construction. Human settlements now occupy several percent of the world's land area and a much higher proportion of the land in densely populated regions. There has also been significant modification within the major classes of land cover. Forests have been extensively thinned and altered in composition. Vegetation decline has been substantial in many grasslands and drylands as a result of human activity, especially livestock grazing. Humans have enjoyed a steadily increasing supply of food and other outputs, which in recent decades has resulted less from the cultivation of new lands than from the more intensive use of lands already farmed. The expansion of cultivated area has thus slowed even in a period of rapidly rising overall output. In some regions of the world there has been a net reversion from cropland to forest cover. Soil degradation in various forms, particularly salinization and nutrient depletion, has been a significant inadvertent consequence of cultivation over much of the Earth. [*See* Salinization.] Soil erosion by wind and running water has in many places been accelerated by human action, though to a degree difficult to quantify. Erosion also causes siltation and sedimentation of the eroded material downwind or downstream. [*See* Erosion.]

The stocks and flows of surface fresh water have been more profoundly altered than has the land surface. Both total and per capita human withdrawals from the hydrologic cycle have risen rapidly during the past several centuries, especially the twentieth. They now claim a substantial fraction of its mean annual volume, by some estimates as much as half of the readily available flow. Globally, irrigation of crops has been and remains the chief activity for which water is withdrawn, but other uses are dominant in many basins and regions, especially those in humid climates. Transfers of water between basins have increased, but they remain minor on global and regional scales. The construction of reservoirs and other regulation of rivers across the globe have made overall flows of water significantly higher than in the past. In some places, however, the trend is partially offset by an increased spread between peak and low flows due to land-cover changes such as deforestation, drainage, and urbanization. As water use has increased, so has the volume of polluted waste water returned to the hydrologic cycle. The variety of pollutants that it contains has expanded as well, with consequences for water composition, biota, and human health. In turn, wastewater treatment and the provision of safe supplies have also expanded, though much more in the developed than in the developing world. [*See* Ground Water.]

The most striking change in the global biota is the great increase in the size and distribution of the human population itself since glacial times and its particularly rapid growth during the past several centuries. The expansion of humans has in turn greatly affected the numbers and distribution of other creatures by extinguishing species and by affecting—usually reducing—the sizes of populations and their genetic diversity. Losses of biodiversity have been heaviest in island and freshwater ecosystems and in tropical forests rich in endemic forms of life. Habitat destruction as a result of land-cover change has been the most powerful human cause of decline. Hunting, pollution, and competition from introduced species have been secondary forces overall, though each has been dominant in some particular cases and regions. Estimates of terrestrial plant and animal extinctions are controversial, but it is generally agreed that the rate of loss as a result of human action far exceeds the natural rate. Extinctions of marine animals have been few, but populations of large marine mammals, especially whales, were drastically reduced by past hunting, and many marine fish stocks have collapsed as an apparent result of overharvesting possibly combined with natural, climate-related population changes. Species transfer by humans, whether deliberate or accidental, is both a cause of extinctions and declines and a major change in its own right.

The environmental history of bacterial and viral pathogens is a distinctive case of human impact on biota. Some social changes have magnified their effects. Once-isolated outbreaks of illness have acquired a worldwide reach as the rate and scale of trade, travel, and migration have increased, leading to what is sometimes called the disease unification of the globe. Other trends, such as improvements in sanitation, nutrition, and medical care, have lessened—though quite unevenly across the world—the burden of infectious illness. Yet some interventions have caused unforeseen consequences: the rapid evolution by selection of strains resistant to common antibiotics, for example, a phenomenon also seen in the evolutionary response of agricultural pests to chemical biocides. [See Disease.]

Human impacts have not been limited to the Earth's surface: they include substantial extraction of ground water from subsurface aquifers, of fossil fuels, and of metal ores and other mineral resources. In each case, the result has been a significant depletion of the resource stock, though one generally difficult to quantify. Global groundwater resources and the net changes that they have undergone are not well documented, but there are many local and regional cases of serious depletion by withdrawal far exceeding rates of recharge. The chief known deposits of high-quality ores of several metals have been exhausted and production shifted to lower-quality ores.

Materials extracted from the surface or the subsurface are released during production, use, or disposal into the air, water, and soil. Many of the chemical flows of the biosphere have thereby been significantly altered, and some entirely new ones have been created. Releases from fossil-fuel combustion, added to those from land-cover changes such as deforestation, have increased the annual flow of carbon through the biosphere by about 10%. Human releases of sulfur to water and atmosphere, mostly from fossil fuels and ore processing, have approximately doubled the natural global flow, with effects including the acidification of precipitation, soil, and surface water. Nitrogen flows have been increased chiefly through the manufacture of synthetic fertilizer and through fossil-fuel combustion, raising agricultural yields while contributing to acidification similar to that resulting from sulfur, to the eutrophication of lakes and coastal waters,

and to certain forms of air pollution. The flow of phosphorus, chiefly mined as another agricultural fertilizer, has also been greatly increased and has also contributed to eutrophication.

Besides altering these great flows of the biosphere, there has been a great human impact on trace constituents of the biosphere. Human action mobilizes many metals—copper, lead, mercury, cadmium, and numerous others—in quantities much larger than do weathering, volcanic activity, and other sources. The current average natural and anthropogenic doses of ionizing radiations in the United States have been estimated as roughly equal. Finally, chemistry has introduced into the biosphere many synthetic substances that did not previously exist, including compounds created by industrial organic chemistry such as pesticides, solvents, and chlorofluorocarbons (CFCs, used as coolants and propellants).

Many of these emissions have contributed to changes in the chemistry of the oceans, especially off populous coastal areas and in enclosed seas, such as the Mediterranean and the Baltic, where human activity is highly concentrated and diluting capacity is small. Nitrogen and phosphorus enrichment through sewage discharge and fertilizer runoff have degraded near-shore waters in many parts of the world. Oil enters the oceans naturally through seeps, but tanker discharges have multiplied the amount many times over, especially along major shipping routes. Much wider-spread but smaller increases in many trace substances from atmospheric deposition have been observed in surface waters across the globe. The accumulation in the ocean of decay-resistant plastic debris, including litter, discarded fish nets, and production residues, is a recent but rapidly expanding phenomenon.

Emissions have also changed the chemistry of the atmosphere. Highly stable CFCs have accumulated in the stratosphere, where their decay products catalyze the breakdown of ozone molecules. The result has been a decline in high-altitude ozone concentrations of 5–10% on global average, that is especially marked over the high latitudes and in winter. Because stratospheric ozone prevents ultraviolet solar rays from reaching the Earth's surface, its depletion increases surface exposure to such high-energy radiation. There have been many localized impacts, in the lower atmosphere. Particulate pollution has increased with industrialization in some places and in other places, especially in the developed world, has been reduced by human intervention. Nitrogen oxides released by fossil-fuel combustion have promoted the formation of ozone smog, especially in sunny low-latitude metropolitan regions where conditions are most favorable. Globally, the atmospheric concentration of carbon dioxide has increased by more than 30% over the preindustrial level, and that of methane, released chiefly by land use, has approximately doubled during the past several centuries.

PATTERNS AND TRENDS OF HUMAN IMPACTS

Taking the necessary caution, several generalizations about human impacts on the environment can be made.

Human impacts have expanded greatly in variety as human activities have multiplied. While such impacts once chiefly involved alterations in the Earth's surface features, they now also include many changes in the biospheric flows of energy and material. Preagricultural impacts were modest and were confined chiefly to the land surface and the biota. They were greatly intensified and expanded by the development of agriculture, but as late as the beginning of the nineteenth century, the chief forms of human impact were forest clearing, land cultivation, and the extinction, depletion, domestication, and transfer of plant and animal species. Biotic impacts aside, they were largely reversible processes; natural recovery could take place if allowed to. A few of these activities affected global material flows. Preindustrial carbon dioxide release from forests and soils and methane release from rice culture and livestock were already substantial fractions of current levels. Global impacts by extractive and industrial processes are largely a phenomenon of the twentieth century. [See Chemical Industry.]

Among those impacts are most global-scale alterations of the major biospheric cycles. There has been an expansion in the geographic extent of impact as many changes once substantial in particular regions have become cumulatively substantial world-wide. Yet most impacts, save for the purest examples of globally systemic change—the atmospheric mixing of relatively stable and long-lived gases—remain highly differentiated across the Earth's surface. In many respects, there are vast differences between advanced industrial societies and less industrialized ones and between the urban and rural areas in each—differences in land cover, in the availability and quality of fresh water, in air quality, and in many other respects. Global trends are only poorly reflected on a subglobal scale.

There has been a striking acceleration in many—probably most—long-term trends of global change as human activity has expanded in scale and scope. Annual freshwater withdrawals, for example, have more than doubled since the end of the World War II. More than half of all anthropogenic sulfur releases, nitrogen fixation, and phosphorus extraction has occurred since 1960 or later. Large-scale synthetic organic chemical manufacturing is chiefly a development of the twentieth century.

On the other hand, a few human impacts have slowed regionally and even globally, whether as the incidental result of a shift in activities taken for reasons of economic or technological change or because of purposeful environmental management. Forest regrowth on once cultivated or grazed land has been extensive in much of the developed world, probably as a result more of the economics of agricultural land abandonment than of deliberate environmental restoration. So too, the clearance of tropical forests has slowed in periods of economic depression, as have global releases of carbon and sulfur from fossil-fuel combustion. But the reductions of some impacts can be credited directly to managerial intervention. They include the decline of radioactive fallout following a international treaty banning atmospheric nuclear testing in the early 1960s, the recovery of many marine-mammal populations following restrictions on harvesting, the declining use of lead additives in gasoline, and

the restriction of persistent pesticides such as DDT. International arrangements have been negotiated to curb chlorofluorocarbon emissions and protect the stratospheric ozone layer, and early agreements have been reached to slow carbon emissions.

Several of these problems addressed by management, however—particularly the impacts of CFCs on stratospheric ozone—are striking examples of the more frequent emergence in recent times of surprise impacts whereby some human action has had unforeseen consequences. Human activities in earlier centuries had unexpected environmental consequences—such as inadvertent transfers of plant and animal species, or planned transfers that got out of hand—but to a much larger degree today the unintended effects may exceed the intended ones. As novel human activities and technological innovations multiply and diffuse much more rapidly than before, many new direct and indirect impacts on the biosphere are created. Substances are mobilized and released in large quantities long before their full range of possible consequences—some of which may be subtle, surprising, or slow but cumulative—can be assessed. Other modern examples have included the worldwide spread of lead as a result of its use in gasoline and that of DDT residues following its development as a pesticide. Prevailing trends suggest many more such surprise environmental impacts in the future. The same trends in innovation and diffusion, however, may also mean that remedies for both novel and long-standing environmental problems and substitutes for activities causing damage can be fashioned and deployed much more rapidly than was possible in the past.

Finally, the increasing variety of human activities and of impacts they produce can greatly complicate the task of dealing with any of them. A measure that alleviates one problem may worsen or create another. When DDT itself was introduced, it was as a means of countering an environmental hazard in some ways worsened by human actions, the prevalence of mosquito-borne malaria in many regions of the world. As its harmful effects on other biota became known, it was widely replaced by more reactive pesticides that did not persist in the environment to such a damaging degree upon release but that posed even more danger to the health of the farmworkers applying them. The replacement of one form of energy generation by another generally replaces one set of environmental impacts with a second. Nuclear power, for example, does not release greenhouse gases but creates a different set of risks that must be weighed against those of fossil fuels. There is every reason to suppose that the trade-offs of this sort involved in managing environmental change will only become more perplexing and challenging in the future.

[See also Anthropogeomorphology; Fire; Global Change History; and Greenhouse Effect.]

BIBLIOGRAPHY

Consequences: The Nature and Implications of Environmental Change, 1995–. (http://www.gcrio.org/CONSEQUENCES/index.htm: accessed June 1, 2008). A quarterly journal presenting articles written and reviewed by specialists that sum up in accessible fashion the current state of knowledge in key areas.

Goudie, A. S. The Human Impact on the Natural Environment. 6th ed. Oxford, U.K., and Malden, Mass.: Blackwell, 2006. A standard textbook on the subject.

Goudie, A. S., and H. Viles. *The Earth Transformed: An Introduction to Human Impacts on the Environment*. Oxford, U.K., and Malden, Mass.: Blackwell, 1997. A comprehensive recent survey.

Goudie, A. S., ed. *The Human Impact Reader: Readings and Case Studies*. Oxford, U.K., and Malden, Mass.: Blackwell, 1997. A useful collection of research papers that illustrate the range of human impacts and the methods used in their study.

Simmons, I. G. *Environmental History: A Concise Introduction*. Oxford, U.K., and Malden, Mass.: Blackwell, 1993. A readable and comprehensive synthesis of the broad sweep of human-nature interactions.

Turner, B. L., II, et al., eds. *The Earth as Transformed by Human Action: Global and Regional Changes in the Biosphere over the Past 300 Years*. Cambridge and New York: Cambridge University Press, 1990. The most detailed and comprehensive inventory of human impact.

Vitousek, P. M., et al. "Human Domination of Earth's Ecosystems." *Science* 277 (1997), 494–499. DOI: 10.1126/science.277.5325.494. A useful short review.

—WILLIAM B. MEYER

HUMAN POPULATIONS

Human populations are among both the causes and consequences of global change. The size of the population, the ways in which it changes—the balance of births and deaths, there being no as yet immigration or emigration on a global scale)—and its internal distribution and redistribution will all affect the type and nature of global change; and the economy, the environment, the state, and society will in turn affect population size, distribution, and rate of change. The broad course of global trends in population over the approximately 3,000 millennia of human history, and the relationships between fertility and mortality, are the starting point for an examination of the causes and implications of a fundamental transition in human population that began only within the last three hundred years and is likely to continue into the next millennium: from an equilibrium of high mortality and high fertility, with crude death and birth rates of 35–40 per thousand, to an equilibrium of low mortality and fertility and rates of 10–15 per thousand. This has been a demographic revolution of dramatic proportions.

SOURCES OF INFORMATION ON HUMAN POPULATIONS

Evidence for the presence of human populations, if not for their size, comes from archaeology. Human remains—typically bones—are the most familiar archaeological source, while DNA evidence is used increasingly to study relationships between human groups, and in particular for identifying long-running patterns of human migration. There is evidence of the volume and type of human activity from its imprint on the land, for example in ancient irrigation and terracing systems. Further evidence is provided by artifacts such as ornaments, weapons, and domestic tools, and by urban and manufacturing remains, especially from metal and stone sources. Archaeological evidence is of necessity partial and geographically patchy, much dependent on where archaeologists have been active—many developing countries remain archaeologically under-investigated—and also on the fact that some materials are less durable than others, especially in hot and wet climates where bacterial decay is rapid and evidence from wood and other organic materials does not survive.

Estimates of population numbers rely heavily on documentary sources. Where early centralized civilizations, mostly associated with the Neolithic revolutions of some 6–8 thousand years ago, developed a literate culture, as in ancient Egypt, there were early estimates of human populations. Rather later, in the Roman Empire for example, population counts in history were associated primarily with taxation, as in the case of the census in Judaea in the late first century BCE, during the reign of Herod the Great. In China, Japan, and India, and in Europe and the Middle East, the primary sources for reconstructing the size and rates of change of populations in history have been national administrative records, such as the Domesday Book for England (1086 CE).

The growth of the economic and political cohesion of European and North American states from the eighteenth century was associated with the first formal national compilations of population data, and the state is now everywhere the prime agency for population enumeration. This takes two forms. The first was the establishment of national registration systems for births, deaths, and marriages, often as a direct derivative of ecclesiastical records of baptisms and burials. In most developed countries, registration has been a continuous source for monitoring population change, and in a few cases (e.g., the Netherlands, Sweden) includes registration of migrants. Registration data are used not only to examine contemporary population trends, but also to analyze historical registers; knowledge of the patterns and causes of the sharp decline in mortality in Europe in the nineteenth century has been largely derived from age and cause-of-death entries in the parish or town registers.

The second was the establishment of regular censuses, usually at 10-year intervals. The essence of any census is that it is cross-sectional, universal, simultaneous, and normative (that is, it asks questions that are relevant to all, such as age, sex, occupation, and place of residence). Census data are valuable in their own right as providing a "snapshot" of the size, distribution, and essential characteristics of a population, but are also used comparatively: successive censuses allow identification of patterns and rates of change between census dates.

Population censuses have been the principal source of population data worldwide over the last 50 years. They have proved relatively simple to collect, even in colonial societies with largely illiterate peoples and no census tradition. The United Nations Population Division has been instrumental in generalizing the census experience, and all countries have now had at least one reasonably reliable national population census within the last 20 years. The results of these censuses and other survey sources permit international comparison, and the United Nations has become the principal source of estimates of past global trends and projections of future trends. These are available in the annual UN Demographic Yearbook and associated publications.

PREMODERN POPULATIONS

Global population change reflects the ratio between births and deaths. Although there is constant redistribution of the global population through migration, both of individuals and of groups, over long and short distances, most populations throughout most of human history have experienced a balance of births and deaths, at least in the medium term (perhaps 25–50 years). In the short term, whether seasonally, annually, or longer, there may be some growth or decline, but in the very long term, over a period of centuries or millennia, growth of the global population has generally been very slow. For most of the period before the last two millennia, the population probably grew no more than 5% in any millennium. Over this long period there has been slow expansion from the earliest foci of human existence in the East African Rift Valley in Tanzania, Kenya, and Ethiopia, some 1.5–3 million years ago, to all habitable areas of the Earth's surface.

During most of this period, life expectancy at birth for most populations was probably less than 30 years, which may be compared with a figure of more than 40 years in the poorest countries today. Life for most people in most groups was nasty, brutish, and short. In particular, in the absence of systematic medical knowledge and with the low and erratic levels of nutrition that were and still are characteristic of hunter-gatherer modes of life, survival rates for infants and children were very low. As food supply became more secure with settled agriculture after the Neolithic revolution, beginning about 10,000 ago, particularly in the riparian civilizations of the Nile, the Tigris-Euphrates, and the Indus between about 5,000 and 3,000 BP and rather later in the rice civilizations of eastern and southern Asia, it is likely that long-term mortality levels improved. Even with settled agriculture, rates remained liable to fluctuate from year to year because of the random occurrence of epidemics or famines and the associated phenomenon of famine mortality. In many cases there will have been an excess of deaths over births, often by a considerable margin, followed by population decline. Some declines may have been spectacular: the most notorious documented example was the Black Death, an outbreak of bubonic plague that killed an estimated one-third of the population of Europe in the middle of the fourteenth century. The nearest twentieth-century equivalent was the global influenza pandemic in 1918–1919, which killed an estimated 30 million people in a twelve-month period (more than three times as many as were killed in World War I, 1914–1918).

The high and fluctuating mortality of the premodern period was accompanied by equally high but much less volatile levels of natural fertility. In theory, women could have at least 20 pregnancies during their biologically productive years—roughly between the ages of 15 and 50—but the highest recorded mean fertilities for whole groups are between 12 and 14 children per woman. Some 3–5% of women in most populations are naturally infertile, a further and much more variable proportion become infertile through infection and disease, especially sexually transmitted disease, and there are periods of biological infertility for all women for several months after childbirth. These infertile periods are extended by social constraints on fertility, notably those associated with marriage and sexual abstinence before, during, or after marriage. These biological and social proximate determinants of fertility reduced the number of children to 4–8 children per woman for most preindustrial societies. Even where there is a strong tradition of early marriage, as in contemporary India, Bangladesh, and Pakistan, there is not necessarily a correlation with high fertility because there is an equally strong tradition of long birth intervals, which are good for the health of mothers as well as for their newborn infants. The demographic benefits of traditional practices associated with long birth intervals, especially breastfeeding, are integral to contemporary maternal and child-health programs in developing countries.

Unlike mortality, fertility is not governed principally by factors beyond individual control. Even in early historical periods, social norms—notably marriage—are likely to have given relative stability to fertility rates, for these norms evolve only slowly. Wrigley and Schofield's classic analysis, *The Population History of England, 1541–1871* (1981) showed, for example, that marital fertility was relatively stable in England between the sixteenth and nineteenth centuries, rising gradually, with some fluctuations, over a period of substantial annual fluctuations in mortality, especially before 1700—with upturns in fertility during some periods of relative economic prosperity.

Although it is not normally possible to reconstruct directly the demographic balance in premodern populations, the apparent outcome of very slow growth for most populations suggests that high but relatively stable fertility, and high but annually and seasonally fluctuating mortality, have been the norm for the greater part of human history. This "natural" regime seems to have been underpinned by social institutions and economic and political systems, and also by generally fragile food-production systems, resulting in inadequate nutrition, variable from place to place and from season to season, as manifested in the universal evidence for famine mortality (although the likelihood of famine over large areas was itself also a function of environmental conditions, notably variable rainfall). The long-term trend was for the slow overall growth to be incorporated in situ or else to fuel migrations to colonize new land.

THE DEMOGRAPHIC TRANSITION AND MODERN POPULATIONS

This long-established high-level global demographic equilibrium has changed very fundamentally and rapidly over the last third of the present millennium. There are now much lower levels of fertility and mortality in developed countries, where there are greater short-term fluctuations in fertility than in mortality. The net global effect of the period of the changing balance between fertility and mortality has been a much higher and, for the most part, continually rising rate of overall population growth, to the extent that the world population has grown from an estimated 300 million 2,000 years ago, to approximately 1 billion by 1800, to 1.65 billion by 1900, and to nearly 6 billion at the century's close (Figure 1). By July 2007 the world's population had reached 6.6 billion. There has clearly been a fundamental shift from a high-level equilibrium of births and deaths to a lower level of both that seems to mark a new low-level equilibrium in some countries. The transition from high to low demographic equilibrium was first evident in Europe. Over a

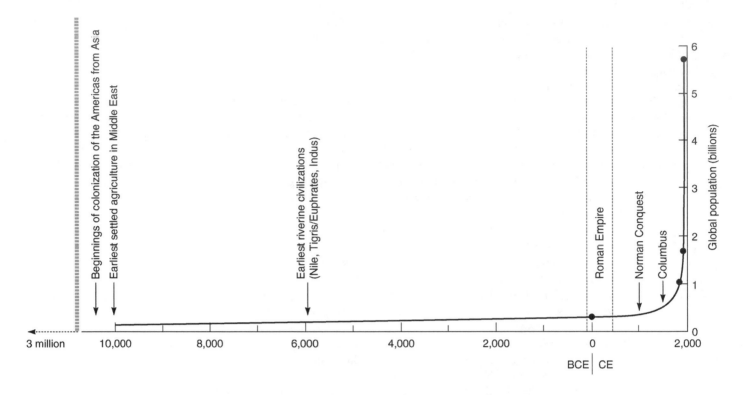

Human Populations. Figure 1. Growth of World Population.

period of two hundred years, from 1700 to 1900, there was very rapid population growth throughout Western Europe as mortality fell but fertility remained at its pre-eighteenth-century level. The sharp and consistent declines in mortality seem to have been triggered in the first instance by improved nutrition. Medieval and Renaissance Europe experienced economic prosperity, with urban growth and relative political stability. The agricultural revolution brought increased local availability of food, and greater interregional and international trade in food was able to reduce greatly the incidence of famine mortality. After 1500, new foods brought from the New World, notably the potato, began to enter the European diet. By the nineteenth century, medical science had also advanced, with direct effects on infant and childhood mortality, especially through vaccinations. Private and public incomes were also rising at this time of rapid urbanization and industrialization, creating a greater purchasing power in the mass of the population, allowing greater food "entitlements," to use Amartya Sen's terminology (Sen, 1981). An "urban penalty" in mortality had emerged throughout Europe, whereby rural areas, with less crowded and less unsanitary conditions for the mass of the population, experienced lower levels of mortality than urban and industrial populations. The quality of the environment in overcrowded and poorly managed towns had deteriorated seriously, but, during the second half of the nineteenth century in particular, substantial public resources were directed to improvements in urban housing and sanitation. By the early years of the twentieth century,

rural and urban mortality levels were low and continued to decline in developed countries.

For most of this period, fertility remained high in Europe, with a growing gap between fertility rates and mortality rates that resulted in high rates of natural increase. Some of that increase fed the large-scale migrations to the New World, but most of it was absorbed in the growing urban populations in Europe, with substantial rural-urban internal migrations that continued well into the twentieth century. Only by the last quarter of the nineteenth century and into the twentieth century did fertility begin to fall in Europe and North America, a fall that was fairly continuous until it approached levels of mortality, and therefore produced very low or even negative rates of natural population growth. This occurred from the 1930s in a few countries (for example, Britain and France), but in most of them by the end of the twentieth century.

Why did fertility fall in these countries at the time it did? It happened in the absence of two features currently associated with contemporary developing-world fertility decreases. First, there was no sense of national population policy, and no direct intervention by governments to facilitate fertility decline. Second, there was no general use of artificial means of contraception: neither barrier methods, including condoms (in widespread use only from the 1920s), nor pharmacological methods, principally the contraceptive pill (which became available only in the 1960s). It happened spontaneously—as a result of decisions of individual couples to limit their family size, either through sexual abstinence or by such means as the rhythm method or coitus interruptus.

Thus, while mortality in industrial populations fell as a result of structural causes, such as health improvements or economic and environmental conditions beyond individual control but affecting everyone (though not necessarily equally), fertility fell as a result of individual choice, a human response to changing economic and social conditions. Life in towns meant overcrowded housing and children who were much more of an economic burden—attending school and, after the enforcement of legislation limiting the employment of children, not direct contributors to the household economy—than they were in rural areas, creating effective incentives for limiting family size. Couples seem to have responded to these new social and economic conditions by reducing mean family size to levels that would allow low or even negative population growth: a lagged response to earlier mortality decline.

This historical experience of Western as well as some Eastern populations (including Japan) of moving from high-level equilibrium to low-level equilibrium has been generalized into the demographic transition model: an empirical generalization based on historical experience, used to describe the general course of population change (Figure 2). All populations began in the high equilibrium stage, with fluctuating mortality and rather more stable fertility, and remained thus until recently. The underlying presumption of the demographic transition model is that all countries will progress through these stages to the low-level equilibrium now evident in the developed countries, but will do so at different rates and perhaps even for different reasons. Thus there is a predictive implication: all populations will progress through the transition, and populations with high rates of growth with currently excess fertility are merely lagging in the process of global change.

Twentieth-century development largely sought to replicate elsewhere the structural conditions that were associated with falling mortality in nineteenth-century Europe: industrialization and associated urbanization and rising personal incomes; the application of medical science and healthcare systems; environmental improvements in clean water supply, sanitation and

better housing; and social improvements such as modern education. Global development has taken place through the diffusion of these structural features out of western Europe and North America, first into eastern Europe and the Mediterranean countries, and subsequently into the less developed areas of Africa, Asia, and Latin America. This was implicit in the colonial objectives of European powers in bringing "civilization" to the colonized populations, and it brought evident, though not necessarily immediate, success as mortality fell almost universally in the twentieth century.

Global modernization had been presumed by the development strategies of the major bilateral and multilateral development agencies, notably the World Bank, which, in its 1984 *World Development Report*, famously argued an explicitly diffusionist explanation of the global demographic transition. There have been very effective medical interventions, as in the eradication of smallpox—the last recorded case was in 1974—and in immunization programs urged by such agencies as UNICEF and Save the Children. There is much less malnutrition globally: the proportion of the world's population living in countries with mean dietary energy supplies below the WHO recommended level fell from 83% in 1961–1963 to 44% in 1990. Food is now much better distributed, both internally (in most countries) and globally, and, with better food security and much greater warning of potential problems, the occurrence of famine mortality is much reduced. Although there is still a long way to go in the poorest countries, mortality rates, especially in children under five, have fallen in all countries of the world in the twentieth century. In many developing countries they are beginning to approach the levels and stability of developed countries.

As we have seen, fertility levels are the result of individual choice and cultural factors rather than the structural conditions associated with development. There are, however, important similarities in the factors affecting fertility in nineteenth-century populations of countries now defined as developed and in contemporary developing-country populations, notably the increasing proportion of the population that is urban and

Human Populations. FIGURE 2. The Demographic Transition Model.

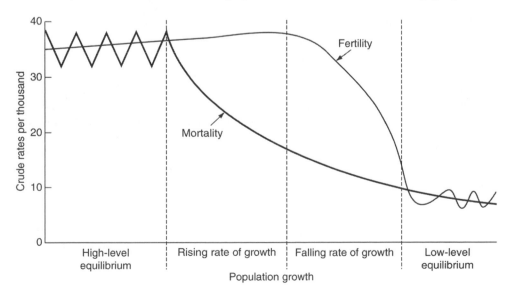

the increasing number of women who have had a modern education and have access to modern health care and contraception. However, there are also important differences in the cultural and economic roles of children, such that many developing-country populations may be more resistant to reduced family size. A higher proportion of such populations remain predominantly rural, winning a marginal living from the land. Children are more likely to be net contributors to the household economy from an early age, whether on the farm in weeding, harvesting, bird-scaring or cattle-herding, or in the domestic sphere in fetching water or caring for younger siblings. In such conditions, large families bring more hands to work rather than more mouths to feed, and weaken economic incentives for lower fertility. Furthermore, in societies that are tied to the land, large families cement inheritance systems and social obligations.

In sub-Saharan Africa, with its strong cultural legacy of traditional landholding and land management systems, the evidence for rural fertility decline has been most elusive, but even here most recent data do indicate falling fertility in all countries. The decline is small in most cases, although much larger in some of the richer countries (South Africa, Botswana, Zimbabwe, Kenya) than in poorer countries with recurring political instability, but overall the annual rate of population growth in this region is still over 2.5%. This would suggest that even sub-Saharan Africa is now exhibiting a lagged fertility response, proceeding through a transition to levels of fertility that approximate to its levels of mortality, themselves considerably higher than elsewhere.

Stronger support for a universal demographic transition is offered by the experience of Latin America and Asia. Latin America is a much more urbanized and industrialized continent that Asia or Africa, and much more exposed to Western economic and cultural attributes and values. There were substantial falls in mortality in the region between 1930 and 1970, and there have also been substantial reductions in fertility, especially since the 1970s. National annual rates of growth, rising to over 2% in the 1970s, are now mainly between 1 and 2%, and fertility continues to fall more rapidly than mortality, such that the achievement of a low-level equilibrium seems likely. The Asian experience has been even more dramatic. Mortality declines have proceeded slowly, especially in India and China, but they have been general, such that by the 1970s the Asian population was growing at a rate of over 2% each year, with little evidence of fertility decline. Since then, however, there have been sharp fertility declines, characteristically in this region associated with direct population policies. The case of China, with its "one child" policy backed by strongly coercive measures and severe economic penalties for exceeding individual or group targets, is the most extreme example of government intervention. Most interventions in the region have taken the form of family-planning programs, with success in relatively poor countries—Bangladesh, Indonesia, and Thailand—as well as in the Asian "tigers" of rapid economic growth—Singapore, Hong Kong, South Korea, Taiwan, and Malaysia.

The rationale for direct intervention in family planning, principally to increase the prevalence of contraception, has been underpinned by the empirical evidence of an apparent universal relationship between total fertility rate (TFR, an index of the number of children each woman can expect to bear) and contraceptive prevalence rate (CPR): as contraceptive prevalence rises, so fertility falls. The most effective government-mediated means of reducing fertility, therefore, is to raise contraceptive usage through effective family-planning programs. Governments of developing countries have been provided with massive international assistance to expand contraceptive availability and knowledge, usually in conjunction with maternal and child-health programs that target birth-spacing as much as the use of contraceptives to prevent further conception.

There seems little doubt that there has been a global reproductive revolution in recent decades. Contraceptive use is everywhere rising rapidly, even in sub-Saharan Africa, and, although this is not the sole factor in fertility decline, it is most effective when applied in economically and politically stable societies. Where women and couples have assured contraception and a high likelihood of survival of existing children, together with a higher income, they usually choose to reduce their family size.

AGE AND SEX STRUCTURE

A major effect of these recent trends in fertility and mortality has been the differentiation of age and, to a lesser extent, sex structures of populations. On the global scale, differentials in sex (as a biological characteristic) have not been of major significance, for in all populations the numbers of males and females have been roughly the same. Females have a longer life expectancy (roughly 5–10% longer than males in most societies), but about 5% more boys than girls have typically been born. There is now, however, considerable potential for the sex ratio at birth to be altered significantly by technology that enables couples to ascertain the sex of unborn children in the womb, and to exercise what is usually a preference for male children either by differential abortion, increasingly common in India, or else by differential infanticide at birth, a practice said to have been fairly widespread in China at the height of its one-child campaigns in the 1980s, resulting in a reported sex ratio at birth of 118 males per 100 females in 1991.

As a result of these trends in fertility and mortality, intercontinental variability in age structures has become large. In Europe and North America, after at least three generations of low fertility and mortality, the proportion of the population under 15 years of age is much lower than the global average, but the proportion aged over 65 is more than double the global average of 6%. In these populations, the proportion in the economically active age groups, commonly defined as 15 to 64 is higher than the global average. This is in clear contrast to Asia and Africa, where continuing high fertility, especially in Africa, keeps the proportion of under-fifteens very high, and the poor quality of healthcare will keep the proportion of those over 65 low.

While it is certainly the case that, in these continents, age is a far less rigid determinant of economic activity, the fact that the proportion aged 15 to 64 remains low, and dependency ratios—the ratio of the dependent population, the young and the old, to the nondependent population—are adverse, has clear implications for the productive potential to generate economic activities to support development expenditures, including the large educational and health expenditures consumed disproportionately by the young and the old. However, as fertility falls, the proportion of under-fifteens will fall, and they will progress into the labor force. In China, the absolute number of 15-year-olds entering the labor force is already less than it is in India, with its higher fertility but smaller overall population. These children will also be entering the reproductive age groups, creating a population momentum: although fertility continues to fall, the reproductive population will keep on growing, albeit at a declining rate. By contrast, improved health care and medical knowledge are allowing adults to live longer. Even in the poorest countries, the proportion of old people is rising.

POPULATION DISTRIBUTION AND DENSITY

As a result of the joint effects of differential population growth and migration, the global distribution of the human population has been in constant change. Humans have spread to occupy all continents, but with very different continental as well as local population densities. Particularly in the period of very rapid growth in the last 300 years, the distribution has altered substantially. A. M. Carr-Saunders (1936) estimated that, in 1650, just before major growth of the European population, just over half the world's population was in Asia, and over 20% in each of Europe and Africa. By 1900, Africa's share had more than halved, but Europe's share had risen to nearly 25%. Growth in the twentieth century has raised the proportion in the Southern Hemisphere to over 80%, with further rises to over 90% within 100 years anticipated by current population projections (Table 1). The current global distribution of population by size of national population and national population density remains highly uneven.

TABLE 1. Shares of World Population by Continent, 1650, 1900, 2007, 2050

	1650*	1900*	2007+	2050+
Europe	21.5	24.2	11.0	8.4
North America	0.2	2.4	5.1	4.8
Oceania	0.4	0.4	0.5	0.5
South America	2.6	3.9	8.6	8.4
Africa	21.5	7.4	14.5	21.7
Asia	53.8	58.3	60.4	57.3
Global North	22	27	18.3	13.5
Global South	78	73	81.7	86.5
Total Population	0.465 billion	1.6 billion	6.671 billion	9.191 billion

* Wilcox, estimated in Carr-Saunders (1936, p. 42). Includes Central America in South America.

+ United Nations World Population Prospects 2006. Revision (2007). Includes Central America in North America.

Within each country, the most important global feature of recent redistribution has been a dramatic change in the proportion of rural to urban populations. The rapid increases in population in nineteenth-century Europe were associated with increases in the proportion of the population living in urban areas, and urbanization has been a major feature in all countries within the present century. It was estimated that, in 1995, 45% of the global population lived in urban areas (Figure 3). This proportion was still as low as 26% in Asia and 31% in Africa, but these are where recent urban growth is most rapid. By 2005, for the first time in human history, the global urban population exceeded the rural population.

WORLD POPULATION CONFERENCES

Global concern for the growth, structure, and distribution of population, first voiced in the League of Nations before World War II, has been a matter of concern for the United Nations throughout its existence. The critical technical role of the UN Population Division in collecting and analyzing population data (discussed above) has in recent years tended to be overshadowed by its broader role in considering global population issues through a series of World Population Conferences.

At Bucharest in 1974, attitudes to "the population problem" were ambivalent. Although this conference took place just after the first UN Conference on the Human Environment (held in Stockholm in 1972) and the publication of the strongly neo-Malthusian *The Limits to Growth* (1972), it was also a time when many developing countries were still experiencing economic optimism after independence, believing that development would come quickly, especially when associated with a global redistribution of wealth. It was generally, although not universally, recognized that population growth rates (then typically over 2% per annum) were too high in developing countries, but that "development is the best contraceptive": direct intervention in population control is generally unnecessary because fertility falls spontaneously with development, as it did in the developed countries. Furthermore, the Green Revolution was by then having an effect on crop yields in Asia, increasing the food supply and reducing the threat of local and regional famines. There was, therefore, an implicit acceptance of the demographic transition model.

By 1984, however, the global economy had deteriorated sharply after the oil shocks of the 1970s, and environmental concerns were becoming more evident. There were droughts and famines in Africa, where annual rates of population growth were already over 3% in some countries and generally continuing to rise. There were recurring food crises in China. Green Revolution technologies had been important in increasing global food supplies, but there were clearly limits to the technological improvement and agricultural intensification. National population growth was now seen as a major problem for many governments, even those previously hostile to direct intervention, as in Africa. The Mexico Conference in 1984 saw the acceptance by the majority of governments of the need for direct intervention to control population growth, and especially through family-planning programs.

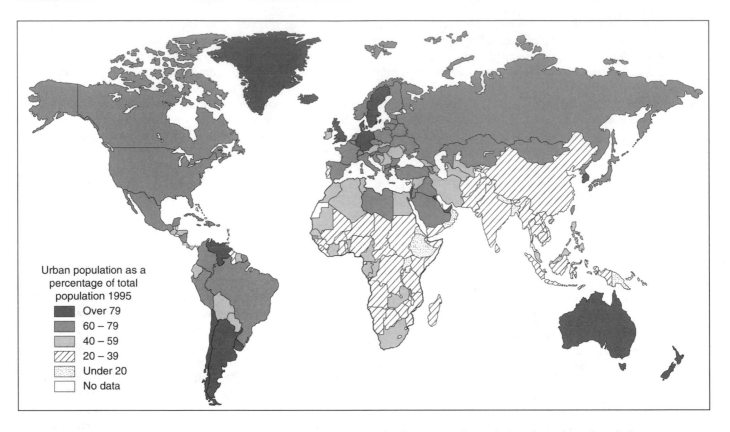

Human Populations. FIGURE 3. Urban Proportion of Natural Populations, 1995.

As indicated above, the close statistical correlation between national TFR and CPR had been used to justify intervention, but now governments, supported by international agencies, would be able to allocate additional resources to fertility reduction. Fertility began to fall in almost all developing countries in the 1980s, and in some with great speed, even to below replacement level (TFR of 2.1), as in China.

Coming after the Rio Conference on Environment and Development (1992), at which many population issues were raised directly, the Cairo Conference (1994) was styled, unlike its predecessors, a conference on Population *and Development*. Nevertheless, the main issue remained direct fertility control, and particularly the extent to which the contraceptive revolution that had allowed much greater choice over reproductive outcomes could be generalized, and in what form. There was criticism of the fairly crude application of family planning in the 1980s, often equated with fairly coercive "pill-pushing." Support was directed toward a more sensitive approach in which family planning could be part of maternal and child-health programs aimed at meeting the expressed needs of the majority of women for smaller families.

These world conferences have been particularly important in two respects: they have encouraged a global view of population questions, in which national governments have been able to place their own policies in the broader context of international population trends; and they have broadened the recognition that population seldom constitutes a problem in itself, but that the problem arises when population size, growth, and/or distribution interact with particular economic, political, and environmental circumstances.

POPULATION PROJECTIONS

It is clear that the universal downturn in fertility, resulting in a fall in the estimated annual increment to the global population from 87 million in the late 1980s to 81 million by the late 1990s, has encouraged some limited optimism. The unprecedented growth rate of the last 100 years has now peaked, and a consistent fall through the early years of the next millennium is confidently expected. Current UN projections of global population change suggest that the population will continue to grow for the next 150 years. High, medium, and low projections are estimated, with the medium variant identifying a population stabilizing at approximately 11 billion people, roughly double its present level, by 2150. Then, some four hundred years after the first major signs of mortality decline in Europe, a new low-level global equilibrium will be reached. The transition to the low equilibrium will be complete, but the world population will have risen more than tenfold.

Like all population projections, the UN projections are inherently open to a range of outcomes, even though only two variables are modeled, namely, birth trends and mortality trends. Of the two, mortality trends are the easier to predict. As we have seen, the joint impact of medical science, of better living conditions, and of better nutrition has been to bring mortality levels to less than 10 per 1000 in developed countries and to reduce the large short-term fluctuations. Mortality levels are low and stable in the richest countries, and development policies elsewhere seek to reduce mortality to these levels. The World Health Organization has set targets for mortality, especially in its *Health for All by the Year 2000*, that assume this downward trend. However, even in developed countries, there may be a limit to improvement in life expectancy, although what that limit might be remains a matter of dispute. In developing countries, mortality levels still have a long way to fall to reach developed-country levels, and in poor tropical countries, with high levels of bacterial infection and many conditions still beyond medical control, there is no guarantee of the triumph of medical science—even where, unfortunately in a minority of countries, increased resources are likely to be available for health provision. Furthermore, new diseases are appearing, and further global epidemics may occur, now much more easily spread in a world of effortless personal transport. The global HIV–AIDS pandemic is the most obvious case. It was responsible for an estimated 18.5 million deaths from 1980 to 1995, and 2–3 million people currently die from HIV-AIDS each year.

The unpredictability of fertility projections is acknowledged by the UN in its population projections. Since fertility is inherently more volatile than mortality in contracepting populations, the experience of the last two decades of negative or near-zero population growth and fertility below replacement levels in developed countries does not necessarily provide assurance of global trends over the next two centuries. For developing countries, the pace and extent of any future fertility decline must remain uncertain, although the projections assume that fertility will fall everywhere to replacement level by the end of the twenty-first century. The recent experience of sharp fertility declines in eastern Asia certainly seems to support an optimistic scenario, although even here there may be some possibility for reversals if economic performance continues to slump after the recent decades of unprecedented economic growth that was able to finance intensive family-planning programs as well as rising personal incomes and increasing urbanization.

However uncertain these projections might be, they do seem to suggest continuous growth in human populations, perhaps a doubling overall in the next 100–150 years, with a very sharp increase in the proportion in developing countries. Is such a population, with such a distribution, sustainable? In an absolute sense it probably is: 11 billion people could probably survive at the low levels of consumption of those currently in India or Ethiopia. However, fertility and mortality declines have been associated with rising levels of wealth and education, and, by implication, rising levels of consumption and production. With Western energy-consumption levels and lifestyles in Africa and Asia, can the global environment support 11 billion people? Furthermore, can this be sustained

where most of that population increment remains in the developing countries, or might there be a necessity for substantial intercontinental migration? Clearly the problems associated with this projected population growth are larger than those of population size alone.

Human populations have been successful in reproducing themselves while achieving rising living standards, but does that success contain the seeds of their own destruction in the longer term? A comparison with change in various plant and animal populations suggests that it does. However, the biological analogy is inappropriate to a fertility revolution based on the general use of contraception that offers human populations, for the first time, an immediate choice about levels of fertility not available to other species. The future of population may be less about Malthusian checks—war, famine, disease, although these will surely continue—than about human choices in family size and family location and about broader societal choices concerning production and consumption.

[*See also* Agriculture and Agricultural Land; Carrying Capacity; Catastrophist-Cornucopian Debate; Climate Change and Societal Development; Economic Levels; Human Ecology; Migrations; Resources; *and* Urban Areas.]

BIBLIOGRAPHY

Bongaarts, J. "A Framework for Analyzing the Proximate Determinants of Fertility." *Population and Development Review* 4.1 (1978), 105–132. This journal, published by the Population Council, is one of the main sources of discussion of population change, and contains many of the most authoritative discussions of global population change, both general, such as this reference, and country-specific, such as Martine (1996), see below.
Bongaarts, J. "Global Trends in AIDS Mortality." *Population and Development Review* 22.1 (1996), 21–45.
Carr-Saunders, A. M. *World Population: Past Growth and Present Trends.* Oxford: Clarendon Press, 1936.
Cleland, J. "Population Growth in the 21st Century: Cause for Crisis or Celebration?" *Tropical Medicine and International Health* 1.1 (1996), 15–26. DOI: 10.1046/j.1365-3156.1996.d01-8.x.
Coleman, D., and R. Schofield. *The State of Population Theory: Forward from Malthus.* Oxford: Blackwell, 1986. A collection of essays by leading authors on population trends in a range of historical and contemporary contexts.
Douglas, R. M., G. Jones, and R. M. D'Souza, eds. *The Shaping of Fertility and Mortality Declines: The Contemporary Demographic Transition. Health Transition Review.* Supplement to vol. 6. Canberra, Australia: Australian National University, Health Transition Centre, 1996.
Gould, W. T., and M. S. Brown. "A Fertility Transition in Sub-Saharan Africa?" *International Journal of Population Geography* 2.1 (1996), 1–22. Discusses in full detail the controversies surrounding the relevance of the demographic transition model to explanations of population trends in Africa. This relatively new journal also contains many contributions on the various themes explored in this entry, e.g., Thomas (1995), see below.
Grigg, D. *The World Food Problem.* 2d ed. Oxford, U.K., and Cambridge, Mass.: Blackwell, 1993. Grigg's studies, also available in the journal literature (e.g., Grigg, 1997, see below), consistently relate population growth to food production and consumption.
———. "The World's Hunger, A Review: 1930–1990." *Geography* 82.3 (1997), 197–206.
Hardin, G. *The Ostrich Factor: Our Population Myopia.* New York: Oxford University Press, 1998.
Jones, H. *Population Geography.* 2d ed. London: Chapman; New York: Guilford Press, 1990. A very readable and informative introduction to a range of population issues.

Livi-Bacci, M. *A Concise History of World Population.* 4th ed. Oxford, U.K., and Malden, Mass.: Blackwell, 2006. A standard history of world population.

Martine, G. "Brazil's Fertility Decline, 1965–95." *Population and Development Review* 22.1 (1996), 47–75.

Meadows, D. H., et al. *The Limits to Growth: A Report for the Club of Rome's Project on the Predicament of Mankind.* New York: Universe Books, 1972.

Robey, B., et al. *The Reproductive Revolution: New Survey Findings. Population Reports* Series M, no. 11 (1992).

Ross, J. A., ed. *International Encyclopedia of Population.* 2 vols. New York: Free Press, 1982. A definitive exploration of all aspects of population change.

Rumsey, G. W., ed. *Readings in Population Research Methodology.* 8 vols. Chicago: Social Development Center, 1993. Technical manuals and readings for all aspects of population analysis, reproduced by the UN Population Fund.

Sen, A. *Poverty and Famines.* Oxford: Clarendon Press; New York: Oxford University Press, 1981.

Simon, J. L. *The Ultimate Resource 2.* Princeton, N.J.: Princeton University Press, 1998.

Thomas, N. "The Ethics of Rural Population Control in China." *International Journal of Population Geography* 1.1 (1995), 3–18.

United Nations. *Demographic Yearbook.* An annual compilation of national statistics, with a standard format, but with special features each year. This is the most widely used of a large range of summary and technical publications of the UN Population Division.

United Nations. *World Population Projections to 2050.* New York: UN Population Division, 1998.

United Nations Children's Fund (UNICEF). *The State of the World's Children.* New York: UNICEF, annual.

Whitmore, T. M., et al. "Long-Term Population Change." In *The Earth as Transformed by Human Action: Global and Regional Changes in the Biosphere over the Past 300 Years,* edited by B. L. Turner, et al., pp. 25–39. Cambridge and New York: Cambridge University Press, 1990.

World Bank. *World Development Report.* New York: Oxford University Press, annual. This publication has a large data appendix of population and other data, and the main text is devoted to a particular theme each year

World Health Organization. *Health for All by the Year 2000.* Geneva: World Health Organization, 1990.

Wrigley, E. A., and R. S. Schofield. *The Population History of England, 1541–1871.* London: Arnold; Cambridge, Mass.: Harvard University Press, 1981.

—W. T. S. GOULD

HUNTING AND POACHING

Since its origin, humankind has fed itself by hunting. Humans shifted to agriculture and animal domestication only 7–8 thousand years ago. As hunters, early humans competed successfully with other mammalian carnivores by being fleet-footed and coordinating their actions. The development of weapons such as stone-bladed spears and throwing sticks enabled humans to kill prey as large as mammoths and mastodons (Ward, 1997).

Humans in historic times have sometimes engaged in the wanton killing of prey animals, exceeding the hunters' needs. The slaughter of 60 million American bison between 1865 and 1884 is a classic example (Matthiessen, 1959). Capricious killing by other mammals is rare, but if it is characteristic of *Homo sapiens,* such behavior could account in part for the massive Pleistocene extinctions in North America 10–12 thousand years ago when about 20–40 bird species and 40 large mammal species disappeared.

The Pleistocene overkill theory blames human hunters from the Old World for the extermination of all species of horses and North American camels, mammoths, mastodons,

Hunting and Poaching. Hunted Species.

Hunting and poaching are very important causes of animal declines and extinctions. Rhino, for example, are extensively hunted because of the supposed aphrodisiacal qualities of their horns.

giant ground sloths, and woolly rhinos; these animals lacked time to develop an effective defense to a newly arrived, intelligent predator. With their prey gone, carnivores and scavengers such as saber-toothed tigers, dire wolves, and giant condors also died out (Van Valkenburgh, 1994). If such excessive hunting occurred, it would have been the greatest human-caused mammal extinction ever. The evidence is sketchy, but man's arrival in the New World coincides with the disappearance of these animals. Climatic and other factors may have contributed to these New World extinctions, but human intervention was probably an important element (Flannery, 1999).

The effect of these extinctions on the biological diversity of the Americas was almost immeasurable, because along with each mammal and bird species that disappeared went its species-specific parasites and ecological dependents. The loss of seed-disseminating animals affected plant and tree distribution, which then influenced the survival of the invertebrates dependent on them for their life cycle. Scientists can only surmise the ecological changes that occurred with the extirpation of so many birds and mammals.

Today humans hunt for both sustenance and sport, with the former having the greater impact on the hunting area's biodiversity. Sustenance hunting generally concentrates on species that are easily harvestable. For example, many West African forest species such as duikers (antelopes) and primates that evolved unthreatened by hunters with dogs and guns are now heavily harvested for bush meat.

Sustenance hunting can be wasteful and may have caused the extinction of species such as the great auk, Atlantic gray whales, dodos, and Steller's sea cow. These animals were generally slow-moving and easily killed. If they were already dying out when they first came in contact with humans, then a sudden reduction in their fragile populations could have accelerated their extermination. The long human history of sustenance hunting has contributed to the elimination of prey species and their parasites and symbionts, thereby resulting in reduced biodiversity.

Sport hunting thrived under Assyrian kings and Egyptian pharaohs, but so few engaged in the sport that the killing had little effect on biodiversity. By the seventeenth century, rulers set aside large natural areas as exclusive hunting reserves and maximized quarry populations. Local farmers, however, now precluded from sustenance hunting, began poaching, and their illegal harvests eventually affected biodiversity. Today, European royal hunting reserves are credited with maintaining such large ungulates (hooved mammals) as the wisent (European bison). Similar efforts in India have helped the Asian rhino survive, and in China, Père David's deer.

Hunting organizations are actively involved in conservation. Ducks Unlimited promotes breeding of waterfowl in the United States and Canada by saving and restoring wetlands. Anglers, too, have increased the use of catch-and-release fishings to maintain quantities of heavily caught game fish. Finally, hunting and fishing license fees are used to restore and protect wild populations and habitats.

Despite hunters' conservation efforts to save prey species, modern poachers thwart these attempts by hunting and selling endangered species. A large-scale, profitable, commercial trade exists in poached rhino horn, tiger parts, ivory, and even caviar from Caspian Sea sturgeon. To curtail this illegal harvest, producer and consumer nations of protected animals and their products have signed the Convention on International Trade in Endangered Species (CITES), which has significantly reduced the international market for these commodities.

Illegal trade has been curbed by the efforts of the Trade Records Analysis of Flora and Fauna in Commerce, a program of the WWF (formerly the World Wildlife Fund) that monitors trade in wild plants and animals and their products through an international network, and by the U.S. Customs Service and Fish and Wildlife Service. Negative publicity about poaching is also an effective deterrent to illegal trade in animal parts and stimulates calls for legislative action. Poaching has decimated populations of tigers, elephants, rhinos, and other mammals to the extent that some of them may be so scattered already that the critical minimum population necessary for long-term survival no longer exists.

Policy conflicts arise when a country with a well-managed elephant herd wants to sell ivory culled from animals to help finance its management, while its neighbor suffers from a declining, heavily poached population. Advocates believe that ivory sales will encourage management and legitimize its international trade, while opponents believe that such sales will encourage poaching because accurate identification of an ivory's source is not yet practical. In time a compromise solution may be found, as it was in the trade of crocodile hides. Poaching declined when entrepreneurs started farming crocodiles to produce better-quality skins and even developing hybrid strains for rapid growth and easy hide identification (Webb et al., 1987; Thorbjarnarson, 1992).

BODY PARTS AND TRADITIONAL MEDICINE IN ASIA

Significant advances in wildlife conservation have been made recently throughout much of Asia: there is increasing awareness of the value of forests and wildlife; more protected areas have been set aside than ever before; and governments have enacted laws and signed international conventions that discourage trade in endangered species. Yet a strong market for body parts used in medicines continues to motivate the hunting and trapping of many large animals and threatens many with extinction.

Animal	Body Part	Medicinal Use
NATIVE TO ASIA		
Musk deer	Musk gland	Malaria, convulsions, and general tonic
Malayan sun bear	Bile	Liver disease, blood disorders, and digestive ailments
Malayan tapir	Skin	Boils, infections
Pig-tailed macaque	Flesh	Malaria, general tonic
Saiga antelope	Horn	Colds, fever, liver
Pangolin (anteater)	Scales	Infections, limb stiffness
Tiger	Bone	Rheumatism, arthritis, muscles
	Many other parts	Variety of complaints
ASIA AND AFRICA		
Leopard	Bone	Substitute for tiger bone
Rhinoceros	Horn	Fever, headache, delerium
ASIA AND NORTH AMERICA		
Black bear	Gall bladder	Fevers, convulsions, skin lesions
	Paw	General tonic
PACIFIC COASTS		
Seal	Penis, testes	Impotence, kidney

BIBLIOGRAPHY

Gaski, A. L., and K. Johnson. Prescription for Extinction: Endangered Species and Patented Oriental Medicines in Trade. Washington, D.C.: TRAFFIC USA (World Wildlife Fund), 1994.

McCracken, C., D. Rose, and K. Johnson. Status, Management, and Commercialization of the American Black Bear. Washington, D.C.: TRAFFIC USA (World Wildlife Fund), 1995.

Rabinowitz, A. "Killed for a Cure." Natural History (April 1998), 22–24.

Robbins, C. An Overview of World Trade in Cervid Antler with an Emphasis on the United States and Canada. Washington, D.C.: TRAFFIC USA (World Wildlife Fund), 1997. Antlers of the deer family.

—DAVID J. CUFF

Another conflict arises when federal authorities forbid hunting endangered species whose products play a religious or cultural role. Bald-eagle feathers, for example, have traditionally adorned Native American objects and clothing. The U.S. government decided that Native Americans could use feathers from confiscated, illegally killed eagles or those found dead from natural causes. A more complicated conflict is the Inuits' insistence on hunting rare bowhead whales off Alaska's north coast. Annual quotas are now set and when reached, whaling must cease. As a result, quotas are seldom reached and the bowhead population is increasing (Marine Mammal Commission Report, 1999).

As nations become politically and economically stable, they begin to husband their natural resources. Legislation is enacted to protect endangered species, and reserves are established. Governments regulate hunting and forbid poaching, but enforcement of game laws is often erratic. As the Earth's wildlife competes with humans for a declining habitat, we have an increasing responsibility to preserve the Earth's biodiversity.

[*See also* Biological Diversity; Carrying Capacity; Deforestation; Extinctions of Animals; Fisheries; *and* Trade and Environment.]

BIBLIOGRAPHY

Flannery, T. F. "Debating Extinction." *Science* 283 (1999), 182–183. DOI: 10.1126/science.283.5399.182.
Marine Mammal Commission. *Annual Report to Congress 1999.* Bethesda, Md.: Marine Mammal Commission, 2000. See pp. 23–26.
Matthiessen, P. *Wildlife in America.* New York: Viking Press, 1959.
Thorbjarnarson, J., comp. *Crocodiles: An Action Plan for Their Conservation.* Edited by H. Messel, F. W. King, and J. P. Ross. Gland, Switzerland: International Union for Conservation of Nature and Natural Resources, 1992. See pp. 51–52.
Van Valkenburgh, B. "Tough Times in the Tar Pits." *Natural History* 103.4 (1994), 84–85.
Ward, P. D. *The Call of Distant Mammoths: Why the Ice Age Mammals Disappeared.* New York: Copernicus/Springer, 1997.
Webb, G. J. W., S. C. Manolis, and P. J. Whitehead, eds. *Wildlife Management: Crocodiles and Alligators.* Chipping Norton, New South Wales, Australia: Surrey Beatty, 1987. See pp. 369–371.

—David Challinor

HURRICANES

See Tropical Cyclones in a Warming World.

ICE SHEETS

The Greenland and Antarctic ice sheets cover 10% of the Earth's land area and contain 77% of the world's fresh water and 99% of all the glacier ice. Their average thicknesses are both approximately 2,100 meters, but the Antarctic Ice Sheet (14 million square kilometers) contains about ten times the ice volume of the Greenland Ice Sheet (1.7 million square kilometers; Figure 1). [*See* Antarctica and Climate Change *and* Greenland ice sheet.] Unlike the small mountain glaciers, which flow through channels bounded on their sides by land, ice sheets rest on land that is relatively flat in comparison with the ice thickness. Icecaps are similar in structure to ice sheets, but much smaller. Although the Earth's crust is depressed by hundreds of meters by the weight of the ice, the bases of the ice sheets are on average close to sea level. However, the West Antarctic Ice Sheet, which is the portion (about 12%) of the Antarctic ice that lies mostly in the Western Hemisphere, is grounded as much as 2,500 meters below sea level. If all of the ice were to melt, sea level would rise by nearly 80 meters.

During the last few million years, ice sheets have waxed and waned (Anderson et al., 2007) with major climate changes occurring about every 100,000 years in response to changes in the Earth's position relative to the Sun. [*See* Causes

---

Ice Sheets. Figure 1. Topography of Greenland and Antarctica.
(A) Greenland is characterized by distinct ridges that define hydrologic and climatologic boundaries, with undulating surfaces in between. (B) Antarctica is characterized by these ice ridges and undulations as well, but also contain ice shelves (the large light gray areas without texture in the figure). Surface elevations for these maps are measured by radar altimeters on the European ERS-1 and 2 satellites (except near the center of the Antarctic, where only aircraft measurements have been made). Ice sheet thicknesses are measured by airborne radars that penetrate as much as 4,000 meters of ice to map the bedrock. In the future, ice thickness changes as small as one centimeter will be measured by a laser altimeter on NASA's ICESat (Ice Cloud and Land Elevation Satellite).

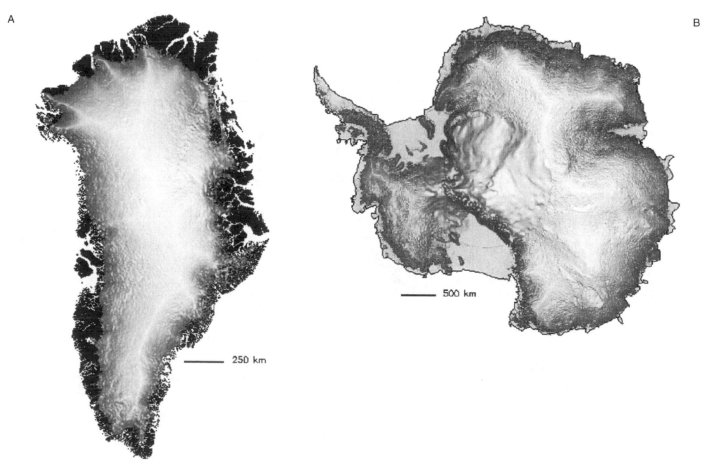

A

B

—— 250 km

—— 500 km

of Climate Change.] Before the end of the last ice age approximately 15,000 years ago, huge ice sheets also covered parts of Eurasia and much of North America, extending as far south as Pennsylvania. As the climate warmed, sea level rose by about 125 meters at an average rate of 2.5 centimeters per year for roughly 5,000 years. As the Northern Hemisphere ice sheets melted, several episodes of massive outbreaks of ice from the Hudson Bay region spread many icebergs over the North Atlantic Ocean. During this time, the Antarctic Ice Sheet decreased by only about 10%. The last interglacial warm period, approximately 120,000 years ago, was even warmer than today's climate; sea level may have been 6 meters higher, and the West Antarctic Ice Sheet may have disintegrated and/or much of Greenland may have melted.

Although the current rate of sea level rise is as much as 2 millimeters per year, it is not known whether the present ice sheets are growing or shrinking. Each year, about 8 millimeters of water from the entire surface of the Earth's oceans accumulates as snow on Greenland and Antarctica. The average ice accumulation is about 26 centimeters per year on Greenland and 16 centimeters per year on Antarctica (measured in centimeters of water equivalent, or about five times greater in terms of snowfall). However, we do not know to better than ±25% whether the amount of water returned to the oceans in icebergs and meltwater runoff equals the snow accumulation. This large uncertainty exists because there is little direct information on ice-sheet volume change.

MASS BALANCE AND THE FORMATION OF ICE SHEETS

The term "mass balance" refers to the difference between the mass input to a glacier or ice sheet and the mass loss. Mass balance governs the development and decay of these bodies of ice. Glacier formation occurs when, for a sustained period of time, the snow deposition in an area consistently exceeds the amount of snow that is lost (i.e., the mass balance is positive). In the case of ice sheets, this occurs over prolonged cold periods on the order of 10,000 years. Snow falls on a large area of land, such as Greenland and Antarctica, at various times of the year depending on local climate conditions (Figure 2). During the summer months, some, but not all, of this snow is removed by melting and evaporation. When snow remains beyond one melt season, it becomes denser as the grains bond to each other and increase in size; such snow is called firn. As the cycle is repeated year after year, the previously fallen snow becomes buried deeper and deeper relative to the surface. Under the increased pressure of the overlying snow, the grains become larger and more intergrown, and the density continues to increase. Eventually, the process reaches a point where the pressure and sintering (agglomeration) are so great that the air between particles is closed off, and ice is formed. As this process continues, older ice is pushed deeper and outward by virtue of the increasing pressure of the overlying ice and firn. As a result, the ice sheets are generally thicker, with higher surface elevations, near their center, and thinner, with lower surface elevations, near their edges.

Ice Sheets. Figure 2. Schematic Diagram of an Ice Sheet.

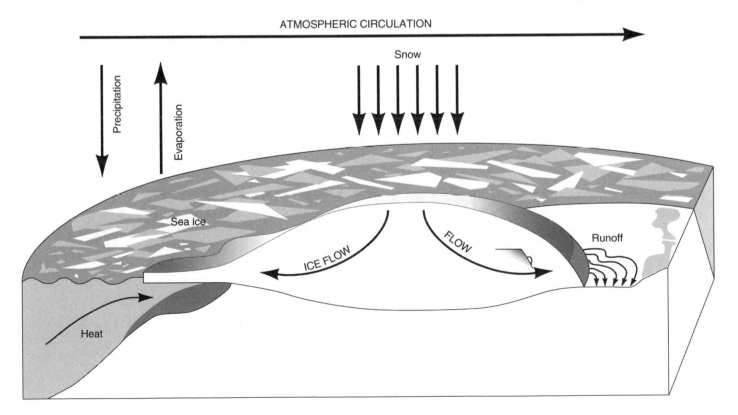

Snow accumulates in the higher central regions, sinks, and is transformed to ice over time. The figure shows the flow processes (at and below the surface as well as in ice streams), iceberg calving, flow in ice streams, ice shelves, the ablation and accumulation areas of an ice sheet, and the equilibrium line.

While the only mass gain to the ice sheets as a whole comes from the accumulation of snow on the surface, the mechanisms of mass loss are somewhat more complicated. As ice flows along the elevation gradient toward the edge of the ice sheet, it is transported to the lower elevations, and in most cases lower latitudes, where temperatures are warmer. In the case of Greenland, the temperatures are sufficiently warm over about half of the ice sheet that surface melting occurs. In Antarctica, typically less than 5% experiences melting. The difference is a result of Antarctica's more polar location. When the snow melts, the water that forms may evaporate, be discharged as surface or subsurface runoff, or percolate into the firn, where it refreezes at greater depths. The first two processes clearly result in mass loss by the system, but the last is simply a redistribution representing no net decrease in mass. There is also some additional loss due to sublimation (the transition from dry snow to water vapor without passing through the liquid state). This occurs because the air is very dry and there is sustained solar radiation during the summer, which provides the energy for the conversion.

Finally, as the remaining ice approaches the outer portions of the ice sheet, the most dramatic and most significant form of loss—calving—occurs. The topography and characteristics of the underlying bedrock are such that the ice tends to flow in major streams, or drainage basins, in which it is carried out to the surrounding seas. Because of the mechanical strength and buoyancy of the ice, it can extend well beyond the water-land boundary as a solid unit. When ice is discharged through singular narrow channels or ice streams, as is generally the case in Greenland, the floating ice is referred to as a glacier tongue. In instances where the discharge from several ice streams merges into a single frozen table of ice, or where ice is discharged over wide areas, as is generally the case in Antarctica, the floating ice is referred to as an ice shelf. Eventually, the stresses on the floating ice that result from its weight and buoyancy, and the erosion from warm water in contact with its base, cause it to break into icebergs that are carried out to sea. The size of these icebergs can range from a few meters to tens of kilometers across. Iceberg calving is believed to account for roughly 40% of the mass loss in Greenland and 80–90% in Antarctica. In addition, the underside of the floating ice experiences melt as a result of its contact with the warmer water. This basal melting also contributes substantially to mass loss, and affects ocean circulation by adding cold fresh water, lowering the salinity of the ocean water.

The relative magnitudes of the accumulation and mass loss components determine the sizes and shapes of the ice sheets, as well as their impact on sea level and their role in the changing climate.

ICE SHEET HISTORY

Of particular importance in the understanding of ice sheets and climate, past and present, is the record contained beneath its surface. Changes in atmospheric conditions affect the physical and chemical structure of the firn. These changes can be observed in ice cores and related to temperature, accumulation, atmospheric circulation, and other phenomena. Physically, the changes appear in the core as horizontal bands of varying clarity and texture that are related to an annual signal. Temperature, radiation, and wind characteristics vary considerably from summer to winter, and they affect the structure of the surface snow differently in different seasons. During the summer, the temperature gradients in the snow can be very high, which can cause snow grains to become very large and faceted, a condition known as hoar formation. These low-density, faceted crystals metamorphose differently from the rest of the snow pack, so that, when they are transformed into ice, the resulting layer appears more cloudy than the rest. In this way, they provide annual markers, and the ice between these layers represents the year-to-year snow accumulation. Additional information is contained in the chemical makeup of the snow. Various chemical compounds and isotopes vary with temperature at the time of ice formation (oxygen-18 and deuterium), with the source of moisture (salt compounds), and with volcanic activity (sulfur dioxide). These amounts vary seasonally and interannually, and, through their combined analyses, a past climate history can be reconstructed.

To date, approximately ten deep ice cores 2–3 kilometers long have been extracted from Greenland and Antarctica. These span a period of tens and even hundreds of thousands of year. The oldest record is from Vostok in Antarctica, which dates back 220,000 years. These cores provide an invaluable record of ice sheet histories.

ICE SHEETS AND CLIMATE CHANGE

The Greenland and Antarctic ice sheets are of great importance to sea level and global climate, both through their impact on and their response to climate changes. However, the precise role of the ice sheets in the climate system and their interaction with global change are complex. In the short term, changes in atmospheric temperature, winds, clouds, precipitation, and radiation balance affect the surface snow accumulation, temperature, and meltwater runoff from the ice sheets, which in turn have long-term effects on the dynamics of the ice sheet and the rates of ice flow and iceberg discharge into the ocean. Changes in ocean temperatures and circulation beneath the antarctic ice shelves also have long-term effects on the rates of ice discharge from the grounded ice sheets.

Recent estimates suggest that, in Greenland, the mass loss associated with increased melting and calving will exceed the increased input caused by enhanced accumulation in the warmer environment. It is expected that the Greenland Ice Sheet, which already experiences melt over roughly half of its surface, will shrink, contributing to an increase in sea level. Antarctica, on the other hand, which is situated much closer to the pole than Greenland, has very few areas that experience temperatures that are even close to the melting point. As a result, increased global temperatures are not expected to change significantly the amount of melt on the ice sheet, and the increased accumulation is presumed to be the dominant phenomenon. Consequently, the Antarctic Ice Sheet is expected to increase in size and help lower the amount of sea-level rise. The extent to which these estimates are true and the relative magnitudes of each are currently the subject of scientific investigation, using satellite technology, improved ice models, and a number of comprehensive field campaigns.

[See also Global Warming; and Sea Level Future.]

BIBLIOGRAPHY

Anderson, D. E., A. S. Goudie, and A. G. Parker. *Global Environments through the Quaternary*. Oxford and New York: Oxford University Press, 2007.
Bindschadler, R A. "Monitoring Ice-Sheet Behavior from Space." *Reviews of Geophysics* 36.1 (1998), 79–104.
Colbeck, S. C., ed. *Dynamics of Snow and Ice Masses*. New York: Academic Press, 1980.
Hambrey, M., and J. Alean. *Glaciers*. 2d ed. Cambridge and New York: Cambridge University Press, 2004.
Paterson, W. S. B. *The Physics of Glaciers*. 3d ed. Oxford, U.K., and Tarrytown, N.Y.: Pergamon, 1994.
Van der Veen, C. J. "Land, Ice, and Climate." In *Climate System Modeling*, edited by K. E. Trenberth, pp. 437–450. Cambridge and New York: Cambridge University Press, 1992.
Warrick, R. A., et al. "Changes in Sea Level." In *Climate Change 1995: The Science of Climate Change*, edited by J. T. Houghton et al., pp. 361–405. Cambridge and New York: Cambridge University Press, 1996.

—H. JAY ZWALLY AND WALEED ABDALATI

ICE SHELVES

See Antarctica and Climate Change.

IMPACTS BY ASTEROIDS

See Extraterrestrial Impacts.

IMPACTS OF CLIMATE CHANGE

Much attention is paid to the emissions reductions that might be achieved by global climate policy. But it is also important, when considering the equity implications of such policies, to take account of the distribution of impacts that will result from climate change if no action is taken. While it has been recognized for some time that developing nations in tropical countries will suffer more damage than developed nations in temperate zones, this article highlights the distribution of climate impacts around the world. The impact sectors covered are water stress, agriculture, coastal flooding, human health, infrastructure, and natural ecosystems. The article provides an overview of major climate change impacts that is based on a wide range of references, not only those cited herein. A more comprehensive list of potential impacts may be found in IPCC (2007), from which much of the material in this chapter is taken.

ECOSYSTEMS

Impacts of climate change are already being seen within ecosystems across the globe (Root et al., 2003) with increases in coral-bleaching events, the earlier arrival of spring (e.g., the dates of leaf-bud burst and of the arrival of migrant birds) and changes in species distributions. Changes in the plankton and fish communities of the North Sea are the probable cause of dramatic reductions in the breeding success of sea birds in Scotland. Impacts, including extinction risks, are expected to escalate quickly as temperatures rise, taking off strongly at temperatures around 1.5°C above 1990 levels (or 2°C above pre-industrial levels) in all continents.

Acidification of the ocean, a direct consequence of increased atmospheric carbon dioxide concentrations, has the potential to disrupt the marine ecosystem, at the very least halting the growth of corals (which is likely to occur at an atmospheric concentration of 500 ppm CO_2) and damaging mollusks and plankton at the base of the food chain. [See Ocean Acidification.]

Once temperatures climb above 2°C above 1990 levels, the terrestrial biosphere carbon-sink will be saturated and begin its transition to a carbon source, causing worldwide forest declines. In this temperature range, the Amazon rainforest could lose its carbon and begin a transition to savanna, with concomitant enormous losses of biodiversity (Cox et al., 2004; Scholze et al., 2006).

Coral reefs are the ecosystem at greatest risk of complete loss, with bleaching expected worldwide for a 1°C rise in sea surface temperature (corresponding to a global temperature rise of only about 1.2°C above 1990), while for a 2°C rise in sea surface temperature they are projected to be entirely lost and replaced by algal mats. Arctic, alpine, and mountain ecosystems are also particularly vulnerable. For example, 50% of the Arctic tundra may be lost for a global mean temperature increase of less than 2.5°C above 1990, impacting the populations of the millions of the world's waterfowl and shorebirds that migrate to the tundra to nest each year. Forty to 100% of Arctic summer sea ice would be lost for a global temperature rise of between 2–2.5°C above 1990, putting the polar bear at high risk of extinction.

In mountain ecosystems, losses of glaciers will affect the hydrology of upland areas and related ecosystems. [See Mountains.] In temperate regions such as the Alps, increases of 2.5°C globally above 1990 may cause extinctions of alpine plants. In New Zealand one- to two-thirds of the alpine flora (200–300 species) are projected to become extinct if temperatures increase globally by 3.5°C above 1990 levels, while in Australia the alpine zone would be severely depleted for a 2.8C rise in global temperature, endangering species such as the alpine sky lily. In tropical regions, cloud forests and their rich biodiversity are particularly at risk, as the envelope of climate suitability for cloud forest is forced to higher altitudes, causing the ecosystem area to shrink (because mountaintops are smaller than their bases), and (with a sufficiently large rise in temperature) to disappear completely. A prime example is Australia's Queensland rainforest, 50% of which is projected to be lost for a global temperature rise of 1.5°C above 1990, causing extinction risks for endemic reptiles and frogs, and for the golden bowerbird. In Hawaii, honeycreepers dependent on cloud forest fragments on mountaintops would be at risk of extinction with a 2°C rise in local temperature matching a global temperature rise of approximately 2.8°C above 1990. Indeed, amphibian extinctions caused by climate-change-induced disease outbreaks have already been seen in Costa Rica, Spain, and Australia.

Globally, biomes will shift as the climate becomes unsuitable for the existing biomes. [See Biomes.] Hence some ecosystems will lose area and others will eventually gain. A sufficiently slow rate of change of 0.05–0.1°C per decade would allow ecosystems to adapt, but the present rate of climate change is much faster—0.13°C per decade, and in Arctic regions 0.46°C per decade—and is considered sufficient to cause serious ecosystem disruption. Because of the slow rate of adaptation, "transformed" areas will be rapidly colonized by weedy, aggressive species, and generalists—leading to a large reduction of biodiversity in these regions. The largest biome losses are projected in tundra, wooded tundra (taiga), cool conifer forest, and temperate deciduous forests. For example, with a 3°C rise in temperature (above 1990), each biome loses variously 7–74% of its extent such that 22% of the land surface is transformed and will support low diversity (Leemans and Eickhout, 2004). At this point, half of nature reserves would no longer be able to fulfill their designated conservation objectives, such as preserving major populations of rare or endemic species, or unique ecosystem types, because of unsuitable climates.

DIVERSITY HOT SPOTS

All extinction rates projected for temperature rises of 1.5°C above 1990 greatly exceed current extinction rates. A doubling of atmospheric carbon dioxide levels has severe implications for global biodiversity hot spots, with those in South Africa, the Caribbean, Indo-Burma, the Mediterranean, central China, and the tropical Andes, being particularly vulnerable. [See Biological Diversity.] Vertebrate extinctions have been projected to reach 42–737 species in the tropical Andes, 21–377 in the Caribbean, and 10–214 in Indo-Burma, while plant extinctions are projected in over 2,000 species in South Africa, Caribbean, Indo-Burma, Mediterranean, southwestern Australia and the tropical Andes (Malcolm et al., 2006). In the worst case 39–43% biota could be lost in the hot spots, leading to the loss of some 56,000 endemic plants species and 3,700 endemic vertebrate species. Numerous regional studies support this analysis: for example in South Africa local temperature increases of 2–3°C (corresponding to global increases of 2°C above 1990) would remove at least 50% of the Fynbos botanical area and 80% of the Karoo, placing 2,800 plant species there, and 20–40% of the famous Proteaceae plant family, at risk of extinction. These areas harbor as large a floral diversity as some entire continents. Similarly, extinction risks would accrue for 25–50% of mammal species in the famous Kruger National Park. Overall, the losses of species from biodiversity hotspots due to climate change could number in the thousands or tens of thousands of species for various scenarios of CO_2-doubling; such a concentration could easily be reached by 2050 (Stern, 2006). But extinctions are also expected away from hot spots—for example, 4–24% of European plants would be critically endangered or extinct for a global temperature rise of about 3.5°C above 1990, and globally 18%, 24%, and 35% respectively of terrestrial species are committed to extinction for low, medium, and high climate-warming scenarios in 2050 corresponding to global mean temperature increases of 1.1, 1.7, and 2.4°C with respect to 1990, based on a study of 20% of the earth's land area (Thomas et al., 2004).

As sea levels rise, 22% of coastal wetlands have been projected to be lost if temperatures increase by 3°C above 1990. Significant losses of migratory bird habitat are expected particularly in the Baltic, the Mediterranean, and the United States. Temperature rises of 1–3°C would cause extensive loss of the Kakadu National Park in Australia through saltwater intrusion. Mangroves are thought to be intolerant to rates of sea-level rise above 5 mm/yr; the current rate is 1.3–2.3 mm/yr (Solomon, et al., 2007). [See Mangroves.] In freshwater ecosystems 63 of the world's 165 major rivers are expected to lose more than 10% of their fish species for a global temperature rise of 2°C, with freshwater fish habitat declining by 24% in North America.

A number of climate-change-induced impacts of ecosystems may have very large ramifications for human systems. For example, predator-prey and pollinator-plant relationships do not shift in concert as climate changes. This means that pest outbreaks and extinctions may occur. There may be negative impacts upon agriculture if key pollinators are lost. As the temperature increases, forest ecosystems are increasingly disrupted by pests, especially in boreal and temperate zones such as Eurasia and North America. As the temperature increases—and in some areas precipitation is reduced—forest ecosystems are also increasingly disrupted by fire. This is especially significant in boreal regions such as Canada, Alaska, and Russia, and also in areas which are drying as a result of climate change, such as the Mediterranean basin. Vulnerability to pests, diseases, and fire is greater at higher rates of change of temperature.

Land-use change and climate change will act synergistically to stress ecosystems and species. This means that species extinctions are likely to proceed more rapidly, because overall ecosystems will be impacted by a combination of climate change, land-use change, invasive species, acid deposition, and eutrophication. A significant reduction in native vegetation (principally forest) in nonindustrialized countries and arid regions is expected because of the expansion of agricultural or urban land use driven principally by population growth, especially in Africa, South America, and South Asia, where a reduction in native habitat will result in biodiversity loss. Globally, biodiversity (represented by species richness and relative abundance) may decrease by 12–16% by 2050 (Millennium Ecosystem Assessment, 2005), because of a combination of climate change and land-use change, in virtually all biomes. Tropical forest and woodland, savanna, and warm mixed forest are expected to account for 80% of the species lost (about 30,000 species) by 2050.

Climate change will affect areas currently being preserved from land use change as conservation regions. While in the absence of climate change, extinctions might be prevented through careful nature conservation policy, this will be more difficult as conservation areas become unsuitable for the species they are designed to protect. Existing and future land-use change will also impede the migration of species as they attempt to adapt their geographical ranges to account for changes in temperature and precipitation.

Overall, countries in the Arctic and those with coral reef ecosystems will experience the largest impacts of climate change, because change will be very rapid in the Arctic and complete losses of coral reef ecosystems are projected. [*See* Arctic Warming *and* Reefs.] Large impacts will also be felt by tropical countries, which will experience large losses of species in biodiversity hotspots. South African and Brazilian ecosystems are particularly at risk owing to the coincidence of high biodiversity and high vulnerability to climate change.

HUMAN SYSTEMS

Climate change affects humans in many ways, but especially in water resources, agriculture, and human health.

Water stress

Climate change affects hydrological regimes. The volume and timing of streamflow through the year will be affected by changes in the amount of precipitation, whether that precipitation falls as snow or rain, and changes in the rate of evaporation; changes to catchment land cover caused by climate change will also affect the rate of interception and infiltration and influence the processes by which water reaches river channels and aquifers.

At the global scale, the pattern of change in the volume of runoff follows changes in precipitation, although percentage changes are typically larger. [*See* Rivers: Impacts of Climate Change.] Under most climate-change scenarios, average annual runoff is reduced in southern Europe and much of the dry tropics, and increased in Southeast Asia and in high latitudes (Arnell, 2003; Milly et al., 2005; Kundzewicz et al., 2007). By the end of the twenty-first century, average runoff in these areas could change by more than ±25%. The estimated magnitude of change, however, varies between climate models, and in some regions, such as southern Asia, the direction of change is uncertain.

Where winter precipitation currently falls as snow, higher temperatures tend to lead to changes in the seasonality of river flows, with a shift from spring peaks caused by the melting of stored snow to peak flows during winter. The effect of higher temperatures depends on the current climate regime. If winters are extremely cold, higher temperatures will simply delay slightly the onset of snow and lead to slightly earlier melt; effects on flow regimes will therefore be small. If winter temperatures are much closer to 0°C, higher temperatures will have a much more dramatic impact on the proportion of precipitation that falls as snow, and therefore on flow regimes. Higher temperatures will tend to lead to accelerated glacier retreat, although this may be offset by increased accumulation in winter if winter snowfall

increases substantially. Accelerated retreat is already occurring in parts of the Hindu Kush and Andes, and by the end of the twenty-first century, the glacier-fed water supplies of large populations in India and Peru may be effectively eliminated. Accelerated melting of glaciers, particularly in the Hindu Kush, is also leading to the formation of moraine and ice-dammed lakes, which may be suddenly released as glaciers retreat, leading to extremely damaging floods.

A consistent result of climate modeling is an increase in the intensity of the hydrological cycle, with increases in the frequency of extreme precipitation events, particularly in mid and high latitudes. The effects on extreme riverflows depend on catchment characteristics (such as the amount of available storage and the responsiveness of the catchment), and while the frequency of floods may increase in some catchments, it may fall in others. The more intense hydrological cycle also manifests itself in more prolonged dry periods in some parts of the world, leading to increased frequency of drought (in some areas in addition to increases in flood risk at other times of the year). In southern Europe, for example, the low flows currently experienced once in a hundred years on average may occur more frequently than once in ten years by the end of the century (Lehner et al., 2005).

Changes in the quality of river and groundwater will occur for three reasons, with the relative impact of each varying from place to place and with changes in chemistry. First, changes in the volume and timing of flows may alter the dilution of loads, leading either to increases or decreases in concentration. Second, changes in processes in the catchment, such as increased mineralization of organic nitrogen with higher soil temperatures, may lead to changes in the load of material delivered to the river. Third, changes in water temperature may alter chemical reactions. Warmer water, for example, holds less dissolved oxygen, and both nitrification and denitrification rates are dependent on water temperature.

Such changes in the volume, timing, and quality of water will affect users of water resources, affecting the reliability of water supply, exposure to flood risk, power generation (both hydropower and thermal, via the availability and temperature of cooling water), and navigation, as well as the availability of irrigation water; changes will also affect aquatic ecosystems, which in turn may impact human society through changing ecosystem productivity. However, climate change is just one of many drivers affecting water resources and their uses, and its impacts may be masked by, or may exaggerate, affects of population and economic change. On a local scale, the effects of climate change on water resources will therefore depend on these other challenges, and on how the water system is managed. Other things being equal, a system under greatest pressure and with the least storage and flexibility will be most exposed to the impacts of a given change in hydrological regime.

Globally, climate change is likely to adversely affect large numbers of people already exposed to water scarcity. By the 2080s, 1–3 billion people living in water-stressed watersheds (less than 1,000 m³ per capita per year) would see a reduction in water availability, with the numbers depending not just on how climate change actually translates into changes in water availability, but also on the total world population (Arnell, 2004). People will be at increased risk of water scarcity in Africa, southern and eastern Europe, large parts of central Asia and the Middle East, and Central America. Whether these people are actually adversely impacted will depend on the measures in place in a watershed to manage water availability. Climate change also means that water availability apparently increases in some water-stressed areas—largely in southern and eastern Asia—but this extra water may occur during increased wet-season floods and thus not appreciably alleviate water problems during the dry season.

Agricultural systems

Impacts of climate change on agriculture may already be occurring, for example through the extensive 2007 drought in Australia, and recent increases in drought in southern Africa, the Sahel, parts of Asia, and southwestern Australia. Though individual drought events cannot be attributed directly to climate change, it is projected to cause continued increases in drought and could render large areas of Australia and Russia unsuitable for agricultural production.

As temperatures increase and precipitation patterns change in response to increasing carbon dioxide concentrations, crops which are not close to their thermal tolerances may benefit from a carbon dioxide fertilization effect (CO_2 f.e.). Hence, in non-drought areas under climate change, a crop yield may increase as temperatures begin to rise, and then fall as thermal tolerances are approached. The CO_2 f.e., however, simultaneously results in lower calorific value per gram of crop harvested and may not manifest in the field to the same degree as it does in the laboratory (Royal Society, 2005). Soil nutrient availability will also affect yields. As climate changes, soil nutrient levels and crop pollinator abundance may be affected, and if emissions of fossil fuels continue at current levels or exceed them, levels of tropospheric ozone in the atmosphere will increase, causing crop damage.

In Africa, many crops are already grown close to their thermal limits. Cereal yields are projected to decline most rapidly under climate change in Africa, South and Central America and in the absence of CO_2 fertilization, China. Areas with severe impacts are North Africa (where yields of wheat, the dominant crop, are expected to fall strongly even with CO_2 fertilization); and southern and western Africa, where large losses of the regionally dominant crop maize are expected. This responds only slightly to the CO_2 f.e., hence 35–500 additional millions of people could be at risk of hunger by the 2080s because of climate change (depending on population and GDP growth scenarios), most of them (23–419) in Africa (Parry et al., 2004), with others in Asia, where cereal production is likely to be affected (Fischer, 1996).

Simulating impacts on agriculture

Many of the above projections depend on modeling studies and their assumptions with respect to: 1) the future socioeconomic scenario, in particular the future population; 2) the GCM (general circulation model) used to model the climate change; 3) the degree to which the CO_2 fertilization occurs; and 4) the degree to which humans can adapt agricultural systems to climate change, including a realistic assessment of the potential to shift agriculture geographically to "new land" as climate changes. (New land is that which becomes newly suitable for cultivation under climate change.) Some modelers use statistical approaches to link current production or farm values to current climate and then assume these relationships hold in the future climate as this climate moves to new geographical areas. This is in effect an assumption of perfect adaptation not only at the farm and policy level, but also on a continental scale, and it entails significant increases in world cropland and consequent stresses on ecosystems, which will themselves have a greater need for conservation of remaining natural habitat, especially to allow migration of fauna and flora to cooler locations. Such optimistic approaches have been questioned on both econometric and economic grounds (Schlenker, 2004). Other modelers base calculations on the physical reductions in yields of the various crops as climate changes, feeding these into assessments of global trade in cereals and the resultant cereal prices, using standard assumptions about probable levels of adaptation.

Though some of the modeling approaches account for the possible different values of the CO_2 f.e., none of the modeling approaches listed takes into account the potential impacts of extreme weather events (flooding and drought) on agriculture. By the 2080s a dramatic increase in climate variability is expected. A few days of high temperatures just as wheat, peanuts, and soybeans are flowering can drastically reduce yield, while heavy precipitation and floods resulting from climate change-induced changes in climate variability and precipitation could double the current flood-related losses in maize yields in the U.S. (Challinor et al., 2006; Rosenzweig, et. al., 2002). Neither do models take account of the way in which agriculture in coastal areas will also be adversely impacted by increases in salinization as sea levels rise, and demand for crops may increase as climate impacts freshwater and marine ecosystems such as warm and cold water coral reefs, thereby reducing fish stocks.

Human health

Climate change will have direct impacts on the distribution of vector-borne diseases and cardiovascular disease, and will cause increases in mortality associated with heat stress and decreases in mortality associated with cold stress. [See Disease.] Indirect effects of climate change will increase deaths due to exposure to tropospheric ozone and skin cancer. Allergies may also increase, as may respiratory illness from exposure to emissions from forest fires if these increase as projected. Climate will also have indirect impacts through increases in malnutrition, additional deaths due to flooding associated with river- or sea-level rises, diseases linked to flooding, and health problems associated with environmental refugees. Climate change has been modeled to have caused the loss of 150,000 lives and 5.5 million days-of-life each year since 1970 (McMichael et al., 2003a).

About 400–500 million cases of malaria and a million deaths occur every year. Early studies projected that malaria would extend into Europe and North America, but these studies mostly referred to the distribution of the mosquito and did not take into account the past control measures leading to the present absence of the disease from these areas, which implies that even in the presence of the mosquito the disease is unlikely to become established without a pool of infected human hosts (Rogers and Randolph, 2000). In some areas in parts of Eastern Europe, however, there could be localized outbreaks under poor socioeconomic conditions. A study of the African continent (where 90% of the world's malaria cases are found) projects a 5–7% increase in the land area where malaria can be found, a 13–19% increase in the number of people exposed, and a 15–28% increase of person-months exposure by 2070–2099, compared to the present day in which 445 million people are exposed (Tanser et al., 2003). Most of the increase in area is altitudinal not latitudinal, and even if zero increase in area is assumed, the person-months exposure still rises by 28–42%. This study assumes a static population (which means that the increases are underestimated) and the current state of development (which means that the increases could be overestimated). Rogers and Randolph (2000) estimate an increase in exposure of 23 million people globally to falciparum malaria by 2050 if the global population remains at 5.6 billion as it was in 1994. This is a much lower estimate than Tanser's, but it is based on a much more simplistic model. Tanser's model (MARA, Mapping Malaria Risk in Africa), which is one of only two models that have been verified to account for the observed effect of climate variables on vector and parasite population biology, has a more rigorous spatial calibration to today's exposure based on 3,791 surveys. Thomas (2004) used the same model and estimates little increase in the area of stable malaria zones over the next 30–40 years in Africa, but by the second half of the century strong altitudinal increases in stable areas are expected, agreeing with Tanser et al. (2003).

Concurrently in 1990, 30% of the world's population (1.5 billion people) lived in regions with a dengue risk of >50%. By 2085, 5–7 billion people could be at risk of dengue compared to 3.5 billion in the absence of climate change (Hales et al., 2002). This takes into account future population growth.

2,800 heat deaths per year in the U.K. are projected for the 2050s (a 250% increase) under a moderate climate-change scenario while greater reductions in cold-related mortality are expected (Keatings et al., 2002). Excess mortality from heat in five U.S. cities in 2020 is projected to increase, variously from 0 to 682%. Also expected are small increases in the risk of cardiovascular disease, significant increases in diarrhea, and large increases in deaths due to inland and coastal floods (McMichael et al., 2003).

Experimental studies have linked higher temperatures to enhanced carcinogenesis related to ulcerative colitis in rats. Finally, it is estimated that for every degree of warming there is a 5% increase in skin cancer for a given solar ultraviolet flux.

Human mortality can ensue from exposure of vulnerable individuals to concentrations of tropospheric ozone above a certain threshold. This threshold is exceeded in some areas for varying numbers of days each year. Under climate change, the frequency of these high ozone episodes is expected to increase because increased temperature enhances tropospheric ozone production. Hence, mortality caused by these air pollution episodes is likely to increase. For example, in the New York region, a 4.5% increase in ozone deaths is expected for a high climate-change scenario (Knowlton et al., 2004).

COASTAL FLOODING

Sea-level rise has a wide range of impacts, the most serious of which is submergence of land and increased flood risk as extreme water levels rise. [See Sea Level Future.] More intense storms may exacerbate these impacts (Nicholls et al., 2007). This has serious consequences because of the large population in the coastal zone, where population densities are the largest on earth. It is estimated that at least 200 million people were exposed globally to flooding from storm surges in 1990, with more than half of this exposed population being in South, Southeast, and East Asia. Under scenarios of rising sea levels, these regions continue to be the most threatened through the twenty-first century, although Africa is expected to be increasingly at risk because of its large population growth (e.g., Nicholls, 2004).

It has been estimated that in 1990 10 million people per year experienced flooding from storm surge (or about 5% of the exposed population). The risk of flooding depends on climate (sea-level rise and other factors), land subsidence (which can produce local rises in sea level), population and socioeconomic scenarios, and most especially on assumptions about adaptation, which for densely-populated areas is normally protection in the form of hard dikes or soft engineering/natural features such as dunes and beaches (Nicholls, 2004). Sea-level rise always increases the number of people at risk. Development pathways are also important: in general wealthy futures with smaller population growth are less vulnerable than poorer futures with higher population growth. Increased protection can, however, offset increases in flood risk, and the biggest uncertainty for the future concerns the nature and the success of the adaptation responses to increased flood risk. Taking an economic-efficiency viewpoint, protection looks widely affordable and rational for much of the world's developed coasts for the twenty-first century (Nicholls and Tol, 2006; Anthoff et al., 2006). These papers point out, however, that the results are idealized and the actual adoption of protection remains uncertain, and the barriers to protection in coastal areas remain a major gap in our understanding. Further protection will degrade coastal wetlands due to coastal squeeze and enhance the risk of flooding as their protective function is degraded. The most recent estimates for all coastal wetlands (excluding sea grasses) suggests global losses of 33% and 44% given a 36-cm and a 72-cm rise in sea level from 2000 to 2080, respectively (Nicholls et al., 2007).

Regionally, South Asia, Southeast Asia, and Africa appear to be in absolute terms the most threatened by flooding caused by sea-level rise. East Africa with its large population growth and tropical storms may be especially vulnerable (Nicholls et al., 2007). While impacts are small in global terms, the small-island regions stand out as especially vulnerable to sea-level rise, including the high islands such as are found in the Caribbean.

Sea levels are expected to continue to rise for centuries due to the thermal inertia of the oceans. The rise could be substantial (many meters) if the Greenland and West Antarctic ice sheets disintegrate. This represents a major challenge for coastal societies. It suggests an ongoing need to adapt to sea-level rise and emphasizes the need to understand better the trade-offs between coastal management policies that "hold the line" and those that "retreat the line" in the face of sea-level rise (Nicholls et al., 2007).

In addition to the effects of sea-level rise, hurricanes and typhoons are expected to become more intense because of global warming and possibly expand the regions that are affected (Solomon, et al., 2007). This implies much greater damage to coastal infrastructure, especially as these extremes will be exacerbated by sea level rise. Many of the world's largest coastal cities are threatened, including Tokyo, Mumbai (Bombay), Dhaka, Karachi, New York, Kolkata (Calcutta), Metro Manila, Shanghai, Osaka, Tianjin, Bangkok, Seoul, and Chennai (Madras) (Klein et al., 2003). Extreme weather will in general damage an increasing amount of infrastructure as the climate changes, imposing large financial costs on developed countries and leading to potential loss of life and livelihoods in developing countries.

[*See also* Regional Patterns of Climate Change.]

BIBLIOGRAPHY

Anthoff, D., et al. "Global and Regional Exposure to Large Rises in Sea-Level: A Sensitivity Analysis." Working Paper 96. Norwich, U.K.: Tyndall Centre for Climate Change Research, 2006. A research report prepared for the *Stern Review*.

Arnell, N. W. "Effects of IPCC SRES Emissions Scenarios on River Runoff: A Global Perspective." *Hydrology and Earth System Sciences* 7.5 (2003), 619–641.

———. "Climate Change and Global Water Resources: SRES Scenarios and Socio-Economic Scenarios." *Global Environmental Change* 14 (2004), 31–52.

Challinor, A. J., T. R. Wheeler, and J. M. Slingo. "Assessing the Vulnerability of Crop Productivity to Climate Change Thresholds Using an Integrated Crop-Climate Model." In *Avoiding Dangerous Climate Change*, edited by H. J. Schellnhuber, et al., pp. 187–194. Cambridge and New York: Cambridge University Press, 2006.

Cox, P. M., et al. "Amazonian Forest Dieback under Climate-Carbon Cycle Projections for the 21st Century." *Theoretical and Applied Climatology* 78.1–3 (2004), 137–156. DOI: 10.1007/s00704-004-0049-4.

Fischer, G., et al. "Impacts of Potential Climate Change on Global and Regional Food Production and Vulnerability." In *Climate Change and World Food Security*, edited by T. E. Downing, 115–160. Berlin, Heidelberg, and London: Springer, 1996.

Hales, S., et al. "Potential Effect of Population and Climate Changes on Global Distribution of Dengue Fever: An Empirical Model." *Lancet* 360 (2002), 830–834.

Keatinge, W. R., et al. "Heat-and-Cold-Related Mortality and Morbidity and Climate Change." In *Health Effects of Climate Change in the U.K.*, prepared by the Expert Group on Climate Change and Health in the U.K., pp. 70–80. London: Department of Health, 2001.

Klein, R. J. T., R. J. Nicholls, and F. Thomalla. "The Resilience Of Coastal Megacities To Weather Related Hazards: A Review." In *Building Safer Cities: The Future of Disaster Risk*, edited by A. Kreimer, M. Arnold, and A. Carlin, pp. 111–137. Washington, D.C.: World Bank, 2003.

Knowlton, K., et al. "Assessing Ozone-Related Health Impacts under a Changing Climate." *Environmental Health Perspectives* 112.15 (2004), 1557–1563. DOI: 10.1289/ehp.7163.

Kundzewicz, Z. W., et al. 2007. "Freshwater Resources and Their Management." In *Climate Change 2007: Impacts, Adaptation and Vulnerability: Contribution of Working Group II to the Fourth Assessment Report of the Intergovernmental Panel on Climate Change*, edited by M. L. Parry, et al., pp. 173–210. Cambridge and New York: Cambridge University Press, 2007.

Leemans, R., and B. Eickhout. "Another Reason for Concern: Regional and Global Impacts on Ecosystems for Different Levels of Climate Change." *Global Environmental Change* 14.3 (2004), 219–228.

Lehner, B., et al. "Estimating the Impact of Global Change on Flood and Drought Risks in Europe: A Continental, Integrated Analysis." *Climatic Change* 75.3 (2005), 273–299. DOI: 10.1007/s10584-006-6338-4.

Malcolm, J. R., et al. "Global Warming and Extinctions of Endemic Species from Biodiversity Hotspots." *Conservation Biology* 20.2 (2006), 538–548. DOI: 10.1111/j.1523-1739.2006.00364.x.

McMichael, A., et al. *Human Health and Climate Change in Oceania: A Risk Assessment 2002.* Canberra: Commonwealth Department of Health and Ageing, 2003a.

McMichael, et al., eds. *Climate Change and Human Health.* Geneva: World Health Organization, 2003b.

Millennium Ecosystem Assessment. *Living beyond Our Means: Natural Assets and Human Well-Being.* 2005. http://www.millenniumassessment.org/en/BoardStatement.aspx (accessed June 2, 2008).

Milly, P. C. D., K. A. Dunne, and A. V. Vecchia. "Global Pattern of Trends in Streamflow and Water Availability in a Changing Climate." *Nature* 438 (2005), 347–350. DOI: 10.1038/nature04312.

Nicholls, R. J. "Coastal Flooding and Wetland Loss in the 21st Century: Changes under the SRES Climate and Socio-Economic Scenarios." *Global Environmental Change* 14.1 (2004), 69–86. DOI: 10.1016/j.gloenvcha.2003.10.007.

Nicholls R. J. and R. S. J. Tol. "Impacts and Responses to Sea-Level Rise: A Global Analysis of the SRES Scenarios over the Twenty-First Century." *Philosophical Transactions of the Royal Society A* 364 (2006), 1073–1095.

Nicholls, R. J., et al. "Coastal Systems and Low-Lying Areas." In *Climate Change 2007: Impacts, Adaptation, and Vulnerability: Contribution of Working Group II to the Fourth Assessment Report of the Intergovernmental Panel on Climate Change*, edited by M. L. Parry, et al., pp. 315–356. Cambridge and New York: Cambridge University Press, 2007.

Parry, M., et al. "Effects of Climate Change on Global Food Production under SRES Emissions and Socio-Economic Scenarios." *Global Environmental Change* 14.1 (2004), 53–67. DOI: 10.1016/j.gloenvcha.2003.10.008.

Rogers, D. J., and S. E. Randolph. "The Global Spread of Malaria in a Future, Warmer World." *Science* 289 (2000), pp. 1763–1766.

Root, T. L., et al. "Fingerprints of Global Warming on Wild Animals and Plants." *Nature* 421 (2003), 57–60. DOI: 10.1038/nature01333.

Rosenzweig, C. E., et al. 2002. "Increased Crop Damage in the U.S. from Excess Precipitation under Climate Change." *Global Environmental Change* 12.3 (2000), 197–202. DOI: 10.1016/S0959-3780(02)00008-0.

Royal Society. "Food Crops in a Changing Climate." Policy Document 10/05. 2005. http://royalsociety.org (accessed June 2, 2008). Report of a Royal Society Discussion Meeting, April 2005.

Schlenker, W., M. Hanemann, and A. Fisher. "Will U.S. Agriculture Really Benefit from Global Warming? Accounting for Irrigation in the Hedonic Approach." Department of Agricultural and Resource Economics, Working Paper 941. Berkeley: University of California, 2004. http://repositories.cdlib.org/are_ucb/941 (accessed June 2, 2008).

Scholze, M., et al. "A Climate Change Risk Analysis for World Ecosystems." *Proceedings of the National Academy of Sciences* 103.35 (2006), 13116–13120. DOI: 10.1073/pnas.0601816103.

Solomon, S., et al., eds. *Climate Change 2007: The Physical Science Basis: The Physical Science Basis: Contribution of Working Group I to the Fourth Assessment Report of the Intergovernmental Panel on Climate Change.* Cambridge and New York: Cambridge University Press, 2007.

Stern, N. *The Economics of Climate Change: The Stern Review.* Cambridge and New York: Cambridge University Press, 2006.

Tanser F. C., B. Sharp, and D. Le Sueur. "Potential Effect of Climate Change on Malaria Transmission in Africa." *Lancet* 362 (2003), 1792–1798.

Thomas, C. D., et al. "Extinction Risk from Climate Change." *Nature* 427 (2004), 145–148. DOI: 10.1038/nature02121.

Thomas, C. J., G. Davies, and C. E. Dunn. "Mixed Picture for Changes in Stable Malaria Distribution with Future Climate in Africa." *Trends in Parasitology* 20.5 (2004), 216–220. DOI: 10.1016/j.pt.2004.03.001.

—RACHEL WARREN, NIGEL ARNELL AND ROBERT NICHOLLS

INDIA AND ENVIRONMENTAL CHANGE

On a world map in which a country's size is proportional to its population, India looms large. If on that same map countries with higher rates of population growth are colored pink, and those with lower rates of growth are colored green, India becomes even more prominent than China, inviting Malthusian concerns over environmental pressures. Ten percent of the human race (half of India's population) lives in the Ganges valley, and the world's greatest concentration of human poverty is centered in the downstream states of Uttar Pradesh, Bihar, West Bengal, and neighboring Bangladesh. The Indian economy in aggregate is growing very fast, but much of the new wealth has passed these states by. In a few states, such as Punjab and Haryana, new wealth has come from agriculture. Mostly, however, it has come from rapidly growing cities.

Both stagnation and development are taking place against a dramatic backdrop. Himalayan South Asia is the product of one of the world's great collisions between tectonic plates, and it is a zone of intense seismic activity—with earthquakes causing spasmodic massive damage not only in the mountains, but in the riverine plains as well. The Himalayas have the greatest extent of nonpolar glaciers, and their role in supplying water to the plains beneath is a matter of significant interest. South Asia experiences the world's most dramatic monsoon (Arabic, *mawsim* "season"), with a layer of moist air 6,000 meters thick suddenly ending the intensely hot dry season. The combination of great (and still rising) mountains and heavy monsoons has produced the massive sediment flux that has deposited the world's biggest alluvial plains, and the world's greatest delta in Bengal, whose alluvial cone extends 2,000 nautical miles into the bay of Bengal. The great rivers have shifted courses within historical time, eroding whole towns, and displacing swaths of population. Sometimes these shifts, as with the Brahmaputra and Tista, have been provoked by earthquakes or tectonic movements. Floods are commonplace. Whether and to what extent one can add to this overview the prospect of regional climate change derived from global climate change, is debatable. Many in India believe that the country already experiences extremes of drought and flood and that there is little in prospect that could makes things worse. There are however, others who worry in particular that water supplies will become increasingly critically short.

This is the background for a discussion of environmental change. The following are some of the questions to be asked:

- Does the size alone of the population create damaging environmental pressures?
- Does the poverty of large areas create environmental pressures?
- Do the new large cities have damaging ecological footprints?
- Is India's unique environment particularly "difficult" or "fragile"?

POPULATION

We know that before the British raj, there were major famines in India, which were to a certain extent accepted as natural calamities—indeed the Hindi/Urdu word *sukha* (dry) means both drought and famine. During the raj, famines were seen as politically destabilizing, and large-scale canal engineering was both reintroduced in Tamil Nadu—some decayed works dated back thousands of years—and developed for the first time in the Punjab and (modern) Uttar Pradesh. Many of these schemes were specifically "protective." These, together with the movement of food stocks by railway, mitigated but did not eliminate famine. The government of India instead took the view that famine was a colonial problem—until disaster struck in 1965 and 1966. Already committed to increasing the amount of irrigation, it built large dams in the Himalayas for the first time and extended huge canals into marginal regions (for example the Indira Gandhi Canal in the Thar Desert of Rajasthan). Currently a massive scheme is being developed to take water from the Narmada River into Gujarat—a scheme subject to international protest and with redoubtable Indian campaigners tirelessly opposing it. These schemes provide water for irrigation and for power, and increasingly for urban consumption. There is no doubt they have contributed to the success of the Green Revolution, which has fed India's population even though it has trebled since Independence, and even though the rates of financial return from canal schemes have been poor. Increasingly, however, water is provided by powered tube-wells. In the Deccan these are now mining water, because they extract water at greater rates than it is replenished. There has also been agricultural colonization of new land, although the high-water mark was probably reached in the 1970s, since when there has been no more suitable land to bring under the plow.

In addition to water, the Green Revolution has used agrochemicals. It is claimed by many that soils have been damaged ("addicted" to fertilizer) and groundwater contaminated. There are plenty of anecdotal reports of these effects, but little hard quantitative evidence. There is evidence that the increases in yields that were achieved in the last few decades have now started to tail off. Agrochemicals used in paddy fields have affected the coproduction of fish in Bengal. With no new land available, attention is turning to the idea of a second green revolution, in which genetic engineering will play a part.

Water "wars," or rioting and police gunfire, with resultant deaths, are annual events in Haryana and Uttar Pradesh. There have been skirmishes between the police forces of Karnataka and Tamil Nadu over the waters of the river Kaveri. These scenarios have prompted Indian engineers to propose a river linkage on a truly subcontinental scale—shipping water from the Brahmaputra across the Ganges and down into the peninsula as far as Chennai. The outcry against the proposal is not simply by environmentalists, but also by neighboring Bangladesh, which claims to have suffered already from India's Farakka Barrage on the Ganges.

Thus, to answer the first question, the size of the population alone has prompted major schemes with both negative and positive impacts, and a potentially damaging agrochemical form of agriculture. Malthus has been thwarted so far, but the future probably hinges on more sustainable technical advances in agriculture.

POVERTY

There is poverty both in the cities, where up to 40% of the population may live in slums, and in rural areas, where levels of poverty are actually more acute. Rural incomes are lower, diets worse, death rates higher, medical facilities fewer, and labor productivity worse, than in the towns. Indian farms everywhere tend to be small, in part because of multiple inheritances, in part because of land-ceiling legislation enacted to limit the growth of large landholdings. The poor are small, marginal farmers and landless laborers, often in areas of high settlement density. The fuels for cooking are mostly animal dung and wood. The vegetation has been stripped from the land (in part by foraging goats) and the soil denied manure. In the major riverine plains it is soil impovrishment rather than soil loss that is the greatest problem.

As with the Nile delta in ancient times, floods are not an unalloyed disaster. In parts of the lower Ganges-Brahmaputra-Meghna flooding does bring rejuvenating silt, but in hilly areas, excluding rice paddies, the exploitation has resulted in erosion and soil loss. In the north Deccan this has been a cause of the degradation of some of India's important forests. To answer the second question above, the conclusion is that poor and dense rural populations are not well equipped for the sustainable management of their areas.

CITIES

India's large cities are growing rapidly—even cities of a million can double in a decade. Kolkata (Calcutta), Delhi, Mumbai (Bombay), and Chennai (Madras) are all over 10 million in population. Around any of them the first and most visible sign of their logistic demands is thousands of acres of brick-pits. Deep clay beds are rare: the pits use alluvium containing enough clay, and machinery is little used. Given the use of human labor and the superficial geology, the excavations are shallow. Much is made by environmental campaigners of this ravaging of agricultural land, but the real story is more complex. The alluvium exposed may have a better mineral content than that which has been removed, even if it lacks organic matter. Pits can be dug with an eye to improving irrigation. In other words, reversion to agriculture is not necessarily difficult and does occur—in some cases even on a seasonal basis, because the monsoon makes firing of the bricks in sunken pits too difficult.

Other major footprints of the cities include the demands for water and energy. The problems are city-specific—in general the cities of the northwest (like Delhi) and the Deccan, as far as Chennai, are those which have the greatest water problems. In the case of Delhi and other cities of the north, dams such as the Tehri on the Ganges have been constructed in the Himalayas in order to increase the dry-season flow of rivers. There are other sites available, particularly in Nepal, for example on the Kosi. These sites have huge potential for hydroelectric generation as well, but the wisdom of pursuing such schemes on very silty rivers in a major earthquake zone is hotly disputed. Overall, per capita water availability is low, flush sanitation unavailable for most, and even major water courses are polluted and nearly stagnant by the end of the dry season. The urban poor may have limited access to electricity, even for cooking, usually cannot obtain bottled gas, and hence rely on biofuels for cooking. Delhi's demand for charcoal extends to Assam, from which whole trains of charcoal depart daily. In the areas where the charcoal is produced, there is little regulation of forest clearance. The cities also demand timber for construction, and the demand for timber extends into the Himalayas as well as to the northeast and the Deccan. There are extensive debates about whether this is prompting continued deforestation or not. There has been a major shift in policy, from state management of forests, to joint management with local communities. The Forest Department claims that forest cover nationally has stabilized at about 14%. This does not mean that "original" forest necessarily survives. In places eucalyptus is planted on arable fields, and proves as valuable a crop as cereals. Everywhere, bamboo is cultivated for its myriad uses from implements to housing and water pipes. To answer the third question, the logistic demands of the cities are indeed impacting on many rural areas, even distant ones.

ENVIRONMENT

India's environment does present particular problems in development. Coastal areas may be windy at most times of the year, and one of the world's largest wind-farms is to be found at the southern tip of the peninsula. But inland, for much of the year there is little wind, no rain, and in the winter in the north, there are temperature inversions. All of this means that for much of the year the atmosphere is little cleaned, and little moved. Add to this an explosion in the use of motor vehicles, many with polluting two-stroke engines or truly dirty diesel engines, domestic use of soft coal, and coal-burning power stations within urban areas, and the result is some of the world's worst air pollution. Smog in Delhi in winter is not only demonstrably killing its inhabitants, it can ground aircraft movements for days. Moves to improve the situation are enacted and planned—starting usually with the conversion of some motor vehicles to LPG/CNG. However, the crisis has not peaked, as power generation increases and more vehicles clog the roads. Indian cities are contributors to Asia's "brown cloud." To answer the fourth question, India's environment does pose specific problems.

Since the beginning of the current interglacial warm period, there have been significant changes to the South Asian environment. The monsoons have always been a feature, but they have changed in strength in the last 10,000 years, and so have precipitation patterns. The Thar Desert on the Indian-Pakistani border has been both larger and smaller than it is now. Glaciers have retreated in the Himalayas, and sea levels have risen from 150 meters below the current level, initially very fast, but much more slowly in the last few centuries. The current concern over global climate change has to be set against this backdrop.

India is of course both culprit and victim of climate change. Western nations are terrified at the prospects of India's use of its massive coal reserves, and the resulting CO_2 emissions. India is also eyed because of the methane emissions from its paddy fields. On the second point there is conflicting evidence about the seriousness of the problem, and in any case rice cultivation provides the staple food for more than half the population. On the first point, India argues that its per capita CO_2 emissions are very small, less in fact than each person's per capita share of known global carbon sequestration. Thus, if personal equity rather than national equity is the rule on this planet, then India can increase CO_2 emissions, and it is up to the oil-guzzling West to decrease its per capita levels.

The other side of the coin is India as victim. There are concerns that the dry-season flow of the Ganges and other northern rivers will decline because of the disappearance of the glaciers. Indeed in Nepal many glaciers are continuing their long retreat; in the Karakorum, however, they have been advancing because of increased precipitation. In any event, much of the dry-season flow of the rivers comes from snow melt, not glacier melt. The Bengal delta is also at risk from rising sea levels—yet it has been built precisely because of the rising sea levels providing "accommodation" for the sediments. What is more likely than simple inundation is changing river courses and increased silt deposition—in short new land, but not in "old" places. Because the Bay of Bengal in particular is at risk of tropical cyclones, if sea surface temperatures do increase, there will probably be an increase in cyclone frequency and intensity. Losses due to cyclones increased throughout the twentieth century, but mostly as a result of increasing populations of land-hungry people settling on exposed land, and as a result of the clearance of protective mangrove swamps.

Mangrove swamps are increasingly being cleared for shrimp cultivation—a valuable crop, but one which has proved unsustainable, as after about ten years, most brackish ponds become irremediably infected with pathogens. (Near Kolkata the abandoned farms usually become brick-pits.) The mangrove forests are a reserve of biodiversity—and in Bengal are home to the highly endangered Bengal tiger. Peninsular India, which was an island for 200 millions years as it journeyed from Africa (Gondwanaland) to Asia, has some of the world's most important biodiversity hot spots. Development, particularly near the Western Ghats, threatens these. These precious wildernesses are perhaps most at risk as India successfully develops for the sake of its more than one billion people.

BIBLIOGRAPHY

Centre for Science and Environment, New Delhi. http://www.cseindia.org/ (accessed June 1, 2008).
Down to Earth (Science and Environment Magazine). http://www.downtoearth.org.in/ (accessed June 1, 2008).
M. S. Swaminathan Research Foundation, Chennai. http://www.mssrf.org/ (accessed June 1, 2008).
The Energy Research Institute, New Delhi. http://teriin.org/ (accessed June 1, 2008).

—GRAHAM CHAPMAN

INDUSTRIAL ECOLOGY

Many people believe that industrial systems are not part of the natural order of things, or in other words, that economy and ecology do not mix. Industrial ecologists view industrial systems as one type of ecosystem, albeit one that is highly modified by human activity.

In fact, the first references to ecology trace back to Linnaeus in 1749 who refers to it as "nature's economy" (Worster, 1977). "Ecology" is derived from the Greek word *oikos* which can be interpreted as the *structure* of the household while "economy" describes the *management* of the household (Costanza et al., 1992). Both structure and management have much to do with relationships and systems. Ecology, in the biological sense, is the study of the interrelationships among species and communities of organisms and the physical environment in which they live (Odum, 1993).

HISTORY

Although many authors have attributed the birth of industrial ecology to the article by Frosch and Gallopoulos in a 1989 special issue of *Scientific American* devoted to industrial ecosystems, its underpinnings can be found much earlier. In fact, industrial symbiosis can be traced back to the late 1800s when Simmonds described potential uses of waste products by other enterprises (1862) and reviewed progress made in the economic utilization of waste products over a quarter century (1876). In the early 1900s, Conover (1918) discussed the salvage and use of wastes and scrap by various industries while Koller (1918) discussed the recovery and remanufacture of waste paper. Clemen (1927) described the use of byproducts in the meat-packing industry and in fact, entire clusters of small industries evolve around the meat-packing plants. These were arguably the first manifestations of eco-industrial clusters.

In the 1960s, studies in material flows were described in the literature by Ayres and Kneese. Systems ecologists such as Odum began writing about the industrial system as a subset of the ecosystem or biosphere. This is possibly the basis for the term "industrial ecology." The Japanese had been exploring the concept in the early 1970s. American ecologist Charles Hall of New York State University lectured about industrial ecosystems in the early 1980s, and a Belgian research group published a paper titled "The Belgian Ecosystem: An Industrial Ecology Experiment" (Erkman, 1983).

The watershed event, however, was the publication of the article by Frosch and Gallopoulos (1989) that described "industrial ecosystems" but actually referred to "industrial metabolism."

TERMINOLOGY

Several terms and concepts have emerged in the past 20 years that have begun to frame the field of industrial ecology. These include "industrial ecosystem," "industrial metabolism," "industrial symbiosis," and "life-cycle analysis and management." In addition, terms such as "eco-industrial development," "eco-industrial park," "eco-industrial clusters," and "eco-industrial network" have appeared in the literature. Eco-industrial networks range from limited symbiotic relationships involving a few materials (e.g., when the heated cooling water from a coal- or oil-fired generating station is used to heat adjoining buildings), to fully mature industrial ecosystems in which infrastructure, buildings, and products are designed and used in cyclical and sustaining ways.

There has been much debate about what is encompassed in the four most common terms in the current literature, "industrial ecosystem," "eco-industrial park," "eco-industrial development," and "eco-industrial network." "Industrial ecosystem" has been widely used since it was popularized by the seminal article by Frosch and Gallopoulos in 1989. This is not surprising, because ecosystems are the cornerstones of the conventional field of ecology. "Eco-industrial park" has been used to describe almost any kind of community of businesses which features some ecological characteristics and is located within the boundaries of a traditional industrial park.

There is some consensus about the characteristics and goals of eco-industrial development. One definition describes it as a "community of manufacturing and service businesses seeking enhanced environmental and economic performance through collaboration in managing environmental and resources issues including energy, water and materials. By working together, the community of businesses seeks a collective benefit which is greater than the sum of the individual benefits each company would realize if it optimized its individual performance only" (Lowe et al., 1996). The President's Council on Sustainable Development of the United States (1996) also recognizes that the community of businesses must cooperate with the local community, the resources which should be shared include information, infrastructure, and the natural habitat, and the sharing must be equitable.

PRINCIPLES

In their book, *Discovering Industrial Ecology: An Executive Briefing and Sourcebook*, Lowe et al. (1997) identify a number of principles of eco-industrial development. Such development must:

- connect individual firms into industrial ecosystems
- close loops through reuse and recycling
- maximize efficiency of material and energy use
- minimize waste generation
- consider wastes as potential products
- balance inputs and outputs to natural ecosystem capacities
- reduce the environmental burden created by releases
- design the industrial interface with sensitivity to the natural environment

- minimize creating and transporting toxic and hazardous materials
- design industrial use of materials and energy
- redesign processes
- substitute technologies and materials
- do more with less
- align policy with a long term (multi-generational) perspective

These principles focus almost exclusively on technical matters. The human and social dimensions have received much less consideration but have been addressed by Côté and Cohen-Rosenthal (1998) and Cohen-Rosenthal (2000), among others. They identify a number of networking possibilities which should be considered in fostering eco-industrial development. In addition to symbiotic relationships involving materials and energy, they point to networking in transportation (carpooling), human resource management (training), information and communications (management information systems), marketing (joint promotions), environment, health and safety (emergency response planning), production (equipment pooling), and quality of life (integrated volunteer programs). Many of these require social as well as technical networking.

The current state of affairs may be a reflection of the fact that our industrial systems are still in a very early stage of evolution (i.e., hundreds rather than millions of years) and therefore understandably immature. The linear thinking in our industries and the high flow-through of materials and energy testify to this fact. Chertow (1998) uses a different analogy, referring to the state of eco-industrial parks as similar to that of VisiCalc, an early spreadsheet program.

INDUSTRIAL SYMBIOSIS

Many authors equate industrial ecology with industrial symbiosis. To many people, the notion that the wastes of one company can become the raw materials of another is still central to industrial ecology. In some industrial sectors, the byproducts represent a larger percentage of the materials or energy than does the main product, as in the case of oil- and coal-fired electricity generating stations. And while industrial symbiosis, or byproduct synergy as it is called by industrial organizations such as the World Business Council for Sustainable Development, is an important concept, it is only one among many.

In a column in the *Journal of Industrial Ecology*, Chertow (2007) suggests a continuum of industrial symbioses which describe interrelationships among businesses. These are:

- waste exchanges involving two or more companies
- life-cycle management of all materials used by one facility or company
- multiple exchanges of resources among several firms in an industrial park
- material- and energy-based relationships among firms within a industrial zone or part of a city or region
- a virtual ecosystem in which networking of various types occurs over a larger area.

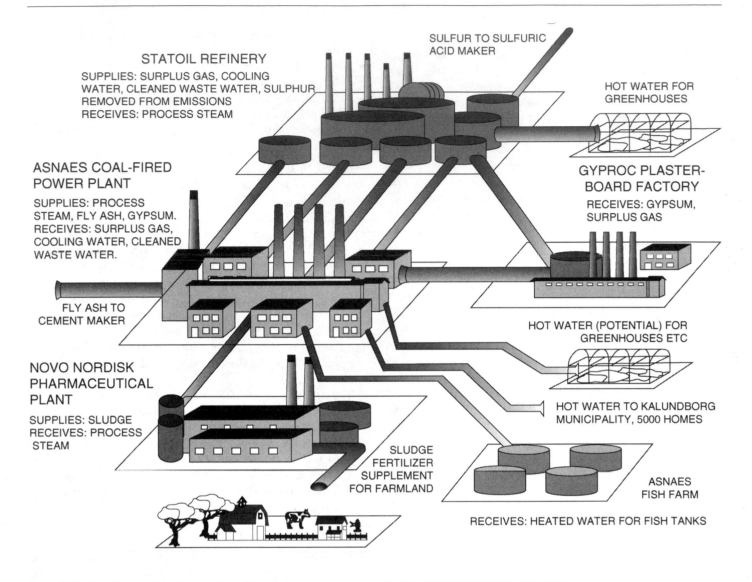

STATOIL REFINERY
SUPPLIES: SURPLUS GAS, COOLING
WATER, CLEANED WASTE WATER, SULPHUR
REMOVED FROM EMISSIONS
RECEIVES: PROCESS STEAM

SULFUR TO SULFURIC
ACID MAKER

HOT WATER FOR
GREENHOUSES

ASNAES COAL-FIRED
POWER PLANT
SUPPLIES: PROCESS
STEAM, FLY ASH, GYPSUM.
RECEIVES: SURPLUS GAS,
COOLING WATER, CLEANED
WASTE WATER.

GYPROC PLASTER-
BOARD FACTORY
RECEIVES: GYPSUM,
SURPLUS GAS

FLY ASH TO
CEMENT MAKER

HOT WATER (POTENTIAL) FOR
GREENHOUSES ETC

NOVO NORDISK
PHARMACEUTICAL
PLANT
SUPPLIES: SLUDGE
RECEIVES: PROCESS
STEAM

HOT WATER TO KALUNDBORG
MUNICIPALITY, 5000 HOMES

SLUDGE
FERTILIZER
SUPPLEMENT
FOR FARMLAND

ASNAES
FISH FARM

RECEIVES: HEATED WATER FOR FISH TANKS

Industrial Ecology. FIGURE 1. Kalundborg Industrial Symbiosis.

There are many examples of symbioses and synergies described in the academic, technical, and Internet literature. The most famous of these is the Kalundborg industrial symbiosis in Denmark in which 24 different symbioses have been explored over a 30-year period. This evolution has been particularly successful, both economically and environmentally (Ehrenfeld and Gertler, 1997; Jacobsen, 2006). For this reason, Kalundborg has served as a model that many other industrial areas have attempted to emulate (Figure 1).

Another early example that spawned the byproduct-synergy concept was developed by Chaparral Steel in Texas. This synergy involved a steel mill, a cement plant, and a car-shredding company. The highly successful venture has not only reduced costs and environmental impacts associated with the three companies but also created new opportunities including a patented process which is being marketed (U.S. PCSD, 1996).

ECO-INDUSTRIAL PARKS

Côté and Hall (1995) were among the first to investigate industrial parks as ecosystems. They have suggested characteristics of an industrial park operating as an ecosystem. In their view, an industrial area operating as a mature ecosystem would require that:

- the industrial activity take into account the ecological capacity of the area, paying particular attention to the assimilative capacity of the air, water (surface and ground), and soil to absorb emissions
- energy production be based increasingly on renewable resources and at least increase the efficiency of current energy production and use through cogeneration and district heating
- buildings be designed and built to optimize conservation of heat and water, while enabling disassembly for reuse and recycling at the end-of-life
- landscaping use indigenous plants and be designed to support building heating and cooling

- industries and businesses be selected based in part on their compatibility for symbiosis
- management of the development encourage a web of businesses involving not only producers and consumers but scavengers and decomposers to support cycling of materials
- redundancy in materials sources be built into the structure of the system
- dissipative uses of materials and energy be discouraged
- management establish a common information-management system which would facilitate networking and symbioses.

In their paper on Kalundborg, Ehrenfeld and Gertler (1997) reviewed a number of emerging eco-industrial park initiatives and concluded that the key elements of successful eco-industrial networking include a regulatory framework which emphasizes flexibility, continuous improvement, and community participation; financing and taxes that are flexible and promote the reduction of waste and enhanced efficiency; transportation logistics that encourages efficiency and sharing of facilities; sharing of information on operations especially on products and byproducts; and a mixture of small, medium and large industries, and finally, private and public sector champions to lead the effort. Although much has been written about eco-industrial parks, very few satisfy these guidelines. Hinton, Alberta, and Devens, Massachusetts, have evolving eco-industrial parks.

ASSESSMENT

Some evolution and maturation must still occur in defining and implementing eco-industrial development, but it is clear that it should involve multiple organizations, not only businesses but other institutions within communities, multiple materials (and energy), and multiple relationships. As a start, a symbiosis may be initiated by collaboration between two facilities involving one material, for example hot water, but an eco-industrial development or industrial ecosystem must eventually grow into a more complex web in which resources are conserved.

Sustainable industrial development will require attention not only to ecological and economic aspects but also to social dimensions. In this way, we can perhaps be assured that the whole will be more than the sum of its parts, a functioning interdependent system.

BIBLIOGRAPHY

Ayres, R. U., and L. W. Ayres, eds. *A Handbook of Industrial Ecology.* Cheltenham, U.K.: Elgar, 2002.
Chertow, M. R. "The Eco-Industrial Park Model Reconsidered." *Journal of Industrial Ecology* 2.3 (1998), 8–10. DOI: 10.1162/jiec.1998.2.3.8.
———. "Industrial Symbiosis: Literature and Taxonomy." *Annual Review of Energy and Environment* 25 (2000), 313–337. DOI: 10.1146/annurev.energy.25.1.313.
———. "'Uncovering' Industrial Symbiosis." *Journal of Industrial Ecology* 11.1 (2007), 11–30. DOI: 10.1162/jiec.2007.1110.
Chertow, M., and M. Portlock, eds. *Developing Industrial Ecosystems: Approaches, Cases, and Tools.* Yale School of Forestry and Environmental Studies Bulletin 106. New Haven, Conn., 2002.
Clemen, R. A. *By-Products in the Packing Industry.* Chicago: University of Chicago Press, 1927.
Cohen-Rosenthal, E. "A Walk on the Human Side of Industrial Ecology." *American Behavioral Scientist* 44.2 (2000), 245–264. DOI: 10.1177/0002764200044002007.
———. *Eco-Industrial Strategies: Unleashing Synergy between Economic Development and the Environment.* Sheffield, U.K.: Greenleaf Publishing, 2003.
Conover, W. R. "Salvaging and Utilizing Wastes and Scrap in Industry." *Industrial Management* 55.6 (1918), 449–451.
Costanza, R., B. G. Norton, and B. D. Haskell. *Ecosystem Health: New Goals for Environmental Management.* Washington, D.C.: Island Press, 1992.
Côté, R. P., and E. Cohen-Rosenthal. "Designing Eco-Industrial Parks: A Synthesis of Some Experiences." *Journal of Cleaner Production* 6.3–4 (1998), 181–188. DOI: 10.1016/S0959-6526(98)00029-8.
Côté, R., and J. Hall. "Industrial Parks as Ecosystems." *Journal of Cleaner Production* 3.1–2 (1995): 41–46. DOI: 10.1016/0959-6526(95)00041-C.
Côté, R., et al.. *Designing and Operating Industrial Parks as Ecosystems.* Halifax, N.S.: School for Resource and Environmental Studies, Dalhousie University, 1994.
Ehrenfeld, J., and N. Gertler. "Industrial Ecology in Practice: The Evolution of Interdependence at Kalundborg." *Journal of Industrial Ecology* 1.1 (1997): 67–79. DOI: 10.1162/jiec.1997.1.1.67.
Erkman, S. "Industrial Ecology: A Historical View." *Journal of Cleaner Production* 5.1–2 (1997), 1–10.
Frosch, R. A., and N. E. Gallopoulos. "Strategies for Manufacturing." *Scientific American* 261.3 (1989), 144–153.
Graedel, T. E., and B. R. Allenby. *Industrial Ecology.* Englewood Cliffs, N.J.: Prentice Hall, 1995.
Jacobsen, N. B. "Industrial Symbiosis in Kalundborg, Denmark: A Quantitative Assessment of Economic and Environmental Benefits." *Journal of Industrial Ecology* 10.1–2 (2006), 239–256.
Lowe, E. A., J. L. Warren, and S. R. Moran. *Discovering Industrial Ecology: An Executive Briefing and Sourcebook.* Columbus, Ohio: Battelle Press, 1997.
Odum, E. P. *Ecology and Our Endangered Life-Support Systems.* Sunderland, Mass: Sinauer, 1993.
Simmonds, P. L. *Waste Products and Undeveloped Substances.* London: Hardwicke, 1862.
———. *Waste Products and Undeveloped Substances: A Synopsis of Progress Made in Their Economic Utilization during the Last Quarter Century at Home and Abroad.* 3d ed. London: Harwicke and Bogue, 1876.
U.S. PCSD (President's Council on Sustainable Development). *Eco-Efficiency Task Force Report.* Washington, D.C., 1996.
Worster, D. *Nature's Economy: The Roots of Ecology.* San Francisco: Sierra Club Books, 1977.

—Raymond P. Côté

INDUSTRIAL METABOLISM

See Industrial Ecology.

INSURANCE

Substantive discussions of the enhanced greenhouse threat, often known as global warming, began in the financial sector only in 1990. Concern is now growing rapidly in the financial institutions, fueled by billion-dollar losses from extreme windstorms, wildfires, and floods (Mills, 2005). The first book specifically on this subject did not appear until 1996 (Leggett, 1996). In it, senior financial-sector managers and executives from a broad range of institutions express their concerns. Among the insurers, the manager of operations at General Accident concludes that "there is no doubt to me that weather patterns are changing. There is also no doubt from historical study that small climate changes have very big effects on society... I am sure that climate change will speed up. I am also sure there will be major consequences for insurers... And I am absolutely certain there will be long term international effects." Among the bankers, the head of environmental affairs at the Union Bank of Switzerland describes global warming as the most serious of all environmental problems: "we must recognize that the financial markets will be affected by climate change... Site contamination and lender liability are only the tip of the banker's 'environmental iceberg.' Climate change is from my perspective the mass underneath the water line and we can't ignore this part... [It] will probably surface soon."

The threat pertains at two levels: the baseline and the worst case. The baseline threat involves the impacts of mid-range estimates of global average temperature rise and sea-level rise by the world's climate scientists, as laid out by the authoritative Intergovernmental Panel on Climate Change (IPCC) in its various reports to governments. This means that, for insurers, the past is no longer a guide to the future. This makes actuarial work, on the basis of which premium rates are set, difficult. For bankers, the concerns are somewhat different and relate to the security of investments. A September 1995 British Bankers Association paper on climate change (Blackman, 1995) spells this out: "as climate change takes place it will have significant adverse effects upon the activities of banks' customers; their operations will fail or become not viable... Within the lifetime of loans granted today climate change is forecast to have a dramatic impact on industrial operations within 20 to 40 years."

The worst-case threat has been summarized best on the public record by the president of the U.S. Insurance Institute for Property Loss Reduction. His view of the threat to the insurance industry in 1993 makes grim reading (Lecomte, 1993): "Despite the fact that the industry is financially healthy, and has some $160 billion in surplus, in two events you could take 70 billion, or maybe 80 billion of that surplus away, and you'd cripple the industry. It wouldn't be able to take on new risks. It wouldn't have the capacity to underwrite the business of the future. We'd have massive, massive availability problems." This is, in other words, a global insurance crash. The kinds of events referred to include potential megacatastrophes such as a Category Five hurricane hitting Miami and New Orleans, a typhoon hitting Tokyo, a drought-related wildfire burning out of control in an urban center such as Los Angeles or Sydney, or a failure of London's Thames barrier under a storm surge. The critical point is that such events become ever more likely as heat-trapping greenhouse gases continue to be emitted into the atmosphere in large quantities. Nor does the risk of a potential wipeout of global surplus—the amount kept by the industry to hedge against property catastrophe losses in any one year, globally—extend just to unlucky hits on large cities. As one analyst for the reinsurance group Swiss Re put it in 1993, the industry could suffer "a machine-gun fire" of smaller catastrophes in a warming world, which would have the same effect (Leggett, 1993).

This potential for a global wipeout of property catastrophe reserves is emphasized by a growing number of on-the-record,

worst-case prognoses within the industry. As the president of the Reinsurance Association of America has bluntly said to *Time* magazine (1994), "the insurance business is first in line to be affected by climate change... It could bankrupt the industry." As an official from the Marine and Fire Association of Japan has put it (Shimbun, 1993), "if more disasters like [Typhoon Mireille] follow, it could affect the industry's very existence." More recently, Munich Re wrote of the 1996 catastrophe record (Munich Re, 1997) that "according to current estimates, the possible extent of losses caused by extreme natural catastrophes in the one of the world's metropolises or industrial centers would be so great as to cause the collapse of entire countries' economic systems and could even bring about the collapse of the world's financial markets."

Deep cuts in greenhouse-gas emissions provide the only route to meaningful risk abatement and loss reduction for financial institutions. Changes to business practice can buy an insurer interim risk management. The insurance industry would have no future if, as the global greenhouse crisis deepened, it simply retreated serially from areas of perceived threat. Nor would it be allowed to; this is a heavily regulated industry. After the full extent of the losses from Hurricane Andrew became clear, 30 insurance companies tried to pull out of Florida altogether. Had they been permitted to do so, economic growth in the state would probably have come to a halt. But the state legislated and forced the companies to stay, permitting them to retreat only at the rate of 5% of capacity per year. In Japan, the situation is even more stringent. Insurers are bound to offer coverage if it is requested and are required to seek the agreement of the Ministry of Finance for every rate increase. The message is clear: if the financial services industry wants to cut the risk from global warming, its interests lie in cutting global warming itself.

The first serious business interest is now arising, both in the financial and energy sectors, in the opportunities involved in greenhouse-risk abatement and loss reduction. Significant reductions in global greenhouse-gas emissions will have to involve the progressive replacement of fossil-fuel energy markets and energy profligacy, with burgeoning new markets in renewable energy and energy-efficiency technologies. The first major players are aware of this, as well as the implications for investments in the years ahead. For example, the Chartered Insurance Institute's Society of Fellows (the UK insurance industry's premier professional body) concluded that "the industry has a limited breathing space in which to gather its wits [on climate change], and plan in a truly long-term timeframe." It recommended many options, one of which was that "all investment managers should modify their investment policies to take account of the potential direct and indirect effects of global warming" (Chartered Insurance Institute, 1994). Swiss Re is among the financial giants that seem to agree, having written of global warming that "there is no shortage of practical suggestions, especially with regard to a drastic reduction of greenhouse gases" (Swiss Re, 1994).

Some effort has been made by financial institutions toward risk abatement at the source. In November 1995, insurance companies from Europe and Japan signed the UNEP Statement of Environmental Commitment by the Insurance Industry, placing climate change high on their list of concerns and reasons to pledge action, but this initiative was criticized by environmentalists as too little, too late.

The devastation from Hurricane Katrina in the U.S. Gulf Coast in August of 2005, caused the insurance industry to reevaluate the risks of natural disasters (see articles by Ceres; Mills; and RMS).

[*See also* Extreme Events; Global Warming; *and* Natural Hazards.]

BIBLIOGRAPHY

Blackman, P. "Environmental Issues: Liability, Climate Change." British Bankers Association paper for the Annual Meeting of Officers, September 20–23, 1995. Oiso, Japan.

"Burned by Warming." *Time*, March 14, 1994. An article based on the U.S. College of Insurance conference referred to in the present article. The *Time* correspondent concluded his article by observing that "these risks and the crucial role played by the $1.41 trillion insurance industry in the world economy could change the dynamic of the debate about global warming."

Ceres. "Availability and Affordability of Insurance Under Climate Change." Ceres press release, Sept. 8, 2005. http://www.ceres.org (accessed June 1, 2008).

Chartered Insurance Institute. "The Impact of Changing Weather Patterns on Property Insurance." Chartered Insurance Institute Special Report, May 1994.

Lecomte, E. Speech given at the U.S. College of Insurance, November 1993.

Leggett, J. K. "Climate Change and the Insurance Industry: Solidarity among the Risk Community?" Greenpeace International Special Publication, February 1993.

Leggett, J. K., ed. "Climate Change and the Financial Sector: The Emerging Threat, the Solar Solution." Munich: Gerling Akademie Verlag, 1996.

"Insurance Industry Concerned about the Earth." *Asahi Shimbun*, February 3, 1993.

Mills, E. "Insurance in a Climate of Change." *Science* 309 (2005), 1040–1044. DOI: 10.1126/science.1112121.

Munich Re. "Topics: Annual Review of Natural Catastrophes 1996." Munich Re Special Publication, 1997.

RMS. "Hurricane Katrina: Profile of a Super Cat: Lessons and Implications for Risk Management." Risk Management Solutions, August 2005. http://rms.com/publications/katrinareport_lessonsandimplications.pdf (accessed June 1, 2008).

Swiss Re. "Element of Risk." Swiss Re Special Publication, 1994.

—JEREMY LEGGETT

INTERGENERATIONAL EQUITY

The central question posed by the ethical concept of intergenerational equity is what, if any, are the current generation's obligations to future generations. Underpinning the answers to the question are beliefs about whether future generations have interests and/or rights. Arguments in favor of such an assignment of interests and rights sometimes seek support via the analogy with contemporary strangers by which future generations and contemporary strangers are entitled to broadly similar ethical treatment. As long as it is feasible to assume that some people will definitely exist in the future and will be in no relevant way unlike current people (right-holders), then they are worthy of equal moral consideration.

Arguments against giving equal moral consideration to future generations have been based on some combination of the following points:

- the temporal location of future generations, and the asymmetry of power between generations that do not overlap
- uncertainty or complete ignorance of distant future peoples' wants and needs
- the contingency of future people, that is, future people may not exist at all, and their actual number depends in large measure on current actions and decisions.

Some versions of utilitarian philosophy favor, at best, a weak form of intergenerational equity and support the argument that the current generation's moral duties are limited to designated people and by the requirement not deliberately to harm future prospects without good cause. The difficulty for these utilitarians is that, on the basis of an individualistic philosophy, the distinction between potential people in the future and actual individuals who will exist at some subsequent time is problematic. Thus it is argued that the assignment of rights to all possible people is an inadequate basis for an environmental ethic focused on sustainable development. If all possible people have a right to life, or to other rights hypothetically, then a current policy based on environmental conservation and growth moderation may not be morally supportable. Some utilitarians will go as far as to coclude that the present generation has no obligation to future generations, arguing that a person has not been wronged by another unless he or she has been made worse off by the other's act. Nothing the current generation can do can wrong future actual people (brought about by our actions), unless what is done results in such a "poor" future world that these actual future generations turn out to wish they had never been born at all.

If, however, the individualistic viewpoint is moderated by a more collectivist approach, then a number of points in support of intergenerational equity obligations can be made. While there will always be uncertainty about the precise form and extent of future individual preferences, it seems reasonable to conclude that basic needs (e.g., clothing, food, shelter, community) will exist and will not be radically different from contemporary ones for the foreseeable future.

A strategy that satisfies these basic needs will be a prerequisite of the satisfaction of most other wants and interests of future generations regardless of their precise configuration. Further, it does not necessarily follow that our obligations to the future require us to know the identity of individual members of succeeding generations, only that there will be future generations of humans. If we accept the existence of future generations as given, then the contingency problem alone does not provide sufficient ground for subordinating future generations' interests to those of existing contemporaries. A "total utility" variant of utilitarianism could therefore be deployed to support a normative ethic in favor of positive obligations to future generations. Members of the current generation have a collective obligation to ensure that human existence continues at a fairly high level of general (total) utility, by maximizing basic-needs provision. If population can be stabilized, this ethical position would require equal provision for the basic needs of each generation. The "generalized obligations" serve to maintain an inheritance of at least a constant flow of resources into the future to ensure ongoing human life.

A number of attempts have been made by philosophers to utilize a contractarian approach to suggest criteria for intergenerational equity. In particular, John Rawls' (1972) "Theory of Justice" has, in amended form, been used as the basis for a number of theories of intergenerational equity and resource-use strategies. But the Rawlsian case that can be made out for the formulation of a principle governing the just distribution and rate of resource usage over long periods of time requires the bringing together of different philosophical principles (e.g., in the tradition of Immanuel Kant as well as John Hume) that are not necessarily complementary. The dual aspects of the theory—justice as rational cooperation (Hume) and justice as hypothetical universal assent (Kant)—may conflict as soon as the analysis moves away from the self-contained society of contemporaries.

The contractarian approach is based on actual or hypothetical negotiations that are said to be capable of yielding mutually agreeable principles of conduct, which are also binding upon all parties. Rawls has formulated an idealized decision model to produce procedural rules for a just society peopled by contemporaries. Rational and risk-averse individual representatives form contemporary society in an "original position" (the negotiations) and operating from behind what is called the "veil of ignorance" (individuals are assumed not to know to which stratum of society they themselves belong) choose the principles of justice. According to this model, among the agreed rules would be equal opportunity for all individuals as well as the "difference principle" (or "maximin criterion"), which requires an acceptable standard of living for the least well off in society.

A number of analysts have sought to apply the difference principle intertemporally to guarantee future generations an adequate natural-resource endowment and a habitable environment. If the representatives were deprived of the knowledge about which generation they were part of, it could be argued that a maximin rule would again be rationally chosen. The rule could translate into a contract that mandated a bequest of a constant capital stock (human, reproducible, and natural capital elements) across generational time. It turns out, however, that "veil of ignorance" conditions may need to be drawn even more tightly, and strictly speaking should leave the individual representative unsure about the total number of generations, as well as about his or her status as a possible or actual person and which species he or she represents.

Pushing the Kantian approach to intergenerational fairness further, the "justice as opportunity" argument can be deployed. The preservation of "opportunities" for future generations becomes a minimal notion of intergenerational fairness. The present generation does not have a right to deplete the economic and other opportunities afforded by the biospherical resource base since it does not "own" it. Sustainability criteria should be imposed as prior constraints on the maximization of social preferences concerning the distribution of welfare across generations. Each successive generation may be charged with a duty to ensure that the expected welfare of its offspring is no less than its own

perceived welfare. The passing-on over time of the resource base "intact" does not necessarily mean literally intact; in cases where depletion occurs, this must be compensated for by capital investment in alternative options and/or technological innovation to increase resource productivity, the combined effect of which is to offset the depletion of both source and sink capacities.

This moral rule also supports a bias against actions that generate current benefits while simultaneously imposing the risk of irreversible future losses if the maintenance of options would allow for improved discussions as new information becomes available. It suggests that precautionary action, such as the protection of biological diversity and the ozone layer, has much to recommend it. Nevertheless, from a weak sustainability position, some depletion of natural resource stocks can be compensated for through capital substitution and is not necessarily inconsistent with the sustainable development policy objective. But, given the level of socioeconomic and scientific uncertainty that pervades our current and foreseeable future societies, it may be better to work toward strong sustainability, conserving the maximum feasible amounts of natural capital to maintain the options for the future.

[*See also* Belief Systems; Conservation; Environmetal Bioethics; Environmental Law; Ethics; Gaia Hypothesis; *and* Human Impacts.]

BIBLIOGRAPHY

Attfield, R. *The Ethics of Environmental Concern.* Oxford: Blackwell, 1983.
Brown, P. G., and D. MacLean, eds. *Energy and the Future.* Totowa, N.J.: Rowman and Littlefield, 1983.
Howarth, R. B. "Sustainability under Uncertainty: A Deontological Approach." *Land Economics* 71 (1995), 417–427.
Norton, B. G. "Intergenerational Equity and Environmental Decisions: A Model Using Rawls' Veil of Ignorance." *Ecological Economics* 1 (1989), 137–159.
Page, T. *Conservation and Economic Efficiency.* Baltimore: Johns Hopkins University Press, 1977.
Parfit, D. "Future Generations: Further Problems." *Philosophy and Public Affairs* 11.2 (1982), 113–172.
Rawls, J. *A Theory of Justice.* New York and Oxford: Oxford University Press, 1972.

—R. KERRY TURNER

INTERNATIONAL ENVIRONMENTAL AGREEMENTS

See Appendix.

INTERNATIONAL GEOSPHERE-BIOSPHERE PROGRAMME

A cooperative research program that became the International Geosphere-Biosphere Programme (IGBP) was proposed by the executive board of the International Council for Science (ICSU) at its meeting in Stockholm, Sweden, in February 1983. It was envisioned as the centerpiece of a number of initiatives under way in the world scientific community to develop and to integrate the knowledge required for sound decision-making in an era in which human activity on planet Earth had already begun to reach a scale that introduced perturbations in the physical, chemical, and biological processes that had been driving global environmental change.

Global environmental change, in turn, was jeopardizing the life-supporting capabilities of the environment. Assessments by ICSU's Scientific Committee on Problems of the Environment had underscored the need to interrelate these processes and determine the impact of human activity on them.

IGBP was launched in 1986 as a result of an international symposium in Ottawa, Canada, in 1984. Its mission is to describe and understand the interactive physical, chemical, and biological processes that regulate the total Earth system, the unique environment that system provides for life, the changes that are occurring in this system, and the manner in which these changes are influenced by human action.

IGBP has inaugurated eight core projects in the atmospheric sciences, terrestrial ecology, oceanography, and hydrology, and three cross-cutting activities on data, modeling, and regional networks linking analysis, research, and training. Each initiative is guided by a scientific steering committee. By 1997, forty-two major reports had been published through the collective efforts of over a thousand scientists in more than 76 countries.

IGBP concluded in 1990 that research focused on the natural and social sciences must be carried out in regions characterized by diverse climates and biogeography, particularly in developing countries. This step was necessary to achieve the understanding of global change processes required to develop and put into use the practical predictive capability essential for sound policy responses.

An array of regional networks called the global change System for Analysis, Research, and Training (START) was established for these purposes. START is now under the joint sponsorship of IGBP, the interinstitutional World Climate Research Programme (WCRP), and the International Human Dimensions Programme on Global Environmental Change (IHDP), the latter jointly sponsored by ICSU and the International Social Science Council.

After the first ten years of IGBP operations, major new scientific results have emerged, effective high-level networks have been formed, and liaisons strengthened with social scientists. The emphasis in all IGBP program activities is shifting toward synthesis, publication, and communication of research results and their implications for public and private policy.

Secretariats for IGBP and START, respectively, are maintained at the Royal Swedish Academy of Sciences in Stockholm, Sweden, and at the American Geophysical Union, Washington, D.C. Both secretariats publish quarterly newsletters.

[See also Earth System Science.]

BIBLIOGRAPHY

Fuchs, R. "START: The Road from Bellagio." Global Environmental Change 5.5 (1995), 397–404. The background for START. DOI: 10.1016/0959-3780(95)00053-Q.

International Geosphere-Biosphere Programme. A Study of Global Change: The Initial Core Projects. IGBP Report No. 12. Stockholm: IGBP, 1990. Available from the IGBP secretariat.

Malone, T. F., and J. G. Roederer, eds. Global Change. Proceedings of the ICSU Symposium, Ottawa, Canada, September 25, 1984. Cambridge and New York: Cambridge University Press, 1985. The background for IGBP.

Turner, B. L., II, et al., eds. The Earth as Transformed by Human Action. Cambridge and New York: Cambridge University Press, 1990. The overall context.

—THOMAS F. MALONE

INTERNATIONAL HUMAN DIMENSIONS PROGRAMME ON GLOBAL ENVIRONMENTAL CHANGE (IHDP)

The International Human Dimensions Programme on Global Environmental Change (IHDP) is an international, interdisciplinary, social-science program dedicated to promoting, catalyzing, and coordinating research, capacity development, and networking on the human dimensions of global environmental change (GEC) (that is, the way people and societies contribute to, are influenced by, and mitigate and adapt to GEC). The growing recognition of the complex economic, social, political, and cultural implications of possible impacts and responses to environmental change have pushed human-dimensions issues higher on the agenda of both the research and the policy communities.

In 1996, the International Council of Scientific Unions (ICSU, now the International Council for Science) and the International Social Science Council (ISSC) cosponsored the IHDP. In 2007, the United Nations University (UNU) joined them to become the third institutional sponsor and host of the Secretariat in Bonn. IHDP is also a member of the Earth System Science Partnership (ESSP) and collaborates on joint projects with the International Geosphere-Biosphere Programme (IGBP), DIVERSITAS (an international program of biodiversity science), and the World Climate Research Programme (WCRP). The IHDP is guided by the Scientific Committee representing different geographic and scientific backgrounds, but with the common objective of strengthening links and synergies between individual researchers and institutions working on human-dimensions issues. National human-dimensions committees are essential to IHDP's research strategy, emphasizing a bottom-up approach, and the IHDP is presently working with over 70 national committees, national contact points, and programmes at various levels of development and activity. These activities are facilitated by the publication of triannual IHDP Update newsletter, a Website, and a triannual e-zine.

CUTTING-EDGE SCIENCE

As defined within the IHDP, the human dimensions of GEC encompass the full range of social and natural sciences disciplines necessary to analyze and understand the role of humans as both probably causing and suffering from global environmental change. IHDP Science Projects are used to generate IHDP research activities in priority areas, to promote international collaboration of researchers, and to link policy makers and researchers. Projects evolve from proposals by the Scientific Committee or via proposals to the IHDP made directly by one or more National Human Dimensions Committees or programs. There are presently five IHDP science projects: the Global Land Project (GLP, a joint project with IGBP), Global Environmental Change and Human Security (GECHS), Urbanization and Global Environmental Change (UGEC), Industrial Transformation (IT), and Land-Ocean Interactions in the Coastal Zone (LOICZ, a joint project with IGBP).

The Global Land Project, successor to the Land Use and Land Cover Change Project (LUCC), provides a framework to measure, model, and understand the changes in the coupled socio-environmental terrestrial system and how these have affected, and may in the future affect, the sustainability of the Earth System. It addresses the main biophysical and societal forces, dynamics, and feedbacks of these changes and evaluates their consequences for the vulnerability and sustainability of various coupled land systems on different scales.

Global Environmental Change and Human Security (GECHS) focuses on five themes: conceptual and theoretical issues; environmental change, resource use, and human security; population, environment, and human security; modeling of regions of environmental stress and human vulnerability; and institutions and policy development in environmental security. GECHS seeks to develop a better understanding of the links between these issues by advancing interdisciplinary and international research and policy efforts in issues such as human vulnerability to global environmental change, the role of cooperative agreements in conflicts over water management, effects of land degradation and climate change on human life and security, and the interactions of global environmental change with other changes closely linked to human security.

Urbanization and Global Environmental Change (UGEC) is a science project focused on understanding the nature of the interactions between global environmental change and urban processes, the direction, rate, intensity, and scale of these processes as well as the challenge of global environmental change to the functioning, stability, and sustainability of urban areas.

Industrial Transformation (IT) presents an innovative way of organizing research into the societal mechanisms and human influences that could facilitate a transformation of the industrial system towards sustainability. The project studies energy and material flows, food consumption and production systems, cities (with focus on transportation and water), governance and transformation processes, and information and communication. IT's global research focuses on regions where concentrated and large populations and strong economic development clash with vulnerable environments.

The Land-Ocean Interactions in the Coastal Zone (LOICZ) project investigates the transport and changes in sediments and nutrients from rivers to the sea and along shorelines. These materials shape the coastline and the space available for humans to live and work, as well as providing the resources that many societies depend on for food and building materials. LOICZ undertakes research that informs the scientific community,

policy makers, managers and stakeholders on global environmental change in the coastal zone and its ramifications for humans and the environment.

IHDP also cosponsors projects within the Earth System Science Partnership (ESSP) such as the Global Carbon Project (GCP), Global Environmental Change and Food Systems (GECAFS), the Global Water System Project (GWSP), and the nascent Global Environmental Change and Human Health project (GECHH). Furthermore, IHDP officially endorses the Population-Environment Research Network (PERN), the Mountain Research Initiative (MRI), and the Young Human Dimensions Researchers (YHDR).

In the near future, IHDP will undertake several new projects, including the new core project Earth System Governance (ESG), the Vulnerability, Resilience, and Adaptation project (VRA), and the Integrated Risk Governance project (IRG), and will join the Integrated History and Future of People on Earth (iHOPE), an IGBP project.

CAPACITY DEVELOPMENT

An important part of IHDP's work in strengthening and broadening the network of researchers working on global environmental change is capacity development. Being a "network of networks," IHDP is in an excellent position to play this role on behalf of the entire human-dimensions research community. IHDP's capacity development activities are an effective tool for enhancing its reputation and an avenue for incorporating new researchers and research into the network, as evidenced by the International Human Dimensions Workshops (IHDW), first established in 1998. Training seminars, national workshops, and regional network activities have also contributed to the Programme's capacity-development portfolio.

IHDP also works to reinforce regional and national networks in efforts to promote capacity development. IHDP focuses its regional and national network building activities in developing countries and regions through the establishment of national committees, national inventories of human-dimensions-of-GEC (HDGEC) researchers, and national contact points. The establishment of communities of HDGEC researchers on national and regional levels promotes collaboration, community building, best-practice and experience sharing, and allows for workshops on regionally relevant themes.

IHDP also has a visiting-scholars program with the University of Bonn with participation from UNU. Another initiative involving collaboration with individual member countries sends postdoctoral researchers to the IHDP Secretariat with the goal of training scientists and bridging the science-policy gap.

SCIENCE-POLICY-PRACTICE INTERACTION

Science-policy interaction is a top priority for IHDP. Through the experience of its network members, IHDP has come to believe that ongoing and substantive interaction between scientists and practitioners is necessary to improve both the conduct of research and the implementation of policy and practice. This interaction must be regular and ongoing, with policy perspective

TABLE 1. Member Nations for the Fourth Assessment Report (2007)

		IPCC Chair India	
Kenya		*IPCC Vice-Chairs* Sri Lanka	Russian Federation
Working Group I *Co-Chairs*	*Working Group II* *Co-Chairs*	*Working Group III* *Co-Chairs*	*Task Force Bureau* *Co-Chairs*
China	Argentina	Sierra Leone	Brazil
USA	UK	The Netherlands	Japan
Vice-Chairs	*Vice-Chairs*	*Vice-Chairs*	
Gambia	Australia	Cuba	
France	Belgium	Denmark	
Italy	Canada	Indonesia	
New Zealand	Mexico	Peru	
Thailand	Morocco	Saudi Arabia	
Venezuela	Slovenia	Sudan	

input beginning at the start of the research process and continuing throughout the scientific investigations. Similarly, practitioners should consult with scientists before making a policy decision, during implementation, and when evaluating results. The worlds of science and policy need to know one another better, learn to speak each other's languages, benefit from their respective expertise, know each other's priorities, and ultimately improve each other's endeavors.

Following the example set in Berne in 2006, IHDP organized a Science-Policy Symposium at the University of California, Santa Barbara, in the spring of 2008 on the themes of energy, greenhouse-gas emissions, and climate change illustrated by case studies from California, China, and Germany. The meeting will involve key scientists and policymakers from both industry and government.

IHDP also holds biannual expert and public roundtables called "The Bonn Dialogues." The first, held in April of 2007, was "Climate Change: Control, Adapt, or Flee?" and the second, in November of 2007, was "Melting Ice, Vanishing Life: The Impacts of Environmental Change on Human Society and Biodiversity."

—DOUGLAS F. WILLIAMSON

IPCC: INTERGOVERNMENTAL PANEL ON CLIMATE CHANGE

The Intergovernmental Panel on Climate Change (IPCC) was established in 1988 by two United Nations organizations, the World Meteorological Organization (WMO) and the United Nations Environment Program (UNEP). It was awarded the Nobel Peace Prize (jointly with former Vice President Al Gore) in October 2007. The IPCC assesses the scientific basis of the risk of human-induced and natural climate change, the potential impacts of climate change and options for adaptation to them, and the mitigation of greenhouse-gas emissions.

ORGANIZATION AND PROCEDURES

The major functions of the IPCC are carried out by three Working Groups and a Task Force, each consisting of specialists representing various member nations. Working Group I assesses scientific aspects of the climate system and climate change. Working Group II assesses the vulnerability of socio-economic systems and natural systems to climate change, and the negative and positive consequences of climate change and options for adapting to them. Working Group III assesses options for limiting greenhouse-gas emissions and otherwise mitigating climate change. The Task Force on National Greenhouse Gas Inventories is responsible for defining methodologies and practices for greenhouse gas inventories.

The panel, consisting of hundreds of officials and experts from the relevant ministries, agencies, and research institutions of member countries and from international organizations, meets in plenary sessions about once per year to discuss the work program and to elect the bureau, which comprises the IPCC chair; three vice-chairs; and co-chairs and vice-chairs of the working groups and the Task Force.

The Bureau for the Fourth Assessment (2007) comprises thirty nations represented at four levels. Members of the Bureau serve for the period during which an assessment is being prepared, often 5–6 years. Each working group and the Task Force has two co-chairs, one from a developing nation and one from a developed nation, and a technical-support unit provided by the developed nation.

The IPCC does not conduct research nor does it monitor climate data—it bases its assessment on the study of published literature (mostly peer-reviewed). Once the outline and scope of a report have been established, governments and participating organizations nominate experts as authors, reviewers, and review editors. From those nominated (and other recognized experts), the relevant working group selects teams of authors and experts who will write and review the report. The writing proceeds through a series of drafts and reviews until the report is accepted by the bureau.

At the end of an assessment period, each of the working groups releases its own report accompanied by its own Summary for Policymakers published in the six official UN languages. Each summary is reviewed first by government representatives, then line-by-line in a session of the working group to ensure that its statements are consistent with material in the full report.

THE ASSESSMENT REPORTS AND THEIR IMPLICATIONS

In 1989, at its 44th session, the United Nations General Assembly requested the IPCC to prepare a report as a basis for negotiating a framework convention on climate change. The *First Assessment Report* (1990) concluded that human activities are substantially increasing the concentrations of greenhouse gases and enhancing the greenhouse effect. This led the UN General Assembly to launch the United Nations Framework Convention on Climate Change (UNFCCC), which entered into force in March 1994.

The *Second Assessment Report: Climate Change 1995* (SAR) was begun in 1991. It addressed the ultimate objective of the UNFCCC, to stabilize greenhouse-gas concentrations at a level that would prevent dangerous anthropogenic interference with the climate system. The report provided scientific, technical, and socioeconomic information that could be used to evaluate the projected range of plausible impacts from increasing greenhouse-gas concentrations and to evaluate adaptation and mitigation options. This report was made available to the Second Conference of the Parties to the UNFCCC, and provided input to negotiations for the convention's Kyoto Protocol, which was adopted in 1997 and entered into force in 2005.

The *Third Assessment Report: Climate Change 2001* (TAR) consists of three working group reports and a Synthesis Report. The TAR broke new ground by explicitly placing climate change in the context of sustainable development, placing greater emphasis on regional dimensions of climate change, recognizing linkages with other regional and global environmental issues such as loss of biodiversity, land degradation, stratospheric ozone depletion, and regional acid deposition, and by providing policy advice to governments.

The *Fourth Assessment Report: Climate Change 2007* (FAR) comprises three working-group reports and a Synthesis Report released in stages during 2007, the first being *The Physical Science Basis* (from Working Group I; Solomon et al., 2007), which was represented by a Summary for Policymakers released in February, 2007. That summary reported improved understanding of the human and natural components of climate change and emphasized that since the previous report (TAR), new and more comprehensive data and more sophisticated analysis have led to more certain statements about the human roles in climate change and more reliable predictions of climate change. Later in the year, the two remaining Working Group reports were released: Working Group II, *Impacts, Adaptation, and Vulnerability*; and Working Group III, *Mitigation of Climate Change*. These were followed by the *AR4 Synthesis Report* that represents the Fourth Assessment more generally.

OTHER IPCC REPORTS

In addition to the Assessment Reports, there are three other types of publication made available by the IPCC: Special Reports, Methodology Reports, and Technical Papers. These, along with Assessment Reports, can be obtained through the IPCC website.

[*See also* Climate Models; Global Warming; *and* Greenhouse Effect.]

BIBLIOGRAPHY

This article is based almost entirely upon materials available on the IPCC website (http://www.ipcc.ch).

Solomon, S., et al., eds. *Climate Change 2007: The Physical Science Basis. Contribution of Working Group I to the Fourth Assessment Report of the Intergovernmental Panel on Climate Change.* Cambridge and New York: Cambridge University Press, 2007.

—DAVID J. CUFF AND XIANFU LU

IRRIGATION

Irrigation is any human-induced change in the natural flow of water for the purpose of growing plants. This includes water conservation measures such as bunding (impounding water in a field using small earthen dikes), mulching, and furrowing that increase the quantity of water available and the reliability of the supply, whether from rainfall or runoff. Irrigation water is usually delivered to farm fields through canals or pipes. Sources of water include rivers and streams (either through direct diversion, or after storage in a natural or artificial lake) and underground aquifers (lifted from open wells or pumped from tube wells). Drainage is the removal of excess water from the land to reduce yield losses due to flooding, waterlogging, and salinity.

Irrigation water made it possible for the earliest forms of civilization to develop in the arid lands of the Middle East and Asia along the major rivers—the Nile, Euphrates, Tigris, Indus, and Yellow (Huang)—by producing the food surpluses needed for these civilizations to survive and flourish. More recently, the colonial powers developed irrigation not only to increase food production and prevent famine, but also to produce crops for export—cotton, sugarcane, and rice. The rapid growth in food production during the Green Revolution, from the mid-1960s to the present, was accomplished largely by expanding irrigated area. During this period, much of the increase in global food production came from increased yields on an expanded area of irrigated land.

Rice is grown on approximately one-third of the world's irrigated cropland and half of Asia's irrigated cropland. Most rice is grown in areas with a monsoon climate. In the main rice-growing season (the wet season) heavy rains often result in an excess of water. Rice is very tolerant of flooding, hence its widespread cultivation in monsoon zones. In these areas, drainage facilities are needed to remove excess water and prevent yield losses due to waterlogging and salinity. In the dry season and in drier climates, most irrigated agricultural production comprises crops other than rice, ranging from grain crops such as wheat and maize to cash crops such as cotton, vegetables, and fruit.

WORLDWIDE EXPANSION OF IRRIGATION

In the half-century after World War II, the irrigated area of the world tripled from approximately 90 million hectares to 270 million hectares, an annual compound growth rate of over 2.5%. Most of the irrigated land is in the developing countries; over half is in Asia. There is a wide variation among regions in the fraction of cropland irrigated. Almost all of the cropland in North Africa and the Middle East is irrigated, over 20% in Asia, but 12% or less in the rest of the world.

The growth of irrigated areas in the developing world during this period was strongly influenced by two periods of severe drought: the drought in the Indian subcontinent in the mid-1960s, and the more general drought and shortfall in grain production accompanied by the energy crisis and fertilizer shortages in the mid-1970s. The Green Revolution—the development and spread of higher-yielding, shorter-season, fertilizer-responsive varieties—was closely associated with the expansion of irrigation.

The expansion of irrigation has been based mostly on the construction of new dams and reservoirs or, where ground water is readily available, through the use of tube wells. These reservoirs help to assure water supplies and allow carry-over of surplus flows in the rainy season for use in the dry season. Of the more than 40,000 large dams (defined by the International Commission on Large Dams as measuring 15 meters from foundation to crest), all but 5,000 have been built since 1950. [See Dams.]

The World Bank has been the largest foreign financier of irrigation projects, having lent over U.S.$58 billion for more than 600 dams in 93 countries. However, in most countries, domestic resources dominated the financing of irrigation development. In India, for example, which alone has more than 3,000 large dams, foreign funding of irrigation accounted for only about 10% of total expenditure in any year. Since the 1960s, net irrigated area served by wells has grown more rapidly than that served by reservoirs and canals, and wells now account for over half of the total irrigated area in India and China.

The growth of irrigation slowed in the 1980s. At least three factors have influenced the recent decline in the rate of new irrigation developments. First, and perhaps foremost, has been the steady decline in cereal-grain prices, which in real terms are about half of 1960 levels, largely because of the very success of the irrigation strategy of previous decades. Second, costs of new dam and canal construction have been rising steadily; several countries have reported cost increases of 50–100% over the past two decades. This has been due in large measure to the fact that the more easily irrigated areas have already been brought into production, and suitable new dam sites are not readily available. Finally, there has been growing pressure from environmental groups and local communities against the construction of new large dams because of concerns about their ecological and social impacts.

For most of modern history, the world's irrigated area has grown faster than the population. Since 1980, however, the irrigated area per person has declined, and per capita cereal-grain production has stagnated. The debate regarding the world's capacity to feed a growing population, brought to the fore by the writings of Malthus two centuries ago, continues unabated. But the growing scarcity and competition for water add a new element to this debate over food security. Most of the gains in crop production over the past three decades have come from higher yields on expanding irrigated land area. While irrigated area grew at about 2% per year during much of this period, the period of major construction of new systems has come to an end. Future growth in irrigated cropland is projected to be less than 1% per year, and, with losses in irrigated land from salinity, urbanization, and other factors, the net irrigated area in the world may already be declining.

A NEW PARADIGM

To meet the challenge posed by the growing scarcity and competition for water, a new paradigm of water resource management is gradually emerging from the work of researchers. This paradigm has two components. First, there is increased recognition of the need to recycle and reuse water in river basins. When water is withdrawn for a particular use, only a fraction of it is used up, or lost to the river basin, through evaporation or contamination. The balance flows to other surface and subsurface areas, where it may be recaptured and reused. Because of this recycling, a "water multiplier effect" occurs, whereby the sum of all the withdrawals in a river basin may exceed the initial amount of water entering the basin by several times. Recognition of the fact of water recycling has profound implications for water resource planning and policies.

The second component of the paradigm concerns recent advances in information technologies. The rapid development of techniques such as remote sensing and geographic information systems will enable water managers to determine water needs and availability, both in the surface and subsurface areas, at the scale of the river basin. Through observation of actual evapotranspiration via remote sensing, it will be possible to determine how well irrigation water is being managed, thus increasing yields and reducing water needs. Further development of this paradigm and of information technologies combined with a better understanding of the social, institutional, and economic aspects of water management can result in dramatic increases in water productivity and equity of water use.

ENVIRONMENTAL CONCERNS

The benefits of irrigation included lower food prices, higher employment, and more rapid agricultural and economic development. But irrigation development has also led to social and environmental problems such as salinization of soils, pollution of aquifers by agrochemicals, loss of wildlife habitats, and the forced resettlement of those previously living in areas submerged by reservoirs. The result has been a growing conflict between those who see the potential benefits of continued irrigation development and those who view further development as a threat to the environment and even to human health. [See Salinization.]

There are valid arguments to support both views, and both the positive and negative effects must be considered in the development of any project. Careful analysis of the benefits and costs of alternatives is needed to assist policy makers in making informed judgments. The long-term, diverse, and complex nature of the impacts of irrigation development make it especially hard to balance these views within a simple cost-benefit framework. For example, the stability of employment for agricultural laborers is hard to weigh against real or potential loss of wetlands or species.

Environmental problems arise largely as a consequence of efforts to intensify agricultural production in irrigated areas. Most forms of environmental degradation represent a cost to society that is borne neither by the suppliers nor by the users of irrigation water. This reinforces the rationale for a new focus on water-basin planning and management in which these external (offsite) costs are taken into account.

COMPETITION FOR WATER

Of the world's total water resources, over 97% is in the oceans and seas and is too salty for productive use. Two-thirds of the remainder is locked in icecaps, glaciers, permafrost, swamps, and deep aquifers. The remainder, less than 100,000 cubic kilometers, is found in the rivers and lakes that constitute the bulk of usable supply.

Global demand for water has grown at 2.4% per year since 1970. Agriculture currently accounts for approximately 70% of global water withdrawals. However, on a smaller geographic scale this figure ranges from as high as 90% in the lowest-income developing countries to less than 50% in some developed countries. But the demand for water for industrial and municipal use is expected to double in the next 25 years, leading to growing competition with agricultural water needs. Agriculture's share may decline as a result.

Many countries are entering a period of severe water shortage. None of the projections of the global food situation, such as those done for the World Bank, the Food and Agriculture Organization, and the International Food Policy Research Institute, has explicitly incorporated water as a constraint. There will be an increasing number of water-deficit countries and regions, including not only the Middle East and North Africa, but also some of the major breadbaskets of the world such as the Indian Punjab and the north-central plain of China. A recent study by Seckler et al. (1998) estimates that about half of the increase in demand for water by the year 2025 might be met by increasing the effectiveness of irrigation. This study suggests, however, that the remainder must be met by the expansion of irrigated area, which will almost certainly necessitate the construction of some new dams.

INCREASING PRODUCTIVITY

The productivity of water can be increased by any one or a combination of the following: increasing output per unit of consumed water; reducing water losses to sinks (including the ocean); reducing the pollution of water; and reallocating water from lower- to higher-valued crops or uses.

There is a wide range of farming practices and technologies available to increase irrigation water productivity, including recharge of aquifers, more intensive control and management of water in canal systems, use of efficient sprinklers and drip irrigation, and recycling. The suitability of any given technology or practice will vary according to the particular physical, economic, and institutional environment.

Eventually, however, as demand increases, the fresh water available in the river basin is fully used: that is to say, all remaining flows are of sufficiently poor quality, the cost of recovery is too high, or they are committed to meet environmental needs. When this happens, since there is no more surplus water to be developed, water-related activities in the river basin become wholly competitive. More water consumed upstream makes less water available downstream, and more pollution upstream reduces quality for all downstream users. At this stage, the basin is "closed," a phenomenon that is increasingly common, either at the low-flow season or throughout the year, for many of the most populated river basins in the world.

DEMAND

As the demand for water increases and its value rises, there is increasing pressure to treat water as an economic good, subject to market forces, with the price to be determined by some form of market. While there are situations where this is desirable, irrigation water is not a good that can be easily traded or bought and sold. So-called market failure calls for government intervention. Furthermore, it must be recognized that minimum levels of water, like food, are a necessity of life to which even the poorest should have access. In the design and management of systems, close attention should be paid to cost effectiveness and economic efficiency. As suggested above, greater efficiency in planning and management is best achieved at the river basin level, where overall effects on productivity and the environment can be taken into account.

PRIVATIZATION

Private systems include individually owned wells and various forms of canal irrigation managed by user groups or by private entities that own systems and provide services on behalf of users. Despite the fact that much of the recent expansion of irrigation has involved the use of public funds for the construction and operation of large irrigation systems, much of the irrigated area in the world is privatized.

Some public systems have not performed well, and their productivity of water use could be increased. Privatization of these publicly managed systems is now often viewed as the best strategy for improving performance. The aim of privatization is to create markets for the management and allocation of water. Elements of a privatized system might include one or more of the following: charges to users for services; pricing that varies with volume of use; water markets; tradable water rights; and management of irrigation systems by local user groups. The small farm size in most developing countries and the absence of established water rights presents a major constraint to volumetric pricing and development of water markets in most developing countries. Hence, the current trend is to turn over the management of public irrigation systems to local entities. While this typically results in reduced government expenditures in the short run, there is no widespread evidence that significant productivity increases are achieved, and there is growing concern that the private sector pays insufficient attention to support services and long-term expenditures for major rehabilitation and repairs.

THE FUTURE OF IRRIGATION

Until very recently, increased food production needs have been met by applying modern technology to an expanding area of irrigated cropland, but opportunities for further expansion are increasingly limited. The growing scarcity and competition among users for finite renewable water resources means that less water per capita may be available for agriculture in the future.

Increased food production and maintenance of food security will thus depend increasingly on the more productive use of existing water resources. As the new paradigm indicates, water resource management must include a river basin perspective, taking into account social objectives in allocating water among competing uses. Efficient irrigation technologies (for example, drip irrigation), biological technologies, and agronomic practices that save water and/or improve its quality will be adopted more widely in the future. Information technologies such as remote sensing, geographic information systems, and better models can assist in management and intersector water resource allocation at the basin level. Much more work needs to be done to assess the relative costs of these various alternatives and their potential for increasing the productivity of irrigated agriculture.

[*See also* Agriculture and Agricultural Land; Erosion; Famine; Land Use; Methane; Nitrous Oxide; Pest Management; Salinization; Soils; Water; *and* Water-Quality Trends.]

BIBLIOGRAPHY

Falkenmark, M., et al. "Macro-Scale Water Scarcity Requires Micro-Scale Approaches: Aspects of Vulnerability in Semi-Arid Development." *Natural Resource Forum* 13.4 (1997), 258–267. A pioneering work in the definition of measurement of water scarcity.

Food and Agriculture Organization. *Crop Water Requirements*. FAO Irrigation and Drainage Paper 24. Rome: FAO, 1984. A standard text for determining crop water requirements and their application in planning, design, and operation of irrigation projects.

Gleick, P. H., ed. *Water in Crisis: A Guide to the World's Fresh Water Resources*. New York and Oxford: Oxford University Press, 1993. This important reference contains, in Part I, a series of essays on freshwater issues and, in Part II, a comprehensive set of data covering irrigation, agricultural production, environment, human health, and other related issues.

Molden, D. "Accounting for Water Use and Productivity." System-Wide Initiative for Water Management, Paper No. 1. Colombo, Sri Lanka: International Irrigation Management Institute, 1997. Of interest principally to researchers, this paper presents a conceptual framework for water accounting and provides generic terminologies and procedures to describe the status of water resource use and consequences of actions related to water resources. The framework applies to water resource use at three levels: a use level such as an irrigated field or household; a service level such as an irrigation or water supply system; and a water basin level that may include several uses.

Pearce, F. *When the Rivers Run Dry*. Boston: Beacon Press, 2006.

Pingali P. L., et al. *Asian Rice Bowls: The Returning Crisis?* Wallingford, U.K.: CAB International, 1997. There are two excellent chapters on the environmental problems associated with intensification of agriculture through irrigation. Unlike many works dealing with environment, the authors present data and research findings to support their arguments.

Postel, S. *Last Oasis: Facing Water Scarcity*. New York: Norton, 1992. A readable account of the growing scarcity and competition for water, its implications for the production of food, and related issues.

Postel, S. *Pillar of Sand: Can the Irrigation Miracle Last?* New York and London: Norton, 1999.

Rosegrant, M. *Water Resources in the Twenty-First Century: Challenges and Implications for Action*. Food, Agriculture and the Environment Discussion Paper 20. Washington, D.C.: International Food Policy Research Institute, 1997. (http://www.ifpri.org/2020/dp/dp20.pdf; accessed June 1, 2008). A comprehensive look at the growing competition for water for irrigation and other purposes, and its implications for policy.

Seckler, D. *The New Era of Water Resources Management: From "Dry" to "Wet" Water Savings*. Research Report No. 1. Colombo, Sri Lanka: International Irrigation Management Institute, 1996. This report contains the rationale for a new paradigm emphasizing a water basin perspective for water resource and irrigation management.

Seckler, D., et al. *World Water Demand and Supply, 1990 to 2025: Scenarios and Issues*. Research Report No. 19. Colombo, Sri Lanka: International Irrigation Management Institute, 1998. This report establishes the methodological framework and the basic set of data for analyzing the present and future water supply situations of major countries of the world. The work to date highlights the national and regional disparities in water resources and provides a basis from which to begin to assess the future supply and demand for this vital natural resource.

—RANDOLPH BARKER AND DAVID SECKLER

J

JOINT IMPLEMENTATION

In the context of a global climate change policy, the concept of Joint Implementation (JI) was discussed for the first time in September 1991, during the negotiations that preceded the establishment of a Framework Convention on Climate Change (FCCC). In the FCCC, which was signed by 154 nations at the UN Conference on Environment and Development (UNCED) in Rio de Janeiro (1992), JI was included in Article 4.2(a): "developed country Parties and other Parties included in Annex I . . . may implement . . . policies and measures *jointly* with other Parties and may assist other Parties in contributing to the objective of the Convention."

The idea is that since greenhouse gases (GHGs) are uniformly mixed gases, that is, one ton of GHG emitted by party A does the same global damage as one ton emitted by party B, it does not make a difference whether a particular GHG emission reduction takes place in the territory of party A or party B.

Although there were still many uncertainties surrounding the concept at the time, the JI concept essentially enables Parties (countries that have ratified the FCCC) to fulfill a part of their greenhouse-gas emission-reduction commitments through abatement action in the territory of another party (the JI host country). The rationale for such cooperation is that for Parties with high marginal costs of abatement—for example, because of their already relatively high level of energy efficiency—it is cost effective to invest in cheaper emission-reduction measures abroad than in expensive measures domestically. If the host countries also benefit from the same cooperation (for example, via financial compensation, technology transfer, or credit sharing), both parties can gain from JI. If, moreover, a larger cost-effectiveness of abatement through JI would enhance the acceptability of actual commitments, JI may also benefit the global economy and climate. Economic theory would suggest that, if the scale of application of JI were not restricted, JI cooperation would proceed to the point at which the marginal abatement costs for all Parties are equal.

FCCC NEGOTIATIONS AND JI

The negotiations on the interpretation of the FCCC text, and therefore also of Article 4.2(a), continued after 1992, and especially after 1994, when a sufficient number of ratifications had been registered for the FCCC to enter into force. JI attracted increasing attention, but also turned out to be controversial. Opponents argued, for example, that JI would allow industrialized-country parties to postpone abatement action and the development of technology to save fossil-fuel energy domestically and would absorb the most attractive abatement opportunities in the host countries.

At the first Conference of the Parties to the FCCC (COP-1, Berlin, 1995), the debate yielded a compromise: to develop the JI concept further during a pilot phase. To remove any sensitivities, it was decided that JI activities should be referred to as Activities Implemented Jointly (AIJ) during this phase. Moreover, it was agreed that, during this phase, developed-country parties could not use AIJ to fulfill their obligations under the FCCC to stabilize their emissions of greenhouse gases by the year 2000. In other words, AIJ investments would earn no credit.

As of April 2000, 126 AIJ projects of various kinds had been reported to the FCCC Secretariat. Thirty of the pilot projects will take place in Latin America, 78 in Central and Eastern Europe, 6 in Africa, and 12 in Southeast Asia.

On December 10, 1997, in Kyoto (Japan) the Kyoto Protocol was adopted by COP-3. Under this Protocol industrialized countries agreed to reduce the emissions of six greenhouse gases by at least 5% below the levels of 1990 in the first commitment period, 2008–2012. Industrialized countries are allowed to achieve part of their GHG emission reduction commitments through cooperation with other countries via three flexibility mechanisms: GHG abatement-project cooperation between industrialized countries (Article 6 of the Protocol); project cooperation between industrialized countries and developing countries under a multilateral regime called the Clean Development Mechanism (CDM, Article 12); and a system of international emissions trading (Article 17). The first two types of cooperation are based on the JI concept. In the following, both the Article 6 and the CDM project-cooperation are referred to as JI.

TECHNICAL ISSUES

For a successful implementation of the JI concept under the Kyoto Protocol, the following technical issues need to be worked out.

Baseline determination

To measure the GHG emission reduction through a JI investment, a baseline must be established that indicates what the emissions would have amounted to in the absence of the investment. This implies that projections must comprise factors such as economic growth, (energy) price developments, and structural changes in the JI host country for the project lifetime, which may be quite long (in the case of forestry, for example).

Such projections may not be easy, especially because of the counterfactual character of a project baseline (i.e., because of the JI project the situation that is described by the baseline will never exist). The FCCC negotiations focus on several approaches to baseline determination, varying from completely unstandardized and project-specific to standardized baselines based on category-wide information.

In order to ensure environmental integrity, baseline calculation should not overstate the emission reduction of a JI project because this would result in a transfer of too many credits from the host to the investor country. This is particularly relevant for projects implemented in countries without emission quota under the Kyoto Protocol (i.e., for CDM projects). In the case of Article 6 project cooperation, the environmental integrity is likely to be safeguarded better as emission-reduction credits from such projects are deducted from the emission budget of the host country (which is also an industrialized country with an emission reduction commitment). There is, therefore, a built-in checking mechanism in Article 6 of the Kyoto Protocol that is not present in the CDM.

JI project monitoring and verification

The GHG emission reductions achieved (or carbon sequestered) through a JI project have to be included in the national governments' reports to the FCCC. The Conference of the Parties will then decide on the credits to be issued. With respect to monitoring and verification of a JI project's performance, some experts suggest that project monitoring should be left to the project parties involved (either national or local governments, or private-sector parties); others suggest that this task should be delegated to independent experts (to prevent parties from cheating to inflate the credits' volume). Most experts agree that the verification of the reported GHG emission reduction (carbon sequestration) should be left to an international third-party auditing body.

Credit sharing

Once the JI project's abatement impact has been verified, it must be decided how the JI credits collected at the country level will be shared among the parties. During the pilot phase for JI (see above), this question has remained a theoretical one because crediting is not yet allowed, but it becomes a relevant issue under the Protocol. The discussion of this question is still in its infancy. It may well be that the credit-sharing issue will be left to negotiations between participants of individual JI projects (i.e., investors and host countries) It is also possible that some general guidelines will be agreed upon, such as distinguishing between categories of host countries according to the stringency of their emission-reduction commitments.

Sustainable development of CDM projects

According to the Kyoto Protocol, one of the purposes of the CDM is to assist developing countries in achieving sustainable development, but the Protocol does not define sustainable development. The question is whether it should be left to developing countries to define sustainable development, given countries' different priorities and circumstances, or whether the term should be defined by the COP, for example, through a list of required project criteria. The risk of the first option is that some developing countries may opt for projects that they consider sustainable, but which the international community considers unsustainable (e.g., nuclear energy). A risk of the second option is that it may conflict with developing countries' sovereignty.

JI in the Second Sulphur Protocol

In 1994 the Second Sulphur Protocol (SSP) to the 1979 Convention on Long Range Transboundary Air Pollution was signed in Oslo. Article 2.7 of this Protocol (covering Europe and the economies in transition) enables parties to implement their obligations jointly. The cost-saving potential of JI in SSP, however, is rather limited (Foundation JIN, 1995). First, since sulfur is a nonuniformly mixed gas, third-party effects have to be taken into account (in the SSP these parties are therefore given an important say). Second, the parties' (differentiated) emission-reduction obligations under SSP were determined using a cost-minimization model, more or less equalizing the marginal sulfur dioxide abatement costs across the countries. Because of this, the cost-savings potential through sulfur dioxide trading—essentially equivalent to the JI concept discussed above—was largely undermined. To date there is only limited experience with JI-like mechanisms that is directly applicable to the design and operation of sulfur or greenhouse-gas trading mechanisms.

[See also Emissions Trading; Framework Convention on Climate Change; and Global Warming.]

BIBLIOGRAPHY

Foundation JIN. "Progress Report on the Role of JI in Acidification Abatement." *Joint Implementation Quarterly* 1.0 (1995), 12.
Jepma, C. J., ed. *The Feasibility of Joint Implementation.* Dordrecht, The Netherlands and London: Kluwer, 1995.
Jepma, C. J., and M. Munasinghe. *Climate Change Policy.* Cambridge and New York: Cambridge University Press, 1997.
Jepma, C. J., and W. van der Gaast, eds. *On the Compatibility of the Flexible Instruments.* Dordrecht, The Netherlands, and London: Kluwer, 1999.
Kuik, O., P. Peters, and N. J. Schrijver, eds. *Joint Implementation to Curb Climate Change: Legal and Economic Aspects.* Dordrecht, The Netherlands: Kluwer, 1994.
Lazarus, M., et al. "Evaluation of Benchmarking as an Approach for Establishing Clean Development Mechanism Baselines." Boston: Tellus Institute, Stockholm Environment Institute, and Stratus Consulting, 1999.

—CATRINUS J. JEPMA

K

KYOTO PROGRESS

With ratification by the required number of countries—accounting for 55% of 1990 industrial carbon dioxide from industrial countries—the Kyoto Protocol entered into force on February 16, 2005. As of June, 2007, a total of 172 countries or other governmental entities had ratified the agreement; of these, however, 137 are developing nations which, like India and China, have no obligation beyond monitoring and reporting emissions.

The 15 nations of the European Union (EU) ratified the Protocol earlier, in 2002, and it appears they will reach their target of cutting greenhouse-gas (GHG) emissions by 8% below 1990 levels during the first test period 2008–2012. [*See* Kyoto Protocol.] To continue their success, members of the European Commission, at a summit in Brussels on March 9, 2007, endorsed a plan for the years following 2012 when Kyoto's targets expire. (International talks on a treaty for post-2012 began in May of 2007.) The commission proposed that under a future worldwide agreement developed countries should cut GHG emissions to an average of 30% below 1990 levels by the year 2020, and asserted that worldwide emissions will need to be cut to half the 1990 levels by the year 2050 (see press release Jan. 1, 2007).

Meanwhile, developing nations (such as China and India), which were exempted from targets in the Protocol, continue to grow economically and to emit GHG at increasing rates: China is expected to match the United States in total annual carbon dioxide emissions in 2007 or 2008. The United States and Australia, which declined to ratify the Protocol, are emitting GHG at record rates; and some industrial nations like Canada, which did ratify the agreement, are emitting at rates that are far beyond the 1990 level.

In this regard, there is a great range of performance. Figures for the period 1990–2004 show that while some European nations have cut emissions to 20–60% below 1990 levels, some nations are at levels 20–60% above the 1990 level. The United States, for instance in 2004 was at 16% above, and Australia and Canada at roughly 25% above 1990 levels (Figure 1). When the data for those Annex I countries are divided to show those with Economies in Transition (EIT Parties) it appears that EIT countries have led the way in reducing GHG emissions (Figure 2). This may be partly because these countries qualify for emission-reduction projects which generate carbon credits that can be sold to Annex I (developed country) buyers, who find it difficult to accomplish significant improvements in their own industries, but it is more likely that the reduced emissions since 1990 reflect the economic disruption that followed the breakup of the Soviet Union. [*See* Emissions Trading.]

In Figures 1 and 2, the emissions reported exclude any effects of land use, land-use change, and forestry (LULUCF) such as deforestation or afforestation. Including such influences has a drastic effect on net emissions, changing Norway's emissions from up 10.3% to down 18.7% in relation to the year 1990, while Canada's numbers change from up 26.6% to up 52.2% (UNFCC, 2006).

The Asia-Pacific Partnership on Clean Development and Climate (AP7) comprises the United States, Canada, India, Australia, China, South Korea, and Japan. The idea is said to be Australian-inspired but U.S.-led and is intended to bring together the world's largest emitters of greenhouse gases, India and China being exempted from the 2008–2012 targets, and Australia and the United States being Annex I nations that declined to ratify the treaty because India and China were not compelled to monitor and reduce their emissions. The group of 7 nations now accounts for over half of the world's emissions per year.

One of the stated goals is to help India and China to advance economically while using the most environmentally-sound technologies available. This is a worthy goal, but the scheme as yet sets no emissions targets and no deadlines, and therefore creates no incentives for change.

Canada joined this group in 2007 (AP6, 2007). In October 2006 a new clean air act was enacted whose regulations will not take effect until 2010 (CBC News, Feb. 14, 2007). Canada faces great difficulty in reducing it GHG emissions because almost one-third of those emissions are produced in the province of Alberta where oil-sands development is growing rapidly. [*See* Oil Sands.]

A cynical view of the Asia-Pacific Partnership points out that both Australia and Canada, as large producers and exporters of coal, would benefit immensely from an arrangement with India and China whose dependence upon coal for electrical generation and steel production will continue, regardless of new technologies.

[*See also* Carbon Taxes; *and* Energy Strategies.]

BIBLIOGRAPHY

AP6. "Asia-Pacific Partnership on Clean Development and Climate." Second Ministerial Meeting and Fourth Policy and Implementation Committee Meeting, October 15, 2007. New Delhi, India. http://www.asiapacificpartnership.org/2ndministerialmeeting.htm (accessed June 1, 2008).

CBC News. (Canadian Broadcasting Corporation). "Kyoto Protocol FAQs." *CBC News Online*, Feb. 14, 2007. http://www.cbc.ca/news/background/kyoto/ (accessed June 1, 2008).

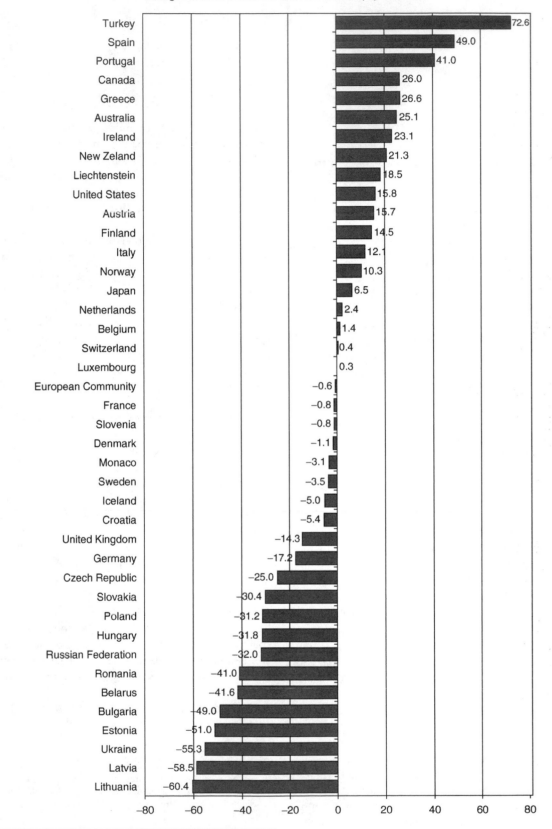

Changes in GHG emissions without LULUCF (%) 1990–2004

Turkey	72.6
Spain	49.0
Portugal	41.0
Canada	26.0
Greece	26.6
Australia	25.1
Ireland	23.1
New Zeland	21.3
Liechtenstein	18.5
United States	15.8
Austria	15.7
Finland	14.5
Italy	12.1
Norway	10.3
Japan	6.5
Netherlands	2.4
Belgium	1.4
Switzerland	0.4
Luxembourg	0.3
European Community	−0.6
France	−0.8
Slovenia	−0.8
Denmark	−1.1
Monaco	−3.1
Sweden	−3.5
Iceland	−5.0
Croatia	−5.4
United Kingdom	−14.3
Germany	−17.2
Czech Republic	−25.0
Slovakia	−30.4
Poland	−31.2
Hungary	−31.8
Russian Federation	−32.0
Romania	−41.0
Belarus	−41.6
Bulgaria	−49.0
Estonia	−51.0
Ukraine	−55.3
Latvia	−58.5
Lithuania	−60.4

Kyoto Progress. Figure 1. Changes in GHG Emissions 1990–2004.

Without Land Use, Land-use Change and Forestry. Using base years other than 1990: Bulgaria (1988), Hungary (1985–87), Poland (1988), Romania (1989), and Slovenia (1986). (Source: UNFCCC website: GHG Emissions Data.)

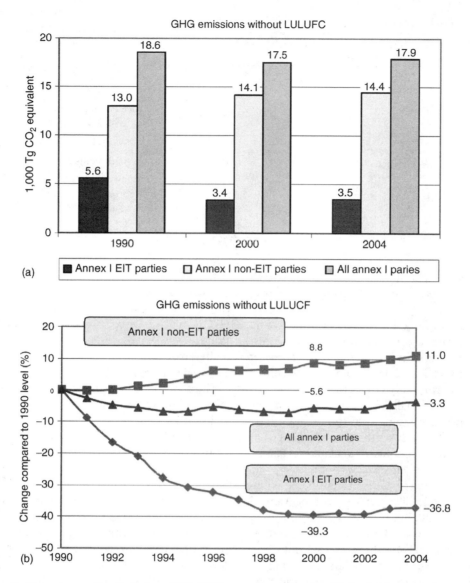

Kyoto Progress. Figure 2. Greenhouse Gas Emissions 1990–2004.

Without land use, Land-Use Change and Forestry. Base years as in Fig. 1. (Source: UNFCCC website: GHG Emissions Data.)

Envocare. "Global Warming, Kyoto Protocol and Climate Change." http://www.envocare.co.uk/energy_and_ecology.htm (accessed June 1, 2008).

European Commission Press Release. "Commission Proposes an Integrated Energy and Climate Change Package to Cut Emissions for the Twenty-First Century." Jan. 1, 2007. http://www.europa.eu/press_room/presspacks/energy/index_en.html (accessed June 2, 2008).

European Environment Agency (EEA). "Projected Progress Towards Kyoto Protocol Targets." http://www.dataservice.eea.europa.eu/atlas/viewdata/viewpub.asp?id=844 (accessed June 2, 2008).

Stavins, R., and J. Aldy, eds. *Architectures for Agreement: Addressing Climate Change in the Post-Kyoto World*. Cambridge and New York: Cambridge University Press, 2007.

—David J. Cuff

KYOTO PROTOCOL

At the Rio Conference on Environment and Development in 1992, governments created an institution for regulating global warming, the United Nations Framework Convention on Climate Change (FCCC). In 1995, the governments that had ratified the FCCC held their first Conference of the Parties (COP) in Berlin, where they adopted the Berlin Mandate, which declared that the FCCC was inadequate to contain the threat of global warming. The Berlin Mandate set COP-3, slated for December 1997 in Kyoto, as the deadline for adopting a new agreement with more stringent commitments. Governments established the Ad Hoc Group on the Berlin Mandate (AGBM) to manage the negotiations. During most of its lifetime, AGBM's deliberations were unfocused. With the threat of failure looming, national delegations hurriedly assembled an agreement late in 1997, which they finalized at Kyoto in a ten-day negotiating session attended by ten thousand delegates and observers.

The Kyoto Protocol obliges industrialized nations—listed in Annex I of the FCCC—to cut their emissions on average by 5% below 1990 levels during the five-year "first budget period" of 2008–2012. The target is comprehensive, which means that it applies to all anthropogenic sources and sinks of all major

TABLE 1. Gases Included in the Kyoto Protocol

Gas	Percentage of Total Global Warming in 1990s	GWP	Anthropogenic Sources
Carbon dioxide (CO_2)	70	1	Fossil fuels, cement, deforestation, and other land use changes
Methane (CH_4)	20	21	Rice paddies, domestic animals, fossil fuels, biomass burning, landfills
Nitrous oxide (N_2O)	6	310	Nitrogen fertilizers, fossil fuels
Hydrofluorocarbons (e.g., CHF_3, CH_3CHF_2)	<1 (rising rapidly)	11,700 (CHF_3)	Replacements for ozone-depleting substances (e.g., refrigerants, solvents)
Perfluorocarbons (e.g., CF_4, C_2F_6)	<1 (rising rapidly)	6,500 (CF_4)	Byproduct of aluminum smelting, semiconductor production
Sulfur hexafluoride (SF_6)	<1 (rising rapidly)	23,900	Electrical equipment, magnesium smelting

greenhouse gases (Table 1). Through negotiation, the overall goal of a 5% cut was distributed among the Annex I countries (Table 2).

Developing countries (not listed in Annex I) adamantly and successfully resisted any formal controls on their future emissions, arguing that they must spend scarce resources on other more pressing problems such as alleviation of poverty, and that global warming is caused principally by emissions from industrialized nations. Some industrialized countries, led by the United States, are pushing developing countries to limit their future emissions at least voluntarily on the grounds that greenhouse warming is a global problem caused by all nations and no solution to the problem can be effective without widespread participation. Indeed, total emissions from developing countries are growing rapidly and will overtake those of Annex I nations by approximately 2030, but per capita emissions from virtually all developing countries will remain lower than those in nearly all industrialized nations for the foreseeable future.

Although the Kyoto Protocol targets are specific and stringent, the Protocol also includes several measures that will make it easier and less costly for Annex I countries to comply. First, because the target is comprehensive, it allows countries to focus controls on those sources and sinks for gases that are least costly to regulate. In practice, the most important advantage of this comprehensive approach is that it allows countries to offset emissions of carbon dioxide due to combustion of fossil fuels—the largest source of global warming—with carbon absorbed in biomass through afforestation and other changes in land use. However, measurement of the growth of these carbon sinks is difficult; in Kyoto, negotiators deferred agreement on the detailed accounting rules needed to put this provision into practice.

Second, industrialized nations have the flexibility of selecting favorable base years. Instead of 1990, several countries in the midst of transition from command economies selected base years in the late 1980s when emissions were at their peak before economic collapse. In addition, the Kyoto Protocol allows any industrialized nation to select 1990 or 1995 as the base year for the synthetic gases—hydrofluorocarbons (HFCs), perfluorocarbons (PFCs), and sulfur hexafluoride (SF_6). Emissions of HFCs—replacements for gases phased out under the Montreal Protocol—were rising especially rapidly in the early 1990s. With higher base-year emissions, a given percentage cut can be achieved more easily.

Third, potentially the most important flexibility mechanism is the Protocol's provision for several types of emission trading. In principle, emission trading cuts the cost of complying with the Protocol by allowing nations and firms to trade the right to emit greenhouse gases—permits will be sold and abatement focused where regulation of sources and sinks is the least costly. Several industrialized countries are planning emission trading systems with Russia, which could allow them to purchase Russia's surplus emission rights at low cost. In Kyoto, Russia agreed to cap its emissions at 1990 levels in the first budget period, but it is unlikely that, even with a modest recovery of the Russian economy, emissions will reach even that level. The case illustrates the large value at stake when targets (and permits) are distributed. As controls on greenhouse gases tighten, the value of these permits will rise, making negotiations over permit allocations increasingly contentious. Moreover, no emission trading system of this scale and complexity has ever been attempted under international law. The Kyoto Protocol includes provisions for monitoring, accounting, enforcement, and other critical functions, but they have yet to be tested. [*See* Emissions Trading.]

The Kyoto Protocol also includes two more limited forms of emission trading. One, known as joint implementation (JI), allows credits to be earned and traded on a project-by-project basis, which gives an incentive for cost-effective international emission control without necessarily confronting the difficulty of allocating permits and administering a full-blown emission trading system. [*See* Joint Implementation.] Through the JI mechanism, Annex I countries may make investments in other Annex I countries and earn credit if lower greenhouse gas

TABLE 2. Emission Targets for Annex I Countries

Kyoto Target (percent)	Annex I Country (or Regional Economic Integration Organization)
−8	European Community
	Austria
	Belgium
	Denmark
	Finland
	France
	Germany
	Greece
	Ireland
	Italy
	Luxembourg
	Netherlands
	Portugal
	Spain
	Sweden
	United Kingdom
−8	Bulgaria
−8	Czech Republic
−8	Estonia
−8	Latvia
−8	Liechtenstein
−8	Lithuania
−8	Monaco
−8	Romania
−8	Slovakia
−8	Slovenia
−8	Switzerland
−7	United States **
−6	Canada
−6	Hungary
−6	Japan
−6	Poland
−5	Croatia
0	New Zealand
0	Russian Federation
0	Ukraine
+1	Norway
+8	Australia **
+10	Iceland

** United States and Australia have not ratified the protocol

emissions result. The other limited trading system is the Clean Development Mechanism (CDM), which allows Annex I nations to earn credits from investments in developing countries. However, implementing the CDM operation is more difficult than implementing the JI because the Protocol does not set limits for emissions from developing countries. Thus, for the CDM, it is especially important to determine the level of emissions that would have occurred without the investment so that proper credit can be given for the difference between (lower) actual emissions and the baseline level that would have existed otherwise. Technically and politically, this counterfactual calculation is extremely difficult to perform. Rules for operating and accounting under the CDM were left unresolved at Kyoto—the deferral of the details explains in part the widespread agreement at Kyoto on the need for the CDM. Experience with JI-like emission offset programs in the United States shows that if the rules are too cumbersome the system will fail to encourage such trading.

In addition to establishing new commitments, the Protocol is an integral part of the institutions established by the FCCC. Parties to the Protocol must be parties to the FCCC. The FCCC and the Kyoto Protocol will share the same secretariat, based in Bonn, Germany. The Protocol's supreme decision-making body—the Meeting of the Parties (MOP)—will meet at the same time as the FCCC's COP. The subsidiary bodies that serve the latter (for example, the Subsidiary Body for Implementation and the Subsidiary Body for Scientific and Technological Advice) will also serve the Protocol's MOP. The Kyoto Protocol also strengthens and clarifies the obligation, first codified in the FCCC that each party report inventories of its emissions of greenhouse gases. Without extensive reporting and review of reports, it will be nearly impossible to verify whether parties have actually complied with the stringent obligations of the Protocol.

Entry into force of the Protocol requires ratification by 55 Parties to the FCCC, representing 55% of the emissions of industrial carbon dioxide from Annex I countries in 1990. For many industrialized nations, the Kyoto commitments will be costly to implement, and it may prove difficult to garner sufficient political support to assure that the treaty is binding under international law. If ratification falters, then the FCCC will remain in place as a backstop and as a framework for future efforts to slow global warming.

[See also Framework Convention on Climate Change; Global Warming; Greenhouse Effect; and Kyoto Progress.]

BIBLIOGRAPHY

Bartsch, U., and B. Müller. Fossil Fuels in a Changing Climate: Impacts of the Kyoto Protocol and Developing Country Participation. Oxford: Oxford University Press, 2000.

Victor, D. The Collapse of the Kyoto Protocol and the Struggle to Slow Global Warming. Princeton, N.J.: Princeton University Press, 2001.

—DAVID G. VICTOR

L

LAKES

Lakes vary in shape, size, depth, and degree of openness, and therefore so does their response to environmental change. Closed lakes—those with no functioning outlets—are particularly sensitive, but even the world's largest lakes (Table 1) are not immune.

Humans have a range of impacts on lake basins, which include eutrophication because of the addition of nutrients to their catchments, acidification because of acid precipitation or land-use changes, contamination by chemical pollutants and heavy metals, explosive invasion by exotic organisms, siltation because of land use and land-cover changes, and changes in their water balance because of such processes as interbasin water transfers and changes in land use (Kira, 1998).

ANTHROPOGENIC EFFECTS ON LAKE LEVELS

Changes in lake levels brought about by human activities have been known for a long time. A basin for which there are particularly long records of change is the Valencia Lake Basin in Venezuela (Böckh, 1973). It was its declining level that so struck Alexander von Humboldt in 1800. He recorded its level as about 422 meters above sea level, whereas previous observations, made by Antonio Manzano in 1727, had established it at 426 meters. The 1968 level was about 405 meters, representing a fall of no less than 21 meters in about 240 years. Humboldt believed that the cause of the declining level was deforestation, and this was supported by Böckh (1973), who pointed also to the withdrawal of water for irrigation. This remarkable fall in level meant that the lake ceased to flow into the Orinoco River. It has as a consequence become subject to salinization and is now eight times more saline than it was two and a half centuries ago.

Even the world's largest lake, the Caspian Sea, has been modified by human activities. The most important change was the

fall of 3 meters in its level between 1929 and the late 1970s (see Figure 1). This decline was undoubtedly partly the product of climatic change (Micklin, 1972). Nonetheless, human actions have contributed to this fall, particularly since the 1950s, because of reservoir formation, irrigation, municipal and industrial withdrawals, and agricultural practices. In the 1970s, 1980s, and early 1990s the Caspian saw a rise in its levels, caused by a decrease in the difference between evaporation and precipitation over its catchment. But for anthropogenic effects its level would have returned to pre-1930 levels (World Meteorological Organization, 1995, p. 124). However, a further fall began in 1995.

Perhaps the most severe change to a major inland sea has taken place in the Aral. Since 1960 it has lost more than 40% of its area and about 60% of its volume, and its level has fallen by more than 14 meters (Kotylakov, 1991). This has lowered the artesian water table across a strip of land 80–170 kilometers wide, exposed 24,000 square kilometers of former lake bed to desiccation, and created salty surfaces from which salts are blown by the wind to be transported in dust storms, to the detriment of soil quality. The mineral content of what remains has increased almost threefold over the same period. It is probably the most dire ecological event to have afflicted the states of the former Soviet Union, and as with the Caspian's decline, much of the blame rests with excessive use of water that would otherwise replenish the sea.

The withdrawal of water from the Jordan River for irrigation purposes has caused a decline in the level of the Dead Sea at a rate of about 0.8 meters per year. The level dropped 20 meters during the twentieth century and may fall a further 100 to 150 meters over the next 400 years (Yechieli et al., 1998). Under natural conditions, fresh water from the Jordan constantly fed the less salty layer of the sea, which occupied roughly the top 40 meters of the 320-meter-deep body of water. Because the amount of water entering the lake via the Jordan was more or less equal to the quantity lost by evaporation, the lake maintained its stable, stratified state, with less salty water resting on the waters of high salinity. With the recent human-induced diminution in Jordan discharge, however, the sea's upper layer has thinned because of intense evaporation. Its salinity has approached that of the older and deeper waters. As a consequence the layered structure has collapsed, causing increased precipitation of salts. Moreover, now that circulating waters carry oxygen to the bottom, the characteristic "rotten-egg" smell of hydrogen sulfide has largely disappeared (Maugh, 1979).

TABLE 1. Major Lakes of the Continents

Lake	Continent	Area (km²)
Victoria	Africa	63,000–69,000
Caspian	Europe	374,000–378,400
Aral	Asia	64,100
Superior	North America	82,100–83,300
Eyre	Australia	up to 40,000
Maracaibo	South America	13,000–14,3000

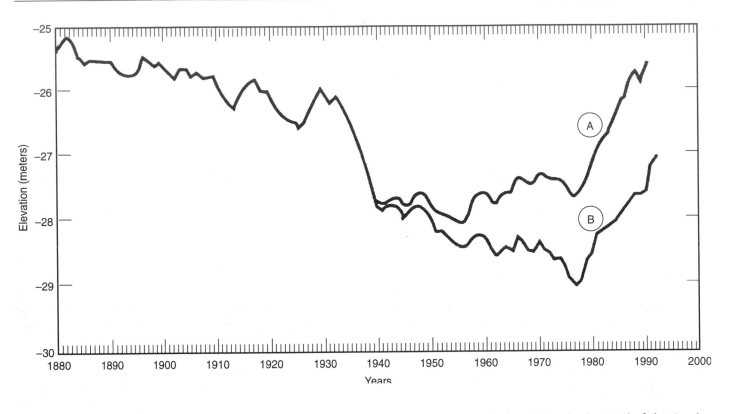

Lakes. Figure 1. Annual Fluctuations in the Level of the Caspian Sea, 1880–1993.

Curve A shows the changes in level that would have occurred but for anthropogenic influences, while curve B shows the actual observed levels. (Modified from World Meteorological Organization, 1995, Figure 15.3.)

RECENT CLIMATE CHANGES AND LAKE LEVELS

Lake levels respond to changes in rainfall inputs and to the outputs of moisture by evaporation and transpiration, which are largely controlled by temperature. One of the most interesting examples of environmental change in the twentieth century has been the fluctuating level of lakes in the tropics. In particular, many equatorial lakes in Africa showed a dramatic increase in level in the early 1960s, which led to the flooding of port installations, deltaic farming land, and the like (Butzer, 1971). This rise contrasted sharply with the frequently low levels encountered in the previous decades.

The Great Salt Lake in Utah has an impressive record of fluctuating levels dating back to the middle of the nineteenth century (Figure 2). The lake rose from an elevation of about 4,200 feet in 1851 to a peak of around 4,210 feet (1,284 meters) in 1873. Thereafter it declined markedly, reaching the lowest recorded level in 1963. By 1986–1987, as a result of a run of wet years, it had risen from around 4,194 feet (1,279 meters) back to the sort of elevation achieved in the 1870s. However, drought conditions caused it to fall again to below 4,198 feet (1,280 meters) in 2002–2003. There has thus been a total fluctuation of this great lake on the order of 5 meters over that time period (Stockton, 1990).

El Niño warming in 1997 led to an increase in rainfall over East Africa that caused Lake Victoria to rise by about 1.7 meters and Lake Turkana by about 2 meters (Birkett et al., 1999). The abrupt change in the level of the Caspian (2.5 meters between 1978 and 1995) has also been attributed to ENSO phenomena (Arpe et al., 2000). Similarly, the 3.7-meter rise in the level of the

Great Salt Lake between 1982 and 1986 was at least partly related to the record rainfall and snowfall in its catchment during the 1982–1983 El Niño (Arnow and Stephens, 1990). The enormous changes that occur in the volume of Lake Eyre (South Australia) result from ENSO-related changes in inflow, with the greatest flooding occurring during La Niña phases (Kotwicki and Allan, 1998) such as those of 1949–1952 and 1974.

LONGER-TERM CLIMATE CHANGES AND LAKE LEVELS

Lakes, like the oceans, can preserve a long record of sedimentation. Arid regions have many closed depressions, and these lake basins, as Russell (1885) and Gilbert (1890) noted over a century ago with reference to lakes Bonneville and Lahontan, are rich depositories of paleoenvironmental information. Ancient shorelines demonstrate that what are now shrunken, salty relicts were once fine, large, freshwater bodies. In addition, lake basins, if they have not suffered wind erosion sufficient to erase the record, can provide a long history from their sediments. At various times in the Quaternary huge water bodies occurred in the Sahara, including Mega-Chad, Mega-Fezzan, and Mega-Chotts. [See Tropical Climate Change.]

Since the late 1960s, at least two main developments have taken place in the study of tropical lake basins. The first of

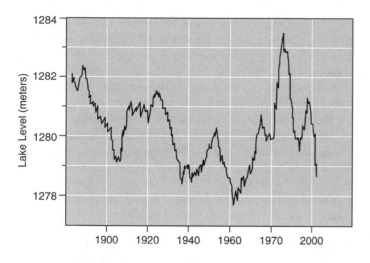

Lakes. Figure 2. The Changing Level of the Great Salt Lake

(Data from Great Salt Lake Basin Hydrologic Observatory, University of Utah, 2004 in http://greatsaltlake.utah.edu/description/, accessed February 8th 2007.)

these has been the radiocarbon dating of former high stands of lake level. The remarkable result of such work was the recognition that in low latitudes glacial and pluvial events were not synchronous and that, if anything, the late glacial maximum could be equated with aridity and the early Holocene interglacial with humidity. This was pointed out for tropical Africa by Grove and Goudie (1971) and shortly thereafter by Butzer et al. (1972).

The second development, which builds upon the first, has been the construction of a global database of lake status that permits interregional comparisons to be made (Street and Grove, 1979). This work shows that while the midlatitude lakes of the American southwest may have been high at the time of the last glacial maximum, those of the tropics and monsoonal lands (e.g., West Africa, East Africa, southern Arabia, northwestern India, and tropical Australia) were low at that time and reached very high levels in the early Holocene, around 9,000 years ago (Goudie, 2002).

Recently, such databases have been developed for more parts of the world (see, for example, Fang, 1991, on China). Their temporal resolution has also improved as more dates have become available, and this improvement has enabled some investigators to suggest correlations between tropical lake fluctuations and short-lived events such as the Younger Dryas of the Late Glacial (Gasse et al., 1990; Sirocko et al., 1996; Roberts et al., 1993). [*See* Younger Dryas.*]

THE RESPONSE OF LAKES TO POTENTIAL GLOBAL WARMING

Just as lakes have responded to past climatic changes, so it is clear that they will respond to the temperature and precipitation changes that may result from global warming. An example of such responses is provided by models that have been developed for the Great Lakes of North America by Croley (1990)

and Hartmann (1990). They suggest that for a doubling of carbon dioxide levels there may be a 23–51% reduction in net basin supplies of water to all the Great Lakes, and that as a result lake levels will fall at rates ranging from 13 millimeters per decade (for Lake Superior) to 93 millimeters per decade (for Lake Ontario). Major falls of up to 9 meters by the end of the present century have been predicted for the Caspian (Elguindi and Giorgi, 2006).

BIBLIOGRAPHY

Arnow, T., and D. Stephens. *Hydrologic Characteristics of the Great Salt Lake, Utah, 1847–1986.* U. S. Geological Survey Water-Supply Paper 2332, p. 32. Denver, Colo.: USGS, 1990.

Arpe, K., et al. "Connection between Caspian Sea Level Variability and ENSO." *Geophysical Research Letters* 27 (2000), 2693–2696.

Birkett, C., R. Murtugudde, and J.A. Allan. "Indian Ocean Climate Event Brings Floods to East Africa's Lakes and the Sudd Marsh." *Geophysical Research Letters* 26 (1999), 1031–1034.

Böckh, A. "Consequences of Uncontrolled Human Activities in the Valencia Lake Basin." In *The Careless Technology,* edited by M.T. Farvar and J.P. Milton, pp. 301–317. London: Tom Stacey, 1973.

Butzer, K.W. "Recent History of an Ethiopian Delta." University of Chicago, Department of Geography, Research Paper 136 (1971), 184.

Butzer, K.W., et al. "Radiocarbon Dating of East African Lake Levels." *Science* 175 (1972), 1069–1075. DOI: 10.1126/science.175.4026.1069.

Croley, T.E. "Laurentian Great Lakes Double-CO_2 Climate Change Hydrological Impacts." *Climatic Change* 17 (1990), 27–47. DOI: 10.1007/BF00148999.

Elguindi, N., and F. Giorgi. "Projected Changes in the Caspian Sea Level for the 21st Century Based on the Latest AOGCM Simulations." *Geophysical Research Letters* 33, L08706 (2006). DOI: 10.1029/2006GL025943.

Fang, J.-Q. "Lake Evolution during the Past 30,000 Years in China, and Its Implications for Environmental Change." *Quaternary Research* 36 (1991), 37–60. DOI: 10.1016/0033-5894(91)90016-X.

Gasse, F., et al. "The Arid-Humid Transition in the Sahara and the Sahel during the Last Deglaciation." *Nature* 346 (1990), 141–146. DOI: 10.1038/346141a0.

Gilbert, G.K. *Lake Bonneville.* U.S. Geological Survey Monograph 1, 1890.

Goudie, A.S. *Great Warm Deserts of the World.* Oxford and New York: Oxford University Press, 2002.

Grove, A.T., and A.S. Goudie. "Late Quaternary Lake Levels in the Rift Valley of Southern Ethiopia and Elsewhere in Tropical Africa." *Nature* 234 (1971), 403–405. DOI: 10.1038/234403a0.

Hartmann, H.C. "Climate Change Impacts on Laurentian Great Lakes Levels." *Climatic Change* 17 (1990), 49–67. DOI: 10.1007/BF00149000.

Kira, T. "Major Environmental Problems in World Lakes." In *Central Eurasian Water Crisis,* edited by I. Kobori and M. Glantz, pp. 13–21. Tokyo and New York: United Nations University Press, 1998.

Kotlyakov, V.M. "The Aral Sea Basin: A Critical Environmental Zone." *Environment* 33.1 (1991), 4–9, 36–38.

Kotwicki, V., and R. Allan. "La Niña de Australia: Contemporary and Palaeo-Hydrology of Lake Eyre". *Palaeogeography, Palaeoclimatology, Palaeoecology* 144 (1998), 87–98. DOI: 10.1016/S0031-0182(98)00122-9.

Maugh, T.H. "The Dead Sea Is Alive and, Well…" *Science* 205 (1979), 178. DOI: 10.1126/science.205.4402.178.

Micklin, P.P. "Dimensions of the Caspian Sea Problem." *Soviet Geography* 13 (1972), 589–603.

Roberts, N., et al. "Timing of the Younger Dryas Event in East Africa from Lake-Level Changes." *Nature* 366 (1993), 146–148. DOI: 10.1038/366146a0.

Russell, I.C. *Geological History of Lake Lahontan.* United States Geological Survey Monograph 11, 1885.

Sirocko, F., et al. "Teleconnections between the Subtropical Monsoons and High-Latitude Climates during the Last Deglaciation." *Science* 272 (1996), 526–529. DOI: 10.1126/science.272.5261.526.

Stockton, E.W. "Climatic Variability on the Scale of Decades to Centuries." *Climatic Change* 16 (1990), 173–183. DOI: 10.1007/BF00134655.

Street, F.A., and A.T. Grove. "Global Maps of Lake-Level Fluctuations since 30,000 Years BP." *Quaternary Research* 12 (1979), 83–118.

World Meteorological Organization. *Climate System Review: Climate System Monitoring, June 1991–November 1993.* Geneva: World Meteorological Organization, 1995.

Yechieli, Y., I. Gavrieli, B. Berkowitz, and D. Ronen. "Will the Dead Sea Die?" *Geology* 26 (1998), 755–758.

—Andrew S. Goudie

LAND PRESERVATION

Caring for the land means more than simply protecting pristine places. Land preservation involves biodiversity, habitats, watersheds, forests, recreational areas, cultural values, environmental services, food production, and buffering against climate change and other hazards. [*See* Biological Diversity.] While maintaining one of these often helps maintain another, it sometimes happens that efforts work at cross purposes. Land preservation takes on dramatically different characteristics in industrialized and less-industrialized regions. [*See* Parks and Preserves.]

PROTECTED LANDS WORLDWIDE

Worldwide, according to the United Nations Environment Programme (UNEP) and the International Union for the Conservation of Nature (IUCN), 11.6% of terrestrial surface area is protected. [*See* United Nations Environment Programme.] Central America and South America are leaders, with approximately 25% of their lands in protected status, while Africa, Oceania, and much of Asia come in under 10%. Nature conservation and biological diversity are the main themes in the UNEP/IUCN protected-areas classification scheme, which includes categories ranging from I (scientific and wilderness preserves) to VI, in which lands are managed for sustainable use (distinct from preservation) of ecosystems. ("Non-categorized" lands also are included in the UNEP/IUCN data.) Growth in protected-area acreage in all the world's major biomes has been steady and substantial over the past several decades. Twenty-three percent of tropical humid forests are in protected status as of 2003, a dramatic rise from the previous UNEP/IUCN assessment, conducted in 1997. By contrast, less than 5% of temperate grassland area is protected. IUCN's goal is a minimum of 10% protected land in each of the world's major biomes, and this has already been achieved for 9 of 14 biomes (Chape et al., 2003). Yet even as that 10% goal is being achieved and exceeded, many of the protected lands face severe management challenges, including lack of political support, inadequate financial resources, pollution and climate-change impacts, and limited law-enforcement capacity.

Land-conservation efforts may play only a small part in slowing land conversion overall. [*See* Conservation.] Despite increased protected-land designations in recent decades, total forest land cover declined at an average annual rate of 0.2% between 1990 and 2000 (World Resources Institute, 2007a). The greatest losses were in Central America and the Caribbean (1.1%), Sub-Saharan Africa (0.9%), and South America (0.4%). More telling are losses in "natural" forest lands, that is, non-plantation forests consisting mainly of indigenous species.

[*See* Deforestation.] Central America–Caribbean losses were 1.2% and South America's were 0.5% annually. In both categories—natural forests and total forested land—developing countries sustained losses, while developed countries held steady or gained slightly. Because of large-scale government afforestation efforts, China's forest cover—in contrast with most of East and Southeast Asia—has increased in the new millennium. Among the main causes of forest loss is land conversion for agricultural and grazing use. Asia and South America registered dramatic increases in acreages of plantation forests, at annual rates exceeding 5%. Between 1992 and 2002, agricultural land use expanded in developing countries and held steady in developed countries (World Resources Institute, 2007b).

NATIONAL AND CROSS-NATIONAL IMPACTS

While conversions to agricultural use threaten biodiversity, loss of arable land also is a significant concern, globally as well as regionally. One region that has no overall shortage of agriculturally productive land is North America. Indeed, in some parts of the United States, too much land is under cultivation; land-conservation programs are designed to retire farm acreage through large parts of the Midwest and Great Plains. Other areas, however, are losing their capacity to produce food locally, especially near major metropolitan areas, whose patterns of sprawling development are consuming ever-increasing acreages, much of it prime farmland. A Brookings Institution analysis (Fulton et al., 2001) revealed that while the amount of urbanized land in the U.S. increased by 47% between 1982 and 1997, population growth was only 17%. Just 17 of the 281 metropolitan regions analyzed in the study experienced an increase in population density. Sprawl is less prevalent in Europe and Japan, where land has long been in comparatively short supply and development is more strictly controlled. But land-extensive development patterns are increasingly a concern even in countries where the supply of arable land already falls well short of national needs for food self-sufficiency. China, for example, is facing serious land-conversion issues associated with new housing developments for the elite, and highways, golf courses, resorts, and shopping centers built on prime farmland.

Sustainability, amenity, and ecological concerns are drivers of land-preservation efforts in and around major metropolitan regions, but most of the ecologically valuable and resource-rich land is located in rural and remote areas. These lands are threatened by forestry, ranching, mining, amenity migration, and intensive recreational uses. Rising global timber demand, as well as demand for oil palms for ethanol production, are creating enormous pressure for land conversion and intensive exploitation, especially in parts of Southeast Asia, South America, and Siberia. These demands are generated mainly in the developed countries, whose "ecological footprints" are proportionately enormous. The ecological footprint is a quantitative measure, expressed as the biologically productive area needed to provide food, energy, and material resources—as well as to absorb wastes—on such scales as the city, country, and region. [*See* Ecological Footprint.] While the footprint is actually a proxy for land impacts rather than a direct measure, it does give a sense of the huge disparities in the impacts that different societies have on the land base. The U.S. footprint, for example, is 109 global hectares per capita (ghp), while its "biocapacity" is estimated at only about 20 ghp. For Mongolia, by contrast, the respective figures are 27 and 190. Most of the world's poorer countries run modest to substantial ecological "surpluses" (Venetoulis and Talberth, 2006).

These imbalances among nations can be expressed in another way, as the "ecological shadows" cast by high-consuming countries. Japan's ecological shadow, for instance, has had devastating effects on Southeast Asia's forests. China now casts a very long shadow in Southeast Asia, the Congo and Amazon basins, and Siberia. This means that land preservation is an international issue, not only because wealthier countries can afford to bear a greater share of the costs, but also because they are responsible for a large proportion of the global impacts. It also means that land preservation in one country may be offset by its shadow impacts elsewhere. Japan is about two-thirds forested, with as much as 25% of its land in some kind of formally protected status. Though the ecological quality of much of that land may be marginal—indeed, plantation forests are widespread—Japan's forest lands are minimally exploited for timber today: its land impacts are transferred elsewhere. And while the Americas have more than 20% of their land base in protected status—high by global standards—the U.S. and its neighbors are responsible for major impacts within the region and around the globe.

PROTECTION STRATEGIES

Large protected areas are generally designated by national governments. Some of these are recognized internationally, in the form of World Heritage Areas, Biosphere Reserves, and Wetlands of International Importance (commonly known as Ramsar sites). But land protection is achieved in diverse ways: state, provincial, regional, and local governments all manage protected areas, and many preserved areas are under multiple levels of governmental administration. Moreover, not all preserved lands are managed by government agencies.

The cultivation of an individual and institutional land ethic can play a vital part in protecting lands and landscapes. In the United States, nonprofit organizations have assumed a markedly increased role in land protection in recent decades. As federal funding has shrunk, various public-private efforts have sought to fill the void. Land trusts and watershed conservancies, in particular, have experienced dramatic growth in numbers as well as acreage managed. Agreements with private landowners, generally in the form of conservation easements, are cost-effective and politically acceptable means for protecting lands. Financing comes also from local and state ballot initiatives. While ecological protection is the predominant value, lands are also protected to sustain working farms and forests, as well as highly valued amenity landscapes.

At the international level, wealthy countries are increasingly underwriting land preservation in poorer countries. Large international nongovernmental organizations (NGOs), such as The Nature Conservancy and Conservation International, are lead actors in these efforts. Conservation International (CI) focuses on biodiversity hotspots around the world; CI purchases lands, collaborates with governmental and nongovernmental stakeholders, and provides incentives for conservation management on private lands. CI's major funding partners include the Starbucks Coffee company, the World Bank, the WWF (formerly the World Wildlife Fund), the Global Environment Facility, the U.S. Agency for International Development, the government of Japan, several foundations, and many other national, multilateral, corporate, and nonprofit organizations.

Debt-for-nature swaps are, increasingly, accepted means for creating protected areas in developing countries. In exchange for debt-relief by the creditor nation, the debtor government agrees to set aside nature-reserve lands and adopt sustainable-management practices. NGOs such as CI, The Nature Conservancy, and WWF, contribute funds for debt relief. Begun in the 1980s, debt-for-nature swaps have found particular favor in Central and South America.

Forest certification also is affecting land management worldwide. Though forest certification programs come under frequent criticism for their limited reach and effectiveness, several national and international initiatives are in place. These programs promote sustainable forestry practices and may also prohibit logging on ecologically important lands or encourage logging on other less critical lands, such as plantation areas, where it is easier to meet sustainability conditions. The most expansive effort is managed by the Forest Stewardship Council (FSC), which works with a variety of corporate and nonprofit stakeholders to develop forest-product certification programs. Approximately 2% of the world's forested lands are covered by some kind of certification scheme, and certified acreages have increased dramatically since the mid-1990s. FSC-certified lands account for most certified forests in developing countries, while many other programs predominate in developed countries.

The greatest promise for protecting forest lands may be through carbon-offset initiatives. These programs can be debt-for-nature exchanges, or simply corporate or government payments—often part of developed-country emissions-trading schemes—that underwrite land protection. A *New York Times* article characterizes this phenomenon as "carbon ranching" (Powers and Hurowitz, 2007). The practice seems to be gaining momentum and will probably expand substantially in coming years. In exchange for foreign aid, the Democratic Republic of Congo recently cancelled 3 million acres of illegal forest concessions and may cancel as much as 12 to 15 million additional contracted acres. At the G8 summit in June 2007, a multistakeholder Forest Carbon Initiative was proposed.

Finally, efforts to reduce human-induced climate change may yield land-protection benefits. A United Nations report (Adeel et al., 2007) suggests that if desertification is not checked, there will be massive displacements of human populations. To the extent that forecasted climate changes are slowed, arable lands, coastal wetlands, and other critical lands may be preserved.

Land preservation, then, is important but immensely challenging. Across the globe, critical portions of the land base face threats from climate change, population migration, and growing demands for fossil fuels, biofuels, forest products, minerals, and arable land. Social and environmental justice issues emerge in skewed land-ownership patterns and indigenous land-rights issues, as well as in the many instances when land is confiscated—with little or no compensation to it occupants—for commercial centers, highways, golf courses, resorts, and even environmental improvements, such as Shanghai's green belt. But several of the initiatives described here bode well for the future of land preservation. Most promising is the role that preserved lands can play in carbon sequestration schemes and in buffering against the negative effects of a changing global climate.

BIBLIOGRAPHY

Adeel, Z., et al. *Re-thinking Policies to Cope with Desertification.* Hamilton, Ontario: United Nations University International Network on Water, Environment and Health, 2007.

Brewer, R. *Conservancy: The Land Trust Movement in America.* Lebanon, N.H.: University Press of New England, 2003.

Chape, S., et al. *2003 United Nations List of Protected Areas.* Gland, Switzerland, and Cambridge, U.K.: International Union for Conservation of Nature and Natural Resources and United Nations Environment Programme World Conservation Monitoring Centre, 2003. http://www.unep-wcmc.org/wdpa/unlist/2003_UN_LIST.pdf (accessed June 2, 2008).

Conservation International. *Conservation International 2004 Annual Report.* Washington, D.C.: Conservation International, 2004.

Convention on Biological Diversity. *Global Biodiversity Outlook 2.* Montreal: Convention on Biological Diversity, 2006. http://www.cbd.int/GBO2/ (accessed June 2, 2008).

Daniels, T., and M. Lapping. "Land Preservation: An Essential Ingredient in Smart Growth." *Journal of Planning Literature* 19 (2005): 316 329. DOI: 10.1177/0885412204271379.

Dauvergne, P. *Shadows in the Forest: Japan and the Politics of Timber in Southeast Asia.* Cambridge, Mass: MIT Press, 1997.

EastSouthWestNorth. 2007. *Conspicuous Consumption in China.* http://www.zonaeuropa.com/20041225_1.htm (accessed June 2, 2008).

Forest Certification Resource Center. 2007. *Introduction to Certification Programs.* http://www.metafore.org/index.php?p=introduction_to_Certification_Programs&s=167 (accessed June 2, 2008).

Fulton, William, Rolf Pendall, Mai Nguyen, and Alicia Harrison. *Who Sprawls Most? How Growth Patterns Differ across the U.S.* Washington, D.C.: Brookings Institution Center on Urban & Metropolitan Policy, 2001. http://www.knowledgeplex.org/kp/facts_and_figures/facts_and_figures/relfiles/bi_fulton_sprawls.pdf (accessed June 2, 2008).

Mason, R.J. *Collaborative Land Use Management: The Quieter Revolution in Place-Based Planning.* Lanham, Md: Rowman & Littlefield, 2008.

Planet Ark. 2007a. "Chinese Demand Drives Global Deforestation Crisis." June 12, 2007. http://www.planetark.com/dailynewsstory.cfm/newsid/42513/story.htm (accessed June 2, 2008).

Planet Ark. 2007b. "Congo to Cancel Logging Deals to Protect Forests." June 25, 2007. http://www.planetark.com/avantgo/dailynewsstory.cfm?newsid=42775 (accessed June 2, 2008).

Powers, W., and G. Hurowitz. "Home on the Rainforest." *New York Times* op-ed. June 16, 2007. http://www.nytimes.com/2007/06/16/opinion/16powers-hurowitz.html (accessed June 2, 2008).

Venetoulis, J., and J. Talberth. *Ecological Footprint of Nations: 2005 Update.* Oakland, CA: Redefining Progress, 2006. http://www.rprogress.org/publication/2006/Footprint%20of%20Nations%202005 pdf (accessed June 2, 2008).

World Resources Institute. 2007a. *Forests, Grasslands, and Drylands 2003.* http://www.earthtrends.wri.org/pdf_library/data_tables/for1_2003.pdf (accessed June 2, 2008).

World Resources Institute. 2007b. *Land Use and Human Settlements 2005.* http://www.earthtrends.wri.org/pdf_library/data_tables/for1_2005.pdf (accessed June 2, 2008).

—ROBERT J. MASON

LAND RECLAMATION

Land reclamation is the improvement of land that was damaged or left inferior by human action or by natural processes. The latter is the older sense. Synonyms coined recently and used primarily to denote the repair of areas damaged by human activity include land restoration, rehabilitation, and remediation. Older synonyms for reclamation denoting mostly the improvement of naturally poor or useless lands include land development, improvement, betterment, and beneficiation. Lands that invite reclamation are often described in such terms as badlands, disturbed lands, derelict lands, deserts, and wastelands. The closest antonym to "land reclamation" is land "degradation," though that term is used to refer more often to human-induced damage to land than to its devaluation by such natural states or processes as aridity or permanent or seasonal inundation.

Traditionally, the term "land reclamation" referred chiefly to two activities: irrigation and wetland drainage. In the first case, it denoted the transformation to productive use of land that the natural climate had left too dry for ordinary farming. In the second, it denoted the creation of solid ground for cultivation or construction out of "swamp" or "overflowed" lands that had been left by nature in a useless state halfway between land and water, and often unsightly and disease- and vermin-ridden. The development and improvement of other lands that fell into the category of waste or unproductive ground—moorland, forest, scrub land—was also often described as land reclamation. So was protection of land from periodic overflow through flood control, as was the fertilization with macro- or micronutrients of land previously ill-suited to productive use for farming or grazing. [*See* Irrigation.]

All of these transformations continue to occur on a large scale around the world, though they are now less widely seen as clear cases of land improvement by human intervention. As the side effects of irrigation, drainage, and similar interventions have become better understood, activities and outcomes still considered by some as reclamation, development, or improvement are now considered by others as land degradation. The terms have not changed in meaning—they still refer to the "bettering" of land—but the meanings of "better" and "worse" have changed. The principal forms of reclamation in the older sense, irrigation and wetland drainage, are discussed in separate entries in this volume. The focus of this entry is on the more recent meaning of land reclamation, the repair of lands damaged by human use.

Damage of this sort would ideally be avoided by proper use instead of being repaired by costly and imperfect efforts. There are often perverse incentives built into tax systems, property-rights structures, and other social institutions that promote careless and destructive exploitation. Correcting them and developing more efficient techniques for land use will help prevent degradation at the outset. Yet from a practical point of view, many activities will continue to degrade land for the foreseeable future. The immediate (if not long-term) returns from doing so are often too large to be forgone. Developing tools and strategies for reclamation helps to ensure that some areas, at least, can be repaired or restored in compensation for those lost, disturbed, or impoverished.

In the simplest sense, reclamation of this sort has long been ubiquitous in ordinary farming practice. When land depleted by cropping is fallowed for a season or longer, or when legumes are planted or fertilizers are applied to restore its fertility, it is being reclaimed. Other forms of agricultural impact are more profound than the removal of nutrients through harvesting and require more elaborate interventions to restore the land affected.

SALINIZATION

Soil salinization is a frequent unintended result of irrigation. It occurs when salts introduced in irrigation water or drawn up by it from the subsurface are left behind in the topsoil when the water evaporates. As salts accumulate, the land is rendered less productive and in extreme cases becomes entirely unfit for cultivation. Salinization is a serious problem in lands irrigated without the proper precautions. It has been a problem since antiquity in some regions. It may have been a cause of large-scale land abandonment in Mesopotamia several millennia ago. Areas severely affected by salinization are currently most extensive in the Middle East, South and Central Asia, and western North America. The problem is better avoided by proper design at the outset than remedied by subsequent reclamation efforts. Technical measures to deal with some forms of salinization do exist, but they tend to be expensive and difficult. Chief among them are chemical treatment and flushing of the soil with water to remove excess salinity, but the fresh water required for the latter is likely to be scarce, and drainage works may have to be constructed at the same time to avoid waterlogging. The operation may also pollute downstream waters. Growing salt-tolerant plants for productive use or for ground cover is a less ambitious means of adapting or adjusting land use to moderate salinization.

DESERTIFICATION

Another form of land degradation (associated chiefly with drylands) is desertification. The single most widely accepted indicator of desertification is a decline in plant biomass. Desertification is generally attributed to overgrazing of dryland vegetation, although the actual cause may in some cases be short- or medium-term fluctuations in climate. Technical measures for the reclamation of desertified land concentrate on the restoration of vegetation cover. Longer-term solutions address various underlying social factors, ranging from growth in human and livestock populations to the pressure of political and economic forces. [See Desertification.]

SURFACE MINING AND DUMPING OF WASTE MATERIALS

Far more drastic alterations are caused by surface mining, especially of stone, gravel, sand, and coal. These activities are often economically attractive if judged only by their immediate returns compared to those available from other uses of the land. They may, however, leave behind a disturbed or derelict landscape that is unsuited to uses such as agriculture, forestry, or construction. Mining may physically disrupt, chemically alter, or completely remove soil; reconfigure the terrain of the site; alter or destroy the previous plant cover and the conditions necessary for spontaneous revegetation; and create a scarred and unsightly landscape. It may release chemical pollutants into local waters through runoff and sediment erosion into streams. In extreme cases, it may create a risk to nearby areas of landslides caused by the slope failure of unstable accumulations of soil. Many of these problems are replicated in the dumping of large amounts of any sort of waste: mine spoil itself, dredge spoil from navigation channels, and the large quantities of coal ash produced by electric power plants.

Efforts to reclaim lands thus disturbed usually focus on restoring a vegetation cover. The addition of topsoil, if it had been removed, and the treatment of the ground with nutrients to repair deficiencies or counteract contamination—liming to neutralize acidity, for example—may have to be undertaken. The area may need to be colonized with plant and tree species selected for their tolerance of the physical and chemical conditions peculiar to its disturbed state. Successful revegetation lessens the problems of erosion, slope instability, and visual pollution, but the land may remain unsuitable for many uses.

Air pollution can have severe effects on nearby lands. Ore smelters release toxic trace metals and acid precipitation that may kill vegetation over large surrounding expanses and leave the land bare and prone to erosion. Like mines, smelters often produce returns so much higher than those of agriculture that their activities are allowed to continue more or less unchecked despite the damage they do to their surroundings. Many of the rehabilitative measures used to reclaim land disturbed by mining can be applied also to land damaged by smelter pollution. [See Mining.]

A small but rapidly increasing part of the world's land surface is devoted to human constructions such as buildings and pavement. Such lands left derelict by abandonment themselves represent a small but rapidly growing share of lands needing reclamation. Vacant buildings, lots, and tracts, and the larger phenomenon of central-city decay are problems in much of the developed world. They frequently occur in combination with a second and equally problematic process, that of rapid, sprawling land development on the metropolitan fringe that consumes open space and forest and agricultural land. Policy remedies for both problems include greenbelts and farmland preservation to stem sprawl and urban renewal programs and tax incentives for redevelopment of derelict central-city space. Chemical pollution is often a serious problem at derelict industrial sites, and measures for rehabilitating them include the removal and burial or incineration or the bioremediation in situ of the waste materials.

WETLANDS

Wetland drainage, one of the two classic forms of the reclamation of naturally inferior land, continues at a rapid rate worldwide, despite many measures intended to slow it. Yet the term "land reclamation" can now be applied also to a new form of change—wetland restoration or creation. The Netherlands, for centuries the world's leader in drainage, has in recent years begun a policy of returning large areas to their previous state. In the 1980s, the U.S. government adopted a policy of "no net loss" of wetlands to offset continued wetland losses judged necessary for various development activities. The benefits of creation and restoration include ones as direct and practical as streamflow and groundwater regulation and wildlife habitat; their success can also be measured by the degree to which they succeed in replicating the full range of natural wetland conditions.

ECOLOGICAL RESTORATION

Recent years have seen a rapid growth of interest in the in ecological restoration, which is the attempt to recreate as far as possible the landscapes and ecosystems that existed in an area prior to significant human disturbance. Restoration projects undertaken by ecologists have been useful as scientific experiments in shedding light on the variety of factors that help to form ecosystems and the conditions needed for their maintenance. At the same time, they have clarified some of the problems and paradoxes of restoration as a program of action. It is impossible to restore any previous ecosystem entirely, given all of the wider external environmental changes necessarily impinging on it. Species subsequently introduced to the area, for example, cannot be excluded from the restored landscape though they were not part of the original. Restoration projects have also underlined the need to choose some point in the natural history of an area to restore, and thus the dominance of human choice in the very act of attempting to restore nature. No piece of land has a single natural character or an inherent ecological identity; it always has a past consisting of many different ones.

Because different things may be desired of the land at any one time, land degradation and land reclamation are both largely in the eye of the beholder. The same projects of irrigation and wetland drainage may be classified in both ways by different observers. Many conflicts have therefore arisen over land reclamation in the newer sense of the term. Restrictions on resident and user populations in national parks and preserves, meant to restore and protect the land and its biota, may hinder activities vital to residents and may in a sense degrade the land by making it less productive. The most ambitious ecological restoration project to be discussed so far, that of converting much of the North American Great Plains to a "Buffalo Commons" closer to its preagricultural state has, not surprisingly, aroused the strongest antagonism in the region itself.

[*See also* Land Use; Salinization; *and* Wetlands.]

BIBLIOGRAPHY

Bradshaw, A.D., and M.J. Chadwick. *The Restoration of Land: The Ecology and Reclamation of Derelict and Degraded Land*. Berkeley, Calif.: University of California Press, 1980. A classic treatment of the repair of disturbed and derelict land.

Harris, J.A., P. Birch, and J. Palmer. *Land Restoration and Reclamation: Principles and Practice*. Harlow, U.K.: Longman, 1996. A fundamental technical text.

Jordan, W.R., III, M.E. Gilpin, and J.D. Aber, eds. *Restoration Ecology*. Cambridge and New York: Cambridge University Press, 1987. A classic survey of the chief issues in ecological restoration.

Mitsch, W.J., and S.E. Jørgensen. *Ecological Engineering and Ecosystem Restoration*. Hoboken, N.J.: Wiley, 2003.

Urbanks, K.M., N.R. Webb, and P.J. Edmonds, eds. *Restoration Ecology and Sustainable Development*. Cambridge and New York: Cambridge University Press, 1997. A fine recent collection addressing technical and social dimensions.

—William B. Meyer

LAND SURFACE PROCESSES

The study of rates of land-surface change has always been a central focus of geomorphologic research (Goudie, 1995). How important are such factors as climate and tectonic setting as controls of geomorphologic processes? To what extent are humans influencing landform development? What is the potential useful life of a particular engineering structure? How much time is required for a particular landscape to develop? What is the relative significance of different land-forming processes? And, how can environments be transformed by future environmental changes? We shall consider here some of these issues in the context of certain key exogenic geomorphologic mechanisms: weathering, general fluvial denudation, mass movements on slopes, glacial activity, and coastal change.

Two main types of weathering are recognized. Mechanical or physical weathering involves the breakdown of rock without a substantial chemical change in the minerals that make up the rock. It includes such processes as frost and salt weathering (caused by the expansion of ice and salt crystals respectively) and organic or biological processes such as root wedging. Chemical weathering, in which biological processes may play a major role, involves the decomposition of rock minerals through such processes as hydration, hydrolysis, oxidation and reduction, carbonation, and chelation. Both types of weathering may operate together, though in differing proportions and one may accelerate the other. For example, the physical disintegration of a rock will expose a greatly increased surface area to chemical attack.

Methods employed in the study of rates of weathering include analyses of soil and weathering-profile development on landforms or monuments of known age, laboratory simulations, and direct monitoring using instrumentation (e.g., microerosion meters and the reweighing of rock tablets embedded in the ground). On a global scale, the most important method of determining rates of weathering is to determine the amounts of dissolved material being transported in river water.

THE DISSOLVED LOAD OF RIVERS

Analysis of river discharge and the concentration of dissolved material in it makes it possible to establish both the rates of chemical denudation and the relative efficiency of mechanical and chemical erosion.

A detailed global analysis has been undertaken by Walling and Webb (1983), who assembled a database for 490 rivers in which pollution was absent or limited. The mean load was found to be 38.8 metric tons per square kilometer per year ($t\,km^{-2}\,yr^{-1}$), and values typically lie in the range 5–100 $t\,km^{-2}\,yr^{-1}$.

The data also demonstrated a weak positive relationship between annual dissolved load and mean annual runoff.

A partial explanation for the positive trend may be that increasing moisture availability increases the rate of chemical weathering and solute evacuation, but other factors control solute delivery, including temperature, seasonality, rock type, and vegetation. Of these, rock type may be the most important, for the dissolved loads of rivers draining igneous rocks are lower than those found in areas of sedimentary rocks.

A third major finding was that the transport of dissolved load to the oceans is on a global scale considerably less than the transport of particulates. The ratio is about 3.6:1. Values of the ratio range from over 100 to less than 0.5, and the particulate component exceeds the dissolved component in more than 60% of cases. Given that the chemical load may include a large input contributed by precipitation and that large amounts of particulate sediment may not be delivered through the catchment and into the oceans, Walling and Webb (1983, p. 16) believe that mechanical erosion may be of greater importance in landscape development than is indicated by a simple comparison of particulate and dissolved loads. Indeed, they believe that the ratio of 3.6:1 may need to be increased "by an order of magnitude in order to produce a meaningful estimate of the relative important of mechanical and chemical erosion" (p. 17).

High rates of chemical denudation are invariably observed in high mountains (Summerfield, 1991, p. 385), and minimal rates of chemical denudation are recorded in dry regions where runoff is low (Table 1). Rivers that drain semiarid regions have low rates of solute transport in relation to total transport. This contrasts markedly with basins from humid and subarctic regions which have high rates of solute transport in relation to total transport. In the case of the St. Lawrence River, the relatively high proportion carried in solution may be attributed to the large proportion of particulate sediment trapped in the Great Lakes.

Meybeck (1979; Table 2) attempted to classify rates of chemical denudation according to climatic zonation. As can be seen, the highest rates occurred in pluvial temperate zones, many of which have very high rainfall amounts associated with high relief conditions. Only slightly less important was the very humid tropical mountainous zone. But, surprisingly, the lowest rates occurred in dry environments (tundra and taiga, the seasonal tropics, and arid lands).

Meybeck (1987) has quantified the lithological control on rates of denudation that was considered by Walling and Webb to be one of the prime reasons for the weak relationship between climate and rate of denudation at the zonal scale. Drainage basins underlain by metamorphic and plutonic rocks tend to have lower values of chemical transport for a given runoff level than do volcanic rocks. The highest rates occur for sedimentary rocks. Meybeck also established a relative erosion rate normalized to the rate for granite: granite, gneiss, and mica schist, 1; gabbro and sandstone, 1.3; volcanics, 1.5; shales, 2.5; miscellaneous metamorphics (including serpentinites, marbles, and amphibolites), 5; carbonates, 12; gypsum, 40; rock salt, 80.

GENERAL FLUVIAL DENUDATION

General rates of fluvial denudation can be obtained by measurements of material carried by streams and of volumes of material deposited in lakes, reservoirs, and on continental shelves, by apatite fission-track dating, and by the use of cosmogenic nuclides. The first of these has been most useful for assessing global and regional rates.

The most comprehensive attempt to relate sediment yield to climate was that of Walling and Kleo (1979). They identified three zones in which rates may be especially high: the seasonal climatic zones of the Mediterranean type, monsoonal areas with large amounts of seasonal tropical rain, and semiarid areas (Figure 1).

A global map of suspended sediment yield was constructed by Walling (1987), based on more than 1,500 measuring stations (Figure 2). The pattern relates to the sediment yields from intermediate-sized basins of 10^4–10^5 square kilometers and is both generalized and complex. The high yields for the Mediterranean area, the southwestern United States, and parts of East Africa may be related to semiarid climatic conditions with seasonal rainfall and limited vegetation cover. On the other hand, the high sediment yields of the Pacific Rim may reflect the combined influence of high rainfall, tectonic instability, and high relief. Relief is a highly important control: high, steep areas in the Himalayas, Andes, Alaska, and the Mediterranean lands produce high yields. Low rates are evident for much of the old shield areas of northern Eurasia and North America, with their low relief and resistant substrates, and for equatorial Africa and South America, with their subdued topography and dense rainforest vegetation.

In some parts of the world, suspended sediment yields can be extraordinarily high (Walling, 1987), exceeding $10,000$ t km^{-2} a^{-1}. The probable reasons for such high values vary greatly and include the presence of erodible material (e.g. loess, glacial drift, volcanic ash), high relief and recent tectonic uplift, intense human pressures on the land surface which have caused accelerated erosion in the late Holocene, and either a semiarid climate (with a limited vegetation cover) or highly erosive rainfall regimes dominated by tropical storms or very high annual totals.

Most of the data discussed so far have involved primarily suspended sediment. Comparative data on bedload transport (transport of particulate material in the water immediately above the streambed) under different climatic conditions are sparse. This applies especially to the world's arid zones where, because of infrequent and unpredictable floods, there is a paucity of reliable field data. A study by Laronne and Reid (1993) in the Negev Desert, Israel, based on monitoring of bedload movement in during flash floods, indicates just how important continuous monitoring of bedloading in such environments can be. Their data show that ephemeral desert rivers could be up to 400 times more efficient at transporting coarse material than perennial rivers in humid zones. They argue that this may be because of the relative lack of bed armoring (a layer of rocks covering the streambed and inhibiting erosion) in desert streams. They suggest that the limited development of armoring could be a function of the rapid rise and fall in discharge that is

TABLE 1. Estimated Denudation Rate for the World's 35 Largest Drainage Basins Based on Solid and Solute Transport Rates

	Drainage area (10⁶ km²)	Total denudation (mm 1,000 a⁻¹)	Chemical* denudation (mm 1,000 a⁻¹)	Chemical denudation as % of total
Amazon	6.15	70	13	18
Zaire (Congo)	3.82	7	3	42
Mississippi	3.27	44	9	20
Nile	2.96	15	2	10
Paraná (La Plata)	2.83	19	5	28
Yenisei	2.58	9	7	80
Ob	2.50	7	5	70
Lena	2.43	11	9	81
Chang (Yangtze)	1.94	133	37	28
Amur	1.85	13	3	22
Mackenzie	1.81	30	10	33
Volga	1.35	20	13	64
Niger	1.21	24	11	47
Zambezi	1.20	31	3	11
Nelson	1.15	–	–	–
Murray	1.06	13	2	18
St. Lawrence	1.03	13	12	89
Orange	1.02	58	3	5
Orinoco	0.99	91	13	14
Ganges	0.98	271	22	8
Indus	0.97	124	16	13
Tocantins	0.90	–	–	–
Chari	0.88	3	1	29
Yukon	0.84	37	10	28
Danube	0.81	47	16	35
Mekong	0.79	95	20	21
Huang (Yellow)	0.77	529	11	2
Shatt-el-Arab	0.75	104	11	11
Rio Grande	0.67	9	3	38
Columbia	0.67	29	13	46
Kolyma	0.64	5	2	31
Colorado	0.64	84	6	7
São Francisco	0.60	–	–	–
Brahmaputra	0.58	677	34	5
Dnieper	0.50	6	5	88

*Allowance made for nondenudational component of solute loads.

SOURCE: After Summerfield, 1991, Table 15.6. Reprinted by permission of Pearson Education Limited.

characteristic of flash floods, the high rates of sediment transport, and the extended intervals of dormancy between flood events. These characteristics reduce the tendency toward the size-selective transport of clasts (rock fragments) and the winnowing of fine-grained material, both of which are thought to promote armoring in perennial channels.

Milliman (1990, 1991) has drawn attention to the particularly large amounts of sediment transported to the oceans from

TABLE 2. The Geographical Origins of Dissolved Loads to the Oceans and Variations of Chemical Erosion According to Morphoclimatic Region

Climatic region	Area of exoreic Runoff*	Exoreic Runoff[†]	Transport of Silica		Transport of Ions		Chemical erosion ($t\ km^{-2}\ a^{-1}$)
			Dissolved Load to Oceans ($10^6\ t\ a^{-1}$)	%	Dissolved Load to Oceans ($10^6\ t\ a^{-1}$)	%	
Tundra and taiga	20.0	10.7	15.0	3.9	466	13.1	14
Humid taiga	3.15	3.4	5.0	1.3	74	2.1	15.5
Very humid taiga	0.2	0.6	1.1	0.2	9	0.25	32
Pluvial temperate	4.5	15.3	45	11.8	540	15.4	80
Humid temperate	7.45	7.75	17.5	4.6	407	12.0	35
Temperate	6.7	3.35	9.4	2.5	301	8.8	28
Semi-arid temperate	3.35	1.05	2.7	1.0	130	3.7	24
Seasonal tropical	13.25	5.85	31.1	8.2	119	3.4	6.4
Humid tropical	9.2	8.85	38.2	10.2	239	8.0	15.5
Very humid tropical (plains)	6.9	18.45	78.6	20.8	165	4.8	22
Very humid tropical (mountains)	7.95	24.05	130	34.4	908	25.6	67
Total of tropical zone	37.3	57.2	278	73.6	1431	41.8	—
Arid	17.2	0.65	3.9	1.0	3457	2.8	3
Pluvial regions of strong relief	12.65	40	176	47	1457	42	≈74

*Percentage of total land surface area.   [†]Percentage of total exoreic runoff quantity.   SOURCE: After Meybeck, 1979.

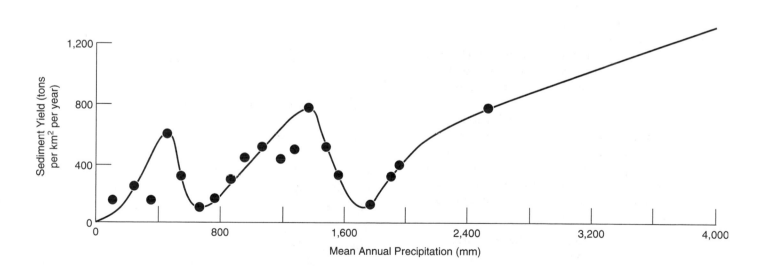

Land Surface Processes. FIGURE 1. Relationship between Mean Annual Sediment Yield and Mean Annual Precipitation.

(After Walling and Kleo, 1979.)

southeastern Asia and Oceania. These areas account for only about 15% of the land area draining into the oceans but contribute about 70% of the flux of suspended sediment. In contrast, rivers draining the Eurasian Arctic, a basin area similar in size to southern Asia and Oceania combined, contribute about two orders of magnitude less sediment.

Milliman and Syvitski (1992) believe that the sediment fluxes from small mountainous rivers, many of which discharge directly onto active continental margins, may have been largely neglected in the past, but that their contribution of sediment to the oceans may be very important. They point out, for example, that in North America the loads of the Susitna, Copper, Stikine,

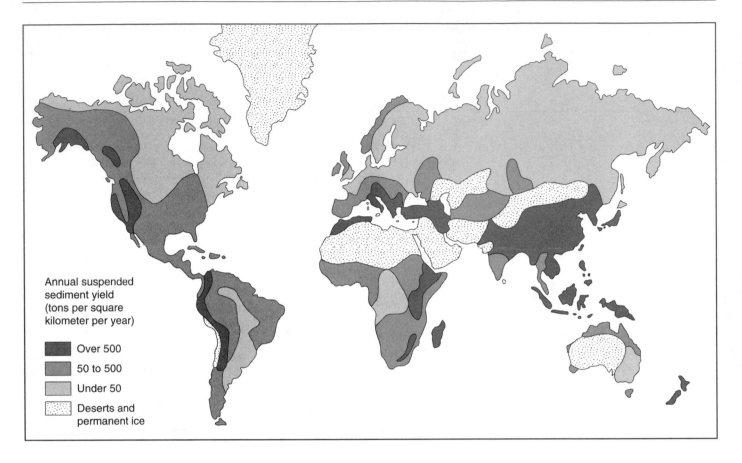

Land Surface Process. FIGURE 2. A Global Map of the Pattern of Specific Suspended Sediment Yield Based on Data from over 1,500 Measuring Stations.

(After Walling, 1987, Figure 4.4. Copyright John Wiley & Sons Limited. Reproduced with permission.)

and Yukon collectively exceed that of the Mississippi. In Europe the Seman River of Albania discharges more than twice as much sediment as do the Garonne, Loire, Seine, Rhine, Weser, Elbe, Oder, and Vistula combined.

It is probably topographic relief rather than elevation (altitude) per se that is the crucial control of the rate of denudation. There is no necessary relationship between elevation and either mean slope-gradient or local relief.

Sediment yield is scale-dependent, tending to be greater per unit area for small basins than for large, at least for basins up to 2,000 square kilometers. The basin-area effect may largely disappear in very large basins because the topographic controls tend to become less variable between basins at this scale. The inverse relationship is due to the following properties of smaller basins in relation to larger ones:

- They commonly have steeper gradients, which encourage more rapid rates of erosion.
- Small streams lack floodplains, which restricts sediment storage, resulting in a higher sediment-delivery ratio.
- Small basins are more likely to be blanketed by individual high-intensity storms, giving high maximum erosion rates per unit area.

The inverse relationship between sediment yield and basin area suggested above is not invariable. For example, Church and Slaymaker (1989) found a positive correlation between sediment and basin area in glaciated basins in British Columbia

at all scales up to 30,000 square kilometers (see also Owens and Slaymaker, 1992). They explained this by the secondary remobilization of Quaternary sediments along river valleys.

GLACIAL DENUDATION

Several methods have recently been used to measure amounts of glacial erosion:

- The use of artificial marks on rock surfaces later scraped by advancing ice.
- The installation of platens in front of an advancing glacier to measure abrasional loss.
- Measurements of the suspended, solutional, and bedload content of glacial meltwater streams and of the area of the respective glacial basins.
- The use of sediment cores from lake basins of known age that are fed by glacial meltwater.
- Reconstructions of preglacial or interglacial land surfaces.
- Estimates of the volume of glacial drift in a given region in comparison with the area of the source region of that drift.

The first four methods apply to present-day glacierized regions and the last two to regions of Pleistocene glaciation. It is not obvious whether the two different periods will yield comparable results, and thus whether it will be possible to use present-day rates of glacial denudation to make historical inferences. As Harbor and Warburton (1992, p. 751) have remarked, "During full-glacial times, … basins would have higher percentage glacier cover, but also far greater ice thickness, discharges, velocities, basal shear stresses, and basal water pressures." Modern glaciers, the majority of which are decaying and retreating, are not necessarily satisfactory analogues for the vastly more active and substantial glaciers and icecaps of full glacial times.

It is also difficult to know how much of the debris transported by glaciers was originally glacially entrained. Much material

---

Land Surface Processes. Hunza Valley, Pakistan.

The combination of climate and tectonics determines the rate of operation of geomorphological processes. In the Hunza Valley, rapid uplift, combined with a severe glacial climate at high altitudes and a desert climate at lower altitudes, mean that the river carries an enormous sediment load.

falls onto glaciers as a result of nonglacial processes (e.g., rockfalls). In some high-relief, high-altitude areas, rates of denudation might be high in the absence of glaciation.

Embleton and King (1968) suggested that erosion rates for active glaciers were 1,000 to 5,000 m³ per km² per year, several times greater than for rivers. However, they drew an important distinction between the role of glaciers and the role of icesheets on low-angle surfaces, suggesting that the latter would be relatively ineffective.

Andrews (1975) came to rather different conclusions than Embleton and King. He believed that a rate of erosion by active glaciers in the range 1,000–5,000 millimeters per thousand years (mm 1,000 a⁻¹) was probably too high by a factor of between 2 and 10 and that a more reasonable estimate was 50–1,000 mm 1,000 a⁻¹, broadly the same as for normal fluvial catchments. He noted, moreover, that most of the data on rates determined from current meltwater streams are biased in favor of high mountain environments and are largely restricted to valley glaciers whose bases are characterized by liquid water and by alternate freezing and thawing and the associated erosion. He argues (p. 122) that these "cannot be considered typical of values for the erosion of bedrock floors by a large ice sheet."

Drewry (1986) again stressed the inadequacy of data and presented some published data on erosion rates for selected glaciers based on the measurement of suspended-sediment transport and total particulate transport (suspended and bedload). The values range from 73 to 30,000 mm 1,000 a⁻¹ (with a mean of about 4,000 mm 1,000 a⁻¹).

An example of the use of stratigraphic methods to determine long-term rates of glacial erosion is provided by Bell and Laine (1985). They estimated the erosion effected by the glaciation of the Laurentide region of North America through a study of sediment volumes determined by seismic studies and Deep Sea Drilling Project boreholes. They calculated that over three million years—the approximate duration of mid-latitude glaciation in the Late Cenozoic—between 120 and 200 meters (400 and 650 feet) of erosion would be required over the glaciated Canadian Shield to produce the observed volume of sediment. This is equivalent to a rate of 40–67 mm 1,000 a⁻¹. The region was not, of course, glaciated throughout the whole three-million-year period, but even so, these rates are lower than most of the short-term rates determined from meltwater-load studies.

Geographical location is clearly an important control of the rate of glacial erosion. Some areas would have had characteristics that limited the power of glacial erosion (e.g., resistant lithologies, low relief, frozen beds), while other areas suffered severe erosion (e.g., nonresistant lithologies, proximity to former fast ice streams, thawed beds, etc.).

OTHER TYPES OF EXOGENIC CHANGE

In addition to the major types of denudation discussed so far are the changes that may take place on slopes and on coasts. There is a great deal of information on rates of soil movement on slopes and on the operation of processes such as soil creep (Young and Saunders, 1986). [*See* Soil Erosion.] There is likewise a great deal of information on rates of coastal change, including cliff retreat. Sunamura (1992), using data from many parts of the world, found a general lithological (rock-type) control of the rates of cliff recession over periods that generally last from 10 to 100 years: 10^{-3} to 10^{-2} meters per year (m a^{-1}) for limestone; 10^{-2} m a^{-1} for flysch, a sedimentary facies comprising marls, shales, sandstones, conglomerates, etc.; 10^{-1} to 1 m a^{-1} for Quaternary deposits; and 10 m a^{-1} for unconsolidated volcanic ejecta.

Rates of coastal erosion for the United States have been plotted by Dolan and Kimball (1985). Retreat is dominant around much of the coastline, particularly the eastern seaboard, much of which is retreating at between 0.1 and 2.9 m a^{-1}. There are, however, a few local stretches (e.g., in Georgia and North Carolina) where accretion has been taking place, and there are a few small stretches where the rate of retreat is 3–5 m a^{-1}. The Gulf Coast is dominated by retreat, most notably in the vicinity of the Mississippi delta and to its west. The rates of change appear to be markedly lower on the West Coast, probably because of its very different tectonic and lithological situation from the Atlantic and Gulf coasts. The rates of retreat are thus almost always less than 1 m a^{-1}. Some accretion has been taking place in southern California and along the southern coast of Washington State, but even in these areas there are locations where cliff retreat is occurring at rates of up to 0.5 m a^{-1}. Dolan and Kimball found that coasts with fine-grained sediments, deltas, and mudflats that offer low levels of resistance to wave attack have the highest mean erosion rates (approximately 2.0 m a^{-1}). Most sandy beaches and barrier islands erode at slightly lower rates (roughly 0.8 m a^{-1}).

HUMAN-INDUCED CHANGES

This discussion of rates of land surface process operation has been concerned essentially with long-term rates of change under predominantly natural conditions, but natural rates have been greatly modified by human activities. [*See* Anthropogeomorphology *and* Desertification.] Sediment yields have been transformed by land-use and land-cover changes, rates of weathering have been modified by such processes as acid deposition, mass movements on slopes have been generated by such actions as loading and undercutting, coasts have suffered accelerated erosion because of sediment starvation created by engineering structures (e.g., dams), and wind erosion has been stimulated by vegetation removal and surface disturbance.

[*See also* Coastlines; Erosion; Mobile Earth; *and* Natural Hazards.]

BIBLIOGRAPHY

Andrews, J.T. *Glacial Systems: An Approach to Glaciers and their Environments.* North Scituate, MA: Duxbury, 1975.
Bell, M., and E.P. Laine. "Erosion of the Laurentide Region of North America by Glacial and Glaciofluvial Processes." *Quaternary Research* 23 (1985), 154–174. DOI: 10.1016/0033-5894(85)90026-2.
Church, M., and O. Slaymaker. "Disequilibrium of Holocene Sediment Yield in Glaciated British Columbia." *Nature* 337 (1989), 452–454. DOI: 10.1038/337452a0.
Dolan, R., and S. Kimball. "Map of Coastal Erosion and Accretion." In *National Atlas of the United States of America.* Reston, Va.: U.S. Geological Survey, 1985.
Drewry, D. *Glacial Geologic Processes.* London: Arnold, 1986.

Embleton, C., and C.A.M. King. *Glacial and Periglacial Geomorphology.* London: Arnold, 1968.
Goudie, A.S. *The Changing Earth: Rates of Geomorphological Processes.* Oxford, U.K., and Cambridge, Mass.: Blackwell, 1995, p. 302. A general review of available information on a wide spectrum of geomorphologic processes.
Harbor, J., and J. Warburton. "Glaciation and Denudation Rates." *Nature* 356 (1992), 751. DOI: 10.1038/356751a0.
Laronne, J.B., and I. Reid. "Very High Rates of Bedload Sediment Transport by Ephemeral Desert Rivers." *Nature* 336 (1993), 148–150. DOI: 10.1038/366148a0.
Meybeck, M. "Concentrations des eaux fluviales en éléments majeurs et apports en solution aux océans." *Revue de Géologie Dynamique et de Géographie Physique* 21 (1979), 215–246.
Meybeck, M. "Global Chemical Weathering of Surficial Rocks Estimated from River Dissolved Loads." *American Journal of Science* 287 (1987), 401–428.
Milliman, J.D. "Fluvial Sediment in Coastal Seas: Flux and Fate." *Nature and Resources* 26 (1990), 12–22.
Milliman, J. "Flux and Fate of Fluvial Sediment and Water in Coastal Seas." In *Ocean Margin Processes in Coastal Change*, edited by R.F.C. Mantouva, J.-M. Martin, and R. Wollest. Chichester, U.K., and New York: Wiley, 1991.
Milliman, J.D., and J.P.M. Syvitski. "Geomorphic/Tectonic Control of Sediment Discharge to the Ocean: The Importance of Small Mountainous Rivers." *Journal of Geology* 100 (1992), 525–544.
Owens, P., and O. Slaymaker. "Late Holocene Sediment Yields in Small Alpine and Subalpine Drainage Basins, British Columbia." *IAHS Publication* 209 (1992), 147–154.
Summerfield, M.A. *Global Geomorphology.* Harlow, U.K.: Longman; New York: Wiley, 1991.
Walling, D.E. "Rainfall, Runoff and Erosion of the Land: A Global View." In *Energetics of Physical Environment*, edited by K. J. Gregory. Chichester, U.K., and New York: Wiley, 1987, pp. 89–117.
Walling, D.E., and B.W. Webb. "The Dissolved Loads of Rivers: A Global Overview." International Association of Hydrological Sciences Publication 141 (1983), 3–20.
Walling, D.E., and A.H.A. Kleo. "Sediment Yields of Rivers in Areas of Low Precipitation: A Global View." International Association of Hydrological Sciences Publication 128 (1979), 479–493.
Young, A., and I. Saunders. "Rates of Surface Processes and Denudation." In *Hillslope Processes*, edited by A.D. Abrahams, pp. 1–27. Boston: Allen and Unwin, 1986.

—ANDREW S. GOUDIE

LAND USE

Change in land use and land cover is a central component of global environmental change. It significantly affects the structure and function of the biosphere through its impact on terrestrial ecosystems and global biogeochemical cycles. Land-use and land-cover change also affects almost sustainability, biodiversity, disease vectors, potable water sources, and agricultural production. The central importance of land use and land-cover changes stems from humankind's derivation of the majority of resources for its material existence and well-being from the surface of the earth. In addition, the history of the human-Earth relationship is one of ever increasing pace, magnitude, and spatial reach of changes in the biosphere, including the land surface (Meyer and Turner, 1994).

LAND USE AND LAND COVER

"Land cover" refers to the biophysical condition of the terrestrial surface of the Earth. Forests, grasslands, wetlands, deserts, and settlements are broad categories of land cover. "Land use" refers to the human management of the biophysical environment. This management may be direct and highly manipulative, as in farming, or obscured through decisions to preserve or not to develop, as in the case of biosphere reserves or lands perceived as marginal and left "underused." Cultivation, pastoralism, recreation, nature reserves, transportation infrastructure, and housing are broad categories of land use.

Management of land covers in order to extract resources is ancient and probably began with the use of fire in the hunt of wildlife. Burning for this purpose may have contributed to worldwide Quaternary extinctions (Martin and Klein, 1984), and to the extension of grasslands and fire-dominated ecosystems in Africa, Australia, and elsewhere (Pyne, 1995). Large-scale use and cover changes, however, awaited the domestication of biota, the "agricultural revolution." Evolving in its complexity and reach, the worldwide effects of this agrotechnological transformation were dramatic, if difficult to measure. Between 1700 and 1980, as much as 1,162,000 hectares of forest cover, 72,000 hectares of grassland (Richard, 1990), and an unestimated area

of wetlands (Williams, 1990) had been converted to farmland throughout the world. These figures do not consider the apparently large land area devoted to shifting cultivation—cycling between crops, brush, and forest—which may have been far more prevalent than previously believed in vast reaches of the tropics. Indeed, some regions of the world, especially in the Americas, are only today beginning to be used as extensively for cultivation as they were before the global expansion of European cultures and economies in the fifteenth century (Denevan, 1992; Turner and Butzer, 1992). Early livestock activities also had significant impacts on use and cover through the use of fire, as pastoralists sought to increase the forageable biomass for their herds.

European colonialism from the fifteenth century to the nineteenth profoundly affected global land uses and covers through the transoceanic transfer of flora, fauna, people, diseases, and technologies (Crosby, 1986). Crop species exchanges, especially between the Western and Eastern Hemispheres, forever changed dietary patterns and, with them, land-use strategies and land covers. Foremost among these changes were the spread of the plow and European livestock. The plow gave plants access to nutrients stored deep within soils and opened American grasslands to extensive cultivation. The introduction of horses, cattle, and sheep, meanwhile, changed uses and cover across a wide range of environments.

Land Use. Effects of Over-grazing.

Changes in land use and land cover are two of the main drivers of environmental change in the world today. In central Zimbabwe at St Michael's Mission, over-grazing has exposed a valley floor to erosion, producing a series of large gullies.

The pace, magnitude, and spatial reach of land use and land cover change continued to escalate during the Industrial Revolution. As the industrial world stretched its reach, the global synergism between technological capacity, population, and affluence increased dramatically, as did the demand for food, fiber, and living space. The resulting changes in land use and land cover were key elements in promoting an even more dramatic population growth in the middle of the twentieth century. In the nineteenth century, massive land use and land cover changes took place in North America and Australia, where cultivation and livestock became the dominant land uses, forcing land-cover change. By the middle of the twentieth century, the major trends were toward increased intensification of use in the middle latitudes and semitropics and, more recently, widespread deforestation of the tropics and Siberia (Richards, 1990). Intensification is registered by the spread of irrigated cultivation (cautiously estimated at about 2.5 million square kilometers; L'vovich et al., 1990, p. 242), especially that of wet rice (a large source of methane, CH_4), and the adoption of modern hybrids and their demands for fertilizers, herbicides, and pesticides that affect various critical trace cycles (e.g., methane, nitrogen dioxide; Dale, 1997), as well as tropospheric pollution (Chameides et al., 1994). And while the developed world undergoes forestation, especially in western Europe and northeastern North America, international agricultural and timber markets shift production to lower-cost areas of the tropics or Siberia. Even where command economies remain intact, such as China, significant changes in land use and land cover remain, caused by increasing stress on land resources.

CURRENT STATE

The current global state of different land uses and covers is not well known, despite international programs for global observations from satellites and other remotely sensed imagery. The Intergovernmental Panel on Climate Change (Leemans et al., 1996), for example, concludes that various aggregate land-cover global datasets disagree by as much as 2.5 million hectares, a margin of error that increases significantly if the location of the different land use and covers is considered. Global ground-based inventories collected by international agencies rely on country-produced information, frequently inaccurate and politicized. Nevertheless, global land-use and land-cover changes appear to be increasing dramatically, with variations in kind and location.

If the current trajectories of change continue well into the twenty-first century, as seems likely, most significant changes in land use and land cover, independent of potential climate warming, will probably be: (1) the expansion of urban and periurban (suburban) settlement, including roads and recreation spaces, everywhere but especially in Asia and frequently at the cost of prime agricultural lands; (2) increasing forest cover in the periurban developed world and decreasing agricultural uses of marginal lands; (3) the loss of natural wetlands to settlement and agriculture and the growth of anthropogenic wetlands, especially in the developed world; (4) the intensification of land management in agriculture, from satellite- and computer-assisted farming to the spread of modern-input, wet rice

cultivation; (5) significant timber extraction in tropical and Siberian forests; (6) large-scale tropical deforestation; (7) the expansion of mining in frontier lands; (8) increasing livestock activities in developing regions; and (9) near-term stress on semi-arid landscapes by impoverished peoples and by government-sponsored irrigation. As the twenty-first century progresses, little land will remain unclaimed or not under some form of management, even if set aside as reserves. [*See* Agriculture and Agricultural Land.]

IMPLICATIONS FOR GLOBAL CHANGE

The past and current trends in land use and land cover have significant implications for global environmental change. Use and cover, for example, serve as sources and sinks of trace gases (e.g., deforestation and forestation). In 1980, 1,500 petagrams (1 petagram equals 10^{15} grams, or one billion metric tons) of carbon were estimated to be stored in the soil and another 560 petagrams in biomass (Houghton and Skole, 1990). Human uses (e.g., plowing, planting, deforesting) release this carbon to the atmosphere, while forestation takes it back. In the late twentieth century, approximately 50% of human-released CO_2 in the atmosphere was attributable to changes in land use and land cover. Industrial production and consumption now dominate carbon emissions, but land changes contribute as much as 30% (Houghton and Skole, 1990) and are the largest source of human-released methane, mass for mass the most potent greenhouse gas. The condition of global land use and cover also affects the hydrologic cycle, especially through impacts on the Walker circulation in the atmosphere over the Pacific (Henderson-Sellors and Gornitz, 1984). Finally, human uses of the land may usurp as much as 40% of the Earth's net primary productivity (Vitousek et al., 1990).

Impacts on biochemical cycles are more than matched by those on landscape fragmentation and biotic diversity. The fragmentation of tropical forests into small patches may endanger their function, productivity, and diversity (e.g., Laurance et al., 1997). The fracturing of landscapes in general by complex combinations of cropping, grazing, and settlement uses, especially in periurban areas, raises serious questions about species migration in the face of potential climate change (Root and Schneider, 1995). Also, the transformation of complex ecosystems, such as wetlands and tropical forests, into biotically simple intensive cropping or grazing systems leads to soil degradation and loss and to increased fluvial sedimentation. For example, intensive land uses may lead to salinization, an important and difficult-to-reverse form of land degradation. These processes tend to decrease biotic diversity, either directly by anthropogenic changes in the vegetation or indirectly through the regeneration of vegetation. Habitat loss (land-cover change) is estimated to lead to the annual loss of 14,000 to 40,000 species (Hughes, Daily, and Ehrlich, 1997), a rate labeled by some as "mass extinction" (Myers, 1997).

With the movement of the science and policy of global change toward the sustainability of the human-environment relationship, the prominence of changing land uses and covers increases (Vitousek, 1994). The sustainability principle implies the maintenance of an increasing human population at higher levels of material consumption with minimal impacts and drawdowns on the biosphere. These aims are largely achieved in land-based production systems in economic contexts in which it is difficult to reconcile the often incongruent environmental impacts between individual actions and social benefits and between immediate and longer-term needs. It is increasingly difficult to identify which land-use systems are sustainable because of "substitutability"—the availability of replacements for nature, land, labor, and capital. The environmentally sustainable becomes intimately intertwined with the economically viable.

THE ARAL SEA

These issues notwithstanding, changes in land use and cover involve not only "hot spots" of environmental degradation but also critical regions of human-environment relationships—those in which the trajectory of change is toward environmental drawdowns linked to the decreasing material condition of the occupants (Kasperson, Kasperson, and Turner, 1995). The death of the Aral Sea is perhaps the most dramatic modern-day case of human-environment collapse caused by land use. Not only were the sea's area and volume reduced in the late twentieth century by 60% and 66%, respectively, its once thriving fishing industry is also dead, symbolized by the decaying fishing fleet stranded in the sands that were once the lake's margin (Kotlyakov, 1991; Micklin, 1988). These impacts are directly related to the development of massive and poorly constructed irrigation systems on the two rivers that sustain the Aral Sea. The cropping systems were so mismanaged, and their efficiency in terms of water use and production so poor, that farming was sustainable only through state subsidies, and their chemical inputs were so inappropriate that infant mortality rose, apparently from contamination of potable water. Yet these immediate land-use causes hide others embedded more deeply in the fabric of the command economy that conceived and orchestrated the Aral Sea irrigation systems: state needs for stable international currencies, unchecked state authority, distant production and management decisions, and rapid local population growth demanding employment opportunities.

ASSESSMENT

The synergistic complexity of the changes causing the Aral Sea crisis typify those of case-specific land use and land-cover change everywhere. They tend to be lost, however, as the spatial and temporal scale of analysis enlarges. Over the long term and at regional and global scales, the so-called PAT variables (population, affluence, and technology) move to the statistical forefront (Meyer and Turner, 1992). The explanatory separation of the short term and local from the long term and global is foreboding: it illustrates divergent modes of understanding. Those studying the long-term global condition and seeking to model and project human-environment impacts typically find power in PAT and related variables. Others focus on more localized effects (e.g., recent regional changes), and consider different causal variables, such as policy and institutional limitations.

The two positions need not be as polarized as they have been in the past, and various integrations are under way in regionally scaled projects designed to elucidate their connections.

[*See also* Albedo; Biological Diversity; Biomes; Deforestation; Desertification; Ecosystems; Fire and Global Warming; Forestation; Human Impacts; International Geosphere-Biosphere Programme; International Human Dimensions Programme on Global Environmental Change (IHDP); Land Preservation; Land Reclamation; Parks and Preserves; Sustainable Growth; United Nations Environment Programme; *and* Wilderness and Biodiversity.]

BIBLIOGRAPHY

Chameides, W.L., et al. "Growth of Continental-Scale Metro-Agro-Plexes, Regional Ozone Pollution, and World Food Production." *Science* 264 (1994), 74–77. DOI: 10.1126/science.264.5155.74.

Crosby, A.W. *Ecological Imperialism: The Biological Expansion of Europe 900–1900.* Cambridge and New York: Cambridge University Press, 1986.

Dale, V.H. "The Relationship between Land-Use Change and Climate Change." *Ecological Applications* 7 (1997), 753–769. DOI: 10.1890/1051-0761(1997)007[0753:TRBLUC]2.0.CO;2.

Denevan, W.M. "The Pristine Myth: The Landscape of the Americas in 1492." *Annals Association of American Geographers* 82 (1992), 369–385.

Henderson-Sellers, A., and V. Gornitz. "Possible Climatic Impacts of Land Cover Transformations, with Particular Emphasis on Tropical Deforestation." *Climate Change* 6 (1984), 231–257. DOI: 10.1007/BF00142475.

Houghton, R.A., and D.L. Skole. "Carbon." In *The Earth as Transformed by Human Action: Global and Regional Changes in the Biosphere over the Past 300 Years,* edited by B.L. Turner, et al., pp. 393–408. Cambridge: Cambridge University Press, 1990.

Hughes, J.B., G.C. Daily, and P.C. Ehrlich. "Population Diversity: Its Extent and Extinction." *Science* 278 (1997), 689–692. DOI: 10.1126/science.278.5338.689.

Kasperson, J.X., R.E. Kasperson, and B.L. Turner II. *Regions at Risk: Comparisons of Threatened Environments.* Tokyo: United Nations University Press, 1995.

Kotlyakov, V.M. "The Aral Sea Basin: A Critical Environmental Zone." *Environment* 33.1 (1991), 4–9, 36–38.

Laurance, W.F., et al. "Biomass Collapse in Amazonian Forest Fragments." *Science* 278 (1997), 1117–1118. DOI: 10.1126/science.278.5340.1117.

Leemans, R., et al. "Mitigation: Cross-Sectoral and Other Issues." In *Impacts Adaptation and Mitigation Options: Working Group 2 Contribution to IPCC 2nd Assessment Report,* edited by R.T. Watson, M.C. Zinyower, and R.H. Moss, pp. 799–819. Cambridge and New York: Cambridge Univeristy Press, 1996.

L'vovich, M.I., et al. "Use and Transformation of Terrestrial Water Systems." In *The Earth as Transformed by Human Action: Global and Regional Changes in Biosphere over the Past 300 Years,* edited by B. L. Turner II, et al., pp. 236–252. Cambridge and New York: Cambridge University Press, 1990.

Martin, P.S., and R.G. Klein, eds. *Quaternary Extinctions: A Prehistoric Revolution.* Tuscon: University of Arizona Press, 1984.

Meyer, W.B., and B.L. Turner II. "Human Population Growth and Global Land-Use/Cover Change." *Annual Review of Ecology and Systematics* 23 (1992), 39–61. DOI: 10.1146/annurev.es.23.110192.000351.

Meyer, W.B., and B.L. Turner II, eds. *Changes in Land Use and Land Cover: A Global Perspective.* Cambridge and New York: Cambridge University Press, 1994.

Micklin, P.P. "Desiccation of the Aral Sea: A Water Management Disaster in the Soviet Union." *Science* 241 (1988), 1170–1176. DOI: 10.1126/science.241.4870.1170.

Myers, N.J. "Mass Extinction and Evolution." *Science* 278 (1997), 597–598. DOI: 10.1126/science.278.5338.597.

Pyne, S.J. *World Fire: The Culture of Fire on Earth.* New York: Holt, 1995.

Richards, J.F. "Land Tranformation." In *The Earth as Transformed by Human Action: Global and Regional Changes in Biosphere over the Past 300 Years,* edited by B.L. Turner II, et al., pp. 163–177. Cambridge and New York: Cambridge University Press, 1990.

Root, T.L., and S.H. Schneider. "Ecology and Climate: Research Strategies and Implications." *Science* 269 (1995), 331–341. DOI: 10.1126/science.269.5222.334.

Turner, B.L., II, and K.W. Butzer. "The Columbian Encounter and Land-Use Change." *Environment* 43 (1992), 16–20, 37–44.

Vitousek, P.M., P.R. Ehrlich, A.H. Ehrlich, and P. Matson. "Human Appropriation of the Products of Photosynthesis." *BioScience* 36 (1990), 368–373.

Williams, M., ed. *Wetlands: A Threatened Landscape*. Oxford, U.K., and Cambridge, Mass.: Blackwell, 1990.

—B. L. Turner II and Eric G. Keys

LITTLE ICE AGE IN EUROPE

The Little Ice Age in Europe was a period of several centuries during the last millennium, in which glaciers grew and their fronts oscillated about advanced positions. [*See* Holocene.] The term refers to the behavior of glaciers, not the climatic circumstances that caused them to expand. The Little Ice Age was not a time of prolonged, unbroken cold; in Europe, certain periods within it (e.g., 1530–1560 CE) were almost as benign as the twentieth century. European annual mean temperatures over the whole period varied by less than 2°C, although there were particularly cold years or clusters of years. Very cold decades—the 1590s and 1690s, for example—saw prolonged snow cover, frozen rivers, and extensive sea ice around Iceland. The characteristics, meteorological causes, and physical and human consequences of this period, which was global in its impact, can be traced in the most detail in Europe. Here, the availability of historical data and concentrated field investigations have permitted the reconstruction of many glacier chronologies. Documentary information, ranging from ice cover around Iceland, sea surface temperatures, and the state of fisheries in the North Atlantic to the timing of the rye harvest in Finland and the incidence of drought in Crete, is unusually substantial (Figure 1). Deliberate monitoring of glacier behavior, initiated in Switzerland in 1880, and some exceptionally long series of meteorological measurements, including that reconstructed for central England (Manley, 1974), assist interpretation of earlier, more fragmentary information.

CHRONOLOGY

The Little Ice Age has commonly been seen as occurring during the last three hundred years, during which glaciers from Iceland and Scandinavia to the Pyrenees have advanced, in some cases across pastures or near high settlements. Evidence is accumulating, however, that these advances, culminating in the seventeenth and nineteenth centuries, were preceded by others of comparable magnitude, culminating in the fourteenth century (Holzhauser, 1995). The intervening period was not sufficiently long, and the effect of loss of ice volume over gain was not great enough, to cause withdrawal to positions held in the tenth to early thirteenth centuries. It is therefore logical to see the whole period from about the mid-thirteenth century to the beginning of recession in the late nineteenth and early twentieth centuries as one Little Ice Age. It was the most recent of several century-scale fluctuations that affected Europe during the Holocene (the period extending from 10,000 BP to the present).

GLACIAL ADVANCE

Glaciers grow when accumulation of snow and ice exceeds loss. The primary controls are temperature, especially in summer, and accumulation, especially in winter. Temperatures were not low through the entire Little Ice Age; warmer and colder, wetter and drier decades followed each other. Advances occurred when volumes increased sufficiently for the lowest parts of glaciers near their fronts to be affected. Mapping and dating of moraines makes it possible to trace many past fluctuations in terminal position and extent. Moraines are accumulations of rock debris, formed alongside glacier tongues or around their fronts when they halt for a time or advance, pushing debris before them. It is because the three main culminations of the Little Ice Age were on a similar scale that the physical evidence from the earlier part of the Little Ice Age has only been recognized as long-concealed evidence has been exposed during ice recession (Grove, 2004).

THE ALPS

The glacial history of the Alps is outstandingly rich because of the wealth of documentary and pictorial evidence as well as extensive dating of moraines and stratigraphic sections (Holzhauser and Zumbühl, 1996). Because glaciers have frequently extended below treelines, wood, sometimes still in situ, is often found beneath or within moraines, permitting radiocarbon dating and sometimes making absolute dating possible by allowing correlation with tree-ring chronologies. In Scandinavia, especially in the north, less documentary evidence is available, so greater reliance has to be placed on moraine-dating using soil or plant samples and lake sediments of glacial origin. Lichenometric dating of moraines by the sizes of lichens of species with known growth rates has helped in disentangling Scandinavian glacial history, but it has important limitations, particularly because it depends on the existence of dated surfaces for construction of growth curves over time. The glacial history of the Pyrenees is currently known only from the late eighteenth century, and chronologies from elsewhere in southern and eastern Europe are even more fragmentary.

The most complete fluctuation history of any glacier in the world is that of the Grosser Aletsch glacier in the Swiss canton of Valais, achieved by assembling data from absolutely dated tree stumps in situ, the heights and radiocarbon dates of numerous samples found in lateral positions above the glacier surface, and modern measurements. The Aletsch front advanced as far in the fourteenth as in the seventeenth and nineteenth centuries

Little Ice Age in Europe. Figure 1. Locations Mentioned in the Text.

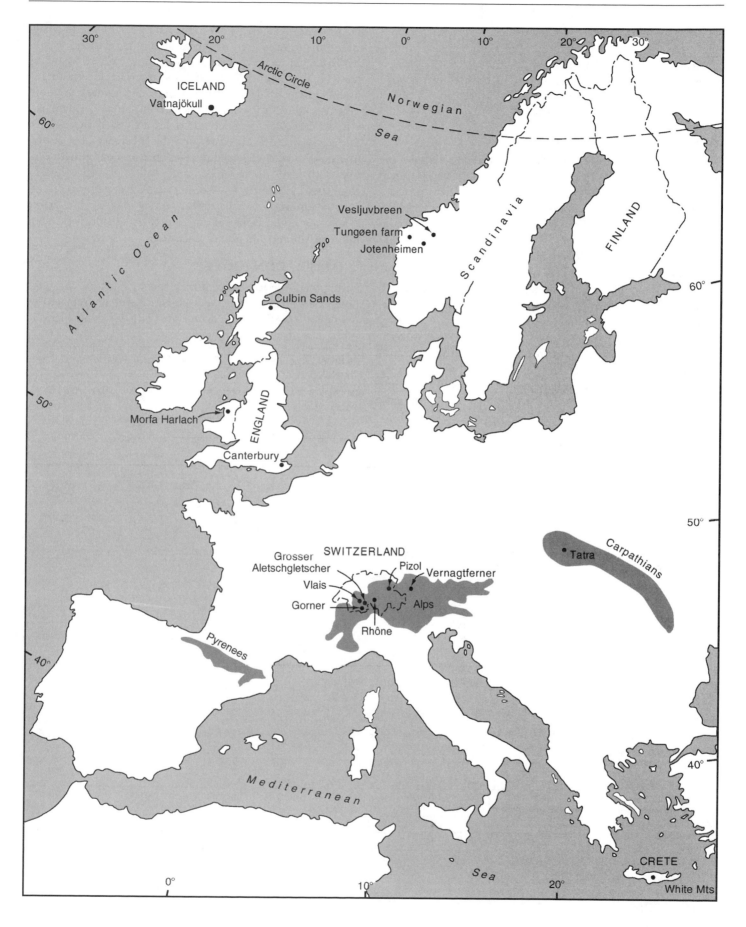

30°   20°   10°   0°   10°   20°   30°

Arctic Circle

ICELAND
Vatnajökull

Norwegian

Sea

Atlantic Ocean

60°

Vesljuvbreen

Tungøen farm
Jotenheimen

Scandinavia

FINLAND

60°

Culbin Sands

ENGLAND

50°

Morfa Harlach

Canterbury

50°

Carpathians

Tatra

SWITZERLAND
Grosser
Aletschgletscher   Pizol
Vlais   Vernagtferner
Gorner   Alps
Rhône

Pyrenees

40°

Mediterranean

40°

Sea

CRETE

White Mts

0°   10°   20°

(Holzhauser, 1984). Other large Swiss valley glaciers, including the Rhône and the Gorner, advanced to similar extents in the fourteenth century (Holzhauser and Zumbühl, 1996). Variations since the sixteenth century can be traced from contemporary documentary accounts, pictures, and measurements in even greater detail than their predecessors (Figure 2).

SCANDINAVIA AND ICELAND

The history of the Grosser Aletsch can be taken as a model for the behavior of European glaciers, although the dates at which advances began and ended varied slightly from glacier to glacier. Within this framework, exceptions and variations are caused by the sizes and response times of glaciers, particular locational and climatic influences, and abnormal flow characteristics. In Iceland, many glaciers did not reach their maximum extents until the late nineteenth century. The outlets of Jostedalsbreen in western Norway, the largest icecap in continental Europe, did not expand as much in the fourteenth or sixteenth centuries as they did in the eighteenth, probably because of the time required for the ice mass to accumulate (Grove, 1988). The glaciers of western Scandinavia obtain more nourishment from westerly air streams than do those in the east, and so may advance, as in recent years, while those to the east are still dwindling in response to rising temperatures. Because of favorable combinations of altitude, relief, and aspect, small, high-altitude cirque glaciers such as Vesljuvbreen in Jotunheimen (in southern Norway) or Pizol in

the Swiss Alps (Figure 1) are immediately responsive to small-scale climatic variations. Advances of surging glaciers, such as the Vernagtferner in Austria and several in Iceland, including many outlets of Vatnajökull, Europe's largest ice sheet, relate to instability associated with bed shape and temperature conditions rather than directly to climatic fluctuations. But the general pattern of Little Ice Age fluctuations has extended right across Europe, as might be expected from the coherence of measurements of frontal change and mass balance in the twentieth century (Grove 1988, fig. 6.7). Large valley glaciers typically lengthened by as much as 1–2 kilometers. A clear pattern emerges from the timing of advance, retreat, and stationary phases across all the monitored fronts of alpine glaciers in Europe, despite minor variations from glacier to glacier.

CLIMATIC CONTROLS

During the Little Ice Age centuries, zonal circulation, bringing moist, maritime air from the west, was frequently replaced by meridional (north-south) circulation with blocking highs in

Little Ice Age in Europe. FIGURE 2. Frontal Positions of Lower Grindelwald, 1590–1970.

Note the minor fluctuations of the front during phases of glacier extension and during retreat.
(From Grove, 1988, Figure 6.4. With permission of International Thomson Publishing Services Ltd.)

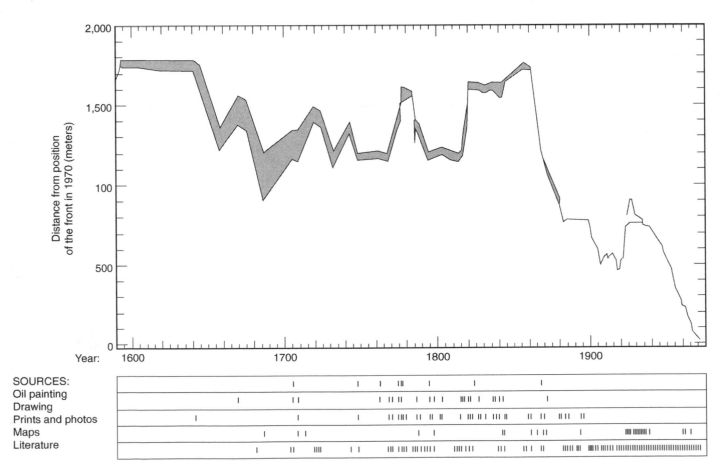

northern and central Europe. All parts of the continent were affected by such low-index (nonzonal) situations, with northerly or northeasterly flows of very cold, dry, Arctic, or polar continental air masses extending over large parts of Europe (Figure 3). The Mediterranean was not immune. In the eastern basin, outbursts of cold air from the north were associated with cyclone formation, bringing occasional bursts of torrential rain. Such conditions alternated with the invasion of warm, dry air from the south, causing long droughts even in winter and spring (Figure 4). In the western Mediterranean too, there were departures from mean twentieth-century values of temperature and precipitation lasting for several years or decades, but not necessarily at the same time as in the eastern basin.

North Atlantic thermohaline circulation appears to have been disturbed, because when sea surface temperatures were

periodically low and sea ice extensive, formation of the dense, saline North Atlantic Deep Water current was interrupted. This had long-distance effects on ocean circulation, reducing heat exchange between high and low latitudes. The large-scale alternation of pressure between the Azores region and the subpolar region east of Greenland (the North Atlantic Oscillation) was evidently involved in these switches from zonal to meridional circulation (Intergovernmental Panel on Climate Change, 1995, pp. 166–167). The extent to which century-scale climatic events such as the Little Ice Age are manifestations of periodic adjustments in the interaction between oceanic and atmospheric circulation (Grove, 1988, chap. 11), or responses of the global climatic system to external forcing caused by factors such as variations in geomagnetism or decreased solar input, remains to be clarified. A full explanation must involve the combined influence of several factors, including the part played by volcanic eruptions. [*See* Thermohaline Circulation; *and* North Atlantic Oscillation.]

The ending of the Little Ice Age cannot be attributed simply to anthropogenic warming following the Industrial Revolution, in view of evidence of comparable warming in the Medieval Warm Period and a series of similar century-scale events, such as the Löbben, earlier in the Holocene (Grove, 1996). Just as Little Ice Age climate consisted of decadal and seasonal departures from longer-term means, it was itself but one of several fluctuations within the Holocene, each lasting several centuries. The Little Ice Age has to be seen as one of many natural climatic fluctuations on a scale that must be expected to continue to occur, modulating to some extent future warming induced by human activity (Wigley et al., 1990). Since evidence of its characteristics, especially in Europe, is more plentiful than that of any of its predecessors, its investigation there is especially worthwhile.

More details of Little Ice Age climatic characteristics, which are essential if its causes are to be identified, are emerging from the increasing sophistication of climatic reconstruction since it was developed by Lamb (1977). This approach now depends on the cross-dating of different types of proxy data, including information relating to stages in the development of plants, with descriptive evidence drawn from contemporary sources, making it possible to extend meteorological time-series into the past (Pfister et al., 1996). The information assembled in the Euro-ClimHist database has already enabled synoptic patterns and even monthly weather maps for Europe to be constructed for the Maunder Minimum period between 1645 and 1715, when sunspots were absent (Frenzel et al., 1994).

GEOMORPHOLOGIC AND BIOLOGICAL EFFECTS

Little Ice Age climatic conditions affected highlands and lowlands as well as coastal areas. Snow cover was extended, and semipermanent snow appeared on midlatitude uplands, as in Scotland, and on high mountains in the Mediterranean, including the White Mountains of Crete. Snowlines fell; avalanches and mass movements increased greatly, as did floods (Figure 5), some caused by damming of main valleys by ice protruding

---

Little Ice Age in Europe. FIGURE 3. Circulation Patterns.

(a) in the winter of 1674–1675, when westerly winds were frequent; (b) in the winter of 1690–1691, when westerly winds were rare.

(From Grove, 2004. With permission of International Thomson Publishing Services Ltd.)

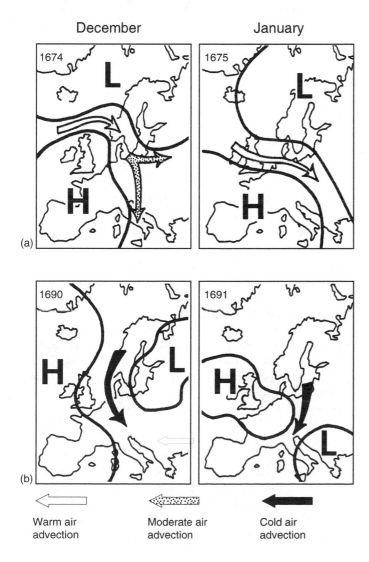

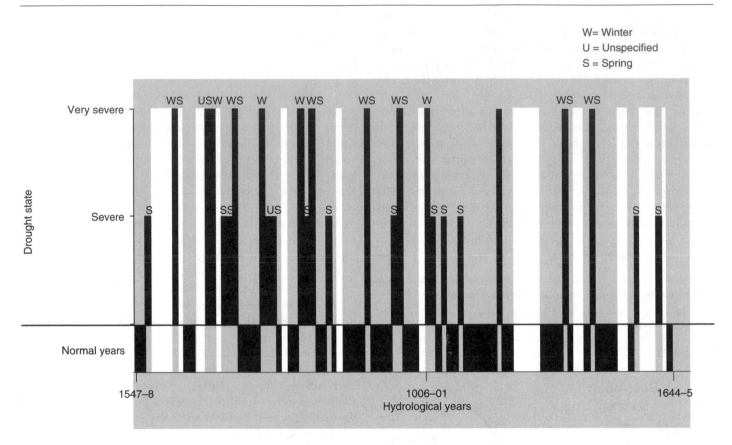

Little Ice Age in Europe. Figure 4. The Incidence of Droughts in Crete, 1547–1548 to 1644–1645.

White indicates years with no data.
(From Grove, in press. With permission of International Thomson Publishing Services Ltd.)

from tributary valleys. Periods of glacial advance were generally associated with increased flooding and sediment transport. Regime changes of proglacial streams and rivers led in the short term to both degradation and aggradation, according to the balance between meltwater sediment load and stream competence (ability to transport the sediment). In the longer term, increased flooding and glacial erosion led to increased sedimentation rates and deposition of valley-fills and deltas. Greater storminess caused flooding of low-lying coasts and the formation of belts of sand dunes, as at Morfa Harlech in northwest Wales. (Lamb, 1977, p. 452; Lamb, 1982, p. 208).

Little Ice Age climatic fluctuations were sufficient to have biological consequences, ranging from shifts in treeline altitude to changes in fish distribution in response to displacement of water masses. The disappearance of cod (*Gadus morhua*) from the Norwegian Sea area in the late seventeenth century, associated with the expansion of polar water, is attributable to the inability of the cod's kidneys to function in water below 2°C. The northward extensions of the range of European birds during twentieth-century warming, such as the establishment of European starlings (*Sturnus vulgaris*) in Iceland after 1941, implies that more substantial changes in the distribution of birds and insects must have occurred during the most marked phases of the Little Ice Age.

HUMAN EFFECTS

The consequences for European populations ranged from ice advance onto farms and farmland, such as the obliteration

in 1743 of Tungøen farm in Oldedalen, western Norway, the overwhelming of nine farms and extensive farmland by the Culbin Sands in Scotland around 1694 (Lamb, 1982), and the fourteenth-century loss to the sea of over a thousand acres of farmland belonging to Christ Church, Canterbury (England), together with many cattle and sheep (Grove, 1996).

The human consequences of Little Ice Age climate were particularly marked in highland regions and areas near the limits of cultivation. When summer temperatures declined and growing seasons shortened, both grass and cereal crops suffered, and the upper limits of cultivation descended. The viability of upland farming decreased as the probability of harvest failure increased. If harvests failed in successive years, leading to the consumption of seed, the results were disastrous. Failure of the grass crop limited the number of cattle that could be overwintered, thus decreasing the quantity of manure, which was at that time essential for successful arable farming. Farm desertion was especially common in Iceland and Scandinavia, although it was not confined to such northern regions. In Iceland, migration out of the worst-affected North in the seventeenth century caused increased impoverishment in the South. A gradual decline in resources could increase sensitivity

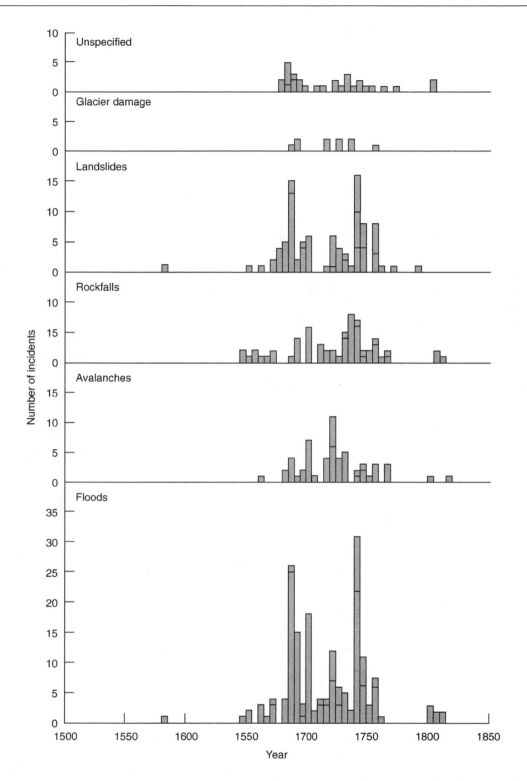

Little Ice Age in Europe. FIGURE 5. The Incidence of Mass Movements and Floods in Western Norway.

(After Grove, 1988, Figure 12.2. With permission of International Thomson Publishing Services Ltd.)

to other factors, including disease and unrelated economic problems, making the impact of a sequence of particularly hard years, such as occurred in the 1690s, much more serious. Crop failure was most dire if several staples were affected simultaneously, or if alternative supplies were unobtainable.

The human consequences of Little Ice Age climate were generally coincident with other social and economic factors from which they must be disentangled if they are to be assessed reliably. In the early fourteenth century the impact was enhanced, even in lowland regions in southern England, by the population growth encouraged by the rarity of harvest failures in the

preceding Medieval Warm Period. Adverse weather in England between 1314 and 1322, coinciding with the rapid advance of the Swiss glaciers (Figure 1), had major economic and social effects, including famine, their severity varying from place to place and social class to social class (Grove, 1996). More resilient societies or those in prosperous regions, such as the Netherlands, were less affected.

Little Ice Age in Europe. FIGURE 6. The Mer de Glace in 1823.

Painted by Samuel Birmann (*Au village des Prats*, Öffentliche Kunstsammlung Basel, Kupferstichkabinett, Inv. B1. 30.125).
(From Grove, 1988, Plate 4.1. With permission of International Thomson Publishing Services Ltd.)

BIBLIOGRAPHY

Bradley, R.S., and P.D. Jones. *Climate Since A.D. 1500*. London and New York: Routledge, 1992. The last half millenium is presented as a period of complex climatic anomalies by detailed studies of high-resolution data. Dismissal of the "Little Ice Age" as a useful term was based on the idea that it was a long period of unbroken cold.

Frenzel, B., C. Pfister, and B. Gläser, eds. *Climatic Trends and Anomalies in Europe 1675–1715*. Stuttgart and New York: G. Fischer, 1994.

Grove, J.M. *The Little Ice Age*. London and New York: Methuen, 1988. Presents the Little Ice Age as a global phenomenon, and includes chapters on its possible causes and consequences.

———. *Little Ice Ages: Ancient and Modern*. London: Routledge, 2004. A greatly expanded and updated global treatment, building upon the 1988 edition.

———. "The Century Timescale." In *Time-Scales and Environmental Change*, edited by T.S. Driver and G.P. Chapman, pp. 39–87. London and New York: Routledge, 1996. Places the Little Ice Age in its Quaternary and Holocene context and provides brief examples of the historical impact of climatic fluctuations.

Holzhauser, H. "Zur Geschichte des Aletschgletscher und des Fieschergletscher." *Physische Geographie* 13 (1984), 1–448.

———. "Fluctuation of the Grosser Aletsch Glacier and the Gorner Glacier during the Last 3200 Years: New Results." *Paläoklimaforschung/Palaeoclimate Research* 24 (1997), 35–58.

Holzhauser, H., and H.J. Zumbühl. "To the History of the Lower Grindelwald Glacier During the Last 2800 Years: Paleosols, Fossil Wood and Pictorial Records: New Results." Translated by M. Joss, C. Bern, and T. Wachs. *Zeitschrift für Geomorphologie* 104 (1996), 95–127.

Houghton, J.T., et al., eds. *Climate Change 1995: The Science of Climatic Change: Contribution of Working Group I to the Second Assessment Report of the Intergovernmental Panel on Climatic Change.* Cambridge and New York: Cambridge University Press, 1996. Contains information on past climatic changes and includes data on influences such as the North Atlantic Oscillation.

Lamb, H.H. *Climate Present, Past and Future.* Vol. 2. London: Methuen, 1977.

——. *Climate, History, and the Modern World.* London and New York: Methuen, 1982. A good introduction for the nonspecialist; see especially Chapters 3, 8, 11, 12, and 13.

Manley, G. "Central England Temperatures: Monthly Means 1659–1973." *Quarterly Journal of the Royal Meteorological Society* 100 (1974), 389–405. A classic paper, providing full details of the ways in which this, the longest European temperature series, was derived.

Pfister, C., G. Schwarz-Zanetti, and M. Wegmann. "Winter Severity in Europe: The Fourteenth Century." *Climatic Change* 34.1 (1996), 91–108. DOI: 10.1007/BF00139255. A reconstruction of some of the European climatic conditions during the early part of the Little Ice Age.

Wigley, T.M.L., M.J. Ingram, and G. Farmer, eds. *Climate and History: Studies in Past Climates and their Impact on Man.* Cambridge and New York: Cambridge University Press, 1981. One of the first works concerned with the interrelations between climate and history.

Wigley, T.M.L., M.J. Ingram, and P. M. Kelly. "Holocene Climatic Changes, [14]C Wiggles, and Variations in Solar Irradiance." *Philosophical Transactions of the Royal Society of London* 330.1615 (1990), 547–560. Little Ice Age-type fluctuations must be expected to continue to influence future climate.

—JEAN M. GROVE

Loess. FIGURE 1. A thick loess section at Khonako, Republic of Tajik in central Asia.

The horizontal layers are paleosols that formed at times when aeolian dust was accumulating at a relatively slow rate.

LOESS

Loess is largely nonstratified unconsolidated silt, containing some clay, sand, and carbonate. It is markedly finer than eolian sand and consists chiefly of quartz, feldspar, mica, clay minerals, and carbonate grains in varying proportions. It has been the subject of great debate ever since Lyell (1834) drew attention to the loamy deposits of the Rhine Valley. Many theories have been advanced to explain its formation. It was, however, von Richthofen (1882, pp. 297–298) who cogently argued that these deposits probably were eolian in origin and that they were produced by dust storms transporting silts from deserts and depositing them on desert margins. The silt may also have been derived from glaciated regions and their outwash plains. Quaternary loess covers as much as 10 % of the Earth's land surface (Muhs et al., 2004). Over vast areas these blanket preexisting topographic relief. Many parts of the world possess long sequences of loess and paleosols (ancient soils; Rutter et al., 2003), and together these provide a major source of paleoenvironmental information that can be correlated with that obtained from ocean cores.

The loess deposits of the U.S. have recently been reviewed by Bettis et al. (2003), who suggest that the last glacial (Peoria) loess is probably the thickest in the world, being more than 48 m thick in parts of Nebraska, and 41 m thick in western Iowa. The Bignell Loess of the Great Plains is of Holocene age (Jacobs and Mason, 2005). Miao et al. (2005) believe that much of the Holocene loess, most of which dates from approximately 10,000 to 6,500 years ago, was produced in dry phases as a result of the winnowing of dune fields.

In South America, loess profiles thicker than 50 m are known from the Pampas of Argentina (Kröhling, 2003). A combination of semiarid and arid conditions in the Andes rain shadow, combined with glacial outwash from those mountains, created near ideal conditions (Zarate, 2003). The Argentinian loess region is the most extensive in the Southern Hemisphere. New Zealand has the other major loess deposits of the Southern Hemisphere. They cover large areas, especially in eastern South Island and southern North Island (Eden and Hammond, 2003). The loess has been derived mainly from dust deflated by westerly winds from the many broad, braided river floodplains.

In Europe the loess is most extensive in the east, where, as in the case of America, there were plains and steppe conditions. The German loess shows a close association with outwash, and in France the same situation is observed along the Rhône and Garonne. These rivers carried outwash from glaciers in the Alps and Pyrenees, respectively. The Danube was a major source of silt for loess in eastern Europe. Britain has relatively little loess and its maximum depth is only about two or three meters. In southern Europe, Late Pleistocene loess, up to 10 m thick, occurs in souteastern Spain.

Loess is probably more widespread in South Asia than has often been realized. Given the size of the Thar Desert (in India) and the large amounts of sediment that are transported to huge alluvial plains by rivers draining from the mountains of High Asia, this is scarcely surprising.

One of the most striking features of Central Asia, one it shares with China (Bronger et al., 1998), is the development of very thick (some more than 200 m), complex loess deposits dating back to the Pliocene (Ding et al., 2002). They are well displayed in both Tajikistan (Mestdagh et al., 1999) and Uzbekistan (Zhou et al., 1995), where rates of deposition were very high in the late Pleistocene. The nature of the soils and pollen grains preserved in the loess profiles suggests a progressive trend towards greater aridity through the Quaternary which may be related to progressive uplift of the Ghissar and Tian Shan mountains (Davis et al., 1980). As in China, the loess profiles contain a large number of paleosols that formed during periods of relatively moist and warm climate (Figure 1).

Loess reaches its supreme development in China, most notably in the Loess Plateau, a 450,000 km² area in the middle reaches of the Yellow (Huang) River (Liu, 1988). In Gansu Province, a thickness of 505 m has been reported (Huang et al., 2000), but over most of the plateau 150 m is more typical. Loess deposits also occur elsewhere, including the mountainous regions, the Tibetan Plateau, parts of northern Mongolia, and Korea. In general terms, periods of loess deposition are associated with cold phases (which by implication were dry) while the palaeosols are associated with warmer phases (An et al., 1990; Sartori et al., 2005), indicating their origin as products of deflation and subsequent transport and deposition by dust storms. Along with ice cores and ocean floor sediments, loess deposits provide a long and detailed picture of past environmental changes.

BIBLIOGRAPHY

An, Z., et al. "The Long-term Paleomonsoon Variation Recorded by the Loess-Paleosol Sequence in Central China." *Quaternary International* 7–8 (1990), 91–95. DOI: 10.1016/1040-6182(90)90042-3.

Bettis, E.A., et al. "Last Glacial Loess in the Conterminous USA." *Quaternary Science Reviews* 22 (2003), 1907–1946. DOI: 10.1016/S0277-3791(03)00169-0.

Bronger, A., R. Winter, and T. Heinkele. "Pleistocene Climatic History of East and Central Asia Based on Paleopedological Indicators in Loess-Palaeosol Sequences." *Catena* 34 (1998), 1–17.

Davis, R.S., V.A. Ranov, and A.E. Dodonov. "Early Man in Soviet Central Asia." *Scientific American* 243 (1980), 91–102.

Ding, Z.L., et al. "The Loess Record in Southern Tajikistan and Correlation with Chinese Loess." *Earth and Planetary Science Letters* 200 (2002), 387–400. DOI: 10.1016/S0012-821X(02)00637-4.

Eden, D.N., and A.P. Hammond. "Dust Accumulation in the New Zealand Region since the Last Glacial Maximum." *Quaternary Science Reviews* 22 (2003), 2037–2052.

Huang, C.C., J. Pang, and J. Zhao. "Chinese Loess and the Evolution of the East Asian Monsoon." *Progress in Physical Geography* 24 (2000), 75–96. DOI: 10.1177/030913330002400104.

Jacobs, P.M., and J.A. Mason. "Impact of Holocene Dust Aggradation on A Horizon Characteristics and Carbon Storage in Loess-Derived Mollisols of the Great Plains, USA." *Geoderma* 125 (2005), 95–106. DOI: 10.1016/j.geoderma.2004.07.002.

Kröhling, D.M. "A 54 m Thick Loess Profile in North Pampa, Argentina." Geological Society of America Abstracts with Programs, 2003, p. 198.

Liu, T. *Loess in China.* 2d ed. Beijing: China Ocean Press; Berlin and New York: Springer, 1988.

Lyell, C. *Principles of Geology.* London: J. Murray, 1834.

Mestdagh, H., et al. "Pedosedimentary and Climatic Reconstruction of the Last Interglacial and Early Glacial Loess-Paleosol Sequence in South Tadzhikistan." *Catena* 35 (1999), 197–218.

Miao, X., et al. "Loess Record of Dry Climate and Aeolian Activity in the Early- to Mid-Holocene, Central Great Plains, North America." *The Holocene* 15 (2005), 339–346. DOI: 10.1191/0959683605hl805rp.

Muhs, D.R., et al. "Holocene Loess Deposition and Soil Formation as Competing Processes, Matanuska Valley, Southern Alaska." *Quaternary Research* 61 (2004), 265–276. DOI: 10.1016/j.yqres.2004.02.003.

Richthofen, F. von. "On the Mode of Origin of the Loess." *Geological Magazine* 9.2 (1882), 293–305.

Rutter, N.W., et al. "Correlation and Interpretation of Paleosols and Loess across European Russia and Asia over the Last Interglacial-Glacial Cycle." *Quaternary Research* 60 (2003), 101–109.

Sartori, M., et al. "The Last Glacial/Interglacial Cycle at Two Sites in the Chinese Loess Plateau: Mineral Magnetic, Grain-Size and ¹⁰Be Measurements and Estimates of Palaeoprecipitation." *Palaeogeography, Palaeoclimatology, Palaeoecology* 222 (2005), 145–160.

Zarate, M.A. "Loess of Southern South America." *Quaternary Science Reviews* 22 (2003), 1987–2006. DOI: 10.1016/S0277-3791(03)00165-3.

Zhou, L.P., A.E. Dodonov, and N.J. Shackleton. "Thermoluminescence Dating of the Orkutsay Loess Section in Tashkent Region, Uzbekistan, Central Asia." *Quaternary Science Reviews* 14 (1995), 721–730. DOI: 10.1016/0277-3791(95)00056-9.

—Andrew S. Goudie

M

MANGROVES

Mangroves are halophytic (salt-tolerant) trees and woody shrubs that grow in the upper part of the intertidal zone on shores not exposed to strong wave action or tidal scour. More than 70 species have been identified. They form extensive communities bordering deltas, estuaries, inlets, tidal lagoons, and sheltered embayments, and are occasionally found behind beaches on coral islands (Hogarth, 2007).

DISTRIBUTION AND SETTING

Mangroves attain their greatest extent, diversity, and luxuriance on tropical coasts, where they can form forests several kilometers wide with trees up to 30 meters (100 feet) tall. A few species extend beyond the tropics, often associated with salt marshes, which occupy a similar intertidal zone, and replace mangroves entirely on cooler coasts. The *World Mangrove Atlas* (Spalding, Blasco, and Field, 1997) indicates that mangroves occupy a total of 181,000 square kilometers (km²), the largest stands being in Indonesia (42,550 km²), Brazil (13,400 km²), Australia (11,500 km²), and Nigeria (10,515 km²). The present latitudinal limits of mangroves on the Pacific coasts of the Americas are about 28° north latitude in the Gulf of California but only 3° 30' south at Tumbes in Peru, where sea temperatures are lowered by the cold Peruvian current. On the Atlantic coast of the Americas they extend north to Florida and the Mississippi delta (Barataria Bay, 29°20' north) and south to Florianópolis in Brazil (27°35'south). In West Africa they extend north to the Senegal River (16° north) and south to Lobito in Angola (12°20' south). On the eastern coast of South Africa mangroves occur south to the Bashee River (32°59' south). They are found on the shores of the Red Sea almost as far north as the Gulf of Aqaba (28° north) and in western Australia south to Bunbury (33°20' south). In the western Pacific there are mangroves as far north as the Min River (26° north) in China and on the Satsuma Peninsula in southern Kyushu, Japan (31°37' north). On the North Island of New Zealand mangroves extend south to Raglan (Whaingaroa) Harbour on the western coast (37° 48' S) and Ohiwa Harbour on the eastern coast (close to 38° S), while in (eastern) Australia they reach their southernmost limit in Corner Inlet, Victoria (38°55' S).

Mangroves typically occur on muddy substrates and are structurally and physiologically adapted to survive in a marine tidal environment, although some species can also grow in fresh water. Adaptations by various species include networks of pneumatophores (snorkels that protrude vertically from the roots through the mud), and prop-root systems. Mangroves are often arranged in clearly defined zones of a single species or group of species parallel to the coastline or the shores of an estuary, the zones being related to the depth and duration of tidal submergence. Some species (especially those with pneumatophores) influence patterns of sedimentation, intercepting and trapping mud and peat (the organic products of the mangrove ecosystem) to build up a depositional terrace, eventually to high-tide level. As the terrace builds up, the mangrove zones migrate seaward, and other vegetation (such as rainforest) displaces them on the newly formed land as the high-tide line advances seaward. Such vegetation successions have occurred, for example, on the Amazon delta and in the Gulf of Papua. In Westernport Bay, Australia, cutting of mangroves was followed by dissection and degradation of the depositional terrace, but this terrace was rebuilt when the mangrove fringe revived. In terms of biological productivity, mangroves are among the richest of natural ecosystems, sustaining a varied flora and fauna, including fish, shellfish, reptiles, insects, and birds, and the world's mangrove forests have absorbed carbon from, and contributed oxygen to, the global atmosphere on a large scale, thereby contributing to global change. Mann (1982) estimated primary productivity (organic matter) in mangroves at up to 2,000 grams per square meter per year.

DISTRIBUTION HISTORY

To explain the existing global distribution of mangroves it is necessary to take account of several major climatic fluctuations and sea level oscillations that occurred during Quaternary times. Mangroves are closely related to existing intertidal levels, and must have migrated in response to rising and falling sea levels, subject to climatic and other constraints. They have thus survived large-scale global changes. About 20,000 BP, during a very cold phase of the Pleistocene when sea level was at least 120 meters (400 feet) lower than it is now and the coastline lay close to the outer margins of the continental shelves, mangroves must have occupied sites on the lowered coastline where the sea was still sufficiently warm to permit their growth. It is possible—bearing in mind the occasional inland occurrence of mangroves (as near Broome in Western Australia) that have survived since Late Pleistocene phases of higher sea level—that some mangroves persisted in wetlands on the emerged continental shelf. [*See* Wetlands.]

Subsequently, between about 18,000 and 5,000 BP, there was a major worldwide sea-level rise (the Late Quaternary or Flandrian [Holocene] marine transgression), in the course of which the coastline advanced across what is now the continental shelf up to its present position. Mangroves must have migrated with this sea level rise, occupying suitably sheltered sites and incorporating any mangrove outliers on the submerging shelf. Stratigraphic studies in northern Australia and southeastern Asia have shown that mangroves grew in accreting estuaries when sea level was rising between 7,000 and 5,500 BP, and that when the Late Quaternary marine transgression came to an end they spread out to embayments and other sheltered sites of muddy accretion along the coast. During the past five thousand years, sea level has been relatively stable, with minor oscillations in some places and a slow rise in others, and mangroves have spread on sites where there has been continuing accretion of sediment (as on tropical deltas) or held their position where a peaty substrate has been maintained by the accumulation of their own organic products (as on the Florida coast). They may have disappeared from some sectors of coastline as the result of erosion, but during the past few centuries a relatively stable sea level and substantial sedimentary accretion has enabled mangroves to occupy extensive areas on tropical and warm temperate coastlines.

HUMAN IMPACT

Mangrove communities have been modified extensively by human activities, especially during the last few decades. They have been destroyed in the course of land reclamation for agriculture, urban and industrial development, and port construction. In southeastern Asia there has been large-scale reclamation of mangrove areas for land development, particularly around Penang and Melaka in Malaysia and Jakarta and Surabaya in Indonesia. It is possible to manage mangrove forests on a sustained yield basis by careful extraction of timber and promotion of natural regeneration, but in many areas mangroves have been depleted by excessive cutting for timber and fuel wood, especially in Arabia and Africa. Elsewhere they have been cleared for the dredging of placer deposits, such as the tin that occurs beneath mangroves on the western coasts of Thailand and Malaysia, and generally they have failed to regenerate on the worked-over terrain. The most extensive clearance of mangroves in recent decades has been carried out for the establishment of aquaculture (fish and shrimp ponds) and salt pans in such countries as Ecuador and Brazil, and especially in southeastern Asia. Mangroves have also been damaged or destroyed by pollution, especially oil spills near port areas, and by defoliating herbicides such as Agent Orange, as during the war in Vietnam. Globally, mangrove losses have already been substantial. Spalding (see bibliography) noted that in Thailand, for example, reclamation and aquaculture have reduced the mangrove area to less than half its natural extent, and similar reductions have occurred in the Philippines (60%), Vietnam (37%), and Malaysia (12%).

Where mangroves are still spreading, they show an unbroken rising canopy, the trees increasing in age and size landward; but where there has been erosion, there is a sharp margin in which the trunks of mature mangroves are exposed and undermined. Reduction of mangrove fringes by erosion has occurred where they are undercut by meandering river channels or where wave action has intensified on coasts on which previously there had been accretion and spreading mangroves. Once a protective mangrove fringe has been lost, low-lying hinterlands are exposed to erosion, and banks built to enclose reclaimed areas require strengthening and elaboration to solid sea walls. Mangroves are still spreading seaward on the fringes of growing deltas and alongside accreting estuaries, but elsewhere erosion has become prevalent, either because of diminishing sediment supply from the land (as where rivers have been dammed, or backing embankments have impeded runoff from reclaimed hinterlands) or where sea level is now rising, perhaps because of coastal land subsidence.

CLIMATE CHANGE

The consequences of possible global warming and worldwide sea-level rise are discussed by Bird (1993). Mangroves will respond to global warming by expanding their latitudinal range, provided that suitable coastal habitats are available and that coastal currents enable seeds to reach them. Mangroves are likely to spread northward along the northeastern coast of Florida, for example, and into Mauritania. Climatic changes that result in increased runoff and sedimentation from the land will also increase the available habitats and stimulate the expansion of mangrove areas if this is not prevented by other factors, such as human activities. However, the accompanying global sea-level rise is likely to prove damaging to mangroves, except where it is offset by tectonic uplift of coastal land, or at least compensated for by accelerating intertidal accretion, which is most likely in estuarine and deltaic regions. Some possible responses are shown in Figure 1. The response of mangroves to a rising sea level can already be seen on coasts that are subsiding, as in the Amazon delta, the Bight of Bangkok, the Adelaide region of South Australia, and northern New Guinea.

It is possible that global warming and a rising sea level will result in the enrichment of intertidal areas with nutrients derived from erosion elsewhere, or enhanced runoff from the hinterland, thereby invigorating mangrove growth and producing sufficient peat to build up the substrate as fast as the sea level rises. Ellison and Stoddart (1991) decided that in the absence of sediment accretion, mangroves could maintain themselves on their accumulating peat while sea level was rising by up to 9 centimeters per century but would be impeded by a faster submergence and collapse when sea level rise exceeded 12 centimeters per century. Mangroves that grow on coral-reef islands, such as the Low Isles off northern Queensland, are unlikely to survive as sea-level rise proceeds because rates of sediment accretion are very low.

In the absence of sustained accretion, coastal submergence by a rising sea level is likely to cause die-back and undercutting of the seaward mangroves. As larger waves arrive through deepening water, a cliff is cut in the intertidal mudflats, and this recedes through the mangroves, consuming the muddy terrace on which they grew (Figure 1). Where such erosion is already in progress, as on the coast of West Johor in Malaysia, a rising sea level will accelerate it.

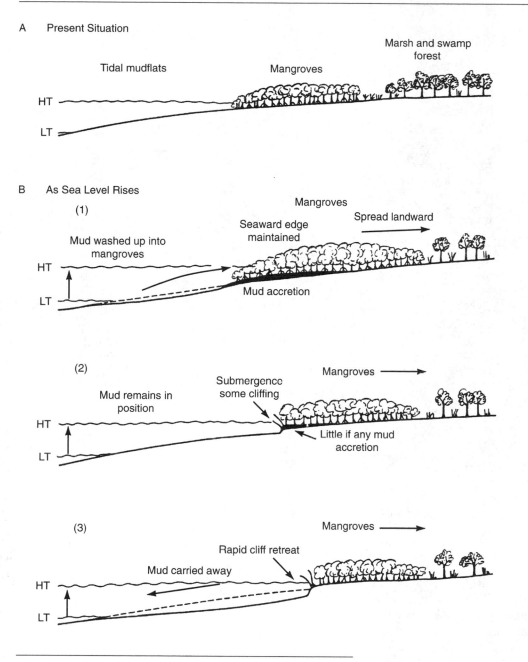

A   Present Situation

Marsh and swamp
forest

Tidal mudflats   Mangroves

HT

LT

B   As Sea Level Rises

(1)   Mangroves

Seaward edge   Spread landward
maintained

Mud washed up into
mangroves

HT

LT   Mud accretion

(2)   Mangroves ⟶

Submergence
some cliffing
Mud remains in
position

HT

LT   Little if any mud
accretion

(3)   Mangroves ⟶

Rapid cliff retreat
Mud carried away

HT

LT

Mangroves. FIGURE 1. Sea-Level Rise.

(A) Mangroves have spread forward on to tidal mudflats, and as the mud level is built up they are succeeded by other vegetation. (B) As sea level rises there are three possibilities: (1) that there will be sufficient mud accretion to maintain the seaward edge while the mangroves spread landward; (2) that in the absence of a sufficient sediment supply the seaward margin will become cliffed as the mangroves spread landward; and (3) that removal of mud will result in a deepening of nearshore waters and stronger wave action, causing rapid retreat of the seaward cliff as the mangroves spread landward. (After Bird, 1993. Reproduced with permission of John Wiley & Sons Limited.)

As submergence proceeds, mangrove zones will tend to migrate landward, invading a low-lying hinterland. In humid regions they will invade backing rainforest or formerly freshwater swamps, as on the Mamberamo delta in Irian Jaya, while in drier areas they will colonize backing salt marsh and bare saline flats, as at Port Adelaide in South Australia. As this migration proceeds, it is likely that some mangrove species will become more abundant and extensive, while others will diminish or even disappear.

In many places the landward migration of mangroves in response to a rising sea level will be prevented because the inner margin abuts a rising slope: the mangrove fringe will become narrower and eventually disappear. Where a bank has been built at the inner margin to protect reclaimed land or enclose ponds for aquaculture or pans for salt production, there will be a similar response: if the wall is maintained, the mangrove fringe will be reduced, and eventually destroyed as sea level rises.

Mangroves are important because they are biologically rich and productive and play a significant role in sustaining estuarine and marine fish and crustaceans. As long as they persist, they protect low-lying hinterlands, intercept sediment and

Mangroves. Mangrove Swamps on Indian Ocean.

Swamps such as those on the east coast of Mauritius offer a degree of coastal erosion control and protection against storms. They are also important in terms of providing an important and productive habitat for many organisms.

nutrients, and provide a habitat for associated plant and animal life. Mangrove areas yield timber, firewood, charcoal, and a variety of other products, especially for the use of people who live in or near them, and, in a world where marine inundation and dryland salting are increasing problems, they provide genetic stock from which halophytic trees and crops could be developed. Unfortunately, mangroves are still widely regarded as waste areas awaiting reclamation, particularly in southeastern Asia and Latin America, where governments are not yet implementing effective conservation programs.

The conservation of mangroves as sea level rises requires the raising of their substrates by artificial nourishment. On the subsiding coast of the Bight of Bangkok, Thailand, the mangrove fringe is diminishing, and in places has disappeared, but there has been vigorous growth and spread of mangroves in an intertidal area where mud dredged from the Chao Phraya (Me Nam) River was dumped. This suggests that mud could be deposited to renourish mangrove swamps in much the same way as sand has been placed to renourish beaches. Planting (or replanting) of mangroves has recently been attempted on eroded muddy shores in Bangladesh and Vietnam and in abandoned fishponds in Thailand.

BIBLIOGRAPHY

Bird, E. C. F. "Mangroves and Intertidal Morphology in Westernport Bay, Victoria." *Marine Geology* 69 (1986), 251–271. Discusses Australian evidence for mangroves causing sediment accretion.
———. *Submerging Coasts.* Chichester, U.K., and New York: Wiley, 1993.
Chapman, V. J. *Mangrove Vegetation.* Vaduz, Liechtenstein: Cramer, 1976. A useful ecological study, a little out of date.
Ellison, J., and D. Stoddart. "Mangrove Ecosystem Collapse during Predicted Sea-Level Rise: Holocene Analogs and Implications." *Journal of Coastal Research* 7.1 (1991), 151–165.
Hogarth, P. *The Biology of Mangroves and Seagrasses.* Oxford and New York: Oxford University Press, 2007.
Kunstadter, P., E. C. F. Bird, and S. Sabhasri, eds. *Man in the Mangroves: The Socio-Economic Situation of Human Settlements in Mangrove Forests.* Tokyo: United Nations University, 1986. A collection of papers on mangrove utilization.
Mann, K. H. *Ecology of Coastal Waters: A Systems Approach.* Berkeley: University of California Press, 1982.
Robertson, A. I., and D. M. Alongi. *Tropical Mangrove Systems. Coastal and Estuarine Studies* 41. Washington, D.C.: American Geophysical Union, 1992.
Spalding, M., F. Blasco, and C. Field, eds. *World Mangrove Atlas.* Okinawa: University of the Ryukus (International Society for Mangrove Ecosystems), 1997.
Woodroffe, C. D. "The Impact of Sea-Level Rise on Mangrove Shorelines." *Progress in Physical Geography* 14.4 (1990), 483–520. DOI: 10.1177/03091333 9001400404. An analysis including evidence of mangrove responses to past sea-level changes.

—ERIC C. F. BIRD

MARGINAL SEAS

Marginal seas are semienclosed bodies of water open to the ocean. The Mediterranean and the Caribbean are marginal Atlantic seas, the South China Sea and the Sea of Japan are marginal to the Pacific, and the Red Sea and the Timor Sea to the Indian Ocean. Some (shelf seas) are shallow, less than 200 meters deep (e.g., Hudson Bay and the North Sea), while others are deep, connected to the ocean only at the surface and bounded at depth by submarine ridges (e.g., the Yellow Sea and the Mediterranean).

Their proximity to the continents influences the physical, chemical, and biological characteristics of marginal seas. Land runoff contributes nutrients, so marginal seas tend to be areas of high biological activity, but association with the land can have disadvantages. The increasing human migration to the edge of the sea brings extensive coastal development for urban and industrial growth, resulting in widespread destruction of habitats by the concreting of shorelines, the drainage of wetlands, the erection of hotels and marinas for tourists, and the construction of shrimp ponds—at the expense of mangrove forests—for aquaculture. This increasing human activity produces a diversity of polluting inputs. These include heavy metals, synthetic organic compounds (from industrial chemicals and pesticides), hydrocarbons, and radionuclides. Another problem is sewage, which carries, among other things, pathogenic organisms that bring diseases to recreational users of the shore and to consumers of seafood. Marginal seas are thus much more polluted than the open oceans. Those that are regularly flushed by the ocean are the least at risk, but others that are relatively enclosed may suffer major degradation.

In addition to these continental influences, marginal seas are polluted by shipping and from the atmosphere. Disposal of wastes at sea is now tightly regulated, and shipping inputs today are mainly from accidental spills and operational discharges, but pollution from the atmosphere is continuous. Contaminants from a wide range of sources are carried in the air and deposited in the oceans, but the concentrations are low and the inputs diffuse, so effects are reduced.

Eutrophication, the overenrichment of waters, has become a global concern. A moderate addition of nutrients has a fertilizing effect, but excessive inputs cause abnormal blooms of seaweeds on the shore and phytoplankton in the upper waters. When these plants die, their decay results in conditions that can cause massive kills of fish and shellfish. The main sources of nutrients are sewage, agricultural runoff from heavy fertilizer use, and wastes from intensive livestock rearing and fish farming. If there is good mixing with the open sea, these inputs are quickly diluted and dispersed, but in more enclosed areas the nutrients can build up to dangerous concentrations. In marginal seas of northern Europe, eutrophication occurs in the Baltic Sea and in the southern North Sea. Parts of the Mediterranean, particularly the Gulf of Lion, the Lake of Tunis, and the Gulf of zmir, often show extreme effects, and in the northern Adriatic,

heavy algal blooms seriously interfere with fisheries and tourism. In the Pacific, Tokyo Bay, Ise Bay, and parts of the Inland Sea are affected, and the important fish-farming industry is greatly disrupted. Increasingly frequent algal blooms (red tides) can kill other marine organisms, damage aquaculture, and sicken or kill humans who eat contaminated seafood.

A significant pressure on marginal seas stems from the exploitation of nonliving resources, particularly oil and gas, and this will increase as more accessible reserves are depleted. Effects on the environment are associated particularly with production operations during which drill cuttings and various chemical effluents are discharged. However, their impacts are mainly restricted to the immediate vicinity of the installations. Much greater pressure on the environment arises from the exploitation of living resources. Fishing is a major activity in marginal seas and in most is now so intensive that all commercial stocks are at risk. The ecological balance of the populations is upset, and continuous trawling with heavy gear causes physical changes in the seabed. Studies of global warming indicate temperature increases in marginal seas which will affect not only fish stocks but also corals and other marine organisms.

[*See also* Coastlines; Ocean Acidification; *and* Ocean Disposal.]

BIBLIOGRAPHY

Newman, P. J., and A. R. Agg. *Environmental Protection of the North Sea.* London: Heinemann, 1988. A good coverage of the issues in one particular marginal sea.

Postma, H., and J. J. Zijlstra, eds. *Continental Shelves.* Amsterdam, Oxford, and New York: Elsevier, 1988. Useful descriptions of a number of marginal seas.

Shepard, C. R. C., ed. *Seas at the Millennium: An Evironmental Evaluation.* Amsterdam, Oxford, and New York: Pergamon, 2000. Addresses a range of marginal seas round the world

Sinclair, M., and G. Valdimarsson, eds. *Responsible Fisheries in the Marine Ecosystem.* Rome: Food and Agriculture Organization, 2003. Comprehensive coverage of fisheries issues.

Tolba, M. K., and O. A. El-Kholy, et al., eds. *The World Environment 1972–1992.* London and New York: Chapman and Hall, 1992. A comprehensive examination of the global environment, covering sea, air, and land, with much on marginal seas.

Van den Bergh, J. C. J. M., et al. "Exotic Harmful Algae in Marine Ecosystems: An Integrated Biological-Economic-Legal Analysis of Impacts and Policies." *Marine Policy* 26.1 (2002), 59–74. DOI: 10.1016/S0308-597X(01)00032-X. A useful introduction.

—A. D. MCINTYRE

MEDIEVAL CLIMATE OPTIMUM

This case study focuses on a controversial late Holocene period of possibly warmer conditions that occurred before the Little Ice Age.

The Holocene has witnessed a series of climatic fluctuations. [*See* Holocene.] In the early to mid-Holocene there was a phase of prolonged relative warmth (the Climate Optimum), and at other times there have been phases of relative cold (neoglacials). One of these neoglacials, the Little Ice Age, occurred between the end of the Middle Ages and the later nineteenth century.

Another proposed climate fluctuation is a period of warmth in early medieval or pre-Renaissance times. This has been called the "Medieval Climate Optimum," "Medieval Warm Period," or "Little Climate Optimum."

Proponents of this idea, including Lamb (1966), argued that from 750 to 1200–1300 CE there was a period of glacial retreat that appears to have been slightly more marked than that of the twentieth century. The trees of this phase, which were eventually destroyed by the cold and the glacial advances from about 1200 CE on, grew on sites where, at the present time, trees have not had sufficient time or the necessary conditions to grow again. Medieval documents suggest that the most clement period of this optimum, with mild winters and dry summers, was around 1080–1180 CE. At this time the coast of Iceland was relatively unaffected by the ice, and settlements were established in what are now inhospitable parts of Greenland. It is also believed that the relative heat and dryness of the summers, which led to the drying-up of some peat bogs, were responsible for the locust plagues which spread at times over vast areas, occasionally reaching as far north as Hungary and Austria. In northern Canada, west of Hudson Bay, fossil forest has been discovered up to 100 km north of the present forest limit, and radiocarbon dates show that this forest was living about 870–1140 CE. It is also interesting that the Camp Century ice core from Greenland has revealed a cold wave after about 1130–1160, but that the five centuries preceding this were quite warm. This has also been confirmed by an ice core from Crete in central Greenland (Dansgaard et al., 1975).

An additional line of evidence is the presence of vineyards in Britain, as far north as York. Lamb (1966) regarded this as indicating summer temperatures 1–2°C higher than today, a general freedom from May frosts, and mostly good Septembers. It has also been maintained that favorable conditions of the Little Optimum coincided with radical changes in the fortunes of farmers in various parts of the U.S. Considerable growth and development occurred from 700 to 1200 CE (Malde, 1964), whereas shortly before the thirteenth century agriculture declined rapidly as a result of cold dry conditions (Woodbury 1961). The response of the Anasazi people of Colorado to the Medieval Warm Period is discussed by Grove (1996). It also appears to have had an impact in China, where three of the most successful dynasties in Chinese history coincide closely with warm wet years (Li et al., 2006).

However, some recent tree-ring analyses for Fennoscandia by Briffa et al. (1990) have failed to find unambiguous evidence for this warm phase or for extended warm periods. They conclude (p. 438) that their reconstruction "dispels any notion that summers in Fennoscandia were consistently warm throughout that period. Although the second half of the twelfth century was very warm, the first half was very cold. For most of the eleventh and thirteenth centuries, summers were near normal (relative to the mean for 1951–70)." They suggest that the significance of the Medieval Climate Optimum has been overstated and that much of the historical evidence upon which the concept was based was sketchy.

Doubts of this sort were expressed during the early 1990s, and fundamental questions were asked, such as whether the medieval warm period actually existed, whether it was a global phenomenon, whether it was continuous or discontinuous, and whether it spanned the entire period identified by Lamb and others (Dean, 1994). In a review of the evidence Hughes and Diaz (1994, p. 109) came to a somewhat equivocal but probably reasonable set of conclusions:

> For some areas of the globe (for example, Scandinavia, Chile, the Sierra Nevada in California, the Canadian Rockies, and Tasmania), temperatures, particularly in summer, appear to have been higher during some parts of this period than those that were to prevail until the most recent decades of the twentieth century.

> These warmer regional episodes were not strongly synchronous. Evidence from other regions (for example, the Southeast United States, Southern Europe along the Mediterranean, and parts of South America) indicates that the climate during that time was little different to that of later times, or that warming, if it occurred, was recorded at a later time than had been assumed. Taken together, the available evidence does not support a *global* Medieval Warm period, although more support for such a phenomenon could be drawn from high-elevation records than from low-elevation records.

Similar doubts have been expressed by Oglivie and Farmer (1997), who reanalyzed much of the available documentary evidence. They argue that the period was one of climatic complexity, and they throw doubt on Lamb's basic scheme. It is interesting that at the same time as the concept of a Medieval Climate Optimum has come under closer scrutiny, so too, the succeeding Little Ice Age is being seen as less clear-cut than previously thought. [*See* Little Ice Age in Europe.] As Jones and Bradley (1995, pp. 659–60) write:

> The last 500 years was a period of complex climatic anomalies, the understanding of which is not well-served by the continued use of the term "Little Ice Age." . . . The period experienced both warm and cold episodes, and these varied in importance geographically. There is no evidence for a world-wide synchronous and prolonged cold interval to which we can ascribe the term "little Ice Age."

There is still a great deal of uncertainty about the climate fluctuations of the past millennium.

BIBLIOGRAPHY

Briffa, K. R., et al. "A 1,400-Year Tree-Ring Record of Summer Temperatures in Fennoscandia." *Nature* 346 (1990), 434–439. DOI: 10.1038/346434a0.

Dansgaard, W., et al. "Climatic Changes, Norsemen, and Modern Man." *Nature* 255 (1975), 24–28. DOI: 10.1038/255024a0.

Dean, J. S. "The Medieval Warm Period on the Southern Colorado Plateau." *Climatic Change* 26.2–3 (1994), 225–241. DOI: 10.1007/BF01092416.

Grove, J. M. "The Century Time-Scale." In *Time-Scales and Environmental Change*, edited by T. S. Driver and G. P. Chapman, pp. 39–87. London and New York: Routledge, 1996.

Hughes, M. K., and H. F. Diaz. (1994) "Was There a 'Medieval Warm Period,' and If So, Where and When?" *Climatic Change* 26.2–3 (1994), 109–142. DOI: 10.1007/BF01092410.

Jones, P. D., and R. S. Bradley. "Climatic Variations over the Last 500 Years." In *Climate Since A.D. 1500*, edited by R. S. Bradley and P. D. Jones, pp. 649–665. London: Routledge, 1995.

Lamb, H. H. *The Changing Climate: Selected Papers.* London: Methuen, 1966.

Li, Y. Y., et al. "The Impact of Ancient Civilization on the Northeastern Chinese Landscape: Palaeoecological Evidence from the Western Liaohe River Basin, Inner Mongolia." *The Holocene* 16.8 (2006), 1109–1121. DOI: 10.1177/09596 83606069403.

Malde, H. E. "Environment and Man in Arid America." *Science* 145 (1964), 123–129. DOI: 10.1126/science.145.3628.123.

Oglivie, A., and G. Farmer. "Documenting the Medieval Climate." In *Climates of the British Isles: Present, Past and Future,* edited by M. Hulme and E. Barrow, pp. 112–133. London: Routledge, 1997.

Woodbury, R. B. "Climatic Changes and Prehistoric Agriculture in the Southwestern United States." *Annals New York Academy of Sciences* 95.1 (1961), 705–709.

—Andrew S. Goudie

MEDITERRANEAN ENVIRONMENTS

The impacts of global environmental changes on Mediterranean environments are likely to be very marked, and many changes are already manifest. Five widely-spread regions of the world have a Mediterranean-type climate; these occur between approximately 30 and 40 degrees north and south of the equator, incorporating parts of the Mediterranean basin, California, central Chile, southwestern Africa, and southwestern and southern Australia (Figure 1). This distinctive climate is marked by pronounced summer aridity and cool moist winters, with mean annual precipitation varying from around 300 millimeters to more than 1,000 millimeters in the uplands. The dry summer climate, which is a product of seasonal fluctuations in the position of the high-pressure zones centered on the tropical deserts at around 20 degrees latitude, brings hot, windy conditions so that the ecosystems are prone to fire, especially in the late summer months. Fire frequency varies from region to region but may indeed be the dominant ecosystem disturbance factor and determinant, as modeled by Bond et al. (2005).

Soils and geomorphology are distinctive, and these regions are typically characterized by high relief, although Australia and the eastern Mediterranean exhibit somewhat more subdued landscapes. Soils are usually poor in nutrients, especially nitrogen and phosphorus; the availability of potassium, calcium, and magnesium depends on regional geology. For example, soils of the southwestern Cape of South Africa are especially low in calcium, while those of the Mediterranean basin itself, derived from limestone, have elevated levels of calcium.

Summer aridity and fire are prominent selective pressures and are reflected in the uniformity of vegetation structure; all five regions are characterized by sclerophyllous shrubs with hard, waxy, drought-resistant leaves. These shrublands are known by a variety of local names: *maquis* or *macchia* (Mediterranean basin), *chaparral* (California), *matorral* (Chile), *mallee* or *kwongan* (Australia) and *fynbos* (South Africa) (Dallman, 1998). The woody shrubs are fire-resistant or fire-dependent, with evergreen leaves that are generally broad, stiff, and sticky or waxy; other species adopt reduced leaf size in response to the lack of summer moisture. Geophytes (perennial plants that reproduce vegetatively from buds below the soil surface), too, are prominent elements, particularly immediately after fire. Woodlands occur around the Mediterranean basin, where cork oak, *Quercus suber*, forms a distinctive overstory while, in Australia, various species of *Eucalyptus* make up the canopy. The similarity of vegetation structure between regions contrasts with their floristic distinctiveness, since the actual plant species that make up the vegetation differ very markedly according to geography. For example, the Mediterranean basin maquis shrublands are characterized by woody shrubs belonging to the Asteraceae (daisy family) with an overstory of oak. In South Africa, the fynbos has extraordinary levels of plant-species diversity, especially among the Ericaceae (heath), Proteaceae (protea), and Restionaceae (Cape reed) families. Australian mallee is typified by numerous *Eucalyptus* and *Banksia* species.

A QUATERNARY LEGACY

The Mediterranean-type climate is, in geological terms, a relatively recent phenomenon and, while elements of the vegetation (e.g., the Proteaceae) are undoubtedly ancient, the various ecological associations were only assembled during the later Tertiary and Quaternary, that is, over the last few million years. Perhaps the most significant environmental changes to influence Mediterranean-type ecosystems took place in the late Pleistocene and Holocene in response to large-scale fluctuations of climate associated with the advance and retreat of ice sheets and glaciers, and in response to the increasing impact of humans. Repeated Pleistocene glaciations, while they did not affect the five regions (except Chile) directly, were accompanied by markedly reduced temperatures and lowered sea levels. The Quaternary temperature changes in these regions were intermediate between the major oscillations of the temperate and polar latitudes and the attenuated changes of the tropics and subtropics. Quaternary environmental change has been the focus of considerable research effort in all five regions and is best illustrated by comparing the situations that prevailed at the time of the last glacial maximum (LGM) with those of the mid-Holocene climatic optimum.

Temperatures during the LGM were substantially cooler in all regions of Mediterranean climate. In general, mean annual temperatures appear in some places to have been considerably lower, perhaps by as much as 9°C around 21,000 BP. With the exception of isolated refugia, much of the Mediterranean basin of Europe was steppe shrubland dominated by *Artemisia* (wormwood, shrubs similar to North American sagebrush) accompanied by a marked decline in tree taxa, and it was only after 10,000 BP that significant woodland expansion took place around the Mediterranean. Unglaciated parts of central Chile, such as Isla de Chiloé (42° south latitude), were occupied at this time by Magellanic moorland, a kind of vegetation that currently occupies the coast of Chile between 48° and 56° south latitude; pollen evidence is thus indicative of mean temperatures cooler by some 4°C (Villagrán, 1990). Palaeoenvironmental evidence for the LGM in the southwestern Cape of South Africa is scarce but consistent with cooling of the same order of magnitude. Precipitation conditions are more difficult to reconstruct and

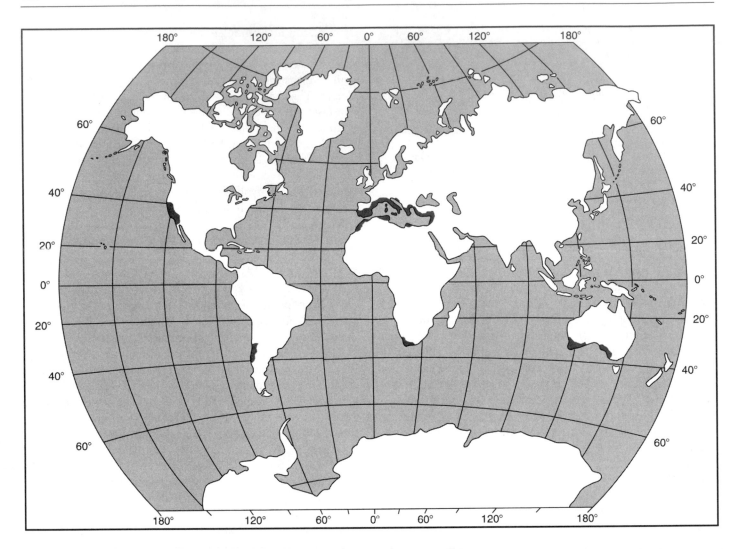

Mediterranean Environments. Figure 1. Distribution of Mediterranean Ecosystems and Representative Climate Conditions.

(After Archibold, 1995.)

vary strongly with geographical position. Thus the mean annual rainfall values of much of the Mediterranean basin during the LGM may have been marginally less than or almost the same as those of today, whereas in Chile, southwestern California, and southwestern South Africa, considerably more moisture may have been available, which cannot be completely accounted for by the reduction in evaporation brought about by temperature reduction. Still other Mediterranean climate regions, such as southeastern Australia, may then have been more arid than they are today.

Climate warming and sea-level rise accompanied the onset of the Holocene in regions of Mediterranean climate and, at such latitudes in the Northern Hemisphere, incident solar radiation was 7% higher in the summer months and correspondingly lower in the winter months than it is today. The resulting climate and environmental patterns, however, were complex. In at least two of the five Mediterranean-type regions,

South Africa and Chile, cooler periods during the Holocene are associated with increased rainfall. Conditions in the *fynbos* biome of the southwestern Cape of South Africa were probably somewhat warmer and drier by 5,000 BP, but parts of the Mediterranean basin remained cooler than the present day until later in the Holocene. Nevertheless, the cold and dry climates of the glacial period were ultimately replaced, and trees, especially oaks, and shrubs typical of maquis became abundant across much of the Mediterranean basin by about 6,000 BP. Warmer temperatures in Chile were also accompanied by drier climates, dry enough, apparently, to result in human abandonment of some areas because of the desiccation of lakes and the loss of food sources (Núñez et al., 2002). In Australia too, in at least parts of the winter-rainfall zone, warmer Holocene climates appear to have been associated with enhanced aridity. These mid-Holocene conditions do not, however, provide a reliable analog for globally warmed Mediterranean-type environments in part because of the different forcing factors operating and in part because of uncertainties regarding chronology and interpretation. We do learn from these studies, however, the highly dynamic nature of climate in these regions and the fact that fluctuations in moisture availability, brought about by changes in rainfall and temperature, have a strong impact on ecosystems.

THE NATURE AND DEGREE OF HUMAN IMPACT

In the Mediterranean basin in particular, human activity and significant anthropogenic impact on the environment have a long history. Nevertheless, it is frequently difficult to distinguish between those environmental changes in which direct human agency is involved and those in which "natural" climate forcing predominates. While climate change has had an obvious influence on ecosystems, much of the recent environmental history of the Mediterranean basin has been shaped by human-induced disturbances. There is also growing evidence to suggest longer-term impacts of humans on landscapes in Mediterranean climate regions extending back almost a million years. For example, fire was first used by humans in northern Greece between 500,000 and one million years ago (Conacher and Sala, 1998), and such practices probably had an impact on vegetation, intentionally or otherwise. But it is during the last few thousand years that human activity, particularly in the form of natural vegetation clearance for agriculture, becomes more pronounced; there is now convincing pollen evidence of large-scale vegetation clearance in the later half of the Holocene at sites in southern France (Roberts et al., 2001). Charcoal and pollen evidence reveals the part played by humans in determining the characteristic vegetation patterns of the region from about 6,000 BP on. Deciduous oak woodland is known to have become degraded and replaced by evergreen oak, juniper, and pine as a result of the establishment of agriculture and livestock. In eastern Spain, pine forest is replaced by oak scrub following clearance. In the eastern Mediterranean, the domestication and widespread introduction of the triad of wheat, olive, and vine, along with the cultivation of other trees such as walnut is a common pattern of disturbance. The tree cover of the Mediterranean basin, once 40% forested, has been literally decimated by humans so that forests now occupy just 4% of the area; even where woodland survives, its species composition may be markedly different from that which existed before clearance, cultivation, and arboriculture. The natural vegetation has also been affected by accelerated erosion. Nevertheless, rates of fluvial erosion suggest relatively low rates of contemporary sediment yield from catchments in the Mediterranean basin itself, a conclusion that points either to the efficacy of modern soil conservation methods or to the fact that vulnerable soils have already been removed by past erosion. Anthropogenic changes in the fire regime have also had a profound influence on biodiversity (Rundel et al., 1998).

Elsewhere, human occupation of Mediterranean-type landscapes may have had less impact, at least until the period of colonial occupation. This is certainly true of South Africa, where the impact of prehistoric cultures has been limited in comparison with the Mediterranean basin. The influence of European settlers, however, has been very marked. For example, widespread changes in vegetation in the catchment of the Verlorenvlei River in the western Cape lowland fynbos occurred as a result of the colonial introduction of winter wheat and livestock grazing. A similar picture emerges from western Victoria, Australia, where no significant aboriginal impact on the landscape appears to have taken place but where marked changes in fire regime, habitat fragmentation, loss of tree cover and biodiversity, and increased soil erosion and salinity were all consequences of European settlement. Colonial occupation here, as in South Africa, brought a marked change in the nature and scale of human impact (Hobbs, 2002).

One of the most obvious recent human impacts on the Mediterranean-type regions involves the introduction of alien plant and animal species, and their impacts appear to have been unusually severe. Indeed, Mediterranean-type ecosystems are generally occupied by introduced plant species to the extent that the native vegetation is almost entirely displaced from its habitat; the impacts of such invasions on biodiversity and other ecosystem properties, such as hydrology, have been very marked. Indeed, so intense is the overall effect of human exploitation of these ecosystems that the term "desertification," previously only associated with desert margins, is used increasingly of Mediterranean-type environments, especially those of the Mediterranean basin itself (Geeson et al., 2002). Even in the southwestern Cape, where the extent of soil erosion is limited, the impact of other forms of degradation, in particular the spread of alien invasives, represents a major threat to the continued survival of its great plant diversity. Mediterranean-type ecosystems are already subject to a high degree of anthropogenic disturbance (Conacher and Sala, 1998).

THE FUTURE

The influence of natural climate variation and industrial, agricultural, demographic, social, and political change on the Mediterranean-type ecosystems has been substantial, but what of the future? The complexities of the ecosystems themselves, together with the dynamics of the environmental changes, are significant impediments to reliable prediction. A number of recent major reviews address this issue (Moreno and Oechel, 1995; Jeftic et al., 1996; Giupponi and Schechter, 2003). Although regional downscaling of atmospheric General Circulation Models has proved challenging, the latest IPCC Fourth Assessment scenarios (IPCC, 2007) do produce regional-scale predictions for climatic conditions in the various Mediterranean-climate areas for the end of the twenty-first century. Two major factors need to be considered: changes in values of climatic parameters per se, including temperature, moisture, humidity, windiness, and their seasonal dynamics; and impacts of elevated carbon dioxide concentrations, the so-called CO_2 fertilization effect.

For the Mediterranean basin, regional warming of 2.5–4.0 °C is likely by the late twenty-first century, a value that is higher than the global mean temperature increase predicted by the IPCC suite of models. Warming is expected to be more pronounced in the summer months and to be associated with higher maximum daily temperatures and heat waves that are more intense, more frequent, and of longer duration. Furthermore, the models suggest that, by the end of the twenty-first century there will be substantial reductions in both winter and annual rainfall totals across the Mediterranean region, with an associated increase in the length of dry spells and drought risk in response to reduced soil moisture storage. Evapotran-spiration is likely to increase substantially: simulation of the expected change in potential evapotranspiration in response to the higher mean temperatures reveals that all localities in the European Mediterranean basin show an increase, while in some areas the values are double those of the present day.

In the other Mediterranean climate regions a similar picture is emerging. Overall reduction in annual precipitation is anticipated over the winter-rainfall area of South Africa and there may be changes in the distribution of the precipitation. In Australia, the pattern of elevated temperatures coinciding with drier climates is also very pronounced. The exceptions to this pattern are in western North America and southern South America where, although temperature increases are in line with rising global temperatures, annual mean rainfall over the Mediterranean climate areas of these continents is not expected to vary much from the present. Given the nature of temperature increase, however, the scenarios for the year 2100 for each of the five Mediterranean-climate regions suggest significantly lower soil moisture and consequent severe ecological and agricultural challenges.

Because Mediterranean-type systems are geographically small and are not significant carbon sinks or sources, the implications of global climate change for the five regions are more important than the feedback effects that these systems have, or will have, on the climate system itself. The implications of predicted changes need to be considered in the context of the complex ecological interactions between climate, soil moisture regime, and fire that characterize the Mediterranean-type ecosystems. Relatively small changes in climate and the subsequent changes in the fire regime can result in rapid shifts in pattern and process at landscape scales. Fire resilience is spatially variable in Mediterranean-type shrub communities, although most are resistant to fire at return intervals of 20 to 50 years. Given the probable future increase in the degree of human disturbance, drier winters and reduced soil moisture may increase fire frequencies and favor shrub species that resprout over those that reseed. The impact of climate change on plant communities has been modeled for southern Africa, and the great plant diversity of fynbos in the southwest is markedly threatened (Midgley et al., 2002), an indication of which is the predicted loss of around 10% of all members of the Proteaceae family. The attendant problems are more than ecological (Meadows, 2006), because reduced streamflow in the future, together with elevated water demand on a limited supply, may

soon result in a permanent inability to supply needs in the area's largest city, Cape Town.

Further impacts of global change will probably be caused by the invasion by alien plant species, which may respond more positively to increased levels of ecological stress than do the natural Mediterranean communities. Gritti et al. (2006) simulate the impacts of climate change on invaded Mediterranean ecosystems and conclude that in the longer term such communities, widespread across the region, may become dominated by exotic species unless there is significant intervention. Land-use changes will also have a significant impact on the runoff and soil erosion under Mediterranean-type conditions. The highest sediment loss today occurs under vines and wheat, so any future increase in either form of land use may cause problems.

Any potential positive impacts of the carbon dioxide fertilization effect appear to be minor. The response of *fynbos* shrubs to elevated carbon dioxide is limited, although it is marginally higher on plants grown on basic soils. For evergreen oaks, there may be a slightly improved drought resistance, and there may be a statistically insignificant increase in root biomass in, for example, Californian ponderosa pines. Although global-change impacts are largely negative for the vegetation of the Mediterranean basin, the model simulations of Osborne et al. (2000) suggest that CO_2 fertilization may already have significantly affected the productivity, structure, and water relations of sclerophyllous shrub vegetation and has tended to offset the negative effects of climate change.

Climate change is a serious threat to the Mediterranean-type climate regions as a whole and to their associated ecosystems, both natural and anthropogenic. Elevated mean annual temperature, reduced moisture availability, and increased fire frequency, coupled with increased intensity of land use, may accelerate land degradation and desertification in the Mediterranean environments of the world. Global climate change is a significant challenge for these systems, which are emerging as among the most vulnerable on the planet.

[*See also* Fire and Global Warming.]

BIBLIOGRAPHY

Archibold, O. W. *Ecology of World Vegetation.* London and New York: Chapman and Hall, 1995.
Bond, W. J., F. I. Woodward, and G. F. Midgley. "The Global Distribution of Ecosystems in a World Without Fire." *New Phytologist* 165 (2005), 525–538.
Conacher, A. J., and M. Sala, eds. *Land Degradation in Mediterranean Environments of the World.* Chichester, U.K., and New York: Wiley, 1998.
Dallman, P. R. *Plant Life in the World's Mediterranean Climates: California, Chile, South Africa, Australia, and the Mediterranean Basin.* Berkeley: University of California Press, 1998.
Geeson, N. A., C. J. Brandt, and J. Thornes, eds. *Mediterranean Desertification.* Chichester, U.K., and Hoboken, N.J.: Wiley, 2002.
Giupponi, C., and M. Schechter. *Climate Change in the Mediterranean: Socio-Economic Perspectives of Impacts, Vulnerability, and Adaptation.* Cheltenham, U.K., and Northampton, Mass.: Elgar, 2003.
Gritti, E. S., B. Smith, and M. T. Sykes. "Vulnerability of Mediterranean Basin Ecosystems to Climate Change and Invasion by Exotic Plant Species." *Journal of Biogeography* 33.1 (2006), 145–157. DOI: 10.1111/j.1365-2699.2005.01377.x.

THE FYNBOS HOT SPOT

The southwestern cape of South Africa has a distinctive low heath type of vegetation called *fynbos*. It is particularly well developed on nutrient-poor, highly leached, acidic, sandstone-derived soils. It displays little or no development of woodland, is naturally subject to fire and drought, and has relatively low biomass per unit area. Its most striking characteristic is its extraordinary plant diversity. There are some 8,500 plant species crowded into a very small geographic area (90,000 square kilometers). The level of endemism—68% of the species are native—has rendered the flora sufficiently distinctive for it to be accorded the status of floristic kingdom, one of only six in the world.

The beautiful and diverse *fynbos*, typified by its many protea species, is, however, under threat, especially by the introduction of alien plant species. The apparently vacant tree niche in the *fynbos*, for example, seems to have provided an opportunity for a number of aggressive introduced shrubs and trees of the genus *Acacia* from Australia to supplant *fynbos* over extensive areas. There are other threats as well, including the spread of cities, forestry, and agriculture. This area qualifies as one of the hottest of all hot spots in both its diversity and the extreme threats to its habitat.

BIBLIOGRAPHY

Cowling, R. M., ed. *The Ecology of Fynbos: Nutrients, Fire, and Diversity.* Cape Town: Oxford University Press, 1992.

—ANDREW S. GOUDIE

Hobbs, R. J. "Synergisms among Habitat Fragmentation, Livestock Grazing, and Biotic Invasions in Southwestern Australia." *Conservation Biology* 15.6 (2002), 1522–1528.

IPCC (Intergovermental Panel on Climate Change) *Climate Change 2007.* http://www.ipcc.ch (accessed June 2, 2008). Comprises the contributions of three Working Groups and a Synthesis Report.

Jeftic, L., S. Kečkeš, and J. C. Pernetta, eds. *Climatic Change and the Mediterranean.* Vol. 2. *Environmental and Societal Impacts of Climate Change and Sea Level Rise in the Mediterranean Region.* London and New York: Arnold, 1996.

Meadows, M. E. "Global Change and Southern Africa." *Geographical Research* 44.2 (2006), 135–145. DOI: 10.1111/j.1745-5871.2006.00375.x.

Midgely, G. F., et al. "Assessing the Vulnerability of Species Richness to Anthropogenic Climate Change in a Biodiversity Hotspot." *Global Ecology and Biogeography* 11.6 (2002), 445–451. DOI: 10.1046/j.1466-822X.2002.00307.x.

Moreno, J. M., and W. C. Oechel, eds. *Global Change and Mediterranean-Type Ecosystems.* Berlin and New York: Springer, 1995.

Núñez, L., M. Grosjean, and I. Cartajena. "Human Occupations and Climate Change in the Puna de Atacama." *Science* 298 (2002), 821–824. DOI: 10.1126/science.1076449.

Roberts, N., M. E. Meadows, and J. R. Dodson. "The History of Mediterranean-Type Environments: Climate, Culture, and Landscape." *The Holocene* 11.6 (2001), 631–634. DOI: 10.1191/09596830195663.

Osborne, C. P., et al. "Modelling the Recent Historical Impacts of Atmospheric CO_2 and Climate Change on Mediterranean Vegetation." *Global Change Biology* 6.4 (2000), 445–446.

Rundel, P. W., G. Montenegro, and F. M. Jaksic, eds. *Landscape Disturbance and Biodiversity in Mediterranean-Type Ecosystems.* Berlin and New York: Springer, 1998.

Villagrán, C. "Glacial Climates and Their Effects on the History of the Vegetation of Chile: A Synthesis Based on Palynological Evidence from Isla de Chiloé." *Review of Palaeobotany and Palynology* 65.1–4 (1990), 17–24. DOI: 10.1016/0034-6667(90)90052-K.

—MICHAEL E. MEADOWS

METHANE

Methane (CH_4) is a minor but very significant organic gas in the atmosphere. Its concentration is the largest among the several hundred hydrocarbons present in the atmosphere. An important component of the carbon cycle, methane is second only to carbon dioxide in contributing to the greenhouse effect. The current average concentration in the atmosphere is 1.774 parts per million (Solomon et al., 2007).

Analysis of methane concentrations in air bubbles in ice cores from Antarctica and Greenland indicates that, before 1900 CE, methane remained constant at about 0.8 parts per million by volume (ppmv). After the Industrial Revolution, methane concen-trations increased exponentially (see Figure 1), more than doubling in one hundred years. The increase in methane concentration correlates strongly with the increase in global population. The changes in atmospheric methane over the last century reflect human activities and a variety of sources. The total amount of methane presently in the atmosphere is about 3.5 billion metric tons of equivalent carbon. While this amount is a small percentage of that for carbon dioxide (750 billion metric tons), the impact of methane on climate change is nevertheless considered significant.

SOURCES AND SINKS

Table 1 presents the major sources and sinks of methane. Natural sources, such as wetlands, oceans and lakes, and termites, provide about 25% of methane emissions to the atmosphere, mainly through decay processes. Agriculture and animal husbandry emit a further 32%, mainly from rice paddies (especially in Southeast Asia and China), ruminants (cattle, sheep, and goats), and human beings. Methane escapes from rice paddies, as it does from wetlands, through decay and fertilization. Ruminant emissions, mostly by belching, are caused by inefficient digestion of fibrous grazing material. Burning and leakage associated with deforestation and fossil fuels add another 27% to annual methane emissions. The natural gas used for heating and cooking is almost entirely methane, and methane is emitted from oil- and gas-fired power stations and from oil wells. The remainder comes from landfills and waste emissions, including those from coal mining.

The average lifetime of a methane molecule in the atmosphere is on the order of 10–12 years. There are three major sinks shown in Table 1. The most important removal mechanism is reactions in the troposphere and stratosphere with the hydroxyl radical (OH). OH and other radicals are fragments of molecules with lifetimes on the order of fractions of a second. They are extremely important as triggers in atmospheric chemistry. Methane and OH combine to form water and the methyl radical, CH_3. About

TABLE 1. Major Sources and Sinks of Methane*

Sources	Rate† (Range)	Sinks	Rate† (Range)
Methanogenesis		Reactions with hydroxyl radical	320 (260–380)
Natural wetlands	85 (75–150)		
Rice paddies	80 (45–130)	Atmospheric accumulation	35 (30–40)
Bovines	60 (45–75)		
Natural gas leakage	75 (60–90)	Soil uptake	20 (15–25)
Landfills/waste	60 (60–80)		
Biomass burning	40 (35–75)		
Termites	15 (5–75)		
Oceans and lakes	10 (5–15)		
Totals	425 (310–765)		375 (305–445)

*Numbers are approximate. †Units are millions of metric tons of carbon equivalent per year.

SOURCE: Turco, 1997, p. 376. With permission of Oxford University Press.

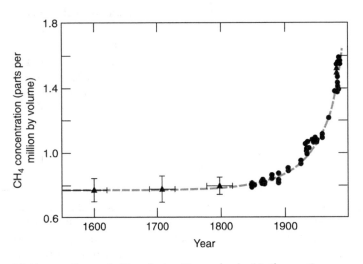

Methane. FIGURE 1. Trends in Atmospheric Methane Concentrations from 1600 to the Late 1980s.
The exponential increase after 1880 is strongly correlated with the increase in global population.

(After Turco, 1997, p. 375. With permission of Oxford University Press.)

85% of methane loss is caused by this reaction. CH_3 is unstable and reacts rapidly to form other compounds, including peroxyacetyl nitrate, an important component of photochemical smog. Another, much smaller sink is methane uptake by soil.

About 35 million metric tons of carbon per year accumulates in the atmosphere, creating an annual average increase in concentration of about 0.6%. In 1992, growth stopped in some parts of the globe. Suggested causes include a decrease in biomass burning and a decrease in the burning of fossil fuels across the globe, enhanced exchange between the troposphere and stratosphere associated with the Mount Pinatubo eruption, and lower emissions from wetlands. The growth rate returned to the usual level in the following year.

The source and sink totals in the table do not match, creating an imbalance in the overall annual methane budget which may perhaps be explained by the uncertainties in the estimates, indicated by the ranges in Table 1. Future research will improve the accuracy of the numbers and ensure a better understanding of the relationships between sources and sinks.

METHANE AS A GREENHOUSE GAS

Methane is a greenhouse gas, and continuing annual increases in atmospheric concentrations add to the threat of anthropogenic impacts on the Earth's climate though artificial global warming. The International Panel on Climate Change rates the global warming potential—the impact compared with that of carbon dioxide on a molecule-by-molecule basis—of methane as ranging from 56 times higher over a 20-year period to 21 times higher over a 100-year period. Methane absorbs longwave radiation in wavelengths with respect to which the atmosphere is not yet saturated, for example, around 7.7 micrometers. Increasing methane concentrations will be able to absorb in this wavelength band to maximum effect. Methane concentrations in the atmosphere are an order of magnitude lower than those of carbon dioxide, and the methane atmospheric lifetime is estimated to be at least five times lower than that of carbon dioxide. The overall impact of carbon dioxide on global warming remains about three times higher than that of methane.

LIMITING EMISSIONS

The complex mix of sources listed in Table 1 indicates that control of methane emissions is very difficult. There are, however, some potential benefits from waste methane. One example on a local or regional scale is to tap methane stored in solid waste facilities (dumps, landfills) for use as an energy source. Landfill gas (LFG), of which methane is a major component, is formed by the anaerobic decay of organic matter and with proper environmental management can be collected with minimal loss to the atmosphere. It is estimated that about 0.18 cubic meters of LFG is produced per kilogram of municipal solid waste, depending on the rate of decomposition of the organic matter and the age and fill rate of the facility. The LFG can be piped to an energy facility where it is burned to generate heat or electricity. From a landfill generating 4 million cubic meters of LFG per year, it is possible, assuming a 50% methane content, to generate about 5,000 megawatt hours of electricity. When methane is completely burned, it turns into carbon dioxide and water, but the equivalent emissions and greenhouse-gas impacts are much lower than if the methane is released into the atmosphere.

SEA-FLOOR DEPOSITS

Another example is the relatively recent discovery of methane gas trapped in hydrates on the sea floor. Methane hydrate is formed in ocean-floor sediments under extreme pressure and low temperatures, where the water is compressed, leaving a solid gray mass similar to ice. It is estimated that about 160 cubic centimeters of methane (at standard atmospheric conditions) is contained in a compressed state in 1 cubic centimeter of methane hydrate. Estimates of the amount on the ocean floor indicate that there is enough energy to replace all the gas, oil, and coal reserves on land. However, methane hydrate is extremely unstable, and, once removed from its natural location, dissolves quickly, releasing methane to the atmosphere. There is a potential danger of a mass release of this greenhouse gas from the ocean floor to the atmosphere if major changes in ocean temperature and pressure occur. Much research is needed in the future if methane hydrate is to be used safely as a source of energy.

[See also Agriculture and Agricultural Land; Biomes; Deforestation; Fossil Fuels; Global Warming; Greenhouse Effect; Methane Hydrates; Nitrogen Cycle; and Wetlands.]

BIBLIOGRAPHY

Environment Australia. Methane Capture and Use: Waste Management Workbook. Canberra: Environment Protection Group, Environment Australia, 1997.

Houghton, J. T., et al., eds. Climate Change 1995: The Science of Climate Change. United Nations Intergovernmental Panel on Climate Change. Cambridge and New York: Cambridge University Press, 1996.

Solomon, S., et al., eds. Climate Change 2007: The Physical Science Basis: Contribution of Working Group I to the Fourth Assessment Report of the Intergovernmental Panel on Climate Change. Cambridge and New York: Cambridge University Press, 2007.

Steele, L. P., et al. "The Global Distribution of Methane in the Troposphere." Journal of Atmospheric Chemistry 5.2 (1987), 125–171. DOI: 10.1007/BF00048857.

Turco, R P. Earth Under Siege. Oxford and New York: Oxford University Press, 1997. The second edition was published in 2002.

—HOWARD A. BRIDGMAN

METHANE HYDRATES

Recently, an unconventional source of natural gas has been recognized. It may require drastically different exploration and production methods, and may therefore never be exploited, but the potential resource is so large that it must be mentioned. In two very different environments—permafrost regions of the Arctic, and sediments of the modern sea floor—methane and other constituents of natural gas occur in a crystalline form bound to ice molecules as gas hydrates (especially methane hydrates). These hydrates belong to the class of substances called clathrates, in which molecules of one substance (the gas) are trapped in cavities in the crystal lattice of another (water ice).

Whether this gas is geologically old enough to be called a fossil fuel is not clear. In the marine setting, the gas may be generated by the decomposition of organic material in the sediments, but these occurrences are not the same as conventional gas in offshore fields. That gas has been formed at high temperature from decomposition of organic material in ancient sediments and then trapped in gaseous form in deeply buried rock. Gas hydrates, on the other hand, are buried within 600 meters of the ocean floor, in unconsolidated sediments, not sedimentary rock. Their thickness appears to be limited by the local temperature gradient, the lower boundary being controlled by the depth where above-freezing temperatures begin (temperature rises with greater depth in the Earth) while the upper boundary

is where the overlying water and sediment depth provide enough pressure for the hydrates to form and survive. On land in the Arctic, the maximum depth is, again, roughly 600 meters, near the bottom limit of permafrost.

Studies to date suggest that the larger part of the total resource is on the ocean floor, not in the Arctic permafrost. Some hydrates in the ocean sediments occur in discrete nodules and patches that would be difficult to exploit, but they also occur in thicker and more continuous beds that could possibly be tapped by modern drilling and production methods, although the water depth in some areas may be prohibitive. Some estimates suggest that gas in all the deposits combined—not recoverable, but in-place amounts—may be ten times that in the world's conventional natural gas reserves (Boswell, 2005).

Methane trapped in these hydrates may be significant in another way. As a potent greenhouse gas, methane would promote global warming if it were released by the melting of hydrates, either in the Arctic or in ocean sediments. It may, in fact, be implicated in past episodes of climate warming (Kennett et al., 2003). The possibility that methane release would promote warming, which then would promote melting, which would release more methane in a feedback loop, is enough to make anyone cautious about drilling to capture methane (ORNL, 2000). There is some evidence that warming may already have caused release of sea-floor methane in the Canadian Arctic (Paull et al., 2007).

In 2001 the U.S. Department of Energy funded a four-year project to develop technologies to locate and safely drill hydrate deposits (USDOE) and the U.S. Naval Research Laboratory has studied occurrences in the Gulf of Mexico, near Vancouver Island, and near Japan.

[See also Arctic Warming; Fossil Fuels; Global Warming; Greenhouse Gases; Methane; and Natural Gas.]

BIBLIOGRAPHY

Boswell, R. "Buried Treasure." Power and Energy 2.1 (2005). http://www.memagazine.org/suppparch/pefebo5 (accessed June 2, 2008).

Kennett, J., et al. Methane Hydrates in Quaternary Climate Change: The Clathrate Gun Hypothesis. American Geophysical Union (AGU) Special Publication 54 (2003).

ORNL. "Methane Hydrates: A Carbon Management Challenge." Oak Ridge National Laboratory Review 33.2 (2000). http://www.ornl.gov/info/ornlreriew (accessed June 2, 2008).

Paull, Charles K., et al. "Origin of Pingo-like Features on the Beaufort Sea Shelf and Their Possible Relationship to Decomposing Methane Gas Hydrates." Geophysical Research Letters 34, L01603 (2007). DOI: 10.1029/2006GL027977.

U.S. Department of Energy. Methane Hydrate: The Gas Resource of the Future. http://www.fossil.energy.gor/program/aligar/hydrates (accessed June 2, 2008).

—DAVID J. CUFF

MIGRATIONS

Migration encompasses all forms of human spatial mobility, ranging from local exchanges of partners for marriage to transcontinental movements associated with job transfers or settlement. Movements within countries and those across national boundaries, as well as voluntary and forced movements, all fall within the ambit of the study of human migration. Within such a vast and complex topic we can identify three broad divisions:

- Population redistribution, which covers internal movements and, most importantly, rural to-urban migration.
- International movement, which encompasses emigration and immigration and issues as diverse as brain-drain and labor migration.
- Forced movements of political refugees and also, increasingly, those in flight from environmental hazards or environmental change.

By bringing peoples of very different backgrounds together and concentrating populations in particular locations, these three broad types of migration are among the most powerful forces of global change. These three types are not mutually exclusive; there are close interrelationships among them. For example, the issue of the loss of talent (brain-drain) can be as relevant at the village level as at the national level, and the flows of wealth from destinations to origins in the form of remittances can result from internal as well as from international migrations. There are also important, if as yet poorly understood, links between internal and international migrations. For example, the arrival of immigrants may increase competition for jobs and be a factor in pushing native populations out of certain areas, and the arrival of rural migrants in cities may precede their movement overseas. Both, however, are voluntary movements, thus distinguishing them from the forced movements of refugees. Voluntary and forced movements fall into separate analytic and policy categories, but the difference between an economic migrant and a refugee can be as much a matter of Realpolitik and definition as it is of the factors behind the move. Voluntary migration has been shown to be controlled more by institutional factors such as company transfers, labor contracts, and availability of housing than by individual decisions; hence, clear, logical divisions between forced and free migrations become difficult to sustain. Despite intuitive differences among the three broad divisions, it is increasingly important that they be examined in a unified framework and their interrelations specified.

CURRENT TRENDS

Major changes have occurred recently in the pattern of global migration, and four main sets of factors can be identified that brought these changes about. First, the expansion of free-market economic activities created nuclei that drew the rural populations to metropolitan areas through the creation of national, and later international, divisions of labor in a process that has come to be known as globalization. Second, the spread of more open, stable forms of government has allowed the international division of labor to function more effectively. Third, the decline in fertility to levels below replacement level in the most developed parts of the world has created tight local labor markets. The response of entrepreneurs has been to export labor-intensive industries, to import labor, or to move from labor-based to knowledge-based industrialization, or some combination of

these. Fourth, developments in technology have allowed the mass transportation of population over long distances and at great speed.

In 1800, only about 12% of Europe's population and around 5% of the population of the United States lived in towns and cities. By 1950, these proportions had risen to 51 and 57% respectively and by 2005 had reached around 72 and 81%. In 2005, 48.7% of the world's population (3.15 billion) was classified as urban. More people are being added every year to the world's urban population than to the rural population. Migration is but one component of urban growth—natural increase and reclassification being the others—but it has been a major cause of the increase in the proportion of urban population worldwide and in the concentration of populations in the largest cities yet seen in human history, with all their environmental and infrastructural problems. The number of urban agglomerations having populations over 10 million increased from three in 1975 to 20 in 2005, with 15 of these in the developing world.

As the world has become more urban, so too has the global system of migration been transformed. International migration from the nineteenth to the mid-twentieth century was dominated by movements from Europe west across the Atlantic to the Americas, or east across Eurasia to Siberia and Central Asia. There were also significant movements out of global centers of population in southern China and India. As fertility declined in Europe from the 1960s, and as Europe experienced the post–World War II economic boom, it became a continent of net immigration rather than of net emigration. The migration to the main settler societies of Australia, Canada, New Zealand, and the United States, on the other hand, shifted from streams dominated by European origins to those dominated by Asian and Latin American origins. The reasons for these changes were not solely demographic; in the case of the settler societies, the triumph of liberal democratic systems of government at the end of World War II had made anathema the maintenance of racist immigration policies that excluded the entry of non-Europeans. These discriminatory laws were finally abolished during the third quarter of the twentieth century.

Other regional systems emerged: from South and Southeast Asian countries to the oil-rich countries of West Asia after the rise in oil revenues from 1973; to Southeast and East Asian countries as Japan and other rapidly growing economies shifted from labor-surplus to labor-deficit; and to smaller nuclei of regional attraction in southern Africa, Israel, northern Venezuela, and central Argentina. More people are moving in more ways than ever before even if, on a per capita basis, international movements from Asian and Latin American countries today do not yet rival those from Europe during the Great Migration of the late nineteenth and early twentieth centuries. The United Nations has estimated that, during the last half of the 1980s, 750 million to one billion people migrated. We are in an age of migration, even if the vast majority moved within their countries of origin. Only a minority have moved from the poorest countries of the South, primarily in Africa, to the rich countries of the North.

ISSUES AND CONSEQUENCES

Modern migrants are of many types: those going for long-term settlement, short-term laborers, students, the highly skilled, and professionals. The majority flow through legal channels, but significant numbers move through irregular channels, with many smuggled or trafficked into destinations where they are vulnerable to exploitation and abuse, providing a challenge to governments in both origins and destinations of the movement. If there is one universal characteristic of migration, it is that the majority of movers are young adults who tend, initially at least, to be better educated and more innovative than the average for the population from which they come.

Since the mid-1990s, issues of migration and development have risen to prominence. Initially, migration was seen as negative for development as the best and brightest left their places of origin for cities or the developed world. Recent research, however, suggests a more nuanced approach by drawing attention to ways in which migrants can assist their countries of origin. Attention has focused on three linked themes: remittances, brain-drain, and diasporas.

Remittances currently surpass foreign aid and, in 2004, reached $214 billion, having doubled over the previous ten years. Almost 70% of this amount flowed to developing countries. While the contribution of remittances to long-term development is contested, there seems little doubt that they can contribute to the alleviation of poverty and the promotion of education in the communities in which migrants originate. Remittances also help to compensate developing countries for the loss of skilled personnel. However, much of the present migration of the highly skilled occurs within the developed world itself or from a relatively small number of middle-income developing countries such as China, India, Mexico, or the Philippines. Small and island populations do indeed appear to suffer from the loss of their skilled, although clear association between the loss of medical personnel and a decline in basic health indicators is not usually clear cut.

The spread of migrants from any area of origin creates a network of communities at various destinations to form a diaspora that can be drawn on as a resource. Migrants not only send remittances but may also return on a long- or short-term basis to assist with development by helping to train those who remained behind or by establishing businesses and creating employment in origin economies; the Overseas Chinese, Non-resident Indians, and the Viet Kieu are examples. Not all migrants, however, will seek to support governments in their countries of origin, and the diaspora is not necessarily a force for sustainable development.

Recent migrations have brought about a mixing of cultures that has been most intense in the traditional settler societies and in Europe, but they have also affected the once more homogeneous societies of Japan, Korea, and Taiwan. However, in many parts of the developing world, the pressures have been to create homogeneous units, and expulsion, ethnic cleansing and forced migration have been common. Although numbers of refugees declined fairly steadily from 18 million in 1993 to 8.7 million in

2005, they increased to 9.9 million in 2006 primarily because of the conflict in Iraq, according to United Nations estimates. The internally displaced have emerged as the most rapidly growing category of forced migrants, bringing those of concern to the United Nations High Commissioner for Refugees to 32.9 million at the end of 2006, up from 21 million a year earlier. Conflicts in Sudan, Uganda, Somalia, Sri Lanka, and Colombia, as well as Iraq, have contributed to this increase in the numbers of internally displaced.

Just as the international migration systems have changed significantly over the last decades, so too have the ways of viewing and conceptualizing human movements. Initially, migration was seen as a relatively simple economic response to variable opportunities available both nationally and internationally. Migrants moved to places where they could best maximize their return, and they moved on the basis of an individual decision. Later research, however, has highlighted the significance of institutional constraints and family linkages in the process of movement, with migration thus conceptualized as a group rather than an individual phenomenon. The significance imputed to structural, large-scale economic and political factors, while justified, does downplay the fact that migration flows are made up of individuals, all with their own hopes and aspirations. The most recent approaches tend to focus on the experience of migration, exile, and identity. Thus, the trend has been from rigorous and objective, if fairly simple, economic models of migration toward much more complex, subjective approaches that highlight the significance of large-scale political and social factors as well as the individual experience of movement.

The consequences of migration for human development have inserted other highly contested variables into the equation, for example, the significance of transnational corporations and the new international division of labor in drawing unskilled labor into factories in locations spread around the world, and in moving the highly skilled from country to country. The incorporation of women into these labor forces has had a marked effect, not just by reducing fertility, but by raising the status of women in what were once conservative, male-dominated societies. But migration can also bring disaster through the transfer of pathogens, not just of the more dramatic viruses such as AIDS, but also of significantly greater and traditional killers such as malaria.

Among the global threads being woven into the increasingly complex fabric of migration are the causes of environmental change. Migration, through the concentration of people in cities, is a major factor contributing to urban and industrial effluent and emissions, and the movement of people into tropical forests and the clearance of these forests by burning contribute to increased CO_2 in the atmosphere. As contributors to global warming, these movements in turn promote a rise in sea level, which might be of the order of one meter by 2100, forcing hundreds of thousands to move in Bangladesh, China, and Egypt, as well as in the island world of the Pacific. Associated climate change and increased aridity in some parts of the world and increased precipitation in others are also likely to force people to move. While these scenarios are largely speculation, the increasing migrations that are already being observed at both ends of the development spectrum will transform societies of origin, as well as societies of destination, to produce a very different world.

BIBLIOGRAPHY

Castles, S., and M. J. Miller. *The Age of Migration: International Population Movements in the Modern World.* 4th ed. Basingstoke, U.K.: Palgrave Macmillan, 2007. A useful introduction to the main trends in international migration.

Cohen, R., ed. *The Cambridge Survey of World Migration.* Cambridge and New York: Cambridge University Press, 1995. A massive review of international migration consisting of a series of short, high-quality essays based on regions rather than topics.

Cornelius, W. A., et al., eds. *Controlling Immigration: A Global Perspective.* 2d ed. Stanford, Calif.: Stanford University Press, 2004. A useful analysis of the migration policies of the developed countries.

Hoerder, D. *Cultures in Contact: World Migrations in the Second Millennium.* Durham, N.C.: Duke University Press, 2002. One thousand years of global migration—a tour de force.

IOM. *World Migration 2005: Costs and Benefits of International Migration.* Geneva: International Organization for Migration, 2005. The third volume in a biennial series by a leading international organization.

MPI. *Migration Information Source.* Washington, D.C.: Migration Policy Institute. http://www.migrationinformation.org/ (accessed June 2, 2008). An online source of information on all aspects of international migration.

OECD. *International Migration Outlook.* Paris: Organisation for Economic Co-operation and Development, 2007. An annual review of migration data and issues in the most developed countries.

Özden, Ç., and M. Schiff, eds. *International Migration, Economic Development, and Policy.* Washington, D.C.: World Bank: Basingstoke, U.K., and New York: Palgrave Macmillan, 2007. The third in a series of major studies of migration and development carried out by the World Bank.

Skeldon, R. *Migration and Development: A Global Perspective.* London: Addison-Wesley Longman, 1997. An attempt to consider, within a unified framework, internal and international migration, and movements in developed and developing countries.

United Nations. *Trends in Total Migrant Stock: The 2005 Revision.* New York: United Nations, Department of Economic and Social Affairs, Population Division, 2006. The standard global database on international migration.

—RONALD SKELDON

MINING

Life today requires products of mining such as precious metals, nonferrous metals, iron and ferroalloy metals, radioactive metals, minor metals, fuels, ceramic clays, building materials, metallurgical and refractory materials, industrial and manufacturing materials, chemical materials, abrasive minerals, fertilizer minerals, and gemstones. All human activities, such as farming, construction, transportation, communication, and space exploration, consume the products of mining. Because the earth is currently the only practical source of these raw materials, their economic extraction, processing, and utilization will continue to be an essential, productive human activity for the foreseeable future.

As one of the primary industries—the other two are agriculture and forestry—the mineral industry provides raw materials that are essential inputs to the secondary industries for manufacturing products demanded by society. Tertiary industries provide the communities with essential services such as infrastructure, transportation, banking, education, and recreation. The continued success of a thriving economy depends on the uninterrupted flow of materials and services to and from the three levels of industry (Gregory, 1980).

Mining activities, in addition to high direct contributions to GDP (gross domestic product), can attract land, capital, and labor, all essential for industrialization and economic development, particularly in developing countries. However, the possession of rich mineral resources and their exploitation alone does not ensure strong and stable economic growth. The use of the mineral revenues to serve the larger goals of the country's development programs and to contribute to the evolution of the other sectors of the economy must be planned and implemented. Abandoned mine sites of the past are a constant reminder that mining without control results in serious blights and hazards to the public, contaminates air and water resources, adversely affects land values, creates public nuisances, and generally interferes with community development (Ramani, 1995). An undeveloped deposit, on the other hand, contributes little, directly or indirectly, to a country's economy, and may even lose all its potential value as a result of technological advancements (Vogely, 1985).

SCOPE OF MINING ACTIVITIES

Figure 1 diagrams the scope of mining activities, from finding a mineral deposit through exploration and mining to processing and marketing the final product. The stages of mining include prospecting, exploration, development, extraction, processing, decommissioning, and rehabilitation of mined lands. The time from preliminary prospecting to start of mining can be long (10 to 15 years) and from start of mining to decommissioning and rehabilitation even longer (several decades). Therefore, the considerations of investment, financial and technical risks, and environmental impacts on the profitability of a mining venture assume greater importance in all the stages.

Exploration

Prospecting and exploration constitute the various methods for locating, defining, and describing the mineral deposits. Minerals occur in diverse environments. Gold and gemstones are found in streambeds, but they also occur in veins thousands of meters deep. Beach sands contain valuable minerals, as do sands in shallow and deep ocean beds. Minerals are found as consolidated and unconsolidated deposits in ocean floors and in solution in sea water. Coal is widely distributed throughout the world in both surface and underground deposits. Salt occurs as evaporites in laminar beds, and huge domes. Porphyry deposits containing copper are huge and low-grade, often 4–8 kilometers across and containing less than 1% copper. As a consequence, prospecting and exploration methods for mineral deposits are diverse.

Extraction

Ore can be extracted by surface mining, underground mining, and nonentry mining. In surface mining, the overburden (soil

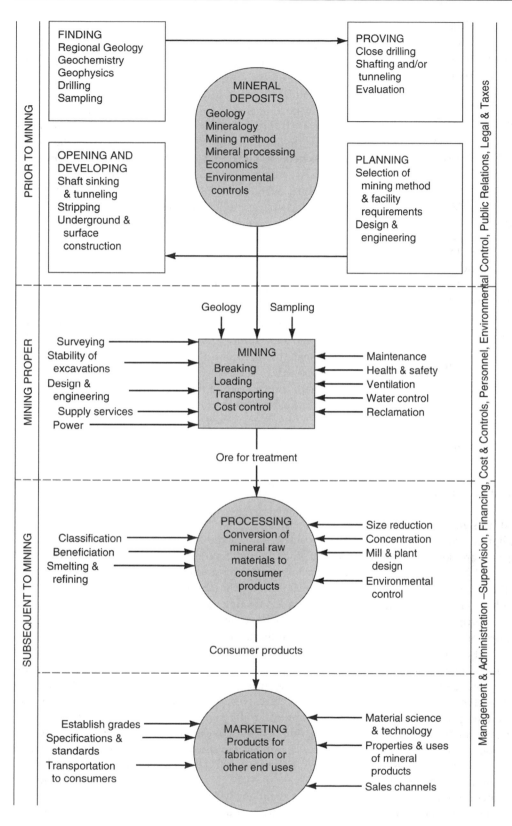

Mining. FIGURE 1. Scope of Mining Activities.

(After Beall, 1973, with permission of the Society for Mining, Metallurgy, and Exploration, Inc.)

and rock above the deposit) is removed, exposing the ore body for its removal. In underground mining, the deposit is first accessed by a suitable opening from the surface, and a network of openings is driven in the surrounding rocks and the deposit for the installation of service facilities for the transport of miners, materials, ventilating air, water, etc., and for the subsequent extraction of the deposit itself. In nonentry mining, the deposit is accessed from a suitable opening on the surface but the extraction process does not require the miners to go underground (Hartman and Mutmansky, 2002).

There are numerous variations in each type of mining, each one most effective for a particular combination of the types of rock above and below the mineral deposit, and the thickness, depth, inclination, extent, and type of mineral deposit. The difficulty of extraction increases tremendously with increases in depth and inclination. Great difficulties are presented by very thin or very thick deposits, and also by steep topography.

Surface mining is superior to underground mining in terms of ore-body recovery, ore quality control, operational flexibility, safety, productivity, and cost. However, when the removal cost of the soil and strata above the deposit becomes prohibitive, it is common practice to switch to underground mining of the deposit. Surface-mining methods can be broadly classified as open-pit mining, quarrying, stripping, and placer mining. Tremendous technological developments in earth-moving equipment have enabled surface mining of deeper deposits.

In underground mining, extensive development of the ore body is required to create blocks of ore that are either not extracted, or are partially or fully extracted, according to the mining plan. Underground mining methods are classified—according to the manner in which the stability of openings and the systematic control of the strata above the deposit are maintained for the duration of mining—as unsupported, supported, and caving.

Special health and safety considerations in underground mining include the problems of toxic, noxious, and explosive atmospheres caused by gases and dust. Design of stable structures in the rock and their support, lighting of the workings, and control of noise in confined spaces are some problems unique to underground mining.

Nonentry mining is widely practiced for the extraction of oil, natural gas, and coal-bed methane. Underground gasification of coal and oil-shale deposits and in situ retorting (distillation of volatile materials in a vessel called a retort) of oil shale have also found application in the recovery of oil and combustible gas. In the nonentry mining methods, in situ solution mining of deposits is a primary method of production, whereby the valuable minerals are recovered by dissolving, melting, leaching or slurrying the minerals in place, and transporting the resulting fluidized product to the surface for further processing. Ocean mining refers to mining in the marine environment. The technology for the recovery of dissolved minerals in sea water is well advanced. While offshore drilling for oil and gas has been remarkably successful, mining of solid mineral deposits, even in shallow water is not common.

Decisions on whether an ore body will be mined or not, and the mining method to be practiced, depend on many technological, economic, and social factors. Often the technological factors constrain the mining engineer to a particular extraction technique, while the economic and social factors determine whether the ore body can be mined at all.

Processing

The processing of the mined ore can vary from simple to complex. It may involve only crushing and sizing, as is usually the case with stone that is mined for use as a construction aggregate. For metalliferous (metal-bearing) ores, the processes include concentration, smelting, and refining before the metal is ready for casting. It is common practice to site the mill or concentrator near the mine to produce the concentrate from the mined ore. Smelters are placed in locations where energy is abundant and less expensive than at the mine site. In some cases, such as coal mining, where conditions are favorable, the mining, processing, and utilization facilities are sited next to each other, in so-called mine-mouth power plants. In other cases, transport of mined products over thousands of kilometers and across the oceans cannot be avoided.

Reclamation and rehabilitation

Reclamation and rehabilitation refers to activities directed at reducing the impacts of mining and processing operations both during and after mining. The global footprint of mining is relatively small, of the order of 1% of the land surface (MMSD, 2002). In the U.S., it is about 2.5%. While this is very small compared with those of agriculture and forestry, mining, as a temporary and nonrenewable use of land, impacts profoundly the future development potential of mineral-bearing lands. The assessment of the on-site and off-site effects of mining operations on air, water, land, social, and cultural resources and the efforts to reduce or eliminate the negative impacts, are part of the reclamation and rehabilitation stage of mining.

ENVIRONMENTAL IMPACTS OF MINING

The impacts of mining on the environment may be felt on-site (on the property of the mine) and off-site and on varying time scales, from the near term to long into the future. The impacts are physical, affecting the land, water, air, wildlife, and vegetation, and economic, affecting such things as the supply and demand of minerals/metal commodities, revenues, tax base, and employment. The impacts have health and safety implications for individuals and communities. Environmental impacts also arise from operations upstream to mining (prospecting, exploration, development, etc.) and from those downstream to mining (processing, transport, concentration, smelting, refining, etc) and continue after the mine has been closed and rehabilitated. The lifetime of a mine is variable, from a few years to several decades. The impacts on the other resources differ at different stages of mining, are affected by the extraction methods used, and continue into the post-mining period, even if the mined land is not abandoned. These impacts, however, are not mutually exclusive, because air pollution may eventually lead to water pollution, and both combined can render on- and off-site lands uninhabitable (Ramani, 1995).

Factors influencing the extent of environmental impacts are both natural and cultural. Among the important natural factors are geographic and geological location, the characteristics of the minerals being mined, topography, and climate. Cultural factors include the method of mining, the scale of operation, and the existing and planned land uses. Mining and processing of gold and silver ores may use cyanide and mercury. Pyrites and sulfide ores are sources of sulfur dioxide and sulfuric acid. High concentrations of salts are associated with the mining of sodium and potassium ores. Uranium mining presents unique problems of tailings management for the containment of radionuclides. High concentrations of heavy metals (aluminum, iron, manganese, lead, nickel, etc.) are likely to occur in the mining and processing of metallic ores. Mining of asbestos, silica sands, and mica presents challenging health, safety, and environmental problems. The impact of ground movements from underground caving methods requires detailed consideration in environmental planning. Deep open pits present numerous challenges for safe decommissioning. Stone, sand, and gravel operations near urban areas present different opportunities for reclamation and land use planning compared with mining operations in remote places where the climate is harsh and the soil not very fertile. Environmental concerns arising from mining and planning for adequate attention to these concerns are site specific.

Effects on air

Mining by itself may not be a major contributor to the air pollution problem, but downstream processes such as the burning of oil and coal and the roasting and smelting of metalliferous ores are major contributors to atmospheric emissions. There are many areas in which mining and related operations emit particulate and gaseous substances to the atmosphere. Dust rising from haul roads, screens in processing plants, blasting in surface mines, and mine exhaust from underground mines also causes air pollution.

Recognition of the air pollution problem has been increasing rapidly, and air-quality criteria have been established not only for suspended particulates, but for sulfur dioxide, sulfates, fluorides, nitrogen oxides, hydrogen sulfide, carbon monoxide, mercury, and other pollutants. Well proven and effective technology is readily available to remove particulates and gaseous contaminants before atmospheric discharge, and most current operations incorporate advanced emissions control technology. [See Acid Rain and Acid Deposition.]

Effects on water

Wherever mining has been practiced, mining engineers have been confronted with water issues. In surface and underground mining, as minerals and fuels are removed, the disruption of the overlying rock affects normal drainage patterns. Seepage and rain water, and abandoned mines with little or no drainage control are a continuous source of water. Fine solid particles from mining sites and preparation plants can be carried to neighboring streams and waterways. Water pollution can result from the solubility of the minerals in the ore body and the associated strata. The water can be acidic and contain large amounts of sulfates and dissolved iron, or it can be alkaline. Mill tailings and waste banks, including coal-refuse and overburden piles, contain significant amounts of dissolved minerals. Factors affecting the quality and quantity of the drainage include the chemical composition of rocks in and around the ore body, their access to air, the water infiltration rate, the bacterial inhabitants of the mine, and the processes of chemical, electrochemical, and biochemical oxidation and biochemically catalyzed reactions. The fitness of water for drinking and industrial use and for flora and fauna can be limited by the undesirable pH levels, ionic content, and suspended solids. Streams and sites affected by water pollution are also aesthetically undesirable. [See Water-Quality Trends.]

Most of the water-pollution problems have sound engineering solutions. The many techniques to mitigate the effects of mine drainage include at-source control by prevention or reduction of the formation of acid mine-drainage, dispersion or dilution of pollutants; treatment of polluted waters, and permanent containment or isolation of polluted waters. Where prevention is not possible, treatment of polluted water to meet sanitary standards is necessary. Neutralization (chemical counteration of pollutants), flash distillation, reverse osmosis, ion exchange, and desulfating are some of the methods developed to treat polluted water. Neutralization is at present the most common.

Carefully designed mine and plant layouts significantly reduce uncontrolled discharges and minimize the water pollution problem. Closed water circuits, covered material transport, silo storage, proper catchment areas and drains, settling ponds, and treatment plants all help to control water pollution.

Effects on land

Mining as a land use is often in competition with uses of land for soil and water, living space, recreation, and industry. Mineral exploration, development, extraction, and processing all have different impacts and conflict with these uses, at least in the short term. Land damage from underground mining has been due mainly to ground movement and surface subsidence. In shallow mines, the disrupted rock may allow air and water access to the workings, which can result in mine fires and drainage problems.

Land disturbances from surface mining are caused mainly by the destruction of pre-mining surface topographies and soil conditions. After mining, the potential of the soil for plant growth can be greatly reduced. Soils disturbed by the operations can be chemically active and toxic. A much larger area may also be affected by the preparation and processing of plant wastes, particularly where low-grade ores are processed. These sites, if not properly rehabilitated, present a safety hazard in inhabited neighborhoods. The scars of mining from the distant past reveal that the altered physical, chemical, and biological systems are not repaired by nature alone in a reasonable time or to a desirable state.

In recent years, with suitable planning, a more productive land use has been achieved on mined lands. In fact, the planning of reclamation and postmining uses of land is required by law in several countries. The reclamation of closed underground and surface mines and affected sites (waste piles, buildings, plants, etc.) to defined standards is mandated. Mined lands and waste dumps that can be revegetated present minor problems and have great potential for development. The possibilities for development under these conditions are limited only by cost-benefit considerations. There are, however, marginal and problem spoils (acid, toxic, etc.) that require special attention and additional planning.

Mining modifies the existing physical environment and the preexisting distribution of metals, minerals, and energy. Among the often-cited undesirable, long-term environmental effects of mining are disruption of the hydrologic cycle, deforestation, desertification, loss of biological diversity, loss of industrial activity, and reduced economic-development potential. The effects of these alterations on the stability of regional ecosystems are not well understood.

THE FUTURE OF THE MINING INDUSTRY

Today's mining industry has achieved much in health, safety, and productivity, innovative applications of high technology, large vertically integrated conglomerates, and impressive achievements in the mining and processing of low-grade ores. New tools and technologies for exploration, mining and mineral processing, have enhanced understanding of geology, the physics of processes, mine-design requirements, mine production, product recoveries, and environmental issues.

Almost all mining operations are conducted under several environmental laws that are either specific to the mining industry or applied to all industrial activities. Mining operations in several countries today are much more environmentally friendly than ever before. At the same time, there has been a growth in artisanal and small-scale mining (ASM) in various countries. The orderly development of the ASM sector is a major concern as operations here operate on marginal deposits, usually with substandard health, safety, productivity and environmental performances.

At the societal level, fundamental questions are being raised about the assumptions and consequences of growth, and these have stimulated intellectual discussions on the role of science, technology, and society. All this has altered fundamentally the acceptance of industrial growth as a necessity for national economic well-being. While it is widely recognized that societal aspirations cannot be satisfied without a mining industry to provide the basic needs of energy and materials, the challenges of global warming, acid rain, solid waste disposal, deteriorating hydrologic resources, and conflicting land uses, will require new approaches. It is evident that demands on available lands will continue to increase because of population increases and industrial expansion. Though there is an upper limit on available lands for human use, the multiuse nature of lands will make it possible to meet these demands. Mining, as opposed to agriculture, is a nonrenewable use of land, consumes land in a real sense, and must come to an end because the resources it exploits

are finite. The economic and cultural catastrophes which have befallen some mining districts in the past and have led to the loss of life-supporting habitats vividly demonstrate the need for a new paradigm in mine planning.

National and international environment

The future promises a world in which the search for top-quality mineral resources, the competition from international producers, and the pressures of substitution and environmental conservation are likely to be more intense than ever before. Issues of improved health and safety, burgeoning ecological considerations, and enhanced quality of life will continue to demand more attention from the mineral industry. The mining industry of the future will be characterized by an intense search for high-grade deposits, greater exploitation of poorer ores, significant competition from substitutes, and accelerating progress toward development of environmentally friendly "green" technologies. Increased efforts are required to:

- Enhance resource-characterization techniques for in situ resources and for various stages of resource exploitation to improve understanding of heterogeneities, thus reducing the high risk of operations.
- Improve resource conservation and recovery through novel resource-exploitation schemes.
- Develop advanced technological systems to encompass multiple resource use and wasteless mineral-extraction technologies.
- Advance health and safety and productivity of mineral-engineering activities through innovative applications of monitoring and control technology.
- Assess and abate the potentially negative environmental impacts of mineral-related activities on the ecosystem.

Artisanal and small-scale mining

In all countries, there is usually a small-scale mining sector that is an important component of the local and rural economy. Among the positive aspects of small-scale mines are the promotion of mineral output from marginal deposits and creation of jobs and life supporting activities in rural communities though some of the social and community problems associated with these mines have to deal with women and child employment. While small-scale mining may represent somewhat a better organized and a more formal and mechanized mining system, artisanal mining is mostly manual, less formal, and may involve families and individuals. Small-scale mining in industrialized nations is subject in many cases to the same standards as larger mines. Artisanal and small-scale mines (ASM) in less developed nations share several same characteristics (MMSD, 2002). Among these are exploitation of marginal or small deposits, lack of capital and support services, low standards of health and safety, low rates of recovery, poor access to markets, and significant negative effect on the environment. There are efforts under way in many countries to support ASM operators and encourage them to generate wealth through improved practices that are environmentally friendly and health-and-safety conscious, and that contribute to community well-being.

Mining. The huge hole produced by the excavation of material at the Rossing Uranium Mine in Namibia.

Sustainable mineral development

The principal focus of the mineral industries will continue to be on the safe and economic extraction and processing of minerals. However, it will be increasingly necessary to consider mineral-industry development in the context of natural ecosystems and the effect on other industrial systems and to integrate the activities of the energy and mineral sectors with geologic, biological, ecological, cultural, and socioeconomic considerations. To continue in operation, the industry will have to address larger issues of ecosystems stability and the role of the mineral industry in ecosystem management. More knowledge is needed on the effects of mining on ecosystem properties such as energy flow, climate, food webs, structure, diversity, biogeochemical cycles, and life-sustaining capacity (Ripley et al., 1996). Questions on cause-and-effect relationships, the safe upper limits for pollutant concentrations, and the transformations and transmutation in the environment must be addressed through research and development.

While the effect of natural processes on health is fairly well recognized, the effect of technologic processes is often subtle. There is also a growing awareness of the relationship between the two processes. The relationship between the disturbance of the earth's environment by the natural and industrial processes and the long term effects on public safety and health is often less well understood.

There is a need for greater understanding of the complex issues of ecosystem stability and for the integration of industrial development (and industrial systems) with natural ecosystems. Since the middle of the last century, there has been growing awareness of the effect of industrial systems on the environment, and in recent years, of the drastic disturbance of land and natural ecosystems. The applications of the new concepts of industrial metabolism and industrial ecology need to be explored and developed (Allenby and Richards, 1994; Schulze, 1996). [*See* Industrial Ecology.]

The concept of sustainable development—development that meets the needs of the present generation without compromising the ability of future generations to meet their own needs—is widely accepted as essential in all endeavors (WCED, 1987). Planning for the sustainable development of the minerals industry requires that mineral companies not only remain competitive but also grow with other industries to enhance industrial metabolic and industrial ecological concepts to advance sustainable development (Ramani, 2001). Until the full impact of mining on the ecological balance and sustainable development is understood, it is only prudent that mining in the future be conducted in a manner that reduces the potential for drastic imbalances by minimizing its impacts on the local and regional environment.

[*See also* Coal; Fossil Fuels; Land Reclamation; Land Use; *and* Nuclear Power.]

BIBLIOGRAPHY

Allenby, B. R., and Richards, D. J. *The Greening of Industrial Ecosystems.* Washington, D.C.: National Academy Press, 1994.

Beall, J. V. "Mining's Place and Contribution." In *SME Mining Engineering Handbook*, vol 1. sect. 1, pp. 2–13. New York: Society of Mining Engineers of AIME, 1973.

Gregory, C. E. *A Concise History of Mining.* New York: Pergamon, 1980. A revised edition was published in 2001.

Hartman, H. L., and J. M. Mutmansky. *Introductory Mining Engineering.* 2d ed. Hoboken, N.J.: Wiley, 2002.

MMSD. *Breaking New Ground: Mining, Minerals, and Sustainable Development.* London, U.K., and Sterling, Va.: Earthscan, 2002. See pp 313–334.

Ramani, R. V. "Mining Disasters Caused and Controlled by Mankind: The Case for Coal Mining and Other Minerals. I. Causes of Mining Disasters." *Natural Resources Forum* 19.3 (1995), 233–242.

———. "Mining Disasters Caused and Controlled by Mankind: The Case for Coal Mining and Other Minerals. II. Control of Mining Disasters." *Natural Resources Forum* 19.4 (1995), 309–319.

———. "Environmental Planning in the Mineral Industry: Problems and Prospects." *International Mining and Minerals* 41 (2001), 5–12.

Ripley, E. A. et al. *Environmental Effects of Mining.* 2d ed. Delray Beach, Fla.: St. Lucie, 1996.

Schulze, P. C., ed. *Engineering within Ecological Constraints.* Washington D.C.: National Academy Press, 1996.

Vogely, W. A., *Economics of the Mineral Industries.* 4th ed. New York: American Institute of Mining, Metallurgical, and Petroleum Engineers, 1985.

WCED (World Commission on Environment and Development), *Our Common Future.* Oxford: Oxford University Press, 1987.

—RAJA V. RAMANI

MOBILE EARTH

Although there had been ideas about continental drift since before the nineteenth century, the first serious proponent of this hypothesis was Alfred Wegener, in 1912 (Wegener, 1966). He used a wide variety of data to suggest mobility of the continents. Although many of his ideas have been proven correct, he was wrong in one major respect, the rate of motion: his speeds were more than a factor of ten larger than those now known to exist. Early supporters of his ideas were Alexander du Toit (1937) and Arthur Holmes (1944). The field advanced greatly when paleomagnetic data became available and confirmed sea-floor spreading, a mechanism essential to understanding the movement of continents. For a recent review of the history of ideas and the concept of plate tectonics, see Oreskes (2003).

SEA-FLOOR SPREADING

Harry Hess (1962) is credited with the first detailed description of sea-floor spreading. He based his ideas on paleomagnetic results, mantle convection currents as suggested by Holmes, the sparse sediment cover of the ocean basins (suggesting that they were much younger than the continents), the high heat flow over the oceanic ridges, the frequency of seamounts (undersea volcanic edifices) in the ocean basins, and the uniform thickness of the oceanic crust.

Vine and Matthews (1963) sought to explain the magnetic anomalies seen near small topographic features and close to the ocean ridges, where zones of normal and reversed magnetization alternate symmetrically on each side of the ridge crest. Vine and Matthews proposed a magnetized layer 8–14 kilometers thick. Later, Vine and Wilson (1965) and Vine (1966) expanded this hypothesis in a more rigorous theory that called for sea-floor spreading at the ridge crests and magnetization of the rock so produced by the Earth's magnetic field. Reversals of the field leave their signals in the rocks, as in a gigantic tape recorder, which can then be "played back" by ships towing magnetometers. Others were also thinking about sea-floor spreading, for example, Schmalz (1961) and Morley (unpublished paper, 1963, published in 1981). Emiliani (1981) lays out a useful history of the events leading up to the Deep Sea Drilling Project, which is continuing more than 30 years later as the Integrated Ocean Drilling Program. One of the major tasks of DSDP was to test the hypothesis of sea-floor spreading.

The theory of sea-floor spreading (SFS) was developed to explain the bands of magnetic anomalies observed on either side of the ridge crest. The spacing of these magnetic anomalies close to the ridge crest was shown to be in the same ratio as the dates of reversals of the Earth's magnetic field during the past few million years, thus proving that the ocean floor was acting as a "tape recorder" for the field, moving at a rate of 10–100 kilometers per million years, which is well suited for recording reversals, which currently happen randomly at a rate of about five every million years. In many cases this results in magnetic anomalies that are symmetrical about the ridge crest, the best example being shown by Pitman and Heirtzler (1966). Other phenomena explained by the theory of SFS include the pattern of heat flow observed in well sedimented portions of the oceanic crust, the large-scale features of ocean-basin bathymetry (sea-bottom topography), the pattern of earthquakes seen on the midocean ridges and transform faults (transverse breaks along which portions of a ridge are offset), and the increase, with distance from the ridge crests, in sediment thickness and in the age of the sediments immediately overlying the sea-floor volcanic rocks. The theory of sea-floor spreading has proved to be very powerful. It has allowed the history of magnetic field reversals to be documented in considerable detail for most of the Neozoic (younger than 180 million years). Although the direct dating of reversals from continental rocks can be done only for the past 10 million years, it is occasionally possible to obtain dates from oceanic crustal rocks that can be identified with specific reversals of the field, or from basal sediments that can be dated biostratigraphically. The reversal history has shown that the rate of reversals has changed considerably in the past, with periods of several tens of millions of years when no reversals occurred. In contrast, the average rate of reversals today is about five per million years.

The first attempt to date the reversal time scale using magnetic anomalies was by Heirtzler et al. (1968). A more recent time scale of reversals for the Late Cretaceous and the Cenozoic is by Cande and Kent (1992, 1995). This time scale has benefited from the accurate dating of lavas that were erupted during specific reversal events, and also from the application of astrochronology, which is the dating of sediments by the use of precessional, obliquity, or ellipticity signals characteristic of the Earth's orbit. A Mesozoic time scale was presented by Gradstein et al. (1994) and tabulated by Opdyke and Channell (1996).

Once the reversal time-scale was developed, scientists were able to date most parts of the oceanic crust with considerable confidence, because it was usually possible to determine which set of reversals was recorded in the oceanic crust under consideration. An example of this is the map showing the age of the oceanic crust by Müller et al. (1997). Areas of oceanic crust formed during a long period of no reversals (120–83 million years ago) during the Cretaceous, however, cannot be dated accurately. This important period in Earth history is known as the Cretaceous quiet zone and has never been satisfactorily explained. Because of the ability to date oceanic crust (with the Cretaceous exception), it is possible to reconstruct the positions of the continents fairly accurately for the Neozoic. This is done by notionally unspreading the oceanic crust sequentially. Knowledge of the positions of the subduction zones then allows the continents to be placed on the globe in their correct relative positions. However, their absolute position (i.e., their paleolatitude) is not defined by this process. To put the continents in their correct paleogeographic location, further information is needed. Three approaches have been suggested: paleomagnetism, hot-spot locations, and paleolatitude measurements.

Measurements of paleolatitude, such as the locations of deposits characteristic of deserts, can frequently be useful but often lack the accuracy of the other two methods. One method that appeared to give good results was the location of the equatorial band of high sedimentation in the Pacific, caused by high productivity resulting from equatorial upwelling. This band of rapid sedimentation could be seen in sediments of different ages, and appeared to show a northward motion of the Pacific plate similar to what was expected from hot-spot and paleomagnetic observations. However, the fact that the present-day band of high sedimentation is displaced from the equator indicates that this method has systematic errors that cannot at the moment be compensated for. So we are left with paleomagnetism and hot spots.

Hot spots are linear manifestations of volcanic activity caused by the motion of the lithosphere over a mantle plume, the source of the hot-spot volcanism. The best example of a hot-spot trace is the Hawaii–Emperor seamount chain which extends about 3,600 miles from Hawaii to the Aleutian Islands. Hot-spot traces can give some idea of absolute plate motions but also suffer from systematic errors. One piece of dogma that has crept into the literature and which has recently come under criticism, is that hot spots remain fixed with respect to each other. This cannot be true if the whole mantle is convecting, as scientists now believe. Whole-mantle convection is necessary to remove the heat generated within the core as a consequence of processes required to produce the Earth's magnetic field. With all of the mantle convecting, there can be no region in which the source of hot spots can be sought that is not in lateral motion.

Proponents of the fixed-hot-spot hypothesis claim that the origin of hot spots is in a portion of the mantle that is moving very slowly, and that though the hypothesis is not absolutely correct, it is practically useful.

Tarduno and Cottrell (1997) have recently shown that, during the Cretaceous and early Tertiary, there was relative hot-spot motion of more than 30 centimeters per year. At other times, they suggest, hot-spot motion may have been smaller. However, 30 centimeters per year is equivalent to 30° of arc in 10 million years and so will give erroneous paleoclimatic information if neglected.

PLATE TECTONICS

Plate tectonics supposes that the Earth is divided up into a small number—roughly a dozen—of plates. The plates are generally thought to be about 100 kilometers thick (equivalent to the relatively rigid lithosphere) resting on the weaker and more mobile asthenosphere. Within each plate there is little or no deformation, although plates can change their shape by addition (through sea-floor spreading) or subtraction (through subduction) at their edges. Figure 1 shows the current boundaries of the plates (Duxbury and Duxbury, 1997). Plate boundaries can be narrow, or wide and diffuse (Robaudo and Harrison, 1993; Gordon, 1998).

Plates move with respect to each other, and there are three types of interaction at plate edges. Where plates move away from each other, the normal boundary is a midoceanic ridge at which sea-floor spreading takes place, such as the Mid-Atlantic Ridge or the East Pacific Rise. This is marked by high heat flow and elevated topography. In some cases, extensional boundaries (two plates moving away from each other) occur in continental regions, in which case the boundary may be marked by rift valleys, as in present-day East Africa and Iceland and, in "fossilized" form, the failed billion-year-old Midcontinent Rift of North America. Rift valleys also occur in most slow-spreading midoceanic ridges. Ridges are marked by earthquake activity, which is normally shallow and can often be shown to be caused by extensional faulting. The oceanic crust formed at ridge crests is made of basalt and gabbro.

When two oceanic plates move toward one other or collide, the result is subduction, in which one plate plunges beneath the other. Subduction, unlike normally symmetrical spreading, is asymmetrical. Subduction zones are marked by many large earthquakes (the strongest on Earth), some of which can be as deep as 650 kilometers. Deep earthquakes occur only in these places because the material at these depths elsewhere is too plastic to store the elastic energy that is released in earthquakes. In contrast, a subducting plate can retain for a long time the cool temperature it acquired at the surface of the Earth, because of the slow rate at which rock-forming silicate minerals conduct heat. One example of the many subduction zones surrounding the Pacific plate is the Mariana Trench, at 11,000 meters, the deepest known depression of the surface of the Earth. Volcanic activity is high and leads to the creation of island arcs in these locations. The volcanoes are formed mainly of andesite, a fine-grained volcanic rock. [See Volcanoes.]

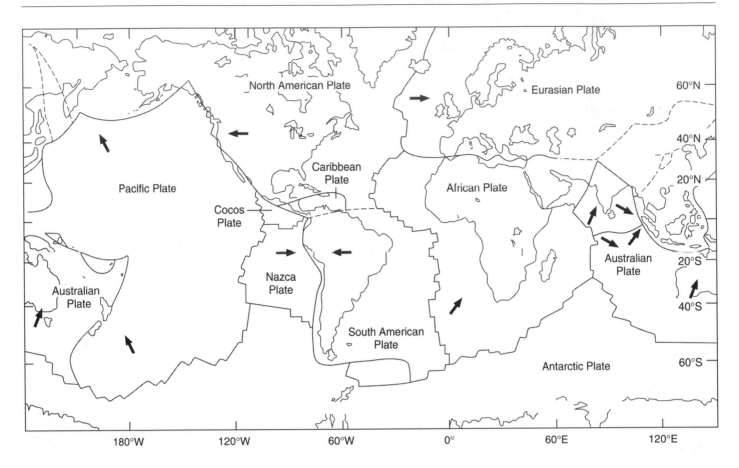

Mobile Earth. FIGURE 1. Lithospheric Plates in Existence Today.
Between the African and Australian plates are the Arabian and Indian plates. There is a small plate to the west of North America and north of 40° north latitude called the Juan de Fuca plate. The Philippine plate is split up by the edges of the map. The jagged pattern of the midoceanic ridges is caused by alternating ridge crests (usually perpendicular to the relative plate motion) and transform faults (parallel to relative plate motion). The East African Rift Valley (not shown) is sometimes considered as a plate boundary separating the Nubian plate (to the west) from the Somalian plate (to the east). The black arrows show the directions of motion of the plates. Note that the North American plate stretches all the way to Siberia and is thought to run down to the Lena River delta and then across to Kamchatka. The plate boundaries are marked by earthquakes, but only the subducting boundaries have intermediate and deep earthquakes.

(After Duxbury and Duxbury, 1997.)

When an oceanic and a continental plate collide, the oceanic plate is usually the one subducted (e.g., the Nazca plate beneath South America), but in rare cases the continental plate is subducted, as is apparently happening in Taiwan today. Andesitic volcanic activity in these areas is intense, and produces mountains such as the Cascades in western North America and the Andes in South America (for which andesite is named). There is much seismic activity, with earthquake foci varying from shallow to very deep.

When two continental plates collide, the result is collision and mountain building, because of the resistance of continental crustal material to subduction. The major example today is the collision of India with Asia, resulting in the Tibetan plateau and the Himalayas. Some elevated areas in South America (the Altiplano and Puna plateaus of Bolivia and Argentina respectively) are caused by collision (Norabuena et al., 1998). Seismic activity is high in these regions and is often spread over a wide area.

The third type of plate boundary occurs where plates move past each other, resulting in no increase or decrease in area. These transform faults occur mostly at ridge offsets (ridge-ridge transform faults), where they are marked by elongated topographic features (ridges and valleys) running parallel to the direction of relative motion. Good examples are the Romanche fracture zone on the equator in the Atlantic and the San Andreas fault in California. Figure 2 illustrates some of the basic processes in plate tectonics and the three types of plate boundary.

Instantaneous plate motions

McKenzie and Parker (1967) showed that earthquake slip vectors (showing directions of initial motion) taken from plate boundaries around the Pacific Ocean agreed with the plate-tectonic theory. They also confirmed that transform fault azimuths (directions of lineation) agreed with the directions seen in slip vectors, but they did not use any information about spreading rates in their model. Morgan (1968) was the first person to use both directional and rate information to determine some present-day plate motions. By analysis of relative plate-motion direction and relative plate speed it is possible to calculate the current velocities of the major plates of the Earth.

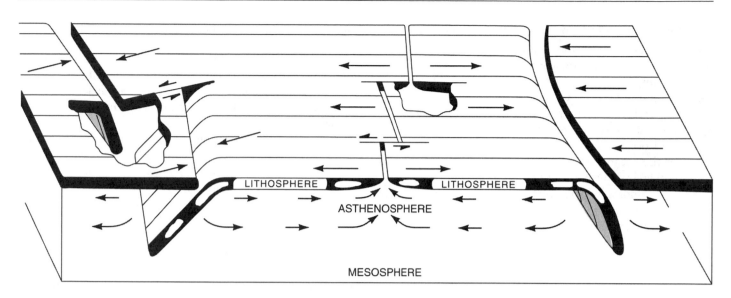

Mobile Earth. Figure 2. Plate Tectonic Processes.

The more rigid lithosphere is 100–150 kilometers thick and is underlain by the more plastic asthenosphere. In the middle of the diagram there are sections of ridge crest joined by ridge–ridge transform faults. To the left there are two sections of trench, in which subduction goes in opposite directions, joined by a trench–trench transform fault. To the right there is a simple trench with subduction all in one direction. The three types of plate boundary are all marked by earthquakes, but ridges and transform faults do not have any deep earthquakes. Volcanoes are common on the nonsubducting side of consuming plate boundaries.

(After Isacks et al., 1968.)

Plate speeds are measured by determining the distance between magnetic anomalies straddling the midoceanic ridges. The anomaly caused by the same reversal pattern on each side of the ridge crest is used to remove any error due to asymmetrical sea-floor spreading, where one limb of the spreading center grows at a rate different from the other.

Plate directions are measured either by transform azimuths or earthquake slip vectors. The end result is a model in which the relative motions of eleven plates are described. These plates are the Pacific, Nazca, Cocos, North America, South America, Caribbean, Antarctica, Africa, Eurasia, Arabia, and Australia plates. DeMets et al. (1990) used information from other sources to describe the motions of two additional plates (Philippine and Juan de Fuca), and there are several microplates.

Finite plate motions

Bullard et al. (1965) introduced the idea of rotating portions of the Earth's crust on the surface of the Earth around Euler poles, to match up the shape of the continental boundaries on either side of the Atlantic. Their jigsaw-puzzle fit is shown in Figure 3. The instantaneous rotations discussed in the previous section are not adequate for this type of operation, and finite rotations have to be used. Finite plate motions are much more complex to deal with than instantaneous plate motions

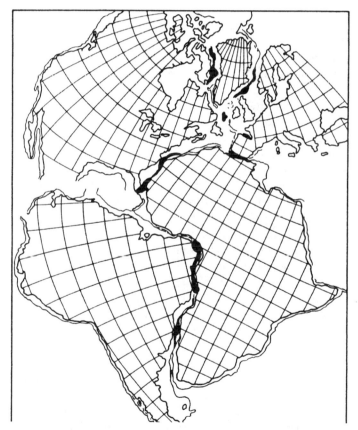

Mobile Earth. Figure 3. The fit of the continents around the Atlantic Ocean proposed by Bullard et al. (1965), and shown by Van der Voo (1990) to be the best fit available.

The dark areas show overlap or underlap. Spain has been rotated to close the Bay of Biscay. Iceland has been neglected because it has been formed since the opening of the North Atlantic. Central America has also been neglected. The fit was done to the continental slope, not the shoreline.

because they cannot easily be combined. Graphical and arithmetic methods of dealing with the addition of finite rotations are given by Le Pichon et al. (1973) and Cox and Hart (1986).

Other phenomena influenced by plate tectonics

Plate tectonics can have a large influence on continental free-board (the amount that the continents are exposed above sea level). Many phenomena affect the continental freeboard through time, but the one with the largest effect is the variation in the time-rate of oceanic crustal production (Harrison, 1988). Because of the topography of the ocean ridges, more rapid production of oceanic crust results in the ridges taking up more space in the ocean basins, causing the water to be displaced upward, thereby reducing continental freeboard.

Another important sea-level effect produced by plate tectonics is caused by the formation and breakup of supercontinents. [See Sea Level Future.] During the formation of supercontinents, the rate of continental collisions is much higher than average. These collisions cause continents to thicken at their edges, the continents occupy less area, and their average elevation increases. The ocean basins become larger in area, and the water level falls. Supercontinents therefore have a larger freeboard than do continents during periods when the continents are more widely dispersed on the globe (Harrison, 1994).

Plate-tectonic processes produce volcanic activity and attendant release of gases both at ridge crests and at subduction zones. Since sea-floor spreading rates are known to vary, this variation might be expected to cause a change in atmospheric composition and hence influence climate through the greenhouse-gas effect. Berner (1994) has produced a model (GEOCARB II) of atmospheric carbon dioxide in which carbon dioxide is released at subduction zones when calcium and magnesium carbonates in sediments are converted to silicates at high temperatures. This phenomenon seems not to have been studied for other gases.

The carbon dioxide released from the subduction zones is essentially a recycling of atmospheric and crustal carbon dioxide, but volcanic activity at ridge crests and hot spots brings up mantle volatiles that might also have an effect on climate. Carbon dioxide outgassing is estimated at between 40 and 400 teragrams (trillion grams) per year (Arthur et al., 1985). A more recent estimate, using the ratio of carbon dioxide to the helium-3 isotope (Sedwick et al., 1994; Craig and Lupton, 1981), yields a flux from the mantle of 335 teragrams per year.

The flow of hydrothermal fluids (hot, mineral-rich aqueous solutions in rock) through the ocean crust has a significant effect on ocean chemistry, so the rate of crustal production could change ocean chemistry through time (Elderfield and Schultz, 1996).

Hay (1996) has discussed many ways in which plate tectonics can influence climate. For example, models suggest that the effect of an opening in Central America would have a major influence on ocean currents in the Atlantic and Pacific oceans. If the Drake Passage (between Cape Horn and the South Shetland Islands) were closed at the same time, a condition that probably existed between the mid-Cretaceous and the Oligocene, the amount of Antarctic Bottom Water (AABW) produced is likely to have been more than three times its present value. The enhanced upwelling of AABW in the northern Atlantic reduces the salinity and prevents the formation of North Atlantic Deep Water. [See Thermohaline Circulation.] Such changes in ocean circulation could have profound effects on global climate. It is well known that the closing of the Strait of Gibraltar in the Messinian resulted in the formation of evaporite deposits in the Mediterranean and must have had a large influence on local climate.

Vertical tectonic events can also have large climatic results. The best known is the formation of the Tibetan plateau and the Himalayas. The high Tibetan plateau is responsible for the development of the monsoonal circulation, which does not occur in models without a plateau at least 2.5 kilometers high, half the present elevation of the Tibetan plateau (Hay, 1996). The effect of the elevation of the Andes (roughly 25–30 million years ago) does not seem to have been studied.

On a longer time scale, plate tectonics can cause more profound changes in the way the Earth works. Radioactive decay produced more heat early in Earth history. Because the Earth loses most of its radiogenically produced heat through sea-floor spreading, it follows that SFS must have been much more active during the earliest period of geological history than it is today. More rapid sea-floor spreading will bring increased rates of mountain building because of continental collision and subduction. To balance the higher rates of mountain building, increased mechanical erosion is necessary, and this can only be achieved over the long term by increasing the freeboard of the continents (Harrison, 1994), because mechanical erosion is highly dependent on elevation relative to sea level.

ASSESSMENT

Plate tectonics has a profound effect on many geological and geophysical phenomena on time scales of tens to hundreds of millions of years. Of most significance are changes in sea level or continental freeboard as a function of the rates of spreading and of continental collision. Also important are oceanographic and climatic effects produced by horizontal tectonic processes such as the opening and closing of oceanic gateways, and vertical tectonic processes produced by continental collisions or subduction volcanism. The effect on climate (through greenhouse mechanisms) of variable volatile production associated with plate-tectonic volcanic activity at the ridge crests has scarcely been explored, but it may be profound.

BIBLIOGRAPHY

Arthur, M. A., et al. "Variations in the Global Carbon Cycle During the Cretaceous Related to Climate, Volcanism, and Changes in Atmospheric CO_2." In The Carbon Cycle and Atmospheric CO_2: Natural Variations, Archean to Present, edited by E. T. Sundquist and W. S. Broecker. Washington, D.C.: American Geophysical Union, 1985.

Berner, R. A. "GEOCARB II: A Revised Model of Atmospheric CO_2 over Phanerozoic Time." American Journal of Science 294 (1994), 56–91.

Bullard, E. C., et al. "The Fit of the Continents around the Atlantic." Philosophical Transactions of the Royal Society A 258 (1965), 41–51. A historic paper showing that the jigsaw fit of the continents around the Atlantic is very good.

Cande, S. C., and D. V. Kent. "A New Geomagnetic Polarity Time Scale for the Late Cretaceous and Cenozoic." Journal of Geophysical Research 97 (1992), 13917–13951. The geomagnetic reversal time-scale for the past 80 million years; a slight revision is presented in Cande and Kent, 1995.

———. "Revised Calibration of the Geomagnetic Polarity Timescale for the Late Cretaceous and Cenozoic." *Journal of Geophysical Research* 100.B4 (1995), 6093–6095.

Cox, A., and R. B. Hart. *Plate Tectonics.* Palo Alto, Calif.: Blackwell, 1986.

Craig, H., and J. E. Lupton. "Helium-3 and Mantle Volatiles in the Ocean and the Oceanic Crust." In *The Sea*, vol. 7, *The Oceanic Lithosphere*, edited by C. Emiliani, pp. 391–428. New York: Wiley, 1981.

Demets, C., et al. "Current Plate Motions." *Geophysical Journal International* 101.2 (1990), 425–478. A detailed description of the current relative motions of the plates.

Du Toit, A. L. *Our Wandering Continents.* Edinburgh and London: Oliver and Boyd, 1937.

Duxbury, A. C., and A. B. Duxbury. *An Introduction to the World's Oceans.* 5th ed. Dubuque, Iowa: Brown, 1997. The sixth edition was published in 2000.

Elderfield, H., and A. Schultz. "Mid-Ocean Ridge Hydrothermal Fluxes and the Chemical Composition of the Ocean." *Annual Review of Earth and Planetary Science* 24 (1996), 191–224. DOI: 10.1146/annurev.earth.24.1.191.

Emiliani, C. "A New Global Geology." In *The Sea*, vol. 7, *The Oceanic Lithosphere*, edited by C. Emiliani, pp. 1687–1728. New York: Wiley, 1981. Includes history of the Deep Sea Drilling Project.

Gordon, R. G. "The Plate Tectonic Approximation: Plate Nonrigidity, Diffuse Plate Boundaries, and Global Plate Reconstructions." *Annual Review of Earth and Planetary Science* 26 (1998), 615–642. DOI: 10.146/annurev.earth.26.1.615.

Gradstein, F. M., et al. "A Mesozoic Time Scale." *Journal of Geophysical Research* 99.B12 (1994), 24051–24074.

Hardie, L. A. "Secular Variation in Seawater Chemistry: An Explanation for the Coupled Secular Variation in the Mineralogies of Marine Limestones and Potash Evaporites over the Past 600 m.y." *Geology* 24.3 (1996), 279–283.

Harrison, C. G. A. "Eustasy and Epeirogeny of Continents on Time Scales between About 1 and 100 m.y." *Paleoceanography* 3.6 (1988), 671–684.

Harrison, C. G. A. "Rates of Continental Erosion and Mountain Building." *Geologisches Rundschau* 83.2 (1994), 431–447. DOI: 10.1007/BF00210556.

Hay, W. W. "Tectonics and Climate." *Geologisches Rundschau* 85.3 (1996), 409–437. DOI: 10.1007/s005310050086.

Heirtzler, J. R., et al. "Marine Magnetic Anomalies Geomagnetic Field Reversals and Motions of the Ocean Floor and Continents." *Journal of Geophysical Research* 73.6 (1968), 2119–2136. The first reversal time-scale derived from marine magnetic anomalies.

Hess, H. H. "History of Ocean Basins." In *Petrologic Studies: A Volume in Honor of A. F. Buddington*, edited by A. E. J. Engel, et al., pp. 599–620. Geological Society of America, 1962. A classic early description of sea-floor spreading.

Holmes, A. *Principles of Physical Geology.* London and New York: Nelson, 1944. This textbook has some discussion of sea-floor spreading.

Isacks, B., J. Oliver, and L. R. Sykes. "Seismology and the New Global Tectonics." *Journal of Geophysical Research* 7318 (1968), 5855–5899.

Le Pichon, X., J. Francheteau, and J. Bonnin. *Plate Tectonics.* Amsterdam: Elsevier, 1973.

McKenzie, D. p., and R. L. Parker. "The North Pacific: An Example of Tectonics on a Sphere." *Nature* 216 (1967), 1276–1280. DOI: 10.1038/2161276a0. One of the first papers on plate tectonics.

Morgan, W. J. "Rises, Trenches, Great Faults, and Crustal Blocks." *Journal of Geophysical Research* 73.6 (1968), 1959–1982.

Morley, L. W. "An Explanation of Magnetic Banding on Ocean Basins." In *The Sea*, vol. 7, *The Oceanic Lithosphere*, edited by C. Emiliani, pp. 1717–1719. New York: Wiley, 1981.

Müller, D., et al. "Digital Isochrons of the World's Ocean Floor." *Journal of Geophysical Research* 102 (1997), 3211–3214.

Norabuena, E., et al. "Space Geodetic Observations of Nazca-South America Convergence across the Central Andes." *Science* 279 (1998), 358–362. DOI: DOI: 10.1126/science.279.5349.358.

Opdyke, N., and J. E. T. Channell. *Magnetic Stratigraphy.* San Diego: Academic Press, 1996.

Oreskes, N., ed. *Plate Tectonics: An Insider's History of the Modern Theory of the Earth.* Boulder, Colo.: Westview Press, 2003.

Pitman, W. C., III, and J. R. Heirtzler. "Magnetic Anomalies over the Pacific-Antarctic Ridge." *Science* 154 (1966), 1164–1171. DOI: 10.1126/science.154.3753.1164.

Robaudo, S., and C. G. A. Harrison. "Measurements of Strain at Plate Boundaries Using Space-Based Geodetic Techniques." *Geophysical Research Letters* 20.17 (1993), 1811–1814.

Schmalz, R. F. "A Case for Convection." *Mineral Industries* 30.5 (1961), 8.

Sedwick, P. N., et al. "Carbon Dioxide and Helium in Hydrothermal Fluids from Loihi Seamount Hawaii, U.S.A.: Temporal Variability and Implications for the Release of Mantle Volatiles." *Geochimica et Cosmochimica Acta* 58 (1994), 1219–1227.

Siever, R. "The Dynamic Earth." *Scientific American* 249.3 (Sept. 1983), 46–55.

Stanley, S. M., and L. A. Hardie. "Secular Oscillations in the Carbonate Mineralogy of Reef-Building and Sediment-Producing Organisms Driven by Tectonically Forced Shifts in Seawater Chemistry." *Palaeogeography, Palaeoclimatology, Palaeoecology* 144.1–2 (1998), 3–19. DOI: 10.1016/S0031-0182(98)00109-6.

Tarduno, J. A., and R. D. Cottrell. "Paleomagnetic Evidence for Motion of the Hawaiian Hotspot during Formation of the Emperor Seamounts." *Earth and Planetary Science Letters* 153.3–4 (1997), 171–180. DOI: 10.1016/S0012-821X(97)00169-6.

Van der Voo, R. "Phanerozoic Paleomagnetic Poles from Europe and North America and Comparisons with Continental Reconstructions." *Reviews of Geophysics* 28 (1990), 167–206.

Vine, F. J. "Spreading of the Ocean Floor: New Evidence." *Science* 154 (1966), 1405–1415. DOI: 10.1126/science.154.3755.1405. The keystone paper of sea-floor spreading.

Vine, F. J., and D. H. Matthews, "Magnetic Anomalies Over Ocean Ridges." *Nature* 199(1963), 947–949.

Vine, F. J., and J. T. Wilson. "Magnetic Anomalies over a Young Oceanic Ridge off Vancouver Island." *Science* 150 (1965), 485–489. DOI: 10.1126/science.150.3695.485.

Wegener, A. *The Origin of Continents and Oceans.* Translated by John Biram from the 4th revised edition of *Die Entstehung der Kontinente und Ozeane* (1929). New York: Dover, 1966.

Wilson, J. T. "A New Class of Faults and their Bearing upon Continental Drift." *Nature* 207 (1965), 343–347. The basic description of transform faults, which were vital in understanding ridge crests and sea-floor spreading.

—CHRISTOPHER G. A. HARRISON

MOUNTAINS

Mountains occupy nearly a quarter of the land surface of the Earth. Their importance in relation to global change derives from their role in influencing regional and global climates, particularly through the interception of atmospheric moisture, and from the evidence they provide of climate change (the retreat of glaciers and the upward migration, or extinction, of plants and animals).

Because most of the world's major rivers rise in mountain regions, changes in mountain climates, and especially in runoff, will affect a large proportion of the global population. In addition, mountains are core areas of global biodiversity and the origin of many of the world's food crops. In many regions, this global heritage is significantly endangered by changes in land use driven by a range of economic and political pressures. Climate change may further exacerbate these processes.

Although mountains can be identified immediately by anyone who visits or flies over them, there is no uniform definition of mountains; they are best defined as regions of accentuated relief (that is, with steep slopes) and altitude. Mere altitude is not a defining characteristic; many mountains start at sea level and, while mountains are the highest features of all of the continents, there are also many high-altitude areas that are not steep, for example, the Tibetan (Xi-zang in Chinese) Plateau, the South American altiplano, and the high plains and plateaus of North America and Africa. Twenty-seven percent of the Earth's land surface is above 1,000 meters, and 11% is above 2,000 meters.

Created by tectonic forces, mountains are dynamic environments whose relief is determined by glacial and fluvial action, mass movement, and weathering. Although the mountains originating in the Caledonian and Hercynian-Appalachian orogenies (mountain-building periods) are now largely characterized by rounded relief, those that began their development during the Alpine orogeny, starting during the Tertiary (from 65 million years ago), are still growing. These include the Alps, the Himalayas, the Rocky Mountains, and the Andes: long mountain systems originating in the collision of continental plates. Other mountains are of volcanic origin, particularly around the Pacific Rim. The world's highest mountain, from base to summit, is not Mount Everest but Mauna Loa, the highest peak of Hawaii, a volcano rising from the bed of the Pacific Ocean.

GLACIERS, GEOMORPHOLOGY, AND CLIMATE

During the Pleistocene (from about 1.8 million to 11,000 years ago), many of the world's mountains were far more glaciated than at present, and those that were not glaciated experienced far cooler climates. Many ranges in temperate and high latitudes were largely ice-covered, with only the highest peaks extending above ice sheets and glaciers. In the postglacial period, starting approximately 10,000 years ago, the higher parts of these mountains have been exposed and subjected to a variety of geomorphic processes. The long, steep slopes of mountain regions promote rapid movement under gravity, not only of water and snow, but also of rocks and soil. While some processes are very rapid—floods, avalanches, rockslides, rockfalls, debris flows, lava and ash flows—gradual processes, such as soil erosion, can also endanger mountain people and affect water quality. Soil erosion is caused not only by the steepness of slopes, but also by human mismanagement, often combined with other dynamic processes such as heavy rainfall, strong winds, and changes in temperature.

The former positions are shown by moraines (accumulations of material transported by ice), where these have not been removed by subsequent denudation. In the postglacial period, the world's glaciers have not retreated uniformly. There have also been periods of advance, notably during the Little Ice Age from the fourteenth to the eighteenth century CE. However, in recent decades, most glaciers have been retreating. This appears to be linked to atmospheric warming, which has been measured in a number of subtropical and tropical mountain regions. Only along the margins of continents, such as Scandinavia and the Pacific Northwest of North America, have glaciers advanced in response to increased winter precipitation. If recent trends continue, most glaciers will continue to retreat—for example, the ice mass in the Alps in 2025 might be as little as 25% of that in 1850. Some glaciers, especially in tropical areas, will disappear; and the catastrophic release of large volumes of water from ice-dammed lakes could become more frequent. In addition, the melting of permafrost and residual ice in rock glaciers will lead to surface subsidence and, possibly, large debris flows. [*See* Glacier Retreat Since the Little Ice Age *and* Little Ice Age in Europe.]

Records of mountain climates are limited in length and representativeness even in the regions with the best measurement networks (the Alps, parts of the Carpathians), not least because most recording stations are in valleys, which are not representative of regional climates. Outside Europe and North America, information on current mountain climates is very limited. In addition, our understanding of many processes of mountain meteorology and the altitudinal variability of climates is poor. Given this lack of knowledge, projection of future mountain climates is highly uncertain; especially because the computer models typically used to predict future climates have too coarse a resolution to depict mountains. However, the application of statistical approaches and regional models provides an important step toward understanding of probable future mountain climates.

HYDROLOGY

For the people and ecosystems of mountain regions, and also the vast number of people downstream who depend on mountain water, changes in the hydrologic regime are of particular concern. However, existing computer models suggest a wide range of future trends—in both magnitude and direction—in precipitation and evaporation. Three key predictions, with reasonable agreement between models, are that winter precipitation in higher latitudes, the intensity and frequency of extreme events, and annual precipitation in the Asian monsoon region are all likely to increase. Nevertheless, the models provide little information concerning changes in the relative proportions of precipitation falling as rain or snow.

At least in the short term, the wasting of glaciers leads to increased runoff. However, the result over the long term, as the supply dwindles, is decreased runoff, as is already apparent in parts of the Alps and the Pamirs. Even before climate change becomes a factor, the quality and quantity of water supplies in many mountain regions are already limiting factors, especially in winter. Semiarid and arid regions are likely to be particularly sensitive to climate change, especially where irrigated

Mountains. The French Alps.

Shown here near Chamonix, are a major tourist attraction and their melting snows and glaciers are also a vital source of water. They are an environment which will be substantially modified by climate change.

agriculture is a basis of local economies. Overall, climate change is likely to increase the uncertainty of water supplies for mountain people, and there will be great need for adaptation and flexibility in both the infrastructure and the institutions used to manage and allocate water supplies. These challenges will often be heightened by demands for storing and releasing water to provide increased supplies of hydroelectricity in response to the policy imperative of decreasing the combustion of carbon-based fuels.

AGRICULTURE AND FORESTRY

In principle, global warming could have positive impacts for mountain farmers and foresters, as higher temperatures permit crops to be grown at higher altitudes, and increasing levels of carbon dioxide lead to increased agricultural and forest production. However, to grow at higher altitudes, crops and trees also require appropriate soil conditions. These may often not be available, either because the soils have unsuitable physical or chemical characteristics, or because of their deterioration as a result of human activities such as leaching following the removal of trees—to create pasture, fodder, and fuelwood—below the current anthropogenic timberline, which is hundreds of meters below its climatic optimum (maximum altitude under current climate) in many temperate and tropical mountain areas. Soil characteristics are likely to change gradually in response to climate changes. Other factors that may limit the ability of domesticated plants to become established and thrive at higher altitudes include increased competition from other species such as weeds, diseases, and pests, a lack of obligate species (species biologically essential for survival, for example, pollinators), and changes in the frequency and timing of extreme events (particularly frosts) and cloud cover. Nevertheless, the great variety of crop varieties developed by generations of mountain farmers and adapted to a wide range of microclimates may provide a vital resource for ensuring food security. This is more likely to be endangered in regions in which native crops have been largely or entirely displaced by varieties that only give high yields under restricted climate conditions, often with high inputs of fertilizer.

Similarly, it is not possible to make unequivocal predictions concerning the probable impacts of climate change on mountain forests. These provide the primary fuel source of most mountain people and are also important for providing fodder and shade for grazing animals, as well as diverse societal benefits such as protection from landslides and floods and places for recreation. While increasing levels of carbon dioxide may promote increased growth of mountain trees, this may not all be directed to the most valued parts of trees and, as with crop species, may be offset by increased competition and predation. The frequency of fires may increase in many regions, a problem likely to be exacerbated in many parts of Europe and North America by the high fuel loading resulting from decades of fire suppression and decreasing harvests. [See Fire and Global Warming.] Consequently, forest management strategies will have to be increasingly flexible, considering not only the diverse functions of forests but also the likely environmental changes. In addition,

as with crops, there is a clear need to maintain genotypes adapted to a wide variety of conditions.

MOUNTAIN ECOSYSTEMS

Natural and seminatural mountain ecosystems will also be affected by climatic changes. As with domesticated species, the natural vegetation of most mountains can be classified into altitudinal zones. There are many classifications, depending primarily on latitude and altitude; the European colline-montane-alpine-nival model has been widely applied. The highest two of these zones are characterized by a lack of trees; in the nival zone, only species that are particularly adapted to the prevailing harsh conditions can survive. While such classifications are useful for summarizing ecological knowledge, larger mountain systems cannot easily be described by a simple vertical zonation, because the limits of the zones depend on factors including latitude, orientation (e.g., south versus north), the position of massifs within a group of ranges, and exposure to prevailing winds (e.g., windward/oceanic versus leeward/continental).

Mountain ecosystems are of global importance as core areas of biological diversity, especially in the tropics, but also in the subtropics. In the temperate zone, mountains are typically centers of biodiversity, not only because many species have been extirpated in adjacent lowlands, but also because many mountains provide the last habitats for relic species from the last ice age, and the complexity and diversity of ecological niches provide particular opportunities for the evolution of species and subspecies. Many of the mountain areas with the greatest biological and landscape diversity have been recognized by their designation as protected areas (national parks, nature reserves, etc.), often with additional international status awarded by UNESCO: some 70 natural and "mixed" (having natural and cultural values) World Heritage Sites and 200 Biosphere Reserves are in mountain regions. Protected areas are valuable not only for protecting endemic and threatened species, but also as test cases for sustainable development in collaboration with local people, for recreation and tourism, and for monitoring of environmental changes.

The diversity of species, with many strategies for survival, means that mountain plant and animal communities are resilient. At the same time, they are also fragile because they require long periods of time to recover when damaged or stressed beyond a certain point, or when key species or soils are removed. In a period of global warming, the optimum habitat for most species will probably move upslope. This presents particular challenges for the conservation of mountain species, as the area available for a particular species or ecosystem will generally decrease with altitude; changes in vegetation zones are usually not symmetrical along altitudinal gradients; and, at the tops of mountains, the coolest habitats may disappear. These constraints on the ability of wild species to adapt and respond to global warming may be relaxed or tightened by human actions. For example, while migration corridors could be established and kept open by appropriate land-use practices and policies, the expansion of agriculture to higher altitudes could decrease possibilities for dispersal. In addition, management strategies must recognize that each species responds individual-istically to changes in climate, so that animal and plant communities tend to disassemble. Consequently, while it is possible to surmise the potential distribution of broad ecoclimatic zones, many of today's plant and animal communities may no longer exist in the future. Climate change has already been identified as a cause of extinction, as of the golden toad (*Bufo periglenes*) in Costa Rica.

ANTHROPOGENIC CHANGES

The prospect of changes in natural and seminatural ecosystems resulting from climate change must be evaluated in the appropriate context. In many mountain regions, direct anthropogenic causes of change are, and are likely to continue to be, as great a threat to biological diversity. In tropical and subtropical mountains, the introduction of exotic species has already greatly changed the species composition of many plant and animal communities, often leading to species extinction, especially on islands. With growing demographic and economic pressures, clearing for agriculture and logging for timber threaten mountain forests; the rate of deforestation in tropical upland forests is 1.1% per year, greater than in any other forest biome. In addition, fire and over-grazing endanger grasslands such as the paramo of the Andes.

Overgrazing is also of particular concern in arid and semiarid mountains, where the genetic diversity of native ungulates (hoofed mammals) is being lost through hybridization with domesticated stock. In temperate mountains, large-scale logging, fire, and the fragmentation of habitats are all direct threats to biological and landscape diversity. To these may be added the changes in, and loss of, habitats through air pollution and soil acidification in regions downwind from major industrial areas. It appears likely that, for some decades at least, the forces of global change that drive changes in land use and cover in the mountains of Europe are likely to derive at least as much from government policies and market forces as from global climate change.

TOURISM

The biological and landscape diversity of mountain regions is one of the prerequisites for tourism, an economic sector of growing and, in some cases, overwhelming importance in these regions, and the world's largest industry. [*See* Tourism.] Tourism is already a major agent of environmental change in mountains around the world, both directly—for example, through the construction of infrastructure, disturbance of plant and animal species, and production of artificial snow—and indirectly, that is, through changes in land use related to the availability of employment in the tourist sector, demands for products, land prices. Climate change is also likely to affect mountain tourism directly, as through changes in the amounts and timing of snowfall and in the timing of good weather, and indirectly, as through changes in landscapes and in patterns of demand for specific activities, and concern about the health risks of ultraviolet radiation at high altitudes. Finally, rises in fuel prices resulting from the likely taxes on the consumption of fossil fuels would affect mountain tourism disproportionately, because the costs of access to mountain regions tend to be a relatively high proportion of total costs. Increasingly, policies for the development of mountain regions will have to consider the complex interactions between all sectors of local, regional, and global economies and the uncertainty of the future environment.

BIBLIOGRAPHY

Barry, R. G. *Mountain Weather and Climate*. 3d ed. London and New York: Routledge, 2008. The most detailed review of the subject.
Huber, U. M., H. K. M. Bugmann, and M. A. Reasoner, eds. *Global Change and Mountain Regions: An Overview of Current Knowledge*. Dordrecht: Springer, 2005. A state-of-the-art collection of papers.
Messerli, B., and J. D. Ives, eds. *Mountains of the World: A Global Priority*. New York and Carnforth, U.K.: Parthenon, 1997. An excellent overview of mountain issues, organized thematically.

—MARTIN F. PRICE

N

NATIONAL ENERGY POLICY IN THE UNITED STATES

Over the next five decades progress to address the risk of significant climate change in a meaningful way will require a reduction in the global emissions of greenhouse gases (GHG) estimated at 80% or more. From the 2007 baseline of over seven billion tons of GHG emissions, three-quarters of which comes from fossil-fuel combustion (and the remainder largely from land conversion and forest burning), the reductions required are from global emissions that are currently increasing. The United States, as the largest current emitter—roughly 25% of the global total—and, more importantly, as the nation with the largest energy-resource and research base to effect change, is poised to play a critical role in our collective climate future, a fact that raises great concern, given U.S. inaction on climate protection in recent years.

There are various technologies that can protect the environment and improve our economic and political security—in many cases with greater political and economic benefits than costs to the nation in the form of reasserted tecnological and financial leadership, through increased geopolitical stability and flexibility, and through job growth in the clean-energy sector (Kammen et al., 2004). To accomplish these goals, we will need, in addition to a comprehensive strategy (Augustine, 2007; Kammen and Nemet, 2005), a balanced approach that recognizes that replacing the vast infrastructure and economic machinery developed to exploit fossil fuels will be a central challenge of the twenty-first century, and one where the fun damental mindset of large, centralized energy monopolies will need to evolve to one of a decentralized clean-energy marketplace. This is the climate-change issue—more than any set of technologies or economic incentives—that causes the most uncertainty, justifiable fear, and adverse reaction.

Developing a balanced program of energy research, development, and deployment (R&D) projects is central to meeting the challenge of climate change, but it is equally clear that "technology push" projects must be accompanied by "demand pull" measures. Among the most important demand-pull—market-creating or -enabling—options available to us today are:

- A national commitment to saving money and energy by implementing energy-efficiency measures throughout the economy.
- A steady rise in renewable-energy standards, and in the cities, states, and regions with mandates to pursue more aggressive policies, the addition of "feed-in" laws to diversify and expand the number and type of clean-energy producers.
- Low-carbon fuel standards that evolve into sustainable fuel standards (Kammen, 2007).
- The use of carbon taxes or cap-and-trade systems under which carbon emission rights are limited.
- Developing and using carbon-footprint analyses for business, industrial, municipal and, most importantly, personal purchases.
- International collaborations designed to commercialize clean-energy technologies.

This is a simple list, but one that has enough teeth, and economic opportunities, to harness the innovative power of the superpower economy. It is also a plan that is simple enough for a suitably committed president to put into action.

DEVELOPING A NATIONAL ENERGY STRATEGY

Before exploring particular technologies, funding decisions, and economic measures, it is important to recognize that we do not currently have an energy plan. In the United States there has arguably been nothing remotely resembling an energy plan since the efforts by presidents Ford and Carter (1974–1981).

Recently, however, integrated planning on climate and energy has begun to emerge, though largely at the state and regional level. The precedent for such a change in a national policy initiated from below is a strong one. Supreme Court Justice Louis D. Brandeis wrote in 1932 that "a single courageous state may, if its citizens choose, serve as a laboratory; and try novel economic and social experiments."

Courageous experiments are now being carried out in a number of U.S. states and can form the basis of necessary federal legislation and leadership. The Global Warming Solutions Act of 2006 (Assembly Bill [AB] 32) in California, as well as the Regional Greenhouse Gas Initiative (RGGI) in the Northeast and Mid-Atlantic States are such examples. By contrast, the federal government's current target will require only a slight change from business as usual (Figure 1) (EPA 2005). Reaching this target would actually allow emissions to grow by 12 to 16%, a larger increase than the 10% growth that occurred in the previous decade. If we are serious about meeting the climate challenge we need to set a goal consistent with the Department of Energy's Climate Change Technology Plan (CCTP) long-term (e.g., about 2050) objective of an 80% reduction in net emissions. In fact, the CCTP actually mentions a zeroing of net emissions at some time after mid-century.

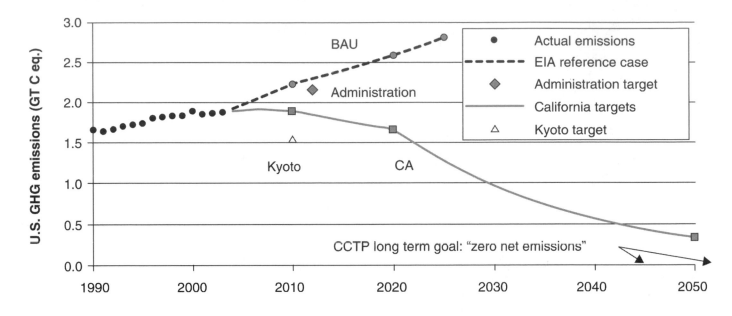

National Energy Policy in the United States. FIGURE 1. Historical U.S. GHG Emissions and Targets.

Actual U.S. GHG emissions from 1990 through 2003 (EPA 2005) in giga-tons of carbon equivalent. Four future paths for future U.S. emissions are shown; circles show the business-as-usual (BAU), or "reference case," as calculated by the Energy Information Agency (EIA). The diamond shows the Administration's GHG intensity target for 2012 of 18% below 2002 level in tons of carbon per unit of GDP, or a 3.6% reduction in emissions from BAU. The squares show U.S. emissions if the nation were to meet the percentage reductions that have been announced in California for 2010, 2020, and 2050 (California Executive Order 3-05, and California AB32). The triangle shows the U.S.'s target for 2010 under the Kyoto Protocol. Arrows indicate the levels required to meet the U.S. Department of Energy's Climate Change Technology Plan (CCTP) long-term goal of "levels that are low or near zero".

A sustained commitment to emissions reductions and a time scale that conveys to the country the urgency of the need for future options are required. The California plan, for example, extends beyond AB32 with a set of mutually reinforcing laws and executive orders. The most recent, the Low Carbon Fuel Standard (Executive Order S-1-07), is a significant advance in our regulatory power to discriminate among liquid fossil fuels and electricity to power plug-in hybrid vehicles.

The California plan represents only one such path to a low-carbon society, but it embodies the key features that are required in federal legislation, an integrated, consistent approach that initiates early action and clarifies the long-term roadmap to a decarbonized future.

RENEWABLE ENERGY AND A ROADMAP TO A DE-CARBONIZED ECONOMY

The U.S. has under-invested in energy RD&D for decades. This history is shown in Figure 2: federal energy research and development investment is today back at pre-OPEC levels—despite the fact that energy dependence and insecurity, and the climatic impact of our energy economy are, for many reasons, dominating local economics and geopolitics, and causing environmental degradation.

As an example of the "commitment" to clean energy, consider the U.S. federal energy budget. At $2.7 billion for energy research, the overall federal energy research and development budget request for 2008 request is $685 million higher than the 2006 appropriated budget. Half of that increased request is accounted for by increases in fission research, and the rest is in moderate increases in funding for biofuels, solar, FutureGen (a U.S. public-private partnership to design, build, and operate the world's first coal-fueled, near-zero-emissions power plant), and $147 million increase for fusion research. However, the National Renewable Energy Laboratory's (NREL) budget is to be cut precisely at a time

when concerns over energy security and climate change are at their highest level.

The larger issue, however, is that as a nation we invest less in energy research, development, and deployment than do a few large biotechnology firms in their own R&D budgets. This is unacceptable on many fronts; we know that investments in energy research pay off at both the national and private-sector levels.

A series of papers (Margolis and Kammen, 1999; Kammen and Nemet, 2005; Nemet and Kammen, 2007) has documented a disturbing trend away from investment in energy technology—both by the federal government and by the private sector, which largely follows the federal lead (Figure 3). The U.S. invests about $1 billion less in energy R&D today than it did a decade ago. This trend is remarkable, because the levels in the mid-1990s were already dangerously low, and because the decline is pervasive—across almost every energy-technology category, in both the public and private sectors, and at various stages in the innovation process. In each of these areas investment has been stagnant or declining. Moreover, the decline in investment in energy has occurred while overall U.S. R&D has grown by 6% per year, and federal R&D investments in health and defense have grown by 10 and 15% per year, respectively.

Figure 2 shows all federal R&D programs since 1955. Note the thin strip showing the small energy R&D program relative to other sectors. The current budgets for energy R&D would continue this situation or even reduce R&D investment (Kammen and Nemet, 2005). This is not in the best interests of the nation (Figures 2 and 3).

Tracking actual investment histories shows that there is a strong correlation between investment in innovation and demonstrated changes in performance and cost of technologies available in the market (Figure 5). This correlation applies not to one technology alone but across the spectrum, in solar, wind, nuclear fission and fusion, and fuel cells. This result—that innovation as measured by patenting closely follows the pattern set by research funding—is hardly surprising, but it is important to note the consistency of the trend: we get what we pay for.

A more detailed look at one sector is also illustrative. A 50% increase in solar photovoltaic (PV) efficiency occurred immediately after an unprecedented $1 billion global investment in PV R&D (1978–1985). Figure 4 shows that significant efficiency improvements account for fully 30% of the cost reductions in PV over the past two decades. Increased plant size, also related to the economic viability of PV, accounts for the largest segment, 40% of the cost decline over the same period of time.

An energy R&D action plan: investing in the most promising sectors

How feasible would it be to raise investment to levels commensurate with the energy-related challenges we face? Scaling up R&D by 5 or 10 times from current levels is not an unrealistic

proposal; in fact, it is consistent with the scale of several previous federal programs (Tables 1 and 2), each of which was a response to a clearly articulated national need. While expanding energy R&D by a factor of 5 or 10 would be a significant initiative, the fiscal magnitude of such a program is well within the range of previous programs, each of which has produced demonstrable economic benefits beyond the direct program objectives.

It is useful to focus not on the entire energy research and development portfolio, but on a subset of technologies that are low- and no-carbon emitters on a life-cycle basis, and where the U.S. could reclaim global leadership and generate significant job growth as a clean-energy dividend. Kammen, Kapadia, and Fripp (2004) estimated that tens of thousands of new domestic jobs would result from an effort to achieve a federal goal of 20% renewable energy. The estimated 30,000–50,000 new jobs in the wind and solar sectors alone would be significant. The total increases would be even more significant, however, when matched by similar-sized increases if energy efficiency were also made a part of widespread state or federal clean energy policy (Apollo Alliance).

"Major R&D initiatives" in this study are defined as federal programs in which annual spending either doubled or increased by more than $10 billion during the program lifetime. For each of these eight programs we calculate a baseline level of spending based on the 50-year growth rate of U.S. R&D, 4.3% per year. The difference between the actual spending and the baseline during the program we call "additional program spending" (Kammen and Nemet, 2005).

Technology push to match demand pull

A set of targeted increases in clean energy programs instead of a simplistic and largely unworkable effort to develop an across-the-board increase makes the most scientific and operational sense. Table 2 shows the 5- and 10-times scenarios based on the Kammen and Nemet (2005) analysis—which should be considered over a four- to five-year period—for some of the most promising technologies to help states meet their Renewable Energy Portfolio Standards.

National Energy Policy in the United States. FIGURE 2. Overall Federal Investment in Science and Technology.

Energy highlighted as the third sliver from the bottom. Note the comparison with the Health R&D budget, directly over the energy component. The federal health R&D budget experienced a doubling from the mid-1980s to today, and at the same time, private sector health investment increased by a factor of 15. (Source: Margolis, R. and Kammen, D. M., 1999.)

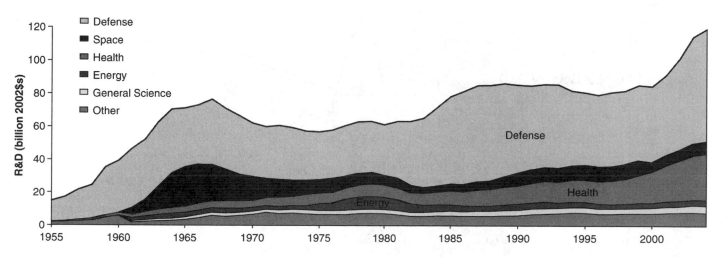

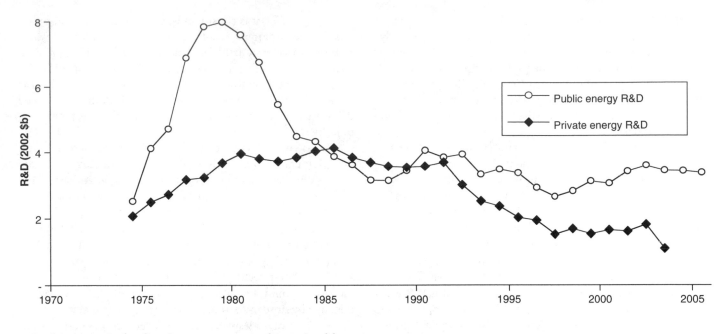

In this scenario funding increases are not determined by a political battle over appropriation levels but are based on an evaluation of what funding level for key technology areas would dramatically expand their market share, saving the nation carbon emissions and significantly advancing these technologies (Duke and Kammen, 1999). This matches the market creation and growth in installed solar power seen in programs already successfully implemented for photovoltaics in Japan, and for solar and wind in Germany. This level of funding is also found to be optimal in stabilizing GHG concentrations according to researchers at the Lawrence Livermore National Laboratory (Schrock et al., 1999).

ENERGY EFFICIENCY

Energy efficiency has a unique role to play in a secure, low-carbon, cost-effective energy policy. Not only is energy efficiency the lowest-cost way to reduce energy demand and

National Energy Policy in the United States. Figure 3. Declining Energy R&D Investment by Both Public and Private Sectors.

(Source: Kammen and Nemet. 2005.)

carbon emissions, but it is the facilitator of every other innovation. Lower energy demand reduces the amount of new, low-carbon energy systems that must be installed. California, New York, and a number of states have been able to keep electricity use per capita virtually unchanged for the past three

National Energy Policy in the United States. Figure 4. Benefits of R&D Investments in Improving Products in the Market.

Directly after a significant increase in federal funding for solar photovoltaics, a 50% rise in cell efficiency occurred. This increase in efficiency has been shown to be the second largest single contributor to the cost effectiveness of solar cells. (Source: Nemet, G. F. (2006).)

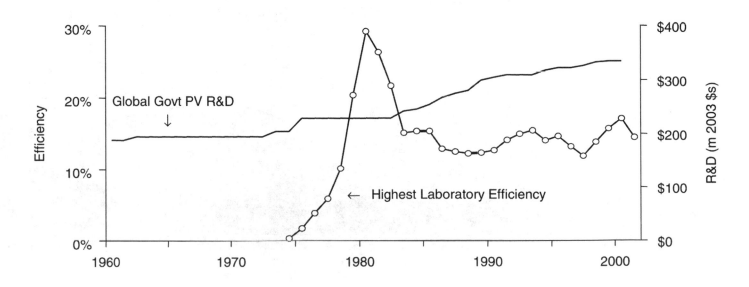

TABLE 1. Comparison of Energy R&D Scenarios and Major Federal Government R&D Initiatives

Program	Sector	Years	Additional Spending over Program Duration (2002$ Billions)
Manhattan Project	Defense	1942–45	25.0
Apollo Program	Space	1963–72	127.4
Project Independence	Energy	1975–82	25.6
Reagan defense	Defense	1981–89	100.3
Doubling NIH	Health	1999–04	32.6
War on Terror	Defense	2002–04	29.6
5× energy scenario	Energy	2005–15	47.9
10× energy scenario	Energy	2005–15	105.4

TABLE 2. Current and forecast future spending on clean energy technologies under the U.S. federal energy research plan, and required levels were a five- or ten-fold increase to be implemented

Current ($m)	2006 Actual	FY2008 Request	5× Scale Up	10× Scale Up
Solar	82	148	409	818
Wind	38	40	192	383
Biomass	90	179	449	898
Battery technology, storage, transmission	146	103	730	1,459
Totals	356	470	1,780	4,199

decades, a remarkable achievement that has saved billions of dollars per year.

One of the simplest energy-efficiency measures is to support and reward states that exempt Energy Star products from a sales tax. A number of state legislatures are considering or have already enacted such measures. States enacting sales-tax waivers for Energy Star products (e.g., energy-efficient water heaters and other appliances) approved by the U.S. Environmental Protection Agency should be eligible for federal rebates. A federal direct rebate could also be implemented to reward the customer for the purchase of the most efficient appliances.

BIOFUELS

The recent dramatic increase in work on biofuels, including ethanol and biodiesel, has been a major advance in diversifying our transportation fuels markets. A calculator available at provides a calculator to compare the GHG benefits of ethanol derived from a range of input biofuels and produced in distilleries powered by different fuels (e.g., coal, natural, gas, and renewables). It is evident from these calculations that biofuels are not created equal in terms of their carbon content. The next logical steps are to rank and then regulate fuels according to their carbon content.

In January 2007, California Governor Arnold Schwarzenegger signed Executive Order S-1-07 to establish a GHG standard for fuels sold in the state. The new Low-Carbon Fuel Standard (LCFS) requires a 10% decrease in the carbon intensity of California's transportation fuels by 2020. The state expects the standard to more than triple the size of the state's renewable-fuels market while placing an additional 7 million hybrid and alternative-fuel vehicles on the road. The standard will help the state meet its GHG reduction goals set by AB32.

On February 21, 2007, Governor Schwarzenegger and U.S. Senator John McCain called for a federal LCFS. An important piece of the LCFS should be the inclusion of electricity as a fuel to support the development and use of plug-in hybrid vehicles in areas where the average grid power is sufficiently low-carbon to result in a net reduction in GHG emissions.

NUCLEAR POWER

One hundred four nuclear reactors provided almost 20% of U.S. electricity generation in 2005, but no new reactors have been approved for construction by the U.S. Nuclear Regulatory Commission (NRC) since 1978. Rising and volatile petroleum prices, geopolitical conflicts in fossil-fuel rich regions, increasing energy demand from emerging economies, and climate change have all brought renewed interest in nuclear power for its potential to promote energy security without emitting carbon dioxide or regional pollutants.

Significant questions remain, however, about waste management and proliferation from nuclear power, and even in a carbon-constrained world, nuclear power may be more expensive than some decentralized energy-efficiency and distributed-generation technologies. It is universally agreed that nuclear

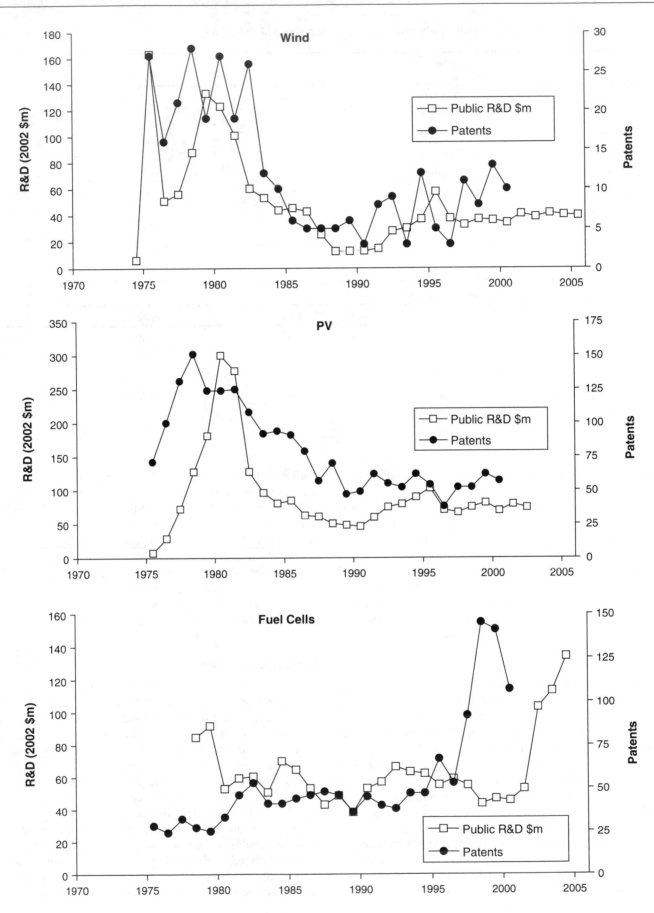

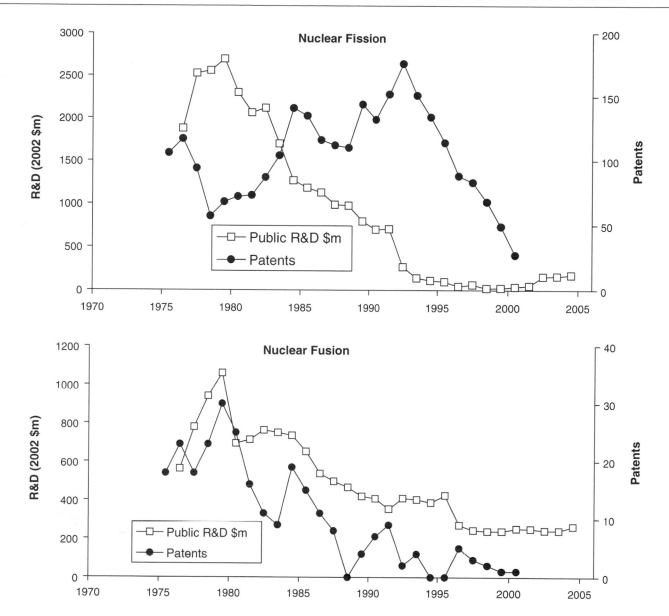

National Energy Policy in the United States. Figure 5. The relationship between federal funding levels (open squares) and patenting (black) for a number of energy technologies.

(Source: Kammen and Nemet, 2005; Nemet and Kammen, 2007.)

power's role in our energy future will be shaped by the framing of debate and the process of evaluation, and by thoughtful integration of this discourse into policy.

For nuclear power to play a significant role, countries would need not only to build new reactors to replace those approaching the end of their service lives, but also to expand significantly the number of commercial reactors in service. Our 60-year experience with nuclear energy has underscored that policy formulation requires not only an estimate of future nuclear costs, benefits, and risks, but also a recognition of the complex technical and social factors that influenced the costs of existing nuclear plants.

Hultman et al. (2007) found that the price per kilowatt-hour for nuclear power varies significantly among U.S. nuclear

reactors. Significant subsidies now in place under the federal Energy Policy Act of 2005 (EPACT 2005) have already resulted in commitments and plans to build a number of new nuclear plants. The experience with the licensing, review, operation, and risk management of these facilities, and the public response to them, will determine the role new nuclear power will play in our future energy mix.

MARKET-BASED SCHEMES AND FUNDING METHODS TO MAKE THE PRICE OF GREENHOUSE-GAS EMISSIONS REFLECT THEIR SOCIAL COST

Both GHG taxes and tradable-permit programs provide simple, logical, and transparent methods to permit industries and households to reward clean-energy systems and tax that which harms our economy and environment. Cap-and-trade schemes have been used with great success in the U.S. to reduce other pollutants (e.g., sulfur dioxide), and several northeastern states are experimenting with GHG emissions trading. Taxing carbon emissions to compensate for negative social and environmental impacts would simplify the national tax code while remaining essentially revenue-neutral. Part of the revenue from a carbon tax could also be used to offset any regressive aspects of the tax, for example by helping to compensate low-income individuals and communities reliant on jobs in fossil-fuel extraction and production.

There are various innovative ways to ease the implementation of a tax on GHG or carbon. One is to institute a national program of energy savings accounts under which everyone pays—for example on gasoline purchases and via utility bills—a federally agreed GHG fee. Instead of simply sending this to the U.S. Treasury in the form of a tax, the funds could be put into individual energy savings accounts that can be used by each individual or family on purchases from a list of federally approved investments. The U.S. Department of Energy and the U.S. Environmental Protection Agency could be charged with developing a list of approved investment areas—such as high efficiency, hybrid vehicles, solar photovoltaic, or solar thermal home-energy systems (Gruener and Kammen, 2007).

FEDERAL CLEAN ENERGY MANDATES: THE RENEWABLE ENERGY PORTFOLIO STANDARD

Clean-energy technologies on the demand-side are a natural complement to clean-energy development strategies. Twenty-three U.S. states and the District of Columbia have now enacted Renewable Energy Portfolio Standards (RPS) which specify the percentage of electric power that is to be generated from renewable resources. Federal legislation could support state action, especially by enacting a federal standard. Several U.S. Senate bills proposing a 20% federal RPS by 2020 have been debated, but each has been defeated. There are additional ways to expand the renewable-energy market-share in ways that could reinforce the RPS.

A feed-in tariff is a renewable-energy law that obliges energy suppliers to buy electricity produced from renewable resources at a fixed price, usually over a fixed period. These legal guarantees ensure investment security and the support of all viable renewable energy technologies. The *Stern Review* concluded that a feed-in tariff was the best policy tool currently available for quickly reducing the cost of deploying renewable-energy technologies. Germany's dramatic expansion in renewable energy manufacturing, domestic and overseas sales, job creation, and installation results largely from the use of feed-in tariffs. More than one thousand megawatts of solar-electric generating capacity was installed in 2006 in Germany alone, compared to 170 megawatts in the U.S.

A concern with clean-energy mandates such as renewable energy portfolio standards (RPS)—as important as they are—is that their effect is focused on the largest institutional investors, along with those best positioned to work with the financial markets and to negotiate the sales contracts necessary to interest the largest power consumers.

Feed-in tariffs can be used to augment RPS standards and/or can be used to open the clean-energy-generation business to new (often smaller) classes of providers. In addition, they often include a built-in sunset clause: the price a specific generator gets for providing power is fixed in the year of installation (e.g., for 20 years), but each year the price is decreased by a fixed amount (e.g., in Germany by 5% for new solar photovoltaic systems). The result is that the feed-in price dips below the energy price paid by the consumer at some known future date (which varies based on how rapidly traditional energy prices rise). It is estimated that the cross-over will occur in Germany in roughly 10–15 years).

In California in the early twenty-first century, the average generation price for photovoltaic based on current crystalline silicon technology is $0.25 per kilowatt-hour (assuming cells for $2.5–3 per watt of peak capacity, modules including installation for $5–6 per watt and 2000–2500 watt-hours per year for each installed watt). As a result, an initial feed-in rate could be below the current peak-rate charged in some utility districts—for example, time-of-use customers served by Pacific Gas & Electric in northern California pay $0.32 per Kilowatt-hour. Programs such as this could also be designated as investment sites to support small businesses or targeted to become residential or commercial feed-in programs.

THE FUTURE

Clean-energy deployment strategies can be tailored to a wide range of local energy-resource and political conditions. The development of new renewable-energy systems is finally at a

---

A SELF-CONSISTENT ENERGY PLAN: RECENT CALIFORNIA ENERGY AND CLIMATE LEGISLATION

California Renewable Energy Portfolio Standard (RPS)
Renewables to constitute 20% by 2010 (and 33% by 2020).

AB1493 (Pavley)
A 30% reduction in automobile GHG emissions (MY2016).

Executive Order S-3–05
Statewide GHG emission reduction targets (about 25% in 2020).

AB32 (Pavley/Nuñez—The California Climate Solutions Act of 2006)
A 25% GHG reduction from stationary sources, a statewide plan.
CPUC action further requires that electricity sold into California meet a carbon standard based, today, on the current generation of natural gas-fired power plants.

AB1007 (Pavley 2)
Develop a comprehensive strategy for alternative fuels and measure the clean-energy jobs dividend.

Executive Order 06–06
Statewide biofuels production targets (40% in 2020).

Executive Order 1–07
California Low-Carbon Biofuel Standard (and State of the State address, January 2007).

stage where deployment to meet a significant fraction of the total energy demands is now possible.

We are left with a number of conclusions and—more importantly—questions. First, can the nations and states that have made these commitments meet and exceed these levels? The global scientific consensus is that an 80% or larger reduction in emissions will be needed by roughly the middle of the twenty-first century. With clean-energy technologies now growing at significant rates, can this trend be matched actual reductions in market share by carbon-intensive sources so that we reverse the century-long trend of emissions increases? The magnitude of this challenge can not be overstated: impressive rates of growth on a percentage basis by the emerging low-carbon technologies mean little or nothing to the climate if the fossil-fuel baseline cannot be reduced—precisely at a time when global investment in fossil-fuel systems is accelerating to meet forecast increases in demand.

Technological innovation is fundamental to increasing the competitiveness of low-carbon energy systems, but the critical driver are the policies we establish to move clean energy sources and systems into the mainstream.

[*See also* Energy Strategies *and* Renewable Sources of Energy.]

BIBLIOGRAPHY

Augustine, N.R. *Rising above the Gathering Storm: Energizing and Employing America for a Brighter Economic Future.* Washington, D.C.: National Academies Press, 2007.

Bailis, R., M. Ezzati, and D.M. Kammen. "Mortality and Greenhouse Gas Impacts of Biomass and Petroleum Energy Futures in Africa." *Science* 308 (2005), 98–103. DOI: 10.1126/science.1106881.

Duke, R.D., and D.M. Kammen. "The Economics of Energy Market Transformation Initiatives." *The Energy Journal* 20.4 (1999), 15–64.

Farrell, A.E., et al. "Ethanol Can Contribute to Energy and Environmental Goals." *Science* 311 (2006), 506–508. DOI: 10.1126/science.1121416.

Gruener, G, and D.M. Kammen. "How to Save the Planet? You Decide." *Los Angeles Times*, January 31, 2007.

Houghton, J.T., et al., eds. *Climate Change 2001: The Scientific Basis: Contribution of Working Group I to the Third Assessment Report of the Intergovernmental Panel on Climate Change.* Cambridge and New York: Cambridge University Press, 2001.

Hultman, N.E., J.G. Koomey, and D.M. Kammen. "What History Can Teach Us about the Future Costs of U.S. Nuclear Power." *Environmental Science and Technology* 40.7 (2007), 2088–2094.

Jacobson, A., and D.M. Kammen. "Science and Engineering Research That Values the Planet." *The Bridge: Journal of the National Academy of Engineering* 35.4 (2005), 11–17.

Kammen, D.M. "September 27, 2006: A Day to Remember." *San Francisco Chronicle*, September 27, 2006.

Kammen, D.M. "Transportation's Next Big Thing is Already Here." http://www.greenbiz.com/column/2007/05/31/transportations-next-big-thing-already-here (accessed June 3, 2008).

Kammen, D.M., K. Kapadia, and M. Fripp. *Putting Renewables to Work: How Many Jobs Can the Clean Energy Industry Generate?* RAEL Report. Berkeley: University of California, Renewable and Appropriate Energy Laboratory, 2004. http://rad.berkeley.edu/renewable-jobs (accessed June 3, 2008).

Kammen, D.M., and G.F. Nemet. "Reversing the Incredible Shrinking Energy R&D Budget." *Issues in Science and Technology* 22.1 (2005), 84–88.

Margolis, R.M., and D.M. Kammen. "Underinvestment: The Energy Technology and R&D Policy Challenge." *Science* 285 (1999), 690–692. DOI: 10.1126/science.285.5428.690.

Nemet, G.F. "Beyond the Learning Curve: Factors Influencing Cost Reductions in Photovoltaics." *Energy Policy* 34.17 (2006), 3218–3232.

Nemet, G.F. and D.M. Kammen. "U.S. Energy Research and Development: Declining Investment, Increasing Need, and the Feasibility of Expansion." *Energy Policy* 35.1 (2007), 746–755.

Schock, R.N., et al. "How Much is Energy Research and Development Worth as Insurance?" *Annual Review of Energy and Environment* 24 (1999), 487–512.

—DANIEL M. KAMMEN

NATIONAL PARKS

See Parks and Preserves.

NATURAL GAS

Natural gas is a widely consumed fossil fuel, supplying just over 20% of the global primary energy in 2006. Natural gas is a mixture of hydrocarbon gases, primarily methane (CH_4), but also ethane (C_2H_6), propane (C_3H_8), and butane (C_4H_{10}), as well as small amounts of carbon dioxide (CO_2), oxygen, nitrogen, and hydrogen sulfide (H_2S).

Natural gas is prized as the cleanest burning fossil fuel, releasing 45% less carbon dioxide (CO_2) than coal and 30% less than oil per unit of usable energy, because of the higher ratio of hydrogen to carbon in natural gas, the combustion of hydrogen generating water rather than CO_2. Natural gas-fired turbines are also more efficient than coal-fired turbines at turning this usable energy into electricity, further enhancing gas's advantage in CO_2 emissions. Natural gas also has significantly lower emissions of regional air pollutants like sulfur oxides (SO_x), nitrogen oxides (NO_x), particulate matter, and mercury.

Although natural gas has been used in the United States for over a century, it has only emerged as a major fuel globally since the 1950s. Technological advances in gas transportation, along with heightened interest in the efficient and clean burning properties of natural gas, have driven demand in a range of uses worldwide.

MAJOR USES OF NATURAL GAS

Today natural gas is consumed in most countries around the world. Some of the major applications of natural gas are described below.

Centralized electricity generation

Electric power generators consume about 40% of the natural gas produced in the world today. Globally, approximately 20% of the world's electricity is produced from natural gas, making it the second largest fuel for power generation behind coal. Most projections expect a large increase in natural gas consumption for electric power generation over the next 30 years. These projections predict coal and natural gas will meet the majority of new global electricity demand, along with smaller contributions from nuclear, and increasingly, renewables.

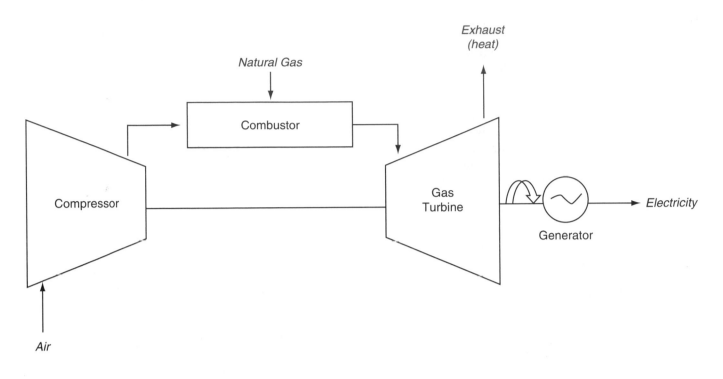

Natural Gas. Figure 1. Open-Cycle Natural Gas Plant.

There are two major natural gas power-plant designs—open-cycle and combined-cycle. Open-cycle natural gas systems are similar in design to aircraft jet engines (see Figure 1). In these systems, natural gas is combusted in compressed air, causing the gas to expand rapidly. This expanding gas spins a turbine, and a generator converts this spinning mechanical energy into electricity.

Open-cycle designs are 25–35% efficient, and are capable of quickly ramping up and down, enabling them to respond to rapidly changing electricity demands. As a result, they are often used on the electricity grid to provide power during peak electricity demand times.

Combined-cycle natural gas plants capture the waste heat from a simple cycle, and use it to drive a steam cycle (see Figure 2). As the figure shows, the exhaust from the open-cycle heats circulating water to produce high-pressure steam. When this steam expands and spins a steam turbine, it too drives a generator to produce electricity. The water is then cooled in a condenser and passed back through the cycle.

Combined-cycle natural gas plants can have efficiencies as high as 60%. However, they are slower to ramp up and down to follow electricity demand and are generally used to provide baseload power. Further efficiency can be gained if the plant is located near a facility which is able to use the waste heat released from the condenser. In these cogeneration applications—so-called because the plant is generating both useful electricity and heat—efficiencies can rise to 70–90%.

Because combined-cycle natural gas plants emit approximately 60% less carbon dioxide per unit of electricity produced than coal plants, a large shift from coal to natural gas would dramatically reduce CO_2 emissions. Because major global energy consumers—including the United States, China, and India—are endowed with plentiful domestic coal resources, such shifts to natural gas will be an important component to effective efforts to address climate change.

Figure 3 quantifies the impact on CO_2 emissions of a hypothetical shift from electricity generated by coal to natural gas. To put these figures in context, the 50 gigawatts in the figure is equivalent to approximately 4% of the new coal-fired capacity expected to be installed in the world to 2030. The quantity of gas required to meet this demand, 70 billion cubic meters (bcm), is only about 2% of global natural gas demand in 2030. Yet the carbon dioxide emission reduction indicated here, 220 million tons, is approximately the size of the European Union's emissions reduction required under the Kyoto Protocol.

Distributed power generation

Natural gas turbines can operate cost-effectively at small scales, making natural gas a widely-used fuel in distributed generation applications. The clean-burning attributes of natural gas allow generation units to be collocated with manufacturing and industrial facilities in and around large population centers.

Medium-sized turbines on the order of 10–50 megawatts are common throughout the world for such onsite generation—providing backup power, and in some cases, highly reliable primary power. India, for example, has seen a proliferation of small natural gas units to provide a reliable supply of electricity in a country with a notoriously unreliable electricity grid.

In recent years, natural-gas-fired microturbines, generating less than one megawatt, have also become available. While they are only used in limited applications to date, it is hoped that

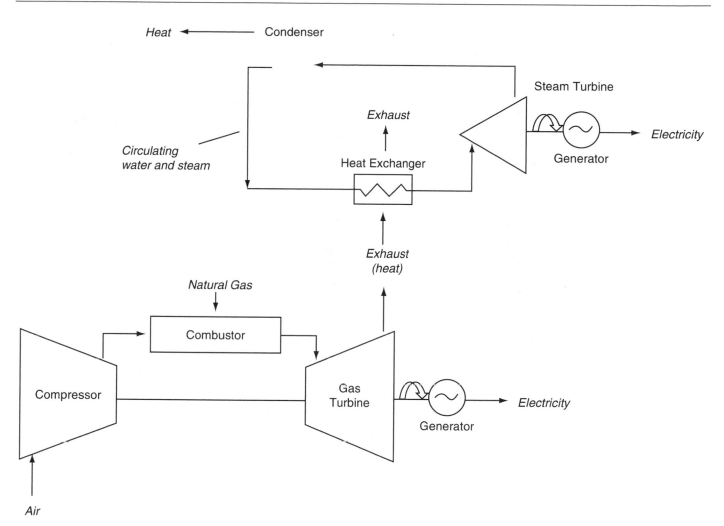

Natural Gas. FIGURE 2. Combined Cycle Natural Gas Plant.

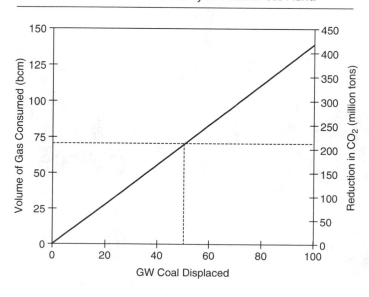

Natural Gas. FIGURE 3. Carbon Dioxide Reductions from a Shift From Coal to Natural Gas.

these small units might be able to provide electricity, space heating, and water heating to residential and commercial buildings, realizing huge efficiency gains over centralized generation.

Industrial applications

Approximately 30% of all natural gas consumed globally is used in industrial applications. In some applications—such as the manufacture of steel, glass, paper, and cement—natural gas is burned to provide process heat. In many of these examples, natural gas competes with coal and oil as the heating fuel of choice.

In other industrial applications, methane in natural gas is chemically converted to other compounds rather than being burned. One of the most widespread such applications is the production of nitrogenous fertilizers, through the Haber-Bosch process. A simplified description of this process, focusing only on the role of natural gas, is described below.

First, methane (CH_4) from natural gas is reacted with steam to produce hydrogen:

$$CH_4 + H_2O \quad CO + 3H_2.$$

This hydrogen is then mixed with nitrogen from air—air is 78% nitrogen by volume—to produce ammonia (NH_3):

$$N_2 + 3H_2 \quad 2NH_3.$$

Ammonia is then used to make the main nitrogenous fertilizers including urea ($[NH_2]_2CO$) and ammonium nitrate (NH_4NO_3).

Residential heating and cooking

Natural gas is a major fuel in home heating applications, including furnaces, water heaters, and stoves. Most residential natural gas use worldwide occurs in urban areas and largely in the colder climates of North America and Europe. Figure 4 shows how this residential use causes overall natural gas consumption to vary over the course of a year, spiking in winter months and declining during the summer.

Increased use of natural gas—as well as other modern heating fuels like liquefied petroleum gas (LPG), and electricity—could provide tremendous health benefits in many parts of the developing world, where these fuels would displace traditional biomass. Over half the world's population relies on wood, dung, and coal for their heating and cooking needs. When burned indoors, the smoke and soot from these fuels cause dangerous levels of indoor air pollution, which annually kills an estimated 1.6 million people worldwide. It is hoped that the spread of cleaner, modern fuels could help prevent many of these unnecessary deaths.

TRANSPORTATION

The uses described above consume most of the natural gas worldwide. Very small amounts are also used as a transportation fuel, and experts debate whether or not natural gas will play a major role in the transportation sector in the future. A few key technologies, which could become significant over the coming decades, are described below.

Compressed natural gas (CNG) vehicles

Compressed natural gas can be used in specially designed engines in cars, buses, and trucks. These engines can be designed to operate exclusively on natural gas, or in combination with gasoline and diesel. Natural gas vehicles are appealing because they are cleaner burning than gasoline and diesel, virtually eliminating particulate and sulfur emissions. However, because CNG refueling stations are sparse and the economics of CNG for drivers is often unfavorable without significant government subsidy, there are only a few million CNG vehicles worldwide today.

Natural Gas. Figure 4. Natural Gas Consumption Over Time in OECD Countries.

OECD stands for Organization for Economic Cooperation and Development. Its members are listed below but are generally the major developed countries around the world.

- OECD Pacific: Australia, Japan, South Korea, New Zealand
- OECD Europe: Austria, Belgium, Czech Republic, Denmark, Finland, France, Germany, Greece, Hungary, Iceland, Ireland, Italy, Luxembourg, Netherlands, Norway, Poland, Portugal, Slovak Republic, Spain, Sweden, Switzerland, Turkey, and United Kingdom.
- OECD North America: Canada, Mexico, United States

Gas consumption data from: International Energy Agency. "Monthly Natural Gas Survey – January 2007." Available at:
http://www.iea.org/Textbase/stats/surveys/natgas.pdf.

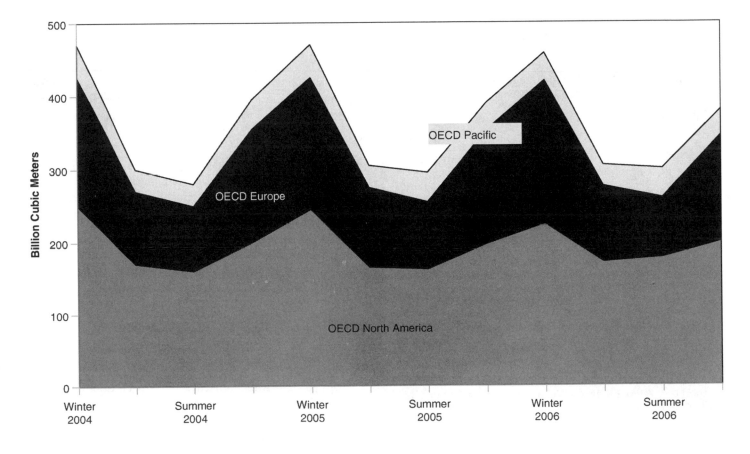

Perhaps the most visible example of CNG vehicles is in Delhi, India. In 1998, in an attempt to alleviate horrendous air quality in the city, the Supreme Court of India mandated that all taxis, buses, and rickshaws in Delhi convert from diesel to CNG. The result, admittedly aided by other environmental rules as well, has been a dramatic improvement in the air quality of Delhi.

Synfuels/gas-to-liquids (GTL)

The short hydrocarbon molecules that make up natural gas can be linked together in a refinery to produce long hydrocarbon chains with properties similar to diesel fuel. This liquid product is often called synthetic fuel, or simply synfuel. In addition to natural gas, synfuels can also be produced from coal or biomass.

Synfuels are prized because they reduce emissions of local air pollutants like sulfur and particulate matter. They can be distributed in the same pipelines as other petroleum products, and burned in automobiles without any modification. Lastly, they are an alternative to oil imports for countries lacking major oil reserves. Indeed, much of the historic development of synfuels has occurred in countries isolated from global oil supplies—most notably South Africa during apartheid and Germany during World War II.

However, because synfuels are very energy intensive to produce, they result in higher carbon dioxide emissions than conventional gasoline. The future of synfuels will be dependent on how policymakers, consumers, and industry prioritize the advantages of synfuels against concerns over climate change.

Fuel cell vehicles

Natural gas can also be used to power a hydrogen fuel cell. When mixed with steam, methane reacts to form hydrogen through a process called steam reformation. The hydrogen then reacts with oxygen in a fuel cell to produce electricity to power the vehicle.

The major advantage to this approach is that the reformation of natural gas to hydrogen can occur onboard the vehicle, obviating the need to develop a new hydrogen infrastructure. Instead, refueling facilities could use the existing natural gas infrastructure. The major disadvantage is that the reformation process releases carbon dioxide, so the fuel cell is not carbon neutral. The process does, however, reduce carbon dioxide emissions relative to gasoline by nearly 60%.

NATURAL GAS SUPPLIES

An ongoing obstacle to increased consumption of natural gas in the future is the difficulty in transporting natural gas from gas fields to consumers. Natural gas is a fossil fuel, composed of the remains of plants and animals that died millions of years ago. As this organic matter was buried and subjected to high temperatures and pressures underground, the long carbon chains that make up organic matter were broken down into ever shorter chains. The short carbon molecules that comprise natural gas and and the somewhat longer ones in oil are the products of this process.

As oil and natural gas formed underground, it rose toward the surface because it is less dense than the surrounding rock. Over millions of years, much of this oil and gas reached the surface and dissipated—the famous La Brea tar pits in Los Angeles are an example of these hydrocarbons bubbling to the surface. However, some oil and gas became trapped under impermeable rock layers that prevented it from rising to the surface. The resulting underground reservoirs are the oil and gas fields we know today. [See: Fossil Fuels]

Natural gas is extracted by drilling through the impermeable rock layer and constructing a well through which the gas can flow to the surface. While much of the gas flows on its own because it is less dense than air, engineers sometimes inject acids or water at high pressure to create cracks in the reservoir to allow the gas to flow more easily.

TABLE 1. Rank Order of Major Gas Resources and Production

Proved Reserves* (trillion cubic meters)		% of total	Production (billion cubic meters)		% of total
1) Russia	47.8	27%	1) Russia	598	22%
2) Iran	26.7	15%	2) United States	526	19%
3) Qatar	25.8	14%	3) Canada	186	7%
4) Saudi Arabia	6.9	4%	4) United Kingdom	88	3%
5) United Arab Emirates	6.0	3%	5) Algeria	88	3%
6) United States	5.5	3%	6) Iran	87	3%
7) Nigeria	5.2	3%	7) Norway	85	3%
8) Algeria	4.6	3%	8) Indonesia	76	3%
World	179.8		*World*	2,763	

* Proved reserves are gas resources that can be profitably extracted with existing market prices.

SOURCE: BP. *Statistical Review of World Energy, 2006.* Available at: http://www.bp.com/productlanding.do?categoryId=6842&contentId=7021390.

Natural gas reserves and production worldwide

Table 1 identifies the countries with the largest natural gas reserves and the major gas-producing countries. Interestingly, many of the countries with large gas resources are not major gas producers. There are a number of explanations for this, probably the most significant being that natural gas is very expensive and difficult to transport. As a result, resources near major demand centers in Europe and the United States have historically been more readily exploited. This explains why Canada, Norway, the United Kingdom, and the United States are all major gas producers despite their relatively small reserves.

Natural gas transportation

Most natural gas worldwide is transported through pipelines. Some examples of major international pipelines are those that connect Russia and Algeria to Western Europe, Canada to the United States, and Bolivia to Chile, Argentina, and Brazil. Other pipelines transport natural gas within countries—the United States, for example, has over 200,000 miles of interstate natural gas pipelines.

When transported long distances or across oceans, natural gas is cooled to below −163°C (−261°F), to condense the gas to a liquid (liquefied natural gas, or LNG), shrinking its volume to 1/600 that at 25°C. The LNG is then shipped in cryogenic tankers to destinations around the world. LNG receiving-terminals slowly warm the LNG back to ambient temperature and distribute the natural gas to consumers.

While only about 6% of the natural gas consumed worldwide today is shipped as LNG, LNG will probably play an increasingly important role in the global natural gas market over the coming decades. The world's major natural gas resources are located in the Middle East and Africa, far from the demand in North America, Europe, and East Asia, and LNG appears to be the most viable option for connecting the producers and consumers.

CHALLENGES TO FUTURE NATURAL GAS USE

Most experts agree that natural gas will continue to play an important role in the global-energy scenario over the coming few decades. There is enough natural gas in the ground to sustain today's rate of natural gas consumption for at least another 65 years, even if no new gas fields are discovered. Some of the major challenges to natural gas use in the future are described below.

Price of natural gas vs. competitors

In today's energy market, natural gas competes mostly with coal in electricity generation and industrial use. In the future, as renewable energy technologies like wind and solar become cheaper, natural gas will be forced to compete with these as well. Through the 1990s, natural gas prices worldwide were low, comparable to coal prices. However, over the last five years, natural gas prices have risen to 2–4 times higher per unit of energy than coal prices, making coal a more attractive option in many applications. If natural gas remains expensive, demand for it will likely be stunted.

Investment in transportation infrastructure

Growth in natural gas consumption will require billions of dollars of new pipelines and LNG facilities to transport the gas. Typical LNG liquefaction and regasification facilities can cost $2 billion each. Major international pipeline projects can cost even more—a pipeline currently under consideration between Iran, Pakistan, and India would cost over $7 billion. Investment in natural gas infrastructure will require the cooperation of governments and industry to pay these upfront costs and guarantee the safety of this infrastructure.

Emerging clean alternatives

Lastly, new technologies cleaner than natural gas are expected to become increasingly cost competitive over the coming few decades. Although natural gas power plants have lower carbon dioxide emissions than conventional coal plants, coal with carbon sequestration, wind, solar, and nuclear power would all have much lower emissions than even natural gas. If climate-change policies become more stringent around the world in the coming decades, these lower carbon technologies could compete successfully with natural gas.

BIBLIOGRAPHY

American Council for an Energy-Efficient Economy. "Combined Heat and Power: The Efficient Path for New Power Generation." http://www.aceee.org/energy/chp.htm (accessed June 3, 2008).

BP. *Statistical Review of World Energy*. http://www.bp.com/ (accessed June 3, 2008). A report issued annually.

Energy Information Administration. "Additions to Capacity on the U.S. Natural Gas Pipeline Network: 2005." http://www.eia.doe.gov/pub/oil_gas/natural_gas/feuatrue_articles/2006ngpipeline/ngpipeline. pdf (accessed June 3, 2008).

Energy Information Administration. "The Global Liquefied Natural Gas Market: Status and Outlook." http://www.eia.doe.gov/oiaf/analysispaper/global/index.html (accessed June 3, 2008).

GE Energy. "GE's First 7H Gas Turbine Heading For Inland Empire Project In California." http://www.gepower.com/about/press/en/2006_press/092606_a. htm (accessed June 3, 2008).

International Energy Agency. "Monthly Natural Gas Survey." http"//www.iea.org/Textbase/stats surveys/natgas.pdf (accessed June 3, 2008).

Jackson, M., et al. "Greenhouse Gas Implications in Large Scale Infrastructure Investments in Developing Countries: Examples from China and India." Working Paper 54. Stanford, Calif.: Stanford University, Program on Energy and Sustainable Development, 2006 (http://iisdb.standford.edu/pubs/21061/China_and_India_Infrastructure_Deals.pdf; accessed June 3, 2008).

Narain, U., and A. Krupnick. "The Impact of Delhi's CNG Program on Air Quality." *Resources for the Future* (February 2007). http://www.rff.org/Documents/REF-DP-07-06.pdf (accessed June 3, 2008).

Victor, D.G., et al. *Natural Gas and Geopolitics: From 1970 to 2040*. Cambridge and New York: Cambridge University Press, 2006.

Wang, M. "Updated Well-to-Wheel Analysis of Energy and Emission Impacts of Fuel-Cell Vehicles." Argonne, Ill.: Argonne National Laboratory, 2005. http://www.hygrogen.energy.gov/pdfs/pr gress05/iii_12_wang.pdf (accessed June 3, 2008).

World Health Organization. "Indoor Air Pollution and Health." Fact Sheet #292. Geneva: World Health Organization, 2005 (http://www.who.int/mediacentre/factsheets/fs292/en/index.html; accessed June 3, 2008).

—MICHAEL P. JACKSON

NATURAL HAZARDS

Natural hazards are created by environmental processes that pose a danger to people and the things they value. The most severe hazards are a threat to human life and economic development. Typically, natural hazards result from concentrated releases of energy or materials from the Earth-atmosphere system that have a rapid onset and short duration, although there are notable exceptions, such as drought. Many natural hazards arise from extreme geophysical events of tectonic origin, such as earthquakes or volcanic eruptions, but atmospherically created events (climatic variations, storms and floods) are the most frequent natural hazards worldwide. Other natural hazards, such as disease epidemics or plant and animal invasions, are primarily dependent on biological processes. In some cases, it is difficult to distinguish between natural processes and processes modified by human activity. For example, a landslide may be generated by a combination of heavy rainfall and unwise land-use practices, such as the deforestation of a slope. When long-term episodes of either human-induced environmental pollution or land degradation occur, complex hazards that endure for decades may result. For example, the burning of fossil fuels leads to global warming, which, in turn, produces sea-level rise and greater risks from coastal flooding. [*See* Drought.]

Natural hazards include a wide variety of interactions between people and their environment. Many events are seen as hazardous because they impose stresses on human society that, under more normal environmental conditions or in other locations, would be perceived as natural resources, as when a river in spate unexpectedly floods an urbanized flood plain rather than providing the expected water supply. However, such spates are necessary to maintain high biological diversity in the river and its adjacent flood plain. To this extent, entirely "natural" hazards have never existed. A landslide in a remote, unpopulated region may be of interest to geomorphologists but does not constitute a natural hazard because it poses no threat to humans.

As the world becomes increasingly settled and transformed by humans, the hazard potential grows. Most commentators now agree that natural hazards are really quasi-natural or hybrid events reflecting diverse interactions between environmental, technological, and social processes. The term "na-tech hazard" has been used to describe the combination of environmental and technological processes when, for example, an earthquake results in urban fires after the rupturing of gas pipelines.

The importance attached to natural hazards by victims, policy makers, and governments tends to mirror the perceived scale of the negative socioeconomic impacts on communities and nations. Some natural hazards have only a minor—or nuisance—value, as when snowfalls temporarily disrupt road and rail communications. On the other hand, when either the number of people killed and injured or the direct economic losses are sufficiently large to prompt widespread reporting through the international media, the event is usually termed a disaster. Unfortunately, a direct link between

the physical scale of the relevant environmental processes and the socioeconomic significance of the resulting disaster is often lacking. Many natural hazards can be scaled according to measurable scientific criteria that may suggest the likely extent of loss, such as their predictability, intensity, rate of onset, and duration. But an earthquake of the same Richter-scale magnitude will have widely different consequences for mortality and property loss according to local cultural factors such as the density of population, the level of earthquake preparedness in the community, the time of day the earthquake occurs, and the types of building materials and methods near the epicenter.

There are further complications, because no general agreement exists on the minimum level of loss that has to occur before a disaster is officially declared. Once again, absolute measures such as the number of people killed or the cost of direct damage do not always reflect the real significance of the event. While the death of 20 people accompanied by economic costs of U.S.$1 million may be catastrophic for a small, remote fishing community, the same losses may hardly affect the functioning of a large industrial city. The Centre for Research on the Epidemiology of Disasters (CRED) at the University of Louvain, Belgium, has standardized an international hazards database called EM-DAT that can be used to identify the relative significance of disasters for each country: number of deaths per event—at least one hundred; direct damage—at least 1% of national GNP; adversely affected people—at least 1% of national population.

The field of natural hazards is conceptually and empirically diverse. Throughout the history of both theory and practice, there has been a progressive trend away from an emphasis on extreme geophysical events and a policy response aimed at the physical controls of hazards toward a more multidisciplinary view that recognizes hazards as an intrinsic part of the social fabric and recommends stronger elements of human responsibility and avoidance at the personal level.

THE ACTS-OF-GOD PARADIGM

Initially, natural hazards were seen as isolated and random events in an acts-of-God paradigm. Because these events were thought to be controlled by some higher being external to society, there was a fatalistic attitude on the part of victims and the absence of positive management responses. This view is still retained by a few traditional cultures. Eventually some environmental processes, mainly those dependent on the passage of the seasons, such as annual floods, became better understood, and primitive flood-control dams were first constructed in the Middle East 4,000 years ago. This was the start of the engineering paradigm that interpreted natural hazards as unpredictable geophysical events disrupting the normal order of society. Because the problem was now perceived to originate in nature, it was logical to believe that the control and prediction of natural events, through the application of science and technology, would provide a solution. Flood defense has always been at the forefront of this response, as illustrated as early as 1802 by the creation of the U.S. Army Corps of Engineers, dedicated to the construction of large-scale flood control projects.

THE ENGINEERING PARADIGM

The engineering paradigm soon predominated throughout the developed world. It has been much favored by government bodies wishing to confront hazards in a visible way. Environmental monitoring, scientific explanation, and managerial control are the hallmarks of this strategy, which has led to widespread defensive structures as varied as river dams, levees, coastal barriers, avalanche sheds, and antiseismic building construction. Advances in communications technology have also been adopted—often very successfully—to mitigate natural hazards. For example, the advent of the telephone, computers and the Internet, satellites, radar, and telemetry transformed weather forecasting in the twentieth century. On the other hand, some important natural hazards such as earthquakes, volcanic eruptions, and drought have resisted scientific forecasting and control.

THE BEHAVIORAL PARADIGM

A major shift occurred around the middle of the twentieth century when American geographers promoted what became known as the behavioral paradigm. This view still emphasized extreme geophysical events as a disruption of normal life but also recognized the contributing role played by the victims. For example, in the developed countries, ill-informed human behavior was thought to include poor hazard perception, which allowed further settlement in unsafe areas such as flood plains and seashores. In the developing countries, human actions such as deforestation and overgrazing increased the hazard potential. Proponents of the behavioral paradigm argued that technical solutions alone were inappropriate for hazard mitigation and that a broader mix of options designed to modify human behavior, such as financial measures and land-use controls, should be adopted. In turn this led to a greater study of the perception of extreme events and the choice of hazard-mitigation adjustments by individual and corporate decision makers.

THE STRUCTURAL PARADIGM

In the mid-1970s, the emergence of the structural paradigm provided a more radical and political interpretation. It was pointed out that the emphasis on the choice of mitigation strategies ignored the structural constraints imposed on people by historical, cultural, and institutional forces that transcend local decision-making. For example, in the developed countries, national governments, regional authorities, and financial bodies—rather than individuals—control many land-use decisions, while in the developing countries, the legacy of colonialism and economic underdevelopment precludes many hazard adjustments possible in richer nations. Workers with field experience in developing countries also questioned the largely Western assumption that extreme geophysical events disrupted normal life. They argued that, in these countries, hazards occupy an integral—rather than an exceptional—place in human livelihoods that are often permanently fragile. For the poorest

people, therefore, extreme natural events are merely triggers that expose deep political, social, and economic problems. The structural paradigm thus recognizes a link between hazard impact and human vulnerability created by disadvantage, and its advocates envisage solutions based on the redistribution of wealth and power in society rather than the application of science.

This political-economic view of hazards has been expressed most powerfully in relation to developing countries in which large-scale global processes associated with the expansion of global capitalism lead to the blight of underdevelopment. Other constructs illuminate different aspects of human vulnerability. For example, sociologists in the United States have extended the concept into the developed countries with surveys of household-scale social inequalities, such as poverty, gender, age, ethnicity, and language and literacy issues following events such as Hurricane Andrew (1992) and the Northridge earthquake (1994). Other researchers have explored human vulnerability to natural hazards in the historical context of the colonial legacy and the spatial context of the geographical region.

DAMAGE TRENDS

The 1990s International Decade for Natural Disaster Reduction (IDNDR) is the most determined attempt yet made to mitigate hazards, mainly by assisting developing countries to assess hazard potential and deploy relevant early-warning schemes and hazard-resistant structures. The IDNDR was established by the United Nations to address two problems: the apparent increasing frequency of natural hazards worldwide, and the unacceptable burden of loss in the developing countries. Time series of natural hazards are available from the 1960s on but are difficult to interpret because of environmental and social changes over recent decades, including new technology, population growth, and more comprehensive disaster reporting by the news media. Nevertheless, some trends do exist. According to the CRED database, the number of disasters claiming at least 100 lives has more than doubled from the late 1960s to the early 1990s, while the number of people affected adversely has grown from less than 50 million per year to around 250 million per year. Economic losses also tend to increase. Even after allowing for price inflation (indexed to 1990 U.S. dollars), average annual flood losses in the United States rose from some U.S.$100 million in 1925 to about U.S.$4 billion in 1995. Disaster losses are not evenly spread throughout the world. For example, it is believed that over 90% of hazard-related deaths occur among the two-thirds of the world population that lives in the developing countries. Although three-quarters of the direct economic damage is confined to the developed countries, the relative effect—expressed as a proportion of gross national product—is many times more severe in the poorest countries.

NATURAL HAZARDS

Few of the recorded increases in hazard impact can be attributed entirely to natural processes. For example, no evidence exists for a greater frequency of earthquakes or volcanic eruptions. On the other hand, there is a growing awareness that human activity is changing atmospheric processes and that such effects may well create increased human vulnerability in the future. Much atmospheric pollution is now intercontinental, or even global, in scale. As a consequence, climatic hazards as varied as acid deposition (leading to the corrosion of buildings and the contamination of water supply systems) and the depletion of stratospheric ozone (leading to greater human exposure to harmful UV-B radiation and the risk of skin cancer) have already been documented. The most publicized threat is that of global climate change due to increased concentrations of radiatively active gases in the atmosphere. Global warming is likely to lead to sea-level rise and increased danger from hurricane winds and storm surges along coasts, and to a more energetic hydrologic cycle with prospects for more damaging floods and droughts.

Pressure on natural resources due to population increase, economic development, and modernization is raising basic questions about the ability of the Earth to sustain future growth. Environmental degradation and the further intrusion of unsafe zones have many implications for natural hazards in the future. Consider, for instance, the 300 cities with populations in excess of one million in the world, and the eighteen megacities containing over 10 million people. Many of these cities have expanded with little regard for the biophysical environment and are located on low-lying shorelines, river flood plains, or unstable slopes or in topography that accentuates any risk from air, ground, or water pollution. These very large cities are under threat because they contain unprecedented concentrations of people who are dependent on commercial, industrial, and transportation infrastructures vulnerable to hazard. Many of the fundamental support services are inadequate, especially in the developing countries, and there are few resources available for hazard reduction.

On the other hand, the threat from natural hazards is declining in some areas. In practice, many authenticated decreases in hazard impact are the result of improved forecasting and warning procedures and the ability to construct better hazard-resistant structures. For example, the increasing efficiency with which low-lying coastland communities in the United States can be evacuated has reduced the number of hurricane deaths per decade from over 8,000 in 1900–1909 to around 250 in 1980–1989. In Bangladesh, specially built cyclone refuges provide limited safety from severe storms. Rapid deployment teams, with skills as varied as disaster medicine and the restoration of electricity supplies, are now stationed around the world, poised to maximize the life-saving opportunities of the first few hours following a disaster. [See Coastlines.]

In the postindustrial age, natural hazards and their effective mitigation are the focus of considerable debate. Science and technology will continue to make vital contributions toward a safer world, as envisaged by the IDNDR, but the primary need is not for more science but for a better deployment of the science that already exists. For example, there is

a growing awareness of the adverse side-effects of some classic environmental engineering schemes, such as river dams and coastal defenses, that interfere with sediment supplies and related ecological processes. Other schemes are criticized for being economically unrealistic, especially in the less developed parts of the world. Increasingly, natural hazards are seen as an indicator of unsustainable growth and as obstacles to future economic well-being, even in wealthy countries. For example, the Kobe earthquake of 1995 killed over 6,000 people in Japan, injured 35,000, and rendered a further 300,000 homeless, with national economic losses estimated at U.S.$100 billion.

THE LIVING-WITH-HAZARDS PARADIGM

Because natural hazards can never be completely eliminated, a new living-with-hazards paradigm is likely to emerge. This is based on the fact that economic development and modernization will not, in themselves, mitigate natural hazards. Indeed, such trends may well erode traditional lifestyles and indigenous hazard responses and encourage more investment of a community's wealth in physical infrastructure that is susceptible to damage. Future hazard-reducing technologies will have to be more sensitive to the ecological, financial, and social framework in which they operate. For example, this means encouraging "softer, environmentally friendly" engineering defenses in coastal-zone and river-basin management plans, together with more self-reliant responses from people at risk. Such responses will need to be supported by better risk communication, practical first-aid training, more help for strengthening weak dwellings and, where necessary, assistance for a managed retreat of people and property from the most hazardous areas.

[See also Insurance and Sea Level Future.]

BIBLIOGRAPHY

Alexander, D. *Natural Disasters*. London: UCL Press; New York: Chapman and Hall, 1993. A wide-ranging introduction to the subject with an emphasis on natural processes.

Blaikie, P., et al. *At Risk: Natural Hazards, People's Vulnerability, and Disasters*. London and New York: Routledge, 1994. A thought-provoking and innovative statement of human vulnerability in the developing countries.

Bolin, R., and L. Stanford. *The Northridge Earthquake: Vulnerability and Disaster*. London and New York: Routledge, 1998. Explores the role of community vulnerability to hazard in one of the wealthiest parts of the world.

Bryant, E.A. *Natural Hazards*. Cambridge and New York: Cambridge University Press, 1991. A geophysical interpretation of hazards firmly in the tradition of the engineering paradigm. The second edition was published in 2005.

Burton, I., R.W. Kates, and G.F. White. *The Environment as Hazard*. 2d ed. New York and London: Guilford Press, 1993. An update of the behavioral perspective by the pioneers of the human-ecology view of hazards.

Gross, E.M. "The Hurricane Dilemma in the United States." *Episodes* 14 (1991), 36–45. A good illustration of how the impact of a specific hazard can be evaluated.

Hewitt, K., ed. *Interpretations of Calamity*. Boston and London: Allen and Unwin, 1983. Seminal case studies that marked the arrival of the structural perspective on hazards.

———. *Regions of Risk: A Geographical Introduction to Disasters*. Harlow, U.K.: Longman, 1997. A critical appraisal of the geography of natural hazards and other risks.

Mitchell, J.K., ed. *Crucibles of Hazard: Mega-Cities and Disasters in Transition.* Tokyo: United Nations University Press, 1999. Authoritative case studies on the growing threat of natural hazards to the largest cities in the world.

Peacock, W.G., B.H. Morrow, and H. Gladwin, eds. *Hurricane Andrew: Ethnicity, Gender, and the Sociology of Disasters.* London and New York: Routledge, 1997. Presents a sociopolitical interpretation of natural hazard impact, with a focus on the city of Miami.

Pielke, R., Jr., and R. Pielke Sr. *Storms.* 2 vols. London and New York: Routledge, 2000.

Sapir, D.G., and C. Misson. "The Development of a Database on Disasters." *Disasters* 16.1 (1992), 74–80. A good description of the strengths and weaknesses of the CRED database.

Smith, K. *Environmental Hazards: Assessing Risk and Reducing Disaster.* 3d ed. London and New York: Routledge, 2000. A comprehensive and accessible introduction to the theoretical study and practical mitigation of hazards. The fourth edition was published in 2004.

Smith. K., and R. Ward. *Floods: Physical Processes and Human Impacts.* Chichester, U.K., and New York: Wiley, 1998. Illustrates differing perspectives on, and human responses to, the most common of all natural hazards.

White, G. F., and J. E. Haas. *Assessment of Research on Natural Hazards.* Cambridge, Mass. and London: MIT Press, 1975. Reviews the classic geophysical and sociological systems material at the core of the behavioral approach.

—Keith Smith

NITROGEN CYCLE

The availability of nitrogen (N) often determines the rate of plant growth on land and in the sea. Nitrogen is an integral part of proteins, especially enzymes, which mediate all biochemical reactions, including photosynthesis. Changes in the availability of N probably controlled the size and activity of the biosphere through geologic time.

A large number of biochemical transformations of nitrogen are possible, because nitrogen is found at valence states ranging from -4 (in NO_4^+) to $+5$ (in NO_3^-). Microbes convert nitrogen between these different forms and use the energy released by the movement of electrons to fuel their life processes. Collectively, these microbial reactions drive the global cycle of nitrogen (Figure 1).

The most abundant form of nitrogen on Earth, N_2, is the least reactive species. Nitrogen fixation converts atmospheric N_2 to one of the forms of "fixed" nitrogen that can be used by biota (e.g., NH_4^+ and NO_3^-). Nitrogen-fixing species are most abundant in nitrogen-poor habitats, where their activity increases the availability of nitrogen for the biosphere. At the same time, denitrifying bacteria return N_2 to the atmosphere, lowering the overall stock of nitrogen readily available for life on Earth. The balance between nitrogen fixation and denitrification through geologic time has determined the nitrogen available to biota and the global nitrogen cycle.

NITROGEN FIXATION

The atmosphere contains about 3.9×10^{21} grams of nitrogen (Figure 1). Relatively small amounts of nitrogen are found in land plants (3.5×10^{15} grams) and soil organic matter (95×10^{15} grams). The nitrogen in the atmosphere is not available to most organisms because the great strength of the triple bond in N_2 makes this molecule practically inert. All nitrogen that is available to biota was originally derived from nitrogen fixation, either by lightning or by free-living and symbiotic microbes. The rate of nitrogen fixation by lightning, which produces momentary conditions of high pressure and temperature allowing N_2 and O_2 to combine, is poorly known but relatively small. Most recent estimates are less than 3×10^{12} grams of nitrogen per year globally.

A widely cited estimate of biological nitrogen fixation in soils is 140×10^{12} grams of nitrogen per year. This is equivalent to about 10 kilograms of nitrogen per year for each hectare of the Earth's land surface. This flux is not, however, distributed uniformly among natural ecosystems; the greatest values are often found in areas of disturbed or successional vegetation. Each year about 40×10^{12} grams of nitrogen are added to agricultural fields as a result of the cultivation of nitrogen-fixing crops (e.g., soybeans). In any case, in the modern world, nitrogen fixation by soil bacteria dwarfs lightning as the source of fixed nitrogen on land. Taking all forms of nitrogen fixation as the only source, the mean residence time of nitrogen in the terrestrial biosphere is about 700 years.

Assuming a global terrestrial net primary production of 60×10^{15} grams of carbon per year and a mean carbon-to-nitrogen ratio of 50 in plant tissues, the nitrogen requirement of land plants is about $1,200 \times 10^{12}$ grams per year. Thus nitrogen fixation supplies only about 12% of the nitrogen that is assimilated by land plants each year. The remaining nitrogen is derived from internal recycling and by the decomposition of dead materials in the soil. When the turnover in the soil is calculated with respect to the input of dead plant materials, the mean residence time of nitrogen in the soil is greater than 100 years.

Humans have a dramatic impact on the global nitrogen cycle. In addition to planting nitrogen-fixing species for crops, humans produce nitrogen fertilizers through the Haber process, that is,

$$3CH_4 + 6H_2O \quad 3CO_2 + 12H_2$$
$$4N_2 + 12H_2 \quad 8NH_3,$$

in which natural gas is burned to produce hydrogen, which is combined with N_2 to form ammonia under high temperature and pressure. Today's fertilizer production supplies more than 80×10^{12} grams of nitrogen per year to agricultural ecosystems worldwide.

Every year fossil-fuel combustion releases about 20×10^{12} grams of nitrogen as NO_x. Some of this is derived from the organic nitrogen contained in fuels, which is best regarded as a source of new, fixed nitrogen for the biosphere because in the absence of human activities, this nitrogen would remain inaccessible in the Earth's crust. A small portion of this NO_x undergoes long-distance transport in the troposphere, accounting for the rising levels of NO_3^- deposited in Greenland snow (Figure 2). The presence of NO_x in the lower atmosphere allows the formation of ozone (O_3), a major air pollutant and health hazard downwind of industry. Because of the short residence time of NO_x in the atmosphere, most of this nitrogen is deposited by precipitation over land, where it enters biogeochemical cycles. Forest ecosystems downwind of major population

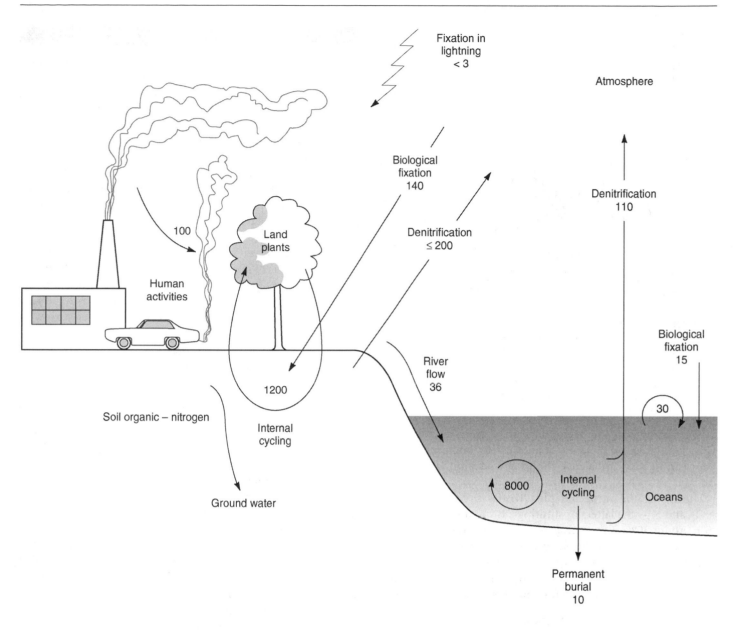

Nitrogen Cycle. Figure 1. The Global Nitrogen Cycle, Showing Annual Flux in Units of 10^{12} Grams of Nitrogen per Year.

(From Schlesinger, 1997, with permission of Academic Press.)

centers now receive enormous nitrogen inputs that may be related to their decline.

DENITRIFICATION

In total, about 240×10^{12} of grams of newly fixed nitrogen is delivered from the atmosphere to the Earth's land surface each year—40% by natural and 60% by anthropogenic sources. In the absence of processes removing nitrogen, a very large pool of nitrogen would accumulate on land in a relatively short time. Each year rivers carry at least 36×10^{12} grams of nitrogen from land to the sea. Globally, humans may account for as much as half of the present-day transport of nitrogen in rivers. Human additions of fixed nitrogen to the land have also resulted in marked increases in the nitrogen content of ground waters, especially in many agricultural areas. The global loss of nitrogen to ground waters may approach 11×10^{12} grams per year. Despite these large transports, riverflow and ground water cannot account for all of the nitrogen that is deposited on land. The remaining nitrogen is assumed to be lost by denitrification in wet soils, wetlands, and forest fires.

Estimates of global denitrification in terrestrial ecosystems range from 13 to 233×10^{12} grams of nitrogen per year. At least half of the denitrification on land occurs in wetlands. If nitrogen-fixation and denitrification were once in balance, then a terrestrial denitrification rate of at least 70×10^{12} grams of nitrogen per year was most likely in the preindustrial world (i.e., fixation minus riverflow). Most of the loss occurs as N_2, but a small fraction is lost as N_2O, which contributes significantly to the global budget of this gas. The current rise in atmospheric

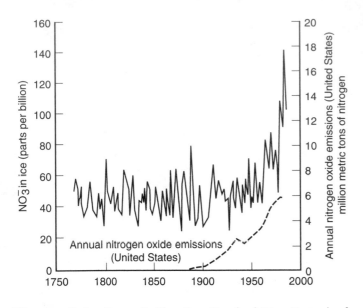

Nitrogen Cycle. FIGURE 2. The Two-Hundred-Year Record of Nitrate in Layers of the Greenland Ice Pack and the Annual Production of Nitric Oxides by Fossil Fuel Combustion in the United States.

(Modified from Mayewski, 1990. Reprinted with permission from *Nature*. Copyright 1990 Macmillan Magazines Limited.)

NITRATES IN RIVERS AND ICE CORES

Human activities such as the use of synthetic fertilizers and the burning of fossil fuels have changed the amounts of nitrates present in soils, rivers, and the atmosphere. This can now be identified at the global scale through the study of river water and ice core chemistry. In 1991, Peierls et al. demonstrated that the quantity of nitrates in world rivers appears to be closely correlated to human population density. Using published data for 42 major world rivers, they found a highly significant correlation between annual nitrate concentration and human population density in their catchments that explained 76% of the variation in nitrate concentration for these rivers. They maintained that "human activity clearly dominates nitrate export from the land."

In 1990, Mayewski et al. studied the nitrate concentration in the upper layers of an ice core retrieved from the Greenland Ice Sheet. They found that nitrate levels were low and relatively stable until around 1900 but that they have climbed since then and are now about 2.5 times their natural background levels.

BIBLIOGRAPHY

Peierls, B. L., et al. "Human Influence on River Nitrogen." *Nature* 350 (1991), 386–387. DOI: 10.1038/350386b0.

—ANDREW S. GOUDIE

N_2O indicates that the overall loss of N_2 from denitrification may have increased by as much as 90×10^{12} grams of nitrogen per year, helping to balance the present-day nitrogen budget on land.

During fire, the nitrogen in plant tissues is volatilized as NH_3, NO_x, and N_2—the latter constituting a form of pyrodenitrification. About 30% of the nitrogen in fuel is converted to N_2, and globally, biomass burning may return as much as 50×10^{12} grams of nitrogen per year to the atmosphere as N_2. To the extent that the rate of biomass burning has increased in recent years, this form of denitrification may have increased as well.

OCEAN NITROGEN FLOWS

Each year, the world's oceans receive about 36×10^{12} grams of nitrogen per year in dissolved forms in rivers, at least 15×10^{12} grams of nitrogen per year from biological nitrogen fixation, and about 30×10^{12} grams of nitrogen in precipitation. While the flux in rivers is a small component of the terrestrial cycle, it contributes about 40% of the total nitrogen delivered annually to the sea. The river flux of nitrogen assumes its greatest importance in coastal seas and estuaries, whereas nitrogen deposited from the atmosphere is most important over the open oceans. Despite these inputs, the pool of inorganic nitrogen in the surface ocean at any time is very small. Most of the net primary production in the sea is supported by nitrogen recycling in the sea. The deep ocean contains a large pool of inorganic nitrogen (570×10^{15} grams of nitrogen) derived from the decomposition of sinking organic materials. Permanent burial of organic nitrogen in sediments is small, so most of the nitrogen input to the oceans must be returned to the atmosphere as N_2 by denitrification. Important

areas of denitrification are found in the anaerobic deep waters of the eastern tropical Pacific Ocean and the Arabian Sea. Globally, marine denitrification may account for the yearly return of more than 110×10^{12} grams of nitrogen to the atmosphere as N_2.

With respect to nitrogen fixation, the mean residence time of atmospheric nitrogen is about 20 million years. This is much shorter than the history of life on Earth, and it speaks strongly for the importance of denitrification in returning N_2 to the atmosphere over geologic time. Denitrification closes the global biogeochemical cycle of nitrogen, but it also means that nitrogen remains in short supply for the biosphere. In the absence of denitrification, most nitrogen on Earth would be found as NO_3^- in seawater, and the oceans would be quite acidic.

Human activities have now disrupted steady-state conditions in the nitrogen cycle. Humans have greatly accelerated the natural rate of nitrogen fixation; the current production of nitrogen fertilizers is increasing at an exponential rate. Elevated levels of nitrogen added to the environment reduce the number of species that can persist in many plant communities, rivers, and coastal seawaters. Enrichments of nitrogen in terrestrial ecosystems, stimulating the rates of nitrification and denitrification, are likely to account for the rapid rise in the atmospheric content of N_2O, which is a greenhouse gas and a cause of ozone destruction in the stratosphere. On the other hand, accelerated nitrogen deposition may have a positive impact on temperate and boreal forest growth and thus on carbon sequestration (Magnani et al., 2007).

[*See also* Acid Rain and Acid Deposition; Agriculture and Agricultural Land; Deforestation; Nitrous Oxide; *and* Water-Quality Trends.]

BIBLIOGRAPHY

Galloway, J.N., et al. "Nitrogen Fixation: Anthropogenic Enhancement-Environmental Response." *Global Biogeochemical Cycles* 9.2 (1995), 235–252.

Magnani, F., et al. "The Human Footprint in the Carbon Cycle of Temperate and Boreal Forests." *Nature* 447 (2007), 848–850. DOI: 10.1038/nature05847.

Mayewski, P.A., et al. "An Ice-Core Record of Atmospheric Response to Anthropogenic Sulphate and Nitrate." *Nature* 346 (1990), 554–556. DOI: 10.1038/346554a0.

Schlesinger, W.H. *Biogeochemistry: An Analysis of Global Change.* 2d ed. San Diego: Academic Press, 1997.

Vitousek, P.M., et al. "Human Alteration of the Global Nitrogen Cycle." *Ecological Applications* 7 (1997), 737–730.

—William H. Schlesinger

NITROUS OXIDE

A natural biogenic and anthropogenic atmospheric trace gas, nitrous oxide (N_2O) is active as a modulator of the Earth's protective stratospheric ozone layer and as a greenhouse gas. A relatively unreactive atmospheric gas, it represents an intermediate oxidation state of nitrogen in the biological nitrogen cycle. Its presence in the atmosphere was discovered in 1939 from its effect on the solar spectrum. Its mean global tropospheric abundance in January 2000 was 314 parts per billion (ppb, expressed on a molecular basis in dry air) and is increasing at about 0.7 ppb per year, presumably because of anthropogenic activity; its mean interhemispheric gradient is about 2 ppb, with the Northern Hemisphere being higher. Model calculations and measurements of air trapped in polar ice cores fix the preindustrial abundance of tropospheric nitrous oxide at about 275 ppb. Precise atmospheric measurements of tropospheric nitrous oxide carried out since the middle 1970s show that its abundance has increased continuously over this period, although there have been variations in the rate of increase and in the interhemispheric gradient that have not been explained.

Most natural nitrous oxide is as a byproduct of bacterial denitrification and nitrification processes, mainly in soils but also in the oceans and other natural waters. Its principal anthropogenic sources are the enhancement of these bacterial processes through agricultural activity and the use of anthropogenic fertilizers, releases of organic wastes, changes in land use, and, to a lesser degree, industrial activity and some forms of combustion. Its principal natural sink is through gradual upward mixing into the stratosphere, where it is destroyed primarily by dissociation by solar ultraviolet radiation, and, to a lesser degree, by reaction with excited atomic oxygen atoms. Because the ultraviolet radiation required to initiate these destruction processes is absorbed by the stratospheric ozone layer, tropospheric (i.e., lower atmosphere) destruction of nitrous oxide is minor and occurs primarily through uptake on some land and water surfaces. The lifetime of tropospheric nitrous oxide is thus believed to be about 120 years, based primarily on modeling calculations of its stratospheric destruction rate.

The preindustrial atmospheric nitrous oxide abundance and lifetime fix the preindustrial total natural source at about 17 teragrams (1 teragram = 10^{18} grams) of nitrous oxide per year (containing about 11 teragrams of nitrogen). Of this total, about one-third is believed to come from the oceans by air-sea gas exchange, based on global measurements of nitrous oxide in surface oceans and models of the gas-exchange rate, and the remaining two-thirds is believed to be of terrestrial origin. Because of the latitudinal distribution of tropospheric nitrous oxide, tropical sources are believed to dominate the terrestrial budget. The mean rate of increase in atmospheric abundance over the past two decades fixes the mean total anthropogenic source strength at about one-third of the total natural sources, about 6 teragrams per year (containing about 4 teragrams of nitrogen), or about the same magnitude as the global oceans. Attempts to reconcile the detailed global budget of nitrous oxide by equating the sum of specific identified sources with the sum of specific identified sinks have been only partially successful, and the errors are large enough that the existence of significant unidentified sources and sinks cannot be ruled out.

When nitrous oxide is destroyed in the stratosphere, approximately 95% of its nitrogen forms unreactive nitrogen gas, and about 5% forms nitric oxide (NO) and nitrogen dioxide (NO_2) that act together in a catalytic cycle to convert ozone (O_3) to molecular oxygen (O_2). In 1970, P. J. Crutzen showed that this catalytic process serves to regulate the abundance of stratospheric ozone in the natural atmosphere. Similarly, the anthropogenic production of nitrous oxide can reduce the abundance of stratospheric ozone below natural levels, with model calculations showing a mean reduction in ozone abundance of about 1% for every 10% increase in nitrous oxide abundance. However, in the presence of elevated levels of stratospheric chlorine due to anthropogenic chlorofluorocarbons, the effects can be far more complex because of the formation of compounds such as chlorine nitrate ($ClNO_3$) that have the effect of temporarily sequestering reactive chlorine and nitrogen species from reaction with ozone. Although nitrous oxide is an ozone-depleting substance, its production has not been regulated by the Montreal Protocol.

Nitrous oxide is also an effective greenhouse gas. According to model calculations using current atmospheric composition, nitrous oxide is about 300 times as effective per added molecule or per added unit mass as carbon dioxide in warming the Earth's surface (nitrous oxide and carbon dioxide have the same molecular weight). This is primarily because the lower abundance of nitrous oxide in the atmosphere makes its infrared absorption spectrum less saturated than is the case for carbon dioxide. The net warming effect of increases of nitrous oxide since preindustrial times is estimated to be about one tenth that of carbon dioxide increases over the same period. Because of the long lifetime of atmospheric nitrous oxide, these effects are expected to continue to be significant well into the next century. Nitrous oxide is among the greenhouse gases that are to be regulated under the Kyoto Protocol.

[*See also* Biomes; Deforestation; Global Warming; Greenhouse Effect; Greenhouse Gases; Nitrogen Cycle; Ozone; *and* Water Vapor.]

BIBLIOGRAPHY

Crutzen, P. J. "The Influence of Nitrogen Oxides on the Atmospheric Ozone Content." *Quarterly Journal of the Royal Meteorological Society* 96 (1970), 320–325. Pioneering work on the catalytic role of nitrous oxide in modulating the ozone layer, which earned the author the 1995 Nobel Prize in Chemistry.

Graedel, T. E., and P. J. Crutzen. *Atmospheric Change: An Earth System Perspective.* New York: Freeman, 1993. A basic text on the chemistry of the changing atmosphere.

Houghton, J. T., et al., eds. *Climate Change 1995: The Science of Climatic Change: Contribution of Working Group I to the Second Assessment Report of the Intergovernmental Panel on Climatic Change.* Cambridge and New York: Cambridge University Press, 1996. An overview for scientists and policy makers on the state of research on greenhouse gases and their impact on climate change.

Wayne, R.P. *Chemistry of Atmospheres.* 2d ed. New York: Oxford University Press; Oxford: Clarendon, 1991. A general textbook on the principles of atmospheric chemistry.

Weiss, R.F. "The Temporal and Spatial Distribution of Tropospheric Nitrous Oxide." *Journal of Geophysical Research* 86 (1981): 7185–7195. The discovery that global tropospheric nitrous oxide is increasing.

World Meteorological Organization. *Scientific Assessment of Ozone Depletion: 1998.* WMO Report No. 44. Geneva, 1999. An overview of the state of research on atmospheric ozone chemistry for scientists and for policy makers.

—RAY F. WEISS

NONGOVERNMENTAL ORGANIZATIONS

Nongovernmental organizations (NGO) play critical roles in the management of global change. Despite their importance, however, it has been difficult to categorize the types of NGOs and identify exactly the many ways in which they operate, because NGOs have been defined principally by what they are not—they are not formal entities of the state. What they are is a complex array of actors with a wide array of goals and strategies.

Wherever the state has not had complete control over economic and social life, various types of NGOs have been influential. Within countries, political parties and religious organizations have long influenced public and private life. Many of these have also operated across borders to form multinational enterprises, such as Socialist International or the Catholic Church. In addition, commercial firms have long organized into associations to pursue their common interests. Under a broad definition, the firm itself is a form of nongovernmental organization.

Although the phenomenon of NGOs is as old as society, several factors have elevated their importance in recent decades. One is the increased number of interests, narrow and broad—with the progress of science, culture, and society, we are aware today of many new concerns that simply were not knowable in the past. Another factor is the increased ease of identifying and organizing around common interests, even when those interests are highly dispersed. Concentrated special interests tend to be well organized and to pursue their causes in the political system (Olson, 1965). But diffuse interests are more difficult to mobilize because each member gains only marginally from collective action—no individual has a sufficiently strong interest to take on the task of organizing the group. With greater ability to communicate information at lower cost—for example, through television, specialized publications produced with desktop publishing, lower-cost travel, and mass mailings by post and the Internet—it is easier for entrepreneurs to identify and organize people and organizations with common interests. Because NGOs often form networks and alliances based on common ideas, these effects typically compound. Thus the number of NGOs and awareness of their influence have grown exponentially. These effects, because they include transnational links, are one manifestation of globalization.

TYPES OF NGO

NGOs take many different forms; Table 1 shows a typology based on the goals and types of issue they pursue. The most general classification typically used for an NGO is based on goals—public interest, commercial, and scientific. Over the last decade, public interest groups have attracted the most attention from practitioners and scholars who have observed the rising power of NGOs as organizers and promoters of mass public movements, but the phenomenon is hardly new. Since the 1960s, many analysts have speculated that transnational networks of corporations—some formally organized—had eclipsed the power of the state. And even earlier during European colonization, entities that were part state and part nonstate—quasi-nongovernmental organizations (QUANGOs), such as the Dutch East Indies Company—dominated or supplanted local governance.

The broad groups shown in Table 1 are often further subdivided according to the issue that they pursue—for example, environmental NGOs (ENGOs), human rights groups, and so on. The goals and issues of an NGO partially determine the resources that are available to the group. In turn, goals, issues, and funding affect tactics and strategy. For example, as Bonner (1993) shows, groups that depend on dues from broad memberships must select issues (e.g., the ban on trade in elephant ivory) and tactics (e.g., campaigns based on salient images) that appeal to the broad nature of the resources that they tap. Thus Table 1 associates funding, tactics, and strategy with the different types of NGOs. Note that the table is intended only to indicate tendencies, as there are many exceptions and complications.

Fundamentally, the many different types of NGO all face similar challenges and tasks. Typically an NGO is formed—or an existing NGO takes on an issue—because it is inefficient for individual interests to act alone. The NGO exists to provide a collective benefit to its supporters. When the benefits of NGOs are commonly available, they often face the problem of free riders. Thus NGOs often attempt to restrict their benefits to supporters, for example by providing informative newsletters and magazines only to dues-paying members. Often NGOs exist in highly competitive environments, with many strategies for survival and growth. Some groups are highly specialized—they pursue one issue, with one source of funding and a single set of tactics. Other groups generalize, often building up their reputation with a small number of issues and trading on their brand to expand. The environmental group Greenpeace, for example, earned its reputation with protests against whaling and nuclear testing in the 1960s and 1970s; since then, Greenpeace has

TABLE 1. Goals, Funding, Strategy, and Tactics of NGOs

Type of NGO	Goals	Funding Sources	Strategy and Tactics
Public interest, such as environmental, human rights, development (e.g., Greenpeace, Amnesty International, Pugwash, Friends of the Earth)	Promote "public interest"	Dues and donations; grants from foundations and like-minded governments; in-kind contributions	Exposure of offending actions and other means of increasing transparency of behavior; mobilizing consumers; lobbying; provide community atmosphere
Commercial associations (e.g., Chemical Manufacturers Association, Global Crop Protection Federation, Global Climate Coalition)	Promote common profit interest	Dues and donations	Lobbying; research; education of members
Scientific and analytic associations (e.g., American Geophysical Union, International Council of Scientific Unions, Pugwash)	Promote science and scientific research; promote use of "independent" analysis	Grants from governments; dues from individuals and organizations; in-kind contributions	Provide forum and platform for experts; provide coordinated and consensus research plans (thus making fundraising easier); provide consensus expert views on complex topics
Spiritual associations (e.g., World Council of Churches)	Promote spirituality and spiritual organizations	Dues (tithing); assessments on member organizations; in-kind contributions	Represent God or other spiritual authority; provide community
Political parties	Get elected	Donations; government contributions; in-kind contributions	Campaigns to mobilize public interest generally and for particular candidates

grown into a multinational NGO active on most major environmental issues. In Europe, green political parties have gained power by specializing on issues (the environment) that attract voters and forming alliances with other parties to form governing parliamentary majorities.

FUNCTIONS OF NGOS

When NGOs act in public forums, such as through lobbying, all typically claim that they are acting in the public interest. Terminology that is widely used to classify and discuss NGOs, such as that in the table, may be somewhat biased—fundamentally, all interest groups act for some segment of the public. Identifying the true public interest in that collection of views is a perennial challenge for democratic political systems.

The density of NGOs is greatest in pluralistic democracies, notably the United States. Those societies favor the creation of private special interests. In some cases they reward successful NGOs directly, as by awarding court fees and damages in citizen suits brought by NGOs. Governments in these countries often fund NGO activities, both inside their own borders and in other countries that advance the government's policies. Examples include direct funding and political support for human rights and dissident groups in countries that have been deemed oppressive or otherwise contrary to the interests of the supporting country's interests. Government support of NGOs, working inside other countries, is an extension of power politics by other means. The rising number and influence of NGOs are both cause and consequence of spreading democratic principles of government, such as the freedom of speech, the right of association, and the protection of human rights.

Indeed, the line between government and nongovernment is increasingly blurred. NGOs were seen traditionally as instruments for giving a voice to interests—for example, an NGO would identify issues, expose injustices, or lobby for action by government. But NGOs also play an important and perhaps growing role by implementing policy. For example, debt-for-nature swaps—in which public debt is bought and extinguished at a discount price in exchange for governmental promises to protect environmental assets such as rainforests—were conceived and mainly implemented by NGOs such as Conservation International.

Often partnerships between public (government) and private (NGO) bodies are most effective, especially for the complicated task of implementing public policies. For example, the Global Environment Facility (GEF) of the United Nations Development Programme, the United Nations Environment Programme, and the World Bank includes a program for small grants conceived by NGOs. Moreover, the standard practice for implementing projects—whether or not the project is initiated by NGOs—entails the active participation of local public-interest groups to shape the design and carry out the elements of the project. These experiences are relatively recent; extensive public participation in World Bank projects has been common only since the 1980s. Over the long run, this approach probably empowers NGOs, which may lead to a further weakening of governmental monopoly on power, further blurring the line between government and nongovernment actors.

NGOS AND THE STATE

NGOs raise many important issues with respect to how society organizes itself. Many celebrate the rising influence of NGOs as a sign of a new form of stakeholder democracy. The logical extension of that argument holds that not only should a wide array of NGOs influence public policy decisions, but NGOs should also implement those decisions, perhaps funded by tax revenues transferred from the state. The function of the state, itself, may change—from that of the single central actor in political life to that of a clearinghouse. However, it is hardly clear that NGOs are eclipsing the state or that they are always democratic. Indeed, the rising importance of NGOs also raises many challenges for democracy. Nongovernmental actors can often perform governmental functions more efficiently; but this blurring of government and nongovernment, public and private, leads many to fear that critical functions of government are being captured by special interests. Moreover, not all interests are equally well organized and heard, as Olson (1965) correctly argued; minority and diffuse interests especially may be trampled by stakeholder democracy.

Truly balanced NGO participation is not easy to achieve. Much of the debate over how to promote the creation and participation of NGO has focused on rights of participation, such as access to policy debates, access to information, and the right to be heard. Those factors are important, but access often does not translate into influence, and often the opening of a decision-making forum to outsiders merely results in the shifting of decision making to other, closed forums.

[*See also* Chemical Industry *and* Environmental Movements.]

BIBLIOGRAPHY

Bonner, R. At the Hand of Man: Peril and Hope for Africa's Wildlife. New York: Knopf, 1993.

Charnovitz, S. "Two Centuries of Participation: NGO and International Governance." *Michigan Journal of International Law* 18 (1996), 183–286.

Olson, M. The Logic of Collective Action. Cambridge, Mass.: Harvard University Press, 1965.

Princen, T., and M. Finger. *Environmental NGOs in World Politics: Linking the Local and the Global.* London and New York: Routledge, 1994.

United Nations Center for Human Settlements (HABITAT). *An Urbanizing World: Global Report on Human Settlements.* New York and Oxford: Oxford University Press, 1996.

Victor, D. G., K. Raustiala, and E. B. Skolnikoff, eds. *The Implementation and Effectiveness of International Environmental Commitments: Theory and Practice.* Cambridge, Mass.: MIT Press, 1998.

Weale, A. The New Politics of Pollution. Manchester, U.K.: Manchester University Press, 1992.

Wirth, D. "Reexamining Decision-Making Processes in International Environmental Law." *Iowa Law Review* 79 (1994), 769–802.

World Bank. *The World Bank Participation Sourcebook.* Washington, D.C., 1996.

—DAVID G. VICTOR

NORTH ATLANTIC OSCILLATION

The North Atlantic Oscillation (NAO), first named and described by Sir Gilbert Walker in the 1920s, is the alternation of atmospheric mass between the subpolar and subtropical portions of the North Atlantic. It is characterized by variations in the regional sea-level pressure gradient, sea-surface temperatures, and the midlatitude westerly winds (Perry, 2000).

In the positive mode of the NAO, such as occurred in the late 1980s and early 1990s, the Azores subtropical high is anomalously strong, while the Icelandic low is simultaneously very deep. The Atlantic westerlies are then abnormally strong,

and warm surface ocean water and mild air masses move northeastward across the Atlantic toward Europe and the Atlantic Arctic. Western Greenland and Labrador are unusually cold, and large amounts of sea ice may be transported southward from Davis Strait.

In the negative mode, the two pressure centers are both anomalously weak. The Icelandic low is displaced to the southwest, near Newfoundland, while atmospheric blocking patterns occur in the flow aloft, and polar anticyclones push southward over the eastern Atlantic and Europe. The winters of this mode are comparatively mild in Greenland, but they are unusually severe in northern and western Europe (e.g., the winters of 1941–1944, 1962–1963, and 1968–1969). It has been argued that the negative mode of the NAO is a good analogue to the atmospheric circulation that prevailed during both the European Little Ice Age, from about 1450 to 1850, and the last ice age glacial maximum at around 18 to 20 thousand years ago.

The winter index of the NAO varies on an approximately biennial basis when one considers a run of years, but it also shows some variability from decade to decade. The 1960s displayed an extreme negative phase whereas a prolonged positive phase occurred in the late 1980s and early 1990s (Hurrell, 1995). Major negative phases similar to those of the 1960s occurred in 1759–1777, 1549–1562, 1528–1539 and 1445–1460 (Glueck and Stockton, 2001). Changes in the strength of the NAO can be traced back over 1,000 years by means of stalagmite studies (Proctor et al., 2000). It may also be possible to reconstruct past NAO behavior through tree-ring analysis (Briffa, 2000) and the Greenland ice-core record (Glueck and Stockton, 2001). Among the responses to changes in the NAO are the distribution, intensity and prevalence of storms, wave climate (Wang and Swail, 2001), sea-ice volume, and iceberg flux (Dickson et al., 2000).

BIBLIOGRAPHY

Briffa, K.R. "Annual Climate Variability in the Holocene: Interpreting the Message of Ancient Trees." *Quaternary Science Reviews* 19 (2000), 87–105. DOI: 10.1016/S0277-3791(99)00056-6.

Dickson, R.R., et al. "The Arctic Ocean Response to the North Atlantic Oscillation." *Journal of Climate* 13 (2000), 2671–2696. DOI: 10.1175/1520-0442(2000)013<2671:TAORTT>2.0.CO;2.

Glueck, M.F., and C.W. Stockton. "Reconstruction of the North Atlantic Oscillation, 1429–1983." *International Journal of Climatology* 21 (2001), 1453–1465. DOI: 10.1002/joc.684.

Hurrell, J.W. "Decadal Trends in the North Atlantic Oscillation: Regional Temperatures and Precipitation." *Science* 269 (1995), 676–679. DOI: 10.1126/science.269.5224.676.

Perry, A. "North Atlantic Oscillation: An Enigmatic See-Saw." *Progress in Physical Geography* 24 (2000), 289–294.

Proctor, C.J., A. Baker, W.L.Barnes and M.A.Gilmour. "A Thousand Year Speleothem Proxy Record of North Atlantic Climate from Scotland." *Climate Dynamics* 16 (2000), 815–820. DOI: 10.1007/s003820000077.

Wang, X.L., and V.R. Swail. "Changes of Extreme Wave Heights in Northern Hemisphere Oceans and Related Atmospheric Circulation Regimes." *Journal of Climate* 14 (2001), 2204–2221. DOI: 10.1175/1520-0442(2001)014<2204:COEWHI>2.0.CO;2.

—ANDREW S. GOUDIE

NUCLEAR POWER

Soon after atomic bombs were used at the end of World War II, Albert Einstein observed, "The unleashed power of the atom has changed everything save our modes of thinking, and we thus drift toward unparalleled catastrophe." More than 60 years later, our thinking and behavior will have to change further to make the world safer for nuclear energy. The peaceful atom will be forever linked to the warlike atom because the same technologies that can make fuel for civilian reactors can also produce material for bombs. These technologies are uranium enrichment, which increases the concentration of the fissile isotope uranium-235, and plutonium reprocessing, which extracts plutonium from irradiated, or spent, nuclear fuel. Plutonium and uranium containing high concentrations of uranium-235 can power nuclear bombs.

While the nuclear-bomb threat has always cast a shadow over nuclear power, increasing global demands for electricity and concerns about climate change have renewed interest in harnessing the peaceful atom. Nuclear energy emits very few greenhouse gases that cause global warming. With mounting fears of catastrophic climate change, many politicians, pundits, and environmentalists are calling for greatly expanded use of nuclear energy. But can countries build nuclear power plants fast enough to make a significant contribution to curbing climate change? Calls for increased use of nuclear energy have spurred political leaders and analysts to clamor for stronger measures to control technologies that can produce nuclear explosive materials. But can countries manage the risks of nuclear proliferation and and radioactive waste disposal and satisfy safety concerns?

MEETING ELECTRICITY DEMAND AND COUNTERING CLIMATE CHANGE

More than 2 billion of the earth's more than 6 billion people do not have reliable access to electricity. Global population is predicted to soar to 9 billion by mid-century. Also, by 2050, electricity demand may triple. Presently, burning of fossil fuels produces most of the world's electricity. Nuclear energy generates one-sixth (about 16%) of global electricity. According to the U.S. Energy Information Administration (EIA), the world's net electricity generation will almost double by 2030. Most of this projected growth will occur in the developing world. Coal and natural gas, two fossil fuels, are predicted to provide for 80% of the increased electricity demand. While nuclear-energy use is expected to increase by 2030, its share of the electricity production mix is predicted to decrease. In recent years, nuclear power accounted for about 370 gigawatts of electrical power capacity, but the EIA estimates an increase to only 481 gigawatts by 2030. For nuclear power to maintain its proportion of the mix, it would have to almost double in capacity to about 700 gigawatts by 2030.

Such estimates of energy demand and nuclear growth call into question nuclear energy's ability to make a further substantial contribution to countering climate change. Nuclear-energy use over the past 50 years has doubtless prevented massive amounts of greenhouse gases from entering the atmosphere. If the world could deploy an additional 700 gigawatts of nuclear power plants by mid-century, it could prevent about one billion tons of carbon dioxide every year from being emitted. This amount of nuclear energy would constitute one "wedge" in Stephen Pacala and Robert Socolow's wedge model. [See Stabilizing Carbon Emissions.] Pacala and Socolow have identified fifteen approaches (energy sources, technologies, and efficiencies) that can reduce the emissions of greenhouse gases. According to Pacala and Socolow, if seven wedges were deployed by mid-century, the world could keep its greenhouse-gas emissions at 2004 levels. Unfortunately, there is no easily deployable wedge. To illustrate this daunting challenge for nuclear energy, the 700 gigawatts of nuclear power to fill a wedge would be in addition to the need to replace almost all of the 370 gigawatts of current capacity by 2054 because of power-plant retirement. Thus, about 1,000 gigawatts of nuclear power plants would need to be built. Currently, a large commercial nuclear reactor generates about 1 gigawatt, or 1,000 megawatts, of electrical power. In the future, many reactors will produce around 1,500 megawatts. Assuming an average power production per reactor of 1,250 megawatts between now and 2054, about 800 reactors will be needed to fill a greenhouse-gas displacement-wedge and to replace most of the current reactors. At least three large commercial reactors would have to come online every two months to meet this goal.

Presently, several barriers would block such a rapid expansion. In particular, only a few companies are now equipped to make vital nuclear power plant components such as reactor pressure vessels. Anticipated growth in power plant orders in the coming decade has resulted in a backup in the queue for pressure-vessel manufacturers in France and Japan. In addition to critical manufacturing shortages, there is a lack of qualified personnel in construction engineering, nuclear-plant operations, quality-assurance inspections, and safety and regulatory oversight. If demand for new nuclear power plants continues, the market will eventually resolve these supply-and-demand bottlenecks. But the lag time could result in several years or even decades of delay. If many climate scientists are correct that the crucial time to act to avert catastrophic climatic effects is within the next ten years, a major expansion of nuclear energy could come too late to have a substantial effect. Nonetheless, many countries will expand their use of nuclear energy in the forthcoming decades.

DEVELOPED WORLD

The Group of Eight (G8) major industrialized countries dominate the nuclear sector with more than 300 of the world's approximately 440 commercial reactors. The G8 includes Canada, France, Germany, Italy, Japan, Russia, the United Kingdom, and the United States. Italy is the only G8 country that does not have a nuclear power plant. To assess the current and projected future status of nuclear energy in the G8, let's examine each country in order of the largest to smallest number of reactors:

United States

The United States leads the world in the number of reactors with 104, which produce about 20% of the country's electricity. Despite not having a new reactor order since the 1970s, the United States has been able to increase nuclear power production. First, several power plants have received from the Nuclear Regulatory Commission power upratings, which allow a slight increase in the amount of power generated by the plant. Second, the capacity factor—the amount of electricity produced compared to the maximum achievable—rose significantly during the past 30 years to more than 90% for many of today's operating plants. Third, and related to the second issue, the amount of time a plant is shut down for performing refueling and maintenance has decreased significantly. Fourth, and boding well for future performance, more than 40 reactors have in recent years received 20-year operating-license extensions. Most U.S. reactors are expected to qualify for these extensions as they near their nominal 40-year license expirations.

However, by 2030 as several 20-year license-renewals expire, the United States will experience a decline in reactor numbers if no new reactors are built. To stimulate further construction, the U.S. Congress passed the Energy Policy Act of 2005, which provides financial incentives for a handful of new reactors—up to 6,000 megawatts. By the end of 2008, several utilities will probably file for operating licenses of new reactors to try to qualify for these incentives. Such financial stimulus might spur even further construction. But because of the relatively large capital costs, which can comprise a significant fraction of a utility's market value, and typically long lead time for reactor construction, many additional reactors might not be built. Further subsidies or a fee levied on greenhouse-gas emissions could make nuclear power plant construction competitive with coal-fired plant construction. Nuclear power-plant operating costs are already competitive with coal-fired electricity production.

France

France leads the world in producing the largest proportion (almost 80%) of its electricity from nuclear power, with 59 reactors. There is little room for further nuclear use in this country unless France decides to overhaul its transportation sector to hybrid plug-in electric cars and trucks in the coming decades. Presently, France exports some nuclear-generated electricity to neighboring European countries. Because most of the French nuclear power plants were built in the 1980s, these plants will not reach their nominal 40-year license expiration until the 2020s. As of early 2007, France was planning for one new nuclear reactor in the near term. Unlike the United States, in which the federal government does not own utilities, the government of France had owned the utility company Electricité de France (EDF), which was responsible for ordering power plant construction. While EDF claims that it did not receive government subsidies, government backing of the utility's debt load during the construction ramp-up, standardized reactor designs, and widespread public acceptance contributed to France deriving a large share of electricity from nuclear power production.

Japan

Despite its legacy as the only country to experience nuclear war, Japan has embraced the use of nuclear energy. Lacking significant indigenous energy resources, Japan has turned to nuclear power to strengthen its energy security. With 55 commercial reactors, Japan leads Asia in the number of nuclear power plants. While Japan currently produces 29% of its electricity from nuclear power, this share could increase to as much as 40% by 2050 if current plans materialize. By mid-century, Japan aims to use breeder reactors to generate electricity and breed plutonium for reactor fuel.

Breeder reactors are designed to allow a blanket of uranium-238, a fertile isotope, to absorb excess neutrons produced during the nuclear reaction. Neutron absorption transforms uranium-238 to uranium-239, which decays rapidly to the isotope neptunium-239. Then another rapid radioactive decay converts neptunium-239 to plutonium-239, which is useful as nuclear fuel.

Like Japan, France, India, and Russia have plans to make great use of breeder reactors. But this reactor technology has been generally much more expensive to operate than the nonbreeder, or thermal, reactor technology that comprises practically the entire world's operating commercial reactors. Still, Japan is especially interested in employing breeder reactors because of its concerns about energy security. Japan relies on foreign suppliers for the uranium used to fuel its present reactors. To harvest plutonium from these reactors, Japan has recently completed construction of an industrial-scale reprocessing plant at Rokkasho-mura. Reprocessing is a chemical technique for separating plutonium from highly radioactive spent nuclear fuel. There is concern that separated plutonium could pose a risk for use in nuclear bombs constructed by nations or nonstate actors such as terrorist groups.

Russia

Russia produces 16% of its electricity from 31 reactors. Eleven of these reactors are Chernobyl-type plants. (Lithuania also operates a Chernobyl-type plant, and the European Union has linked closure of this plant to Lithuania's admittance into the EU.) After the 1986 Chernobyl accident in Ukraine, financial and technical assistance from the European Union and the United States helped improve the safety of the remaining Chernobyl-type plants. Despite this assistance, these plants do not meet Western standards. Russia plans to continue operating its Chernobyl-type reactors until their planned end-of-life, but the more than 10 plants ordered or projected to be built by 2020 will employ safer and more modern designs. In addition to this indigenous construction, Russia's state-owned Rosatom is vigorously marketing to developing-world countries. One of Rosatom's most controversial projects is the construction of the Bushehr plant in Iran.

United Kingdom

The United Kingdom has 19 reactors generating 20% of its electricity. With an aging fleet of reactors, the United Kingdom would likely experience a decline in the number of nuclear power plants from now until at least 2020, when new plants could make up for reactor retirements. The previous Blair government in its energy policy review of 2006 had indicated support for new nuclear construction to complement growth of all zero- and low-greenhouse-gas-emission energy sources. The U.K. has backed the recent development of an EU Emissions Trading Scheme that, if successful, would set a high enough price on greenhouse-gas emissions to make nuclear plant construction competitive with fossil fuel sources.

Canada

Having decided in the 1940s not to invest in uranium-enrichment plants, Canada has relied on indigenously developed heavy-water reactors that can be fueled with natural uranium. Canada has marketed this reactor technology to some other countries, notably India and South Korea. Currently, Canada produces about 15% of its electricity from 18 reactors. It plans on bringing two laid-up reactors back online as well as constructing two new reactors in the coming years. Canada is also considering using slightly enriched uranium. With huge uranium reserves, reactor manufacturing capability, and possible development of uranium enrichment plants, Canada could become well-positioned as a major supplier of all major aspects of nuclear power plants.

Germany

A previous German government dominated by socialist and green parties had decided to phase out this country's nuclear power plants by not renewing operating licenses and not building new plants. But with the rise to power of conservative Chancellor Angela Merkel, that decision could change to allow expansion of nuclear energy. Currently, Germany produces 31% of its electricity from 17 reactors.

OTHER PARTS OF THE DEVELOPED WORLD

To understand nuclear energy's prospects in other parts of the developed world, two case studies are briefly examined.

South Korea

The Republic of Korea generates 45% of its electricity from 20 reactors. It aims to build an additional eight reactors by 2015. Despite its massive investment in nuclear power production, South Korea has refrained from investing in uranium enrichment or plutonium reprocessing because of American pressure. For decades, the U.S. government has worked to convince South Korea not to perform these dual-use (reactor-fuel and bomb-making) activities because of the fear of stimulating a nuclear arms race between South and North Korea; North Korea had used plutonium reprocessing to extract plutonium for its nuclear weapons program. In 2006, the Bush administration invited South Korea to take part in developing a reprocessing technology, called pyroprocessing, which is claimed to be proliferation-resistant, that is, difficult to use for the production of materials used in nuclear bombs.

Australia

Australia stands out as one of the few major industrialized countries without a single nuclear power plant. But in 2006, an Australian government-sponsored report projected that Australia could have as many as 25 reactors by 2050. These reactors could supply up to one-third of Australia's electricity needs. The government report pointed out that nuclear construction costs are 25–50% greater than coal-fired power plant construction costs. The report estimated that a fee of U.S.$12–30 per ton of carbon dioxide could make nuclear cost competitive with coal. Even if Australia decided to build nuclear power plants, the first reactor would probably not come online until 2020.

DEVELOPING WORLD

The greatest growth in nuclear energy in the coming decades will likely take place in the developing world, especially in Asia, where China and India have ambitious plans for a major nuclear expansion. These two countries presently derive only a small proportion of their electricity from nuclear energy: in China about 2% from 10 reactors and in India about 3% from 16 reactors. China and India each have about a half-dozen reactors under construction. China wants to build as many as 50 reactors by 2030, and India wants to add another 15 reactors in that time period. Because of construction constraints, these plans will probably not fully materialize. Even if they do, both countries will rely much more heavily on new coal-fired plants for electricity.

While China and India have become mature users of nuclear power, numerous countries have recently expressed interest in acquiring their first nuclear power plants. In particular, several Arab countries have launched or renewed feasibility studies for commercial reactors. Many security analysts believe that one of the motivations of these countries, aside from a professed need for electricity, is to hedge against a nuclear-armed Iran. Iran, according to the U.S. and some allied governments, is using the cover of a civilian nuclear program to produce a latent or actual nuclear-weapons capability. Countries in South America (e.g., Chile and Venezuela) and in Southeast Asia (e.g., Indonesia, Malaysia, Thailand, and Vietnam) have expressed interest in nuclear power plants but have little or no experience in nuclear regulations. These new nuclear developments could further strain safety and security risks.

CONTROLLING THE SAFETY AND SECURITY RISKS

If a major nuclear power expansion occurs, the demand for nuclear fuel making will increase. Under some aggressive growth scenarios, the demand for uranium enrichment could soar to greater than six times current capacity. The International Atomic Energy Agency is already stretched thin in safeguarding some 1,000 nuclear facilities. The current safeguards budget is about $100 million. If the expansion takes place, the IAEA will need more resources and greater authorities to detect possible clandestine use of peaceful nuclear technologies for weapons purposes. Countries that benefit from nuclear power have a vested interest in ensuring that the IAEA is adequately funded. But it remains uncertain whether they will provide the necessary funding.

The buzz about a nuclear renaissance has led to a reincarnation of proposals to offer fuel assurances. Such assurances would guarantee that a country will receive nuclear fuel as long as it is in good standing with its safeguards commitments and does not enrich uranium or reprocess plutonium. In early 2006, for example, the Bush administration proposed the Global Nuclear Energy Partnership (GNEP), which offered fuel services to client countries so that they would not need to do fuel making themselves. Critics pointed out that this partnership would divide the world into haves (fuel suppliers) and have-nots (fuel clients). Under the Bush administration's plan, the fuel suppliers would comprise China, France, Russia, the United Kingdom, and the United States, the 5 original nuclear-armed countries, and Japan. But this group leaves out countries such as Argentina, Brazil, and South Africa that want to pursue fuel-making. In contrast to GNEP's double standard, Mohammed ElBaradei, the director-general of the IAEA, has proposed a less discriminatory multinational approach to fuel-making. In the coming years, the debate about fuel assurances will continue, and it remains uncertain whether a solution acceptable to all countries will be found.

Another uncertainty hanging over nuclear power is what to do with the tens of thousands of tons of nuclear waste that has already been produced. A major nuclear expansion would generate much more radioactive waste. No country has yet to store its nuclear waste in a permanent repository. An approach to buy time to reach political and technical consensus about repositories is to store spent nuclear fuel in hardened, dry-store casks. Such casks could safely and securely store spent nuclear fuel for many decades. Other approaches favor reprocessing spent fuel to remove the long-lived radioactive isotopes and then consuming these materials in fast reactors, which are based on breeder-reactor technology. Nonetheless, even if this recycling works, large amounts of radioactive waste will require safe and secure storage.

These challenges pose an opportunity for the global community to take a serious examination of nuclear energy's prospects. On the verge of a possible nuclear resurgence, it is time to heed Einstein's admonition to change our modes of thinking to avert "unparalleled catastrophe" in both nuclear war and climate change.

[See also Coal; Coal Gasification; Energy Strategies; Nuclear Waste; and Stabilizing Carbon Emissions.]

BIBLIOGRAPHY

Department of Trade and Industry, U.K. "The Future of Nuclear Power: The Role of Nuclear Power in a Low Carbon UK Economy." October, 2007 (http://www.berr.gov.uk/consulations/pages39704.htmll; accessed June 2, 2008).
Ferguson, C.D. "Nuclear Energy: Balancing Benefits and Risks." Special Report No. 28, Council on Foreign Relations, April, 2007 (http://www.crf.org/publication/13104/nuclear_energy.html; accessed June 2, 2008).
Greenpeace International. "The Economics of Nuclear Power." May 1, 2007 (http://www.greenpeace.org/usa/press-center/reports4/the-economics-of-nuclear-power; accessed June 2, 2008).
Interdisciplinary MIT Study Group. The Future of Nuclear Power. Massachusetts Institute of Technology, July, 2003 (http://web.mit.edu/nuclearpower/; accessed June 2, 2008).
Parker, L., and M. Holt. "Nuclear Power: Outlook for New U.S. Reactors." Congressional Research Service, March 9, 2007 (http://www.fac.org/sgp/crs/misc/RL33442.pdf; accessed June 2, 2008).
Smith, B. Insurmountable Risks: The Dangers of Using Nuclear Power to Combat Global Climate Change. Takoma Park, Md.: IEER; Muskegon, Mich.: RDR, 2006.
Sokolski, H. "Does Nuclear Nonproliferation Have a Future? Market-Based Atomic Power." Harvard International Review, February, 2007 (http://hir.harvard.edu/articles/1475/; accessed June 2, 2008).

—CHARLES D. FERGUSON

NUCLEAR WASTE

There is considerable controversy as to the best means of disposing of nuclear long-lived intermediate-level wastes (ILW) and high-level wastes (HLW). On the one hand, some advocate on-site storage (i.e., at the nuclear facility), where no long-distance transport is required, where monitoring is relatively simple, and where one does not have the technical uncertainties that are attached to deep underground disposal. Others advocate deep disposal in underground caverns, on the grounds that this does not expose workers and the local community to the risk of radioactivity, it is safe from terrorist attack, theft, or some accident (e.g., a plane crash), it concentrates the waste at a few (usually remote) locations, and it provides a long-term solution. It is argued that deep disposal in stable geologic formations with a series of containment measures will prevent escape of radionuclides over the periods of time that it will take for them to decay to harmless levels. Against this, however, it has been argued that over the time scales involved (10,000 to one million years), climatic and geologic stability is unlikely. To find geologically suitable conditions in areas that are politically acceptable seems to be a nearly insuperable problem in many countries.

BIBLIOGRAPHY

Blowers, A., and D. Lowry. "The Politics of Radioactive Waste Disposal." In Energy, Resources, and Environment, edited by J. Blunden and A. Reddish. London: Hodder and Stoughton and Open University, 1996.
Canadian Nuclear FAQ. "How is High-level Nuclear Waste Managed in Canada?" http://www.nuclearfaq.ca/cnf-section.E.htm (accessed June 2, 2008).
Ojovan, M. I., and W. E. Lee. An Introduction to Nuclear Waste Immobilization, Amsterdam and Boston: Elsevier, 2005.
Saling, J. H., and A. W. Fentiman, eds. Radioactive Waste Management. New York: Taylor and Francis, 2001.

—ANDREW S. GOUDIE

NUCLEAR WINTER

Nuclear winter comprises a constellation of physical and chemical effects associated with the wholesale detonation of nuclear weapons (Robock et al., 2007). Aside from the extensive direct destruction and intense radioactive fallout accompanying nuclear explosions, it has been postulated that accompanying changes in the atmosphere and climate might prove worse. Massive emissions of smoke and dust would lead to unprecedented pollution of the troposphere, strong attenuation of sunlight, strong surface cooling in continental areas—up to 10–20°C in the northern midlatitudes—heating of the atmosphere, sharply reduced rainfall in some regions, accelerated interhemispheric transport of nuclear debris, and global stratospheric ozone depletion.

Our knowledge of these potential widespread environmental impacts of a nuclear war has advanced considerably since the earliest work on this subject (e.g., Crutzen and Birks, 1982; Turco et al., 1983; NRC, 1985; Pittock et al., 1986). The basic mechanisms that occur in nuclear winter have been studied and modified through increasingly sophisticated theoretical and experimental analyses. The magnitude of predicted land-temperature perturbations has decreased from original estimates, as values of key physical parameters have been refined over time. Meanwhile, the severity of other effects—such as potential ozone depletion and exposure to radioactivity—have been projected to be greater. While the most recent forecasts of a nuclear winter are not as dire as the earlier ones, they nevertheless point to enormous global human casualties—probably greater than those from the direct effects of the nuclear detonations, owing in large part to disruptions in food production and distribution, and the destruction of health facilities and services (Harwell and Hutchinson, 1985; Solomon and Marston, 1986). Significant uncertainties will always remain in such analyses, and these forecasts should be considered merely as qualitative or indicative.

The demise of the Soviet Union as a superpower has reduced concerns about global nuclear warfare, but thousands of nuclear weapons remain at the ready and continue to pose a threat. Moreover, new nations are achieving nuclear capability, most recently India, Pakistan, Iran, and, North Korea. Thus, none of the dangers associated with existing nuclear arsenals regarding national security or nuclear winter—either from the viewpoint of national security or of nuclear winter—have been resolved. Indeed, to avoid the possibility of nuclear winter, it has been suggested that almost total disarmament is needed (Sagan and Turco, 1990). In this regard, it is debatable whether the realization of nuclear winter has stimulated a fundamental reevaluation of strategic policy and doctrine or played a role in the recent movement toward nuclear arms reductions, although their coincidence is apparent.

Effects comparable to nuclear winter have been associated with historical volcanic explosions ("volcanic winter") and large meteor impacts on the Earth ("meteorite winter"), both of which inject large quantities of particles into the upper atmosphere. For example, following the eruption of the Indonesian volcano Tambora in 1815, the weather in the Northern Hemisphere was highly unusual, and 1815 is remembered as the "year without a summer" (Stommel and Stommel, 1979). Farmers in the northeastern United States suffered frosts throughout the spring; in western North America, the unseasonable weather was recorded as frost damage to tree rings in the hearty bristlecone pines. Across Europe, crops failed under stressful climatic conditions.

Anecdotal evidence from China testifies to strange weather and poor agricultural output. [See Volcanoes.] These events are thought to reflect the impacts of a mild nuclear winter. In another related phenomena, the smoke palls from forest fires and other large fires (such as those in Kuwait during the Persian Gulf War of 1991) have been shown to cool land surfaces rapidly, and often strongly, by tens of degrees Celsius. In the case of nuclear detonations (and the resultant firestorms in cities), such cooling could be exacerbated by the larger extent of the smoke clouds and their greater height of injection.

The widespread effects described above are largely related to the microscopic particles—so-called aerosols—that are generated by nuclear detonations and fires. Airborne smoke and dust particles scatter and absorb solar radiation and absorb and emit heat radiation. The overall energy budget of the underlying surface is thus altered, in some instances resulting in an "antigreenhouse" effect accompanied by temperature drops. The magnitude of the aerosol-induced cooling is determined by the spatial distribution and radiative properties of the particles. Smoke, especially sooty smoke, has optical constants most likely to produce cooling. Soot is the black carbonaceous byproduct of combustion and is one of the most efficient light-absorbing materials in nature. [See Aerosols.]

Field experiments and numerical simulations focusing on the behavior of large fires suggest that sooty smoke from nuclear-ignited city fires (like those caused in Hiroshima and Nagasaki by the first atomic bombs) can be directly lofted into the upper atmosphere, where the smoke will have a relatively long residence time. Moreover, other experiments have shown that soot clouds exposed to direct sunlight warm and rise further into the atmosphere—an effect referred to as "self-lofting." This process, in turn, may enhance the geographic dispersion and residence time of the soot. Consequently, surface cooling beneath a large soot cloud may be deeper and longer-lasting. Other experiments indicate that precipitation, which is normally very efficient at removing most types of particles from the atmosphere, might be less efficient at washing out soot, allowing the soot to remain suspended for a longer time.

Continental land masses would cool much more rapidly than the oceans under nuclear winter conditions. Though surface temperatures in coastal regions and on smaller land areas would be moderated by the advection of heat through the atmosphere from neighboring oceans, land temperatures in the deep interiors of continents, such as in North America and Eurasia, could drop rapidly and deeply.

Agriculture is essential to the survival of human civilization as we know it—some estimates place the fraction of the human population supported by agriculture as opposed to natural ecosystems at 99%—so agricultural performance in response to nuclear winter climatic (and socioeconomic) perturbations has been a focus of investigation (Harwell and Hutchinson, 1985). Most domestic crops have semitropical origins and are vulnerable to even modest temperature decreases of several degrees on average during the growing season. Hence, nuclear winter forecasts pointing to month-long temperature drops of 5–10°C represent a clear danger to agriculture—and therefore to much of the human population. Another profound climatic alteration that appears consistently in nuclear winter predictions is the failure of the Asian monsoons, which would have strong implications for agriculture over much of the southern range of that continent.

Many of the basic physical concepts and processes associated with nuclear winter have been successfully incorporated into modern climate models. Particularly important has been the recognition—heightened by nuclear-winter studies—of the importance of aerosols in the global climate system and their role in modifying atmospheric radiation and chemistry.

[*See also* Extreme Events; *and* Extraterrestrial Impacts.]

BIBLIOGRAPHY

Crutzen, P. J., and J. W. Birks. "The Atmosphere after a Nuclear War: Twilight at Noon." *Ambio* 11 (1982), 114–125.
Harwell, M. A., and T. C. Hutchinson. *Environmental Consequences of Nuclear War.* Vol. 2. *Ecological and Agricultural Effects.* SCOPE-28. Chichester, U.K.: Wiley, 1985.
National Research Council (NRC). "The Effects on the Atmosphere of a Major Nuclear Exchange." Washington, D.C.: National Academy Press, 1985.
Pittock, A. B., et al. *Environmental Consequences of Nuclear War.* Vol. 1. *Physical and Atmospheric Effects.* SCOPE-28. Chichester, U.K.: Wiley, 1986.
Robock, A. "Enhancement of Surface Cooling due to Forest Fire Smoke." *Science* 242 (1988), 911–913.
Robock, A., et al. "Climatic Consequences of Regional Nuclear Conflicts." *Atmospheric Chemistry and Physics* 7 (2007), 2003–2012.
Sagan, C., and R. P. Turco. *A Path Where No Man Thought: Nuclear Winter and the End of the Arms Race.* New York: Random House, 1990.
Solomon, F., and R. Q. Marston, eds. *The Medical Implications of Nuclear War.* Washington, D.C.: Institute of Medicine and National Academy of Sciences, National Academy Press, 1986.
Stommel, H., and E. Stommel. "The Year without a Summer." *Scientific American* 240.6 (1979), 176–186.
Turco, R. P., et al. "Nuclear Winter: Global Consequences of Multiple Nuclear Explosions." *Science* 222 (1983), 1283–1292. DOI: 10.1126/science.222.4630.1283.
———. "Climate and Smoke: An Appraisal of Nuclear Winter." *Science* 247 (1990), 166–176. DOI: 10.1126/science.11538069.
World Health Organization (WHO). "Effects of Nuclear War on Health and Health Services." Geneva, 1988.

—RICHARD P. TURCO

O

OCEAN ACIDIFICATION

A proportion of the extra carbon dioxide being released into the atmosphere by the burning of fossil fuels and biomass is absorbed by sea water. As carbon dioxide combines with water it produces carbonic acid. An increase in carbonic acid in sea water will cause that water to become more acidic (i.e., it will have a lower pH).

The absorption of carbon dioxide has already caused the pH of modern surface waters to be about 0.1 lower (i.e., more acidic and less alkaline) than in pre-industrial times. Ocean pH may fall an additional 0.3 by 2100 (Caldeira and Wickett, 2003), which means that the oceans may be more acidic than they have been for 25 million years. Several centuries from now, if we continue to add carbon dioxide to the atmosphere, ocean pH will be lower than at any time in the past 300 million years (Doney, 2006). This will be particularly harmful to those organisms (corals, mollusks, and plankton) that depend on the presence of carbonate ions to build their shells or other hard parts out of calcium bicarbonate (Orr et al., 2005a); and it will affect low latitudes as well as high (Orr et al., 2005), and the rate of change in acidity will be very rapid. This is still a greatly underresearched field, but it is clear that changes in plankton production could have feedbacks on global climate and that there are implications for fisheries and tourism (Royal Society, 2005).

BIBLIOGRAPHY

Caldeira, K. and M.G. Wickett. "Anthropogenic Carbon and Ocean pH." *Nature* 425 (2003), 365. DOI: 10.1038/425365a.
Doney, S.C. "The Dangers of Ocean Acidification." *Scientific American* 294.3 (2006), 38–45.
Orr, J.C., S. Pantoja, and H.-O. Pörtner. "Introduction to Special Section: The Ocean in a High-CO_2 World." *Journal of Geophysical Research* 110, C09S01 (2005a). DOI: 10.1029/2005JC003086.
Orr, J.C., et al. "Anthropogenic Ocean Acidification over the Twenty-First Century and its Impact on Calcifying Organisms." *Nature* 437 (2005b), 681–686. DOI: 10.1038/nature04095.
Royal Society. *Ocean Acidification due to Increased Atmospheric Carbon Dioxide.* Policy document, June, 2005. London: Royal Society, 2005.

—ANDREW S. GOUDIE

OCEAN-ATMOSPHERE COUPLING

Ocean-atmosphere coupling is a concept of climate dynamics essential for understanding a large number of climate phenomena including the El Niño–Southern Oscillation (ENSO) and climate variability on multidecadal timescales. The concept originated in the work of Bjerknes (1964, 1972) and Wyrtki (1973, 1974). Understanding ocean-atmosphere coupling is critical for predicting changes in global temperature patterns and climate variability with global warming.

The idea behind active ocean-atmosphere coupling is straightforward: a large-scale anomaly of sea surface temperature (SST) induces heating or cooling of the atmosphere, which alters atmospheric circulation and hence the effect of winds on the ocean surface (wind stress) and heat exchange between the ocean and the atmosphere (heat fluxes). In turn, the wind stress variations modify the ocean thermal structure and circulation, giving rise to feedbacks that can reinforce the initial SST anomaly. One can no longer treat the ocean and atmospheric circulations independently of each other: ocean surface temperature becomes the link between the two.

The degree to which the ocean and atmosphere are coupled varies between regions. In the tropics, for instance, the coupling is very strong because tropical wind stress is largely controlled by tropical sea-surface temperatures. In mid-latitudes, however, atmospheric circulation depends to a much smaller extent on ocean local temperatures, which implies a weak dynamical coupling. The temporal and spatial scales of coupling vary greatly as well. For instance, ocean wind-waves are generated by air-sea interactions at scales ranging from 1 cm to 100 m. ENSO and the seasonal cycle in the tropical Pacific involve the entire tropical basin and operate on timescales from annual to interannual. Here, we will concentrate only on such large-scale phenomena.

THE TROPICS

In the tropics, moist air rises into cumulus towers over the warmest regions, causing heavy rainfall. Aloft, the air, drained of its moisture, diverges from these regions and subsides over the colder regions that get little precipitation. Surface winds, the easterly (i.e., westward-flowing) trades in the case of the Pacific, restore moisture to the air by means of evaporation while converging to the warmest regions. The convergence of moist air and the release of latent heat through condensation drive this direct thermal circulation. Because the tropical circulation is largely driven by latent heat supplied by evaporation from the warm ocean surface, anomalies in sea surface temperatures have a profound effect on rainfall, winds, and other atmospheric characteristics.

Perhaps, the most striking example of active ocean-atmosphere coupling is El Niño—the warm phase of a natural oscillation (Figure 1a) driven by tropical ocean-atmosphere interactions and associated with unusually high temperatures (Figure 1b) in the eastern equatorial Pacific (Philander, 1990).

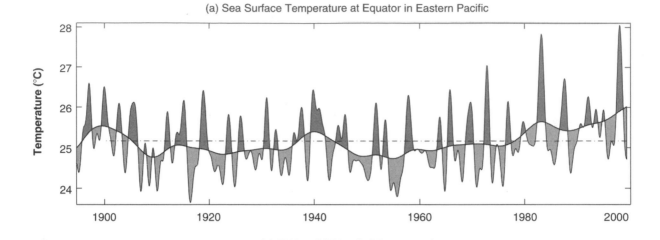

(a) Sea Surface Temperature at Equator in Eastern Pacific

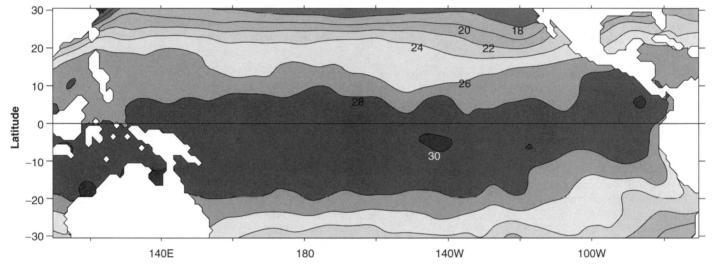

(b) El Niño SST in °C (March 1983)

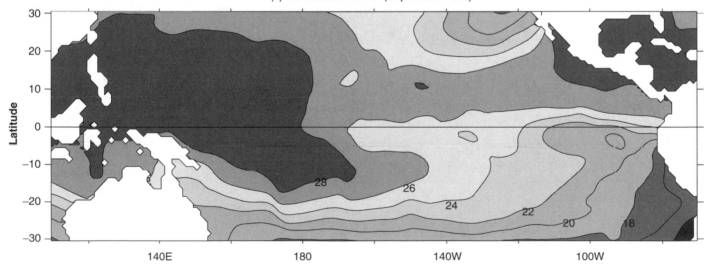

(c) La Niña SST in °C (September 1955)

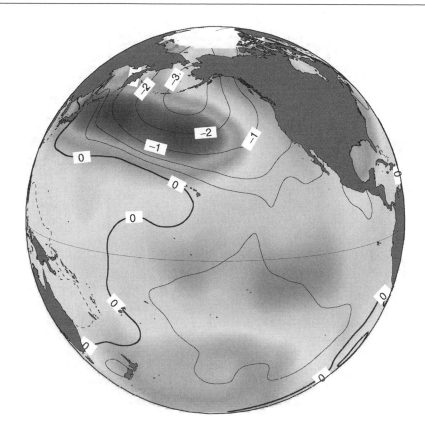

Ocean-Atmosphere Coupling. FIGURE 2. The Typical Pattern of Sea-Level Pressure Anomalies Associated with Positive Phase of the PDO.

Units are millibars. Dark zone in North Pacific represents lower temperatures. After Mantua et al., 1997.

Ocean-Atmosphere Coupling. FIGURE 1. Natural Oscillation (facing page).

(a) Interannual oscillations in sea surface temperature (SST) at the equator in the eastern Pacific shown on the background of the decadal fluctuation after removal of the annual cycle and higher frequency variability. The horizontal dot-dashed line is the time average for the record. Sea surface temperatures (°C) at the peaks of El Niño (b) and La Niña (c). Some of the differences between (b) and (c), such as high temperatures that extend far north in September and far south in March, are attributable to the seasonal cycle. The mean state of the tropical Pacific resembles a weak La Niña. (After Fedorov and Philander 2000.)

[*See* El Niño–Southern Oscillation.] During El Niño, a positive SST anomaly (up to 6°C) develops in the eastern equatorial Pacific, which induces anomalous heating of the atmosphere, anomalous air flow convergence to this region, and hence an eastward wind anomaly. During the cold phase of the oscillation—La Niña—the temperature in the eastern equatorial Pacific becomes a few degrees colder than normal (Figure 1c).

Such variations of ocean temperatures are possible because, in the tropics, the warm surface waters constitute only a shallow layer floating on the cold water below. The winds, by causing variations in the depth of this temperature boundary (the thermocline), can either shield cold water from or expose it to the surface. Intense trade winds along the equator normally drive the warm waters westward along the equator while bringing cold water to the surface in the east, thus contributing to the colder surface temperature in the eastern part of the basin (Figure 1c). A relaxation of these winds allows water to flow eastward, reducing the zonal temperature gradient along the equator and creating positive feedbacks that give rise to warm temperature anomalies associated with El Niño.

Thus, the explanation for El Niño and its cold counterpart La Niña, and for the mean zonal (west-east) SST gradient along the equator, involves a circular argument: changes in sea-surface temperature are both the cause and consequence of wind fluctuations (Zebiak and Cane, 1987; Battisiti and Hirst, 1989; Djakstra and Neelin, 1995). Consider, for example, conditions during La Niña, when intense trade winds keep the warm surface waters along the equator in the far west, thus maintaining a zonal temperature gradient that contributes to the intense winds. A modest disturbance in the form of a westerly wind anomaly near the dateline can generate currents that transport some of the warm water eastward, thus decreasing the zonal temperature gradient. The resultant weakening of the trades will cause even more warm water to flow eastward, reducing the upwelling of cold water to the surface and setting a strong SST anomaly in the eastern equatorial Pacific. Negative feedbacks associated with the ocean dynamics that cause a delay in ocean response to wind forcing explain the cyclicity of El Niño which occurs roughly every 4–5 years.

THE MID-LATITUDES

Ocean-atmosphere coupling in mid-latitudes remains a subject of intense research and even heated debate. Climate variability in mid-latitudes is determined to a large extent by random atmospheric variability, also called the atmospheric "noise," and passive oceanic response to the atmospheric forcing. However, simple stochastic climate models (Frankignoul and Hasselmann 1977; Barsugli and Battisti 1998) do not describe specific climate modes, such as the North Atlantic Oscillation (NAO) and the Pacific Decadal Oscillation (PDO). Various mechanisms based on active ocean-atmosphere coupling in mid-latitudes have been proposed to describe the physics of these modes, even though the observational evidence for such coupling remains not as strong as in the tropics.

It is clear that atmospheric variability can induce significant large-scale SST anomalies in the ocean. In fact, ocean response to varying winds in mid-latitudes includes changes in wind-induced upwelling, changes in the depth of the thermocline and in ocean circulation (e.g., shifts in the paths of the Gulf Stream in the North Atlantic and the Kuroshio in the western Pacific caused by wind stress anomalies), and variations in heat exchange across the ocean surface caused mostly by changes in evaporation. Because of ocean thermal inertia, the induced temperature anomalies can persist for several months or even years.

The dominant mode of multidecadal climate variability in the Pacific is usually referred to as the Pacific Decadal Oscillation (PDO). The PDO has a horseshoe-like signature in sea-surface temperatures and affects a large region extending from the North Pacific to the equatorial region to the Southern Hemisphere (e.g., Zhang et al., 1997; Mantua et al., 1997; see Figures 2 and 3).

The North Atlantic Oscillation may also involve ocean-atmosphere coupling (e.g., Hurrell, 1995). The NAO is related to variations in the pressure difference between an atmospheric low-pressure system over Iceland (the Icelandic Low) and a high-pressure system over the Azores (the Azores High). These variations, especially pronounced in winter, are associated with changes in wind, precipitation and temperature patterns that strongly affect the climate of Europe and the North Atlantic (Figure 4). A larger than normal pressure difference (the positive phase of the NAO) leads to increased westerly winds, a poleward shift of the storm tracks and, consequently, mild and wet winters over most of Europe. A smaller pressure difference (the negative phase of the oscillation) leads to weaker westerlies; the storm tracks move closer to the Mediterranean Sea, and most of Europe (except for its southern portions) experiences cold and dry winters.

Subduction Mode

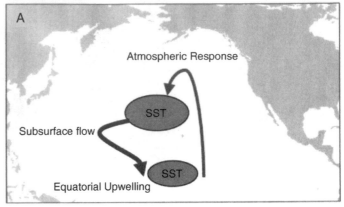

Midlatitude Gyre Mode

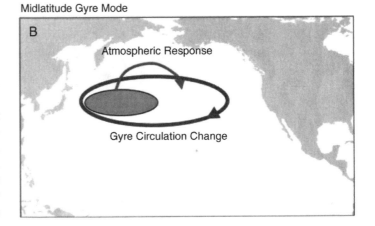

Ocean-Atmosphere Coupling. FIGURE 3.

A schematic description of (A) the subduction mode and (B) the mid-latitude gyre mode proposed to explain decadal climate variability in the Pacific. The subduction mode involves a mid-latitude SST anomaly that subducts into the thermocline, slowly travels towards the tropics, and then upwells in the eastern equatorial Pacific, forcing an SST anomaly of opposite polarity in mid-latitudes. The gyre mode involves the atmosphere responding to a mid-latitude SST anomaly in the western part of the basic, which is driven by a delayed response of the subtropical gyre circulation to antecedent atmospheric forcing with opposite polarity.
(After Miller et al., 2003.)

One of the key issues related to ocean-atmosphere coupling and the NAO is whether variations in the position and strength of the Gulf Stream can affect the North Atlantic Oscillation. Marshall et al. (2001), for example, proposed a conceptual model that couples ocean thermohaline and wind-driven circulations to the atmospheric jet stream. [See Thermohaline Circulation.] The model identifies nondimensional parameters that control whether the ocean responds passively to NAO forcing or actively couples to the NAO. Yet, which regime better describes the actual ocean-atmosphere system in the North Atlantic remains unclear.

(a) Sea level pressure anomalies (mb)

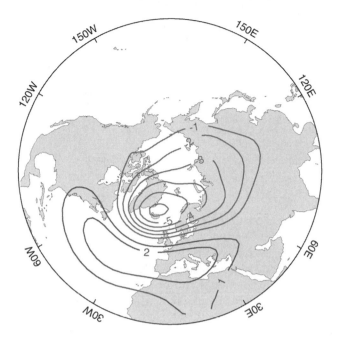

(b) Temperature anomalies (°C)

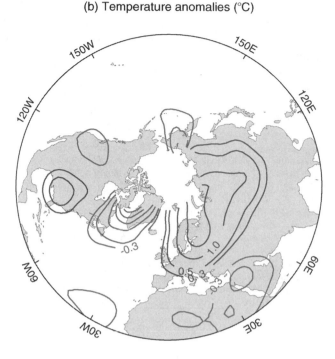

Ocean-Atmosphere Coupling. Figure 4.

Typical pressure and temperature anomalies associated with positive phase of the NAO. Courtesy of Tim Osborn, Climatic Research Unit, University of East Anglia (http://www.cru.uea.ac.uk/cru/info/nao/).

CLIMATE CHANGE

In recent decades, there has been dramatic progress in our understanding of and ability to model Earth's climate. Studies of ocean-atmosphere interactions have been instrumental in this progress, and yet we still do not fully understand the role of these interactions in climate change. In recent years, we have experienced the most intense and devastating El Niño episodes (1982 and 1997) in more than a century. An extraordinary heat wave occurred in France in 2003. The year 2005 showed the most active Atlantic hurricane season on record. Since the 1970s, the winter NAO index characterizing mid-latitude climate has stayed predominantly positive, which occurred on the background of persistent global warming trends over the second half of the twentieth and the beginning of the twenty-first century. These factors raise a number of important questions regarding the characteristics of ocean-atmosphere interactions in a changing climate.

One question concerns the connection between the NAO and global warming. Some studies suggested that the North Atlantic climate change since 1950 is linked to a gradual warming of tropical SSTs over the Indian and Pacific oceans (Hoerling et al., 2001). Changes in ocean temperatures modified rainfall patterns and surface heating of the atmosphere in low latitudes, which affected the North Atlantic Oscillation remotely and

forced it into the positive phase during the past half-century. These results, however, contradict other studies indicating that much of the decadal variability of the winter North Atlantic Oscillation over the same time interval can be reconstructed from the knowledge of North Atlantic sea-surface temperatures of (Rodwell et al., 1999).

Another question concerns the severity and frequency of hurricanes in a warmer climate, especially in the context of feedbacks that the hurricanes could provide for the climate system by affecting ocean vertical mixing and poleward heat transport (Sriver and Huber, 2007). Although there have been suggestions that the potential intensity and impacts of hurricanes have been increasing over the past half-century (Emanuel, 2005), the entire subject remains highly controversial.

Possible changes in the properties of El Niño are another important issue (e.g., Fedorov and Philander, 2000). Is the occurrence of strong El Niño events in the last 30 years a premonition of what to expect as global temperatures continue to rise? Can the climate system shift towards continuous, or permanent, rather than intermittent El Niño events? Imagine conditions similar to El Niño of 1997 lasting for many decades. Proxy temperature records show that the climate system was locked into a permanent El Niño state during the early Pliocene, approximately 3–5 million years ago, when the Earth was experiencing greenhouse conditions similar to today's (e.g., Fedorov et al., 2006). A permanent El Niño would imply very different characteristics of ocean-atmosphere coupling.

Unfortunately, the modeling results on changes in the properties of ENSO and other climate modes with global warming are not yet very reliable—differences between climate models are much larger than changes predicted by each particular model in greenhouse-warming simulations (e.g., Guilyardi, 2006). Similarly, projections for changes in the mean state of the climate system vary greatly from one model to the next. While many such problems remain unresolved, our continuing progress in understanding ocean-atmosphere interactions and the greater computational power available to researchers are very encouraging.

BIBLIOGRAPHY

Barsugli, J.J., and D.S. Battisti. "The Basic Effects of Atmosphere-Ocean Thermal Coupling on Midlatitude Variability." *Journal of the Atmospheric Sciences* 55 (1998), 477–493. DOI: 10.1175/1520-0469(1998)055<0477:TBEOAO>2.0.CO;2.

Battisti, D.S., and A.C. Hirst. "Interannual Variability in a Tropical Atmosphere-Ocean Model: Influence of the Basic State, Ocean Geometry, and Nonlinearity." *Journal of the Atmospheric Sciences* 46 (1989), 1687–1712.

Bjerknes, J. "Atlantic Air-Sea Interaction." In *Advances in Geophysics*, Vol. 10, pp. 1–82. New York: Academic Press, 1964.

Bjerknes, J. "Large-Scale Atmospheric Response to the 1964–65 Pacific Equatorial Warming." *Journal of Physical Oceanography* 2 (1972), 212–217.

Chelton, D.B., et al. "Satellite Microwave SST Observations of Transequatorial Tropical Instability Waves." *Geophysical Research Letters* 27 (2000), 1239–1242.

Chang, P., L. Ji, and H. Li. "A Decadal Climate Variation in the Tropical Atlantic Ocean from Thermodynamic Air-Sea Interactions." *Nature* 385 (1997): 516–518. DOI: 10.1038/385516a0.

Dijkstra, H.A., and J.D. Neelin. "Ocean-Atmosphere Interaction and the Tropical Climatology. Part II: Why the Pacific Cold Tongue is in the East." *Journal of Climate* 8 (1995), 1343–1359.

Emanuel, K.A. "Increasing Destructiveness of Tropical Cyclones over the Past 30 Years." *Nature* 436 (2005), 686–688. DOI: 10.1038/nature03906.

Guilyardi, E. "El Niño–Mean State–Seasonal Cycle Interactions in a Multi-Model Ensemble." *Climate Dynamics* 26.4 (2006), 329–348. DOI: 10.1007/s00382-005-0084-6.

Fedorov, A.V., et al. "The Pliocene Paradox (Mechanisms for a Permanent El Niño)." *Science* 312 (2006), 1437–1443. DOI: 10.1126/science.1122666.

Fedorov, A.V., and S.G.H. Philander. "Is El Niño Changing?" *Science* 288 (2000), 1997–2002. DOI: 10.1126/science.288.5473.1997.

Frankignoul, C., and K. Hasselmann. "Stochastic Climate Models. Part II: Application to Sea-Surface Temperature Anomalies and Thermocline Variability." *Tellus* 29 (1977), 289–305.

Hoerling, M.P., J.W. Hurrell, and T. Xu. "Tropical Origins for Recent North Atlantic Climate Change." *Science* 292 (2001), 90–92. DOI: 10.1126/science.1058582.

Hurrell, J.W. "Decadal Trends in the North Atlantic Oscillation: Regional Temperatures and Precipitation." *Science* 269 (1995), 676–679. DOI: 10.1126/science.269.5224.676.

Kushnir, Y., et al. "Atmospheric GCM Response to Extratropical SST Anomalies: Synthesis and Evaluation." *Journal of Climate* 15 (2002), 2233–2256. DOI: 10.1175/1520-0442(2002)015<2233:AGRTES>2.0.CO;2.

Marshall, J., H. Johnson, and J. Goodman. "A Study of the Interaction of the North Atlantic Oscillation with Ocean Circulation." *Journal of Climate* 14 (2001), 1399–1421. DOI: 10.1175/1520-0442(2001)014<1399:ASOTIO>2.0.CO;2.

Mantua, N.J., et al. "A Pacific Interdecadal Climate Oscillation with Impacts on Salmon Production." *Bulletin of the American Meteorological Society* 78 (1997), 1069–1079.

Miller, A.J., et al. "Potential Feedbacks between Pacific Ocean Ecosystems and Interdecadal Climate Variations." *Bulletin of the American Meteorological Society* 84 (2003), 617–633. DOI: 10.1175/BAMS-84-5-617.

Philander, S.G.H. *El Niño, La Niña, and the Southern Oscillation.* San Diego: Academic Press, 1990.

Rodwell, M., D. Rowell, and C. Folland. "Oceanic Forcing of the Wintertime North Atlantic Oscillation and European Climate." *Nature* 398 (1999), 320–323. DOI: 10.1038/18648.

Samelson, R.M., et al. "On the Coupling of Wind Stress and Sea Surface Temperature." *Journal of Climate* 19 (2006), 1557–1566. DOI: 10.1175/JCLI3682.1.

Sriver, R.L., and M. Huber. "Observational Evidence for an Ocean Heat Pump Induced by Tropical Cyclones." *Nature* 447 (2007), 577–580. DOI: 10.1038/nature05785.

Wyrtki, K. "Teleconnections in the Equatorial Pacific Ocean." *Science* 180 (1973), 66–68. DOI: 10.1126/science.180.4081.66.

———. "Equatorial Currents in the Pacific 1950 to 1970 and Their Relations to the Trade Winds." *Journal of Physical Oceanography* 4 (1974), 372–380. DOI: 10.1175/1520-0485(1974)004<0372:ECITPT>2.0.CO;2.

Zhang, Y., J.M. Wallace, and D.S. Battisti. "ENSO-Like Interdecadal Variability: 1900–93." *Journal of Climate* 10 (1997), 1004–1020. DOI: 10.1175/1520-0442(1997)010<1004:ELIV>2.0.CO;2.

Zebiak, S.E., and M.A. Cane. "A Model El Niño/Southern Oscillation." *Monthly Weather Review* 115 (1987), 2262–2278.

—ALEXEY V. FEDOROV

OCEAN DISPOSAL

Pollutants are introduced or disposed of into the ocean from point sources and nonpoint sources. Point sources are deliberate discharges from outfalls and ocean dumping. Oil drilling platforms, more than a thousand of which are in use or abandoned worldwide (GESAMP, 1990), are also point sources of a variety of pollutants. Nonpoint sources include runoff from land surfaces (e.g., streets, parking lots, agricultural lands, lawns), seepage through aquifers, and wet and dry atmospheric deposition. Rivers entering coastal waters usually contain pollutants from both point and nonpoint sources.

POINT SOURCES

Sewage treatment plant (STP) effluent is usually discharged through outfalls to the ocean. Industrial waste can be treated on site and discharged through an outfall or discharged to a municipal STP for treatment and discharge. Storm water is diverted primarily from paved areas and eventually discharged through stormwater outfalls, gullies, and ditches. In many coastal cities, storm water is combined with domestic sewage for treatment in a sewage treatment plant. During dry weather or low flow conditions, sewage is treated and discharged as sewage effluent; but, during a heavy rainfall, the combined sewage and stormwater flow may exceed the capacity of the STP, and some fraction of the total flow may be discharged, untreated, through a combined sewer outfall.

Ocean dumping is the intentional release, for the sole purpose of disposal, of waste materials into the sea from a vessel. Sewage sludge (the solid, semisolid, and liquid residue from sewage treatment), dredge spoil (sediments removed from navigational channels and harbors as they are constructed or maintained), industrial wastes, low-level radioactive wastes, construction debris, and garbage have all been dumped in the ocean, usually at specifically designated sites. In the United States, low-level radioactive wastes and garbage have not been ocean-dumped for decades. The Soviet Union is the only country thought to have dumped high-level nuclear wastes in the ocean. Dumping of sewage sludge and industrial waste was banned by the United States in the early 1990s, leaving dredge spoil as the only waste that may legally be ocean-dumped.

NONPOINT SOURCES

Coastal-water pollution from nonpoint sources is ubiquitous, and the sources are elusive. Runoff not channeled through an outfall is considered to come from a nonpoint source. It may come from city streets and other impervious surfaces, suburban lawns, golf courses, agricultural activities, construction sites, landfills, septic systems, and cesspools. There are many nonpoint sources of pollution discharging directly into coastal waters. Commercial shipping and recreational boating and their support facilities, shipyards, mooring facilities, and marinas are sources of a variety of contaminants including oil and grease, metals (such as copper and tin) from antifouling paints, and sewage. The atmosphere quickly disperses pollutants such as automobile exhaust, stack gases, and sprays used in pesticide control and agriculture. Many of these fall out onto the ocean surface through dry and wet deposition.

ACCIDENTAL RELEASES

Unintentional releases of polluting materials can reach the ocean even through well-regulated and well-managed facilities. Treatment plant breakdowns and malfunction of processing facilities occasionally occur, releasing excessive quantities of permitted discharges and perhaps substances prohibited from legal discharge. There are also dramatic accidental discharges such as oil spills from supertankers. Devastating as they are, oil spills are responsible for only a small fraction of the total amount of oil reaching the ocean from anthropogenic activities (Clark, 1992).

POLLUTANTS OF CONCERN

Pollutants that are discharged into the marine environment from various sources reflect the nature of society. Among these are particulate material, microorganisms (including pathogens), trace elements such as metals (cadmium, mercury, silver, copper, chromium, iron), synthetic organic compounds (e.g., DDT, PCBs), petroleum-derived compounds, and radionuclides. These pollutants are introduced primarily to harbors, particularly those with industrial facilities. They are also introduced along populated stretches of the coastal zone. Because most of the industrialized world is in the Northern Hemisphere, many of the world's polluted harbors are located there. However, many harbors in the developing world are also badly polluted because they may lack regulations to restrict polluting materials from entering waterways, and they may not have facilities to treat polluted waste streams before they enter the marine environment. Today, because of the availability of cheap labor and also because of inadequate regulation, some industries are relocating from developed nations to developing nations. The primary pollution concerns in the developing world are of sewage contamination and perhaps sedimentation from poor agricultural practices. In the future, pollution in these harbors may rival the worst of the developed world.

As of the early 1990s, the United Nations estimated the percentage contribution of all pollutants entering the world's oceans as follows (GESAMP, 1990): runoff and land-based discharges, 44%; atmosphere, 33%; maritime transportation, 12%; dumping, 10%; offshore production, 1%.

IMPACTS OF POLLUTION

The impacts of disposal on the oceans and their biota depend upon the physical and chemical nature of the disposed material and also upon the location of disposal. Some locations may be dispersive, others may tend to accumulate wastes. Some chemical constituents may dissolve, others may have an affinity for particles and tend eventually to settle with the particles to the sea floor. Because the oceans are interconnected, disposed material may be transported globally. Synthetic organic chemicals that do not readily degrade (such as many pesticides) are a particular concern in this regard.

Ecosystem impacts experienced by organisms could include smothering, toxicity, carcinogenicity, and reproductive failure. Some pollutants, such as synthetic organics, can be bioconcentrated and passed up the food web. Excess nutrients can lead to eutrophication in coastal waters.

Discharged contaminants can also impact humans. Pathogens as well as toxic and potentially carcinogenic materials can reach people through consumption of seafood. Direct contact via swimming in contaminated waters can lead to gastroenteritis and possibly other illnesses as well.

The United Nations (GESAMP, 1990) determined that the most important threats to the marine environment are: nutrient contamination; microbial contamination in seafood; debris; synthetic organic compounds in sediment; oil; trace contaminants such as cadmium, lead, and mercury; and radioactive contamination.

REDUCING AND REGULATING MARINE DISPOSAL

There is a considerable body of legislation in the United States that encourages reduction of wastes entering the marine environment, requires treatment of those that do, and restricts the concentration of pollutants in waste streams approved for disposal. Among these are the Marine Protection, Research and Sanctuaries Act (1972), the Federal Water Pollution Control Act (1948, popularly known as the Clean Water Act), and the Ocean Dumping Ban Act (1988). The latter put an end to ocean dumping of all materials except some dredge spoil.

Internationally, the most significant mechanism for reducing and controlling marine disposal is the Convention on the Prevention of Marine Pollution by Dumping of Wastes and Other Matter. Also known as the London Dumping Convention, it requires member states (more than 90) to adhere to minimal standards for ocean disposal of wastes seaward of signatories' territorial seas. It prohibits dumping of a number of blacklisted substances (such as organohalogen compounds, and mercury and cadmium and their compounds), permits others to be dumped with special care, and encourages members to develop individual protocols and regional agreements to improve the quality of marine waters (Office of Technology Assessment,

1987; GESAMP, 1990). Important regional environmental conventions include the Oslo Convention, the Paris Convention, the Barcelona Convention, the Helsinki Convention, and the Bonn Agreement. The United Nations Environment Programme has also established the Regional Seas Programme, which encourages pollution control and protection of living marine resources. Currently there are ten such regional-seas programs, including those for the Mediterranean, the Caribbean, and the Red Sea.

BIBLIOGRAPHY

Clark, R.B. *Marine Pollution.* 3d ed. Oxford: Clarendon Press, 1992. A clear introductory text, broadly covering pollution sources and effects with useful examples.
GESAMP (Joint Group of Experts on Scientific Aspects of Marine Pollution). *The State of the Marine Environment.* UNEP Regional Seas Reports and Studies No. 115. Nairobi, 1990. Provides a general status of the health of the marine environment, as compiled by some of the world's leading scientists in marine pollution, and ranks marine pollution sources and problems; easy to read.
Office of Technology Assessment. *Wastes in the Marine Environment.* Washington, D.C., 1987. A comprehensive overview of marine pollution in the United States, with some excellent examples; includes descriptions of pertinent laws and agency responsibilities.
Swanson, R.L. "A History of Ocean Dumping." *MSRC Bulletin.* Stony Brook, N.Y.: Marine Sciences Research Center, The University at Stony Brook, 2000. An up-to-date discussion of ocean dumping primarily in the United States.

—ROBERT LAWRENCE SWANSON

OIL SANDS

With the expected decline in conventional crude oil production in this century there has been renewed interest in unconventional sources of crude. [*See* Crude Oil Supply.] These include oil shales, such as those in Colorado, Utah, and Wyoming, and various deposits of heavy oil and bitumen. [*See* Fossil Fuels.] There has not been not been any large-scale production of crude from oil shales, but there are now projects producing significant amounts of heavy oil and bitumen, both of which require special production techniques and chemical upgrading to make the product suitable as refinery feedstock.

The resources of heavy oil and bitumen are very large on the basis of barrels of "oil in place" and estimates of volumes that are "technically recoverable," without considering price. One estimate puts world total heavy oil resources (technically recoverable) at 434 billion barrels, and that for natural bitumen at 651 billion. Together they exceed the current conventional crude recoverable reserves of roughly 900 billion barrels (Meyer and Attanasi, 2003). Those conventional reserves are economically recoverable using today's technologies, however, and not comparable to "technically recoverable" amounts.

Although deposits of heavy oil and bitumen occur worldwide, each of these categories is dominated by a single massive accumulation. The Orinoco Belt of Venezuela contains 90% of the world's extra-heavy oil: when combined with other heavy-oil deposits in South America, that continent accounts for roughly 60% of the world's technically recoverable heavy oil. For bitumen, the distribution is even more restricted: roughly 80% of the world's recoverable bitumen is in the oil sands of northern Alberta, Canada (Meyer and Attanasi, 2003).

ALBERTA OIL SANDS

Rising crude-oil prices have encouraged rapid development of the Alberta oil sands, revitalizing the Canadian oil industry that has seen conventional reserves and production decline in recent decades. One recent estimate puts economically recoverable amounts at 174 billion barrels (Alberta Energy and Utility Board, 2005). That compares to Saudi Arabia's crude reserves of 264 billion barrels and Canada's conventional crude reserves of 17 billion barrels (BP Statistical Review, 2007). Production from Alberta oil sands in 2006 had risen to 1.26 million barrels per day (bopd), roughly 40% of Canada's total crude production, and nearly 10% of North American production; production of heavy oil in the Orinoco belt of Venezuela was 0.45–0.50 million bopd in 2007. Planned expansions and new projects in Alberta suggest production will reach 3 billion bopd by 2020. That scale of operation has captured the interest of a number of national governments seeking a reliable supply of crude. Oil-sands production cannot satisfy the world—consumption 83.7 million bopd in 2006 and growing at roughly 2%—but it would be roughly one-seventh of current U.S. consumption (20.6 million bopd in 2006) and would be equivalent to Canada's total need (2.2 million bopd in 2006).

IMPACTS OF ALBERTA PRODUCTION ON THE ENVIRONMENT

Rapidly growing production affects water supply, the atmosphere, and the boreal forest in ways that depend partly on whether the production is by mining or by in situ processes. Overriding any local effects is the issue of greenhouse-gas emissions (see below).

In a relatively small area extending 55 miles along the Athabasca River north of Fort McMurray, bitumen-saturated sands are near the surface and can be mined after removal of overlying soil and rock (Figure 1). After mining, the saturated sand and intermixed clay are churned with hot water to extract the bitumen, some of which is sold while most is upgraded to synthetic crude oil shipped to refineries.

In most of the oil-sands areas the saturated material is buried too deeply for mining and is suited to various forms of in situ extraction in which the deposits are left in place and penetrated by drillholes (Figure 1). Steam is usually introduced to thin the bitumen which can then be pumped to the surface. In 2006, mining accounted for 61% of bitumen produced, while in situ extraction produced the balance.

Mining operations

When large areas are stripped and mined, much of the devastated landscape is restored and reforested; but artificial lakes, or tailings ponds, are required to handle large volumes of waste water from the hot-water extraction. Sand settles out of the water promptly, but clay may require decades to settle; the lakes,

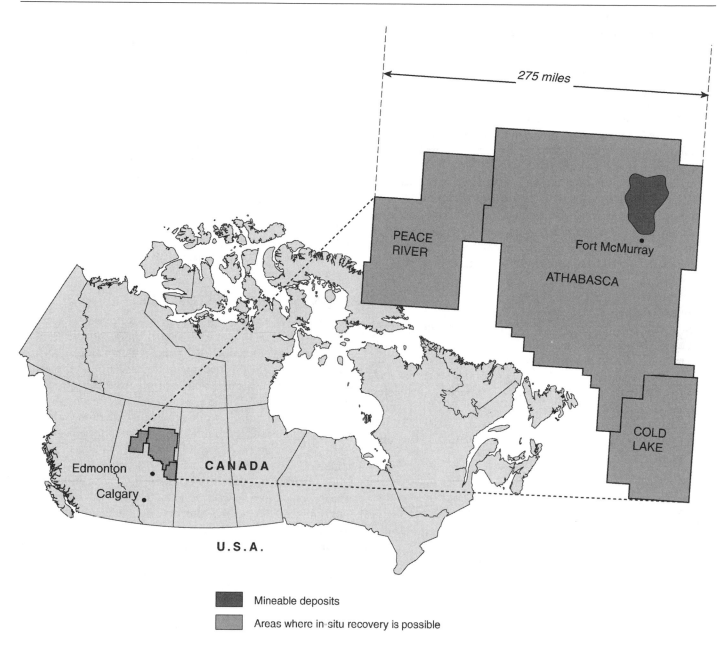

Oil Sands. FIGURE 1. Areas of Alberta's Oil Sands Deposits.

Mineable deposits

Areas where in-situ recovery is possible

meanwhile, are considered unsafe for birdlife because of other contaminants. This water for processing is drawn almost entirely from the Athabasca River, and while some from the tailings ponds is reused, the withdrawals in winter, when river flow is low, may eventually threaten fish populations (Pembina Institute, 2005). Natural gas is used to heat water for the extraction of bitumen from the mixture of sand and clay.

In situ operations

This approach does not disrupt the surface as mining does, but the network of roads and drilling pads does affect large areas of boreal forest because each drilling-heating-and-pumping operation can extract bitumen from only a small area of buried saturated sands, requiring, therefore, many drilling sites regularly spaced through the forest. Natural gas is used to produce steam injected to thin the bitumen.

Upgrading

Whatever the extraction process, most of the resulting bitumen is upgraded to synthetic oil by hydrogenation, using hydrogen derived from natural gas (primarily methane, CH_4). This use, together with gas for heat in mining and in situ operations used roughly 5% of Canada's natural gas production in 2004. With planned expansion in the next 10 years, it is likely that oil-sands production will use most of the Arctic gas expected to come to market via a new pipeline to Alberta (Isaacs, 2004).

OIL SANDS AND CANADA'S GREENHOUSE GAS EMISSIONS

Under the Kyoto Protocol, ratified by Canada in 2002, the nation pledged to cut greenhouse-gas emissions by 6% from 1990 levels by the year 2012, but emissions are now 35 % *above* the 1990 levels (*Planet Ark*, June 13, 2006). Oil-sands production may bexthe single largest contributor to growth in Canada's greenhouse-gas emissions. The carbon dioxide emissions are from diesel-fueled mining machines and trucks, from natural gas burned for heat in both mining and in situ operations, and from natural gas consumed in upgrading the bitumen. In a business-as-usual scenario the oil sands are projected to contribute up to 47% of Canada's total emissions growth in the period 2003 to 2010. It is possible, though, through greater fuel efficiency, carbon dioxide capture and storage, and purchasing carbon offsets, that the entire oil-sands industry could be carbon-neutral by the year 2020 at a cost of U.S.$10–13 per barrel (Pembina Institute, Oct.23, 2006).

The heavy use of natural gas for oil sands production is controversial. Natural gas, with its high hydrogen-to-carbon ratio, is a premium fuel whose impact on global warming is less than that of coal, gasoline, or diesel fuel. [*See* Greenhouse Effect *and* Greenhouse Gases.] The extraction of hydrogen from the gas and using it to upgrade bitumen to synthetic crude oil is a symptom of our current dependence on gasoline and diesel fuel.

[*See also* Biofuels; Global Warming; Natural Gas; *and* Transportation.]

BIBLIOGRAPHY

Isaacs, E. *Canadian Oil Sands: Development and Future Outlook*. Alberta Energy Research Institute, 2004. http://www.aeri.ab.ca (accessed June 3, 2008).
Meyer, R.F., and E.D. Attanasi. *Heavy Oil and Natural Bitumen: Strategic Petroleum Resources*. U.S. Geological Survey Fact Sheet 70-03, Aug. 2003. http://pubs.usgs.gov/fs/fs070-03/ (accessed June 3, 2008).
Oil and Gas Journal. *Alberta Bitumen Development Continues Its Rapid Expansion*. July 9, 2007.
Planet Ark. *Canada Wrests Oil from Sands, But at What Cost?* June 13, 2006.
The Pembina Institute. *Blueprint for Responsible Oil Sands Development*. Drayton Valley, Alberta, April 2, 2007. http://www.pembina.org/pub/1404 (accessed June 3, 2008).
———. *Carbon Neutral by 2020: A Leadership Opportunity in Canada's Oil Sands*. Drayton Valley, Alberta, Oct. 23, 2006. http://www.bembina.org/pub/1316 (accessed June 3, 2008).
———. *Death by a Thousand Cuts: Impacts of In-Situ Oil Sands Development on Alberta's Boreal Forest*. Drayton Valley, Alberta, Aug. 1, 2006. http://wwwenergy.pembina.org/pub/1262 (accessed June 3, 2008).
———. *Oil Sands Fever: The Environmental Implications of Canada's Oil Sands Rush*. Drayton Valley, Alberta, Nov. 23, 2005. (http://www.pembina.org/bub/203 accessed June 3, 2008).

—David J. Cuff

OPTIMISM

See Catastrophist-Cornucopian Debate.

OZONE

Ozone (O_3) is a rare constituent of the Earth's atmosphere. Ninety percent of the ozone in the atmosphere is in a layer from 10 to 50 kilometers in altitude, the stratosphere, with a maximum ozone concentration between 20 and 27 kilometers, which corresponds to absolute values on the order of 2.5–5.1×10^{12} molecules per cubic centimeter, or relative values of 4–8 parts per million, corresponding to 4–8 molecules of ozone for one million air molecules. The remaining 10% of the ozone is in the lower region of the atmosphere, the troposphere, which extends from the Earth's surface up to 10–12 kilometers. Ozone is continuously formed at altitudes above 30 kilometers by the photodissociation of molecular oxygen (O_2) by solar radiation. The ozone balance in the stratosphere is maintained by destruction of ozone through catalytic cycles that involve nitrogen, hydrogen, chlorine, and bromine species. The chemistry of the stratosphere, with respect to the production and catalytic destruction of ozone, is thus a complex system, involving a large number of chemical reactions.

OZONE IN THE STRATOSPHERE

Ozone plays a major role in the Earth's atmosphere because it absorbs solar radiation at wavelengths shorter than 300 nanometers that is not absorbed by molecular nitrogen (N_2) or molecular oxygen, the two main constituents of the atmosphere. It thus shields the Earth's surface from damaging high-energy ultraviolet (UV-B) radiation. Indeed, if ozone were not present in the stratosphere, this energetic radiation emitted by the Sun would reach the surface and destroy molecules such as DNA and proteins that constitute the living material of the biosphere. Life on Earth is thus directly dependent on the existence of the ozone layer. In addition, the absorption of UV radiation by ozone between 10 and 50 kilometers releases heat and thus creates a positive temperature gradient in the stratosphere, that is to say temperature increases with height, suppressing vertical movement and transport of energy. This distinguishes the stratosphere from the troposphere where declining temperature with height promotes vertical circulation.

OZONE IN THE TROPOSPHERE

In contrast to its beneficial role in the stratosphere, ozone in the troposphere interacts directly with living matter, with potential detrimental effects on ecosystems and human health. These effects arise from ozone's properties as a powerful oxidant, even at the low concentrations—20 to 50 parts per billion (ppb)—currently observed. The harmful effects of ozone on forest growth and crop production have been clearly demonstrated, while, at the higher concentration levels observed in polluted areas (where relative concentrations can reach hundreds of ppb), ozone can directly affect human health. Also, ozone in the troposphere is a greenhouse gas with an efficiency on a per molecule basis in the atmosphere 1,200 times larger than that of carbon dioxide, the main contributor to the greenhouse effect. Ozone is thus responsible, directly and indirectly (through chemical processes that affect other greenhouse gases such as methane), for about 20% of the increase in the greenhouse effect observed since the beginning of the twentieth century. [*See* Greenhouse Effect.]

HUMAN INFLUENCE

Continuous atmospheric observations over more than three decades show that the vertical distribution of ozone is strongly perturbed by human activities. Since the early 1970s, the increase of chlorine and bromine compounds in the stratosphere, linked to the continuous increase in anthropogenic production of chlorofluorocarbons (CFCs) and halons (brominated hydrocarbons, some also containing other halogens), has led to a decrease in the thickness of the ozone layer. CFCs and halons are destroyed by solar radiation once they have reached the stratosphere through vertical diffusion, thereby liberating chlorine and bromine atoms, which further enhance the efficiency of ozone-destroying catalytic cycles. The most recent evaluation of the long-term evolution of the ozone layer shows negative trends in the total ozone content, with the largest deficits observed in the high latitudes of both hemispheres in winter. In the high latitudes of the Southern Hemisphere, the springtime ozone deficit is now a permanent feature of the stratosphere, and a direct link has been established between anthropogenic chlorine and the large decrease in the ozone concentration, up to 90%, observed between 15 and 20 kilometers. Similar decreases have appeared since 1995 in the Arctic winter stratosphere, where record low temperatures (relative to the average values recorded over the last 20 years) have been observed. These measurements constitute additional evidence of the destructive effects of CFCs and halons on the stratospheric ozone layer. They are also a clear indication of the fragility of the ozone balance in the atmosphere and of the nonlinearities that can occur in complex chemical and dynamical systems.

In the troposphere, the background ozone concentration, relative to the concentration observed at the Earth's surface during the last decades of the nineteenth century in nonpolluted areas, has increased threefold in the Northern Hemisphere and twofold in the Southern Hemisphere. These changes, together with increased frequency of ozone pollution episodes in large urban areas, can be related unambiguously to increased emissions of nitrogen oxides and hydrocarbons. Because the lifetime of ozone molecules in the lower atmosphere ranges from a few days to a few weeks, this additional ozone is not transferred to the stratosphere. And because the regions in which ozone increases in the troposphere (mainly the middle latitudes of the Northern Hemisphere) are geographically distinct from those regions in which ozone decreases rapidly in the stratosphere, the two human-induced perturbations to the vertical distribution of atmospheric ozone do not compensate for each other.

The detrimental effects on atmospheric ozone of emissions from industry, transport, and agriculture represent departures from the natural balance of ozone in the stratosphere and the troposphere. Although the chemistry of these two atmospheric regions is very different, ozone is always created by the recombination reaction of atomic oxygen with molecular oxygen in the presence of a third body M, whose role is to carry away the energy released in the reaction:

$$O + O_2 + M \rightarrow O_3 + M.$$

The variation with altitude in the chemical processes governing the concentration of ozone relates to the origin of the oxygen atoms required for this reaction and to the chemical and photochemical reactions involving other minor constituents of the atmosphere that also affect the ozone balance.

THE PERTURBED STRATOSPHERE

Perturbation of the ozone balance in the stratosphere occurs because of increased emission of source species at the surface. Chlorine species play a dominant role, and the main source of stratospheric chlorine is anthropogenic—the result of emissions of stable organic chlorine as chlorofluorocarbons (CFCs) or chlorinated hydrocarbons. The most significant species are $CFCl_3$ (CFC-11), CF_2Cl_2 (CFC-12), carbon tetrachloride (CCl_4), and methylchloroform (CH_3CCl_3). The total chlorine level in the stratosphere has increased from 0.6 ppb in the 1950s, a value that can be considered as the background level, to 3.8 ppb in 1997. The bromine-containing halons also reach the stratosphere, but the present total abundance of bromine in the stratosphere is much lower than that of chlorine, reaching 15 parts per trillion in 1997.

These increased levels of chlorine and bromine lead to additional ozone destruction at 40 kilometers, where the chlorine-controlled destruction cycles are the most efficient. Based on a simple consideration of CFC and halon emissions, the estimated decrease in the thickness of the ozone layer resulting from these gas-phase processes should have been limited to 1–2% per decade over the period 1975–1995. But much larger effects identified in the mid-1980s completely changed our understanding of ozone chemistry in the presence of high chlorine levels in the stratosphere.

IN THE ANTARCTIC

The seasonal ozone depletion that occurs over Antarctica during the Southern Hemisphere spring was discovered by Farman et al. (1985). This phenomenon, which has recurred every spring since the early 1980s, when total chlorine in the stratosphere reached a threshold value of about 2 ppb, was completely unexpected and could not be accounted for by chemical models that incorporated only gas-phase chemistry. This was the first recorded evidence of a large change in ozone climatology. It corresponded to a change in the seasonal cycle of column ozone, as the spring minimum of 270 Dobson units (DU, a measure of atmospheric ozone concentration), observed since the late 1950s at various stations in Antarctica, plunged to values as low as 100 DU during October. Ozone is completely depleted at altitudes from 15 to 20 kilometers. As a result of several coordinated campaigns conducted in the Antarctic since 1987, a clear picture has now emerged of the combination of dynamical, radiative, and chemical processes that are responsible for the Antarctic ozone depletion.

The dynamic processes in the Antarctic winter stratosphere are dominated by strong westerly zonal winds—the polar vortex—surrounding a region of very cold air at latitudes higher than 65° south. These winds are generated by the large temperature gradient between the midlatitude regions and the polar-night areas, where very low temperatures, below −83°C, are reached as a result of radiative equilibrium in the absence of sunlight. The Southern Hemisphere vortex is very stable because of the circular symmetry in the troposphere, which is dominated by regions of low pressure in the 50–60° south latitude belt. In the very cold area over Antarctica, polar stratospheric clouds can form at altitudes between 15 and 20 kilometers as a result of the condensation of either nitric acid trihydrate ($HNO_3 \cdot 3H_2O$) at -83°C, or of water vapor itself when the temperature drops below -88°C. Polar stratospheric clouds provide sites for chemical reactions that convert inactive chlorine compounds into ozone-destroying radicals—specifically, active chlorine. When sunlight returns to the Antarctic stratosphere in spring it initiates a series of photochemical reactions that convert ozone molecules to oxygen. These mechanisms are a direct cause-and-effect link between anthropogenic chlorine (which represents 90% of the chlorine reservoir in the stratosphere) and ozone depletion.

IN THE ARCTIC

In the Arctic, the dynamical conditions are different: the polar vortex is less stable because of a continuously varying tropospheric forcing related to the alternation of continents and oceans that characterizes the midlatitude regions of the Northern Hemisphere. Air is continuously mixed during winter between the colder polar regions and the warmer midlatitude regions, resulting in average temperatures about 15–20°C higher than those in the Antarctic stratosphere. Until the early 1990s, the early breakdown of the vortex and the subsequent warming that occurs in the north polar stratosphere prevented the occurrence of large depletions similar to those observed over Antarctica. Nevertheless, heterogeneous processes similar to those occurring over Antarctica are also taking place at the surface of polar stratospheric clouds in the Arctic, resulting in high levels of active chlorine in January and February. Since 1994, lower temperatures have been observed in the Arctic stratosphere, and these have led to increased ozone depletion during the spring. Observations from several field experiments confirm that large ozone losses, reaching about 25% by the end of March, are now occurring in the northern high latitudes over surface areas similar to those observed in Antarctica.

STRATOSPHERIC OZONE DEPLETION

Despite the difficulty of determining trends from instruments that have not all been specifically designed for that purpose, there is evidence from both ground-based and satellite measurements that large variations have occurred in the ozone concentration in the lower and upper stratosphere over the last few decades. These downward trends, which cannot be explained by natural causes such as the solar cycle, are much larger than the values predicted from our present knowledge of the chlorine catalytic cycles, for both gas-phase and heterogeneous (multiphase) chemistry. In contrast to the Southern Hemisphere, where the Antarctic ozone hole has been related directly to the presence of anthropogenic chlorine in the stratosphere, no such

direct cause-and-effect link has yet been established between the Northern Hemisphere ozone depletion and the emission of halocarbons into the atmosphere. Although mechanisms involving chlorine and bromine from anthropogenic sources appear to be largely responsible for the measured ozone losses, the main difficulty resides in quantifying the relative importance of the various processes that are thought to be acting in the stratosphere. These include local heterogeneous chemistry acting on the surface of sulfate particles, transport of ozone-depleted air masses from the polar regions towards the middle latitudes, and transport of chemically perturbed polar air with high levels of reactive chlorine and low levels of nitrogen species towards the midlatitude regions.

The June 1991 eruption of the Mount Pinatubo volcano in the Philippines, which released a large quantity of sulfate particles directly into the stratosphere, has provided an opportunity to test some of these hypotheses. From observations made in the years following this large perturbation, it is known that heterogeneous reactions can also occur on the surface of such sulfate aerosols, especially in the cold stratosphere. Evidence that the stratospheric ozone layer has been strongly perturbed by this eruption as a result of the high level of anthropogenic chlorine in the stratosphere, which in turn induces chlorine-catalyzed ozone destruction, is provided by the low values of total ozone content obtained from ground-based and satellite measurements in 1992 and 1993. The 1993 values are about 15% lower than the lowest values recorded over the decade 1980–1990.

ULTRAVIOLET RADIATION AT THE SURFACE

In the absence of other interfering absorbers or scatterers of UV radiation such as clouds or pollution, decreases in stratospheric ozone content lead to an increase in surface UV-B radiation (280–315 nanometers). This inverse relationship has been established firmly by both theory and measurements. It is confirmed by several experiments conducted in Antarctica over the last decade. These are large effects; for example, in ozone-hole conditions, the UV-B intensity at the Palmer Station in Antarctica in late October is more intense than that observed in San Diego, California, at any time of the year. However, such observations are currently restricted to areas in which large ozone depletions (more than 60%) have been observed. In other areas, UV-B increases are more difficult to detect because they are complicated by changes in cloudiness or by local pollution, as well as by the difficulty of keeping the detection instruments in precisely stable observation conditions over long periods. Prior to the late 1980s, instruments with the necessary accuracy and stability were not available. Hence the record of ground-based measurements is not long enough for the reliable determination of decadal changes in UV fluxes. However, as the effects of altitude, aerosols, and geographic differences have become better understood, estimates have been made from satellite observation using the TOMS (Total Ozone Mapping Spectrometer); these show increases in UV-B fluxes at latitudes above 35°, in agreement with the observed ozone decreases. As a result of such observations, public interest in UV exposure has been addressed in many countries by the establishment of a standardized UV index to provide daily information about the intensity of UV radiation based on ozone measurements and weather forecasting.

TROPOSPHERIC OZONE

Until the 1970s, photochemical production of ozone in the troposphere was considered to be important only in highly polluted areas. This ozone buildup in urban smog was known to be caused by the oxidation of methane, carbon monoxide, and volatile organic compounds (VOCs) in the presence of nitrogen oxides and solar radiation. Early studies demonstrated that in situ photochemical production of ozone from the same precursors—nitrogen oxides and VOCs—could also occur in remote areas, induced by both natural and artificial causes. This additional production of ozone is likely to have changed the oxidation efficiency of the atmosphere during the past century.

Oxides of nitrogen are a central element of the oxidation scheme because they affect the switching reaction and are the only source of ozone and thus of OH radicals. Natural sources of nitrogen oxides include microbial activity in the soils, oxidation of biogenic ammonia, and lightning discharges in the atmosphere. [See Nitrogen Cycle and Nitrous Oxide.] The other ozone precursors—methane, carbon monoxide, and VOCs—also have natural sources, mainly linked to biogenic processes and further oxidation processes in the atmosphere. In particular, terpenes and isoprenes (volatile hydrocarbons) are found over regions with high densities of citrus or pine-family trees. Anthropogenic sources that have been superposed over time on these natural sources, affect not only densely populated areas, but also remote sites. In 1995, these anthropogenic sources dominated the global emissions of methane, accounting for 63% of the total sources (World Meteorological Organization, 1998), carbon monoxide (65%), and nitrogen oxides (75%). They are linked to industry (fossil-fuel burning, combustion processes, natural gas emissions), agriculture (soil fertilization, rice paddies, cattle), and transport (terrestrial, aviation). Although the anthropogenic sources of hydrocarbons and other VOCs predominate in polluted areas (industry and transport through combustion processes), natural sources linked to biogenic emissions still predominate on the global scale, accounting for 80% of the total emissions.

The global budget of tropospheric ozone is thus influenced by ozone produced directly by photochemical processes in urban and industrialized regions and transported downwind, as well as in situ production such as that resulting from biomass-burning in the tropics. Almost 80% of present tropospheric ozone is thought to be of photochemical origin, whereas the downward transport from the stratosphere only accounts for 20%. An average yearly increase in tropospheric ozone content of 0.5–2% in the temperate Northern Hemisphere is one of the many indications that the photochemistry of the troposphere is changing, with potential consequences for plant life, human health, and climate change.

ASSESSMENT

Clear evidence has emerged over the last two decades that the distribution of ozone in the atmosphere, both in the stratosphere and the troposphere, is directly affected by human activities. Considering the huge volume of the Earth's atmosphere and the magnitude of the changes occurring in ozone content, in particular the ozone depletion in the stratosphere, possible cures for the problem have proven to be far too expensive, impractical, and potentially damaging to the global environment. The alternative is to apply the precautionary principle as reflected in the internationally agreed Montreal Protocol (1987) and its further amendments made in London (1990), Copenhagen (1992), Vienna (1995), and Montreal (1997). These agreements call for a total elimination of the production and use of CFCs and other ozone-damaging substances. In addition, regulatory measures have been proposed or adopted in many developed countries to reduce emissions of ozone precursors in the troposphere, especially nitrogen oxides.

[See also Chemical Industry; Chlorofluorocarbons; Greenhouse Effect; and Precautionary Principle.]

BIBLIOGRAPHY

Brasseur, G., and S. Solomon. *Aeronomy of the Middle Atmosphere.* Dordrecht, Netherlands: Reidel, 1984.
Chapman, S. "A Theory of the Upper Atmospheric Ozone Layer." *Memoirs of the Royal Meteorological Society* 3 (1930), 103–125.
Farman, J.C., B.G. Gardiner, and J.D. Shanklin. "Large Losses of Total Ozone in Antarctica Reveal Seasonal ClO$_x$/NO$_x$ Interaction." *Nature* 315 (1985), 207–210. DOI: 10.1038/315207a0.
Götz, F.W.P. "Zum Strahlungsklima des Spitzbergen Sommers." *Gerlands Beiträge zur Geophysik* 31 (1931), 119–154.
Solomon, S. "The Mystery of the Antarctic Ozone 'Hole'." *Reviews of Geophysics* 26 (1988), 131–148.
Wayne, R.P. *Chemistry of Atmospheres.* Oxford: Clarendon Press, 1985.
World Meteorological Organization. *International Ozone Assessment: 1989.* World Meteorological Organization Global Ozone and Monitoring Network, Report 20. Washington, D.C., 1990a.
———. *Report of the International Ozone Trends Panel: 1988.* Report 18. Washington, D.C., 1990b.
———. *International Ozone Assessment: 1991.* Report 22. Washington, D.C., 1992.
———. *International Ozone Assessment: 1994.* Report 37. Washington, D.C., 1994.
———. *International Ozone Assessment: 1998.* Report 44. Washington, D.C, 1999.

—GÉRARD J. MÉGIE

OZONE FLUCTUATIONS IN THE STRATOSPHERE

Much attention is given to anthropogenic damage to stratospheric ozone in polar regions by release of industrial chemicals. This damage takes place against a background of normal fluctuations and a persistent gradient from higher to lower latitudes.

Figure 1, which resembles a map, shows how the normal ozone content of the stratosphere varies with latitude and with the seasons. Because of transport poleward from equatorial

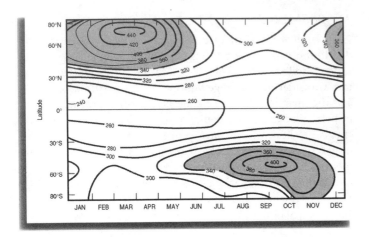

Ozone Fluctuations in the Stratosphere. Figure 1. Total Ozone (Average 1957–1975) Showing Seasons and Latitudes of Greatest Normal Concentration.

Values over 340 Dobson units are shaded. After London and Angell, in Morris and Barras, 1978. Copyright American Society for Testing and Materials. Reprinted with permission.

regions, ozone concentration is highest in high latitudes; it is stored there during the polar night and then appears strongly in the spring months (February-May in the Northern Hemisphere, October-November in the Southern Hemisphere). In connection with recent concern about the ozone layer and its interception of harmful ultraviolet radiation, two points are worth noting:

• It is the polar springtime maxima of ozone concentration (in which values of 400 Dobson units are normal) that are disrupted by ozone holes, as sunlight returns after the polar night and drives chemical reactions in which chlorine and bromine rapidly destroy ozone.
• Labeled isolines show that, under normal conditions, the lowest concentrations of ozone (and the least protection from ultraviolet radiation at the Earth's surface) year around are in lower latitudes, not at the poles.

BIBLIOGRAPHY

BASIC REFERENCE

Morris, A.L., and R.C. Barras, eds. *Air Quality Meteorology and Atmospheric Ozone*. Philadelphia: American Society for Testing and Materials, 1978.

OTHER SOURCES

Barry, R.G., and R.J. Chorley. *Atmosphere, Weather, and Climate*. 6th ed. London and New York: Routledge, 1992.
Goddard Space Flight Center (NASA). *Stratospheric Ozone Electronic Textbook*, edited by R.M. Todaro. (accessed June 3, 2008).
National Oceanic and Atmospheric Administration (NOAA). Earth System Research Laboratory. *Stratospheric Ozone Layer*. (accessed June 3, 2008).

—DAVID J. CUFF

P

PALEOCLIMATE

The climate of the world has changed repeatedly and substantially throughout geological time, before and during the presence of humans on the face of the Earth. Changes have ranged from the minor fluctuations within the period of instrumental record—with a duration of the order of a decade or decades in events such as the Sahel drought beginning in the mid-1960s—to those with durations of many millions of years (Table 1). For example, over the last billion years there have been at least 6 major ice ages when ice caps have covered substantial parts of the Earth's surface. Such extensive phases of glacial activity appear to have been separated by millions of years of relative warmth when ice caps and glaciers were largely absent. This variability is illustrated in Figure 1. General reviews of climatic change are provided by Crowley and North (1991), Williams et al. (1998), Wilson et al. (2000) and Anderson et al. (2007), while Bradley (1985) and Lowe and Walker (1997) provide good surveys of the techniques used to date and reconstruct past environments. The IPCC (Solomon et al., 2007, chapter 6), provides a succinct summary of past climates.

EVIDENCE FOR PAST CLIMATIC CHANGES

There are five main types of evidence that can be used to reconstruct past climatic conditions (Table 3). First is the evidence that can be derived from drill cores extracted from ice sheets. This has been particularly useful for understanding climates for as much as 800,000 years. Second is geological evidence derived from the study of sediments and landforms, both marine and terrestrial (e.g., coral reefs, sand dunes, and glacial hills). Third is the biological evidence provided by the remains of organisms. Past vegetation cover, for example, can be estimated by pollen analysis (palynology). Fourth, there is historical evidence for the last few thousands of years, and fifth, there is archaeological evidence. Extensive archaeological remains in the heart of the Sahara, for instance, may indicate moist climatic phases. [*See* Climate Reconstruction; Dating Methods; *and* Proxy Data for Environmental Change.]

CLIMATIC CHANGES IN THE GEOLOGICAL RECORD

The long-term history of climate is progressively more difficult to decipher as one goes further back in time and the resolution diminishes. Nonetheless, Crowley and North (1991) have divided the Earth's 4.6-billion-year history as follows:

1) From 4.6 to about 2.5 billion years ago, Earth was probably ice-free, despite a substantially lower solar luminosity. An enhanced greenhouse effect may account for this paradox by having compensated for the decreased insolation.
2) At around 2.5 billion years ago, atmospheric temperatures appear to have dipped, producing the first glaciation.
3) Between then and 900 million years ago Earth was again largely ice free.
4) From 900 to 600 million years ago, at least three major phases of glaciation occurred, and Precambrian rocks from virtually all regions of the Earth show evidence for glaciation during this time. Glaciation appears to have penetrated into low latitudes.
5) From 600 to 100 million years ago, climates were generally milder but were punctuated by two major phases of ice growth. In the Ordovician, for example, there was extensive glaciation in what is now the Sahara Desert, which was then located in the South Polar regions.
6) From 100 to 50 million years ago, a mild nonglacial climate prevailed. There is, for example, considerable evidence for warmer temperatures in high latitudes during the Mid-Cretaceous, and dinosaurs of presumed warm-weather affinity ranged north of the Arctic Circle. Relative warmth continued into the Cenozoic (Paleocene and Eocene), and plant fossils reflect such conditions in the high latitudes of both the Northern and Southern Hemispheres.
7) In the late Cenozoic a climatic decline started that led to the ice ages of the Plio-Pleistocene.

THE CENOZOIC CLIMATE DECLINE

During the Tertiary era, which followed the Cretaceous about 65 million years ago, Earth's climate underwent one of its longer-lasting changes—the Cenozoic climate decline (Figure 2). Temperatures generally fell throughout the world. The warmth of the first half of the Tertiary (the Paleogene) in Western Europe had both local and global causes. Locally, Western Europe was 10–12° further south than today. Globally, the oceans and continents had very different shapes and locations, affecting ocean currents and monsoon circulations, and atmospheric carbon dioxide may have been much higher, creating a greenhouse effect. There may also have been a marked reduction in the angle of tilt of the earth's axis which would have affected the impact of incoming solar radiation.

At the end of the Eocene (36 million years ago) there was a climatic shift, and in the ensuing Oligocene the climate of

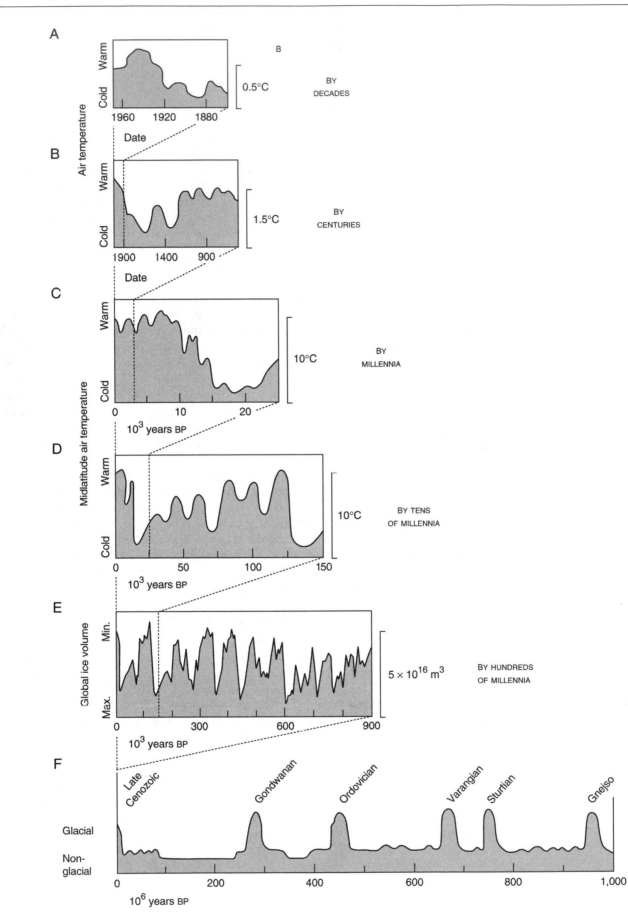

TABLE 1. Orders of Climatic Variation

Time Scale Unit	Duration (Years)	Typical Phenomena	Principal Bases of Evidence
1. Minor fluctuations within the instrumental record	10	Minor fluctuations that give the impression of operating over intervals on the order of 25–100 years, with somewhat irregular length and amplitude	Instrumental; behavior of glaciers; records of riverflow and lake levels; noninstrumental diaries; crop yields, tree rings
2. Postglacial and historic	10^2	Variations over intervals on the order of 250–1,000 years	Earlier records of extremes: fossil tree rings; archaeological finds; lake levels; varves and lake sediments; oceanic core samples; pollen analysis
3. Glacial	10^4	The phases within an ice age, e.g., the duration of the last glacial was about 9×10^3 years	Fauna and flora characteristics of interglacial deposits; pollen analysis; variation in height of snow line and extent of frozen ground; oceanic core samples
4. Minor geologic	10^6	Duration of ice ages as a whole, periods of evolution of species	Geologic evidence: character of deposits; fossil fauna and flora
5. Major geologic	10^8	Intervals between ice ages	Geologic evidence: character of deposits; fossil fauna and flora

Western Europe may have been comparable to that of the southeastern United States. Major ice sheets were permanently established on Antarctica approximately 34 million years ago (Edgar et al., 2007). By Pliocene times (5.5 million years ago) the cooling was such that a more temperate flora was present in the North Atlantic region, and at 2.4 million years ago glaciers started to develop in mid-latitude areas, and many of the world's deserts came into being.

THE QUATERNARY (Begins with Pleistocene)

In the Quaternary the gradual if uneven progression toward cooler conditions which had characterized the Earth during the Tertiary gave way to extraordinary climatic instability. Temperatures oscillated wildly from values similar to or slightly higher than today's (in interglacials) to levels that were sufficiently cold to treble the volume of ice sheets on land (during glacials). Not only was the extent of change remarkable but so, according to evidence from the sedimentary record retrieved from deep-sea cores, was the frequency of change. There have been about 17 glacial/interglacial cycles in the last 1.6 million years. The cycles tend to be characterized by a gradual buildup of ice volume (over a period of about 90,000 years), followed by a dramatic termination in only about 8,000 years. Furthermore, over the 3 million years

Paleoclimate. **FIGURE 1. The Different Scales of Climatic Change.**

(A) Changes in the five-year average surface temperatures over the region of 0–80°N. (B) Winter severity index for eastern Europe. (C) Generalized Northern Hemisphere air temperature trends, based on fluctuations in alpine glaciers, changes in tree lines, marginal fluctuations in continental glaciers, and shifts in vegetation patterns recorded in pollen spectra. (D) Generalized Northern Hemisphere air temperature trends, based on midlatitude sea surface temperature, pollen records, and worldwide sea level records. (E) Fluctuations in global ice volume recorded by changes in isotopic composition of fossil plankton in a deep-sea core. (F) The occurrence of ice ages in geological time. (After Goudie, 1992.)

or so during which humans have inhabited the earth, conditions such as those we experience today have been relatively short-lived and atypical of the Quaternary (Bowen, 1978). Figure 3 illustrates the changes that have taken place over the last 850,000 years.

The last glacial cycle reached its peak (the so-called Last Glacial Maximum) about 18,000–20,000 years ago, with ice sheets extending over Scandinavia to the north German plain, over all but the south of Britain, and over North America to 39°N (Figure 4). To the south of the Scandinavian ice sheet was a tundra steppe underlain by permafrost, and forest was relatively sparse north of the Mediterranean.

Ice covered nearly one-third of the land area of the earth, but the additional ice-covered area in the last glacial was almost all in the Northern Hemisphere, with only about 3 per cent in the Southern, though substantial ice cover did develop over Patagonia and New Zealand. The thickness of the ice sheets may have exceeded 4 km, with typical depths of 2 to 3 km. The total ice-covered area at a typical glacial maximum was 40×10^6 km².

Significant changes also took place in the oceans. During the present interglacial (the Holocene), the Atlantic is at least seasonally ice-free as far north as 78°N in the Norwegian Sea because of the advection of warm water into this region by the Gulf Stream. During the Last Glacial Maximum, however, the oceanic polar front probably lay at about 45°N, and north of this the ocean was mainly ice-covered during winter.

The temperature change over land was especially large near the great ice sheets. Evidence of permafrost in southern Britain suggests a temperature about 15°C lower than that present. The decline in mid-latitude areas was probably smaller—perhaps 5–8°C. In areas subject to maritime air masses, temperatures were probably reduced by 4–5°C.

The transfer of large volumes of water from the oceans to the ice caps caused a global fall in sea levels. The degree of

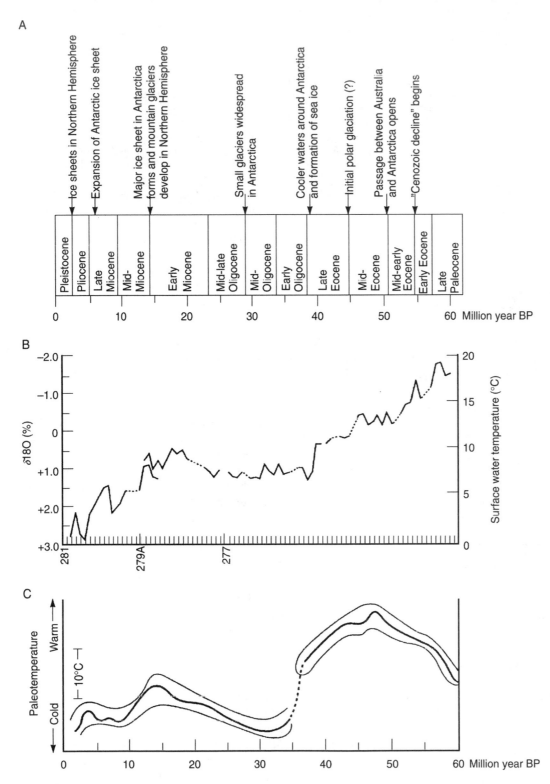

Paleoclimate. Figure 2. The Cenozoic Climate Decline.

(A) A generalized outline of significant events in the Cenozoic climate decline. (B) Oxygen isotopic data and paleotemperature indicated for planktonic foraminifera at three subantarctic sites (277, 279A, and 281). (C) Temperature changes calculated from oxygen source values of shells in the North Sea.

(After Goudie, 1992.)

this worldwide (eustatic) change at the time of glacial maxima is the subject of some debate but may have been of the order of 120 to 150 m.

In addition to their global effect, the ice sheets had a more localized effect on sea levels through the process of glacial isostasy: the weight of the ice depressed the Earth's crust and caused upward displacement in unglaciated areas peripheral to

TABLE 2. Examples of Climate Oscillations

1) *At less than century to millennial scales*

Antarctic Circumpolar Wave

Antarctic Oscillation

Arctic Oscillation

El Niño

Interdecadal Pacific Oscillation

La Niña

Madden-Julian Oscillation

North Atlantic Oscillation

Northern Hemisphere Annual Mode

Pacific Decadal Oscillation

Pacific-North American Teleconnection/Pattern

Quasi-Biennial Oscillation

Southern Annular Mode

Southern Oscillation

2) *At century to millennial time scales*

Bond cycles

Dansgaard-Oeschger Cycles

Heinrich Events

Neoglaciations (e.g. Little Ice Age)

3) *At longer time scales*

Major glacials

Major interglacials

Milankovitch cycles

TABLE 3. Principal Sources of Proxy Data for Paleoclimatic Reconstructions

(1) Glaciological (ice cores)
- (a) oxygen isotopes
- (b) physical properties (e.g., ice fabric)
- (c) trace element and microparticle concentrations

(2) Geologic
- (A) Marine (ocean sediment cores)
  - (i) Organic sediments (planktonic and benthic fossils)
    - (a) oxygen isotopic composition
    - (b) faunal and floral abundance
    - (c) morphological variations
  - (ii) Inorganic sediments
    - (a) Mineralogical composition and surface texture
    - (b) Accumulation rates and distribution of terrestrial dust and ice-rafted debris
    - (c) Geochemistry
- (B) Terrestrial
  - (a) glacial deposits and features of glacial erosion
  - (b) periglacial features
  - (c) glacio-eustatic features (shorelines)
  - (d) eolian deposits (loess and sand dunes)
  - (e) lacustrine deposits and erosional features (lacustrine sediments and shorelines)
  - (f) speleothems (age and stable isotope composition)

(3) Biological
- (a) tree rings (width, density, stable isotope composition)
- (b) pollen (type, relative abundance or absolute concentration)
- (c) plant macrofossils (age and distribution)
- (d) insects (type and assemblage abundance)
- (e) modern population distribution (refuges and relict populations of plants and animals)

(4) Historical
- (a) written records of environmental indicators (parameteorological phenomena)
- (b) phenological records

(5) Archaeological
- (a) stone tools
- (b) pottery, coins, metal objects

SOURCE: Bradley, 1985 (Table 1.1), with modifications.

---

the ice sheets. When the ice load was removed upon deglaciation the reverse occurred; parts of northeastern Canada, for instance, have rebounded by more than 300 m during the Holocene.

The glacials had many impacts on the landscape. The ice sheets produced characteristic landforms such as cirques, arêtes, U-shaped valleys, and roches moutonnées and transformed drainage patterns, as the lacustrine landscapes of the Canadian Shield and Scandinavia testify. Elsewhere they deposited till and outwash gravels, some as sheets and some as distinctive landforms such as moraines and eskers. Beyond the glacial limit, fine particles blown from outwash plains settled to produce belts of loess in areas like Central Europe, Tajikistan, China, New Zealand, and the Mississippi valley. [*See* Loess.]

Areas equatorward of the great ice caps were also changed. Cyclone-bearing westerlies brought rain to what are now the arid lands of the southwest United States, creating a freshwater body—Lake Bonneville, of which Great Salt Lake is a relict—the size of present-day Lake Michigan. Conversely, because the oceans were cooler, the tropical circulation was weaker, causing the Sahara, the Thar of India and Pakistan, and the Australian deserts and their dune fields to expand. Large tracts of what is now savanna were transformed into sand seas, and the great rainforests of the Amazon and Congo basins were fragmented. [*See* Tropical Climate Change.]

STADIALS AND INTERSTADIALS

Each glacial cycle was internally complex, with phases of intense glacial activity and advance (stadials) being separated by slightly

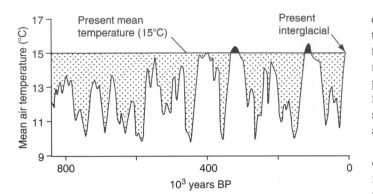

Paleoclimate. Figure 3. Temperature of the Earth for the last 85,000 Years.

Inferred from ice volume derived by oxygen isotope measurements from ice cores.

(After Gates, 1993.)

Paleoclimate. Figure 4. The Possible Maximum Extent of Glaciation in the Pleistocene in the Northern Hemisphere.

C = Cordilleran ice; L = Laurentide ice; S = Scandinavian ice; and A = Alpine ice. (After Goudie, 1992.)

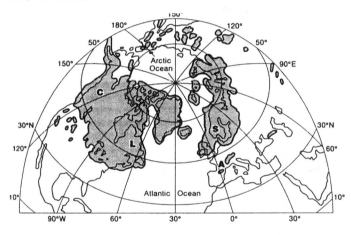

warmer periods (interstadials) when glacial retreat occurred. Short, warm phases called Dansgaard-Oeschger events have been identified in ice-core records: 24 of them have been recognized in the period from 115,000 to 14,000 years ago. [See Dansgaard-Oeschger Cycles.] The nature and causes of such abrupt climatic fluctuations within glacials have been discussed by Adams et al. (1999). Some cold snaps, termed Heinrich events (Andrews, 1998), have been identified in ocean-sediment cores through the evidence of debris rafted by icebergs. At least seven Heinrich events occurred between 66,000 and 12,000 years ago. [See Heinrich Events.]

INTERGLACIALS

The Quaternary interglacials were generally short-lived but appear to have been essentially similar in their climate, fauna, flora, and landforms to the present Holocene interglacial. It was

during the interglacials, perhaps 1–2 degrees warmer than today, that the great ice sheets rapidly retreated and decayed and that forests replaced tundra over the now temperate lands of the northern hemisphere. Much information on conditions in the previous interglacial (the Eemian) has recently been obtained from ice cores extracted from polar ice caps. In particular, their stable isotopic composition provides a means of calculating past atmospheric temperatures.

Birks (1986) has described the general sequence of vegetation development during an interglacial. The first, or cryocratic, phase, represents cold glacial conditions, with sparse assemblages of pioneer plants growing on chemically basic skeletal mineral soils under a dry, continental climate. In the second, or protocratic, phase, there is the onset of interglacial conditions. Rising temperatures allow the base-loving, shade-intolerant herbs, shrubs and trees to migrate and expand quickly to form widespread species-rich grasslands, scrub, and open woodlands, which grow on unleached, fertile soils with a still low humus content. In the third, or mesocratic, phase, temperate deciduous forest and fertile, brown-earth soils develop under warm conditions, allowing the expansion of shade-giving forest genera such as *Quercus* (oak), *Ulmus* (elm), *Fraxinus* (ash), and *Corylus* (hazel), followed by slower immigrants such as *Fagus* (beech) and *Carpinus* (hornbeam). In the fourth and last (retrogressive) telocratic phase, soil deterioration and climatic decline led to the development of open conifer-dominated woods, ericaceous heaths, and bogs growing on less fertile humus-rich podzols and peats.

THE TRANSITION FROM LATE GLACIAL TIMES

The Last Glacial Maximum occurred at around 18,000–20,000 years BP. Studies of the oxygen-isotope composition of ocean sediments suggest that deglaciation started at around 15,000 to 14,500 years BP in the North Atlantic and at 16,500 to 13,000 years BP in the Southern Ocean (Bard et al., 1990). The years between the maximum and the beginning of the Holocene are usually termed the Late Glacial; they were marked by various stadials and interstadials.

The character, identification and correlation of the Late Glacial interstadials need clarification (Anderson, 1997). The classic threefold division of the Late Glacial into two cold zones (I and III) separated by a milder instadial (II) comes from a type section at Allerød, north of Copenhagen in Denmark, where an organic lake mud was exposed between an upper and lower clay, both of which contained pollen of *Dryas octopetala* (mountain avens), a plant tolerant of severely cold climates. The lake muds contained a cool-temperate flora including some tree-birches, and the milder stage which they represented was called the Allerød interstadial. The interstadial itself and the following Younger Dryas temperature reversal are sometimes called the Allerød Oscillation. The Younger Dryas is thought to have started at around 12,700 BP and to have lasted for 1,300 years. [See Younger Dryas.] It was a time when glaciers readvanced in Scotland, and it may have been caused by a rapid cooling of the ocean

Paleoclimate. Glacial Excavation.

During glacial phases of the Quaternary, glaciation was much more extensive than today. This classic U-shaped valley was excavated by glaciers that formed in the mountains of central Portugal.

caused by the breakup of large ice shelves from the Arctic (Ruddiman and McIntyre, 1981), or by a sudden influx of meltwater from the Laurentide ice sheet into the Atlantic via the St. Lawrence River causing salinity changes in the ocean. These in turn affected seawater density and currents, and thus climate (Broecker and Denton, 1989). [*See* Thermohaline Circulation.]

THE HOLOCENE

The end of the Last Glacial period was not the end of environmental change. Indeed, as the Holocene progressed the impact of climatic change was augmented by the increasing role of humans (Roberts, 1998). The Holocene witnessed cold phases when glaciers advanced (neoglaciations), interspersed with warm phases (climatic optima). [*See* Holocene.]

CONCLUSIONS

The history of the Earth demonstrates that climates have been highly variable through time at a range of temporal scales. The precision and resolution of paleoclimatic reconstruction become greater as the present is approached. The causes of these changes are extremely complex but included variations in output of radiation from the Sun, changes in the altitude, extent, and configurations of the continents and oceans in response to plate tectonic activity, changes in the nature of the Earth's orbit with respect to the Sun, and changes in the gas and aerosol content of the atmosphere. Our ability to explain particular climatic changes becomes increasingly speculative as we go back in time. Given the degree, frequency, and (in some cases) the abruptness of changes, it is certain that they have played a major role in evolution and extinction of organisms and that they have, more recently, affected human affairs. For example, the transition from Pleistocene glacial to Holocene interglacial may have been a stimulus for domestication and may have contributed to the demise of some of the Earth's megafauna around 11,000 years ago.

BIBLIOGRAPHY

Adams, J., M. Maslin, and E. Thomas. "Sudden Climate Transitions during the Quaternary." *Progress in Physical Geography* 23 (1999), 1–36. DOI: 10.1177/030913339902300101.

Anderson, D. "Younger Dryas Research and its Implications for Understanding Abrupt Climatic Change." *Progress in Physical Geography* 21 (1997), 230–249. DOI: 10.1177/030913339702100203.

Anderson, D. E., A. S. Goudie, and A. G. Parker. *Global Environments through the Quaternary.* Oxford and New York: Oxford University Press, 2007.

Andrews, J. T. "Abrupt Changes (Heinrich Events) in Late Quaternary North Atlantic Marine Environments." *Journal of Quaternary Science* 13 1998, 3–16. DOI: 10.1002/(SICI)1099–1417(199801/02)13:1<3::AID-JQS361>3.0.CO;2–0.

Bard, E., et al. "The Last Deglaciation in the Southern and Northern Hemispheres." In *Geological History of the Polar Oceans: Arctic versus Antarctic,* edited by V. Bleil and J. Thiede, pp. 405–415. Dordrecht, The Netherlands, and Boston, Mass.: Kluwer, 1990.

Birks, H. J. B. "Quaternary Biotic Changes in Terrestrial and Lacustrine Environments, with Particular Reference to Northwest Europe." In *Handbook of Holocene Palaeoecology and Palaeohydrology,* edited by B. E. Bergland, pp. 3–65. Chichester, U.K., and New York: Wiley, 1986.

Birks, H. J. B. "Changes in Vegetation and Climate during the Holocene in Europe." In *Landscape-Ecological Impact of Climatic Change,* edited by M. M. Boer and R. S. de Groot, pp. 133–158. Amsterdam: IOS Press, 1990.

Bowen, D. Q. *Quaternary Geology.* Oxford: Pergamon, 1978.

Bradley, R. S. *Quaternary Paleoclimatology.* Boston: Allen and Unwin, 1985.

Broecker, W. S., and G. H. Denton. "The Role of Ocean–Atmosphere Reorganizations in Glacial Cycles." *Geochimica et Cosmochimica Acta* 97 (1992), BIO,13917–13951.

Cande, S. S., and D. V. Kent. "A new geomagnetic polarity time scale for the late Cretaceous and Cenozoic." *Journal of geophysical Research* 97 (1992), B10, 13917–13951.

Cronin, T. M. *Principles of Paleoclimatology.* New York: Columbia University Press, 1999.

Crowley, T. J., and G. R. North. *Paleoclimatology.* New York: Oxford University Press, 1991.

Edgar, K. M., et al. "No Extreme Bipolar Glaciation during the Main Eocene Calcite Compensation Shift." *Nature* 448 (2007), 908–911. DOI: 10.1038/nature06053.

Gates, D. M. *Climate Change and Its Biological Consequences.* Sunderland, Mass.: Sinauer, 1993.

Goudie, A. *Environmental Change.* 3d ed. Oxford: Oxford University Press, 1992.

Lowe, J. J., and M. J. C. Walker. *Reconstructing Quaternary Environments.* 2d ed. Harlow, U.K.: Longman, 1997.

Ritchie, J. C., C. H. Gyles, and C. V. Haynes. "Sediment and Pollen Evidence for an Early to Mid-Holocene Humid Period in the Eastern Sahara." *Nature* 314 (1985), 352–355. DOI: 10.1038/314352a0.

Roberts, N. *The Holocene: An Environmental History.* 2d ed. Oxford, U.K., and Cambridge, Mass.: Blackwell, 1998.

Ruddiman, W. F. and A. McIntyre. "The North Atlantic Ocean during the Last Deglaciation." *Palaeogeography, Palaeoclimatology, Palaeoecology* 35 (1981), 145–214. DOI: 10.1016/0031–0182(81)90097–3.

Solomon, S., et al. *Climate Change 2007: The Physical Science Basis. Contribution of Working Group I to the Fourth Assessment Report of the Intergovernmental Panel on Climate Change.* Cambridge and New York: Cambridge University Press, 2007.

Williams, M. A. J., et al. *Quaternary Environments.* 2d cd. London: Arnold, 1998.

Wilson, R. C. L., S. A. Drury, and J. L. Chapman. *The Great Ice Age. Climate Change and Life.* London and New York: Routledge and the Open University, 2000.

—ANDREW S. GOUDIE

PALEOMAGNETIC EVIDENCE OF CRUSTAL MOVEMENT

When an iron-rich igneous rock, such as basalt, solidifies from lava, magnetic particles in the lava align with the magnetic field of that location on the Earth in a way that is consistent with the polarity of the field at that time in Earth history.

Location is expressed in two ways in the magnetic texture of a rock. First is the compass direction of alignment toward a magnetic pole: if the rock's magnetic texture does not align with

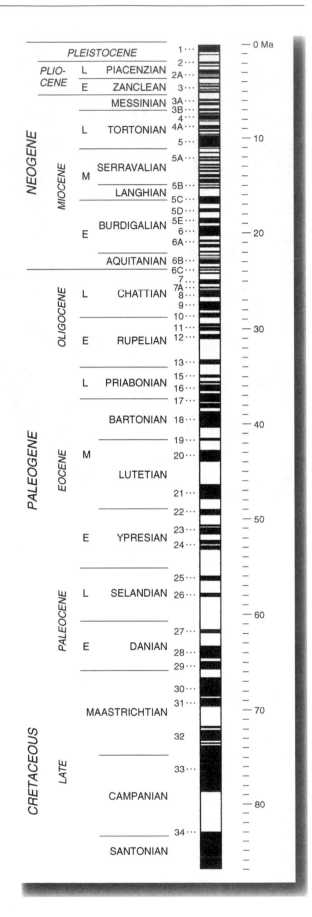

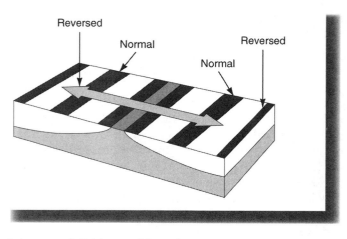

Palemagnetic Evidence of Crustal Movement. FIGURE 2. The Ocean Floor, Showing Polarity Stripes Schematically.

the direction of today's magnetic field in that location, this indicates some movement of the continent (or of the magnetic pole) since the rock was formed. Second is the vertical dip of the alignment. Near a magnetic pole, the rock particles will align with a force field that plunges steeply into the Earth, whereas, near the equator, the field lines run parallel to the Earth's surface. If an ancient basalt in a midlatitude location shows horizontal magnetic alignment, then the rock and its host continent have probably drifted poleward. These two manifestations of paleomagnetism provide vital evidence for the movement of continents but do not suggest a mechanism for that movement.

It is the polarity of the magnetic field at the time of imprint that provides evidence to clinch the idea of plate movement and sea-floor spreading. In certain periods, the Earth's magnetic field has been normal (as today), while in other periods it has been reversed, with north polarity at the south magnetic pole. Before the reversal occurs, the intensity of the Earth's magnetic field declines; then it strengthens again as the new polarity is adopted. Study of hundreds of volcanic rocks of various ages has revealed a series of normal and reversed periods extending back to 85 million years ago (see Figures 1 and 2). When, in the 1960s, magnetic surveys of the Atlantic sea floor showed normal and reversed rocks in a striped pattern symmetrical about the Mid-Atlantic Ridge, it became apparent that outlying pairs of stripes, matching in polarity, were older, while innermost matching pairs were formed most recently. Sea-floor spreading and the continual birth of new ocean floor at the ridge were demonstrated (Figure 2).

Paleomagnetic Evidence of Crustal Movement. FIGURE 1. Geomagnetic Polarity Time Scale. Black periods: normal polarity; White periods: reversed.

(After Cande and Kent, 1992, pp. 13, 935. Copyright by the American Geophysical Union.)

BIBLIOGRAPHY

Monastersky, R. "Earth's Heart Beats with a Magnetic Rhythm." *Science News* (Nov. 20, 1993, 327.

—DAVID J. CUFF

PARKS AND PRESERVES

Parks and preserves are social and cultural institutions as well as natural entities. The word *park*, from Old French and Middle English *parc* (an enclosure for hunting), and the original parks (discounting the Garden of Eden) were the hunting preserves of Persian royalty in Asia Minor between 550 and 350 bce. Another antecedent was the landscaped garden estate of eighteenth-century England—a privatized space dominated by a pastoral idea of nature. A further influence on modern versions, the city park, is the ancient Greek *agora*, a place of public relaxation and shaded recreation.

Public access to exclusive parklands in western Europe, a response to industrialization and urbanization and a function of democratization, began with the opening of London's royal parks in the eighteenth century. Victoria Park in London's East End was the first park of any kind specifically acquired and designed for public use (1842). But Birkenhead Park near Liverpool, established soon after, is better known because, with its informal style, it inspired the world's most famous example, New York City's Central Park (1861). North America's urban park movement was related to the "rural" cemetery phenomenon. From the 1830s, urbanites frequented cemeteries on city outskirts to stroll and picnic. The prototype was Mount Auburn, near Boston, and by the 1970s, cemeteries constituted 35% of the open space in Greater Boston. These enclosures also functioned as de facto wildlife sanctuaries; a 1974 study located 95 species of bird and 20 species of mammal.

NATIONAL PARKS

The national park dominates current conceptions. It is one of ten major categories of nature conservation recognized by the International Union for Conservation of Nature and Natural Resources (World Conservation Congress, IUCN) in 1978, as protected area category number 2. The IUCN definition stresses the national park's ecological role, referring to preservation "in a natural state" of "representative samples of physiographic regions, biotic communities and ... species in danger of extinction to provide ecological stability," and envisaged parks being established in ecosystems "not materially altered by human exploitation and occupation." Yet the conservation of ecological diversity is a relatively recent (largely post-1960s) objective. Moreover, though over 100 countries now boast national parks, many fall far short of IUCN ideals.

The part of the royal forest of Fontainebleau near Paris designated a nature reserve and public recreational area in 1853 (complete with marked hiking trails) was another precursor, but the term "national park" was first employed in the proclamation of Royal National Park near Sydney, Australia (1879). Both Canada and New Zealand had reserved national parks before the words "national park" were first used in the United States (1899). These technicalities aside, the national park as idea and institution is rightly associated with the United States, many nations having been inspired directly by U.S. example. The first national park in all but name was Yellowstone (1872), which differed from previous parks by virtue of its wilder scenery and larger size, the greater measure of public access envisaged, and its ownership by the national government.

The pioneering wave of parks served as surrogates for "Old World" cultural heritage, sources of national pride, and outlets for a desire for contact with nature in its more rugged manifestations. Early parks encompassed lands that possessed what later generations would recognize as wilderness value and biodiversity. But their main aim was to protect monumental scenery from private acquisition or exploitation by extractive industries as "pleasuring ground[s] for the benefit and enjoyment of the people" (to quote the Yellowstone Park Act). Economic development was by no means proscribed, but roads and resort facilities were privileged over logging and mining. During the 1960s, African national parks became vital components of national economies. By 1968, Murchison Falls generated 70% of Uganda's tourist revenue.

Before the 1930s, the only serious contenders for park status beyond Africa (where wildlife spectacle was more often the raison d'être) were dramatic topographies—often alpine. Florida's Everglades National Park (authorized in 1934) marked a sharp departure: biological splendor was placed before scenic feast. Yet Everglades also involved incomplete ecosystem protection; park flora and fauna remained affected by drainage and other agricultural policies beyond the park boundaries. Political and economic requirements usually dictated boundaries, bestowing "island" status. Some African parks and preserves resorted to elephant culling in the late 1970s and early 1980s to deal with overpopulation in confined spaces. Wildlife in Kenya's Amboseli National Park (1947) migrates seasonally onto the lands of Maasai pastoralists.

The birthplace of Europe's first national parks in the early 1900s was northern Scandinavia. This was the continent's last region largely devoid of agriculture, however, and it was hard to replicate similar parks elsewhere in Europe. According to IUCN specifications regarding ownership, environmental conditions, degree of protection, and range of permissible activities, the nine national parks designated in England and Wales during the 1950s are neither national nor parks. These patches of high moorland and mountain, which deviate radically from the central principle of public ownership, encompass not only towns, roads, farms, reservoirs, and quarries but even a nuclear power plant and live artillery ranges, catering to more powerful constituencies than conservationists and recreationists (not least the military). The IUCN classifies them as "Protected Landscapes."

GAME PRESERVES AND OTHER PROTECTIVE UNITS

The distinction between nature preserves (IUCN protected area category 1) and national parks, often blurred, has been clearest in the former Soviet Union. *Zapovedniki* (forbidden areas) were identified in the 1920s specifically to protect rare plants and animals, and use was restricted to ecological study (a major innovation). *Zapovedniki* served as specimens of healthy environments to guide land usages elsewhere. Soviet national parks—sites for outdoor amusement—were installed in the 1960s in response to public pressure for recreational access to *zapovedniki*.

Wildlife preservation was a concern in some national parks during the formative years, and the roles of wildlife preserve and national park have overlapped. Italy's first national park, Gran Paradiso (established in 1922), hitherto a royal hunting reserve, aimed to protect alpine ibex. But wildlife refuges were essentially game reserves, spaces where production of economically valuable species or those prized by sports hunters was maximized regardless of cost to predators. Late nineteenth-century sportsmen in North America and sub-Saharan Africa spearheaded efforts to secure their sport's future by protecting birds and mammals they hoped would spill over into hunting areas. These reserves and refuges were generally smaller than parks (perhaps limited to a few acres covering breeding grounds) and not intended for recreation.

Parks and preserves usually occupied emptied rather than empty spaces. Medieval Europe's peasantry raged against hunting reserves that excluded their traditional activities. Central Park displaced the shacks and piggeries of Irish immigrants, while national parks such as Glacier and Yosemite were carved out of the domain of American Indians. From Italy's Abruzzo National Park (established in 1923) to Amboseli, locals have perceived them as colonial impositions catering to outside interests and resented the loss of opportunities to graze livestock, cut timber, and hunt. The tensions characterizing relations with locals were exemplified by the controversy in India over the creation of tiger reserves that excluded all human use and occupation. Project Tiger (launched 1973) was highly effective; India's Bengal tigers increased from 1,827 in 1972 to 3,015 in 1979. But the project also displaced 40 villages, affecting 6,000 people and their livestock. Villagers denounced it as a collaboration between discredited local elites and international wildlife conservationists that condemned them to perpetual underdevelopment. Resentment was inflamed by a spate of killings by tigers in the late 1970s and early 1980s (conversion of grassland to sugarcane fields south of Dudhwa National Park impinged on tiger habitat).

Parks and preserves have become increasingly sensitive to the interests of indigenous peoples. In the late 1970s, aborigines in Australia's Northern Territory leased their lands to create Kakadu National Park, which incorporated their customary subsistence pursuits. The mission statements of the ten Alaskan parks, preserves, and monuments designated in 1980 refer to the protection of both natural values and traditional cultures by allowing gathering, fishing, and hunting to continue. Native hostility gives way to a new appreciation of parks and preserves as a valuable means to protect the natural resources that constitute their lifeblood.

CONFLICTS BETWEEN USE AND CONSERVATION

Conflicts have also stemmed from the parks' equivocal dual mandate of preservation and public access. The challenge faced by early managers in the developed world, that of providing adequate facilities to persuade people to visit in numbers sufficient to ensure their viability, has been supplanted by that of guaranteeing the survival of treasures in danger of being "loved to death." Though the 1972–1982 period saw unprecedented expansion (new units boosted the protected area by over 80%), the use-versus-preservation conflict intensified. In the 1970s, 25,000 people climbed Japan's Mount Fujiyama daily, and permits and quotas for rafting through the Grand Canyon were introduced. Unregulated rock climbing in the German-Luxembourg Nature Park (established in 1965) nearly wiped out a rare fern, and a surfeit of canoeists threatened its freshwater pearl mussel. Whereas rangers in Africa might risk their lives to protect endangered species such as the white rhinoceros from poachers, their counterparts in the United States formulate plans to ban private vehicles, replacing them with free, locally nonpolluting electric minibuses.

[*See also* Biological Diversity; Biomes; Carrying Capacity; Wilderness and Biodiversity; *and* Wilderness Debates.]

BIBLIOGRAPHY

Anderson, D., and R. Grove, eds. *Conservation in Africa: People, Policies, and Practice*. Cambridge and New York: Cambridge University Press, 1987. Part 2 (pp. 103–186) contains essays analyzing relations between wildlife, parks, and pastoralists in Ethiopia, Kenya, and Tanzania in a historical context.

Beinart, W., and P. Coates. "Nature Reserves and National Parks." In *Environment and History: The Taming of Nature in the USA and South Africa*. London: Routledge, 1995. A concise, properly integrated comparative history of parks and reserves in the United States and South Africa.

Carruthers, J. *The Kruger National Park: A Social and Political History*. Pietermaritzburg, South Africa: University of Natal Press, 1995. This examination of South Africa's premier national park (established in 1926) situates its story within the wider currents of South African history, paying particular attention to relations with local peoples.

Elliott, H., ed. *Second World Conference on National Parks*. Morges, Switzerland: International Union for Conservation of Nature and Natural Resources, 1974.

Federation of Nature and National Parks of Europe (FNNPE). *Loving Them to Death? Sustainable Tourism in Europe's Nature and National Parks*. Grafenau, Germany: FNNPE, 1993. A watchdog organization's report on visitation pressures and proposed solutions.

Greenprints for the Countryside? The Story of Britain's National Parks. London: Allen and Unwin, 1987. A popularized and updated version of MacEwen and MacEwen (1982) focusing on developments since 1981.

Hendee, J. C., G. H. Stankey, and R. C. Lucas. "International Concepts of Wilderness Preservation." In *Wilderness Management*. Washington, D.C.: U.S. Department of Agriculture, Forest Service, 1978. A survey of attitudes to wilderness and wilderness area management from Japan to East Africa that contains considerable insight into national parks and their historical backgrounds.

MacEwen, A., and M. MacEwen. *National Parks: Conservation or Cosmetics?* London: Allen and Unwin, 1982. Part 1 discusses the origins of parks in England and Wales. The rest of the book is a vigorous indictment of their inadequacies. See *Greenprints for the Countryside?* (1987) for a more recent version.

Machlis, G. E., and D. L. Tichnell. *The State of the World's Parks: An International Assessment for Resource Management, Policy, and Research*. Boulder, Colo.: Westview Press, 1985. The first systematic treatment of the various threats facing parks in the early 1980s, based on data from 135 parks in over fifty countries.

McNeely, J. A., and K. R. Miller, eds. *National Parks, Conservation, and Development: The Role of Protected Areas in Sustaining Society*. Washington, D.C.: Smithsonian Institution Press, 1984. Edited by members of the Commission on National Parks and Protected Areas, International Union for Conservation of Nature and Natural Resources (IUCN). These are the proceedings of the Third World Congress on National Parks, Bali, Indonesia, 1982. The second world congress (held in Grand Teton/Yellowstone National Parks, 1972) also resulted in a useful publication (see Elliott, 1974).

Nash, R. "The Confusing Birth of National Parks." *The Michigan Quarterly Review* 16 1977, 216–226. Examines Australian claims and seeks to explain why the term *national park* was not attached to Yellowstone in 1872.

Nelson, J. G., R. F. Needham, and D. L. Mann, eds. *International Experience with National Parks and Related Reserves*. Waterloo, Ontario: University of Waterloo, Department of Geography, 1978. Containing individual papers on a range of countries and types of protected unit (from Israel to Iran) and a wealth of figures and tables, this is the first comparative study of the purposes, effects, and management of nature reserves, past, present, and future.

Runte, A. *National Parks: The American Experience*. 2d ed. Lincoln: University of Nebraska Press, 1987. Still the most authoritative history of U.S. parks from the standpoint of cultural and intellectual history. See Sellars, 1997.

Sellars, R. *Preserving Nature in the National Parks: A History*. New Haven: Yale University Press, 1997. An insider's critique.

Waycott, A. *National Parks of Western Europe*. Southampton, U.K.: Inklon, 1983. A popular guide to eighty-four parks in fifteen countries that contains snippets of useful historical information.

—PETER COATES

PEAK OIL

See Crude Oil Supply.

PERMAFROST

Perennially frozen ground (permafrost) is a unique characteristic of polar regions and high mountains that is fundamental to geomorphic processes and ecological development in tundra and boreal forests. Permafrost-affected regions cover about 23% of the exposed land in the Northern Hemisphere, and the stability of permafrost is important to the fate of ecosystems and human development in Russia, Canada, the United States, and China. Because permafrost properties are temperature-dependent and ice-rich permafrost settles upon thawing, the degradation of the permafrost in response to climate change has important consequences for human infrastructure. Also, thawing permafrost affects surface hydrology by impounding water in sinking areas and draining upland areas, leading to habitat changes for vegetation and wildlife emissions of greenhouse gases, and coastal erosion. The consequences range from site-specific ground collapse to possible global contribution of greenhouse gases.

NATURE OF PERMAFROST

Permafrost is defined as earth material having a temperature below 0°C for two or more years—although most permafrost is hundreds to tens of thousands of years old—and in which most water present remains as ice. Some liquid water may be present, however, depending on the temperature and on the extent to which soil texture and salinity lower the freezing point of water. The upper horizons of soil with permafrost react to seasonal climatic variations by developing a seasonally thawed layer, termed the active layer, above the permafrost table (surface) (Figure 1). In places where permafrost is thawing from above, a talik (perennially unfrozen zone) may develop between the active layer and the permafrost, or around a zone where groundwater has penetrated. Permafrost thickness can vary from a few meters below the surface at the southern margins of permafrost to hundreds of meters below in the continuous permafrost zone.

Permafrost. Figure 1.

Stratigraphy of soil and ice morphology in fine-grained, ice-rich permafrost, illustrating the active layer (A), transient layer (B), intermediate layer with ataxitic ice formed during decrease of the active layer depth with accumulation of organic on the soil surface (C), deeper permafrost with lenticular ice (D), a young ice wedge developed in the intermediate layer, and old ice wedge formed during an earlier period (F). The organic layer (1), permafrost table (2).

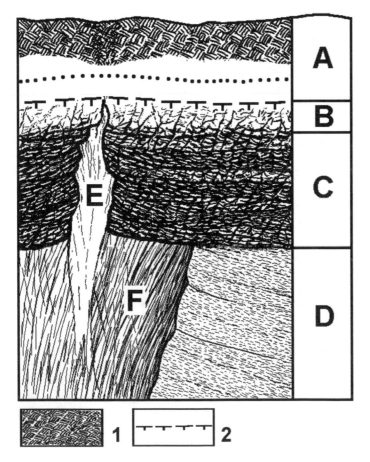

Permafrost properties depend on the geological origin of the soil and the cryogenic origin of the permafrost. Permafrost can form in two ways. Epigenetic permafrost forms when the soil slowly freezes downward after soil deposition has ended. At the depth of initial permafrost formation below the active layer (typically 1–1.5 m), the permafrost slowly freezes downward into unfrozen material, although there is some minor upward freezing as the active layer thins in response to changes in surface vegetation and soil. In contrast, syngenetic permafrost is formed simultaneously with soil deposition. Consequently, two fronts are moving upward: the surface of the accumulating sediment and peat, and the permafrost table at the bottom of the readjusting active layer. Epigenetic and syngenetic permafrost also can develop concurrently in newly exposed sediments with continuing sediment accumulation as frost penetrates downward from the permafrost base, while syngenetic permafrost grows upward into the accumulating sediments.

Ice in permafrost strongly influences the properties of frozen and thawing soil (Johnston, 1981). Ground ice varies widely in size, from microscopic inclusions to large masses up to 50 m, and in distribution within the soil, because of differences in soil texture, moisture, and thermal regime (Figure 2). Ice morphology is classified according to whether it is visible or not and whether it is segregated within a soil matrix or in massive bodies, and by how it is formed. Ice in the soil pore-space may be invisible if the soil is fine-grained. When ice volume exceeds the pore space, the ice is referred to as segregated ice. Lenticular ice (or cryogenic structure) occurs as tiny lenses within a continuous soil matrix and generally forms during rapid freezing of soils. Layered ice occurs as thin to thick, nearly continuous horizontal layers (belts) of ice and typically forms during slow freezing under low-temperature gradients. Reticulate ice has a net-veined appearance and forms during periods of slow adjustment of a thinning active layer. Ataxitic (or suspended) ice is an irregular or chaotic ice matrix containing small, suspended soil inclusions and typically forms in the upper permafrost during long periods of active-layer stability in very cold climates. Segregated ice usually occurs in distinctive vertical sequences in syngenetic permafrost (Figure 1). Massive ice likewise occurs in many forms. Most massive ice forms inside soil, although some forms at the surface and is later buried by sediments. Pingos and palsas (two types of ice-cored mound) have intrusive ice formed by movement of water from areas of high to low pressure. Other massive ice forms when water fills cracks and cavities inside frozen soil. Ice wedges, the most widespread type of massive ice, typically are 2–3 m across the top and extend 2–4 m down into fine-grained soils. They are formed by spring snowmelt filling in the cracks caused by seasonal contraction and expansion of permafrost in cold climates. These ice types vary in their volume and distribution, which greatly affect the sensitivity of permafrost to climate warming.

DISTRIBUTION

Permafrost in the northern hemisphere is divided into four zones based on the abundance of the permafrost (Brown et al.,

Permafrost. Figure 2. Massive Ice from Exposures.

Photograph of the ice wedges is from northern Alaska, the ice complex from the Shirokastan Peninsula, Russia (courtesy M. Grigoriev), and the buried glacial ice from the Alaska Range.

1997): continuous (>90% area with permafrost), discontinuous (50–90%), sporadic (10–50%), and isolated (>0–10%) (Figure 3). These zones are closely related to mean annual air temperatures (MAAT), with approximate temperatures of -6 °C, -6 to -2 °C, -2 to 0°C, and 0 to 2 °C, respectively.

The complex interaction of climatic and ecological processes in permafrost formation and degradation is closely associated with these permafrost zones and can be differentiated into five types of formation (Shur and Jorgenson, 2007). Climate-driven permafrost is formed in the continuous zone, where permafrost forms immediately after the surface is exposed to the atmosphere and even under shallow water. Climate-driven,

ecosystem-modified permafrost occurs in the continuous zone when vegetation succession and organic-matter accumulation lead to development of an ice-rich layer at the top of syngenetic permafrost. During warming climates, permafrost that formed initially as climate-driven can persist in the discontinuous zone for a long time as ecosystem-protected. Climate-driven, ecosystem-protected permafrost, and its associated ground ice, cannot be reestablished (under existing conditions) in the discontinuous zone once degraded, although the near surface can recover as ecosystem-driven permafrost. Ecosystem-driven permafrost forms in the discontinuous zone in poorly drained, low-lying and north-facing landscape conditions under strong influence of ecological processes. Its distribution is greatly affected by the presence of surface water, groundwater movement, topography, soil properties, vegetation, snow, and natural and human disturbance. Finally, ecosystem-protected permafrost persists as sporadic patches under warmer climates, but cannot be reestablished after disturbance.

RESPONSE OF PERMAFROST TO CLIMATE CHANGE

Permafrost has been responding to climatic change over millions of years, and most current permafrost is of Pleistocene age (Sumgin, 1927). The large increase in air temperature (approximately 20°C) at the Pleistocene-Holocene transition led to a large contraction of the permafrost regions; ice-wedge casts have been found as far south as Iowa in North America, whereas at that longitude, permafrost presently extends no further south than the latitude of James Bay. Permafrost degradation during this transition period caused the formation of the contemporary discontinuous zone, where permafrost used to be continuous; the formation of taliks under lakes and rivers; and the reduction of permafrost thickness by thawing of permafrost upward from its base. Permafrost stability thus depends on climate changes over various periods and of varying magnitudes, which can cause permafrost to persist over hundreds to thousands of years, or to be newly formed during cold, snow-poor winters and persist only for years to decades.

Temperature monitoring of deep boreholes in northern Alaska indicates that permafrost warmed 2–4°C in the early 1900s and warmed an additional 3–4°C (Figure 4) at the end of the century (Osterkamp, 2007). In contrast, borehole monitoring in the discontinuous zone of Alaska since the 1980s indicates that permafrost generally has warmed only 0.3–1°C, but temperatures in this zone are already near thawing.

Permafrost is not connected directly to the atmosphere because its thermal regime is mediated by topography, surface water, groundwater movement, soil properties, vegetation, and snow. Topography affects the amount of solar radiation to the soil surface, causing permafrost in the discontinuous zone to occur generally on north-facing slopes that receive less direct radiation and in flat, low-lying areas where vegetation has a greater insulating effect and where air temperatures tend to be colder during winter inversions. Surface water impounded in sinking depressions provides an important positive feedback that enhances degradation. Groundwater in the active layer or

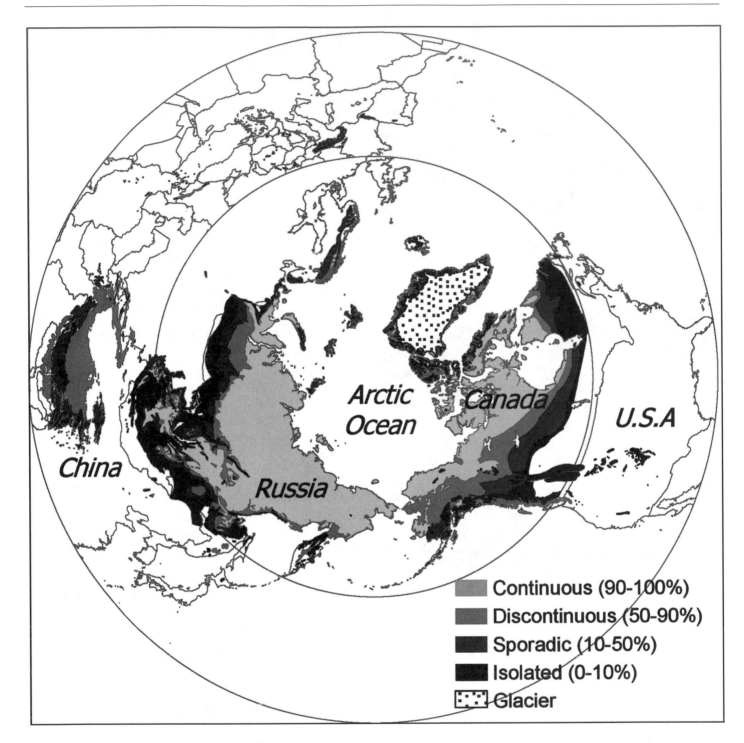

Permafrost. Figure 3. Distribution of Permafrost Zones in the Northern Hemisphere.

(Adapted from Brown et al. 1997).

within permafrost delivers heat and is often surrounded by thawed zones. Soil texture affects soil moisture and thermal properties with the result that gravely soils tend to be well-drained with little difference between thermal conductivities when frozen or thawed. In contrast, surface organic soils, and to a lesser extent clayey and silty soils, tend to be poorly drained and to have much higher thermal conductivities when frozen than when thawed in summer. This difference leads to rapid heat loss in winter and slower heat penetration in summer. Vegetation has a particularly important effect in flat areas through interception of solar radiation, growth of mosses and accumulation of organic matter, and interception of snow by trees and shrubs. Snow protects soil from cooling in winter. Thus, the seasonality (e.g., deep snow in early winter) and depth of snow are extremely important. Because permafrost is

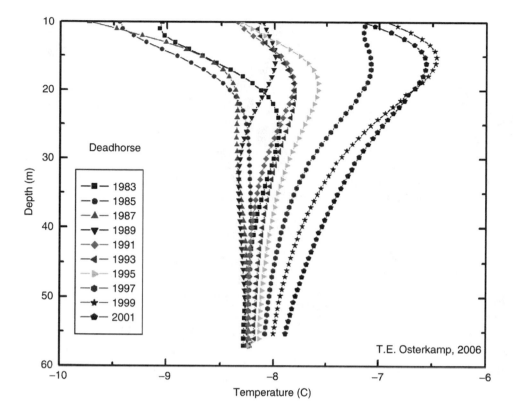

Permafrost. Figure 4. Temperature Profiles at the Healy, Alaska, Site for 1985, 1989, and Subsequent Odd Years to 2005.

greatly affected by these ecological components, permafrost properties evolve along with the successional patterns of ecosystem development. In turn, the patterns of ice growth and degradation influence the patterns of vegetation and soil development. This coevolution of permafrost and ecological characteristics at the ground surface is most evident after disturbance such as river channel migration, lake drainage, and fire (Shur and Jorgenson, 2007).

The dependence of permafrost stability on both air temperatures and ecological factors greatly complicates the prediction of the effects of climate change. Permafrost is more sensitive to climate change in areas without a protective organic layer, such as high Arctic ecosystems. Other regions sensitive to climate change are areas where massive ice is close to the soil surface. Ice wedges are particularly sensitive because the top of ice wedges just below the active layer is constantly adjusting to active layer dynamics. Thus, ice wedges formed during colder climates are not in equilibrium with the contemporary warming climate, as indicated by the recent observations of the abrupt degradation of ice wedges in northern Alaska (Jorgenson et al., 2006). In contrast, shifts in vegetation and rapid accumulation of peat in some ecosystems may act to protect permafrost. For example, at the transition from the Pleistocene to the Holocene, extremely ice-rich permafrost (yedoma) in eolian silt deposits (loess) in many permafrost regions has been preserved despite large temperature increases (Shur and Jorgenson, 2007). Significant

thawing can also occur at the base of the permafrost. The thickness of Pleistocene-age permafrost, in particular, was determined by the balance of the geothermal heat flux upward through the permafrost and heat loss from the surface during the earlier colder climate. With a constant heat input in the bottom and less heat lost from the top, permafrost thickness is out of equilibrium with the contemporary climate and surface conditions.

The thawing of ice-rich soils causes the surface to subside, creating depressions in the ground surface called thermokarst (Figure 5). The types of thermokarst and the ecological implications are extremely variable depending on climate, topography, soil texture, hydrology, and amounts and types of ground ice (Jorgenson and Osterkamp, 2005). Thawing can occur downward from expansion of the active layer, laterally because of heat flow from surface and groundwater, internally from groundwater intrusion, and upward from the bottom near surface water.

Disturbance of vegetation and soil by human activity and wildfire are important factors contributing to permafrost degradation. Stripping vegetation by fire or human activities leads to an increase in the active layer and degradation of permafrost, which in many cases can be irreversible. Mining, oil development, settlements, logging, and farming that have become widespread since the beginning of the twentieth century have been important in localized degradation of permafrost (Brown and Grave, 1979). Even more widespread are the effects of fire on eliminating the vegetation canopy and moss layer, removing a portion of the surface peat and reducing the albedo (Van Cleve and Viereck, 1983). Large wildfires in recent years have been attributed to warming and drying climates in boreal forest

Permafrost. FIGURE 5. Thermokarst Modes.

Photographs of common thermokarst modes in Alaska: (A) thermokarst lakes and shore bogs; (B) collapse-scar fens; (C) collapse-scar bogs; (D) thaw slump; (F) polygonal troughs; (F) thermokarst pit with drowing birch trees.

regions. This combination of increased wildfire and climate change greatly increases the vulnerability of permafrost in the discontinuous zone.

Substantial effort has been made to model the effects of climate change on permafrost distribution. Site-specific models (Romanovsky and Osterkamp, 1997) have shown that changes in snow depth can be as important as warming temperatures. Landscape-level models that incorporate topography, vegetation, and soils and that reasonably approximate permafrost distribution in the discontinuous zone, have been developed, but these have focused only on vertical heat transfer through soils and have ignored the lateral degradation of permafrost critical to many of the common types of thermokarst (Wright et al., 2000). Finally, numerical models have attempted to predict the changes in permafrost distribution in the northern hemisphere based on regional climatic patterns. Of five models used to simulate permafrost changes, the GFDL-R30_c model with intermediate results predicts the total extent of near-surface permafrost will decrease 23% by 2080 (ACIA, 2005). Accuracy of the models has been limited, however, by the difficulties associated with the critical role played by small-scale variation in vegetation, soil, and permafrost properties (ACIA, 2005).

Progress in understanding the response of permafrost to climatic change will depend, in part, on recognizing permafrost as an interacting component of dynamic ecosystems. Current efforts to assess the effects of global warming on permafrost have focused on the direct linkage of increasing air temperature, snow thickness, and permafrost temperature. To improve the accuracy of projections of permafrost temperature and distribution, models will need higher-resolution regional climatic input, more explicit vegetation and soil components, and increased resolution of differences in upper soil layers, and must be validated in a more spatially comprehensive manner (ACIA, 2005). An additional challenge is that vegetation, soil, and snow characteristics will also be changing in the future.

CONSEQUENCES OF THAWING PERMAFROST TO SOCIETIES AND ECOSYSTEMS

The societal and ecological consequences of permafrost degradation include damage to human infrastructure, changes in the hydrologic regime and freshwater discharge, changes in habitat for fish and wildlife, increased emissions of methane and alteration of carbon sequestration, potential effects on gas hydrates in subsea permafrost, thaw-slumping on slopes, and accelerated coastal erosion. The magnitude of these changes will depend on thermal changes and ground ice conditions.

Threats to human facilities from permafrost degradation include decreased bearing capacities of pile foundations of buildings and aboveground pipelines, impairment of road surfaces, compromising of large mine-tailings impoundments that rely on permafrost to minimize groundwater leaching, reduced use of ice- and snow-roads for transportation in winter, damage of structures from landslides, and contamination of runoff or groundwater from failure of industrial and military waster sumps and village sewage lagoons that are critical to isolating

Permafrost. FIGURE 6. Thermokarst Damage.

Damage from thermokarst to the Old Richardson Highway in central Alaska (photo by Alaska Department of Transportation), to the Copper River Railroad (1960 photo by O. Ferrians), and from coastal erosion at Shishmaref, Alaska (photo by Alaska Corps of Engineers).

wastes (Figure 6). The costs associated with this damage are already large (ACIA, 2005).

Hydrologic changes caused by degrading permafrost alter Arctic and boreal ecosystems (Woo, 1990). Permafrost prevents subsurface drainage and affects abundance of water runoff. In upland areas, degradation of permafrost can lead to subsurface drainage and loss of wetlands on hillslopes. Loss of this impermeable barrier allows rainfall to infiltrate deeper into the soil and percolate down to groundwater instead of running off the surface or evaporating. Increased freshwater discharge in springs and streams, particularly during winter, may be related to increased infiltration of water into the groundwater system. In low-lying areas, initial permafrost degradation in fine-grained, ice-rich soils can create isolated waterbodies that increase evaporation and reduce runoff. The reduction of surface runoff in favor of groundwater input is likely to change the chemistry of freshwater discharge from high in dissolved organic carbon to high in dissolved minerals (Fey et al., 2007).

Habitats affected by thawing permafrost become drier in upland areas and wetter in lowland areas as forests are converted to lakes and bogs (Jorgenson and Osterkamp, 2005). With drying soils, black spruce and larch (tamarack) forests will be replaced by birch, aspen, white spruce, and lodgepole pine that are better adapted to well-drained soils. Birds and mammals adapted to late-successional forests will be replaced by those adapted to more productive vegetation on permafrost-free sites. Thermokarst lakes in flat boreal and tundra regions are already habitats important to a wide range of waterbirds, and these habitats are likely to expand in low-lying landscapes. If there is too little ground ice for thermokarst lake development, or if accumulation of sphagnum mosses is rapid, nutrient-poor bogs develop. Although bogs support a diverse moss flora, they are poor habitats for most vascular plants, birds, and mammals. Collapse-scar fens that develop in degrading areas with groundwater movement have more productive herbaceous vegetation useful to herbivores.

Methane emissions from thermokarst lakes, fens, and bogs are likely to increase with their expansion and contribute to atmospheric concentrations of methane (Christensen et al., 2004). The net effect of permafrost degradation on the carbon balance of tundra and boreal soils associated with CO_2 release, a release that occurs from drying soils and from sequestration in carbon in peat of wetter ecosystems remains unclear (ACIA, 2005). The fate of the large reservoir of methane sequestered in gas hydrates in subsea permafrost is uncertain (Judge and Majorowicz, 1992).

Coastal erosion of permafrost soils along the margins of the Arctic Ocean contributes to the loss of habitat, endangers villages, and contributes long-sequestered carbon to marine ecosystems (Rachold et al., 2000). Permafrost soils initially are resistant to erosion, but with thawing of ground ice they become highly erodible. Erosion rates are greatest where ground ice volumes are high and cliffs are exposed to large stretches of open ocean at the end of summer, when the sea ice has retreated its, maximum distance from the shore. Long-term average erosion rates as high as 10 m/yr have been observed along some exposed, ice-rich sections of the Beaufort Sea coast. The shore erosion is a hazard to many villages, such as Shishmaref and Kivalina, Alaska, and Tuktoyaktuk, Northwest Territories.

BIBLIOGRAPHY

ACIA (Aretic Climate Impact Assessment). Impacts of a Warming Arctic: Arctic Climate Assessment. Cambridge, Cambridge University Press, 2005.

Brown, J., and N. A. Grave. *Physical and Thermal Disturbance and Protection of Permafrost*. Special Report 79–5. Hanover, NH: U.S. Army Cold Regions Research and Engineering Laboratory, 1979.

Brown, J., et al. *Circum-Arctic Map of Permafrost and Ground Ice Conditions*. Circum-Pacific Map Series CP-45. Reston, VA: U.S. Geological Survey, 1997.

Christensen, T. R., et al. "Thawing Sub-Arctic Permafrost: Effects on Vegetation and Methane Emissions." *Geophysical Research Letters* 31, L04501 2004. DOI: 10.1029/2003GL018680.

Frey, K. E., D. I. Siegel, and L. C. Smith. "Geochemistry of West Siberian Streams and Their Potential Response to Permafrost Degradation." *Water Resources Research* 43, W03406 (2007). DOI: 10.1029/2006WR004902.

International Permafrost Association. http://www.ipa-permafrost.org/ (accessed June 3, 2008).

Johnston, G. H., ed. *Permafrost: Engineering Design and Construction*. Toronto and New York: Wiley, 1981.

Jorgenson, M. T., and T. E. Osterkamp. "Response of Boreal Ecosystems to Varying Modes of Permafrost Degradation." *Canadian Journal of Forest Research* 35 (2005), 2100–2111.

Jorgenson, M. T., Y. Shur, and E. R. Pullman. "Abrupt Increase in Permafrost Degradation in Arctic Alaska." *Geophysical Research Letters* 33, L02503 (2006). DOI: 10.1029/2005GL024960.

Judge, A. S., and J. A. Majorowicz. "Geothermal Conditions for Gas Hydrate Stability in the Beaufort-Mackenzie Area: The Global Change Aspect." *Global and Planetary Change* 6 (1992), 251–263. DOI: 10.1016/0921–8181(92)90041–8.

Osterkamp, T. E. "Characteristics of the Recent Warming of Permafrost in Alaska." *Journal of Geophysical Research* 112, F02S02 (2007). DOI: 10.1029/2006JF000578.

"Permafrost." Geological Survey of Canada. http://gsc.nrcan.gc.ca/permafrost (accessed June 3, 2008).

Permafrost Laboratory, University of Alaska Fairbanks. http:// www.gi.alaska.edu/snowise/permafrost-lab/(accessed June 3, 2008).

Rachold, V., et al. "Coastal Erosion vs Riverine Sediment Discharge in the Arctic Shelf Seas." *International Journal of Earth Sciences* 89 (2000), 450–460. DOI: 10.1007/s005310000113.

Romanovsky, V. R., and T. E. Osterkamp. "Thawing of the Active Layer on the Coastal Plain of the Alaskan Arctic." *Permafrost and Periglacial Processes* 8 (1997), 1–22. DOI: 10.1002/(SICI)1099–1530(199701)8:1<1::AID-PPP243>3.0.CO;2-U.

Shur, Y. L., and M. T. Jorgenson. "Patterns of Permafrost Formation and Degradation in Relation to Climate and Ecosystems." *Permafrost and Periglacial Processes* 18 (2007), 7–19. DOI: 10.1002/ppp.582.

"State of the Cryosphere: Permafrost." National Snow and Ice Data Center. (accessed June 3, 2008).

Sumgin, M. I. *Permafrost in USSR*. [In Russian.] Vladivostok: Far-East Geophysical Observatory, 1927.

Van Cleve, K., and L. A. Viereck. "A Comparison of Successional Sequences Following Fire on Permafrost-Dominated and Permafrost-Free Sites in Interior Alaska." In *Permafrost: Fourth International Conference Proceedings*. Washington, D.C.: National Academy Press, 1983.

Woo, M. "Consequences of Climatic Change for Hydrology in Permafrost Zones." *Journal of Cold Regions Engineering* 4 (1990), 15–20. DOI: 10.1061/(ASCE)0887–381X(1990)4:1(15).

Wright, J. F., M. W. Smith, and A. E. Taylor. "Potential Changes in Permafrost Distribution in the Fort Simpson and Norman Wells Areas." In *The Physical Environment of the Mackenzie Valley, Northwest Territories: A Baseline for the Assessment of Environmental Change*, GSC Bulletin 547, edited by L. D. Dyke and G. R. Brooks. Ottawa: Geological Survey of Canada, 2000.

—M. Torre Jorgenson and Yuri L. Shur

PESSIMISM

See Catastrophist-Cornucopian Debate.

PEST MANAGEMENT

Organisms are considered to be pests when they cause problems in crops or livestock, compete with humans for food and fiber, or otherwise cause economic or other problems for humans. The range of pests is wide, including insects, nematodes, mites, plant pathogens, vertebrate pests, and weeds. Their distribution and economic effects depend on a wide range of factors that include changes in farming patterns and in agroclimatic and ecological conditions. Pests have coexisted with humans from the beginning of civilization. Whenever humans engage in agriculture, pest problems emerge, particularly weeds, to the extent that in the tropics most of the cultural practices associated with crop production are directly or indirectly related to the control of weeds; hence the assertion that "every field always has a weed problem."

Pest management should aim to manipulate the pests and their environment in such a way as to maintain populations below levels that cause economic crop losses, thereby protecting crops from pest damage and/or destruction. Pest management requires the designing of cropping systems or the development of productive farming systems that minimize farmers' economic, health, and environmental risks by using a combination of control practices such as host-plant resistance, high-quality seeds, crop rotation, field sanitation, sound farming practices, and judicious use of pesticides (herbicides, insecticides, nematocides, etc.) at critical periods during the cropping period. Pest management takes into consideration the agroecosystem, the interaction of weather with farming practices, and the population dynamics of coexisting organisms (including humans and their environment) to avoid altering the delicate balance of the ecosystem.

CROP LOSSES

Estimates of crop losses vary widely by location and by year, but about one-third of potential global agricultural production in the form of food, fiber, and feed in developing countries is destroyed annually by over 20,000 pest species. Total annual losses are estimated at about U.S.$300 billion. Estimates of average yield loss range from 30 to 40%. Crop losses are generally much higher in many tropical and subtropical countries; total losses are not uncommon in such countries because of a climate favorable to the proliferation and growth of pests, limited resources for crop protection programs, and the continuing intensification of agricultural production to meet food demands and income needs.

USE OF AGROCHEMICALS

The need for rapid increases in agricultural productivity to meet the food demands of growing human populations has caused agricultural scientists to develop higher-yielding crop varieties. Many such crop varieties are grown intensively in vast areas in monocultures with complementary yield-enhancing inputs such as fertilizers and irrigation. Pest attack under such conditions can be damaging, especially if new pests have emerged for which resistant crop varieties are not available. However, host-plant resistance to insects and diseases in particular should always be the first line of defense in pest management, and the belief that traditional varieties have more resistance to pests than modern varieties is mostly unfounded. Farmers have in the past used mixtures of crops or crop varieties to try to fend off pest attack.

Pesticides are used in pest management as one of several practices to keep pest populations below levels that would cause damage. Pesticides can also help to protect the crops from total loss or damage due to pests. Agrochemicals are used not only in agriculture but also to control residential pests. Inappropriate use of pesticides has sometimes caused problems including toxicity to nontarget organisms, among them humans and animals; residue on crops or environmental contamination; pest resistance to pesticides; and the need for frequent subsequent applications.

Pesticide use in agriculture increased after World War II, as agriculture became more intensive and crop yields continued to improve. Also, a wide array of chemicals became available in most Western countries, offering immediate, cheap, and reliable protection against pests. Most of these chemicals are petroleum-based and were affected when oil prices began to rise in the early 1970s. Also, the potential environmental costs of chemical pest control began to be recognized, and public awareness of the economic, health, and environmental risks of pesticides increased. Policy- and decision-makers in a number of countries are thus faced with growing public environmental concerns along with rising concern about higher costs of pest protection in highly specialized farming operations in developed countries.

Today, it is not only environmentalists who are concerned about pesticide availability and use. Farmers are increasingly worried that in the future many inputs on which they depend may not be available, or may not be as effective or as affordable as in the past. Farmers are therefore searching for farming systems and related practices that are more sustainable, yet productive and profitable, through intensive management of available internal resources.

RECENT AND FUTURE STRATEGIES

Pesticides are often a necessary means of protecting crops and ornamental plants from complete loss or damage by pests, and their proper use can be a low-risk practice. Nevertheless, there are still risks, including increasing resistance of some pests to certain pesticides and environmental contamination or damage to nontarget species. For these reasons, farmers and scientists are seeking more effective ways to combat pests in production systems. Integrated pest management (IPM) was developed as a way to combat pests by using a combination of tried-and-tested and new technologies in a rational, integrated way. Practices used include (1) varietal resistance, (2) new-generation pesticides, sometimes biodegradable, with short life spans in the field, (3) sex attractants (substances that attract males or females of the target pests to traps, baiting stations, or other control systems), (4) juvenile hormones that interfere with pest maturation, and (5) modifications of cropping patterns and practices. IPM is knowledge- and management-intensive, and involves training of extension workers and farmers in target areas to help

them in its implementation. Key areas of training include recognition of pests in the field, identification of beneficial and harmful organisms, determination of when proper treatment thresholds have been attained, and setting of harmful and beneficial pests against each other to the point of restoring an ecological balance.

Diversified farming and multiple cropping systems traditionally adopt crop rotations to control pests, conserve moisture, and maintain adequate productivity. The adoption of integrated cropping and livestock systems has often resulted in lower feed costs, recycling of waste, and stabilized farm incomes. In turn, such systems can lead to a more stable environment that allows the density and variety of beneficial parasites and predators alike to increase.

Hopes for future success lie in finding ways of combining sound management practices with emerging tools and technologies, such as biotechnology and microcomputers, along with traditional knowledge of farmers that can contribute to IPM. An example of such traditional knowledge is the neem tree (*Azadirachta indica*), which from African and Asian experience is known to have pest-control properties derived from natural plant chemicals. Such plants are used in their natural forms at the village level by farmers with limited resources.

Biotechnology has much to offer in pest management. It has already produced diagnostic tools for identifying and managing pests in crops, and genetic engineering shows great potential for new approaches to pest management. For example, scientists recently discovered the gene that causes the *Bacillus thuringiensis* (Bt) bacterium to produce a protein that is active against certain insect pests. This gene was inserted into cotton to enable the plant to produce the protein on its own, but without changing the plant's composition. The Bt protein in transformed cotton is able to repel or kill budworms, thus eliminating the need for artificial chemical pesticides. Also, new, less hazardous chemicals can be sprayed in fields prior to planting of crops to kill the weeds, without affecting the crop later on. This eliminates the need to plow and thus minimizes soil erosion.

[*See also* Agriculture and Agricultural Land; *and* Chemical Industry.]

BIBLIOGRAPHY

Grainge, M., and S. Ahmed. *Handbook of Plants with Pest-Control Properties.* New York: Wiley, 1987.
Hahn, S. K., and F. E. Caveness, eds. *Integrated Pest Management for Tropical Root and Tuber Crops.* Proceedings of the Workshop on Global Status and Prospects for Integrated Pest Management of Root and Tuber Crops in the Tropics. Ibadan, Nigeria: IITA, 1987.
Haney, P. B., et al. *Reducing Insecticide Use and Energy Costs in Citrus Pest Management.* Davis: University of California, 1997.
Magretta, J. "Growth Through Global Sustainability: An Interview with Monsanto's CEO, Robert B. Shapiro." *Harvard Business Review* (January–February 1997).
Waage, J. "Making IPM Work: Developing Country Experience and Prospects." In *Agriculture and Environmental Challenges: Proceedings of the Thirteenth Agricultural Sector Symposium*, edited by J. P. Srivastava and H. Alderman. Washington, D.C.: World Bank, 1993.
Wiebers, U.-C. *Integrated Pest Management and Pesticide Regulation in Developing Asia.* Washington, D.C.: World Bank, 1993.

Yudelman, M., A. Ratta, and D. Nygaard. *Pest Management: Looking to the Future.* Washington, D.C.: International Food Policy Research Institute, 1998.

—DONALD L. PLUCKNETT AND ROBERT B. KAGBO

PHOSPHORUS CYCLE

The global phosphorus cycle has four major components: (1) tectonic uplift and exposure of phosphorus-bearing rocks to the forces of weathering; (2) physical erosion and chemical weathering of rocks, producing soils and providing dissolved and particulate phosphorus to rivers; (3) riverine transport of phosphorus to lakes and the ocean; and (4) sedimentation of phosphorus associated with organic and mineral matter that is buried in aquatic sediments The cycle begins anew with uplift of sediments into the weathering regime.

Phosphorus is an essential nutrient for all life forms. It is a key element in fundamental biochemical reactions involving genetic material (DNA, RNA) and energy transfer (ATP), and in structural support of organisms provided by membranes (phospholipids) and bone (the biomineral hydroxyapatite [hydroxy calcium phosphate]). Photosynthetic organisms utilize phosphorus, carbon, and other essential nutrients to build their tissues, using energy from the sun. Biological productivity is contingent upon the availability of phosphorus to these organisms, which constitute the base of the food chain in both terrestrial and aquatic ecosystems.

Phosphorus locked up in bedrock, soils, and sediments is not directly available to organisms. Conversion of unavailable forms to dissolved phosphate, which can be directly assimilated, occurs through geochemical and biochemical reactions at various stages in the global phosphorus cycle. In environments with adequate phosphorus, production of biomass results in the deposition of organic matter in soil and sediments, where it acts as a source of fuel and nutrients for microbial communities. Microbial activity in soils and sediments, in turn, strongly influences the concentration and chemical form of phosphorus incorporated into the geological record.

TERRESTRIAL PHOSPHORUS CYCLE

In terrestrial systems, phosphorus resides in three pools: bedrock, soil, and living organisms (biomass). Weathering of continental bedrock is the principal source of phosphorus to the soils that support continental vegetation; atmospheric deposition is relatively unimportant. Phosphorus is weathered from bedrock by the dissolution of phosphorus-bearing minerals such as apatite ($Ca_{10}[PO_4]_6[OH,F,Cl]_2$), the most abundant primary phosphorus mineral in crustal rocks. Weathering reactions are driven by the exposure of minerals to acids mainly derived from microbial activity. Phosphate solubilized during weathering is available for uptake by terrestrial plants and is returned to the soil by the decay of dead plant material.

Low phosphate concentrations are found in soil-pore solutions as a result of phosphorus sorption by various soil constituents, particularly oxyhydroxides of ferric iron and aluminum. Sorption is considered the most important process controlling the terrestrial bioavailability of phosphorus. Plants have different physiological strategies for obtaining phosphorus despite low soil-solution concentrations, including increasing root volume and surface area, the secretion by plant roots or associated fungi of chelating compounds that solubilize phosphorus bound with ferric iron and calcium, and the release of enzymes or acids in the root vicinity to solubilize phosphate. Plants also minimize phosphorus loss by resorbing from their leaves much of their phosphorus prior to litterfall, and by efficient recycling of phosphorus from fallen litter. In extremely unfertile soils (e.g., in tropical rainforests) phosphorus recycling is so efficient that topsoil contains virtually no phosphorus; it is all tied up in biomass.

Systematic changes in the total amount and chemical form of phosphorus occur during soil development. In initial stages, phosphorus is present mainly as primary minerals such as apatite. In midstage soils, the reservoir of primary apatite is diminished; less soluble secondary minerals and organic phosphorus make up an increasing fraction of soil phosphorus. In highly weathered soils, phosphorus is partitioned mainly between refractory minerals and organic phosphorus. At this latest stage of soil development, atmospheric phosphorus deposition can take on disproportionate importance as a source of bioavailable phosphorus.

TRANSPORT OF PHOSPHORUS FROM CONTINENTS TO THE OCEAN

Phosphorus is transferred from the continental to the oceanic reservoir primarily by rivers. Deposition via atmospheric dust is a minor flux. Groundwater seepage to the coastal ocean is a potentially important but undocumented flux.

Riverine phosphorus derives from weathered continental rocks and soils. Dissolved phosphorus in rivers occurs in both inorganic and organic forms. The scant data on dissolved organic phosphorus suggests that it may account for 50% or more of dissolved riverine phosphorus. By most estimates, over 90% of the phosphorus delivered by rivers to the ocean is in particulate form. The chemical form of phosphorus associated with riverine particles is variable and depends on drainage basin geology and topographic relief, and on climatically controlled factors such as runoff. Available data suggest that approximately 20–40% of phosphorus in suspended particulate matter is organic. The majority of inorganic phosphorus is found in ferric oxyhydroxides and apatite, but aluminum oxyhydroxides and clays may also be significant carriers of the element.

The fate of phosphorus entering the ocean via rivers is variable. Some phosphorus is deposited in estuarine and coastal sediments by the coagulation of humic-iron complexes and by biological uptake and sedimentation of biogenic matter. A portion of suspended and sedimented phosphorus is released into the water column by various biogeochemical reactions, including desorption from freshwater particles entering high-ionic-strength marine waters, release of phosphorus from decaying organic matter, and dissolution of phosphorus-containing minerals. Estimates of the flux of dissolved phosphorus entering the ocean must take into account the amount of particulate phosphorus released to solution when rivers enter the ocean.

THE MARINE PHOSPHORUS CYCLE

Phosphorus in its simplest form, dissolved orthophosphate (PO_4^{3-}), is taken up by photosynthetic organisms (phytoplankton) at the base of the marine food web. When this pool of phosphorus is exhausted, organisms may utilize more complex forms by converting them to orthophosphate by means of enzymatic and microbiological reactions. In the open ocean, most phosphorus contained in biogenic particles is recycled in the upper water column. Efficient stripping of phosphate from surface waters by photosynthesis, combined with a buildup of phosphate at depth, where it is released by the decay of biogenic particles, results in markedly lower concentrations in waters less than 1,000 meters deep. The progressive accumulation of respiration-derived phosphate at depth along the global deep-water circulation trajectory results in higher phosphate concentrations in the deep Pacific Ocean than in the North Atlantic, where deep water is initially formed by the sinking of cold surface waters in polar regions.

The sole means of phosphorus removal from the oceans is by burial in marine sediments. The phosphorus flux to shelf and slope sediments is by most estimates larger than the phosphorus flux to the deep sea for several reasons. Coastal waters receive continentally derived nutrients via rivers, which stimulate high rates of primary productivity relative to the open ocean. The resulting higher flux of organic matter to sediments is accompanied by a larger terrigenous flux and higher sedimentation rates. Because of the shorter water column in coastal waters, less decay of organic matter occurs prior to deposition. These factors combine to enhance the retention of sedimentary phosphorus. During high sea level stands, the sedimentary phosphorus reservoir on continental margins expands, increasing the phosphorus removal flux and therefore shortening the oceanic element's residence time.

Predominantly terrigenous shelf and slope (hemipelagic) sediments and abyssal (pelagic) sediments have distinct phosphorus distributions. All are dominated by authigenic (formed in place) calcium-phosphate compounds (mostly apatite), but this reservoir is more important in pelagic sediments. Phosphorus is also found bound with ferric iron (mostly oxyhydroxides) and in organic forms in both environments, although detrital apatite (formed by mechanical disintegration of rock) is important only in hemipelagic sediments. Certain coastal environments characterized by extremely high, upwelling-driven biological productivity and low terrigenous input are enriched in authigenic apatite; these are proto-phosphorite deposits. A unique process contributing to the loss of phosphorus from sea water in pelagic environments is the sorptive removal of phosphate onto ferric oxyhydroxides created in midocean ridge hydrothermal systems.

Solubilization of particulate phosphorus by microbial activity in sediments causes dissolved phosphate to accumulate in sediment pore waters, promoting the release of phosphate to bottom waters. The combined flux from coastal and abyssal sediments to sea water is estimated to exceed the total riverine phosphorus flux to the ocean. Reprecipitation of pore-water phosphorus in secondary minerals in sediments can also occur, effectively reducing the return flux of phosphate to overlying sea water. The balance between these two processes impacts the marine phosphorus cycle by affecting the amount of phosphorus available for primary productivity in oceanic surface waters.

PHOSPHORUS AS A LIMITING NUTRIENT

In terrestrial soils and in the surface waters of lakes and the ocean the concentration of dissolved orthophosphate is typically low. When bioavailable phosphorus is exhausted before more abundant nutrients, it limits biological productivity. Phosphorus limitation in lakes is widely accepted, and terrestrial soils are often phosphorus-limited. In the oceans, however, phosphorus limitation is the subject of controversy.

The prevailing wisdom favors nitrogen as the limiting nutrient in the oceans. Limitation by phosphorus can also occur in marine systems, however, there sometimes being a seasonal shift from nitrogen to phosphorus limitation in concert with changes in environmental factors such as upwelling and river runoff. Whereas an abundant reservoir of nitrogen (gaseous N_2) in the atmosphere can be rendered bioavailable by nitrogen-fixing organisms, phosphorus supply to the ocean is limited to that weathered off the continents and delivered by rivers. Because continental weathering controls phosphorus supply to the oceans, phosphorus limitation is more likely than nitrogen limitation on geological time scales.

HUMAN IMPACTS ON THE GLOBAL PHOSPHORUS CYCLE

The mining of phosphate rock (mostly from phosphorite deposits, ancient marine sediments enriched in phosphorus) for use as agricultural fertilizer increased dramatically in the latter half of the twentieth century. In addition to fertilizer use, deforestation, increased cultivation, and urban and industrial waste disposal all have enhanced phosphorus transport from terrestrial to aquatic systems, often with deleterious results. For example, elevated phosphorus concentrations in rivers resulting from these activities have resulted in eutrophication in some lakes and coastal areas, stimulating nuisance algal blooms and promoting hypoxic or anoxic conditions harmful or lethal to natural populations.

Increased erosion due to forest clear-cutting and widespread cultivation has increased riverine suspended-matter concentrations, and the riverine flux of particulate phosphorus has increased as a result. Dams, in contrast, decrease sediment loads in rivers and therefore diminish phosphorus flux to the sea. The overall effect has been a large increase in riverine phosphorus flux to the oceans as a result of human activities.

LINKS TO OTHER BIOGEOCHEMICAL CYCLES

The biogeochemical cycles of phosphorus and carbon are linked through photosynthetic uptake and release during respiration. During times of elevated marine biological productivity, enhanced uptake of carbon dioxide by photosynthetic organisms results in increased uptake of atmospheric carbon dioxide by oceanic surface waters, which persists until the supply of the least abundant nutrient is exhausted. On geologic time scales, phosphorus is likely to function as the limiting nutrient and thus regulate atmospheric carbon dioxide by limiting its draw-down by marine photosynthetic activity. This connection between nutrients and atmospheric carbon dioxide may have played a role in triggering or enhancing the global cooling that resulted in glacial episodes in the geologic past. [*See* Biogeochemical Cycles.]

The phosphorus and oxygen cycles are linked through the chemistry of iron. Unstable at the Earth's surface in the presence of oxygen, reduced (ferrous) iron oxidizes to form ferric iron oxyhydroxides, which are extremely efficient scavengers of dissolved phosphate. The resupply of phosphate to surface waters, where it can fertilize biological productivity, is reduced when oceanic bottom waters are well oxygenated and ferric oxyhydroxides are present. During times in Earth's history when oxygen was not abundant in the atmosphere (the Precambrian), and when expanses of the deep ocean were anoxic (e.g., the Cretaceous), there may have been much higher concentrations of dissolved phosphate in the deep sea owing to the diminished importance of sequestration with ferric oxyhydroxides. This iron-phosphorus-oxygen coupling produces a negative feedback that may have kept atmospheric O_2 within the narrow range of concentrations required to sustain aerobic life throughout the Phanerozoic. Thus, it is in the oceans that the role of phosphorus as a limiting nutrient has the greatest repercussions for the global carbon and oxygen cycles.

[*See also* Carbon Cycle; Mining; *and* Soils.]

BIBLIOGRAPHY

Chadwick, O. A., et al. "Changing Sources of Nutrients during Four Million Years of Ecosystem Development." *Nature* 397 (1999), 491–497. DOI: 10.1038/17276.

Colman, A. S., and H. D. Holland. "The Global Diagenetic Flux of Phosphorus from Marine Sediments to the Oceans: Redox Sensitivity and the Control of Atmospheric Oxygen Levels." In *Marine Authigenesis: From Global to Microbial*, edited by C. R. Glenn, L. Prévôt-Lucas, and J. Lucas, pp. 53–75. Tulsa, Okla.: Society of Economic Paleontologists and Mineralogists Special Publication No. 66, 2000.

Delaney, M. L. "Phosphorus Accumulation in Marine Sediments and the Oceanic Phosphorus Cycle." *Global Biogeochemical Cycles* 12.4 (1998), 563–572.

Duce, R. A., et al. "The Atmospheric Input of Trace Species to the World Ocean." *Global Biogeochemical Cycles* 5 (1991), 193–259.

Jahnke, R. A. "The Phosphorus Cycle." In *Global Biogeochemical Cycles*, edited by S. S. Butcher, et al., pp. 301–315. San Diego: Academic Press, 1992.

Karl, D. M. "A Sea of Change: Biogeochemical Variability in the North Pacific Subtropical Gyre." *Ecosystems* 2 (1999), 181–214. DOI: 10.1007/s 100219900068.

Lerman, A., F. T. Mackenzie, and R. M. Garrels. "Modeling of Geochemical Cycles: Phosphorus as an Example." *Geological Society of America Memoir* 142 (1975), 205–218.

Mackenzie, F. T., et al. "C, N, P, S Global Biogeochemical Cycles and Modeling of Global Change." In *Interactions of C, N, P, and S Biogeochemical Cycles and Global Change*, edited by R. Wollast, F. T. Mackenzie, and L. Chou, pp. 1–61. Berlin: Springer, 1993.

Meybeck, M. "Carbon, Nitrogen, and Phosphorus Transport by World Rivers." *American Journal of Science* 282.4 (1982), 401–450.

Tiessen, H., ed. *Phosphorus in the Global Environment: Transfers, Cycles, and Management.* Chichester, U.K., and New York: Wiley, 1995.

Petsch, S. T., and R. A. Berner. "Coupling the Geochemical Cycles of C, P, Fe, and S: The Effect on Atmospheric O_2 and the Isotopic Records of Carbon and Sulfur." *American Journal of Science* 298 (1998), 246–262.

Richey, J. E. "The Phosphorus Cycle." In *The Major Biogeochemical Cycles and Their Interactions*, edited by B. Bolin and R. B. Cook, pp. 51–56. Chichester, U.K., and New York: Wiley, 1983.

Ruttenberg, K. C. "Reassessment of the Oceanic Residence Time of Phosphorus." *Chemical Geology* 107 (1993), 405–409.

Ruttenberg, K. C., and R. A. Berner. "Authigenic Apatite Formation and Burial in Sediments from Non-Upwelling, Continental Margin Environments." *Geochimica et Cosmochimica Acta* 57.5 (1993), 991–1007.

Sverdup, H. V., M. W. Johnson, and R. H. Fleming. *The Oceans, Their Physics, Chemistry, and General Biology.* New York: Prentice Hall, 1942.

Tyrell, T. "The Relative Influences of Nitrogen and Phosphorus on Oceanic Primary Production." *Nature* 400 1999, 525–531. DOI: 10.1038/22941.

Walker, T. W., and J. K. Syers. "The Fate of Phosphorus during Pedogenesis." *Geoderma* 15 (1976), 1–19.

—K. C. RUTTENBERG

PLATE TECTONICS

See Mobile Earth.

POLAR BEARS

See Arctic Warming.

POLLUTION

In its broadest sense, pollution is any human impact on the natural environment. Pollution is a complex problem that can influence all aspects of the environment. Its impact is normally assessed by the level of damage to human health, to quality of life, to the well-being of other planetary organisms, and to aesthetics and impacts on inanimate structures. This discussion considers pollution associated with the atmosphere, water, soil, and the ocean.

Sources of pollution are classified as point-source—which comes from identifiable specific locations, such as a chimney attached to a factory, a sewage discharge pipe into a river, a damaged oil tanker on the ocean, or an accident at a nuclear power station—and nonpoint pollution sources that include the mix of individual sources from an area or region. Examples include smog over cities and polluted river water entering the ocean. In both cases the term "emission" means the release of pollutants to the environment.

Pollution. Pollution from Mineral Processing.
The very tall smoke stacks at the smelting complex at Sudbury in Ontario, Canada, attempt to reduce the impact of pollutants in the immediate vicinity, but mineral processing produces large quantities of pollutants that are transported in the atmosphere and deposited downwind.

AIR POLLUTION

Pollution emitted to the atmosphere can cause respiratory health problems, damage to vegetation and buildings, and aesthetic degradation. Air pollutants consist of gases and particulate matter (aerosols) and can be divided into three categories by their scale: global, national and/or regional, and local/regional.

Air pollutants influencing the global environment are gases that contribute to greenhouse warming and stratospheric ozone depletion. The major gases involved are carbon dioxide, methane, chlorofluorocarbons (CFCs), and nitrous oxide. With the exception of CFCs, all of these gases occur naturally in the atmosphere and have been increasing steadily in concentration since the industrial revolution. The increase in methane is directly linked to the increase in global population and that of carbon dioxide to increased burning of fossil fuels. [See

Greenhouse Effect; *and* Greenhouse Gases.] Extra nitrous oxide is created mainly by the use of agricultural fertilizers. CFCs are artificial compounds created for refrigeration, aerosol spray cans, and foam mattresses. [*See* Chlorofluorocarbons.]

CFCs also damage the stratospheric ozone layer, which protects organisms on the Earth's surface from potentially fatal ultraviolet radiation. After the CFCs enter the stratosphere from the troposphere, the chlorine in the CFCs is released by ultraviolet irradiation and then reacts to destroy the ozone. In springtime over Antarctica, satellite and ground-based measurements have shown an ozone loss of over 95% in some layers of the stratosphere. There is evidence of loss over the Arctic as well. An increased flux of ultraviolet radiation at the Earth's surface will incread the incidence of melanoma, cataracts, and possible reproductive and other biological problems throughout the food chain. [*See* Ozone.]

On a national or regional scale, air pollutants are transported from point and nonpoint sources over thousands of kilometers. Pollutants from point sources in Europe and Siberia cross the north polar region to Alaska and northern Canada during March and April each year as Arctic haze. In eastern North America, northern Europe, and parts of China, the interaction of pollutants with clouds during transport leads to significant acidification of rain and fog. While clean rainwater is moderately acidic with a pH between 5.0 and 5.6, polluted rain has a pH of 3.5–4.5, or 50–150 times more acidic. This increased acidity is caused by chemical reactions involving sulfur dioxide and nitrogen oxides, which are emitted from tall chimneys associated with industry and power stations. Acid rain and acid deposition can kill fish in lakes, damage vegetation, and cause soil-quality problems through leaching of toxic metals into the ecosystem. [*See* Acid Rain and Acid Deposition.]

On the local/regional scale, the most important air pollution problems originate from internal combustion engines used in urban transportation. Extensive emissions of hydrocarbons and nitrogen oxides into a stable urban atmosphere (i.e., one with little vertical mixing and resultant dispersion of pollutants), with the addition of strong sunlight, create photochemical smog in the summertime. The major pollutant in photochemical smog is ozone, which in high concentrations can cause burning eyes and respiratory problems in sensitive people, as well as damage to vegetation. Photochemical smog has been the major pollution problem in cities such as Los Angeles and Athens for decades. As large cities have expanded in developing countries, photochemical smog has become uncontrollable. Air pollution levels in Mexico City, Bangkok, São Paulo, and Jakarta are among the worst in the world.

WATER POLLUTION

Pollution of water supplies by human populations causes disease, illness, and sometimes death. Water-based sanitation is the main method by which human sewage is removed as waste. In developed countries, legal requirements for proper sewage removal and disposal require local councils and water authorities to invest heavily in treatment infrastructure to avoid water pollution and ensure public safety and health. The greatest concern is bacteria (e.g., streptococci) and viruses, but excess nutrients and other water quality concerns also require various means of monitoring and testing. Treated sewage is often discharged into oceans, rivers, or lakes. Other, more controversial methods include the drying of sewage to form sewage sludge for use as a fertilizer on forests or pastures. Unfortunately, untreated sewage may also be discharged, especially during heavy rains, but also from leaking or poorly maintained septic systems and pipes, through accidental release from pumpout systems, or through system breakdowns. In many developing countries, sewage-control systems do not exist, and sewage is discharged untreated into open drains, streams, and rivers, making the water unusable for any other purpose.

Near industrial locations, water quality can be threatened by the discharge of undesirable chemicals into rivers and oceans. Heavy metals such as lead, copper, cadmium, zinc, and mercury are extremely hazardous and may accumulate in bottom sludge in riverbeds and lake bottoms, to be re-released, perhaps many years later, by some disturbance. Metals can also enter the food chain. Mercury in uncontrolled discharges into Minamata Bay in Japan was taken up by shellfish and fish, which, when eaten by the local population, caused birth defects. Oil spills from boats and ships can also create a pollution hazard, damaging local wildlife populations and interfering with normal life cycles.

Other forms of water pollution include increased temperatures in lakes caused by thermal discharges from powers stations and industries, and increased salinity from a range of activities, including liquid discharges from coal, metal, and mineral mining. Runoff from agricultural practices such as fertilization and application of pesticides adds excess nutrients and poisons to rivers, lakes, and streams. Under hot, dry conditions large areas (blooms) of blue-green algae may develop, which are extremely toxic to animals and humans and make untreated water undrinkable. [See Water; and Water-Quality Trends.]

Trash often pollutes waterways in and near population centers. Trash accumulates because the discharge of unwanted materials is not controlled. These materials consist predominantly of plastic and paper, along with bottles and cans. Especially during heavy rains, when runoff removes much of the ground trash into drains, streams, and rivers, such pollution is a major aesthetic problem and a health hazard.

Nuclear hazards can result from accidental spillage or discharge from nuclear power plants, or from a nuclear explosion. Pollutants include various radioactive elements and compounds, including daughter elements of uranium, plutonium, cesium, and iodine. Radioactive materials are injurious to human health, can contaminate large areas for decades or centuries (depending on the half-life of the radioactive element), and can cause genetic abnormalities in humans and other animals. The most infamous nuclear accident occurred at Chernobyl in the former Soviet Union in April 1986. The accident was caused by human error. Nuclear accidents are extremely rare, but older reactors such as Chernobyl's are hazardous because of obsolete and degraded equipment. Modern nuclear power stations have a range of protection devices designed to prevent discharges in case of accident. [See Chernobyl; and Nuclear Waste.]

SOIL POLLUTION

Apart from problems caused by acid rain and nuclear accidents, pollution of the soil tends to be local and is caused mainly by industrial and manufacturing activities, agriculture, and solid-waste disposal. The improper disposal of hazardous chemicals and poisons can result in leakage and contamination of ground water and may interfere with the normal structure and life cycle of the soil. Such contamination can create major health hazards many years after the industrial or disposal activity has ceased. Housing developments have been built on old industrial sites, only to have contaminants seep out of the ground, affecting health and aesthetics alike. For example, in the famous Love Canal incident in New York State in 1976 whole families were exposed to hazardous chemicals when a new housing development was built on the site of a chemical dump; major environmental and health problems resulted.

In their efforts to control insects and other pests that affect agricultural production, farmers have used a variety of organic and inorganic poisons. The potential impacts of these on the environment first gained international recognition in the 1960s through Rachel Carson's book Silent Spring (1962). The major focus of this work was on the role of pesticides, especially DDT, in harming the reproduction of songbirds. Carson also described how the transport of pesticides through ground and surface water spread destructive impacts well away from the original point of use. She also showed that DDT and similar pesticides did not disappear from the environment after use but remained a threat for decades. Most modern pesticides are less harmful, breaking down rapidly after use, but there is a tendency for pesticides to be overused by the farming community, to the potential long-term detriment of the environment. [See Pest Management.]

Solid waste disposal, especially that associated with the massive urban populations, can also be a major source of soil pollution. In the past, solid waste was simply dumped into open pits on the landscape, allowing leaching of toxins by rainfall into ground water or adjacent waterways. The breakdown of organic refuse can produce undesirable gases such as methane and hydrogen sulfide, which can cause explosions and poisoning if not properly controlled. Such dumps still exist in many developing countries. In cities such as Manila in the Philippines, people live on the dump by scavenging waste material discarded by others.

A modern, well-maintained solid-waste-management facility provides extensive controls to minimize pollution to waterways and the soil. Waste pits may be lined with impermeable plastic or rubber to prevent leaching. Excess water after rain events is captured in holding ponds where pollutants are allowed to settle to the bottom, to be removed later. Solid waste dumped at the facility is covered daily with soil and gravel to minimize the spread of vermin and other pests. Most solid waste can be recycled, including green waste (to garden mulch), paper, cans, bottles, and certain types of plastic. Methane gas buildup is monitored and the gas may be tapped as an energy source for heating homes and businesses. [*See* Waste Management.]

OCEAN POLLUTION

Apart from coastal problems associated with polluted river and sewage discharges, the main cause of marine pollution is oil, through deliberate or accidental discharge and oil-well leaks and blowouts. Other important sources include ocean disposal of solid waste and contaminated material. The impact of oil on the ocean environment can be catastrophic, depending strongly on the length of time the contamination persists. The most spectacular and well publicized discharges of oil to the oceans occur when supertankers suffer accidents during transit. Examples include the *Torrey Canyon* off the coast of Cornwall, United Kingdom, in 1967, the *Exxon Valdez* in Alaska in 1989 (discharge 41,600 metric tons), and the *Braer* in the Shetland Islands off the northern coast of Scotland in 1992 (discharge 85,000 tons). It is estimated that about 6 million tons of oil are spilled into the ocean every year, the majority from undetected sources such as the flushing of oil tanks with sea water, which may discharge millions of gallons of oil into the open ocean. Small discharges of oil can be dispersed by natural ocean processes. Since oil floats on the surface, large discharges may cause long-term damage to the surface environment by destroying elements of the ocean food chain, especially plankton, fish, and birds. Living organisms coated with oil seldom survive. Oil is a continuing threat to a range of highly sensitive ocean environments, including coral reefs, coastal wetlands, and fish spawning areas.

Ocean disposal has been used for urban garbage and hazardous waste from large cities such as New York, Seoul, and Tokyo. While such disposal is now regulated by the London Dumping Convention (1972), the corrosion of existing storage containers allows slow leakages, causing an unknown amount of continuous contamination of the ocean. [*See* Ocean Disposal.]

POLICY REGULATION ISSUES

Pollution and problems on a global scale are extremely difficult to control, especially for the ocean and the atmosphere. International agreements may be signed, but monitoring to ensure adherence is almost impossible. There have been a few successes. The Montreal Protocol, signed in 1987 and followed by updates in London (1990), Copenhagen (1992), Vienna (1995), and Montreal (1997), recognized CFCs as the major cause of stratospheric ozone depletion and constituted an international agreement to phase out production and use. On national, regional, and local scales, regulation of pollution depends very much on political will and the recognition that pollution control is as essential as economic development.

BIBLIOGRAPHY

Aplin, G., et al. *Global Environmental Crises: An Australian Perspective.* Melbourne: Oxford University Press, 1995. A useful introduction to a wide range of pollution issues.

Bridgman, H. A., R. Warner, and J. Dodson. *Urban Biophysical Environments.* Melbourne: Oxford University Press, 1995. Focuses on pollution and environmental problems in cities.

Elsom, D. M. *Atmospheric Pollution: A Global Problem.* 2d ed. Oxford, U.K, and Cambridge, Mass.: Blackwell, 1992. An excellent review of air pollution and its problems.

Intergovernmental Panel on Climate Change. *Climate Change 1994: Radiative Forcing of Climate Change.* Cambridge and New York: Cambridge University Press, 1994. A definitive discussion of anthropogenic impacts on the global climate.

Mannion, A. M., and S. R. Bowlby, eds. *Environmental Issues in the 1990s.* New York: Wiley, 1992. A series of chapters on pollution and environmental problems from a global perspective.

O' Riordan, T., ed. *Environmental Science for Environmental Management.* London and New York: Longman, 1995. An excellent overview of a range of global pollution problems.

Seager, J. *The State of the Environment Atlas.* London: Penguin, 1995. A brief, well packaged overview of global environmental problems with very interesting maps.

World Health Organization and United Nations Environment Programme. *Urban Air Pollution in Megacities of the World.* Oxford, U.K., and Cambridge, Mass.: Blackwell, 1992. The definitive evidence on air pollution in the world's twenty largest cities.

World Resources Institute. *World Resources 1994–95.* New York: Oxford University Press, 1994. An excellent overview of the state of the world environment.

—HOWARD A. BRIDGMAN

POPULATION POLICY

Population policies are sets of principles, strategies, programs, and spending plans devised by governments—and sometimes by intergovernmental, nongovernmental, and private organizations—chiefly to influence human population growth and distribution. Scientifically, a population is the aggregate of specified organisms in a habitat or area. This article will limit the term to the number of human beings on the planet and in nations. In a few cases population policies aim either to enlarge family size in order to accelerate population growth (for example, Romania during the era of Nicolae Ceausescu) or to restrict family size in order to slow population growth (for example, China in the 1980s and 1990s). More often, population policies guide the funding or distribution of contraceptive information and supplies along with the overall care of reproductive and sexual well-being. This subset of public health (reproductive health) is strongly associated with population outcomes. People who use these services, however, rarely have a direct interest in such outcomes. Their interest is rather to avoid or delay pregnancy, plan families, have healthy babies, and maintain health through their reproductive lives. Reproductive-health providers, too, share these objectives for their clients. Population policy nonetheless remains the overarching term that most often covers the dissemination, expansion, and improvement of these reproductive health services worldwide. This seeming paradox serves as a useful reminder that a set of policies and programs that directly benefits individuals and couples also has the side benefit of slowing population growth. To the extent that population dynamics influence natural resources and the natural environment, population policies also indirectly slow human-induced environmental change.

This article will deal primarily with these linkages and the evolution of policies related to them.

Population policies could in theory go beyond reproductive health programs, but they rarely do in practice. The education of girls through secondary school and the economic empowerment of women also contribute to slower rates of population growth, but governments tend not to associate these two objectives with population trends, and thus today they lie largely outside the realm of population policy. Similarly, laws and regulations that influence migration within and among nations could qualify as population policies, but these are typically driven not by demographic ends but by economic, cultural, political, and other social considerations. In 1998 the Sierra Club, a major U.S. environmental organization, polled its membership on whether the organization should advocate more restrictive immigration policies in order to slow U.S. population growth; the membership opposed the idea by a modest margin.

Policymakers and analysts in some industrialized countries have expressed concern about falling (subreplacement) birth rates (that is, birth rates too low to replace parental generations) among their populations. Indeed, the populations of Japan and most of Europe have national fertility rates significantly below the replacement level of two and a fraction births per woman. (The national fertility rate is the number of children born to the average woman, assuming current national birth patterns are sustained through her lifetime.) These trends have undoubtedly fueled political support for policies favoring parents in France and some other European nations. In 2000, the United Nations Population Division issued a report on developed-country population trends arguing that some should consider increasing immigration to maintain population size and possibly current ratios of workers to retirees. Yet few governments have instituted policies expressly aimed at increasing fertility or attracting immigrants for demographic purposes. Although factors outside of family planning and reproductive health are now infrequently addressed in population policies, they may well be addressed more often in the future. The balance of this article, however, will consider population policies related to family planning and reproductive health services.

It is important to distinguish the population policies of the world's relatively wealthy and industrialized developed countries from those of the less wealthy, less industrialized developing countries. Most developed countries have low or even negative population growth, and none of their governments has seen fit to develop policies to influence domestic population growth. Population policy, in these nations, means their direct funding or technical assistance to developing countries to expand the reach of family planning and related services. By contrast, most of the world's developing nations have national policies related to domestic population growth and the need for services to help couples and women space or limit births. Hence, there are two broad types of population policies: those

involving foreign aid in developed countries, and those involving domestic population policy and provision of reproductive-health services in developing ones.

POPULATION HISTORY AND CURRENT TRENDS

Demographically, the millennium just ended differed dramatically from the one that preceded it. From 1–1000 c.e., world population was essentially stable, with increases eventually balanced by equal decreases. By demographers' best estimates, the first millennium began with 300 million people on the planet and ended with about the same number. As the second millennium closed, by contrast, there were 20 times more people on the planet, and no way to be certain when or at what number population growth will end.

Demographic trends today are contradictory. Human numbers are still rising at a pace that, if maintained, would lead to 12 billion people by the middle of the twenty-first century. In much of the world, per capita income and natural-resource consumption are increasing even more rapidly. Many analysts fear the twenty-first century will witness growing scarcities of key natural resources that could lead to conflicts and increases in death rates. Yet at the same time, population growth rates are now declining significantly. This has led to concerns that populations will become progressively older and may even begin to decrease in the twenty-first century.

Current demographic patterns vary considerably between regions and levels of economic development, and demographic predictions should be treated warily. We can examine likely outcomes, but we cannot know the future. The range of most likely outcomes calculated by United Nations demographers suggests the twenty-first century will end with 5–16 billion people, but we cannot be sure even of this. Projections of population change are simply straightforward calculations based on current population trends and assumptions about future rates of births, deaths, and migration.

Critically, population projections assume continued declines in both birth and death rates. Yet neither of these trends may continue for long without major new investments in education and health care, especially reproductive health programs that encourage lower birth rates through family planning and prolong life by curbing transmission of the HIV/AIDS virus. Whatever happens to world population tomorrow depends critically on what governments and individuals decide to do today.

At the opening of the new millennium there are more than 6 billion human beings, almost four times as many as in 1900. Life expectancy has soared, especially the survival prospects for infants and children, which was the dominant factor in the population growth of the 1900s. Settlements and farm fields dominate much of the six habitable continents, and human beings are almost as likely to live in a city or suburb as in a village. On average, each person is or will become a parent to 2.5 children, and world population grows by about 1.3% annually. The planet is home to roughly 78 million more people each year, 215,000 more each day, 9,000 more each hour.

All but 3% of this growth occurs in developing countries, yet many industrialized countries—especially the United States—also contribute to world population growth. The average age of human beings is rising as birthrates decline and life expectancy increases. Yet 1 billion of the planet's inhabitants are 15–24 years old, and in many countries school construction barely keeps pace with the need for new classrooms.

It is increasingly a demographically uneven world, mirroring to some extent the economically skewed world in which one-fifth of the population, mostly living in industrialized countries, earns the vast majority of monetary income. Life expectancy continues to rise in much of the world. But over the last quarter century it fell in 18 countries, most of them, in sub-Saharan Africa, overwhelmed by the HIV/AIDS pandemic. In Europe and Japan, subreplacement fertility sets the stage for current or future population declines. In the United States, Canada, and Australia, fertility rates are closer to replacement level, and due both to high proportions of young people and to net immigration, population growth averages around 1% annually in these countries. In Latin America and in Asia—the continent on which most human beings live—fertility rates have fallen by half in little more than a generation. Population growth rates in these regions resemble that of the world as a whole.

In most of Africa and in the Middle East the transition to later childbirths and small families has not yet advanced very far. Family size still averages 5–6 children, and population projections envision a doubling or even a tripling of population in some countries, many of them already critically short of cropland, forests, and renewable fresh water. Population growth rates tend to exceed 2.6%, twice the global rate, in many countries where governments have the fewest resources for critically needed education and health care.

POPULATION AND ENVIRONMENTAL CHANGE

These relationships between changing population size and the natural resources on which human well-being depends contribute to policymaker concerns about population growth. It may be that human resources are the most important for development and prosperity, yet history and current experience demonstrate that this is most true when natural resources are abundant, cheap, and accessible to all. In the case of most critical natural resources, supplies are diminishing or being degraded as more human beings use them with greater intensity. The finite resources must be shared among more people, and this can begin a sequence of competing claims and rising anxieties that challenge governments and other institutions. The long debate over the impact of population growth on the environment is gradually converging on overall agreement that contemporary population growth is among a handful of factors that strongly influence the sustainability of natural-resource use in many or most places. The relationship is never simple, and population never acts alone in causing such environmental problems as water scarcity and global warming.

Yet its influence cannot be severed from such direct causes as overdrawn aquifers and rising greenhouse-gas emissions.

Consumption patterns also influence relationships between population and natural resources. The average individual in the United States and other industrialized countries consumes a volume of natural resources dozens of times larger than the amount consumed in many developing countries. If every one of the world's 6 billion inhabitants consumed as much paper and petroleum as do each of the United States' 277 million inhabitants, the damage to forests, soils, air, and climate would be catastrophic. The logical place to begin to transform this simple equation is within the wealthy countries that promulgate the high-consumption, high-waste model of happiness and prosperity. No wealthy countries, however, have begun to contemplate even the concept of "consumption policy".

The role of population growth is also impossible to sever from the management of human affairs by governments and other legal, social, and economic institutions. Analysts of population-environment interactions often consider how much of a particular natural resource is available—in the sense of simply "being there"—to each person in a country. Also important is how much of a resource people are actually extracting from the earth, processing, using, and disposing of. But mediating the flow of natural resources between the earth and human beings are the social regulating valves known as institutions. These may be governments and their policies and programs. They also may be rules of law, economic markets, and such legal principles as the right to hold and dispose of property.

The development of these social structures and processes plays a critical role in the management and conservation of natural resources worldwide. Institutions may work well or poorly. Acknowledging disparities in institutional development is essential to understanding the effects of population change, and indeed population change itself plays important roles in institutional development. One linkage may connect population growth, scarcities of essential natural resources, and the weakening of vulnerable institutions.

How do institutions, population growth, economic growth, and the environment interact? Several economists suggest that poorly developed institutions and high fertility reinforce each other in a cycle of social and economic stagnation. Such a vicious cycle could explain why high fertility is frequently associated with low levels of institutional development. It may also help us understand how declines in fertility can stimulate institutional and economic development and be stimulated themselves by the same development.

THE EVOLUTION OF POPULATION POLICY

Should governments actually do anything to influence population growth? That question first emerged in the nineteenth century, after English economist and clergyman Thomas Robert Malthus hypothesized that without adequate individual or collective restraint, population growth tends always to outstrip the natural resources on which human beings depend. Malthus continually reworked his 1798 *Essay on the Principle of Population*. At the end of his life the final essay, published posthumously in 1830, suggested (far more optimistically than his more famous initial essay) both that human beings could adapt under many conditions to growing population and that the right social policies might even slow the increase of human numbers. His writing engendered philosophical debate that continues to this day, and he may be considered the author of the concept of population policy.

As a staunch opponent of contraception, however, Malthus can in no sense be considered a pioneer of contemporary population policy, which rests on the foundation of contraceptive availability and use. A handful of mid-twentieth-century social scientists and policy analysts were the true pioneers, arguing that couples would have fewer children if governments subsidized or otherwise supported the distribution of safe and effective contraceptives, including sterilization for those who wanted no more children at all.

As early as 1951 India began such a program in an effort to stem the rapid rise of its post-independence population. A half century later, despite some success at helping to lower national fertility from roughly six children per woman to 3.4 in the late 1990s, India's government continues to experiment in an effort to expand the reach of its population program.

In instituting a population program so early, India set a precedent that few other developing countries followed until the 1960s. In developed countries, a number of demographers and government officials argued beginning in the 1950s and early 1960s that the post–World War II efforts to stimulate economic development in the former colonies of European powers should include assistance with family planning services. The reasoning was chiefly that such assistance would slow the increase of population resulting from dramatic declines in infant and child mortality after the war's end. By 1965 the United States had instituted such a foreign assistance program through its Agency for International Development (USAID). By 1969, the United Nations Fund for Population Activities (UNFPA) was accepting contributions from many developed nations for the purposes of helping to disseminate family planning assistance worldwide. (The agency later adopted the name the UN Population Fund but still uses its original acronym.)

Population policies have been controversial from the beginning, though the nature of the controversy has changed. Dozens of developing countries asked USAID and UNFPA to help with national family-planning programs in the late 1960s and early 1970s. (Eventually the World Bank became a major lender for family-planning programs in developing countries.) Yet when the world's nations gathered under UN auspices in 1974 in Bucharest for the World Population Conference, most developing nation delegations repudiated the concept of population policies and population assistance. "Development is the best contraceptive" was the slogan that dominated the conference, reflecting still-popular views in developing-country intellectual circles that poverty, not population, is the root issue to be addressed and that family planning is less important than prosperity in lowering birthrates. The idea of population policies based on family planning lost further luster after an overzealous Indian population program, based on assigning family-planning worker quotas for sterilization procedures and other types of contraceptive acceptance, contributed to the 1977 fall of Prime Minister Indira Gandhi's government.

By the next decade's population conference, however, the simplistic view that wealthy countries wanted to foist "population control" on unwilling developing countries was no longer tenable. Almost all developing-country governments had promulgated population policies and family-planning programs by the 1984 International Conference on Population in Mexico City. Developing-country delegations agreed that family-planning programs were critical to their economic and social development, and most asked for more assistance from industrialized "donor" country governments to help pay for these programs and expand their reach. But now a new element came into play. Under President Ronald Reagan, the U.S. government, long the world's leader in providing population assistance, tempered its own involvement by declaring that population growth was a "neutral factor" in economic development. Reagan issued a presidential order that no U.S. foreign-aid money go to nongovernmental organizations providing abortion services or counseling. Because many of the NGOs providing contraceptive assistance in developing countries also used their own funds for abortion-related services, this prohibition reduced the effectiveness of U.S. population assistance until President Bill Clinton reversed the doctrine, as one of his first presidential acts, in 1993.

In the 1980s China emerged as a special case in the evolution of population policies. During the long reign of Mao Zedong, the prevailing communist government view of China's population—which included, then as now, about one in five of the planet's human beings—was that there could never be too many Chinese. Contraception was available only to a favored few, and fertility averaged more than five children per woman. After Mao's death in 1976, however, China's new leaders considered with alarm the challenge the country faced in feeding and housing its rapidly growing population. They instituted a population policy based largely on expanding the availability of contraceptive services. The policy also encouraged late marriages, avoiding childbirths before age 20 and after age 40, and greater employment of women in collective farms and state factories. The result was a precipitous decline in fertility to roughly three children per woman.

By the early 1980s, however, China's leaders feared that this population policy was insufficient to lead to a manageable population maximum in the twenty-first century and sustainable economic growth. They altered the policy to one requiring that most Chinese couples should have no more than a single child, and granted local authorities relatively free reign in enforcing this one-child policy. The result was a far less impressive decline in fertility—and numerous reports of coercion, including forced abortions. By the late 1990s, the central government of China was insisting it was working to eliminate such excesses. China's experience illustrated the extremes to which a highly demographically-focused population policy can go that will not soon fade from view.

CAIRO AND THE NEW PARADIGM OF POPULATION POLICY

The 1990s was a period of optimism in population policy. Demographic researchers were beginning to converge on key findings that have since come to guide that policy internationally. One was that fertility rates were falling significantly worldwide, and that the 30-year international movement to expand access to a range of contraceptive services was largely responsible for this trend. Another was that popular acceptance and continued use of family planning was more likely when service providers focused on the overall reproductive-health needs of their clients, rather than on government fertility preferences and demographic goals. These findings began to shape a new approach to population based less on numbers and more on the reality of people's lives— especially the lives of women—and the need to encourage access to health care, to education and the economic opportunities.

In 1994, delegations from almost every government converged in Cairo, Egypt, for the third of the United Nation's decadal population meetings, this time called the International Conference on Population and Development. The world was spending roughly $4 billion on family planning services in the developing world, up from just $50 million a year in 1965. These figures include money contributed by donor countries, the developing countries themselves, and consumers in developing countries. Two years earlier, delegates to the Earth Summit in Rio de Janeiro had agreed that demographic trends were an important element in global environmental change but had failed to recommend concrete steps to build on that linkage. At the same time, many social scientists and an increasingly influential community of nongovernmental organizations representing women were insisting that women had a right to make their own decisions about reproduction and sexuality without outside interference, regardless of governmental interest in population trends. In the United States and elsewhere, several private foundations were directing substantial resources to raising public and policymaker awareness about the potential for slowing global population growth through support for international family planning.

These independent and even contradictory strands of thought converged in Cairo. There, despite opposition from the delegations of some countries—and of the Vatican, which enjoys the status of a national government at such UN conferences—the world's nations worked out a historic agreement on population and development likely to guide international population policies for some time to come. The strategies endorsed in Cairo were designed to attract popular and government support regardless of whether population growth is a decisive factor in environmental change and human well-being or a mere footnote to history. Population policies and programs consistent with this agreement are grounded not so much in demographic objectives as in the development of each person's capacity to decide for herself or himself when to have a child and how many to have. In Cairo the governments of 179 nations agreed to allocate $17 billion annually to assure universal access to basic reproductive health services by the middle of the century's second decade. Five years later, in 1999, the same governments renewed this pledge and specified the importance of including young people among those who deserve such access to reproductive health services. Except for some developing-country governments, however, most have failed to live up to their commitments. Population program spending in 1997 amounted to about $10 billion, but only around $2 billion of this came from donor nations. The U.S. government, torn internally over the side issue of abortion, is contributing less than it did in 1995. In 1999 a conservative-dominated U.S. Congress forced President Clinton to accept statutory restrictions on U.S. population assistance that are similar to those President Reagan imposed administratively in 1984. Such developments cast doubt on whether sufficient funding will emerge for the kind of widespread reproductive health services that would enable the world to follow the path suggested by the "median variant" UN population projection, which estimates world population at 8.9 billion in 2050.

The primary objective of reproductive health providers is not to alter global demographic trends but to improve the lives of individuals directly. Access to good reproductive health care, to decent schools, and to opportunities to earn a living can mean the difference between happiness and misery—sometimes even between life and death—for women and their children. But an important side benefit of addressing these individual needs is that population growth will slow and eventually end, not because of more deaths but fewer births. At what level and in what decade population growth halts, and what kind of societies will witness this peak, will depend very much on how seriously governments and other social institutions take the commitments agreed to in Cairo in 1994.

[See also Belief Systems; Catastrophist-Cornucopian Debate; Economic Levels; Ethics; Human Populations; and Religion.]

BIBLIOGRAPHY

Ahlburg, D. A., et al. *The Impact of Population Growth on Well-Being in Developing Countries.* Berlin and New York: Springer, 1996. A series of essays by experts in demographics, economics, and other social sciences on linkages between population dynamics and aspects of human well-being.

Ashford, L. S. "New Perspectives On Population: Lessons From Cairo." *Population Bulletin* 50.1 (1995) 1–44. An analysis of and commentary on the Program of Action agreed to by the nations participating in the 1994 International Conference on Population and Development.

Bongaarts, J. "Population Policy Options in the Developing World." *Science* 263 (1994), 771–776. DOI: 10.1126/science.8303293. A consideration of the role of population policy in fertility decline and population change in developing countries, including an influential analysis of the role of maternal age of childbearing on population trends.

Bongaarts, J., et al. "The Demographic Impact of Family Planning Programs." *Studies in Family Planning* 21.6 (1991), 299–310. Quantifies the impact of international family-planning efforts on world population dynamics, calculating that the global total at the time of publication would have been at least 400 million higher without the programs. (In 1999 Bongaarts revised the number to 700 million for that year.)

Casterline, J. B., and S. W. Sinding. *Unmet Need For Family Planning in Developing Countries and Implications for Population Policy*. Population Council Policy Research Division Working Paper No. 135. New York: Population Council, 2000. A discussion of the meaning of "unmet need" for family planning (referring to the unrealized intentions of many women to delay or otherwise limit pregnancy) with a defense of its importance as a concept in population policy.

Cincotta, R. P., and R. Engelman. *Economics and Rapid Change: The Influence of Population Growth*. Washington, D.C.: Population Action International, 1997. Summarizes and expands upon existing literature on the impact of population growth on economic growth in developing countries, with special considerations of the link to the environment and the role of institutions in demographic, economic, and environmental change.

Cohen, J. E. *How Many People Can the Earth Support?* New York: Norton, 1995. A comprehensive overview of the work of those who have pondered the question the title poses, from before Malthus to the present.

Conly, S. R., and S. de Silva. *Paying Their Fair Share? Donor Countries and International Population Assistance*. Washington, D.C.: Population Action International, 1999. An overview of industrialized-country financial assistance for developing-country population programs and a country-by-country assessment of donor performance in the mid-1990s.

Donaldson, P. J. *Nature Against Us: The United States and the World Population Crisis, 1965–1980*. Chapel Hill: University of North Carolina Press, 1990. A historical review of the early development of U.S. population policy and its role in shaping international population.

Engelman, R., et al. *People in the Balance: Population and Natural Resources at the Turn of the Millennium*. Washington, D.C.: Population Action International, 2000. A comprehensive updating of data on population and natural resources along with an original essay on global population trends and population policy.

Kelley, A. C., and R. M. Schmidt. *Population and Income Change: Recent Evidence*. World Bank Discussion Paper No. 249. Washington, D.C.: The World Bank, 1994. An examination of the accumulated research of the last few decades of the twentieth century on the influence of population dynamics on economic growth.

Malthus, T. R. *On the Principle of Population*. 2 vols. New York: Dutton, 1993. A modern edition including Malthus' first and last versions of his essay on population.

Mazur, L., ed. *Beyond the Numbers: A Reader on Population, Consumption, and the Environment*. Washington, D.C.: Island Press, 1995. Essays on the linkage between population and the environment and its implications for population policy, published at the time of the International Conference on Population and Development.

Moffett, G. D. *Critical Masses: The Global Population Challenge*. New York: Viking, 1994. A consideration of the hazards of population growth and the benefits of policies addressing it, published on the eve of the 1994 United Nations International Conference on Population and Development.

Piotrow, P. T. *World Population: The Present and Future Crisis*. New York: Foreign Policy Association, 1980. A dated but still useful overview of the beginnings of international population assistance. Its foreword was authored by George W. Bush, who as president later refused to support international assistance to slow rapid population growth.

Robey, B., et al. "Fertility Decline in Developing Countries." *Scientific American* 269.6 (1993), 60–67. An examination of the reasons for the decline in human fertility in recent decades in developing countries, including a consideration of the role of family-planning programs and population policy in this decline.

United Nations Department of Economic and Social Affairs, Population Division. *World Population Prospects*. Vol. 1. *Comprehensive Tables*. Vol. 2. *The Sex and Age Distribution of the World Population*. New York: United Nations. Definitive estimates of past and current population in the world, its regions and each of its nations, along with various projections of future population change to the year 2050. The United Nations population estimates and projections, published every two years, are those most commonly used in scientific and policy work related to population trends.

—ROBERT ENGELMAN

POST-GLACIAL PERIOD

See Holocene.

PRECAUTIONARY PRINCIPLE

The precautionary principle is a legal and policy principle addressing the problem of scientific uncertainty in environmental decision-making. Although numerous formulations have been advanced, the core idea is expressed in the familiar adage, better safe than sorry. The principle has implications for both the timing and substance of environmental measures: states should anticipate and respond to potential environmental harms, rather than only known or proven harms, and environmental risks should be managed with a margin of error in case they are more serious than originally expected.

The importance of precaution is recognized in many national environmental laws—for example, the 1970 U.S. Clean Air Act, which requires regulators to apply an "ample margin of safety" in setting emissions limits for hazardous pollutants—and is reflected in international actions such as the 1982 moratorium on commercial whaling. However, as an explicit precept, the precautionary principle originated in Germany and made its way into international environmental law in the mid-1980s. The principle has been included in numerous policy declarations, as well as in most recent environmental treaties, including the Climate Change and Biological Diversity conventions. [*See* Biological Diversity *and* Climate Change and Societal Development.] The most widely cited international formulation is Principle 15 of the 1992 Rio Declaration on Environment and Development, which states:

> In order to protect the environment, the precautionary approach shall be widely applied by States according to their capabilities. Where there are threats of serious or irreversible damage, lack of full scientific certainty shall not be used as a reason for postponing cost-effective measures to prevent environmental degradation.

The precautionary principle's applicability is a function of both the severity and the evidence of environmental risk. Most formulations of the principle address these issues only in somewhat general terms. Typically, application of the principle is limited to risks of serious or irreversible harm. With regard to evidence, lack of full scientific certainty is not an excuse for delay. Instead, precautionary action depends only on prima facie grounds for concern. Some formulations assert more specifically that precautionary action is warranted when there is knowledge that an effluent is persistent, toxic, and liable to accumulate in the environment, even though no environmental harm has yet been proven, or when there is knowledge of an environmental harm, even though the causal link with an activity is only suspected, not proven.

Like other international environmental principles such as sustainable development and intergenerational equity, the precautionary principle does not dictate particular environmental measures but serves instead as a general orientation or guide. Different formulations frame the principle in more or less absolute terms. The Rio Declaration incorporates the notion of cost-benefit balancing, but some treaty formulations are oblivious to cost. At a minimum, the precautionary principle would appear to entail environmental-impact assessment. Beyond that, a precautionary approach may involve clean production techniques, best available technology, or a reversal of the burden of proof. An example of the latter is the reverse-listing procedure of the 1996 Protocol to the London (Dumping) Convention, which forbids the dumping of wastes at sea unless a material is specifically determined to be safe.

Outside the context of treaty law, the legal status of the precautionary principle is controversial. Although the principle has been included in many international agreements and policy declarations, as well as in European Union law and some national statutes and court decisions, scholars disagree about whether the principle has attained the status of customary international law, given the variety of formulations and the lack of consistent national practice.

[*See also* Environmental Law.]

BIBLIOGRAPHY

Bodansky, D. "Scientific Uncertainty and the Precautionary Principle." *Environment* 33.7 (1991), 4–5, 43–44. A critical appraisal of the precautionary principle's ambiguities and difficulties of application.

Cross, F. B. "Paradoxical Perils of the Precautionary Principle." *Washington and Lee Law Review* 53 (1996), 851–925. Criticism of the precautionary principle as a simplistic rhetorical device that may increase rather than decrease overall environmental risk.

Freestone, D., and E. Hey, eds. *The Precautionary Principle and International Law*. The Hague, London, and Boston: Kluwer, 1996. An excellent collection of essays focusing on how to put the precautionary principle into practice.

Hickey, J. E., Jr., and V. R. Walker. "Refining the Precautionary Principle in International Environmental Law." *Virginia Environmental Law Journal* 14 (1995), 423–454.

Kriebel, D., et al. "The Precautionary Principle in Environmental Science." *Environmental Heath Perspectives* 109.9 (2001), 871–876.

O' Riordan, T., and J. Cameron, eds. *Interpreting the Precautionary Principle*. London: Cameron May, 1994. A multidisciplinary collection of essays on scientific, policy, and legal aspects of the precautionary principle.

—DANIEL BODANSKY

PROXY DATA FOR ENVIRONMENTAL CHANGE

Land-based proxy data for past environmental changes include records from peat bogs, growth patterns of trees with seasonal rings (dendroclimatological data), the orientation of desert dunes, the growth and geochemistry of speleothems (secondary calcareous deposits in caves, including stalactites and stalagmites), changes in fluvial (river) regimes, the extensive loess deposits that cover vast areas of continental Europe, Asia, and the Americas, and deposits related to mountain glaciers. [*See* Loess.] Glacial varves, annual layers that are found in lakes near the glacial margin and result from the summer melting of glaciers, are another significant source of data. [*See* Climate Reconstruction.] Deep-ocean sediments—including marine organisms (principally radiolarians, foraminifera, and other microorganisms) and the inorganic sedimentary detritus supplied from continental areas as river sediment, eolian (wind-borne) dust, and ice-rafted detritus transported from high latitudes by icebergs—are also important. Over the past three decades the records of snow chemistry, quantity, and aerosol components (such as dust, salt, and volcanic ash), and greenhouse gases as recorded in ice cores from the high latitudes and high altitudes, have provided some of the most detailed records of the past few hundred thousand years of climate change. While such proxy records rarely provide a direct index of climatic parameters, they can provide indirect qualitative or quantitative indices (Lowe and Walker, 1997; Anderson et al., 2007).

The main basis for stratigraphic correlation and interpretation of Quaternary environmental records, whether on land or offshore, is the numbered series of more than 20 glacial-interglacial cycles defined principally on the basis of oxygen isotopic evidence from deep-sea cores (Hillaire-Marcel and de Vernal, 2007). There are three stable isotopes of oxygen, of which oxygen-16 is the most abundant and oxygen-17 and oxygen-18 much rarer. Of the two minority species, oxygen-18 is the more abundant, but its ratio to oxygen-16 is only 0.0019–0.0021 in natural materials. Although the isotopes are similar in chemical behavior, there are some temperature-dependent processes that reduce the incorporation of the heavier isotopes into the material being formed (e.g., ice) and some that give preference to them. The net result of such fractionation processes is that the ratio of oxygen-18 to oxygen-16 in glaciers is slightly lower than in sea water—that is, the oxygen in the water of glaciers is isotopically lighter. During glacial times, because of the greater amount of water locked up in glaciers, sea water is isotopically heavier. Shells formed in this water are heavier still because there is further fractionation during the formation of shell carbonate, lower temperatures favoring incorporation of oxygen-18.

Past oxygen and carbon isotope ratio values are recorded in calcareous skeletons (commonly called shells) of marine organisms (usually foraminifera) in deep-sea sediments. Samples are obtained in coring tubes up to 50 meters in length. The continuous sediment cores so obtained also carry a magnetic-polarity record that allows correlation of the climatic variations with the magnetic polarity time scale. [*See* Dating Methods.]

One of the first records of marine oxygen isotopes was obtained by Cesare Emiliani during the 1950s (Emiliani, 1961). This showed variations initially interpreted as reflecting primarily the temperature of the water in which the shells had been formed, but it was later argued that the influence of glacier volume was dominant and that the isotope variations could be considered as a paleoglaciation record. This core showed evidence of 13 phases, warm and cold. These were numbered from the top down, with odd numbers corresponding to warm stages and limited global ice volumes and even numbers to cold stages with greater global ice volumes. They are now referred to as marine isotope stages (MIS).

The stage numbers allocated by Emiliani continue to be used but have been refined so as to include substages. These are commonly designated by letters—for example, the warm substages of MIS 5 are named 5a, 5c, and 5e, and the intervening cool periods are named 5b and 5d. A decimal system has also been developed for the naming of additional layers or horizons within the marine isotope stages in which subtle isotopic variations occur so as to give greater flexibility in dealing with the complexities of the isotope curve. Boundaries between pronounced isotopic maxima (full glacials) and consecutive pronounced minima (peak interglacials) are called terminations. These are numbered by roman numerals in order of increasing age. The most recent period of full glacial conditions was at a maximum around 21,000 BP.

Because of the slow sedimentation rate on the ocean floor, and sometimes because of bioturbation (the mixing of sediments on the sea floor by the actions of animals and plants), there is a tendency for any short-term changes to be smoothed out, so that, in most cores, changes persisting for less than a few thousand years are unlikely to be seen, and the record is primarily one of long-term changes.

BIBLIOGRAPHY

Anderson, D. E., A. Goudie, and A. G. Parker. *Global Environments through the Quaternary*. Oxford: Oxford University Press, 2007.

Emiliani, C. "Cenozoic Climatic Changes as Indicated by the Stratigraphy and Chronology of Deep-Sea Cores of Globigerina-Ooze Facies." *Annals of the New York Academy of Science*, 95 (1961), 521–536.

Hillaire-Marcel, C., and A. de Vernal, eds. *Proxies in Late Cenozoic Paleoceanography*. Amsterdam: Elsevier, 2007.

Lowe, J. J., and M. J. C. Walker. *Reconstructing Quaternary Environments*. London and New York: Longman, 1997.

—STEPHEN STOKES

R

RAINFORESTS

See Tropical Forests and Global Change; and Amazonia and Deforestation.

REEFS

Reefs are accumulations of carbonate derived largely from the skeletal materials of marine organisms. The principal reef-building organisms are algae and corals. Algal reefs can develop in most oceans, but corals are restricted to those in which surface temperatures remain in the range 18°–36°C (optimally, 26°–28°C) and in which salinity is 3.3–3.6%. In terms of size and importance in global-change studies, coral reefs significantly outweigh other types of reef, and are thus the focus of this entry.

Living coral reefs occupy over 600,000 square kilometers of the Earth's surface, confined mostly to tropical oceans. Exceptions occur when warm water is continuously moved into higher latitudes; examples include the northwestern Hawaiian islands, Lord Howe Island in the southwestern Pacific, the Ryukyu Islands of Japan, and Bermuda in the western Atlantic.

Reefs are most simply classified into fringing reefs, barrier reefs, and atoll reefs (Figure 1). Fringing reefs tend to be young and surficial, rising from comparatively shallow depths on the submerged flanks of the land. Barrier reefs rise from greater depths and, because they rise almost vertically, they break the ocean surface at some distance from the coast. Atoll (or ring) reefs rise upward from a submerged edifice, typically a sunken volcanic island.

In 1842, Charles Darwin was the first to recognize that fringing reefs could develop into barrier reefs, which could develop into atolls by the progressive subsidence of a reef-fringed volcanic island (Figure 1). This subsidence theory of atoll formation was largely corroborated when atoll-reef drilling confirmed that such reefs rose from submerged volcanic foundations. Yet to insist—as Darwin did not—that every atoll must have once been a barrier reef and that every barrier reef must have once been a fringing reef has proved unhelpful, especially in tectonically active parts of the coral seas in the Caribbean and southwestern Pacific.

Islands exist on reefs in many places. These may be surficial and transient (cays), often created and removed in successive storm events, or they may be more enduring (motus) as the result of having developed beachrock or other armor. In places where slight emergence has taken place, reef islands will be even more enduring, a good example being the low emerged reef Aldabra in the western Indian Ocean.

Although coral reefs have existed since the Ordovician (500–440 million years ago), most of those living in the world today have foundations of Neogene age (since 25 million years ago). These reefs have proved to be sensitive recorders of many environmental changes and have thus been the object of studies by many global-change researchers.

Reefs have, for instance, been accurate recorders of tectonic changes. Most ancient midocean atolls, such as those in the northwestern Pacific, have been subsiding slowly for several million years. In response to this subsidence, the veneer of living reef that caps the dead reef below has been growing slowly upward. Hence dated cores through the reef can provide information about the long-term subsidence rate.

SEA-LEVEL CHANGE

Knowledge of subsidence rates can also help in understanding past sea-level changes. Solution unconformities found in reef cores represent times when sea level fell below the reef surface, which was exposed and eventually eroded and lowered by subaerial (rainwater) solution. By measuring the depths of unconformities of particular ages, it has been possible to determine precise levels of former low stands of global sea level relative to the present.

The comparatively rapid recurrence of sea-level oscillations during the later Neogene (Quaternary) caused the frequent exposure of reef surfaces during times of low sea level, approximately coincident with glacial maxima. At such times, the regions within which coral reefs were able to grow shrank markedly. As temperatures warmed again and sea level began rising, the surfaces of the reefs became gradually flooded and corals once more became established.

There has been considerable debate about the relationship between such periods of sea-level rise and the shape of modern atolls. When an atoll reef has been exposed during a Neogene sea-level low, subaerial solution has caused it to develop a characteristic rim-and-basin morphology in its highest parts. When flooded by rising sea level, most reef growth has taken place along the rim rather than in the basin. Thus the form of most modern atolls reflects the form of the most recent rim to have developed on its submerged reef foundation (Figure 2).

In some places, a combination of uplift and sea-level fall has caused the emergence of a reef edifice. Most high limestone islands in the world are emerged reefs, yet only a few of these appear to be authentic "elevated atolls," despite their characteristic rim-and-basin form. On account of their often remote, midocean locations, emerged reefs have often been a focus for

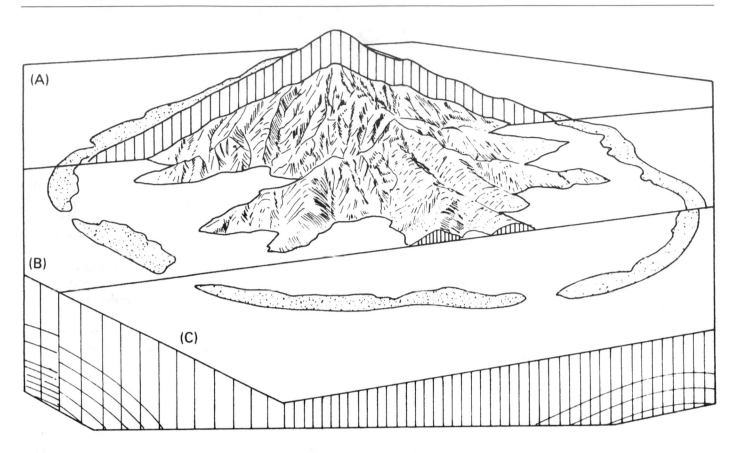

seabird colonization, which has led to the development of phosphate-rock (phosphorite) deposits on islands such as Christmas Island in the Indian Ocean and Nauru and Banaba (Ocean Island) in the Pacific.

IMPACTS ON REEFS

Corals, the principal warm-water reef-builders today, are sensitive to changes in water temperature, salinity, and turbidity. While clearly resilient in the long term, many coral reef ecosystems have been adversely affected by human and nonhuman activities in the recent past.

Through nearby land-use changes, typically logging, large amounts of sediment have been released onto neighboring reefs. This has increased turbidity to such an extent that insufficient light penetrates to the reef surface for photosynthesis to take place, so that the corals and their dependent organisms die and the reef surface becomes barren. Clearance of mangrove forests along many tropical coasts has also contributed to reef death, largely by releasing large amounts of sediment, formerly held together by the root systems of the mangroves, onto nearby reefs. Human demands on reef ecosystems have often led to their overexploitation (particularly where subsistence demands have been replaced by commercial ones), physical damage (from trampling, anchors, and dynamite), and chemical pollution (from fish poisons and industrial and domestic waste).

Coral mining is increasingly contributing to the degradation of reefs. On island nations that have no other source of rock for construction, reefs are routinely blasted or excavated by hand.

Reefs. Figure 1. Darwin's Theory of Atoll Formation.

Through submergence, a volcanic island with a fringing reef (A) may become an island with an embayed coast and a barrier reef (B), and finally an atoll reef (C). (After Nunn, 1994.)

Increasing demand for reef fish has also led to the overexploitation of reefs in many countries.

Nonhuman causes of reef stress are also common. They include predation by occasionally massive numbers of crown-of-thorns starfish (*Acanthaster planci*). Storms often cause significant structural damage to reefs, and may occasionally cover them with detritus carried up their underwater faces from depth. Reefs can generally recover from structural damage; the reefs off Florida recovered within 7 years of the passage of a hurricane with winds of 200 kilometer per hour. Indeed, it has been suggested that periodic storms are necessary for the rejuvenation and extension of reefs. Conversely, many reef flats appear to have been denuded beyond recovery as the result of storm damage. The increasing frequency of such storms in some places over recent decades implies that the normal recovery of reefs, following such events, may increasingly be inhibited.

Although the El Niño–Southern Oscillation has affected the Earth for most of the Holocene, its impacts on reefs have been understood only recently. One major effect is the prolonged low sea levels, which may cause reef surfaces to be exposed for several weeks. These cause the living veneer of reefs to be exposed for so long that it dies. El Niño also involves temperature changes,

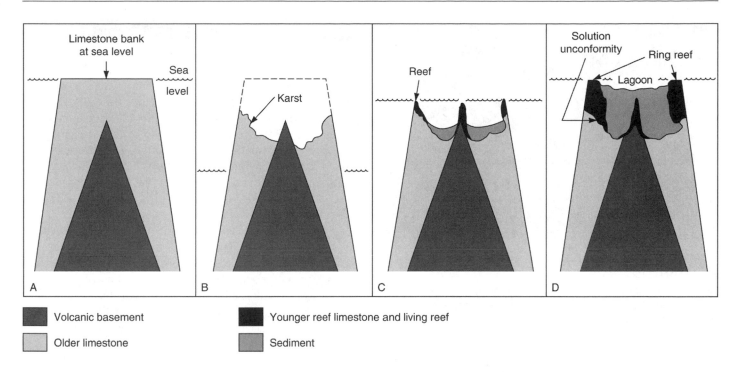

Volcanic basement

Older limestone

Younger reef limestone and living reef

Sediment

Reefs. FIGURE 2. Atoll Formation Following a Fall and Rise in Sea Level.

(A) A limestone bank exists at a relatively high (interglacial) sea level. (B) Sea level falls (during the subsequent glacial period) and subaerial erosion causes the exposed limestone bank to develop a saucer shape. (C) Sea level begins to rise (during the early postglacial period), reef is established and begins growing upward (as sea level continues rising) on the highest parts of the island. (D) As sea level continues rising (to its interglacial maximum), upward reef growth continues around the periphery but is gradually stifled by sediment accumulation in the center of the drowned saucer; an atoll develops. (After Nunn, 1994.)

which must be distinguished in their cause from those associated with global warming, although the effect is the same.

The severe storms and widespread coral death associated with El Niño, for example, may allow the initiation of other processes that complete the degradation of a particular reef. Bioerosion on eastern Pacific reefs that experienced widespread coral death in the 1982–1983 El Niño now exceeds carbonate buildup, a process that will convert the reef framework into sediment if it continues.

As the Earth's surface has warmed in recent decades, so too has the uppermost ocean. Increased temperatures in some places have increased stress on coral reefs to the point where coral bleaching has occurred. This phenomenon is a response to a high level of stress—to which temperature rise is but one contributor—and involves the corals expelling the symbiotic algae (zooxanthellae) within them and dying as a consequence. Since the algae give most corals their color, this process causes an easily recognizable bleaching.

If Earth surface temperatures increase as predicted, reefs throughout the world are likely to experience increases in stress that may will in some cases prove fatal. Yet even if Earth surface temperatures rise less than predicted, increases in stress will still

occur on many reefs. Many reefs are located in places where economic growth takes precedence over environmental conservation. In much of the developing world, at both the national and the individual level, reef protection is sometimes perceived as a preoccupation of the developed world to which only lip service need be paid. Approximately 10% of the world's people live within 100 km of a coral reef, and 91% of them live in the "developing" world. Reef degradation will therefore disproportionately affect these nations and will compound future global inequities.

As much as 85% of the sediment entering the ocean comes off land in the tropical western Pacific, where the greatest diversity of coral reef ecosystems also occurs. The threats to coral reef diversity in this region—particularly in the Philippines, Indonesia, and Papua New Guinea—are manifest, and they are spreading. The Solomon Islands, for example, are a large group of reef-fringed tropical islands with one of the highest population densities in the Pacific, where most of the people live on the coasts and depend on coral reefs for their daily sustenance. In 1997, the Australian government withdrew certain aid from the Solomon Islands on the grounds that if deforestation continued at its present rate, there would be no forests left within 15 years. In addition to depriving people of their terrestrial resources, the effects on nearby reef systems of terrestrial sediment released from the land as a result of logging would lead to their degradation.

Coral reefs are also tourist attractions. More than 3 million tourists visit Hawaii's reefs each year. The effect of such pressure has been understood and legislated for in a few countries, but many of the countries in the Caribbean and the South Pacific have little foreign income beyond that from tourism, so are reluctant to impose constraints that they fear may drive tourists away.

Reefs. Sharks Bay, Eqypt.

Reefs are hugely important ecosystems, but they are also subject to a large number of human pressures. This notice asks tourists to take care of the coral reefs at Sharks Bay, Sharm El Sheik, on the Red Sea in Egypt.

THE FUTURE

Future temperature rise is predicted to be accompanied by sea-level rise. Although predictions of the magnitude of this rise have been downgraded considerably in recent years, it still seems likely that sea level will rise perhaps 30 centimeters in the next 50 years or so. The effects of this rise on reef ecosystems have been discussed by a few authors. A minority avers that reefs will be able to grow upward at the same rate as sea level rises and thus maintain reef-fringed shorelines much as they are now. This view has encouraged complacency among government planners and bodes ill for the future of many reefs. An alternative view recognizes that, although reef surfaces grew upward during the Holocene sea-level rise at rates far in excess of that needed in the next 50 years to keep pace with predicted sea-level rise, they may not continue to do so, partly because sources of stress (see above) exist today that did not exist thousands of years ago, and partly because modern reefs have not had to grow upward for several millennia. Thus the types of coral that are critical for upward reef growth are rarer today, and there will need to be a significant change in species composition on many reefs before they will be able to respond optimally to sea-level rise. How long this change will take is unclear, particularly in reef ecosystems that are already stressed for other reasons.

Increasing degradation of coral reefs in the future will greatly impact the biodiversity of the oceans, both directly through reef species loss and indirectly through the loss in many places of a habitat that is essential to the life cycle of various other organisms. For example, fisheries dependent on coral reefs total about 9 million metric tons per year, around one-tenth of total marine fisheries. Specialist fish species are likely to be the first casualties of increased coral-reef degradation.

About half the calcium entering the ocean every year is incorporated at least temporarily into a coral reef. Since calcium combines with carbon dioxide in this process, it has been

CORAL BLEACHING

Increased sea-surface temperatures resulting from global warming could have deleterious consequences for corals, which are near their thermal maximum of tolerance, and increased temperatures in recent years have been identified as one cause of coral bleaching. This involves the loss of symbiotic zooxanthellae or a decrease in the photosynthetic pigmentation in these zooxanthellae. This in turn has an adverse effect on the coral host because these photosynthetic symbionts typically supply about two-thirds of the coral's nutrients and also facilitate calcification. Those corals thus stressed by a rise in temperature or by various types of pollution, will probably find it more difficult to cope with rapidly rising sea levels than would healthy corals. Moreover, it is possible that increased ultraviolet radiation due to ozone depletion could aggravate bleaching and mortality caused by global warming. Various studies have addressed the issue of coral bleaching (e.g., Brown, 1990), and some have demonstrated an increasing incidence of bleaching events during the warm years of the 1980s and 1990s (e.g., Glynn, 1996).

Indeed, Goreau and Hayes (1994) have produced maps of global coral bleaching episodes between 1983 and 1991 and have related them to maps of sea-surface temperatures over that period. They find that areas of severe bleaching are related to what they describe as ocean "hot spots" where marked positive temperature anomalies exist. They argue that coral reefs are ecosystems that may be uniquely prone to the effects of global warming:

> If global warming continues, almost all ecosystems except the warmest ones can be replaced by migration of species from lower latitude, as corals have no source of immigrants already adapted to warmer conditions. Their species must evolve new environmental tolerances if their descendants are to survive—a much slower process than migration.

A more recent survey of the future of the world's coral reefs (Hoegh-Guldberg, 1999), based on modeling changes in sea-surface temperatures using various general circulation models, is even more pessimistic, concluding that "bleaching events are projected to increase in frequency until they become yearly events by 2050 in most oceans" (p. 15). Noting that previous bleaching events (since 1979) have been triggered by unseasonably high temperatures associated with El Niño events, the author goes on to note that "in 20–40 years from now, bleaching is projected to be triggered by seasonal changes in water temperature and will no longer depend on El Niño events to push corals over the limit" (p. 15).

BIBLIOGRAPHY

Brown, B.E. "Coral Bleaching." *Coral Reefs* 8 (1990), 153–232.
Goreau, T.J., and R. L. Hayes. "Coral Bleaching and Ocean 'Hot Spots'." *Ambio* 23 (1994), 176–180.
Glynn, P.W. "Coral Reef Bleaching: Facts, Hypotheses and Implications." *Global Change Biology* 2.6 (1996), 495–509. DOI: 10.1111/j.1365-2486.1996.tb00063.x.

—ANDREW S. GOUDIE

calculated that around 700 billion kilograms of carbon is sequestered in coral reefs annually. The conservation of the reefs is thus vital, because their degradation would release massive amounts of carbon dioxide which might then be transferred to the Earth's atmosphere where it would probably exacerbate the effects of global warming.

The future of the world's coral reefs is in serious doubt. Stress levels on many modern reefs are at unprecedented levels, and the most authoritative predictions of the future suggest that the principal sources of stress—direct human impact, temperature rise, and sea-level rise—are likely to increase, at least over the next century or so. Increased awareness of the fragility of the world's living reefs, especially among people who interact with them on a daily basis, is probably the best long-term hope for their conservation.

[See also Coastal Protection and Management; Marginal Seas; and Sea Level Future.]

BIBLIOGRAPHY

Birkeland, C., ed. Life and Death of Coral Reefs. New York: Chapman and Hall, 1997. A first-rate compilation on the workings of coral reefs and the concerns about their future.

Brown, B.E., and J.C. Ogden. "Coral Bleaching." Scientific American 268 (1992), 64–70. A concise review of the main occurrences of coral bleaching.

Carpenter, R.A., and J.E. Maragos. How to Assess Environmental Impacts on Tropical Islands and Coastal Areas. Honolulu: Environment and Policy Institute, East-West Center, 1989. A practical guide that incorporates many examples of poor practice and illustrates realistic solutions.

Darwin, C. The Structure and Distribution of Coral Reefs. 2d ed. London: Smith, Elder, 1874. The first systematic scientific observations of coral reefs and the classic statement of subsidence theory, still largely valid in its essentials.

Davis, W.M. The Coral Reef Problem. Washington, D.C.: American Geographical Society, 1928. An exhaustive account of reef genesis, adhering uncritically to subsidence theory. Although many of the conclusions have since been invalidated (particularly as the complexity of Neogene sea level changes has become apparent), this remains a reference classic for many reefs.

Donner, S.D., and Potere, D. "The Inequity of the Global Threat to Coral Reefs." BioScience, 57.3 (2007), 214–215.

Guilcher, A. Coral Reef Geomorphology. Chichester, U.K., and New York: Wiley, 1988. A geographically well-balanced and systematic account of reefs and the various forms they assume.

Hoegh-Guldberg, O. Climate Change, Coral Bleaching and the Future of the World's Coral Reefs. Amsterdam: Greenpeace International, 1999.

Hopley, D. The Geomorphology of the Great Barrier Reef: Quaternary Development of Coral Reefs. New York: Wiley, 1982. A thorough description of the world's largest living reef system, with good summaries of ideas about Neogene reef genesis and development.

Munday, P.L. "Habitat Loss, Resource Specialization, and Extinction on Coral Reefs." Global Change Biology 10.10 (2004), 1642–1647. DOI: 10.1111/j.1365–2486.2004.00839.x.

Nunn, P.D. Oceanic Islands. Oxford, U.K., and Cambridge, Mass.: Blackwell, 1994. Includes a chapter on coral reefs and islands, with examples worldwide.

Nunn, P.D. Keimami sa vakila na liga ni Kalou = Feeling the Hand of God: Human and Nonhuman Impacts on Pacific Island Environments. 3d ed. Suva, Fiji: University of the South Pacific, 1997. Includes a discussion of the various causes of reef damage and degradation in the Pacific Islands.

Pandolfi, J.M., et al. "Global Trajectories of the Long-Term Decline of Coral Reef Ecosystems." Science 301 (2003), 955–958. DOI: 10.1126/science.1085706.

Raloff, J. "Sea Sickness: Marine Epidemiology Comes of Age." Science News 155 (January 30, 1999), 72–74.

Smith, S.V. "Coral-Reef Area and the Contributions of Reefs to Processes and Resources of the World's Oceans." Nature 273 (1978), 225–226. DOI: 10.1038/273225a0. An unsurpassed set of statistics about reefs.

Sorokin, Y.I. Coral Reef Ecology. Berlin and New York: Springer, 1995.

Wiens, H.J. Atoll Environment and Ecology. New Haven, Conn.: Yale University Press, 1962. A comprehensive account of the subject.

—PATRICK D. NUNN

REFLECTIVITY

See Albedo.

REGIONAL ASSESSMENT

Regional assessment is the process of making integrated interdisciplinary research available to decision-makers in response to global environmental change at regional levels. It is a systematic approach to the analysis of regional contributions to global change, and it identifies regional impacts and possibilities for adaptation to change and mitigation of harmful activities. In the context of climate change, regional assessment includes, on the one hand, local contributions to greenhouse gases and, on the other, downscaling from general circulation models to local climate change, tracing the consequences of that change, suggesting the resulting impacts on society, and specifying possible responses.

Human effects on environment and environmental change impacts on society do not occur in a vacuum. Thus regional assessment examines the interactions of these factors with other regional factors—such as impacts of economic globalization, development of local policy in the context of national and international policy, land-use change, and population dynamics. Integrated assessment at the regional level is meant to inform local policy and adaptation and to elucidate the ways in which global processes affect humans.

THE RATIONALE FOR REGIONAL ASSESSMENT

Regional assessments are vital to policymakers, stakeholders, and scientists. Since 1995, reports of the Intergovernmental Panel on Climate Change have recognized the importance of variations in contributions to and impacts of climate change at the scale of major geographical regions. Global integrated-assessment models bring together interdisciplinary research but do not effectively capture the reality of transitional and developing economies or processes occurring at regional scales. Thus national and international organizations have called for and sponsored climate-change research at a regional scale.

Why should policymakers and stakeholders want regional assessments? Human activities vary in their vulnerability to climate change. Whereas industry and energy production may be less sensitive to climate change, agriculture, forestry, water resources, recreation, and health may be more sensitive, and all sectors differ greatly from region to region. Some elements important to policymakers and stakeholders include the following:

- regional and national security.
- judging the importance of climate change relative to other challenges.

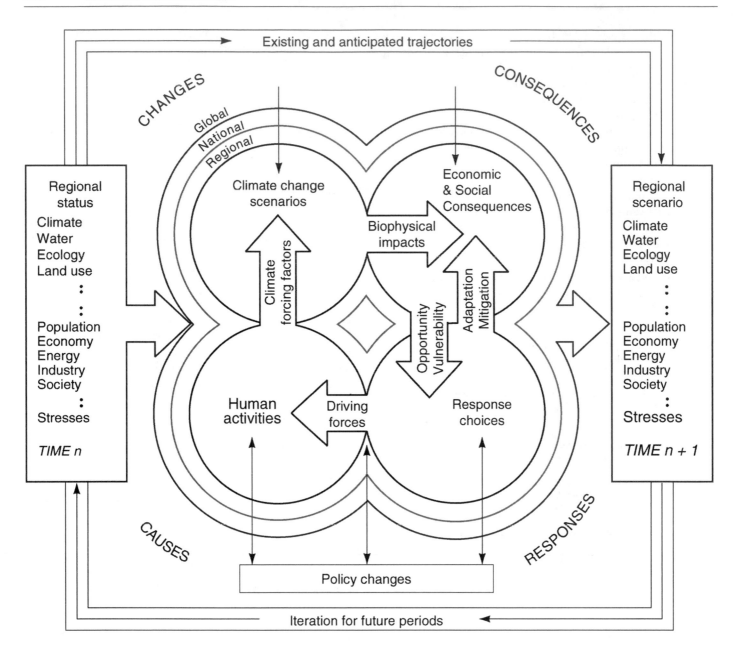

Regional Assessment. Figure 1. A Framework for Integrated Regional Assessment of Global Climate Change.

(After Knight et al., 2008.)

- understanding, anticipating, and exploiting regionally unique opportunities to meet the exigencies of national and international commitments.
- selecting regionally appropriate mitigation and adaptation strategies.
- judging when and where actions must be taken in the face of limited social, technological, and economic choices.
- determining socially and spatially marginal areas and possible differential impacts on them.
- addressing local inequities in mitigation and adaptation.
- helping to resolve the different viewpoints of scientists, policymakers, and lay persons.

Why are regional assessments vital to scientists? The spatial variability of changing weather and climate at the regional scale is not captured in global climate models, and, similarly, the temporal as well as spatial variability of hydrological processes may be obscured by the use of low-resolution approaches. Regional assessments are consistent with the use of environmental- and social-science models, providing the proper scale for matching social and environmental data and interactions. Moreover, a regional scale is more appropriate for process (versus statistical) modeling. Social and amenity values as expressions of local culture and society are captured only at a regional or local level. There have been increasing calls for a cyclical regional-global modeling approach in which regional and global models would interact. Such a strategy would allow testing of the regional components of the global assessment, provide bounds for the regional model, and permit the synergistic advancement of assessment methods and knowledge.

REGIONAL ASSESSMENT

Many specific regional assessments have been undertaken, including the Missouri–Iowa–Kansas–Nebraska (MINK) study (Rosenberg, 1993) and the Mackenzie River Basin Impacts Study (Cohen, 1997). Country reports to the United Nations Framework Convention on Climate Change are becoming more integrated in their assessment of climate impacts.

Key concepts for regional assessment are integration in place, interdependencies between places, and interdependencies among scales. Examples of integration in place include society-environment dynamics (e.g., land-use change) as well as the distinctiveness of individual places, both of which are important in understanding the impact of global change in specific places. Interdependency between places recognizes that external events affect causes and effects within the region. Finally, the recognition of interdependency among scales identifies processes otherwise obscured by analysis at the wrong scale. Thus "critical questions for science in understanding global change include clarifying the scale(s) at which change should be observed and analyzed, and tracing linkages between processes that operate at macro- and microscales" (National Academy of Sciences, 1997).

"Formal regions" are defined by common factors—soil types, climate, biomes, transitional and developing countries, and island nations are examples. Such regions need not be spatially contiguous. "Functional" or "nodal" regions, in contrast, are united by interaction such as hydrological systems, trade, communication, or other human interaction: the idea of spatial contiguity is implicit. Both formal and functional regions can also be seen from a hierarchical perspective, with regions of more local extent being part of more general regions at a wider geographical scale. In everyday language, the word "region" is ambiguous in scale and character. Some regions are officially recognized with accepted nomenclature and definite boundaries (a river basin, a political jurisdiction); others are vernacular, informal, or indefinite. In scale, regions can range from a neighborhood of a few city blocks or a mountain valley to multicountry domains (e.g., sub-Saharan Africa). For START (System for Analysis, Research, and Training) or the Inter-American Institute, a region consists of geographically contiguous countries (e.g., the Mediterranean Basin). Global-change studies also focus onsubnational entities (e.g., states), nations (e.g., the Netherlands), or river basins (e.g., the Nile).

For regional assessment, an overlapping spatial scale extends from individual places, at scales of perhaps $10–10^4$ square kilometers, to less than the global scale (10^8 km^2). "Localities" cover $10^3–10^5$ km^2, on the order of the equatorial degree square (10^4 km^2) as used in some global-change studies. "Regions" and "basins" focus on areas of $10^4–10^7$ km^2; "countries" range upward to 10^6 km^2; and multicountry "domains" (such as those used in START) range from 10^6 to 10^7 km^2, a level of regionalization used in some global models. Within are embedded varying degrees of spatial and temporal resolution, with a subregional resolution appropriate to the topic of analysis (perhaps 1–4 km^2) and a temporal resolution appropriate to the phenomena being modeled (perhaps days to a year, although as coarse as decades in some scenarios).

One of the most difficult challenges to the regional assessment of climate change is the development of climate scenarios at a suitable scale and resolution. Thus climate downscaling by process modeling or statistical approaches is important; some assessments have instead used historical climate as an analogy (Rosenberg, 1993). Regional assessments can be quantitative (using mathematical models), qualitative, or, most frequently, a combination. There are areas of scientific understanding relevant for regional assessment, including the long tradition of human-environment studies in geography and anthropology; environmental perception and behavior in psychology and geography; interdisciplinary natural-hazards studies; environmental and social impact analysis; political economy; spatial change and diffusion; and postmodern criticism of resource knowledge and management.

There is currently no well-developed prototype for regional assessment. Regional assessment is an emerging field of research, drawing on the traditions of integrated assessment in general and of the more recent integrated assessment of climate change at the global scale. The future of this approach to understanding global climatic change will probably evolve through a multiplicity of activities at various scales in different places. The opportunity to compare approaches, to develop and elaborate frameworks, and to synthesize across geographical locations and spatial scales lies ahead, providing a tantalizing inducement for the participation of scientists and policymakers alike.

[*See also* Climate Change and Societal Development; Global Change History; *and* Human Impacts.]

BIBLIOGRAPHY

Cohen, S.J., ed. *Mackenzie Basin Impact Study (MBIS): Final Report.* Downsview, Ont.: Atmospheric Environment Service, Environment Canada, 1997. Summary of an early and important regional assessment.

Easterling, W.E. "Why Regional Studies are Needed in the Development of Full-Scale Integrated Assessment Modeling of Global Change Processes." *Global Environmental Change* 7.4 (1997), 337–356. Discusses the importance of the regional dimension for research on global change.

Ghan, S.J., et al., eds. *Regional Impacts of Global Climate Change: Assessing Change and Response at the Scales that Matter.* Columbus, Ohio: Battelle, 1996. Illustrates the importance of regional-scale analysis.

Knight, C.G., et al. "A Framework for Integrated Regional Assessment." In *Integrated Regional Assessment of Climate Change*, edited by C. G. Knight and J. Jäger (forthcoming). One possible protocol for integrated regional assessment.

Knight, C.G., and J. Jäger, eds. *Integrated Regional Assessment of Climate Change.* Cambridge and New York: Cambridge University Press, (forthcoming). Key issues in integrated regional assessment are presented with examples.

National Academy of Sciences. *Rediscovering Geography: New Relevance for Science and Society.* Washington, D.C.: National Academy Press, 1997. See p. 99.

North, G.R., J. Schmandt, and J. Clarkson, eds. *The Impact of Global Warming on Texas.* Austin: University of Texas Press, 1995. An example of a state-level assessment of global change.

Parry, M.L., et al. *Climate Change 2007: Impacts, Adaptation, and Vulnerability: Contribution of Working Group II to the Fourth Assessment Report of the Intergovernmental Panel on Climate Change.* Cambridge and New York:

Cambridge University Press, 2007. The latest IPCC report on regional and sectoral impacts, partially integrated, with citations to regional and national studies.

Rayner, S., and E.L. Malone, eds. *Human Choice and Climate Change*. 4 vols. Columbus, Ohio: Battelle, 1998. A collaboration examining the interactions among society, technology, and policy related to climate change.

Rosenberg, N.J., ed. *Towards an Integrated Impact Assessment of Climate Change: The MINK Study*. Dordrecht, Netherlands, and Boston, Mass.: Kluwer, 1993. Summary of a now-classic study.

Rotmans, J., and H. Dowlatabadi. "Integrated Assessment Modeling." In *Human Choice and Climate Change*, edited by S. Rayner and E.L. Malone, pp. 291–377. Columbus, Ohio: Battelle, 1998.

Schmandt, J., and J. Clarkson. *The Regions and Global Warming*. New York: Oxford University Press, 1992.

Smith, J.B., and R. Mendelsohn. *The Impact of Climate Change on Regional Systems: A Comprehensive Analysis of California*. Cheltenham, U.K., and Northampton, Mass.: Elgar, 2007. Example of state-level impact analysis.

Yarnal, B. "Integrated Regional Assessment and Climate Change Impacts in River Basins." *Climate Research* 11.1 (1998), 65–74. Review of the rationale and progress of regional assessment at the river basin scale.

—C. Gregory Knight

REGIONAL PATTERNS OF CLIMATE CHANGE

The evidence is by now overwhelming that increasing concentrations of greenhouse gases (GHG) of anthropogenic origin have affected the Earth's climate in the twentieth century and will continue to do so increasingly throughout the twenty-first (Solomon et al., 2007). The radiative forcing due to increased GHG concentrations induces global warming of the Earth system, which in turn modifies the general circulation of the atmosphere and regional climates (Solomon et al., 2007). In order to predict the impacts of climate change on human societies and natural ecosystems it is thus necessary to quantify the regional patterns of climate change associated with global-warming projections. Traditionally, the uncertainty in regional climate change projections has been very large (Giorgi et al., 2001), but in recent years the scientific community has conducted more coordinated climate-change experiments that are starting to show emerging robust patterns of regional climate change. This article presents a review of such patterns along with a discussion of the main sources of uncertainty affecting them.

DATA AND METHODS

The material presented in this article makes use primarily of the CMIP3 data set recently completed in support of the Fourth Assessment Report of the Intergovernmental Panel on Climate Change (IPCC). This consists of simulations of twentieth- and twenty-first-century climate by 22 coupled atmosphere-ocean general circulation models (AOGCMs) from laboratories worldwide. The twentieth-century simulations employ historical GHG concentrations along with reconstructed natural forcings (solar activity and major volcanic eruptions). The twenty-first-century simulations employ GHG concentrations from three IPCC (Nakicenovic et al., 2000) SRES (Special Report on Emissions Scenarios) emission scenarios, the B1, A1B, and A2. These scenarios lie near the lower end (B1, CO_2 concentration

of about 550 ppm by 2100), the middle (A1B, 700 ppm by 2100), and the upper end (A2, 850 ppm by 2100) of the full SRES scenario range. Details on the models and simulations can be found at the CMIP3 web site (http://www.pcmdi.llni.gov).

We divide the year into two periods, April-September (A-S), the boreal warm (austral cold) season, and October-May (O-M), the boreal cold (austral warm) season. For each of these seasons we calculate the surface air temperature, precipitation, and sea-level pressure (SLP) climate-change signals defined as the difference between averages in the future 30-year climate period of 2071–2100 and the reference present-day period of 1961–1990. We note that, because of the regional pattern scaling properties found in the change signals of various surface climate variables (e.g., Giorgi and Bi, 2005a), changes in earlier decades of the twenty-first century, when the GHG concentration are lower, are similar in pattern to and smaller in magnitude than those shown here. In addition, for illustrative purposes we analyze here only results from the A1B scenario. However, for the above mentioned scaling properties, similar conclusions are valid for the other scenarios, the change patterns being similar across scenarios and depending on the GHG concentration levels (Giorgi and Bi, 2005a).

REGIONAL PATTERNS OF CLIMATE CHANGE

Figures 1 and 2 show the change in surface air temperature and precipitation (2071–2100 minus 1961–1990) for the two 6-month seasons and the scenario A1B. Prominent regional features in the change signals can be summarized as follows:

Temperature

- Warming occurs everywhere, but it is greater for land areas than ocean areas.
- The greatest warming is found over the Arctic and the Himalaya Plateau in O-M (cold season). This can be attributed to snow and sea-ice melting and the associated snow-albedo feedback mechanism. More generally, warming tends to increase with elevation during the cold season.
- Maximum warming in the A-S season is found over the Mediterranean Basin, western Sahara, Middle East, Tibetan Plateau, interior continental U.S., central Amazon Basin and southern Africa regions. These areas of maximum warming, occurring mostly in the local warm season, are associated with the general drying of continental interiors found in different generations of climate change experiments (Giorgi et al., 2001 and Soloman et al., 2007) and/or occur in correspondence of areas of projected decrease in precipitation (see below).

Precipitation

- Maximum increase in precipitation over high-latitude regions of both hemispheres. This is related to a poleward migration of storm tracks projected by most global models (see below).
- Precipitation increase along the ITCZ (intertropical convergence zone) over oceans, which is associated with the increased evaporation from the warmer underlying waters.

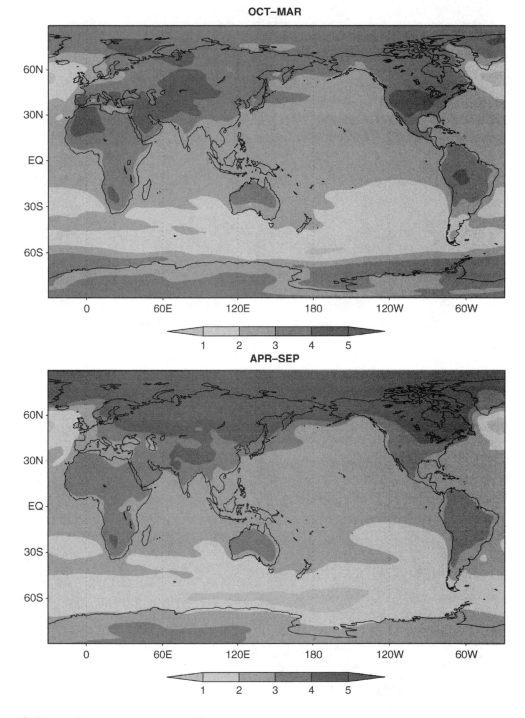

Regional Patterns of Climate Change. FIGURE 1. Ensemble Average Temperature Change (2071–2100 Minus 1961–1990) for October–March and April–September.

Periods from the CMIP3 models; A1B scenario. Units are degrees C.

- Marked precipitation decreases in both seasons over the Mediterranean and Central America regions.
- Decreased warm season precipitation over western Europe and the western United States.
- Pronounced decrease of precipitation over southern Africa and the eastern Amazon basin in A-S.

- Increased summer monsoon precipitation in South Asia and East Asia.
- Increased precipitation over equatorial East Africa in O-M (encompassing the short rainy season).
- Widespread decrease of precipitation over Australia in A-S, particularly in its westernmost regions.

Some of the regional precipitation change patterns of Figure 2 are related to changes in global circulation patterns. Figure 3 shows the CMIP3 ensemble average change in SLP for the A-S and O-M seasons. The most prominent feature emerging from

OCT–MAR

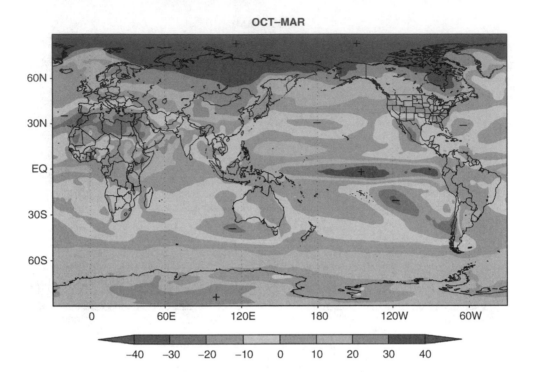

APR–SEP

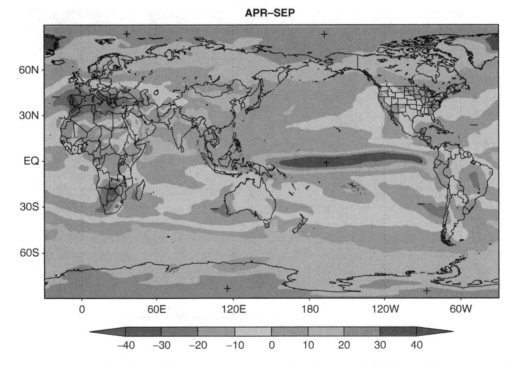

Figure 3 is the presence of bands of increased SLP between 30–60° latitude, both in the northern and southern hemispheres, with decreased SLP at higher latitudes. These are the result of a poleward shift of the mid-latitude jets and storm tracks, which is in turn due to greater mid-tropospheric warming in the tropics than at high latitudes that forces the regions of maximum meridional temperature gradients towards the poles (Solomon et al., 2007). Many areas of increased (decreased) precipitation are correlated with these areas of decreased (increased) SLP, because decreased (increased) SLP

Regional Patterns of Climate Change. FIGURE 2. Same as FIGURE 1 but for precipitation change. Units are % of 1961–1990 precipitation.

is an indication of greater (lesser) storminess. Also note that the land-ocean SLP contrast over Asia decreases in future climate conditions, which indicates a weakening of the South and East Asia monsoon circulations. Monsoon rain still increases, however, due to the greater water-holding capacity of the warmer future atmosphere.

OCT–MAR

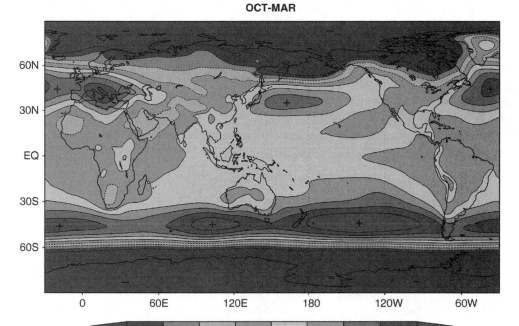

APR–SEP

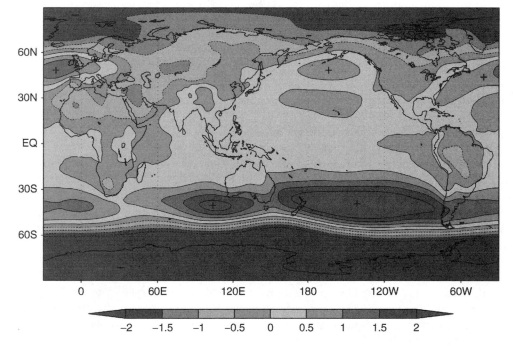

Regional Patterns of Climate Change. FIGURE 3. Same as Figure 1 but for sea level pressure (SLP). Units are hPa.

UNCERTAINTIES IN REGIONAL CLIMATE CHANGE PATTERNS

Regional climate change projections are affected by a number of uncertainty sources, which accumulate through all steps of the climate prediction process (Giorgi, 2005; Mearns et al., 2001).

At the top of this uncertainty "cascade" is the uncertainty due to GHG emissions and subsequent concentrations. This has been addressed by using a range of emission and concentration scenarios associated with different assumptions of socio-economic development (Nakicenovic et al., 2000).

Once the GHG concentrations from different scenarios are determined, they are fed into the AOGCMs to simulate the corresponding climate response. Sources of uncertainty in this step are associated with the different model representations of dynamical and physical processes (or model "configuration") and with the models' internal variability. The model-configuration uncertainty manifests itself in the responses of different models to the same GHG forcing. Conversely, the uncertainty due to the model internal variability is related to the effects of different initial states of the slowly evolving components of the climate system and can be explored by initializing a climate-change simulation with different ocean and biosphere states.

Once the AOGM simulations are completed, different regionalization techniques can be used to downscale the AOGCM fields and produce fine-scale climate information (e.g., regional climate models or statistical downscaling tools; Giorgi et al., 2001). This adds further uncertainty to the climate-change prediction.

Past evaluations (Houghton et al., 2001) have identified the largest sources of uncertainty in the emission/concentration scenarios and the different AOGCM configurations. Of the full uncertainty range of projected global warming by IPCC (Houghton et al., 2001: Solomon et al., 2007), about half is due to the range in scenarios and the other half to the range in AOGCM response. Although, as mentioned, ensemble average regional changes show remarkable scaling properties, the change signal at the regional scale often changes substantially across different models, especially for precipitation. In addition, multi-decadal variability and chaotic behavior are more pronounced at the regional than the global scale, and this can also mask the change signal. The uncertainty in regional climate changes is thus generally higher than at the large or global scale. For example, if we take the intermodel standard deviation as a measure of model configuration uncertainty, the temperature changes of Figure 1 are much greater than the standard deviation over the vast majority of the globe (not shown), indicating a high level of robustness. By contrast, the precipitation changes are greater than the intermodel standard deviation only over relatively small regions where the changes are largest (mostly the high latitudes, the Mediterranean and some portions of eastern and southern Africa, not shown). This indicates a large uncertainty in the regional precipitation change signal.

Finally, regional climate models simulations have shown that the change signal (e.g., for precipitation) can be substantially affected by local forcings, such as those caused by precipitation or land-use change (Giorgi et al., 2001). This adds a further level of uncertainty to the projection of regional climate change.

OTHER PROJECTED CHANGES

Concerning changes in additional climatic variables, IPCC (Solomon, et al., 2007) places high confidence in the following projected changes: increase in the frequency and intensity of heat waves and drought events, increase in the intensity of precipitation events; increase in the intensity of extratropical and tropical storms, and increase in the storm peak intensity (implying also an increase in peak wind intensity). These changes are general; their magnitude can vary substantially from region to region (for example, changes in tropical storms).

Different studies, using both global and regional models, have analyzed changes in interannual variability and found a widespread increase in variability, in both temperature and precipitation, in warm climate regimes (Raisanen, 2002; Giorgi and Bi, 2005b; Schär et al., 2004). This is consistent with an intensified hydrologic cycle and a greater efficiency of land-atmosphere feedbacks in the drier future continental interiors (Seneviratne et al., 2006). In cold climate regimes (winter season at mid and high latitudes), interannual variability in precipitation is still projected to mostly increase, while temperature variability is projected to mostly decrease. This has been attributed to the reduction of snow cover and the snow-albedo feedback mechanism (Raisanen, 2002).

DISCUSSION AND CONCLUSIONS

This article has provided a concise review of the basic patterns of regional climate change for the twenty-first century emerging from the latest set of AOGCM simulations. Some of these patterns show robust features, often associated with changes in general circulation patterns. The paper does not address the issue of observed trends, but some of the features shown by the projections are indeed consistent with observed trends, for example, the regional temperature warmings (Stott, 2003), the poleward shift of storm tracks, and the increase in heat waves and droughts (Solomon et al., 2007).

The analysis presented here makes use of the latest-generation CMIP3 AOGCM results, but many of the patterns found here are consistent with previous generations' model results (Giorgi et al., 2001). This increases their robustness. Despite a tremendous increase in computer power in the last decade, the horizontal resolution of current AOGCMs is still of the order of a few hundred kilometers, so that the patterns identified here can be considered as valid mostly for the broad regional to subcontinental scale (on the order of 1000 km and larger).

Regionalization techniques have been developed to produce fine-scale climate information (of the order of a few tens of kilometers or less). To date, regionalization experiments have been too scattered and targeted to provide a coherent picture of climate change over different regions. New coordinated regional model experiments involving relatively large numbers of models (e.g., Takle et al., 2007) and the increased maturity of all regionalization techniques (Giorgi et al., 2001), however, augur well for the use of such techniques in providing fine-scale climate information for use in impact assessment studies.

Although there are still large uncertainties in the prediction of regional climate changes, we have seen that some robust patterns are emerging. In order to reduce the uncertainties associated with the quantification of these change patterns we need to improve models, increase their resolution, and produce large ensembles of simulations. This appears possible with the rapid increase in computer power foreseen in the near future. More reliable regional climate change information will thus probably soon be available for use in impact, risk, adaptation, and mitigation studies.

BIBLIOGRAPHY

Giorgi, F. "Climate Change Prediction." *Climatic Change* 73.3 (2005), 239–265.

Giorgi, F., and X. Bi. "Updated Regional Precipitation and Temperature Changes for the 21st Century from Ensembles of Recent AOGCM Simulations." *Geophysical Research Letters* 32, L21715 (2005a). DOI: 10.1029/2005GL024288.

———. "Regional Changes in Surface Climate Interannual Variability for the 21st Century from Ensembles of Global Model Simulations." *Geophysical Research Letters* 32, L13701 (2005b). DOI: 10.1029/2005GL023002.

Giorgi, F., et al. "Regional Climate Information: Evaluation and Projections." In *Climate Change 2001: The Scientific Basis: Contribution of Working Group I to the Third Assessment Report of the Intergovernmental Panel on Climate Change*, edited by J.T. Houghton, et al., 583–638. Cambridge and New York: Cambridge University Press, 2001.

Houghton, J.T., et al., eds. *Climate Change 2001: The Scientific Basis: Contribution of Working Group I to the Third Assessment Report of the Intergovernmental Panel on Climate Change* . Cambridge and New York: Cambridge University Press, 2001.

Mearns, L.O., et al. "Climate Scenario Development." In *Climate Change 2001: The Scientific Basis: Contribution of Working Group I to the Third Assessment Report of the Intergovernmental Panel on Climate Change*, edited by J.T. Houghton, et al., 739–768. Cambridge and New York: Cambridge University Press, 2001.

Nakićenović, N., et al., eds. *Special Report on Emission Scenarios*. Intergovernmental Panel on Climate Change. Cambridge and New York: Cambridge University Press, 2000.

Raisanen, J. "CO_2-Induced Changes in Interannual Temperature and Precipitation Variability in 19 CMIP2 Experiments." *Journal of Climate* 15.17 (2002), 2395–2411. DOI: 10.1175/1520–0442(2002)015<2395:CICIIT>2.0.CO;2.

Schär, C., et al. "The Role of Increasing Temperature Variability in European Summer Heatwaves." *Nature* 427 (2004), 332–336. DOI: 10.1038/nature02300.

Seneviratne, S.I., et al. "Land-Atmosphere Coupling and Climate Change in Europe." *Nature* 443 (2006), 205–209. DOI: 10.1038/nature05095.

Solomon, S., et al., eds. *Climate Change 2007: The Physical Science Basis. Contribution of Working Group I to the Fourth Assessment Report of the Intergovernmental Panel on Climate Change*. Cambridge and New York: Cambridge University Press, 2007. The Summary for Policymakers is available at http://www.ipcc.ch/pdf/assessment-report/ar4/syr/ar4_syr_spm.pdf (accessed June 3, 2008).

Stott, P.A. "Attribution of Regional Scale Temperature Changes to Anthropogenic and Natural Causes." *Geophysical Research Letters* 30.14 (2003), 1728. DOI: 10.1029/2003GL017324.

Takle, E.S., et al. "Transferability Intercomparison: An Opportunity for New Insight on the Global Water Cycle and Energy Budget." *Bulletin of the American Meteorological Society* 88 (2007), 375–384. DOI: 10.1175/BAMS-88-3-375.

—Filippo Giorgi

REGULATION

Regulations are frequently necessary to achieve a desired level of environmental protection, but they need to be designed carefully and in full recognition that they often have unintended or perverse consequences. For example, the imposition of stringent new pollution-control standards for electric utilities may have made pollution worse by encouraging existing high-emitting sources of electricity to stay open longer. The potential for remedying market failure through government intervention must be weighed carefully against the potential for government failure.

An important justification for regulation is that unrestrained competition may fail to yield a socially efficient outcome. In the case of pollution, for example, if producers are not required to account for the costs of environmental degradation imposed on others, this could lead to excessive levels of pollution. The problem is particularly acute where environmental costs are spread over a large population, but the benefits of polluting are concentrated with a few producers. One approach to this problem is through direct regulation, whereby the government specifies a level of pollution reduction a firm must achieve and sometimes specifies the technology that must be used. An example of such command-and-control regulation is the requirement that zero-emitting vehicles be sold.

As concerns over air and water quality have grown, various laws have been passed to improve the state of the environment. The main instruments in efforts by the United States to curb pollution are major federal laws enacted by Congress. The implementation of these laws is left to the executive agencies, which pass rules that the private sector and state and local governments are required to follow. Those rules are compiled in the *Code of Federal Regulations*. The primary administrator of environmental laws is the Environmental Protection Agency (EPA), which is charged with implementing mandates to improve environmental quality. The Department of the Interior and the Department of Agriculture also play important roles by administering regulations to implement the Endangered Species Act and the conservation provisions of the Farm Bill. In some cases, the specifics of implementing the laws are left to the states. In addition, some states, most notably California, often pass regulations that are more stringent than the federal government's. The courts also play a role in the regulatory process by forcing agencies to comply with statutory deadlines and imposing major penalties if they are not met.

When the EPA was established in 1970, it was given the task of administering existing environmental statutes such as the Federal Insecticide, Fungicide, and Rodenticide Act, the Water Pollution Control Act (Clean Water Act), and the Air Pollution Control Act (Clean Air Act). The authority of the EPA has increased considerably since its inception through the addition of new environmental statutes as well as amendments to existing laws. There are now at least ten major U.S. federal laws that address environmental quality administered by the EPA. Some of those laws are media-specific—aimed, for example, at improving air or water quality. Others cover the use of specific chemicals such as pesticides or toxic pollutants. The largest in terms of the estimated cost of recent regulations is the Clean Air Act, second is the Resource Conservation and Recovery Act, and third is the Safe Drinking Water Act (Hahn, 1998).

Over the last three decades, as the number of environmental laws and the resulting regulations have increased, the total annual cost of those mandates has increased considerably. Indeed, according to the first comprehensive government report on the benefits and costs of federal regulation produced by the Office of Management and Budget, the direct costs of federally mandated environmental quality regulations is now approximately U.S.$150 billion in 1996 dollars (Office of Management and Budget, 1997). This is more than half of total federal government spending on all domestic discretionary programs. Estimates of direct and indirect costs using general-equilibrium economic modeling suggest that the costs are substantially higher (Hazilla and Kopp, 1990; Jorgenson and Wilcoxen, 1990). The benefits from those laws are less certain. Some estimates suggest that aggregate benefits are approximately equal to costs (Freeman, 1990; Hahn and Hird, 1991; Office of Management and Budget, 1997); others suggest that they substantially exceed costs (Environmental Protection Agency, 1997).

The aggregate analysis of benefits and costs masks some important information on individual regulations. It appears that many environmental regulations would not pass a standard benefit-cost test, even when the government's own estimates are used. For example, from 1980 to 1995, more than two-thirds of the federal government's environmental quality regulations failed a strict benefit-cost test (Hahn, 1998). As the EPA attempts to regulate even smaller risks in the future, there is a real danger that a larger fraction of rules could fail such a test. At the same time, there is reason to believe that more flexible regulations could save substantial amounts of money while reducing health risks. For example, one study found that a reallocation of mandated expenditures toward those regulations with the highest payoff to society could save as many as 60,000 more lives a year at no additional cost (Tengs and Graham, 1996).

One reason for the relatively high level of inefficient environmental regulation is that many of the laws prohibit the balancing of economic benefits and costs (Crandall et al., 1997; Fraas, 1991; Portney and Stavins, 1990). There have, however, been some recent attempts by Congress to place a greater emphasis on the balancing of benefits and costs. For example, under the Unfunded Mandates Reform Act of 1995, executive-branch agencies must prepare benefit-cost analyses for major rules. In addition, under the 1996 Safe Drinking Water Act Amendments, the EPA Administrator is required to publish a finding of whether the benefits of a maximum-contaminant-level standard justify the costs. Some scholars suggest that all major regulations, including environmental regulations, be required to pass a broadly defined benefit-cost test (Crandall et al., 1997). Others express more skepticism about the extent to which benefit-cost analysis should be relied upon in developing regulatory policy (e.g., Lave, 1996).

Another significant problem with environmental regulation is that current laws are overly prescriptive. The EPA has traditionally used a command-and-control approach to set uniform technology-based or performance-based standards. Both statutes and regulations frequently specify a preferred technology or set of technologies for achieving a given policy goal. For example, scrubbers were effectively required for some power plants as part of a compromise reached under the 1977 Clean Air Act Amendments (Ackerman and Hassler, 1981). Uniform performance standards are slightly more flexible, allowing a regulated entity to choose its own method for achieving a particular emission limit. While these approaches have been successful in meeting some environmental goals, they are unduly costly because they do not take into account differences in pollution-control costs across firms.

Economists have long recommended more flexible approaches, such as an emissions tax or a marketable-permit scheme that could achieve the same or similar environmental results at much lower cost (for example, see Bohm and Russell, 1985; Tietenberg, 1985). These market-based approaches create economic incentives that encourage firms to find cleaner and less expensive technologies to reach the environmental goal. For example, a firm that faces a tax on its air pollution has an incentive to reduce its emissions up to the point at which the cost of abatement is equal to the tax. By ensuring that each firm controls its emissions at the same marginal cost, the result is a cost-effective allocation of the overall burden of achieving the aggregate emissions-reduction goal. Many factors, such as the rising cost of environmental regulation and the increased importance of productivity and competitiveness in an increasingly global economy, have led to wider political support for market-based approaches (Hahn and Stavins, 1991). In recent years, tradable-permit schemes and taxes have been used to implement programs such as the phaseout of ozone-depleting chemicals and the reduction of sulfur dioxide emissions.

In general, economists agree that market-based mechanisms can help meet specified environmental goals cost-effectively. In addition, the use of economic analysis in balancing the costs and benefits of regulations can help ensure that environmental goals are set at desirable levels. But there is also widespread agreement that the practical application of these tools needs to be studied carefully to see how they can be designed and implemented most effectively.

The problem of selecting the right mix of regulatory instruments is formidable. In general, the appropriate regulatory tool will vary with the nature of the problem. If, for example, pollution results in local "hot spots," direct regulation may be the most effective tool. In contrast, for problems covering a broad area with a large number of sources, taxes or tradable permits may be more appropriate. The regulator will want to consider a number of factors in designing and implementing a policy, including economic efficiency, equity, transparency, and ease of administration.

[See also Environmental Law; and Joint Implementation.]

BIBLIOGRAPHY

Ackerman, B.A., and W.T. Hassler. *Clean Coal/Dirty Air: Or How the Clean Air Act became a Multibillion-Dollar Bail-Out for High-Sulfur Coal Producers and What Should Be Done About It.* New Haven, Conn.: Yale University Press, 1981.

Bohm, P., and C. Russell. "Comparative Analysis of Alternative Policy Instruments." In *Handbook of Natural Resource and Energy Economics*, edited by A.V. Kneese and J.L. Sweeney, vol. 1, pp. 395–460. Amsterdam and New York: North-Holland, 1985.

Council of Economic Advisers. "*Economic Report of the President.*" Washington, D.C.: U.S. Government Printing Office, 1998.

Crandall, R.W., et al. "*An Agenda for Reforming Federal Regulation.*" Washington, D.C.: AEI Press and Brookings Institution Press, 1997.

Environmental Protection Agency. *Environmental Investments: Cost of a Clean Environment.* EPA-230–11–90–083. Washington, D.C, 1990.

Environmental Protection Agency. *The Benefits and Costs of the Clean Air Act: 1970 to 1990.* Washington, D.C., 1997.

Fraas, A.G. "The Role of Economic Analysis in Shaping Environmental Policy." *Law and Contemporary Problems* 54.4 (1991), 113–125.

Freeman, A.M. III. "Water Pollution Policy." In *Public Policies for Environmental Protection*, edited by P.R. Portney. Washington, D.C.: Resources for the Future, 1990. The second edition was published in 2000.

Hahn, R.W. "United States Environmental Policy: Past, Present, and Future." *Natural Resources Journal* 34.2 (1994), 305–348.

———. "Regulatory Reform: Assessing the Government's Numbers." In *Reviving Regulatory Reform: A Global Perspective*, edited by R.W. Hahn. New York: AEI Press, 1998.

Hahn, R.W., and J.A. Hird. "The Costs and Benefits of Regulation: Review and Synthesis." *Yale Journal on Regulation* 8.1 (1991), 233–278.

Hahn, R.W., and R.N. Stavins. "Incentive Based Environmental Regulation: A New Era from an Old Idea?" *Ecology Law Quarterly* 18 (1991), 1–42.

Hazilla, M., and R.J. Kopp. "The Social Cost of Environmental Quality Regulations: A General Equilibrium Analysis." *Journal of Political Economy* 98.4 (1990), 853–873.

Jorgenson, D.W., and P.J. Wilcoxen. "Environmental Regulation and U.S. Economic Growth." *Rand Journal of Economics* 21.2 (1990), 314–340.

Lave, L.B. "Benefit–Cost Analysis: Do the Benefits Exceed the Costs?" In *Risks, Costs, and Lives Saved: Getting Better Results from Regulation*, edited by R.W. Hahn. Oxford and New York: Oxford University Press; Washington, D.C.: AEI Press, 1996.

Office of Management and Budget. *More Benefits, Fewer Burdens*. Washington, D.C., 1996.

Office of Management and Budget. *Report to Congress on the Costs and Benefits of Federal Regulation*. Washington, D.C., 1997.

Portney, P.R., and R.N. Stavins, eds. *Public Policies for Environmental Protection*. Washington, D.C.: Resources for the Future, 1990.

Tengs, T.O., and J.D. Graham. "The Opportunity Costs of Haphazard Social Investments in Life-Saving?" In *Risks, Costs, and Lives Saved: Getting Better Results from Regulation*, edited by R.W. Hahn, 167–182. New York: Oxford University Press; Washington, D.C.: AEI Press, 1996.

Tietenberg, T.H. *Emissions Trading: An Exercise in Reforming Pollution Policy*. Washington, D.C.: Resources for the Future, 1985.

—ROBERT W. HAHN AND FUMIE YOKOTA

RELIGION

The vast majority of humans identify with one or another of the world religions. The *International Bulletin of Missionary Research*, which provides estimates of world religious identifications, lists only 225 million atheists and 886 million nonreligious among the globe's six billion inhabitants. While there are great gaps between nominal identification and active practice among those listed, the major religions influence cultures far beyond the immediate sphere of committed members.

Reckoning by nominal identification, one-third of humanity is Christian, with 2 billion followers, while Islam is growing rapidly, having attracted one-seventh of the global population at midcentury, and moving toward one-fifth, or 1.15 billion people, near the century's end. Judaism—the third member of what are often called the Abrahamaic, Jerusalemaic, or Peoples of the Book communities—is comparatively small, about fifteen million, but is influential far beyond its numbers. Meanwhile, faiths classified as "Eastern" attract hundreds of millions: 806 million are listed as Hindu, 328 million are Buddhist, while Sikhs claim 20 million. The new-religionist and tribal-religionist movements, which are harder to classify, number 125 million and 100 million, respectively.

Given such large constituencies, what religions teach and do about global change, whether constructively or destructively, has enormous implications, and is like to reveal more as the decades pass. Adherence and participation in the various religions mean vastly different things in different cultures, but those numbers of estimated adherents themselves suggest how vital it is for those who think of population, development, and environmental responsibilities to make attitudes toward and the actions of religion an important consideration.

WHAT RELIGIONS SIGNIFY

Religion in these contexts does not mean only dogma or doctrine—many religions around the world have no formal versions of these—attendance at sanctuaries for sacred rites, or membership in congregations that can be numbered in yearbooks or encyclopedias. Religion instead deals first with what theologian Paul Tillich called people's "ultimate concern." Normally, people form communities that reinforce such concern. They prefer mythic language and symbolic forms to pragmatic expression, and enhance these with rites and ceremonies that relate to the passages of life, the changing seasons of the year and their import, as well as presumed historic events at the root of such religions. Most imply or specify what might be called a metaphysical backdrop, which would mean a claim that, behind the ordinary visible human scene, a cosmic drama is occurring. All of this also calls for prescribed or encouraged behavioral forms.

RELIGIOUS IMPLICATIONS

This picture of religion suggests why so many people relate to natural and anthropogenic change through religion, and why topics such as population, development, and the environment cannot be exhausted by resort only to political, scientific, or practical agendas.

Population, for example, alludes to the intimate and vital processes relating to love and marriage, birth and death, themes in which all religions specialize as humans try to make sense of an often mysterious world and their part in it. Development implies concern for the resources of the Earth and their cultivation, distribution, and stewardship. The myths and symbols, rites and ceremonies of the various faiths relate to precisely these themes. And environmental responsibility is integral to most religious proclamations and commandments.

However otherworldly some faiths may be, they survive also because they address the ordinary daily lives of people who are dependent upon resources of water, air, and earth. If what might be called "merely secular forces and impulses" address these zones of concern, they will meet resistance from religious leaders or be ignored by many informed and obedient followers. If, however, they tap into the religious impetuses, they will also be advanced by religious forces.

Thus Judaism and Christianity, on the first page of their sacred scriptures in the book of Genesis, hear of divine commands to the storied first human pair. These commands are ambiguous; they can be interpreted in ways that may either enhance or be destructive of care. "Be fruitful and multiply, and fill the Earth and subdue it; and have dominion over ... every living thing that moves upon the Earth." Though long cherished as a divine charter for parental responsibility in an underpopulated world and a call to vocational creativity in the natural environment, in recent decades—especially after an influential essay by critic Lynn White (1967)—this passage has been seen as destructive. Under its influence, it was said, humans interpreted global life far too anthropocentrically and rendered nature exploitable by believers who thought they had a sacred charter for using environmental resources to the point of despoiling and depleting them.

When religious beliefs and practices are monitored or disciplined by effective religious authority, they acquire special power. A modern dictator, Joseph Stalin, is said to have sneered at formal churchly authority with a disdainful question, "How many divisions has the pope?" The pope, as head of the 992-million-member Catholic Church, did not need military divisions to wield power at the 1994 Cairo Conference on Population and Development. In tandem with spokespersons for some schools of Islamic thought, particularly those often classified as "fundamentalist," the Vatican, Catholicism's headquarters and a state that has a voice in the United Nations, attracted headlines and redirected the agenda for days. Its actions were in opposition to most methods of birth control and family planning that are advocated by the non-Catholic, non-Muslim-fundamentalist majorities. So long as the Vatican opposes what is often called "artificial means of birth control," it is difficult for the United Nations or private sources to be effective in population planning, especially in poorer regions of the world. It might be noted that in nations such as the United States, the vast majority of Catholic women, when polled, make clear that they do not follow Catholic strictures against birth control, but that does not lessen the energy or do much to limit the influence of Catholic authority on the global scene.

At the same time, Pope John Paul II, traveling around the world proclaiming a familiar theme of his papacy, *dignitatis humanae* (of human dignity), argued that the needs of expanding populations can be met if nations develop policies that make the best use of the resources of the Earth and enlarge their potential and production.

RELIGIOUS DIVERSITY

When religious leadership convenes to address development and environmentalism, authorities who cannot agree on God—who God is, whether God is, how one interacts with the sacred, and who determines truth about relations to the sacred—tend to concur that religions are chartered to support human dignity. Critics see most religion as focused on other-worldliness and thus irresponsible about the global environment. It was true that many religions, by encouraging asceticism as religious discipline or offering hope to the hopelessly poor in this life (by promising compensation and reward in the life to come), devalued earthly concerns. So it was that many spiritual agencies were late to address the dangers of exploitation in the world of nature and human endeavor.

As movements encouraging sustainable development and global environmental responsibility have spread in the last third of the twentieth century, however, many religious leaders have explored anew their scriptures and tenets and have begun to accent underemphasized and overlooked themes. In the world of Western religion, often characterized as too devoted to human dominion over the nonhuman scene, this new exploration has encouraged the uncovering of scriptural and traditional devotion to the beauties of creation as gifts of the divine.

In an age of increasingly rapid communication and efficient use of media, populations have become aware of environmental attitudes of religions that had once seemed remote and had been regarded merely as competitors to their own cherished and exclusive faiths. So Westerners were taught by others to listen to and to respect as sacred the voices of earth, sky, and stream and to live in harmony with the rhythms of the year and the cycles of nature. Meanwhile, Western gospels of efficiency and productivity, many of them religiously informed, spread worldwide. As technological medicine led to increased population and the importation of exploitative practices to places where nature had not previously been regarded as a resource to be despoiled by humans, new problems arose. As an illustration, Native American attitudes to tribe, nature, and spirit, long dismissed as superstition by Christian and secular Americans, came to be regarded as offering valuable lessons far beyond the reservations in which American Indians had been segregated.

On the global scene, with world religions coming into ever closer contact, whether in conflict or agreement on ethical issues, Westerners are showing more interest than before in attitudes to the environment of "non-Western" faith communities, which are also increasingly present internationally. Islam teaches responsibility to others, also in the use of resources. Thus Muslims drew on the Qur'an (Koran), their holy book, to advance environmental conservation in Pakistan in 2001. Buddhists have drawn and can draw on teachings that one should consume as few goods as necessary, and promote well-being through proper use of resources. While Buddhism and Hinduism can lead toward attitudes of passivity to the environment because adherents are to seek release from the world or to find Nirvana, in recent generations environmentally concerned members of such religious communities are also revisiting their sacred books and using formerly underemphasized teachings to inspire concern for forests and rivers.

ON BALANCE

At the end of the twentieth century, any balance sheet on which religious influence is to be appraised would reveal drastic changes and developments. Forces conventionally labeled "secularizing" have increased in strength. There has been an increase in the influence of industry, technology, and commerce. Encroaching ideological forces—such as Communist materialism in the former Soviet Union and China, or post-Enlightenment thought prevailing in European and American universities—have increased their hold on human imagination and practice. Religion, then, has been expected progressively to dwindle, if not to disappear. If religion was to survive, it was often foreseen that only smaller defensive movements, of the sort that remained in the totalitarian world, or compromising and genteel versions in the free world, would endure. Instead, religion has, by all reckonings, prospered, and its burgeoning versions are often those that make intense demands, possess strong holds on emotions, and are expressed in hard-line versions with which political forces have had to reckon.

While these versions of religions have often blocked a full range of approaches to population, development, and environmental issues, concurrently there has spread on the global scene both an awareness of religions that urge the celebration of the environment and concern for the nonhuman world, just as they promote population planning and sustainable development as pleasing to God or congruent with the sacred, and an awareness of the fragility of the environment and human responsibility to prosper and share intelligent use of resources.

[*See also* Belief Systems; Human Populations; *and* Population Policy.]

BIBLIOGRAPHY

Gardner, G.T. *Inspiring Progress: Religions' Contributions to Sustainable Development*. New York: Norton, 2006

Gottlieb, R.S. *The Oxford Handbook of Religion and Ecology*. Oxford and New York: Oxford University Press, 2006

Kurtz, L.R. *Gods in the Global Village: The World's Religions in Sociological Perspective*. Thousand Oaks, Calif.: Pine Forge Press, 1995. The second edition was published in 2007.

White, L. Jr. "The Historical Roots of Our Ecologic Crisis." *Science* 155 (1967), 1203 1207. DOI: 10.1126/science.155.3767.1203.

—MARTIN E. MARTY

RENEWABLE SOURCES OF ENERGY

There is a wide range of renewable energy sources, some of which depend on the sun's energy to grow crops, while others entail the direct use of solar radiation, and still others harness the continuous flows of wind and water that depend ultimately on solar radiation.

RENEWABLE LIQUID FUELS (BIOFUELS)

These offer the potential for a secure supply of fuels for vehicles, and for diminished emissions of carbon dioxide. Technologies for biofuels production are well established, but net energy efficiency varies with the types of feedstock employed, and competition with food crops is a serious issue. [*See* Biofuels; *and* Ethanol.]

OTHER BIOMASS

Wood chips and other biomass are used to fuel some electrical generating plants. Significant amounts of methane gas can be retrieved from landfills: this source is referred to as municipal solid wastes (MSW) and landfill gas (LFG).

SOLAR HEAT FOR BUILDINGS AND HOT WATER

"Solar energy" is a general term often applied to electrical generation, while "solar heat" encompasses low-tech, low-cost installations that, combined with adequate insulation and sun-oriented building design, can displace substantial amounts of fuel and electricity now used to heat buildings and water for domestic or industrial use.

Passive design in buildings employs orientation to the sun, shade trees, and overhangs (to take advantage of low winter sun and high summer sun), insulation, and simple heat storage in massive walls, rock, or water. Active designs use solar collectors that heat water to be stored and circulated in winter, or used for domestic hot water.

ELECTRICAL GENERATION

Various forms of noncombustion electrical generation promise, hypothetically, electric power free from air pollution and greenhouse gases. In fact, the manufacture of solar or wind-powered devices currently consumes fuels and fuel-generated electricity; so careful life-cycle analysis is needed to reveal the net environmental benefit. If the manufacturing were accomplished with combustion-free electricity, then the ideal would be accomplished, the only limitation being the energy cost of materials.

Solar-electric

There are two kinds of solar-electric generation. The first is solar-thermal, in which the sun's rays are focused by lenses and concentrated to heat water or other fluids that ultimately drive a turbine and dynamo. This concentrated solar power may be gathered and used in a number of ways that have been tested in experiments and pilot plants around the world. The applications are usually assumed to be utility-scale operations that require large areas in regions of clear skies and direct sun that can be concentrated. The various technologies and their potential for large-scale development in coming decades are explained in a study published in 2005 (Greenpeace).

The second kind of solar-electric is photovoltaic, in which solar radiation falls on light sensitive materials that immediately create a flow of electrons. The devices are modular and can be assembled into small or large arrays for residences, larger buildings, or utility-scale installations. This is the technology often assumed for distributed electrical generation versus central power plants and long transmission lines. Although they perform best under clear skies, they do not require concentration, so they work adequately on a cloudy day.

Germany, Japan, and the United States now lead in photovoltaic generating capacity. At the end of 2005, Germany and Japan each had roughly 38% of the world total and the United States roughly 13%; the German capacity was the equivalent of one and a half large nuclear power plants (International Energy Agency). The history of photovoltaic power in world nations (Figure 1) shows not only rapid growth in recent years but also a shift from isolated, off-grid, installations to utility-scale and other grid-connected projects. Research continues to improve the efficiency of photovoltaic devices and to make them competitive with conventional sources of electricity.

Wind power

As wind-electric generators become more reliable and less expensive they assume greater importance. Measured by total

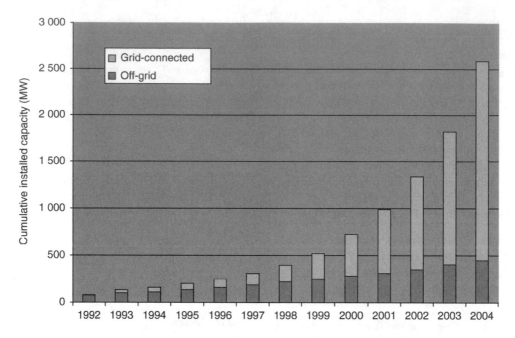

Renewable Sources of Energy. Figure 1. World Cumulative Installed Photovoltaic Capacity, 1992–2004.

(Source: International Energy Agency, 2007).

installed generating capacity in 2006, Germany, Spain, and the United States stand out, with 20,650, 11,610, and 11,570 megawatts respectively—1,000 megawatts being the rating of a typical large nuclear plant. The U.S. wind farms are mostly in California and Texas.

Measured by electrical output as a proportion of national electrical consumption, nations line up very differently: Denmark gets 21.4% of its electrical needs from the wind, Spain 8.8%, Portugal 7.0%, Germany 7%, and the United States 0.8% (see DOE Annual Report). In the United States all wind farms now are land-based, though several projects are proposed for offshore locations in Massachusetts, Texas, Delaware, New Jersey, New York, and Georgia.

Hydroelectric Power

Hydropower has always been the leading provider of renewable electricity. Recently it has provided about 16% of the world's electrical output, and 89% of its renewable electrical output. Canada and the United States report roughly the same annual hydro output—Canada 334 billion KWh, U.S. 276 billion KWh—but for Canada that is 58% of total output and for the U.S. only 7%. Hydro accounts for 97% of renewable electrical output in Canada, and 75% in the United States (raw data from EIA, 2004).

Although the U.S. hydro potential still is only half developed, there are barriers to further growth because of environmental effects such as fish mortality and changes to water quality downstream from the dam, as well as flooding of valuable lands by the reservoir. [*See* Dams.] The U.S. National Renewable Energy Laboratory (NREL) now is working on advanced hydropower technologies that promise to reduce environmental impacts. NREL estimates that if advanced systems were applied the nation could add 15,000–20,000 megawatts of capacity at existing dams and 30,000 mW at undeveloped sites. If 45,000 mW were added, this would increase the U.S. hydro capacity by 45%, from 99,000 to 144,000 mW (NREL, March 2006).

Geothermal electric

Geothermal resources are classified as low-temperature or high-temperature. Many hot springs can be used to heat buildings, as in Boise, Idaho, and in 16 other district-heating systems in the United States. There are many others around the world, the best known being in Iceland. Even the average ground temperatures at shallow depth can be used—as a heat source for heat pumps—because a persistent subsurface temperature of 50°F (10°C) is attractive when the winter air temperature at the surface is 20 to 30°F (−7 to −1°C).

A more significant contribution comes from high-temperature geothermal systems that produce steam or hot water that can be used to generate electricity. The occurrences are restricted to geologically younger areas of a continent, as in the southwestern U.S. A steam-driven electrical generating complex has operated at the Geysers in California since 1960; and by the mid-1980's geothermal-electric plants were operating also in Hawaii, Utah, and Nevada. Generating capacity in the U.S. peaked at 2,900 mW in the period 1996–1998 and diminished to roughly 2,200 mW in 2004, when it was roughly 28% of the world total. U.S. nonelectric (direct-use) geothermal capacity is roughly 25% of world total (NERL *Energy Data Book*, 2007).

CONTRIBUTIONS OF RENEWABLE SOURCES

One way to assess the value of renewable sources of energy is by the amounts of fossil fuel they displace. One analysis, using installed renewable-electric capacities as of 2006 and making a number of assumptions about their output, results in tonnages of coal being displaced annually (Table 1). An important

TABLE 1. Amounts of Coal Now Displaced by Renewable Electrical Generation

	Million Short Tons	Capacity Factor (Percent)
Hydropower	150.125	44
Biomass	22.883	80
Wind	18.049	36
Geothermal	8.716	90
Solar thermal	0.412	24
Solar photovoltaic	0.274	22

SOURCE: NREL, *Energy Data Book*, 2007

TABLE 2. Projected Renewable Electricity Net Generation (billion kilowatt hours) and Carbon Dioxide Emissions Saved (million metric tons of carbon)

	2015		2025	
	Net Gen.	CO_2 Svd.	Net Gen.	CO_2 Svd.
Geothermal	15.60	2.88	35.00	5.37
Wind	64.60	11.93	558.60	85.69
Solar	12.80	2.36	151.10	23.18
Hydroelectric	303.70	56.10	304.30	46.68
Biomass	29.60	5.47	39.30	6.03
MSW & LFG	27.80	5.13	28.60	4.39
Total	454.70	83.99	927.90	142.34

SOURCE: NREL Power Technologies Energy Data Book (Edition #4) www.nrel.gov/analysis/power

element in the calculation is the extent to which a generating facility produces at its rated capacity, its so-called capacity factor. This varies from 90% for geothermal to 22% for photovoltaic, illustrating a weakness of solar and wind power installations: their output is intermittent and variable, making storage technologies extremely important. Research on batteries, flywheels, and chemical-flow storage is continuing at a number of centers including Sandia National Laboratories.

Future benefits of renewable electric generation can be assessed by projecting the electrical output and deducing the carbon dioxide emissions saved by displacing fuel-burning generation of electricity (Table 2). The analysis represented here made projections for 2010, 2015, 2020, 2025, and 2030; we show data for only two of those years and for the model that assumes strong growth in geothermal, wind, and solar power. That growth will depend partly on federal funding of research and development, and incentives for reducing emissions from coal-burning power plants. [*See* Appendix; Carbon Taxes; Emissions Trading; *and* National Energy Policy in the United States.]

READINGS AND INFORMATION SOURCES

GENERAL
U.S. National Renewable Energy Laboratory (NREL) www.nrel.gov

SOLAR
American Solar Energy Society www.ases.org
Greenpeace, *Concentrated Solar thermal Power-Now.* Sept., 2005. An excellent review of various technologies and their potential for growth. www.greenpeace.org

WIND
Gipe, Paul. *Wind Power: Renewable Energy for Home, Farm, and Business.* White River Junction, VT: Chelsea Green Publishing Co., 2004.
American Wind Energy Association www.awea.org
World Wind Energy Association www.wwindea.org

HYDROELECTRIC
U.S. National Renewable Energy Laboratory (NREL) *Power Technologies Data Book,* March 2006

GEOTHERMAL
U.S. Department of Energy (DOE) *Geothermal Program* www.eere.energy.gov/geothermal

ENERGY STORAGE
Sandia National Laboratories, *Energy Storage Systems.* www.sandia.gov/ess/Technology

—DAVID J. CUFF

RESOURCES

If human economic activities are viewed as an integral part of the environment, which provides materials and absorbs waste products (Figure 1), then resources are essentially identical to the environment. Although fuels, building materials, and raw materials for industry are useful, air and water are even more important as resources essential to life. The equivalence of natural resources and the environment is demonstrated when newly-discovered plant species are found to be sources of medicines and chemicals.

Because resource use is intimately entwined with pollution of air and water and the accumulation of solid wastes, an important issue is whether extraction and processing of certain resources can continue without regard for environmental costs. If the price of a refined metal were to include the costs of preventing or remediating damage to land, air, and water, then higher prices for the metal would presumably reduce the amounts of the raw resource being mined. [*See* Externalities.] High prices would, of course, tend to reduce standard of living. This conundrum complicates the question of how to encourage development while developing a more harmonious relationship with the environment than has been maintained by the now-industrial nations. [*See* Sustainable Growth.]

ATTITUDES TOWARD RESOURCES

The ways humans interact with resources are determined by social, cultural, and ideological factors, which filter our perception of the resources and affect how profoundly we alter them (Figure 2). The most potent cultural factor is scientific or technological level: an early human traveling on foot may have regarded an oil seep as a barrier to be crossed, a person traveling by canoe might use the gummy stuff to patch holes in the hull, while a twentieth-century technologist sees it as a clue to crude oil for numerous applications—and, furthermore, has the drilling rigs to extract oil in immense quantities. The cultural filter

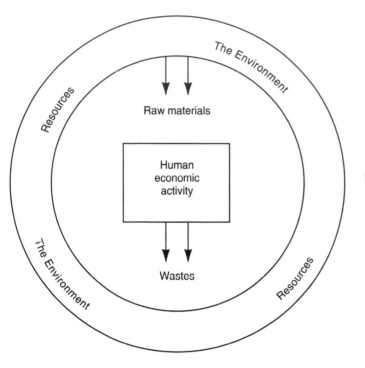

Resources. Figure 1. Resources (the Environment) and Human Activity.

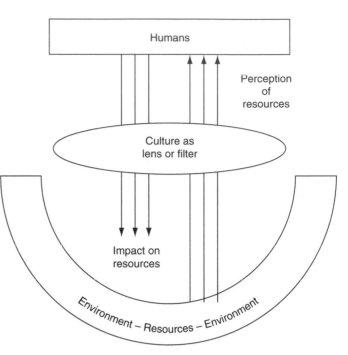

Resources. Figure 2. Culture Intervening between Humans and Resources.

(Derived from ideas of Alfred L. Kroeber, Berkeley anthropologist.)

determines human impact on the environment mainly through differences in technological level and affluence whose effects are multiplied by population. The combined result can be summarized by the simple IPAT expression: Impact = Population × Affluence × Technology.

In the absence of organization or regulation, individuals (or groups, or industries) may satisfy their own needs without regard for others who also need the same resource. Any such natural resources—and there are few that do not qualify—are considered common-pool resources, or common-property resources. Grazing lands, or a particular groundwater aquifer, are examples. On a global scale, the atmosphere, oceans and all natural endowments, including mineral deposits, forests, fishing grounds, and wildlife, may be considered common, regardless of national boundaries, because any citizen, or the descendants of that person, may be compromised by the loss of a scarce metal or a threatened plant species. [*See* Commons; *and* Tragedy of the Commons.]

While some resource uses such as ocean fishing are regulated by international arrangements, it is usually national policy that controls the extraction of mineral or forest resources. In North America there still are policies that encourage exploration for and production of these resources and perpetuate a frontier attitude toward the land. One such policy is the depletion allowance that permits companies to deduct from their taxable income the value of resources produced. The private company therefore benefits from depletion of its assets, the same minerals or forests whose production yields income. However, in the United States and most other nations, this depletion of natural resources is not considered when

calculating net national product—unlike capital assets like factories and equipment, whose depreciation is charged against the value of national production. Thus, "A country could exhaust its mineral resources, cut down its forests, erode its soils, pollute its aquifers, and hunt its wildlife and fisheries to extinction, but measured income would not be affected as these assets disappeared" (Repetto et al., 1989).

RENEWABLE VS. NONRENEWABLE RESOURCES

Generally, air, water, animals and plants, including crops, are considered renewable, while mineral resources are nonrenewable. That simple division can be enhanced by applying a scale of renewability that accounts for the time required for regeneration of a resource (Figure 3).

At the renewable end of the scale are constant-flow resources— solar radiation, air, wind, and surface water. Requiring only a few years for renewal are plant and animal life, such as annual crops, trees that are pruned each year for fuel, and livestock that mature within a few years. At the next level are trees for lumber that require decades to regrow. Geothermal heat in shallow, exploitable occurrences can be quenched in three or four decades of use and may require a similar time to recover, although in some discussions this energy is considered renewable because the ultimate source is practically inexhaustible. Ground water, if mined to exhaustion, will require decades or centuries to be replenished, depending on climate and exposure of the aquifer. Half a meter of soil lost to erosion would be replaced only after thousands of years, even in a moist climate.

When economic minerals such as metals and fossil fuels are considered, the scale shifts drastically to hundreds of millions of

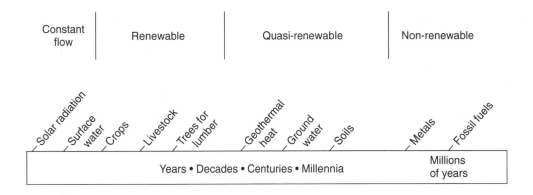

Resources. FIGURE 3. The Spectrum of Resource Renewability.

years. Such resources are all clearly in the nonrenewable category, but there is a useful distinction: whereas metals, once refined, can be reused, fossil fuels yield their energy just once.

Serious deterioration of resources can occur even at the renewable end of the scale. Although their volumes are renewable, rivers, lakes, and estuaries can be so degraded by pollutants that decades are required for recovery; and severe poisoning may exceed nature's ability to restore their natural state. Ground water, while less exposed to most pollutants, may require centuries to recover, because its flow rates are so low. [*See* Water.]

MINERALS: THE NONRENEWABLES

While uneven, the distribution of minerals on a global or continental scale is not random but follows the patterns of the major rock types that make up every continent. Most metals, for instance, occur in crystalline rocks that occur in mountain belts and in ancient shield areas that are the cores of continents. Fossil fuels occur in sedimentary rock that overlies crystalline basement rock, obscuring it and making it unavailable for prospecting for most metals. Nations of continental size, such as Canada, the United States, Russia, and Australia, have greater potential for both metals and fossils fuels, while an island nation such as Japan has more limited possibilities.

AMOUNTS OF NONRENEWABLE RESOURCES REMAINING

While estimates of renewable resource amounts, such as cubic meters of lumber or metric tons of biomass, are not simple, they do involve straightforward assessment of land areas that are evident and measurable. The same is not true of nonrenewable (mineral) resources. Our mineral endowment is often said to be finite, implying that it is strictly limited and that it will not grow. That is true, but the amounts available are indefinite because of two uncertainties. The first arises from incomplete exploration: there will always be some possibility of undiscovered deposits of metallic ores or crude-oil accumulations, and those undiscovered amounts can only be estimated. The second uncertainty arises from changing economic factors and technological advances, both of which can alter the definition of a usable or economic deposit.

Both uncertainties can be recognized and dealt with if a rectangle encloses all existing amounts of some mineral substance in

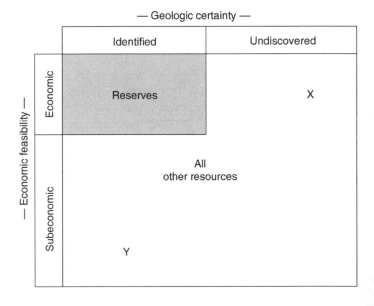

Resources. FIGURE 4. General Scheme for Classifying Mineral Resource Amounts.

(From United States Geological Survey, 1975.)

a specified region or nation, whether those resources are discovered or undiscovered (Figure 4). The horizontal dimension expresses how thoroughly defined the deposits or occurrences are: identified amounts are toward the left, undiscovered amounts are on the right. The vertical dimension accommodates differences in economic feasibility: rich deposits that are shallow, or otherwise easily recovered and processed, are placed toward the top and classed as economic, while deposits less rich, more deeply buried, or otherwise difficult to attain are toward the lower end of the scale, and classed as subeconomic. The criterion for economic amounts is that they be recoverable at current prices and with current technology. This general framework can be applied to any mineral resource, but when used for some specific mineral, both the geologic and economic dimensions are divided more finely to account for gradations in certainty and in economic feasibility.

Amounts that are both identified and economic are considered reserves (amounts in the ground, not in stockpiles). Other resources of the same substance do not qualify as reserves: they may be attractive economically but have not yet been discovered (position X in Figure 4), or they may be well defined geologically but uneconomic (position Y).

Although reserves are firmly defined, their magnitude changes through time. Obviously, production from a deposit will diminish reserves, but two processes augment them. First is the discovery of suitable resources that allow the reserve category to expand toward the right. Equally important are rising prices or new technologies, both of which can lower the economic threshold and transform known subeconomic amounts into reserves. When estimating the life of a mineral resource, it is necessary to recognize this potential for expansion of reserves. Any estimate of resource life that uses only current reserve figures will produce a short estimate that is unrealistic and will brand the author an alarmist.

The life of a particular nonrenewable resource can be estimated by dividing total resources remaining (deduced by geological principles) by current production rate or by a rate assumed to increase through time. If rates of use increase continually at a fixed percentage, the impact upon resource amounts is staggering. For instance, if production increases steadily at 3.5% per year (a rate consistent with world energy use in the 1990s), then the cumulative amount used will double in twenty years, implying that if some mineral resource were half gone by the year 2010, it would be exhausted by 2030.

THE METALS

Two main factors determine which metallic ores are easily obtained and processed to meets the needs of an industrial society. First is the metal's abundance in rocks of the earth's crust. Second is the ease with which the mineral that contains the metals can be separated from host rock and then broken down chemically to release the metal. Only five metals occur in average crustal rock at concentrations greater than 0.1%: they are aluminum, iron, manganese, magnesium, and titanium. These are the abundant metals; among them aluminum and iron stand out, with respective concentrations of 8.0 and 5.8% in average rock. The scarce metals vary greatly in concentration: zinc is 0.005%, lead 0.0039%, copper 0.0024%, silver 0.000004%, gold 0.000002%, and platinum 0.0000005%. Of course, average rock is not mined for these metals, but iron and aluminum ores need be only 5–10 times background concentration, while ores of platinum and gold must be on the order of 1,000 times as rich as background rock (Skinner, 1986, p. 96).

Many scarce metals are commonplace—zinc, lead, and copper, for instance, are widely used and often discarded. Platinum, with six zeroes in its abundance rating, is used in catalytic converters of millions of vehicles. Lead is used in auto batteries replaced every few years and sometimes consigned to landfills. Some of these scarce metals may be in very short supply during the twenty-first century. Such alarms have been sounded before, but the circumstances may be different now that very large populations are becoming more industrial and may soon use these metals at rates currently enjoyed by wealthy nations. Platinum's role in catalytic converters may become obsolete if internal combustion engines are phased out, but platinum is a vital component of fuel cells. Gallium and indium are scarce metals used to make indium-gallium arsenide, the semiconducting material essential to a new generation of more efficient photovoltaic cells. Other metals that appear threatened include zinc, hafnium (in computer chips), and terbium used in fluorescent light bulbs (Cohen, 2007).

The dates when these metals will run low are difficult to predict because of limited information on reserves and additional resources that may become available when prices rise. Many experts agree, however, that substitution, conservation, and more recycling will be essential, because "virgin stocks of several metals appear inadequate to sustain the modern 'developed world' quality of life for all of Earth's people under contemporary technology" (Gordon et al., 2006).

CONFLICTS OVER RESOURCES

Conflicts over water supply have been part of human history wherever people share a river system. Today, conflicts occur between national groups in the Nile watershed, the Jordan, Tigris-Euphrates, and the Indus (Klare, 2001). Conflicts between regions within a country and between agricultural and urban interests erupt when the limited river volume must be shared, as with the Colorado River in the United States.

Nonrenewable resources are the cause of major conflicts between nations: oil in the Persian Gulf region; oil and gas in the Caspian Sea region; and oil in the South China Sea. Intertribal conflicts centered on metals and diamonds have plagued countries in sub-Saharan Africa, while gold and copper mining companies have clashed with indigenous peoples in Papua New Guinea (Klare, 2001).

[See also Boreal Forests and Climate Change; Crude Oil Supply; Fisheries; Forests and Environmental Change; Fossil Fuels; and Tropical Forests and Global Change.]

BIBLIOGRAPHY

Cohen, D. "Earth Audit." *New Scientist* 2605 (May 23, 2007), 34–41.

Craig, J.R., D.J. Vaughan, and B.J. Skinner. *Resources of the Earth: Origin, Use, and Environmental Impact.* 2d ed. New York: Prentice-Hall, 1996. A textbook covering the occurrence and availability of resources and how human activities impact the environment. The third edition was published in 2001.

Gordon, R.B., M. Bertram, and T.E. Graedel. "Metal Stocks and Sustainability." *Proceedings of National Academy of Sciences* 103.5 (2006), 1209–1214.

Holland, H.D., and U. Petersen. *Living Dangerously: The Earth, Its Resources, and the Environment.* Princeton, N.J.: Princeton University Press, 1995.

International Energy Agency. *Key World Energy Statistics.* Published annually. www.iea.org (accessed June 3, 2008).

Klare, M.T. *Resource Wars: The New Landscape of Global Conflict.* New York: Metropolitan, 2001. A thorough account of resource conflicts, in principle and in numerous case studies illustrated with maps.

Repetto, R., et al. *Wasting Assets: Natural Resources in the National Income Accounts.* Washington, D.C.: World Resources Institute, 1989. Promotes improved natural-resource accounting, using Indonesia's petroleum and soil resources as examples.

Skinner, B.J. *Earth Resources.* 3d ed. Englewood Cliffs, N.J.: Prentice-Hall, 1986.

United States Geological Survey. "Mineral Resource Perspectives." Professional Paper 940. Washington, D.C.: USGS, 1975. A review of resource concepts, developing the summary diagram used in Figure 4.

World Resources Institute. *World Resources Annual Report, 2006–2007.* www.wri.org/puldication/wri-annual-report-2006 (accessed June 3, 2008).

—David J. Cuff

RESOURCES FOR CITIZENS

See Appendix.

RIVERS: IMPACTS OF CLIMATE CHANGE

Climate change will bring a new era of human influence on rivers. Temperature increases of 1.5–6°C by the year 2100 will melt snow and ice and promote greater soil-moisture loss through increased evapotranspiration. There will also be changes in the amount, intensity, duration, type, and timing of precipitation, which will affect river flows. On a global basis it is possible that runoff will increase in a warmer world because of a global increase in atmospheric humidity (Willett et al., 2007) and precipitation (Douville et al., 2002). Historical discharge records indicate that global runoff increases about 4% for each 1°C rise in temperature (Labat et al., 2004). There will, however, be regional differences. In the subtropics an enhanced Hadley circulation (which transports heat and moisture poleward from the equatorial region) and associated accentuation of air subsidence may cause drying to occur. In some parts of the world increasing tropical storm intensities may create more flooding, whereas in others stream flows will be reduced as a result of more severe droughts. Furthermore, vegetation cover will respond to fire frequency and to temperature and precipitation changes, with concomitant impacts on flows. Climate change will also promote further human interventions in fluvial systems, as with greater use of irrigation in areas subjected to increased drought (Conway et al., 1996). Elevated atmospheric CO_2 levels may stimulate plant growth and lead to changes in plant water-use efficiency and thus in transpiration and runoff (Morgan et al., 2004). Betts et al. (2007) suggest that the physiological effect of doubled CO_2 concentrations on plant transpiration may increase global mean runoff by 6% relative to preindustrial levels.

RAINFALL INTENSITY

There are various reasons to expect increases in extreme precipitation if and when significant warming occurs. There will be more moisture in the atmosphere, and probably greater thermodynamic instability (Kunkel, 2003). There is evidence that rainfall events have become more intense during recent warm decades in some locations in the United States, Canada, Australia, Japan, South Africa, and Europe (Goudie, 2006). [*See* Twentieth-Century Climate Change.] In their analysis of flood records for 29 large river basins from high and low latitudes, Milly et al. (2002) found that although increases in flooding had only occurred in certain decades and places, the frequency of great floods had generally increased during the twentieth century, particularly during its warmer later decades. Analysis of general circulation models (GCMs) by Palmer and Räisänen (2002), applied to western Europe and the Asian monsoon region, shows under global warming an increase in extreme winter precipitation for the former and for extreme summer precipitation for the latter.

In addition, an increase in hurricane intensity and frequency would accentuate river flooding and coastal surges. [*See* Tropical Cyclones in a Warming World.]

RUNOFF RESPONSE

Studies of the response of runoff to climate change suggest that annual runoff volume is more sensitive to changes in precipitation than to changes in potential evapotranspiration and that a given percentage change in precipitation results in a greater percentage change in runoff (Najjar, 1999), with arid catchments showing a greater sensitivity than humid ones (Gordon and Famiglietti, 2004). An increase in annual precipitation of 10% is enough to offset the higher evaporation associated with a 2°C temperature rise.

Historical records show that higher than average annual precipitation leads not only to higher stream flows but also to higher floods. In Canada, for example, Ashmore and Church (2001) found that in the southern prairies and along the Atlantic coast the magnitude of large floods (with a 10-year recurrence interval) increases by up to 50–100% for increases of only 5–15% in annual precipitation. Flood discharges increase proportionately much more than mean flows. Wetherald and Manabe (2002) suggest that given predicted changes in evapotranspiration and rainfall, runoff will increase globally by about 7.3% by mid-century. What is striking, however, is the variability of responses in different regions. Some areas will have reduced annual runoff (e.g., New England [Huntington, 2003]), while others will see an enhancement of flows, including extreme events (e.g., Sierra Nevada, California [Kim, 2005]). However, the global pattern indicates that by the 2080s, high latitudes in the Northern Hemisphere, together with parts of central Africa and central Asia, will have higher annual runoff levels, whereas Australia, southern Africa, northwestern India, the Middle East and the Mediterranean basin will show reduced runoff. There is a tendency for some major deserts to become even drier. There will also be shifts in the seasonality of river flows. Models suggest that in California there will be decreases in summer flows, increases in winter flows, and a shift of flow to earlier in the year (Maurer and Duffy, 2005).

Some dry regions will suffer particularly large reductions in soil moisture (Wetherald and Manabe, 2002) and annual runoff (sometimes 60% or more), and significant runoff changes may be anticipated for the semiarid southwestern United States (Thomson et al., 2005). [*See* Deserts.] Revelle and Waggoner (1983) suggest that the effects of increased evapotranspiration losses as a result of a 2°C rise in temperature would be particularly serious where the mean annual precipitation is less than about 400 millimeters. Summer dryness in such areas may be accentuated by a positive feedback process involving decreases in cloud cover and associated increases in radiation absorption on the ground caused by a reduction in soil moisture. Shiklomanov (1999) has suggested that in drylands as a whole an increase in mean annual temperature by 1–2° and a 10% decrease in precipitation could reduce annual river runoff by up to 40–70%.

Various factors will determine the response of cold-region hydrological systems (Rouse et al., 1997). [*See* Arctic Warming.] In the Arctic, the amount of moisture in the atmosphere is expected to increase as it warms, leading to a general increase in precipitation and in discharges. Peterson et al. (2002) have analyzed records for the six largest Eurasian rivers that flow into the Arctic Ocean and have shown that as air temperatures have increased so has the average annual discharge of freshwater; it grew by 7% from 1936 to 1999. They suggest that with increased levels of warming there would be an 18–70% increase in Eurasian Arctic river discharge over the present.

Snow pack also affects on hydrological conditions in cold regions (Nijssen et al., 2001), and winter snow accumulation in alpine watersheds provides most of the stream runoff in western North America and similar regions of the world. In an analysis of future global discharge trends, Nijssen et al. (2001) suggested that the largest changes will be in snow-dominated basins of middle to higher latitudes and that there will probably be marked changes in the amplitude and phase of the annual water cycle (Arora and Boer, 2001). Lapp et al. (2005) have modeled the likely response of snow-pack accumulation to global warming in the Canadian Rockies and have suggested that there will be a decline in the overwinter snow accumulation in most years, and that spring runoff volumes may decrease with the decline in snow packs.

Rapid retreat and melting of glaciers may for a period of years cause a greater incidence of summer melt floods, but when the glaciers have disappeared, river flow volumes may be drastically reduced (Braun et al., 2000). This is of great concern for many great rivers. Melting glaciers account, for example, for 70% of the summer flow in the Ganges. As Barnett et al. 2005, p. 306) have remarked, "It appears that some areas of the most populated region on Earth are likely to 'run out of water' during the dry season if the current warming and glacial melting trends continue for several more decades."

Permafrost regions may also suffer from the effects of climate change. *See* Permafrost.] First, the permafrost itself—which is an important control of a wide range of processes and phenomena, including slope stability, groundwater flow and recharge, rates of river bank erosion, ground subsidence (thermokarst), and surface runoff—is by its very nature and definition susceptible to the effects of warming. Second, the temperature increase predicted for high latitude environments is greater than the global mean. Third, the nature (e.g., rain rather than snow) and amount of precipitation may also change.

THE U.K. AND EUROPE

Arnell (1996) has studied the changes that may occur in the U.K. With higher winter and lower summer rainfalls (particularly in the southeast) he forecasts for the 2050s:

- An increase in average annual runoff in the north of Britain of 5–15%.
- A decrease in the south of 5–15%, but up to 25% in the southeast.

- An increased seasonal variation in flow, with proportionately more of the total runoff occurring during winter.
- High flows increased in northern catchments and decreased in the south.

In southern England, lower summer rainfall, coupled with increased evaporation, means that stream flows will probably decrease during summer, whereas in the catchments in northern Britain, stream flow will increase in winter but change little in summer.

In mainland Europe, vulnerability to flooding seems to be increasing because of such factors as floodplain occupation by more people and their engineering structures. Unusually severe floods affected much of the continent during the 1990s and early 2000s (Mitchell, 2003). Therefore, a major question is the extent to which flooding might be exacerbated by climate change. Planton et al. (2005) have suggested that extreme winter precipitation events may become more common.

More generally, Arnell (1999) has modeled potential changes in hydrological regimes for Europe, using four different GCM-based climate scenarios. While there are differences between them, they all indicate a general reduction in annual runoff south of about 50°N and an increase north of there. The decreases could be as great as 50% and the increases as mcuh as 25%. A model by Eckhardt and Ulrich (2003) for the Rhenish Massif in western Germany found that in summer mean monthly groundwater recharge and stream flow may be reduced by up to 50%.

Rising temperatures will affect snowfall and snowmelt (Seidel et al., 1998). *See* Snow Cover.] Under milder conditions, even a modest temperature rise might mean that snow becomes very rare, being replaced by rain, so that the spring snowmelt peak would be eliminated, to be replaced by higher winter flows. Under more extreme conditions, all winter precipitation would still fall as snow, even with a rise in temperature. As a consequence, the snowmelt peak would still take place, although it might occur earlier in the year.

Models suggest that the discharge of the Rhine will become more seasonal by the end of the century, with discharge decreases of about 30% in summer (Shabalova et al., 2003). The decrease in summer discharge is related mainly to predicted decreases in precipitation and increases in evapotranspiration. Increases in winter discharge will be caused by a combination of increased precipitation, reduced snow storage, and increased early melt. Glacier melting in the Alps also contributes to the flow of the Rhine.

OUTLOOK

River systems will respond to global warming in some significant ways, notably in cold, tropical and arid regions, but also more generally. Some areas will experience overall increases in runoff, while others will experience decreases. More intense rainfall may cause more widespread flooding in some catchments. The annual flow regimes will be modified by changes in such phenomena as snow packs.

BIBLIOGRAPHY

Arnell, N.W. *Global Warming, River Flows and Water Resources.* Chichester, U.K. and New York: Wiley, 1996.

———. "The Effect of Climate Change on Hydrological Regimes in Europe: A Continental Prospective." *Global Environmental Change* 9.1 (1999), 5–23. DOI: 10.1016/S0959-3780(98)00015-6

Arora, V.K., and G.J. Boer. "Effects of Simulated Climate Change on the Hydrology of Major River Basins." *Journal of Geophysical Research* 106.D4 (2001), 3335–3348.

Ashmore, P., and M. Church. *The Impact of Climate Change on Rivers and River Processes in Canada.* Geological Survey of Canada Bulletin 555. Ottawa, 2001.

Barnett, T.P., J.C. Adam, and D.P. Lettenmaier. "Potential Impacts of a Warming Climate on Water Availability in Snow-Dominated Regions." *Nature* 438 (2005), 303–309. DOI: 10.1038/nature04141.

Betts, R.A., et al. "Projected Increase in Continental Runoff Due to Plant Responses to Increasing Carbon Dioxide." *Nature* 448 (2007), 1037–1041. DOI: 10.1038/nature06045.

Braun, L.N., M. Weber, and M. Schulz. "Consequences of Climate Change for Runoff from Alpine Regions." *Annals of Glaciology* 31 (2000), 19–25.

Conway, D., et al. "Future Availability of Water in Egypt: The Interaction of Global, Regional and Basin Scale Driving Forces in the Nile Basin." *Ambio* 25.5 (1996), 336–342.

Douville, H., et al. "Sensitivity of the Hydrological Cycle to Increasing Amounts of Greenhouse Gases and Aerosols." *Climate Dynamics* 20.1 (2002), 45–68. DOI: 10.1007/s00382-002-0259-3.

Eckhardt, K., and U. Ulbrich. "Potential Impacts of Climate Change on Groundwater Recharge and Streamflow in a Central European Low Mountain Range." *Journal of Hydrology* 284.1–4 (2003), 244–252.

Gordon, W.S., and J.S. Famiglietti. "Response of the Water Balance to Climate Change in the United States over the 20th and 21st Centuries: Results from the VEMAP Phase 2 Model Intercomparisons." *Global Biogeochemical Cycles* 18, GB1030 (2004). DOI: 10.1029/2003GB002098.

Goudie, A.S., "Global warming and fluvial geomorphology." *Geomorphology* 79 (2006), 384–394.

Huntington, T.G. "Climate Warming Could Reduce Runoff Significantly in New England, USA." *Agricultural and Forest Meteorology* 117.3 (2003), 193–201. DOI: 10.1016/S0168-1923(03)00063-7.

Kim, J. "A Projection of the Effects of the Climate Change Induced by Increased CO_2 on Extreme Hydrologic Events in the Western U.S." *Climatic Change* 68.1–2 (2005), 153–168. DOI: 10.1007/s10584-005-4787-9.

Kunkel, K.E. "North American Trends in Extreme Precipitation." *Natural Hazards* 29.2 (2003), 291–305. DOI: 10.1023/A:1023694115864.

Labat, D., et al. "Evidence for Global Runoff Increase Related to Climate Warming." *Advances in Water Resources* 27.6 (2004), 631–642.

Lapp, S., et al. "Climate Warming Impacts on Snowpack Accumulation in an Alpine Watershed." *International Journal of Climatology* 25.4 (2005), 521–536.

Maurer, E.P., and P.B. Duffy. "Uncertainty in Projections of Streamflow Changes Due to Climate Change in California." *Geophysical Research Letters* 32, L03704 (2005). DOI: 10.1029/2004GL021462.

Milly, P.C.D., et al. "Increasing Risk of Great Floods in a Changing Climate." *Nature* 415 (2002), 514–517. DOI: 10.1038/415514a.

Mitchell, J.K., "European river floods in a changing world." *Rick Analysis* 23 (2003), 567–574.

Morgan, J., et al. "Water Relations in Grassland and Desert Ecosystems Exposed to Elevated Atmospheric CO_2." *Oecologia* 140.1 (2004), 11–25. DOI: 10.1007/s00442-004-1550-2.

Najjar, R.G. "The Water Balance of the Susquehanna River Basin and Its Response to Climate Change." *Journal of Hydrology* 219.1 (1999), 7–19. DOI: 10.1016/S0022-1694(99)00041-4.

Nijssen, B., et al. "Hydrologic Sensitivity of Global Rivers to Climate Change." *Climatic Change* 50.1–2 (2001), 143–175.

Palmer, T.N., and J. Räisänen. "Quantifying the Risk of Extreme Seasonal Precipitation Events in a Changing Climate." *Nature* 415 (2002), 512–514. DOI: 10.1038/415512a.

Peterson, B.J., et al. "Increasing River Discharge to the Arctic Ocean." *Science* 298 (2002), 2171–2173. DOI: 10.1126/science.1077445.

Planton, S., et al. "Impact du réchauffement climatique sur le cycle hydrologique." *Comptes Rendues Geoscience* 337.1–2 (2005), 193–202.

Revelle, R.R., and P.E. Waggoner. "Effects of a Carbon Dioxide-Induced Climatic Change on Water Supplies in the Western United States." In *Changing Climate: Report of the Carbon Dioxide Assessment Committee*, 419–432. Washington D.C.: National Academy Press, 1983.

Rouse, W.R., et al. "Effects of Climate Change on the Freshwaters of Arctic and Subarctic North America." *Hydrological Processes* 11.8 (1997), 873–902.

Seidel, K., C. Ehrler, and J. Martinec. "Effects of Climate Change on Water Resources and Runoff in an Alpine Basin." *Hydrological Processes* 12.10 (1998), 1659–1669.

Shabalova, M.V., W.P.A. van Deursen, and T.A. Buishand. "Assessing Future Discharge of the River Rhine Using Regional Climate Model Integrations and a Hydrological Model." *Climate Research* 23 (2003), 233–246.

Shiklomanov, I.A. "Climate Change, Hydrology, and Water Resources: The Work of the IPCC, 1988–1994." In *Impacts of Climate Change and Climate Variability on Hydrological Regimes*, edited by J.C. van Dam, pp. 8–20. Cambridge and New York: Cambridge University Press, 1999.

Thomson, A.M., et al. "Climate Change Impacts for the Conterminous USA.: An Integrated Assessment. Part 4. Water Resources." *Climatic Change* 69.1 (2005), 67–88. DOI: 10.1007/s10584-005-3610-y.

Wetherald, R.T., and S. Manabe. "Simulation of Hydrologic Changes Associated with Global Warming." *Journal of Geophysical Research* 107.D19 (2002). DOI: 10.1029/2001JD001195.

Willett, K.M., et al. "Attribution of Observed Surface Humidity Changes to Human Influence." *Nature* 449 (2007), 710–712. DOI: 10.1038/nature06207.

—ANDREW S. GOUDIE

S

SALINIZATION

Salinization is a natural process in soils and water, especially in areas of water deficit (Szabolcs and Varallyay, 1979), but various human activities are increasing its extent and severity—a process called accelerated or enhanced salinization (Table 1) (Goudie, 2003). This has a range of undesirable consequences. For example, as irrigation water is concentrated by evapotranspiration, calcium and magnesium precipitate as carbonates, leaving sodium ions dominant in the soil solution. The sodium ions tend to be absorbed by colloidal clay particles, disaggregating them and leaving the resultant structureless soil impermeable to water and unfavorable to root development. The death of vegetation in areas of saline patches (salt scalds), caused by poor soil structure and toxicity, creates bare ground, which becomes a focal point for erosion by wind and water. Probably the most serious impact of salinization is on plant growth. This takes place partly through its effect on soil structure, but more significantly through its effects on osmotic pressures and its direct toxicity. When a water solution containing large quantities of dissolved salts comes into contact with a plant cell, it causes a shrinkage of the protoplasm. The phenomenon is due to the osmotic movement of water from the cell into the more concentrated soil solution. The cell collapses and the plant dies. Toxicity varies with different plants and different salts. Sodium carbonate, by creating highly alkaline soil conditions, may damage plants by a direct caustic effect. Nitrate may promote undesirable vegetative growth in grapes or sugarbeets at the expense of sugar content. Boron is injurious to many crop plants at solution concentrations of more than 1 or 2 parts per million. Salinity limits the use of drinking water for humans and their domestic stock.

Increasing salinity accelerates the weathering of buildings and engineering structures (Goudie and Viles, 1997). Salts crystallize, hydrate, and expand in stone and concrete (with resultant mechanical damage), cause mineralogical changes in cements, and corrode steel reinforcements. This has caused the decay of some of the world's great cultural treasures, including the Pharaonic temples and the Sphinx in Egypt, the city of Mohenjo-Daro in Pakistan, and the Islamic treasures of Uzbekistan. The same applies to the fabric of some of the great new cities of the Middle East.

Soil and water salinity are spreading for several reasons. First, and most importantly, the area of irrigated land has increased from roughly 8 million hectares (20 million acres) at the end of the eighteenth century to 250 million hectares at the end of the twentieth (Thomas and Middleton, 1993). The extension of irrigation and the use of a wide range of different techniques for water abstraction and application can lead to a buildup of salt in the soil through the raising of ground water so that it is near enough to the ground surface for capillary rise through the soil and subsequent evaporative concentration to take place. Table 2 provides some data on the rise of ground water following the introduction of irrigation. In the case of the semiarid northern plains of Victoria in Australia, for instance, the water table has been rising at around 1.5 meters per year, so that now in many areas it is almost within 1 meter of the surface. When ground water comes within 3 meters of the surface in clay soils (less for silty and sandy soils), capillary forces bring moisture to the surface, where evaporation takes place.

Second, irrigation schemes require the addition of large quantities of water to the soil. This is especially true for rice cultivation. Such surface water is readily evaporated, so salinity builds up. Third, the construction of large dams and barrages to control water flow and to give a head of water creates large reservoirs from which further evaporation takes place. Fourth, especially in areas of permeable soils, water seeps laterally and downward from irrigation canals, resulting in further evaporation.

Increases in soil and water salinity are not restricted to irrigated areas. In certain parts of the world, such as Australia,

TABLE 1. Causes of Accelerated Salinization

1. Irrigation salinity
   a. Rise in ground water
   b. Evaporation of water from fields
   c. Evaporation of water from canals and reservoirs
   d. Waterlogging produced by seepage losses
2. Dryland salinity
   a. Vegetation clearance
3. Urban salinity
   a. Water importation and irrigation
   b. Faulty drains and sewers
4. Inter-basin water transfers
   a. Mineralization of lake waters
   b. Deflation of salts from desiccating lakes
5. Coastal zone salinity
   a. Over-pumping
   b. Reduced freshwater recharge
   c. Sea-level rise
   d. Ground subsidence

TABLE 2. Increase in Level of Water Table Due to Irrigation

Irrigation Project	Country	Water Table (meters)	
		Original Depth	Rise/Year
Nubariya	Egypt	15–20	2.0–3.0
Beni Amir	Morocco	15–30	1.5–3.0
Murray-Darling	Australia	30–40	0.5–1.5
Amibara	Ethiopia	10–15	1.0
Xinjang Farm 29	China	5–10	0.3–0.5
Bhatinda	India	15	0.6
SCARP 1	Pakistan	40–50	0.4
SCARP 6	Pakistan	10–15	0.2–0.4

SOURCE: Tolba and El-Kholy, 1992, p. 91.

salinization has resulted from vegetation clearance (Peck, 1978). This is called "dryland salinity." The removal of native forest vegetation allows a greater penetration of rainfall into deeper soil layers, which causes groundwater levels to rise, creating seepage of saline water in low-lying areas. Similar problems exist in North America, notably in Manitoba, Alberta, Montana, and North Dakota. The clearance of the native evergreen forest (predominantly eucalyptus forest) in southwestern Australia has led to an increase in recharge rates of ground water and to an increase in the salinity of streams. Replanting can reverse the process (Bari and Schofield, 1992).

Salinity can also be increased by translocation of saline materials from lake beds that dry out as a consequence of interbasin water transfers. Around 30–40 million metric tons per year are blown off the exposed bottom of the shrunken Aral Sea, for example, and these add to the salt content of soils downwind.

In coastal areas, salinity problems are created by seawater incursion brought about by the overpumping of fresh water. This can be explained as follows. Fresh water has a lower density than salt water, so a column of sea water can support a column of fresh water approximately 2.5% higher than itself (or a ratio of about 40:41). So where a body of fresh water has accumulated in a reservoir rock that is also open to penetration from the sea, it does not simply lie flat on top of the salt water but forms a lens, whose thickness is approximately 41 times the elevation of the water table above sea level (the Ghyben-Herzberg principle; see Figure 1). It follows that if the hydrostatic pressure of the fresh water falls as a result of overpumping, the underlying salt water will rise by 40 times the amount by which the freshwater table is lowered.

Urbanization can also lead to changes in groundwater conditions. In some large desert cities, the importation of water and its usage, wastage, and leakage can feed this phenomenon. This is a problem, for example, in Cairo and its immediate environs. The rapid expansion of Cairo's population has outstripped the development of its municipal infrastructure. In particular, leakage losses from water pipes and sewers have led to a substantial rise in the groundwater level.

In those areas of the world with severe winter freezes, salts can build up in the environment from another source. Rock salt (sodium chloride) is used to deice roads and sidewalks. With the rise in the number of vehicles there has been a corresponding increase throughout Europe and North America in the use of salt for deicing purposes (e.g., Howard and Beck, 1993).

Future global changes in climate and sea level could have implications for salinity conditions. For example, increasing drought risk in Mediterranean Europe could lead to a substantial increase in salinization-prone areas (Imeson and Emmer, 1992; Szabolcs, 1994), while higher sea levels in geomorphologically susceptible locations (e.g., coastal deltas, and the sebkhas [flat, salty depressions] along the coast of the Arabian Gulf) could change the position of the all-important salt/freshwater interface and the height of the water table.

At present, however, it has been estimated that the area of salt-affected and waterlogged soils amounts to 50% of the irrigated area in Iraq, 23% of all Pakistan, 50% in the Euphrates valley of Syria, 30% in Egypt, and over 15% in Iran (Worthington, 1977, p. 30). In Africa, on the other hand, less than 10% of salt-affected soils are so affected by human action (Thomas and Middleton, 1993). Table 3 presents data on the extent of salt-affected lands by continent and subcontinent, and for individual countries.

The calculations of Rozanov et al. (1991) on global salinization are grim. They estimate (p. 120) that "From 1700 to 1984, the global areas of irrigated land increased from 50,000 to 2,200,000 km^2, while at the same time some 500,000 km^2 were abandoned as a result of secondary salinization." They believe that in the last three centuries total soil loss due to irrigation is 1 million km^2 of land destroyed, plus 1 million km^2 of land with diminished productivity due to salinization.

Given the seriousness of the problem, a range of techniques for the eradication, conversion, or control of soil salinity have been developed (Rhoades, 1990). They can be divided into three main types: eradication, conservation, and control.

Eradication involves the removal of salt, either by improved drainage or by the addition of quantities of fresh water to leach

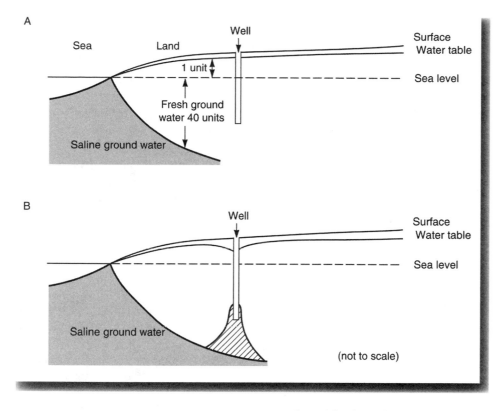

Salinization. FIGURE 1. Fresh and Saline Ground Water.
(A) The Ghyben–Herzberg relationship between fresh and saline ground water.
(B) The effect of excessive pumping from the well, showing the increasing incursion of saline water.
(After Goudie and Wilkinson, 1977, Figure 63. With permission of Cambridge University Press.)

TABLE 3. Extent of Salt-Affected Soils by Continent and Subcontinent*

Region	Millions of Hectares
North America	15.7
Mexico and Central America	2.0
South America	129.2
Africa	80.5
South Asia	84.8
North and Central Asia	211.7
Southeast Asia	20.0
Australia	357.3
Europe	50.8
Total	952.0

*Note that "salt-affected" includes both saline soils and alkaline soils.

SOURCE: After Szabolcs and Varallyay, 1979.

the salt out of the soil. Both solutions involve considerable expense and pose severe technological problems in areas of low relief and limited freshwater availability. Improved drainage can either be provided by open drains or by the use of tube wells to reduce groundwater levels and associated salinity and waterlogging. A minor eradication measure that may have some potential is the biotic treatment of salinity through the harvesting of salt-accumulating plants such as *Suaeda fruticosa* (shrubby sea blite).

Conversion involves the use of chemical methods to convert harmful salts into less harmful ones. For example, gypsum is frequently added to sodic soils to convert caustic alkali carbonates to soluble sodium sulfate and relatively harmless calcium carbonate.

Some of the most effective ways of reducing the salinity hazard involve the less wasteful and lavish application of water through the use of sprinklers rather than traditional irrigation methods; the lining of canals to reduce seepage; the realignment of canals through less permeable soils; and the use of more salt-tolerant plants. Because salinity is a particularly serious threat at the time of germination and for seedlings, various strategies can be adopted during this critical phase of plant growth: plots can be irrigated lightly each day after seeding to prevent salt buildup; major leaching can be carried out just before planting; and areas to be seeded can be bedded in such a way that salts accumulate at the ridge tops, with the seed planted on the slope between the furrow bottom and the ridge top.

To conclude, accelerated salinization created problems for Mesopotamian farmers 4,000 years ago, and it remains an environmental problem today. Land-cover changes, the spread of irrigation, the exploitation of ground water, and the application of salts for deicing purposes are all involved in the process. Several methods are available for reducing the problem that accelerated salinization creates, but some parts of the world may suffer in the future if sea levels rise and rates of evapotranspiration increase.

[*See also* Aral Sea; Desertification; Irrigation; *and* Soils.]

TABLE 4. Global Estimate of Secondary Salinization in the World's Irrigated Land

Country	Cropped Area (Mha)	Irrigated Area (Mha)	Share of Irrigated to Cropped Area (Percent)	Salt-Affected Land in Irrigated Area (Mha)	Share of Salt-Affected to Irrigated Land (Percent)
China	96.97	44.83	46.2	6.70	15.0
India	168.99	42.10	24.9	7.00	16.6
Commonwealth of Independent States	232.57	20.48	8.8	3.70	18.1
United States	189.91	18.10	9.5	4.16	23.0
Pakistan	20.76	16.08	77.5	4.22	26.2
Iran	14.83	5.74	38.7	1.72	30.0
Thailand	20.05	4.00	19.9	0.40	10.0
Egypt	2.69	2.69	100.0	0.88	33.0
Australia	47.11	1.83	3.9	0.16	8.7
Argentina	35.75	1.72	4.8	0.58	33.7
South Africa	13.17	1.13	8.6	0.10	8.9
Subtotal	842.80	158.70	18.8	29.62	20.0
World	1473.70	227.11	15.4	45.4	20.0

SOURCE: Ghassemi et al., 1995, Table 18. With permission of the Centre for Resource and Environmental Studies, The Australian National University, Canberra.

Salinization. Effects of Irrigations.

The spread of irrigation in the Indus Plains of Pakistan has caused severe waterlogging and the buildup of salts in the soil.

BIBLIOGRAPHY

Bari, M.A., and N.J. Schofield. "Lowering of a Shallow, Saline Water Table by Extensive Eucalypt Reforestation." *Journal of Hydrology* 133.3–4 (1992), 273–291.

Ghassemi, F., A.J. Jakeman, and H.A. Nix. *Salinisation of Land and Water Resources.* Wallingford, U.K.: CAB International, 1995. A full analysis of the problem in a global context.

Goudie, A.S. "Enhanced Salinisation." In *Water Resources Perspectives: Evaluation, Management, and Policy,* edited by A. Alsharhan and W.W. Wood, pp. 287–294. Amsterdam, London, and Boston: Elsevier, 2003.

Goudie, A.S., and H.A. Viles. *Salt Weathering Hazards.* Chichester, U.K., and New York: Wiley, 1997. An analysis of salt attack on buildings in a wide range of environments.

Goudie, A.S., and J. Wilkinson. *The Warm Desert Environment.* Cambridge and New York: Cambridge University Press, 1977.

Howard, K.W. F., and P.J. Beck. "Hydrogeochemical Implications of Groundwater Contamination by Road De-Icing Chemicals." *Journal of Contaminant Hydrology* 12.3 (1993), 245–268.

Imeson, A., and I.M. Emmer. "Implications of Climatic Change on Land Degradation in the Mediterranean." In *Climatic Change and the Mediterranean,* edited by L. Jeftic, J.D. Milliman, and G. Sestini, pp. 95–128. London: Arnold, 1992.

Peck, A.J. "Salinization of Non-Irrigated Soils and Associated Streams: A Review." *Australian Journal of Soil Research* 16 (1978), 157–168. DOI: 10.1071/SR9780157.

Rhoades, J.D. "Soil Salinity: Causes and Controls." In *Techniques for Desert Reclamation,* edited by A.S. Goudie, pp. 109–134. Chichester, U.K., and New York: Wiley, 1990.

Rozanov, B.G., V. Targulian, and D.S. Orlov. "Soils." In *The Earth as Transformed by Human Action,* edited by B. Turner et al., pp. 203–214. Cambridge and New York: Cambridge University Press, 1991.

Szabolcs, I. "State and Perspectives on Soil Salinity in Europe." *European Society for Soil Conservation Newsletter* 3 (1994), 17–24.

Szabolcs, I., and G. Varallyay. *Review of Research on Salt-Affected Soils.* Paris: UNESCO, 1979.

Thomas, D.S.G., and N.J. Middleton. "Salinization: New Perspectives on a Major Desertification Issue." *Journal of Arid Environments* 24.1 (1993), 95–105.

Tolba, M.K., and O.A. El-Kholy. *The World Environment 1972–1992.* London and New York: Chapman and Hall, 1992.

Worthington, E.B. *Arid Land Irrigation in Developing Countries: Environmental Problems and Effects.* Oxford and New York: Pergamon, 1977.

—ANDREW S. GOUDIE

SAVANNAS

Savannas (also spelled "savannahs") comprise the most important vegetation formation of the lowland seasonal tropics and subtropics. The word comes from the sixteenth-century Spanish *çavana* or *zavana* (modern Spanish *sabana*) recorded in 1515 and thought to be from the Taino language of the West Indies (Corominas, 1983, p. 518).

Ecologically, the term is used to describe a continuum of tropical and subtropical vegetation types in which there is codominance between a fairly continuous grass cover and a range of woody plants from dwarf shrubs to trees. The tree/grass ratio, however, varies enormously between different savanna types. Certain savannas look just like parklands. By contrast, in some virtually treeless savannas, such as the Serengeti Plain of Tanzania, the woody cover may be as low as 2%; in others, such as the dipterocarp savanna forests of mainland Southeast Asia and the eucalyptus savanna woodlands of northern Australia, the canopy cover, when in full leaf, may be as high as 50 to 80%. Nevertheless, even these wooded savannas are clearly distinguishable from true forests by their continuous ground cover of grasses, sedges, and herbs. The absence of a grass cover also separates savannas from semidesert and desert communities at the opposite end of the climatic spectrum. Fire is a key factor in savanna ecology, partly because of this grass cover, which, when cured in the dry season, forms—along with the leaf litter from the trees—an easily ignitable fuel. Some savannnas are relatively dry habitats, but others may be subject to inundation, at least seasonally, and so have some of the characteristics of wetlands.

The open grassy character of the savannas is frequently associated with a distinctive and often very visible mammal fauna of predators, such as the lion (*Panthera leo*) and the cheetah (*Acinonyx jubatus*), and large herds of grazers and browsers, including wild cattle, antelope, and deer, as well as a variety of highly characteristic savanna mammals, such as the zebras (*Equus grevyi* and *E. burchelli*) and giraffe (*Giraffa camelopardalis*) of Africa. The flat umbrella silhouette of many savanna trees reflects the basic browsing pattern of these herbivores. Certain savannas are also noted for their more specialized animals, including the endangered Gouldian finch (*Erythrura gouldiae*) in northern Australia, the Komodo dragon (*Varanus komodoensis*), the largest living lizard, in eastern Indonesia, and the giant anteater (*Myrmecophaga tridactyla*) in the *cerrado* of Brazil. Yet the most important animal of all savannas undoubtedly is the insects, especially the ants and the termites, which play a vital role in herbivory and seed dispersal. The landscapes of many savannas are punctuated by tall termite mounds.

Savannas occupy a very wide area of the tropics and subtropics where there is a combination of a relatively low total annual rainfall of 400–1,500 millimeters (with extremes of 200–2,000 millimeters) and a marked seasonality in the rainfall distribution, with a normal dry season of 4–8 months of the year (extremes of 2–10 months). Under such monsoonal climatic conditions, fire is a common annual or biennial phenomenon during the dry season, and both natural fires (started by lightning) and human-caused fires are endemic to nearly all savanna areas—although fire is not itself necessarily a determining factor. Nevertheless, in certain locations, protection from fire will trigger succession to a more wooded environment, while too frequent or intense fires may force the system into a grassless thorn-scrub.

Biologically, savanna plants exhibit a wide range of adaptations to both fire and drought, including thick bark, thorns, reduced and leathery (sclerophyllous) leaves, sunken and protected stomata, subterranean stems, complex lateral roots, deep terminal roots, underground storage organs (geophytes), and specialized life cycles. Most of the perennial grasses are hemicryptophytes, plants that are able to resprout from the surface of the ground within a very short period after a fire. Such plants are also well adapted to heavy grazing pressures. Many of the tree species shed their leaves under water stress, and woody plants possess various strategies for germinating fruits: some fruits and seeds requiring the scarifying (breaking open by heat) effects of fire, whereas other species disperse their fruits after the fires have gone through.

Savannas are further distinguished by the fact that their dominant grass species use the C4 photosynthesis pathway. They initially fix carbon dioxide as a four-carbon compound (oxaloacetic acid) and are especially adapted to hot and dry environments, such as the savannas, their optimum temperature for carbon dioxide fixation lying between 30 and 45°C. Savannas are therefore clearly differentiated from tropical grasslands, which tend to be dominated by C3 grasses, which fix CO_2 initially as a three-carbon compound (phosphoglyceric acid). Tropical grasslands also tend to have fewer woody species and to occur on higher, cooler plateaus and mountains, such as in the Drakensberg range in southern Africa.

SAVANNA DISTRIBUTION

It is the very wide climatic tolerance of the savannas that accounts for their areal dominance throughout the tropics and the subtropics (Figure 1). Savannas occupy no less than 45% of South America (including the grassy llanos of Venezuela and the woody *cerrado* of Brazil), 65% of Africa (acacia savannas, *Burkea africana* savannas, bottle-tree [baobab, *Adansonia*] savannas), and the *miombo* woodland of central southern Africa), and 60% of Australia (with eucalyptus and acacia savannas). Savannas range from Louisiana (the Big Thicket) and Texas north of the Tropic of Cancer, to well south of the Tropic of Capricorn, near Port Elizabeth in South Africa. They are also widespread in the Caribbean, on the Indian subcontinent (sal [*Shorea robusta*] savanna woodlands) and in both mainland and maritime Southeast Asia, especially east of Wallace's Line (the notional line that separates the distinctive floras and faunas of Australia and Southeast Asia). It is often forgotten that savanna forests are the most widespread formation in Burma, Thailand, Laos, and Cambodia; the Buddha is thought to have been born under a savanna forest tree.

The majority of people in the tropics, at least one-fifth of the world's population, live in the savannas, which form the core of the world's monsoon lands that, overall, support some 50% of the global population. Savannas are therefore the single most important terrestrial biome, and to gain an understanding of their role in global environmental change, both past and present, is unquestionably a vital ecological task.

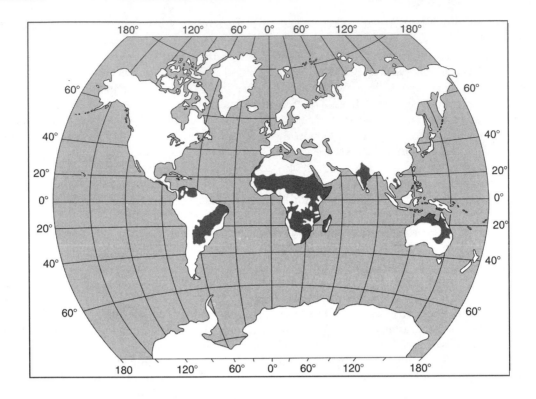

Savannas. Figure 1. Worldwide Savanna Distribution.

(After Archibold, 1995, p. 60, Figure 3.1. With permission of Kluwer Academic Publishers.)

SAVANNA ECOLOGY: PAST AND PRESENT

Until the mid-1980s, savanna studies were based on ecological concepts first developed in Europe and North America between 1910 and 1940. In these concepts, plant communities were essentially seen as "organisms," or ecosystems, the equilibrium state of which would be ultimately determined by one prime ecological factor such as climate or geology. However, there was marked disagreement as to the main ecological determinant of savannas. German scholars working in South West Africa (now Namibia) and South America tended to view savannas as climatically determined formations, whereas British foresters living in West Africa thought them to be anthropogenic (human-generated) communities, created from the forests by cutting and burning. French workers in Indochina (Laos, Cambodia, and Vietnam) saw savannas as essentially fire climaxes, while certain geographers tried to interpret them as formations determined by soil or geology. There was little debate or agreement among proponents of the different theories, and savanna studies became somewhat nationalistic, regionally limited, and outdated.

In the last two decades by contrast, savanna research has grown increasingly interdisciplinary and international, and it is now thought that all savannas are determined by the complex interplay of at least six main ecological factors: plant available moisture (PAM), plant available nutrients (PAN), fire, herbivory, major historical anthropogenic (human) events, and, at certain locations, special regional factors (such as frost or wind). PAM and PAN are seen as the prime determinants of savanna form, which is then modified by fire, herbivory, and any relevant special factors or historical anthropogenic events (such as the abandonment of human settlement or enhanced global warming) triggering savannas into new ecological states. The relationships among these variables are analyzed using ecological modeling or hierarchy theory, and the PAM/PAN plane (a plane whose axes are defined by measurements of PAM and PAN) can be used to make basic international, national, and regional comparisons among savannas.

Still more importantly, however, savannas are no longer regarded as representing simple equilibrium communities, but rather as formations that are always changing, with their biology driven by both continuous and catastrophic variations in the six ecological determinants. Some scholars think of savannas as constantly moving between what are termed multiple equilibrium states, such as open savanna, wooded savanna, and woodland, whereas other scholars, including the present author, are more radical and see savannas as intrinsically non-equilibrium systems, in which every savanna organism is responding individualistically to the changes in the ecological determinants. These new approaches place savannas at the very center of the discussion of global change, because the six ecological determinants link savannas directly with both world-scale and local-scale environmental fluctuations. Any ecological change, of any scale, will work through those determinants to adjust the tree/grass ratios, the C3/C4 grass mixes, the species complements, and the geographic ranges of the world's savannas, which in turn will affect the ecological processes in question.

SAVANNA CHANGE: PAST AND PRESENT

Until recently, many ecologists and conservationists, particularly in the United Kingdom and North America, have regarded large areas of savanna as a recent byproduct of the processes of tropical deforestation, brought about largely by cutting and burning for agricultural development. These writers have also seen the burning of savanna plant biomass as a major factor in the links between gas and aerosol emissions and global atmospheric change, particularly because carbon dioxide (CO_2) is the dominant emission from biomass flame combustion, along with nitric oxide (NO), nitrogen dioxide (NO_2), sulfur dioxide (SO_2), and water vapor. (Carbon monoxide [CO] is the main emission from smoldering combustion.) According to one estimate, savanna fires contribute 75% of all the CO_2 emitted to the atmosphere through biomass burning in the tropics, a figure that rises to around 85% for sub-Saharan Africa.

On both counts, however, these arguments are fundamentally flawed. With regard to the effects of savanna fires, it is essential to remember that savannas have always burned, originally through lightning strikes and other natural causes, then with an intensification of fire use by hominids taking place as early as 1.4 million years ago, and with a further intensification and spread by *Homo sapiens* some 50,000 years ago. Few scholars have bothered to include these historical patterns in their calculations.

There may even have been more emissions in the past than there are today, especially because it is now well substantiated that, despite popular misconceptions, the savannas have largely retreated during the period since the end of the last ice age. Around 18,000 years ago, tropical climates were much drier and cooler than they are now, and areas in both Amazonia and Southeast Asia currently covered by tropical rainforests were then savannas. There was, for example, a savanna corridor, with its own savanna fauna, running through the peninsula of Malaysia, linking the presently disjunct savannas of mainland Southeast Asia and maritime Southeast Asia. In South America, there is growing evidence that savanna animals and plants once occupied areas long thought to have been rain-forest refuges during the last ice age. Moreover, even in more recent times, the story is not always one of forest loss. Work in Gambia, West Africa, by foresters and anthropologists has clearly demonstrated a pattern of constant forest-savanna alternation since 1900 CE. Finally, in many parts of the tropics, subtropics, and Mediterranean climatic zones, such as in southern Africa,

Savannas.

A savanna area in the tropical Kimberley area of north Western Australia, composed of a mixture of grasses and trees (mainly Eucalypts). Fire is a major factor in controlling the nature of such savannas in the seasonal tropics.

savannas—along with other nonforest formations, including tropical grasslands, the fynbos, and the Karoo—have been the dominant formations for millions of years. There is no record of there being any significant forest cover in these areas.

Most savannas, therefore, have wide ancient cores, which have ebbed and flowed constantly at their margins and around forest islands, in response to environmental change, the changes being mediated through the complex ecological determinants of PAM, PAN, fire, herbivory, human agency, and local factors. The process continues today. Traditionally, human populations in the savannas, particularly pastoralists like those in East Africa, have responded to these changes in an opportunistic manner, well attuned to the essential nonequilibrium character of the savanna biome. Such equilibrium concepts as overstocking, overgrazing, and carrying capacity are now seen to be problematic when applied to development in these environments. Some savanna areas are also experiencing rapid urbanization, as around the Pretoria/Johannesburg complex in South Africa and Brasilia in Brazil, while pasture improvement is a significant factor in places such as Queensland, Australia.

More specific environmental-change problems facing savanna ecologists include the potential effects of CO_2 enhancement on the relative performance of C3 and C4 grasses, because C4 plants show little response to elevated concentrations of carbon dioxide. This may mean that their competitive advantage is reduced under increased atmospheric CO_2, leading to significant effects on both the composition and the productivity of the grass stratum in tropical savannas. However, predictions are difficult because of the complicating influence of the other ecological factors, especially temperature and PAM.

Savannas are also increasingly seen as one of the most biodiverse formations in the tropics. Like tropical rainforests, they show, for many groups of organisms, a direct relationship between the extent of the area sampled and the number of species inhabiting it. This intrinsic biodiversity partly reflects the fundamental nonequilibrium of savannas, an inverse relationship having been established between stability and diversity, but also their heterogeneous patch structure, created by the codominance of grasses and trees. There are also important intercontinental and regional differences, with, for example, the *cerrado* of Brazil exhibiting noteworthy diversity in its woody element, a diversity with enormous potential for food and drug production. Insects, by contrast, appear to be biodiverse in all savanna areas.

Plants and animals introduced from other savannas and from different habitats are also a significant feature of savanna environments, and, as with the Asian water buffalo (*Bubalus bubalis*) in the eucalyptus savannas of northern Australia and various African grass species in the savannas of Latin America, they can greatly alter both local ecology and biodiversity. There are also important debates on the conservation of many large savanna mammals, such as the discussion over whether the conservation of big game, like the African elephant (*Loxodonta africana*), should have to pay for itself through controlled commercial hunting.

Change is therefore at the very heart of all savanna ecology, both past and present. During the next decades, the careful management of savannas will be vital for the future of both wildlife and the fifth of the world's population that inhabits these important environments. The ecological resilience and persistence of savannas lie above all in their biodiversity and in the opportunistic response of this biodiversity to nonequilibrium change. In linking savannas with global change, we should bear in mind the recent words of Sian Sullivan in the *Journal of Biogeography* (1996). She argues that we must celebrate "variability as well as average values, process and pattern as well as structure, stasis and order, and creative as well as conservative behaviour."

BIBLIOGRAPHY

Archibold, O.W. *Ecology of World Vegetation.* London: Chapman and Hall, 1995.

Bourlière, F., ed. *Tropical Savannas.* Amsterdam and New York: Elsevier, 1983. A good, if slightly dated, general world survey.

Bullock, S.H., et al., eds. *Seasonally Dry Tropical Forests.* Cambridge and New York: Cambridge University Press, 1995. Detailed studies of the more wooded and forested savannas, as well as the monsoon forests.

Cole, M.M. *The Savannas: Biogeography and Geobotany.* London and Orlando, Fla.: Academic Press, 1986. An idiosyncratic survey, stressing the importance of geology and soils.

Corominas, J. *Breve diccionario etimológico de la lengua castellana.* 3d ed. Madrid: Gredos, 1983.

Furley, P.A., J. Proctor, and J.A. Ratter, eds. *Nature and Dynamics of Forest-Savanna Boundaries.* London and New York: Chapman and Hall, 1992. A series of detailed studies of savanna–forest boundary determinants, especially in Latin America.

Huntley, B.J., and B.H. Walker, eds. *Ecology of Tropical Savannas.* Berlin and New York: Springer, 1982. A useful world survey, if now a little dated.

Leach, M., and J. Fairhead. *Second Nature: Building Forests in West Africa's Savannas.* Haywards Heath, U.K.: Cyrus Productions, 1997. An important video examining the human use of forest and savanna in West Africa. Highly recommended.

Mistry, J. *World Savannas: Ecology and Human Use.* London and New York: Prentice Hall, 2000. The most up-to-date survey of the world's savanna ecosystems.

Sarmiento, G. *The Ecology of Neotropical Savannas.* Translated from the Spanish by O. Solbrig. Cambridge, Mass.: Harvard University Press, 1984. Remains one of the best detailed studies of plant life cycles in savannas; focuses on Latin America, especially Venezuela.

Scholes, R.J., and B.H. Walker. *An African Savanna: Synthesis of the Nylsvley Study.* Cambridge and New York: Cambridge University Press, 1993. The best and most up-to-date detailed ecological study of any savanna ecosystem, that of South Africa. Highly recommended.

Solbrig, O., ed. *Savanna Modelling for Global Change. Special Issue 24 of Biology International.* Paris: International Union of Biological Sciences, 1991. An essential introduction to savanna ecological determinants and savanna modeling.

Stott, P. "Recent Trends in the Ecology and Management of the World's Savanna Formations." *Progress in Physical Geography* 15.1 (1991), 18–28. DOI: DOI: 10.1177/030913339101500102. A relatively simple guide to some of the new ideas in savanna ecology.

———. "Savanna Landscapes and Global Environmental Change." In *The Changing Global Environment*, edited by Neil Roberts. Oxford, U.K., and Cambridge, Mass.: Blackwell, 1994, pp. 287–303. A detailed analysis of savanna landscapes, particularly in relation to global climate change; also helpful on hierarchy theory and C3 and C4 grasses.

Sullivan, S. "Towards a Non-Equilibrium Ecology: Perspectives from an Arid Land." *Journal of Biogeography* 23.1 (1996), 1–5. A short, useful introduction to nonequilibrium ideas and their implications.

Tothill, J. C., and J. J. Mott, eds. *Ecology and Management of the World's Savannas.* Canberra: Australian Academy of Science, 1985. A useful general survey, focused on Australia.

Walker, B.H., and J.C. Ménaut, eds. *Research Procedure and Experimental Design for Savanna Ecology and Management.* Melbourne: CSIRO, 1988. A helpful guide to research methods in savanna ecology.

Werner, P.A., ed. *Savanna Ecology and Management: Australian Perspectives and Intercontinental Comparisons.* Oxford, U.K., and Boston, Mass.: Blackwell, 1991. One of the more up-to-date surveys of current problems in savanna ecology, emphasizing Australia and Latin America.

Young, M.D., and O.T. Solbrig. *Savanna Management for Ecological Sustainability, Economic Profit, and Social Equity.* Man and Biosphere 13. Paris: UNESCO, 1992. A useful introduction to the applied ecology and economics of savannas.

Young, M.D., and O.T. Solbrig, eds. *The World's Savannas: Economic Driving Forces, Ecological Constraints, and Policy Options for Sustainable Land Use.* Man and Biosphere 12. Paris and Carnforth, U.K.: UNESCO and Parthenon, 1993. A more advanced study of the applied ecology and economics of savannas.

—Philip Stott

SEA LEVEL FUTURE

Sea level has been both higher and lower on the world's coasts in the geological past. In the Last Glacial phase of the Pleistocene the expansion of snowfields, ice sheets, and glaciers resulted in a global lowering of sea level, and when the climate grew warmer in the late Pleistocene and early Holocene, partial melting of the ice led to a world-wide marine transgression (Flandrian). Eighteen thousand years ago global sea level was about 140 meters (m) lower, but during the Flandrian transgression it rose to roughly its present level about 6,000 years ago. The last 6,000 years have been a period of sea-level stillstand (with only minor oscillations of 2–3 m) on much of the world's coastline, but sea level has continued to rise on coasts where the land is subsiding and to fall on coasts where the land is rising.

Sea level is determined largely by the volume of water in the oceans, the size and shape of the ocean basins, and prevailing climatic conditions. It can vary because of changes in any of these, but a major factor is the amount of ice in polar and mountain regions. If the ice cover were to increase, sea level would again fall, while if it were to diminish, more water would be released into the oceans and sea level would rise. It has been estimated that melting of all the world's glaciers and ice sheets would raise sea level by about 60 m around the world's coasts.

There is now concern about sea-level rise as a consequence of global warming. The Intergovernmental Panel on Climate Change (Solomon et al., 2007) forecast that global warming will result in an average sea-level rise of 0.18–0.59 m between 1980–1999 and 2090–2099. This is partly because of expansion of the oceans with rising temperature (the steric effect) and partly because of the melting of snow and ice. The higher rate implies that average global sea level will stand a meter higher before the end of the twenty-second century. Measurements from tide gauges (to 1993) and satellite altimetry (since 1993) indicate that average global sea level has risen at the rate of 0.18 ± 0.05 meters per century in 1961–2003, accelerating to 0.31 ± 0.07 meters per century in 1993–2003.

Predictions of changes on particular coasts should take into account the known variability of sea-level changes related to upward or downward movements of the land and with changes in the shape of the geoid, factors that could increase or diminish sea-level rise. Although there has already been extensive melting of glaciers and ice sheets, many coasts still show little if any sea-level rise so far. This may be due to these factors, or to a delay between the loss to the atmosphere of water vapor from melting ice and its precipitation onto the land and into the oceans.

IMPLICATIONS

A rising sea level will lead to coastal changes. Submerging coastlines, now confined mainly to sectors where the land has been subsiding (Figure 1), will become more extensive, and emerging coastlines more restricted. In the Gulf of Bothnia postglacial isostatic recovery has been raising the land by up to a centimeter per year, and the coastline has been advancing. As sea level rises at a rate equaling and then exceeding the rate of land uplift, this coastline advance will be halted and then give way to recession. In time, all of the world's coastline will be submerging as the result of sea-level rise.

As sea level rises on low-lying coastal areas high- and low-tide lines will advance landward, and at least part of the present intertidal zone will be completely submerged. On vertical hard-rock cliffs where there is little or no marine erosion, submergence will simply raise the high- and low-tide lines and the coastline will remain where it is.

There may be slight changes in tide range around the world's coastline as tidal amplitude adapts to changing coastal and near-shore configuration. Deepening nearshore seas may increase tide range at the coast. It is also possible that the additional load of water on submerging coasts will result in isostatic depression of the nearshore sea floor, thereby increasing relative sea-level rise.

On many coasts the high-tide line will move landward because of more severe erosion as nearshore waters deepen and larger and more destructive waves break on the shore. As sea level rises erosion will begin on coasts that are at present stable and accelerate on coasts that are already receding, while on prograding coasts (coasts that are being built out into the sea) the advance of the coastline will be curbed, and then reversed. This has occurred around the land-locked Caspian, where progradation during several years of falling local sea level has given way to extensive submergence and erosion since sea level began to rise in 1977 (Kaplin and Selivanov, 1995).

Erosion will be augmented where climatic changes that accompany the rising sea level lead to more frequent and severe storms, generating surges that penetrate further inland than they do now. Coasts already subject to storm surges, such as the hurricane-prone Gulf and Atlantic coasts of the United States, will have more frequent and extensive marine flooding as submergence proceeds, with more rapid erosion and structural damage by larger waves.

While erosion will increase on most coasts, some may receive sufficient sediment from eroding cliffs or river discharge to maintain, or even raise, the nearshore profile as the sea rises. On such coasts wave energy will not intensify, and there may be little, if any, coastline erosion; there may even be progradation.

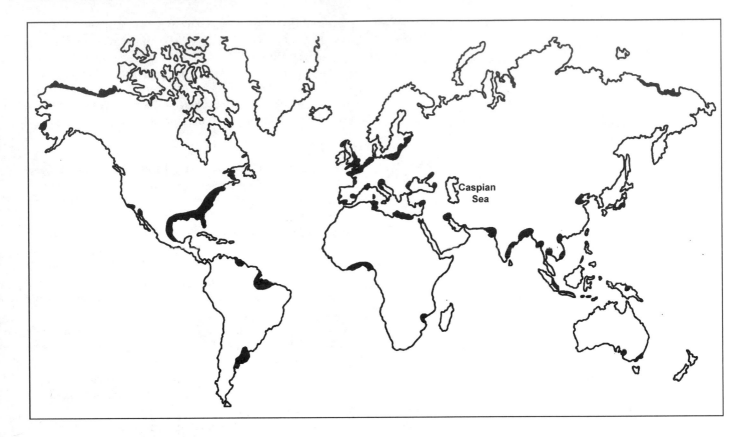

Assessments of the effects of a rising sea level (Bird, 1993; Douglas et al., 2001; Cracknell, 2005) remain speculative because of the imprecision of available models. A major difficulty is the prediction of an accelerating sea-level rise, with no early prospect of stabilization. If global warming can be curbed by managing the atmosphere, sea-level rise could be halted at a higher level or even returned to its present position.

If the sea continues to rise, coastal erosion will accelerate and become more widespread. Pictures showing St. Paul's Cathedral in London and the Eiffel Tower in Paris standing in the sea and maps showing the extent of submergence expected in various regions with sea level raised by up to 60 m (flooding most of the world's capital cities) have drawn attention to the scale of the problem.

EFFECTS OF CLIMATE CHANGE

The predicted sea-level rise will be accompanied by other responses to global warming. In addition to raising temperatures, global warming will cause the migration of climatic zones, tropical sectors expanding as temperate sectors migrate poleward and the domain of Arctic coasts shrinks. Tropical cyclones will become more frequent and severe, extending into higher latitudes and bringing storm surges and torrential downpours to coasts that now lie outside their range. Coastal climates will also be modified by changes in ocean currents, as already shown by the El Niño–Southern Oscillation, which has led to heavy rain and river flooding in China, Ecuador, and Peru, and droughts in Australia.

Sea Level Future. Figure 1. Subsiding Coasts.

Sectors of the world's coastline (in black) that have been subsiding (as shown by tide gauge records and satellite sensing), and thus show a relative rise in sea level. They include the tectonically sinking Gulf and Atlantic coasts of the United States and areas where ground water extraction (e.g., Venice, Bangkok) or oil extraction (e.g., Long Beach, California) have caused subsidence. In addition, sea level has been rising since 1977 in the Caspian.

Effects on cliffed coasts

As sea level rises on cliffed coasts, deepening nearshore waters will submerge shore platforms and rocky shores and allow larger waves to reach the coast and attack the base of the cliff, thereby accelerating erosion. Cliffs cut in soft sediments around the Great Lakes in North America receded more rapidly during phases of rising water level. On resistant rock outcrops there will be little change.

Effects on beaches

There is already widespread erosion on the world's beaches. More than 70% of sandy coastlines retreated and less than 10% advanced between 1880 and 1980, the remainder having remained stable or shown no net change (Bird, 1985). Beach erosion will intensify where a rising sea level deepens nearshore water, so that larger waves break on the shore.

The effects of a sea-level rise can already be seen on beaches where there has been submergence as a result of land subsidence in recent decades, as on the Atlantic seaboard of the United

States (Douglas et al., 2001). Submergence has contributed to beach profile erosion on these coasts, much as predicted by the Bruun rule (Figure 2), though it needs to be remembered that this rule has certain limitations and only applies, for example, to sandy beaches without substantial longshore drift.

Beaches will persist, migrating landward, where the rising sea encounters sand or gravel deposits on the subsiding land. The formation of existing beaches during and after the Flandrian marine transgression occurred because the rising sea advanced across a land surface that was strewn with Pleistocene beach deposits left stranded during a preceding emergence. Where there are sand and gravel deposits in coastal regions a rising sea could move some of them shoreward to form beaches at higher levels, but existing beaches would by then be submerged.

One prediction of the Bruun rule is that a beach profile will recede 50 to 100 times the dimensions of a rise in sea level, so that a one-meter rise would cause the beach to retreat by 50 to 100 m. Since many seaside resort beaches are no more than 30 m wide, the implication is that these will have disappeared by the time the sea has risen 15 to 30 cm, unless they are artificially replaced. Beach nourishment at higher sea levels may be preferable to building sea walls, which tend to deplete fronting beaches by the scouring caused by waves reflected from the walls.

Effects on coastal dunes

Coastal dunes behind eroding beaches will show increased cliffing of the backshore (the shoreward, usually dry zone of the beach) by storm waves as sea level rises. As the coastal dune fringe is cut back, blowouts will be initiated, and some of these will grow into large transgressive dunes as sand is excavated and blown landward. If at the same time the climate becomes drier and windier, coastal dunes that are at present stable and vegetated may become unstable as the vegetation cover is weakened and sand mobilized; dunes that are already active will become more mobile. A wetter and calmer climate could aid vegetation growth and dune stabilization.

Effects on salt marshes and mangroves

A rising sea level will submerge existing intertidal areas, and as the nearshore water deepens, stronger wave action will initiate or accelerate erosion on the seaward margins of salt marshes and mangroves. Microcliffs will form and recede through the marshland. Tidal creeks that intersect salt marshes and mangrove areas will be enlarged, and extend headward (landward) as they are submerged. As submergence proceeds the retreat of the seaward margin will be matched by a diachronous transgression (one that advances with time as the sea advances) of the landward margin of salt marsh or mangroves on to the hinterland at a rate related to the transverse elevation gradient of the shore.

Where the hinterland is low-lying, salt marshes or mangroves will migrate landward to displace freshwater or terrigenous vegetation communities, or invade backing salt flats. Vegetation zones will move to maintain their position relative to the shifting intertidal zone. Where the hinterland rises more steeply vegetation zones will be compressed (coastal squeeze) as sea level rises, and the salt marsh or mangrove fringe will disappear completely where these communities are backed by a steep slope or a sea wall. Where there is a continuing supply of muddy sediment, however, the salt marshes or mangroves could be maintained, or even extended seaward despite a rising sea level. There is the possibility that salt marsh and mangrove fringes could be maintained by dumping mud in the nearshore area, whence it can be washed onshore and into the vegetated areas, raising the substrate to match a sea-level rise.

Changes can be seen in salt marshes and mangroves on coasts that are already submerging. On the Atlantic seaboard of the United States salt-marsh islands in Chesapeake Bay have diminished in area or disappeared as the result of sea-level rise, and submergence has resulted in salt-marsh plants invading backing meadow land. Similar features are seen on subsiding areas of mangrove-fringed coast, as on the Mamberamo delta in Irian Jaya, Indonesia.

Sea Level Future. Figure 2. Bruun Rule.

The Bruun Rule states that on beaches that had attained a profile of equilibrium, the response to a sea-level rise will be erosion of the upper beach (R) and withdrawal of sediment from the beach to the adjacent sea floor ($V_1 \rightarrow V_2$) in such a way as to restore the previous profile in relation to the higher sea level.

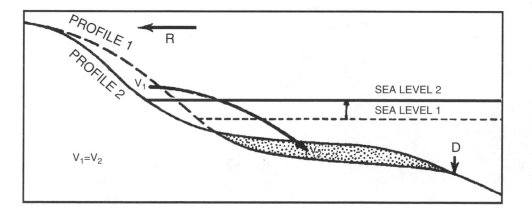

Marine organisms that are vertically zoned in relation to specific intertidal levels will migrate upward on rocky shores and artificial structures such as sea walls as sea level rises.

Effects on estuaries and lagoons

Estuaries and lagoons will generally become wider and deeper as sea level rises; their shores will be submerged and eroded. Tides will penetrate farther upstream and tide ranges may increase. Entrances to coastal lagoons are likely to be enlarged and deepened, increasing the inflow of sea water during rising tides and drought periods. This will raise the salinity of lagoons that were previously relatively fresh. Erosion of enclosing barriers may lead to breaching of new lagoon entrances and could eventually reopen the lagoons as marine embayments. On the other hand, new lagoons may be formed by sea-water incursion or rising water tables in low-lying areas behind dunes on coastal plains. This has occurred around parts of the Caspian coast as the sea level has risen since 1977.

The Lagoon of Venice has been maintained partly by continuing subsidence accelerated by groundwater extraction and partly by the diversion of rivers such as the Po and Brenta, which had been carrying sediment into it. A sea-level rise in the Lagoon of about a meter during the past century has led to more frequent storm surges (*acqua alta*) in the Venice region, and further sea-level rise will worsen this situation.

Effects on deltas and coastal plains

Most large deltas already show isostatic subsidence under the weight of accumulating sediment, leading to the submergence of areas no longer being maintained by sedimentation. This is obvious on the Mississippi delta, where former lobes of the delta no longer maintained by sedimentation have subsided beneath the sea. A rising sea level will increase submergence and erosion of deltas and coastal plains, except where there is sufficient accretion to maintain progradation.

Effects on coral reefs

Growth of corals and algae on the surface of intertidal reefs will be stimulated by a rising sea level, providing other ecological conditions remain suitable. Growth may be curbed by increased turbidity from rivers or coral bleaching caused by higher temperatures. Much will depend on the rate at which the sea rises (Spencer, 1995). A slowly rising sea (<1 cm/yr) should stimulate the revival of coral growth on reef platforms, so that some reefs will maintain upward growth with a rising sea level. Others may survive to grow up to the surface when the sea-level rise slows or stops. A more rapid sea level rise

Sea Level Future. Effects of Tectonic Activity.

A submerged Lycian tomb in southern Turkey indicates that subsidence has occurred as a result of tectonic activity.

(>2 cm/yr) would lead to the drowning of corals and the submergence of inert reef formations.

Islands on coral reefs will be modified by a rising sea level. Many cays and low wooded islands will be eroded by larger waves approaching through deepening waters, and may disappear, overwashed by storm surges, especially if there is an increasing frequency and severity of tropical cyclones as sea and atmospheric temperatures rise. Inhabitants of low islands in Kiribati in the western Pacific are already concerned about erosion and submergence by a rising sea level and are facing eventual evacuation.

Effects on developed coasts

As the sea level rises coasts will be greatly affected by human impacts, and there will be a demand for larger and higher coast-protection structures. Land levels can be raised and buildings elevated to prevent submergence by the rising sea, as at Galveston in Texas.

Coastal land reclamation and coastal protection have made many coastlines artificial, bordered by sea walls. As the sea rises alongside such structures there is a risk that they will be overwashed or breached by storm surges, while the associated rise in the water table will lead to waterlogging and flooding of reclaimed areas. In recent years a number of areas of formerly reclaimed coast have been deliberately abandoned, a procedure called managed retreat or coastal realignment. In Britain, Freiston in Lincolnshire and Porlock Bay in Somerset are examples of coastal lowlands that have been abandoned to marine invasion. More broadly, some coastal structures have been moved inland in response to the threat of coastline recession (McGlashan, 2003). As the sea rises, great modifications will have to be made to cities, ports, and low-lying areas along the world's coastlines.

[*See also* Emerging Coasts.]

BIBLIOGRAPHY

Bird, E.C.F. *Coastline Changes: A Global Review.* Chichester, U.K, and New York: Wiley, 1985.

———. *Submerging Coasts.* Chichester, U.K, and New York: Wiley, 1993.

Cracknell, B.E. *Outrageous Waves: Global Warming and Coastal Change in Britain through Two Thousand Years.* Chichester, U.K.: Phillimore, 2005.

Douglas, B.C., M.S. Kearney, and S.P. Leatherman, eds. *Sea Level Rise, History, and Consequences.* San Diego: Academic Press, 2001.

Kaplin, P.A. and A.O. Selivanov. "Recent Coastal Evolution of the Caspian Sea As a Natural Model for Coastal Responses to the Possible Acceleration of Global Sea-Level Rise." *Marine Geology* 124:1–4 (1995), 161–175. DOI: 10.1016/0025–3227(95)00038-Z.

McGlashan, D.J. "Managed Relocation: An Assessment of Its Feasibility." *Geographical Journal* 169.1 (2003), 6–20. DOI: 10.1111/1475–4959.04993.

Solomon, S., et al., eds. *Climate Change 2007: The Physical Science Basis. Contribution of Working Group I to the Fourth Assessment Report of the Intergovernmental Panel on Climate Change.* Cambridge and New York: Cambridge University Press, 2007. The Summary for Policymakers is available at http://www.ipcc.ch/pdf/assessment-report/ar4/syr/ar4_syr_spm.pdf (accessed June 3, 2008).

Spencer, T. "Potentialities, Uncertainties, and Complexities in the Response of Coral Reefs to Future Sea-Level Rise." *Earth Surface Processes and Landforms* 20.1 (1995), 49–64.

—Eric C. F. Bird

SECURITY AND ENVIRONMENT

National security has traditionally focused on maintaining the territorial integrity and political sovereignty of nations. In turn, the security issues of the nation-state are linked to broader issues of international security. Hence threats to the security of states can also be considered threats to international security. In recent years, increased emphasis has been placed on expanding the traditional conception of security to include nonconventional threats. Such threats include resource scarcity, human-rights abuses, outbreaks of infectious disease, and environmental degradation caused by toxic contamination, ozone depletion, global warming, water pollution, soil degradation, and the loss of biodiversity.

HISTORY

The interest in linking environment and security emerged strongly in the mid-1980s, although discussions on the issue of environmental change and security occurred without explicit use of the term "environmental security" as early as the 1950s. The U.S. military's use of defoliants in Southeast Asia during the Vietnam War focused international attention on both the intentional and unintentional environmental damage caused by war. Protocol I on the Protection of Victims of International Armed Conflicts (1977), additional to the 1949 Geneva Convention, was the first of two treaties with major environmental importance that stemmed from international concern over excessive environmental degradation in Vietnam.

Efforts to develop more stringent definitions for "widespread, long-term and severe damage to the natural environment" continued with the 1977 Convention on the Prohibition of Military or Any Other Hostile Use of Environmental Modification Techniques (the ENMOD Convention), the second of the post-Vietnam treaties.

By the early 1980s, various institutions and writers began addressing security issues beyond strictly military concerns that affect the state. The UN Commission on Disarmament and Security Issues made a distinction between collective security (the more traditional interstate military security issues) and common security (nonmilitary threats, including economic, resource scarcity, population growth, and environmental degradation). This was followed by the new political thinking of Russian President Mikhail Gorbachev, which promoted the concept of comprehensive security as a cornerstone of international politics. Comprehensive security included various threats, including nuclear war, poverty, and global environmental issues.

At the same time, numerous writers began to address the issue of expanding the definition of security to include nonmilitary threats. The following example is from Ullman (1983):

A threat to national security is an action or sequence of events that (1) threatens drastically and over a relatively brief span of time to degrade the quality of life for the inhabitants of a state, or (2) threatens significantly to narrow the range of policy choices available to the government of a state or to private, nongovernmental entities (person, groups, corporations) within the state.

While still circumscribing security within state boundaries, such analysts sought to expand the range of threats to security beyond the traditional military concerns.

The suggestion to broaden the definition of security to include environmental threats was by no means limited to American sources. The report of the World Commission on Environment and Development, *Our Common Future* (1987), which was best known for its definition of sustainable development, also called for recognition that security was partly a function of environmental sustainability. The Commission highlighted the role that environmental stress can play in conflict and asserted that a "comprehensive" approach to international and national security must transcend the traditional emphasis on military power and armed competition. Norman Myers (1993) argued similarly for moving from security as a "freedom from" various threats to security as a "freedom to" access environmental services. Others point out that comprehensive security has two intertwined components, political security, with its military, economic, and humanitarian subcomponents, and environmental security, including the protection and use of the environment.

The importance of this distinction became obvious after the 1986 nuclear accident at Chernobyl placed health considerations squarely in a security framework for many people. The next year, President Gorbachev proposed "ecological security" as a top priority that would serve as a de facto means of advancing international confidence-building.

INTO THE POLITICAL REALM

It should be noted that discussion of the links between environment and security has extended far beyond an academic debate. Warren Christopher, former U.S. Secretary of State, has explicitly linked the two, noting that "natural resource issues [are] frequently critical to achieving political and economic stability." Former Norwegian Defense Minister Johan Jørgen Holst was even more explicit when he noted that "environmental degradation may be viewed as a contribution to armed conflict in the sense of exacerbating conflicts or adding new dimensions."

Some confusion still exists among academics and in public-policy circles over how environment and security are linked. This confusion persists not only within disciplines, but within government departments as well. Many researchers avoid the term "security" altogether, preferring to focus on environmental change and social adaptation and/or armed conflict.

At least part of the confusion in identifying the links between environment and security results from different institutional interpretations of the terms "environment" and "security." At present, these interpretations include the following.

- Security of the environment (or security of services provided by the natural environment). This has also been interpreted as nondiminishing natural capital. This includes military and defense intelligence institutions monitoring and enforcing international environmental agreements; gathering, analyzing, and disseminating scientific data on the natural environment; responding to environmental crises and disasters; implementing environmental sustainability programs; guaranteeing access to natural resources; spinning off environmental-cleanup technologies; and protecting natural parks and reserves.
- Environmental degradation or depletion stemming from military preparation for armed conflict, from the conduct of armed conflict, and from the disposal of military waste.
- Environmental degradation and resource depletion as potential causes of violent conflict.
- Institutional infringement on the principle of sovereignty to mitigate environmental degradation.
- Environmental degradation and resource depletion as threats to national welfare (and, therefore, to national security).
- A broad notion of environment embedded in a range of factors that affect "human" security.

The discussions have become even more difficult because of their interdisciplinary nature; participants range from environmentalists, who may interpret a secure environment as one in which there is no further decline in the stocks of natural capital, to the military, which sees certain environmental issues as new threats, or environmental security as a "greening" of their operations. Adding to the confusion are specialists who interpret "security" differently from members of the international-relations community or the defense establishment. Conversely, the introduction of new terms (such as "environmental scarcity" and "environmental refugees") can frustrate researchers and policy makers for whom similar terms may have specific, important, and sometimes legal, meanings.

RELATIONS BETWEEN ENVIRONMENT AND SECURITY

Assessments of the nature of linkages between environment and security have proven difficult. The complexity of the relationship sets up tremendous empirical and methodological hurdles. The ambiguous and controversial nature of the term "security" also complicates research and policy in the area of environment and security. A number of researchers have tried to circumvent this problem by ignoring the term altogether and concentrating specifically on the role of environmental change and resource depletion as potential causes of violent conflict. Such conflict, in turn, could pose a serious threat to the security of individuals, regions, and nations. The general discussions on the nature of security and the role of environmental degradation as a contributor to insecurity and conflict have been labeled by Marc Levy (1995) as the "first wave" of environment and conflict research. The empirical research that attempted to prove a link between environment and conflict has been labeled by Levy as the "second wave" of environment and conflict studies.

The state of environment and conflict research that defined this "second wave" is by no means complete or definitive, but from this research has emerged a coherent set of causal claims that provides a basis for debating the potential role of environmental and demographic stress as contributors to conflict. These claims also allow a further discussion of policies that incorporate the links between environment and conflict and provide a basis for pursuing further investigation of the complex and still poorly understood linkages and for taking action.

Several types of environmental threat may contribute to insecurity and produce conflict. Constraints on resources are a crucial factor. Rapid industrialization and population growth in many regions have resulted in an increased demand for both renewable and nonrenewable natural resources, and competition for resources has historically been a major cause of conflict. This seems intuitively reasonable, but some feel that it overstates the importance of resources and the environment as contributors to conflict. At first glance, the availability of water in the Middle East, the depletion of fish stocks off the eastern coast of Canada, and deforestation in Brazil, Thailand, and elsewhere have all been, or have the potential to be, sources of conflict. It has further been suggested that atmospheric change—including global warming and ozone depletion—has the potential to cause significant societal disruption. In addition, land degradation—or land-use change in general—may directly affect society's ability to provide food resources for a growing population, or may indirectly affect other changes, such as global warming. Homer-Dixon (1994) provides some evidence of these relationships and concludes that "environmental scarcity" (which includes environmental change, population growth, and an unequal distribution of resources) can cause violent conflict. While this contention remains open to debate, it is increasingly accepted that environmental degradation and resource factors are at least a contributor to conflict and insecurity.

[*See also* Environmental Law; Migrations; Sustainable Growth; *and* Water.]

BIBLIOGRAPHY

Canadian Global Change Program. *Environment and Security: An Overview of Issues and Research Priorities for Canada.* Report No. 96–1.Ottawa: Royal Society of Canada, 1996. Outlines the key arguments for and against linking environment and security.
Deudney, D. "Environment and Security: Muddled Thinking." *Bulletin of Atomic Scientists* 47.3 (1991), 22–28. The second part of a debate on how environment and security are linked (see also Gleick, 1991).
Gleick, P. "Environment and Security: The Clear Connections." *Bulletin of Atomic Scientists* 47.3 (1991), 17–21. The first part of a debate on how environment and security are linked (see also Deudney, 1991).
Homer-Dixon, T. "On the Threshold: Environmental Changes as Causes of Acute Conflict." *International Security* 16.2 (1991), 76–116. A conceptual and theoretical article on how environment may affect conflict.
Homer-Dixon, T.F. "Environmental Scarcities and Violent Conflict." *International Security* 19.1 (1994), 5–40.
Levy, M. "Is the Environment a National Security Issue?" *International Security* 20.2 (1995), 35–62.
Mathews, J.T. "Redefining Security." *Foreign Affairs* 68.2 (1989), 162–177. One of the classic articles on expanding the definition of security.
Myers, N. "Environment and Security." *Foreign Policy* 74 (1989), 23–41. An overview article on the relationship between environment and security.
———. *Ultimate Security.* New York and London: Norton, 1993.
Ullman, R.H. "Redefining Security." *International Security* 8.1 (1983), 129–153.
World Commission on Environment and Development. *Our Common Future.* New York and Oxford: Oxford University Press, 1987.

—STEVE LONERGAN

SNOW COVER

Snow cover is the most spatially extensive and seasonally variable component of the global cryosphere (that part of the Earth system comprising frozen water in its various forms). On average, snow covers almost 47 million square kilometers, or half, of the Northern Hemisphere land surface in late January, with an August minimum of one million km^2. In addition, there is perennial snow cover over the Antarctic ice sheet (12 million km^2), and at the higher elevations of the Greenland Ice Sheet (about 0.6 million km^2).

Information on snow cover has been collected routinely at hydrometeorological stations, with records beginning in the late nineteenth century at a few stations, and more widely since the 1930–1950s. The ground is considered to be snow-covered when at least half of the area visible from an observing station has snow cover. Since 1966, snow cover has been mapped by satellites, initially using visible-band data, which are limited by illumination and cloud cover, and since 1978 by multichannel passive microwave sensors, which are not limited by these factors. Reliable hemispheric snow-cover data have been available since 1972 from the Advanced Very High Resolution Radiometer (AVHRR). The visible images are interpreted manually, and snow extent is mapped over the Northern Hemisphere on a daily basis (formerly weekly). The charts have been digitized for grid boxes varying in size from 16,000 to 42,000 km^2, and these data have also been remapped to a 25×25 kilometer grid for 1978–1995 and combined with the extent of Arctic sea ice mapped from passive microwave data to display the seasonal cryosphere in the Northern Hemisphere. There is a more limited record from AVHRR data for 1974–1986 in the Southern Hemisphere, where the snowcover extent in South America varies between about 1.2 million and 0.7 million km^2 in July. There is a negligible cover in January in the Southern Hemisphere apart from Antarctica.

Snow cover plays an important role in the climate system. The best-known effect involves the albedo-temperature positive feedback, whereby an expanded (reduced) snow cover increases (decreases) the reflection of incoming solar radiation, reducing (increasing) the temperature and thereby encouraging an expansion (reduction) of the snow cover. Fresh snow has a spectrally integrated albedo of 0.8–0.9, making it the most reflective natural surface. [*See* Albedo.] This value decreases with age to 0.4–0.7 as the snow density increases through settling and snow metamorphism and is reduced still further by impurities in or on the snow (e.g., mineral dust, soot, aerosols, biogenic matter). The cooling effect of snow cover is illustrated by the fact that, in the Upper Midwest of the United States, winter months with snow cover are about 5–7°C colder than the same months without snow cover. Snow, a poor conductor of heat, also insulates the soil surface and sea ice. The storage of water in the seasonal snow cover introduces into the hydrological cycle an important delay of weeks to months, causing a peak in the annual runoff in spring and early summer when the river water is agriculturally more valuable.

Snowfall is reported in routine meteorological observations. The catch of solid and mixed precipitation in precipitation gauges is melted and total precipitation is usually reported. In windy environments especially, gauge totals may underestimate snowfall by 20–50% or more. Snow depth and the corresponding snow-water equivalent (SWE) are measured at ground stations. Depth is routinely measured at fixed stakes, or by a ruler inserted into the snow pack, and this depth is reported in daily weather observations at 0900 hours. Average maximum snow depths vary from 30 to 40 centimeters on Arctic Sea ice to several meters in maritime climates such as the mountains of western North America. The SWE along snow courses is measured from depth and density determinations made at weekly to monthly time intervals. These records are used in runoff forecasting. Such networks are decreasing because of their cost, and satellite passive-microwave data are beginning to be used in combination with other techniques for estimating SWE. The basis of this approach is that microwave radiation emitted by the land surface is attenuated by snow cover, but the effects of any liquid water due to snow melt, the obscuring of the snow surface by the vegetation canopy, changes in the grain size of the snow, and terrain irregularities greatly complicate such determinations. Moreover, the typical satellite footprint is of the order of 12–25 kilometers, meaning that the signal is a complex spatial average and hard to relate to point measurements. Nevertheless, such methods are being used for operational SWE mapping over the high plains and prairies of North America. In the western United States, SWE is determined by "pressure pillows" that record the weight of the overlying snow packs. There are more than 500 such stations in the western cordilleras.

Observational records from satellites indicate that between 1972 and the present, the annual snow-covered area in the Northern Hemisphere decreased by about 7%. The changes are especially marked in spring and summer, with little or no change in winter. These reductions are highly correlated with increasing air temperature. For North America, approximately −0.6 million km² of snow-cover area is lost per degree Celsius rise in temperature. Calculations also suggest that the reduced hemispheric snow cover corresponds approximately to 0.5°C of warming as a result of feedback effects on the energy balance. Global-warming trends especially affect winter temperatures, and in high latitudes, warmer winters, may be snowier as a result of increased atmospheric moisture content. This effect has been observed on maritime glaciers in Norway and Alaska and is projected to occur over coastal Antarctica under future global warming.

[*See also* Global Warming.]

BIBLIOGRAPHY

Armstrong, R.L., and M.J. Brodzik. 2005 "Northern Hemisphere EASE-Grid Weekly Snow Cover and Sea Ice Extent Version 3." Boulder, Colo.: National Snow and Ice Data Center. www.nside.org (accessed June 4, 2008).

Gray, D.M., and D.H. Male, eds. *Handbook of Snow: Principles, Processes, Management, and Use.* Toronto: Pergamon, 1981.

Groisman, P. Ya., T.R. Karl, and R.W. Knight. "Observed Impact of Snow Cover on the Heat Balance and the Rise of Continental Spring Temperatures." *Science* 263 (1994), 198–200. DOI: 10.1126/science.263.5144.198.

Robinson, D.A., K.F. Dewey, and R.R. Heim Jr. "Global Snow Cover Monitoring: An Update." *Bulletin of the American Meteorological Society* 74.9 (1993), 1689–1696. DOI: 10.1175/1520–0477(1993)074<1689:GSCMAU>2.0.CO;2.

Sevruk, B., ed. *Snow Cover Measurements and Areal Assessment of Precipitation and Soil Moisture.* Geneva: World Meteorological Organization, 1992.

—Roger G. Barry

SOILS

Soils are the products of the breakdown of rocky and organic components of the Earth's surface by interactions among the lithosphere, atmosphere, hydrosphere, and biosphere. Soils play essential roles in supporting the terrestrial biosphere and in element cycling and are fundamentally important to the well-being of all humans. They are increasingly used for a range of economic purposes—including food production, and mining and quarrying—and are suffering degradation and pollution.

All soils consist of solids, liquids, and gases. They include organic and mineral materials, and each soil has its own combination of inherent properties of texture (relative abundances of sand, silt, and clay), fabric (pattern of particles and voids), and mineralogy, which influence strength, porosity, permeability, moisture retention, chemistry, plasticity, frost resistance, shrinkage and swelling (shrink/swell), and numerous other properties.

Because there are no universally agreed definitions of soil, description and understanding depend on the interests of the observer. A pedologist (soil scientist) may take a theoretical view in an attempt to understand the genesis of soils. An agronomist will see soils as a natural medium for plant growth and be most concerned with chemistry and physics. An engineer will consider soil as a material to be built upon or as construction material and will be more interested in particle size, fabric, drainage, and mechanics. A ceramicist may be interested only in the clay fraction as a raw material for the manufacture of cement, bricks, china, and high-technology engine components.

These people all describe and classify soils according to their own needs, and there is little overlap in their perceptions and jargon. Such fragmented views are a barrier to communication and understanding that needs to be broken down if we are to manage our soil resources more effectively.

SOIL FORMATION

Mineral soils are derived from the breakdown of primary rock minerals. The processes of formation include: weathering; leaching; the formation of new minerals; erosion, deposition, and sorting; and interactions with the biosphere.

Weathering

The effects of weather may break down rock minerals into simpler constituents through reaction with water. Hydrolysis is the basis of this process, and different elements show varying resistance to it. Sodium and potassium react readily; calcium, magnesium, and ferrous iron react more slowly; ferric iron and aluminum are resistant; and silicon is very resistant. Of the common rock-forming silicates, ferromagnesians (olivine, augite, etc.) break down quickly and completely; feldspars form chain silicate fragments as a precursor to clays; micas disintegrate along their cleavage planes to form new sheet-structured silicates; and quartz does not change other than to break into smaller particles.

Leaching

Taking place in aqueous solution, leaching moves the products of weathering over distances of microns to the external surface of the rock mineral, or over meters when more soluble elements such as sodium and calcium leave the soil environment in solution. Leaching rates increase with water availability. The depth of calcium carbonate accumulation within a soil can be a guide to leaching intensity; it is quite shallow in an arid-zone soil and absent in a humid-zone soil. Even stronger patterns may be seen in the accumulation of common salt, but these minerals are quite ephemeral and may be indicative only of present-day processes.

On a geographical scale, leaching is the process responsible for the separation of mobile elements (sodium, potassium, calcium, and magnesium) from the relatively insoluble elements (iron, aluminum, and silicon).

Formation of new minerals

The entities formed and concentrated by weathering and leaching may recombine into new minerals that are stable at surface conditions. Most new minerals are clays, fine-grained silicates with sheet structures. Different clays have different chemical and physical properties that are important to soil users. The nature of the clay depends on the chemical composition of the original rock mineral and on the intensity of the weathering and leaching environment.

The end products of weathering, leaching, and new-mineral formation—a set of processes that in combination are called epimorphism—are resistant rock silicates (especially sand-sized quartz), fine-grained insoluble oxides of iron and aluminum, and clays. In most cases of simple epimorphism the end products tend to have a bimodal size distribution, with residual sands (0.2–2.0 mm in diameter) and fine-grained (>0.002 mm in diameter) clays or oxides being dominant. Particles of intermediate size (silt) are rare in environments subject to normal epimorphism but more common where rock minerals have been comminuted.

Particle size is an important factor in controlling soil chemistry, physics, and mechanics. Sand, for example, has a specific surface area of 0.1–0.01 square meters per gram, whereas clay can range from 10 (kaolinite) to as much as 800 (montmorillonite). The finer the soil, the greater its ability to retain nutrients, pollutants, and water. Reactive clays also have a higher shrink/swell potential, a characteristic especially important in engineering. The packing of all particles is the key to porosity and most mechanical properties.

The nature of the end products of epimorphism is strongly affected by properties of the original lithospheric minerals: our understanding of soil materials must take account of inheritance from parent material. This applies both in the case of epimorphism of original igneous or metamorphic rock minerals and, even more importantly, in the secondary epimporphism of sedimentary rocks or sediments. Inheritance may influence soil mineralogy, texture, and fabric.

Erosion, deposition, and sorting

All epimorphism takes place on a land surface that is subject to geomorphic processes. Like the other components of this model, the landscape is itself complex, and no one landscape is totally erosional or depositional. On any hill slope, the movement of materials and soil water varies spatially and temporally. An appreciation of flow patterns can improve our understanding of the soil materials on that slope.

The importance of erosion processes has long been obvious to geomorphologists studying landscape evolution, but pedologists have tended not to consider them a normal part of soil genesis. The two most important erosion processes on a global scale are probably rainwash (raindrop-agitated surface flow) on hill slope mantles and wind erosion in moving and sorting fine materials (especially sands) in any environment with limited vegetation cover. Processes of mass movement and glaciation often occur on such a large scale that they disrupt soil formation to create or redistribute raw materials for a new soil cycle.

Interactions with the biosphere

The biosphere is involved in epimorphism by adjusting pH conditions through the release of organic acids and respiratory carbon dioxide, and it is an essential part of leaching and the cycling of nutrients through plants and animals. Elements stored in plant biomass may be released slowly to the soil through litter decay or rapidly during a wildfire. In either event, the elements are not returned to the same point on the slope from which they were derived, and there is a net vertical movement of nutrients from weathering bedrock to the surface and a downslope concentration toward stream lines. The most important physical process in the biosphere is bioturbation—the mixing, mounding, and overturn of soil material by treefall and burrowing organisms such as ants, worms, termites, and some vertebrates. Although the importance of such processes was recognized by Charles Darwin more than a century ago, they have only recently begun to be incorporated in soil-genesis models. The combination of rapid bioturbation of a surface soil mantle and rainwash erosion creates a relatively coarse biomantle, as finer mineral particles are winnowed from the slope. Bioturbation is usually depth-limited, and many soils exhibit a marked contrast in fabric and texture between the biomantle (topsoil) and underlying saprolite (subsoil or weathered rock in which the fabric of the original rock is preserved).

SOIL IDENTIFICATION AND CLASSIFICATION

In the late nineteenth century, soils were recognized as independent natural bodies of earth that supported terrestrial plants. Each had a unique morphology, represented in layers (horizons)

Soils. Soil Erosion.

Most soils take a very long time to form, but can be eroded quickly if the vegetation cover is removed. In northwestern Australia, overgrazing by cattle has caused the surface soil to be stripped off by intense tropical storms, exposing tree roots.

which were believed to be genetically determined and which reflected the integration of all the processes of soil genesis. This concept still underpins the discipline of pedology, which has become tied to horizonation and profile maturity.

By convention, soil horizons are the essential attribute of soils whose characteristics include texture, fabric, color, pH, and the presence of pans (hard layers), concretions, and salts. Particular horizon combinations make up accepted soil types, which are the basis of most soil surveys.

The most widely used classification of soils is that of the U.S. Department of Agriculture. The text *Soil Taxonomy* (Soil Survey Staff, 1984; 2d ed. 1999; http://soils.usda.gov/technical/classification/taxonomy/) divides soils into mineral and organic types. Mineral soils are further classified on the presence or absence of six diagnostic surface horizons (epipedons) and seventeen diagnostic subsurface horizons.

At a lower level, *Soil Taxonomy* considers soil moisture and temperature regimes, parameters that hark back to older concepts of the importance of climate in controlling zonal soil profiles.

The *Soil Taxonomy* classification is a hierarchy: at the top are ten orders (alfisols, aridsols, entisols, histosols, inceptisols, mollisols, oxisols, spodosols, ultisols, and vertisols), fifty suborders, and about two hundred great groups; further down are descriptions of subgroups, families, series, and finally soil types with a specific geographic distribution.

Perhaps the best example of the difficulties this zonalist and hierarchical approach has created can be seen in the geography of soil with a classic podzol morphology. Most workers agree on the general nature of such a profile. It is a soil with an acid plant-litter horizon and an organic sandy topsoil over a prominent bleached horizon (eluvial zone). Beneath the bleaching, iron oxides or humic materials or both have accumulated as complex pans in the sandy subsoil (illuvial zone). The same workers, however, do not agree on a nomenclature for the podzol profile, or on the genesis of this soil.

In the current *Soil Taxonomy* classification, podzol profiles are recognized as spodosols; in other classifications they have been given different names, such as placosols and podosols. Very commonly they are grouped with other superficially similar profiles as podzolized soils, implying that the eluvial and illuvial processes are pervasive.

Early pedologists noted the close relationship between the podzol and the climate and vegetation of the regions where it was found. From these and other observations was developed a genetic model that emphasized the dominant role of the "active factors" in soil formation, namely, vegetation (or the biosphere) and climate, which acted over time on the parent material of the soil at a particular site (topography) to form zonal profiles. The podzol was accepted as such a profile.

Consideration of the recent geological history of the Earth and the patterns of Northern Hemisphere soil-distribution can explain the initial success and subsequent failure of the zonal-genesis model. Those parts of Northern Hemisphere high latitudes that were extensively glaciated during the Pleistocene ice ages are exactly the regions in which the first successful correlations were made between soil profiles, vegetation, and climate. Thus the podzols were identified in the cool, humid, coniferous forests, and the chernozems ("black earths") in the cold, semiarid, prairie grasslands (steppes). Geologically, these are respectively the regions of outwash sands beyond the front of the ice sheets and the areas blanketed by windblown loess. Taking parent material into account, it is apparent that podzols are linked to deep sand bodies and chernozems to deep silts.

In Australia, ice-age glaciation was very limited, but profiles identical to the classic podzol are widely distributed along the east coast from Tasmania to Cape York. Clearly, there is no obvious link to the "active factors" of soil formation here, but there is a link to the parent material. In every case, the podzol profile is formed in deep quartz sands. In extreme cases, the key features of the podzol (bleached horizons and pans) can develop in porous, inert quartz sandstone. Such a profile in rock would not ordinarily be recognized as a soil; this illustrates the difficulty in demarcating pedology from the related disciplines of geology, geomorphology, and ecology.

It should be emphasized that parent material is a major factor in the nature of the soils formed at any place, and that the transfer of explanations from one part of the world to another, with the transfer of descriptive jargon from its original context, has done more to confuse pedology than to elucidate it.

SOIL GEOGRAPHY

An alternative global model of soil genesis is based on the distribution of rock types and plate-tectonic megageomorphology. This model defines regions where particular combinations of the environmental factors and the balance of soil-formation processes have led to similar assemblages of soil materials.

Plate centers

Australia is a good example of a province located in the center of a tectonic plate where the landscape has been subject to soil formation for a long time with minimal tectonic activity and landscape rejuvenation. Many of the soil-genesis processes are approaching their end points. The topography is subdued, there is no active volcanism, and Quaternary glaciation affected limited areas. Typical soils exhibit the effects of extreme epimorphism. Profiles of contrasting fabrics and textures are common on hill slopes. Completely weathered red and yellow soils are typical of the tropics. Extensive areas of well-sorted sandy soils have accumulated in the coastal zone and in deserts, and deep alluvial clay soils are found along the inland drainage lines. Similar soil assemblages caused by the same combination of factors can be recognized in India, much of Asia, Africa, South America, and smaller regions of Europe and North America.

Plate margins

A different assemblage of soil materials is associated with the fold-mountain belts that ring the Pacific and extend through Indonesia, Southeast Asia, the Himalayas, the Middle East, the Mediterranean, and the West Indies. Topographic instability is so great that erosion processes operate on a different scale. The continuous addition of primary rock minerals from volcanic eruptions makes early-stage products of epimorphism much more common.

The soils of New Zealand have been formed in this environment. All of the processes of soil formation have a different emphasis and relative balance in New Zealand than in nearby Australia, and the following points are critical to understanding the nature and distribution of soil materials:

- Over most of the country, topographic relief is considerable and slopes are steep to very steep, and mass-movement processes are common.
- Active tectonism, extensive volcanism, an abundance of metamorphic rocks, and a dominance of the sedimentary rock graywacke containing high proportions of feldspars and partly-altered mafic minerals constitute a complex surface geology from which the soils are derived. Mineralogic and fabric inheritance is therefore important in almost all situations. In the North Island, twenty-six Holocene tephra (pyroclastic volcanic) units blanket the landscape, ranging in composition from rhyolite to basalt. In the South Island, Pleistocene glaciofluvial sediments (formed by streams flowing from glaciers) and eolian sediments (eroded and deposited by wind) are widespread. Most soil profiles exhibit little epimorphism and a dominance of slope-movement processes. Paleosols (buried soils) are common.
- Rainfall is high to very high in most parts of the country, so fluvial erosion and leaching are very active. At altitudes above 1,300–1,500 meters, snow accumulation is sufficient to cause valley glaciation, and in the drier rainshadow regions east of the Southern Alps, freeze/thaw processes are important in the breakdown of rock and the mass movement of regolith (unconsolidated material overlying bedrock).
- Several features of the natural vegetation and animals have had a greater effect on soil formation processes than is common elsewhere. These include an abundance of earthworms; the absence of large native herbivores; the rarity of wildfire; the leaching of soils promoted by polyphenol compounds from kauri trees which can live for many centuries; and Polynesian deforestation beginning about one thousand years ago.

Areas subject to Pleistocene glaciation

A completely different assemblage of soil materials is found in those areas of the world, particularly in the Northern Hemisphere, where the longer-term processes of soil genesis have been disturbed by Quaternary ice-age conditions and the renewed operation of those processes on homogenized and unconsolidated material has spanned only a few thousand years. The soil materials in these regions include all the classic profiles of the peatlands, podzols, and chernozems. The distribution of these soils reflects latitudinal patterns of glacial advance and sediment accumulation and parallels modern climates and vegetation.

Soils affected by human activity

Humans have had a major impact on natural soils in areas throughout the world, and several resulting soil profiles have been identified. For example, *Soil Taxonomy* describes anthropic and plaggen epipedons, which have been strongly influenced by long periods of intensive human activity. These are most common in Northern Hemisphere regions with long histories of cultivation.

An anthropic epipedon is typically dark and well structured and generally has moderate to high levels of plant nutrients, having been managed by the repeated application of shells or lime (for calcium) and bone or phosphate fertilizers (for phosphorus). A plaggen epipedon is a sod soil formed by frequent cultivation with the incorporation of large amounts of animal manures and straw. These additives raise the organic carbon content and increase water-holding capacity, soil biota, and plant growth.

Paddy soils also have been extensively modified by continued human use over centuries and even millennia in the cultivation of rice. They include a wide variety of natural soil types modified by cultivation and flooding to the extent that they are puddled, saturated, almost anoxic, and have a specialized soil biota. With this treatment paddy soils typically increase in acidity, and although the availability of some nutrients may increase, the crops rely on blue-green algae and Azolla (water fern, mosquito fern) to provide nitrogen. There are estimated to be more than 100 million hectares of potential paddy soil undeveloped in Asia because they are naturally too acidic or too saline. It is possible to change these conditions if the need is great enough.

In many coastal regions of the world, shallow estuaries have been diked and drained and the sediments converted to arable soils in polder lands. The best-known examples are in the Netherlands and Belgium, where the techniques of polder development have been developed over centuries. Within ten years of drainage, polder lands can carry productive forests, and estuarine sediments begin to become soils and support an expanding and dynamic terrestrial biota. One of the most important steps in this conversion process is the colonization of the sediments with soil biota, especially earthworms; the process of converting sediment to soil has been described as "zoological ripening."

These environments are emerging and developing ecosystems. They provide a salutary reminder that not all human interference with soils is harmful.

SOILS AND GLOBAL CHANGE

Given our universal dependence on soils for agriculture, their value as a construction material, the importance of their related biodiversity, and their critical roles in essential element cycles, any environmental or management change that accelerates soil pollution and degradation threatens human well-being.

The threats include all forms of physical, chemical, and biological damage to soils. Soil erosion at rates exceeding natural soil genesis is probably the most important problem on a global scale, but unlike the greenhouse threat of increasing atmospheric carbon dioxide, this problem is occurring at many local sites. Degradation of the soil as a growth medium through salinization, depletion of soil fauna, increased acidification, inappropriate use of fertilizers, and physical damage to soil fabric are also major threats. These land-degradation processes commonly enter negative feedback loops when a threshold of degradation is reached. For example, the loss of soil organic matter by any means usually leads to a decrease in soil moisture capacity. With reduced soil moisture there is reduced growth, less input to soil organic matter, loss of soil structure, further reductions in soil moisture, and then increased soil erosion. Breaking these loops and reversing the degradation depends on our recognition and understanding of the processes, and remedies can be effected only in favorable economic, social, and political climates (Fullen and Catt, 2004).

Following are some of the major types of soil degradation most likely to be affected by global changes in the next century.

Desertification

This term can include all forms of land degradation but is also specifically applied to degradation in marginal arid zones experiencing the spread of desert conditions. Changes in aridity have been a problem since ancient times but accelerated in the twentieth century with increased human pressure on the soil, the advent of mechanized agriculture, and the breakdown of traditional land management. The future of the more than 1 billion people who live in these environments is at risk, from their continued inappropriate range management and from harmful climate change. [*See* Desertification.]

Soil erosion

Loss of soil by erosion occurs from all unprotected surfaces subject to the effects of water and wind; it is a natural and inevitable part of the rock cycle. It is worst on steep slopes and in unvegetated sands. It is estimated that global soil-erosion rates are 20–100 times greater than average rates of soil renewal. In the long term, this relationship must be checked through appropriate soil management. In farming, this means using practices such as zero tillage, strip-cropping, intercropping, and the construction of soil-conservation works. In urban areas, soil losses from construction sites also need to be controlled because of the impact of sediments and turbidity in urban streams. [*See* Erosion.]

Salinization

Increased salinity and waterlogging of soils in irrigated lands has been a problem for humans for 6,000 years, and it is still occurring through inadequate irrigation-scheme design and water management. About one-third of the world's irrigated land is presently salinized; although this loss is not enormous in terms of total land degradation, the land affected was some of the most productive and the capital costs of its development were considerable.

The problem can be avoided by providing adequate drainage, but once salinization is established it is difficult to reverse. Some sodic soils can be reclaimed by exchanging sodium ions with calcium ions through the addition of gypsum, calcium chloride, iron sulfate, aluminum sulfate, sulfuric acid, sulfur, or pyrite. Effective leaching and safe disposal of drainage water is essential if this treatment is done because the exchange process liberates salts. This may be impractical because large-scale irrigation areas are in inland basins with low topographic relief, where the lack of good drainage was part of the problem in the first place. [See Salinization.]

Soil acidification

Increasing acidity in soils is a serious problem in both tropical and temperate regions and has three causes. Acidification results in a decline in agricultural production, because when pH falls below 5.0, most plant nutrients become less available and the levels of soluble iron, aluminum, and manganese in the soil can become toxic.

In the tropics, the primary cause is inappropriate clearing of forests growing on extremely weathered soils. These ecosystems normally operate on a rapid nutrient cycle through plants, litter, and topsoil with very small soil reserves. After removal of the forest and depletion of the litter by fire and cultivation, the system collapses, with an increase in soil erosion, establishment of weedy but stable monocultures of poor grasses, and an increase in the acidity of streamflow that can impact offshore fisheries and coral reefs. Reversion of the system to forests is slow and difficult.

In temperate regions, the causes are an excessive use of superphosphate fertilizer in conjunction with leys of nitrogen-fixing clover in grain crops without maintaining a neutral pH by liming and acid rain from industrialized countries. [See Acid Rain and Acid Deposition.]

The total impact of induced soil acidity is largely unknown, because most soils have several other sources of acidity and it is difficult to rank the role of any anthropogenic cause. The impact of an additional source of acid will largely depend on the buffering capacity of the soil; that is, how much basic material is available in the soil to neutralize acids. In a limestone soil, for example, this will be considerable, but in a soil that is near neutral (pH 7) and only has limited amounts of calcium or organic matter, increased acidity can occur quickly.

Laterization and podzolization

Much has been written about these processes as agents of soil degradation, but their global extent and importance are difficult to evaluate. "Laterization" is a term that refers loosely to the irreversible hardening of some soil materials that are naturally rich in oxides and hydroxides of iron and aluminum. Such profiles are the product of extreme epimorphism and are common in tropical environments. They are not confined to tropical regions, and not all iron-rich soils behave in this way, but extensive clearing of tropical forests and woodlands has often resulted in the abandonment of agricultural development allegedly because of widespread development of laterites, iron pans, or plinthites (soil materials rich in clay, quartz, and oxides such as Fe_2O_3 and Al_2O_3). The fact that such lands were unsuitable for large-scale agriculture in the first place tends to be ignored when invoking laterization as an excuse for the failure.

The process of accelerated podzolization is more subtle. Many plant species enhance the leaching of iron and aluminum and increase soil acidity, contributing to the formation of podzol profiles; in a soil material with limited buffering capacity, a single generation of pine forest (for example) can acidify the soil and strip the limited plant nutrients from it. Second-generation forests have slower growth rates. Again, the problem becomes an explanation for economic failure rather than a means of recognizing the agricultural inadequacies of those environments and management practices. Unlike the laterization problem, an increase in soil acidity can at least be counteracted with the application of lime or other chemically basic materials.

Soils and greenhouse gases

Soils are an integral part of the global carbon budget. The flux of carbon through soil organic matter is both vital to ecologically sustainable development and a significant part of the problem of greenhouse climate change. [See Global Warming.]

It is uncertain how large a part soils play in the global carbon budget. Several computer models have been developed, but all lack reliable data on carbon partioning into above- and below-ground biomass and provide only a rough indication of the scale of turnover processes. Intensive agriculture contributes carbon dioxide to the atmosphere through the loss of soil organic matter, and intensive rice cultivation has been identified as an important source of methane, another greenhouse gas. Reversal of soil organic-matter loss could allow us to use soils as a sink for greenhouse gases, but this depends on achieving a good balance between biospheric processes in the soil and good soil structure. The potential for increasing soil-carbon stores as a hedge against atmospheric carbon dioxide buildup is limited; it is more important in the short term, at least, to substantially increase carbon storage in growing forests. Carbon sequestration in forests is greatest in tropical regions of rapid growth, where vast areas of forests have been cleared and the soils seriously degraded. Reversing this trend in the next few decades will be a great challenge. [See Carbon Cycle.]

Global climate change will bring land-use change, but the human response will not be instantaneous, because it is individual farmers and ranchers who must respond to the pressures. Farmers are by their nature optimists and will maintain traditional practices for years or even decades in the expectation that good times will return. The 1930s dust bowl of the prairie states of the United States and the famine conditions in the Sahel in the 1970s have shown that farmers and ranchers are slow to change when their opportunities are limited by political and social factors beyond their control.

A core project of the International Geosphere-Biosphere Programme involves global change and terrestrial ecosystems. This project includes a soil-research program intended to determine the impacts of global change on soil organic-matter dynamics, predict changes in soil erosion caused by interactive changes in land use and climate, and review the greenhouse-gas emissions from agricultural soils. [See International Geosphere-Biosphere Programme.]

Soils themselves will also change in the short term, especially where a particularly ephemeral or mobile constituent is a key constituent. For example, solonchaks may be leached and create new soil types; conversely, salts may accumulate in other profiles and create solonchaks. These salts that can be mobilized in decades, as demonstrated in polder lands, or in the vast expanses of salinized soil in irrigation areas throughout the world.

Soil-erosion rates and other forms of physical degradation are likely to change, driven largely by extreme climatic events (rainfall, floods, drought, frost, etc.), and global climate change will affect such events. All global climate models suggest a general increase in extreme events (e.g., tropical cyclones) and their areas of occurrence. Wherever the soils are presently under land-use pressure, any change in the frequency of large events might increase soil losses.

POSITIVE CHANGES IN SOILS AND THEIR MANAGEMENT

Perhaps the best examples of positive change can be seen in the way engineers have increasingly utilized soils as construction materials in the past fifty years.

Soil stabilization has become more scientific. Traditionally, it was achieved by mechanical compaction, which increased soil density and strength by rolling, ramming, vibrating, or blasting. Soil mechanical properties can also be changed by the addition of components such as cement, lime, sodium silicate, salt, synthetic resins, or bitumen, and in recent years there has been a boom in the use of geotextiles.

The concept of reinforcing soils with fibrous materials goes back to ancient times with the use of straw in sun-dried mud bricks and fascines for swamp drainage. Mechanically, the principles are the same as the natural reinforcement of soils on slopes by plant roots, but in the last 20 years the rapid development of synthetic geotextiles (synthetic fabrics) and geogrids (more rigid materials) has created entirely new approaches. Geosynthetics are now routinely used for the separation and isolation of different soil materials, for spreading loads on weak substrates, for filtering fine particles, for sealing and containing fluids, for enhancing drainage, and to control soil erosion.

OUTLOOK

Soils will change with enhanced greenhouse warming in the next century, but vegetation and land use will change first, and these changes will have an immediate feedback on soils. Pedologists can make a contribution to these studies, and humans can adjust by deliberately manipulating soils to meet our changing requirements.

Our goal must be to achieve an ecologically sustainable pattern of land use based on a respect for the dynamics of the soils. We are at present a long way from an adequate understanding of soils. We need to make concerted international efforts to address innumerable issues:

- An appreciation of the role of soil biota.
- An understanding of biological fertility.
- Effective means of reversing soil acidification.
- Adequate quantification of soil-carbon dynamics.
- New approaches to tillage and erosion control.
- Application of intercropping and other polyculture techniques.
- Improved modeling of salinization and its control.
- Better social and political approaches to land reform.
- Changed global economics with respect to cash crops and tropical forestry.
- Developing means of accelerating soil formation and regenerating degraded lands.
- Tightening planning regulation to prevent the sterilization of fertile and valuable soils by other land uses.

[See also Agriculture and Agricultural Land.]

BIBLIOGRAPHY

Bal, L. *The Zoological Ripening of Soils.* Wageningen, Netherlands: Centre for Agricultural Publishing and Documentation, 1982. A detailed account of the development of polder lands, with an emphasis on biological processes.

Barrow, C.J. *Land Degradation: Development and Breakdown of Terrestrial Environments.* Cambridge and New York: Cambridge University Press, 1991. A comprehensive global review of all forms of land degradation.

CSIRO. *Soils: An Australian Viewpoint.* Melbourne: CSIRO and Academic Press, 1983. A detailed and technical account of the soils of a plate center region written largely from theoretical and agricultural viewpoints.

Fullen, M.A., and J.A. Catt. *Soil Management: Problems and Solutions.* London: Arnold, 2004.

Ghassemi, F., A.J. Jakeman, and H.A. Nix. *Salinisation of Land and Water Resources: Human Causes, Extent, Management, and Case Studies.* Sydney: University of New South Wales Press, 1995. A detailed global review of one of the intractable soil and land degradation problems.

Gillott, J.E. *Clay in Engineering Geology.* Amsterdam: Elsevier, 1987. A technical overview of clay as an engineering material.

Holtz, R.D., ed. *Geosynthetics for Soil Improvement.* Geotechnical Special Publication 18. New York: American Society of Civil Engineers, 1988. Summary technical document describing the different types of geotextiles and their uses.

McLaren, R.G., and K.C. Cameron. *Soil Science: Sustainable Production and Environmental Protection.* Auckland: Oxford University Press, 1996. A general agricultural text dealing with the soils of New Zealand.

Paton, T.R., G.S. Humphreys, and P.B. Mitchell. *Soils: A New Global View.* London: University College of London Press, 1995. The source of the basic soil genesis model outlined in this entry.

Rounsevell, M.D. A., and P.J. Loveland, eds. *Soil Responses to Climate Change.* NATO ASI Series Series 1; Vol. 23, *Global Environmental Change.* Berlin:

Springer, 1994. Conference papers regarding all aspects of the role of soils in global climate change.

Soil Survey Staff. *Soil Taxonomy: A Basic System of Soil Classification for Making and Interpreting Soil Surveys*. U.S. Department of Agriculture Handbook no. 436. New York: Wiley, 1984. The most widely used soil classification scheme in the world today. A very technical document with an excess of jargon.

—P. B. MITCHELL

SOLAR ENERGY

See Renewable Sources of Energy.

SOLAR VARIABILITY AND CLIMATE

Variations in solar activity have been observed in numbers of sunspots since ancient times, but the extent to which solar variability may affect global climate has been controversial. Solar radiation is the fundamental energy source for the atmosphere, so any change in total solar irradiance (TSI) has the potential to influence climate but—although many papers have been written on relationships between sunspot numbers and the weather—the topic of solar influences on climate has until recently been considered somewhat suspect by meteorologists. A major reason for this was the lack of reliable measurements indicating that solar radiation did indeed vary. There was also mistrust of the statistical validity of the evidence, and there were no established scientific mechanisms whereby the apparent changes in the Sun might induce detectable signals near the Earth's surface. Now, however, with improved measurements of solar and climate parameters, evidence for an influence of solar variability on the climate of the lower atmosphere has emerged from the noise. Furthermore, the current need to distinguish between natural and anthropogenic causes of climate change, combined with developments in both climate and solar science, are driving advances in our understanding of the processes involved.

SOLAR VARIABILITY

The most obvious signal of variation in solar activity is given by the cycle of appearance, transit, and decay of groups of spots on the Sun's surface with a period of approximately 11 years. It is not immediately apparent how these might influence the Earth, although it might be anticipated that the dark spots would reduce the amount of light and heat emitted. Observations from the Earth's surface have not been able to measure any systematic changes in the total radiation emitted by the Sun (the solar constant) because they are subject to uncertainties and fluctuations in atmospheric absorption that swamp the solar variability signal. But satellite-borne absolute radiometers since the late 1970s has produced indisputable evidence that total solar irradiance varies systematically with the 11-year sunspot cycle, with more radiation being emitted when the sunspot number is higher (Fröhlich and Lean, 1998). The variation is small, being from peak-to-peak of the cycle only about 0.08% of

the total irradiance, but this magnitude corresponds approximately to the radiative forcing of the climate being produced per decade by increases in the concentration of atmospheric carbon dioxide and is thus not insignificant in this context. A remaining serious uncertainty is in the absolute value of the irradiance: the measurements made by contemporaneous radiometers currently differ by up to 5 watts per square meter, or about 0.4% of the total. This problem with the intercalibration of the instruments also means that it is difficult to determine the existence of any underlying trend in solar irradiance during the satellite era. That the Sun is brighter at sunspot maximum is due to the simultaneous increase in bright patches (or faculae) which are less obvious to the naked eye. An understanding of the compensating contributions of these two components to the TSI has resulted in the development of empirical models of solar irradiance as a function of sunspot number, thus enabling time series of past TSI to be estimated from sunspot records. These reconstructions are quite uncertain, especially in the longer-term secular variation, as can be seen from Figure 1.

Another measure of solar activity is the intensity of galactic cosmic rays. These high-energy particles arrive at Earth from deep in space but their path is altered by the Sun's magnetic field so that their incidence is less when the Sun is more active. Estimates of cosmic-ray intensity can be made from measurements at the Earth's surface of their decay products (e.g., neutrons), and such records are available dating back about half a century. Much longer records of cosmic-ray flux are available from cosmogenic radionuclides: these include beryllium-10, carbon-14, and chlorine-35, which are produced in the Earth's atmosphere by the interaction of the cosmic rays with nitrogen, oxygen, and argon and are laid down in natural archives such as ice sheets, ocean sediments and tree trunks. Although dating the samples is not without difficulty, these media can provide records of solar magnetic activity up to 10,000 years in the past (Beer et al., 2006). There is accumulating evidence of correlation between such measures of solar activity and climate on timescales of several millennia; for example Bond et al. (2001) show a relationship between beryllium-10 and the quantity of ice-rafted debris in sediment cores from the North Atlantic. However, the relationship between solar magnetic activity and solar irradiance is not well understood, so it is not yet clear to what extent the cosmogenic-isotope records provide a direct measure of solar forcing of climate (Lockwood, 2006).

On even longer timescales the amount of solar radiation received by the Earth is modulated by variations in its orbit around the Sun. The distance between the two bodies varies during the year due to the ellipticity of the orbit, which varies with periods of around 100,000 and 413,000 years due to the gravitational influence of the Moon and of other planets. At any point on the Earth the amount of radiation striking the top of the atmosphere also depends on the tilt of the Earth's axis to the plane of its orbit, which varies cyclically with a period of about 41,000 years, and on the precession of the Earth's axis, which varies with periods of about 19,000 and 23,000 years. Averaged over the globe the solar energy flux at the Earth

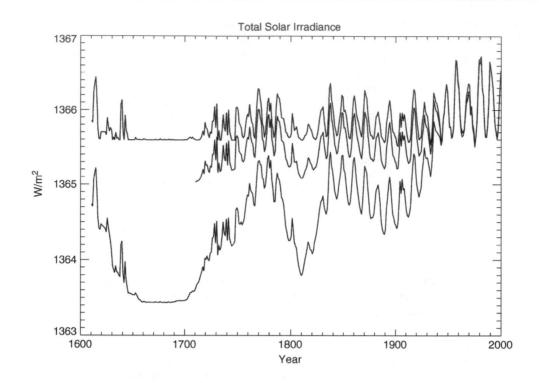

Solar Variability and Climate. FIGURE 1. Estimates of Total Solar Irradiance, 1610–2000. Based on the known relationship between sunspot number and TSI over the past 2 solar cycles.

All the reconstructions show lower values coinciding with the Maunder Minimum in sunspot numbers during the latter part of the 17th century, but there is a wide range of possible values. The top curve shows variations due solely to the 11-year sunspot cycle; the bottom curve has a long-term evolution inferred from brightness changes in Sun-like stars (Lean and Rind, 1998) while that in the middle curve is based on a model of the solar magnetic field (Wang et al., 2005).

depends only on the ellipticity, and evidence from ice cores does, indeed, show that glacial and interglacial periods occur with a period of about 100,000 years, but seasonal and geographical variations of the irradiance depend on the tilt and precession. These are important because the intensity of radiation received at high latitudes in summer determines whether the winter growth of the ice cap will recede or the climate will be precipitated into an ice age. Thus changes in seasonal irradiance can lead to much longer-term shifts in climatic regime.

SOLAR SIGNALS IN RECENT CLIMATE

Records of global mean surface temperature dating back 2,000 years have been constructed from instrumental data and proxy indicators (such as the width of tree rings). [See Proxy Data for Environmental Change.] An example is shown by the curve in Figure 2 beginning below O.O°C, which indicates significant variability on multidecadal timescales overlying longer-term trends. One approach to the detection of a solar signal in such a record is to seek a statistical relationship between it and a parameter representing solar variability, examples of which are given below. An alternative approach, which tests our understanding of how the solar influence might take place, is to incorporate a potential mechanism into a climate model and assess to what extent it is able to reproduce the observations. An example of this approach also appears in Figure 2, which shows results from experiments with an energy-balance model. This model includes radiative forcing by total solar irradiance, volcanic aerosol, greenhouse gases, and anthropogenic aerosol and is able to simulate well the long-term trends, and the amplitude of the variability, when all these forcings are all included. This suggests that variations in the global average preindustrial climate on millennial timescales can be explained quite well by the radiative forcing of solar and volcanic activity.

There is evidence, however, that the response to changes in solar activity is not uniform world-wide. The coincidence of the Little Ice Age in the latter part of the seventeenth century with the Maunder Minimum in sunspot numbers has frequently been cited as evidence for a solar influence on climate. [See Little Ice Age in Europe.] It is now clear that the significantly colder temperatures experienced in western Europe during this period were not a global phenomenon (Jones and Mann, 2004) but represented anomalously frequent recurrence of the negative phase of the North Atlantic Oscillation. This suggests that the Sun can influence this mode of atmospheric variability. Further evidence is provided by an apparent modulation of the NAO on both shorter (11-year solar cycle, Kodera, 2002) and much longer (millennial, Bond et al., 2001) timescales. [See North Atlantic Oscillation.]

There is also evidence that variations in tropical sea-surface temperatures are associated with solar activity. The pattern of the mean anomaly in January/February temperatures in the Pacific Ocean of the years at the peaks of the 11 solar-activity cycles that occurred between 1880 and 1995 is very similar to that of a Cold Event (negative phase of the ENSO cycle). The statistical robustness of this result is still uncertain, but a similar

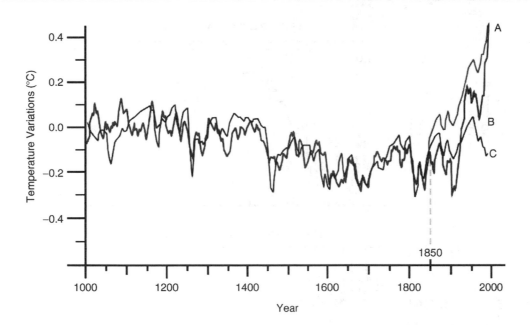

Solar Variability and Climate. FIGURE 2. Global Average Surface Temperature Variations (11-Year Running Means) Over the Past Millennium.

(A) Observational record (Crowley and Lowery, 2000). (B) Energy balance model calculations with natural forcings (solar and volcanic). (C) Anthropogenic forcings (greenhouse gases and aerosols) are included after 1850. Solar forcing is a TSI reconstruction based on sunspot numbers 1610–1998 (see Figure 1) spliced to a cosmogenic isotope (^{14}C) record for earlier dates. After Crowley (2000).

pattern has been produced by a coupled ocean-atmosphere model in a study of the response to changes in solar irradiance (Meehl et al., 2003).

The Sun affects the climate not just at the Earth's surface but throughout the depth of the atmosphere. When the Sun is more active the air warms (by about 0.5°C) in the low-latitude lower stratosphere and in vertical bands through the troposphere in midlatitudes (Haigh, 2003). Similar analysis of wind data suggests that jet-stream winds are slightly weaker and positioned further poleward (Haigh et al., 2005). These results are consistent with a weaker, broader (Hadley) cell of meridional overturning in the tropics and a poleward shift of the midlatitude storm tracks. This provides further evidence that the response of climate to solar activity will be found in certain preferred geographic regions.

Such localized signals cannot be explained by the direct absorption of solar radiation, and several theories have emerged of how the patterns of response may be produced. Meehl et al. (2003) speculate that they arise through spatial asymmetries in the solar heating of the sea surface produced by the contrast between cloudy and clear sky regions. Other ideas have involved the effects of varying solar ultraviolet radiation (UV) and the impact of ionization by cosmic rays (see below). The proposed mechanisms have varying degrees of maturity, but they are not mutually exclusive and it may be that all of them contribute, to a greater or lesser degree, to the overall influence of the Sun on the climate.

SOLAR ULTRAVIOLET RADIATION

Although TSI varies only by about 0.1% over the 11-year cycle, variations at the UV end of the spectrum are much larger. Figure 3 indicates that between 300 and 100 nanometers, the increase ranges from about 1% to 100%. Radiation of these wavelengths is absorbed high in the atmosphere (between about 20 and 100 km altitude) so that the solar signal in temperature increases markedly with height at and above these altitudes. UV radiation is also important in controlling the concentration of stratospheric ozone: both observational records and model calculations show approximately 2% higher concentrations of (vertically-integrated) ozone at 11-year solar cycle maximum relative to minimum. The ozone thus produced modulates the magnitude of the solar stratospheric heating.

It is not obvious that this upper-air heating would affect the climate near the Earth's surface, but there is growing evidence that disturbances (from whatever cause) to the stratosphere may have an impact lower in the atmosphere through dynamical coupling. For example, the strength of the stratospheric winter polar vortex may propagate downward to the surface, although there is no consensus on how such propagation takes place (Baldwin and Dunkerton, 2005). Variations in stratospheric solar heating are very likely to influence the strength of the vortex, so this provides a plausible route for variations in UV to influence high-latitude climate, including, for example, the state of the NAO.

Some climate models show changes in the tropical troposphere in response to varying TSI, probably via thermodynamic processes (such as the effects on the North Atlantic Oscillation). Those studies, however, used a spectrally flat increase in irradiance so that preferential warming of the stratosphere could not occur. Other model experiments show that inclusion of the spectral composition, and particularly of the concomitant ozone changes, produces the shifts of the storm tracks and impact on the Hadley cells suggested by observations (Haigh, 1996) and a stronger response in the hydrological cycle (Shindell et al., 2006).

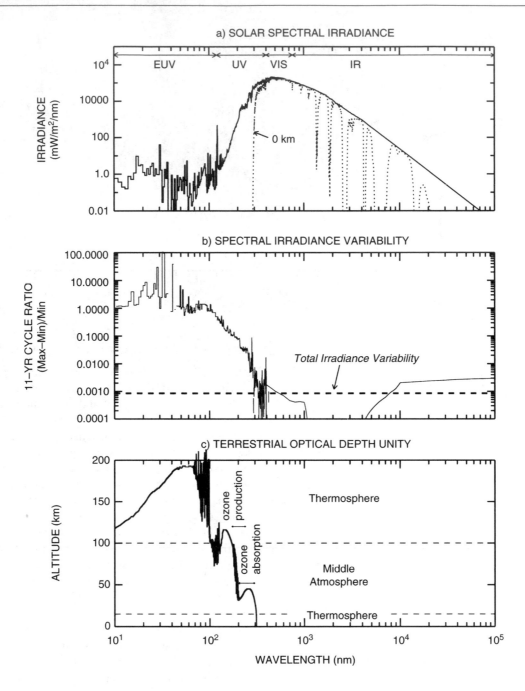

Solar Variability and Climate. Figure 3.

(a) Solar spectrum. (b) Fractional increase in solar spectral irradiance from minimum to maximum of the 11-year cycle (NB logarithmic scale). (c) Altitude of peak absorption of solar spectral radiation. From Lean and Rind, 1998.

GALACTIC COSMIC RAYS

It has been proposed that atmospheric ionization by cosmic rays may influence cloud cover by increasing the effectiveness of aerosol particles to act as condensation nuclei. The modulation of solar activity by cosmic-ray intensity would provide a mechanism whereby solar variations could produce an impact on climate through changes in the Earth's albedo, with lower solar activity resulting in more cosmic rays, more clouds, greater reflectivity and potential surface cooling. Evidence for a solar modulation of cloud cover is not well established, and the processes involved are complex. Nevertheless, there have been several studies designed to investigate potential mechanisms.

Laboratory and atmospheric measurements show that ultrafine particles can be formed from ions, and microphysical models show that particles large enough to act as cloud condensation nuclei can grow from these within hours. There will, however, usually be competing effects, so that the fraction of new aerosol that ultimately grows into cloud drops is likely to be small (Harrison and Carslaw, 2003).

THE FUTURE

Climate change over the past half century has been dominated by warming caused by the increased concentrations of greenhouse gases, but solar variability has played a significant role in climate in the past. Thus the prediction of future climate should ideally also involve a prediction of solar activity. This science is, however, in its infancy: there is in the early twenty-first century no consensus among experts even on the magnitude and timing of the next 11-year cycle maximum (due in about 2012; see http://www.sec. noaa.gov/solarCycle/SE24/PressRelease.html), let alone over longer periods. On the timescale of centuries it is likely that the Sun will slump into another grand minimum (like the Maunder Minimum), but it is impossible to forecast exactly when this will happen or how deep it will be (Nigel Weiss, personal communication).

BIBLIOGRAPHY

Baldwin, M.P. and T.J. Dunkerton. "The Solar Cycle and Stratosphere-Troposphere Dynamical Coupling." *Journal of Atmospheric and Solar-Terrestrial Physics* 67 (2005), 71–82. DOI: 10.1016/j.jastp.2004.07.018.

Beer, J., M. Vonmoos, and R. Muscheler. "Solar Variability over the Past Several Millennia." *Space Science Reviews* 125 (2006), 67–79. DOI: 10.1007/s11214–006–9047–4.

Bond, G., et al. "Persistent Solar Influence on North Atlantic Climate during the Holocene." *Science* 294 (2001), 2130–2136. DOI: 10.1126/science.1065680.

Crowley, T.J. "Causes of Climate Change over the Past 1000 Years." *Science* 289 (2000), 270–277. DOI: 10.1126/science.289.5477.270.

Crowley, T.J., and T.S. Lowery. "How Warm Was the Medieval Warm Period?" *Ambio* 29 (2000), 51–54.

Fröhlich, C., and J. Lean. "The Sun's Total Irradiance: Cycles, Trends, and Related Climate Change Uncertainties since 1976." *Geophysical Research Letters* 25 (1998), 4377–4380.

Haigh, J.D. "The Impact of Solar Variability on Climate." *Science* 272 (1996), 981–984. DOI: 10.1126/science.272.5264.981.

———. "The Effects of Solar Variability on the Earth's Climate." *Philosophical Transactions of the Royal Society A* 361 (2003), 95–111. DOI: 10.1098/rsta.2002.1111.

Haigh, J.D., M. Blackburn, and R. Day. "The Response of Tropospheric Circulation to Perturbations in Lower Stratospheric Temperature." *Journal of Climate* 18 (2005), 3672–3691. DOI: 10.1175/JCLI3472.1.

Harrison, R.G., and K.S. Carslaw. "Ion-Aerosol-Cloud Processes in the Lower Atmosphere." *Reviews of Geophysics* 41 (2003), 1012. DOI: 10.1029/2002RG000114.

Jones, P.D., and M.E. Mann. "Climate over Past Millennia." *Reviews of Geophysics* 42, RG2002 (2004). DOI: 10.1029/2003RG000143.

Kodera, K. "Solar Cycle Modulation of the North Atlantic Oscillation: Implication in the Spatial Structure of the NAO." *Geophysical Research Letters* 29 (2002), 1218. DOI: 10.1029/2001GL014557.

Lean, J., and D. Rind. "Climate Forcing by Changing Solar Radiation." *Journal of Climate* 11 (1998), 3069–3094. DOI: 10.1175/1520–0442(1998)011<3069: CF BCSR>2.0.CO;2.

Lockwood, M. "What Do Cosmogenic Isotopes Tell Us about Past Solar Forcing of Climate?" *Space Science Reviews* 125 (2006), 95–109. DOI: 10.1007/s11214–006–9049–2.

Meehl, G.A., et al. "Solar and Greenhouse Gas Forcing and Climate Response in the Twentieth Century." *Journal of Climate* 16 (2003), 426–444. DOI: 10.1175/1520–0442(2003)016<0426:SAGGFA>2.0.CO;2.

Shindell, D.T., et al. "Solar and Anthropogenic Forcing of Tropical Hydrology." *Geophysical Research Letters* 33, L24706 (2006). DOI: 10.1029/2006GL027468.

Van Loon, H., G.A. Meehl, and D.J. Shea. "Coupled Air-Sea Response to Solar Forcing in the Pacific Region during Northern Winter." *Journal of Geophysical Research* 112, D02108 (2007). DOI: 10.1029/2006JD007378.

Wang, Y.M., J.L. Lean, and N.R. Sheeley. "Modeling the Sun's Magnetic Field and Irradiance since 1713." *Astrophysical Journal* 625 (2005), 522–538. DOI: 10.1086/429689.

—JOANNA D. HAIGH

STABILITY

The concept of stability is central to global change. It is important to distinguish between stability and the concepts of constancy, equilibrium, steady-state, persistence, resistance, control and controllability, and recurrence. It is also important to understand the concepts of positive and negative feedback.

The classic idea of stability, sometimes referred to as "classic static stability," attributes two qualities to a system: a system, undisturbed, remains in a constant condition; and when disturbed from this constant condition but released from the disturbing influence, a system returns to an original constant condition. The pendulum of a mechanical clock has this kind of stability. The belief that this kind of stability is a characteristic of nature has an ancient lineage, expressed in the myth of the balance of nature.

One of the common confusions is to equate stability with equilibrium, but systems can have stable and unstable equilibria. An equilibrium is a rest point and can be stable or unstable. While a pendulum has a point of stable equilibrium in that it returns to its vertical position after being disturbed, a pencil balanced on its point is in unstable equilibrium; once deflected from that position, it will not return.

Systems can be stable locally or globally. A point of local stability is one in which the system is stable against some finite, typically small, disturbance but not against all disturbances. A point of global stability is one in which the system is stable to all disturbances. A pinball game has points of local stability (curved surfaces where the ball can rest unless the side of the table is pushed hard enough to move the ball over the edge of the surface) and one of global stability (the bottom of the game board). A seed, temporarily lodged in a swale on a mountainside where it is moved about by light winds, is within a region of local stability. A strong gust can blow the seed outside the swale and down the mountainside to the valley, where it germinates and is then located at a point of global stability.

STABILITY VS. CONTROL

It is typically assumed that all ecological systems that have classic static stability are most likely to persist and that most are easily controlled. This is not necessarily true. An analogy with the invention of aircraft is helpful here. During the early development of airplanes, there was a concern with making them both stable and controllable. A stable airplane is one that will continue to fly straight and level in spite of small gusts of winds and changes in air density. A simple way to improve one aspect of the stability of an airplane is to design the wings in the form of an inverted "V" (a dihedral). This shape is intrinsically stable against forces such as gusts of wind that would push one wing down and the other up. The wing pushed upward, more to the vertical, loses lift while the other wing, made more horizontal, increases in lift. The lower wing, with more lift, rises; the more vertical wing, with less lift, descends. As a result, the plane rights itself automatically.

During the early development of the airplane, it was soon discovered that the more stable the plane, the harder it was to turn and therefore the harder it was to control. A plane whose wings were so stable that the force of the pilot's hands on the stick would not allow it to bank would be uncontrollable and would crash. This experience made clear that there was a tradeoff between stability and controllability. The less stable an airplane, the easier it was to control, but the greater need for rapid response and constant attention. Gradually, by trial and error, pilots and engineers worked out a compromise between stability and controllability that worked best in practice. A plane moves in three dimensions, pitching, rolling, and yawing. Aircraft have different degrees of stability for each of these dimensions—there is no single answer to the tradeoff between stability and controllability. Today, this is integrated into the theory and practice of aeronautical engineering. Until the invention of computers, the reflexes of a pilot limited the instability that could be designed into an airplane. Today, some aircraft are designed to be highly unstable and therefore highly maneuverable. This is made possible by onboard computers that constantly readjust the controls, faster than a pilot could do it manually. This experience suggests that a natural system that is best controlled may not be the most stable in the classic sense, and that there is a tradeoff between controllability and stability.

Steady-state is a condition of a dynamic system with inputs and outputs analogous to equilibrium. A system in steady-state is one for which inputs equal outputs of some variable of interest. For instance, a lake for which the inflow of water from rain, and surface and subsurface water transport is equal to the output of water from evaporation and surface and subsurface flow losses, is in steady-state in regard to water quantity.

A system with feedback is one for which there is a detection of some change in the system and a response to that change. Sometimes the change is in a quantity or rate of some input or output. Sweating is an example of negative feedback related to body temperature. When the body temperature begins to rise, detecting mechanisms open pores in the skin and the rate of water evaporation increases, cooling the body. This is an example of negative feedback. The growth of a population of bacterial cells is an example of positive feedback: although the rate of cell division can be constant for all cells, the more cells there are the faster the total growth of the mass of bacteria. In the Arctic, the shrinking of sea ice leads to reduced reflectivity of the surface (albedo) which, in turn, leads to more warming and greater shrinking of sea ice. Whether the Earth system is characterized by classic stability, steady-state, control, and positive and negative feedback has long been debated.

The concepts described thus far apply to systems that are deterministic, without randomness or change. Systems that are characterized by stochastic properties might have negative feedback mechanisms and therefore might be stable in the classic sense described earlier. But there are additional concepts that apply only to probabilistic system, pertinent to the Earth system. Systems with randomness may be characterized as having a set of states which the system revisits. States that are

revisited indefinitely are referred to as "recurrent." States that are visited a finite number of times and therefore have a last time are called "nonrecurrent." It is also possible to speak of a system as "persistent within bounds," meaning that the system varies within some finite and definable range. It is becoming common in discussions of environmental variables to speak of the "historic range of variation," meaning the range that is known from either scientific monitoring of a variable over time or reconstruction of that variation through a variety of means. These include written, historical records or records left in the growth rings of trees, in trapped gases in pockets in glacial ice, the ratios of isotopes in marine sediments. This information can be used to reconstruct the historic range of variation for factors important to global change.

BIBLIOGRAPHY

Botkin, D.B. *Discordant Harmonies: A New Ecology for the Twenty-First Century.* New York: Oxford University Press, 1990.

—Daniel B. Botkin

STABILIZING CARBON EMISSIONS

To avoid runaway global warming, carbon dioxide concentration in the atmosphere must not exceed 500–550 parts per million (ppm), which is less than double the pre-industrial value of 280 ppm (Environmental Defense, 2002; Royal Commission, 2000). [See Global Warming.] As of 2006 the concentration was near 430 ppm, and at the present rate of increase it will double in roughly 50 years.

A number of strategies can be implemented to counter the continued increase in carbon dioxide concentration: some require experimental new technologies and most lack specific goals—each being assumed to work, somehow, in concert with the others. [See Energy Strategies; *and* Geoengineering.]

STABILIZATION WEDGES

The task was illuminated in 2004 by a paper that clarifies the daunting scale of the task but also offers a number of prescriptions for attaining the goal using technology and practices that are well-established. The ideas were presented by Steven Pacala and Robert Socolow (*Science*, Vol. 305, No. 5686, August 13, 2004, pp. 968–972). The main concepts are presented here by paraphrasing sections of the article but omitting technical details available in the article and its references.

Very roughly, stabilization at 500 ppm requires that emissions be held near the present level (2004 level) of 7 billion tons of carbon per year (gigatons [Gt] per year) for the next 50 years, even though they are on course to more than double (Figure 1). The upper curve in Figure 1 is a representative business-as-usual (BAU) emissions path for carbon emitted as CO_2 from fossil-fuel combustion and cement manufacture: emissions grow at 1.5% per year starting at 7 Gt per year. The lower curve is a carbon-emissions path consistent with stabilizing CO_2 at

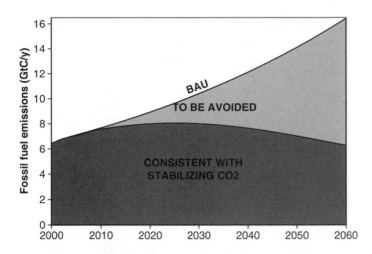

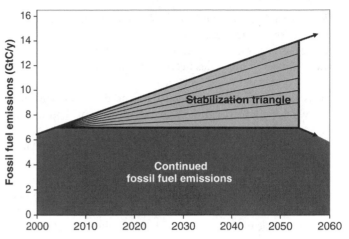

Stabilizing Carbon Emissions. Figure 1.
(A) Projected growth in carbon emissions (business as usual) and the avoided emissions needed for stabilization. (B) Idealized projection, dividing the stabilization triangle into seven wedges.

(Source: Pacala and Socolow, Fig. 1A and B.)

500 ppm by the year 2125, making assumptions about the declining ability of ocean and land areas to absorb CO_2 (see notes in Pacala and Socolow). The area between the two curves represents the avoided carbon emissions required for stabilization.

The elements of the graph are simplified to show the gap as a stabilization triangle of avoided emissions resting on a plateau of emissions that continue at 7 Gt per year. The stabilization triangle is divided evenly into seven wedges, each of which grows in linear fashion to a rate of one Gt per year by 2054. Collectively, the seven triangles reduce emissions by 25 Gt of carbon, or one-third of the total implied by the BAU rate.

The avoided emissions required have been reduced to an arbitrary seven wedges that must be "filled" by applying technologies and/or life-style changes immediately, and continuing those changes for 50 years. Wedges can be filled, for instance, through energy efficiency, by decarbonizing the generation of electricity, or by using nuclear or renewable sources of electricity. Twelve of the authors' 15 options are listed below, each being equivalent to one wedge. Hypothetically, then, it should be possible to select only seven from the list, or to mix and match the wedges to build the required stabilization triangle. The experience of making these choices in a group of people, each building a "portfolio" of wedges, is provided by a hands-on game available through Princeton University's Carbon Mitigation Initiative (www.princeton.edu/~cmi/resources/stabwedge.htm).

WAYS TO FILL WEDGES

- *Efficiency and Conservation.* If carbon emissions per unit of gross domestic product (carbon intensity) were reduced in the U.S. by 2.11% per year (rather than the 1.96% goal announced in 2002) and all countries boosted their reduction goals to the same extent, this would fill one wedge.

- *Improved Vehicle Fuel Economy.* Assuming 2 billion cars in 2054 (four times today's total) and an average of 60 mpg, rather than 30 mpg, and an average 10,000 miles driven per year, the carbon displaced would be equivalent to one wedge.

- *Reduced Reliance on Cars.* A wedge would be filled, even at 30 mpg, if the annual distance traveled were 5,000 rather than 10,000 miles. Combining higher mileage with reduced distance would displace even more carbon.

- *More Efficient Buildings.* Applying established approaches to more efficient space-heating and cooling, lighting, and refrigeration in residential and commercial buildings. Roughly half the savings would be in developing countries.

- *Improved Power Plant Efficiency.* Even if coal-based electricity output in 2054 were twice that of today's, a wedge would be filled by increasing plant efficiency from 40% to 60%.

- *Substituting Natural Gas for Coal.* Because carbon emissions from natural gas are lower per BTU than for coal, displacing 700 thousand-megawatt coal plants with gas-fired plants would fill one wedge. That power shifted to gas is roughly four times the world's current gas-based electric power.

- *Storing Carbon Dioxide Captured in Power Plants.* Installing carbon capture and storage systems in 800 coal-fired thousand-megawatt baseload plants, or 1600 such gas-fired plants, would fill one wedge.

- *Nuclear Fission.* If nuclear power plants displaced 700 thousand-megawatt coal-fired power plants (roughly twice the world's present nuclear power capacity) one wedge would be filled.

- *Wind Electric.* Considering the intermittent output of wind turbines, it would require 2,000 thousand-megawatts (peak capacity) to displace enough coal-fired plants and their carbon emissions. A wedge, therefore, requires roughly 700 times today's deployment of wind generators.

- *Photovoltaic Electric.* Assuming the electricity produced displaces coal-fired power plants as in "Wind Electric," the required 2,000 gigawatts of capacity would be needed by the year 2054. Again, that is roughly 700 times today's deployment: like wind-electric, however, photovoltaic installation is growing at roughly 30% per year.

- *Renewable Hydrogen for Vehicles.* Because of energy lost in the conversion of electricity to hydrogen, using hydrogen to displace gasoline or diesel fuel in vehicles would require roughly twice the wind machines needed to displace coal in coal-fired power plants in "Wind Electric."
- *Biofuels.* Displacing enough gasoline and diesel fuel with ethanol would require roughly 50 times the 2004 world production, most of which comes from Brazilian sugar cane and U.S. corn.
- *Forest Management.* At least a half wedge would be filled if the current rate of clear cutting of primary tropical forest were reduced to zero over 50 years. A second half-wedge would be filled by reforesting or afforesting roughly 250 million hectares in the tropics or 400 million in temperate zones (currently tropical forests cover 1,500 million hectares, and temperate forests 700 million hectares). A third half-wedge could be filled by establishing roughly 300 million hectares of plantations on land that is not now forested.

[*See also* Biofuels; Carbon Capture and Storage; Coal; Coal Gasification; Ethanol; Nuclear Power; Renewable Sources of Energy; Transportation; *and* Tropical Forests and Global Change.]

BIBLIOGRAPHY

Environmental Defense. *Adequacy of Commitments: Avoiding "Dangerous" Climate Change: A Narrow Time Window for Reductions, and a Steep Price for Delay*, 2002. http://www.edf.org/documents/2422_COP_time.pdf (accessed June 4, 2008).
Royal Commission on Environmental Pollution. *Energy: The Changing Climate*, 2000. http://www.rcep.org.uk/newenergy.htm (accessed June 4, 2008).

—David J. Cuff

STERN REPORT *See* Economics and Climate Change.

SULFUR CYCLE

Sulfur is abundant, essential for life, and present in many oxidation states, from sulfides to sulfates. Like many nonmetals, sulfur is highly mobile in most environments, which leads to large annual movements of sulfur in the global cycle at the Earth's surface. Metallic sulfides (e.g., iron sulfide, FeS_2) are insoluble but unstable at high temperature, giving rise to gaseous emissions from volcanoes. The higher oxidation states of sulfur are encountered as oxyanions (sulfates, sulfites, etc.) at the Earth's surface; with a few important exceptions such as barium sulfate, these are soluble in water.

Sulfur was mobilized at the very beginning of the Earth's history, and sulfate evaporites are evidence of abundant sulfur in the Ancient Ocean of Precambrian time (over 610 million years ago). Even without oxygen in the ancient atmosphere, sulfur-oxidizing microbiota could easily oxidize sulfur, possibly in early sulfur-based photosynthetic pathways:

$$H_2S + 2CO_2 + 2H_2O \rightarrow 2CH_2O + 2H^+ + SO_4^{2-} \tag{1}$$

EVAPORITE SULFATES

Since Phanerozoic times (less than 610 million years ago), sulfur has moved between the oceans and the crust, largely through the reduction of seawater sulfate by anaerobic sulfur-reducing bacteria. This leads to the deposition of pyrite (FeS_2) in sedimentary rocks. Evaporation of sea water also leads to the deposition of sulfate in sedimentary rocks (evaporites). These processes take place on geologic time scales and at variable rates. Evaporite formation requires the formation of basins that are filled on short geologic time scales, so that the ocean, at any given time, could easily be out of steady state with respect to inputs and losses of sulfate.

Evaporite deposition from sea water in basins is a simple process that gives a predictable sequence of salts as sea water evaporates. Calcium carbonate precipitates first, but there is relatively little carbonate in sea water compared with the amount of sulfate, which produces gypsum ($CaSO_4 \cdot 2H_2O$), the next salt to deposit. Presently, there are no large isolated basins that are accumulating evaporites. The few arid tidal flats such as those on the coast of the United Arab Emirates of the Persian Gulf suggest that current evaporite deposition is several orders of magnitude less than during periods in the past.

SULFATE REDUCTION TO SULFIDES

Sulfide deposition requires reduction of seawater sulfate to sulfide. This is typically a biological process that occurs in sediments, most commonly at the continental margin where the accumulation or organic material is fastest, encouraging the activities of sulfate-reducing bacteria:

$$2CH_2O + SO_4^{2-} \quad 2HCO_s^- + HS^- + H^+ \tag{2}$$

The sulfide is converted to pyrite (FeS_2) in a poorly understood process consuming thiosulfate and producing bisulfite (hydrogen sulfite) that can be summarized as follows:

$$Fe^{2+} + HS^- + S_2O_3^{2-} \quad FeS_2 + HSO_3^- \tag{3}$$

Sulfur-isotope ratios indicate the relative importance of the deposition of gypsum and pyrite in marine sediments over geologic time. They suggest that the Permian period was one of pervasive oxidation of sulfide to sulfate, while a massive reduction of sulfate to sulfide characterized early Palaeozoic times.

THE NATURAL SULFUR CYCLE

The sulfur cycle in the absence of human activities is shown in Figure 1. The atmosphere and the surface of the Earth are probably close to steady state. Each year, input and output to the atmosphere are almost in balance; however, the volcanic flux can show significant annual variations. A single explosive volcanic eruption can inject large quantities of sulfur dioxide (SO_2) into the stratosphere, where it remains for a few years. This sulfur is slowly transformed to sulfuric acid (H_2SO_4), which exists as small droplets (aerosols) at high altitude. These droplets can affect the radiation balance of the Earth and are responsible for the slight global cooling following very large eruptions. The eruption of Tambora in 1815 was perhaps the most noticeable in historical times. The following summer was so cool that widespread crop failure resulted. Stratospheric sulfate particles can also affect the ozone layer by enhancing the formation of polar stratospheric clouds, which are important in springtime ozone destruction.

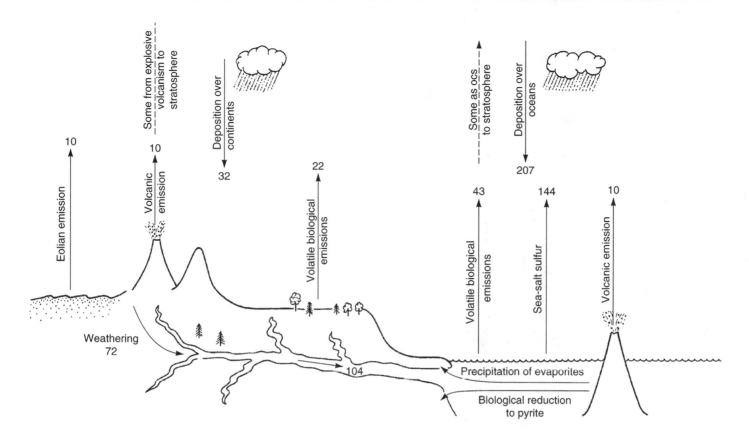

Sulfur Cycle. FIGURE 1. Natural Sulfur Cycle.

Volcanoes also make important contributions to sulfur in the troposphere, mostly as sulfur dioxide. Although we frequently associate the rotten-egg smell of hydrogen sulfide with volcanic regions, H_2S becomes important only where the gases are vented at relatively low temperatures.

Biological emissions of sulfur to the atmosphere from both land and sea take the form of reduced sulfur gases, dimethyl sulfide ($[CH_3]_2S$), carbon disulfide (CS_2), and carbonyl sulfide (COS). The dominant emission from the sea is dimethyl sulfide, a product of osmoregulatory activities by marine algae. Once in the atmosphere, dimethyl sulfide is rapidly oxidized to compounds such as sulfuric and methanesulfonic (CH_3SO_2OH) acids. Terrestrial biogenic sulfur emissions are much smaller and probably dominated by carbonyl sulfide. Carbonyl sulfide is relatively stable in the lower atmosphere, so that some escapes to the stratosphere where, like volcanic sulfur dioxide, it is involved in the production of sulfuric acid aerosols. Much of the sulfur returns to the Earth's surface as sulfates dissolved in rain (wet deposition), although some sulfur dioxide sticks directly to surfaces such as plant leaves (dry deposition).

HUMAN IMPACTS ON THE SULFUR CYCLE

The Earth's surface has always delivered sulfur to the atmosphere as part of windblown dusts. The development of grazing over the last few millennia has led to a decrease in the plant cover that normally restricts wind erosion in arid regions. Plowing and, more recently, river diversion have also increased the amount of sulfate material carried aloft as dust. The Aral Sea is now so reduced in size that its exposed bottom sediments contribute 0.1–1.0 million metric tons of sulfur each year to the atmosphere. [*See* Aral Sea.]

This is just one of many human impacts on the sulfur cycle, which is illustrated in Figure 2. Large amounts of sulfur are mobilized every year in mineral and fossil-fuel extraction. Because many minerals are bound in sulfide ores, refining (roasting) of the ore releases sulfur to the atmosphere or to waste waters. Fossil-fuel combustion creates the largest human emission of sulfur to the atmosphere, amounting to almost 100 million metric tons per year. Despite a reduction in emissions from North America and Europe in recent years, the growing economies of Asia are emitting increasing amounts of sulfur dioxide to the atmosphere.

Some sulfur is applied to the land as fertilizer, because it is such an important biological element. Ironically, the application of sulfates to European agricultural soils has increased in recent years because of the reduction of sulfur emissions by power stations and heavy industry, resulting in soil-sulfur deficiencies for plants such as cereals, so that sulfur must be added in fertilizers.

The sulfur that falls in continental rain or is applied to the land moves into drainage waters. Rivers and lakes can accumulate large amounts of sulfate, a process carried to the extreme in closed basins such as the Dead Sea. Much of the sulfur in rivers

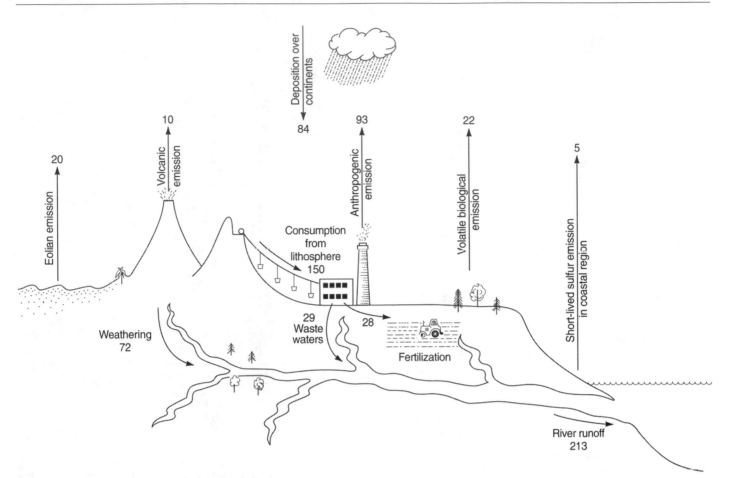

Sulfur Cycle. FIGURE 2. Sulfur Cycle as Modified by Humans.

derives from the weathering of sedimentary rocks, but anthropogenic sources such as acid mine drainage also contribute. Deposited sulfur also accumulates in snow packs and, when the snow melts in the spring, much of the sulfur is highly concentrated in the early acidic meltwaters. Despite the large human impact on the sulfur content of fresh water, the sulfate concentrations of sea water are so high that human inputs to riverflow have no measurable effect on oceanic sulfur concentrations.

In the atmosphere the human impact is more significant. Our contributions of sulfur to the atmosphere are larger than the natural emissions. This imbalance is worsened by the fact that human emissions are land based and located largely in the mid-latitudes of the Northern Hemisphere. The emissions are further concentrated in cities or industrial regions, so that deposition is enhanced in highly industrialized areas widely spread across the globe. This generally appears as acid rain, contaminated most often with sulfuric acid.

The formation of sulfuric acid in rain takes about a day because the reactions proceed most effectively when sulfur dioxide has first dissolved in raindrops. Naturally occurring strong oxidants (hydrogen peroxide or ozone), or oxygen in the presence of catalysts (Fe^{3+} or Mn^{2+}), convert this to sulfate. The reaction in solution can be represented as follows:

$$HSO_3^- + H_2O_2 \rightarrow H^+ + SO_4^{2-} + H_2O \qquad (4)$$

$$HSO_3^- + O_3 \rightarrow H^+ + SO_4^{2-} + O_2 \qquad (5)$$

$$HSO_3^- + \tfrac{1}{2}O_2 \rightarrow H^+ + SO_4^{2-} \text{ (reaction catalyzed)} \qquad (6)$$

Although sulfuric acid has been the most important acidifying agent in rainfall, reduced sulfur dioxide emissions in Europe and North America (Cooper and Jenkins, 2003; Malm et al., 2002) have meant that nitric acid makes proportionately greater contributions to acid rain in these regions.

Sulfates in the atmosphere not only cause acid rain, they also have the potential to influence climate, because sulfate particles in the atmosphere affect the radiation balance of the Earth. Higher concentrations of sulfate particles can mean more cloud condensation nuclei and thus more clouds. This in turn would mean greater reflection of solar radiation, potentially leading to a cooler world. If a cooler Earth meant less biological emission of sulfur to the atmosphere, then biological processes could reduce the cooling and help establish a constant temperature for the Earth. Indeed, there is a possibility that this is a natural regulatory process and that it forms part of the well-known Gaia hypothesis. Although it is not yet possible to establish whether sulfur biogeochemistry controls Earth temperature, it represents an interesting postulate concerning the interconnection between biology and global processes.

[*See also* Acid Rain and Acid Deposition; Aerosols; Biogeochemical Cycles; Desertification; Gaia Hypothesis; *and* Ozone.]

BIBLIOGRAPHY

Andreae, M. O. "Ocean–Atmosphere Interactions in the Global Biogeochemical Sulfur Cycle." *Marine Chemistry* 30 (1990), 1–29. DOI: 10.1016/0304–4203(90)90059-L.

Bates, T. S., et al. "The Biogeochemical Sulfur Cycle in the Marine Boundary Layer over the Northeast Pacific Ocean." *Journal of Atmospheric Chemistry* 10 (1990), 59–81. DOI: 10.1007/BF01980038.

Cooper, D. M., and A. Jenkins. "Response of Acid Lakes in the UK to Reductions in Atmospheric Deposition of Sulfur." *The Science of the Total Environment* (2003), 91–100. DOI: 10.1016/S0048–9697(03)00263–8.

Malm, W. C., et al. "A 10-Year Spatial and Temporal Trend of Sulfate across the United States." *Journal of Geophysical Research* 107 (2002), 4627. DOI: 10.1029/2002JD002107.

Schlesinger, W. H. *Biogeochemistry: An Analysis of Global Change.* 2d ed. San Diego: Academic Press, 1997.

—P. BRIMBLECOMBE

SUSTAINABLE GROWTH

In the last 200,000 years or so, humans have vaulted from being just one edible ape on the African savanna to being a species with both the power to disrupt virtually every ecosystem on Earth and the intellect to realize we are doing it. Today there are more than 6 billion people on Earth, and the United Nations expects that number to rise to around 9 billion by the middle of the twenty-first century. By any standard, humanity has been extraordinarily successful.

Humans have dramatically transformed the planet. The rise of humanity is now precipitating what some ecologists consider a new age of mass extinction comparable to that caused by the meteorite that wiped out the dinosaurs. This is an ironic testament to humanity's decisive influence on the world.

At the same time, the quality of life for much of humanity (excepting especially parts of sub-Saharan Africa) has greatly improved. It is easy to forget how fast a wonderful invention becomes indispensable. Only 100 years ago inventors were trying to win over a skeptical public as to the merits of electricity. Today, the fact that one third of the world's people lack access to electrical power is seen as a massive failure in development.

SUSTAINABLE GROWTH

This surge of prosperity seems so miraculous that it is worth asking whether it can be sustained. It faces a number of challenges. First, the depletion of key natural resources such as fish stocks, crude oil, and soil fertility threatens food supplies and access to other goods such as energy. Second, excessive pollution threatens ecosystems all humans depend on, degrading drinking water and compromising the stability of the world's climate. Third, technological advances have given humanity the ability to destroy itself, particularly through the use of weapons of mass destruction.

We here define sustainable growth as the material development of humanity consistent with staying within critical ecological or social limits to that development. It is an elusive concept. Whether growth can be sustained depends more on the range of human policies and capabilities that surround it than on the characteristics of that growth.

The concept of sustainable growth does not address another fundamental concern, that of equity and other social considerations. It may be morally repugnant that vast numbers of people live in poverty, but that does not keep humanity as a whole from undergoing both population and economic growth. Some of the world's poorest countries have had zero or negative economic growth since the early 1980s (Easterly, 2002) while global growth has continued apace. Equity and development have not always been closely linked.

These issues remain vitally important, however, as moral questions and as threats to broader global stability as globalization brings world populations into ever closer contact. Although it has so far been possible for the world economy to develop very unevenly, migration, information technologies, and greater economic integration may reduce these disparities in the future.

SO FAR, SO GOOD?

Humanity has achieved a great deal but has failed in important ways on both sustainability and equity. Consider just a few indicators (UNEP, 2005):

- The Earth is losing 15 million hectares of tropical forest every year.
- Nearly 70% of world fish stocks have been overfished or fished to their biological limits.
- Over the last century, soil degradation has affected two-thirds of the world's agricultural land.
- It is estimated that one species disappears from the planet every 20 minutes.
- Two billion people have no access to electricity.
- In 1998 more than 45% of the world's people lived on $2 a day or less.

Many of these trends are accelerating and are expected to continue to do so. Climate change exacerbates many of them, as well as worsening problems with water availability, agricultural production, and other resources. Perhaps the most pessimistic conclusion from these trends is that of James Lovelock (2006), who argues that the climate problem has become so severe that we will see a catastrophic collapse of human populations, with remnants eking out an existence at the poles and in the mountains. Although Lovelock himself denies that his analysis is cause for despair, it seems unlikely that human societies and the natural world have the capacity to respond to such dramatic changes.

Others are quick to point out that we have been through this before. The original proponent of such a scenario, Thomas Malthus, argued in 1798 that human population growth must soon run up against the limits of agricultural production, leading to mass starvation. In the more than two centuries since, humanity has become both vastly more numerous and so well fed that obesity is as widespread a problem as undernourishment. So spectacularly wrong were Malthus' predictions that his name is sometimes (unfairly) invoked to ridicule the idea that humanity is, this time, really running up against ecological limits to growth.

In principle, his observation that there is an upper limit to the number of people that the Earth can maintain is correct. Humanity has so far always found some way to increase population and prosperity at the same time. These adjustments have sometimes been painful, but the concept of sustainable growth does not demand that everyone be happy, merely that humanity as a whole grow in population and prosperity. So far, so good.

Perhaps, though, we face a new class of threat that undermines or overwhelms our ability to cope as well as we have in the past. Climate change, declining supplies of fresh water, and the depletion of the world's fisheries are often cited as such threats. Climate change in particular causes Lovelock's deep pessimism. Feedback effects in the world's climate system may indeed lead us into accelerating warming, and melting Arctic ice may lead to an interruption of the thermohaline circulation that warms western Europe, paradoxically plunging it into Siberian conditions. [See Thermohaline Circulation.]

Signs of shortage are not far to seek. Supplies of many vital minerals are reaching their limits, with known resources of metals such as iridium, hafnium, silver, zinc, and platinum expected to be exhausted in 5 to 20 years (Gordon et al., 2005). Known reserves of uranium will last perhaps 30 to 40 years. Oil, perhaps more scrutinized than any other resource, is nonetheless poorly understood. Some observers argue that world resources are much lower than thought, and that the world is nearing peak production. [See Crude Oil Supply.] Others insist that geological resources are abundant. All, however, acknowledge that issues such as political control may mean supplies remain restricted. Even food shortages, the Malthusian bugbear that the green revolution seemed to have banished, no longer seem far-fetched. World grain consumption has exceeded production in 7 of 8 recent years (FAO, 2006).

The Millennium Ecosystems Assessment (United Nations Foundation) identified a variety of growing stresses on the earth and its resources. Animal species are becoming extinct, and we are degrading the ecosystem services which the world relies on in order to fulfill basic needs such as water, soil, and wood. This degradation has been accelerated by global warming, desertification, overfishing, and environmental problems caused by industrialization. This degradation is not only a result of growth of population and economy; it is also a limit to that growth.

Such resource constraints have led to the collapse of earlier civilizations (Diamond, 2005). The fact that modern civilization in the West has so far managed to remain a step ahead of disaster does not mean that will always be the case.

DOOM OR BOOM?

The first thing to realize is how little we know. In the case of climate change, for instance, the basic science is not in doubt. The world is getting warmer, our emissions are causing it, and the effects will be painful. But our understanding of exactly how and where those impacts will be felt is rudimentary. The nature of some incremental impacts, such as the steady rise in sea level caused by thermal expansion, is well understood. But the threat to sustainable growth comes also from nonlinear responses that are difficult to predict. When and how fast will the ice sheets of Greenland or West Antarctica melt? Will major ocean currents be disrupted? Will the melting permafrost of Russia and Canada release increasing amounts of trapped greenhouse gases leading to runaway warming? All these catastrophic impacts are possible, but none is well understood.

We also understand little of how technology develops. Innovation has repeatedly helped societies out of seemingly intractable problems. Perhaps the best known example is the green revolution that occurred in the developing world, as fertilizers, pesticides, and irrigation doubled grain production in poor countries from 1965 to 1980. Some are banking on the promise of genetic modification to repeat that success. Perhaps even more pressing is the need to find alternative energy sources that can help reduce carbon emissions while avoiding the risks associated with large-scale handling of nuclear fuels and wastes. Renewable energy technologies such as wind and solar power have boomed in recent years, but it is likely that the final push will come from technologies that are now just laboratory experiments. It is difficult to see where the next innovation will come from and how it will help or harm us in the long run.

Threats to the long-term sustainability of growth can come from many quarters. We may run out of some crucial resource, such as oil, fertile land, or usable water. Some countries will face drought and hunger while others thrive: water will not run out everywhere. This is simply a more dramatic manifestation of the inequities existing around the globe. A second and related possibility is that pollution, whether contaminating water supplies or changing the world's climate, will make parts of the world unlivable.

Finally, just as technological innovation has repeatedly come to our rescue, it may also prove our ruin. The invention and propagation of weapons of mass destruction, particularly biological and nuclear weapons, give us for the first time the capability to render much of the globe uninhabitable. The end of the Cold War has allayed concerns about nuclear winter, but the reprieve is illusory: in the next few decades many more countries will have nuclear weapons, and nuclear materials will be widely available. [See Nuclear Winter.]

All these threats are to some degree interlinked. Resource constraints will exacerbate inequities and worsen poverty. The social reactions to these inequities and disputes over natural resources increase the risk of conflict with hideously dangerous weapons. The 6 billion people on the Earth already lack elbow room. What will decide how much further we can go?

THE DECIDING FACTORS

Sooner or later, Malthusian limits to growth will impose themselves. Larger populations of more avid consumers must eventually exhaust vital natural resources unless they are able to shift to increasingly efficient and less resource-hungry lifestyles. Human societies will have to have the requisite institutional and economic structures to make the necessary changes. Perhaps more fundamentally, they will have to make those changes in a world in which both threats and solutions will be hard to predict.

The market economy is in some cases an excellent tool for doing this. As prices of certain commodities rise, people are spurred to find new sources or alternative technologies. A period of sustained high oil prices, for instance, calls forth increased efficiency from consumers and investment in new fuels.

In other instances, the market lacks the proper signals. In the case of greenhouse gases, for instance, polluters do not pay for the damage done by their emissions and so have little incentive to reduce them. Intelligent government policy can help, by mandating limits to emissions or by using taxes to make sure that the polluter pays. [See Carbon Taxes; and Emissions Trading.] Many countries are adopting such measures, but they have so far only scratched the surface. The appeal of such measures is that rather than predicting how a problem will be solved they leave the decision to individuals and companies, unleashing the tremendous innovative power that has always been humanity's best defense.

When dealing with other fundamental threats, even mechanisms such as these do not work. The prevention of nuclear war, for instance, is something that the world has achieved through a combination of diplomacy, fear, and luck. It may be of little comfort to know that our continued prosperity relies on such uncertain grounds, but uncertainty has always been humanity's lot. There is no magic formula for ensuring sustainable growth: as with liberty, its price is eternal vigilance.

[See also Agriculture and Biodiversity; Human Populations; Industrial Ecology; and Resources.]

BIBLIOGRAPHY

Diamond, J. Collapse: How Societies Choose to Fail or Succeed. New York: Viking, 2005.

Easterly, W.R. The Elusive Quest for Growth. Cambridge, Mass.: MIT Press, 2002.

FAO (United Nations Food and Agricultural Organization). The State of Food Insecurity in the World, 2006. http://www.fao.org/SOF/sofi (accessed June 4, 2008).

Gordon, R.B., M. Bertram, and T.E. Graedel. "Metal Stocks and Sustainability." Proceedings of the National Academy of Sciences 103 (2005), 1209–1214. DOI: 10.1073/pnas.0509498103.

Lovelock, J. The Revenge of Gaia: Earth's Climate in Crisis and the Fate of Humanity. New York: Basic Books, 2006.

UNEP (United Nations Environment Programme). One Planet, Many People: Atlas of Our Changing Environment, 2005. http://www.na.unep.net/OnePlantManyPeople/ (accessed June 4, 2008).

United Nations Foundation. The Millennium Ecosystems Assessment, 2005. http://www.maweb.org (accessed June 4, 2008).

ADDITIONAL READING

Adams, W.M. "Sustainable Development?" In Geographies of Global Change, edited by R.J. Johnston, P.J. Taylor, and M.J. Watts. Oxford, U.K., and Cambridge, Mass.: Blackwell, 1995.

Weizsäcker, E. von, A.B. Lovins, and L.H. Lovins. Factor Four: Doubling Wealth, Halving Resource Use. London: Earthscan, 1997.

—ROBERT BRADLEY AND DAVID J. CUFF

SYNFUELS

The term "synfuel" (synthetic fuel) has been applied to liquid fuels derived from oil sands, extra-heavy oil, or oil shales. [See Oil Sands.] Currently, though, and especially in the eyes of the U.S. Department of Energy, it refers to liquid fuels produced from coal by coal-to-liquids processes (CTL), natural gas (gas-to-liquids, GTL), or biomass (biomass-to-liquids, BTL). Because world coal resources are large in comparison to crude-oil resources there is great interest in processes that convert coal to liquid fuels. [See Coal Liquefaction.]

Liquid fuels produced from edible crops (biofuels) are distinguished from liquids produced by BTL processes using wood wastes and other inedible plant matter. [See Biofuels.] The term "syngas" is applied to gas (especially methane) produced from various feedstocks, including coal. Emissions of carbon dioxide from existing coal-burning electrical plants are spurring development of technologies that convert coal into gas for gas-turbine generators. [See Coal Gasification.]

At the same time, there are around the world substantial reserves of natural gas not close to markets (stranded gas) waiting for a gas pipeline to reach them. One alternative is to convert this gas chemically to liquid fuel by gas-to-liquid (GTL) processes. Another is to liquefy the natural gas at high pressure and ship it as liquefied natural gas (LNG), as is already extensively done. [See Natural Gas.] There are small GTL operations now in Malaysia and South Africa. In the United States the first such plant may be built in Alaska where substantial reserves of natural gas are stranded.

BIBLIOGRAPHY

U.S. Department of Energy, Energy Information Adminstration (DOE/EIA). Annual Energy Outlook 2006, pp. 52–60. http://www.eia.doe.gov/oiaf/archive.html (accessed June 4, 2008). A thorough review of technologies for production of synfuels, syngas, and biofuels.

—DAVID J. CUFF

T

TAR SANDS

See Oil Sands.

TECHNOLOGY AND ENVIRONMENT

"Unlike resources found in nature, technology is a man-made resource whose abundance can be continuously increased, and whose importance in determining the world's future is also increasing" (Starr and Rudman, 1973).

Technology is the aspect of our culture that, more than any other, defines how we are limited by our physical environment and at the same time how deeply we impact that environment. There are ideological factors, such as the anthropocentric view that nature is ours to subdue (see White, 1967), but technology always has been central to our relationship with the environment. [*See* Belief Systems *and* Resources.]

It was tools, or technology, that defined the stages of prehistory and the evolution of the human ability to survive and prosper as scavenger and hunter-gatherer. It was a decline in heavy industry that caused population to diminish in Pittsburgh, Pennsylvania, and technological enterprise that attracted thousands to Silicon Valley, California.

The rate of change in technologies today is startling. Innovations like the telephone, aircraft, and automobile made a big difference to society, and then advanced slowly and predictably. More recent technologies, however, seem to be self-accelerating: new computer chips, for instance, spawn the next generation of even faster chips. And the technologies interact: computers make gene-sequencing possible, and simultaneously, DNA is being considered as a medium for computation (Brand, 2000).

THE PARADOX OF TECHNOLOGICAL DEVELOPMENT

While technology may be the cause of many of our environmental ills, it can also provide solutions, not simply technical fixes but profound changes in energy sources, or transportation, or communication. This capacity of technology to be both detrimental and beneficial is a recurrent theme in discussions of technology and global change (Gray, 1989).

In the first Industrial Revolution, access to coal-fired steam power simply worsened some impacts that had been of concern before the end of the eighteenth century—loss of forests, coal mining disturbance, and decline in the quality of urban air. Subsequently, and especially in the late twentieth century, there emerged new substances—petrochemicals, plastics, and various toxins—that accumulate in the biosphere, and unprecedented expenditure of fossil-fuel energy in electrical generation, mining, forestry, agriculture, and transportation with serious impacts on the land and the atmosphere at local, regional and global scales. The future will require decisions about whether and how to intervene, especially with regard to energy technologies, and whether to encourage developing nations to embrace technologies more sustainable than those employed by the now-industrial nations. [*See* China and Its Environment; Global Warming; India and Environmental Change; Sustainable Growth; *and* Transportation.]

Technological advances, however, have already greatly reduced the impacts of industrial activity. One example is the reduction in materials used per unit of industrial output (dematerialization). Another is improvements in energy efficiency, expressed as reduction in the energy intensity of output (see Grübler, 1998, pp. 238–242, 284–290). Without these advances the stress on resources and the alteration of the atmosphere would be far more serious than they are now.

Further gains in this regard, especially the reduction of waste in materials and energy, can be attained through new technologies and by collaboration among complementary industries. [*See* Industrial Ecology.] Unhappily, all the economies realized through dematerialization and reduced energy intensity have in the past been outweighed by the rebound effect, the overall growth in production as populations grow and economies expand.

Another benefit of advanced technology is that we have an ever-improving ability to measure and monitor environmental change though new instruments and methods for analysis of air and water, and satellites to map changes in land cover and ocean temperatures. Furthermore, in recent decades computer models have allowed us to use our knowledge of processes in the atmosphere and oceans to predict changes in temperature, precipitation, ocean currents, and sea ice. [*See* Climate Models and Uncertainty; Global Warming; *and* Greenhouse Effect.]

TECHNOLOGY EXAMINED

Early in the nineteenth century, voices were raised against the advance of technology and the transformation of society by machines. Organized textile workers, the Luddites, resisted machinery in textile mills in 1811; their counterparts opposed horse-drawn threshing machines in the 1830s; and in 1829 Thomas Carlyle observed that mechanization had disrupted traditions and caused workers to lose faith in individual endeavor (Carlyle, 1957).

In the twentieth century, the social and political ramifications of technology were examined by Lewis Mumford (1970) and Jacques Ellul (1964), among others. Perhaps most influential for nonspecialists was E. F. Schumacher's book *Small Is Beautiful: Economics as if People Mattered* (1973), which proposed methods of economic advance in harmony with the existing conditions of traditional societies. The implicit concept, appropriate technology, was taken up by a number of organizations during the 1970s, applying the idea to industrial nations as well as traditional societies (Winner, 1986, pp. 62–74).

More recently, ethical and philosophical implications of technology have been explored by Mitcham (1994) and Winner (1986). Winner's book presents a strong statement of the need to steer technology toward goals that will benefit society. A similar stance is taken by Freeman Dyson (1999), whose chapter "Technology and Social Justice" deals with the revival of villages through solar energy, bioengineered crops, and Internet connections. The concept of soft technology, emphasizing human culture—especially as it applies to China—is further developed in a recent book (Jin, 2005).

MATERIALS

An industrial society uses a staggering quantity and variety of materials. In a year an average U.S. citizen consumes directly or indirectly more than 37 tons of wood, stone, gravel, metal, fertilizers, and plastics—in addition to food and fuels. Today's materials draw from all 92 naturally occurring elements, compared to about 20 elements in 1900. Roughly 100,000 synthetic chemicals have been introduced in the twentieth century. Americans alone use about one-third of all the materials that churn through the global economy (see Gardner and Sampat, 1999). Energy-intensive technology has lowered the cost of mining, facilitated the concentration and refining of metals from ores of ever-diminishing grade, and increased efficiency in cutting and processing of trees for paper and lumber. For a thorough study of the role of technology in natural resources, see *Productivity in Natural Resource Industries* (Simpson, chap. 1).

A rational and more sustainable use of materials will require new incentives and policies, such as eliminating subsidies that encourage the use of virgin materials, but there will also be modular products easy to remanufacture or to recycle. There is also the prospect in materials science of working at the molecular level to build substances such as photonics materials, materials for information storage, biomedical materials, new polymers, and diamonds for industrial uses, rather than refining raw materials. Whether this approach can make a substantial impact on our traditional mining and manufacturing remains to be seen (see Ball, 1997).

ENERGY TECHNOLOGIES

Because energy choices are at the root of so many environmental concerns any technologies that offer more benign sources of primary energy or ameliorate the impacts of our present energy sources are worth pursuing

In locating, producing, and using fossil fuels, a number of technological advances have been helpful. There is still an urgent need to find ways to burn coal without releasing greenhouse gases, because more coal-fired power plants are being built and planned across the world in spite of their obvious contribution to global warming. [*See* Coal.] Any "clean coal" system depends on storing (sequestering) carbon dioxide—by pumping the gas into deeply-buried permeable rock, including rock that previously held crude oil or natural gas, or by converting it into solids by using mineral carbonization. These and other methods of storage must be developed very soon.

Equally urgent is improving the efficiency of solar and wind-powered generation of electricity. More efficient photovoltaic devices could validate the vision of distributed electrical generation and less reliance on central power plants. Progress in renewable energy sources depends heavily on government grants and incentives and on reliably high prices for electricity generated by coal and natural gas. [*See* National Energy Policy in the United States.]

The threat of accelerated global warming has renewed interest in nuclear power, despite its serious drawbacks. [*See* Nuclear Power.] Some see an expansion of fission reactors as essential now and a stepping stone to fusion power (Lovelock, 2006). Others are less committed but nevertheless point out that existing nuclear plants displace enough coal-electric plants to prevent the emission of more than one-third of the total CO_2 produced by fossil-fuel combustion in the year 2000: "curiously, this impressive total of avoided emissions is almost never mentioned in current debates about the management of greenhouse gases" (Smil, 2003, p. 313).

Whatever the progress in the technologies of energy production and conversion, there is another urgent need, for a reduction in demand for electricity and transportation fuels. This can to some extent be accomplished by new technologies, such as the compact fluorescent lights now displacing incandescent bulbs, improved appliances and electric motors, and a new generation of cars and trucks. Increased efficiency of a growing fleet of vehicles will not reduce demand for liquid fuels, however, unless high fuel taxes, improved public transport, and other incentives force or enable us to drive less. Insulation, smart glass, and passive solar design already exist and are waiting for building codes to ensure their use. Buildings worldwide account for a third of all human emissions of CO_2: technically, that contribution could be cut by almost 30% in little more than a decade (Harvey, 2007).

Reducing demand in the wealthier nations may be necessary because demand for materials and energy is increasing rapidly in developing nations. According to one estimate, if today's low-income countries were sometime in the future to average one-third of the per capita energy use in affluent nations—in the year 2000 it was less than one-fifth of the rate—and the rich economies limited themselves to a 20% growth in energy demand, the global primary energy supply would be 60% above the 2000 level (Smil, 2003, p. 339). The questionable term in that scenario is not that developing nations will use more energy per capita, but that wealthy nations will continue to increase their energy use per capita. That may not be realistic without some remarkable breakthroughs in clean and sustainable energy sources.

TECHNOLOGY AND DEVELOPMENT

The role of technology in economic growth cannot be explored here but is analyzed in a number of studies (see Grübler, 1998; Steil et al., 2002). One unknown is the role of the rapid spread of computers and the increasing importance of information technology. The Internet especially is credited with providing new opportunities worldwide. Commenting on how the Internet has leveled the competitive playing fields between industrial and developing countries, Thomas Friedman states,

> It is now possible for more people than ever to collaborate and compete in real time with more other people on more different kinds of work from more different corners of the planet and on a more equal footing than at any previous time in the history of the world. (Friedman, 2006)

Some doubt was raised in an earlier article that reported that developing countries are being left behind as the transformation to the new economy takes place in wealthier countries. The authors suggest policies that might accelerate the development of information technology in the poorer countries (Lucas and Sylla, 2003).

A PERSPECTIVE FROM SPACE

In 1969 a long series of triumphs in ballooning, heavier-than-air flight, supersonic flight, rocketry, earth-orbit flights, and moon-orbit flights culminated in landing humans on the Moon—the ultimate expression of how science and technology can work together toward a specific goal, spurred in this case by competition between two world powers. That feat and subsequent excursions to the planets and their moons have revised our view of the earth and altered our attitudes toward it.

The photos of Earth taken by Apollo astronauts emphasized the isolation and sphericity of our globe; while blue oceans under white swirls of cloud made images irresistible to journalists and textbook publishers. These views led readers to see our planet as an extraterrestrial might see it—a moist, fertile sphere, unique in the solar system. The impetus given to environmental movements at the time is impossible to measure, partly because the lunar landings coincided roughly with influential writings of biologists Paul Erlich, Barry Commoner, and Garrett Hardin, and with events such as the conflagration on Cleveland's oil-polluted Cuyahoga River and a crude-oil leak from an offshore well near Santa Barbara, California; nevertheless, those images were an awakening and a milestone marking our entry to a new era.

Roughly ten years later, an even more profound image was sent to earth from a spacecraft, Voyager 1, as it approached the edge of the solar system. Looking back toward the Sun, it captured the tiny Earth, over 3 billion miles away, apparently illuminated by a beam of light, making the view still more dramatic. Seeing that image, Carl Sagan was struck by how isolated and lonely is our planet—the only world that harbors life, as far as we know. This distant view of our tiny world "underscores our responsibility to deal more kindly with one another, and to preserve and cherish the pale blue dot, the only home we've ever known" (Sagan, 1994, p. 7).

Some scientific communities—encouraged by successful space probes—have nurtured the idea of migrating to Mars or colonizing the asteroid belt, while possibly mining distant bodies for mineral resources. There appear to be two reasons to colonize Mars: first, to search for life there; and second, to find a refuge for *Homo sapiens,* whose existence is threatened at home by our own actions.

"We have liberated ourselves from the environment. Now it is time to liberate the environment itself" (Ausubel, 1996).

BIBLIOGRAPHY

Ausubel, J. H. "The Liberation of the Environment." *Daedalus,* 125.3 (1996), 1–17.
Ball, P. *Made to Measure: New Materials for the 21st Century.* Princeton, N.J.: Princeton University Press, 1997.
Brand, S. "Is Technology Moving Too Fast?" *Time,* June 19, 2000, 108–109.
Carlyle, T. "Signs of the Times." In *Selected Works, Reminiscences, and Letters,* edited by J. Symons. Cambridge, Mass.: Harvard University Press, 1957.
Dyson, F. J. *The Sun, the Genome, and the Internet.* New York: Oxford University Press, 1999.
Ellul, J. *The Technological Society.* New York: Knopf, 1964.
Friedman, T. *The World Is Flat: A Brief History of the Twenty-First Century.* New York: Farrar, Straus, and Giroux, 2006.
Gardner, G., and P. Sampat. "Forging a Sustainable Materials Economy." In *State of the World 1999.* Worldwatch Institute. New York: Norton, 1999.
Gray, P. E. "The Paradox of Technological Development." In *Technology and Environment,* edited by J. H. Ausubel and H. E. Sladovich. Washington, D.C., National Academy Press, 1989.
Grübler, A. *Technology and Global Change.* Cambridge: Cambridge University Press, 1998.
Harvey, D. Quoted in "Building for a Cooling Planet." *New Scientist,* July 28, 2007, p. 9.
Jin, Z. *Global Technological Change: From Hard Technology to Soft Technology.* Bristol, U.K.: Intellect, 2005.
Lovelock, J. *The Revenge of Gaia: Earth's Climate in Crisis and the Fate of Humanity.* New York: Basic Books, 2006.
Lucas, H., and R. Sylla "The Global Impact of the Internet: Widening the Economic Gap Between Wealthy and Poor Nations?" *Prometheus* 21.1 (2003), 1–22.
Mitcham, C. *Thinking Through Technology: The Path between Engineering and Philosophy.* Chicago: Chicago University Press, 1994.
Mumford, L. *The Myth of the Machine.* Vol. 2. *The Pentagon of Power.* New York: Harcourt, 1970.
Sagan, C. *Pale Blue Dot.* New York: Random House, 1994.
Schumacher, E. F. *Small Is Beautiful: Economics as if People Mattered.* New York: Harper and Row, 1973.
Simpson, David. "*Productivity in Natural Resource Industries: Improvement Through Innovation,* Washington, D.C.: Resources for the Future Press, 1999.
Smil, V. *Energy at the Crossroads: Global Perspectives and Uncertainties.* Cambridge, Mass.: MIT Press, 2003.
Starr, C., and R. Rudman. "Parameters of Technological Growth." *Science* 182 (1973), 358–364. DOI: 10.1126/science.182.4110.358.
Steil, B., D. G. Victor, and R. R. Nelson, eds. *Technological Innovation and Economic Performance.* Princeton, N.J.: Princeton University Press, 2002.
White, L. "The Historical Roots of Our Ecologic Crisis." *Science* 155 (1967), 1203–1207. DOI: 10.1126/science.155.3767.1203.
Winner, L. *The Whale and the Reactor.* Chicago: University of Chicago Press, 1986.

ADDITIONAL RESOURCES

Deutch, J. M., and R. K. Lester. *Making Technology Work.* Cambridge and New York: Cambridge University Press, 2004.
Smil, V. *Transforming the Twentieth Century: Technical Innovations and Their Consequences.* Oxford and New York: Oxford University Press, 2006.

—DAVID J. CUFF

THERMOHALINE CIRCULATION

Climate is closely linked to ocean circulation, so any change in the pattern of currents is likely to have consequences for climate at a regional and even global scale. Some circulations are driven by water temperature and salinity gradients—the so-called thermohaline circulation, which depends on cooler and more saline waters being more dense and tending to sink. Some of the abrupt climate changes during the last glacial-interglacial cycle (Clark et al., 2002), such as the Younger Dryas, could be explained by the cycling of this circulation, as could the abrupt climate changes at 9,300 and 8,200 years BP (Marshall et al., 2007).

In modern oceans the densest waters occur in the North Atlantic, where a combination of low temperature and high salinity gives rise to the North Atlantic Deep Water. Within the North Atlantic the circulation appears to operate as a conveyor, moving water northward in upper levels of the ocean (including the Gulf Stream or North Atlantic Drift), ultimately to sink at about 60°N. The return limb of the conveyor at depth returns this deep water to the Southern Oceans.

Any warming in high latitudes would increase the melting of glaciers in Greenland and Baffin Island, introducing more fresh water to the North Atlantic, reducing salinity of surface waters, and disrupting the thermohaline circulation. Because northern Europe is warmed now by westerly winds crossing the Gulf Stream it would have colder winters in the absence of that circulation. Whether this is happening now as a result of current global temperature increases, and whether it poses a major future threat as warming intensifies, is a matter of debate, (Schiermeier, 2007).

BIBLIOGRAPHY

Broecker, W. S., and G. H. Denton. "The role of ocean-atmosphere reorganizations in glacial cycles." *Quaternary Science Reviews* 9 (1990), 305–341.

Clark, P. U., et al. "The Role of the Thermohaline Circulation in Abrupt Climate Change." *Nature* 415 (2002), 863–869. DOI: 10.1038/415863a.

Marshall, J. D., et al. "Terrestrial Impact of Abrupt Changes in the North Atlantic Thermohaline Circulation: Early Holocene, UK." *Geology* 35 (2007), 639–642. DOI: 10.1130/G23498A.1.

Schiermeier, Q. "Ocean Circulation Noisy, Not Stalling." *Nature* 448 (2007), 844–845. DOI: 10.1038/448844b.

—ANDREW S. GOUDIE

Thermohaline Circulation. FIGURE 1. The Large-Scale Salt Transport System ("Ocean/Global Conveyor") Operating in Today's Oceans. This compensates for the transport of water (as vapor) through the atmosphere from the Atlantic to the Pacific Ocean. Salt-laden deep water formed in the northern Atlantic flows down the length of the Atlantic and eventually northward into the deep Pacific. Some of this water upwells in the northern Pacific, bringing with it the salt left behind in the Atlantic due to vapor transport. Flow of the "Atlantic Conveyor" may have been interrupted during cold episodes. (Reprinted from Broecker and Denton, 1990. With permission of Elsevier Science.)

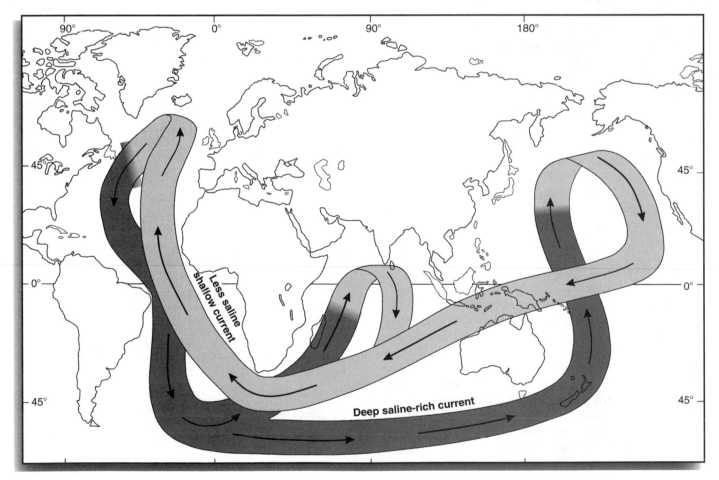

TIPPING POINTS AND GLOBAL CHANGE

As Walker (2006, p. 802) has written,

> The idea that passing some hidden threshold will drastically worsen man-made change has been around for decades, normally couched in technical terms such as "nonlinearity," "positive feedback," and "hysteresis."

Recently, the term "tipping point" has come into vogue to describe the moment at which internal dynamics start to propel change previously driven by external forces. The questions are being asked, "Is climatic change getting out of control?" and "Are we at a point of no return?" For example does the melting of Arctic ice lead to such a change in albedo (surface reflectivity) that it is self-reinforcing? Could increasing melting of Arctic sea ice and the Greenland ice cap cause the thermohaline circulation of the oceans to flip from one state to another? Could a rise in temperature cause the Amazon rainforest to be replaced by scrub or desert, thereby causing the Earth to lose another cooling mechanism (Lovelock, 2006, p. 51)?

As Flannery (2006, p. 83) has argued, global warming may change climate in jerks, during which patterns jump from one state to another. As he put it,

> The best analogy is perhaps that of a finger on a light switch. Nothing happens for a while, but if you slowly increase the pressure a certain point is reached, a sudden change occurs, and conditions swiftly alter from one state to another.

Flannery recognized three potential climatic tipping points: a slowing or collapse of the Gulf Stream, the demise of the Amazon rainforest, and the release of gas (methane) hydrates from the floor of the Arctic. However, there are doubtless more tipping points than these; a map of such locations is provided by Kemp (2005).

BIBLIOGRAPHY

Flannery, T. F. *The Weather Makers*. London: Allen Lane, 2006.
Kemp, M. "Science in Culture: Inventing an Icon. Hans Joachin Schellnhuber's Map of Global 'Tipping Points' in Climate Change." *Nature* 437 (2005), 1238.
Lovelock, J. *The Revenge of Gaia*. London: Allen Lane (2006).
Walker, G. "Climate Change: The Tipping Point of the Iceberg." *Nature* 441 (2006), 802–805. DOI: 10.1038/441802a.

—Andrew S. Goudie

TOURISM

Tourism, in one form or another, has been with us for millennia, but its emergence as a major industry with significant global impacts did not occur until after World War II. The World Travel and Tourism Council estimates world tourism revenues in 2007 at $7 trillion, growing to $13 trillion by 2017. Such a dramatic growth rate is a manifestation of general worldwide socioeconomic and technological change that has resulted in the rise of the tertiary or service sector of the economy.

GROWTH

Contributing to the growth of tourism have been rising standards of living, increased levels of personal mobility, and the global information explosion. The principal generators of tourism have been the advanced economies of Western Europe, North America, and Southeast Asia. It is now the turn of East Asia and the Pacific to lead in the growth and development of tourism.

As individuals have secured more disposable income and leisure time, they have converted them into travel experiences. Since tourists have tended to travel in family groups, we have created a generation of young and experienced travelers who are likely to be more insatiable and demanding than in the past. Indeed, modern tourism is now a collection of special-interest markets.

While the automobile has been the vehicle of choice for most domestic and interregional travel, it was the jet engine that heralded the surge in long-distance international travel: Pan Am entered the jet age with the first purchase of a Boeing 707, flying from New York to Paris in half the time of previous propeller-driven planes.

The rapid diffusion of television has provided a window onto the world that has raised awareness and curiosity about other lands and cultures. As people have traveled they have grown dependent on the existence of an international banking system, the availability of international reservation systems, and, not least, international air traffic control. New technology provides an impetus to new tourism by providing the ability to handle the high volumes of complex information associated with global deregulation practices (Poon, 1993).

IMPACTS OF TOURISM

Tourism's expansion has had a variety of impacts on its destinations. In most cases it has brought the expected benefits of increased employment, increased revenue and taxes, a regional redistribution of income, and an increased appreciation of natural and cultural heritage. In many economies, tourism now represents 5% or more of the gross domestic product and has become a significant socioeconomic component of local life. Because of its ubiquitous nature, however, tourism seldom receives the full economic recognition it deserves and is more often associated with negative impacts resulting from its high visibility.

One of the key issues in tourism is its impact on fragile ecosystems and local cultures. The very size of the modern tourism market places such environments under considerable stress, and they need to be managed carefully if they are to survive as both living communities and tourist attractions. National parks, alpine areas, tropical islands, wetlands, and wilderness areas are some of the sensitive areas showing tourism-induced stress (De Kadt, 1979; Theobald, 1994; Cater and Lowman, 1994). Even the most remote areas can no longer escape: there are now over eight times as many tourists as researchers visiting Antarctica.

In many cases, overloading of the physical environment is associated with stress on the local inhabitants and societal norms. Communities in developing countries and rural and wilderness areas are particularly susceptible to stress and change when invaded by large numbers of tourists who have different lifestyles and expectations (Cater and Lowman, 1994, pp. 78, 81, 177). A common problem faced by all host communities, regardless of size and complexity, is the issue of how much to put on show and how it should be done (Murphy, 1985). Each community needs to decide its local balance on the "authenticity–staged event" continuum, and how much it is willing to commoditize its cultural heritage for visitors (Cohen, 1979).

ECOTOURISM OPTION

One way to ease the problems of environmental and social change is to emphasize ecotourism, an "enlightening natural travel experience that contributes to conservation of the ecosystem while respecting the integrity of host communities" (Wight, 1994, p. 39). It has been promoted as an alternative form of tourism that can match the growing special-interest niches with specific small-scale travel and learning experiences that are less intrusive and stressful (Cater and Lowman, 1994, pp. 3, 32, 36).

While a true ecotourism approach avoids the pitfalls of excessive numbers and offers a more compatible linkage of tourist and destination interests, it is not a panacea. First, its intent and scope will always limit its applicability to a small segment of the tourism market. Second, the inquisitive nature of ecotourists may render them more intrusive than the usual tourist. Third, the small scale and low-key emphasis works against large income-generation opportunities in host communities. Some specific limitations and ill effects have been pointed out (Isaacs, 2000; Vivanco, 2002).

Tourism is both a product of and a contributor to global change. It has benefited from rising living standards in economically developed nations and from technological improvements in transportation and information flows around the world. But in facilitating the movement of millions of people and opening up every corner of the Earth to their examination, it has become a major agent of change in its own right. It is an industry that caters to the best and worst of our travel motives and thereby influences the form and function of every destination in the world, be it a small African village or a major western metropolis.

[See also Parks and Preserves; and Wilderness Debates.]

BIBLIOGRAPHY

Barkin, D., and C. P. Bouchez. "NGO-Community Collaboration for Ecotourism: A Strategy for Sustainable Regional Development." *Current Issues in Tourism* 5.3–4 (2002), 245–253.

Cater, E., and G. Lowman, eds. *Ecotourism: A Sustainable Option?* Chichester, U.K., and New York: Wiley, 1994. A case-by-case study of the growing demand for an environmentally sensitive approach to tourism.

Cohen, E. "Rethinking the Sociology of Tourism." *Annals of Tourism Research* 6.1 (1979), 18–35. An examination of the sociological typologies involved in modern mass tourism.

De Kadt, E. *Tourism: Passport to Development?* New York: Oxford University Press, 1979. A seminal study that examines the social and cultural effects of tourism in developing countries with a view to influencing policy decisions.

Hobson, P. "Growth of Tourism in East Asia and the Pacific." *Tourism Management* 15.2 (1994), 150–155. DOI: 10.1016/0261–5177(94)90009–4. This paper examines the growing level of tourism in this part of the world and its impact on infrastructure, human resources, and environmental degradation.

Isaacs, J. C. "The Limited Potential of Ecotourism to Contribute to Wildlife Conservation." *Wildlife Society Bulletin* 28.1 (2000), 61–69.

Murphy, P. E. *Tourism: A Community Approach*. London: Methuen, 1985. A major work that examines the significance of tourism development from the host-community viewpoint.

Poon, A. *Tourism, Technology, and Competitive Strategies*. Wallingford, U.K.: CAB International, 1993. An innovative examination of the relationships between information technology and tourism.

Theobald, W. F., ed. *Global Tourism: The Next Decade*. London: Butterworth-Heinemann, 1994. A useful review of recent tourism impacts and associated policy and planning.

Vivanco, L. "Ecotourism Paradise Lost: A Thai Case Study." *Ecologist* 32.2 (2002), 28–30.

Wight, P. "Environmentally Responsible Marketing of Tourism." In *Ecotourism: A Sustainable Option?*, edited by E. Cater and G. Lowman, pp. 39–56. Chichester, U.K., and New York: Wiley, 1994. This study examines the potential positive and negative impacts of ecotourism marketing on the sustainability of resources.

—Peter E. Murphy

TRADE AND ENVIRONMENT

There are numerous connections between international trade and environmental quality. Many also link domestic trade and environmental quality. For example, opportunities for trade affect the scale and composition of production, which can have implications for pollution and resource use. But international trade also presents challenges different from those of internal commerce. For example, alien organisms brought in with imported products can disturb ecosystems. Problems also arise when countries with different environmental policies compete with each other in world commerce.

The recognition of connections between trade and environment is not new; some of the earliest international environmental treaties (such as the 1902 treaty on birds) contained trade provisions. In 1972, the Secretariat of the General Agreement on Tariffs and Trade (GATT) prepared a thoughtful study on pollution control and international trade. But it was not until 1990 that trade and environment became a significant focus of attention.

Three largely independent events raised the profile of the trade-environment nexus. First, several European countries, led by Austria, called attention to this issue at the 1990 ministerial conference of the Uruguay Round trade talks. Second, after U.S. President George H. W. Bush launched negotiations for a free-trade agreement with Mexico, critics pointed to the poor environmental conditions along the border between the United States and Mexico as a demonstration of the spillover effects from trade. This forced negotiators to make environment an issue in the ongoing trade talks. Third, in 1991, a GATT panel issued an infamous decision in a dispute between the Mexican and U.S. governments over Mexican tuna-fishing practices that were killing numerous dolphins. At issue was a U.S. law that banned imports of tuna from Mexico because of high dolphin-kill rates. The GATT panel held that international trade law did not permit a government to ban imports in order to protect the environment outside its geographic borders. This decision alarmed environmentalists, who were unexpectedly confronted with an entirely new political threat to environmental law. [*See* Environmental Law.]

Because both trade and environmental policy are broad and expanding, the issues that fall under the rubric of trade and environment are myriad. One approach for exploring these issues is to group them into four categories: (1) effects of trade on environment; (2) effects of environmental policy on trade; (3) effects of trade rules and trade agreements on the environment; and (4) the need for coordination among trade and environmental institutions.

EFFECTS OF TRADE ON ENVIRONMENT

There are several ways in which trade can affect the environment. The clearest is when a traded product causes direct physical effects. For example, toxic waste might be transferred to a country where it will be improperly handled. Services such as transportation can also cause harm. In some circumstances, a traded product can trigger a physical benefit rather than harm. For example, a new technology can facilitate cleaner production in the country obtaining access to it.

Another way in which trade affects the environment is by causing physical effects through the market. This occurs when trading opportunities change the scale or composition of production in the country of export. For example, in the early twentieth century, the demand in the United Kingdom and the United States for feathers in women's fashions led to widespread killing of exotic birds in other countries. Similarly, demand for certain metals in industrial countries has led to mining in fragile ecosystems. Not all changes induced by trade are harmful to the environment. For example, green product specifications in a big market can upgrade industry standards worldwide. Transnational corporations can bring high environmental standards with them when they build new plants.

Trade can also affect the environment by causing economic changes through the market. When it increases economic growth and national welfare, trade can enhance a country's willingness to pay for environmental cleanup. Economists have detected an inverted-U relationship between national income per capita and certain kinds of pollution. That is, pollution initially increases with income and then decreases as income grows higher. Such findings have led to the hypothesis that richer consumers will demand more environmental regulation from government. Some analysts suggest that growth-promoting trade will be beneficial for the environment. Skeptics deny that inverted-U curves have predictive value and point out that, in any event, there are some pollutants and emissions that do not exhibit this relationship to national income.

A public-choice hypothesis posits that environmental regulation is influenced by producers rather than consumers. When domestic corporations compete with foreign corporations operating under lower environmental regulation, domestic corporations will use competitiveness as an argument against higher environmental standards or taxes. Seen in this way, an open economy puts pressure on national standard-setting that might not exist in a less open economy. Skeptics challenge this view by noting that less open economies do not have higher environmental standards. They also note a lack of evidence that lower environmental standards are an important factor attracting new corporate investment into polluter havens.

If governmental environment policies were perfect—that is, if government properly and successfully regulated pollution and resource overuse—then trade liberalization would enrich a country without adversely affecting the environment. In a world with imperfect environmental policies, however, trade liberalization can have either positive or negative effects. Trade economists do not deny this but suggest that the proper response is to seek both open trade and correct environmental policies. But this view ignores the way in which the competition to export can make it harder to set correct environmental policies. This is particularly so when environmental practices have transborder or global effects. For example, large timber-export profits can hinder domestic efforts to set appropriate forest conservation policy. Domestic subsidies on energy, water, coal, agriculture, and fisheries may support inefficient production, including production for export, which causes adverse environmental effects.

EFFECTS OF ENVIRONMENTAL POLICY ON TRADE

Changes in environmental policy affect supply and demand and thus international trade. For example, concern about global warming might decrease demand for carbon-based fuel and therefore reduce exports of coal; and the policies of the International Whaling Commission have nearly eliminated trade in whale products.

The issue of greatest interest to business groups is ecoprotection. This is the use of environmental laws and standards ostensibly to safeguard the environment, but in reality to protect domestic producers from foreign competition. There is no objective way to detect ecoprotection—it is in the eyes of a frustrated exporter. For example, a tax on beer cans in a country where domestic beer is typically produced in bottles might be viewed as unwarranted ecoprotection. When analysts have tried to evaluate ecoprotection, they have found it to amount to only a small percentage of regular protection implemented through tariffs and quotas.

Another way in which environmental practices affect trade is through ecolabels such as "Green Seal" (U.S.), "Blue Angel" (Germany) or "Ecomark" (Japan). Since labeling programs are typically national, there is a concern that criteria can be written so as to favor the products made domestically even though they may not be any more environmentally friendly than products made elsewhere. The growing tendency of labels to take a life-cycle approach—a method of identifying and assessing the environmental effects of products over their entire life cycle from extraction to processing, use and maintenance, to eventual disposal—raises even more concerns because labeling certifiers might not be fair in evaluating environmental practices in other countries.

EFFECTS OF TRADE RULES ON THE ENVIRONMENT

The General Agreement on Tariffs and Trade (GATT) was based on the principle that the imposition of tariffs would be acceptable government behavior if all GATT member nations were treated equally. In other words, a country could impose a tariff on widgets so long as it imposed it on all other signatories. Environmental policy makers can run afoul of trade rules because they care about where imports come from and how they are made. For example, if the import is fish and the fish in one country are caught using a driftnet and those in a second are not, environmental policy might seek to ban the fish from the first country but not from the second.

When a member of GATT objected to a trade barrier in another member country, it was able to lodge a complaint. Panels were then appointed to consider whether the barrier violated GATT rules. In the eight environment-related complaints considered by GATT from 1982 to 1994, panels found five of these measures to be in violation of GATT rules. Several of the cases focused on Article XX of GATT, which provides exceptions for measures "necessary to protect human, animal, or plant life or health" and for measures "relating to the conservation of exhaustible natural resources." The GATT panels interpreted these provisions strictly to deny their applicability to the environmental measures in dispute.

Under the World Trade Organization (WTO)—which succeeded GATT institutionally and incorporated most of its rules—trade-related environmental measures remain subject to challenge. In the first complaint to come before the WTO, the panel found that a United States Clean Air Act regulation violated trade rules. Unlike GATT, however, where compliance with panel reports was effectively voluntary, governments are now required to comply or face possible trade sanctions from the winning party. Following its loss at the WTO, the United States Environmental Protection Agency (EPA) changed its clean air regulation in an effort to comply with trade rules. EPA said it could do so without reducing air quality. Future conflicts may force losing governments to choose between adherence to trade rules and safeguarding their environment.

The power of the new WTO dispute settlement system is worrisome because panelists consider only international trade law, not international environmental law. Moreover, the panelists are typically trade bureaucrats or lawyers with little expertise in environmental regulation. Many environmentalists fear that a complaint will be filed about a trade measure used in a multilateral environmental agreement, and the ensuing adverse decision will undermine the agreement.

Trade measures are included in at least 26 multilateral environmental agreements. For example, the Convention on International Trade in Endangered Species of Wild Fauna and Flora forbids international trade for commercial purposes of species threatened with extinction. The Montreal Protocol on Substances that Deplete the Ozone Layer prohibits imports of controlled substances (such as chlorofluorocarbons), or products containing them, from nonparties (unless the nonparty country has been determined to be in compliance with the protocol). The Basel Convention on the Control of Transboundary Movements of Hazardous Wastes prohibits trade in waste products with nonparties (but allows bilateral arrangements with nonparties that do not derogate from the environmentally sound management required by the convention).

Under GATT Article XX interpretations propounded by recent panels, all of these trade measures might be found to violate GATT, particularly if the complaining country were not a party to the environmental treaty. So far, no complaint has been lodged. The removal of trade measures from environmental treaties would weaken the treaties. For example, the trade provisions in the Montreal Protocol prevent evasion of the Protocol's regulations.

In addition to reinforcing GATT rules with tough dispute settlement, the WTO also limits the ability of governments to use environmental policies to restrict trade. The Agreement on the Application of Sanitary and Phytosanitary Measures requires governments to justify food safety measures that apply to imports. The Agreement on Technical Barriers to Trade contains disciplines on product standards and labeling.

COORDINATION AMONG INSTITUTIONS

The most valuable feature of the trade and environment debate is that the two regimes have learned more about each other. Before 1991, environmental policy makers paid little attention to the trade effects of environmental regulation, and trade policy makers paid little attention to the tools of environmental regulators. Today, there is more mutual understanding and dialogue.

Because they were accustomed to open processes in the UN Environment Programme (UNEP), environmentalists were critical of the lack of transparency at GATT. In the early 1990s, many GATT documents were not publicly released. Panel decisions were not released to the public until after they were debated and approved by the GATT Council. This has now changed: the WTO is a more transparent institution than GATT was. Environmentalists and public interest groups deserve some of the credit for stimulating this reform.

The main institutional innovation for addressing trade and environment was the creation of a GATT/WTO Committee on Trade and Environment in 1994. So far the Committee has accomplished very little. The most critical defect of the committee is one that it shares with the WTO, namely, institutional insularity. Although it carries out joint activities with the UN Conference on Trade and Development, the WTO has made little effort to coordinate its work with other agencies such as UNEP, the International Labour Organization, and secretariats of multilateral environmental treaties. The WTO also continues to resist giving consultative status to nongovernmental organizations such as environment, development, business, and consumer groups.

One of the most salutary suggestions that has surfaced in the trade and environment debate is that proposed trade agreements should receive environmental impact assessments, and proposed environmental agreements should receive trade impact assessments. Despite the potential impact of the Uruguay Round on the environment, no such assessments were carried out before completion of the negotiations. A few governments drafted reports after the trade round, but they were descriptive rather than analytical.

REGIONAL AGREEMENTS

The coordination of trade and environment policy can also occur at the regional level. The increasing number of regional trade agreements offers opportunities for achieving multilateral linkage among like-minded countries. The first major effort to do this arose through negotiations for the North American Free Trade Agreement (NAFTA). Although NAFTA contains a few provisions related to the environment, the most significant development was the approval of the parallel North American Agreement on Environmental Cooperation. This Agreement set up a trinational commission (Canada, U.S., Mexico) to examine environmental protection throughout the region and to promote research and policy coordination. This commission's secretariat may investigate complaints from nongovernmental organizations that one of the parties is not enforcing its environmental laws. For example, several Canadian citizen groups petitioned the commission in April 1997, alleging that the Quebec government was failing to enforce agricultural pollution laws. In October 1999, the secretariat decided that the matter warranted the development of a "factual record." Canada opposes this step, however, and the three governments have withheld approval for any investigation.

The secretariat may also prepare reports on environmental problems. In 1994, about 40,000 birds died at the Silva Reservoir northwest of Mexico City. This triggered a successful request for the secretariat to sponsor an investigation. A panel of scientists found that the deaths were largely caused by botulism and made recommendations to the Mexican government for preventing such disasters.

Building on these NAFTA precedents, many environmental groups have proposed that ongoing regional trade negotiations—such as the Free Trade Area of the Americas and the Asia-Pacific Economic Cooperation Forum (APEC)—should include environmental negotiations. The proponents argue that these negotiations are already projected to be much broader than trade liberalization and should therefore not ignore the benefits of improving coordination of ecological and economic policy. The opponents of linkage worry that industrial countries will try to dictate higher environmental standards to developing countries in order to reduce their competitiveness. As in other forums of the trade and environment debate, the differing perspectives are being poorly integrated.

BIBLIOGRAPHY

Anderson, K., and R. Blackhurst, eds. *The Greening of World Trade Issues.* London: Harvester Wheatsheaf, 1992. The first book on trade and the environment; contains 12 articles mainly by economists.

Andersson, T., C. Folke, and S. Nyström. *Trading with the Environment: Ecology, Economics, Institutions, and Policy.* London: Earthscan, 1995. A survey of trade and environment issues by ecological economists.

Cameron, J., et al., eds. *Trade and the Environment: The Search for Balance.* 2 vols. London: Cameron May, 1994. Two volumes. Volume 1 contains 19 chapters by separate authors about different aspects of the debate. Volume 2 contains a wealth of source material.

Chang, H. F. "Carrots, Sticks, and International Externalities." *International Review of Law and Economics* 17 (1997), 309–324. Demonstrates the difficulty of a "carrots-only" approach to trade and environment bargaining. DOI: 10.1016/S0144–8188(97)00019–7.

Charnovitz, S. "A Critical Guide to the WTO's Report on Trade and Environment." *Arizona Journal of International and Comparative Law* 14 (1997), 342–379.

Copeland, B. R., and M. S. Taylor. *Trade and the Environment: Theory and Evidence.* Princeton, N.J., Princeton University Press, 2005.

Dua, A., and D. C. Esty. *Sustaining the Asia Pacific Miracle.* Washington, D.C.: Institute for International Economics, 1997. Discusses the environmental issues of Asia-Pacific economic integration.

Esty, D. C. *Greening the GATT.* Washington, D.C.: Institute for International Economics, 1994. A comprehensive review of legal and economic issues of the trade and environment debate

Gallagher, K. *Free Trade and the Environment: Mexico, NAFTA, and Beyond.* Stanford: Stanford Law and Politics, 2004.

International Institute for Sustainable Development. *The World Trade Organization and Sustainable Development: An Independent Assessment.* Winnipeg: International Institute for Sustainable Development, 1996.

Johnson, P. M., and A. Beaulieu. *The Environment and NAFTA.* Washington, D.C.: Island Press, 1996. A comprehensive review of NAFTA and the environment.

Organization for Economic Cooperation and Development. *The Environmental Effects of Trade.* Paris: Organization for Economic Cooperation and Development, 1994. A good survey chapter plus chapters on five sectors.

Sampson, G. P. *Trade, Environment and the Millennium.* New York and Tokyo: United Nations University Press, 2002.

Stone, C. D. "Too Many Fishing Boats, Too Few Fish: Can Trade Laws Trim Subsidies and Restore the Balance in Global Fisheries?" *Ecology Law Quarterly* 24 (1997), 505–544.

Tay, S., and D. C. Esty, eds. *Asian Dragons and Green Trade.* Singapore: Times Academic Press, 1996. Contains fourteen chapters by policy makers and leading analysts on trade and environment.

Webster, D. "The Looting and Smuggling and Fencing and Hoarding of Impossibly Precious, Feathered, and Scaly Wild Things." *New York Times Magazine,* February 16, 1997, 26. A good description of the endangered species trade.

—STEVE CHARNOVITZ

TRAGEDY OF THE COMMONS

Garrett Hardin is a biologist trained in genetics. His 1968 article, *Tragedy of the Commons,* is an appraisal of what he calls the population problem. He insists that technological solutions, such as improved agricultural methods, are inappropriate, and he questions the implicit assumption that people have the right to reproduce without restraint in a world of finite resources.

Hardin recognizes that—despite Adam Smith's famous pronouncement in *The Wealth of Nations*—individuals acting to further their own ends do not always advance the public good but instead deplete common resources. Hardin's best-known illustration, taken from an 1833 pamphlet by William Frank Lloyd, describes a common pasture, open to all and grazed by a number of herdsmen. Each herdsman realizes that any effects of overgrazing will be shared by all, while the benefits of a larger herd will be his alone, so each increases his own flock until a tragic destruction of the grazing land results.

Hardin applies the principle to cattlemen grazing in the southwestern United States, to saltwater fishing fleets, to tourists in national parks, and, of course, to individuals who choose to reproduce. He concludes that personal liberty cannot be respected if it threatens the common good: in today's world, regulations and incentives to modify behavior are appropriate and necessary.

[*See also* Commons; *and* Externalities.]

BIBLIOGRAPHY

Hardin, G. "The Tragedy of the Commons." *Science* 162 (1968), 1243–1248. DOI: 10.1126/science.162.3859.1243.

Lloyd, W. F. *Two Lectures on the Checks to Population*. Oxford: Oxford University Press, 1833. Reprinted in part in Hardin, G., *Population, Evolution, and Birth Control*. San Francisco: Freeman, 1964.

Smith, A. *The Wealth of Nations*. London: Ward, Lock, and Tyler, n.d. Originally published in 1776 as *An Inquiry into the Nature and Causes of the Wealth of Nations*.

—David J. Cuff

TRANSPORTATION

Transportation is the moving of people and goods by road, rail, ship, and aircraft. Road transport comprises nonmotorized modes, as well as light-duty vehicles, including automobiles, sport utility vehicles, minivans, small trucks, and two- and three-wheelers and heavy-duty vehicles (buses for mass transit and large trucks for moving freight). Transportation plays a vital role in economic activity and development; improved mobility both results from and enables economic development (WBCSD, 2001). Per capita income is increasing around the world, enabling people to seek a better quality of life, and globalization is shrinking the effective size of the world, playing an important role in the increased demand for movement of goods and people.

In the United States, for example, total transportation-related consumer demand rose by 37% between 1990 and 2001 (in 1996 chained dollars, a measure used to relate buying power to the reference year) from $719.8 billion to $984.1 billion (Bureau of Transport Statistics, 2003). Projections indicate that growth will continue to be strong, driven primarily by continued population growth and rising incomes in developing countries (WBCSD, 2004). Transportation-petroleum demand is forecast to grow an average of 1.4% per year to 2030. This estimate varies by region and by level of economic development. For instance, in OECD (Organisation for Economic Co-operation and Development) countries, projected growth is only 0.8% per year, while in non-OECD countries it is 2.3% per year (EIA, 2006). This growth in travel demand has serious implications for a range of socioeconomic and environmental issues, including climate change and oil demand at a global scale, regional issues such as infrastructure needs, and air pollution, health impacts, safety, equity, traffic congestion, and noise at a local level.

MODES

As increased per capita income fuels growth in transport demand, it also leads to changes in the modes of transport. Automobiles are the dominant mode of passenger transport particularly in the industrialized world. Similarly, in the developing world, light-duty vehicles are the fastest growing mode of transport. The world's transport infrastructure capacity reflects the dominance of automotive transport: there are more than 30 million kilometers of roadways in the world, compared to roughly one million kilometers of railway and fewer than 700,000 km of inland waterway (CIA, 2007).

In developing countries, bicycles, pedestrians, animals, and buses remain important forms of transport, but as incomes rise, people tend to prefer faster modes, particularly personal motorized vehicles. In China, for instance, public transit makes up approximately 50% of urban transportation, while cycling and walking account for another 40% roughly (Ng and Schipper, 2005), but faster modes of transport are increasing. Around the world, the faster the mode of transport, the greater increase in passengers it has seen over the past 50 years (WBCSD, 2001). The number of travelers using the fastest modes—air and high-speed train—has been increasing recently, and these modes could increase to 20 times the 2000 levels by midcentury (DeCicco and Greene, 2000).

TRENDS

The growth in transport has been accompanied by distinctive trends in population growth and distribution, and in the consumer preferences of an increasingly affluent population.

Population growth

Transportation demand has increased steadily as the world's population has continued to grow. At the start of the twentieth century, global population stood at 1.7 billion, by midcentury it had grown to 2.5 billion, by 2000 it had more than doubled to 6.1 billion, and by the first decade of the twenty-first century it was over 6.6 billion (CIA, 2007). This rapid population expansion has resulted in a corresponding increase in the demand for mobility and transportation.

Per capita incomes have also been increasing globally. GDP per capita (in current international dollars) increased over 200% in the 25 years from less than $3,000 in 1980 to more than $9,500 in 2005 (World Bank).

Urbanization and suburbanization

The trend toward increased urbanization around the world is contributing to the increased demand for transportation services. Urban populations have grown from 1.7 billion in 1980 to 3.1 billion in 2005. By 2025, 58% of the world's population will live in urban areas, as opposed to 45% in 1995 (UNUP). This trend is particularly dramatic in the developing world, as urbanites have increased from 18% of developing-country populations in 1950 to nearly 40% by 2000 and are projected to increase to 56% by 2030 (see Figure 1).

As people increasingly move to growing megacities, there is a simultaneous trend toward decreasing population density, meaning large cities today are increasingly spread across larger areas than was the case historically. The modernization of the transportation sector has facilitated this trend, which has, in turn, created greater demand for modern transportation. In many parts of the world, faster transportation has enabled people to extend the distance of their commutes without simultaneously increasing the time they spend traveling, making the prospect of moving to the suburbs much more attractive.

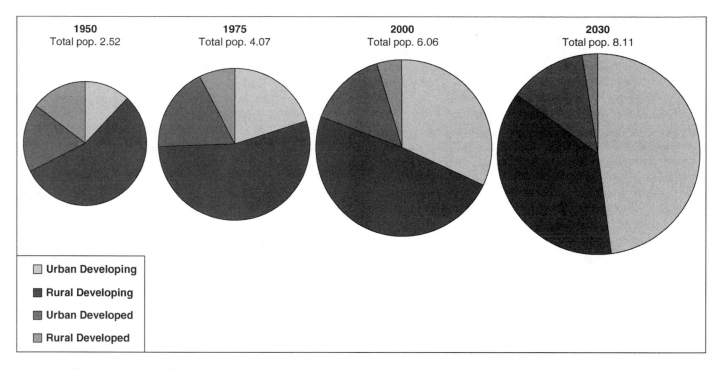

Urban Developing

Rural Developing

Urban Developed

Rural Developed

Transportation. Figure 1. World Population Growth, 1950–2030 (billions of people).

(Source: WBCSD, 2001, from UN World Urbanization Prospects, 1999 Revision.)

Consumer preferences

As incomes rise, people travel further, but there is very little variation around the world in the amount of time people spend traveling per day (WBCSD, 2001). As people's incomes increase and they choose to travel greater distances, they tend to switch modes, selecting faster forms of transportation. The longer distances are therefore covered in the same amount of time, or less. These faster modes, however, are generally more energy intensive: using a motor vehicle requires more energy per passenger-kilometer than walking or biking, and taking an airplane requires more than driving a car.

The popularity of the personal vehicle continues to drive increasing oil consumption and greenhouse-gas emissions from the transport sector. Demand growth in the industrialized world remains strong, but it is mainly developing countries like China and India that are driving the growth of transport demand worldwide (see Figure 2). The rise of middle-class consumers in rapidly developing countries has led to increasing demand for personalized transport options. Less than 25 years ago, for instance, China's streets were crowded with bicycles, but the past decade has witnessed the boom of private-vehicle ownership. Between 2001 and 2006, the Chinese automotive fleet grew by 4.83 million and, even with this enlarged base, growth-rate projections remain around 15% for 2007 and 2008 (Global Insight). Automobile ownership in China is still relatively low: in 2003 there were 10 passenger cars per 1,000 people (WRI), compared to 468 per 1,000 in the European Union (2003 data from UNEOE, 2006) and 815 in the U.S. (ORNL, 2005). While this discrepancy is

large, China actually has more cars relative to income than the U.S. did when it had China's 2007 per capita income, in about 1920 (Ng and Schipper, 2005). With economic growth at 10% per year, China is narrowing the gap in automobiles and total motor vehicles per capita. In China today a new car is sold every six seconds, and vehicle ownership is a status symbol. This is true throughout the world and is unlikely to change dramatically in the near future. According to the World Bank, vehicle ownership is rising 15 to 20% per year in much of the developing world (WRI).

As more people around the world reach the middle class and aspire to own a personal vehicle, they will also increasingly experience the problems associated with personal-vehicle use, such as air and noise pollution, traffic congestion, traffic fatalities, oil insecurity and GHG emissions.

Transportation. Figure 2. Predicted Growth in Number of Passenger Vehicles (millions) 2000–2050.

(Source: Institute for Transportation & Development Policy, 2007, from IEA/SMP 2004 data.)

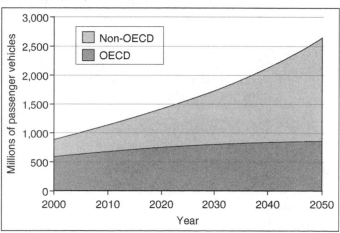

CHALLENGES

The growth in transport demand, particularly in developing countries, poses problems that policy makers must manage; these problems range from planning and logistical issues to longer-term implications such as oil insecurity and climate change.

Congestion

Traffic congestion is increasing as more private vehicles come onto the roadways, and clogged transportation systems struggle to keep pace because of underinvestment, land availability constraints, and other limiting factors. Congestion is not only a nuisance but also poses serious risks to safety and health and imposes a significant economic cost through the inefficiency caused by gridlock.

Safety

Traffic fatalities and safety issues are a primary concern. According to the World Health Organization, traffic injuries are the leading cause of death for people ages 10 to 24 around the world (Brown, 2007), and every year more than one million people die as a result of injuries sustained in road accidents. According to the World Bank, developing countries are disproportionately affected, accounting for roughly 70% of these deaths. As traffic safety in developed countries is improved by regulations and technology improvements, safety in developing countries is declining as more cars and buses enter already taxed infrastructure systems.

From 1980 to 2003, the number of deaths in traffic accidents in the 25-member European Union (EU-25) declined by nearly half to 39,000 per year, and when set against the growth in the number of vehicles on the road, this decline is even more impressive: 557 deaths per million vehicles in 1980 to 193 in 2003. Traffic fatalities per million vehicles have similarly declined in the U.S., from 320 in 1980 to 164 in 2003 (UNEOE, 2006). In developing countries, on the other hand, transport-related fatalities are increasing as access to transport options grows. The populations that are least able to afford access to modern transport modes are most likely to be injured or killed in accidents involving automobiles. For instance, in a collision between a rickshaw or a pedestrian and an automobile, the rickshaw driver and the pedestrian face a much higher risk than the driver of the automobile.

Pollution

Pollutants produced during the combustion of fuel for transport (primarily gasoline and diesel) are environmentally harmful. Pollutants include carbon monoxide (CO), nitrogen oxides (NO_x), particulate matter (PM), sulfur dioxide (SO_2), ammonia (NH_3), volatile organic compounds (VOCs), and air-borne toxins (e.g., lead). These pollutants cause smog in cities and affect the health of the exposed population (e.g., asthma, reduced pulmonary function, cancer). These impacts are particularly severe in densely populated cities, where exposure to these pollutants is higher, and in developing countries, where many people live and work alongside heavily traveled thoroughfares (Ng and Schipper, 2005).

Transport infrastructure (e.g., highways, harbors, airports) also causes damage to surrounding ecosystems in other ways. Vast networks of roads crossing the countryside bring mobility and access to isolated areas, but these roads and the vehicles that use them damage habitats and ecosystems, fragmenting areas ecologically and causing increased runoff and associated erosion. Water-based transportation causes its own problems, as by requiring dredging to enlarge waterways.

An important contribution to pollution in Asia is the tens of millions of two-stroke two- and three-wheeled vehicles running on gasoline with almost no emissions controls. While these are slowly being replaced by vehicles with cleaner (and larger) four-stroke engines, they still contribute significantly to congestion and high levels of fatal accidents. These vehicles give their riders low-cost individual mobility but impose high costs on society as a whole.

Noise pollution

Motorized transport causes noise pollution, from tire-road contact and engines and exhaust systems in road transport to more intrusive noise from freight trains and aircraft (WBCSD, 2001/2004). While technological advances during the past 30 years have reduced noise pollution from vehicles, it remains a significant problem in urban areas, decreasing quality of life and limiting the expansion of these systems (because of public resistance).

Energy security

Given the dominance of road transport over the other modes, and our reliance on the internal combustion engine in vehicles, today's transport sector is dominated by oil. Ninety-six percent of the energy in the transport sector comes from oil (Baumert et al., 2005). In fact, transport is the dominant sector in terms of oil consumption: it has accounted for nearly the entire growth in the use of oil over the past 30 years, and this trend is expected to continue (Fulton, 2004). Natural gas, biomass, and coal are also used as transportation fuels, but to a far smaller degree. This preponderance of petroleum-based fuels is largely the result of the cost-advantage oil-producers have over their rivals, given the huge scale (tens of millions of barrels of oil products a day used in transportation worldwide). This nearly complete reliance on oil for transport is the primary cause of rising concerns about energy security in oil-importing countries.

Domestic oil production is in decline especially in OECD countries, which have historically been important providers. The EIA estimates that while non-OPEC production will grow through 2030, OPEC countries will be responsible for more than half of the increased production in that period. OECD production in the North Sea is expected to decline more rapidly than previously estimated: production in Norway, OECD's largest producer, appears to have peaked in 2001 at 3.4 million barrels per day, and U.K. production peaked in 1999. Production from these countries is projected to continue to decline (EIA, 2006). In the absence of a viable alternative at the scale required, increasing domestic demand coupled with decreasing domestic supply means rising oil imports.

With oil prices over U.S.$100 per barrel—primarily because of tight spare capacity in producing countries, uncertainties in the market, and the declining value of the dollar—imports lead to balance-of-payment concerns in importing countries, as well as concerns about revenue distribution within exporting countries. Estimates place the cost to the U.S. of the instability in the global oil market from 1970 to 2000 at approximately $7 trillion (1998 dollars present value; Greene and Tishchishyna, 2000).

CO_2 emissions

As climate change increasingly worries policy makers and the public around the world, the transport sector is recognized as as a major contributor to the problem. Transport accounts for roughly 14% of global greenhouse-gas (GHG) emissions (Baumert et al., 2005) and 20% of global CO_2 emissions (WRI, CAIT), and it is the sector with the fastest-growing emissions. From 1980 to 2003, world emissions from transport increased by 80%, equivalent to an average annual growth rate of 2.7% (Baumert et al., 2005) (Figure 3). Estimates suggest that global emissions from transport will continue to increase at an average annual growth rate of 1.7% through 2030 (IEA, 2006).

Within the transport sector, the majority of emissions come from road transport (72% of the sector and 10% of global GHG emissions in 2004). Passenger cars and light-duty vehicles in the U.S. emit more than 5 metric tons of CO_2 equivalent per vehicle per year (EPA, 2003), while vehicles in the EU and Japan emit only about half as much. Nonetheless, with over 800 million vehicles on the roads, traveling anywhere from 1,000 km to over 24,000 km per year (depending largely on geography), road-transport emissions contribute substantially to climate-change concerns (Webber, 2005).

With its driving habits, the U.S. continues to be a leader in global transport-sector emissions, accounting for 35% of global emissions from transport in 2003. The U.S. ranks highest in yearly emissions from transport with per capita emissions from transport of 6.2 tons of CO_2 (per person), of which around half is from cars and household light trucks and SUVs. The nearest competitors in the rankings drop off quickly: the EU-25 and

TABLE 1. GHG Emissions from Transport: Top 25, 2003

Country	$MtCO_2$	% of World Total	Tons CO_2 Per Person
United States of America	1794.00	35.02%	6.2
European Union (25)	920.00	17.96%	2
China	267.30	5.22%	0.2
Japan	250.10	4.88%	2
Russian Federation	193.50	3.78%	1.3
Germany	162.40	3.17%	2
Canada	153.20	2.99%	4.8
France	138.60	2.71%	2.3
United Kingdom	133.40	2.61%	2.2
Brazil	125.40	2.45%	0.7
Italy	117.80	2.30%	2
Mexico	113.30	2.21%	1.1
Spain	103.20	2.01%	2.5
Korea (South)	98.00	1.91%	2
India	94.70	1.85%	0.1
Iran	87.60	1.71%	1.3
Australia	77.90	1.52%	3.9
Indonesia	69.60	1.36%	0.3
Saudi Arabia	63.50	1.24%	2.7
Thailand	50.70	0.99%	0.8
South Africa	39.80	0.78%	0.9
Malaysia	36.60	0.71%	1.5

SOURCE: WRI, CAIT, 2007.

Transportation. FIGURE 3. CO_2 Emissions from Transportation Indexed to Each Region's Respective 1980 Values (1980–2003).

(Source: WRI, Climate Analysis Indicators Tool (CAIT), 2006.)

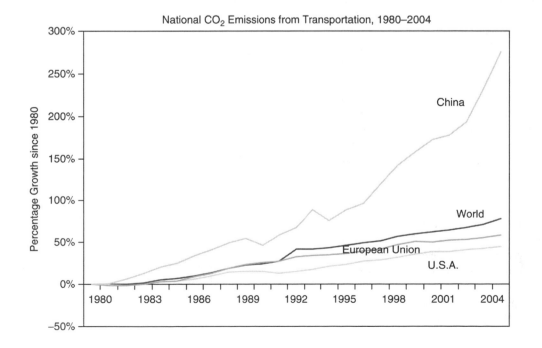

National CO_2 Emissions from Transportation, 1980–2004

China accounted for only 18% and 5.2% of global transport sector emissions respectively, with only 2 and 0.2 tons CO_2 per person, and only 10% of that from automobiles (see Table 1). However, Chinese growth in the sector is outpacing U.S. growth—increasing by 13% between 2002 to 2003, for instance, while the U.S. transport emissions growth rate hovers around 2%, growth rates close to the historical rates for the two countries. Estimates vary, but the Netherlands Environmental Assessment Agency reported in June 2007 that China's total emissions have already surpassed those of the U.S. Given the sheer size of China's population and the country's rapid economic growth, and despite the fact that vehicle miles traveled remain low, China's transport emissions will not long lag behind those of the U.S if Chinese consumers continue to aspire to personal vehicle ownership.

OUTLOOK

As demand for transport continues to grow throughout the world, proliferating transport-related impacts and challenges become increasingly difficult to manage. The technologies and policy tools that will be employed to manage this growing demand and the associated challenges will become increasingly important. Policy makers will need to act quickly to avoid some of the worst impacts of the transport boom in developing countries and to avoid locking in technologies and travel patterns because of the substantial investment they require. Where technologies and systems are already established and entrenched by earlier policy and investment decisions in developed countries, policy makers need to take every effort to lessen the impact of transport systems.

As vehicles are likely to supply a substantial portion of transport demand well into the future, improvements in vehicle technology must be a priority. Vehicle technology improvements can increase the efficiency and cleanliness with which engines use fuel, reducing concerns over oil security and emissions. Alternative fuels can also be used to reduce oil consumption and its associated impacts.

Improvements in technological and system-wide efficiencies will be vital to minimizing the damage, and the growth of demand must be managed and minimized. Policy solutions such as surcharges for vehicle ownership, parking, and congestion are effective demand-side management measures. Efficient, safe, and clean public rapid transit will reduce demand further and avoid many of the challenges associated with individual vehicles. As Fulton et al. (2002) point out, while improvements in emissions controls and fuel quality reduce harmful pollutant emissions, increasing the size of buses and increasing their attractiveness to passengers reduce pollution per passenger-kilometer, while increasing revenue in the system. So while cleaner vehicles are important, they should not be used as substitutes for improved system performance as a whole: clean but empty buses stuck in traffic provide no transport service and save no energy and emissions.

Given the scale of the transport sector and the rapid increase in demand forecast for the coming years, some combination of all of the policies, measures, and technologies available will be needed to manage the growth and minimize the impact.

BIBLIOGRAPHY

Baumert, K., T. Herzog, and J. Pershing. *Navigating the Numbers: Greenhouse Gas Data and International Climate Policy.* Washington, D.C.: World Resources Institute, 2005.

Brown, D. "Traffic Deaths a Global Scourge, Health Agency Says." *Washington Post,* April 20, 2007. Page A09. http://www.washingtonpost.com/wp-dyn/content/article/2007/04/19/AR2007041902409.html (accessed June 6, 2008).

Bureau of Transportation Statistics. *Transportation Statistics Annual Report.* Oct., 2003. http://www.bts.gov/publications/transportation_statistics_annual_report/2003/ (accessed June 6, 2008).

Central Intelligence Agency (CIA). *The World Fact Book.* 2007. https://www.cia.gov/library/publications/the-world-factbook/ (accessed June 6, 2008).

DeCicco, J. M., and D. L. Greene. *Energy and Transportation Beyond 2000.* http://onlinepubs.trb.org/onlinepubs/millennium/00032.pdf (accessed June 6, 2008).

Eads, G. C. *Worldwide Demand for Mobility and Petroleum.* Presentation to the "Modeling the Oil Transition" Workshop. Washington, D.C.: April 20–21, 2006.

Energy Information Administration (EIA). *International Energy Outlook 2006.* EIA, 2006.

EPA. *U.S. Inventory of Greenhouse Gas Emissions and Sinks 1990–2001.* Office of Atmospheric Programs, U.S. Environmental Protection Agency 430-R-03–004. Washington, D.C.: EPA, 2003.

Fulton, L. *Reducing Oil Consumption in Transport.* Paris: IEA/OECD, 2004.

Fulton, L., et al. *Bus Systems for the Future: Achieving Sustainable Transport Worldwide.* Paris: International Energy Agency, 2002.

Global Insight. *Outlook Still Buoyant for Chinese Auto Market Despite Lower 2007 and 2008 Growth Forecasts.* http://www.globalinsight.com/SDA/SDADetail9307.htm (accessed June 7, 2008).

Greene, D. L., and N. I. Tischishyna. *Costs of Oil Dependence: A 2000 Update.* Oak Ridge National Laboratory, 2000.

Institute for Transportation & Development Policy. *Bus Rapid Transit: Planning Guide.* 3d ed. New York: ITDP, 2007.

International Energy Agency (IEA). *World Energy Outlook 2006.* Paris: International Energy Agency, 2006.

IPIECA. Workshop Summary Brochure. *Transportation and Climate Change: Opportunities, Challenges and Long-term Strategies.* October, 2004.

Nakanishi, N. "China Slows Coal-Liquids Push on Water Fear." *Reuters Energy Weekly,* June 18–22, 2007.

Ng, W.-S., and L. Schipper. "China Motorization Trends: Policy Options in a World of Transport Challenges." In *Growing in the Greenhouse: Protecting the Climate by Putting Development First,* edited by K. A. Baumert and R. Bradley. Washington, D.C.: World Resources Institute, 2005.

Oak Ridge National Laboratory (ORNL). *Transportation Energy Data Book: Edition 24.* Figure 3.1. Oak Ridge, Tenn.: ORNL, 2005.

United Nations Economic Commission for Europe (UNEOE). *Handbook of Transportation Statistics in the UNECE Region 2006.* New York and Geneva: United Nations, 2006.

UNUP (Population Division of the Department of Economic and Social Affairs of the United Nations Secretariat). *World Population Prospects: The 2004 Revision and World Urbanization Prospects; The 2005 Revision.* http://esa.un.org/unup. (accessed June 7, 2008).

Webber, F. *Statement of the Alliance of Automobile Manufacturers before the Commerce, Science, and Transportation Committee of the U.S. Senate.* November 15, 2005.

World Bank. *Road Safety.* www.worldbank.org/transport/roads/safety.htm (accessed June 7, 2008).

World Business Council for Sustainable Development (WBCSD). *Mobility 2001: World Mobility at the End of the Twentieth Century and Its Sustainability.* Massachusetts Institute of Technology and Charles River Associated Incorporated, 2001.

———. *Mobility 2030: Meeting the Challenges to Sustainability.* 2004.

World Resources Institute (WRI). *EarthTrends.* http://earthtrends.wri.org. (accessed June 7, 2008).

World Resources Institute (WRI). *Climate Analysis Indicators Tool (CAIT).* http://cait.wri.org (accessed June 7, 2008).

—BRITT CHILDS STALEY

TREE RINGS

See Dendrochronology.

TROPICAL CLIMATE CHANGE

The lower latitudes have not been immune to the many changes that affected higher and middle latitudes during the Quaternary. Tropical lakes, deserts, river and slope systems (Thomas et al., 2007), and forests display abundant evidence of major environmental swings, with conditions having been both wetter and drier than the present. The wet phases are termed pluvials, while the drier phases are called interpluvials.

THE ANTIQUITY OF DESERTS

Many of our present deserts are old (Goudie, 2002), especially the Namib and Atacama coastal deserts. Their climatic development was closely related to plate tectonics in that the degree of aridity must have been largely controlled by the opening of the seaways of the Southern Ocean, the location of Antarctica with respect to the South Pole, and the development of the offshore, cold Benguela and Peruvian currents. Arid conditions appear to have existed in the Namib for some tens of millions of years (Ward, 1988). Likewise the Atacama appears to have been predominantly arid since the late Eocene and possibly since the Triassic (Clarke, 2006), and hyperarid since the middle to late Miocene.

Latitudinal shifts caused by continental drift led to moist conditions in India and Australia during much of the Tertiary, but they entered latitudes where conditions were more arid in the late Tertiary. In China, Miocene uplift and a resulting transformation of the monsoonal circulation caused aridification. The eolian red clays and loess of China may have started to form around 7.2–8.5 million years ago (Qiang et al., 2001). Off the Sahara, sediment cores from the Atlantic contain dust-derived silt that indicates that a well-developed arid area, producing dust storms, existed in North Africa in the early Miocene, around 20 million years ago (Diester-Haass and Schrader, 1979). Schuster et al. (2006) have argued that the onset of recurrent desert conditions in the Sahara started 7 million years ago, with dune deposits accumulating in the Chad basin from that time.

In many regions aridity intensified in the late Pliocene and Pleistocene. DeMenocal (1995) recognized accelerated dust loadings in ocean cores off the Sahara and Arabia after 2.8 million years and attributed this to decreased sea-surface temperatures associated with the initiation of extensive Northern Hemisphere glaciation. Likewise, loess deposition accelerated in China after 2.5 million years ago (Ding et al., 1992).

ANCIENT SAND SEAS

One of the best ways to assess the former extent of Pleistocene deserts during interpluvials is by studying the former extent of major sand seas (dune fields) as evidenced by fossil forms which are often visible on air or satellite photographs. Optical dating is making it increasingly feasible to estimate the ages of periods of dune formation. Features like deep-weathering, intense iron-oxide staining, soil development, calcification, stabilization by vegetation, gully incision by fluvial action, and general degradation indicate that some dunes are fossil rather than active. Sometimes archaeological evidence can be used to show that sand deposition is no longer progressing, while elsewhere dunes have been found to be flooded by lakes, to have had lacustrine clays deposited in interdune depressions, and to have had lake shorelines etched on their flanks.

Sand movement only takes place over wide areas while there is a limited vegetation cover, though small parabolic (hairpin) dunes are probably more tolerant in this respect than the more massive seifs (linear) and barchans (crescentic). Sediment availability is also an important factor in determining dune mobility. It is therefore difficult to establish precisely the rainfall limits to dune development. Nevertheless, studies where dunes are currently moving and developing suggest that vegetation becomes effective in restricting dune movement only where annual precipitation exceeds 100–300 mm. (These figures apply to warm inland areas.)

The extent of old dune-fields compared with currently active dune-fields emphasizes the marked changes in vegetation and rainfall conditions that have taken place in many parts of the tropics, this despite the fact that decreased Pleistocene glacial temperatures would have led to reduced evapotranspiration rates and thus to increased vegetation cover. This would, if anything, have promoted dune immobilization. Dune movement might, however, have been accelerated by apparently higher trade-wind velocities during glacials (Wasson, 1984).

Reviewing such evidence from the different continents, Sarnthein mapped the world distribution of ancient and modern sand seas and summarized the situation (1978, p. 43):

> Today about 10% of the land area between 30°N and 30°S is covered by active sand deserts. Sand dunes and associated deserts were much more widespread 18,000 years ago than they are today. They characterized almost 50% of the land area between 30°N and 30°S forming two vast belts. In between, tropical rainforests and adjacent savannahs were reduced to a narrow corridor, in places only a few degrees of latitude wide.

Fossil dunes have been identified in northwestern India (Goudie et al., 1973) and in southern Africa, where the Kalahari is dominantly a fossil desert, now covered by a dense mixture of woodland, grassland, and shrubs. Relict dunes are widespread in Botswana, Angola, Zimbabwe, and Zambia (Thomas and Shaw, 1991) and may well extend as far north as the Congo rainforest. North of the Equator, the fossil-dune fields extend south into the savannah and forest zones of West Africa. The "Ancient Erg of Hausaland" (present-day northern Nigeria; Grove, 1958) extends into a zone where present annual rainfall is as high as 1,000 mm. Further east, in Sudan, fixed dunes (*qoz, quz, qawz*) extend as far south as 10°N and merge to the north with mobile dunes at about 16°N. They crossed the Nile, which was probably dried up at the time of their formation (Grove and Warren, 1968).

Fossil dune-fields have also been recognized in the U.S., notably in Nebraska and elsewhere in the High Plains. In South America, Tricart (1974) identified an ancient erg in the Llanos, where dunes, partly fossilized by Holocene alluvium, extend southwards as far as latitudes 5°20'N. Recent studies of late Pleistocene dunes in northern Amazonia and the Roraima-Guyana region include that of Latrubesse and Nelson (2001). Another erg was in the valley of the São Francisco River in Bahia State, Brazil. In addition it is likely that eolian activity was also much more extensive in the Pantanal and in the Pampas and other parts of Argentina (Tripaldi and Forman, 2007). In Australia, fossil dunes associated with a counterclockwise continental atmospheric circulation are developed over wide areas (Nanson et al., 1995). Their great extent has been mapped by Wasson et al. (1988).

PLUVIAL LAKES

Pluvial lakes are extinct or remnant bodies of water that accumulated in basins during times of greater moisture availability resulting from changes in temperature and/or precipitation.

During the Pleistocene, the Great Basin of the western U.S. held some 80 pluvial lakes that covered an area at least 11 times greater than they cover today. Lake Bonneville was the largest of the late Pleistocene lakes and was roughly the size of present-day Lake Michigan. It was the predecessor to the now modest Great Salt Lake of Utah. Lake Lahontan was more complicated in form, covered 23,000 km², and reached a depth of about 280 m. It was nearly as extensive as present-day Lake Erie. River courses became linked up, and lakes overflowed from one subbasin to another. For example, the Mojave River drainage, the largest arid fluvial system in the Mojave Desert, fed at least four basins and their lakes (Tchakerian and Lancaster, 2001). The eastern California lake cascade comprises a series of lakes which with sufficient discharge during the Quaternary may have linked up to an eventual sump below sea level in Death Valley. Smith and Street-Perrott (1983) demonstrated that many basins had particularly high stands during the period roughly contemporaneous with the Late Glacial Maximum (LGM), between about 25,000 and 10,000 years ago. Those high levels may have resulted from a combination of factors, including lower temperatures and evaporation rates, and reduced precipitation. Pacific storms associated with the southerly branch of the polar jet stream followed tracks south of those taken by present-day storms.

Pluvial lakes also existed in the Atacama and Altiplano of South America (Lavenu et al., 1984). The morphological evidence for high lake stands is impressive, especially the algal accumulations at high levels above the present saline crusts of depressions like that of Uyuni in southwestern Bolivia (Rouchy et al., 1996).

In the Sahara there are huge numbers of pluvial lakes in the chotts (shallow saline lakes) of Tunisia and Algeria, in Libya (e.g., Lake Mega-Fezzan) (White and Mattingly, 2006), in Mali (Petit-Maire et al., 1999) and in the south (e.g., Mega-Chad, which covered some 350,000 km²) (Leblanc et al., 2006). In the Western Desert of Egypt and the Sudan there are many closed depressions, relict river systems, and abundant evidence of prehistoric human activity (Hoelzmann et al., 2001). Lake sediments indicate that the depressions once contained substantial bodies of water which would have attracted Neolithic settlers. Many of these sediments have now been dated and indicate the

existence of an early to mid-Holocene wet phase, the Neolithic pluvial. A large lake, the West Nubian Palaeolake, formed in the far northwest of Sudan, (Hoelzmann et al., 2001). The record of flow variations is preserved in Nile submarine-fan deposits. In East Africa, the rift valleys are occupied by numerous lakes surrounded by raised Quaternary shorelines. Evidence for the timing of fluctuations across the East African region is relatively uniform. Between 30,000 and 22,000 BP lake levels tended to be high. During the LGM levels fell—Lake Tanganyika was about 350 m lower than present—and some basins dried up, including Lakes Victoria and Albert. The former began to refill around 14,700 years ago and did not achieve open-basin status until about 11,200, when the Victoria Nile was formed (Johnson et al., 1996). Many lakes record a transitional phase between 12,500 and 10,000 BP coinciding with the Younger Dryas in the Northern Hemisphere. Lake levels were high during the early to mid-Holocene period, although there is evidence for some abrupt, short-lived lake-lowering events during this period, for example at 8,200 BP (Gasse, 2000). From 5,000 BP lake levels have generally fallen. In southern Africa, Lake Paleo-Makgadikgadi, now marked by a large salt basin in Botswana, encompassed a substantial part of northern Kalahari. It was over 50 m deep and covered 120,000 km², vastly greater than the present area of Lake Victoria (68,800 km²). This makes Paleo-Makgadikgadi second in size in Africa to Lake Chad at its Quaternary maximum.

In the Middle East, maximum lake levels for the last glacial were achieved at about 25,000 BP (Robinson et al., 2006). In Lake Lisan (the precursor of the Dead Sea), a major lowering was recorded at 24,000 BP. During the LGM, lake levels were generally high but were falling during peak LGM conditions with an increase in regional aridity. Lake levels rose around 15,000 BP with a high stand recorded in Lake Lisan at 13,000 BP. During the Younger Dryas, levels fell, with substantial salt deposition occurring between 13,200 and 11,400 BP. During the Holocene there was a high stand at 8,500 BP followed by lower levels. Also in the Middle East, expanded lakes occurred in the currently arid Rub' al-Khali and in Anatolia (Roberts, 1983; Wood and Imes, 1995). In Central Asia the Caspian Sea expanded. At several times during the late Pleistocene its level rose to around 0 m (present global sea level) compared to -27 m today, and it inundated a huge area, particularly to its north. Earlier it was even more extensive, rising to about 50 m above sea level, linking up to the Aral, extending some 1,300 km up the Volga from its present mouth and covering an area greater than 1.1 million km² (compared to 400,000 km² today).

Large pluvial lakes occurred in the drylands and highlands of China and Tibet, from 40,000 to 25,000 BP (Li and Zhu, 2001). The interior basins of Australia, including Lake Eyre, have likewise shown major expansions and contractions, with high stands tending to occur in interglacials (Harrison, 1993). Generally wetter conditions between 30,000 and 24,000 BP prevailed followed by general aridity at the glacial maximum until 12,000 BP. During the early to mid-Holocene, lake levels rose again.

These regional examples indicate that pluvial lakes were widespread (even in hyperarid areas), reached enormous dimensions, and had different histories in different areas. In general, dry conditions during and just after the LGM and humid conditions during part of the Early to Mid Holocene appear to have been characteristic of tropical regions, though not of the southwestern U.S.

SAPROPELS

Sapropels, organic-rich mud layers in the eastern Mediterranean, were created by enhanced flow of the Nile, which caused the collapse of deep-water ventilation and/or the elevated supply of nutrients, which in turn fuelled enhanced productivity and anoxic conditions (Scrivner et al., 2004). Their development appears to have coincided systematically with Northern Hemisphere insolation maxima related to the orbital cycle of precession, which intensified the African monsoon (Tuenter et al., 2003). Ethiopian rivers, fed by strong summer monsoon rains generated a strong seasonal flood in the Nile (Rossignol-Strick, 1985).

Eleven sapropel events have occurred during the last 465,000 years: while most occurred during interglacials, two formed during glacial periods. Sapropel 1 belongs to Oxygen Isotope Stage (OIS) 1 (the Holocene). It started at about 9,000 BP and ended after about 6,000 years BP and like earlier sapropels, was caused by a massive input of freshwater from the Nile (Freydier et al., 2001), though it was not as intense as Sapropel 5 (Scrivner et al., 2004). Sapropels 3–5 belong to OIS 5 (Last Interglacial), Sapropel 6 occurs within OIS 6 (Masson et al., 2000), Sapropels 7–9 within OIS 7, Sapropel 10 in OIS9, Sapropel 11 in OIS 11, and Sapropel 12 in OIS 12. Sapropels 6 and 8 occurred during colder, drier phases. Although these were cold times, they were still times of higher Northern Hemisphere summer insolation.

FAUNAL AND FLORAL CHANGES IN THE TROPICS

The massive environmental changes described so far led to changes in floral and fauna distribution in the tropics. The substantial degree of change in the altitudinal zonation of vegetation on tropical mountains during cold phases can be demonstrated from the highlands of Latin America, Africa, southwestern Asia and the West Pacific. Analysis of pollen from numerous lakes and swamps (Flenley, 1998) shows that over the last 30,000 years the major vegetation zones have moved through as much as 1,700 m. The boundary between the forest and the alpine zone above it was low before 30,000 BP, showed a slight peak (of uncertain height and imprecise date) between 30,000 and 25,000 BP, reached an especially low point at 18,000 to 15,000 BP (more or less equivalent to the LGM), showed a steep climb as climate ameliorated between 14,000 and 9,000 BP, and reached modern altitudes or slightly above them by about 7,000 BP.

In the 1960s and 1970s it was believed that severe reductions in the extent of the Amazonian rainforest might have had major implications for fauna and flora. In particular, the "refugia hypothesis" suggested that the breaking up of the rainforest into small patches in a sea of savanna might have caused endemism, thereby helping to explain the great biodiversity of the region (Van der Hammen and Hooghiemstra, 2000).

However, the postulated explanation of species diversity in Amazonia by means of the forest refugia hypothesis is controversial. In particular, Colinvaux (1987) has argued that there is little convincing evidence for marked precipitation diminution in Amazonia in the Pleistocene, and he believes that a more likely cause of the species diversity is ongoing geomorphological disturbance and fire in an area which is far from homogeneous.

The extent to which Amazonia dried up at the LGM is hotly debated. Some argue on the basis of geomorphological evidence—such as aeolian dunes and changes in river sedimentology—for sharply reduced moisture conditions (e.g., Filho et al, 2002; Latrubesse and Nelson, 2001). They have been supported by some paleoecologists (e.g., van der Hammen and Hooghiemstra, 2000). Others, using evidence from the organic composition of Amazonian deep sea fan sediments (Kastner and Goñi, 2003) or other forms of paleoecological analysis, argue that extensive forested areas persisted during the LGM (e.g., de Freitas et al., 2001; Colinvaux and De Oliveira, 2000).

Two major concerns in coming years will be the impact of global climate change on tropical forests and the impact of land cover changes in the tropics on global climates (Malhi and Phillips, 2005).

BIBLIOGRAPHY

Clarke, J. "Antiquity of Aridity in the Chilean Atacama Desert." *Geomorphology* 73 (2006), 101–114. DOI: 10.1016/j.geomorph.2005.06.008.

Colinvaux, P. "Amazon Diversity in Light of the Paleoecological Record." *Quaternary Science Reviews* 6 (1987), 93–114. DOI: 10.1016/0277–3791(87)90028-X.

Colinvaux, P., and P. E. De Oliveira. "Palaeoecology and Climate Change of the Amazon Basin during the Last Glacial Cycle." *Journal of Quaternary Science* 15 (2000), 347–356. DOI: 10.1002/1099–1417(200005)15:4<347::AID-JQS537> 3.0.CO;2-A.

De Freitas, H. A., et al. "Late Quaternary Vegetation Dynamics in the Southern Amazon Basin Inferred from Carbon Isotopes in Soil Organic Matter." *Quaternary Research* 55.1 (2001) 39–46. DOI: 10.1006/qres.2000.2192.

DeMenocal, P. B. "Plio-Pleistocene African Climate." *Science* 270 (1995), 53–59. DOI: 10.1126/science.270.5233.53.

Diester-Haass, L., and H. J. Schrader. "Neogene Coastal Upwelling History off Northwest and Southwest Africa." *Marine Geology* 29 (1979), 39–53. DOI: 10.1016/0025–3227(79)90101–4.

Ding, Z., et al. "A Coupled Environmental System Formed at about 2.5 Ma in East Asia." *Palaeogeography, Palaeoclimatology, Palaeoecology* 94 (1992), 223–242. DOI: 10.1016/0031–0182(92)90120-T.

Filho, A. C., et al. "Amazonian Paleodunes Provide Evidence for Drier Climate Phases during the Late Pleistocene-Holocene." *Quaternary Research* 58 (2002), 205–209. DOI: 10.1006/qres.2002.2345.

Flenley, J. "Tropical Forests under the Climates of the Last 30,000 Years." *Climatic Change* 39 (1998), 177–197. DOI: 10.1023/A:1005367822750.

Freydier, R., et al. "Nd Isotopic Compositions of Eastern Mediterranean Sediments: Traces of the Nile Influence during Sapropel SI Formation?" *Marine Geology* 177 (2001), 45–62. DOI: 10.1016/S0025–3227(01)00123–2.

Gasse, F. "Hydrological Changes in the African Tropics since the Last Glacial Maximum." *Quaternary Science Reviews* 19 (2000), 189–211. DOI: 10.1016/ S0277–3791(99)00061-X.

Goudie, A. S. *Great Warm Deserts of the World: Landscapes and Evolution.* Oxford and New York: Oxford University Press, 2002.

Goudie, A. S., B. Allchin, and K. T. M. Hegde. "The Former Extensions of the Great Indian Sand Desert." *Geographical Journal* 139 (1973), 243–257.

Grove, A. T. "The Ancient Erg of Hausaland, and Similar Formations on the South Side of the Sahara." *Geographical Journal* 124 (1958), 528–533.

Grove, A. T., and A. Warren. "Quaternary Landforms and Climate on the South Side of the Sahara." *Geographical Journal* 134 (1968), 194–208.

Harrison, S. P. "Late Quaternary Lake-Level Changes and Climates of Australia." *Quaternary Science Reviews* 12 (1993), 211–231. DOI: 10.1016/0277–3791(93)90078-Z.

Hoelzmann, P., et al. "Environmental Change and Archaeology: Lake Evolution and Human Occupation in the Eastern Sahara during the Holocene." *Palaeogeography, Palaeoclimatology, Palaeoecology* 169 (2001), 193–217. DOI: 10.1016/S0031–0182(01)00211–5.

Johnson, T. C., et al. "Late Pleistocene Desiccation of Lake Victoria and Rapid Evolution of Cichlid Fishes." *Science* 273 (1996), 1091–1093. DOI: 10.1126/science.273.5278.1091.

Kastner, T. P., and M. A. Goñi. "Constancy in the Vegetation of the Amazon Basin during the Late Pleistocene: Evidence from the Organic Matter Composition of Amazon Deep Sea Fan Sediments." *Geology*, 31 (2003) 291–294. DOI: 10.1130/0091–7613(2003)031<0291:CITVOT>2.0.CO;2.

Latrubesse, E. M., and B. W. Nelson. "Evidence for Late Quaternary Aeolian Activity in the Roraima-Guyana Region." *Catena* 43 (2001), 63–80. DOI: 10.1016/S0341–8162(00)00114–4.

Lavenu, A., M. Fournier, and M. Sebrier. "Existence de deux nouveaux épisodes lacustres quaternaires dans l'Altiplano peruvo-bolivien." *Cahiers ORSTOM, ser. Géologie*, 14 (1984), 103–114.

Leblanc, M. J., et al. "Evidence for Megalake Chad, North-Central Africa, during the Late Quaternary from Satellite Data." *Palaeogeography, Palaeoclimatology, Palaeoecology* 230 (2006), 230–242. DOI: 10.1016/j.palaeo.2005.07.016.

Li, B. Y., and L. P. Zhu. "'Greatest Lake Period' and Its Palaeo-Environment on the Tibetan Plateau." *Journal of Geographical Sciences* 11 (2001), 34–42. DOI: 10.1007/BF02837374.

Malhi, Y., and O. L. Phillips, eds. *Tropical Forests and Global Atmospheric Change.* New York and Oxford: Oxford University Press, 2005.

Masson, V., et al. "Simulation of Intense Monsoons under Glacial Conditions." *Geophysical Research Letters* 27 (2000), 1747–1750.

Nanson, G. C., X. Y. Chen, and D. M. Price. "Aeolian and Fluvial Evidence of Changing Climate and Wind Patterns during the Past 100 ka in the Western Simpson Desert, Australia." *Palaeogeography, Palaeoclimatology, Palaeoecology* 113 (1995), 87–102. DOI: 10.1016/0031–0182(95)00064-S.

Petit-Maire, N., et al. "Paléoclimats Holocènes du Sahara septentionale? dépôts lacustres et terrasses alluviales en bordure du Grand Erg Oriental à l'extrême-Sud de la Tunisie." *Comptes Rendus Académie des Sciences*, Series 2, 312 (1999), 1661–1666.

Qiang, X. K., et al. "Magnetostratigraphic Record of the Late Miocene Onset of the East Asian Monsoon, and Pliocene Uplift of Northern Tibet." *Earth and Planetary Science Letters* 187 (2001), 83–93. DOI: 10.1016/S0012–821X(01)00281–3.

Roberts, N. "Age, Palaeoenvironments, and Climatic Significance of Late Pleistocene Konya Lake, Turkey." *Quaternary Research* 19 (1983), 154–171. DOI: 10.1016/0033–5894(83)90002–9.

Robinson, S. A., Black, S., Sellwood, B. W. and Valdes, P.J. "A Review of Palaeoclimates and Palaeoenvironments in the Levant and Eastern Mediterranean from 25,000 to 5,000 Years BP: Setting the Environmental Background for the Evolution of Human Civilisation." *Quaternary Science Reviews* 25 (2006), 1517–1541. DOI: 10.1016/j.quascirev.2006.02.006.

Rossignol-Strick, M. "Mediterranean Quaternary Sapropels, An Immediate Response of the African Monsoon to Variation of Insolation." *Palaeogeography, Palaeoclimatology, Palaeoecology* 49 (1985), 237–263. DOI: 10.1016/0031–0182(85)90056–2.

Rouchy, J. M., et al. "Extensive Carbonate Algal Bioherms in Upper Pleistocene Saline Lakes of the Central Altiplano of Bolivia." *Sedimentology* 43 (1996), 973–993. DOI: 10.1111/j.1365–3091.1996.tb01514.x.

Sarnthein, M. "Sand Deserts during Glacial Maximum and Climatic Optimum." *Nature* 272 (1978), 43–46. DOI: 10.1038/272043a0.

Schuster, M., et al. "The Age of the Sahara Desert." *Science* 311 (2006), 821. DOI: 10.1126/science.1120161.

Scrivner, A. E., D. Vance, and E. J. Rohling. "New Neodymium Isotope Data Quantify Nile Involvement in Mediterranean Anoxic Episodes." *Geology* 32 (2004), 565–568. DOI: 10.1130/G20419.1.

Smith, G. I., and F. A. Street-Perrott. "Pluvial Lakes of the Western United States." In *Late-Quaternary Environments of the United States*, edited by S. C. Porter, pp. 190–212. London: Longman, 1983.

Tchakerian, V. P., and N. Lancaster. "Late Quaternary Arid/Humid Cycles in the Mojave Desert and Western Great Basin of North America." *Quaternary Science Reviews* 21 (2001), 799–810. DOI: 10.1016/S0277–3791(01)00128–7.

Thomas, D. S. G., and P. A. Shaw. *The Kalahari Environment.* Cambridge and New York: Cambridge University Press, 1991.

Thomas, M. F., et al. "Fluvial Response to late Quaternary Climate Change in NE Queensland, Australia." *Palaeogeography, Palaeoclimatology, Palaeoecology* 251 (2007), 119–136. DOI: 10.1016/j.palaeo.2007.02.021.

Tricart, J. "Existence de periodes seches au Quaternaire en Amazonie et dans les regions voisines." *Révue de Géomorphologie Dynamique* 23 (1974), 145–158.

Tripaldi, A., and S. L. Forman. "Geomorphology and Chronology of Late Quaternary Dune Fields of Western Argentina." *Palaeogeograophy, Palaeoclimatology, Palaeoecology* 251 (2007), 300–320. DOI: 10.1016/j.palaeo.2007.04.007.

Van der Hammen, T., and H. Hooghiemstra. "Neogene and Quaternary History of Vegetation, Climate, and Plant Diversity in Amazonia." *Quaternary Science Reviews* 19 (2000), 725–742. DOI: 10.1016/S0277–3791(99)00024–4.

Ward, J. D. "Eolian, Fluvial and Pan (Playa) Facies of the Tertiary Tsondab Sandstone Formation in the Central Namib Desert, Namibia." *Sedimentary Geology* 55 (1988), 143–162. DOI: 10.1016/0037–0738(88)90094–2.

Wasson, R. J. "Late Quaternary Palaeoenvironments in the Desert Dunefields of Australia." In *Late Cainozoic Palaeoenvironments of the Southern Hemisphere*, edited by J. C. Vogel, pp. 419–432. Rotterdam: Balkema, 1984.

Wasson, R. J., et al. "Large-Scale Patterns of Dune Type, Spacing, and Orientation in the Australian Continental Dunefield." *Australian Geographer* 19 (1988), 80–104. DOI: 10.1080/00049188808702952.

White, K. H., and D. J. Mattingly. "Ancient Lakes of the Sahara." *American Scientist* 94 (2006), 58–65.

Wood, W. W., and J. L. Imes. "How Wet is Wet? Precipitation Constraints on Late Quaternary Climate in the Southern Arabian Peninsula." *Journal of Hydrology* 164 (1995), 263–268. DOI: 10.1016/0022–1694(94)02551-L.

—ANDREW S. GOUDIE

TROPICAL CYCLONES IN A WARMING WORLD

Tropical cyclones (hurricanes) are a major hazard for human communities and have a whole series of environmental consequences, including increased river flooding, coastal surges, the triggering of landslides, and accelerated land erosion and siltation. The possibility that their frequency, intensity, and geographical extent might increase in a warmer world became a particular concern after the ravages of hurricane Katrina on the U.S. Gulf Coast in August 2005 which killed at least 1,836 people, caused damage estimated at $81.2 billion, and flooded roughly 80% of New Orleans. Hurricane formation is restricted to warm ocean waters, with a marked increase in intensity when sea-surface temperatures (SSTs) exceed 27°C. Heat provides the energy that enables the storms to develop. Intuitively, therefore, one might expect that a warming of the oceans would lead to an increase in hurricane intensity, frequency, and extent.

It is far from clear, however, whether this will happen. The Intergovernmental Panel on Climate Change (Houghton et al., 2001, p. 606) stressed that there is a great deal of debate, though there is evidence that peak intensity may increase by 5–10% and that precipitation rates may increase by 20–30%. Walsh (2004) has reiterated that there are no detectable changes in tropical cyclone characteristics that can be ascribed to global warming with certainty, that in the future there is likely to be no significant change in regions of formation, and there is little evidence of substantial changes in the poleward extent of active tropical cyclones, once they leave their tropical regions of formation.

Tropical Cyclones in a Warming World. Cyclone Damage.

Tropical cyclones, such as Cyclone Domoina, which hit southern Africa in 1984, cause enormous damage to infrastructure, such as this road bridge over the Usutu River near Big Bend, Swaziland. A major question is whether such cyclones may become more frequent, more widespread and more intense under global warming.

Moreover, as Goldenberg et al. (2001) have pointed out, although SSTs in the North Atlantic have exhibited a warming trend over the last 100 years and cyclone activity was high in the last years of the twentieth century, Atlantic hurricane activity has not exhibited variability tending toward a trend, but rather distinct multidecadal cycles. In other words, factors other than or additional to SST play a role. Trenberth (2005) has argued that these factors include an amplified high-pressure ridge in the upper troposphere across the eastern and central North Atlantic and reduced vertical wind shear over the central North Atlantic (which tends to inhibit vortex formation).

However, Emanuel (1987) used a general circulation model which predicted that with a doubling of present atmospheric concentrations of CO_2 there will be an increase of 40–50% in the intensity of hurricanes. More recently Knutson et al. (1998) and Knutson and Tuleya (1999) simulated hurricane activity for an SST increase of 2.2°C and found that this yielded more intense hurricanes with wind speeds higher by 3–7 m per second, an increase of 5–12%. Similarly, Emanuel (2005) has suggested that tropical cyclones have become increasingly destructive over the last 30 years and that this can be related to higher SSTs. The increase in global hurricane intensity with increasing SST has been confirmed by Hoyos et al. (2006), and Santer et al. (2006) have demonstrated that human factors have caused the increase in SSTs and cyclogenesis in both the Atlantic and Pacific regions. The Inter-governmental Panel on Climate Change (Solomon et al., 2007, p. 239) has argued that, "Globally, estimates of the potential destructiveness of hurricanes show a significant upward trend since the mid-1970s, with a trend towards longer lifetimes and greater storm intensity."

If, as some scientists have suggested (e.g., Trenberth and Hoar, 1997) ENSO (El Niño–Southern Oscillation) events change under conditions of global warming, then this too could affect hurricane activity, variations in which are closely linked to ENSO (Landsea, 2000). [*See* El Niño–Southern Oscillation.]

BIBLIOGRAPHY

Emanuel, K. A. "The Dependence of Hurricane Intensity on Climate." *Nature* 326 (1987), 483–485. DOI: 10.1038/326483a0.
——. "Increasing Destructiveness of Tropical Cyclones over the Past 30 Years." *Nature* 436 (2005), 686–688. DOI: 10.1038/nature03906.
Goldenberg, S. B., et al. "The Recent Increase in Atlantic Hurricane Activity: Causes and Implications." *Science* 293 (2001), 474–479. DOI: 10.1126/science.1060040.
Houghton, J. T., et al., eds. *Climate Change 2001: The Scientific Basis: Contribution of Working Group I to the Third Assessment Report of the Intergovernmental Panel on Climate Change.* Cambridge and New York: Cambridge University Press, 2001.

Hoyos, C. D., et al. "Deconvolution of the Factors Contributing to the Increase in Global Hurricane Intensity." *Science* 312 (2006), 94–97. DOI: 10.1126/science.1123560.

Knutson, T. R., and R. E. Tuleya. "Increased Hurricane Intensities with CO_2-Induced Warming as Simulated Using the GFDL Hurricane Prediction System." *Climate Dynamics* 15 (1999), 503–519. DOI: 10.1007/s003820050296.

Knutson, T. R., R. E. Tuleya, Y. Kurihara. "Simulated Increase of Hurricane Intensities in a CO_2-Warmed Climate." *Science* 279 (1998), 1018–1021. DOI: 10.1126/science.279.5353.1018.

Landsea, C. W. "El Niño/Southern Oscillation and the Seasonal Predictability of Tropical Cyclones." In *El Niño and the Southern Oscillation*, edited by H. F. Diaz and V. Markgraf, pp. 148–181. Cambridge and New York: Cambridge University Press, 2000.

Santer, B. D., et al. "Forced and Unforced Ocean Temperature Changes in Atlantic and Pacific Tropical Cyclogenesis Regions." *Proceedings of the National Academy of Sciences* 103 (2006), 13905–13910. DOI: 10.1073/pnas.0602861103.

Solomon, S., et al., eds. *Climate Change 2007: The Physical Science Basis: Contribution of Working Group I to the Fourth Assessment Report of the Intergovernmental Panel on Climate Change*. Cambridge and New York: Cambridge University Press, 2007.

Trenberth, K. "Uncertainty in Hurricanes and Global Warming." *Science* 308 (2005), 1753–1754. DOI: 10.1126/science.1112551.

Trenberth, K. D., and T. J. Hoar. "El Niño and Climate Change." *Geophysical Research Letters* 24 (1997), 3057–3060.

Walsh, K. "Tropical Cyclones and Climate Change: Unresolved Issues." *Climate Research* 27 (2004), 77–83. DOI: 10.3354/cr027077.

—ANDREW S. GOUDIE

TROPICAL FORESTS AND GLOBAL CHANGE

Tropical forests constitute nearly half of the Earth's total forest cover. Although this amounts to somewhat less than 10% of the earth's land area, estimates suggest that roughly 40% of the carbon in terrestrial biomass is found in tropical forests, and 50–90% of terrestrial species find their homes within them. Nearly 70 million people live deep in remote tropical forest areas, and more than 700 million others live in rural areas within tropical forests or at their margins (Chomitz et al., 2006).

Global changes are driving local and regional changes in tropical forests around the world. Since 1975, overall temperature increases of $0.26 \pm 0.05°C$ per decade and precipitation decreases of $1.0 \pm 0.8\%$ have recorded for tropical regions, along with large temperature anomalies and record droughts during El Niño events in 1982–1983, 1987–1988, and 1997–1998 (Malhi and Wright, 2004). Generally, warmer and drier climates can radically alter habitat suitability and reproductive success of tropical-forest species while increasing the susceptibility of forests to dry-season fires. Projected climate change that is already committed (i.e., unlikely to be affected by future emissions reductions) appears likely to lead to the replacement of a substantial area of tropical forest by biotically impoverished savanna vegetation. Additionally, rising sea levels associated with temperature increases and the retreat of coastal glaciers subject coastal and low-lying riverine forests to flooding (Parry et al., 2007).

Along with the impact of global climate change on the distribution and composition of tropical forests, global demand for wood and agricultural commodities promotes logging and conversion of forest land. Tropical forests are shrinking at a rate of about 5% per decade, as forests are logged and cleared to supply local, regional, national, and global markets for wood products, cattle, agricultural produce, and biofuels to global markets (Chomitz et al., 2006; Nepstad et al., 2006a). Against this bleak scenario, recent increases in designated conservation areas and indigenous lands may slow the expansion of agro-industrial frontiers that have been eating away at the forests (Nepstad et al., 2006b). For example, from 2004 to 2006 over 24 million hectares of new protected areas were created in the Brazilian rainforest. [*See* Amazonia and Deforestation.]

In addition to the substantial impact that global climate change and economic globalization have on tropical forests, tropical deforestation and forest degradation are also responsible for roughly 1–2 billion tons of carbon emissions to the atmosphere (GtC) per year. When emissions associated with cattle production and mechanized agriculture are included, tropical-forest land-use change contributes roughly 25% of global greenhouse-gas emissions (Houghton, 2005). The largest contributors are Indonesia and Brazil, which, unlike the other major carbon-emitting nations, have emission profiles dominated by land-cover change rather than fossil-fuel emissions. The cost of reducing emissions from deforestation and forest degradation is often lower than achieving reductions in fossil-fuel emissions, but this climate-change mitigation strategy was not included in Phase One of the Kyoto Protocol, because of concerns about permanence (i.e., susceptibility of forests to predatory logging, conversion to agriculture, and accidental or intentional fire) and leakage (i.e., displacement of deforestation from one area to another). Recent initiatives suggest growing momentum for the inclusion of compensation for reducing emissions from deforestation in Phase Two (post-2012), a strategy which could benefit the tropical forests, the people who live in them, and the global climate (Santilli et al., 2005; Gullison et al., 2007).

ECOLOGICAL ISSUES

The interaction between tropical forests and global change is not a recent phenomenon. Paleoecological data indicate that the extent of tropical forests has fluctuated throughout the Pleistocene in response to climate changes associated with glacial and interglacial periods in temperate and boreal latitudes. Temperatures in the tropical-forest regions were probably 5–10°C lower during the Last Glacial Maximum (34,000–22,000 years BP), when atmospheric CO_2 levels were about 200 parts per million. Recent research suggests that while the extent of Amazon Basin forests then was not much different from today, carbon storage was 50% lower, and species composition was substantially different, with a greater prevalence of deciduous forest cover, cold-adapted Andean species in the lowlands, and drought-adapted species across the southern Amazon. Even within the last 10,000 years, there have been major shifts in climate—and consequently in vegetation—in the tropical forest regions (Mayle et al., 2004).

Similarly, while deforestation and forest degradation are generally viewed as modern phenomena, archaeologists worldwide are revealing long histories of large-scale manipulation of tropical forests by people—ranging from the more subtle impacts of hunting large herbivores, to thinning and enrichment of standing forests, to replacement of forests by other land uses. Thousands of years of human history predate the European "discovery" of the tropical forests. As an example, extensive investigations of prehistoric human occupation in the lowland Congo basin—the largest block of intact rainforest on the continent—reveal that much of the region was inhabited, cleared, and cultivated for over a thousand years, ending about 1,600 years ago. The chronology of that period overlaps with evidence of iron smelters in what is now Gabon, which could have been fueled only by substantial extraction of wood from the surrounding forests (Willis et al., 2004).

While history provides important context for understanding present-day phenomena, it should not lead to complacency. Current rates of both land-use change and climate change in tropical forest regions are both unprecedented and unsustainable. Two key predictions for 2100: (1) if the rates of clearing recorded in the 1990s are maintained, the world's tropical forests will be largely gone (Houghton, 2005); and (2) if the present, rather consistent, climate projections are close to the mark, average annual temperatures in the tropics will be 3–8° C warmer than today—a 2-million-year high (Malhi and Phillips, 2004).

Biodiversity loss

Current rates of extinction are believed to exceed what they would be in the absence of *Homo sapiens*. The primary cause of extinction is the loss of habitat. As tropical forests are converted to other land-cover types, tropical-forest species are threatened with extinction. The relationship between forest clearing and extinction is nonlinear, and extinction rates are projected to multiply from roughly 0.1% per decade to roughly 5% per decade during the next 50 years (Pimm and Raven, 2000). Much of the endemic biodiversity of tropical forests is concentrated in a relatively small fraction of the total area, and these "hotspots" are disproportionately endangered to the extent that as much as 90% of their area has been cleared (Myers et al., 2000). Conservation of the remaining area in the biodiversity hotspots could substantially reduce the projected extinction rate (Pimm and Raven, 2000).

Climate change puts additional pressure on endemic biodiversity (IPCC, 2002). Direct impacts include changes in the timing of reproduction and alterations in the geographic distribution of species due to warmer regional temperatures, altered precipitation regimes, and higher sea level. These direct impacts are projected to provoke a generally poleward and upward migration of species, with substantial lags for long-lived species (Miles et al., 2004) and substantial losses for isolated populations, especially those in isolated hotspots. For example, the projected twenty-first-century warming corresponds to an 800 m upward migration (Malhi and Phillips, 2004), leaving already threatened tropical cloud-forests with no refuge.

Indirect impacts of climate change on biodiversity include alterations in disturbance regimes (e.g., flooding, hurricanes, wildfire) that alter habitat structure and composition. Depending on their frequency and severity, altered disturbance regimes can result in the wholesale replacement of extant ecological communities with new ones. For example, species-poor savanna-like vegetation is projected to replace the remaining forests of the eastern Amazon (Brazil) by mid-century (Parry et al., 2007).

Carbon uptake and emissions

The impact of increased atmospheric CO_2 concentrations on tropical forests and the interaction of the ongoing changes in CO_2, temperature, and precipitation is complex and subject to conflicting results and interpretation by ecologists and plant physiologists (Malhi and Phillips, 2004). Among other lines of recent evidence, vertical profiles of the atmosphere suggest that old-growth tropical forests are sequestering more CO_2 than previously thought, probably because of the "fertilization effect" of excess CO_2 in the atmosphere (Stephens et al., 2007). The importance of this effect to the carbon balance of tropical forest regions is likely to decrease as deforestation advances. Other evidence indicates that increased temperatures associated with climate change increase night-time respiration with concomitant increased release of CO_2, and there is a strong positive correlation between temperature and interannual variation in tropical-region carbon emissions (Clark, 2007). Furthermore, the growth and mortality of forest trees are strongly linked to changes in temperature and moisture availability. In Costa Rica, for example, tree growth-rates are strongly and negatively correlated with temperature (Clark, 2007). Droughts associated with recent El Niño events have resulted in substantial tree mortality in tropical forests in Panama (Condit et al., 2005), Malaysia (Nakagawa et al., 2000), and Brazil (Williamson et al., 2000). The spread of wildfire in El Niño years can lead to a doubling of tropical-forest carbon emissions; the 1997–1998 ENSO-related fires were responsible for additional emissions of 2.1 ± 0.8 GtC (van der Werf et al., 2004).

Various methods have been used to estimate the contribution of deforestation to atmospheric carbon emissions, and the magnitude of those estimates ranges from 0.5 to 3.0 GtC per year (Houghton, 2007). Uncertainties in the estimates include the rates of deforestation and the biomass of the forests. Net emissions from deforestation, uptake from the standing forest, and river transport have been estimated at 1.5 ± 1.2 GtC per year.

Hydrological implications

Relationships between tropical deforestation and local and regional hydrology are complex and variable. Forests both store and cycle water, hence deforestation may increase stream flows. For example, the Tocantins River in the Brazilian Amazon has experienced a 24% increase in annual discharge associated with an increase of nearly 20% in cleared area in that watershed and no change in regional precipitation (Costa et al., 2003). Effects of deforestation on precipitation patterns are complex, and may include short-term saturation of the atmosphere with smoke-derived condensation nuclei (so that individual cloud water droplets do not coalesce sufficiently to fall to earth), and longer-term reductions in transpiration as forest is replaced by pasture and crops (Nepstad et al., 2001). Net results of these alterations vary substantially with regional topography, hydrological dynamics, and the amount and distribution of deforestation in the landscape. Furthermore, hydrometeorological teleconnections link tropical deforestation to global rainfall patterns, in such a way that deforestation in Amazonia and Central Africa reduces rainfall in the U.S. Midwest whereas deforestation in Southeast Asia reduces rainfall in China and the Balkan Peninsula; combined effects of deforestation throughout these tropical regions decrease precipitation in the winter in California while increasing summer precipitation in the southern Arabian Peninsula (Avissar and Werth, 2005).

SOCIAL CONCERNS

Tropical forests are far from devoid of human inhabitants, although some regions, especially in Africa and Latin America, are probably occupied by fewer people today than before European colonization (Willis et al., 2004). Some tropical forest regions are now highly urbanized—in the Brazilian Amazon, for example, the urban population exceeds the rural population, and the disparity is growing. Poverty is endemic in many tropical forests, in part because of their inaccessibility. Hence rural inhabitants migrate to the cities in search of jobs (Chomitz, 2006).

Nonetheless, there are nearly 70 million people living in remote tropical-forest regions. These are a mixture of indigenous peoples whose cultural histories have been linked to the forests for millennia, and more recent arrivals, some with over 100 years of family history in their respective regions, others who arrived yesterday. In many regions, there is a long history of marginalization, disenfranchisement, and human-rights violations, often at the hands of politically well-connected speculators keen to establish "rights" over large areas. On the positive side, a growing global trend of decentralization and devolution has led to some form of community control over nearly 20% of tropical-forest area (White and Martin, 2002), and such areas seem to serve as a barrier to deforestation (Nepstad et al., 2006b).

The concerns and priorities of marginalized populations in tropical-forest regions often focus on land rights, access to resources, technical assistance, medical services, education, social inclusion, and self-determination. Historically, their needs have been largely ignored by both national development agendas and international conservation agendas, both of which treated the plight of tropical-forest inhabitants as incidental to their larger goals (Chapin, 2004). Beginning with the rubber-tappers movement in the 1980s, increasingly savvy social movements have been forming strategic alliances with conservationists and policymakers to achieve specific objectives. In a recent example from Brazil, a network of small farmers' associations took the lead in establishing a major conservation corridor that serves to protect them from land-grabbers and the advancing frontier of large-scale mechanized agriculture (Campos and Nepstad, 2006). Similarly, Brazil's International Alliance of Forest Peoples has emerged as a major supporter of compensation for reducing emissions from deforestation as a means of achieving environmental-service payments for maintaining forest cover.

Social costs of deforestation extend beyond the forest boundaries. The incidence of emerging infectious diseases has been linked to deforestation and forest degradation as the penetration of new human populations into areas of endemic infectious disease creates many new opportunities for infection, along with conditions conducive to its spread (Wilcox and Ellis, 2006). Additionally, the direct effect of forest fire on human respiratory health has been well-documented. The Indonesian fires associated with the 1997–1998 El Niño resulted in over 500 deaths, and about 1.8 million reports of asthma, bronchitis, and acute respiratory infections. Financial costs associated with the health impacts of the fires were estimated at $1.2 billion (Aditama, 2000).

ECONOMIC CONSIDERATIONS

Economic drivers, including commodity and currency markets, labor availability, access to transportation corridors, subsidies, and rural poverty are important determinants of land-use change in tropical forest regions. The relative importance of these and other drivers varies somewhat systematically as a function of remoteness but also somewhat idiosyncratically, because of local and regional differences (Chomitz, 2006). As remoteness declines with increasing globalization, the importance of macroeconomic drivers grows, and these are remarkably insensitive to the future of tropical forests and the people who live in them—because these are places and people who, for the most part, remain marginal to national and global economies and politics.

Economists refer to the difference between the financial return that can be realized from the highest-value nonforest use, and the financial return that may be realized from conserving the forest as the "opportunity cost" of forest conservation. Unfortunately, returns from forest conservation are often considered to be low or zero, and hence do not provide much counterweight to earnings from timber or agricultural commodities, or from mineral and petroleum extraction. However, such calculations ignore (1) measurable financial benefits that often accrue from intact forests, such as fuelwood, food, and medicinal products; (2) distributional inequities that often result from favoring large-scale, capital-intensive land uses that disproportionately benefit powerful corporate interests at the expense of small-scale enterprises; and (3) the ecosystem-service values of maintaining intact forest, principally for its role in carbon and water storage—this falls under the category of what economists term "externalities" and, in the case of carbon, will be discussed further below.

Although the economic prognosis for tropical forests may seem gloomy, market-based incentives can play a role in promoting conservation. Such incentives include "green" certification of both timber and agricultural production systems. For example, a number of forest products companies in tropical regions benefit from third-party certification of their management practices by the Forest Stewardship Council, which provides them with market access and price premiums in Europe. On the agricultural front, in 2006, a well-orchestrated campaign by Greenpeace forced a moratorium on new deforestation for soy production under the threat of boycotts of Amazonian soybeans by major purchasers. Leading soybean producers in the region are now experimenting with requiring best-practices management on their own landholdings and on those that they pre-finance (Nepstad et al., 2006b). This is a remarkable development considering that thus far there is no "green premium" in the grains commodity market.

In addition, many banks active in tropical forest regions subscribe to the Equator Principles, which are intended to ensure that the projects the banks finance are socially and environmentally responsible. Although the "proof of the portfolio" thus far has not been as positive as the principles would suggest (BankTrack, 2004), making the extension of credit conditional on the adoption of sustainable practices has enormous potential to improve the practices of borrowers that need the capital. A number of major banks and investment companies now have policies in place that prevent them from investing in projects that would result in deforestation.

Nonetheless, as efforts to mitigate global climate change increase in coming years, there will be unforeseen consequences and feedbacks in our globalized world. For example, policy initiatives that promote ethanol production in response to rising oil prices and concern over fossil-fuel CO_2 emissions are intended to increase the areas under sugar cane cultivation in Brazil and under corn cultivation in the U.S. (USDA, 2007), both of which will tend to displace soybean cultivation into Brazil's Amazon region. Since there is now a moratorium on soybean production from new deforestation in the Amazon, this process will probably lead to substitution of soybeans for pasture wherever the terrain permits, and the subsequent migration of the displaced cattle further into the forest. A similar process has previously been documented for the ongoing northward migration of Brazil's cattle herd (Cattaneo, in press). The result of this perverse domino effect is that deforestation for cattle ranching that could otherwise be avoided at costs of less than $20 per ton of CO_2 in Brazil (Gullison et al., 2007) occurs as a result of U.S. government promotion of a carbon offset resulting from ethanol produced by corn that occurs at a cost of about $500 per ton of CO_2 (Koplow, 2006).

POLITICAL OPPORTUNITIES

Tropical deforestation accounts for roughly 20% of global CO_2 emissions, so reducing deforestation has substantial potential to reduce emissions, a potential enhanced by the relatively low cost of reducing emissions from deforestation compared to other emission-reduction strategies (Gullison et al., 2007). Early skeptics of compensated reduction of emissions from deforestation have argued that (1) monitoring forest carbon is difficult, (2) any guarantees of permanent carbon storage are doubtful, (3) "leakage" of deforestation from one area to another is likely, and (4) in the event that the strategy works, too much cheap carbon will flood the market, thereby slowing the reduction of fossil-fuel emissions. While these objections are important to address, they are not insurmountable (Chomitz, 2006). Some countries already have credible, spatially-explicit estimates of

forest-carbon storage, and good measurements of deforestation. Permanent storage may not be necessary, and emission reductions can be rented rather than bought. Leakage between countries is likely to be less than within countries; hence national-level accounting may be most desirable. Finally, forest-carbon emission reductions should be added to, rather than substituted for, fossil-fuel emission reductions.

In 2005, shortly after deforestation rates in the Brazilian Amazon reached a 10-year high of over 25,000 km^2 per year, the Conference of Parties of the United Nations Framework Convention on Climate Change (UNFCCC) began an assessment of avoided deforestation as a carbon-emissions reduction-strategy. By 2007, the annual deforestation rate in the Brazilian Amazon had fallen to a 20-year low of about 10,000 km^2. The Brazilian government has claimed credit for that reduction, as a result of the creation of 24 million hectares of new protected areas, and a systematic crackdown on corruption in the enforcement of environmental crimes. Others have cautioned that, while government policy has had a generally positive effect, much of the deforestation reduction may have resulted from changes in currency and commodity markets that reduced the profitability of agricultural expansion. An upsurge in deforestation associated with improved commodity markets appears likely (Souza et al., 2007).

The UNFCCC assessment of avoided deforestation was undertaken at the request of the Coalition of Rainforest Nations, which now includes 15 developing countries but does not include Brazil and Indonesia, the countries responsible for most tropical deforestation. Historically, Brazil has had the best deforestation monitoring system in the world but, ever protective of its sovereignty over its Amazonian territory, Brazil was unwilling to discuss deforestation within the UNFCCC before 2006. In a series of major policy initiatives, beginning at the Conference of Parties meeting in Nairobi in December, 2006, the Brazilian government has now "recognized the need for positive financial incentives for the full implementation of actions to secure the reduction of emissions from deforestation" according to Minister of the Environment Marina Silva, speaking at the United Nations on September 23, 2007. Brazil's importance to an international process aimed at achieving emission reductions from avoided deforestation is paramount; its absence would be analogous to the absence of U.S. participation in the Kyoto process itself (P. Moutinho, personal communication).

Carbon-offset projects for avoided deforestation are already multiplying, in spite of the lack of inclusion of such projects in the Kyoto Protocol's Clean Development Mechanism (CDM). This is largely the result of the growing availability of capital for investment in climate-change mitigation projects generally, but in the absence of a recognized system for certifying these emission reductions, investment of private capital in avoided deforestation is a high-risk endeavor. Following the lead of the UNFCCC, the World Bank is now launching a Forest Carbon Partnership Facility (FCPF), to initiate a national-level system of compensation for reduced emissions from deforestation. FCPF includes a donor-supported "readiness fund" to help tropical forest countries develop the capacity to plan for and monitor defore-station reductions, along with a "carbon fund" for investment in the purchase of what would be tradable certified emission reductions, analogous to those issued through the CDM.

At the time of this writing, details regarding a growing assortment of "compensated reduction" initiatives remain unresolved, not the least of which is the determination of baselines against which any reductions should be calculated. It is nonetheless clear that we are moving toward a time when financial incentives for forest conservation could begin to compete with the incentives for deforestation that result from global increases in consumption—but time is running out.

[See also Amazonia and Deforestation; Boreal Forests and Climate Change; Forestation; and Forests and Environmental Change.]

BIBLIOGRAPHY

Aditama, T. Y. "Impact of Haze from Forest Fire to Respiratory Health: Indonesian Experience." *Respirology* 5 (2000), 169–174.

Avissar, R., and D. Werth. "Global Hydroclimatological Teleconnections Resulting from Tropical Deforestation." *Journal of Hydrometeorology* 6 (2005), 134–135.

BankTrack. 2004. *Principles, Profits or Just PR? Triple P Investments under the Equator Principles.* (accessed June 8, 2008).

Campos, M. T., and D. C. Nepstad. "Smallholders, the Amazon's New Conservationists." *Conservation Biology* 20 (2006), 1553–1556. DOI: 10.1111/j.1523–1739.2006.00546.x.

Cattaneo, A. "Regional Comparative Advantage, Location of Agriculture, and Deforestation in Brazil." *Journal of Sustainable Forestry.* Forthcoming.

Chapin, M. "A Challenge to Conservationists." *World Watch Magazine* 17.6 (2004), 17–31.

Chomitz, K. M., et al. *At Loggerheads? Agricultural Expansion, Poverty Reduction, and Environment in the Tropical Forests.* Washington, D.C.: World Bank, 2007.

Clark, D. A. "Detecting Tropical Forests' Responses to Global Climatic and Atmospheric Change: Current Challenges and a Way Forward." *Biotropica* 39 (2007), 4–19. DOI: 10.1111/j.1744–7429.2006.00227.x.

Costa, M. H., A. Botta, and J. A. Cardile. "Effects of Large-Scale Changes in Land-Cover on the Discharge of the Tocantins River, Southeastern Amazonia." *Journal of Hydrology* 283 (2003), 206–217. DOI: 10.1016/S0022–1694(03)00267–1.

Gullison, R. E., et al. "Tropical Forests and Climate Policy." *Science* 316 (2007), 985–986. DOI: 10.1126/science.1136163.

Houghton, R. A. "Balancing the Global Carbon Budget." *Annual Review of Earth and Planetary Sciences* 35 (2007), 313–347. DOI: 10.1146/annurev.earth.35.031306.140057.

———. "Tropical Deforestation as a Source of Greenhouse Gas Emissions." In *Tropical Deforestation and Climate Change*, edited by P. Moutinho and S. Schwartzman, pp. 13–20. Belém, Brazil: Amazon Institute for Environmental Research, 2005.

IPCC. *Climate Change and Biodiversity.* IPCC Technical Paper V. Cambridge and New York: Cambridge University Press, 2002.

Koplow, D. *Biofuels at What Cost? Government Support for Ethanol and Biodiesel in the United States.* Geneva: International Institute for Sustainable Development, Global Subsidies Initiative, 2006. (accessed June 8, 2008).

Malhi, Y., and O. L. Phillips. "Tropical Forests and Global Atmospheric Change: A Synthesis." *Philosophical Transactions of the Royal Society of London* B 359 (2004), 549–555. DOI: 10.1098/rstb.2003.1449.

Malhi, Y., and J. Wright. "Spatial Patterns and Recent Trends in the Climate of Tropical Rainforest Regions." *Philosophical Transactions of the Royal Society of London* B 359 (2004), 311–329. DOI: 10.1098/rstb.2003.1433.

Mayle, F. E., et al. "Responses of Amazonian Ecosystems to Climatic and Atmospheric Carbon Dioxide Changes since the Last Glacial Maximum." *Philosophical Transactions of the Royal Society of London* B 359 (2004), 499–514. DOI: 10.1098/rstb.2003.1434.

Miles, L., A. Grainger, and O. Phillips. "The Impact of Global Climate Change on Tropical Forest Biodiversity in Amazonia." *Global Ecology and Biogeography* 13 (2004), 553–565. DOI: 10.1111/j.1466–822X.2004.00105.x.

Myers, N., et al. "Biodiversity Hotspots for Conservation Priorities." *Nature* 403 (2000), 853–858. DOI: 10.1038/35002501.

Nakagawa, M., et al. "Impact of severe drought associated with the 1997–1998 El Niño in a tropical forest in Sarawak." *Journal of Tropical Ecology*, 355–367.

Nepstad, D., et al. "Road Paving, Fire Regime Feedbacks, and the Future of Amazon Forests." *Forest Ecology and Management* 154 (2001), 395–407. DOI: 10.1016/S0378–1127(01)00511–4.

Nepstad, D. C., C. M. Stickler, and O. Almeida. "Globalization of the Amazon Soy and Beef Industries: Opportunities for Conservation." *Conservation Biology* 20 (2006a), 1595–1603. DOI: 10.1111/j.1523–1739.2006.00510.x.

Nepstad, D., et al. "Inhibition of Amazon Deforestation and Fire by Parks and Indigenous Lands." *Conservation Biology* 20 (2006b), 65–73. DOI: 10.1111/j.1523–1739.2006.00351.x.

Parry, M. L., et al., eds. "Summary for Policy Makers." In *Climate Change 2007: Impacts, Adaptation and Vulnerability: Contribution of Working Group II to the Fourth Assessment Report of the Intergovernmental Panel on Climate Change*, pp. 7–22. Cambridge and New York: Cambridge University Press, 2007.

Pimm, S. L., and P. Raven. "Biodiversity: Extinction by Numbers." *Nature* 403 (2000), 843–845. DOI: 10.1038/35002708.

Santilli, M., et al. "Tropical Deforestation and the Kyoto Protocol." *Climatic Change* 71 (2005), 267–276.

Souza, C., Jr, et al. *Boletim Transparência Florestal no Estado de Mato Grosso* (No. 9). Imazon, 2007. http://www.imazon.org.br (accessed June 8, 2008).

USDA. *Soybeans and Oil Crops: Market Outlook.* U.S. Department of Agriculture, 2007. http://www.ers.usda.gov/Briefing/SoybeansOilcrops/2007baseline.htm (accessed June 8, 2008).

Van der Werf, G. R., et al. "Continental-Scale Partitioning of Fire Emissions during the 1997 to 2001 El Niño/La Niña Period." *Science* 303 (2004), 73–76. DOI: 10.1126/science.1090753.

White, A., and A. Martin. *Who Owns the World's Forests? Forest Tenure and Public Forests in Transition.* Washington, D.C.: Forest Trends and the Center for International Environmental Law, 2002. http://www.forest-trends.org (accessed June 8, 2008).

Wilcox, B. A., and B. Ellis. "Forests and Emerging Infectious Diseases of Humans." *Unasylva* 224 (2006), 11–18.

Willis, K. J., L. Gillson, and T. M. Brncic. "How 'Virgin' is Virgin Rainforest?" *Science* 304 (2004), 402–403. DOI: 10.1126/science.1093991.

—Daniel J. Zarin

TWENTIETH-CENTURY CLIMATE CHANGE

Climate change over the last hundred years has been greater than formerly believed: changes in temperature and rainfall have led periodically to great fluctuations in river discharges, glaciers, lake levels, and dust storms (Solomon et al., 2007).

In many parts of the world, warming in the late nineteenth century and early twentieth century ended the Little Ice Age. These changes are illustrated by the dates of the first and last snowfalls in London from 1811 to 1960: in the nineteenth century the mean dates were separated by over 150 days, while by 1931–1960 this figure had declined to 113 days. The period during which snow might fall decreased by around four weeks between 1931–1960 and 1901–1930. This may result partly from the urban heat-island effect. [See Urban Climates.] The length of ice-cover on rivers and lakes in high latitudes also declined appreciably at least until the 1930s as did that of the Arctic Ocean. Off Iceland, there was an average of 12–13 weeks of ice per year in the 1860s and 1880s, but by the 1920s, that was down to 1.5 weeks. The area of drift-ice in the Russian sector of the Arctic Ocean was likewise reduced, by 1 million km^2 between 1924 and 1944 (Diamond, 1958).

The colonization of the continental shelf of western Greenland by cod from Iceland is the best example of the response of fish to the warming trend. Before 1917, except probably for short periods during the nineteenth century, only small local fiord populations of cod occurred in Greenland. After 1917 large numbers of fish appeared as far north as Frederikshåb (62°N) and migrated north through 9° of latitude in 27 years (Ahlmann, 1948).

The distribution of the land flora and fauna of northern Europe also changed. The polecat began spreading into Finland about 1810 and by the late 1930s had occupied the whole southern Finnish interior to about 63°N (Kalela, 1952). The warmer the winter and the smaller its snowfall, the easier it is for the polecat to find its natural food of small rodents, frogs, and the like. In northeastern Greenland the musk ox had plenty of food from 1910 on, and its numbers increased markedly (Vibe, 1967). Likewise, the roe deer, common in southern and central Scandinavia before the Little Ice Age, was almost extinct there by the early nineteenth century, only to reappear and spread strongly northward after 1870. Also in Finland some permanently resident birds such as the partridge, the tawny owl, and many species of tit extended their ranges northward (Crisp, 1959).

In parts of North America, subalpine meadows, which lie at high altitudes between closed forest and treeless alpine tundra, experienced a massive invasion by trees. Although it might be argued that changes in anthropogenic fire or in grazing by domestic animals might be contributing factors, tree-ring studies indicate that the most intense phase of invasion coincided with the temperature peak from the early 1920s to the late 1940s. The increased temperatures and diminished depth and duration of winter snow increased the growing season to the benefit of the trees (Heikkinen, 1984).

COOLING AT MID-CENTURY

About 85% of the Earth's surface experienced increases in mean annual temperature between 1900–1919 and 1920–1939, whereas about 80% of the Earth's surface experienced a net annual cooling between 1940 and 1960 (Mitchell, 1963). Parker and Folland (1988) suggested the cooling affected the Northern Hemisphere from about 1945 to 1970 over the land, and from about 1955 to 1975 over the oceans, but some parts of the world seem never to have experienced the brief cooling episode of the mid-twentieth century. Warming continued without interruption in New Zealand (Salinger and Gunn, 1975) and over much of Australia (Tucker, 1975). The cooling in the middle years of the twentieth century had various consequences including the development of perennial snowbanks and small glaciers in the Canadian Arctic (Bradley and Miller, 1972), an increase in snowfall frequencies and quantities in New England, a decrease in the length of the growing season in Oxford, U.K. (Davis, 1972), and an increase in sea-ice cover in the Baltic.

WARMING IN THE LATE TWENTIETH CENTURY

There is mounting evidence, however, that climatic warming has again become general globally in the last three decades (Jones et al., 1988; Houghton et al., 2001). The 1980s and 1990s were particularly warm decades in most areas. The overall increase in temperature during the twentieth century was about 0.74°C (Solomon et al., 2007), and the IPCC reported (p. 54) that, "It is *very likely* that average NH [Northern Hemisphere] temperatures during the second half of the 20th century were warmer than any other 50-year period in the last 500 years, and *likely* the warmest in at least the past 1300 years."

Associated with the warming has been a tendency toward reduced diurnal temperature ranges over land. Increases in minimum temperature have been about twice those in maximum temperatures. Nights have warmed more than days. The reason for the reduced diurnal range is that cloud cover, which reduces heat loss from the ground at night and obstructs daytime sunshine, has increased in many of the affected areas (Nicholls et al., 1996, pp. 144–146).

There has been considerable debate about the causes of the warming that has been observed during the period of instrumental observation. The degree of change and the temporal pattern cannot be accounted for solely in terms of the enhanced greenhouse effect caused by emissions of greenhouse gases, but when allowance is made for the cooling effect of sulfate aerosols in climate simulations, the simulations agree closely with surface temperature trends (Houghton et al., 1996, p. 33).

PRECIPITATION CHANGES

Globally, precipitation over land has increased by about 2% since the beginning of the twentieth century (Houghton et al., 2001, p. 142), and it is likely that some precipitation trends are the result of human influence (Zhang et al., 2007). Bradley et al. (1987) provide a general picture of precipitation changes over Northern Hemisphere land areas since the middle of the nineteenth century. In Europe they found that annual precipitation totals have increased steadily since the middle of the nineteenth century, with well above average precipitation since a dry spell in the 1940s. Most of the upward trend was caused by winter precipitation, with lesser amounts in autumn and spring. Summer rainfall, on the other hand, has shown a slight decline. Rainfall in the former USSR had increased dramatically since the 1880s, with most of the change occurring before 1900 and after 1940. The increase in annual totals is accounted for mainly by increases in autumn, winter, and spring. Summer totals have displayed very little trend. In the U.S., precipitation totals declined from around 1880, reaching a low in the 1930s, and generally increasing thereafter. Precipitation has increased markedly in the last 30 years, principally as a result of precipitation increases from autumn through spring. In North Africa and the Middle East very little trend was evident until the 1950s, when, after a wet episode, precipitation declined drastically, especially in summer. In Southeast Asia a wet episode in the 1920s and early 1930s separated two dry periods: the former centered on 1900 and the latter extending from the mid-1960s through to the present. The general trend for the last 40 years has been one of decline. Summer rainfall in the area shows virtually no trend since the 1870s.

There is evidence of an increased incidence of heavy rainfall events in various countries over recent warming decades. Examples are known from the U.S. (Karl and Knight, 1998), Canada (Francis and Hengeveld, 1998), Australia (Suppiah and Hennessy, 1998), Japan (Iwashima and Yamamoto, 1993), South Africa (Mason et al., 1999), and Europe (Førland et al., 1998).

In lower latitudes concern has been expressed that climatic deterioration may be contributing to desertification, but the situation appears complex. [See Desertification.] Rainfall data for some arid areas of the Sudan-Sahel zone in Africa, central Australia, northwestern India, and Arizona show little evidence of a downward trend in the last three or four decades, whereas others (e.g., the Sahel) do show some decrease. Climatic deterioration was severe in the Sudan where, in White Nile Province, annual rainfall in 1965–1984 was 40% below 1920–1939 levels, and wet-season length contracted by 39–51% (Walsh et al., 1988). The dry epoch that began in the mid-1960s continued and intensified in the 1980s. Further west, the dry epoch had dramatic effects on Lake Chad. Its area declined from 23,500 km^2 in 1963 to about 2,000 km^2 in 1985. In southern Africa, analyses of long-term precipitation changes were made by Tyson (1986). He could find no statistical evidence that southern Africa is becoming progressively drier but did find evidence for a number of quasi-periodic rainfall oscillations, the most noteworthy of which has an average period of about 18 years. In northwestern India the rainfall trend appears to have been very different from that in the Sahel. Analyses of monsoonal summer rainfall for Rajasthan (Pant and Hingane, 1988) indicate a modest upward trend in precipitation levels between 1901 and 1982. In the drought-prone region of northeastern Brazil, Hastenrath et al. (1984) analyzed rainfall records since 1912 and found no conspicuous evidence of a long-term trend, either up or down. This century has seen decreased winter rainfall over much of southwestern Australia and increased summer rainfall over much of eastern Australia (Nicholls and Lavery, 1992), but Australian precipitation, which is heavily influenced by ENSO, has also been characterized by large interannual fluctuations. Indeed, some of the variability in precipitation that is observed in the historical record is associated with major changes in the interactions between the ocean and the atmosphere (Viles and Goudie, 2003). The most interesting illustrations of these are El Niño and the North Atlantic Oscillation.

The changes in rainfall and temperature that have taken place over the past century would be expected to have consequences for river flow, though it is important to recognize that anthropogenic effects (e.g., land-cover change, dams, and inter-basin water transfers) will have confused the picture. In extreme cases such as the Colorado River of the southwestern U.S., the Yellow River of northern China, and the rivers flowing into the Aral Sea, river discharges may have been substantially reduced by these mechanisms.

Almost all North American rivers showed a general decrease in discharge during the first three or four decades of this century, with the lowest discharges being recorded during the dust bowl years of the 1930s. This was a time of high temperatures and low precipitation over much of North America. Many North American river discharges appear to have varied in response to El Niño–Southern Oscillations (Dracup and Kahya, 1994).

The Blue Nile, fed by rainfall in the Ethiopian highlands, showed a mean annual discharge of 52 km^3 between 1900 and 1989, but the highest 10-year mean discharge at 56.7 km^3 was 9% higher than this long term mean and occurred between 1903 and 1912. The lowest 10-year mean discharge occurred between 1978 and 1987 and was 19% lower than the long-term mean. For the main Nile at Dongola (Sudan) for the period 1890–1990 the mean annual discharge (corrected for upstream withdrawals and reservoir losses) was 89.9 km^3, but 10-year mean flows ranged from 109 km^3 in 1890–1898 (a 21% increase over the long term mean) to only 74 km^3 in 1978–1987 (an 18% decrease over the long-term mean). Fluctuations of such a magnitude have immense consequences for water-resource development (Conway and Hulme, 1993).

Probst and Tardy (1987) analyzed discharge trends for a large number of the world's rivers. Overall they found that global run-off had increased by about 3% over the period 1910–1975. More importantly they showed periods of low and high river flow in different regions. They found that North American rivers tended to have low flows around 1930–1940 and around 1960 and that European rivers showed low flows around 1940–1950. In Australia, there appears to be no clear evidence from the historical flow records to suggest a trend or change in the mean flow volumes of most Australian unregulated streams (Chiew and McMahon, 1993), though there is considerable interannual variability of flows. In their analysis of flood records for basins from high and low latitudes Milly et al. (2002) found that the frequency of great floods had increased substantially during the twentieth century, particularly during its warmer later decades.

GLACIER AND SEA ICE FLUCTUATIONS IN THE TWENTIETH CENTURY

Since the end of the Little Ice Age in the late nineteenth century, many of the world's alpine glaciers have retreated (Oerlemans, 1994). [See Little Ice Age in Europe.] Fitzharris (1996, p. 246) suggested that since then, the glaciers of the European Alps have lost about 30–40% of their surface area and about 50% of their ice volume. In Alaska (Arendt et al., 2002), glaciers appear to be thinning at an accelerating rate, which in the late 1990s amounted to 1.8 meters per year. In China, monsoon-nourished temperate glaciers have lost an amount equivalent to 30% of their modern glacier area since the maximum of the Little Ice Age. Not all glaciers have retreated in recent decades. In the European Alps a general trend toward mass loss—with some interruptions in the mid-1960s, late 1970s, and early 1980s—is observed. In Scandinavia, glaciers close to the sea have seen a strong mass gain since the 1970s, but mass losses have occurred with the more continental glaciers. The mass gain in western Scandinavia could be explained by an increase in precipitation, which more than compensates for an increase in ablation caused by rising temperatures. Western North America showed a general mass loss near the coast and in the Cascade Mountains.

Twentieth-Century Climate Change.

In many parts of the world, the warm decades of the second half of the twentieth century have seen glaciers retreat and thin. This is the Bossons Glacier near Chamonix, France, and shows the trimline which the glacier reached when it was thicker in the Little Ice Age.

The positive mass balance (and advance) of some Scandinavian glaciers in recent decades, notwithstanding rising temperatures, has been attributed to increased storm activity and precipitation inputs coincident with a high index of the North Atlantic Oscillation (NAO) in winter months since 1980 (Zeeberg and Forman, 2001).

Glaciers that calve into water can show especially fast rates of retreat, in some cases over a kilometer per year (Venteris, 1999). In Patagonia in the 1990s, retreat of up to 500 meters per year occurred. The Columbia tidewater glacier in Alaska retreated around 13 kilometers between 1982 and 2000. The terminus of the Mendenhall Glacier, which calves into a proglacial lake, has retreated 3 kilometers in the twentieth century (Motyka et al., 2002). Certainly, calving permits much larger volumes of ice to be lost from the glacier than would be possible simply through surface ablation (van der Ween, 2002). The glaciers of the Antarctic Peninsula, all of which calve into the sea, also show a

pattern of overall retreat, with 87% retreating in the last 50 years (Cook et al., 2005).

Some glaciers at high altitudes in the tropics have shrunk to one-sixth to one-third of the area they had at the end of the nineteenth century (Kaser, 1999). At present rates of retreat, the glaciers and ice caps of Mount Kilimanjaro in Tanzania will disappear by 2010–2020. The reasons for the retreat of the East African glaciers include not only an increase in temperature, but also a relatively dry phase since the end of the nineteenth century (which led to less accumulation of snow) and a reduction in cloud cover (Mölg et al., 2003). In the tropical Andes, the Quelccaya ice cap in Peru has also suffered a drastic and accelerating loss over the last 40 years (Thompson, 2000). In neighboring Bolivia, the Chacaltaya glacier lost at least 40% of its average thickness, two-thirds of its volume, and more than 40% of its surface area between 1992 and 1998. Extinction is expected in 10 to 15 years (Ramirez et al., 2001).

Since the 1970s, the area of sea ice in the Arctic has declined by about 30% per decade (Comiso, 2002). [*See* Arctic Sea Ice; *and* Arctic Warming.] Its thickness may also have been reduced, with an almost 40% decrease in its summer minimum thickness (Holloway and Sou, 2002). By contrast, changes in Antarctic sea ice have been described by the IPCC as "insignificant" (Stocker et al., 2001, p. 446). It has been difficult to identify long-term trends because of the limited period of observations and the inherent interannual variability of Antarctic sea ice extent, but it is possible that there has been some decline since the 1950s (Curran et al., 2003).

[*See also* Antarctica and Climate Change; Arctic Warming; Arctic Sea Ice; Glacier Retreat; *and* Holocene.]

BIBLIOGRAPHY

Ahlmann, H. W. "The Present Climatic Fluctuation." *Geographical Journal* 112 (1948), 165–195.

Arendt, A. A., et al. "Rapid Wastage of Alaska Glaciers and Their Contribution to Rising Sea Level." *Science* 297 (2002), 382–385. DOI: 10.1126/science.1072497.

Bradley, R.S., et al. "Precipitation fluctuations over Northern Hemisphere land areas since the mid-19th century." *Science* 237(1987), 171–175.

Bradley, R. S., and Miller, G. H. "Recent Climatic Change and Increased Glacierization in the Eastern Canadian Arctic." *Nature* 237 (1972), 385–387. DOI: 10.1038/237385a0.

Chiew, F. H. S., and T. A. McMahon. "Detection of Trend or Change in Annual Flow of Australian Rivers." *International Journal of Climatology* 13.6 (1993), 643–653. DOI: 10.1002/joc.3370130605.

Comiso, J.C. "A rapidly declining perennial sea ice cover in the Arctic." *Geophysical Research Letters* 29(2002), doi: 10.1029/2002 FL015650.

Conway, D., and M. Hulme. "Recent Fluctuations in Precipitation and Runoff over the Nile Sub-Basins and Their Impact on Main Nile Discharge." *Climate Change* 25.2 (1993), 127–151. DOII: 10.1007/BF01661202.

Cook, A. J., et al. "Retreating Glacier Fronts on the Antarctic Peninsula over the Past Half-Century." *Science* 308 (2005), 541–544. DOI: 10.1126/science.1104235.

Crisp, D. J. "The Influence of Climatic Changes on Animals and Plants." *Geographical Journal* 125.1 (1959), 16–19.

Curran, M. A. J., et al. "Ice Core Evidence for Antarctic Sea Ice Decline since the 1950s." *Science* 302 (2003), 1203–1206. DOI: 10.1126/science.1087888.

Davis, N.E. "The variability of the onset of Spring in Britain." *Quarterly Journal of the Royal Meteorological Society* 98(1972), 763–777.

Diamond, M. "Precipitation Trends in Greenland during Past 30 Years." *Journal of Glaciology* 3 (1958), 177–180.

Dracup, J. A., and E. Kahya. "The Relationships between U.S. Streamflow and La Niña Events." *Water Resources Research* 30.7 (1994), 2133–2141.

Fitzharris, B. B. "The Cryosphere: Changes and Their Impacts." In *Climate Change 1995: The Science of Climate Change*, edited by J. T. Houghton, et al., pp. 241–265. Cambridge and New York: Cambridge University Press, 1996.

Førland, E. J., et al. "Trends in Maximum 1-Day Precipitation in the Nordic Region." *DNMI Report 14/98*, Klima. Oslo, 1998.

Francis, D., and H. Hengeveld. "Extreme Weather and Climate Change." Downsview, Ontario: Environment Canada, 1998.

Hastenrath, S., W. Ming-Chin, and C. Pao-Shin. "Toward the Monitoring and Prediction of North-East Brazil Droughts." *Quarterly Journal of the Royal Meteorological Society* 118 (1984), 411–425.

Heikkinen, O. "Forest Expansion in the Subalpine Zone during the Past Hundred Years, Mount Baker, Washington, USA." *Erdkunde* 38 (1984), 194–202.

Holloway, G., and T. Sou. "Has Arctic Sea Ice Rapidly Thinned?" *Journal of Climate* 15.13 (2002), 1691–1701.

Houghton, J. T., et al., eds. *Climate Change 2001: The Scientific Basis: Contribution of Working Group I to the Third Assessment Report of the Intergovernmental Panel on Climate Change.* Cambridge and New York: Cambridge University Press, 2001.

Iwashima, T., and R. Yamamoto. "A Statistical Analysis of the Extreme Events: Long-Term Trend of Heavy Daily Precipitation." *Journal of Meteorological Society of Japan* 71.5 (1993), 637–640.

Jones, P. D., et al. "Evidence for Global Warming in the Past Decade." *Nature* 332 (1988), 790. 10.1038/332790b0.

Kalela, O. "Changes in the Geographic Distribution of Finnish Birds and Mammals in Relation to Recent Changes in Climate." *Fennia* 75 (1952), 38–51.

Karl, T. R., and R. W. Knight. "Secular Trends of Precipitation Amount, Frequency and Intensity in the United States." *Bulletin of the American Meteorological Society* 79.2 (1998), 231–241. DOI: 10.1175/1520–0477(1998)079<0231:STOPAF>2.0.CO;2.

Kaser, G. "A Review of the Modern Fluctuations of Tropical Glaciers." *Global and Planetary Change* 22.1 (1999) 93–103. DOI: 10.1016/S0921–8181(99)00028–4

Mason, S. J., et al. "Changes in Extreme Rainfall Events in South Africa." *Climatic Change* 41.2 (1999), 249–257.

Milly, P. C. D., et al. "Increasing Risk of Great Floods in a Changing Climate." *Nature* 414 (2002), 514–517. DOI: 10.1038/415514a.

Mitchell, J. M., Jr. "On the World-Wide Pattern of Secular Temperature Change." *Arid Zone Research* 20 (1963), 161–181.

Mölg, T., C. Georges, and G. Kaser. "The Contribution of Increased Incoming Shortwave Radiation to the Retreat of the Rwenzori Glaciers, East Africa, during the 20th Century." *International Journal of Climatology* 23 (2003), 291–303.

Motyka, R. J., et al. "Twentieth Century Thinning of Mendenhall Glacier, Alaska, and Its Relationship to Climate, Lake Calving, and Glacier Run-Off." *Global and Planetary Change* 35.1–2 (2002), 93–112. DOI: 10.1016/S0921–8181(02)00138–8.

Nicholls, N., and B. Lavery. "Australian Rainfall Trends during the Twentieth Century." *International Journal of Climatology* 12.2 (1992), 153–163.

Nicholls, N. et al., "Observed climatic variability and change." In *Climate Change 1995: The Science of Climate Change*, edited by J.T. Houghton et al., 133–192. Cambridge: Cambridge University Press, 1996.

Oerlemans, J. "Quantifying Global Warming from the Retreat of Glaciers." *Science* 264 (1994), 243–245. DOI: 10.1126/science.264.5156.243.

Pant, G. B., and L. S. Hingane. "Climatic Change in and around the Rajasthan Desert during the 20th Century." *Journal of Climatology* 8 (1988), 391–401.

Parker, D. E., and C. K. Folland. "The Nature of Climatic Variability." *Meteorological Magazine* 117 (1988), 201–210.

Probst, J. L., and Y. Tardy. "Long Range Streamflow and World Continental Runoff Fluctuation since the Beginning of This Century." *Journal of Hydrology* 94.3–4 (1987), 289–311. 10.1016/0022–1694(87)90057–6.

Ramirez, E., et al. "Small Glaciers Disappearing in the Tropical Andes: A Case Study of Bolivia: Glacier Chacaltya (16°S)." *Journal of Glaciology* 47 (2001), 187–194.

Salinger, M. J., and J. M. Gunn. "Recent Climatic Warming around New Zealand." *Nature* 256 (1975), 396–398. DOI: 10.1038/256396a0.

Solomon, S., et al., eds. *Climate Change 2007: The Physical Science Basis: Contribution of Working Group I to the Fourth Assessment Report of the Intergovernmental Panel on Climate Change.* Cambridge and New York: Cambridge University Press, 2007.

Stephens, B.S., et al., "Weak northern and strong tropical land carbon uptake from vertical profiles of atmospheric CO_2." *Science* 316(2007), 1732–1735.

Stocker, T. F., et al. "Physical Climate Processes and Feedbacks." In *Climate Change 2001: The Scientific Basis: Contribution of Working Group I to the Third Assessment Report of the Intergovernmental Panel on Climate Change*, edited by J. T. Houghton et al., 417–470. Cambridge and New York: Cambridge University Press, 2001.

Suppiah, R., and K. J. Hennessy. "Trends in Total Rainfall, Heavy Rain Events, and Number of Dry Days in Australia." *International Journal of Climatology* 18.10 (1998), 1141–1164.

Thompson, L. G. "Ice Core Evidence for Climate Change in the Tropics: Implications for Our Future." *Quaternary Science Reviews* 19.1–5 (2000), 19–35. DOI: 10.1016/S0277–3791(99)00052–9.

Tucker, G. B. "Climate: Is Australia's Changing?" *Search* 6 (1975), 323–328.

Tyson, P. D. *Climatic Change and Variability in Southern Africa.* Cape Town: Oxford University Press, 1986.

Van der Veen, C. J. "Polar Ice Sheets and Global Sea-Level: How Well Can We Predict the Future?" *Global and Planetary Change* 32.2–3 (2002), 165–194. DOI: 10.1016/S0921–8181(01)00140–0.

Venteris, E. R. "Rapid Tidewater Glacier Retreat: A Comparison between Columbia Glacier, Alaska and Patagonian Calving Glaciers." *Global and Planetary Change* 22 (1999), 131–138. DOI: 10.1016/S0921–8181(99)00031–4.

Vibe, C. "Arctic Animals in Relation to Climatic Fluctuations." *Meddelelser om Grønland* 170 (1967), 1–227.

Viles, H. A., and A. S. Goudie. "Interannual, Decadal, and Mutidecadal Scale Climatic Variability and Geomorphology." *Earth-Science Reviews* 61.1–2 (2003), 105–131. DOI: 10.1016/S0012–8252(02)00113–7.

Walsh, R. P. D., M. Hulme, and M. D. Campbell. "Recent Rainfall Changes and Their Impact on Hydrology and Water Supply in the Semi-Arid Zone of the Sudan." *Geographical Journal* 154.2 (1988), 181–198.

Williamson, G. B., et al. "Amazonian tree mortality during the 1997 El Niño drought." *Conservation Biology* 14 (2000), 1538–1542.

Zeeberg, J., and S. L. Forman. "Changes in Glacier Extent on North Novaya Zemlya in the Twentieth Century." *The Holocene* 11.2 (2001), 161–175. DOI: 10.1191/095968301676173261.

Zhang, X., et al. "Detection of Human Influence on Twentieth-Century Precipitation Trends." *Nature* 448 (2007), 461–465. DOI: 10.1038/nature06025.

—Andrew S. Goudie

U

UNCERTAINTY

There are huge uncertainties about the future of global environments. [See Regional Patterns of Climate Change.] This is true, for example, with regard to past, present, and future extinction rates as summarized by Reid (1992, pp. 56–57):

> We do not yet know how many species exist, even to within an order of magnitude; the best data on rates of tropical deforestation are bounded by large uncertainties, and essential information is lacking of endemism, forest fragmentation, and the potential for species persistence in disturbed habitats. Moreover, ecologists can never even know if extinction rate estimates are borne out. It will not be possible to determine at a future date the number of species that went extinct between now and that future date without knowledge of how many species exist today.

This is a view that has been elaborated in the context of tropical forests by Heywood and Stuart (1992), who lay out nine reasons that the prediction of extinction rates is almost impossible:

- Data on the total number of species currently extinct are highly approximate, particularly for very poorly known groups, such as some invertebrates and soil fungi.
- Knowledge of the most important reservoir of species, the tropical rain forests, is fragmentary. Geographical distributions are very incompletely known. The sizes of floras and faunas are very uncertain and the degrees of endemism are only approximations.
- Taxonomic extrapolations may be invalid. Can we extrapolate extinction estimates from mammals and bird data to plants and invertebrates? Could insects be more at risk (because of their narrow ecological specializations) or could large mammals (because of their low densities and large space requirements)?
- Geographical extrapolations may be invalid. Rainforests in different areas have different characteristics, so lessons learned in one area may not be applicable in another.
- The population size of most tropical species is unknown. We need data on population size if probabilities of extinction are to be estimated.
- Our knowledge of the adaptability of primary forest species to secondary forest and habitat fragmentation is scant.
- There is no understanding of the impact that conservation measures have had on rates of extinction globally.
- It is often impossible to confirm that extinction has taken place until long after it has occurred.

- It is possible that extinctions may occur in an area long after deforestation has been stopped.

Another crucial area in which there is great uncertainty is the prediction of climate change and its impacts (Schmiermeier, 2007). The main uncertainties in simulations using global climate models (GCMs) arise from problems of adequately representing clouds and their radiative properties, the coupling between the atmosphere, biota, and the oceans, and the small-scale processes that operate at the land surface. Like all models, GCMs employ assumptions, and they remain relatively coarse in scale. It is thus not surprising that different GCMs give different projections.

The climate-analogue scenario method of climatic prediction, which is based on the use of a suitably defined ensemble of warm years from the recent instrumental record, which is then compared with either the long-term mean or a similarly defined cold-year ensemble, is another imperfect method of prediction. The temperature shifts are relatively modest compared to those that may be anticipated in a world with a doubled greenhouse-gas loading, and forcing mechanisms may be different. Likewise, the use of selected past warm periods (e.g., the Holocene Optimum or the Last Interglacial) has limitations imposed by data gaps, dating uncertainties, changed boundary conditions, and changed forcing mechanisms (Webb and Wigley, 1985).

A potential problem in forecasting climates is that change may take place not only in a gradual and progressive manner but by stepwise changes across thresholds, and positive feedbacks may be involved. The Amsterdam Declaration of 2001 pointed out the role of thresholds and surprises (Steffen et al., 2004, p. 298):

> Global change cannot be understood in terms of a simple cause-effect paradigm. Human-driven changes cause multiple effects that cascade through the Earth System in complex ways. These effects interact with each other and with local and regional changes in multidimensional patterns that are difficult to understand and even more difficult to predict. Surprises abound.

Earth system dynamics are characterized by critical thresholds and abrupt changes. Human activities could inadvertently trigger such changes with severe consequences for Earth's environment and inhabitants.

Why then is there such great environmental uncertainty? The following are possible explanations (Goudie, 1993):

- Environmental change is the result of complex interactions among several closely coupled nonlinear systems. Nonlinearity means that the dimensions of a response are not necessarily directly proportional to the size of the stimulus that causes the change. The presence of thresholds means that effects may increase suddenly and dramatically and intense feedback loops may develop.

- Environmental change is the result of a complex interplay of a large number of variables. This creates problems for modeling—which normally can cope with only a limited number of variables—and for comprehension.

- Prediction of environmental change depends on models, many of which (including GCMs) are imperfect.

- Identification of future trends requires some knowledge of background trends. Often we lack long-term data which enable us to ascertain whether observed trends have happened before and whether they are linear or cyclic in nature.

- Nature always produces surprises (e.g., various types of catastrophic or extreme event) and will continue to do so. These surprises may either counteract or reinforce the effects of human actions.

- Human influences are difficult to quantify given the problems of demographic prediction, economic forecasting, etc. Human responses are also unpredictable (e.g., with regard to energy choice).

- There will always be factors of which we are ignorant (e.g., are there more substances like CFCs that can create an unexpected response like the ozone hole?)

- There are some crucial factors that are more difficult to predict than others and that therefore prevent accurate prediction of changes in phenomena dependent on them (e.g., the problems inherent in the prediction of precipitation make it difficult to predict changes in hydrology, vegetation, etc.)

- Although we suspect that changes may take place (e.g., permafrost degradation in the face of a temperature rise), it is much more difficult to predict the speed of such a response.

- There are problems of definition. Without definition, measurement is difficult, "results" can be meaningless, and changes difficult to identify (e.g., what precisely is desertification and how do you measure it? How much tree removal constitutes deforestation?)

BIBLIOGRAPHY

Goudie, A.S. "Environmental Uncertainty." *Geography* 78 (1993), 137–141.

Heywood, V.H., and S.N. Stuart. "Species Extinctions in Tropical Forests." In *Tropical Deforestation and Species Extinction*, edited by T.C. Whitmore and J.A. Sayer, pp. 91–117. London and New York: Chapman and Hall, 1992.

Reid, W.V. "How Many Species Will There Be?" In *Tropical Deforestation and Species Extinction*, edited by T.C. Whitmore and J.A. Sayer, pp. 55–73. London and New York: Chapman and Hall, 1992.

Schmiermeier, Q. "What We Don't Know about Climate Change." *Nature* 445 (2007), 580–581. DOI: 10.1038/445580a.

Steffen, W., et al. *Global Change and the Earth System.* Berlin and New York: Springer, 2004.

Webb, T. and T.M.L. Wigley. "What Past Climates Can Indicate about a Warmer World." In *Projecting the Climatic Effects of Increasing Carbon Dioxide*, edited by M.C. MacCracken and F.M. Luther, pp. 239–257. Washington D.C.: U.S. Department of Energy, 1985.

—ANDREW S. GOUDIE

UNITED NATIONS ENVIRONMENT PROGRAMME

The United Nations Environment Programme (UNEP), an agency of the United Nations, was created by the UN General Assembly in 1972 to be the "environmental conscience of the UN system," in response to a recommendation from the United Nations Conference on the Human Environment. UNEP coordinates the environmental activities of UN agencies; works to increase national capacity for environmental protection in member states; assists in negotiations over, and provides support to, international agreements; oversees environmental monitoring activities and the gathering of scientific information; and in general works to increase the ability of the UN to deal with environmental problems.

UNEP is overseen by a Governing Council comprising 58 states, elected by the General Assembly to staggered four-year terms. Seats are distributed by region to maintain geographic balance. The organization's secretariat is located in Nairobi, Kenya, making it the first UN agency to be headquartered in a developing country. The budget of the organization has grown from U.S.\$20 million in 1973 to \$239 million in 2007.

UNEP has played an increasingly active role in negotiations of international agreements; nearly half of the multilateral environmental agreements concluded since the organization's creation have been under UNEP auspices. The organization provides secretariat services to many of these agreements, acts as an implementing agency for projects carried out under the Global Environment Facility, and has overseen international conferences on such issues as human settlements, water, desertification, and, most importantly, the United Nations Conference on Environment and Development in 1992. It has drawn up guidelines for addressing a variety of environmental issues, such as the management of shared natural resources, environmental impact assessment, and disposal of toxic waste. UNEP has also been active in creating management arrangements for regional seas, under its Oceans and Coastal Areas and Regional Seas programs.

Assessment and monitoring activities have been an important part of UNEP's mandate, under the Earthwatch program. This program includes the Global Environmental Monitoring System (GEMS), an information-referral program (Infoterra), and the Global Resource Information Database (GRID). Other programs monitor water quality, food contamination, chemicals, concentrations of atmospheric pollutants, and the condition of ecosystems.

UNEP also works to build capacity in countries for improving environmental management. The organization trains officials within countries, sponsors demonstration projects, and provides information.

Although its programs have had mixed success, UNEP has helped to increase the awareness of environmental issues globally and the ability of the United Nations system to manage them effectively.

BIBLIOGRAPHY

Haas, P.M. "Institutions: United Nations Environment Programme." *Environment* 36.7 (1994), 43–45.

Hierlmeier, J. "UNEP: Retrospect and Prospect." *Georgetown International Law Review* 14 (Summer 2002), 767–805.

McCormick, J. *Reclaiming Paradise: The Global Environmental Movement.* Bloomington: Indiana University Press, 1989. See Chapter 6 for a good overview of UNEP's first ten years.

United Nations Environment Programme (UNEP). www.unep.org (accessed June 5, 2008).

—ELIZABETH R. DESOMBRE

URANIUM

See Nuclear Power.

URBAN CLIMATES

"The city is the quintessence of man's capacity to inaugurate and control changes in his habitat" (Detwyler and Marcus, 1972). Urban areas can, with respect to their weather, "have similar impacts as a volcano, a desert, and as an irregular forest" (Changnon, 1973, p. 146). Recent studies occur in Taha (1997), and Souch and Grimmond (2006) provide a recent review of progress in the study of urban climates.

THE HEAT ISLAND

City surfaces absorb more heat from the sun than do rural surfaces, because a higher proportion of the reflected radiation is retained by high walls and dark roofs. Concrete surfaces have great thermal capacity and conductivity, so heat is stored during the day and released by night. By contrast, the plant cover in the countryside acts like an insulating blanket, so rural areas tend to experience lower temperatures by day and night, an effect enhanced by the evaporation and transpiration taking place from soils and vegetation. Another major thermal change in cities, contributing to the development of the "urban heat island," is the large amount of heat produced from industrial, commercial, transport, and domestic sources.

The existence of the urban heat island has a number of implications: snowfall may be less and last a shorter time, city plants may bud and bloom earlier, some birds may be attracted to the thermally more favorable urban habitat, humans may find higher temperatures stressful if the city is already situated in a warm area, higher temperatures during summer heat waves may cause mortality among sensitive members of the population, and less space-heating may be required in winter and more air-conditioning may be necessary in summer. As the world is warmed by the greenhouse effect, the higher urban temperatures in summer will become an increasingly serious problem.

In general the highest temperature anomalies are associated with the densely built-up area near the city center and decrease markedly at the city edge. The form of the urban temperature effect has been likened to an island protruding from the cool sea of the surrounding landscape. The rural-urban boundary exhibits a steep temperature gradient or cliff marking the edge of the urban heat island. Much of the rest of the urban area appears as a "plateau" of warm air with a steadily but less strongly increasing temperature toward the city center. The zone of maximum temperature, occurring usually in the urban core, resembles a peak rising from that plateau. The difference between this value and the background rural temperature defines the urban heat-island intensity (Oke, 1987).

The average annual urban-rural temperature differences for large cities range from 0.6 to 1.8°C. The relationship between city size and urban-rural difference, however, is not necessarily linear. Factors such as the density of buildings are at least as important as city size, and if a city is located in an area with high wind velocities this will tend to eliminate the heat-island effect. Oke (1987) nonetheless found that the urban heat-island intensity is proportional to the logarithm of the population, which he used as a surrogate for city size.

In mid-latitude cities like London, urban heat-island effects are generally stronger in summer than in winter because of the higher levels of solar radiation absorbed by building materials during the day. In winter the contrast between rural and urban areas is weaker because solar-energy absorption is lower and there thus is less energy to radiate, despite higher levels of urban space heating (Wilby, 2003).

PRECIPITATION EFFECTS

The urban-industrial effects on clouds, rain, snowfall and associated weather hazards such as hail and thunder are harder to measure and explain than the temperature changes (Lowry, 1998) but can be related to various influences (Changnon, 1973, p. 143): thermally induced upward movement of air, increased vertical motions from mechanically induced turbulence, increased concentrations of cloud and raindrop nuclei, and industrial increases in water vapor. In general, urbanization leads to increased precipitation and to more intense storms (Solomon et al., 2007, p. 258).

London provides an interesting example of the effects of a major urban area on precipitation. Here it seems that the mechanical effect of the city has been dominant in creating localized maxima of precipitation both by being a mechanical obstacle to air flow and by causing frictional convergence of flow (Atkinson, 1975). A long-term analysis of thunderstorm records for southeastern England is highly suggestive, indicating higher frequencies of thunderstorms over the conurbation compared to elsewhere (Atkinson, 1968). The similarity between the shapes of zones of equal thunderstorm frequency and the shape of the urban area is striking. Moreover, Brimblecombe (1977) showed a steadily increasing thunderstorm frequency as the city has grown. In U.S. cities, summer rainfall is 9–27% greater than in rural areas, the incidence of thunderstorms is 10–42% greater, and hailstorms are more frequent by 67–430%.

WINDS

Cities affect winds; two main factors are involved, the rougher surface they present in comparison with rural areas and the frequently higher temperatures of the city fabric. Buildings, especially those in cities with a highly differentiated skyline such as is provided by skyscrapers, exert a powerful frictional drag on air moving over and around them (Chandler, 1976). This creates turbulence, with characteristically rapid spatial and temporal changes in both direction and speed. The average wind speeds are lower in built-up areas than over rural areas, but Chandler found that in London, when winds are light, speeds are greater in the inner city than outside, whereas the reverse relationship exists when winds are strong. The overall annual reduction of wind speed in central London is about 6%, but for the higher-velocity winds (over 1.5 meters per second) the reduction is more than doubled.

Studies in both Leicester and London, England, have shown that on calm, clear nights, when the urban heat-island effect is at its maximum, there is a surface inflow of cool air towards the zones of highest temperatures (Chandler, 1976). These so-called "country breezes" have low velocities and are quickly decelerated by intense surface friction in the suburban areas. These breezes transport pollution from the outer parts of an urban area into the city center, accentuating the pollution problem during smoggy periods.

BIBLIOGRAPHY

Atkinson, B.W. "A Preliminary Examination of the Possible Effect of London's Urban Area on the Distribution of Thunder Rainfall 1951–60." *Transactions of the Institute of British Geographers* 44 (1968), 97–118.

———. *The Mechanical Effect of an Urban Area on Convective Precipitation.* London: University of London, 1975.

Brimblecombe, P. "London Air Pollution 1500–1900." *Atmospheric Environment* 11.12 (1977), 1157–1162.

Chandler, T.J. "The Climate of Towns." In *The Climate of the British Isles*, edited by T.J. Chandler and S. Gregory, pp. 307–329. London and New York: Longman, 1976.

Changnon, S.A. "Atmospheric Alterations from Man-Made Biospheric Changes." In *Modifying the Weather: A Social Assessment*, edited by W. R. D. Sewell, pp. 135–184. Victoria, B.C.: University of Victoria, 1973.

Detwyler, T.R., and M.G. Marcus. *Urbanization and Environment: The Physical Geography of the City.* Belmont, Calif.: Duxbury Press, 1972.

Lowry, W.P. "Urban Effects on Precipitation Amount." *Progress in Physical Geography* 22.4 (1998), 477–520. DOI: 10.1177/030913339802200403.

Oke, T.R. *Boundary Layer Climates.* 2d ed. London and New York: Methuen, 1987.

Solomon, S., et al. *Climate Change 2007: The Physical Science Basis. Contribution of Working Group I to the Fourth Assessment Report of the Intergovernmental Panel on Climate Change.* Cambridge and New York: Cambridge University Press, 2007.

Souch, C., and S. Grimmond. "Applied Climatology: Urban Climate." *Progress in Physical Geography* 30 (2006), 270–279. DOI: 10.1191/0309133306pp484pr.

Taha, H. "Urban Climates and Heat Islands: Albedo, Evapotranspiration, and Anthropogenic Heat." *Energy and Buildings* 25.2 (1997), 99–103. DOI: 10.1016/S0378-7788(96)00999-1.

Wilby, R.L. "Past and Projected Trends in London's Urban Heat Island." *Weather* 58 (2003), 251–260.

—ANDREW S. GOUDIE

URBAN TRENDS

In 1950, only one-third of the world's population lived in cities, but at some time in 2007, for the first time in history, the urban population of the world exceeded the rural population (ABC [Australian Broadcasting Corporation] News, 2005). Typically, cities grow as a country advances economically, and nonagricultural opportunities arise in and near cities. In the United States, for example, the urban population became the majority a few years before 1920. Now, development is spreading rapidly in the world; and cities in less-developed areas are growing rapidly as people leave the land for real or perceived opportunities in urban areas. With the majority of world population in extended cities and growing fast, Klaus Töpfer, Executive Director of the United Nations Environment Programme (UNEP), stated in June, 2007, "the battle for sustainable development, for delivering a more environmentally stable, just, and healthier world, is going to be largely won or lost in our cities" (ABC News, 2005).

As of 2005, there were 20 urban agglomerations with populations over 10 million, and an additional ten with more than 7 million (Table 1). The agglomerations include metropolitan areas and surrounding urban areas, though definitions may differ from city to city, making comparisons risky. Here, we tabulate only the most recent population estimates, but our source provides data on rates of growth and estimated populations in the year 2015. Delhi, India, at 15 million in 2005, is expected to reach 18.6 million by 2015; and Dhaka, Bangladesh, is expected to grow from 12.4 to 16.8 million by that year.

New York City was the first to attain megacity status (population over 10 million) sometime around 1940. There seems to be a limit to the size of a city with a single downtown or center: growth tapers off when traffic congestion and pollution become prohibitive. Mexico City reached 16 million in the mid-1980s and was expected to double by 2000, but leveled off at 18 million, as did São Paulo, Brazil. Growth often sprawls to create urban regions like those extending west and north from London, and from Tokyo to Osaka (Pearce, 2006, p. 41).

With continuing growth, urban areas are becoming the major source of greenhouse gases from vehicles, industries, and buildings. In addition, cities attract and consume vast amounts of water, metals, fuels, paper, glass, plastics, and building materials, and then produce wastewater, sewage sludge, local air pollution, demolition waste, and municipal waste. In the absence of deliberate plantings on and around buildings, the urban environment becomes hotter in summer than the surrounding countryside and needs more air conditioning, which consumes more fuel for electrical generation and increases emissions of carbon dioxide. Many cities that grew during the post–World War II period were designed with the automobile in mind: public transport was neglected, the emphasis was on roads to distant suburbs, and housing sprawled over prime agricultural land.

In the twenty-first century, the combination of global warming and impending shortages of crude oil have focused attention on ways to modify existing cities and to steer future growth. One manifestation of this thinking is New Urbanism, an organization started in 1998 and derived from an urban design movement in the 1980s. It promotes "smart, good urbanism, transportation, transit-oriented development, and sustainability." The organization recognizes the current convergence of climate change, peaking crude-oil supply, energy-security

TABLE 1. Most Populous Urban Agglomerations, 2005

Rank	Name	Estimated Population
1	Tokyo, Japan	35,197,000
2	Mexico City, Mexico	19,411,000
3	New York–Newark, U.S.A.	18,718,000
4	São Paulo, Brazil	18,333,000
5	Mumbai (Bombay), India	18,196,000
6	Delhi, India	15,048,000
7	Shanghai, China	14.503,000
8	Calcutta, India	14,277,000
9	Jakarta, Indonesia	13,215,000
10	Buenos Aires, Argentina	12,550,000
11	Dhaka, Bangladesh	12,430,000
12	Los Angeles–Long Beach–Santa Ana, U.S.A.	12,298.000
13	Karachi, Pakistan	11,608,000
14	Rio de Janeiro, Brazil	11,469,000
15	Osaka–Kobe, Japan	11,268,000
16	Cairo, Egypt	11,128,000
17	Lagos, Nigeria	10,886,000
18	Beijing, China	10,717,000
19	Manila, Philippines	10,686,000
20	Moscow, Russia	10,654,000
21	Paris, France	9,820,000
22	Istanbul, Turkey	9,712,000
23	Seoul, South Korea	9,645,000
24	Chicago, U.S.A	8,814,000
25	London, U.K.	8,505,000
26	Guangzhou, China	8,425,000
27	Santa Fe de Bogota, Colombia	7,747,000
28	Tehran, Iran	7,314,000
29	Shenzhen, China	7,233,000
30	Lima, Peru	7,186,000

SOURCE: Population Division of the UN Department of Economic and Social Affairs, *Urban Agglomerations 2005* (released 2006). www.unpopulation.org.

needs, traffic congestion, and urban sprawl, and proposes the following ideal solutions to be applied in the United States: (1) a permanent moratorium on major road construction and expansion; (2) increased funding for railways, especially AMTRAK; (3) a moratorium on additional sprawl; (4) a focus by federal, state, and local governments on smart growth and transit-oriented development; (5) tripling of mileage standards for vehicles; (6) a moratorium on airport construction and expansion; (7) a moratorium on construction of coal-fired and nuclear power plants; (8) rapid construction of solar and wind-electric capacity; (9) establishment of organic farms in every

URBAN AREAS

Urban areas are zones of concentrated urban settlement usually defined on the basis of a threshold population size and a minimum population density. These criteria may vary from country to country, and from census to census within countries. In general, urban areas include urban places and their urban expansion zones. They are defined statistically, not legally.

In the vernacular, "built-up area" is sometimes used as a synonym for "urban area." It is the appearance of the landscape that permits designation as an urban area. High population densities yield different built environments than do low densities. Hence, satellite images and aerial photographs are used to supplement geostatistical analyses in defining the boundaries of urban areas. Geostatistical analyses are usually conducted using administrative and statistical areas as a geographic base, and census data (or possibly survey data) to provide information on population size and density. Even in the absence of demographic data, however, urban areas can be quickly delineated on maps using low-altitude photography or high-resolution satellite imagery.

Urban areas are contrasted with rural areas, their less densely settled counterparts. The dividing line between urban and rural, however, has as much to do with economic characteristics as with population size. The economic base of urban areas is tied to commercial exchange, the provision of services, and manufacturing, whereas that of rural areas is tied to agriculture or other primary activities such as forestry or mining. Rural villages, even very large ones, do not qualify as urban until a set proportion of their labor force is employed in the nonagricultural sector. At that point, they are also likely to become more socially diverse and more interactive with other urban areas. Each nation chooses a dividing line between urban and rural based on the size at which an agglomerated settlement's economy is sufficiently independent from the primary sector of the economy. That dividing line often reflects changing national economies. In the United States, for instance, a city or town had to have a population of at least 8,000 to be classified as urban after the 1870 census. By 1910, that threshold had dropped to 2,500 (Gibson, 1998).

BIBLIOGRAPHY

Gibson, C. "Population of the 100 Largest Cities and Other Urban Places in the United States: 1790 to 1990." Population Division Working Paper No. 27. Washington, D.C.: U.S. Bureau of the Census, 1998.

— DONALD J. ZIEGLER

city and town; and (10) planting of millions of trees (www.newurbanism.org).

Some of these ideal elements are being promoted and even adopted, as indicated by the following developments:

- In 2002 urban and environmental thinkers met in Melbourne, Australia, to draw up a set of ten general principles to guide the design of sustainable cities (UNEP).

- Mayors of 15 cities, including New York, Chicago, Karachi, Toronto, and Tokyo, met in New York, in May, 2007, and signed on to a $5 billion program to make older buildings more energy-efficient (New York Times, 2007).
- The Sierra Club Cool Cities Campaign encourages more efficient vehicles, and renewable energy alternatives (McDunn, 2006).
- The City of Vancouver, British Columbia, has developed a model downtown residential area allowing residents to walk or use public transport. It is one of the fastest-growing downtown cores in North America. The principles of "Vancouverism" are being copied by other urban planners (Montgomery, 2006).
- A suburb city being built for Shanghai on the island of Chongming will feature reliance on renewable energy, a street plan that discourages automobiles and favors public transport, bicycles, and walking, and a waste-disposal system that generates biogas for cooking and heating. It will be completed by 2010, in time for the Shanghai World Expo (Pearce, 2006, pp. 43–45).

To improve the social and environmental conditions in cities, it is vital to reduce car use. Even zero-emission cars running on electricity or fuel cells are not enough, because cars still require a massive network of streets, freeways, and parking structures. What is needed is a wholesale rethinking of how new cities are laid out—and how existing ones expand—to minimize the need for cars in the first place (Pearce, 2006, pp. 39–40).

BIBLIOGRAPHY

ABC News (Australian Broadcasting Corporation). *UN Urges Green Planning for Sprawling Cities.* June 5, 2005. http://www.abc.net/au/news (accessed June 5, 2008).

McDunn, Bob. "Cool Cities Campaign is Spreading in State." *Sylvanian* (Sierra Club), July-September, 2006, p. 23.

Montgomery, C. "Futureville." *Canadian Geographic* 126.3 (May-June, 2006), 44–60.

New Urbanism. http://www.newuranism.org (accessed June 5, 2008).

New York Times. "Can Cities Save the Earth?" Editorial. May 19, 2007.

Pearce, F. "Ecopolis Now." *New Scientist* (June 17, 2006), 36–45.

UNEP (United Nations Environment Programme). *Melbourne Principles for Sustainable Cities.* http://www.unep.or.jp/ietc/kms/data/86.pdf (accessed June 5, 2008).

OTHER READINGS AND RESOURCES

American Planning Association, New Urbanism Division. www.planning.org/newurbanism.

A Vision of Europe, sponsored by International Association for the Promotion of Debate on the City, its Architecture, and the Urban Environment. www.avoe.org

Charlesworth, Esther. *City Edge: Case Studies in Contemporary Urbanism,* Bridgewater, N. J.: Elsevier, 2005.

Congress for the New Urbanism (CNU) www.cnu.org

Girardet, Herbert. *Creating Sustainable Cities.* Darlington: Green Books, 1999.

Girardet, Herbert. "Cities, People, Planet," a lecture at Liverpool, April, 2000 www.schumaker.org.uk

Glover, Paul. *Los Angeles: A History of the Future* www.ithacahours.com/losangele

Sierra Club Cool Cities Campaign. www.coolcities.us

U.S. Green Building Council. www.usgbc.org

World Green building Council. www.worldgbc.org

—DAVID J. CUFF

V

VOLCANOES

Volcanoes and volcanic eruptions (Francis and Oppenheimer, 2003) occur in three different settings dictated by plate tectonics and by active molten rock (magma) production zones, or mantle plumes, within the Earth. [*See* Mobile Earth.] While the greatest amount of volcanic activity and the most numerous volcanoes are situated under the oceans, this article concentrates mainly on activity on land. The location and variety of active volcanism control the two issues that most impact humankind—the effect of eruptions on the global atmosphere and environment, and direct volcanic hazards. In the subaerial environment, volcanism is either effusive (lava-producing) or explosive, forming volcanic ash (pyroclastic ejecta). Deep submarine activity is thought to be entirely effusive because hydrostatic pressure inhibits explosive activity.

SITES OF VOLCANISM

Volcanic activity occurring at spreading centers (divergent plate boundaries), where new oceanic crust is created at the midocean ridges, is dominantly submarine. Little of this activity is seen above the ocean surface, but occasional ocean-island volcanoes, such as the Azores in the Atlantic Ocean, are a reminder of this hidden and little-known volcanic realm. Continental rift zones such as the East African Rift Valley are also sites of volcanism controlled by the same process.

Magma generation and rise at spreading plate boundaries are controlled by decompression melting of the upper mantle, caused by divergence of the tectonic plates. Magma may rise from the generation zone (more than 50 kilometers deep) to the surface with only a brief pause for storage in the crust. The magma generated is mostly basaltic (dark, and low in silica), and the eruptions are usually effusive to mildly explosive, forming lava flows and shield volcanoes on land. Effusive venting dominates in the submarine environment, forming pillow lavas (globs of magma quenched by sea water into pillow-shaped masses of rock). Other magma types that can build large cone-like volcanoes and erupt explosively are produced under the continental rift zones.

Subduction zones—collisional (destructive) plate boundaries—are host to a wide variety of volcanism including some of the largest and most explosive eruptions. These long arc-shaped volcanic zones—whether island volcanoes, as the Aleutian chain, or mainly on land as in Japan or the Andes—are the most active volcanic (and seismic) regions on Earth. Melting is caused in the wedge of mantle material caught between the overriding and downgoing plates by the thermal energy released by subduction. Little of this magma, however, reaches the surface in its original state. The rising molten material, charged with volatile components derived from the top of the subducting plate, melts the base of the plate above, giving rise to a wide variety of magma types at the surface. Magma generation processes are complex, but most situations involve storage for some time in crustal reservoirs, thus making possible the mixing of magmas with different compositions. The most common magma type is andesite, which is a mixture of mantle-derived basalt and more silica-rich magmas such as dacite or rhyolite derived from crustal melting.

A third setting for volcanoes is "hot spots," which can apparently occur anywhere on Earth, either in midplate locations (subaerial and submarine) or at spreading plate boundaries. The Hawaiian volcanoes are an example of the former and Iceland of the latter. Hot spots are caused by the rise of mantle plumes, thermal perturbations originating at depths from midmantle (650–1,000 kilometers) to the core-mantle boundary (around 2,900 km). New mantle plumes cause huge floods of basalt lava when they first erupt. Flood-basalt episodes have occurred at intervals of several tens of millions of years throughout most of Earth history (though not at the present), and the flood-basalt provinces of various geologic ages record mantle-plume activity. After initiation, a mantle plume remains more or less stationary and may continue to produce basaltic magma at a hot spot for over 100 million years—the Hawaiian one is at least 70 million years old. The long-term magma production rate is much lower than at the start, and some old hot spots yield just a trickle of lava. As the melting begins deep in the mantle, the plates slide over the rising plume of melt and leave a "hot-spot track," such as the Hawaiian Island–Emperor Seamount (extinct submarine volcano) chain.

Volcanoes also pop up in hard-to-explain places under both continental and oceanic parts of plates, sometimes in short-lived flareups probably related to mountain building. There are thus volcanoes scattered throughout China, and in North America in places like Colorado and New Mexico. Magma generation under hot spots and in these other settings is due either to excess heat or to decompression in the mantle (or both). It is largely basaltic in composition, with other types generated if the magma is stored for a long time in a crustal reservoir or if contiguous parts of the crust are melted. Activity is largely effusive, but with some large explosive events.

611

DISTRIBUTION, ERUPTION FREQUENCY, AND MAGNITUDE

Active volcanoes are distributed in three main latitudinal belts of volcanism determined by the present configuration of plate margins (Figure 1). The first is a tropical-equatorial belt, including volcanoes in Indonesia, New Guinea, the Philippines, Central America, northern South America, and Africa. This zone contains more active volcanoes than any other zone. Ash and gas clouds from explosive eruptions of these volcanoes can attain global atmospheric distribution, depending upon the latitude and season of the activity. Another belt is in the middle to high latitudes of the Northern Hemisphere, consisting of volcanoes in Japan, China, the Kuril-Aleutian island chains, North America, and southern Europe. The third belt comprises volcanoes in the southern Andes and New Zealand, as well as some ocean islands. Eruption clouds from both these volcanic zones will most likely be limited to the one hemisphere.

Most of the world's population lives in the northernmost volcano zone, so this is where volcanic risk is perhaps the greatest, although any population center near an active or potentially active volcano is at risk. Also, more aircraft fly across this same northern hemisphere zone than other regions, so the risk to aircraft from ash and gas clouds is also greatest there. Although there has not been a disaster from an aircraft-ash encounter, there have been some recent close calls.

There are globally 40 to 60 volcanoes active in any given year. This number includes several consistently active ones such as Kilauea in Hawaii and Yasur in Vanuatu (a group of islands in the southwestern Pacific). There are about half as many newly awakened volcanoes per year. Most eruptions are small affairs producing lava and/or low clouds of gas and pyroclastic ejecta, but larger events take place on average a few times per decade. The most rigorous way to estimate the size of an eruption is by the mass of magma yielded (magnitude) or the mass eruption rate (intensity); volumes of magma are more often given, because these are a little easier to gauge. In units of mass or volume, magnitudes and intensities have spanned many orders of magnitude, even in recent decades. The range is from tiny lava outpourings of less than 0.01 cubic kilometers that take years to dribble out (for example, at Oldinyo Lengai, Tanzania) to huge explosive events expelling about 10 cubic kilometers of magma in a few hours, such as Mount Pinatubo (Philippines) in 1991 or Katmai-Novarupta (Alaska) in 1912. Katmai, at 13–15 km³, was the largest eruption of the twentieth century.

The larger the eruption, the fewer there are, and really big events such as Tambora (Indonesia) in 1815, which produced 50 km³ of magma in about one day, occur every few hundred years. Lava-forming events on this scale are not known from the recent geologic past, the largest (in Iceland) having been in the 15–20 km³ range; these occur once every thousand years or so. How big can eruptions get? In the geologic past, lava flows of up to 2–3,000 km³ were produced during flood-basalt episodes, and explosive eruptions of similar size, forming huge sheets of welded ash deposits and a type of collapsed volcano called a caldera, are known from as recently as 75,000 BP (Yellowstone, Wyoming). Such extreme events may occur globally every few hundred thousand years or so. The size of an eruption does not necessarily correlate directly with its violence or with its destructive potential if humans live nearby.

Volcanoes. FIGURE 1. Global Distribution of Active Volcanoes.

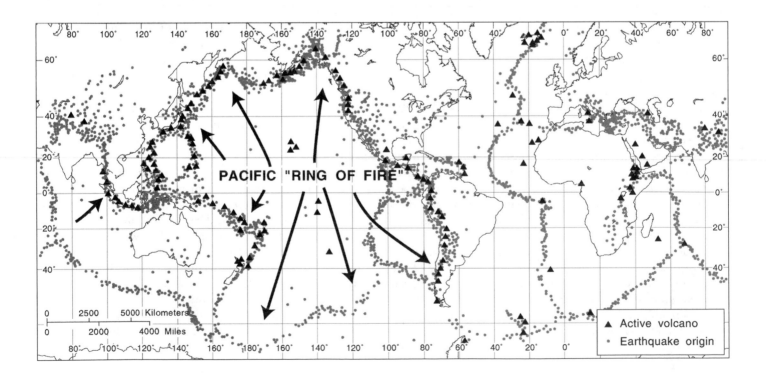

ERUPTION MECHANISMS

Volcanic eruptions are driven by magma—a mixture of silicate melt, crystals, and volcanic gases (mainly CO_2, H_2O, SO_2 [sulfur dioxide], H_2S [hydrogen sulfide], HCl [hydrogen chloride], HF [hydrogen fluoride], H_2, and assorted trace gases). Magma rising under a volcano usually forms a magma chamber. Eruptions occur when the pressure within a part of the magma chamber exceeds the strength of the overlying magma and rock. Pressure builds when the rate at which gases are supplied to the top few kilometers of a magma plumbing system exceeds the rate at which they leak out of that system, when confining pressure decreases (because of magma ascent or fracturing or removal of overlying rock), or when crystallization of magma concentrates gas in a diminishing fraction of melt. The volume of an eruption depends on the amount of gas-charged magma that can be tapped. The explosivity of an eruption depends on the gas content of the magma and how quickly the gas is released once magma reaches the surface. The largest, most explosive, and most dangerous eruptions are those involving large volumes of magma in which gas accumulates to high concentrations until the magma and the gases suddenly break through to the Earth's surface.

ERUPTION TYPES AND HAZARDS

Nonexplosive or weakly explosive volcanic activity produces lava flows, as during most Hawaiian eruptions. Usually, people can escape from lava flows, but structures are destroyed. The volcanic activity known as "Hawaiian" forms widespread, thin, black flows of basalt lava and small cones around the vents. Liquid basalt lava, at one end of the spectrum of physical properties of magma types, is of low viscosity. Stacks of basaltic lava flows build up shield volcanoes. Explosive eruptions fragment the magma into sand- or silt-sized ash, pebble-sized lapilli, and even larger volcanic bombs. The more explosive an eruption, the greater the fragmentation and the smaller the pyroclasts. Strombolian activity (named for the Mediterranean volcanic island of Stromboli) is akin to Hawaiian in that it forms both lava flows and pyroclastic deposits and is characterized by basaltic to andesitic magmas. Magmas forming Strombolian eruptions are slightly more viscous and gas-rich, causing a higher proportion to fragment into pyroclasts. Bigger cones (scoria cones; scoria is rough, vesicular volcanic material) therefore form around Strombolian vents. Strombolian eruptions also display pulsating fire fountains, higher eruption columns, and a wider dispersal of scoria and ash fallout, but they are still not very hazardous unless there is a town immediately nearby, as in the case of the island of Heimaey (Iceland) in 1973.

"Vulcanian" is a catch-all term covering a range of explosive behavior, often accompanied by effusive activity forming lava domes of andesite or dacite magma. Closely related is Pelean activity, named for the notorious Mount Pelée whose eruption killed 30,000 people in the town of Saint-Pierre on Martinique (Lesser Antilles) on May 8, 1902. Vulcanian eruptions involve moderately viscous and gas-rich magma that may shatter with great force, fragmenting the magma into tiny pieces of hot ash.

The force with which the pent-up gases blow the fragments out of the vent leads to towering eruption columns that rise by convection and commonly reach 12–20 kilometers (65,000 feet) in altitude. The pyroclastic material rises high in the column, promoting wide dispersal of fallout as it is blown downwind. However, ash falls are rarely fatal except when roofs collapse under the weight. Sometimes a volcanic explosion can be directed sideways because of a plug of lava over the vent, or for other reasons (e.g., the directed blast at Mount Saint Helens in 1980). This phenomenon, and the ground-hugging, hot flows of pyroclastic material that it spawns, caused the devastation at Saint-Pierre.

Plinian activity (named for the Roman scholar Pliny the Elder who died in the eruption of Vesuvius in 79 CE, and his nephew Pliny the Younger, who observed and wrote about the eruption) occurs when silica-rich, highly viscous, gas-rich magma such as dacite or rhyolite erupts, causing huge columns of ash and gas that rise to heights of 40 kilometers (130,000 feet) into the atmosphere. Great eruptions such as Pinatubo (Philippines, 1991), Krakatoa (Krakatau, Indonesia, 1883), and Tambora (Indonesia, 1815) are most often of this type. Widespread deposits of pumice and fine ash fall downwind of the vent. The lowermost parts of the eruption columns may collapse to form flows of pyroclastic material along the ground, forming rock called ignimbrite (or ash-flow tuff) when solidified. Within areas swept by pyroclastic flows, nearly all life is extinguished and nearly all structures demolished. When mixed with water from crater lakes, snowpack, or heavy rain, loose pyroclastic deposits also form lahars, which are fast-moving, often lethal volcanic mudflows.

DETECTING VOLCANIC ERUPTIONS

The principal precursors of volcanic eruptions are small, often imperceptible earthquakes, deformation of the ground by the expanding magma or heated pore-water in the overlying rock, and emission of magmatic gases. The flux rates of gases, especially SO_2, are a clue to how much unerupted magma is present and degassing beneath the surface; changes in the ratios of various species can suggest the depth and degree of degassing. Gas fluxes and types released can be used to assess the amount of gas remaining and its potential for escape. Less frequently, changes are observed in temperatures of gas vents and hot springs, in local magnetic, gravitational, and electric fields, or in the water table. Seismicity is traditionally measured with seismometers that are designed to measure seismic waves with frequencies of 1–10 hertz, but volcanic seismicity is increasingly tracked over a wider frequency spectrum with broadband seismometers. Ground deformation is measured with high-precision surveying tools, including levels, laser rangefinders, tiltmeters, borehole strainmeters, global positioning systems (GPS), and, most recently, radar interferometry.

Gas emissions were once measured by direct sampling of fumaroles, but such measurements are too infrequent and risky to be useful in forecasting. Sampling of volcanic plumes from manned aircraft is possible but more expensive than most volcano observatory budgets allow. Remote spectroscopic measurement of sulfur dioxide has been possible for over two decades, but remote measurements of CO_2, HCl, H_2S, CO, and SiF_4 (silicon fluoride) are only now becoming possible, principally through lidar (similar in principle to radar but using pulsed laser-light instead of microwaves) and infrared spectroscopic techniques.

ATMOSPHERIC EFFECTS OF VOLCANIC ERUPTIONS

The volcanic emission of gases created a significant portion of the Earth's atmosphere and continues to modify it. Volcanic aerosol clouds are a short-lived, natural atmospheric perturbation that can influence the radiation budget, surface temperatures, and circulation patterns. [*See* Aerosols.] Considerable observational evidence now exists for the connection between explosive volcanism, the generation of volcanic aerosols, and climatic cooling. Other atmospheric effects, such as ozone depletion, are also associated with periods of enhanced atmospheric aerosols. Volcanic aerosols also affect stratosphere stability and tropospheric dynamics and may provide nuclei for upper tropospheric cirrus clouds.

Scientists first recognized and observed volcanic atmospheric dust veils in the year after Krakatoa erupted in 1883, but it was thought at that time that fine-grained silicate dust was the cause. Since the discovery of the stratospheric sulfate aerosol, it has become evident that this layer in the atmosphere, which plays an important role in modulating the net incoming solar radiation, is mostly generated by sulfur dioxide released from erupting magma and injected to stratospheric heights by explosive eruption columns.

Sulfur is released into the atmosphere during eruptions mainly as SO_2 gas, which is oxidized photochemically to sulfuric acid (H_2SO_4) via hydroxyl (OH). Sulfuric acid (70%) and water (30%) are the dominant components. Stratospheric residence time ranges from days through weeks, months, and years for regional, zonal, hemispheric, and global distribution, respectively. The injection of other volatiles such as HCl and H_2O may alter atmospheric composition, but evidence for long-term residence of chlorine compounds from volcanic HCl emission is lacking. Aerosol composition is further altered by heterogeneous reactions on sulfate aerosol surfaces. Depletion of stratospheric ozone in temperate latitudes occurs after volcanic aerosol events; processes involving sulfate aerosols as sites of heterogeneous chemical reactions are implicated, but this phenomenon may have existed only since atmospheric chlorofluorocarbons (CFCs) have been present in our atmosphere. [*See* Ozone.] Recent studies have established a strong correlation between certain types of eruption and climate change, and some workers have suggested that there may be a simple relationship between the sulfur yield of a volcanic eruption and decrease in surface temperature. This may be true for smaller sulfur yields but may not apply to large eruptions. It is known that enhanced levels of aerosols after volcanic eruptions coincide with periods of a few years' duration with lowered incident solar radiation, lower surface and tropospheric temperatures, and stratospheric warming.

Benjamin Franklin is usually credited as the first person to make the association between a volcanic eruption and climate or weather. While he was U.S. Ambassador in Paris in 1783, he theorized that the haze or dry fog, presumably sulfuric acid aerosols, that hung over the city in the latter part of 1783 was caused by an eruption in Iceland. In fact, one of the world's greatest historic lava-producing eruptions occurred at Laki, Iceland, from June 1783 to February 1784. In this event, most of the aerosols generated may have been limited to the troposphere; this is a good example of an eruption of long duration maintaining tropospheric aerosols. Under this haze, as with other aerosol veils, the Sun's rays were dimmed and anomalously cold weather occurred, including bitter cold in August and the coldest winter on record in New England. Crop failures were commonplace the next year and were also experienced after the next large eruption (Tambora), which occurred in 1815.

The year 1816, "the year without a summer," is probably the best known example of a volcanically induced climate cooling event. It was caused largely by the eruption of Tambora, which yielded 100 megatons (10^{14} grams) of sulfuric acid aerosols in one of the largest known eruptions of the past several millennia. The aerosol veil caused cooling of up to 1°C regionally and probably more locally, with effects lasting until the end of 1816 and extending to both hemispheres. It snowed in New England in June, and abnormally cool temperatures in Europe led to widespread famine. The connection to volcanic aerosols was not recognized at the time.

The aftermath of Krakatoa's climactic eruption in August 1883 was probably the first time that scientists widely took notice of a volcanically induced atmospheric event, because the developed world quickly learned of the eruption by telegraphic communication. Observers could ascribe to the eruption the colorful sunsets and other optical phenomena that spread over the Northern Hemisphere during the following months. The Royal Society of London in 1888 published a volume that documented the eruption and the ensuing dust veil. After Krakatoa, scientists measured and reported decreases in incoming radiation following volcanic eruptions in 1902 (Pelée) and 1912 (Katmai-Novarupta).

Several recent eruptions have proven invaluable in improving our understanding of the connection between volcanism, aerosols, and climate change. Eruptions of very sulfur-rich magma at El Chichón, Mexico, in 1982 and Mount Pinatubo, in Luzon, Philippines, in 1991 have been thoroughly documented in terms of the stratospheric aerosols produced, their spread and atmospheric residence time, and their climatic effects. El Chichón was a small-volume eruption of unusually sulfur-enriched magma that produced the first large aerosol veil to be tracked by instruments on satellites. Its impact on surface temperatures has, however, been difficult to assess. Pinatubo was the second-largest eruption in the twentieth century (the largest was Katmai-Novarupta in 1912), and its aerosol veil hung over the Earth for more than 18 months, causing spectacular sunsets and sunrises worldwide. During this period there was more material in the aerosol layer than at any time since Krakatoa erupted.

General circulation models of temperature changes expected under this aerosol cloud predicted Northern Hemisphere surface cooling of as much as 0.5°C, and this appears to have been verified by the meteorological data.

Simple models suggest that eruptions on the scale of large prehistoric events might alter climate to a much greater degree than has been observed following historical events. How large an impact can volcanic eruptions have on surface temperature, precipitation, and weather patterns—through either short-term effects from individual events or longer-term changes controlled by periods of enhanced volcanism? Although large eruptions are less frequent than smaller ones, they are certain to occur in the future. We have an imperfect record of past eruptions and of changes in temperature and weather; future events will provide natural experiments in which we can study the impact of volcanic aerosols, an effort that has already begun.

Perhaps the most important challenge to the research effort on global change for the purposes of making policy decisions will be the early detection of the effects of global warming caused by human activities. It will be essential to recognize and remove effects resulting from natural phenomena, among which volcanic aerosols are significant. Nevertheless, we are still a long way from understanding fully the effects of volcanic eruptions on atmospheric composition, climate, and weather.

BIBLIOGRAPHY

Chester, D.K. *Volcanoes and Society*. London: Arnold, 1993.

Decker, R., and B. Decker. *Volcanoes*. 3d ed. New York: Freeman, 1998. The fourth edition was published in 2006.

Francis, P. *Volcanoes: A Planetary Perspective*. Oxford: Clarendon Press; New York: Oxford University Press, 1993.

Francis, P., and C. Oppenheimer. *Volcanoes*. 2d ed. Oxford and New York: Oxford University Press, 2003.

Harrington, C.R., ed. *The Year without a Summer? World Climate in 1816*. Ottawa: Canadian Museum of Nature, 1992.

Kelly, P.M., P.D. Jones, and J. Pengqun. "The Spatial Response of the Climate System to Explosive Volcanic Eruptions." *International Journal of Climatology* 16.5 (1996), 537–550.

Rampino, M.R., et al. "Volcanic Winters." *Annual Review of Earth and Planetary Sciences* 16 (1988), 73–99.

Scarpa, R., and R.I. Tilling, eds. *Monitoring and Mitigation of Volcano Hazards*. New York: Springer, 1996.

Sigurdsson, H., et al., eds. *Encyclopedia of Volcanoes*. San Diego: Academic Press, 2000.

Sparks, R.S.J., et al. *Volcanic Plumes*. Chichester, U.K., and New York: Wiley, 1997.

Stothers, R.B. "The Great Eruption of Tambora and its Aftermath." *Science* 224 (1984), 1191–1198. DOI: 10.1126/science.224.4654.1191.

Toon, O.B., and J.B. Pollack. "Atmospheric Aerosols and Climate." *American Scientist* 68.3 (1980), 268–278.

—STEPHEN SELF

VULNERABILITY

Vulnerability is an intuitively simple notion that is difficult to define, conceptualize, and measure. Commonly, vulnerability means being susceptible to damage or injury. Given the variety and complexity of global environmental changes, it is not feasible to study vulnerability to global change per se. Rather, researchers have begun to study vulnerability to discrete sets of changes or environmental hazards, such as sea-level rise (e.g., Barth and Titus, 1984) and famine (e.g., Bohle, 1993).

While models of global environmental change remain rudimentary, we do know that the nature and magnitude of environmental changes vary considerably over time and space (Houghton et al., 1992). Some regions, places, groups, and individuals may benefit from these changes, while others may suffer biophysical, socioeconomic, psychological, and cultural harms. Those that are most likely to be harmed are considered to be the most vulnerable. In part, this reflects differences in exposure, but it also reflects differences in the abilities of some nations, groups, and individuals to resist the hazard event and recover afterwards. It is relatively straightforward to identify those most severely affected after a hazardous event (such as flood, drought, or famine). The goal for any analysis of vulnerability in a policy context, however, is to identify in advance who is most likely to be harmed, where, and why, and what to do to prevent or limit such harm. Unfortunately, models of physical and social processes are currently unable to identify in advance precisely those who are most vulnerable.

In the absence of more refined measures, vulnerability is often equated with the extent of exposure and poverty (e.g., Chambers, 1989). In these terms, the global outlook is bleak, because the number of people living in poverty continues to rise (United Nations Development Programme, 1990) and an increasing proportion of the world's population is increasingly exposed (Dow, 1992, p. 418). Poverty and exposure to environmental changes are only rough surrogates for vulnerability, however, and the most vulnerable groups and individuals are not necessarily the most exposed or the most impoverished. Many other factors contribute to vulnerability (e.g., Liverman, 1990), and definitions, terms, and concepts have proliferated, but consensus remains elusive (Cutter, 1996).

Vulnerability is a function of both exposure and coping abilities. Early natural-hazards researchers recognized this ecological relationship and viewed natural hazards as "extreme events of nature that exceed the capabilities of the system to reflect, absorb, or buffer them" (Kates, 1971). This perspective introduced three important concepts (Burton et al., 1978). First, natural hazards cannot be viewed as purely physical events. Second, human systems are dynamic and constantly adapt and adjust to the vagaries of the natural environment. Third, harm occurs when various thresholds are crossed. The notion of vulnerability is essential but remains implicit.

Burton et al. were severely criticized (e.g., Torry, 1979) for their emphasis on exposure to extreme events and on individual perception and behavior (such as choice of coping responses). The critics argued that social marginalization (as through poverty) pushes people into hazard-prone areas and disrupts indigenous coping mechanisms so that vulnerability increases as the ability to resist and recover from hazard events is reduced. From this political economic perspective, vulnerability is conceived as the "degree to which different classes in society are differentially at risk" (Susman et al., 1983). Blaikie et al. (1994) build on this perspective in the development of their disaster "pressure and release" model in which root causes (e.g., limited access to power and resources) generate dynamic pressures (e.g., rapid population growth and urbanization) that create unsafe conditions. Natural-hazard events act as triggers that create disasters. Thus vulnerability is inversely related to the "capacity to anticipate, cope with, resist, and recover from the impact of a natural hazard" (Blaikie et al., 1994, p. 9).

Bohle (1993) integrates entitlement theory (Sen, 1981), empowerment theory (Beck, 1989), and political ecological perspectives (Blaikie, 1985) to develop a synthetic model of the vulnerability of food systems. Long-term structural processes, such as marginalization and disenfranchisement, generate a baseline vulnerability (Downing, 1991) and tendency to crisis (Figure 1). Events external to the food system (such as drought, war, and economic crisis) act as triggers that may lead to escalating vulnerability and ultimately famine unless internal coping strategies and external interventions are sufficient to counteract the crises. The level of resilience and completeness of recovery will determine the new baseline of vulnerability.

Researchers have developed more comprehensive and complex models of vulnerability that are better able to explain and predict social responses to natural hazards and global environmental changes. Nevertheless, the models operate best at regional and local scales and require considerable local knowledge and data to implement in any meaningful fashion. Future research is, therefore, likely to generate hazard- and location-specific analyses of vulnerability rather than generic, global measures. Gross measures, such as poverty and exposure, are likely to remain the best large-scale surrogate measures of vulnerability to most global environmental changes.

[*See also* Famine; Human Dimensions of Global Change; *and* Natural Hazards.]

BIBLIOGRAPHY

Barth, M.C., and J.G. Titus, eds. *Greenhouse Effect and Sea Level Rise*. New York: Van Nostrand Reinhold, 1984.
Beck, J. "Survival Strategies and Power Among the Poorest in a West Bengal Village." *IDS Bulletin* 20.2 (1989), 23–32.
Blaikie, P. *The Political Economy of Soil Erosion in Developing Countries*. London and New York: Longman, 1985.
Blaikie, P., et al. *At Risk: Natural Hazards, People's Vulnerability, and Disasters*. London and New York: Routledge, 1994. The second edition was published in 2004.
Bohle, H.G. "The Geography of Vulnerable Food Systems." In *Coping With Vulnerability and Criticality*, edited by H.-G. Bohle et al., pp. 15–29. Saarbrücken and Fort Lauderdale: Breitenbach, 1993.
Browder, J.O., ed. *Fragile Lands of Latin America: Strategies for Sustainable Development*. Boulder, Colo.: Westview Press, 1989.
Burton, I., R.W. Kates, and G.F. White. *The Environment as Hazard*. New York: Oxford University Press, 1978. The second edition was published in 1993.
Chambers, R. "Vulnerability, Coping and Policy." *IDS Bulletin* 20.2 (1989), 1–7.
Cutter, S.L. "Vulnerability to Environmental Hazards." *Progress in Human Geography* 20.4 (1996), 529–539. DOI: 10.1177/030913259602000407.
Dow, K. "Exploring Differences in Our Common Future(s): The Meaning of Vulnerability to Global Environmental Change." *Geoforum* 23.3 (1992), 417–436.
Downing, T.E. "Vulnerability to Hunger in Africa: A Climate Change Perspective." *Global Environmental Change* 1.5 (1991), 365–380.

Vulnerability. Figure 1. Bohle's Model of Food Crisis.

(After Bohle, 1993. With permission of Verlag für Entwicklungspolitik Saarbrücken GmbH.)

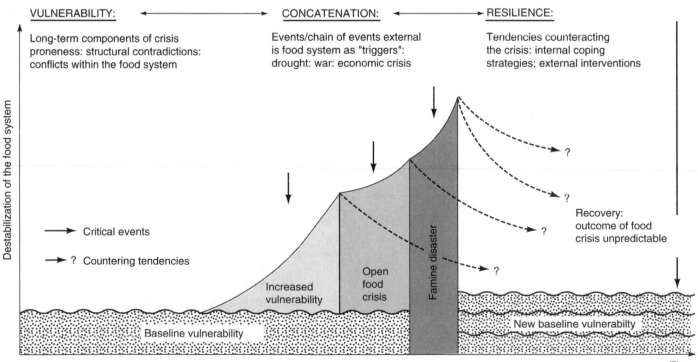

Hewitt, K. "The Idea of Calamity in a Technocratic Age." In *Interpretations of Calamity*, edited by K. Hewitt, pp. 3–32. Boston: Allen and Unwin, 1983.

Houghton, J.T., B.A. Callander, and S. K. Varney, eds. *Climate Change 1992: The Supplementary Report to the IPCC Scientific Assessment.* Cambridge and New York: Cambridge University Press, 1992.

Kates, R.W. "Natural Hazard in Human Ecological Perspective: Hypotheses and Models." *Economic Geography* 47.3 (1971), 438–451.

Liverman, D.M. "Vulnerability to Global Environmental Change." In *Understanding Global Environmental Change,* edited by R.E. Kasperson, et al., pp. 27–44. Worcester, Mass.: Earth Transformed Program, Clark University, 1990.

Sen, A. *Poverty and Famines: An Essay on Entitlement and Deprivation.* Oxford: Clarendon Press; New York: Oxford University Press, 1981.

Susman, P., P. O'Keefe, and B. Wisner. "Global Disasters, a Radical Interpretation." In *Interpretations of Calamity,* edited by K. Hewitt, pp. 263–283. Boston: Allen and Unwin, 1983.

Torry, W.I. "Hazards, Hazes and Holes: A Critique of *The Environment as Hazard* and General Reflections on Disaster Research." *Canadian Geographer* 23.4 (1979), 368–383.

United Nations Development Programme. *Human Development Report 1990: Concept and Measurement of Human Development.* New York and Oxford: Oxford University Press, 1990.

—Dominic Golding

W

WASTE MANAGEMENT

The three basic processes of the global economy, extraction, processing, and consumption, all involve the generation of waste products that eventually return to the environment. Too much waste in the wrong place and/or at the wrong time can cause changes in the environment and harm to animals, plants, and ecosystems. The careful management of waste can limit the damage done to the environment and can conserve scarce resources. To this end, the 1992 Earth Summit in Rio de Janeiro produced several Agenda 21 objectives for the sustainable management of waste, including minimizing wastes, maximizing waste reuse and recycling, promoting environmentally sound waste disposal and treatment, and extending waste services to more people. These areas were seen to be interrelated, and an integrated plan was therefore sought for the environmentally sound management of wastes.

Waste can be defined as a material that has been "left over after use," or that "no longer serves a purpose." It is usually its lack of value that makes it a waste product rather than a useful resource. This lack of value may stem from its mixed state, as in mixed household waste, its potential for pollution, as in hazardous waste, or its location, as in the case of low-value materials that are expensive to transport, such as demolition waste.

WASTE GENERATION

Wastes can be solid, liquid, or gaseous. They are often categorized according to their source; for example, household waste, industrial waste, sewage sludge, hazardous waste. Waste composition can vary considerably, particularly between developed and developing countries. For example, municipal waste in developing countries tends to contain greater quantities of biodegradable kitchen waste, because food is generally purchased unprocessed. In developed countries, greater quantities of processed food are purchased, so that food waste comes from the food industry rather than individual householders. In developing countries there may be low levels of industry and thus less industrial waste, but where industries use old technology, the waste may be more hazardous (Figures 1 and 2).

WASTE COLLECTION

It is estimated that half of the urban population in developing countries is now without adequate solid-waste disposal services. One of the objectives of Agenda 21 is the provision of safe waste collection and disposal to all people. In particular, priority should be given to the extension of waste-management services to the urban poor, especially those in "illegal" settlements. At present it is thought that, globally, approximately 5.2 million people die each year from waste-related diseases, including 4 million children under 5 years of age.

Some of the problems with waste collection in poor urban areas result from inadequate infrastructure combined with the difficulty of access in overcrowded conditions. The problems are exacerbated by the need, in many hot countries, for a daily collection because of the rapid deterioration of the waste, which often has a high biodegradable content. In some areas, low-technology solutions such as hand- and animal-drawn carts are used for the initial collection. The wastes are then transferred to open trucks or refuse vehicles for transport to a transfer station or a waste-disposal facility.

In developed countries the waste is usually collected weekly from the curbside, either in plastic bags or wheeled bins. Waste collection sometimes includes the collection of separated recyclable materials, or this may be carried out independently. Industrial and commercial premises make their own arrangements with waste-disposal companies for waste to be collected, usually in dumpsters. Hazardous wastes need special arrangements for collection and disposal.

WASTE DISPOSAL

There are many different methods of disposing of waste. Many countries have a hierarchy of waste management, which generally favors waste minimization, reuse, and recycling. The least favored methods are landfill and incineration without energy recovery.

In some countries it is now recognized that the waste-management hierarchy should be imposed with some flexibility to take into consideration environmental, economic, and social costs. It is understood that the best practicable environmental option (BPEO) will vary for individual waste streams and local circumstances. However, the European Commission does consider that waste prevention should remain the first priority. In some countries, integrated waste management is promoted, in the realization that there can be several complementary management options for one waste stream: for example, the recycling of noncombustible components of household waste followed by the incineration with energy recovery of the remaining waste stream.

Prevention

Methods of reducing waste at the source vary considerably, from encouraging householders to compost their kitchen and yard

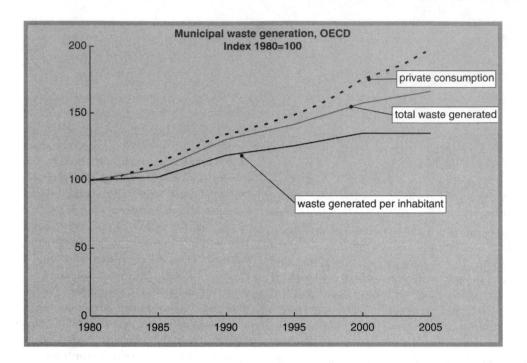

Waste Management. Figure 1. Municipal Waste Generation, OECD Area, 1980–2005.

(Source: Municipal Waste Generation, OECD, OECD Key Environmental Indicators, © OECD 2007, www.oecd.org/env.)

waste at home to improving process efficiency in an industrial unit so that waste is reduced. Some industries have found that they can reduce their waste cheaply, and sometimes even profitably, through good housekeeping methods such as better levels of maintenance, reduction of leaks, and the recycling of non-products within the plant rather than disposing of them (e.g., the cleaning and reuse of solvents). Waste minimization can also be achieved by installing cleaner technology. The harmfulness of the waste must also be taken into account. It may be possible for an industry to change its raw materials or processing so that the waste produced is less damaging to the environment, for example, the reduction of CFC refrigerants. The design of products is also important and can be manipulated to reduce harmfulness (e.g., the replacement of aerosols by pump sprays), to improve recyclability (e.g., so that cars can be dismantled rather than scrapped); and to encourage overall waste prevention (e.g., the reduction of excess packaging).

Recovery

Recovery includes the reuse and recycling of materials and the recovery of energy. There has been considerable debate as to the relative values of materials and energy recovery from waste. The recovery of materials often saves large quantities of energy, but for some materials there are reprocessing and marketing problems.

Composting

Composting is aerobic digestion, the biological decomposition of waste in the presence of oxygen. It can take the form of a garden compost-pile, which reduces household waste and produces useful garden compost. On a larger scale, biodegradable kitchen and garden waste can be collected separately and used to produce compost in a centralized biological treatment plant.

Many industrial and agricultural wastes can also be treated in this way. Some mixed wastes need treatment to remove the majority of the nonorganic fractions prior to composting, and the remainder may still only produce a low-grade product suitable for landfill cover. Separately collected organic material and purely organic waste streams can, however, produce a high-quality product. To obtain a good rate of decomposition, it is important that oxygen be constantly available. This is achieved either by the use of forced air or by a "windrow" system, in which the piles of material are regularly turned to expose them to the air. Further information on composting can be found in White et al. (1995).

ENERGY RECOVERY FROM WASTE

The energy value of waste varies with its composition. Paper and plastics have a high energy value. In many developing countries, municipal waste has a substantial proportion of biodegradable kitchen waste, making it more suitable for composting than for energy recovery.

There are four main methods of recovering energy from waste: (1) the combustion of unsorted waste in a large purpose-built incinerator that uses energy recovery (mass-burn incineration); (2) the burning of partially sorted waste in a purpose-built incinerator (flock fuel or coarse refuse-derived fuel [RDF]); (3) the processing of waste to separate the combustible components to produce an RDF that can be burned in specially designed boilers; and (4) the recovery of methane from landfill sites (landfill gas).

The main difference between the first three methods is the degree of processing that the waste undergoes prior to combustion. Waste entering a mass incinerator generally receives no pretreatment, although ferrous metal is often recovered from the ashes. A flock-fuel system involves the separation and removal of most of the noncombustibles for recycling, leaving a more uniform waste stream with a higher energy value than raw waste. RDF plants have the same or a higher level of sorting, but the fuel is then usually compacted and pelletized so that it can be stored. Other advantages of flock fuel and RDF are that they have a lower heavy-metal content than municipal waste, requiring less stringent air cleaning systems, and that, with a smaller noncombustible fraction, they produce less ash.

Despite these advantages, the predominant method of recovering energy from waste is mass incineration. This is primarily because the technology is reliable and straightforward. It achieves maximum volume reduction of the waste without having to use less-reliable waste separation techniques, and there is no problem marketing the recovered recyclable materials. An alternative method of combustion uses a fluidized bed in which the waste is burned on a bed of inert material such as sand, which is fluidized by currents of air. This method is popular in Japan, but less so in Europe where moving-grate incinerators are well established.

The main benefit of recovering energy from waste is that the recovered energy displaces energy generated by other fuels. In countries where the displaced energy is from fossil fuels, large quantities of carbon dioxide emissions are also displaced. Energy can be recovered as heat or electricity, or as combined heat and power (CHP, or cogeneration). Heat recovery requires that customers be located close to the waste facility, because the cost of installing pipelines to transport hot water is high. Although the generation of electricity is less efficient than heat recovery (20% rather than 60–70%), the electricity is easier to sell because it can be exported directly into the national grid. CHP improves the efficiency (80%) but again requires a pipe network. A mass-burn incinerator recovers 8–10 gigajoules per metric ton of municipal waste.

Gas-cleaning systems are used to control various emissions, including particulate matter, acid gas, dioxins, and nitrogen oxides. In Europe, national and European Union laws now require incineration plants to meet high pollution-control standards.

Landfill

Although the disposal of waste as landfill is the least favored method in the waste hierarchy, it remains the main disposal method in many countries. In the United Kingdom, for example, an estimated 85% of controlled waste is disposed to landfill, while in the United States, 70% of municipal waste goes to landfills. Even in countries where alternative methods of disposal predominate, there is a need for landfill sites to dispose of residues such as incinerator ash. The underlying reason for the popularity of landfill is its relative cheapness, particularly in countries where unregulated landfill is permitted. In recent years, however, there has been increasing awareness of the pollution problems that can arise from these waste dumps, and stringent regulations have been introduced in some countries, resulting in sophisticated landfill sites with leachate collection systems and landfill gas recovery. There has been a consequent increase in cost, but landfill generally remains cheaper than other disposal options.

When organic waste decomposes anaerobically (without oxygen) in a landfill site, it produces a liquid, known as leachate, and landfill gas. Both emissions can be polluting if they escape into the environment. Landfill gas is composed of carbon dioxide and methane—both major greenhouse gases—plus water vapor and trace organic compounds. The decomposition of waste in landfill sites is considered to be one of the main sources of methane. The U.S. Environmental Protection Agency's global-change program has estimated that methane from the decomposition of municipal waste accounts for 7–20% of all anthropogenic methane emissions globally. Migrating landfill gas can also become a local fire or explosion hazard, either at the landfill or in adjacent properties. Landfill gas, especially when it contains hydrogen sulfide, can be an asphyxiation risk in an inadequately ventilated enclosed space. The smell from raw landfill gas can be a nuisance to people living near the landfill.

To mitigate these problems, landfill gas can be collected though a system of perforated pipes and either flared off or used as an energy source. Estimates of the efficiency of gas collection systems range from 40 to 85%, with the remaining gas escaping into the environment. Flaring is an effective method for controlling methane emissions, which are converted into carbon dioxide during combustion. However, a valuable energy source with its environmental and financial benefits is lost. The amount of energy recovered depends on the methane content of the recovered gas, which varies with the waste composition and the environmental conditions of the site. On average, 4 gigajoules of electricity is generated per metric ton of municipal waste in developed countries.

In the past it was not considered necessary to control leachate, and the "dilute and disperse" method was and still is used in many countries, so leachate can pose a serious risk to groundwater supplies. For example, the U.S. Environmental Protection Agency has estimated that approximately 40,000 landfill sites in the United States may be contaminating ground water (Uehling, 1993). In some developed countries, new landfill sites are now operated on a dry containment basis, with multiple liners and leachate collection and treatment systems. This results in a reduction in waste decomposition, so that the landfill sites are regarded as a method for the long-term storage of waste rather than a form of waste treatment.

There is an alternative view that landfill sites should be regarded as bioreactors and the decomposition accelerated by recirculation of the leachate. The argument is that the majority of the gas and leachate production should take place in the beginning of a landfill site's life, when the gas and leachate collection systems are operating effectively (White et al., 1995).

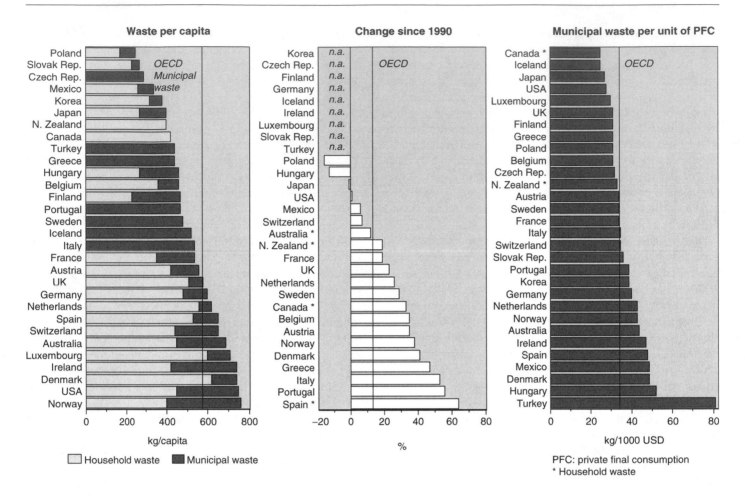

Waste Management. Figure 2. Waste Generation Intensities, OECD and Selected Nations.

(Source: Municipal Waste Generation, OECD, OECD Key Environmental Indicators, © OECD 2007, www.oecd.org/env.)

In Europe, however, this idea may be thwarted by the European Commission's Directive on the Landfill of Waste (1999), which aims to reduce the amount of biodegradable waste disposed in landfills. It also recommends the pretreatment of all waste prior to landfill and the banning of "codisposal," which is the disposal of liquid hazardous waste in trenches cut into landfill sites containing household waste.

NIMBY

Many waste facilities suffer from the NIMBY (not in my backyard) effect, with the main concern being health risks, especially with regard to dioxin emissions from waste incinerators, which have led to several large studies, some with conflicting results. Experts tend to use the relative-risk approach, comparing the risk posed by the chemical exposure from a waste site with risks such as traffic accidents, smoking, and alcoholism. On this basis, the waste site can be shown to present a relatively low risk. However, individuals see the risk from a waste facility as being imposed on them, and there are also problems of misinformation and misperception. Petts (1992) provides further discussion of the risk perception of waste facilities.

Economic Instruments

Waste management policy has traditionally been secured by the use of regulatory standards, with the threat of some penalty if these are not met. [*See* Regulation.] This has resulted in some waste-disposal options being priced without taking environmental costs and benefits into consideration. These costs and benefits are borne by society as a whole and are not accounted for in the decisions made about waste. For example, the cost of disposal to landfill does not include the external costs associated with the global-warming potential of methane emissions. Social costs and benefits (externalities) can include air emissions, water pollution and health impacts, and benefits from the displacement of emissions from energy generated from fossil fuels.

If all waste-management options reflected their true social cost, market forces could produce the optimal combination of waste-management options, but because of market and information failure, this is not the case. The result is that levels of waste minimization and recycling are too low and the level of disposal is too high. Several countries have recognized the limitations of the regulatory approach and have introduced market-based instruments to influence behavior in the direction of sustainable waste management.

There are various economic instruments, including raw material and product charges, deposit-refund systems, waste collection and disposal charges, tradable recycling targets, taxes, and subsidies.

Variable Charging of Household Waste. Householders generally pay an average amount for the collection and disposal of their waste, which is unrelated to the quantity of waste that they dispose of. The fee is often included in a general local tax and not separately identified. Variable charging relates the amount paid to the amount of waste produced, excluding materials separated for recycling. This is also known as "pay by the bag," "volume-based fees," or "unit pricing." Various methods are used, the most common being the purchase of distinctive trash bags by the householder, the cost of which includes the full cost of collection and disposal. Alternatively, stickers can be purchased for placement on ordinary trash bags. It is now also possible for waste in wheeled bins to be weighed as it is being dumped into a garbage truck and for the householder to be charged automatically for the disposal of that quantity of waste.

The countries (approximately 15) that have already introduced this system have experienced increased recycling and decreases in disposal by up to 50%; this offsets landfill demand, rewards recyclers, and fosters long-term changes in consumer behavior. The disadvantages are an increase in the illegal dumping or burning of waste, and the extensive education program that is required. It can also be considered unfair for low-income families and those with children. The system does not work as well in larger apartment buildings and rural areas and is expensive to administer.

Deposit-refund Systems. This approach is essentially a combination of a tax and a subsidy, which may be market-generated or imposed by law. A deposit is added to the price of a product such as a beverage can or bottle, which is refunded to the consumer if the used container is returned. The container can then be refilled or recycled, depending on the material and the contents. This system has been introduced in several U.S. states and in some northern European countries. Experience has shown that the management of deposit-refund schemes is best carried out by beverage producers, the containers being returned by the customers to the retailers. United States beverage-container systems have had return rates of 72–98%, but they have led to relatively small reductions in the volume and cost of waste disposal, and are expensive to operate.

The benefits of deposit-refund systems are a reduction in the cost of waste collection and disposal, reduced litter, and reduced energy and material resources used in container production. The disadvantages are an increase in storage and handling costs and possible inconvenience to the householder. Evidence suggests that return rates are not very sensitive to the size of deposit, and that the number and convenience of return points are more important—although a greater number of return points means higher system-costs for handling, storage, and transportation. In the United Kingdom, where there is no monetary reward, about 20% of all glass bottles are returned, but 95% of milk bottles are returned. These are collected from the doorstep when the milk is delivered, the key factor being convenience. Deposit-refund systems can also be used to help ensure the safe disposal of hazardous household waste such as batteries.

Recycling Credits. Recycling credits are not a subsidy, but they do correct a market failure of the waste-management system. Recycling of household waste obviously removes waste from the disposal stream, saving a proportion of the cost of waste collection and disposal. The aim of recycling credits is to pass on these financial savings to local authorities and third parties who operate the recycling programs. In the United Kingdom, the *Recycling Credits Scheme* was introduced under the *Environmental Protection Act* (1992) to transfer the financial savings to the organizations who collect and sort the waste for recycling. The payments are made by waste-collection and disposal authorities to the recycling operators such as local authorities, private organizations, and community groups.

Landfill Tax. A landfill tax is a disposal charge that internalizes the externalities of landfill, raises revenue, and reduces the amount of waste going to landfill through increased recycling and/or waste minimization. Six European Union countries have landfill taxes: Denmark, France, Germany, Belgium, the United Kingdom, and the Netherlands. In some countries, the tax revenue is dedicated to a specific purpose. In France, for example, it is used to finance the *Modernization Fund for Waste Management*.

[*See also* Environmental Accounting; Industrial Ecology; Land Use; Ocean Disposal; *and* Sustainable Growth.]

BIBLIOGRAPHY

Abduli, M.A. "Solid Waste Management in Tehran." *Waste Management and Research* 13.6 (1995), 519–531. DOI: 10.1177/0734242X9501300603. A good description of waste management in a developing country.

British Medical Association. *Hazardous Waste and Human Health.* Oxford: Oxford University Press, 1991. This book is a useful guide to methods of treatment and disposal of hazardous wastes and links exposure to ill health. Dated but still useful.

Department of the Environment. *Making Waste Work: A Sustainable Waste Strategy.* London, 1995. Discusses the aims and objectives of the U.K. waste strategy.

Environment Canada. *Options for Managing Emissions from Solid Waste Landfills.* Toronto, 1994. An in-depth study of the control and utilization of methane emissions from landfills in Canada.

European Commission. *European Union Strategy for Waste Management.* Brussels: European Commission, 1990.

European Commission. "Review of Community Waste Management Strategy." COM (96) 399, September 10, 1996. Contains full details of the European Community Waste Management Policy.

Henderson, J.P., et al. "Solid Waste Practices in China." *International Solid Waste Association Times* 3 (1997), 16–20. An interesting description of waste management in China.

Petts, J. "Incineration Risk Perceptions and Public Concern: Experience in the U.K. Improving Risk Communication." *Waste Management and Research* 10.2 (1992), 169–182. DOI: 10.1177/0734242X9201000205.

Powell, J., and A.L. Craighill. "The UK Landfill Tax." In *Ecotaxation*, edited by T. O'Riordan, pp. 304–320. London: Earthscan; New York: St. Martin's Press, 1997. Describes in detail the introduction and operation of the landfill tax in the United Kingdom.

Turner, R.K. *Green Taxes, Waste Management, and Political Economy.* Norwich, U.K.: Centre for Social and Economic Research on the Global Environment,

1996. This paper surveys recent developments in the context of waste management policy and the emergence of resources such as recycling credits and the landfill tax.

Turner, R.K., and J.C. Powell. "Solid and Hazardous Waste." In *Blueprint 3, Measuring Sustainable Development*, edited by D. Pearce, pp. 78–97. London: Earthscan, 1993. This chapter looks at the sustainable management of U.K. waste from an economics perspective.

Uehling, M. "Keeping Rubbish Rotten to the Core." *New Scientist* 139 (August 28, 1993), 12–13.

Watson, R.T., M.C. Zinyowera, and R.H. Moss. *Technologies, Policies, and Measures for Mitigating Climate Change*. Geneva: Intergovernmental Panel on Climate Change, 1996.

White, P.R., M. Franke, and P. Hindle. *Integrated Solid Waste Management: A Lifecycle Inventory*. London and New York: Blackie, 1995. A useful and detailed guide to all methods of solid waste management.

—JANE C. POWELL

WATER

Problems associated with access to and the quality of fresh water have become an increasing concern for the world's scientific community and for the public and policymakers. This concern has manifested itself in conferences, studies, analyses, policy meetings, and publications about all aspects of the world's water resources. Those concerned are beginning to understand the intricate connections between water and human well-being, water quality and health, water availability and ecosystem function, water pricing and equity issues, and between economics and politics on the one hand and water policies on the other.

THE WORLD'S STOCKS AND FLOWS OF FRESHWATER

During the twentieth century, the focus of water policymakers and managers was on constructing infrastructure to provide reliable water supplies. In the past few years, however, the emphasis has begun to shift toward a better understanding of water needs and policies in order to improve the management and use of water. At the same time, great uncertainties remain about water availability, the natural variations in the hydrologic cycle, and our freshwater stocks and flows. Despite our increasingly accurate remote-sensing technology, mapping capabilities, and modeling abilities, not even the total amount of water on the planet is known accurately. Water is found in many places and takes many forms, and it is in continuous and rapid transformation from one form and stock to another.

THE BASIC HYDROLOGIC CYCLE

Fresh water is a renewable resource made continuously available by the flow of solar energy reaching the earth. This energy evaporates fresh water into the atmosphere from the oceans and land surfaces and redistributes it around the world in what is known as the hydrologic cycle. Atmospheric water is constantly being diminished by precipitation and replenished by evaporation. Less water falls on the oceans as precipitation than

is lost through evaporation: thus there is a continuous transfer of water to the land, which runs off in rivers and streams or goes into long-term storage in lakes, soils, and groundwater aquifers.

Because of the heterogeneous nature of our atmosphere, land surfaces, and energy fluxes, the distribution of fresh water around the world is uneven in space and time. Some places receive enormous quantities of water regularly; others are extremely arid. At one extreme, regions in India and the rainforests on the island of Kauai may receive more than 10 meters of rainfall per year, while the dry deserts of South America may receive no measurable rainfall for decades.

Highly variable seasonal cycles of rainfall and evaporation are the rule in most regions, and variability from one period to another can be large. Water planners and managers must take all of these characteristics into account when designing and operating water systems. Hydrology and water management have developed over the past millennia to deal with these characteristics.

The principal sources of water for human use are lakes, rivers, soil moisture, and relatively shallow groundwater basins. These stocks hold, on average, only about 200,000 cubic kilometers (km^3) of water—less than 1% of all fresh water on Earth (Table 1).

In addition to stocks of water, the hydrologic cycle consists of continuous flows of water into and out of every stock, under the influence of inputs of solar energy, the dynamics of the atmosphere, gravity, and human activities. The rates of flux of water vary enormously: the average time a molecule of water stays in the atmosphere between evaporation and precipitation is approximately eight days; the residence time of water in glaciers or deep groundwater may be hundreds or

TABLE 1. Major Freshwater Stocks

	Volume (1,000 km3)	Percent of Total Fresh Water
Ground water (fresh)	10,530	30.1
Soil moisture	16.5	0.05
Glaciers and permanent snow cover	24,064	68.7
Ground ice/permafrost	300	0.86
Freshwater lakes	91	0.26
Wetlands	11.5	0.03
Rivers	2.1	0.006
Biota	1.1	0.003
Atmospheric water vapor	12.9	0.04
Total*	35,029	100

* Totals may not add because of rounding; significant figures as in original.

SOURCE: Shiklomanov, 1998.

thousands of years. These cycling rates are of great importance when evaluating the possible use of water for human activities and the impacts of those uses on natural systems.

The major flows of fresh water are evaporation and precipitation. Water evaporates off of, and precipitates onto, land and ocean surfaces. Approximately 505,000 km³ evaporates annually from the oceans, and 72,000 km³ evaporates each year from land surfaces. About 458,000 km³ of precipitation (or approximately 90% of the water evaporated from the oceans) falls over the oceans. The remaining 119,000 km³ of precipitation falls over land. The global totals of evaporation and precipitation thus balance out at 577,000 km³. The difference between precipitation and evaporation on land is runoff and groundwater recharge—approximately 47,000 km³ per year, the same as the amount by which ocean evaporation exceeds precipitation.

These global averages mask considerable variation in both the spatial and temporal distribution of water, variations that are of vital importance in understanding the dynamics of water on Earth and in assessing the consequences of various forms of development. Precipitation and evaporation vary on every time scale, ranging from interannual variations to sharp differences in the intensity of storm events. Nearly 80% of the annual runoff in Asia occurs between May and October; three-quarters of runoff in Africa occurs between January and June; in Australia as much as 30% of runoff may occur in March alone. Nearly 7,000 km³ more water is stored on land in snow, soil moisture, and lakes in March than in September, and 600 km³ more water is stored in the atmosphere in September than in March (van Hylckama, 1970).

Global runoff is very unevenly distributed, even accounting for differences in areal extent. More than half of all runoff occurs in Asia and South America; in fact, an unusually large fraction of all runoff occurs in just a single river—the Amazon—which carries more than 6,000 km³ of water a year. Brazilian rivers all together account for nearly 20% of all global renewable freshwater resources, 35% more than Russia, and about twice as much as both Canada and China, which

have the third and fourth largest average annual runoff volumes.

Table 2 presents water availability per square kilometer of land area and per person. South America and Asia have the largest volumes of runoff annually. South America, however, is considerably smaller in area and population and thus has a much larger amount of water available on an areal or per capita basis. Australia and Oceania (which includes New Zealand and most of the Pacific island nations) receive the least water overall but have the highest per capita availability because of their low populations. Total continental runoff volumes are greatest in Asia, but the greatest per capita availability is in South America, while Asia has the lowest per capita availability of a continental area.

WATER USE

Many of the world's water concerns are related to how much water is available for use in different qualities and at different times of the year, but many of the most serious problems relate to how, when, and where humans use water. Water-resources development around the world has taken many different forms. Huge economic expenditures have been made to modify the natural hydrologic cycle to make water more available for particular uses. Humans move, store, and redirect natural waters to make them more reliable and useful. Because many humans live in cities or in arid and semiarid regions, water supplies have to be brought from distant sources. As early as 5,000 years ago humans were building irrigation canals and ditches to move water from rivers to fields; designers in ancient cities built aqueducts to support dense urban populations.

Human needs for water led to advances in civil engineering and hydrology. The industrial revolution and population growth of the nineteenth and twentieth centuries led to dramatic and extensive modifications of the hydrologic cycle and the construction of massive engineering projects for flood control, water supply, hydropower, and irrigation. The enormous expansion of water-resources infrastructure in the past

TABLE 2. Renewable Water Resources and Water Availability by Continents

Continent	Area (million Sq. Km)	2007 Population (millions)	Average Water Resources (Cu.Km/yr.)	Water Availability (Cu.Km/yr)	
				Per sq. Km	Per Capita
Europe	10.5	733	2,900	277	3.96
Asia	43.5	4,010	13,510	311	3.37
Africa	30.1	944	4,050	134	4.29 r.
North and Central America	24.3	483	7,890	324	16.33
South America	17.9	381	12,030	672	31.57
Oceania	8.9	35	2,360	264	67.43

SOURCES: Shiklomanov, 1998; and Population Reference Bureau, 2007

century has been driven by the dramatic growth of population, industrial development, and irrigated agriculture. Between 1900 and 2000, the population of the world grew from 1.6 billion to more than 6 billion. Land under irrigation increased from around 50 million hectares at the turn of the century to over 260 million hectares in 2000. These and other factors have led to a nearly seven-fold increase in freshwater withdrawals. [*See* Irrigation.]

WATER: USE, WITHDRAWAL, CONSUMPTION

The terms "use," "withdrawal," and "consumption" are not synonymous, and care should be taken when using them. These terms are often used inconsistently and misleadingly. "Water use" encompasses many different ideas, including the withdrawal of water, gross water use, and the consumptive use of water. "Withdrawal" should be used for the taking of water from a source for storage or use. Not all water withdrawn is necessarily consumed. For many processes, water is withdrawn and then returned directly to the original source after use, as with water used for cooling thermoelectric power plants. "Gross water use" is distinguished from water withdrawal by the inclusion of recirculated or reused water. Thus for many industrial processes, water requirements may exceed actual water withdrawn for use because that water is reused. Water "consumption" or "consumptive use" should refer to the use of water in a manner that prevents its immediate reuse, such as through evaporation, plant transpiration, contamination, or incorporation into a finished product. Water for cooling power plants, for example, may be withdrawn from a river or lake, used once or more than once, and then returned to the original source; this should not be considered a consumptive use. Water withdrawn for agriculture may have both consumptive and nonconsumptive uses, as part of the water is transpired into the atmosphere or incorporated into plant material, while the remainder may return to groundwater or the surface source from which it originated.

Freshwater withdrawals worldwide increased from an estimated 580 km^3 per year in 1900 to 3,800 km^3/yr in 1995, a six-fold increase. In the industrialized world, the increases in withdrawals were even more dramatic. In the United States, 56 cubic kilometers were withdrawn for all purposes in 1900. By 1920, this had doubled to over 120 km^3/yr. By 1950 total water withdrawals were 250 km^3/yr. By 1970, withdrawals doubled a third time to over 500 km^3/yr. And water use in the U.S. peaked in 1980 at over 610 km^3/yr (Solley et al., 1998)—a tenfold increase in water withdrawals during a period when population increased by a factor of four (Gleick, 1993).

It is estimated that humans already appropriate 54% of accessible runoff on earth and that future population growth and economic development could lead humans to use more than 70% of accessible runoff by 2025 (Postel et al., 1996).

TWENTY-FIRST CENTURY WATER ISSUES

Problems of scarcity and quality dominated the water agenda in the twentieth century. Many of these problems are still with us and must be addressed in the coming decades. Now, however, there is a new set of issues that must also be factored into water planning, management, and policy. These include the need to meet basic human and ecosystem needs for water, the impacts of climate change for water and water systems, the risks of conflict over scarce water resources, new technology for addressing water problems, and questions of management and planning.

Meeting basic human and ecosystem water needs

Much of the world's population, particularly in developing countries, remains without access to clean drinking water or adequate methods to dispose of human wastes. The lack of clean drinking water and sanitation services leads to hundreds of millions of cases of water-related diseases and 5–10 million deaths annually, primarily of small children. A decade-long effort to deal with these shortcomings began in 1980 with the International Drinking Water Supply and Sanitation Decade, coordinated by the United Nations and international aid organizations. Despite the substantial progress made by 1990, rapid population growth and serious economic problems in Asia and Africa limited the overall gains. According to UN estimates, in the mid-1990s nearly 3 billion people lacked access to adequate sanitation services, while over 1.2 billion people lacked adequate clean drinking water. While most water policymakers agree that the failure to meet basic needs is the most pressing water problem facing nations, there is still little agreement about the most effective ways of meeting those needs.

The water needs of the natural environment are rarely considered or guaranteed. In the United States and Europe, some minimum flow requirements have been set for rivers and some minimum quality or temperature standards have been promulgated to protect environmental assets. In the United States, legislation has protected stretches of certain pristine rivers from development, and some water has been reallocated from major water projects and users to the environment. In California, for example, federal and state laws have set aside nearly 30,000 million cubic meters of annual runoff for environmental purposes, including the protection of wild and scenic rivers, the Sacramento–San Joaquin Delta, and flow protections for fish and waterfowl. Similar legal efforts are underway internationally. Despite these efforts, aquatic ecosystems throughout the world are under severe stress and threat of destruction. Globally, more than 1,000 species of fish, amphibians, and aquatic plants are considered threatened with extinction. [*See* Extinctions of Animals.] Basic water requirements to protect these species and, more broadly, whole ecosystems, must be identified and provided.

Water and climate change

The world's leading climate scientists believe that we are now on the verge of changing our climate through human activities that produce trace gases, including the burning of fossil fuels, the destruction of forests, and a wide range of industrial and agricultural activities. [*See* Global Warming *and* Greenhouse Effect.] Indeed, a growing number of scientists believe that some human-induced climatic changes are already beginning to occur or are unavoidable even if we act now to reduce our emissions of these gases. These climatic changes will have widespread consequences for water resources and water management. The climate determines where and when it rains, the kinds of crops we grow and the water needed for their success, the location, size, and operation of dams and reservoirs, the kinds of structures we build along our coastlines, and how much water we need to drink. Among the most important consequences of the greenhouse effect will be impacts on water resources, including both the natural hydrologic system and the complex water-management schemes we have built to alter and control that system. Changes may be necessary in the design of projects being planned. Modifications may be required to existing facilities to permit them to continue to meet their design objectives. New projects may need to be built or old projects removed, new institutions may need to be created or old ones revamped, in order to cope with possible changes.

There is little doubt that climatic change will alter the hydrologic cycle, but there is little certainty about the form these changes will take, or when they will be unambiguously detected. The hydrologic system—an integrated component of the earth's geophysical system—both affects and is affected by climatic conditions. Changes in temperature affect evapotranspiration rates, cloud characteristics, soil moisture, storm intensity, and snowfall and snowmelt regimes. Changes in precipitation affect the timing and magnitude of floods and droughts, shift runoff regimes, and alter groundwater recharge characteristics. Synergistic effects will alter cloud formation and extent, vegetation patterns and growth rates, and soil moisture.

Among the expected impacts of climatic changes on water resources are increases in global average precipitation and evaporation, changes in the regional patterns of rainfall, snowfall, and snowmelt, changes in the intensity, severity, and timing of major storms, rising sea level and saltwater intrusion into coastal aquifers, and a wide range of other geophysical effects. These changes will also have many secondary impacts on freshwater resources, altering the demand and supply of water and changing its quality. Specifically, in areas dependent on glacier melt for water supply, the rapid loss of glaciers to global warming will have a serious impact on the amount of available water and the timing of water flow during the warm season.

The impacts of climate change on water-resources supply and availability will lead to direct and indirect effects on a wide range of institutional, economic, and social factors. The nature of these effects is not well understood, nor is the ability of society to adapt to them. If water managers and planners can easily and cheaply adapt to any climatic disruptions that may occur, actions to prevent climate change will be less urgent. If we overestimate our ability to adapt, we may ignore inexpensive and successful actions that can reduce the impacts of climate change early.

Adaptation and innovative management will certainly be a useful and necessary response to climatic changes. Several factors, however, suggest that relying solely, or even principally, on adaptation may prove a dangerous policy. First, the impacts of climate change on the water sector will be very complicated and at least partly unpredictable. Second, many impacts may be nonlinear and chaotic, characterized by surprises and unusual events. Third, climatic changes will be imposed on water systems increasingly stressed by other factors, including population growth, competition for financial resources from other sectors, and disputes over water allocations and priorities. Finally, adaptive strategies may help mitigate some adverse consequences of climate change while simultaneously worsening others.

Many difficulties hinder accurate assessments of the impacts of climate changes on global or regional hydrology. Important hydrologic processes occur at fairly small spatial scales and are not yet capable of being accurately modeled. [See Climate Models and Uncertainty.] Limitations in data availability and quality affect our ability to accurately validate models or verify results, and the complex human modifications of watersheds must be incorporated into any detailed analysis of impacts and adaptation.

Conflicts over shared water resources

There is a long history of conflicts over water shared by two or more political entities. Fresh water is vital to all ecological and societal activities, including the production of food and energy, transportation, waste disposal, industrial development, and human health. Yet the uneven distribution of water leads to local and international frictions and tensions. Not all water-resources disputes will lead to violent conflict; most lead to negotiations, discussions, and nonviolent resolutions. But in certain regions water is a scarce resource that is becoming increasingly important for economic and agricultural production and increasingly scarce because of growing population and resource degradation. In these regions, shared water is evolving into an issue of high politics, and the probability of water-related disputes is increasing. In the twenty-first century, water and water-supply systems are increasingly likely to be instruments of political conflict and the objectives of military action as human populations grow, standards of living improve, and global climatic changes make water supply and demand more problematic and uncertain.

There are four major links between water and conflict: Water has been used as a military and political goal. Water has been used as a weapon of war. Water-resources systems have been targets of war. And inequities in the distribution, use, and consequences of water-resources management and use can be a source of tension and dispute. These links can occur at local, subnational, and international levels.

Policymakers must be alert to the likelihood of disagreements over water resources and to possible changes in international water law, regional political arrangements, and patterns of use that could minimize the risk of conflict. Various regional and international approaches exist for reducing water-related tensions. Among the approaches are legal agreements, the application of proper technology, institutions for dispute resolution, and innovative water management. Unfortunately, these mechanisms have never received the international support or attention necessary to resolve many conflicts over water. Efforts by the United Nations, international aid agencies, and local communities to ensure access to clean drinking water and adequate sanitation can reduce the competition for limited water supplies and the economic and social impacts of widespread waterborne diseases. Improving the efficiency of water use in agriculture can extend limited resources, increase water supplies for other users, strengthen food self-sufficiency, reduce hunger, and lower expenditures for imported food. In regions with shared water supplies, third-party participation in resolving water disputes can also help end conflicts.

IMPROVING THE PRODUCTIVITY OF WATER USE

A key approach to water-resources management is the growing focus on using water more productively. In the late 1980s and early 1990s, arguments against developing new supplies of water began to gain favor, driven in part by concerns over the high costs of new large dams and irrigation systems and over the accumulating environmental consequences of past actions. During this period, it was argued that the need to develop new sources of water supply could largely be avoided by implementing intelligent water conservation and demand management programs, installing new efficient equipment, and applying appropriate economic and institutional incentives to shift water among users.

Vast improvements in water-use efficiency appear possible in almost all sectors in both developed and developing countries. While many developing countries could benefit from increases in overall water availability, existing systems often waste much of the available supply through poor distribution systems, faulty or old equipment, and inappropriately designed or maintained irrigation systems. In Jordan, for example, at least 30% of all domestic water supplies never reach users because of flaws and inadequacies in the water-supply network, and the losses reach 50% in Jordan's capital, Amman (Salameh and Bannayan, 1993). It has been estimated that the amount of water lost in Mexico City's supply system is equal to the amount needed to supply a city the size of Rome (Falkenmark and Lindh, 1993). Increased water prices and government restrictions on wastewater discharges encouraged the Zuari Agro-Chemical fertilizer plant in Goa, India, to reduce total daily water use 50% between 1982 and 1988. Similar efforts in Tianjin, China, reduced industrial water use per unit of industrial output there by about 60%, and economic incentives led to improvements in industrial water-use efficiency by 42–62% in three industrial plants in São Paulo, Brazil, in the early 1980s.

Great improvements are possible in the industrialized world as well. Industrial output in Japan has steadily risen since the 1970s, while total industrial water use there has dropped more than 25%. In 1965 Japan used nearly 48,000 cubic meters of water to produce a million dollars of industrial output; by 1989, this had dropped to 13,000 m³ (in real terms, i.e., corrected for inflation)—a tripling of industrial water productivity (Postel, 1997). In California, where water use has been subject to close scrutiny for years, great potential still exists for reducing water use without sacrificing economic productivity or personal welfare. Total industrial water use in California dropped 30% between 1980 and 1990 without any formal or intentional efforts, because of natural economic and technological changes that occurred during the decade. Over the same period, total gross industrial production rose 30% in real terms.

In all economic activities, water demands depend on what is being produced and the efficiency with which it is produced. Total water use thus depends on the mix of goods and services demanded by society and on the processes chosen to generate those goods and services. Making a ton of steel in the 1930s consumed 60–100 tons of water. Today the same steel can be produced with less than 6 tons of water, but a ton of aluminum today requires only 1.5 tons of water. Replacing old steel-making technology with new processes can reduce water needs. Replacing steel with aluminum, as has been happening for many years in the automobile industry for other reasons, can also reduce water needs.

Water-use efficiency can also be improved in gardens, municipal lawns, golf courses, and other features of urban landscapes. In some parts of the United States as much as half of all residential or institutional water demand goes to water gardens and lawns. Improvements in watering efficiency could reduce that demand substantially, as could changes in the composition of these gardens. Xeriscaping, the use of drought-resistant plants in landscaping, is being pursued in many major western U.S. cities. Innovative garden designs, combined with new technology, can reduce outdoor water use in homes by 25–50% or more depending on homeowners' preferences, the price of water, and the cost of alternatives. In some regions, outdoor municipal and institutional landscape irrigation is being done with reclaimed water, completely eliminating the use of potable water for this purpose.

Agriculture is the largest single user of water, and this water use is largely inefficient—water is lost as it moves through leaky pipes and unlined aqueducts, as it is distributed to farmers, and as it is applied to grow crops. Some analysts estimate that the overall efficiency of agricultural water use worldwide is only 40% (Postel, 1997), meaning that more than half of all water diverted for agriculture never produces food. Even modest improvements in irrigation efficiency can free up vast quantities of water for growing more food or for meeting other needs. New sprinkler designs, such as low-energy precision application (LEPA), can increase sprinkler efficiencies from 60 to 70% to as high as 95%. Drip irrigation, invented in Israel to deal with both water scarcity and salinity problems and now watering over half of Israel's irrigated land, has expanded worldwide. In California, more than 400,000 hectares of crops are watered using drip systems, and more crops are being watered by such methods. Where high-valued crops are grown in relatively permanent settings such as orchards and vineyards, drip irrigation is now the dominant irrigation method, and it is being used increasingly for row crops such as strawberries, asparagus, peppers, melons, tomatoes, cotton, and sugar cane.

[*See also* Climate Change and Societal Development; Global Warming; Greenhouse Effect; Ground Water; Impacts of Climate Change; Lakes; Rivers: Impacts of Climate Change; Water-Quality Trends; *and* Water Vapor.]

BIBLIOGRAPHY

REFERENCES CITED

Arnell, N., et al. "Hydrology and Freshwater Ecology." In *Climate Change 1995: Impacts, Adaptations, and Mitigation of Climate Change: Contribution of Working Group II to the Second Assessment Report of the Intergovernmental Panel on Climate Change,* edited by R.T. Watson, M.C. Zinyowera, and R.H. Moss, pp. 325–364. Cambridge and New York: Cambridge University Press, 1996.

Falkenmark, M., and G. Lindh. 1993. "Water and Economic Development." In *Water in Crisis: A Guide to the World's Fresh Water Resources,* edited by P.H. Gleick, pp. 80–91. New York: Oxford University Press, 1993.

Gleick, P.H., ed. *Water in Crisis: A Guide to the World's Fresh Water Resources.* New York: Oxford University Press, 1993.

Gleick, P.H., et al. *California Water 2020: A Sustainable Vision.* Oakland, Calif.: Pacific Institute for Studies in Development, Environment, and Security, 1995.

Postel, S. *Last Oasis: Facing Water Scarcity.* Updated ed. Worldwatch Institute. New York: Norton, 1997.

Postel, S.L., G.C. Daily, and P.R. Ehrlich. 1996. "Human Appropriation of Renewable Fresh Water." *Science* 271 (1996), 785–788. DOI: 10.1126/science.271.5250.785.

Salameh, E., and H. Bannayan. *Water Resources of Jordan: Present Status and Future Potentials.* Amman, Jordan: Friedrich Ebert Stiftung, 1993.

Shiklomanov, I.A. "World Water Resources and World Water Use." Data archive. St. Petersburg, Russia: State Hydrological Institute, 1998.

Solley, W.B., R.R. Pierce, and H.A. Perlman. "Estimated Use of Water in the United States in 1995." *U.S. Geological Survey Circular 1200.* Denver, Colorado: U.S. Department of the Interior, 1998.

Van Hylckama, T.E.A. 1970. "Water Balance and Earth Unbalance." In International Association of Scientific Hydrologicy Publication No. 93, Symposium on World Water Balance, vol. 2, pp. 434–444.

SOURCES DEALING WITH TWENTY-FIRST CENTURY WATER PROBLEMS

de Villiers, M. *Water: The Fate of Our Most Precious Resource.* Boston: Houghton Mifflin, 2001.

Gleick, P.H. "Global Fresh Water Resources: Soft-Path Solutions for the 21st Century." *Science* 302 (2003), 1524–1528. DOI: 10.1126/science.1089967.

Gleick, P.H., ed. *The World's Water 2006–2007: The Biennial Report on Freshwater Resources.* Washington, D.C.: Island Press, 2006.

Natural History [magazine]. *Water, the Wellspring of Life.* Special Issue, November, 2007, pp. 29–70.

Nowak, R. "Australia: The Continent That Ran Dry." *New Scientist* 194 (June 16, 2007), 8–11. DOI: 10.1016/S0262-4079(07)61467-5.

Pearce, F. *When the Rivers Run Dry.* Boston: Beacon Press, 2006.

———. "The Parched Planet." *New Scientist* (February 25, 2006), 32–36.

Planet Ark. "Melting Glaciers Threaten World Water Supply." November 19, 2004. http://www.planetark.com/dailynewsstery.cfm/newsid/28200/stery.htm (accessed June 5, 2008).

Postel, S. *Pillar of Sand: Can the Irrigation Miracle Last?* New York: Norton, 1999.

———. *Liquid Assets: The Critical Need to Safeguard Freshwater Ecosystems.* Washington, D.C.: Worldwatch Institute, 2005.

Postel, S., and B. Richter. *Rivers for Life.* Washington, D.C.: Island Press, 2003.

UNESCO. *Water: A Shared Responsibility.* World Water Development Report No. 2. Paris: UNESCO; New York: Berghan Books, 2006.

Yardley, J. "Beneath Booming Cities, China's Future is Drying Up." *New York Times,* September 28, 2007.

—PETER H. GLEICK AND DAVID J. CUFF

WATER-QUALITY TRENDS

Water quality has many definitions. For geochemists it refers to the chemical composition of a water sample: a set of concentrations, chemical species (such as NO_3^-, NH_4^+, NO_2^-, organic nitrogen), and physical partitions (such as dissolved, colloidal, fine particulate, or coarse particulate matter; Chapman, 1996). For most ecologists it refers to the physicochemical conditions of an aquatic system that may sustain a healthy aquatic biotic community in equilibrium with the local natural conditions. For sanitary engineers, water quality is considered at a given location mostly with regard to human health, including concerns over water-borne and other water-related diseases. Finally, water-management engineers define water quality depending on its potential uses by humans, such as drinking water, irrigation, industrial use, transportation, or power generation. [*See* Irrigation.]

Descriptors of water quality are physical (color, transparency, pH, temperature, and total suspended solids [TSS]), chemical (for water and particulates), bacteriological (total coliform and fecal coliform bacteria), and ecological (chlorophyll, biotic indices, biological oxygen demand [BOD]). Water quality now includes the overall quality of the aquatic ecosystem, based on the water, its suspended particulate matter, the health of the biological communities and organisms, and the nature of the riverbed. Such broad definitions also take into account the time variability of the physicochemical conditions, including water level and water velocity (Chapman, 1996).

In many regions of the world, the most critical health issue is still water-borne and water-related diseases such as malaria, bacterial diarrhea, onchocerciasis, and schistosomiasis (bilharzia). These issues still affect a much greater population than that exposed to severe chemical pollution. Water-related diseases require the treatment of both wetlands (for malaria) and fast-flowing waters (for onchocerciasis) with appropriate pesticides (particularly in densely populated tropical regions), by filtration, or by chemical processes. Neither these issues nor that of radioactive contamination will be discussed here. [*See* Disease; *and* Nuclear Waste.]

Pollution is used here as a generic term for the impacts on natural or artificial aquatic systems caused by human activities that may adversely affect aquatic biota, reduce actual and potential water uses, impair human health, or reduce water-related amenities. [*See* Pollution.]

CONTAMINANTS: ORIGINS AND PATHWAYS

Most pathways of contaminants to surface and ground waters are similar to those of natural compounds: atmospheric pollution (Figure 1, flux G); direct release of treated or untreated wastewaters from mines (H), cities (I), and industries (J); runoff from agricultural land (K), urbanized areas (L), and mine tailings (M); and leaching of contaminated soil waters to ground waters from agriculture (N), mines (O), industries (P), and dumps (Q). Contaminant inputs that can be collected and treated are referred to as point sources, while sources that cannot be collected— typically atmospheric fallout and agricultural runoff—are called diffuse sources. Intermediate types of sources such as cars and scattered housing, that can either be collected or treated individually, may be termed dispersed sources.

River channelization (Figure 1, flux R), wetland filling, river damming (S) associated with reservoir construction, and sand mining in floodplains constitute another category of important impacts on aquatic systems. They all modify the river–groundwater interface that regulates the concentrations of such key compounds as NO_3^- and O_2. Most reservoirs store 70–99% of incoming particulates, with their attached toxins and nutrients, which in turn may be released from the sediments to the bottom water layers if anoxic conditions are established, as is common in deep reservoirs. These modifications have a global impact on aquatic communities, particularly for the thousands of major reservoirs over 15 meters high.

GLOBAL TRENDS IN WATER QUALITY

On a multiyear scale, changes in land and water use, urbanization, industrialization, deforestation, and pollution-control activities (regulation, prevention, waste collection and treatment, water reuse, landscape engineering) gradually change the quality of water bodies. General trends of water quality are difficult to describe because both deterioration and improvements occur (UNEP 1994, 1995, 1996). Yet a broad picture can be drawn on the basis of a few water-chemistry records for 40–100 years, environmental archives of particulate pollution (recorded in sediment cores from river flood plains, deltas, lakes, and estuaries), and expanding water-quality monitoring since the 1970s.

Fecal contamination has diminished in most western countries, especially in Europe and North America. Maximum counts of 10,000–100,000 total coliform bacteria per 100 ml were frequently observed in the 1960s and 1970s. They have decreased as the result of domestic sewage collection and treatment. In such heavily populated and fast-developing countries as China, India, Brazil, Mexico, Indonesia, and Nigeria, fecal contamination may still be the primary water-quality issue. Yet, where wastewater treatment increases faster than population, an improvement can be observed: over the last ten years the peak contamination of total coliform of the Lower Ganges at Rajmahal dropped from

---

Water Quality Trends. Figure 1. Major Natural and Anthropogenic Sources and Pathways of Water-Borne Material.

Natural sources and pathways: A. Oceanic and salt fallout; B. Soil leaching and erosion; C. Mineral dissolution by ground water; D. Biogeochemical processes at ecotones; E. Processes within water bodies; F. Evaporation. Anthropogenic sources and pathways: G. Atmospheric pollution; H. Direct release of mine water; I. Release of urban waste waters; J. Release of industrial waster waters; K. Runoff from agricultural land; L. Runoff from urban areas; M. Runoff from mine tailing; N. Leaching of contaminated soils to ground waters; O. Leaching of mine tailing to ground waters; P. Pollutant dumps leaks; Q. Waste release to ground waters; R. River channelization; S. Damming.

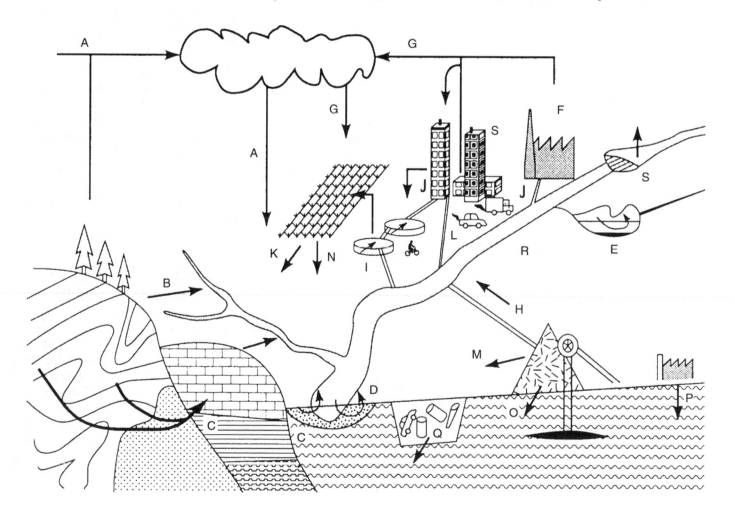

more than 100,000 per 100 ml to fewer than 1,000 per 100 ml, according to the Central Pollution Control Board in Delhi.

In many western European rivers (Rhine, Thames, Seine, Schelde) where the population density is high (greater than 250 people per square kilometer), the dissolved oxygen levels were formerly below the 2 milligrams per liter (mg/L) limit for the survival of fish of the carp family and even near zero downstream of major sources of pollutants. For instance, the Rhine River (basin area 220,000 km^2), with O_2 below 3 mg/L between 1955 and 1975 and BOD_5 (the amount of dissolved oxygen in water consumed in 5 days by the decomposition of organic matter) up to 10 mg/L, saw a spectacular increase in the mid-1970s. Major O_2 problems can still be found during the low-flow season in many rivers exposed to untreated domestic sewage.

The ammonia problem, which concerns both fish and human health, is similar to those of fecal contamination and oxygen demand. For instance, in the Rhine, NH_4^+ peaked in the early 1970s then dropped dramatically in 10 years.

Nitrate originating from nitrogen fertilizers has increased in all river basins affected by agricultural activities: in Western Europe (Rhine, Seine, Po, Danube), in North America (Mississippi), and China (the Yellow [Huang] and Yangtze [Chang] rivers). This trend is also observed in ground waters for the same regions. In some cases the nitrate level may now exceed the WHO drinking water standard (50 mg NO_3^-/L).

Phosphate, not a toxic substance per se but the nutrient primarily responsible for excessive algal growth, is increasing in most populated river basins as the result of domestic sewage collection without tertiary phosphorus removal and phosphorus-detergent use since the 1950s. Where environmental regulations are very strict, as in the North American Great Lakes and the Rhine basin, the PO_4^{-3} level in river and lakes has dropped considerably. These regulations combine a complete ban on phosphorus detergents, the removal of remaining phosphorus from domestic and industrial wastewaters at treatment plants, and the control of total phosphorus leaching from agricultural soils. Where phosphorus control has only begun, as in the Seine basin, the present levels may reach 50 times the preanthropogenic values (700 micrograms of phosphorus per liter, compared to 10–20 μg P/L). In the Seine the resulting algal biomass is responsible for marked hypoxia in the turbid estuarine zone, where bacterial respiration predominates greatly over primary production. In lakes and reservoirs, excessive algal production is responsible for the hypoxia and anoxia of bottom waters with subsequent release of NH_4^+, metals, and PO_4^{-3}, a common feature of eutrophic (overly nutrient-rich) water bodies in western Europe, North America, and now Asia (UNEP, 1994). [See Phosphorus Cycle.]

The inputs of nitrogen and phosphorus to the oceans have increased globally by a factor of three, and by 10–50 times at some regional and local scales. Dissolved silica is not released to aquatic systems by human activities; on the contrary, its uptake by diatoms as a result of eutrophication results in a long-term SiO_2 decrease in eutrophic rivers. The change in the N:P:Si ratio in rivers is one of the fastest and most remarkable global changes and will ultimately affect coastal ecosystems, such as those in Louisiana and Romania.

Many major ions, such as Na^+, Cl^-, and SO_4^{-2}, are increasing steadily in many rivers and lakes. On exceptional occasions they exceed World Health Organization (WHO) guidelines, as in rivers in dry environments—such as the Colorado in the southwestern U.S. and the Amu Dar'ya and the Syr Dar'ya in Central Asia—when much water is withdrawn and then returned after irrigation and subsequent evaporation. For the Lower Amu Dar'ya, SO_4^{-2} increased from its natural range of 200–300 mg/L in the 1950s to its present value of 600–750 mg/L, well above the WHO guideline of 250 mg/L (Tsirkunov, in Kimstach et al., 1998).

Trends in heavy metals are more difficult to assess because of a lack of reliable data. In a few cases, long-term trends have been determined from sediment cores or from analyses of suspended sediments. The greatest increase of metals (tens to hundreds of times above the natural background) are observed in small and medium-sized basins (Seine, Rhine), where the additional metal inputs are little diluted by particulates such as clays and quartz. In bigger basins the contamination is much less obvious, for example, in the major Chinese rivers or the Mississippi, which carry 100 millions tons of suspended solids. A slight (10 μg/g) decrease in particulate lead in the Mississippi sediments from 1970 to the early 1980s implies an enormous change in lead transport of the order of 2,000 tons per year, which has been attributed mostly to the control of atmospheric lead. In a few industrialized regions, waste collection and recycling have been successful. In the Rhine the marked decrease in the 1970s of most inorganic toxins—arsenic, cadmium, mercury, lead—is continuing. In the River Seine, up to 10 μg/g of mercury and 50 μg/g of cadmium—more than one hundred times the natural background levels—were measured downstream of local industrial pollution sources in the 1980s. These extreme peaks are no longer found, but the present metal contents of particulates downstream of Paris are still more than ten times the natural background values for cadmium and mercury, and exceed many national standards for copper, zinc, and lead in sediments.

Trends of organic micropollutants are even less well documented, except in the sedimentary record. Their monitoring is very recent, still expensive, and requires careful and sometimes frequent sampling. Where DDT has been banned there has been a marked drop in its concentration in river and lake particulates after 1970, but there are still traces of DDT in soil particles carried by rivers. The manufacture of PCBs, but not their use, has now been stopped in North America and Europe, and these contaminants are found in all riverine particulates, though concentrations are beginning to decline.

New xenobiotic products, chemicals found in an organism but which are not normally produced or expected to be present in it, appear on the global market every year. Atrazine, a widely used herbicide, was first detected in the 1980s and is now present in many rivers where its short-term peaks may exceed the WHO standard. The new pesticides are less harmful than earlier ones, but there is still much debate between the manufacturers of new chemicals and environmental engineers. It takes more than ten years to detect a new product in environmental samples, control its impacts, and develop the low-cost analysis procedure that permits its routine monitoring. By the time the appropriate monitoring is set up, a new chemical is put on the market.

GLOBAL POLLUTION HOT SPOTS

Some single pollution sources may affect wide areas because of the amount, density, or nature of their pollutant loads. These "hot spots" include megacities, major mining and smelting areas, some industrial regions, and nuclear facilities. The catastrophic Chernobyl accident has reminded the world about the possible global contamination of water from a single facility through the long-range atmospheric transport of radionuclides.

Major mining or smelting can occur anywhere, in densely populated regions (e.g., Sudbury, Ontario) or in such remote places as the Subarctic (e.g., Severonikel in the Kola Peninsula, Noril'sk in the Pyasina basin), South America, central Africa, or New Guinea. In many of these places, environmental regulations either do not exist or are inadequately enforced. The result is that high concentrations and enormous pollution loads can be discharged to the atmosphere and surface waters, some being equivalent to natural loads originating from areas 1,000–100,000 times larger.

Many megacities, such as Delhi, Moscow, Paris, Chicago, and Cairo, are located on rivers and have an enormous impact. The impact of Paris (10 million people) on the River Seine (65,000 km^2) can be taken as an example. About four-fifths of Paris's wastewater is collected and treated at a single plant. This treated sewage is equivalent to a small river with a discharge of 25 cubic meters per second—i.e., 25–35% of the Seine's discharge during droughts—still containing very high levels of BOD$_5$ (38 mg/L), NH$_4^+$ (24.7 mg N/L), and PO$_4^{-3}$ (3.6 mg P/L). Before the wastewater was properly treated in the 1960s, the Seine was sometimes completely anoxic in the summer. The Seine's nitrogen and phosphorus inputs to the ocean are presently equivalent to 2 million km^2 of natural land.

GLOBAL FRESHWATER ISSUES

Table 1 presents a list of mid-1990s water-quality issues for various water bodies found in well-monitored regions of the temperate Northern Hemisphere (Japan, North America, Europe, and Asiatic Russia; Meybeck, 1989; UNEP, 1994, 1995, and 1996). In the fast-developing and densely populated countries of tropical regions, the situation can be worse, whereas in countries with a sparse population or in very humid environments (surface runoff exceeding 500 mm per year), most issues are less critical. These issues can be grouped as chemicals-related problems and as physical, biological, and health issues. Acidification is mostly related to the combination of sensitive local soils and acidic atmospheric fallout.

Global climate change is presently not the most critical issue for water quality. It is much slower than most other global changes, such as water diversion and reservoir building, the global increase of inputs of nutrients, metals, and toxic organic chemicals to oceans and regional seas, and wetland filling. Global climate change will, however, affect semiarid areas that are most sensitive to the modification of their water balance and where severe salinization problems are likely in the future. In coastal zones, seawater intrusion into coastal aquifers resulting from sea level rise will be also a major issue.

TABLE 1. Major Freshwater Quality Issues at the Global Scale, for Populated Regions of the Temperate Northern Hemisphere[*]

Issue	Rivers	Reservoirs	Lakes	Ground Waters
Organic pollution	X (XX)	X(?)	X(?)	X
Eutrophication	X (X)	XX (X)[†]	X (X)	NA
Nitrate pollution	XX (X)	X (?)	O (?)	XXX (XX)
Salinization	X (XX)	O (X?)	O (?)	O (X to XX)
Metal contaminants	XX (XX)	X (?)	X (X)	XX (XX?)
Toxic organic substances	XXX (XX)	X (?)	X (X)	XX (XX?)
Acidification	X (X)	X (?)	XX (X)	O
Microbial pathogens	X (XXX)	X (X?)	X (X?)	X (XX?)
Hydrological changes	XXX (XXX)	NA	X (X)	X
Water-related diseases	O (XXX)	O (XX)	O (XXX)	(XX)
Biological invasion[‡]	X (XX)		X (X)	NA
Relative recovery period[§]	Years to decades	Years	Years to centuries	Decades to centuries

Note: X = Limited issue; XX = Important issue; XXX = Critical issue; O = Very limited or local; NA = Not applicable.

[*] Items in parentheses represent issues for the densely populated tropical zone.

[†] In some cultures eutrophication can be regarded as beneficial.

[‡] Dreissena in temperate waters, Eichhornia in tropical waters.

[§] Higher figure for larger water bodies or high water residence time.

[*See also* Desalination; Environmental Law; Erosion; Salinization; *and* Water.]

BIBLIOGRAPHY

Adriansee, M., H.A.G. Niederlander, and P.B.M. Stortelder. *Monitoring Water Quality in the Future.* Vol. 1. *Chemical Monitoring.* The Hague: Ministry of Housing, Spatial Planning, and the Environment, 1995.

Chapman, D., ed. *Water Quality Assessments: A Guide to the Use of Biota, Sediments and Water in Environmental Monitoring.* 2d ed. London and New York: Spon, 1996. A general presentation of the various approaches to water quality.

Drever, J.I. *The Geochemistry of Natural Waters.* 2d ed. Englewood Cliffs, N.J.: Prentice Hall, 1988. Water quality as seen by a geochemist. The third edition was published in 1997.

Gibbs, R.J. "Mechanisms Controlling World Water Chemistry." *Science* 170 (1970), 1088–1090. A seminal paper on the spatial distribution of major ions. DOI: 10.1126/science.170.3962.1088.

Hem, J.D. *Study and Interpretation of the Chemical Characteristics of Natural Waters.* 3d ed. Water Supply Paper 2254. Reston, Va.: U.S. Geological Survey, 1989. A handy book with many case studies.

Horowitz, A.J. *The Use of Suspended Sediment and Associated Trace Elements in Water Quality Studies.* Special Publication 4. Reading, U.K.: International Association of Hydrological Sciences, 1995. A complete presentation of heavy metal surveys in water and sediments.

Kimstach, V., M. Meybeck, and E. Baroudy, eds. *A Water Quality Assessment of the Former Soviet Union.* London: Spon, 1998. An example of the multiple aspects of water quality issues over an area of 20 million square kilometers.

Meybeck, M. "Surface Water Quality: Global Assessment and Perspectives." In *Water: A* Meybeck, M., D. Chapman, and R. Helmer, eds. *Global Freshwater Quality: A First Assessment.* Oxford, U.K., and Cambridge, Mass.: Blackwell, 1989. The first global overview of water quality issues in rivers, lakes, reservoirs, and ground waters.

Meybeck, M. "River Water Quality, Global Ranges, Time, and Space Variabilities." *Verhandlungen International Vereingung Limnologie* 26 (1996), 81–96. From the natural variability of river water quality to human impacts.

Meybeck, M., and R. Helmer. "The Quality of Rivers: From Pristine Stage to Global Pollution." *Global and Planetary Change* 1.4 (1989), 283–309. DOI: http://dx.doi.org/10.1016/0921-8181(89)90007-6. Discusses pristine river quality and human impacts.

Meybeck, M., and A. Ragu. *River Discharges to the Oceans: An Assessment of Suspended Solids, Major Ions, and Nutrients.* Nairobi: United National Environmental Programme, 1996. The first water quality register of world rivers discharging to oceans, with more than two hundred rivers documented.

Salomons, W., and U. Förstner. *Metals in the Hydrocycle.* Berlin and New York: Springer, 1984. A seminal book on the origins and fate of metals in aquatic systems.

UNESCO. *Water: A Looming Crisis?* Paris: 1998, pp. 173–185. Discusses water quality issue scaling.

United Nations Environment Programme (UNEP). *The Pollution of Lakes and Reservoirs.* UNEP Environment Library, no. 12, Nairobi, 1994; no. 14, Nairobi, 1995. *Ground Water: A Threatened Resource*; no, 15. Nairobi, 1996. Three booklets on water quality issues.

—MICHEL H. MEYBECK

WATER VAPOR

Water vapor, the gaseous form of water (H_2O), is present in the Earth's atmosphere. It plays a central and varied role in the determination of the Earth's climate. Many of the uncertainties in prediction of climate changes—whether they be caused by solar variability or by increase in carbon dioxide (CO_2)—stem from uncertainties in the modeling of the way water vapor affects climate.

LATENT HEAT

The first type of water-vapor effect arises from the energy involved in the phase change between liquid (or solid) water and the vapor state. It takes about 2.5×10^6 joules of energy to change one kilogram of liquid water into a vapor at the same temperature; conversely, when one kilogram of water vapor condenses into a liquid, the same amount of energy is released to the surroundings. Stored energy of this sort is known as latent heat. The latent heat of one kilogram of water vapor is equivalent to the energy released by burning 72 milliliters of gasoline. Put another way, if the tropical Sun on a clear day beats down on the ocean surface with an intensity of three hundred watts per square meter, the solar energy absorbed in the course of a day could be compensated by the evaporation of a layer of water just one centimeter deep. In fact, this is the primary means by which solar energy is communicated to the atmosphere. Only about 20% of the incident solar energy is absorbed directly by the atmosphere. The balance is absorbed at the surface, where it is largely employed in the evaporation of water. The resulting water vapor enters the atmosphere, and the stored solar energy is released where the water vapor condenses back to a liquid. This could be thousands of kilometers from where the solar energy was absorbed. Water vapor is important to energy transport in the atmosphere because it allows the atmosphere to store large amounts of energy without heating up.

Latent heat is released where air rises in large-scale midlatitude storms and in tall convective towers in the tropics and the midlatitudes. The release of latent heat affects the lapse rate, which is the rate at which atmospheric temperature declines with height. An ascending parcel of air cools as it expands, but part of this cooling is offset by the latent heat released through condensation brought on by the cooling. Dry ascent would yield a lapse rate of about 10°K (Kelvin, = 10°C) per kilometer (the dry adiabat), whereas the observed lapse rate is around 6.5 °K/km. The physics determining the lapse rate is not simple, and the lapse rate is affected by many dynamic phenomena as well as by condensation. The lapse rate is important to the greenhouse effect; higher lapse rates favor a stronger greenhouse effect, other things being equal. A higher lapse rate means that for a fixed surface temperature, the upper atmosphere is colder. In this circumstance, the atmosphere radiates to space at a temperature much below that of the surface and thus radiates less heat than does the surface, yielding a large greenhouse effect. In the opposite situation—an atmosphere held at the same temperature as the surface—there would be no greenhouse effect, regardless of the CO_2 concentration, because heat would be lost to space from the top of the atmosphere at the same rate as it is radiated from the surface. Thus the way the lapse rate changes with changing climate affects the response of the system to perturbations.

The maximum amount of water vapor that can be stably held in a fixed volume without condensation is measured by the saturation vapor pressure, which increases roughly exponentially with temperature. Specifically, at saturation the water-vapor concentration is 2.06 parts per thousand (volume) at 260°K (−13°C) and 1,000 millibars pressure, but rises to 6.14 parts per thousand at 273°K (0°C) and 35.9 parts per thousand at 300°K (27°C). For this reason, water vapor is generally much more important in warm regions than in cold regions, with an important exception to be noted below. The ratio of the actual water content of an air parcel to the water content at saturation is known as the relative humidity, generally expressed as a percentage. Air at 100% relative humidity is saturated.

WATER VAPOR AS GREENHOUSE GAS

The second way water vapor affects climate is through its behavior as a greenhouse gas. [See Greenhouse Effect.] A no-atmosphere planet with a surface temperature of 300°K (typical of the Earth's tropics) would radiate infrared energy to space at a rate of 459 watts per square meter (W/m^2). Using a typical tropical temperature profile, adding an atmosphere whose only greenhouse gas is CO_2 at 300 parts per million (volume) brings the radiated energy down to 409 W/m^2. However, if water vapor is added to the atmosphere to achieve 50% relative humidity, the radiated energy drops to 303 W/m^2. For 40% relative humidity the value is 309 W/m^2, whereas for 60% it is 297 W/m^2. Because so much of the greenhouse effect is caused by the presence of water vapor in the atmosphere, climate predictions are sensitive to the way water-vapor content changes as the climate is altered.

This does not mean that the greenhouse effect of CO_2 and other trace gases is negligible compared to that of water vapor. Water vapor has a short lifetime in the atmosphere and therefore responds as a feedback as long-term variables such as CO_2 concentration, Earth's orbital parameters, and solar output are changed. In the simplest picture, water vapor amplifies climate sensitivity. As an atmosphere warms, it can (and therefore presumably does) hold more water vapor. Thus a small warming due directly to, say, doubling CO_2 is boosted to a much larger value by the greenhouse effect of the water vapor added to the atmosphere. In extreme cases, such as presumably occurred on Venus in its early history, the destabilizing effect of water vapor can be so great that the process ends only when all the oceans have evaporated. Even short of a runaway greenhouse of this type, water vapor greatly enhances climate sensitivity. The importance of water-vapor feedback in anthropogenic global warming was first made clear in climate models by the pioneering work of Manabe and Strickler in the late 1960s. Were it not for the water-vapor feedback, the temperature increase due to a doubling of CO_2 would not be a cause for concern.

The temperature of the lower atmosphere decreases with height, so most of the water vapor in an atmospheric column is generally contained in its lowest few kilometers. However, the small amount of water vapor aloft—the upper tropospheric humidity (UTH)—is disproportionately important for the greenhouse effect. UTH is difficult to model accurately, because it represents only a small portion of the water in the climate system and therefore is highly sensitive to moisture sources. The pattern of UTH is complex and is strongly influenced by the disposition of convective-moisture source-regions and by the wind patterns that transport water into dry regions far from the source. Water vapor further affects climate through its control of the formation of clouds.

[See also Climate Models and Uncertainty; Global Warming; Greenhouse Effect; and Ocean-Atmosphere Coupling.]

BIBLIOGRAPHY

Held, I.M., and B.J. Soden. "Water Vapor Feedback and Global Warming." *Annual Review of Energy and the Environment* 25 (2000), 441–475. A modern review emphasizing implications of water vapor feedback for global change.

Manabe, S., and R.T. Wetherald. "Thermal Equilibrium of the Atmosphere with a Given Distribution of Relative Humidity." *Journal of the Atmospheric Sciences* 24.3 (1967), 241–259. DOI: 10.1175/1520–0469(1967)024<0241:TEOTAW>2.0.CO;2. The classic paper that introduced the idea of simple models of water-vapor feedback.

Pierrehumbert, R.T. "Subtropical Water Vapor as a Mediator of Rapid Climate Change." In *Mechanisms of Global Climate Change at Millennial Time Scales*, Geophysical Monograph 112, edited by P.U. Clark, R.S. Webb, and L.D. Keigwin, pp. 339–361. Washington, D.C.: American Geophysical Union, 1999 (http://georci.unchicago.edu/~rtp1). Another review, emphasizing paleoclimate problems as well as global change.

Spencer, R.W., and W.D. Braswell. "How Dry Is the Tropical Free Troposphere? Implications for Global Warming Theory." *Bulletin of the American Meteorological Society* 78.6 (1997), 1097–1106. DOI: 10.1175/1520–0477(1997) 078<1097:HDITTF>2.0.CO;2. Contains satellite images illustrating the role of dynamics in modulating the water vapor field.

—R. T. PIERREHUMBERT

WEATHER MODIFICATION

Deliberate efforts to modify the weather—for example by cloud seeding—will probably be one of the responses to global climate changes in the next few decades. These may include large-scale efforts to modify surface albedo or atmospheric constituents, but substantial advances would be necessary before these became feasible. For the immediate future, modification of clouds and precipitation is a more realistic option.

Weather modification on a local or regional scale can be useful. This has been demonstrated by research and operations already carried out that encompass the range of climatic variations that could be expected with any projected climate changes. Weather changes that have been studied include fog clearance, cloud-cover modifications, the augmentation of orographic (mountain) precipitation, modification of rain, hail, and severe weather from convective clouds, and modification of hurricanes and extratropical storms (Hess, 1974; Cotton and Pielke, 2007).

In the western United States over the past 50 years, research into and implementation of weather modification has been cyclic: very extensive and intense during drought cycles, particularly in the mid-1950s and mid-1970s, and very limited during wet periods. In some areas, specifically in California and Utah, programs have continued since the early 1950s. These are areas in which augmentation of normal levels of precipitation is desirable, or where reservoirs are available to store water from wet years to be used in drier ones. Projects such as these would probably expand if climate change were to produce drier regional climates. Some areas in the western United States already have sufficient mountain precipitation in most years and thus have only occasionally resorted to weather modification during droughts.

At the other extreme, there are areas in which, even during normal or dry years, there would be no significant benefit from slightly increased precipitation, and thus weather modification has not been seriously employed. Other areas fall into an intermediate category that can benefit from increased precipitation in most years, and especially in drought years. In California, as many as 20 programs have been active in a single year. Most of these have been designed to increase snow in the mountain watersheds of the Sierra for enhanced hydroelectric power generation. Others have focused on California agriculture or supplemental water for municipalities. Fifteen programs were active in California during the 1994–1995 season, two of which have operated almost every year for more than 40 years; one has a record of 45 years of continuous operation (Henderson, 1997). These programs operate in a marginal area where, in most years, there is a need for more water. Wetter areas that have more frequent droughts in a future climate-change scenario arc likely to resort to weather modification, which is a technology that can be employed or discontinued with almost no time lag.

ADVANCES IN SCIENCE AND TECHNOLOGY

The technology of cloud modification, precipitation enhancement, and some types of severe-weather abatement is gradually becoming more soundly based as vastly improved tools for research and for operational programs become available. During a discovery period in the late 1940s and 1950s, it was established that it was possible to induce changes in clouds. Statistical experiments during the 1960s and 1970s, supported by physical studies, indicated that economically and socially beneficial effects could be achieved. However, the complex nature of the cloud systems and the treatment processes limited the researchers' physical understanding of the cloud-process changes and the treatment technology and thus their confidence in the statistical results. The understanding of the physical processes and the treatment technology has been greatly enhanced during the past 20 years. The increased investigative capabilities have included laboratory capabilities for describing nucleation modes and specific requirements applicable to different cloud regimes (DeMott, 1995); computer capabilities for studying cloud and treatment models (Farley et al., 1997; Heimbach et al., 1997); multiwavelength and polarized remote-sensing capabilities for continuous observation of cloud and treatment processes; instrumentation for direct in-cloud observations of cloud particles and processes; and enhanced particulate-tracing capabilities for improved cloud-treatment systems. In addition, long-term programs have provided a continuously increasing sample size for statistical analysis. The physical studies and new statistical results generally support the findings of the earlier statistical studies.

CURRENT CAPABILITIES

A number of experiments have shown that artificial treatments can increase mountain precipitation by 10–15%. Many researchers and water users have concluded that this is the type of weather modification most ready for practical application.

The results of experiments on the seeding of convective clouds to increase precipitation or decrease hail have been less consistent. Continuing research is providing knowledge as to which convective clouds are suitable for beneficial treatment and which are not. With the research tools now available, it is likely that more consistent beneficial treatment results will be possible for convective cloud systems within the next few years. Hail suppression is even more complex than precipitation augmentation for convective clouds. While some types of hailstorm are treatable with present technology, some of the more intense supercell storms are not and may remain unsuitable for treatment for hail reduction. However, the indications from both the physical and the statistical studies of hailstorms increasingly support the feasibility of beneficial treatment of many hail-producing cloud systems.

The possibility of beneficial modification of large-scale tropical and extratropical systems must be relegated to the more distant future. Perhaps the most likely option for altering these systems will be in cirrus cloud-cover, which could change the balance of incoming and outgoing radiation. It has been observed that there are sometimes large upper-atmospheric layers that are supersaturated with respect to ice and in which cirrus cloud systems can be created.

In summary, it appears likely that weather modification as a response to climate change will be used to augment water supplies from mountainous areas. It seems probable that, with further advances in our understanding of the dynamic and microphysical processes of convective systems, artificial treatment of these clouds for economically beneficial result will become increasingly feasible. It is unlikely that modification of large-scale weather systems will be a feasible response to climate change in the near future.

[See also Drought; and Geoengineering.]

BIBLIOGRAPHY

Cotton, W.R., and R.A. Pielke. Human Impacts on Weather and Climate. Cambridge and New York: Cambridge University Press, 2007.

DeMott, P.J. "Quantitative Description of Ice Formation Mechanism of Silver Iodide-Type Aerosols." Atmospheric Research 38 (1995), 63–99.

Farley, R.D., D.L. Hjermstad, and H.D. Orville. "Numerical Simulation of Cloud Seeding Effects during a Four-Day Storm Period." Journal of Weather Modification 29 (1997), 49–55.

Heimbach, J.A. Jr., W.D. Hall, and A.B. Super. "Modeling and Observations of Valley-Released Silver Iodide during a Stable Winter Storm over the Wasatch Plateau of Utah." Journal of Weather Modification 29 (1997), 33–41.

Henderson, T.J. "New Assessment of the Economic Impacts from Ten Winter Snowpack Augmentation Projects." Journal of Weather Modification 29 (1997), 42–48.

Hess, W.N., ed. Weather and Climate Modification. New York: Wiley, 1974.

—LEWIS O. GRANT

WETLANDS

Wetlands is the collective name increasingly given to all those types of terrain in which there is an interplay between land and water, and that share the characteristics of both. Swamps, bogs, fens, mires, peatlands, marshes, sloughs, wet meadows, prairie, river bottom lands, and even pothole country and pocosin (the commonly accepted southeastern Algonquian Indian name for evergreen shrub bogs), are all subsumed under the term.

Wetlands were formerly considered wastelands, neither sound land nor good water, and fit only to be filled in for urban or industrial purposes, dredged for harbors or marinas, reclaimed for agricultural land, or used as waste-disposal dumps. Consequently, they have been disappearing at an ever-increasing rate. But, while economic pressures have intensified, wetlands have become a more valued environment as their hydrologic/physical, chemical, biological, and socioeconomic benefits have been investigated and acknowledged and their basic Earth-sustaining qualities and biodiversity recognized. Perhaps above all, wetlands are perceived increasingly as an environment in which air, land, and water, and their fauna and flora, meet in an attractive and delicate environment that has caught the scientific and popular imagination. Demands for their conservation and nonuse are therefore widespread. Their common qualities are emphasized rather than their individual, unique ones, and a pride in achievement at their transformation has given way to concern at their loss.

THE NATURE OF WETLANDS

Wetlands are estimated to cover some 7.8 million square kilometers, or 6% of the world's surface (a little less than tropical rainforests, for example), but they are highly fragmented and diverse. They rarely cover large contiguous stretches of land, except, for example, in the Everglades, the Fens of eastern England, the Dutch polders, and the deltas of major rivers. Most wetlands were formed during the Holocene, about 10,000 BP, many by the deposition, immature drainage, and fluctuating sea levels that followed the retreat of the ice. Others have been formed by human action in the historical era. They are found in every climatic zone from the tundra mires of the Arctic to the tropical mangroves of the equator, and in every continent except Antarctica. [See Mangroves.] Their diversity has been simplified by Cowardin et al. (1979) into (1) the marine and estuarine wetlands of the coast, and (2) the riverine, lacustrine (of or near lakes), and palustrine (of or near marshes, usually topographic lows and areas underlain by impermeable strata) wetlands of the interior, a classification that emphasizes their commonalities.

Hydrology is the key to the formation of wetlands, and they have a distinctive botanical composition that arises from being at the junction between dry terrestrial ecosystems and permanently wet aquatic ecosystems. They are formed and conditioned by water and waterlogging, and are adapted to anoxic biochemical processes. Vegetation is adapted to wet (hydrophytic) conditions because it is water-covered for part of the year and is deficient in oxygen. It decomposes slowly and contributes to the formation of the wetland by trapping silt and forming, in time, actual soil (for example, peat). Much of the fauna is adapted to either deep water (fish and shellfish) or dry land (waterfowl, amphibians), moving seasonally into the wetland.

The physical volatility and constant flux from flooding, nutrient flows, and vegetation growth mean that wetlands are highly diverse ecosystems, the productivity of which is exceeded only by tropical rainforests. Consequently they have been a constant lure to humankind for settlement and use.

ATTITUDES TO WETLANDS

The neglect and denigration of wetlands changed after the early 1960s with greater scientific understanding of their common physical processes and attributes and with a shift in attitude toward them as a unique and valued environment. Interest emanated from the United States, where recreational, hunting, and wildlife enthusiasts, with the active support of the Fish and Wildlife Service (FWS), promoted wetland preservation during the 1930s, as did the duck-hunting lobby, Ducks Unlimited. In total, 1.7 million hectares (4.2 million acres) were purchased, created, or otherwise preserved. In addition, the integrated ecosystems approach stimulated curiosity about wetlands, and research centers focusing on wetland issues were set up at Baton Rouge (Louisiana), Sapelo Island (Georgia), and Miami (Florida). These trends came together as public and administrators alike became concerned at losses through marina dredging, prairie-pothole filling, and flood-control measures. By 1972, many U.S. coastal states had enacted legislation to protect their shores.

The importance of wetlands for water quality control and wastewater treatment, and a growing appreciation of their aesthetic qualities, led to a great deal of U.S. government legislation. Permits were required for dredge-and-fill activities and were only granted after scrutiny by the Environmental Protection Agency (EPA) and the FWS, the objectives and actions of the Corps of Engineers were redefined, and, in 1977, executive orders 11988 (Flood Plain Management) and 11990 (Protection of Wetlands) made wetlands a matter of national policy. By 1986, the Emergency Wetlands Resources Act directed the FWS to acquire wetlands with socioeconomic value, and a national wetlands survey was begun.

There was no equivalent wetlands lobby in Europe; in the postwar drive to maximize food production, wetland drainage was underwritten with generous grants from the Common Agricultural Policy of the European Community. Not until the mid-1970s were concerns voiced about losses.

VALUE OF WETLANDS

The natural processes and functions of wetlands are valuable to humans and are used as a counterargument to their destruction. For example, the physical/hydrologic benefits include flood mitigation, coastal protection, recharging of aquifers, sediment trapping, and possibly effects on atmospheric and climatic fluctuations through trapping of carbon dioxide.

After Hurricane Katrina stuck the U.S. Gulf Coast a number of authorities recognized the importance of preserving wetlands as buffers against storms and flooding: in fact, these values were pointed out well before Katrina (U.S Geological Survey, 2003).

Chemical functions include pollution trapping, removal of toxic residues, and waste recycling, while biological functions include biomass production and wildlife habitats. The socioeconomic consumptive benefits include food production, fuel from organic soils, fiber from hardwood forests, mangroves, and reed swamps, and fish, fowl, and other fauna.

Compared with the above, the nonconsumptive benefits are much more difficult to define, prove, and value in a monetary sense. These include scenic, recreational, educational, aesthetic, archaeological, scientific, heritage, and historical benefits. These are largely subjective. Recreation values can often be quantified by, for example, payment for fishing and hunting licenses, but there is an imperceptible transition between active involvement in the natural environment and passive enjoyment of a scene that can never be valued. A vast literature has attempted to quantify nonconsumptive values (5,600 abstracts in the FWS Value Database by 1988 alone), and there is still no consensus.

Two nonconsumptive aspects have caught the public imagination, namely, wildlife habitats and archaeology. The intensely moving sight of migrating wildfowl was probably the first, and has remained the most powerful, cause for action for preservation. And in Europe in particular, a spate of archaeological finds in wetlands has given tangible evidence of their heritage value. Organic matter is preserved in the waterlogged environment and found in identifiable stratified deposits. The Neolithic villages around Swiss lakes, Romano-British settlements in the Fens, the complex of late Mesolithic and early Neolithic trackways across the Somerset Levels in southwestern England, and the excavations at Key Marco in Florida have put wetlands high on the historical/heritage agenda, although their monetary value is still undetermined.

THE HUMAN IMPACT

Nearly every human activity has an actual or potential effect on wetlands. In the upland portions of watersheds, vegetation change, the surfacing of roads, and soil compaction will accelerate runoff and possibly reduce the recharge of water. Agricultural drainage enhances these processes. Mineral extraction, cultivation, and construction of all kinds increase erosion and transport of sediment. A variety of chemical and thermal discharges come from industry, agriculture, and sewage, such as acid runoff from old coal-mining areas or heated cooling water from power stations. Downstream, wetlands are affected directly by dredging, filling, construction of dams and pipelines, coastal protection works, piers and quays, and the excavation of ditches and canals. Less directly, offshore drilling, gas, water, and mineral extraction, and offshore island construction can all have an effect.

The only quantitative evidence of change is in the United States between 1955 and 1975, when a net loss of 4.625 million hectares was calculated. Of the 5.939 million hectares of freshwater wetlands lost, 80% succumbed to agricultural conversion,

followed by urban infilling (6.3%), and impounding for reservoirs and lakes (4.2%). Of the 0.195 million hectares of saltwater wetlands lost, dredging for canals, ports, and marinas accounted for 56% of the total. However, the volatility of the wetlands is highlighted by the fact that there was a gain of 1.465 million hectares of freshwater wetlands and 0.044 million hectares of saltwater wetlands, the former largely through active succession around the margins of new farm ponds, or through the neglect of existing land drainage, and the latter through the formation of new salt marshes and mud flats. How far these figures can be transferred to other parts of the world is open to question, but agricultural conversion probably accounts for at least four-fifths of losses, and urban-industrial impacts for another tenth.

THE AGRICULTURAL IMPACT

Draining for agriculture and grazing intensification is one of the major process of global change. It accounts for most of the 1.606 million square kilometers of wetlands lost by 1985, although some of that may be connected with the draining of irrigated lands. Nearly three-quarters of the agricultural reclamation has been in the temperate world. The inherent biological wealth of the wetlands bordering the North Sea was important in the transformation of the late medieval economy, and they became some of the most prosperous lands in Europe. In the Netherlands and the English Fens, the shrinkage of organic soils upset drainage patterns, a process exacerbated by fuel stripping, which actually created the lakes of northern Holland and the Norfolk Broads in eastern England. Progressively, new draining techniques of polders, sea walls, and windmills, eventually superseded by steam and then electric pumps, overcame the problem of land below sea level. The creation of most of the Netherlands is a monument to this activity.

In the United States, the reduction of wetlands has been enormous, although the exact extent of the loss is open to question. Three main types of land are affected: the extensive swamps of the Atlantic coast, which merge with the mangroves of the Gulf and the Everglades of Florida; the alluvial, riverine bottom lands of the Mississippi and its tributaries; and the glacially-derived heavy clay soils, with low relief and immature drainage, that stretch across the Midwest from Ohio to Iowa and southern Minnesota, with scattered areas of peat in the three "Lake" states of Wisconsin, Michigan, and Minnesota. The loss has been great. Drainage in the Midwest took place mainly from 1880 to 1930, using buried clay drain-tile, but the accelerating deficit is now in the Mississippi and tributary river-bottom lands that are being cleared of hardwoods, ditched, walled, pumped, and planted to soybean and other crops. Recent losses in the South between 1937 and 1978 may be as much as 2.67×10^6 hectares, with no end in sight.

For millennia, some of the greatest losses have been in the tropical wetlands of southern and eastern Asia. We can only guess their magnitude because these transformations are now an integral part of the "normal" landscape of wet rice or paddy. But the reduction of the Sundarabans of the

Ganges-Brahmaputra, and the deltaic plains of the Irrawaddy, Chao Phraya, Zhu (Pearl), and other Chinese rivers is at least 100,000 square kilometers.

Currently, some of the greatest pressures on wetlands are in Africa, where more than 120 dam and/or irrigation schemes will reduce the magnitude of wet-season floods and the seasonal agriculture and fisheries that they support. Particularly noteworthy are the Jonglie Canal, Sudan, planned to cut off a bend in the White Nile and reclaim the flood plain of the Sudd, and the Bakolori Dam in northern Nigeria, with their detrimental effects on indigenous smallholders.

URBAN AND INDUSTRIAL IMPACTS

Urban and industrial impacts are greatest in coastal locations. The extension of deep-sea port facilities and the development of port-related industries such as petroleum refining, steel making, and bulk handling of various sorts all contribute to the losses. The sediment dredged from channels to keep them open is often dumped on adjacent wetlands to consolidate them for further urban/industrial uses. Classic cases of urban and industrial expansion in wetlands are Rotterdam, Bombay, Tunis, Sydney, Boston, New York, Miami, Saint Petersburg (Florida), Hong Kong, Singapore, and the urban accretions around Tokyo Bay, where over 250 square kilometers have been infilled or new land created. The dumping in San Francisco Bay became a cause célèbre of the environmental movement in California during the 1970s.

RECREATIONAL IMPACTS

The management of recreational impacts is difficult because they are neither uniform nor homogeneous. Canal-based residential dredge and fill, or pollution and bank damage from speedboats, is of a different order from birdwatching, fishing, or ecological study, and most recreational impacts are multiple and their deleterious effect may be synergistic. Moreover, the mix and intensity of impacts vary with population density, affluence, mobility, and even fad (such as dune buggies and windsurfing). It seems, however, that values in Western societies are moving more from the active/consumptive to the passive/appreciative, which makes the outright banning of traditional activities highly contentious.

THE FUTURE OF WETLANDS

The threats to the future of wetlands are internal and external; the two types are intimately connected.

Wetlands.

One of the greatest wetland areas of Africa is the Okavango Swamps of northern Botswana. They are fed by water from the Angolan Mountains and are home to large numbers of birds, reptiles, fish and mammals.

Internally, rising global population numbers mean a greater need for food, and hence potentially productive wetland will continue to be drained and utilized for agriculture. Expanding urbanization and industrialization (which has often begun near coastal and estuarine locations) will put greater pressure on prime lowland sites, so that the apparent wasteland of the wetland is the obvious place to expand.

Externally, global warming will almost inevitably lead to rising sea levels and the drowning of coastal marshes and estuaries, with untold effects on fisheries, storm protection, and recreational facilities. The expense of remedial measures such as the raising of protective walls in the Netherlands, the Fens, and around major urban conurbations may be exorbitant but within the grasp of affluent societies (for example, the Thames flood barrier to protect London). The similar raising of sea walls around Bangladesh, at costs that are variously estimated at between $20 billion and $50 billion, is prohibitively expensive and may never happen, with catastrophic consequences. The Nile Delta may likewise disappear. Similar dilemmas face smaller delta areas around the world.

The fact that wetlands may account for 24% of the primary productivity of the world means that any loss of their biomass, through human activity or as a consequence of global warming and sea-level rise, could have long-range implications for carbon budgets, which may feed back into the global circulatory system and cause further global warming. Against all this gloom, however, is the knowledge that changes in sea level and water tables can also create new wetlands, thereby increasing primary productivity. As ever, the future of wetlands is uncertain.

BIBLIOGRAPHY

WETLAND CHARACTERISTICS, USE, AND MISUSE

Hook, D.D., et al., eds. *The Ecology and Management of Wetlands*. 2 vols. London: Croom Helm; Portland, Oreg.: Timber Press, 1988. A heterogeneous but informative collection of papers about wetland ecology and its management.

Mitsch, W.J., and J.G. Gosselink. *Wetlands*. New York: Van Nostrand Reinhold, 1986. A good general survey of the physical properties and management problems of wetlands.

Williams, M., ed. *Wetlands: A Threatened Landscape*. Oxford, U.K., and Cambridge, Mass.: Blackwell, 1990. A comprehensive review of knowledge of all physical and human/historical aspects of wetlands.

DISTRIBUTION, NATURE, AND PHYSICAL CHARACTERISTICS

Chapman, V.J., ed. *Wet Coastal Ecosystems*. Amsterdam and New York: Elsevier, 1977. The definitive survey of the formation and character of coastal wetlands.

Cowardin, L.M., et al. *Classification of Wetlands and Deepwater Habitats of the United States*. Washington, D.C.: U.S. Department of the Interior, Fish and Wildlife Service, 1979. Probably the most widely used classification for wetland management.

Gore, A.J.P., ed. *Mires: Swamp, Bog, Fen and Moor*. Amsterdam, London, and New York: Elsevier, 1983a. Together with its companion volume (below) the definitive survey on the formation and character of inland wetlands.

———. *Mires: Swamp, Bog, Fen and Moor. Regional Studies*. Amsterdam, London, and New York: Elsevier, 1983b.

Kivinen, E., and P. Pakarinen. "Geographical Distribution of Peat Resources and Major Peatland Complex Types in the World." *Annals of the Academy Sciencia Fennia*, Series A, III Geology-Geography 132 (1981), 1–28. A thorough survey of peat wetlands.

ATTITUDES, VALUES, AND AESTHETICS

Gosselink, J.G., et al. *The Value of the Tidal Marsh*. LSU-SG-74–03. Baton Rouge, La.: Louisiana State University, Center for Wetland Resources, 1974. The classic, integrated ecological study that attempts to assess the functions and values of a wetland.

Greeson, P.E., et al., eds. *Wetlands Functions and Values: The State of Our Understanding*. Technical Publication TPS 79–2. Minneapolis, Minn.: American Water Resources Association, 1979. An excellent survey of opinion on this topic

U.S. Geological Survey, Wetlands Research Center. Press release May 2, 2003 (accessed June 5, 2008).

ARCHAEOLOGY

Coles, J. *The Archaeology of Wetlands*. Edinburgh: Edinburgh University Press, 1984. A preliminary survey of a new topic.

Coles, J.M., and B.J. Coles. *People of the Wetlands*. London and New York: Thames and Hudson, 1989. A well-illustrated review of the human occupants of the wetlands in the past.

HUMAN IMPACTS

Baldock, D. *Wetland Drainage in Europe: The Effects of Agricultural Policy in Four EEC Countries*. London: Institute for European Environmental Policy/ International Institute for Environment and Development, 1984. An analysis of the detrimental effects of agricultural policies.

Clark, J.R., and J. Benforado, eds. *Wetlands of Bottomland Hardwood Forests*. Amsterdam and New York: Elsevier, 1981. Investigates current bottomland losses in the United States.

Council on Environmental Quality. Environmental Quality: 1978. The Ninth Annual Report of the Council on Environmental Quality. Washington, D.C., 1978.

Darby, H.C. *The Changing Fenland*. Cambridge and New York: Cambridge University Press, 1983. The classic historical geography of the draining and management of the fenland.

Lambert, A.M. *The Making of the Dutch Landscape: An Historical Geography of the Netherlands*. 2d ed. London and Orlando, Fla.: Academic Press, 1985. A nontechnical, well illustrated, historical geography of the creation of the Netherlands.

Office of Technology Assessment. *Wetlands, Their Use and Regulation*. Washington, D.C., 1984. Concerned with wetland loss in general and the United States in particular.

Ruddle, K. "The Impact of Wetland Reclamation." In *Land Transformation in Agriculture*, edited by M. G. Wolman and F. G. A. Fournier. Chichester, U.K., and New York: Wiley, 1987, pp. 171–202. The human impact in Asian wetlands.

Tiner, R.W., Jr. *Wetlands of the United States: Current Status and Recent Trends*. Washington, D.C.: U.S. Fish and Wildlife Service, 1984. The definitive survey of U.S. wetlands.

RECREATIONAL IMPACTS

Fish and Wildlife Service. *The 1980 National Survey of Hunting and Wildlife Associated Recreation*. Portland, Oreg.: U.S. Fish and Wildlife Service, 1980. An overview of U.S. wetland recreational uses.

Leitch, J.A., and D.F. Scott. *A Selected Annotated Bibliography of Economic Values of Fish and Wildlife and Their Habitats*. Fargo, N.D.: Department of Agricultural Economics, North Dakota State University, 1977. An indispensable aid to understanding the importance and valuation of consumptive and nonconsumptive values of wildlife.

FUTURE OF WETLANDS

Armentano, T.V., and J.T.A. Verhoven. "The Contribution of Freshwater Wetlands to the Global Biogeochemical Cycles of Carbon, Nitrogen, and Sulfur." In *Wetlands and Shallow Continental Water Bodies*, edited by B. C. Patten. The Hague: SPB Academic, 1989. The relationship between wetlands and climate.

Hoffman, J.S., et al. *Projecting Future Sea-Level Rise: Methodology, Estimates to the Year 2100, and Research Needs*. U.S. Environmental Protection Agency. Washington, D.C., 1983.

Zelazny, J., and J.S. Feierabend, eds. *Increasing Our Wetland Resources*. Washington, D.C.: National Wildlife Federation, 1987. A review of how more wetland might be created.

—MICHAEL WILLIAMS

WILDERNESS AND BIODIVERSITY

Land-use changes have eradicated many wildlife habitats and reduced others to disconnected remnants that may have lost much of their ecological integrity. Although the functional aspects of ecosystems have long been recognized, only recently has this issue become of fundamental concern in conservation. The principal objective of conservation is to maintain or increase a species population. In the past, this was attempted in piecemeal fashion, often relying on zoos or botanical gardens to maintain the species outside its natural habitat. Such efforts mainly focused on large mammals and birds and vascular plants. Today the roles of all species in an ecosystem form the basis of conservation efforts that aim to preserve the entire biotic complex. Such an approach requires that ecological, behavioral, and evolutionary processes be able to operate at various spatial and temporal scales. Wilderness areas that retain their primitive characteristics are essential to this method. In wilderness areas, all life forms contribute to the area's biodiversity and are considered important. However, keystone or system-directing species that have a great influence on overall diversity are usually given highest priority in conservation efforts. Successful wilderness conservation must therefore preserve genetic diversity within a taxon, species diversity within an area, and community diversity within different habitats. For this reason, the design of wilderness areas is critical to their success. [See Conservation.]

Natural-area theory was initially based on ideas adopted from island biogeography and assumed that large reserves would contain more species and have lower extinction rates than small ones. In addition, a single large reserve was expected to favor more species than several smaller ones with the same total area. Groups of reserves were considered to be more efficient if they were close to one another and preferably equidistant and connected by corridors that facilitated population exchange. Because the shape of the reserve is critical for those species that prefer to live in the interior of an ecosystem, a circular boundary with minimal edge effect was preferred. Some of these assumptions have proved flawed in conservation studies. Species diversity is typically higher in several small reserves if they provide more varied habitats than exist in a single larger area. Similarly, smaller reserves may lessen the risk of extinction, especially for rare species with limited distributions. Conversely, larger areas are needed to conserve viable wild populations of species, such as caribou and bison, that move seasonally to different parts of their range. [See Parks and Preserves.]

Ideally, wilderness areas should include substantial populations of endemic species, but it is rarely possible to select sites that provide all of the natural features needed for successful conservation. Frequently, the locations are chosen opportunistically based on land availability and political strategies and traditionally focus on preserving the breeding areas of high-profile species. Consequently, reserves created in the past to protect a species were often poorly designed because of limited emphasis on dispersal and behavior. The long-term survival of a species is threatened when its range becomes limited to a single area or when the population becomes isolated with no effective means of dispersal. Population-viability analysis provides a means of assessing the risk of extinction over a specified time period; it is a way of determining how many individuals, dispersed in what pattern, over which habitats, and throughout what region are needed to prevent extinction due to environmental uncertainty and chance demographic and genetic events (Wilcox, 1990). For mammalian herbivores, 95% population persistence for 100 years requires a minimum viable population (MVP) of 1,000 individuals, while 10,000 are needed for small herbivores (Belovsky, 1987). This is far greater than estimates based solely on genetic data (Lande, 1988). MVP requirements are now available for many species, but they assume that the ecosystem in which they are found will be maintained; this obviously requires persistence of all of its components. The minimum area required for an ecosystem can be estimated by assessing the MVPs of area-sensitive species, which will then provide a protective umbrella for others.

Because the majority of the world's species exist only in the wild, in situ preservation is the most effective way of maintaining biodiversity. An ecosystem approach to conservation can ensure that representative examples of important plant and animal habitats will be protected. The advantage of this approach is that it offers an opportunity to protect species for which there is limited knowledge. In Britain, over 75% of nationally threatened plant species are represented in nature reserves; about 50% of the 3,635 threatened plant species in Australia are in conservation reserves; in southern Africa, practically all of the endangered fynbos (heathland) species occur in protected areas (Groombridge, 1992). Animals are similarly protected in some parts of the world; in southern Africa 92% of amphibian and reptilian, 97% of avian, and 93% of mammalian species native to the region are represented in breeding populations in protected areas (Siegfried, 1989). High percentages of native bird species are reported in protected areas in many other parts of Africa (Sayer and Stuart, 1988), but elsewhere, especially in Oceania, the protected area network is inadequate (Groombridge, 1992). The occurrence of a species in a protected area does not guarantee its survival. Many of these areas are too small to maintain viable populations, and habitat degradation outside of protected areas continues to erode long-term success, as many species must migrate across park boundaries.

Wilderness areas were selected in the past mainly on the basis of aesthetics or simply because they were not suitable for development. Consequently, there is a disproportionately large amount of rugged and ice-covered terrain. Only recently have scientific principles been used in the selection and management of wilderness areas and other landscape-size reserves in order to enhance their role in preserving biodiversity. Efforts to retain tracts of wildland of all ecosystems are increasing worldwide. As well as establishing isolated reserves, there is growing interest in problems of connectivity and the benefits of wilderness recovery networks. These comprise a system of strictly protected areas (core reserves) surrounded by lands used in a manner that is compatible with conservation (buffer zones) and linked in a way that provides functional interconnectivity (Noss, 1992). Visionary plans of this type have been prepared for several regions in North America. The Wildlands Project in Florida proposes to link ecologically sensitive areas including the Everglades, Okefenokee Swamp, and upper Gulf Coast by way of the major river systems. Long-distance dispersal of grizzly bears is a principal objective of the proposed Y2Y project that will link Yellowstone National Park with the Yukon Territories in Canada. The general strategy in these schemes is to build on existing wilderness by expansion and linkages with other areas of high biodiversity.

[See also Biomes; and Sustainable Development.]

BIBLIOGRAPHY

Belovsky, G.E. "Extinction Models and Mammalian Persistence." In *Viable Populations for Conservation*, edited by M. E. Soulé, pp. 35–57. Cambridge and New York: Cambridge University Press, 1987.

Groombridge, B., ed. *Global Biodiversity: Status of the Earth's Living Resources.* London and New York: Chapman and Hall, 1992.

Lande, R. "Genetics and Demography in Biological Conservation." *Science* 241 (1988), 1455–1460. DOI: 10.1126/science.3420403.

Noss, R.F. "The Wildlands Project: Land Conservation Strategy." *Wild Earth*, special issue (1992), 10–25.

Sayer, J.A., and S. N. Stuart. "Biological Diversity and Tropical Forests." *Environmental Conservation* 15.3 (1988), 193–194.

Siegfried, W.R. "Preservation of Species in Southern African Nature Reserves." In *Biotic Diversity in Southern Africa*, edited by B. J. Huntley, pp. 186–201. Cape Town: Oxford University Press, 1989.

Wilcox, B.A. "In-Situ Conservation of Genetic Resources." In *The Preservation and Valuation of Biological Resources*, edited by G. H. Orians, et al., pp. 45–77. Seattle: University of Washington Press, 1990.

—O. W. ARCHIBOLD

WILDERNESS DEBATES

The idea of wilderness has a long history in Western culture, in contrast with cultures that retain aboriginal ways. As farming and herding supplanted hunting and gathering during the Neolithic, an inchoate awareness of distinctions between the artifice of human society and the natural community of life appeared. Refined notions distinguishing the domestic and the wild evolved over subsequent millennia and were reflected in biblical, philosophical, and other ancient texts. Today the wilderness idea is a mélange of competing beliefs, ranging from anthropocentric perspectives such as resource conservation to ecocentric perspectives such as conservation biology. Wild nature is, in the anthropocentric view, valued in instrumental, economic ways; the watchwords of environmental policy are efficiency and utility. In the ecocentric view, wild nature (land, flora, fauna, evolution itself) possesses intrinsic value apart from economic schemes; ecological integrity and the conservation of biodiversity are the watchwords of environmental policy. Viewed prospectively, the idea of wilderness occupies a continuum: one end is a romantic anachronism; the other represents perspectives that value biological and ecological diversity as well as evolutionary processes.

THE IMPORTANCE OF WILDERNESS

As the humanization of the planet continues, driven by population growth and economic development, the wilderness idea paradoxically assumes new importance. Considered inclusively, the idea represents the abundance of life, the diversity of land forms, the biospheric processes upon which life depends, and the processes of evolution. Advocates such as preservationists, deep ecologists, and conservation biologists contend that wilderness conservation is fundamental to the maintenance of life and civilization. In contrast, the culturally dominant ideology (variously termed anthropocentrism, industrialism, or resourcism) makes wilderness "other," that is, antithetical to civilization. So viewed, nature's wildness is evident not only in such phenomena as hurricanes and earthquakes, but in environmental dysfunctions such as the depletion of stratospheric ozone and the collapse of oceanic fisheries; the problems of global change thus reinforce the notion that wild nature must be controlled and bent to human purposes through engineering. In contrast, wilderness proponents contend that there are no technological solutions for the problems of global change, which are largely the consequence of economically misguided technology and the assumption that natural processes are simple and linear rather than complex and nonlinear. Continuing global industrialization, driven by the global market, thus threatens biodiversity and impairs biospheric processes upon which civilization depends.

WILDERNESS PRESERVATION VERSUS SUSTAINABLE DEVELOPMENT

Disputes between those who hold an inclusive idea of wilderness and the supporters of so-called sustainable development are conceptually and politically complicated. Scientists and others who believe that wild nature is a self-sustaining, non-equilibrium process argue that globalist visions for sustainable development are fundamentally self-contradictory, because humans lack the scientific knowledge and the technological means to replace naturally-evolved biophysical processes with artificial life support systems. They also argue that anthropocentrism remains institutionalized in Agenda 21 (United Nations Program of Action for Sustainable Development), and that the political economy of the new world order neither responds to the genuine needs of impoverished people nor advances the conservation of biodiversity; rather, Agenda 21 and other development plans are driven by the imperatives of nationalism, capitalism, and materialism. Advocates of sustainable development believe that environmental dysfunctions and poverty can be mitigated within the dominant conceptual and institutional framework, that human survival depends on refining the processes of economic development (industrialization) and the technological control of nature, and that proponents for wilderness preservation and the conservation of biodiversity are misguided iconoclasts who ignore the causes of and remedies for economic destitution. [*See* Land Preservation; Parks and Preserves; *and* Sustainable Growth.]

Beyond these contested notions involving the role of wilderness in the next century are issues concerning the importance of wilderness experience. Some human ecologists, psychologists, and others believe that isolation from wild nature jeopardizes essential processes of cognitive and psychological development, arguing that dynamic interactions with animals, plants, and natural habitats shaped human intelligence, that the human species has been and remains embedded in the web of life, and that wilderness experience rekindles awareness of living connections between humans and their environments. Thus encounters with land forms and floral and faunal domains outside the bounds of the built environment are critical to the development and continuing nurture of humans. Critics argue that, in the context of urban, industrial society, wilderness experience is at best atavistic, and at worst an evasion of responsibilities of economically privileged individuals to deal with the problems of global change.

THE U.S. WILDERNESS SYSTEM AND THE UN'S MAN AND THE BIOSPHERE PROGRAM

The first officially protected wilderness in the United States was proposed by Aldo Leopold in 1922. Now known as the Aldo Leopold Wilderness, it was established in 1924 under the aegis of the Forest Service and comprises 82,000 hectares (202,000 acres). Today the United States is an international exemplar in preserving wilderness, partly because of the Wilderness Act (1964), which established the National Wilderness Preservation System, and because large areas of relatively unhumanized land existed in the United States long after their disappearance in Europe. The Wilderness Act defines wilderness as a place untrammeled by humans, where humans are visitors, where natural ecological processes operate freely, where the primeval character of the land and natural influences are retained, and where opportunities for solitude and primitive recreation experiences abound. Lewis (2007) provides a new history of the wilderness concept in America.

The federal government controls 29% of the land in the United States. Almost 55% of all designated wilderness is in Alaska, nearly 19% of the state; less than 4% of the 48 contiguous states has been designated as or recommended for wilderness, and 95% of these areas are west of the Mississippi River (Table 1). The Forest Service, the National Park Service, the Fish and Wildlife Service, and the Bureau of Land Management (BLM) are the agencies responsible for preparing and implementing wilderness management plans, and recommending to Congress additional lands for wilderness designation; nearly 40 million hectares (100 million acres) have been added to the original 3.6 million hectares. There are presently more than 630 areas, ranging in size from more than 3 million hectares to less than 1 hectare.

The United Nations Man and the Biosphere (MAB) program (1990), which focuses on ecological research with a conservation policy, resource use, and management orientation, is

TABLE 1. Twenty Large Designated U.S. Wilderness Areas

Name (and Agency)	Location	Total Size (hectares)
Wrangell–St. Elias (NPS)	Alaska	3,675,577
Arctic (FWS)	Alaska	3,238,866
Gates of the Arctic (NPS)	Alaska	2,901,697
Noatak (NPS)	Alaska	2,334,181
Frank Church–River of No Return (FS)	Idaho, Montana	957,305
Togiak (FWS)	Alaska	919,028
Misty Fiords (FS)	Alaska	867,305
Denali (FS)	Alaska	860,236
Selway–Bitterroot (FS)	Idaho, Montana	542,696
Everglades (NPS)	Florida	524,899
Bob Marshall (FS)	Montana	408,646
Admiralty (FS)	Alaska	379,538
Boundary Waters Canoe Area (FS)	Minnesota	323,594
Washakie (FS)	Wyoming	285,131
Teton (FS)	Wyoming	236,938
John Muir (FS)	California	234,949
Glacier Peak (FS)	Washington	231,716
Trinity Alps (FS)	California	201,677
Weminuche (FS)	Colorado	186,075
High Uintas (FS)	Utah	184,901

analogous to the U.S. preservation system in creating more than three hundred protected areas in approximately eighty participating countries. MAB is unlike the U.S. wilderness system, however, in that biosphere reserves include not only core wilderness areas, but buffer zones and zones of transition subject to human development.

TYPES OF DISPUTES

Disputes over the protection and management of wilderness habitats can be classified in three categories. The first concerns disagreements between nations, especially between governments and environmental NGOs in the Northern Hemisphere and the governments of developing nations in the Southern Hemisphere. Northern Hemisphere conservation groups, for example, favor a preservationist stance on policies affecting tropical rainforests, such as Amazonia, which lies primarily within Brazil. Brazilian interests favor a development stance, arguing that it is unfair for developed nations, who have historically and continue presently to exploit their forests economically, to demand that they preserve theirs. Developing nations also argue that the Northern Hemisphere fueled its own economic advance by exploiting the natural resources of developing countries, and that global capitalism continues to exert environmentally destructive pressures; thus, the Northern Hemisphere is ethically obligated to pay for the conservation of biodiversity and wildlands in the Southern Hemisphere. Another issue concerns land management: the Southern Hemisphere argues that indigenous people, including subsistence hunters and gatherers, and traditional agriculturists, are good stewards of natural habitats who should not be excluded from wildlands because of conservation agendas of the Northern Hemisphere.

Disagreements also exist between interest groups within nations, as for example between American preservationists and the wise-use movement or "localists," or between environmentalists and industrialists. Localists argue that urban interests in wilderness preservation reflect selfish desires for recreational playgrounds while denying the rights of people who have traditionally mined, logged, grazed, and ranched the land. Preservationists argue that the Wilderness Act allows mining and grazing for preexisting operations, that the amenity value of wilderness far exceeds traditional economic uses, and that the wise-use movement itself is a very small but highly visible group funded by corporate logging and mining interests. Another issue arises over rights of access between owners of wildlands and groups of people who have traditionally hunted, fished, and gathered on them. Finally, controversies have arisen over the rights of private property holders to develop wildlands, since various agencies have acted to prevent development under the mandate of the Endangered Species Act.

A third area of debate involves the policies and procedures used by federal agencies for designating and managing wilderness. For example, critics argue that wilderness areas are abundant in rock and ice, with scant biodiversity, leaving old-growth ecosystems rich in biodiversity vulnerable to logging; that the zoning of wilderness areas too often designates lands that are too small and too isolated to allow the continuation of evolutionary processes; that fire suppression is rooted in the failure to understand its role in natural ecosystems; that fees for access to wilderness and the granting of licenses to concessionaires (so-called private-public ventures) mark the final chapter in commodifying wilderness; that too many people visit wilderness areas, thereby destroying any possibility of wilderness experience; that the very notion of wilderness management is oxymoronic; and that ecosystem management is more a bureaucratic buzzword than a scientifically grounded procedure.

[*See also* Biomes; *and* Parks and Preserves.]

BIBLIOGRAPHY

Burks, D.C., ed. *Place of the Wild: A Wildlands Anthology.* Washington, D.C.: Island Press, 1994. A collection of essays concerning wilderness and the protection of biodiversity.

Foreman, D., and H. Wolke. *The Big Outside: A Descriptive Inventory of the Big Wilderness Areas of the United States.* Rev. ed. New York: Harmony Books, 1992. A description of large primitive areas and their biological importance.

Forestra, R.A. *Amazon Conservation in the Age of Development: The Limits of Providence.* Gainesville, Fla.: University of Florida Press, 1991. Analyzes the hypothesis that long-term preservation of Amazonia is more likely to succeed outside development initiatives.

Glacken, C. *Traces on the Rhodian Shore: Nature and Culture in Western Thought from Ancient Times to the End of the Eighteenth Century.* Berkeley: University of California Press, 1967. A magisterial study of changing conceptions of the land.

Grumbine, R.E., ed. *Environmental Policy and Biodiversity.* Washington, D.C.: Island Press, 1994. Multifaceted discussions of the role of wilderness in the conservation of biodiversity.

Hendee, J.C., G.H. Stankey, and R.C. Lucas. *Wilderness Management.* 2d ed. Golden, Colo.: Fulcrum, 1990. A comprehensive account of the theory and practice of wilderness management.

Knight, R.L., and K.J. Gutzwiller, eds. *Wildlife and Recreationists: Coexistence through Management and Research.* Washington, D.C.: Island Press, 1995. A scientific analysis of the consequences of wilderness recreation on habitat, flora, and fauna in the United States.

Leopold, A. *A Sand County Almanac, and Sketches Here and There.* New York: Oxford University Press, 1949. An original statement of the scientific and ethical underpinnings for wilderness preservation.

Lewis, M., ed. *American Wilderness: A New History.* Oxford and New York: Oxford University Press, 2007.

Nash, R. *Wilderness and the American Mind.* Rev. ed. New Haven and London: Yale University Press, 1973. A study of the role of the wilderness idea in U.S. public lands policy. The third edition was published in 1982.

Oelschlaeger, M. *The Idea of Wilderness: From Prehistory to the Age of Ecology.* New Haven and London: Yale University Press, 1991. A comprehensive study of the evolution of the wilderness idea in Western culture.

Rudzitis, G. *Wilderness and the Changing American West.* New York: Wiley, 1996. A study of the changing ideas of public lands management in the American West.

Shepard, P. *The Others: How Animals Made Us Human.* Washington, D.C.: Island Press, 1996. An inquiry into the historical and contemporary importance of interactions between wild animals and humans.

Snyder, G. *The Practice of the Wild.* San Francisco: North Point Press, 1990. Essays that deny the cogency of the wilderness-civilization dichotomy and affirm a place for humans in wild nature.

Wright, W. *Wild Knowledge: Science, Language, and Social Life in a Fragile Environment.* Minneapolis: University of Minnesota Press, 1992. An extension of the wilderness idea to the question of what counts as knowledge in the context of environmental crisis.

—Max Oelschlaeger

WILDLIFE MANAGEMENT

Wildlife management is the act, discipline, and profession of managing wildlife populations. The term "wildlife" sometimes refers to all wild species, including fishes and plants. However, in the context of the discipline of wildlife management, it refers to free-ranging birds and mammals. Wildlife management is stewardship of the wildlife resource; it seeks to achieve human goals for wildlife resources by working with wildlife populations, their habitats, and people.

MANAGEMENT OPTIONS

A wildlife manager has four basic options for managing a wildlife population. First, make the population increase. This option usually applies to small, depleted, or decreasing populations. Second, make the population decrease. This usually applies to populations that are judged to be too high or increasing too rapidly. Third, exploit the population by harvesting it for a sustained, continuing yield. Fourth, monitor it but do not seek to manipulate it. The first three options imply manipulative management, which involves changing the population level of the species involved, either through direct methods, such as hunting, or indirectly by changing the habitat, for example, through provision of water or reduction of predators or disease. The fourth option represents custodial management: for example, in the management of a national park or reserve where the objective is to "let nature take its course."

Three decisions must be made in the management of a wildlife population. The first decision, on the goal of the management process, represents a value judgment and is the responsibility of the political system or other decision makers, not that of the wildlife manager. The second decision is to determine which management option is appropriate to achieve the goal, and the third is how to implement that management approach. The second and third decisions are technical judgments, and they are the responsibility of the wildlife manager.

MANAGEMENT GOALS

When wildlife management was developed as a discipline in the early 1930s, the goal was to provide wildlife resources for sport hunting. Aldo Leopold, who is regarded as the father of wildlife management, defined wildlife management as the art of making land produce sustained annual crops of wild game for recreational use. With the exception of predator control, support of sport hunting remained the principal and often the sole goal of wildlife management for nearly 40 years. However, by the 1960s, because of, or as part of, a growing environmental awareness and concern among the public, the attention of the wildlife management profession began slowly to broaden its focus to include nongame wildlife and nonconsumptive uses of wildlife. Gradually the goals were broadened. Today, in addition to providing sport hunting, the goals involve managing wildlife in support of a number of human interests and concerns, including (1) maintenance of the ecosystems of which they are a component and the ecological services that they and their ecosystems provide; (2) protection and restoration of populations of endangered species; (3) maintenance of healthy wildlife populations in national parks and reserves; and (4) encouragement of suitable wildlife species in urban situations. In some countries other than the United States, the provision of a sustainable yield of wildlife for commercial and subsistence purposes is another current goal of wildlife management.

Reduction or elimination of species that are considered undesirable is an important goal of wildlife management in some countries. Examples range from reduction of kangaroo populations that compete with sheep in Australia to control of predators that prey on livestock or even humans in Africa and Asia. In the United States, predator control long predated the establishment of wildlife management as a discipline and profession, and it has continued as an increasingly controversial component of management. Federal and state programs to control predators and other "pest species" existed long before modern wildlife management was developed. In the 1970s, these programs were curtailed somewhat because of public objections to their excesses, but predator control still remains an active, if somewhat minor and increasingly controversial goal of wildlife management.

EVOLUTION OF THE PROFESSION

Historically, wildlife in the United States has been the property of the state and has usually been treated as a common property resource. It was an important resource of food and other animal products in pioneer days, but some forms were also perceived as competitors or threats. Laws that provided bounty payment for killing of predators date from the original colonies. Settlers sought to remove grazing species such as deer, elk, and bison that competed with livestock, and predators such as wolves, bears, and cougars, and by 1900 most such animals were greatly reduced. Several species were exterminated, including the eastern and Oregon bisons, the eastern wapiti (elk), and several subspecies of grizzly bear. Until about 1870, predators were eliminated to assist livestock raisers. After that time such "control" was also promoted as a way to increase game animals. Commercial take of wildlife began early: the fur trade, for example, played a major role in explorations of the American West, and market hunters were a major user of the wildlife resource from the earliest days. The resultant slaughter of the bison and passenger pigeon provided dramatic evidence of the devastating impact of uncontrolled hunting and raised public consciousness of the need for conservation.

Even by the mid-1800s, many forms of wildlife were so decimated that some members of the public sought to bring in conservation measures. Sportsmen's organizations sought laws to stop or limit market hunting, and to ban the hunting and sale of game when the animals were breeding and raising young, and seasonal closure of hunting was the principal form of wildlife management until the late 1800s, when these laws were augmented by the establishment of protected areas (led by the establishment of Yellowstone National Park in 1872). Some of the private sportsmen's clubs developed into the first official state fish and wildlife agencies.

Concern with depletion of wild birds led to the establishment of several bird conservation organizations, notably the American Ornithologists' Union (AOU) in 1883, and the Audubon Society in 1886, both of which became effective instruments for channeling public concern for conservation into government action. In 1885 the AOU was instrumental in convincing Congress to establish what became the Bureau of Biological Survey, much later renamed the U.S. Fish and Wildlife Service. The AOU and Audubon later persuaded President Theodore Roosevelt to create a system of federal bird reservations that became the National Wildlife Refuge System.

In the late 1800s, restocking of depleted game and introduction of exotic species were added to the list of principal methods of wildlife management. Local sportsmen or sportsmen's groups began restocking whitetail deer, which had been virtually eliminated from the eastern United States by overhunting and habitat loss, and, starting with ring-necked pheasants in 1881, foreign game birds were introduced in many parts of the country.

Until the early 1930s, actions undertaken to achieve wildlife management were focused primarily on the species itself. The actions were aimed at reducing mortality by reducing natural enemies (predator control), protecting the populations from hunting (closed seasons and provision of refuges), and increasing game populations by restocking with artificially raised native birds and animals and with exotic species. More recently, it has been recognized that predator control has a negative rather than a positive effect on wildlife; that refuges have limited value, except to protect endangered species; that bounty payments for predators simply do not work; that restocking of depleted species has generally been a failure unless the habitat condition has improved; that, except in a few cases (for example, the ring-neck pheasant), introduced exotics cause more harm than good; and that protection from hunting is often essential, but insufficient to restore depleted wildlife populations unless there is parallel habitat improvement. The whole approach to wildlife management was changed by Aldo Leopold, who put it on an ecological basis.

In 1933, Leopold, a forest scientist, who had retired from the U.S. Forest Service, joined the faculty of the University of Wisconsin. He took the chair in wildlife management, which was the first such academic chair in the country. Leopold taught a theory he was developing, which combined population dynamics of wildlife species with a broad ecological approach, emphasizing the importance of habitat suitability and condition as the basis for supporting wildlife populations. Leopold's work laid the foundations for wildlife management as a discipline and profession.

The following year, Congress authorized the Cooperative Wildlife Research Unit Program, initially with units at ten colleges around the country supported jointly by the state wildlife agency and the college. The program was intended to provide training in the new discipline of wildlife management and to conduct research on key wildlife conservation problems. This program has since been expanded to 22 additional colleges and, in recent years, curricula in wildlife management have been established in colleges and universities throughout the country and abroad.

In 1935 the American Wildlife Institute, since renamed the Wildlife Management Institute, was established as a nongovernmental organization funded largely by sporting arms and ammunition companies. Its objective was to promote wildlife management for sport hunting through support to the wildlife units at colleges, and through research and public education. The following year, the General Wildlife Federation, now the National Wildlife Federation, was established as a federation of local sportsmen's groups throughout the country. And, in 1937, the Wildlife Society was established as the professional society for the new discipline of wildlife management, with a high-quality professional journal.

That year also saw the passage of the Federal Aid in Wildlife Restoration Act, which dedicated a 10% excise tax on sporting arms and ammunition for use by states in approved wildlife research, land acquisition, and management. The act required that the states receiving federal funding pass enabling legislation and apply all revenues from hunting licenses to wildlife conservation. This act was a major milestone in advancing wildlife management.

By World War II, wildlife management was established as a discipline and a profession, with a body of wildlife law, government institutions at federal and state levels, university departments to provide trained staff and to conduct research, a professional society and journal, and a constituency represented by several active nongovernmental supporting organizations. It was also firmly committed to its original goals of supporting sport hunting, which in turn provided virtually all the funds to support wildlife management. However, as discussed above, the focus of the profession is broadening to encompass the whole realm of wildlife and of human interests in it. Until recently, most consumptive use of wildlife was based on the concept of maximum sustainable yield, the maximum production per unit time that can be sustained, estimated from the theoretical growth curve of the target species, calculated without reference to the rest of its ecosystem. But no species exists in isolation from its environment, so this approach does not work, and wildlife management is now moving away from it.

Wildlife management today has become a largely scientific discipline. Research is a vital component, including sophisticated experimental design and treatment of data, advanced field and laboratory techniques, and population and habitat analysis. Management includes research, census, monitoring, law enforcement, habitat acquisition and improvement, protection of species as necessary, and regulated taking. It also must involve public education and interactions with the public and with decision makers. It has shown itself sufficiently flexible to spread beyond the United States and is now practiced throughout the world. Like other resource management professions, it was slow to recognize and adopt the changing goals of the broader public wildlife constituency, but to a large degree it has now done so.

The greatest challenge for the future for wildlife management will be to recognize and adapt to global warming and other changes in biophysical and socioeconomic conditions.

[*See also* Agriculture and Biodiversity; Biological Diversity; Carrying Capacity; *and* Wilderness and Biodiversity.]

BIBLIOGRAPHY

Bookhout, T.A., ed. *Research and Management Techniques for Wildlife and Habitats*. 5th ed. Bethesda, Md.: Wildlife Society, 1996.

Caughley, G., and A.R.E. Sinclair. *Wildlife Ecology and Management*. Boston: Blackwell, 1994. The second edition was published in 2006.

Leopold, A. *Game Management*. New York and London: Scribner's, 1933.

—LEE M. TALBOT

Y

YOUNGER DRYAS

The Younger Dryas (YD) was a cold climatic interval between approximately 12,900 and 11,600 BP (Alley et al., 1993). This pronounced and rapid cooling, identified a century ago in the Scandinavian macrofossil record, is named for the Arctic-alpine herb *Dryas octopetala*, whose preserved leaves and fruits were discovered in terrestrial sediments overlying sediments that contained indicators of a previously warmer climate. This climate change was the third and most extensive reversal to colder climate conditions in Europe following the general climate warming that occurred after maximum ice-age cold conditions, the previous two being the Oldest Dryas and the Older Dryas (Mangerud et al., 1974).

YOUNGER DRYAS IN EUROPE

By 12,900 BP, retreat from maximum glacial conditions resulted in an ice-free British Isles, substantial recession of Scandinavian glaciers, and retreat of the Laurentide Ice Sheet well into Canada. The global sea-level curve from Barbados suggests that ice extent had diminished to less than half of ice-age conditions (Fairbanks, 1989). However, as the YD occurred, glaciers actually reformed in the Scottish highlands, and prominent YD glacial moraines are characteristic of the entire Scandinavian coastline. Montane glacial advances in the western Rocky Mountains of North America have also been correlated with the YD (Osborne and Gerloff, 1997).

The discovery of the Younger Dryas in Scandinavia was followed in the 1930s by pollen investigations into lake and bog sediments throughout Europe (Watts, 1980). Tundra pollen was diagnostic of the YD, because it followed the prevalence of forest pollen that indicated the late-glacial warming. Dramatic changes in vegetation characterized both coastal and inland areas from northern Norway to the Mediterranean (Walker et al., 1994). In the British Isles, birch forest was replaced by shrubs and herbs. Many continental European records show small changes in pollen percentages but a marked change from organic to inorganic deposition and a rise in *Artemisia* (wormwood) pollen, indicating a more open, disturbed landscape. Estimates from botanical data suggest that mean July temperatures as far south as northern Spain may have been as much as 8°C below modern values.

There are indications of an ameliorating climate during the latter part of the YD. While in some areas of Europe, such as Britain and Ireland, the increase in steppe and halophytic (salt-tolerating) taxa may indicate a drier climate, other areas appear to have been slightly wetter. Geomorphologic and lithologic changes as well as faunal (e.g., beetles) and isotopic shifts provide additional evidence for the climatic fluctuation at numerous European sites.

YOUNGER DRYAS IN NORTH AMERICA

At the eastern margin of the Laurentide Ice Sheet, numerous late-glacial buried sequences found more than 50 years ago reveal a sudden oscillation in climate. For many years, problems with conventional carbon-14 dating precluded their correlation with the YD event, but the advent of accelerator mass spectrometry (AMS) carbon-14 dating combined with very detailed macrofossil analysis has resulted in very strong correlation of the changes in North America with those in Europe (Mayle et al., 1993). In northern Nova Scotia, herb tundra replaced shrub tundra as the climate cooled. In southern New Brunswick and central Nova Scotia, shrub tundra replaced spruce forest. The lake sediment itself is characterized by higher levels of silts and sands resulting from erosion. Surface-water temperature reconstructions derived from modern midge-fly larvae indicate temperature declines of 6°–7°C (Walker et al., 1991).

Southern New England also shows a strong regional pattern of late-glacial palynological change (Peteet et al., 1997). Fluctuations in a mixed coniferous-deciduous forest (spruce, fir larch, white pine, oak, ash) are marked at the onset of the YD by a rapid disappearance of the warmth-loving trees and a marked increase in the boreal trees (spruce, fir, larch, paper birch, alder) as the climate cooled. The abundance of the boreal macrofossils indicates their local dominance on the landscape, and their AMS carbon-14 dating agrees with the European chronology, confirming the climatic correlation. The summer cooling inferred for the YD is 3°–4°C, based on the type of vegetational changes and their modern analogues in the Adirondack Mountains. The sharp return to warmer conditions at 11,600 BP is marked by the dominance of white pine and loss of the boreal trees.

In the midwestern United States, a pollen shift in the Till Plains area has been correlated with the YD, showing a rapid recurrence of spruce just before the Holocene warming (Shane and Anderson, 1993). Future attention to AMS dating is needed to refine the chronology. The coastline of the Pacific Northwest shows changes that also correlate with the YD. Mountain hemlock is indicative of cooling in British Columbia, while further north, in southeastern Alaska near Glacier Bay, tundra elements dominate (Mathewes, 1993). On Kodiak Island, Alaska, the dominance of crowberry and loss of ferns along with marked increases in inorganic lake sediments are characteristic of coastal stratigraphy (Peteet and Mann, 1994).

YOUNGER DRYAS IN GREENLAND ICE CORES

The YD event is very well defined in Greenland ice cores (Camp Century, Dye 3, and Renland, confirmed in the GRIP and GISP-2 deep cores; Dansgaard et al., 1993). The signal is observed as a change of several parts per million in oxygen-isotope ratios, corresponding to temperatures about 15°C colder than today (Cuffey et al., 1995). The event is also marked by significantly higher dust levels and chemical concentrations compared to adjacent intervals. The onset of the YD in the ice cores is gradual, and the termination abrupt, occurring in as little as 1–3 years in some indicators. The snow accumulation rate in the YD was about half that of the Preboreal (ca. 10,000–9,000 BP), and about one-third of modern. The changes at the end of the YD were completed in three 5-year steps spread over about 40 years (Taylor et al., 1993), and snow accumulation changed by about 90% in one year (Alley et al., 1993). The discovery of a YD methane signal in Antarctic ice cores (Chappellaz et al., 1990) first showed the global effect of the changes characteristic of this period.

YOUNGER DRYAS AND OCEAN CIRCULATION

In the 1980s, the discovery of North Atlantic faunal changes contemporaneous with the terrestrial European signal led to the conclusion that the North Atlantic polar (airmass) front readvanced to its glacial position at that time (Ruddiman and McIntyre, 1981). Subsequent geochemical analyses indicate that the production of North Atlantic Deep Water (NADW), which today is responsible for bringing heat to Europe, was greatly reduced at this time, as it was during the ice age. [See Thermohaline Circulation.] The cause of this deep-water cessation is still in dispute. Evidence from the Cariaco Basin indicates an increase in wind-induced upwelling during the YD off coastal Venezuela (Hughen et al., 1996). North Pacific investigations show that the YD was also expressed in the Japan Sea as well as off coastal California (Behl and Kennett, 1996).

GEOGRAPHIC EXTENT

The geographic distribution of the YD event is a topic under close scrutiny. While the research of the last three decades has shown that its distribution is not limited to Europe but includes North America and Greenland, its presence in the Southern Hemisphere is highly disputed. Figure 1 shows a global map (generated by an International Geological Correlation Project working group) of the distribution of palynological evidence for the YD cooling (Peteet, 1995). The most convincing evidence outside North America is from Colombia, South America, where many sites show an oscillation that awaits precise AMS carbon-14 dating. Regions where some sites seem to have an oscillation and others do not are Central America, southern South America, and the eastern Mediterranean region. A clear absence of a YD signal is not yet confirmed in any area, because very

high-resolution AMS-dated sites are rare; none has proven the absence of an oscillation during this interval. Regions where existing data exhibit no palynological oscillation include Ecuador, Peru, South Africa, and New Zealand, but in some of these same areas (New Zealand and possibly Peru) glacial advances do indicate a YD correlative.

Today, the most widely accepted hypothesis for the cause of the YD oscillation is a slowdown in NADW production (Broecker et al., 1985; McManus et al., 2004). A colder, fresher North Atlantic would have stopped the sinking of dense, saline water that today is responsible for releasing heat to the atmosphere. Sources for this colder water that would have formed a freshwater "lid" on the northern Atlantic may have been the retreating Laurentide and Scandinavian ice sheets. However, the echo of a YD-type signal throughout the Holocene in marine and ice-core records suggests that the signal may be a complicated recurring climate oscillation that was magnified during the YD by meltwater from receding ice sheets.

Other possible causes include major changes in the hydrologic cycle leading to a freshwater North Atlantic buildup. These may or may not involve ice advances and retreats. Harvey (1989) used an energy-balance model to test various causal hypotheses, including lowered carbon dioxide, and found that a low-salinity lid composed of meltwater led to warming (not cooling) in summer, that lower carbon dioxide levels caused an annual global cooling of about 1°C, and that North Atlantic iceberg floods caused significant summer cooling in the Northern Hemisphere but much smaller temperature declines in the Southern Hemisphere.

CAUSES

Several atmospheric groups have investigated the YD climate using global climate models (GCMs). The first of these experiments used the hypothesis that a colder North Atlantic would have caused the YD through an atmospheric response (Rind et al., 1986). The results of the experiment indicated that the cooling was produced only in the vicinity of the North Atlantic and do not explain a cooling elsewhere around the world. Subsequent experiments with the same Goddard Institute for Space Studies GCM included a 2°C cooling of the North Pacific, which resulted in a widespread Northern Hemisphere cooling and snow expansion along the North Pacific coastline (Peteet et al., 1997). Renssen (1997) obtained similar results using the Hamburg model. Using a coupled ocean-atmosphere model, Mikolajewicz et al. (1997) found a primary atmospheric forcing caused by a shutdown of the thermohaline circulation in the North Atlantic, suggesting that teleconnections may have taken place.

The YD may have contributed to the beginnings of agriculture around the fertile crescent (Moore and Hillman, 1992). On the North Slope of Alaska, the disappearance of humans at the Mesa site argues for the impetus that the severe climate gave migration (Kunz and Reanier, 1996). The YD occurred between times when Greenland was nearly as warm as today. Similar climate changes, although not as large as the YD and much briefer,

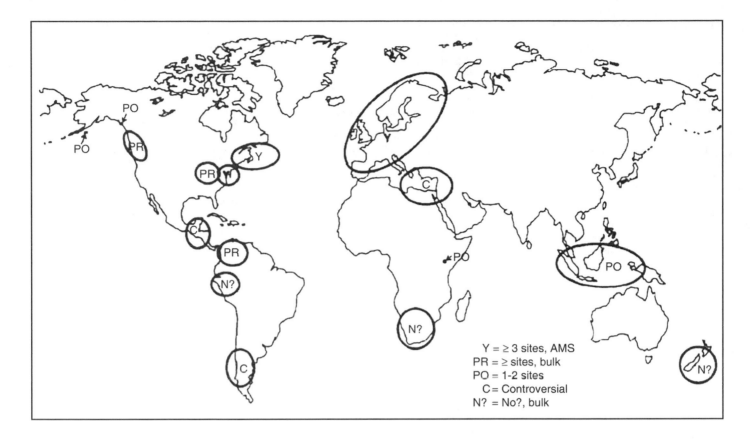

Younger Dryas. Figure 1. Global Map of Distribution of Palynological Evidence for the Younger Dryas Cooling, 12,900–11,600 BP.

Where clear palynological evidence exists for a climate oscillation in three or more sites, with AMS carbon-14 dating, Y denotes a "Yes YD" (e.g., maritime Canada). For regions where three or more sites show a palynological oscillation, but it is not yet AMS-dated, a PR is designated for "Probable YD" (e.g., Colombia). For sites where one or two oscillations exist, a P denotes "Possible YD" (e.g., southern Alaska). For areas where some sites show an oscillation and others do not, a C denotes "Controversial YD". Finally, where evidence for a YD is lacking, an N? is given for "No? YD", unless three or more sites have been investigated, in which case the designation would be N for "No YD."
(After Peteet, 1995. With permission of Elsevier.)

are evident in ice cores, the North Atlantic records, and even on land during the last 10,000 years. Because we do not understand the causes of such climatic reversals, it is difficult to predict their occurrence. One emerging hypothesis, however, suggests that anthropogenic greenhouse warming could produce another YD-type effect as a result of increased precipitation around the North Atlantic basin, leading to weaker NADW production (Manabe and Stouffer, 1997).

[*See also* Climate Models and Uncertainty; Climate Reconstruction; *and* Ocean-Atmosphere Coupling.]

BIBLIOGRAPHY

Alley, R.B., et al. "Abrupt Increase in Greenland Snow Accumulation at the End of the Younger Dryas Event." *Nature* 362 (1993), 527–529. DOI: 10.1038/362527a0.

Behl, R.J., and J.P. Kennett. "Brief Interstadial Events in the Santa Barbara Basin, NE Pacific, During the Past 60 Kyr." *Nature* 379 (1996), 243–246. DOI: 10.1038/379243a0.

Broecker, W.S., D. Peteet, and D. Rind. "Does the Ocean-Atmosphere System Have More than One Stable Mode of Operation?" *Nature* 315 (1985), 21–26. DOI: 10.1038/315021a0.

Chappellaz, J., et al. "Ice-Core Record of Atmospheric Methane over the Past 160,000 Years." *Nature* 345 (1990), 127–131. DOI: 10.1038/345127a0. Measurements from the Vostok ice core.

Cuffey, K.M., et al. "Large Arctic Temperature Change at the Wisconsin-Holocene Glacial Transition." *Science* 270 (1995), 455–458. DOI: 10.1126/science.270.5235.455.

Dansgaard, W., et al. "Evidence for General Instability of Past Climate from a 250-kyr Ice-core Record." *Nature* 364 (1993), 218–220.

Fairbanks, R.G. "A 17,000-Year Glacio-Eustatic Sea Level Record: Influence of Glacial Melting Rates on the Younger Dryas Event and Deep-Ocean Circulation." *Nature* 342 (1989), 637–642. DOI: 10.1038/342637a0.

Harvey, L.D.D. "Modelling the Younger Dryas." *Quaternary Science Reviews* 8.2 (1989), 137–149. DOI: 10.1016/0277-3791(89)90002-4.

Hughen, K., et al. "Rapid Climate Changes in the Tropical Atlantic Region during the Last Deglaciation." *Nature* 380 (1996), 51–54. DOI: 10.1038/380051a0.

Kunz, M., and R. Reanier. "Paleoindians in Beringia: Evidence from Arctic Alaska." *Science* 263 (1996), 660–662. DOI: 10.1126/science.263.5147.660.

Manabe, S., and R.J. Stouffer. "Coupled Ocean-Atmosphere Model Response to Freshwater Input: Comparison to Younger Dryas Event." *Paleoceanography* 12.2 (1997), 321–336.

Mangerud, J., et al. "Quaternary Stratigraphy of Norden, a Proposal for Terminology and Classification." *Boreas* 3 (1974), 109–128.

Mann, D.H., and D.M. Peteet. "Extent and Timing of the Last Glacial Maximum in Southwestern Alaska." *Quaternary Research* 42 (1994), 136–148.

Mayle, F.E., A.J. Levesque and L.C. Cwynar. "Accelerator-Mass-Spectrometer Ages for the Younger Dryas Event in Atlantic Canda." *Quaternary Research* 39 (1993), 355–360.

Mathewes, R.W. "Evidence for Younger Dryas-Age Cooling on the North Pacific Coast of America." *Quaternary Science Reviews* 12.5 (1993), 321–332. DOI: 10.1016/0277-3791(93)90040-S.

McManus, J.F., et al. "Collapse and Rapid Resumption of Atlantic Meridional Circulation Linked to Deglacial Climate Changes." *Nature* 428 (2004), 834–837. DOI: 10.1038/nature02494.

Mikolajewicz, U., et al. "Modelling Teleconnections between the North Atlantic and North Pacific during the Younger Dryas." *Nature* 387 (1997), 384–387. DOI: 10.1038/387384a0.

Moore, A.M.T., and G.C. Hillman. "The Pleistocene to Holocene Transition and Human Economy in Southwest Asia: The Impact of the Younger Dryas." *American Antiquity* 57.3 (1992), 482–494.

Osborne, G., and L. Gerloff. "Latest Pleistocene and Early Holocene Fluctuations of Glaciers in the Canadian and Northern American Rockies." *Quaternary International* 38/39 (1997), 7–19. DOI: 10.1016/S1040-6182(96)00026-2.

Peteet, D. "Global Younger Dryas?" *Quaternary International* 28 (1995), 93–104. DOI: 10.1016/1040-6182(95)00049-O.

Peteet, D., et al. "Sensitivity of Northern Hemisphere Air Temperatures and Snow Expansion to North Pacific Sea Surface Temperatures in the GISS General Circulation Model." *Journal of Geophysical Research* 102.D20 (1997), 23781–23791.

Renssen, H. "The Global Response to Younger Dryas Boundary Conditions in an AGCM Simulation." *Climate Dynamics* 13.7–8 (1997), 587–599.

Rind, D., et al., "The Impact of Cold North Atlantic Sea Surface Temperatures on Climate: Implications for the Younger Dryas Cooling (11-10 k)." *Climate Dynamics* 1 (1986), 3–33.

Ruddiman, W.F., and A. McIntyre. "The North Atlantic Ocean During the Last Deglaciation." *Paleogeography, Paleoclimatology, Paleoecology* 35 (1981), 145–214.

Shane, L.C.L., and K.H. Anderson. "Intensity, Gradients and Reversals in Late Glacial Environmental Change in East-central North America." *Quaternary Science Reviews* 12 (1993), 307–314.

Taylor, K.C., et al. "The 'Flickering Switch' of Late Pleistocene Climate Change." *Nature* 361 (1993), 432–436. DOI: 10.1038/361432a0.

Walker, M.J.C., et al., "The Devensian/Weichselian Late-glacial in Northwest Europe (Ireland, Britain, North Belgium, The Netherlands, Northwest Germany)." *Journal of Quaternary Science* 9 (1994), 109–118.

Watts, W.A. "Regional Variation in the Response of Vegetation to Lateglacial Climate Events in Europe." In *Studies in the Lateglacial of North-West Europe*, edited by J.J. Lowe, J.M. Gary and J.E. Ronison. Oxford: Pergamon, 1980, pp. 1–22.

—Dorothy M. Peteet

RESOURCES FOR CITIZENS

"The immensity of global-scale challenges, their seeming remoteness from everyday life, and the inaccessibility of the policy processes that address them make it hard for individuals to think they can make a difference. The good news is that Web-based resources, outstanding organizations, and other levers make it possible today as never before for citizens to affect the outcome of global challenges"

—James Gustave Speth

The entries that follow are taken from *Red Sky at Morning: America and the Crisis of the Global Environment* (New Haven-London: Yale University Press, 2004), and are grouped by Speth's "eight transitions to sustainability."

1. A STABLE OR SMALLER WORLD POPULATION

People and the Planet www.peopleandplanet.ne
Women's Environmental and Development Organization
  (WEDO) www.wedo.org
WomenWatch www.un.org/womenwatch/ianwge
Center for Development and Population Activities (CEDPA)
  www.cedpa.org
The Planned Parenthood Federation of America
  www.plannedparenthood.or/global/about
The Population Council www.popcouncil.org
Population Action International (PAI) www.populationaction.org
The Population Reference Bureau www.prb.org
  www.popnet.org www.popplanet.org
The Center for Environment and Population www.ccpnet.org
United Nations Population Fund (UNFPA) www.unfpa.org
United Nations Development Fund for Women (UNIFEM)
  www.unifem.org
Association for Women's Rights in Development (AWID)
  www.awid.org/index.pl
Pathfinder International www.pathfind.org
Population Connection (formerly Zero Population Growth)
  www.populationconnection.org

2. FREEDOM FROM MASS POVERTY

United Nations Development Program (UNDP)
  Annual Human Development Report http://hdr.undp.org
  Millennium Development Goals (and to volunteer)
    www.netaid.org www.developmentgoals.org
World Bank Poverty Net www.worldbank.org/poverty
International Centre for Trade and Sustainable Development
  (ICTSD) www.ictsd.org
Center for Global Development www.cgdev.org
World Resources Institute (WRI) www.wri.org
International Institute for Sustainable Development (IISD)
  www.iisd.org
Institute for Environment and Development (IIED) www.iied.or
International Forum on Globalization (IFG) www.ifg.org
Institute for Agriculture and Trade Policy (IATP)
  www.iatp.org
Worldwatch Institute www.worldwatch.org

Sustainable Development
  Enterprise Works www.enterpriseworks.org
  Horizon International www.solutions-site.org
  One World www.oneworld.net

Poverty Alleviation
  Oxfam International www.oxfam.org
  Interaction www.interaction.org
  Microcredit Summit Campaign
    www.microcreditsummit.org

3. ENVIRONMENTALLY BENIGN TECHNOLOGIES

Global Network of Environment and Technology (GNET)
  www.gnet.org
    Cool Companies www.cool-companies.org
    TechKnow www.techknow.org
GreenBiz.com www.greenbiz.com
Sustainable Alternatives Network
  www.sustainablealternatives.net
Rocky Mountain Institute (RMI) www.rmi.org
United Nations Environment Programme www.unep.org
    Cleaner Production Site www.unepie.org
Greening of Industry Network
  www.greeningogfindustry.org
National Pollution Prevention Roundtable www.p2.org
BuildingGreen.com www.buildinggreen.com
USDA Regional Pest Management Centers
  www.ipmcenters.org
Leading-edge Technologies
    Clean Edge www.cleanedge.com
    McDonough and Braungart www.mbdc.com
Solar Today www.solartoday.org
American Wind Energy Association www.awea.org
State Incentives for Renewable Energy Installations
  www.dsireusa.org

4. ENVIRONMENTALLY HONEST PRICES

Subsidy Watch www.iisd.org/subsidywatch
Friends of the Earth www.foe.org

Taxpayers for Common Sense www.taxpayer.net
Public Interest Research Group www.uspirg.org
U.S. Society for Ecological Economics www.oecd.org
International Society for Ecological Economics
  www.ecologicaleconomics.org

Internalizing External Environmental Costs, and Eliminating Perverse Subsidies

  Rocky Mountain Institute www.rmi.org
  World Resources Institute www.wri.org
  International Institute for Sustainable Development
    www.iisd.org
  Wuppertal Institute www.wupperstalinst.org
  OECD Environment Directorate www.oecd.org

5. SUSTAINABLE CONSUMPTION

Co-op America www.responsibleshopper.org
E-The Environmental Magazine www.emagazine.com
Environmental Law Institute www.elistore.org
Consumers International www.consumersinternational.org
United Nations Environment Programme Production and
  Consumption Branch www.uneptie.org
American Council for an Energy-Efficient Economy
  www.aceee.org

Green Certification of Products

  Marine Stewardship Council www.msc.org
  Salmon Safe www.salmonsafe.org
  Forest Stewardship Council www.fscoax.org
  Energy Star www.energystar.gov
  U.S. Green Building Council www.usgbc.org
  Rain Forest Alliance Certified www.rainforest-alliance.org

Sustainable Food Supply

  United States Department of Agriculture's Organic Seal
    www.ams.usda.gov
  Natural Resources Defense Council www.nrdc.org
  Environmental Defense www.environmentaldefense.org

Ecotourism

  International Ecotourism Society (TIES)
    www.ecotourism.org
  Ecotravel Online magazine www.ecotravel.com

6. KNOWLEDGE AND LEARNING

National Environmental Education and Training Foundation
  www.neetf.org
National Academies of Science, of Engineering, of Medicine
  www.nas.edu
International Council for Science www.icsu.org
Second Nature www.secondnature.org
National Council for Science and the Environment
  http://NCSEonline.org
Initiative on Science and Technology for Sustainability
  http://sustsci.harvard.edu

The World Conservation Union (IUCN) www.iucn.org
Millennium Ecosystem Assessment
www.milleniumassessment.org

Independent Research Centers

  Woods Hole Oceanographic Institution www.whoi.edu
  Institute of Ecosystem Studies www.ecostudies.org
  Wildlife Conservation Society www.wcs.org

7. GOOD GOVERNANCE

United Nations Association of the United States of America
  www.unausa.org
The Better World Campaign www.betterwordfund.org

United Nations

  United Nations Environment Program (UNEP) www.unep.org
  U.N. Framework Convention on Climate Change
    www.unfccc.int
  U.N. Convention on Biological Diversity www.biodiv.org
  U.N. Convention to Combat Desertification www.unccd.int

Environmental Non-Government Organizations (NGO's) Based in North America

  Natural Resources Defense Council www.nrdc.org
  Environmental Defense www.environmentaldefense.org
  World Resources Institute www.wri.org
  Environmental Law Institute www.eli.org
  Earth Action www.earthaction.org
  International Institute for Sustainable Development
    www.iisd.org
  World Conservation Union www.iucn.org
  Center for International Environmental Law
    www.ciel.org
  World Wildlife Fund www.worldwildlife.org
  Sierra Club www.sierraclub.org
  Friends of the Earth www.foe.org
  Greenpeace www.greenpeace.org
  National Wildlife Federation www.nwf.org
  International Center for Local Environmental Initiatives
    www.iclei.org
  Pew Climate Center www.pewclimate.org
  Conservation International www.conservation.org
  Nature Conservancy www.nature.org

Support for Voluntary Climate Initiatives

  Safe Climate for Business www.safeclimate.net
  Climate Neutral Network www.climateneutral.com
  Pew Climate Center www.pewclimate.org
  Chicago Climate Exchange www.chicagoclimatex.com

Greening of Business

  Biogems Initiative www.savebiogems.org
  Global Reporting Initiative www.globalreporting.org
  Coalition for Environmentally Responsible Economies
    www.ceres.org
  INFORM www.informinc.org

Greening of Industry Network
  www.greeningofindustry.org
Sustainable Business www.sustainablebusiness.com
Greenpeace www.greenpeace.com
Corporate Watch www.corpwatch.org

Initiatives by Local Communities

Sustainable Communities Network www.sustainable.org
Institute for Local Self-Reliance www.ilsr.org
Local Government Commission wwwlgc.org
E.F. Schumacher Society www.smallisbeautiful.org

Responsible Investing

Investor Responsibility Research Center
  www.irrc.org
Carbon Disclosure Project www.cdproject.net
Clean Yield Group www.cleanyield.com
Socially Responsible Investing www.enn.com
Dow Jones Sustainability Indexes
  www.sustainability-indexes.com
Social Investment Forum www.socialinvest.org
Social Venture Network www.svn.org

Politically Active

REP America www.repamerica.org
MoveOn www.moveon.org

Social and Political Criticism

The Ecologist www.theecologist.org
Turning Point Project www.turnpoint.org
Earth Island Journal www.earthisland.org
Mother Jones www.motherjones.com
The American Prospect www.prospect.org
TomPaine www.tompaine.com
Grist www.gristmagazine.com

Think Tanks and Policy Research Centers (in addition to those based at Universities)

Worldwatch Institute www.worldwatch.org
World Business Council for Sustainable Development
  www.wbcsd.ch
International Forum on Globalization www.ifg.org
American Enterprise Institute www.aei.org
Resources for the Future www.rff.org
Heinz Center www.heinzcenter.org
World Resources Institute www.wri.org
Union of Concerned Scientists www.ucsusa.org
Tellus Institute www.tellus.org
Center for International Sustainable Development Law
  www.cisdl.org
International Institute for Environment and Development
  www.iied.org
Carnegie Endowment for International Peace www.ceip.org
Earth Policy Institute www.earth-policy.org
World Wildlife Fund www.worldwildlife.org
World Conservation Union www.iucn.org

Measures of Sustainability

Environmental Sustainability Index www.ciesin.columbia.edu
Living Planet Index www.panda.org
Ecological Footprint www.rprogress.org
Compass of Sustainability www.iisd.org
Wellbeing Assessment www.iucn.org

8. CULTURE AND CONSCIOUSNESS

National Religious Partnership for the Environment
  www.nrpe.org
Earth Charter Commission www.earthcharter.org
Tellus Institute www.tellus.org

SELECTED INTERNATIONAL AGREEMENTS ON ENVIRONMENTAL ISSUES, LISTED BY DATE OF ADOPTION OR ENFORCEMENT

Date	Agreement
1946	International Convention for the Regulation of Whaling
1959	Antarctic Treaty
1972	Stockholm Declaration on the Human Environment
1972	Convention for Conservation of Antarctic Seals
1972	London Dumping Convention
1973	Convention on International Trade in Endangered Species (CITES)
1973	International Convention for Prevention of Pollution from Ships
1975	Convention on Wetlands of International Importance
1979	Convention on Long-Range Transboundary Air Pollution
1980	Convention on Conservation of Antarctic Marine Living Resources
1982	U.N. Convention on the Law of the Sea
1985	Vienna Convention for Protection of the Ozone Layer
1986	Convention on Early Notification of a Nuclear Accident
1987	Montreal Protocol on Substances that Deplete the Ozone Layer
1988	Convention on Regulation of Antarctic Mineral Resource Activities
1989	Prior Informed Consent in Hazardous Chemicals and Pesticides
1989	Basel Convention on the Control of Trans-boundary Movements of Hazardous Wastes, and Their Disposal
1991	Antarctic Environment Protocol
1992	Rio Declaration on Environment and Development
1992	U.N. Framework Convention on Climate Change
1992	Convention on Biological Diversity (CBD)
1994	U.N. Convention to Combat Desertification in Countries Experiencing Serious Drought and/or Desertification
1995	U.N. Agreement on Straddling Fish Stocks and Highly Migratory Fish Stocks
1997	Kyoto Protocol
1998	Convention for Prior Informed Consent for Trade in Hazardous Chemicals and Pesticides
2001	Convention on Persistent Organic Pollutants
	International Treaty on Plant Genetic Resources for Foods and Agriculture

For details, and for a separate and exhaustive compilation of multinational agreements (1875 to 2005), bilateral agreements (1351 to 2005), and secretariats see: *International Environmental Agreements (IEA) Data Base* available at http://iea.uoregon.edu and described in Ronald B. Mitchell, "International Environmental Agreements: A Survey of Their features, Formation, and Effects" *Annual Review of Environment and Resources*, 28, Nov. 2003.

—DAVID J. CUFF

NATIONS RANKED BY ENVIRONMENTAL PERFORMANCE INDEX, 2008

Source: Yale Center for Environmental Law and Policy (YCELP) and Center for International Earth Science Information Network (CIESIN), Columbia University, with the World Economic Forum, and Joint Research Centre (JRC) of the European Commission (2008). 2008 Environmental Performance Index. Downloaded from http://sedac.ciesin.columbia.edu/es/epi/ (last accessed May 22, 2008).

#	Nation	EPI Score		#	Nation	EPI Score
1.	Switzerland	95.5		43.	Poland	80.5
2.	Norway	93.1		44.	Greece	80.2
3.	Sweden	93.1		45.	Venezuela	80.0
4.	Finland	91.4		46.	Australia	79.8
5.	Costa Rica	90.5		47.	Mexico	79.8
6.	Austria	89.4		48.	Bosnia and Herzegovina	79.7
7.	New Zealand	88.9		49.	Israel	79.6
8.	Latvia	88.8		50.	Sri Lanka	79.5
9.	Columbia	88.3		51.	South Korea	79.4
10.	France	87.8		52.	Cyprus	79.2
11.	Iceland	87.6		53.	Thailand	79.2
12.	Canada	86.6		54.	Jamaica	79.1
13.	Germany	86.3		55.	Netherlands	78.7
14.	United Kingdom	86.3		56.	Bulgaria	78.5
15.	Slovenia	86.3		57.	Belgium	78.4
16.	Lithuania	86.2		58.	Mauritius	78.1
17.	Slovakia	86.0		59.	Peru	78.1
18.	Portugal	85.8		60.	Tunisia	78.1
19.	Estonia	85.2		61.	Philippines	77.9
20.	Croatia	84.6		62.	Armenia	77.8
21.	Japan	84.5		63.	Paraguay	77.7
22.	Ecuador	84.4		64.	Gabon	77.3
23.	Hungary	84.2		65.	El Salvador	77.2
24.	Italy	84.2		66.	Algeria	77.0
25.	Albania	84.0		67.	Iran	76.9
26.	Denmark	84.0		68.	Czech Republic	76.8
27.	Malaysia	84.0		69.	Guatemala	76.7
28.	Russian Federation	83.9		70.	Jordan	76.5
29.	Chile	83.4		71.	Egypt	76.3
30.	Spain	83.1		72.	Turkey	75.9
31.	Luxembourg	83.1		73.	Honduras	75.4
32.	Panama	83.1		74.	Macedonia	75.1
33.	Dominican Republic	83.0		75.	Ukraine	74.1
34.	Brazil	82.7		76.	Viet Nam	73.9
35.	Ireland	82.7		77.	Nicaragua	73.4
36.	Uruguay	82.3		78.	Saudi Arabia	72.8
37.	Georgia	82.2		79.	Tajikistan	72.3
38.	Argentina	81.8		80.	Azerbaijan	72.2
39.	United States	81.0		81.	Morocco	72.1
40.	Taiwan	80.8		82.	Nepal	72.1
41.	Cuba	80.7		83.	Romania	71.9
42	Belarus	80.5		84.	Belize	71.7

		EPI Score			*EPI Score*
85.	Turkmenistan	71.3	117.	Uganda	61.6
86.	Ghana	70.8	118.	Swaziland	61.3
87.	Moldova	70.7	119.	Haiti	60.7
88.	Namibia	70.6	120.	India	60.3
89.	Trinidad and Tobago	70.4	121.	Malawi	59.9
90.	Lebanon	70.3	122.	Eritrea	59.4
91.	Oman	70.3	123.	Ethiopia	58.8
92.	Congo	69.7	124.	Pakistan	58.7
93.	Fiji	69.7	125.	Bangladesh	58.0
94.	Kyrgzstan	69.6	126.	Nigeria	56.2
95.	Zimbabwe	69.3	127.	Benin	56.1
96.	Kenya	69.0	128.	Central African Republic	56.0
97.	South Africa	69.0	129.	Sudan	55.5
98.	Botswana	68.7	130.	Zambia	55.1
99.	Syria	68.2	131.	Rwanda	54.9
100.	Mongolia	68.1	132.	Burundi	54.7
101.	Lao People's Dem. Rep.	66.3	133.	Madagascar	54.6
102.	Indonesia	66.2	134.	Iraq	53.9
103.	Côte d'Ivoire	65.2	135.	Mozambique	53.9
104.	China	65.1	136.	Cambodia	53.8
105.	Myanmar (Burma)	65.1	137.	Solomon Islands	52.3
106.	Kazakhstan	65.0	138.	Guinea	51.3
107.	Uzbekistan	65.0	139.	Djibouti	50.5
108.	Guyana	64.8	140.	Guinea-Bissau	49.7
109.	Papua New Guinea	64.8	141.	Yemen	49.7
110.	Bolivia	64.7	142.	Congo, Dem. Rep.	47.3
111.	Kuwait	64.5	143.	Chad	45.9
112.	United Arab Emirates	64.0	144.	Burkina Faso	44.3
113.	Tanzania, United Rep. of	63.9	145.	Mali	44.3
114.	Cameroon	63.8	146.	Mauritania	44.2
115.	Senegal	62.8	147.	Sierra Leone	40.0
116.	Togo	62.3	148.	Angola	39.5
			149.	Niger	39.1

NATIONS RANKED ACCORDING TO HUMAN DEVELOPMENT INDEX, 2006

Source: United Nations Human Development Report, 2006

1.	Norway	46.	Qatar
2.	Iceland	47.	Seychelles
3.	Australia	48.	Costa Rica
4.	Ireland	49.	United Arab Emirates
5.	Sweden	50.	Cuba
6.	Canada	51.	Saint Kitts and Nevis
7.	Japan	52.	Bahamas
8.	United States	53.	Mexico
9.	Switzerland	54.	Bulgaria
10.	Netherlands	55.	Tonga
11.	Finland	56.	Oman
12.	Luxembourg	57.	Trinidad and Tobago
13.	Belgium	58.	Panama
14.	Austria	59.	Antigua and Barbuda
15.	Denmark	60.	Romania
16.	France	61.	Malaysia
17.	Italy	62.	Bosnia and Herzegovina
18.	United Kingdom	63.	Mauritius
19.	Spain	64.	Libyan Arab Jamahiriya
20.	New Zealand	65.	Russian Federation
21.	Germany	66.	Macedonia, TFYR
22.	Hong Kong	67.	Belarus
23.	Israel	68.	Dominica
24.	Greece	69.	Brazil
25.	Singapore	70.	Columbia
26.	Korea, Republic of	71.	Saint Lucia
27.	Slovenia	72.	Venezuela
28.	Portugal	73.	Albania
29.	Cyprus	74.	Thailand
30.	Czech Republic	75.	Samoa (Western)
31.	Barbados	76.	Saudi Arabia
32.	Malta	77.	Ukraine
33.	Kuwait	78.	Lebanon
34.	Brunei Darussalam	79.	Kazakhstan
35.	Hungary	80.	Armenia
36.	Argentina	81.	China
37.	Poland	82.	Peru
38.	Chile	83.	Ecuador
39.	Bahrain	84.	Philippines
40.	Estonia	85.	Grenada
41.	Lithuania	86.	Jordan
42.	Slovakia	87.	Tunisia
43.	Uruguay	88.	Saint Vincent and the Grenadines
44.	Croatia	89.	Suriname
45.	Latvia	90.	Fiji

91. Paraguay	135. Bhutan
92. Turkey	136. Ghana
93. Sri Lanka	137. Bangladesh
94. Dominican Republic	138. Nepal
95. Belize	139. Papua New Guinea
96. Iran	140. Congo, Dem Rep.
97. Georgia	141. Sudan
98. Maldives	142. Timor-Leste
99. Azerbaijan	143. Madagascar
100. Occupied Palestinian Territories	144. Cameroon
101. El Salvador	145. Uganda
102. Algeria	146. Swaziland
103. Guyana	147. Togo
104. Jamaica	148. Djibouti
105. Turkmenistan	149. Lesotho
106. Cape Verde	150. Yemen
107. Syrian Arab Republic	151. Zimbabwe
108. Indonesia	152. Kenya
109. Viet Nam	153. Mauritania
110. Krgyzstan	154. Haiti
111. Egypt	155. Gambia
112. Nicaragua	156. Senegal
113. Uzbekistan	157. Eritrea
114. Moldova, Republic of	158. Rwanda
115. Bolivia	159. Nigeria
116. Mongolia	160. Guinea
117. Honduras	161. Angola
118. Guatemala	162. Tanzania, United Rep. of
119. Vanuatu	163. Benin
120. Equatorial Guinea	164. Cote d'Ivoire
121. South Africa	165. Zambia
122. Tajikistan	166. Malawi
123. Morocco	167. Congo, Dem. Rep. of the
124. Gabon	168. Mozambique
125. Namibia	169. Burundi
126. India	170. Ethiopia
127. Sao Tome and Principe	171. Chad
128. Solomon Islands	172. Central African Republic
129. Cambodia	173. Guinea-Bissau
130. Myanmar (Burma)	174. Burkina Faso
131. Botswana	175. Mali
132. Comoros	176. Sierra Leone
133. Lao People's Dem. Rep.	177. Niger
134. Pakistan	

TOTAL GREENHOUSE GAS EMISSIONS* AND EMISSION INTENSITY,** 2000

	Million tons CO_2 Equiv.	Percent of World total	Emission Intensity
1. USA	6,928	21	720
2. China	4,938	15	1,023
3. EU (25)	4,725	14	449
4. Russia	1,915	5.7	1,817
5. India	1,884	5.6	768
6. Japan	1,317	3.9	400
7. Germany	1,009	3.0	471
8. Brazil	851	2.5	679
9. Canada	680	2.0	793
10. U.K.	654	1.9	450
11. Italy	531	1.6	369
12. So. Korea	521	1.5	729
13. France	513	1.5	344
14. Mexico	512	1.5	586
15. Indonesia	503	1.5	799
16. Australia	491	1.5	977
17. Ukraine	482	1.4	2,369
18. Iran	480	1.4	1,353
19. South Africa	417	1.2	1,006
20. Spain	381	1.1	471
21. Poland	381	1.1	991
22. Turkey	355	1.1	844
23. Saudi Arabia	341	1.0	1,309
24. Argentina	289	0.9	659
25. Pakistan	285	0.8	1,074
Top 25	27,915	82.9	
Remainder	5,751	17.0	

* Carbon dioxide, methane, nitrous oxide, hydrofluorocarbons, perfluorocarbons, and sulfur hexafluoride

** Emissions per unit of Gross Domestic Product

SOURCE: World Resources Institute, CAIT, *Navigating the Numbers: Greenhouse Gas Data and International Climate Policy*, 2005. Available online

INDEX

Note: Page numbers in **bold** indicate main articles. Page numbers followed by *f* and *t* indicate figures and tables.

A

AB32. *See* Global Warming Solutions Act
Abruzzo National Park, 492
Accelerated salinization, 541, 541*t*
Accounting, environmental, **216–217**
Accumulation rates, Loess, 187, 188*t*
Acetaldehyde, biofuels and, 58
Acidification
  ocean, **469**
  soil, 561
Acid rain and acid deposition, **1–5**
  agriculture and, 13
  air pollution and, 505
  extent of, 2
  health and, 3–4
  history of, 1–2
  impacts of, 2–4
  sulfur trading and, 209–210
Acid Rain Program, 209–210
Activities Implemented Jointly (AIJ), 375
Acts-of-god hazard paradigm, 453–454
Adenosine triphosphate (ATP), 203
Ad Hoc Group of the Berlin
  Mandate (AGBM), 379
Administrative forestry, 266
Admiralty wilderness area, 642*t*
Advanced Very High Resolution Radiometer
  (AVHRR), 555
Aerosols, **5–8**
  albedo and, 19
  climate change and, 7, 8
  cloud formation and, 6
  in geoengineering, 283*t*
  in greenhouse effect, 308
  ice-core record of, 7–8
  sinks of, 6–7, 6*t*
  sources of, 6–7, 6*t*
  stratospheric, 284
Afghanistan, carbon dioxide emissions of, 97*t*
Aforestation, 285
Africa
  coal reserves in, 272*t*
  deforestation in, 160
  deserts and climate change in, 175*t*
  erosion in, 235*f*
  famine in, 259–260
  fertility in, 342
  glaciers in, 603
  hydroelectric generation in, 149*t*
  Mediterranean environment in, 415
  oil reserves in, 273*t*
  salinization in, 543*t*
  savannas in, 545

  sea-level rise and, 356–357
  water resources in, 625*t*
  wetlands in, 638*f*
Africanized honeybee, 248
African Plate, 432*f*
AGBM. *See* Ad Hoc Group of the Berlin Mandate
  (AGBM)
Age, population and, 342–343
Agenda 21
  sustainable development and, 641
  waste and, 619
Agriculture and agricultural land, **9–14**
  acid rain and, 3
  adaptation in, 13–14
  as anthropogeomorphology, 31
  in Australia, 50
  biofuels and, 59
  bioregionalism and, 15
  Chinese famine and, 258–259
  climate change and, 12–13
  cultivation in, 11–12
  deforestation and, 23–24, 160
  demand growth and, 15–16
  desertification and, 167
  erosion and, 234
  fertilizer production for, 449–450, 456
  global warming and, 299–300
  habitat patches and, 17
  history of, 9–11
  impacts on, 355–356
  in India, 358
  irrigation and, **370–373**
  livestock production and, 11
  major trends in, 12
  methane and, 419
  monocultures in, 17
  mountains and, 437
  native species and, 17
  nuclear winter and, 467
  organic, 13, 18
  perennial crops in, 17
  permaculture and, 15
  pesticides and, 500–501
  pests and, 500
  plant protection and, 16
  population and, 16
  precipitation and, 355
  salinization and, 541
  salinization in, 544*t*
  shifting cultivation system in, 18
  soils and, 560
  strategic planning in, 18
  sulfur cycle and, 571

  systems of, 18
  tropical, 596
  urban sprawl and, 15
  watersheds and, 16–17
  water use and, 628
  wetlands and, 637–638
  world food production and, 257–258
Agriculture and biodiversity, **15–18**
Agrochemicals, 500–501
Agroforestry, 12
AIDS, 180, 184
Aircraft, aerosols from, 8
Air pollution. *See* pollution; smog
Alaska, glaciers in, 602
Albania, carbon dioxide emissions of, 96*t*
Albedo, **19–20**
  Arctic warming and, 45–46
  geoengineering and, 283*t*
  snow cover and, 555
  sulfur dioxide and, 283*t*
Alberta oil sands, 476
Alcohol. *See* biofuels; ethanol
Aldo Leopold Wilderness, 642
Algeria
  carbon dioxide emissions of, 95*t*
  natural gas production in, 451*t*
  natural gas reserves in, 451*t*
Alkali, 110
Alliance of Small Island States (AOSIS), 274
Alps
  glacial retreat in, 290*f*
  in Little Ice Age, 400–402
Amazon administrative region, 21
"Amazonas Initiative," 26
Amazon basin, 392*t*
Amazonia and deforestation, **21–26**
Amboseli National Park, 492
American Ornithologists Union (AOU), 645
American Samoa, carbon dioxide emissions
  of, 97*t*
American Wildlife Institute, 645
Amibara irrigation project, 542*t*
Ammonium aerosols, 6*t*
Amphibians, in Australia, 50*t*
Amsterdam Declaration on
  Global Change, 193
Amu Dar'ya delta, 36
Amur River, 392*t*
Anasazis, 121*t*
Anatomy Lesson of Dr. Tulp (Rembrandt), 54
Angara River, 80
Angola, carbon dioxide emissions of, 96*t*
Anhydrite, 252

Animals. *See also* fauna
  antibiotics in, 178
  Arctic warming and, 47
  biological realms and, 69–70, 69*f*
  dams and, 150–151
  exotic, **244–247**
  hantavirus and, 183
  hunting of, **346–348**
  infections from, 177–178
  interhemispheric exchange of, 325
  poaching of, **346–348**
  in savanna, 545
  wildlife management and, **644–645**
Annales school, 331
Antarctica
  ozone and, 479–480
  topography of, 349*f*
Antarctica and climate change, **27–31**
  Eastern, 31
  glaciated land in, 28*f*
  history of, 29
  Northern, 31
  recent, 29–30
  sea levels, global, and, 30–31
  sea levels in, 28*f*
  temperature records, 30
  Western, 31
Antarctic ice sheet, **349–352**
  vs. Greenland ice sheet, 310
  volume of, 349
Anthracite coals, 271
Anthropogenic aerosols, 7
Anthropogenic steppes, 160
Anthropogenic *vs.* natural change, 335
Anthropogeomorphology, **31–35**
  constructional, 32*t*
  definition of, 31
  direct, 32*t*
  excavational, 32*t*, 33*f*, 35
  indirect, 31–32, 32*t*
  subsidence, 32*t*
Antibiotic use, 178
Antigua, carbon dioxide emissions of, 97*t*
Antilles, carbon dioxide emissions of, 96*t*
AO. *See* Arctic Oscillation (AO)
AOGCMs. *See* atmosphere-ocean general
  circulation models (AOGCMs)
AOSIS. *See* Alliance of Small Island States (AOSIS)
AOU. *See* American Ornithologists Union (AOU)
AP7. *See* Asia-Pacific Partnership on Clean
  Development and Climate (AP7)
APEC. *See* Asia-Pacific Economic Cooperation
  Forum (APEC)
Apollo Alliance, 201
Apollo program, 443*t*
Aquaculture, **263–265**
Aquatic ecosystems, acid rain and, 2
Aral Sea, **36–38**
  area of, 383*t*
  land use and, 399
  map of, 37*f*
  salinity of, 38*t*
  shrinking of, 37*f*, 383
  sulfur cycle and, 571
Arctic, ozone in, 480
Arctic Oscillation (AO), sea ice and, 40

Arctic sea-ice, **38–42**
  age of, 39
  Arctic warming and, 43–44, 45*f*
  changes in, 38–39
  effects of reduction in, 43
  extent of, 38–39, 39*f*, 40*f*, 41*f*, 42*f*
  future of, 39
  losses of, 39–40
  polar bears and, 47
  thickness of, 39
Arctic warming, **42–48**
  as accelerated, 43
  global nature of, 44–46, 45*f*
  local effects of, 46–48
  precipitation and, 43
Arctic wilderness area, 642*t*
Argentina
  carbon dioxide emissions of, 95*t*
  salinization in, 544*t*
Aridification. *See also* desertification
  anthropogeomorphology and, 32
  in Australia, 48
  building decay and, 85–86
  deserts and, 170
  in feedback loop, 68*f*
Armenia, carbon dioxide emissions of, 96*t*
Arrhenius, Svante, 293, 306
Arroyos, 32
Art, belief systems and, 53–54
Artisanal fisheries, 263
Artisanal mining, 428
Aruba, carbon dioxide emissions of, 96*t*
Asia
  acid rain in, 5
  "brown cloud" of, 359
  coal reserves in, 272*t*
  dams in, 149
  deforestation in, 160
  deserts and climate change in, 175*t*
  dust storms in, 191*f*
  famine in, 258–259
  hydroelectric generation in, 149*t*
  mangroves in, 410
  oil reserves in, 273*t*
  salinization in, 543*t*
  savannas in, 545
  traditional medicine in, 347–348
  water resources in, 625*t*
  wetlands in, 637–638
Asian water buffalo, 247–248
Asia-Pacific Economic Cooperation Forum
  (APEC), 585
Asia-Pacific Partnership on Clean Development
  and Climate (AP7), 377
Asthma, acid rain and, 3–4
Aswan Dam, 86, 163
Atacama Desert, 167
Athabasca River, 476
Atmosphere
  in carbon cycle, 91, 92*f*, 93
  Gaia hypothesis and, 279
  nitrogen in, 456, 457*f*
  nitrous oxide in, 459
  ocean coupling with, **469–474**
  ozone in, **478–481**
  permafrost and, 495

volcanoes and, 614–615
  water vapor in, **633–634**
Atmosphere-ocean general circulation models
  (AOGCMs), 124, 125–126, 522, 523*f*, 524*f*,
  525–526, 525*f*
Atmospheric models, 124
Atolls, 515, 517*f*
Audobon, John James, 230
Audobon Society, 645
Australasian zoological region, 69*f*
Australia, **48–52**
  carbon dioxide emissions of, 94*t*, 95*t*
  coal reserves in, 272*t*
  deserts and climate change in, 175*t*
  dust storms in, 190*f*
  emissions of, 377, 378*f*
  emissions target under Kyoto, 381*t*
  landscape management in, 198
  mangroves in, 409
  Mediterranean environment in, 415
  nuclear power in, 465
  salinization in, 543*t*, 544*t*
  savannas in, 545, 547*f*
  transportation-related emissions in, 589*t*
Australian Plate, 432*f*
Austria
  carbon dioxide emissions of, 95*t*
  emissions of, 378*f*
  emissions target under Kyoto, 381*t*
  trade and, 582
AVHRR. *See* Advanced Very High Resolution
  Radiometer (AVHRR)
Azerbaijan, carbon dioxide emissions of, 95*t*
Azores subtropical high, 462, 472

B
Bacille Calmette Guérin (BCG) vaccine, 181
Bacon, Francis, 53
Baden Conference, 216–217
Bahamas, carbon dioxide emissions of, 96*t*
Bahrain, carbon dioxide emissions of, 95*t*
Bailey, Liberty Hyde, 55
Bambi, 54
Bangladesh, carbon dioxide emissions of, 95*t*
Barbados, carbon dioxide emissions of, 96*t*
Barents Sea, 40
Barley, as biofuel feedstock, 57*f*, 239*f*
Barrier reefs, 515
Barrows, Harlan H., 330
Basalt carbon storage, 88
Basel Convention, 225
Baseline-and-credit emissions trading, 210
Bates, Marston, 293
BCG. *See* bacille Calmette Guérin
  (BCG) vaccine
Beaches, sea levels and, 550–551
Beef, in Brazil, 23
Behavioral hazard paradigm, 454
Beijing, 609*t*
Belarus
  carbon dioxide emissions of, 95*t*
  emissions of, 378*f*
Belgium
  carbon dioxide emissions of, 95*t*
  emissions of, 378*f*
  emissions target under Kyoto, 381*t*
Belief systems, **53–55**

Belize, carbon dioxide emissions of, 97*t*
Bellini, Giovanni, 53
Beni Amir irrigation project, 542*t*
Benin, carbon dioxide emissions of, 96*t*
Bennett, H. H., 234
Berlin Conference, 275*t*
Berlin Mandate, 379
Bermuda, carbon dioxide emissions of, 97*t*
Bhatinda irrigation project, 542*t*
Bhutan, carbon dioxide emissions of, 97*t*
Bicarbonate, mean residence time of, 61
Bierstadt, Albert, 54
Biocentrism, 218
Biocoenose, 201
Biodiesel
  feedstocks, 57*f*
  production of, 56, 56*f*
Biodiversity, **61–65**
  acid rain and, 2
  agricultural systems and, 18
  agriculture and, 10, 13, **15–18**
  definition of, 61
  deforestation and, 24
  ecotones and, 62
  extinctions and, 63–64
  in feedback loop, 68*f*
  future of, 17–18
  Gaia hypothesis and, 281
  genetic diversity and, 61
  growth in agricultural demand
    and, 16–17
  habitat patches and, 17
  hotspots, 353–354
  importance of, 62–63
  in India, 360
  landscape connectivity and, 17
  livestock and, 17
  measures of, 62
  medicine and, 16
  mountains and, 435, 437–438
  native species and, 17
  organic farming and, 18
  parks and, 196, 197–198
  patterns of, 62
  plant protection and, 16
  population and, 15–16
  protection of, 64–65
  in savannas, 548
  threats to, 63–64
  tropical forests and, 597
  types of, 61–62
  valuation of, 24
  watersheds and, 16–17
  wilderness and, **640–641**
Bioethics, **218–219**
Biofuels, **56–59**. *See also* ethanol
  as renewable, 531
  in U.S. energy policy, 443
  as wedge, 570
Biogenic aerosols, 6*t*
Biogeochemical cycles, **60–61**
Biological cycles, 60–61
Biological ecology, 329
Biological feedback, **65–68**
Biological realms, **69–71**
Biological weathering, 86

Biomass
  burning, U.S. spending on, 443*t*
  in ecosystems, 202
  as renewable, 531
Biomass burning aerosols, 6*t*
Biomass combustion, 57
Biomes, **71–74**
  shifting, 353
Biorefineries, 238
Bioregionalism, agriculture and, 15
Biozones, 154
Birds
  Arctic warming and, 46
  in Australia, 50*t*
  exotic, 245
Birkenhead Park, 491
Birth rates
  decline in, 327
  population policy and, 507–508
Bituminous coals, 271
Black Death, 339
Bleaching, of coral reefs, 518
Bligh Reef, 231
"Blitzkrieg effect," 248
Bloch, Marc, 331
"Blue Angel" program, 216
Blytt-Sernander model, 320
Bob Marshall wilderness area, 642*t*
Bogota, 609*t*
Bogs, 499
Bohle's model of food crisis, 616*f*
Bolivia
  Amazon River in, 21
  carbon dioxide emissions of, 96*t*
Boreal forest, 73, **75–83**
Bosnia-Herzegovinia, carbon dioxide emissions
    of, 96*t*
Bossons Glacier, 603*f*
Botswana, carbon dioxide emissions of, 96*t*
Boundary Waters Canoe Area, 642*t*
Brain-drain, 422
Brandeis, Louis D., 439
Braudel, Ferdinand, 325, 331
Brazil
  Amazon region of, 21*f*
  biofuels in, 57, 58*f*
  carbon dioxide emissions of, 94*t*, 95*t*
  coal reserves in, 272*t*
  ethanol in, 58*f*
  mangroves in, 409
  "Plano Real" program in, 23
  transportation-related emissions in, 589*t*
Brazilian Institute for the Environment and
    Renewable Natural Resources, 25
Breakbone fever, 182
Breeder reactors, 464
Brick-pits, 359
Broadband albedo, 19
Bromofluorocarbons, 119
Bronze, 110
"Brown cloud," 359
Brown tree snake, 246
Brundtland, Gro Harlem, 84, 225
Brundtland Commission, **84–85**, 225
Brunei, carbon dioxide emissions of, 96*t*
Brunn rule, 551, 551*f*

Buddhism, 219
Buenos Aires, 609*t*
Buffon, Count, 292
Building decay, **85–86**
Bulgaria
  carbon dioxide emissions of, 95*t*
  emissions of, 378*f*
  emissions target under Kyoto, 381*t*
Burkina Faso, carbon dioxide
    emissions of, 96*t*
Burning, *vs.* deforestation, 22
Burundi, carbon dioxide emissions of, 97*t*
Bushmeat, 16
Business, green, 217
Butane, in natural gas, 447

C

Cacao production, 17
Cadmium/calcium ratios, 130
Cairo, 609*t*
Cairo Conference, 511, 529
Calcite, 127
Calcutta, 609*t*
California
  energy policy in, 439, 440, 443, 446
  Mediterranean environment in, 415
  photovoltaic energy production in, 446
  water use in, 628
  weather modification in, 635
Caloric intake, daily, 257
Calving
  of glaciers, 603
  of ice sheets, 351
Cambodia, carbon dioxide
    emissions of, 97*t*
Cambrian Period, 155*f*
Cameroon, carbon dioxide emissions of, 96*t*
Canada
  in AP7, 377
  carbon dioxide emissions of, 94*t*, 95*t*
  coal reserves in, 272*t*
  emissions of, 377, 378*f*, 478
  emissions target under Kyoto, 381*t*
  environmental law in, 222
  natural gas production in, 451*t*
  nuclear power in, 465
  oil sands in, 476
  transportation-related emissions in, 589*t*
Canada Geographic Information System (CGIS),
    288
Cancers, microbes and, 177
Canon law, 221
Cap-and-trade emissions trading, 100–101, 210.
    See also emissions trading
Cape Verde, carbon dioxide emissions of, 97*t*
Capital, natural, 216
Capitalism, 325
Capture, of carbon, 285
Carbonate fills, 32
Carbonate oozes, 127
Carbon capture, **87–90**, 133–135, 285, 301
Carbon cycle, 60, **91–97**
  ecosystems and, 202–203
  reservoirs in, 91
Carbon dating, 128, 156, 156*f*, 164–165
Carbon dioxide. *See also* greenhouse gas(es)
  Australian emissions of, 94*t*

Brazilian emissions of, 94*t*
Canadian emissions of, 94*t*
in carbon capture, 87
Chinese emissions of, 94*t*
in coal *vs.* natural gas fired power plants, 448, 449*f*
emissions by country, 95*t*–97*t*
ethanol and, 239–240
European emissions of, 94*t*
forests and, 269
fossil fuels and, 270
French emissions of, 94*t*
in geoengineering, 283*t*
global-warming potential and, 297
in greenhouse effect, 308
as greenhouse gas, 309
historical levels of, 29
Indian emissions of, 94*t*
Japanese emissions of, 94*t*
in Kyoto Protocol, 380*t*
ocean acidification and, 469
phosphorus cycle and, 503
plate tectonics and, 434
savannas and, 547–548
solar radiation management and, 283–284
stabilization wedges, 568–569, 569*f*
taxing of, 204
transportation and, 589, 589*t*
U.S. emissions of, 94*t*
Carbon disulfide, sulfur cycle and, 571
Carbon footprint, **98**
Carboniferous Period, 155*f*
Carbon isotopes, 128
Carbon management, 284–285
Carbon monoxide, transportation and, 588
Carbon offsets, 98
Carbon sequestration, 87, 133–135
Carbon stabilization, **568–570**
Carbon storage, **87–90**
    basalt, 88
    challenges of, 90
    coal and, 133–135
    costs of, 88
    deforestation and, 24
    gaps in science of, 90
    in geoengineering, 285
    geological, 88
    in global carbon sequestration, 87
    hazards, 90
    large-scale commercial deployment, 89–90, 89*t*
    in permafrost, 81–82
    reservoirs, 88
    In Salah site, 89*t*
    sink to source transition of, 352
    Sleipner site, 89*t*
    as wedge, 569
    Weyburn site, 89*t*
Carbon taxes, 24–25, **98–101**, 215
Carbon tetrachloride, 120*t*
Carbon uptake, 597
Caribbean Plate, 432*f*
Caricao Basin, 648
Carlyle, Thomas, 577
Carrying capacity, **101–103**
Carson, Rachel, 55, 230, 294

Carson carbon storage project, 89*t*
Carter, Jimmy, 439
Caspian Sea, 208, 383, 383*t*, 384*f*
Cassava, as ethanol feedstock, 239*f*
Catastrophist-cornucopian debate, **103–105**
Catholicism, 530
Catton, William, Jr., 332
Causes, of climate change, **106–109**
Cayman Islands, carbon dioxide emissions of, 97*t*
Cays, 515
CBD. *See* Convention on Biological Diversity (CBD)
CCNs. *See* cloud condensation nuclei (CCNs)
C3 crops, 13
C4 crops, 13
CCTP. *See* Climate Change Technology Plan (CTTP)
CCX. *See* Chicago Climate Exchange (CCX)
CDM. *See* Clean Development Mechanism (CDM)
Cellulose, 238
Cenozoic climate decline, 483, 485, 486*f*
Cenozoic Era, 155*f*
Censuses, 338
Center-pivot irrigation, 13
Central African Republic, carbon dioxide emissions of, 97*t*
Central England Temperature Record, 126
Central Park, 491
Centre for Research on the Epidemiology of Disasters (CRED), 453, 454
CFCs. *See* chlorofluorocarbons (CFCs)
CGIS. *See* Canada Geographic Information System (CGIS)
Chad
    carbon dioxide emissions of, 97*t*
    famine in, 259
Chardin, Teilhard de, 293
Chemical denudation, 391
Chemical industry, **110–112**
Chemical spills, 111
Chemical weathering, 86
Chemical wonders, **112–113**
Chemostratigraphic units, 154–155
Chernobyl, **113–115**, 464
Chesapeake Bay, salt marshes in, 551
Chestnut fungus, 247
Chiang Jiang River, 392*t*
Chicago, 609*t*
Chicago Climate Exchange (CCX), 212
Chicxulub crater, 251, 252
Chile
    carbon dioxide emissions of, 95*t*
    coastal protection in, 137*f*
    desert in, 173*f*
    Mediterranean environment in, 415
China, **115–118**
    air pollution in, 115–116
    carbon dioxide emissions of, 94*t*, 95*t*
    climate records in ancient, 126–127
    coal reserves in, 272*t*
    contribution to climate change, 116–118
    dams in, 149
    deforestation in, 116
    desertification in, 116, 168*f*
    emissions of, 377
    famine in, 258–259

glaciers in, 602
mangroves in, 409
nuclear power in, 465
population policy in, 342, 510–511
salinization in, 544*t*
transportation in, 586, 587
transportation-related emissions in, 589*t*
urbanization in, 116
water pollution in, 116
Chlorine nitrate, 459
Chlorofluorocarbons (CFCs), **118–121**
    in greenhouse effect, 308
    as halocarbons, 119
    ozone and, 118–119, 479
    as pollutants, 504–505
    specific, 120*t*
    Vienna Convention and, 225
Cholera, 179–180
Chongming suburb, 610
Christianity
    creation story in, 529
    Europeanization of world and, 326
    global change and, 292
    prevalence of, 529
Chronic diseases, 177
Chronostratigraphy, 155–156
Chukchi Sea, 39
Church, Frederick, 54
CI. *See* Conservation International (CI)
Circulation models, 124–126
Cirques, 487
Cirrus clouds, 8. *See also* clouds
CITES. *See* Convention on the International Trade in Endangered Species (CITES)
Cities. *See* entries at urban
City parks, 491
Civil law, 221
Civil liability, 223
Classic static stability, 567
Clathrates, 421
Clay varve chronology, 157
Clean Air Act, 527
Clean Development Mechanism (CDM)
    emissions trading and, 210
    joint implementation and, 375
    Kyoto Protocol and, 381
    sustainable development of, 376
Clean Water Act, 527
Cliffed coasts, sea levels and, 550
Climate change, **295–302**. *See also* weather
    aerosols and, 7, 8
    agricultural impacts of, 355–356
    agriculture and, 12–13, 14
    albedo and, **19–20**
    Antarctica and, **27–31**
    anthropogeomorphology and, 33–34
    in Arctic, **42–48**
    Australia and, 51–52
    belief systems and, **53–55**
    causes of, **106–109**
    Chinese contribution to, 116–118
    coastal consequences of, 34*t*
    cryospheric consequences of, 34*t*
    deforestation and, 13, 24–25, 159
    deserts and, 174, 175*t*

economic levels and, 199–200
eolian consequences of, 34t
exctinctions and, 353
in feedback loop, 68f
fires and, **262**
flooding and, 356–357
forests and, 269
geomorphologic consequences of, 34t
global warming and, 239–241
health and, 355–356
in history, 29
history of thought on, 291–293
human systems and, 354–356
hydrologic consequences of, 34t
ice sheets and, 351–352
impacts of, **352–357**
India as victim of, 360
lakes and, 385
Mediterranean environments and, 417–418
modeling, 29
natural hazards and, 454–455
natural responses to, 308–309
natural *vs.* anthropogenic, 335
permafrost and, 495–498
positive feedbacks in, 66
regional patterns of, **522–526**
rice cultivation and, 13
sea levels and, 550–553, 551f, 552f
societal development and, **121–122**
subsidence and, 34t
tipping points and, 581
twentieth century, **600–603**
uncertainty and, 605–606
vegetational controls and, 34t
water stress and, 354–355
Climate Change Solutions Act, 446
Climate Change Technology Plan (CTTP), energy
    policy and, 439
Climate models, **122–126**
Climate reconstruction, **126–132**
Climate regulation, 281
Climatic Optimum, 295, **413–414**
Closing Circle, The (Commoner), 231
Cloud condensation nuclei (CCNs), 281
Cloud forests, 352
Clouds
    aerosols and, 6, 8
    aircraft and, 8
    albedo and, 19
    algae and, 66, 67f
    cirrus, 8
    in Gaia hypothesis, 281
    in geoengineering, 283t, 284
    global dimming and, 294
    ice, 6
    marine stratocumulus, 284
    weather modification and, 635
CNG. *See* compressed natural gas (CNG) vehicles
Coal, **133–136**
    in China, 115–116
    combustion of, 214
    deposits, 271
    displaced by renewables, 533t
    energy content of, 274
    gasification of, **136–137**

greenhouse gases and, 270
    liquefaction, **137**
    prevalence of, 270
    rise of, 270
    technology, 578
Coalition of Rainforest Nations, 599
Coal Question, The (Jevons), 104
Coal reserves, 271, 272t
Coastal cliffs, sea levels and, 550
Coastal dunes, 551
Coastal erosion, Arctic warming and, 47
Coastal flooding, 356–357
Coastal plains, sea levels and, 552
Coastal protection and management, **137–139**
Coastal subsidence, 550f
Coastal zone salinity, 541t
Coastlines, **139–142**
    human influences on, 141, 141t
    rates of change in, 140
    types of, 139
Coasts, emerging, **207–209**
Coccidioides immitis, 182–183
Coccidioidomycosis, 182–183
Cocos Plate, 432f
Cod colonization of Greenland, 601
Coffee growing, 17
Coke, 271
Cole, Thomas, 54
Colline-montane-alpine-nival model, 437
Colombia, carbon dioxide emissions of, 95t
Colombian Encounter, 325–326
Colorado River, 150
Combined-cycle natural gas electricity generation,
    448, 449f
Combustion
    in carbon capture, 87
    energy and, 214
    of waste, 620
Commoner, Barry, 231, 579
Common law, 221
Commons, global, **142–143**, 305–306
Communist Party, in China, 258–259
Comoros, carbon dioxide emissions of, 97t
Compensated reduction initiatives, 600
Competitive exclusion, 246
Complexity, in climate models, 125–126
Compliance, with international law, 227–228
Composting, 620
Compressed natural gas (CNG) vehicles, 450–451
Concatenation, in food crisis, 616f
Conference of the Parties to the FCCC I, 274, 375
Conflict
    over natural resources, 536
    over water, 627–628
Congestion, transportation and, 588
Congo, carbon dioxide emissions of, 96t
Congo Basin, 392t
Conservation, **143–144**
    coastal, 137–139
    disputes in, 643
    energy, 215
    exctinctions and, 353–354
    land, 386–388
    manifestations of, 143–144
    parks and, 197–198

societies, 230
    soil, 234–235
    species, 64
    strategies, 387–388
    vs. use, 493
    as wedge, 569
Conservation International (CI), 387
Constable, John, 54
Constant-flow resources, 534, 535t
Constructional anthropogeomorphology, 32t
Consumer preference, transportation and, 587
Consumption
    over, 231
    population and, 509
    of water, 626
Contemporary globalization, 304. *See also*
    globalization
Continental drift, 131–132, **430–434**
Contractarianism, 366
Contradiction, 54
Control, *vs.* stability, 567–568
Convention on Biological Diversity (CBD), 243
Convention on International Trade in Endangered
    Species of Wild Fauna and Flora, 584
Convention on Long Range Transboundary Air
    Pollution, 376
Convention on the Control of Transboundary
    Movements of Hazardous Wastes, 225
Convention on the International Trade in
    Endangered Species (CITES)
    belief systems and, 55
    biodiversity and, 64–65
Convention on the Prevention of Marine Pollution
    by Dumping of Wastes and Other Matter,
    475–476
Convention on the Prohibition of Military or Any
    Other Hostile Use of Environmental
    Modification, 553
Cooking, natural gas for, 450
Cook Islands, carbon dioxide emissions of, 97t
Cooling, in Younger Dryas period, 648–649, 649f
Cooperative Wildlife Research Unit Program, 645
COP-1. *See* Conference of the Parties to the FCCC I
Coping, vulnerability and, 615
Copper, 110, 536
Coral reefs, **515–519**
    area of, 515
    barrier, 515
    bleaching of, 518
    classification of, 515
    El Niño and, 516–517
    fringing, 515
    future of, 518–519
    impacts on, 516–517
    loss of, 352, 354
    mining and, 516
    sea levels and, 515–516, 552–553
    sedimentation and, 516
Corn
    as ethanol feedstock, 239f
    in fuel *vs.* food debate, 241
Cosmic rays, 563, 566
Costa Rica, carbon dioxide emissions of, 96t
Côte d'Ivoire, carbon dioxide emissions of, 96t
Count Buffon, 292

"Country breezes," 608
Crawford, Elisabeth, 293
CRED. *See* Centre for Research on the Epidemiology of Disasters (CRED)
Credit sharing, 376
Creosotebush, 168
Cretaceous Period, 155*f*
Cretaceous quiet zone, 431
Cretaceous-Tertiary boundary, 251
Criminal liability, 223
Croatia
    carbon dioxide emissions of, 95*t*
    emissions of, 378*f*
    emissions target under Kyoto, 381*t*
Crookes, Sir William, 104
Crop diversity, 10, 13
Crop loss, 500
Crop rotation, 10
Crown-of-thorns starfish, 516
Crude oil, 272–273. *See also* oil
Crude oil supply, **144–147**
Crustal movement, paleomagnetic evidence of, **490–491**
Crutzen, Paul, 286
Cryosphere, 555
Cuba, carbon dioxide emissions of, 95*t*
Cultivation, 11–12
Culture
    Europeanization of world and, 326–327
    globalization and, 65, 327–328
    migration and, 423
    natural disasters and, 453
    natural resources and, 533, 534*f*
    policy and, 55
    popular, 328
Cuyahoga River, 579
Cyclone Domoina, 595*f*
Cyclones, 254, **594–595**
    climate change and, 455
    El Niño and, 206
    insurance and, 364
    intensification of, 357
    wetlands and, 637
Cyprus, carbon dioxide emissions of, 96*t*
Czech Republic
    carbon dioxide emissions of, 95*t*
    emissions of, 378*f*
    emissions target under Kyoto, 381*t*

D

Dairying, 11
Daisyworld, 279–280, 280*f*
Daly, Herman, 216
Dams, **149–153**
    Aswan Dam, 86, 163
    Edwards Dam, 153
    Hoover Dam, 151
    Hsinfengkiang Dam, 151
    Kariba Dam, 150*f*, 151
    Konya Dam, 151
    Kremasta Dam, 151
    large, 152
    Marathon Dam, 151
    Nurek Dam, 149
    small *vs.* large, 152
    Three Gorges Dam, 86

Dansgaard-Oeschger cycles, **153**, 488
Danube River, 392*t*
Darwin, Charles, 244
Dating methods, **154–157**
Dawkins, Richard, 279–280
DDT, 55, 112–113, 230, 294
Dead Sea, 383
Death control, 327
Debt-for-nature swaps, 387
Decay, of buildings, **85–86**
Deep ecology, 219
Deep sea sediments, 127–128
Deer, 245
Defense research, U.S., 442*f*
Deforestation, **159–162**. *See also* forests
    agriculture and, 13, 23–24
    albedo and, 19
    in Amazonia, **21–26**
    biodiversity and, 24
    vs. burning, 22
    carbon emissions and, 597
    carbon storage and, 24
    causes of, 23–24, 161
    in China, 116
    climate change and, 24–25
    countermeasures to, 25–26
    current efforts against, 25
    definition of, 21–22, 159
    desertification and, 160, 168
    development and, 26, 160–161
    economics and, 598–599
    effects of, 161–162
    extent of, 22–23, 22*f*
    impacts of, 24–25
    livestock and, 23
    locations of, 159–160
    in Mato Grosso, Brazil, 24
    methane and, 419
    natural, 159
    policy changes for, 25–26
    property size and, 26
    protected areas and, 25
    rate of, 22–23, 22*f*, 159–160
    tropical, 596
    water cycling and, 25
Degradation, *vs.* desertification, 167
Dehli
    natural gas vehicles in, 451
    population of, 609*t*
Deltas, **163**
    sea levels and, 552
Demographic Transition, 327, 339–342, 340*f*, 341*f*
Demographic trends, 508–509
Demography. *See* population, human
Denali wilderness area, 642*t*
Dendrochronology, **163–165**
Dengue fever, 182
Dengue hemorrhagic fever (DHF), 182
Dengue shock syndrome (DSS), 182
Denitrification, 457–458
Denmark
    carbon dioxide emissions of, 95*t*
    emissions of, 378*f*
    emissions target under Kyoto, 381*t*
Density, population, 343

Denudation. *See also* erosion
    chemical, 391
    fluvial, 391–394, 392*t*
    glacial, 394–395, 395*f*
Depositional features, 130
Deposit-refund systems, for waste, 623
Desalination, **165–166**
Descartes, René, 53
Desertification, **167–170**
    in China, 116
    deforestation and, 160
    land reclamation and, 389
    soils and, 560
Deserts, **170–176**
    antiquity of, 591
    changes in coverage of, 72*t*
    classification of, 171*t*
    defining, 170
    distribution of, 172*f*
    dunes in, **176**
    extent of, 171
    future of, 174
    global warming and, 174, 175*t*
    human impact on, 173–174
    identification of, 171
    past changes of, 171–172
    Quaternary, 172–173
    in Quaternary, 487
Detection, of global warming, 297–298
Determinism, 330–331
Development
    biodiversity and, 65
    deforestation and, 160–161
    environmental services as, 26
    population and, 341
    sustainable, **573–575**
        vs. preservation, 641–642
        urban, 608–610
    technology and, 579
    UN goals on, 199
    urban, 608–610
Devonian Period, 155*f*
DF1 carbon storage project, 89*t*
DF2 carbon storage project, 89*t*
Dhaka, 609*t*
DHF. *See* dengue hemorrhagic fever (DHF)
Diarrheal diseases, 184
Dickens, Charles, 54
Diderot, Denis, 53
Dimethyl sulfide (DMS)
    in Gaia hypothesis, 279, 281
    as negative feedback loop, 66, 67*f*
    sulfur cycle and, 571
Dimming, global, **294**
Dioxin, 111
Disasters, natural. *See* natural hazards
Discovery, *vs.* production of oil, 144–148
Disease, **176–183**. *See also* health
    Colombian Exchange and, 326
    deaths from, 177
    diarrheal, 184
    environment and, 178–179
    exotic species and, 247
    as impact, 356
    microbes and, 177–178

top 5 killer, 184
vectors, 178
Disposal
    ocean, **474–476**
    of waste, 619–622
Distribution
    biological realms and, 70–71
    population, 343
DIVERSITAS program, 367
Diversity, religious, 530
Diversity hotspots, 353–354
Djibouti, carbon dioxide emissions of, 97*t*
Doctrines, in international law, 224
Documentation, of human impact, 334–335
Domesday Book for England, 338
Domesticated animals, 325–326. *See also* livestock
Domestic law, 221–224
Dominica, carbon dioxide emissions of, 97*t*
Dominican Republic, carbon dioxide emissions of, 95*t*
Dongas, 235*f*
Drilling, oil, 272
Drought, **184–186**
    causes of, 185
    civilization downfall and, 170
    coccidioidomycosis and, 182–183
    definition of, 184
    desertification and, 169
    dust storms and, 188
    environmental mismanagement and, 185–186
    features of, 186
    frequency of, 184–185
    impacts of, 184–185
Drylands, **170–176**
Dryland salinity, 541*t*, 542
DSS. *See* dengue shock syndrome (DSS)
Dunc fields, 591–592
Dunes, **176**
    sea levels and, 551
    stabilization schemes, 32
Dunlap, Riley, 332
Durand, Asher, 54
Dust, in sulfur cycle, 571*f*
Dust additions, 187
Dust aerosols, 6*t*, 186
Dust Bowl, 190
Dust storms, **186–191**
Dynamite, 111
Dyson, Freeman, 578

E

Earth
    carrying capacity of, 101–103
    energy balance in, 306–307
    food production capacity of, 260–261
    in Gaia hypothesis, **279–282**
    human impacts on, 333–334
    impacts in early evolution of, 251
Earth as Transformed by Human Action, The, 294
Earth Day, 231
Earth First!, 231
Earthmoving, 35–36
Earthquake generation, 32*t*
Earthquakes
    coccidioidomycosis and, 182
    dams and, 151

emerging coasts and, 208
phosphorus cycle and, 501
plates and, 431–432, 432*f*
Earth system models of intermediate complexity (EMICs), 125–126
Earth system science, **193**
Earth System Science Partnership (ESSP), 367
Earthwatch program, UNEP and, 606
Easter Island, 248
Eastern religions, 219, 529
East Greenland Sea, 40
East Siberian Sea, 39
East Timor, carbon dioxide emissions of, 97*t*
Eco-forestry, 266
Eco-industrial development, 361
Eco-industrial networks, 361
Eco-industrial parks, 362–363
Ecological footprint, **194**
Ecological integrity, **194–195**
Ecological restoration, 390
Ecological sabotage, 231
Ecology
    biological, 329
    deep, 219
    human, 219, **329–333**
    industrial, 330, **360–363**
    root of word, 329, 360
    social, 219
Ecology-based forestry, 266–267
Ecomanagement, 143
Economic levels, **198–200**
Economics, **200–201**
    agriculture and, 10–11, 14
    Apollo Alliance and, 201
    Aral Sea and, 36
    biodiversity and, 63
    in Brazil, 23
    deforestation and, 23, 598–599
    emissions and, 310
    expansion in, 304
    forests and, 598–599
    in functional theory of resources, 331
    GDP and, 199
    globalization and, 304–305
    greening business and, 217
    insurance and, **363–365**
    mining and, 424
    neoclassical, 105
    Stern Report and, 200–201
    sustainability and, 575
    tourism and, 581
    waste and, 622–623
Economics of Warfare, The (Pigou), 204
Economies in Transition (EIT) Parties, to Kyoto, emissions of, 377
Ecosystems, **201–203**
    definition of, 201
    food web in, 202*f*
    functions of, 201
    impacts on, 352–353
    scale and, 201
Ecotaxation, **203–205**
Ecotheology, 242
Ecotones, biodiversity and, 62
Ecotourism, 582

Ecuador
    Amazon River in, 21
    carbon dioxide emissions of, 95*t*
Edge creep, 66
Edwards Dam, 153
Efficiency
    energy, 215
    as wedge, 569
Egypt
    carbon dioxide emissions of, 95*t*
    climate records in ancient, 126
    emergence of ancient, 121*t*
    salinization and, 542
    salinization in, 544*t*
    sea levels and, 163
Ehrlich, Paul R., 231
EIA. *See* Energy Information Administration (EIA); environmental impact assessment (EIA)
1816 (year), 467, 614
8,200 cal yr event, 322
Einstein, Albert, 463
EIT. *See* Economies in Transition (EIT) Parties, to Kyoto
El Chichón volcano, 614
Electricity generation
    coal in, 271
    demand increase for, 463
    geothermal, 532
    hydroelectric, 532
    natural gas in, 447–448, 448*f*
    nuclear power in, 463–465
    renewable, 531–532
    wind power for, 531–532
Ellul, Jacques, 578
El Niño-Southern Oscillation (ENSO), **205–207**
    Australia and, 48–49
    boreal forests and, 81
    coastlines and, 139–140
    deserts and, 171
    drought and, 185
    effects of, 473
    hurricanes and, 595
    ocean-atmosphere coupling and, 469–472, 470*f*
    reefs and, 516–517
El Salvador, carbon dioxide emissions of, 96*t*
EM-DAT hazard database, 453
Emerging coasts, **207–209**
Emerson, Ralph Waldo, 230
EMICs. *See* earth system models of intermediate complexity (EMICs)
Emissions intensity, **209**
Emissions trading, **209–213**
Emissions Trading Scheme, 209, 212
Emission trading, in Kyoto Protocol, 380–381
Endangered Species Act (ESA)
    belief systems and, 55
    biodiversity and, 63, 64
End-use energy, 213
Energy, **213–215**
Energy balance, 306–307
Energy efficiency, 442–443
Energy Information Administration (EIA), 463
Energy-loss rate, 307
Energy Policy Act of 2005, 445
Energy recovery, from waste, 620–621

Energy strategies, **215–216**
Energy technologies, 578–579
Enforcement
    of domestic law, 224
    of international law, 227–228
Engineering, geo-, **282–287**
Engineering hazard paradigm, 454
Enhanced salinization, 541, 541*t*
ENSO. *See* El Niño-Southern Oscillation (ENSO)
Entitlement theory, 616
Environmental accounting, **216–217**
Environmental bioethics, **218–219**
Environmental Defense Fund (EDF), 230
Environmental determinism, 330–331
Environmental impact assessment (EIA), **220–221**, 223–224
Environmental law, **221–228**
Environmental movements, **228–232**
Environmental NGOs, 460
Environmental Performance Index (EPI), 232
Environmental philosophy, 218
Environmental Protection Agency (EPA), 527–528
Eocene climate, 483, 485
Eolian dust, 186
EPA. *See* Environmental Protection Agency (EPA)
EPI. *See* Environmental Performance Index (EPI)
Epimorphism, 557
Equatorial Guinea, 97*t*
Equilibrium, *vs.* stability, 567
Equity, inter generational, **365–366**
Ergs, 591–592
Eritrea, carbon dioxide emissions of, 97*t*
Erlich, Paul, 579
Erosion, **232–235**. *See also* denudation
    anthropogeomorphology and, 32*t*
    Arctic warming and, 47
    building decay and, **85–86**
    coastlines and, 140
    consequences of, 234
    desertification and, 168
    dust storms and, 188
    estuaries and, 236
    historical perspectives, 234
    mangroves and, 410
    permafrost and, 499
    in phosphorus cycle, 501
    rain and, 232–233
    runoff and, 233
    sea levels and, 549
    sedimentation and, 234
    soil formation and, 557
    wind and, 233–234
Erratics, 127
Eruption, of volcanoes, 613
ESA. *See* Endangered Species Act (ESA)
ESS. *See* earth system science
Essay on the Principle of Population, An (Malthus), 104, 260
ESSP. *See* Earth System Science Partnership (ESSP)
Estonia
    carbon dioxide emissions of, 96*t*
    emissions of, 378*f*
    emissions target under Kyoto, 381*t*
Estuaries, **236–237**
    definition of, 236

recent changes in, 236
    sea levels and, 552
    sensitivity of, 236
Estuarine management, 236–237
Ethane, in natural gas, 447
Ethanol, **237–241**
    as alcohol, 237
    in Brazil, 57, 58*f*
    carbon dioxide and, 239–240
    cellulosic, 238
    demand, 239*t*
    exports of, 57
    feedstocks, 57*f*, 239*f*
    food and, 241
    fossil fuels and, 240
    global warming and, 239–241
    as motor fuel, 237
    production of, 56, 56*f*, 237–239, 238*f*, 239*f*
    in United States, 57, 58*f*
    in U.S. energy policy, 443
Ethics, **241–242**
    environmental bio-, **218–219**
    intergenerational equity and, **365–366**
Ethiopia
    carbon dioxide emissions of, 96*t*
    famine in, 259–260
Ethiopian zoological region, 69*f*
Ethnobiology, **242–243**
Ethnoecology, 242
Ethyl alcohol. *See* ethanol
Eukaryotic cells, 279
Eurasian Plate, 432*f*
Europe
    carbon dioxide emissions of, 94*t*
    coal reserves in, 272*t*
    deserts and climate change in, 175*t*
    environmental impact statements in, 220
    heathlands in, 317, 318
    Holocene in, 322
    hydroelectric generation in, 149*t*
    oil reserves in, 273*t*
    salinization in, 543*t*
    transportation-related emissions in, 589*t*
    water resources in, 625*t*
    Younger Dryas period in, 647
European Commission, Kyoto Protocol and, 377
Europeanization, of world, 326–327
European Little Ice Age, **400–406**
    cooling in, 296
    glacial retreat since, **289–291**, 290*f*
    Greenland ice sheet in, 311
    Holocene and, 323–324
    North Atlantic Oscillation and, 462
    solar variability and, 564
    twentieth century as end of, 600
    warming after, 295
European Union
    biofuels in, 57, 58*f*
    emissions of, 378*f*
    ethanol in, 58*f*
    in Kyoto Protocol, 377
Eutrophication, 413
Evaporation
    deserts and, 171
    of water, 625

Evaporite sulfates, 570
E85 vehicles, 237
Everglades National Park, 492
Everglades wilderness area, 642*t*
Evolution
    impacts and, 251
    of microbes, 177–178
Excavational anthropogeomorphology, 32*t*, 33*f*, 35
Exclusion, competitive, 246
Extinctions, **248–250**
    in Australia, 49–50, 51
    "blitzkrieg effect" in, 248
    climatic hypothesis of, 249
    "innovation effect" in, 248
    land use change and, 353
    minimum viable population and, 640
    modern, 249–250
    potential for, 353
    prehistoric, 248–249
    sea levels and, 353
    uncertainty and, 605
    wilderness areas and, 640
Exotic species, **244–247**
Expansion, economic, 304
Explosives, 111
Exposure, vulnerability and, 615
Externalities, **247–248**
Extrapolation, uncertainty and, 605
Extraterrestrial impacts, **251–253**
Extreme events, **252–255**. *See also* natural hazards
Extremely drug-resistant (XDR) tuberculosis, 181
Exxon Valdez, 217, 231

F

Faeroe Islands, carbon dioxide emissions of, 97*t*
Falkland Islands, carbon dioxide emissions of, 97*t*
Family planning, 342
Famine, **257–261**
    in China, 258–259
    definition of, 257
    in Ethiopia, 259–260
    mitigation, 261
    in North Korea, 260
    regions, 259*f*
    signs of, 258*f*
    urban, 261
"Famine foods," 16
Famines, in India, 358
FAO. *See* Food and Agriculture Organization (FAO)
Fauna. *See also* animals
    biological realms and, 69–70, 69*f*
FCCC. *See* Framework Convention on Climate Change (FCCC)
FCPC. *See* Forest Carbon Partnership Facility (FCPF)
Febvre, Lucien, 331
Federal Aid in Wildlife Restoration Act, 645
Federal clean energy mandates, 446
Federal Insecticide, Fungicide, and Rodenticide Act, 527
Feed-in tariff, 446
Feedstocks
    biofuel, 57*f*
    ethanol, 239*f*
Fens, 499
Fertility, changes in, 340

Fertilization
    ocean surface, 283t, 285
    sulfur cycle and, 571
Fertilization effect, 13
Fertilizer production
    methane in, 449–450
    nitrogen in, 456
Fiji, carbon dioxide emissions of, 96t
Finland
    carbon dioxide emissions of, 95t
    emissions of, 378f
    emissions target under Kyoto, 381t
Fires
    Arctic warming and, 46–47
    in Australia, 50
    biodiversity and, 62
    boreal forests and, 79–81
    global warming and, **262**
    in heathlands, 317–318
    insects and, 79–81
    insurance and, 364
    in Mediterranean environments, 415
    mountains and, 437
    nitrogen and, 458
    permafrost and, 497
Fish
    in Australia, 50t, 51
    cod colonization of Greenland, 601
    dams and, 150–151
    introduction of exotic, 244–245
Fisheries, **263–265**
Fixation, nitrogen, 456, 457f, 458
"Flex fuel" vehicles, 237
Flock fuel, 620
Flood-basalt episodes, 611
Flooding, 253–254
    coastal, 356–357
    dams and, 151
    hydroelectric, 23
    in India, 359
    insurance and, 364
    rivers and, 537–538
    in wetlands, 636
Floristic regions, 69
Fluvial denudation, 391–394, 392t
Food
    Chinese rationing of, 258–259
    daily caloric intake, 257
    ethanol and, 241
    fisheries and, **263–265**
    Malthus and, 104
    population and, 340
    web, 202f
    world production capacity, 260–261
    world production of, 257–258
Food and Agriculture Organization (FAO)
    deforestation and, 22
    ethnobiology and, 243
Food crisis model, 616f
Footprint
    carbon, **98**
    ecological, **194**
Ford, Gerald, 439
Forecasting, uncertainty and, 605
Forestation, **266–269**

Forest Carbon Partnership Facility (FCPF), 599–600
Forest certification, 387
Forestry, **266–269**
Forests, **269**. See also deforestation
    acid rain and, 3
    adaptations of, 79
    aforestation and, 285
    albedo and, 19
    Arctic warming and, 46–47
    biodiversity and, 597
    boreal, **75–83**
    carbon uptake and, 597
    changes in coverage of, 72t
    changing biomes and, 73
    cloud, 352
    ecological issues with tropical, 596–597
    economics and, 598–599
    extinction in and uncertainty, 605
    hydrological impacts and, 597–598
    hydrology in, 269
    loss of, 353
    mountains and, 437
    old-growth, 161, 267–268
    planted, 267
    political opportunities and, 599–600
    populations in, 598
    poverty and, 598
    in Quaternary, 487
    services provided by, 26
    social concerns with, 598
    soil in, 269
    tropical, **596–600**
    as wedge, 570
    in Younger Dryas, 647
Fossil fuel(s), **270–274**
    in carbon cycle, 91
    coal as, 272
    definition of, 270
    distribution of, 273
    energy content of, 274
    in ethanol production, 240
    greenhouse gases and, 270
    methane and, 419
    oil as, 272–273
    reserves of, 273t
    unconventional, 273
Fossil-fuel aerosols, 6t
Fossils
    biological realms and, 71
    dunes as, 591–592
    paleoclimates and, 483
    in wetlands, 637
    Younger Dryas, 647
Fountainebleu forest, 492
Fourier, Joseph, 306
Framework Convention on Climate Change
        (FCCC), **274–277**
    deforestation and, 599
    geoengineering and, 286
    history of, 274
    joint implementation and, 375
    key provisions of, 275–277, 276t
    Kyoto Protocol and, 379, 381
    objective of, 275
    vs. regulatory convention, 274–275

Fram Strait, 40
France
    carbon dioxide emissions of, 94t, 95t
    emissions of, 378f
    heat wave in, 473
    nuclear power in, 464
    transportation-related emissions in, 589t
Frank Church-River of No Return wilderness area,
        642t
Franklin, Benjamin, 614
Freedom, 554
Free Trade Area of the Americas, 585
French Guiana, carbon dioxide emissions of, 97t
French Polynesia, carbon dioxide emissions
        of, 97t
Freshwater carbonate fills, 32
Friedrich, Ernst, 293
Fringing reefs, 515
Frost-free seasons, boreal forests and, 78f
Fuel cell(s)
    natural gas and, 451
    R&D on, in U.S., 444f
    as wedge, 570
Functional theory, of natural resources, 331
Funding
    energy policy and, 445–446
    insurance and, **363–365**
    of NGOs, 461t
FutureGen, 89t, 136–137, 440
Futurists, **277**
Fynbos Biome, 73
Fynbos shrubs, 418, 419

G
Gabon, carbon dioxide emissions of, 96t
Gaia hypothesis, 193, **279–282**
Galactic cosmic rays, 563, 566
Gallium, 536
Gambia, carbon dioxide emissions of, 97t
Game preserves, 492–493
Ganges River, 392t
Gas fluxes, in volcanic eruptions, 613
Gasification, of coal, **136–137**
Gas-to-liquids (GTL), 451
Gates of the Arctic wilderness area, 642t
GATT. See General Agreement on Tariffs and Trade
        (GATT)
GCMs. See global climate models (GCMs)
GCS. See global carbon sequestration
GDP. See gross domestic product (GDP)
GECHS. See Global Environmental Change and
        Human Security (GECHS)
GEF. See Global Environment Facility (GEF)
GEMS. See Global Environmental Monitoring
        System (GEMS)
Gender structure, in population, 342–343
General Agreement on Tariffs and Trade (GATT),
        582, 584
General circulation models, 124–126
General Wildlife Federation, 645
Generation time, microbial, 177
Genetic diversity
    biodiversity and, 61
    natural resources and, 62–63
Geneva Convention, 553
Geoengineering, **282–287**, 301–302

Geographical extrapolation, 605
Geographic information systems (GIS), **288–289**
Geological carbon sequestration, 88
Geologic-climatic units, 154
Geologic time scale, 154, 155f
Geologic time units, 154
Geophytes, 415
Georgia, carbon dioxide emissions of, 96t
Geothermal electric, 532
Germany
    carbon dioxide emissions of, 95t
    emissions of, 378f
    emissions target under Kyoto, 381t
    nuclear power in, 465
    photovoltaic generation in, 531
    transportation-related emissions in, 589t
GGAS. *See* Greenhouse Gas Abatement Scheme
    (GGAS)
Ghana, carbon dioxide emissions of, 96t
Gibraltar, carbon dioxide emissions of, 97t
GIS. *See* geographic information systems (GIS)
Glacial denudation, 394–395, 395f
Glaciations
    evidence of, 127
    as units, 154
Glacier Peak wilderness area, 642t
Glaciers
    in Africa, 603
    in Antarctica, 28f
    calving of, 603
    in China, 602
    formation of, 350
    freshwater stock in, 624t
    Greenland ice sheet and, 311
    vs. ice sheets, 349
    ice shelves and, 30
    in Little Ice Age, 400
    loss of, 352
    mass balance of, 290–291
    mountains and, 436
    retreat of, **289–291**, 290f
    rivers and, 538
    soils and, 560
    tills and, 154
    twentieth century changes in, 602–603
    water stress and, 354
    in West Antarctic ice sheet, 31
Glaciolacustrine varves, 157
Glacken, Clarence, 292
Glass, 110
Glen Canyon, 150
Global carbon sequestration, 87
Global change history, **291–294**
Global climate models (GCMs), **122–126**
    of agricultural impacts, 355
    geographic information systems and, 288–289
    for historic periods, 296
    uncertainty and, 605
    Younger Dryas period in, 648–649
Global commons, 305–306
Global Conveyor, 580f
Global dimming, **294**
    acid rain and, 4
Global Environmental Change and Human
    Security (GECHS), 368

Global Environmental Monitoring System (GEMS),
    UNEP and, 606
Global Environment Facility (GEF), 387, 461, 606
Global Footprint Network, 194
Globalization, **303–306**
    biodiversity and, 64
    contemporary, 304
    culture and, 65
    drought and, 185–186
    economics and, 304–305
    problems of, 305
    society and, 327–328
    trade and, 303–304
Global Land Project (GLP), 368
Global Nuclear Energy Partnership (GNEP), 466
Global Resource Information Database (GRID),
    UNEPS and, 606
Global warming, **295–302**. *See also* weather
    aerosols and, 7, 8
    agricultural impacts of, 299–300, 355–356
    agriculture and, 12–13, 14
    albedo and, **19–20**
    Antarctica and, **27–31**
    anthropogeomorphology and, 33–34
    in Arctic, **42–48**
    Australia and, 51–52
    belief systems and, **53–55**
    causes of, **106–109**
    Chinese contribution to, 116–118
    coastal consequences of, 34t
    cryospheric consequences of, 34t
    current, 296–297
    deforestation and, 13, 24–25, 159
    deserts and, 174, 175t
    detection, 297–298
    in different energy use scenarios, 298f
    economic levels and, 199–200
    eolian consequences of, 34t
    ethanol and, 239–241
    extinctions and, 353
    in feedback loop, 68f
    fires and, **262**
    flooding and, 356–357
    forests and, 269
    geomorphologic consequences of, 34t
    greenhouse gases in, 296–297
    health and, 300, 355–356
    in history, 29
    history of thought on, 291–293
    human systems and, 354–356
    hydrologic consequences of, 34t, 299
    ice sheets and, 351–352
    impacts of, 299–300, **352–357**
    India as victim of, 360
    industry and, 300
    Kyoto Protocol and, 301
    lakes and, 385
    malaria and, 179
    measurement, 297–298
    Mediterranean environments and, 417–418
    migration and, 300
    modeling, 29
    natural hazards and, 454–455
    natural responses to, 308–309
    natural *vs.* anthropogenic, 335

    past trends in, 295–296
    permafrost and, 495–498
    positive feedbacks in, 66
    prediction, 298–299
    regional patterns of, **522–526**
    responses to, 300–302
    rice cultivation and, 13
    sea levels and, 298, 550–553, 551f, 552f
    settlement and, 300
    societal development and, **121–122**
    solutions for, 300–302
    stabilization and, 302
    subsidence and, 34t
    thresholds in, 302
    tipping points and, 581
    twentieth century, **600–603**
    uncertainty and, 605–606
    vegetational controls and, 34t
    vegetation and, 299
    water stress and, 354–355
Global-warming potential (GWP), 297
Global Warming Solutions Act, 439
GLP. *See* Global Land Project (GLP)
GNEP. *See* Global Nuclear Energy Partnership
    (GNEP)
GNP. *See* gross national product (GNP)
Goats, 245
Gold, 536
Gorbachev, Mikhail, 553
Gorgon carbon storage project, 89t
Governments
    in energy strategy, 216
    NGOs and, 461–462
GPP. *See* gross primary production (GPP)
Gran Paradiso park, 492
Grasses
    in heathlands, 319
    in savannas, 546
Grassland, changes in coverage of, 72t
Grazing, desertification and, 167
Great African Famine, 259–260
Great Salt Lake, 384, 385f
Greece
    carbon dioxide emissions of, 95t
    emissions of, 378f
    emissions target under Kyoto, 381t
Green chemistry, 112
Greenhouse effect, **306–309**
Greenhouse gas(es), **309–310**. *See also* carbon
        dioxide; methane; nitrous oxide
    Annex I emissions of, 379f
    biofuel production and, 58
    biofuel use and, 59f
    boreal forests and, 76
    carbon dioxide as, 309
    in China, 377
    in coal *vs.* natural gas fired power plants, 448, 449f
    emissions trading and, **209–213**
    ethanol and, 58
    fossil fuels and, 270
    global dimming and, 294
    in global warming, 296–297
    hydrofluorocarbons as, 309–310
    intensity of emissions, 209
    joint implementation and, 375–376

in Kyoto Protocol, 380*t*
methane as, 309
nitrous oxide as, 309, 459
from ocean sediments, 46
perfluorocarbons as, 310
from permafrost, 46
in permafrost, 81–82
pricing of, 445–446
savannas and, 547
soils and, 561
stabilization of, **568–570**
sulfur cycle and, 572*f*
sulfur hexafluoride as, 310
targets under Kyoto Protocol, 381*t*
transportation and, 589, 589*t*
urban growth and, 608
U.S. emissions of, 440*f*
water vapor as, 634
Greenhouse Gas Abatement Scheme (GGAS), 212
Greenland
    carbon dioxide emissions of, 97*t*
    cod colonization of, 601
    ice accumulation in, 350
    Norse colonization of, 325
    settlement abandonment, 121*t*
    topography of, 349*f*
    in Younger Dryas, 648
Greenland Ice Core Project (GRIP), 133
Greenland ice sheet, **310–313, 349–352**
    Arctic warming and, 46
    bedrock elevation in, 311*f*
    changes in, 311–313, 312*f*
    evolution of, 314*f*
    nitrogen in, 458*f*
    sea levels and, 313
    surface elevation of, 311*f*
    thickness in, 311*f*
    volume of, 349
Green parties, 228
Greenpeace, 231
"Green Seal" program, 216
"Green taxes," 216
Grenada, carbon dioxide emissions of, 97*t*
GRID. *See* Global Resource Information Database (GRID)
GRIP. *See* Greenland Ice Core Project (GRIP)
Gross domestic product (GDP), 199, 209, 217
Grosser Alestsch glacier, 400
Gross national product (GNP), 199
Gross primary production (GPP), 93, 202
Ground water, **305**
Grove, Richard, 292
Growing seasons, boreal forests and, 78
Growth
    limits to, 104–105
    sustainable, 573
    tourism and, 581
GTL. *See* gas-to-liquids (GTL)
Guadeloupe, carbon dioxide emissions of, 96*t*
Guam, 96*t*, 246
Guangzhou, China, 609*t*
Guatemala, carbon dioxide emissions of, 96*t*
Guinea, carbon dioxide emissions of, 96*t*
Guinea Bissau, carbon dioxide emissions of, 97*t*
Gulf of Bothnia, 208

Gulf of Mexico
    biofuels and, 59
    dead zone in, 241
Gulf Stream. *See also* thermohaline circulation
    NAO and, 473
    thermohaline circulation and, 580
    tipping points and, 581
Guyana
    Amazon River in, 21
    carbon dioxide emissions of, 96*t*
GWP. *See* global-warming potential (GWP)
Gypsum, 570

H

Haber process, 456
Habitat change
    in Australia, 51
    biodiversity and, 63–64
    edge creep and, 66
Habitat clearance, in Australia, 50
Habitat conservation, 64
Habitat patches, 17
Hadley, George, 122
Haeckel, Ernst, 329
Hague Summit, 275*t*
Hail, 255
Haiti, carbon dioxide emissions of, 96*t*
Hall, Charles, 360
Halocarbons, 119–120
Halogenated alkanes, 120*t*
Halons, 120*t*
    chlorofluorocarbons and, 119
    in greenhouse effect, 308
    ozone and, 479
Hantaviruses, 183
Harappan civilization, 121*t*
Hardin, Garrett, 142, 579, 585
Hard law, 225
Harz Mountains, 121*t*
Hatcheries, 245
Hauten carbon storage project, 89*t*
Hawaii, volcanic eruptions in, 613
HDI. *See* Human Development Index (HDI)
Health. *See also* disease
    acid rain and, 3–4
    advances in, 327
    global warming and, 300
    heat mortality and, 356
    human ecology and, 330
    impacts on, 355–356
    malaria and, 356
    U.S. spending on research in, 442*f*
Heat
    latent, 633–634
    mortality from, 356
Heathlands, **317–319**
Heating, natural gas for, 450
Heat island, 607
Heinrich, Hartmut, 320
Heinrich events, **320**, 488
Helheim glacier, 313
Hemicellulose, 238
Herbivore niches, new, 246–247
Hess, Harry, 430
Hetch Hetchy Valley, 150
High-level wastes (HLW), 466

High Uintas wilderness area, 642*t*
Himalayan mountains, 358
Hinduism, 219
Histoire Naturelle (Buffon), 292
Historical perspective, 325–328
Historical records, 126–127
Historic climates, **483–489**
History, global change, **291–294**
HIV/AIDS, 180, 184
HLW. *See* high-level wastes (HLW)
Holmes, Arthur, 430
Holocene climatic optimum, **413–414**
Holocene El Niño, 206
Holocene period, **320–324**
Holy Earth, The (Bailey), 55
Honduras, carbon dioxide emissions of, 96*t*
Honeybees, 248
Hong Kong, carbon dioxide emissions of, 95*t*
Hoover Dam, 151
Horticulture, 12
"Hot spots," volcanoes and, 431, 611
Hsinfengkiang Dam, 151
Hudson Bay, 413
Hugo, Victor, 54
Human Development Index (HDI), 199
Human dimensions, of global change, **325–328**
Human ecology, 219, **329–333**
Human history, **121–122**
Human impacts, **333–337**
Human population
    agriculture and, 12, 15–16
    biodiversity and, 15–16
    dams and, 151
    deforestation and, 161
    food production capacity and, 260–261
    growth projection, 16
    in India, 358–359
    natural hazards and, 454
    negative feedback and, 66
    positive feedback and, 66
    sustainability and, 455
    uncertainty and, 605
    urban, **608–610**
    wetlands and, 639
Human systems, climate change and, 354–356
Hume, David, 366
Humidity, upper tropospheric, 634
Hungary
    carbon dioxide emissions of, 95*t*
    emissions of, 378*f*
    emissions target under Kyoto, 381*t*
Hunting, 245, **346–348**
Huntington, Ellsworth, 330
Hurricane Andrew, 253, 364
Hurricane Katrina, 253, 365, 637
Hurricanes, 254, **594–595**
    climate change and, 455
    El Niño and, 206
    insurance and, 364
    intensification of, 357
    wetlands and, 637
Huxley's Line, 69, 70*f*
Hydrates, methane, **421**
Hydrochloric acid, volcanic eruptions and, 614
Hydrochlorofluorocarbons, 120*t*

Hydroelectric flooding, 23
Hydroelectric generation, by region, 149t
Hydroelectric power generation, 532
Hydrofluorocarbons
    as greenhouse gas, 309–310
    in Kyoto Protocol, 380t
    specific, 120t
Hydrological interference, 32t
Hydrologic cycle, 624–625
Hydrology. See also water
    in forests, 269
    global warming and, 299
    in mountains, 436–437
    permafrost and, 499
    tropical forests and, 597–598
    of wetlands, 636
Hydroxyl radical, 419–420
Hyperaridity, 167, 170
Hysteresis, 581

I

IAEA. See International Atomic Energy Agency (IAEA)
IARIW. See International Association for Research
    in Income and Wealth (IARIW)
Ice, sea, **38–42**
    age of, 39
    Arctic warming and, 43–44, 45f
    changes in, 38–39
    effects of reduction in, 43
    extent of, 38–39, 39f, 40f, 41f, 42f
    future of, 39
    losses of, 39–40
    polar bears and, 47
    thickness of, 39
    twentieth century changes in, 602–603
Ice ages, in Gaia hypothesis, 281–282
Ice clouds, 6
Ice-core record
    of aerosols, 7–8
    in Antarctica, 29
    Climatic Optimum in, 414
    Dansgaard-Oeschger cycles and, **153**
    dust deposition in, 187
    Greenland Ice-Core Project and, 133
    of Holocene, 321–322
    ice sheets and, 351
    nitrogen in, 458
    in paleoclimatic records, 130–131
    of Younger Dryas, 648
Iceland
    carbon dioxide emissions of, 96t
    emissions of, 378f
    emissions target under Kyoto, 381t
    Little Ice Age in, 402
Icelandic low, 462, 472
ICESat, 349f
Ice sheets, **310–313, 349–352**. See also Antarctic ice
        sheet; Greenland ice sheet; Laurentide ice
        sheet
    calving of, 351
    climate change and, 351–352
    formation of, 350–351
    vs. glaciers, 349
    history, 351
    prehistoric, 350
    in Quaternary, 487

Ice shelves, 30. See also Antarctica and climate
        change
    in Antarctica, 349f
ICSU. See International Council of Scientific
        Unions (ICSU)
Icthyophonus disease, 78
ICZM. See integrated coastal-zone-management
        (ICZM)
IDNDR. See International Decade for Natural
        Disaster Reduction (IDNDR)
IFPR. See International Food Policy Research
        Institute (IFPR)
IGBP. See International Geosphere-Biosphere
        Programme (IGBP)
IGCC. See Integrated Gasification and Combined
        Cycle (IGCC)
IHDP. See International Human Dimensions
        Programme on Global Environmental
        Change (IHDP)
ILW. See intermediate level wastes (ILW)
Impacts. See extraterrestrial impacts
Impacts of climate change, 299–300, **352–357**
India, **358–360**
    carbon dioxide emissions of, 94t, 95t
    cities in, 359
    coal reserves in, 272t
    dams in, 149
    environment of, 359–360
    mangroves in, 412f
    nuclear power in, 465
    population in, 358–359
    population policy in, 510
    poverty in, 359
    salinization in, 544t
    savannas in, 545
    transportation-related emissions in, 589t
    as victim of climate change, 360
Indigenous communities
    Arctic warming and, 48
    in Australia, 49–50
    biodiversity and, 65
    parks and, 492–493
    religions of, 219
Indira Gandhi Canal, 358
Indirect anthropogeomorphology, 31–32, 32t
Indirect ecotaxation, 204
Indium, 536
Indonesia
    biofuel production in, 59
    carbon dioxide emissions of, 95t
    mangroves in, 409
    natural gas production in, 451t
    transportation-related emissions in, 589t
Indus civilization, 121t
Industrial applications, of natural
        gas, 449–450
Industrial ecology, 330, **360–363**
Industrial fisheries, 263
Industrial hazards, 111
Industrial Revolution, 577
Industrial symbiosis, 361–362, 362f
Industrial Transformation (IT) program, 368
Industry
    chemical, **110–112**
    global warming and, 300

Infectious disease, **176–183**. See also health
    deaths from, 177
    diarrheal, 184
    environment and, 178–179
    as impact, 356
    microbes and, 177–178
    top 5 killer, 184
    vectors, 178
Influenza pandemic, 326, 339
Infoterra, UNEP and, 606
Infrared spectrometry, 279
Infrastructure
    acid rain and, 4
    improvements as wedge, 569
    natural gas, 452
    salinization and, 541
"Innovation effect," 248
In Salah carbon storage site, 89t
Insecticide, 111
Insects
    Arctic warming and, 46–47
    boreal forests and, 76, 79–81
    fires and, 79–81
Insurance, **363–365**
Integrated coastal-zone-management (ICZM),
        137–138
Integrated Gasification and Combined Cycle
        (IGCC), 136–137
Integrated management, 197–198
Integrated pollution control (IPC), 224
Integration, economic, 304–305
Integrity, ecological, **194–195**
Intensity, emissions, **209**
Interdecadal Pacific Oscillation (IPO), 206
Intergenerational equity, **365–366**
Interglaciations, 154, 488
Intergovernmental Panel on Climate Change
        (IPCC), **369–370**
    on Arctic sea ice, 39
    FCCC and, 274
    on modeling, 29
    on sea levels, 30, 549
Intermediate level wastes (ILW), 466
International Alliance of Forest Peoples, 598
International Association for Research in Income
        and Wealth (IARIW), 216–217
International Atomic Energy Agency (IAEA), 465–466
International commerce, 304. See also globalization
International Conference on Population and
        Development, 511
International Council of Scientific Unions (ICSU),
        366, 367
International Decade for Natural Disaster
        Reduction (IDNDR), 454
International Food Policy Research Institute
        (IFPR), 257
International Geosphere-Biosphere Programme
        (IGBP), **366–367**
International Human Dimensions Programme on
        Global Environmental Change (IHDP),
        367–369
International law, 224–228
International Social Science Council (ISSC), 367
International Union for the Conservation of
        Nature, 55, 491

Interstadials, 487–488
Intertropical convergence zone (ITCZ), 522
Introductions, of exotic species, 244–246
Invasive species, **244–247**
IPC. *See* integrated pollution control (IPC)
IPCC. *See* Intergovernmental Panel on Climate
      Change (IPCC)
IPO. *See* Interdecadal Pacific Oscillation (IPO)
Iran
    carbon dioxide emissions of, 95t
    natural gas production in, 451t
    natural gas reserves in, 451t
    salinization in, 544t
    transportation-related emissions in, 589t
Iraq, carbon dioxide emissions of, 95t
Ireland
    carbon dioxide emissions of, 95t
    emissions of, 378f
    emissions target under Kyoto, 381t
Iron, in dust, 186
Irrigation, **370–373**
    agriculture and, 11, 13
    Aral Sea and, 36
    environmental concerns with, 372
    expansion of, 371
    future of, 373
    privatization and, 372–373
    salinization and, 541, 541t
    salinization in, 544t
    water table and, 542t
    water use and, 628
Islam, 530
Isotope climatic records, 128
Isotope dating, 157, 158f
Israel, carbon dioxide emissions of, 95t
ISSC. *See* International Social Science Council
      (ISSC)
Istanbul, 609t
IT. *See* Industrial Transformation (IT) program
Itaipú Reservoir, 150
Italy
    carbon dioxide emissions of, 95t
    emissions of, 378f
    emissions target under Kyoto, 381t
    transportation-related emissions in, 589t
ITCZ. *See* intertropical convergence zone (ITCZ)
IUCN. *See* World Conservation Union (IUCN)

J
Jakarta, 609t
Jakobshavn Isbrae glacier, 313
Jamaica, carbon dioxide emissions of, 96t
Japan
    carbon dioxide emissions of, 94t, 95t
    emissions of, 378f
    emissions target under Kyoto, 381t
    mangroves in, 409
    nuclear power in, 464
    transportation-related emissions in, 589t
    water efficiency in, 628
Japanese Emissions Trading Scheme, 212
Jatropha, as biofuel feedstock, 57f
Jevons, William Stanley, 104
John Muir wilderness area, 642t
John Paul II, Pope, 530
Joint Implementation, 210, **375–376**

Joint liability, 223
Jordan, carbon dioxide emissions of, 96t
Jordan River, 383
Judaism
    constituency of, 529
    creation story in, 529
Jurassic Period, 155f
Jurisdiction, 222
Justice, intergenerational equity and, 365–366

K
Kakadu National Park, 492–493
Kalahari Desert, 170
Kalundborg, Denmark, 362, 362f
Kane Basin, 311
Kangerdlugssuaq glacier, 313
Kant, Immanuel, 366
Karachi, 609t
Kariba Dam, 150f, 151
Katmai-Novarupta volcano, 614
Kaveri River, 358–359
Kazakhstan, 95t, 233
Kennebec River, 153
Kennedy, John F., 230
Kenya, carbon dioxide emissions of, 96t
Kerogen, 273
Kilauea volcano, 612
Killer bees, 248
Kiribati, carbon dioxide emissions of, 97t
Kobe earthquake, 455
Konya Dam, 151
Koran, 530
Krakatoa eruption, 614
Kremasta Dam, 151
K/T boundary. *See* Cretaceous-Tertiary boundary
Kudzu, 245
Kuwait, carbon dioxide emissions of, 95t
Kyoto Conference, 275t
Kyoto Protocol, **379–381**
    deforestation and, 26
    FCCC and, 375
    gases in, 380t
    key provisions in, 276t
    oil sands and, 478
    progress with, **377–379**
    as response, 301
    as solution, 301
Kyrgyzstan, carbon dioxide emissions of, 96t

L
Labels, trade and, 583
Lacustrine landscapes, 487
Lagoon of Venice, 552
Lagoons, sea levels and, 552
Lagos, Nigeria, 609t
Lake Bonneville, 592
Lake Eyre, 383t, 592
Lake Lisan, 592
Lake Maracaibo, 383t
Lake Paleo-Makgadikgadi, 592
Lake Powell, 150
Lakes, **383–385**
    global warming and, 385
    major, 383t
    methane and, 420t
    pluvial, 592–593
Lake Superior, 383t

Lake Tanganyika, 592
Lake Victoria, 383t, 384
Laki volcanic eruption, 614
Land clearance, in Australia, 50
Land cover
    changes in, 72t
    dams and, 150
    land use and, 396–397
Landfill gas (LFG), 420, 621
Landfills, waste in, 621–622
Landfill tax, 623
Land-Ocean Interactions in the Coastal Zone
      (LOICZ), 368
Land preservation, **386–388**
Land reclamation, **388–390**
    definition of, 388
    desertification and, 389
    estuaries and, 236
    salinization and, 389
    wetlands and, 389–390
Landscape connectivity, 17
Landscape management, 198
Land surface processes, **390–396**
Land use, **396–399**
Land Use and Land Cover Change Project
      (LUCC), 368
Land use change, extinctions and, 353
La Niña
    ENSO and, 205–206
    ocean-atmosphere coupling and, 470f, 472
Laos, carbon dioxide emissions of, 96t
Lapse rate, water vapor and, 633
Last Glacial Maximum (LGM), 415, 488, 592, 596
Latent heat, 633–634
Lateralization, 561
Latrobe Valley carbon storage project, 89t
Latvia
    carbon dioxide emissions of, 96t
    emissions of, 378f
    emissions target under Kyoto, 381t
Laurentide ice sheet, Greenland ice sheet and, 311
Law. *See also* regulation
    chemical industry, 111–112
    environmental, **221–228**
    precautionary principle and, **512–513**
Law of the Sea Convention, 225
LCFS. *See* Low-Carbon Fuel Standard (LCFS)
Leachate, 621
Leaching, soil formation and, 557
Lead, 536
Leaf scorch, 80f
Lebanon, carbon dioxide emissions of, 96t
Lena River, 77–78, 392t
Leopold, Aldo, 55, 230, 242, 642, 645
LFG. *See* landfill gas (LFG)
LGM. *See* Last Glacial Maximum (LGM)
LIA. *See* Little Ice Age
Liability, 223
Libby, W. F., 156
Liberia, carbon dioxide emissions of, 97t
Libya, carbon dioxide emissions of, 95t
Liechtenstein
    emissions of, 378f
    emissions target under Kyoto, 381t
Life expectancy, premodern, 339

Lightning, nitrogen and, 456
Lignin, 238
Lignite coal, 271
Lima, 609t
Limits, to growth, 104–105
Linnaeus, 360
Liquefaction, coal, **137**
Liquefied natural gas (LNG), transportation
    of, 452
Literature, belief systems and, 54
Lithosphere, 433f
Lithostratigraphy, 154
Lithuania
    carbon dioxide emissions of, 96t
    emissions of, 378f
    emissions target under Kyoto, 381t
Little Ice Age, **400–406**
    cooling in, 296
    glacial retreat since, **289–291, 290**f
    Greenland ice sheet in, 311
    Holocene and, 323–324
    North Atlantic Oscillation and, 462
    solar variability and, 564
    twentieth century as end of, 600
    warming after, 295
Livestock
    agriculture and, 11
    antibiotics in, 178
    biodiversity and, 17
    in Brazil, 23
    desertification and, 167
    global demand growth for, 16
    methane and, 419, 420t
Living-with-hazards paradigm, 455
Lloyd, William Frank, 585
LNG. See liquefied natural gas (LNG)
Loess, **407–408**, 487
Loess accumulation rates, 187, 188t
Logging, in Australia, 51
LOICZ. See Land-Ocean Interactions in the Coastal
    Zone (LOICZ)
Lombok Strait, 69
London
    heat island in, 607
    population of, 609t
Los Angeles, 609t
"Lost" crops, 13
Love Canal, 231
Lovelock, James, 279
Low-Carbon Fuel Standard (LCFS), 440, 443
Lowdermilk, W. C., 234
Low-tillage cultivation, 13
LUCC. See Land Use and Land Cover Change
    Project (LUCC)
Lung infections, 184
Luxembourg
    carbon dioxide emissions of, 96t
    emissions of, 378f
    emissions target under Kyoto, 381t
Lydekker's Line, 69, 70f

M
Macau, carbon dioxide emissions of, 96t
Macedonia, carbon dioxide emissions of, 96t
Mackenzie River, 392t
Madagascar, carbon dioxide emissions of, 96t

Magma, in volcanic eruptions, 613
Magma generation, 611
Magma rise, 611
Magnetic stratigraphy, 156–157, 158f
Malachite, 110
Malaria, 179, 184, 356
Malawi, carbon dioxide emissions of, 97t
Malaysia
    carbon dioxide emissions of, 95t
    transportation-related emissions in, 589t
Maldives, carbon dioxide emissions of, 97t
Mali
    carbon dioxide emissions of, 97t
    famine in, 259
Malta, carbon dioxide emissions of, 96t
Malthus, Thomas Robert, 104, 260, 573–574
Mammals
    in Australia, 50t, 51
    biological realms and, 69f
*Man and Nature, or Physical Geography as Modified
    by Human Action* (Marsh), 292
Man and the Biosphere reserves, 65
Mangrove swamps, 360, **409–412**, 551–552
Manhattan Project, 443t
Manila, 609t
Manufacturing, natural gas in, 449–450
Marathon Dam, 151
Marginalization, vulnerability and, 615–616
Marginal seas, **413**
Margulis, Lynn, 279
Marine access, Arctic warming and, 47–48
Marine biomes, 72
Marine phosphorus cycle, 502–503
Marine stratocumulus clouds, 284
Market-based funding, 445–446
Mars, 279, 307
Marsh, George Perkins, 292–293
Marshall, Bob, 230
Marshes. See wetlands
Martinique, carbon dioxide emissions of, 96t
Mass balance, 290–291, 350–351
Mass-burn incineration, 620
Materials, technology and, 578
Maunder Minimum, 564
Mauritania, carbon dioxide emissions of, 96t
Mauritius, carbon dioxide emissions of, 96t
Mayan civilization, 121t, 170
McCain, John, 443
ME. See multieffect evaporation (ME) distillation
Mean residence time, 61
Measurement, of global warming, 297–298
Mechanical weathering, 85–86
Mechanization, in agriculture, 10
Medicine. See also disease; health
    biodiversity and, 16
    human ecology and, 330
    poaching and, 347–348
Medieval climatic optimum, **413–414**
Medieval Warm Period (MWP), 295
Mediterranean environments, **415–418**
Mediterranean Sea, 413
Meeting of the Parties, Kyoto Protocol and, 381
Megacities, 608
Mendenhall Glacier, 603
Mesopotamia, 170

Mesosphere, 433f
Mesozoic Era, 155f
Mesquite, 168
Metabolism, industrial. *See* industrial ecology
Metals, as natural resources, 536
Metaphysics, 219
Meteorite winter, 467
Methane, **419–421**. *See also* greenhouse gas(es)
    concentration trends, 420f
    in fertilizer production, 449–450
    fossil fuels and, 270
    in fuel cells, 451
    in greenhouse effect, 308
    as greenhouse gas, 309
    historical levels of, 29
    increase in atmospheric, 297
    in natural gas, 447
    in ocean sediments, 46
    permafrost and, 499
    sinks, 419–420, 420t
    sources of, 419–420, 420t
    from waste, 620–621
Methane hydrates, **421**
Methanogenesis, 420t
Methyl iodide, in Gaia hypothesis, 279
Metropolitan areas, 608
Mexico
    carbon dioxide emissions of, 95t
    salinization in, 543t
    transportation-related emissions in, 589t
    U.S. trade with, 582
Mexico City, 608, 609t
Microbes
    cancer and, 177
    generation times of, 177
    infectious disease and, 177–178
Microfossils, 127–128
Migration(s), **421–424**
    Arctic warming and, 46
    boreal forests and, 75
    global warming and, 300
Millennium Ecosystems Assessment, 574
Miller carbon storage project, 89t
Minamata Bay, 111
Mineral formation, 557
Minerals, 535
Minimum viable population (MVP), 640
Mining, **424–429**
    air and, 427
    anthropogeomorphology and, 32t
    artisanal, 428
    environmental impacts of, 426–428
    exploration, 424, 426
    extraction in, 424–426
    future of, 428–429
    land reclamation and, 389
    nonentry, 426
    oil sands and, 476–477
    processing in, 426
    reefs and, 516
    scope of, 424–426
    small scale, 428
    surface, 426
    sustainable, 428
    tons moved for, 35

types of, 424–426
underground, 426
water and, 427
Miscegenation, 327
Mississippian Period, 155f
Mississippi Basin, 392t
Misty Fiords wilderness area, 642t
Mitigation, in energy sector, 301
Mixed farming, 18
MNCs. See multinational corporations (MNCs)
Mobile Earth, 430–434
Mobility, of sand dunes, 176
Modeling, 122–126. See also global climate models (GCMs)
Modes, of transport, 586
Modification, weather, 634–635
Moldova, carbon dioxide emissions of, 96t
Monaco
    emissions of, 378f
    emissions target under Kyoto, 381t
MONARCH program, 73
Mongolia, carbon dioxide emissions of, 96t
Mongooses, 245
Monocultures, 17
Monsoons, in South Asia, 358
Montague Island, 208
Montreal Protocol, 297, 380
Montserrat, carbon dioxide emissions of, 97t
Moraines, 127, 128f, 436
Morality
    ethics and, 241–242
    intergenerational equity and, 365–366
Moran, Thomas, 54
Morocco, carbon dioxide emissions of, 95t
Moscow, 609t
Mosquitoes
    dengue and, 182
    malaria and, 179
Motus, 515
Mountain ecosystems, 437–438
Mountain pine beetle, 80–81
Mountains, 435–438
Mount Auburn, 491
Mount Pelée volcano, 613
Mozambique
    carbon dioxide emissions of, 96t
    famine in, 259
MSF. See multistage flash distillation (MSF)
Mudflats, mangroves and, 411f
Muir, John, 230
Muller's Line, 70f
Multidrug-resistant (MDR) tuberculosis, 181
Multieffect evaporation (ME) distillation, 165
Multinational corporations (MNCs), 304
Multistage flash distillation (MSF), 165
Mumbai, 609t
Mumford, Lewis, 293, 578
Murray-Darling irrigation project, 542t
Murray River, 392t
Murray's Line, 70f
Muslims, 530
MVP. See minimum viable population (MVP)
MWP. See Medieval Warm Period (MWP)
Myanmar, carbon dioxide emissions of, 96t
Mycobacterium tuberculosis, 180–181

N

NADW. See North Atlantic Deep Water (NADW)
NAFTA. See North American Free Trade Agreement (NAFTA)
Nairobi, Kenya, 606
Namib Desert, 167, 174f
Namibia, carbon dioxide emissions of, 96t
NAO. See North Atlantic Oscillation (NAO)
Napoleonic Code, 221
Nares Strait, 311
National energy policy in U.S., 439–447
    biofuels in, 443
    clean-energy mandates, 446
    energy efficiency and, 442–443
    funding in, 445–446
    future of, 446–447
    nuclear power in, 443.445
    renewable energy and, 440–442
    strategy for, 439–440
    technology and, 439
National Environmental Policy Act, 220
National Environmental Protection Act, belief systems and, 55
National Institutes of Health, 443t
National parks, 491–492
National Renewable Energy Laboratory (NREL), 440
National security, 553–555
National Wilderness Preservation System, 642
National Wildlife Federation, 645
National Wildlife Refuge System, 645
Natural-area theory, 640
Natural capital, 216
Natural disasters. See natural hazards
Natural gas, 447–452
    combustion of, 214
    compressed, 450–451
    electricity generation from, 447–448, 448f
    energy content of, 274
    in energy mix, 270
    exploration for, 272
    greenhouse gases and, 270
    industrial applications of, 449–450
    liquefied, 452
    methane and, 420t
    origin of, 272
    supplies of, 451–452, 451t
    in transportation, 450–451
    transportation of, 452
    unconventional, 273
    uses of, 447–450
    as wedge, 569
Natural hazards, 453–455
    insurance and, 363–365
Natural resources, 533–536
    in Arctic, 42
    attitudes towards, 533–534
    biodiversity and, 62–63
    common pool, 142
    conflict over, 536
    environment and, 533
    functional theory of, 331
    metals as, 536
    minerals as, 535
    natural hazards and, 455
    regulation of, 534

remaining nonrenewables, 535–536
renewable vs. nonrenewable, 534–535, 535t
sustainability and, 574
Nature Conservancy
    belief systems and, 55
    biodiversity and, 64
Nauru, carbon dioxide emissions of, 97t
Nazca Plate, 432f
NDVI. See normalized difference vegetation index (NDVI)
Nearctic zoological region, 69f
Negative externalities, 247
Negative feedbacks, 66, 280, 568
Negev Desert, 391
Nelson River, 392t
Neoclassical economics, 105
Neoglaciations, 323–324
Neolithic revolution, 339
Neotropical zoological region, 69f
NEP. See net ecosystem production (NEP)
Nepal, carbon dioxide emissions of, 96t
Net ecosystem production (NEP), 93
Netherland Antilles, carbon dioxide emissions of, 96t
Netherlands
    carbon dioxide emissions of, 95t
    emissions of, 378f
    emissions target under Kyoto, 381t
Net primary production (NPP), 93, 202
Networking, 579
New Caledonia, carbon dioxide emissions of, 96t
New South Wales Greenhouse Gas Abatement Scheme, 212
New Urbanism, 608–609
New York City, 608, 609t
New Zealand
    carbon dioxide emissions of, 95t
    coal reserves in, 272t
    emissions of, 378f
    emissions target under Kyoto, 381t
    Resource Management Act in, 222
    soils in, 559
NGOs. See nongovernmental organizations (NGOs)
Nicaragua, carbon dioxide emissions of, 96t
Niches, exotic species and, 246–247
Nigardsbreen glacier, 290
Niger, carbon dioxide emissions of, 96t
Nigeria
    carbon dioxide emissions of, 95t
    mangroves in, 409
    natural gas reserves in, 451t
Niger River, 392t
Nile Basin, 392t
Nile Delta, 163
NIMBY. See "not in my backyard" effect
Nitrate aerosols, 6t
Nitric oxide, nitrous oxide and, 459
Nitrogen availability, 456
Nitrogen cycle, 60, 456–458, 457f
Nitrogen dioxide, nitrous oxide and, 459
Nitrogen fixation, 456, 457f, 458
Nitrogen oxide
    agriculture and, 13
    biofuels and, 58
    transportation and, 588

Nitroglycerine, 111
Nitrous oxide, **459**. *See also* greenhouse gas(es)
    in greenhouse effect, 308
    as greenhouse gas, 309
    increase in atmospheric, 297
    in Kyoto Protocol, 380t
Noatak wilderness area, 642t
Nobel, Alfred, 111
Noise pollution, 588
Nomadism, pastoral, 11
Nonentry mining, 426. *See also* mining
Nongovernmental organizations (NGOs), 228,
    460–462
Nonlinearity, 581
Nonpoint source pollution, 504
Nonrenewable resources, 534–535, 535–536, 535t
Noordwijk Conference, 275t
Normalized difference vegetation index (NDVI), 171
Norse colonization, of Greenland, 325
North America
    deserts and climate change in, 175t
    glacial retreat in, 290f
    Holocene in, 322–323
    hydroelectric generation in, 149t
    migration to, 327
    oil reserves in, 273t
    salinization in, 543t
    water resources in, 625t
    Younger Dryas in, 647–648
North American Free Trade Agreement
    (NAFTA), 585
North American Plate, 432f
North Atlantic Deep Water (NADW)
    thermohaline circulation and, 580
    Younger Dryas period and, 648
North Atlantic Drift, thermohaline circulation
    and, 580
North Atlantic Oscillation (NAO), **462**
    Arctic sea ice and, 40
    dust storms and, 188, 189f
    effects of, 473
    Gulf Stream and, 473
    ocean-atmosphere coupling and, 472
    pressure anomaly with, 473f
    solar variability and, 564
North Carolina, dune stabilization in, 32
Northern Sea Route, 48
North Korea
    carbon dioxide emissions of, 95t
    famine in, 260
North Sea, 413
Northwest Passage, 48
Norway
    carbon dioxide emissions of, 95t
    emissions of, 378f
    emissions target under Kyoto, 381t
    Little Ice Age in, 405f
    natural gas production in, 451t
Norwegian Emissions Trading Scheme, 212
No-tillage cultivation, 13
"Not in my backyard" effect, 622
Nova Scotia, in Younger Dryas, 647
NPP. *See* net primary production (NPP)
NREL. *See* National Renewable Energy
    Laboratory (NREL)

Nubariya irrigation project, 542t
Nubian Plate, 432f
Nuclear fission
    U.S. spending on, 445f
    as wedge, 569
Nuclear fusion, U.S. spending on, 445f
Nuclear power, **463–466**
    in Australia, 465
    in Canada, 465
    energy and, 214
    in France, 464
    in Germany, 465
    in Japan, 464
    in Russia, 464–465
    in South Korea, 465
    technology, 578
    in United Kingdom, 465
    in United States, 464
    in U.S. energy policy, 443, 445
Nuclear waste, **466**
    oceanic dumping of, 474–475
Nuclear weapons
    nuclear power and, 463, 465–466
    nuclear winter and, **466–468**
Nuclear winter, **466–468**
Nurek Dam, 149

O
Ocean acidification, **469**
    as impact, 352
Ocean-atmosphere coupling, **469–474**
    in mid-latitudes, 472–473
    in tropics, 469–472
Ocean circulation, Younger Dryas and, 648
Ocean Conveyor, 580f
Ocean desalination, **165–166**
Ocean disposal, **474–476**
Oceania
    hydroelectric generation in, 149t
    water resources in, 625t
Oceanic heat transport, Arctic sea ice and, 40
Ocean nitrogen flows, 458
Ocean phosphorus, 502
Ocean pollution, 507. *See also* pollution
Oceans, in carbon cycle, 92f, 93
Ocean sediments, Arctic warming and, 46
Ocean surface fertilization, 283t, 285
Ocean vaporization, 251
Offsets, carbon, 98
Ogalalla aquifer, 13
Oil
    combustion of, 214
    discoveries *vs.* production rates, 144–148
    energy content of, 274
    exploration for, 272
    as fossil fuel, 272–273
    reserves of, 273t
    rise of, 270
    supply, **144–147**
    transportation and, 588
    unconventional, 273
Oil drilling platforms, 474
Oil sands, **476–478**
Oil shales, 279
Oil spills, 507
Okavango Swamps, 638f

Old-growth forests, 161, 267–268
Oldinyo Pinatubo volcano, 612
Oligocene climate, 483, 485
Oman, carbon dioxide emissions of, 95t
One-child policy, 509
On the Origin of Species by Natural Selection
    (Darwin), 244
Open-cycle natural gas electricity generation, 448, 448f
Optimism. *See* catastrophist-cornucopian debate
Optimum operations, 194
Orbit, solar radiation and, 563
Ordovician Period, 155f
Organic aerosols, 6t
Organic farming, 13, 18
Oriental zoological region, 69f
Orinoco Belt, 476
Orobiomes, 72
Orthophosphate, 502
Osaka, 608, 609t
Our Common Future (Brundtland Commission),
    84–85, 554
Outer Hebrides, 208
Overconsumption, 231
Overgrazing, 167
Overkill theory, 346
Oxygen cycle, phosphorus cycle and, 503–504
Oxygen isotopes, 128
Ozone, **478–481**
    chlorofluorocarbons and, 118–119
    depletion, 480, 482f
    in greenhouse effect, 308
    nitrous oxide and, 459
    in stratosphere, 478, **481–482**, 482f
    in troposphere, 478
    Vienna Convention and, 225

P
Pacala, Stephen, 463
Pacific Decadal Oscillation (PDO), 471f
    dust storms and, 188
    El Niño and, 206
    ocean-atmosphere coupling and, 472
Pacific Plate, 432f
Pakistan
    carbon dioxide emissions of, 95t
    salinization in, 544t
Palau, carbon dioxide emissions of, 97t
Palearctic zoological region, 69f
Paleoaltitude, 431
Paleoclimate, **483–489**
Paleoclimatic records, 127–132
Paleomagnetic dating, 156–157, 158f
Paleomagnetic evidence of crustal movement,
    490–491
Paleozoic Era, 155f
Palme Commission, 84
Palm oil, 57, 59
PAM. *See* plant available moisture (PAM)
PAN. *See* plant available nutrients (PAN)
Panama, carbon dioxide emissions of, 96t
Papua New Guinea, carbon dioxide emissions
    of, 96t
Paraguay, carbon dioxide emissions of, 96t
Parasites, exotic species and, 247
Paris, 609t
Parks, **491–493**

biodiversity and, 197–198
city, 491
eco-industrial, 362–363
function of, 196
human activity and, 196–197
management of, 197–198
national, 491–492
origin of word, 491
value of, **196–198**
Pascal, Blaise, 53–54
Pastoral nomadism, 11
Patterns, regional, **522–526**
PCBs. *See* polychlorinated biphenyls (PCBs)
PDMS. *See* postdepositional modification
      stratigraphy (PDMS)
PDO. *See* Pacific Decadal Oscillation (PDO)
Peak oil. *See* crude oil supply
Peanut, as biofuel feedstock, 57*f*
Peat, coal and, 271
Pedobiomes, 72
Pelean activity, 613
Pennsylvanian Period, 155*f*
Perennial crops, 17
Perfluorocarbons
      as greenhouse gas, 310
      in Kyoto Protocol, 380*t*
      specific, 120*t*
Perfluoroethane, 120*t*
Perfluoromethane, 120*t*
Permaculture, agriculture and, 15
Permafrost, **493–499**
      Arctic warming and, 46, 47
      boreal forests and, 77, 81–82
      carbon in, 81–82
      changes in, 81–82
      climate change and, 495–498
      consequences of thawing, 498–499
      distribution of, 494–495, 496*f*
      fertility and, 81
      freshwater stock in, 624*t*
      hydrates in, 421
      nature of, 494
      rivers and, 538
      soil in, 494
      thickness, 494
      vegetation and, 496–497
      water in, 494
Permian Period, 155*f*
Person-to-person infections, 178
Peru
      Amazon River in, 21
      carbon dioxide emissions of, 95*t*
      El Niño in, 206
Pessimism. *See* catastrophist-cornucopian debate
Pesticides, 55, 111, 230, 294, 500–501
Pest management, **500–501**
Petroleum, 214, 272–273
Pets, 245
Philippines, carbon dioxide emissions of, 95*t*
Philosophy
      belief systems and, 53
      environmental, 218
      intergenerational equity and, **365–366**
Phosphorus, 203
Phosphorus cycle, **501–504**

Photosynthesis
      carbon cycle and, 93
      phosphorus cycle and, 502
Photovoltaic cells, 446, 531, 532*f*, 569. *See also* solar
      energy
Phytoplankton, dimethyl sulfide and, 66, 67*f*
Pigou, Arthur C., 204
Pilot Program to Conserve the Brazilian
      Rainforest, 25
Pipelines, natural gas, 452
"Plano Real" economic reform program, 23
Plant available moisture (PAM), 546
Plant available nutrients (PAN), 546
Planted forests, 267
Plant protection, 16
Plants
      in Australia, 50*t*, 51
      biological realms and, 69
      in carbon cycle, 92*f*, 93
      carbon cycle and, 60
      coastlines and, 141
      exotic, **244–247**
      global warming and, 299
      in heathlands, 317
      interhemispheric exchange of, 325
      in Mediterranean environment, 415
      permafrost and, 496–497
      salinization and, 541
      in savannas, 546
      in wetlands, 636
Plate centers, 559
Plate margins, 559
Plates, 431–434, 432*f*
Plate tectonics, **430–434**
Platinum, 536
Pleistocene deserts, 591–592
Pleistocene dust accumulation, 188*t*
Pleistocene extinctions, 249
Pleistocene mountains, 436
Pleistocene overkill theory, 346
Pleistocene pluvian lakes, 592–593
Pleistocene sea levels, 549
Plinian activity, 613
Pliocene climate, 485
Plunder economy, 293
Pluvial lakes, 592–593
Pneumonia, 184
Poaching, **346–348**
Podzolization, 561
Podzols, 558
Point source pollution, 504
Poland
      carbon dioxide emissions of, 95*t*
      emissions of, 378*f*
      emissions target under Kyoto, 381*t*
Polar bears, sea ice and, 47
Polders, 10
Policy
      culture and, 55
      deforestation, 25–26
      IHDP and, 368–369
      integrity and, 194
      pollution, 507
      population, **507–511**
      trade, 583

U.S. energy, **439–447**
waste management, 622–623
wilderness, 642–643
Politics, geoengineering and, 286
Pollen grains, in paleoclimatic records, 131
Pollution, **504–507**
      acid rain and, **1–5**
      air, 504–505
      in China, 115–116
      ethanol and, 58
      fossil fuels and, 271
      global dimming and, 294
      in India, 359–360
      integrated control of, 224
      mining and, 427
      natural hazards and, 455
      noise, 588
      nonpoint source, 504
      ocean disposal and, **474–476**
      ozone and, 479
      point source, 504
      pollutants in air, 504
      of soils, 506–507
      taxing, 203–204
      traffic and, 588
      transportation of pollutants, 505
Polychlorinated biphenyls (PCBs), 111
Pope, Carl, 201
Pope John Paul II, 530
Popular culture, 328
Population, human, **338–345, 507–511**
      age structure and, 342–343
      agriculture and, 12, 15–16
      archaeology and, 338
      biodiversity and, 15–16
      Black Death and, 339
      carrying capacity and, 101–103
      censuses, 338
      Chinese policy, 510–511
      conferences on, 343
      consumption and, 231, 509
      current trends, 508–509
      dams and, 151
      deforestation and, 161
      demographic transition and, 339–342, 340*f*, 341*f*
      density, 343
      development and, 341
      distribution, 343
      DNA evidence and, 338
      economic levels and, 200
      estimates of, 338
      fertility and, 340
      food production capacity and, 260–261
      forests and, 598
      growth projection, 16
      history, 508–509
      in India, 358–359
      information sources on, 338
      migrations and, **4421–424**
      mortality and, 340–341
      natural hazards and, 454
      negative feedback and, 66
      positive feedback and, 66
      premodern, 338–339
      projections, 344–345

religion and, 529
sex structure in, 342–343
shares of, by continent, 343*t*
sustainability and, 455, 573–574
transportation and, 586
uncertainty and, 605
urban, 344*f*, **608–610**
wetlands and, 639
Population Bomb, The (Ehrlich), 231
Portugal
carbon dioxide emissions of, 95*t*
emissions of, 378*f*
emissions target under Kyoto, 381*t*
Positive externalities, 247
Positive feedbacks, 66, 280, 581
Possibilism, 332
Postdepositional modification stratigraphy
(PDMS), 155
Postglacial climatic optima, 323–324
Potassium-argon dating, 156
Poverty
disease and, 177
economic levels and, **198–200**
environment and, 199
forests and, 598
in India, 359
vulnerability and, 615
P/PET formula, 171
Precambrian Era, 155*f*
Precautionary principle, 143, 226, **512**
Precipitation
agriculture and, 355
Arctic warming and, 43
boreal forests and, 76, 78–79
denudation and, 393*f*
drought and, **184–186**
El Niño and, 206
erosion and, 232–233
Greenland ice sheet and, 310
in India, 360
regional patterns of, 522–524
rivers and, 537
snow-water equivalent and, 556
in sulfur cycle, 571*f*
tropical, 596
twentieth century changes in, 601–602
urban climate and, 607
water stress and, 354
weather modification and, 634–635
Prediction
global warming, 298–299
uncertainty and, 605, 606
Prehistoric climates, **483–489**
Prehistoric extinctions, 248–249
Prehistoric ice sheets, 350
Premodern populations, 338–339
Preservation
as conservation, 143
land, **386–388**
parks and, 196
vs. sustainable development, 641–642
Preserves, **196–198, 491–493**
Prianfar'e region, 80
Pricing, 217
Primary energy, 213

Primary producers, 202
Private energy R&D, 441*f*
Privatization, irrigation and, 372–373
Productivity, in water use, 628
Project Independence, 443*t*
Project Tiger, 492
Prokaryotes, 279
Property law, 222
Property-rights systems, 142–143
Protected lands, 386
Protection of Victims of International Armed
Conflicts, 553
Proxy data, **513–514**
Public-choice hypothesis, 583
Public energy R&D, 441*f*
Puerto Rico, carbon dioxide emissions of, 96*t*
Pyrite, 571*f*

Q
Qatar
carbon dioxide emissions of, 95*t*
natural gas reserves in, 451*t*
Quality, water, **629–632**. *See also* water
QUANGOs. *See* quasi-nongovernmental
organizations (QUANGOs)
Quantification, uncertainty and, 606
Quasi-nongovernmental organizations
(QUANGOs), 460
Quaternary climate, 485, 487
Quaternary deserts, 172–173, 487
Quaternary dust storms, 187
Quaternary lakes, 384
Quaternary Period, 155*f*
Quaternary stratigraphy, 154
Queensland rainforest, 352–353
Qur'an, 530

R
Radiative forcing
aerosols and, 8
greenhouse gases and, 309
solar variability and, 564
Radiometric dating, 156, 156*f*, 164–165
Rain. *See also* precipitation
coccidioidomycosis and, 182
desertification and, 169
El Niño and, 206
erosion and, 232–233
malaria and, 179
rivers and, 537
Rainforests. *See* forests; tropical forests
Ranching, 11
"Range of choice" perspective, 331
Rank, *vs.* coal, 271
RapeSeed oil, 57
Raster approach, to geographic information
systems, 288, 289
Ratification, of treaties, 224–225
Rawls, John, 366
RDF. *See* refuse-derived fuel (RDF)
Reagan defense plan, 443*t*
Realms, biological, **69–71**
Reclamation, after mining, 426
Reconstruction, climate, **126–132**
Records
historical, 126–127
paleoclimatic, 127–132

Recovery, vulnerability and, 616
Recycling credits, 623
Red Sea, 413
Reefs, **515–519**
area of, 515
barrier, 515
bleaching of, 518
classification of, 515
El Niño and, 516–517
fringing, 515
future of, 518–519
impacts on, 516–517
loss of, 352, 354
mining and, 516
sea levels and, 515–516, 552–553
sedimentation and, 516
Reflectivity. *See* albedo
Refuse-bag tax, 204
Refuse-derived fuel (RDF), 620
Regional assessment, 519–521
Regional Greenhouse Gas Initiative (RGGI), 439
Regional patterns, **522–526**
Regional Seas Programme, 476
Regional trade agreements, 585
Regulation, 111–112, 280, 281, **527–528**.
See also law
Reliability, of climate models, 126
Relict dunes, 591
Religion, **529–531**
diversity and, 530
Eastern, 219
ecotheology and, 242
environmental, 219
Europeanization of world and, 326–327
global change and, 292
implications of, 529–530
importance of, 529
natural disasters and, 453–454
population and, 529
significance of, 529
Rembrandt Harmenszoon van Rijn, 54
Renewability, of biofuels, 58
Renewable energy, **531–533**
coal displaced by, 533*t*
contributions of, 532–533
for electricity generation, 531–532
energy and, 214
U.S. energy policy and, 440–442
Renewable Energy Portfolio Standards (RPS), 446
Renewable resources, 534–535, 535*t*
Reproductive health, 507
Reptiles, in Australia, 50*t*
Research and development
benefits of, 442*f*
comparison of major U.S. initiatives, 443*t*
fuel cell, U.S. spending on, 444*f*
nuclear fission, U.S. spending on, 445*f*
nuclear fusion, U.S. spending on, 445*f*
promising sectors for, 441
public *vs.* private, 441*f*
solar, U.S. spending on, 443*t*
U.S. spending on, 442*f*
on wind energy, 444*f*
Reserves
coal, 271, 272*t*

natural gas, 451–452, 451*t*
    in oil sands, 476
Reservoirs
    dams and, 149
    earthquakes and, 151
Resilience, in food crisis, 616*f*
Resource Conversation and Recovery Act, 527
Resource Management Act (New Zealand), 222
Resources, **533–536**
    in Arctic, 42
    attitudes towards, 533–534
    biodiversity and, 62–63
    common pool, 142
    conflict over, 536
    environment and, 533
    functional theory of, 331
    metals as, 536
    minerals as, 535
    natural hazards and, 455
    regulation of, 534
    remaining nonrenewables, 535–536
    renewable *vs.* nonrenewable, 534–535, 535*t*
    sustainability and, 574
Responsible Care plan, 112
Retreat, of glaciers, **289–291, 290***f*
Reunion, carbon dioxide emissions of, 96*t*
RGGI. *See* Regional Greenhouse Gas Initiative (RGGI)
Rice cultivation
    climate change and, 13
    irrigation and, 371
    methane and, 419, 420*t*
    soils and, 560
    wetlands and, 637–638
Rift Valley, 339
Rills, 233
Rinderpest, 247
Rings, tree, **163–165**
Rio Conference. *See* United Nations Conference on Environment and Development (UNCED)
Rio Declaration, 225
Rio de Janeiro, 609*t*
Rio Grande, 392*t*
Riverine phosphorus, 502
River Jordan, 383
Rivers, **537–538**
    dams and, **149–153**
    deltas and, **163**
    dissolved load of, 390–391
    earthmoving and, 35
    flooding and, 537–538
    freshwater stock in, 624*t*
    in India, 358
    mountains and, 435
    nitrates in, 458
    in phosphorus cycle, 501
    precipitation and, 537
    runoff and, 537–538
    water stress and, 354
Romania
    carbon dioxide emissions of, 95*t*
    emissions of, 378*f*
    emissions target under Kyoto, 381*t*
Roman law, 221
Roosevelt, Theodore, 645

RPS. *See* Renewable Energy Portfolio Standards (RPS)
Rubidium-strontium dating, 156
Runoff, 233, 299, 537–538, 625
"Run of river" dams, 152
Rural, *vs.* urban areas, 609
Russia
    carbon dioxide emissions of, 95*t*
    coal reserves in, 272*t*
    natural gas production in, 451*t*
    natural gas reserves in, 451*t*
    nuclear power in, 464–465
    transportation-related emissions in, 589*t*
Russian Federation
    emissions of, 378*f*
    emissions target under Kyoto, 381*t*
Rwanda, carbon dioxide emissions of, 97*t*

S
Sabotage, ecological, 231
Safe Drinking Water Act, 527
Sagan, Carl, 579
Sahara
    dust conditions in, 189*f*
    dust transport from, 169, 169*f*, 186
    expansion of, 167
    pluvial lakes and, 592
Sahel zone, 169, 189*f*
Saint Helena, carbon dioxide emissions of, 97*t*
Saint Kittis, carbon dioxide emissions of, 97*t*
Saint Lucia, carbon dioxide emissions of, 97*t*
Saint Pierre, carbon dioxide emissions of, 97*t*
St. Vincent, carbon dioxide emissions of, 97*t*
Salinity / salinization, **541–544**
    accelerated, 541
    of Aral Sea, 38*t*
    desalination and, **165–166**
    land reclamation and, 389
    mangroves and, 409
    soils and, 561
    thermohaline circulation and, 580
Salten, Felix, 54
Salt marshes, 551–552
Samoa, carbon dioxide emissions of, 97*t*
Sand County Almanac (Leopold), 55, 230
Sand dunes, **176**
Sands, oil, **476–478**
Sand seas, 591–592
São Paulo, 608, 609*t*
Sao Tome, carbon dioxide emissions of, 97*t*
Sapropels, 593
Saudi Arabia
    carbon dioxide emissions of, 95*t*
    natural gas reserves in, 451*t*
    transportation-related emissions in, 589*t*
Sauer, Carl, 293, 332
Savannas, **544–548**
Scale, ecosystems and, 201
Scandinavia
    glacial retreat in, 290*f*
    Little Ice Age in, 402
    national parks in, 492
Scarce metals, 536
SCARP irrigation project, 542*t*
Schelling, Tom, 286
Schumacher, E. F., 216, 578

Schwarzenegger, Arnold, 443
Schweitzer, Albert, 55
Science research, U.S. spending on, 442*f*
SEA. *See* strategic environmental assessment (SEA)
Sea-floor methane, 420–421
Sea-floor spreading (SFS), 430–431
Seafood, **263–265**
Sea ice, **38–42**
    age of, 39
    Arctic warming and, 43–44, 45*f*
    changes in, 38–39
    effects of reduction in, 43
    extent of, 38–39, 39*f*, 40*f*, 41*f*, 42*f*
    future of, 39
    losses of, 39–40
    polar bears and, 47
    thickness of, 39
    twentieth century changes in, 602–603
Sea levels, **549–553**
    Africa and, 356–357
    in Antarctica, 28*f*
    Antarctica and global, 30–31
    Antarctic ice sheet and, 349
    in Aral Sea, 36, 37*f*, 38*t*
    Arctic warming and, 46
    atolls and, 517*f*
    beaches and, 550–551
    cliffed coasts and, 550
    coastal planes and, 552
    coastlines and, 139
    coast line subsidence and, 550*f*
    coral reefs and, 515–516, 552–553
    current rate in rise of, 350
    deltas and, 163, 552
    dunes and, 551
    Egypt and, 163
    emerging coastlines and, **207–209**
    erosion and, 549
    estuaries and, 236, 552
    exctinctions and, 353
    factors in, 549
    flooding and, 356–357
    global warming and, 298
    Greenland ice sheet and, 46, 313
    implications of, 549–550
    lagoons and, 552
    mangrove swamps and, 409, 410, 551–552
    measurement of, 30
    Mediterranean environments and, 416
    in Pleistocene, 549
    in Quaternary, 485
    salt marshes and, 551–552
    tides and, 549
    wetlands and, 639
Sea of Japan, 413
Seas, marginal, 413
Sea salt aerosols, 6*t*
Sea Shepherd Conservation Society, 231
Seasons, disease and, 179
Sea-surface temperatures
    anthropogeomorphology and, 33
    Arctic sea ice and, 39
    boreal forests and, 54
    hurricanes and, 594–595
    ocean-atmosphere coupling and, 469, 471*f*

paleoclimatic records and, 128
in 20th century, 470f
Seawater desalination, **165–166**
Second Sulfur Protocol (SSP), joint
    implementation in, 376
Security, **553–555**
Sedimentary cycles, 60
Sedimentation
    anthropogeomorphology and, 32t
    in carbon cycle, 92f
    coastlines and, 140
    dating and, 154
    erosion and, 234
    fluvial denudation and, 391–394, 392t
    Heinrich events and, 320
    in India, 358
    paleoclimatic records and, 127
    in phosphorus cycle, 501
    reefs and, 516
Sediments, ocean, Arctic warming and, 46
Seed banks, 16
Self-regulation, 280
Selway-Bitterroot wilderness area, 642t
Seminatural heathlands, 317
Semple, Ellen Churchill, 330
Senegal
    carbon dioxide emissions of, 96t
    famine in, 259
Seoul, 609t
Serengeti Plain, 545
Settlement, 300
Settlement transformation, 327
Several liability, 223
Severe weather, 254–255
Sewage treatment plant effluent, 474
Sex structure, in population, 342–343
Seychelles, carbon dioxide emissions of, 97t
Shade-grown coffee, 17
Shale, 272
Shanghai, 609t
Shellfish, cholera in, 179
Shelter Belt, 168f
Shenzhen, China, 609t
Shields, solar, 283t, 284
Shifting cultivation, 18
Shrimp cultivation, 360
Shrublands, 415
Shrubs, desertification and, 168
SIA. See social impact assessment (SIA)
Siberian silkmoth, 80
Sierra Club, 230
Sierra Club Cool Cities Campaign, 610
Sierra Leone, carbon dioxide emissions of, 97t
Silent Spring (Carson), 55, 230, 294
Silkmoth, Siberian, 80
Silurian Period, 155f
Silver, 536
Singapore, carbon dioxide emissions of, 95t
Skuleberget mountain, 207–208
Sleipner carbon storage site, 89t
Slope failure, 32t
Slovakia
    carbon dioxide emissions of, 95t
    emissions of, 378f
    emissions target under Kyoto, 381t

Slovenia
    carbon dioxide emissions of, 96t
    emissions of, 378f
Small is Beautiful: Economics as if People Mattered
    (Schumacher), 960
Small-scale mining, 428
Smith, Adam, 585
Smith, Robert Angus, 2
Smog
    biofuels and, 58
    in China, 115–116
    in India, 359
Snohvit carbon storage project, 89t
Snow cover, **555–556**. See also precipitation
    albedo and, 19
    Arctic warming and, 43
    boreal forests and, 76, 78
    ice sheets and, 351
    rivers and, 538
    sulfur and, 572
Snowstorms, 254–255
Snow-water equivalent (SWE), 556
Soap, 110
Social cost pricing, 445–446, 622
Social ecology, 219
Social forestry, 267
Social impact assessment (SIA), 220
Societal development, **121–122**
Socolow, Robert, 463
Sodium, mean residence time of, 61
Soft law, 225
Soil(s), **556–562**
    acidification, 561
    agriculture and, 560
    albedo and, 19
    biosphere interactions and, 557
    classification of, 557–559
    coccidioidomycosis in, 182
    conservation of, 234–235
    deforestation and, 162
    desertification and, 168, 560
    erosion of, 560
    in forests, 269
    formation of, 556–557
    freshwater stock in, 624t
    geography, 559–560
    greenhouse gases and, 561
    in heathlands, 317
    identification of, 557–559
    lateralization, 561
    leaching and, 557
    makeup of, 556
    in Mediterranean environment, 415
    nitrogen fixation in, 456
    in permafrost, 494
    permafrost and, 495–496
    phosphorus in, 502
    plate centers and, 559
    plate margins and, 559
    Pleistocene glaciation and, 560
    podzolization, 561
    pollution of, 506–507
    rice cultivation and, 560
    salinization and, 541, 543t, 561
    weathering and, 556–557

Soil stratigraphic units, 155
Soil Taxonomy (USDA), 558
Solar energy
    desertification and, 168–169
    in ecosystems, 202
    for electricity generation, 531
    rate of arrival of, 307
    as renewable, 531
    U.S. spending on, 443t
    as wedge, 569
Solar radiation management, 283–284
Solar shields, 283t, 284
Solar-thermal generation, 531
Solar ultraviolet radiation, 565
Solar variability, **563–567**
Solomon Islands, carbon dioxide emissions of, 97t
Somalian Plate, 432f
Sorghum, as biofuel feedstock, 57f, 239f
South Africa
    agriculture in, 18
    carbon dioxide emissions of, 95t
    Mediterranean environment in, 417
    salinization in, 544t
    transportation-related emissions in, 589t
South America
    coal reserves in, 272t
    deforestation and, 160
    deserts and climate change in, 175t
    hydroelectric generation in, 149t
    Mediterranean environment in, 415
    oil reserves in, 273t
    salinization in, 543t
    savannas in, 545
    water resources in, 625t
South American altiplano, 436
South American Plate, 432f
South China Sea, 413
Southern Oscillation, 205–206. See also
    El Niño-Southern Oscillation (ENSO)
South Korea
    carbon dioxide emissions of, 95t
    nuclear power in, 465
    transportation-related emissions in, 589t
Soviet Union
    dams in, 149
    preserves and parks in, 492
Soybean oil, 57
Space research
    Gaia hypothesis and, 279
    technology and, 579
    U.S., 442f
Spain
    carbon dioxide emissions of, 95t
    emissions of, 378f
    emissions target under Kyoto, 381t
    transportation-related emissions in, 589t
Spatial pattern diversity, 62
Special Conference on Environmental Accounting,
    216–217
Species, exotic, **244–247**
Species conservation, 64
Spores, in paleoclimatic records, 131
Sport hunting, 346–348
Sprinklers, 628
Spruce budworm, 79f

Sri Lanka, carbon dioxide emissions of, 96*t*
SSP. *See* Second Sulfur Protocol (SSP)
SST. *See* sea-surface temperatures
Stability, **567–568**
Stabilization, 215, 302, **568–570**
Stades, 154
Stadials, 487–488
Stalin, Joseph, 529
Standards, 223
Starvation. *See* famine
Steady-state condition, 568
Steno's law, 154
Steppes, anthropogenic, 160
Stern Report, 200–201
Steward, Julian, 332
Stockholm Conference, 225
Stockholm Declaration, 225
Stocks, water, 624, 624*t*
Storage, of carbon, 285
Strata, 154
Strategic environmental assessment (SEA), 220
Stratigraphy, 154–156
Stratocumulus clouds, 284
Stratosphere
    aerosols in, 284
    methane in, 419
    ozone in, 478, **481–482**, 482*f*
Strict liability, 223
Strombolian activity, 613
Structural hazard paradigm, 454
Subbituminous coals, 271, **573–575**
Subduction zones, volcanoes and, 611
Subjectivity, 218
Subsidence anthropogeomorphology, 32*t*, 34*t*
Subsidence atoll formation, 515
Suburbanization, transportation and, 586
Succession, forests and, 268
Sudan
    carbon dioxide emissions of, 96*t*
    famine in, 259
Sugarbeet, as biofuel feedstock, 57*f*, 239*f*
Sugar cane, 239*f*, 325
Sulfate aerosols, 6*t*
Sulfides, 570
Sulfur cycle, **570–573**
Sulfur dioxide, 3
    in geoengineering, 283*t*
    in sulfur cycle, 570
    trading, 209–210
    transportation and, 588
    in volcanic eruptions, 614
Sulfur hexafluoride
    as greenhouse gas, 310
    in Kyoto Protocol, 380*t*
Sulfuric acid
    plants, 110
    sulfur cycle and, 572
    volcanic eruptions and, 614
Supercontinents, 434
Superfund Law, 111–112
Surface change, **390–396**
Surface mining, 426. *See also* mining
Surface runoff, 233
Surface temperatures
    Arctic warming and, 43, 44*f*

biomes and, 72*f*
boreal forests and, 76, 76*f*
changes in, 295, 295*f*
forests and, 269
Greenland ice sheet and, 313
heat island and, 607
in last glacial maximum, 415
permafrost and, 496–497
reefs and, 517
tree growth and, 82
Suriname, carbon dioxide emissions of, 96*t*
Sustainability, **573–575**
    economics and, 575
    growth and, 573
    integrity and, **194–195**
    in mining, 428
    natural hazards and, 455
    population and, 573–574
    technology and, 574
Sustainable development
    in Kyoto Protocol, 227
    vs. preservation, 641–642
    urban, 608–610
Sustenance hunting, 346
Swamps. *See* wetlands
Swaziland, carbon dioxide emissions of, 97*t*
SWE. *See* snow-water equivalent (SWE)
Sweden
    carbon dioxide emissions of, 95*t*
    emissions of, 378*f*
    emissions target under Kyoto, 381*t*
Swedish Time Scale, 157
Sweet sorghum, as biofuel feedstock, 57*f*, 239*f*
Switzerland
    carbon dioxide emissions of, 95*t*
    emissions of, 378*f*
    emissions target under Kyoto, 381*t*
Symbiogenesis, 279
Symbiosis, industrial, 361–362, 362*f*
Synfuels, 451, **575**
Syphilis, 326
Syr Dar'ya delta, 36
Syria, carbon dioxide emissions of, 95*t*

T
Taiga, loss of, 353
Tajikistan, carbon dioxide emissions of, 96*t*
Talik, 494
Tambora eruption, 612, 614
Tanana River, 78
Tansley, A. G., 201
Tanzania, carbon dioxide emissions of, 96*t*
Taoism, 219
Targets, under Kyoto, 381*t*
Tar sands. *See* oil sands
Tax(es)
    carbon, **98–101**
    in ecotaxation, **203–205**
    as energy strategy, 215
    green, 216
    indirect, 204
    landfill, 623
Taxonomic extrapolation, 605
Technology, **577–579**
    advantages of, 577
    belief systems and, 54–55

carbon storage, 90
change rates in, 577
coal, 578
development and, 579
drawbacks of, 577
energy, 578–579
energy policy and, 439
as energy strategy, 215
ethanol production, 237–239, 238*f*, 239*f*
examination of, 577–578
in geographic information
    systems, 288–289
hazard-reducing, 455
interhemispheric exchange of, 325
materials, 578
nuclear power, 578
as paradox, 577
parks and, 196
pest management and, 501
space, 579
standards and, 223
sustainability and, 574
weather modification, 635
Tectonic plates, **490–491**
    phosphorus cycle and, 501
    soils and, 559
    volcanoes and, 611
Tehran, 609*t*
TEK. *See* traditional ecological knowledge (TEK)
Television, tourism and, 581
Temperatures
    early records of, 126–127
    regional patterns of, 522
    sea-surface
        anthropogeomorphology and, 33
        Arctic sea ice and, 39
        boreal forests and, 54
        hurricanes and, 594–595
        ocean-atmosphere coupling and, 469, 471*f*
        paleoclimatic records and, 128
        in 20th century, 470*f*
    surface
        Arctic warming and, 43, 44*f*
        biomes and, 72*f*
        boreal forests and, 76–77, 76*f*
        changes in, 295, 295*f*
        forests and, 269
        Greenland ice sheet and, 313
        heat island and, 607
        in Holocene, 321
        in last glacial maximum, 415
        permafrost and, 496–497
        reefs and, 517
        tree growth and, 82
Tephra, 154
Teratogenesis, 111
Terminator, The (film), 54
Terminology, in industrial ecology, 361
Termites, methane and, 420*t*
Tertiary climate, 483, 485
Tertiary Period, 155*f*
Teton wilderness area, 642*t*
Thailand
    agriculture in, 18
    carbon dioxide emissions of, 95*t*

salinization in, 544t
transportation-related emissions in, 589t
Thalidomide, 111
Thermochemical conversion, 239
Thermohaline circulation, **580**
  cooling and, 296
  in Little Ice Age, 403
  Younger Dryas period and, 648
Thermokarst, 497, 498f
Third world, 199
Thoreau, Henry David, 55, 230
Thornthwaite method, 171
Three Gorges Dam, 86
Thresholds, 302
Thunderstorms
  severe, 255
  urban climate and, 607
Tibetan plateau, 434, 436
Tides, sea levels and, 549
Tillich, Paul, 529
Tills, 154
Timber, 161
Times Beach, 231
Time scale, geologic, 154, 155f
Time stratigraphy, 155–156
Time units, geologic, 154
Timor Sea, 413
Tin, 110
"Tipping point," 66
Tipping points, **581**
Tiwanaku state, 121t
Tocantins River, 597
Togiak wilderness area, 642t
Togo, carbon dioxide emissions of, 96t
Toit, Alexander du, 430
Tokyo, 608, 609t
Tokyo Bay, 208
Toncantins-Araguaia Basin, 21
Tonga, carbon dioxide emissions of, 97t
Töpfer, Klaus, 608
Top of the atmosphere (TOA) albedo, 19, 20f
Tornadoes, 255
Toronto Conference, 275t
Tort law, 222
Total solar irradiance (TSI), 563
Tourism, 196, 438, 517, **581–582**
Toxic Substances Control Act (TSCA), 111
Trace elements, in paleoclimatic record, 128–129
Trade, **582–585**
  in biofuels, 57–58
  effects of, 583
  globalization and, 303–304
  in history, 303
  policy, 583
  regional agreements, 585
Trading, **209–213**
  in Kyoto Protocol, 380–381
Traditional ecological knowledge (TEK), 243
Traditional medicine, in Asia, 347–348
Tragedy of the commons, **142–143, 585–586**
Transportation, **586–590**. See also ethanol
  challenges, 588–589
  consumer preference and, 587
  modes, 586
  trends, 586–587, 587f

Travel, 328, 581
Treaties, international law and, 224–225
Tree rings, 131. See also dendrochronology
Trees. See also deforestation; forests
  acid rain and, 3
  adaptations by, 79
  in boreal forests, 78–79
  carbon dioxide and, 269
  cultivation of, 12
  in dendrochronology, **163–165**
  invasions by, 601
  rings in, **163–165**
  snow and, 76
  temperatures favorable to, 82
Triassic Period, 155f
Trinidad and Tobago, carbon dioxide emissions
    of, 95t
Trinity Alps wilderness area, 642t
Trophic complexity, 203
Tropical climate change, **591–593**
Tropical cyclones, 254, **594–595**
  climate change and, 455
  El Niño and, 206
  insurance and, 364
  intensification of, 357
  wetlands and, 637
Tropical forests, **596–600**. See also forests
Tropics, ocean-atmosphere coupling and, 469–472
Troposphere
  humidity in, 634
  methane in, 419
  ozone in, 479–480
True cost pricing, 217
TSCA. See Toxic Substances Control Act (TSCA)
TSI. See total solar irradiance (TSI)
Tuberculosis, 180–181, 184
Tufa fills, 32
Tundra
  changes in coverage of, 72t
  loss of, 353
Tunisia, carbon dioxide emissions of, 96t
Turkey, emissions of, 95t, 378f
Turkmenistan, carbon dioxide emissions of, 95t
Twentieth century climate change, **600–603**
Typhoons, 254, **594–595**
  climate change and, 455
  El Niño and, 206
  insurance and, 364
  intensification of, 357
  wetlands and, 637

U

Uganda, carbon dioxide emissions of, 96t
UGEC. See Urbanization and Global Environmental
    Change (UGEC)
Ukraine
  carbon dioxide emissions of, 95t
  Chernobyl disaster in, **113–115**, 464
  emissions of, 378f
  emissions target under Kyoto, 381t
  famine in, 260
Ultraviolet radiation
  ozone and, 480–481
  solar variability and, 565
UNCED. See United Nations Conference on
    Environment and Development (UNCED)

Uncertainty, **122–126,** 525–526, **605–606**
UNCOD. See UN Conference on Desertification
UN Conference on Desertification, 170
Unconventional fossil fuels, 273
Underground mining, 426. See also mining
UNEP. See United Nations Environment
    Programme (UNEP)
UNESCO Man and the Biosphere reserves, 65
Unfunded Mandates Reform Act, 528
Union Bank of Switzerland, 364
United Arab Emirates
  carbon dioxide emissions of, 95t
  natural gas reserves in, 451t
United Kingdom
  carbon dioxide emissions of, 95t
  coastal management in, 138, 138f
  emissions of, 378f
  emissions target under Kyoto, 381t
  landfill in, 621
  natural gas production in, 451t
  nuclear power in, 465
  transportation-related emissions in, 589t
United Kingdom Emissions Trading Scheme, 212
United Nations Conference on Environment and
    Development (UNCED)
  Brundtland Commission and, 84–85
  joint implementation and, 375
  UNEP and, 606
United Nations Environment Programme (UNEP),
    225, 274, **606**
United Nations Millennium Development
    Goals, 199
United Nations University (UNU), 367
United States, 190
  biofuel production in, 59
  biofuels in, 57, 58f
  carbon dioxide emissions of, 94t, 95t
  coal reserves in, 272t
  dam construction in, 149
  dust storms in, 189f
  emissions of, 377, 378f, 440f
  emissions target under Kyoto, 381t
  energy policy in, **439–447**
  ethanol demand in, 239t
  ethanol in, 58f, 237
  landfill in, 621
  major R&D initiatives in, 443t
  mangroves in, 409
  Mediterranean environment in, 415
  Mexico, trade with, 582
  migration to, 327
  natural gas production in, 451t
  NGOs in, 461
  nuclear power in, 464
  regulation in, 527
  renewable energy in, 440–442
  research and development spending in, 442f
  salinization in, 544t
  sulfur dioxide trading in, 209–210
  transportation-related emissions in, 589t
  wilderness in, 642, 642t
  wildfires in, **262**
  wildlife management in, 644–645
  Younger Dryas in, 647–648
UNU. See United Nations University (UNU)

Upper tropospheric humidity (UTH), 634
Uranium. *See* nuclear power
Uranium enrichment, nuclear power and, 463
Urban areas
    in China, 116
    in India, 359
    vs. rural, 609
    salinization and, 542
    transportation in, 586
    wetlands and, 638
Urban climates, **607–608**
Urban famine, 261
Urban growth, 608
Urban heat island, 607
Urbanization, 327
Urbanization and Global Environmental Change
        (UGEC), 368
Urban migration, 422
Urban parks, 491
Urban population shares, 344*f*
Urban salinity, 541*t*
Urban sprawl, agriculture and, 15
Urban trends, **608–610**
Uruguay, carbon dioxide emissions of, 96*t*
Uruguay Round, 582
U-shaped valleys, 487, 489*f*
Usutu River, 595*f*
UTH. *See* upper tropospheric humidity (UTH)
Utilitarianism, 241–242, 365
Uzbekistan, carbon dioxide emissions of, 95*t*

V

Vancouver, 610
Van Eyck, Jan, 53
Vanuatu, carbon dioxide emissions of, 97*t*
Vapor compression (VC) distillation, 165
Vaporization, of oceans, 251
Variability, solar, **563–567**
Variables, uncertainty and, 606
Varve chronology, 157
VC. *See* vapor compression (VC) distillation
Vector approach, to geographic information
        systems, 288–289
Vectors
    cholera, 179–180
    disease, 178
    malaria, 179
    tuberculosis, 181
Vegetation
    in Australia, 50*t*, 51
    biological realms and, 69
    in carbon cycle, 92*f*, 937
    carbon cycle and, 60
    exotic, **244–247**
    global warming and, 299
    in heathlands, 317
    interhempispheric exchange of, 325
    in Mediterranean environment, 415
    permafrost and, 496–497
    salinization and, 541
    in savannas, 546
    in wetlands, 636
Vegetational controls, 34*t*
Vegetation zones
    Arctic warming and, 46
    shifts in, 72

Venezuela
    Amazon River in, 21
    carbon dioxide emissions of, 95*t*
    Orinoco belt in, 476
Venice Lagoon, 552
Venus, 307
Vernadsky, Vladimir Ivanovich, 293
Vibrio cholerae, 179
Victoria Park, 491
Vienna Convention, 119–120, 225
Vietnam, carbon dioxide emissions of, 95*t*
Villach Conference, 275*t*
Viral vectors, 178
Virgin Islands, carbon dioxide
        emissions of, 96*t*, 97*t*
Visibility, acid rain and, 4, 4*f*
VOCs. *See* volatile organic compounds (VOCs)
Voeikov, Aleksandr Ivanovich, 293
Volatile organic compounds (VOCs)
    ethanol and, 58
    ozone and, 481
Volcanic winter, 467
Volcanoes, **611–615**
    atmospheric effects of, 614–615
    causes of, 611
    dating and, 154
    distribution of, 612, 612*f*
    eruption frequency of, 612
    eruption mechanism of, 613
    hazards of, 613
    sites of, 611
    sulfur cycle and, 571, 571*f*
Volga River, 392*t*
Vulcanian events, 613
Vulnerability, **615–616**
    definition of, 615
    entitlement and, 616
    measurement of, 615

W

Wake Island, carbon dioxide emissions of, 97*t*
Walden (Thoreau), 55
Walker, Sir Gilbert, 462
Wallace's Line, 69, 70*f*
Warming. *See* global warming
War on Terror, 443*t*
Washakie wilderness area, 642*t*
Waste, 506
    categories of, 619
    collection of, 619
    composting of, 620
    disposal of, 619–622
    economic instruments and, 622–623
    energy recovery from, 620–621
    generation of, 619, 620*f*
    in landfill, 621–622
    land reclamation and, 389
    methane and, 420*t*
    NIMBY effect and, 622
    oceanic dumping of, 474–475
    per capita change in, 622*f*
    prevention, 619–620
    recovery, 620
    in waterways, 506
Waste management, **619–623**
Water, 92*f*, 93, **624–628**

agriculture and, 13–14
    in Australia, 51
    in China, 116
    cholera in, 179–180
    conflicts over, 358–359, 627–628
    consumption, 626
    dams and, **149–153**
    deforestation and, 25
    desalination of, 165–166
    global warming and, 299
    ground, **305**
    hydrologic cycle and, 624–625
    in India, 358–359
    irrigation and, **370–373**
    mining and, 427
    in mountains, 436–437
    in permafrost, 494
    pollution, 505–506. *See also* pollution
    population growth and, 16
    productivity in use of, 628
    quality trends, **629–632**
    resources, 625*t*
    salinization and, 541
    stocks of, 624, 624*t*
    stress, 354–355
    21st century issues with, 626–628
    use, 625–626
    wetlands and, 636
    withdrawal, 626
Water buffalo, 246–247
Watershed(s)
    Amazon River, 21
    biodiversity and, 16–17
Water vapor, **633–634**
    in Holocene, 321
WCRP. *See* World Climate Research Program
        (WCRP)
Wealth of Nations, The (Smith), 585
Weather. *See also* climate change
    acid rain, **1–5**
    aerosols and, 5–6
    dengue fever and, 182
    as hazard, 453
    reefs and, 516
    severe, 254–255
    in South Asia, 358
    urban, **607–608**
Weathering
    anthropogeomorphology and, 32*t*
    building decay and, 85–86
    soil formation and, 556–557
    sulfur cycle and, 571*f*
Weather modification, **634–635**
Weber's Line, 70*f*
Wedges, stabilization, 568–569, 569*f*
Wegener, Alfred, 430
Weminuche wilderness area, 642*t*
West Antarctic ice sheet, 31
Western Sahara, carbon dioxide emissions of, 97*t*
West Nubian Paleolake, 592
Wetland cultivation, 11
Wetlands, **636–639**
    agriculture and, 637–638
    attitudes to, 636
    in Australia, 50

definition of, 636
freshwater stock in, 624t
human impact on, 637
land reclamation and, 389–390
methane and, 419, 420t
nature of, 636
sea levels and, 551–552
value of, 636–637
Weyburn carbon storage site, 89t
Wheat, as ethanol feedstock, 239f
White, Gilbert F., 331
Wild and Scenic Rivers Act, 55
Wilderness
    biodiversity and, **640–641**
    debates, **641–643**
    importance of, 641
    preservation, 641–642
    sustainable development and, 641–642
    in United States, 642, 642t
Wilderness Act
    belief systems and, 55
    overview of, 642
Wildfires
    Arctic warming and, 46–47
    in Australia, 50
    biodiversity and, 62
    boreal forests and, 79–81
    global warming and, **262**
    insects and, 79–81
    insurance and, 364
    nitrogen and, 458
    permafrost and, 497

Wildlife management, **644–645**
Wildlife Management Institute, 645
Wind energy
    for electricity generation, 531–532
    U.S. research on, 444f
    U.S. spending on, 443t
    as wedge, 569
Winds
    deforestation and, 162
    desertification and, 168
    erosion and, 233–234
    urban climate and, 607–608
Wine grapes, 325
Winter storms, 254–255
WIPO. *See* World Intellectual Property
    Organization (WIPO)
Withdrawal, of water, 626
WMO. *See* World Meteorological Organization
    (WMO)
Wonders, chemical, **112–113**
Wood, as fuel, 270
Wood shipping, 161
World Bank
    conservation projects and, 387
    irrigation projects and, 371
World Climate Research Program (WCRP), 367
World Commission on Environment and
    Development, **84–85**, 554
World Conservation Union (IUCN), 197
World food production, 257–258
World food production capacity, 260–261
World Future Society, **277**

World Intellectual Property Organization
    (WIPO), 243
World Meteorological Organization (WMO), 274
World Trade Organization (WTO), GATT and, 584
World War II, 111
Wrangell-St. Elias wilderness area, 642t
WTO. *See* World Trade Organization (WTO)

X
Xinjang Farm 29 irrigation project, 542t

Y
Yasur volcano, 612
"Year without summer," 467, 614
Yellow River Basin, 392t
Yellow River Delta, 140
Yellow Sea, 413
Yemen, carbon dioxide emissions of, 96t
Yenisei River, 80, 392t
Younger Dryas (YD), **647–649**
Yugoslavia, carbon dioxide emissions of, 95t
Yukon River, 78

Z
Zaire, carbon dioxide emissions of, 96t
Zambezi River, 150f, 392t
Zambia, carbon dioxide emissions of, 96t
ZeroGen carbon storage project, 89t
Zimbabwe, carbon dioxide emissions of, 96t
Zimmermann, Erich, 331
Zinc, 536
Zonobiomes, 71–72
Zoological mammal regions, 69f
Zoonoses, 178